The Joan Palevsky  Imprint in Classical Literature

In honor of beloved Virgil—

"O degli altri poeti onore e lume . . ."

—Dante, *Inferno*

The publisher gratefully acknowledges the generous support
of the Classical Literature Endowment Fund of the University
of California Press Foundation, which was established by
a major gift from Joan Palevsky.

Sons of Hellenism, Fathers of the Church

TRANSFORMATION OF THE CLASSICAL HERITAGE
Peter Brown, General Editor

I. *Art and Ceremony in Late Antiquity*, by Sabine G. MacCormack

II. *Synesius of Cyrene: Philosopher-Bishop*, by Jay Alan Bregman

III. *Theodosian Empresses: Women and Imperial Dominion in Late Antiquity*, by Kenneth G. Holum

IV. *John Chrysostom and the Jews: Rhetoric and Reality in the Late Fourth Century*, by Robert L. Wilken

V. *Biography in Late Antiquity: The Quest for the Holy Man*, by Patricia Cox

VI. *Pachomius: The Making of a Community in Fourth-Century Egypt*, by Philip Rousseau

VII. *Change in Byzantine Culture in the Eleventh and Twelfth Centuries*, by A. P. Kazhdan and Ann Wharton Epstein

VIII. *Leadership and Community in Late Antique Gaul*, by Raymond Van Dam

IX. *Homer the Theologian: Neoplatonist Allegorical Reading and the Growth of the Epic Tradition*, by Robert Lamberton

X. *Procopius and the Sixth Century*, by Averil Cameron

XI. *Guardians of Language: The Grammarian and Society in Late Antiquity*, by Robert A. Kaster

XII. *Civic Coins and Civic Politics in the Roman East, A.D. 180–275*, by Kenneth Harl

XIII. *Holy Women of the Syrian Orient*, introduced and translated by Sebastian P. Brock and Susan Ashbrook Harvey

XIV. *Gregory the Great: Perfection in Imperfection*, by Carole Straw

XV. *"Apex Omnium": Religion in the "Res gestae" of Ammianus*, by R. L. Rike

XVI. *Dioscorus of Aphrodito: His Work and His World*, by Leslie S. B. MacCoull

XVII. *On Roman Time: The Codex-Calendar of 354 and the Rhythms of Urban Life in Late Antiquity*, by Michele Renee Salzman

XVIII. *Asceticism and Society in Crisis: John of Ephesus and "The Lives of the Eastern Saints,"* by Susan Ashbrook Harvey

XIX. *Barbarians and Politics at the Court of Arcadius*, by Alan Cameron and Jacqueline Long, with a contribution by Lee Sherry

XX. *Basil of Caesarea*, by Philip Rousseau

XXI. *In Praise of Later Roman Emperors: The* Panegyrici Latini, introduction, translation, and historical commentary by C. E. V. Nixon and Barbara Saylor Rodgers

XXII. *Ambrose of Milan: Church and Court in a Christian Capital*, by Neil B. McLynn

XXIII. *Public Disputation, Power, and Social Order in Late Antiquity*, by Richard Lim

XXIV. *The Making of a Heretic: Gender, Authority, and the Priscillianist Controversy*, by Virginia Burrus

XXV. *Symeon the Holy Fool: Leontius's "Life" and the Late Antique City*, by Derek Krueger

XXVI. *The Shadows of Poetry: Vergil in the Mind of Augustine*, by Sabine MacCormack

XXVII. *Paulinus of Nola: Life, Letters, and Poems*, by Dennis E. Trout

XXVIII. *The Barbarian Plain: Saint Sergius between Rome and Iran*, by Elizabeth Key Fowden

XXIX. *The Private Orations of Themistius*, translated, annotated, and introduced by Robert J. Penella

XXX. *The Memory of the Eyes: Pilgrims to Living Saints in Christian Late Antiquity*, by Georgia Frank

XXXI. *Greek Biography and Panegyric in Late Antiquity*, edited by Tomas Hägg and Philip Rousseau

XXXII. *Subtle Bodies: Representing Angels in Byzantium*, by Glenn Peers

XXXIII. *Wandering, Begging Monks: Spiritual Authority and the Promotion of Monasticism in Late Antiquity*, by Daniel Caner

XXXIV. *Failure of Empire: Valens and the Roman State in the Fourth Century* A.D., by Noel Lenski

XXXV. *Merovingian Mortuary Archaeology and the Making of the Early Middle Ages*, by Bonnie Effros

XXXVI. *Quṣayr 'Amra: Art and the Umayyad Elite in Late Antique Syria*, by Garth Fowden

XXXVII. *Holy Bishops in Late Antiquity: The Nature of Christian Leadership in an Age of Transition*, by Claudia Rapp

XXXVIII. *Encountering the Sacred: The Debate on Christian Pilgrimage in Late Antiquity*, by Brouria Bitton-Ashkelony

XXXIX. *There Is No Crime for Those Who Have Christ: Religious Violence in the Christian Roman Empire*, by Michael Gaddis

XL. *The Legend of Mar Qardagh: Narrative and Christian Heroism in Late Antique Iraq*, by Joel Thomas Walker

XLI. *City and School in Late Antique Athens and Alexandria*, by Edward J. Watts

XLII. *Scenting Salvation: Ancient Christianity and the Olfactory Imagination*, by Susan Ashbrook Harvey

XLIII. *Man and the Word: The Orations of Himerius*, edited by Robert J. Penella

XLIV. *The Matter of the Gods*, by Clifford Ando

XLV. *The Two Eyes of the Earth: Art and Ritual of Kingship between Rome and Sasanian Iran*, by Matthew P. Canepa

XLVI. *Riot in Alexandria: Tradition and Group Dynamics in Late Antique Pagan and Christian Communities*, by Edward J. Watts

XLVII. *Peasant and Empire in Christian North Africa*, by Leslie Dossey

XLVIII. *Theodoret's People: Social Networks and Religious Conflict in Late Roman Syria*, by Adam M. Schor

XLIX. *Sons of Hellenism, Fathers of the Church: Emperor Julian, Gregory of Nazianzus, and the Vision of Rome*, by Susanna Elm

Sons of Hellenism, Fathers of the Church

Emperor Julian, Gregory of Nazianzus, and the Vision of Rome

Susanna Elm

UNIVERSITY OF CALIFORNIA PRESS
Berkeley   Los Angeles   London

University of California Press, one of the most distinguished university presses in the United States, enriches lives around the world by advancing scholarship in the humanities, social sciences, and natural sciences. Its activities are supported by the UC Press Foundation and by philanthropic contributions from individuals and institutions. For more information, visit www.ucpress.edu.

University of California Press
Berkeley and Los Angeles, California

University of California Press, Ltd.
London, England

© 2012 by The Regents of the University of California

Library of Congress Cataloging-in-Publication Data

Elm, Susanna.
   Sons of hellenism, fathers of the church : Emperor Julian, Gregory of Nazianzus, and the vision of Rome / Susanna Elm.
      p. cm. — (Transformation of the classical heritage; 49)
   Includes bibliographical references and index.
   ISBN 978-0-520-28754-9 (ppbk : alk. paper)
   1. Church history—Primitive and early church, ca. 30–600.   2. Gregory, of Nazianzus, Saint.   3. Julian, Emperor of Rome, 331–363.   4. Church and state—Rome.   5. Rome—History—Julian, 361–363.   6. Rome—Religion.   I. Title.
BR170.E46   2012
270.2092′2—dc23
                                              2011027434

Manufactured in the United States of America

20 19 18 17 16 15 14 13 12
10 9 8 7 6 5 4 3 2 1

Für Martin

CONTENTS

Abbreviations xiii
Acknowledgments xvii

Introduction 1
   Universalism and Governance 2
   Julian the Emperor and Gregory the Theologian 3
   Gregory and the Bishops 6
   Julian and Gregory in Context 9

PART ONE

1. Nazianzus and the Eastern Empire, 330–361 17
   Nazianzus and Gregory: The Personal and the Local 19
   Constantinople: Emperor, Cosmopolis, and Cosmos 28
   Constantius's Triumph: Unity and Harmony, 358–360 42
   Reversal: Constantius and Julian Augustus, 360–361 53

2. Julian, from Caesar to Augustus: Paris to Constantinople, 355–362 60
   Toward Constantinople: From Caesar to Augustus, 360–361 61
   Julian's Concepts of Leadership: Philosopher and King 71

3. Philosopher, Leader, Priest: Julian in Constantinople, Spring 362 88
   The Context of Julian's Concepts of the True Philosophical Life 90
   A Philosopher as Leader, in Julian's Own Words: Against the Cynic Heraclius 106
   A Universal Divinity for a Universal Empire; or, How to Interpret Myth:
   Hymn to the Mother of the Gods 118

    How to Achieve True Philosophy: Against the Uneducated Cynics   136
    The Law Regarding Teachers   139

PART TWO

4. On the True Philosophical Life and Ideal Christian Leadership: Gregory's Inaugural Address, *Oration* 2   147

    A High-Wire Act: The True Philosophical Life as the Model of Priesthood in Late Antiquity   153
    The Codes of Aptitude   166

5. The Most Potent *Pharmakon:* Gregory the Elder and Nazianzus   182

    The Other High-Wire Act: Fathers and Sons   183
    The Royal Road: Gregory the Elder's Opponents at Nazianzus   201

6. Armed like a Hoplite—Gregory the Political Philosopher at War: Eunomius, Photinus, and Julian   213

    Oikeiōsis pros Theon *as Political Philosophy*   215
    The Enemy on the Inside: Photinus and Eunomius   228
    What Do Words Mean?   245
    Oikeiōsis pros Theon: *Oration* 2 *against Eunomius*   259

PART THREE

7. A Health-Giving Star Shining on the East: Julian in Antioch, July 362 to March 363   269

    The Emperor as Priest   273
    Julian's Divine Mandate   286
    The Platonic Philosopher-King: The Misopogon and Julian's Universal Vision   327

8. The Making of the Apostate: Gregory's *Oration* 4 against Julian   336

    The Pillar of Infamy: An Inverted Fürstenspiegel   344
    Imperial Decrees and Divine Enactments: Julian and Constantius   365

9. A Bloodless Sacrifice of Words to the Word: *Logoi* for the *Logos*   378

    Myth and Allegory   380
    Logoi: *The Theological Implications*   387
    Apostasis *versus* Theōsis; *or,* True Oikeiōsis pros Theon   413
    Oration 6, On Peace: *Unity and Concord*   422

10. Gregory's Second Strike, *Oration* 5   433

    The Pagan Context   435
    Gregory's Second Strike against the Pagans   445
    Procopius versus Valens   465

Conclusion: Visions of Rome 479
   Governing the Oikoumenē 480
   Authority and Kinship of the Elites 483
   Competing Universalisms 485

Bibliography 489
Index 529

ABBREVIATIONS

In the text and notes of this book, titles of journals are abbreviated as in *L'Année Philologique* and G. Krause, G. Müller, H. R. Balz, et al., eds., *Theologische Realenzyklopädie* (Berlin 1977–); authors and their works are abbreviated as in H. G. Liddell, R. Scott, H. S. Jones, et al., eds., *A Greek-English Lexicon,* 9th ed. (Oxford 1940); G. W. H. Lampe, *A Patristic Greek Lexicon* (Oxford 1961); and P. G. W. Glare, ed., *Oxford Latin Dictionary* (Oxford 1982). Apart from those abbreviations, the following are used in this book.

AH   The Arian Historiographer (or Homoian Historiographer). See *Philostorgius: Kirchengeschichte, mit dem Leben des Lucian von Antiochien und den Fragmenten eines arianischen Historiographen,* ed. J. Bidez and F. Winkelmann, 2nd ed., 151–76. Berlin 1972.
BHG *Bibliotheca Hagiographica Graeca.* 3 vols. 3rd ed. Ed. F. Halkin. Brussels 1957.
CA   *Les constitutions apostoliques: Introduction, texte critique, traduction et notes.* 3 vols. Ed. M. Metzger. Paris 1985–86.
CAG *Commentaria in Aristotelem Graeca.* 23 vols. Berlin 1882–1909.
CCG Corpus Christianorum, Series Graeca. Turnhout 1977–.
CCL Corpus Christianorum, Series Latina. Turnhout 1953–.
CG   Julian, *Oratio contra Galilaeos.* [*Against the Christians.*] *Giuliano imperatore: Contra Galileos.* Ed. and trans. E. Masaracchia. Rome 1990. [English translation: W. C. F. Wright, *The Works of Emperor Julian,* vol. 3, 311–427. (Cambridge, Mass., 1923; reprint 1998.)]
CIL *Corpus Inscriptionum Latinarum.* 16 vols. Berlin 1863–.

CJ *Corpus iuris civilis*, vol. 2, *Codex Justinianus*. 11th ed. Ed. P. Krüger. Berlin 1954.
CPG *Clavis Patrum Graecorum*. 5 vols. and suppl. Ed. M. Geerard and J. Noret. Turnhout 1974–98.
CSCO Corpus Scriptorum Christianorum Orientalium. Paris 1903–.
CSEL Corpus Scriptorum Ecclesiasticorum Latinorum. Vienna 1866–.
CTh *Theodosiani libri XVI cum Constitutionibus Sirmondianis*. Ed. T. Mommsen. Berlin 1905.
Dig. *Digesta*. Ed. T. Mommsen. In *Corpus iuris civilis*, vol. 1. Berlin 1893.
D-K *Die Fragmente der Vorsokratiker*. Ed. H. Diels and W. Kranz. 3 vols. 5th ed. Berlin 1934.
FGrH *Die Fragmente der griechischen Historiker*. 4 vols. Ed. F. Jacoby. Berlin 1923–.
GCS Die griechischen christlichen Schriftsteller der ersten drei Jahrhunderte. Berlin and Leipzig 1897–.
GNO *Gregorii Nysseni Opera*. 11 vols. Ed. W. Jaeger et al. Berlin 1921–2009.
ILS *Inscriptiones Latinae selectae*. 3 vols. Ed. H. Dessau. Berlin 1892–1916.
Lampe *A Patristic Greek Lexicon*. Ed. G. W. H. Lampe. Oxford 1961.
LC Eusebius of Caesarea, *Oration in Praise of Constantine*. [*De laudibus Constantini*.] Trans. H. A. Drake, *In Praise of Constantine: A Historical Study and New Translation of Eusebius' Tricennial Orations*, 83–102. Berkeley and Los Angeles 1976.
LSJ *A Greek-English Lexicon*. 9th ed. Ed. H. G. Liddell, R. Scott, H. S. Jones, et al. Oxford 1940.
MoG Julian, *Hymn to the Mother of the Gods. Giuliano imperatore: Alla madre degli dèi*. Ed. and trans. V. Ugenti. Lecce 1992. [English translation: W. C. F. Wright, *The Works of Emperor Julian*, vol. 1, 443–503. (Cambridge 1930; reprint 1980.)]
PG *Patrologiae cursus completus*, Series Graeca. 161 vols. Ed. J. P. Migne et al. Paris 1857–66.
PL *Patrologiae cursus completus*, Series Latina. 221 vols. Ed. J. P. Migne et al. Paris 1844–1900.
PLRE *The Prosopography of the Later Roman Empire*. 2 vols. [Vol. 1, A.D. 260–395, ed. A. H. M. Jones, J. R. Martindale, and J. Morris; vol. 2, A.D. 395–527, ed. J. R. Martindale.] Cambridge 1971–80.
POxy *The Oxyrhynchus Papyri*. Ed. B. P. Grenfell, A. S. Hunt, et al. London 1898–.
PPO *Praefectus Praetorio Orientis*
RE *Real-Encyclopädie der classischen Altertumswissenschaft*. Ed. A. F. von Pauly, G. Wissowa, W. Kroll, et al. Stuttgart 1894–1972.

SC   Sources Chrétiennes. Paris 1941–.
SC   Eusebius of Caesarea, *Oration on the Church of the Holy Sepulchre*. [*De sepulchro Christi.*] Trans. H. Drake, *In Praise of Constantine: A Historical Study and New Translation of Eusebius' Tricennial Orations*, 103–27. Berkeley and Los Angeles 1976.
SVF   *Stoicorum veterum fragmenta*. 4 vols. Ed. H. von Arnim. Leipzig 1903–24.
VC   Eusebius of Caesarea, *Life of Constantine* [*De vita Constantini*]: *Introduction, Translation, and Commentary*. Ed. and trans. A. Cameron and S. Hall. Oxford 1999.

ACKNOWLEDGMENTS

This book began to take shape in the summer of 1998. At the time, I was immersed in research for a project on the relevance of slavery for the formulation of late Roman Christian notions of leadership: that is, for the role of the bishop. Gregory of Nazianzus's second oration soon emerged as a central source, and I was already working on a number of papers devoted to it when Martin Nettesheim suggested I write instead a short little book on Gregory. Over a decade later, this short little book has accumulated an enormous debt of gratitude from friends, students, and colleagues. During a year spent at the Shelby Cullom Davis Center for Historical Studies at Princeton in 2000–2001, I formulated a first draft of what have become the first six chapters. It was an enormously fruitful and enjoyable time, for which I thank Anthony Grafton and Kenneth Mills. A semester as Ellen Maria Gorrissen Berlin Prize Fellow at the American Academy in Berlin in the spring of 2007 allowed me to finish chapters 8, 9, and 10 in such splendor as I imagine Gregory and his peers enjoyed, *mutatis mutandis,* at their estates; no one who has had the privilege of Gary Smith's and the Academy's hospitality will ever forget the spirit of excited engagement with culture in all its depth and variety. I completed the final revisions as Visiting Professor and Fellow of the Center for Advanced Study at the Ludwig-Maximilians-Universität, Munich, during the fall of 2009, yet another extraordinary place of intellectual engagement embodying the classical ideal of *otium cum dignitate.* I am deeply grateful to Dr. Annette Meyer, Dr. Sonja Asal, and Prof. Dr. Bernd Huber, Prof. Dr. Hans van Ess, and, above all, Prof. Dr. Barbara Vinken. I owe a very special debt of gratitude to the directors of the Historische Seminar at the Eberhard Karls Universität, Tübingen, Prof. Dr. Frank Kolb and Prof. Dr. Mischa Meier, and to PD Dr. Hilmar Klinkott for their generous hospitality, giving me room and board nearly every summer and during two semesters, in their wonderful Seminarbibliothek, where the memory of Prof. Dr. Hildegard Temporini Gräfin Vizthum is ever present.

At the University of California Press, I very much thank Eric Schmidt and Cynthia Fulton. Stephanie Fay and Paul Psoinos transformed my text, and I thank the two readers, Harold Drake and John McGuckin, for their extravagant encouragement. And I owe far more than the footnotes suggest to my many conversations with Glen Bowersock, Peter Brown, William C. Jordan, Michael Maas, Philip Rousseau, and above all with Rebecca Lyman and Neil McLynn. Many thanks are also due my friends and colleagues in the University of California Multi-Campus Research Group "Late Antiquity": Emily Albu, Ra'anan Boustan, Catherine Chin, Elisabeth Digeser, Hal Drake, Dayna Kalleres, Claudia Rapp, Michele Salzman, and the late, much-missed Thomas Sizgorich. At Berkeley, my friends and colleagues Erich Gruen, Carla Hesse, Thomas Laqueur, Maureen Miller, and Randolph Starn read the manuscript and gave me excellent advice. Boris Rodin Maslov and Laura Pfuntner were far more than the words "research assistant" suggest; they know how much I owe them. My very special thanks are due to my father, Kaspar Elm, who made me appreciate the importance of small differences in ways that I am only now beginning to understand, and to my daughter, Clara Cecilia, my constant source of joy. This book is dedicated to my husband, Martin Nettesheim, the light of my life.

Berkeley, December 2010

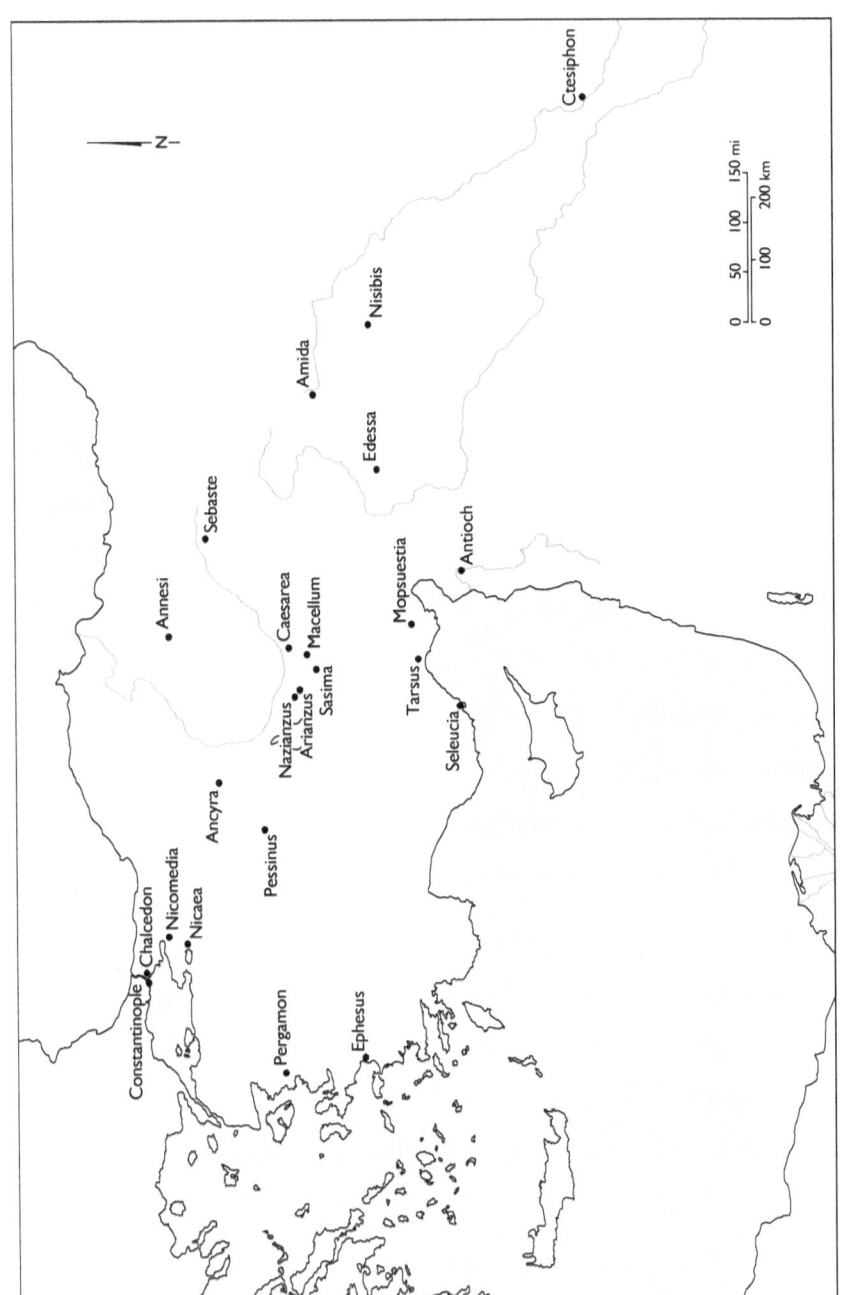

Asia Minor

Introduction

Occorre diffidare del quasi-uguale . . . del praticamente identico, del pressa-poco, dell'oppure. . . . Le differenze possono. essere piccole, ma portare a conseguenze radicalmente diverse.
—PRIMO LEVI, IL SISTEMA PERIODICO

If we have treated this subject with a few words, it is to illustrate the difficulty involved in attempting to find the word that has the power to restore the entire world and to illuminate it with the light of knowledge.[1]
—GREGORY OF NAZIANZUS, ORATION 2.39

This is a book about two powerful, enduring, and competing visions of universalism in the fourth century: Christianity and the Roman Empire. Yet, I will argue that these visions were in fact one, since Christianity was essentially Roman. Christianity's universalism lasted because it was, from the beginning, deeply enmeshed in the foundational ideologies granting Rome's supremacy. In the crucial fourth century of imperial patronage and religious conflict, Christian universalism was even more profoundly influenced by those ancient Roman ideological foundations. The book demonstrates these claims through the figures of one of Rome's ancient foundations' defenders, the pagan emperor Julian the Apostate, and of one of Julian's Christian attackers, Gregory of Nazianzus. Focusing on these protagonists and their vision of (Greek) Rome, the book engages these questions: What made Christianity last? How did it adapt to continuously changing external circumstances while retaining a core message? I will argue that the Roman Empire provided Christianity the ideological and social matrix without which its longevity and dynamism would have been inconceivable. This matrix was Rome's universalism. By what means was that universalism expressed, and how did Christian Romans adapt it? How did Greek Roman Christians integrate Christian norma-

---

1. Levi, *Sistema*, "Potassio," 63, Gr. Naz. Or. 2.39, εὑρεῖν τινα τὸν πάντας καταρτίσαι δυνάμενον λόγον καὶ λαμπρῦναι τῷ φωτὶ τῆς γνώσεως.

tive writings of Gospel and salvation into the matrix that Rome provided? What aspects did Christians retain, which ones jettison, and why? Only by observing this process in the literary duels between Julian and Gregory may we see the adaptation and transformation of traditional Roman themes in Christian self-definition, theology, and political theory.

UNIVERSALISM AND GOVERNANCE

Roman universalism, *Romanitas* properly understood, has many facets, not least the proper hierarchical arrangement of the various ethnicities Rome encompassed. What mixture of Greekness, or Hellenism, and Romanness best expressed Rome's supremacy? Even more crucial, what constellation of (ethnically connoted) divinities had caused Rome's greatness and was thus the guarantor of its security, prosperity, and permanence? After Constantine had granted Christianity the status of a legal religion, such questions were far from resolved. The gods of the Greeks and the Romans preserved their influence and power for many who belonged to the empire's elite. Yet, for those who were Christian it was not certain how the Christian God should be understood and how the God as Trinity would safeguard the power of the Romans. All agreed that Rome's power was divine in origin and that appropriate comprehension of the divine was essential to governing Rome's *oikoumenē*. Under intense debate in the fourth century was the nature of that divinity. Since to misread the divine will could spell disaster for all, even small theological differences could have significant impact, if misunderstood by those who ruled the empire, the emperor and the elites. These rulers ensured the continued protection of the divine at the root of Rome's power, because all had been originally created and instituted by that divinity, from each individual human being to the manner in which (just) wars should be fought and cities governed, buildings and temples built or destroyed, public festivals enacted, emperors honored, laid to rest, and divinized.

Thus, because of the cosmic dimension of Rome's universal power, and hence the necessity to comprehend the divine will precisely, it is not surprising that much of the discussions among those engaged in leading the empire in the fourth century, especially in the Greek-speaking part of the realm, focused on normative, if not socially canonical, texts by Plato and Aristotle on proper rule in its relation to the divine. Here, the philosopher as leader played a central role. How and in what manner should the emperor rule as philosopher? What philosophical life, in what composition of active engagement and retreat devoted to contemplation of the normative texts, could best ascertain the good rule of the realm and thus the salvation of all its inhabitants? Debates concerning the true philosophical life were in essence debates about the correct governance of the Roman Empire, the equivalent of the known world. Especially because by the time of Julian and Gregory Rome's allegiance to the divine that had caused and guaranteed its greatness had recently shifted—from the gods of the Greeks and the Romans, as expressed by the Egyptians, Phoenicians, Gauls, or Hebrews, to the Trinity—the true philosopher's privileged access to the divine was of particularly vital importance. Only a true philosopher, whether as emperor or as an emperor's advisor, could achieve the purity necessary to comprehend the divine to the degree possible for humans. Only such a figure could mediate appropriately between the divine and the rest of mankind, and therefore only he, either as emperor, public official, or advisor to those in office, could guide all in the manner appropriate to guarantee Rome's continued well-being.[2] An increasing number of the elite men engaged in discussing the correct philosophical life, either as public officials or as advisors to public officials, including the emperor, were Christian: men better known as bishops (or presbyters and priests).[3] Thus, this is also a book about the role and function of the bishop in the later Roman Empire.

JULIAN THE EMPEROR AND GREGORY THE THEOLOGIAN

Two elite men are central to my argument, Flavius Claudius Iulianus, emperor from 361 to 363, the last scion of the second Flavian dynasty, who entered history as Julian the Apostate, and Gregory of Nazianzus, bishop of Constantinople from 380 to 381, better known by his honorific, the Theologian. I have chosen these men because they stand as paradigmatic for their generation and their time, and for the empire of the Romans (*hē archē tōn Rhōmaiōn*) after the Tetrarchs and before Theodosius I, a world in the process of adjusting to the shift in its religious affiliation. These men also stand as paradigmatic for the way in which modern scholars conceptualize and discuss this period: pagan versus Christian.[4]

Julian the Apostate is familiar to many. From the moment of his death, on a Persian battlefield, in 363, to today there has been hardly a year when he was not the subject of a written work in one genre or another.[5] As I have shown elsewhere, the extensive scholarly focus on his role as emperor and as pagan has made him into

---

2. Philosophers, a specific group among the elite, were considered by birth, education, and personal charisma particularly close to the divine, and because these men were able to elaborate what the divine intended an emperor to do, good emperors consulted them as advisors, as Dominic O'Meara has shown in *Platonopolis*. Hahn, *Philosoph*.

3. Rapp, *Holy Bishops*, 26, 44–45, shows that the sources rarely differentiate between priest and bishop.

4. By using two persons as a case study, my book belongs to a recent historiographic trend reinserting individual agency back into a more structural analysis.

5. Rosen's last chapter in *Julian* discusses Julian's reception in the West until the present. Julian's reception in the Byzantine and Russian East remains a desideratum (though Rosen mentions V. Mayakovsky).

an ambivalent figure.[6] Because he was an emperor, modern scholars of ancient history study him for the manner in which he governed, but because he was first Christian and then pagan, he was anomalous among Roman emperors of the fourth century, so that not even the manner in which he governed is seen as representative of later Roman imperial governance.[7] Though he may be attractive for ancient historians as emperor, Julian's religious affiliation makes him an outsider; he is studied as entirely sui generis. Not even his extensive writings, more than we possess of any other Roman emperor, have received the in-depth scholarly analysis one would expect, in part because they discuss topics often not considered the purview of modern ancient historians: that is, philosophy and religion. For most modern historians Julian the emperor is, thus, not a person representative of his status and time, while modern scholars of church history and even more so theology consider him, as emperor and pagan, of little relevance to the history of Christianity.

Gregory of Nazianzus also occupies an ambivalent position as object of much scholarly interest yet also an outsider, for different reasons. Born, in 329 or 330, into the Greek-speaking provincial elite, he became known, with Basil of Caesarea and Gregory of Nyssa, as one of the three Cappadocian Fathers of the Church. He was the principal architect of Neo-Nicene orthodoxy, and his formulation of the nature of the Trinity, "to preserve God as in essence one [*homoousios*] and to profess three persons [*hypostaseis*], each with its own characteristics," became the official expression of orthodoxy in the Nicene creed for generations.[8] Gregory's impact as a theological thinker was such that in 451 the council of Chalcedon honored him officially as "the Theologian," a title previously bestowed only on John the Evangelist. Scripture serves as a good barometer of Gregory's influence. Throughout the Byzantine realm, the scriptures were the only writings published more widely than those of Gregory, whose immense oeuvre soon became part of the school curriculum.[9] Gregory's impact is not limited to the Greek-speaking world of the Roman East and its successor, medieval Rus. His *Orations* formed part of Ambrose of Milan's library, were translated into Latin by Rufinus of Aquileia, read by Augustine, and taken to heart by Gregory the Great.[10] Not surprisingly, it was Gregory the Theologian who wrote Julian the emperor into Julian the Apostate.

Paradoxically, however, Gregory of Nazianzus's rhetorical mastery and his

---

6. S. Elm, "Hellenism."

7. See Schmidt-Hofner's excellent analysis of scholarly approaches to late Roman imperial governance, *Reagieren*, 80–102.

8. Gr. Naz. *Or.* 2.36.

9. Forty-four orations in all rhetorical genres, from *apologiae* to panegyrics; 249 letters; and about 19,000 lines of poetry in all meters.

10. S. Elm, "Hellenism," 493–94.

fluency as a theologian contributed to his marginal position in scholarly and historiographic traditions emerging out of the Latin West. Though Gregory holds a firm place among French, Italian, and German theologians and Patristic scholars (though slightly less so among church historians), he has until recently been relatively neglected in the English-speaking world, and often treated as an adjunct to the more widely known Basil of Caesarea.[11] Despite the current renaissance of scholarship concerning Gregory, the basic assumptions regarding him have changed less than one might imagine.[12] This Gregory is passionately devoted to withdrawal, retreat, and retirement, so much so that he was incapable of operating successfully in the real world. In Raymond van Dam's words, Gregory, "whom contemporaries and subsequent readers admired for the fluency of his theological treatises about the nature of the Trinity . . . , 'stuttered' as he remembered and recorded memories about himself."[13]

For most scholars, Gregory of Nazianzus was an abject ecclesiastical failure as reluctant priest and lackluster adjunct bishop to his father, the bishop of Nazianzus. After his ordination as bishop of Sasima he refused to assume his duties and disappeared for three years to Seleucia, emerging as the leader of the Nicene (that is, orthodox) congregation at Constantinople in 379. Less than a year later, the new emperor, Theodosius I, within three days of his arrival, made him bishop of the capital city. A mere nine months later, however, Gregory, while presiding over the first ecumenical council in 381, resigned and retired to his country estate, forced out by rival bishops from Alexandria and Antioch.[14] French and Italian scholars attribute such fits and starts to Gregory's sensitive soul as *romantique avant la lettre*. English scholars see an indecisive, pusillanimous, labile man.[15] As a consequence, scholars concerned with the role and function of the bishop in late antiquity rarely consider Gregory's writings for their purposes. Unlike, say, Basil of Caesarea, he is not seen as a representative of the office.

Such near-canonical characterizations of Gregory as gifted theologian but weak man and disastrous bishop piqued my curiosity. Would Theodosius I—the emperor,

---

11. McGuckin, *St. Gregory*; Holman, *The Hungry*; Van Dam, *Kingdom*; idem, *Families*; idem, *Becoming Christian*; Gautier, *Retraite*; Daley, *Gregory*, 1–61; Sterk, *Renouncing the World*, 119–40.

12. Lugaresi's and especially McLynn's important work on Gregory, now collected in *Christian Politics*, set a different agenda.

13. Van Dam, "Self-Representation," 140.

14. McLynn, "'*Genere Hispanus*'"; Villegas, *Gregorio*.

15. McGuckin, *St. Gregory*, 34. For Daley, *Gregory*, 2, Gregory is "oversensitive, self-pitying, demanding, dark in his views of humanity." Daley characterizes the contradictions in Gregory's self-presentation as those of "a pacific loner ill-suited to the conflicts of public administration" while active as bishop. Van Dam, *Families*, 6, 46, and 93, attributes Gregory's stuttering to his "image of himself primarily as a son," whose "one true love had always been his mother."

who by law mandated *katholikos* (universal) Christianity as the *religio* of all Romans at a time of high tension—have made bishop of Constantinople, the New Rome, a man so weak, insecure, and indecisive? Could a man who stuttered about his private life, overwhelmed by his desire for retreat and abhorrence of public office—and that is how he characterized himself in his writings—become and remain the foremost Christian authority for centuries? Gregory's pronouncements on what he did and did not consider orthodox gained him the bishop's see of Constantinople over and against intense competition from others poised to occupy that position, and his speeches on the topic informed Theodosius's imperial legislation on heresy.[16] What does that much influence on a ruling emperor by a soul so malleable, romantic, and entirely apolitical say about the relation of power and authority, the nature of orthodoxy and heresy in late antiquity? What does it tell us about the empire of the Romans and Christianity? Perhaps that it was no wonder that it declined and fell so speedily?[17]

GREGORY AND THE BISHOPS

If we are to assume that a Roman emperor selected his top personnel, how plausible is it that Theodosius chose as bishop of the New Rome such a loser, devoid of what one would call today a sense of political power?[18] My answer is that Gregory was no such man. This a priori assessment required a different perspective on Gregory's writings.[19] If his self-presentation—as a man caught between his desire to live the true philosophical life and his assumption of the very public office that ostensibly repelled him—did not prevent him from being called to the capital and gaining imperial attention and approval, then this true philosophical life must be investigated in a context other than that proposed by most scholars of Christianity.

16. McLynn, "Moments."
17. The topic has been injected with new vigor by Liebeschuetz, Ward Perkins, Heather, and others, reacting against scholarship that, in their view, overemphasizes continuity given the dramatic changes that affected Rome's West in the fourth and early fifth century. Though the Mediterranean world by 750 had undergone profound changes, the fourth-century East was transformed, and did not decline; Wickham, *Framing the Early Middle Ages*, 10–13.
18. The role of merit in late-antique imperial patronage networks and in the choice of high administrators remains debated: Kelly, *Ruling the Later Roman Empire*.
19. In what follows I use Gregory's writings primarily as edited in the Sources Chrétiennes series, based on Tomas Sinko's editorial principles. New editions may alter specifics of the texts. Gregory edited and revised his works in the 380s in Nazianzus. Contrary to McGuckin, and to Beeley, *Gregory*, I do not seek to identify what parts of the orations Gregory may have altered in the 380s; the manuscripts give no indications of his editorial hand. Daley, *Gregory*, 259–63, lists editions, ancient commentaries and *Lives*, and the most recent English translations. Unless otherwise specified, all translations in the following are mine.

For if, as scholars have argued, late-antique bishops professed a troubled, ambivalent relation to public power, bound to their cities and sees, but derived their true legitimacy from the spiritual authority gained in the monastic life, then why, like Gregory, were so many of these monk-bishops at or near the centers of power?[20] Did bishops—as most modern studies of the office of the bishop argue, critiqued in Claudia Rapp's seminal work *Holy Bishops in Late Antiquity*—become increasingly involved in nonreligious responsibilities and duties, which then had to be aligned with their spiritual and ascetic virtues as private persons, virtues considered to be the true source of their authority and derived from the New Testament?[21]

My first encounter with Gregory of Nazianzus's *Oration 2, On the Priesthood*, suggested different causal sequences.[22] The men who led the church both before and after Constantine derived their authority from their social position, as members of the provincial elites. Members of that group, made homogeneous through shared education, or *paideia*, were groomed for positions of power and authority: that is, for the activities Peter Norton described as "non-religious."[23] Rather than reconciling nonreligious functions with a prior (private) spiritual and ascetic dimension that had emerged out of the New Testament, Gregory's work suggests that elite men born to rule the empire integrated their understanding of scripture into the matrix of their world, which was shaped by the classic discourse of political power that formed the ideological, divinely authorized foundation of Rome's supremacy.[24]

As a consequence, such elite persons as Christian leaders—that is, bishops and presbyters—were at or near centers of power because they wished to be there. As

---

20. As Sterk shows in *Renouncing the World*, the figure of the monk-bishop is a later evolution. Most studies of the late Roman imperial court and its administration exclude bishops, despite Drake's *Constantine* and the work of T. D. Barnes, in particular his *Athanasius*; Schmidt-Hofner, *Reagieren*, 80–102.

21. Norton, *Episcopal Elections*, 8; Rapp, *Holy Bishops*, 3–22, criticizes scholars' separation of religious and secular in discussing episcopal leadership; at 24–33 she observes that a bishop's personal virtues, important before Constantine, remained so.

22. *Oration 2*, composed in 362/3, is the earliest theoretical reflection on the topic. Ps.–Maximus the Confessor's *loci communes* most frequently cite *Or.* 2, even though it does not belong to the so-called liturgical sequence that became the most widely circulated of Gregory's orations. For Beeley, *Gregory*, 237, *Or.* 2 is "the fountainhead of pastoral reflection in both Eastern and Western Christendom." It is required reading for aspiring Russian Orthodox priests; S. Elm, "Diagnostic Gaze," 86, 99; Maslov, "*Oikeiosis*," 38.

23. Norton, *Episcopal Elections*, 8. Brown's discussion of *paideia* in *Power and Persuasion* remains unsurpassed. For a detailed analysis of scholarly notions of private and public episcopal authority, Sessa, *Formation*.

24. Lizzi Testa, *Potere*, and Leyser, *Authority*, are foundational for the evolution of the role of the bishop.

the chapters that follow show, they were frequently on the move from see to see, eager to be as close as possible to the imperial court and those associated with it. The desire for such closeness shaped the lives of many of the late-antique bishops whom we know sufficiently well to grasp their movements and interests—those bishops who wrote or were written about (and hence belonged to the social elites)—even though their rhetoric persistently and pervasively extolled ascetic retreat and contemplation.[25]

Once we establish as the methodological starting point Gregory's role as a member of the provincial-Greek Roman elite on the make—and not as Gregory the Theologian, bishop, and saint—we see that his asceticism in fact establishes his authenticity and authority in the competition to outdo his peers and opponents, who also advocated a life of retreat and involvement. Both Gregory's peers and his principal audience were the local elite, including the new service aristocracy that was then spreading throughout the empire. These men became prosperous serving in the military or civilian imperial bureaucracy and increased their wealth by acquiring large landed estates and running them for profit. They helped fuel the economic growth and urban expansion of the East in the fourth century. These *novi homines*, "new men," many of whom sat in the new Constantinopolitan senate, were scions of the native municipal elites, like Gregory and his brother, Caesarius (one of Julian's physicians), or they took over the social roles previously held by the municipal elite to become the new ruling class. Most were Christian, and for their benefit Gregory formulated the Christian rules for public conduct and the affairs of the *politeia*.[26] In so doing, he also defined what it meant to be a bishop: to lead the true philosophical life of active involvement in the affairs of the *politeia* for the benefit of the *oikoumenē* of the Romans now Christian.

That Gregory managed to write himself into the capital, where he was noticed by the emperor's advisors and eventually by the emperor, means that he used all the

---

25. I use "elites" because most of the men I discuss did not belong to the aristocracy, a term more apt for Western senatorial families: Salzman, *Making of a Christian Aristocracy*; S. Elm, "Programmatic Life." Members of the clergy came from a variety of social strata, but the majority of those present in the historical record (including inscriptions) belonged to the elite, including the elite's lower end. Inscriptions show a degree of upward social mobility, but in the main the move was lateral: those who joined the clergy often acquired an ecclesiastic position—measured more by influence than as part of a *cursus honorum*—of a social status similar to what they already held, though some advanced higher as clerics than they otherwise might have. Here, the clergy parallels the upward mobility of other branches in the imperial administration. Geographic differences need to be taken into account. For Italy, Sotinel, "Recruitement"; for Asia Minor, S. Hübner, *Klerus*, an analysis based on a small sample of inscriptions; Haensch, "Römische Amtsinhaber"; idem, "Inscriptions"; idem, "Rolle."

26. Sarris, "Rehabilitating the Great Estate"; Banaji, *Agrarian Change*, 20–22; Heather, "New Men."

rhetorical means available to elite men of his time to attain prestige through his writings. His impact was so enormous not because he differed from his peers but because he was better than most at writing himself prestige.[27] What then to make of his statements of perpetual tension between his desire for contemplation and the loathsome duty to assume office and to act? When read in their immediate elite context rather than in a literary genealogy that connects them back to Origen, Clement, and Philo, Gregory's writings do not reveal the psyche of a troubled man torn between contemplative retreat and public office, and in conflict with his father.[28] Taking Gregory's highly praised rhetorical mastery seriously shows that in adopting that persona, Gregory evoked all the elite's notions of prized and shared stability as normative ideals, and fashioned himself a life that embodied and presented authority, even power, beyond what he was entitled to by birth: the true philosophical life. Gregory persuaded his audience with lasting effect. His concept of the true philosophical life is the blueprint of episcopal leadership for the orthodox bishop, suggesting that our modern conceptions of power and authority, specifically ecclesiastical power and authority, narrow unduly our perception of what ecclesiastical authority might have looked like then.[29]

JULIAN AND GREGORY IN CONTEXT

To arrive at such a reading of Gregory's writings required placing them and Gregory rigorously into the contemporary context and to write what I call a "microsocial history of ideas."[30] This context included men such as Themistius, Libanius, Eunomius, Aetius, Basil, Caesarius, Eustathius, and, last but not least, Gregory's father and men of his generation. The years when Gregory emerged on the scene as presbyter and advisor to his father, the bishop of Nazianzus, were, however, dominated by the figure of the emperor Julian. Yet, modern scholars have never brought

---

27. I have profited enormously from Sailor, *Writing*, 6–50.
28. Because this has been excellently done by others, I purposely do not emphasize Gregory's intertextual place in relation to Philo, Clement, Origen, and Gregory the Wonder-worker, nor do I compare him explicitly to Basil of Caesarea and Gregory of Nyssa. Though those authors undoubtedly influenced Gregory, this influence has dominated scholarly analysis to the exclusion of most else (e.g., Beeley, McGuckin, Spidlik, Plangieux).
29. See also S. Elm, "'Pierced by Bronze Needles,'" "Asket," "The Dog That Did Not Bark," and "Diagnostic Gaze."
30. Recent research demonstrates the degree to which episcopal authority is locally defined. Differences between the city of Rome and Italy, Alexandria and Egypt, Antioch and its hinterland are significant, as is the geographic origin, educational background, and social position of the officeholder, who created authority in accordance with his world, as Brown observed in *Authority*. Conversely, comparisons between, say, Paulinus of Nola and John Chrysostom highlight the shared cultural notions of *paideia*.

into dialogue the writings of Julian and of Gregory, divided by their prima facie historiographic identities as pagan Roman emperor and Christian theologian.

Both men belonged to the first generation born in a Roman Empire in which Christianity was legal, supported and even sponsored by the imperial court. Both were deeply engaged in the dynamic process of formulating the consequences of that recent shift in religious affiliation in theory and in practice, fully aware of the actions of their elders (such as the elder Gregory and the emperor Constantius), during whose lifetime Christianity had become legalized. Both understood that to formulate the meaning of being a Roman Greek and a Christian required what each despised in his opponents: innovation.[31] Both engaged in an intense search for the right words as consequential acts with the power to order their world and to restore to order what they thought had gone amiss.[32] Both men belonged to the governing elites of the Roman Empire, one the nephew of the emperor Constantine the Great, the other a scion of the first family of a provincial town on the route linking Constantinople and Antioch. One eventually became sole emperor; the other, bishop of Constantinople. Each held his position for a brief time, Julian twenty-two months and Gregory a mere nine; but the impact of both, especially on posterity, stands in inverse proportion to their short sojourns on the summits of their careers.

When Julian and Gregory are read together, the extent to which Gregory laid the foundations of his intellectual oeuvre in direct counterpoint to Julian's writings and actions becomes apparent. Nothing less than the vision of Rome—how the empire should be led—was at stake. That vision included good governance as the right way to deduce the divine through analysis of its mediation between its transcendent self and its material creation, the cosmos and man, to permit those in leadership positions to safeguard the *oikoumenē* of the Romans by guiding it back to the divine: that was the supreme duty of God's first slave, the emperor as philosopher and priest, and that of his philosopher-priests as advisors (bishops and presbyters, if the emperor was Christian).

Julian and Gregory both claimed to have been divinely chosen philosophers, endowed with the mandate to mediate between the divine and mankind for the common good and the salvation of all in their keep, the *oikoumenē* of the Romans. Both argued that their gods represented the true universality of Rome. To honor their gods in the right way was thus the only means for all to achieve salvation, and hence the sole guarantor of the *imperium* of the Romans. For one of them, the gods of the

---

31. Innovation (καινοτομία, lit. "cutting freshly into something") was fraught with tensions in a society as devoted to harmony, order, stability, and tradition as the Roman Empire. Though innovation could restore order and stability when correct, it more often caused disorder, instability, and civil war—and in such cases represented a misreading of the divine will, supremely expressed through order, stability, harmony, and unity.

32. Gregory uses καταρτίζειν, "to order" or "to restore" or "to form": LSJ s.v.

Greeks and the Romans embodied the correct mixture of both Greekness (*Hellēnismos*) and *Romanitas,* which had made Rome great and kept it that way; whereas for the other, the power of the Romans had grown together with belief in Christ. In the event, Gregory saw Julian's death as a clear sign of who was right. Yet, the differences between Julian and Gregory were small, though significant. Because Julian claimed, by imperial letter, that Christians had voluntarily abandoned the universality of Greek Rome for the limited and exclusionary God of the Galileans, Gregory was forced to refute the emperor on all counts. That refutation made Gregory into the Theologian, the Father of the Church. Thus God, in his inexplicable wisdom, made Julian too a Father of the Church.

Focusing on what unites rather than divides Julian the emperor and Gregory the Theologian reveals that the boundary between pagan and Christian was so porous that these terms lose their analytical value. Gregory, paradigmatic of his elite contemporaries, was not alone in wishing to influence those in power. Others, pagans as well as Christians, had the same wish. After all, when Constantine made Christianity legal, very little differentiated Christian intellectuals from their non-Christian intellectual neighbors; what separated them were nuances. Constantine's edict, however, made Christianity an option for the men who governed, and that changed the equation. As more elite intellectuals became Christian, they had to transform Christianity into a religion for rulers. Here, the shared heritage comes into play.

Arguments over who truly owned *logoi,* the heritage of Homer, Hesiod, Plato, Aristotle, and so on (that is, Hellenism), were central for Julian and Gregory as well as for all the others fighting over that vision as the paramount source of ascetic and spiritual authority, the primary font of the true philosophical life. This was the matrix to which scripture was added (by almost all participants) to formulate what became, through Gregory's writings, the intellectual foundation of the Byzantine world, including Nicene orthodoxy.[33] Because this was the common matrix, divisions and alliances formed over the right and wrong ways to apply, for example, Aristotelian language theory and logic rather than along pagan versus Christian lines. These right and wrong ways of using the technical apparatus of advanced *paideia* also, I argue, marked the difference between orthodox and heretical. Gregory thus used against (the heretic) Eunomius the very arguments that he had used to cast the deceased emperor as the Apostate: neither Julian nor Eunomius comprehended grammar and rhetoric—never mind Aristotelian logic—the right way.

---

33. Greek Christians thus did not conquer, adopt, or appropriate *logoi* and *paideia* (that is, Hellenism or pagan culture), because one does not adopt, conquer, or appropriate what one possesses by birth, education, and divine design. Averil Cameron's desiderata in *Christianity and the Rhetoric of Empire,* 120–41, remain, calling for different scholarly approaches to discuss the relation of Christian author to classical culture. Kaldellis, *Hellenism.*

Closeness to Julian, or to Constantius, and then later on to Jovian, Procopius, and Valens, was not primarily a matter of religious affiliation either, for all these emperors sponsored Eunomius, and especially Caesarius, Gregory's brother and one of Julian's physicians, and like Themistius, a successful new man. The degree to which those engaged in these arguments presented their expertise, how much they persuaded their peers and managed to write themselves close to the emperors and their advisors, in turn, determined who and therefore what would be considered right (orthodox) teaching. The emperor and his advisors determined what Christian doctrinal formulation (or what form of paganism, in Julian's case) won at any given moment, and the thinking of the emperor and his advisors changed. Emperors reacted to what their advisors declared were correct deductions of the divine and its will, and their reaction, often expressed in edicts, affirmed the selected pronouncement as right (*orthos*).

Placing Gregory and Julian into their shared context therefore required a tightened focus and, at the same time, an opening of the perspective. Thus, what follows is about Julian as much as it is about Gregory (albeit Julian as seen from Gregory's perspective). I present a close reading of Julian's writings and of those Gregory composed during and immediately after the emperor's reign, his first six orations, to show how these writings were in dialogue.[34] Gregory formulated his theological writings in direct response to the writings and actions of Julian, engaging in the process not only Julian and his friends and advisors, high-ranking public officials as philosophers and rhetoricians, including the Christian Eunomius, but also those against whom Julian set himself, most important among them Constantius and his (pagan) philosopher Themistius.[35] All these men engaged the earlier debates about the correct interpretation of the divine will (in part known as Christological debates) that were reflected in the writings of Porphyry, Iamblichus, Eusebius of Caesarea, and others. All used the same methods—those of *paideia*, the normative foundation of Greek Rome's supremacy, as epitomized in the writings of Homer, Plato, Aristotle, Demosthenes, Dio Chrysostom, and the scriptures—to achieve excellence and to claim a level playing field, even with emperors, and to define their own positions over and against their friends' and competitors'.[36]

Bringing together these two men and their writings dramatically crystallized scholarly approaches to pagan Rome and its Christian successor. Scholars writing

---

34. I do not argue that Julian responded to Gregory directly. I do argue, however, that the emperor was familiar with current theological debates and those associated with them, and that he intervened in these debates. Gregory, in turn, need not have read the emperor's works; he knew them well enough to construct his Julian.

35. Gregory's political, philosophical, and theological writings are one and the same.

36. Because I foreground Gregory's relation to his contemporaries and their shared classical matrix, I highlight scriptural passages in his work only as required by the context.

on Julian do not read Gregory's writings—as a Christian theologian and a failed bishop he is assumed to have little to say about how later Roman emperors ruled and managed their courts. Julian's philosophical works have received far less attention than one would expect given the enormous scholarly interest in him. Nevertheless, it is here that the emperor theorized the implications of his role as the philosopher, priest, and emperor: how he should lead the true philosophical life that would enable him to lead the realm as mandated by the gods.[37] Similarly, though Gregory of Nazianzus continues to receive a great deal of attention from theologians, and increasingly also from church historians and historians interested in the social history of the later Roman Empire, they do not consider relevant the life and work of Julian, the apostate emperor. This attitude reflects a general (though diminishing) tendency to limit the impact of classical philosophy and rhetoric on Gregory to questions of form rather than content, ignoring Julian's potential effect on the contours of Gregory's evolving concepts, philosophical, theological, and nonreligious. Social and church historians know of Julian's impact on Gregory's life but are unaware of his effect on Gregory's theology, perhaps for reasons similar to those that keep historians from considering Julian's philosophical writings.[38] Yet, both men shared far more than divided them, even if their small differences were at the same time highly significant.

Bringing Julian and Gregory into close dialogue has, I hope, accented another key point. Although I have attempted to decipher and present the debated themes and concepts as codes rich with intertextual allusions, notions of decorum, and the subtleties of social stratification, I know that I have missed a great deal. I might be able to point back to Plato, Aristotle, Dio Chrysostom, and other authors of the Second Sophistic, or to imperial notions of the Tetrarchs, even to Trajan, Aurelian, and Augustus, for some of the ideas, themes, and messages in play, but I have often felt tone-deaf among the ancient persons who were able not only to differentiate between, say, Bach and Chopin, but to point to the conductor, soloists, and recording date; I imagine that *paideia* functioned that way, so that it was enough to hear a bar to identify a work, its composer, and all the nuances that distinguish the interpreters. In my translation, above all of Gregory's work, I therefore took pains to stress his classical heritage: that is, I consciously sought to retranslate him from a Christian saint back into a classical philosopher, by translating key words that both he and Julian use the same way. For example, I render *to koinon* or *ta koina* as "realm" or "commonwealth," and not, when Gregory uses it, as "congregation." That way (and

---

37. Modern scholars of philosophy largely disregard Julian's philosophical writings as neither innovative nor systematic.

38. Even Demoen, in *Pagan and Biblical Exempla*, argues that Gregory's formation in *paideia* offered him only formal material that did not affect the content of his theology.

by citing a fair amount of Greek technical terminology) I hope to underscore the enormous sophistication with which all these men (pagan, Christian, orthodox, heretical) used the *instrumentarium* of *paideia* to make their points, some subtle and others less so.[39] As a side effect I hope to remove Constantius, Julian, Gregory, Eunomius, Themistius, Libanius, and others from their corsets—heretical Arian Christian emperor; idiosyncratic pagan revivalist emperor; sensitive apolitical Christian ascetic and monk theologian; heretic; pagan philosopher; and rhetorician—and bring them to life as persons entirely of their own time, improvising on a common theme.

39. Critical commentaries on Gregory's orations, such as those on *Orations* 4 and 5 by Kurmann in *Gregor* and by Lugaresi in Gregory of Nazianzus, *Contro Giuliano* and *Morte,* remain desiderata.

PART ONE

1
Nazianzus and the Eastern Empire, 330–361

"I have been beaten, and I recognize my defeat: I have surrendered to the Lord and have come to supplicate him" (Gr. Naz. *Or.* 2.1).[1] With these words Gregory the Younger of Nazianzus begins his second oration, delivered probably on Easter 363 and circulated soon thereafter. This oration represents the earliest systematic treatment of the Christian priesthood propagated by a member of the Greek-speaking Roman elite.[2] Gregory's treatise on the nature of Christian leadership had a profound and lasting impact, for example on John Chrysostom, another member of that elite and bishop of Constantinople. Chrysostom's work on the priesthood, based on Gregory's, then influenced another bishop in an imperial residence, Ambrose of Milan, through whom it gained purchase in the West. Rufinus's Latin translation of Gregory's oration influenced Western writers directly, including Augustine and Jerome, who had heard Gregory speak in Constantinople, as well as Paulinus of Nola and Julian of Eclanum. Gregory the Great's work on the priesthood also reflects his acquaintance with Gregory of Nazianzus's, gained either during the former's stay in Constantinople or through Rufinus's translation. In sum, Gregory's *Oration* 2,

---

1. Ἥττημαι καὶ τὴν ἧτταν ὁμολογῶ· ὑπετάγην τῷ Κυρίῳ καὶ ἱκέτευσα αὐτόν (*Grégoire de Nazianze: Discours 1–3*, ed. and trans. Bernardi). This oration is best known under the somewhat misleading title *Apology for His Flight*, a later addition of the manuscripts: *Grégoire de Nazianze: Discours 1–3*, ed. and trans. Bernardi, 84 n. 1.

2. Gr. Naz. *Epp.* 7 and 8. Mossay, "Date," suggests 364. I am following Gautier, *Retraite*, 292–317. McGuckin, *St. Gregory*, 101–2, dates the ordination itself to Christmas 361, and *Or.* 2 to Easter; *Grégoire de Nazianze: Discours 1–3*, ed. and trans. Bernardi, 11–17. For a detailed discussion, see below, Chapter 5.

On the Priesthood, became immensely influential in the East and permeated the Western tradition. But in 363 this was all in the future.[3]

When Gregory spoke the opening words (or words very similar to those he chose to preserve for posterity), he had just returned to his ancestral city of Nazianzus from a sojourn at Annesi, a small village in Pontus where the family of his friend Basil, later bishop of Caesarea, owned an estate.[4] Ostensibly, his departure and return are the key themes of the second oration. Given its length, however—117 chapters—we can surmise that Gregory's reasons for leaving and coming back were complex. Indeed, they range from his own affairs to those of the *oikoumenē* of the Romans and to the very cosmos and its genesis. All these reasons, personal, local, and the global and cosmic, were seamlessly intertwined in *Oration* 2, the principal focus of Part II of this book. But not only in *Oration* 2. Gregory in all his writings from the early 360s—that is, his first six orations—formed a densely woven tapestry that included the same elements, from the personal to the cosmological. These orations were composed like an instrument with many different strings (to use his own intertextual metaphor), each one activated at appropriate moments but all sounding together in harmony as a comprehensive whole. As such these six orations contain the nucleus of Gregory's interpretation of the nature of the divine; its relation to the sensible, material world; and the consequences of that relation for humans seeking to guide others toward the divine. In these orations Gregory delineates which persons had been divinely entrusted to lead mankind and how they ought to comport themselves to approach the divine so that they could lead others to it. In short, these orations are the foundational work that made Gregory "the Theologian."

Gregory formulated most of these concepts in Nazianzus, and they were in the first instance intended for a local audience. But Nazianzus was not an island. Gregory's thoughts and positions engaged some of the most intense debates then gripping men of the Greek-speaking elites of the Eastern Roman Empire and reverberating among their Western contemporaries. These debates revolved around the nature of the divine and its interaction with the material world and humanity, crystallized in the way in which the divine was thought to speak to humans. How the divine and these interactions were understood affected the qualities considered nec-

---

3. John Chrysostom, *Sur le sacerdoce*, ed. and trans. Malingrey. John Chrysostom's treatise was one of the models for Ambrose's *De officiis*; Cicero another. Ruf. *Orationes*, CSEL 46.1; Moreschini, "Rufino," 228–30, and E. A. Clark, *Origenist Controversy*, 137–51 and 159–93 for the translations of Gregory's *Orations* 166 and 167; Julian of Eclanum may have read the copy owned by Melania the Elder, or by Melania the Younger. Jer. *De vir. ill.* 117; *Ep.* 50.1; *In Isaiam* 3. Markus, "Gregory."

4. Today's Sonusa or Uluköy, near the confluence of the Yeçil Irmak (Iris) and the Kelkit Çayi (Lycos); S. Elm, *Virgins*, 63, 78–81; Rousseau, *Basil*, 62 n. 7.

essary to lead the *oikoumenē* and its inhabitants to salvation. To understand Gregory's second oration and its impact we need to know first what the state of the debate was in the late 350s and early 360s. Who were Gregory's contemporaries, and what were they debating in the 360s? How had these debates evolved in the preceding decade, and why did they matter? And who was Gregory of Nazianzus?

NAZIANZUS AND GREGORY: THE PERSONAL AND THE LOCAL

"I, Diocaesarea, am a small town." Gregory's description, placed rhetorically into the mouth of his native city, was certainly accurate.[5] Diocaesarea, Nazianzus in the native tongue, was a small town. In western Cappadocia, however, a small town was not necessarily insignificant. Diocaesarea, like Caesarea, Tyana, and Archelaïs, actually had municipal or city status, in a region exceptional for its lack of such cities.[6] Diocaesarea-Nazianzus's territory, the Tiberine, was considerable. It included Venasa, some fifty kilometers to the north; Karbala, about ten kilometers south; and Sasima, twenty-five kilometers east.[7] Furthermore, it was located on one of the major west-east routes of the empire, linking the imperial residences Constantinople and Antioch, a route Ammianus described as the *usus itineribus solitis*.[8] It passed from Antioch to Issus, Mopsuestia, and Tarsus, and then crossed the mountains at the Cilician Gates to descend to Tyana, passing via Sasima and Nazianzus to Ancyra and then Constantinople. In fact, the only mention of Nazianzus prior to Gregory's occurred in two itineraries designating it in Latin either as a "mansio Anathiango" or as Nandianulus.[9] Nazianzus was (or, rather, parts of it were) indeed a *mansio* (Greek *monē*) or *stathmos*, a posting station between Archelaïs (Civitas Colonia)

---

5. Gr. Naz. *Epigr.* 135 (*Greek Anthology*, ed. Paton, vol. 2, 459); *Epp.* 141, 142, To Olympius (*Saint Grégoire de Nazianze: Lettres*, ed. Gallay, vol. 2, 30–33), were written in response to the threatened loss of Diocaesarea's city status; see Gr. Naz. *Or.* 17, *Or.* 19.11, *Carmen* 2.1.19.25–26.

6. That Diocaesarea and Nazianzus are the same city is not universally accepted; Talbert, ed., *Barrington Atlas*, considers them two different cities. Gallay, *Vie*, 12–16; Le Nain de Tillemont, *Mémoires*, vol. 9, 309, 692; Mitchell, *Anatolia*, vol. 1, 97–98, notes the scarcity of cities in western Cappadocia. He, too (at vol. 2, 66), locates Diocaesarea at some distance from Nazianzus. Mossay, "Nazianze," and Van Dam, *Kingdom*, 31, identify the two as one.

7. For the extent of the territory, Hild and Restle, *Kappadokien*, 150–51 (Arianzus), 171–72 (Doara), 200–201 (Karbala), 302 (Venasa).

8. Amm. Marc. 22.9.14. Hild and Hellenkemper, *Kilikien*, 131–33; den Boeft, Drijvers, et al., eds., *Philological and Historical Commentary on Ammianus Marcellinus 22*, 173, 176.

9. Philost. *HE* 8.11. Nazianzus first appeared as "Nandianulus" in the late third-century *Antonine Itinerary*, and as "mansio Anathiango" (i.e., *ab Nathiango*) in the *Bordeaux Itinerary*, dating from 333 C.E.: Cuntz, ed., *Itineraria*, 20, 93. McLynn, "Gregory the Peacemaker," 192; Douglass's thesis in "A New Look," that the itinerary was written by a woman, has not yet been accepted.

and the next *mansio* on the main highway between Constantinople and Antioch, the said Sasima, twenty-four Roman miles distant.[10]

As a *mansio*, Nazianzus was equipped with inns offering "meals and sleeping quarters; [a] change of clothing for the drivers and postilions; [a] change of animals [stabling as many as forty horses, mules, or both], carriages, and drivers . . . ; grooms . . . ; escorts for bringing back vehicles and teams to the previous station . . . ; porters . . . ; veterinarians . . . [and] cartwrights."[11] *Mansiones* had to accommodate ordinary travelers passing through, all those who held permission to use the *cursus publicus*, and the large imperial traveling parties.[12] Numerous inscriptions and literary sources attest to the effort and personnel an emperor required as he moved across his realm. During the late 350s and the early 360s, imperial travel between Constantinople and Antioch was especially frequent, because Antioch was the traditional staging place for Persian campaigns, and the size of the entourage only increased when the emperor was en route to a military campaign.[13]

Thus, while neither a Caesarea nor an Archelaïs, Nazianzus was no isolated hamlet. A *polis* with a *mansio* on a major route traversed by the imperial court, numerous public officials, and other men of letters, Nazianzus had regular contact with the wider world.[14] Although Gregory had reason to refer to Nazianzus-Diocaesarea as insignificant, such a characterization was also a well-known rhetorical topos. Authors who considered themselves members of a well-established provincial elite expressed pride in their ancestral cities in rhetorical formulations that, paradoxically, stressed their very insignificance. Thus Plutarch, Aelius Aristides, and Galen, like Gregory, frequently evoked the smallness of their native cities.[15] The artfully constructed context, however, leaves no doubt that these writers, Gregory included,

---

10. The Greek, μονή, appeared around 215 in conjunction with Caracalla's journeys and repeatedly in relation to Diocletian's visit to Egypt in 298: Skeat, ed., *Papyri*, 28, 34, no. 1, ll. 223, 262, 263; Ath. V. *Anton.* 86.

11. Casson, *Travel*, 185.

12. Permission to use the *cursus* was a privilege reserved for members of the army and the imperial administration that could be extended to the well-connected. It included amenities such as beasts for transport and the option to rest in a *mansio*. For Julian's reform of the *cursus publicus*, A. Kolb, "Kaiser"; Hyland, *Equus*, 252, 261; Matthews, *Roman Empire*, 253–54.

13. Di Paola, *Viaggi*, esp. 41–60 for the *praepositura mansionum*; Halfmann, *Itinera*, esp. 65–89; Millar, *Emperor*, 31–40; Ando, *Imperial Ideology*, 190–93.

14. Van Dam, *Kingdom*, 97–115, discusses emperors in Cappadocia. For the movement of poets through the later empire, see Alan Cameron, "Wandering Poets."

15. Plu. *Dem.* 1 and 2 on Chaeronea, in *Plutarch's Lives*, ed. and trans. Perrin, vol. 7, 2–6; Aelius Aristides provides numerous examples. Though born at Hadrianoi in Mysia, both Aelius and his father were granted citizenship at Smyrna. The unifying theme is the tension between citizenship in one's native polis and spatial and social mobility, in this case to Rome. Men. Rh. *Treatise* 1.2 (*Peri epideiktikōn*, ed. Spengel, 344–51) discusses how to praise a country and a city: *Menander Rhetor*, ed. and trans. Russell and Wilson; Swain, *Hellenism*, 65–79, 83–100; Nutton, "Galen"; Rizzi, "Cittadinanza." For Gregory's

intended to contrast the insignificance of the city with the importance of the author who hailed from it and whose praise would immeasurably augment its prestige.[16]

Indeed, Gregory expressed civic pride through such literary topoi naturally. His family belonged to Cappadocia's landholding elite, and his father had been one of the most prominent citizens (a *principalis* or leading *curialis*) of Nazianzus, a rank to which his son could also lay claim.[17] Born around 329 or 330, most likely at Arianzus, one of his family's estates at Karbala located in the hills about ten kilometers south of Nazianzus, Gregory was the older son of Gregory the Elder and his wife Nonna's three children, Gorgonia, Gregory, and Caesarius.[18] Arianzus was also where he spent the years of his retirement after Constantinople.[19] This and the family's other estates contained vineyards, orchards, and flowering fields, and were pleasant and fertile despite occasional severe droughts.[20]

Caesarea and Athens

To this Nazianzus Gregory returned in 363. It was not his first return. In 358 or 359 he had come home after nearly a decade spent in Athens in pursuit of higher education. Athens had not been the first stop on his educational journey. Gregory and his younger brother, Caesarius, like most of their social peers, were first trained in grammar at home by a *paidagōgos*, Carterius, who also accompanied the brothers to the provincial capital, Caesarea, for further training in grammar and rhetoric, probably during the year 345/6.[21] About a year later they proceeded to Caesarea Maritima, in Palestine. This city housed the remarkable library of Origen, continued by Pamphilus and Eusebius. John McGuckin proposed even that Gregory and

---

indebtedness to the intellectual milieu of the Second Sophistic, Demoen, *Pagan and Biblical Exempla*, 21; Ruether, *Gregory*, 18.

16. When Diocaesarea-Nazianzus's city status was under threat in the 380s, Gregory used the opposite approach to emphasize that his city had been "founded by kings, safeguarded through time, and preserved by generations [and was] an ancient and venerable city that had made its mark on history": Gr. Naz. *Epp.* 141, 142; Kopecek, "Cappadocian Fathers."

17. Gr. Naz. *Ep.* 141.7. Eventually, the elder Gregory became one of the ἀξιωματικοί: McLynn, "*Curiales.*" See also Gautier, *Retraite*, 257–58.

18. The date of his birth is not entirely certain, but most scholars opt for 325 or, more likely, 329/30: *Gregory of Nazianzus: Autobiographical Poems*, ed. and trans. White, xii–xiii; Gregory of Nazianzus, *Faith*, intro. Norris, 1; *Grégoire de Nazianze: Discours 1–3*, ed. and trans. Bernardi, 9.

19. Gr. Naz. *Ep.* 203; *Ep.* 123 and his testament, *PG* 37.92A; Gallay, *Vie*, 16–17; Coulie, *Richesses*, 14–17, lists the other estates that Gregory owned by the 380s. The debate is ongoing whether Arianzus is an estate within which Karbala is located, or whether Karbala is the name of the estate located near Arianzus, as Daley, *Gregory*, 3, and Talbert, ed., *Barrington Atlas*, suggest. Hild and Restle, *Kappadokien*, 150–51; Szymusiak, "Sites."

20. Gr. Naz. *Ep.* 57, *Epigr.* 30, *Or.* 16, *Carm.* 2.1.1.143–64, 2.1.44.2–4, 13–17; Gallay, *Vie*, 17.

21. Gr. Naz. *Epigr.* 142–46; not identical with the father of Philostorgius (*HE* 9.9), born around 368. Gregory's Carterius died ca. 374. For the role of the *paidagōgos*, Cribiore, *Gymnastics*, 47–49, 160–76.

his brother were sent there because it "was the closest thing in the fourth century to a Christian university town."[22]

Indeed, Gregory's stay at Caesarea in Palestine marks a decisive period in modern scholarly accounts of his Christianization. Because of the city's excellent Christian library dating back to Origen, scholars have assumed that Gregory received here his first profound introduction to Origen's thought and method as well as to the theological debates then surrounding them, and that the decisive influence of Origen on his later thought began with his sojourn in Caesarea. Scholars support this assumption by pointing to the so-called *Philocalia,* excerpts of Origen's writings that Gregory supposedly made together with Basil in the late 350s or early 360s.[23] While Gregory probably had contact with the library and its Christian milieu, his scant remarks on his time in Caesarea praise only his pagan teacher Thespesius. Even though Gregory calls him a grammarian, Thespesius was a well-known rhetorician in the tradition of the Second Sophistic, who also counted among his students a certain Euzoius, who would renovate Eusebius's library after he had succeeded Acacius as bishop of the city.[24] Gregory's praise of Thespesius and Libanius's complaint that Caesarea's reputation as a center of rhetorical education rivaled Antioch's suggest that this excellent education exercised at least as much pull as Origen's library (which Gregory does not mention). Still, Gregory may have purchased the excerpts of Origin's writings later known as the *Philocalia* while he was at Caesarea.

---

22. McGuckin, *St. Gregory,* 36–44 (quotation 36). For the library, Carriker, *Library.*

23. Most scholars consider the *Philocalia* "a *vade mecum* of useful texts, to offer in response to different inquiries" (Rousseau, *Basil,* 84), "devoted to making available the central texts of a tradition, in a form that could be consulted quickly, prior to or even during some dialogue or confrontation" (Beeley, *Gregory,* 10) that Gregory and Basil had excerpted from Origen's writings while they were together in Cappadocia, either at Annesi or later in Caesarea; McGuckin, *St. Gregory,* 102–4; Gautier, *Retraite,* 289. There is, however, no consensus. In *Ep.* 115 Gregory says that he presented the *Philocalia,* "extracts of things useful for *philologoi,*" in the early 380s to a certain Theodore as a present and a souvenir of Basil. Already Junod ("Basile" and "Particularités") questioned whether Basil and Gregory actually made these extracts themselves. As the most recent editors, Harl (Origen, *Philocalie 1—20*) and Junod (Origen, *Philocalie 21—27*), point out, Gregory nowhere stated that he made them, and they suggest instead that he acquired ready-made excerpts of Origen's writings while in Caesarea (Origen, *Philocalie 1-20,* ed. Harl, 1–32). McLynn ("What Was the *Philocalia?*") argues convincingly that content and arrangement of the collection points indeed to set excerpts made in-house in the library at Caesarea, perhaps by members of Eusebius's staff, and intended for sale to interested parties (in transit) who had no direct access to Origen's corpus. Gregory's copy of the *Philocalia,* though evidently used by him and Basil, would then have been purchased while he was at Caesarea rather than excerpted from the twenty-two works of Origen that the traditional interpretation presupposed as in his or Basil's possession (or at least easily accessible), or both, at Annesi. McLynn, "Disciplines," 37–40.

24. Gr. Naz. *Or.* 7.6 (*Grégoire de Nazianze: Discours 6–12,* ed. and trans. Calvet-Sébasti); and Gr. Naz. *Epitaphion* 4, *PG* 38.12, *For Thespesius.* For Thespesius and Euzoius Jer. *De vir. ill.* 113, *PL* 23.707A; Gallay, *Vie,* 33. Kaster, *Guardians,* 435. McGuckin, *St. Gregory,* 41–43, discusses why Gregory called him a grammarian. See Lib. *Or.* 31.42 for Caesarea's increasing competitiveness.

But it is important to keep in mind that assumptions about Gregory's immersion in an Origenist milieu at that time, however tempting they may be in explaining his education as Christian, are unverified, notwithstanding Origen's notable influence on Gregory's later oeuvre.[25] After about a year in Caesarea, toward the end of 348, Gregory and Caesarius moved on to Alexandria. Here, the brothers parted ways, Caesarius remaining in Alexandria to study medicine, and Gregory proceeding to Athens, evidently without having met either Didymus the Blind or Athanasius in Alexandria (i.e., again having established no demonstrable connections to the local Christian circles).[26]

Gregory arrived in Athens in 348 or 349 and remained there for nearly a decade. He did not fail to record in his later writings the imprint of Athens on his formation, though he said little or nothing of that of either Caesarea in Palestine or Alexandria. "O Athens, the glory of Greece; O Athens, the golden city of learning!" With these words he celebrated his own and Basil's time in Athens many years later in his eulogy for the deceased bishop of Caesarea.[27] As Samuel Rubenson has noted, Gregory's evocation of that city "is the longest extant passage on contemporary Athens in the entire literature of the Patristic period," and certainly not by accident.[28] Gregory left no doubt that he enjoyed his stay at Athens thoroughly and that he embraced and was prepared to defend the "passionate love of letters" that he had deepened in "the golden city of learning."[29] Among those who fostered his passion were the rhetoricians Himerius, as Socrates and Sozomen tell us, and Prohaeresius, as Gregory himself confirms in a later epigram.[30] Himerius, who came from Prusias, in Bithynia, was so famous for his harmoniously poetic style as to be compared to Aelius Aristides. The Armenian Prohaeresius, who had spent time in Cappadocian Caesarea prior to coming to Athens, was famous for his extemporaneous speeches and renowned as a mentor. He was a Christian and as such an exception in Athens and among Gregory's teachers. A certain Priscus, a disciple of Iamblichus, also lectured there at that time, and Gregory may have heard him too.[31] Although

---

25. Beeley, *Gregory*, 271–73. Origen's impact on Gregory requires further study.

26. McGuckin, *St. Gregory*, 44–48, makes evocative suggestions about whom Gregory may have met during that period, how they may have influenced his Christian evolution, and what his Christian mother may have thought about this education; Daley, *Gregory*, 4–5.

27. Gr. Naz. *Or.* 43.14.

28. Rubenson, "Cappadocians," 113. Rubenson notes that Gregory refers to Athens thirty-eight times, of which thirty refer to the contemporary rather than the classical city. For the shape of post-Herulian Athens, Frantz, *Athenian Agora*, 12–48; Watts, *City*, 24–78.

29. Gr. Naz. *DVS* 112–13, 211; *Or.* 43.14.

30. Gr. Naz. *Epit.* 5, *PG* 38.13; Socr. *HE* 4.26.6 and Soz. *HE* 6.17.1 extol both as Basil and Gregory's teachers: Sozomen, *Kirchengeschichte*, ed. Bidez and Hansen.

31. Eun. *VS* 484–85 (*Philostratus and Eunapius*, ed. and trans. Wright); Himerius, *Man*, ed. and trans. Penella, 1–16, for Himerius's life. Born in 276, and thus almost a generation older than Himerius, Pro-

Gregory heaped lavish praise on Athens as a center of learning, he was, again, rather reticent about his Christian formation there. A single reference to "our sacred buildings" asserts a preference for these rather than the teachers outside (Gr. Naz. Or. 43.21). Things Christian were not on Gregory's mind when he recalled his time at Athens, except for the preternaturally mature Basil (Or. 43.23).[32] Basil arrived in Athens a few years after Gregory. The two men may have already known each other from Caesarea in Cappadocia, or they may have met in Athens as Cappadocians tending toward companions and teachers with connections to Cappadocia or at least Asia Minor. In any event, in Athens the two became "all in all" to each other, one soul in two bodies, sharing room, table, and all their days and nights (Or. 43.19).[33]

In Athens both men also made a momentous decision: to cultivate excellence or virtue (*aretē*) with a twist. "Philosophy was the object of our zeal," as Gregory would later say (Or. 43.19–20), though exactly what he meant by that will occupy us for much of the subsequent chapters. For now it suffices to note Gregory's recollection that he and Basil had already in Athens attempted to combine the goal of philosophy with a Christian formation, basing their attempt solely on the scriptures and each other as inspiration and "measuring rod" (Gr. Naz. Or. 43.17–22). To have at hand a collection of excerpts from Origen's writings on questions such as the nature of free will and "the divine inspiration of the divine scripture, and how it is to be read and understood; and what is the reason for the obscurity in it, and for what is impossible in some cases when it is taken literally, or what is unreasonable," may well have been of great value in this endeavor, which would further support Neil McLynn's suggestion that Gregory had purchased such a collection at Caesarea.[34] As he points out, the *Philocalia,* which throughout suggests an individual ap-

---

haeresius had spent time in Antioch and perhaps in Caesarea in Cappadocia before coming to Athens. (The *Suda,* II 2375, suggests that Prohaeresius was from Caesarea, but that may merely reflect his connection to the Cappadocians, or the fact that his teacher Julianus was from Caesarea.) Penella, *Greek Philosophers,* 79–94, 97–100; Watts, *City,* 48–78. T. D. Barnes, "Himerius," 209, addresses the difficulty of dating Himerius; Goulet, "Prohérésius"; Gregory of Nazianus, *Faith,* intro. Norris, 3–5; Gallay, *Vie,* 31–37.

32. McGuckin, *St. Gregory,* 47–83, provides an excellent picture of Gregory's stay at Athens, but I cannot find evidence for his claim that there was a thriving ascetically minded Christian community under the leadership of Prohaeresius. McGuckin dates Gregory's baptism just prior to his time in Athens, thus providing a Christian basis for his time there; Daley, *Gregory,* 6; Rubenson, "Cappadocians," 114.

33. For the erotic aspect of Gregory's description, Børtnes, "Eros."

34. The quotation continues "From Volume IV of *On Principles* and Various Other Works of Origen," the heading that introduces the first part of the *Philocalia* (Origen, *Philocalie 1–20,* ed. and trans. Harl, 182). The manuscript tradition suggests that these *kephalaia* go back to the original version handed to Theodore and may thus be Gregory and Basil's: Origen, *Philocalie 1–20,* ed. and trans. Harl, 24–31; Junod, "Particularités," 186–89.

proaching the divine writings without reference to institutional settings such as a teacher or a community, would have been ideal for such enterprising students as Gregory and Basil.[35]

Gregory and Basil were not alone in these experiments. Gregory's connections to men such as Sophronius, eventually a magistrate (*magister officiorum*) at the court of Valens in Antioch and then prefect of Constantinople; Eustochius, a future professional rhetor at Caesarea; Hellenius, eventually equalizing the taxes at Nazianzus (as *peraequator*); Julian, another tax assessor responsible for Nazianzus and perhaps also *praeses*, or governor, of Phrygia; and Philagrius, a fellow student of Caesarius, all date back to his student days.[36] These friendships were forged, according to Gregory's later reminiscences, in an atmosphere of intense rivalry and correspondingly tight-knit groups of like-minded students, a brotherhood based on common geographic origin and further enhanced by allegiance to specific teachers, often with the same regional background, who "initiated" their flock to the Muses (*Or.* 43.22).[37] Rivalries between such brotherhoods involved public displays of individual *aretē*, which was understood as the capacity to endure blows, to devise appropriate rhetoric to accompany such skirmishes, and to maintain face on all occasions. For those who trained in Athens, such public displays gained from the opportunity there to reenact the famous bouts of a Demosthenes or Callimachus at the very site— a heady experience, no doubt, even for someone like Gregory, who had learned, as he later claimed (in the process of establishing once and for all his superiority while verbally beating his opponents to the ground), to sublimate his competitive streak through his desire for the philosophical life (*Or.* 43.20).[38] Competition in public and between close friends such as Gregory and Basil was an essential feature of rhetorical training; after all, those who received such an education had to learn how

---

35. McLynn ("What Was the *Philocalia?*") lists one reference to a bishop and four vague references to a church.

36. His connection with some friends dates back to Caesarea in Cappadocia: Gr. Naz. *Epp.* 26–27, 98, 192. His acquaintance with Stagirius, a rhetorician at Caesarea, dates to a later period: *Ep.* 188. Hauser-Meury, *Prosopographie*, s.vv.; Van Dam, *Families*, 140–42, 146–48; idem, *Kingdom*, 88–92. It is not clear whether Julian the *peraequator* and Julian the governor of Phrygia are the same: *PLRE*, vol. 1, 471–72, Iulianus 14, Iulianus 17. Van Dam, *Kingdom*, 225 n. 26, considers them two different people.

37. Himerius frequently exhibited the characteristic pride of his native city and addressed Prusian students as fellow citizens; he also dedicated orations to students from a common regional background: for example, *Or.* 18 to his Cappadocian students. Himerius is a good example of a teacher who took initiation to the Muses and its attendant responsibilities very seriously: e.g., *Or.* 69.7–9. McLynn, "Disciplines," 32–37; Himerius, *Man*, ed. and trans. Penella, 1–2 and especially 66–113. For the importance of nonnatural adoptive brotherhood in Byzantine social relations, Rapp, "Ritual Brotherhood."

38. Callimachus and Cynagirus, mentioned in Gr. Naz. *Epp.* 233 and 235, addressed to two professional rhetoricians, were depicted on the Painted Stoa, reconstructed just before Gregory's arrival; Frantz, *Athenian Agora*, 26–28.

to confront as well as collaborate with each other, and with those ranking above and below them in the public forum of the empire and its administration.[39]

Indeed, while Gregory and Basil's decision to search for ways "to become more pleasing to God" (to use words attributed to Libanius in his correspondence with Basil) did not represent a common path for young men of their background and education, both men began after Athens to do what Gregory's friends did—to become professional rhetoricians, advocates, and public officials.[40] As Gregory's later autobiographical writings and letters exchanged after Basil's return to Cappadocia in the mid-350s and Gregory's about three years later confirm, Gregory in fact engaged in the profession of rhetorician more decisively than Basil.[41]

Although Gregory makes scant reference to how he spent his time upon returning to Nazianzus around 358, his letters and his autobiographical poem *De vita sua* reveal that he instructed students "in the Attic training" and had "shown off *logoi*" and "danced for friends."[42] There is little doubt among scholars that Gregory became a teacher of rhetoric. It is very probable, however, that he held that position longer than the few months or one year that have usually been assumed, at least until his ordination in late 361 or early 362 and potentially even to mid-363. Gregory's social status and that of his family support this probability. As members of the curial class, Gregory and his father were affected by the complex and improvisational imperial legislation regulating curial exemptions and membership in the clergy.[43] As mentioned, Gregory the Elder had been among the *principales*, the leading *curiales* of his city, prior to becoming a bishop. He retained his properties and upon his ordination, at least according to a law issued in 349, his privileges and his fiscal responsibilities would have devolved upon his sons.[44] Caesarius, who had returned to Nazianzus at the same time as Gregory, took a highly popular route to escape these responsibilities: he moved up the social ladder and on to Constantinople and a position in the senate there (Gr. Naz. *Or.* 7.9). Gregory as an Athens-trained rhetor pursued another proven method to alleviate his and his family's fis-

---

39. Gr. Naz. *Or.* 43.20–22; *DVS* 215–27; *Ep.* 192; Cribiore, *Gymnastics*, 220–44, recreates Libanius's classroom.

40. Lib. *Ep.* 336: ὅπως ἂν γένοιο Θεῷ μᾶλλον φίλος. While it is accepted that Basil studied with Libanius, the authenticity of their correspondence remains debated: *Ep.* 335–59 in Basil of Caesarea, *Saint Basil*, ed. and trans. Deferrari, vol. 4; Rousseau, *Basil*, 57–61; Cadiou, "Problème."

41. Bas. *Ep.* 210.2; Gr. Naz. *Ep.* 3, *DVS* 265–76; Gr. Nyss. *Ep.* 13.4, *V. Macr.* 6; Lib. *Ep.* 336.1. Basil's years just after his return are difficult to reconstruct.

42. Gr. Naz. *Ep.* 3, *To Evagrius* (359), and *DVS* 265, 274; see also *Ep.* 188.1 for his and Stagirius's Attic training.

43. Kopecek, "Social Class"; Van Dam, *Families*, 22–24; C. Drecoll, *Liturgien*, 13–77, for membership conditions for the curial class and the corresponding duties; S. Hübner, *Klerus*, 147–54, 162–68; Rapp, *Holy Bishops*, 282–87, provides a wider context.

44. *CTh* 16.2.9 (349); Gr. Naz. *Or.* 18.6 for his father's position. Van Dam, *Families*, 41, downplays Gregory the Elder's rank unduly.

cal burdens: for any city would happily have granted relief from fiscal responsibilities in exchange for boasting such a figure among its citizens, as an enhancement of its status and as an exemplar of its connection to the wider world.[45]

Nazianzus in 358–361

Fiscal and other obligations go a long way toward explaining Gregory's moves in the late 350s and early 360s, as reflected in a famous exchange of letters between Gregory and Basil. I return to this exchange in Chapter 6 but sketch its general contours and their standard interpretation here. According to scholarly consensus, by the time Gregory returned to Cappadocia, around 358/9, Basil had already made a start on the philosophical life of retreat that both men envisioned at Athens. Prompted by the example of his younger brother Naucratius, who had just renounced his position as an advocate and rhetor, Basil moved to his country estate, Annesi, to dedicate himself to the pursuit of philosophy.[46] Almost immediately, he began to persuade or to pressure Gregory to join him in that pursuit, in accordance with their plans. Gregory, however, wavered (already in keeping with his scholarly depiction as a labile character), torn between his desire for retreat with Basil and the pressures that his father put on him to remain in the world. "I must confess it. I have gone back on my promise to be with you and live the philosophical life with you as I had promised as far back as our Athenian days.... One law has won out over another [*nomou nomon nikēsantos*], the one that prescribes care for one's parents [over] that of loving friendship and togetherness."[47]

While these letters appear to corroborate the scholarly characterizations of the protagonists, with Basil steadfast and committed and Gregory wavering and tormented, in fact Gregory himself later chose and edited his own letters together with Basil's responses, presumably to present to posterity a cameo of a forceful Basil and a deliberating (or wavering) Gregory, carefully examining his options and obligations as early as the late 350s and the beginning of the 360s. And he may well have had reasons for shaping his own historiographic persona as well as Basil's in this manner.[48]

---

45. This is not to suggest that he held a formal municipal chair, which was automatically exempt. As McLynn points out ("Among the Hellenists," 220–21), such a chair at Nazianzus may at that time have been held by Gregory's uncle Amphilochius, in whose school he may have taught in an unpaid position, thereby easing his curial obligations; Gr. Naz. *Anth. Pal.* 8.132, 135–36. Kaster, *Guardians*, 221–26, discusses teachers' immunities.

46. For the location and character of Annesi, the circumstances of Basil's retreat, and Gregory's return and visit, Daley, *Gregory*, 8–9; McGuckin, *St. Gregory*, 86–96; S. Elm, *Virgins*, 63–67, 78–91, 102–11, 124; Rousseau, *Basil*, 61–68, 72–73; and Ruether, *Gregory*, 19–28. V. H. Drecoll, *Entwicklung*, 1–5, finds no evidence for Basil's stay at Annesi before 362.

47. Gr. Naz. *Ep.* 1. White, *Christian Friendship*, 70–72.

48. Bas. *Epp.* 1, 14, and 2 (in that order); Gr. Naz. *Epp.* 4 (response to Bas. *Ep.* 14), followed by 5 and 6 (and perhaps 2).

"May we forgive each other, I who have been the victim of this beautiful tyranny . . . , and you who have exercised this beautiful tyranny upon me."[49] However attractive the idea of the retreat (*apragmosynē*) in Pontus may have been, however sweet and powerful the bonds of friendship, Gregory, as his own preserved contemporary writings make clear, wanted it known that between 358 and 363 the duty to serve one's parents was paramount.[50] He had in fact joined Basil at Annesi for a brief period before being called back by the laws circumscribing the duties toward his parents and his city, and the specific requirements that they placed on him at that moment. In the event, Basil's philosophical sojourn at Annesi did not last long either. By late 359, Basil had left Annesi, first for Constantinople and then for Caesarea, and Gregory was in Nazianzus, teaching as a rhetorician and "dancing" his Attic training for his friends.[51] To appreciate fully what this position and his duties to his father entailed, however, it is necessary to step back in time and outwards geographically, to retrace what other than curial obligations were at stake for Basil in Constantinople and for Gregory and his father in Nazianzus in the late 350s and early 360s: it is time to place the personal and the local into the wider context of the *oikoumenē*.

CONSTANTINOPLE: EMPEROR, COSMOPOLIS, AND COSMOS

Constantius II as Sole Ruler, 353–358

With the defeat and subsequent suicide of the usurper Magnentius at Mons Seleuci in the Alps in August 353, Constantius II, the son of the *Divus Constantinus* of *iusta veneranda memoria,* became the sole ruler of the empire, the first since 337. Constantius immediately began to focus on the task that was his by right of inheritance as well as military superiority: to consolidate and secure a united *orbis Romanus*.[52] As sole Augustus, he immediately offered amnesty to the usurper's followers and

---

49. Gr. Naz. *Or.* 1.1.5–6, ἐγώ τε ὁ τυρρανηθεὶς τὴν καλὴν τυραννίδα . . . οἱ καλῶς τυραννήσαντες, and *Ep.* 1.

50. Gr. *Ep.* 1: τοῦ θεραπεύειν κελεύοντος τοὺς γεννήτορας. For the meaning of *therapeuein*, see also *Ep.* 16.7, where Gregory recommends it to Basil and his bishop.

51. Gr. Naz. *Ep.* 1. Gregory visited Basil at least once, most likely during the winter of 358. Further, he proposed a compromise arrangement whereby both men would alternate stays at Annesi and Karbala (Arianzus); Rousseau, *Basil,* 66–67; S. Elm, *Virgins,* 66–67.

52. Amm. Marc. 14.1.1 (Ammianus Marcellinus, *History,* vol. 1, *Books 14–19,* ed. and trans. Rolfe); Aur. Vict. *Caes.* 41–42 (Aurelius Victor, *Livre des Césars,* ed. and trans. Dufraigne; and *Liber de Caesaribus,* trans. Bird); Them. *Or.* 2.37a–b (Themistius, *Themistii Orationes,* ed. Dindorf). Until 350 the Western part of the empire had been under the control of his brother Constans: Eutr. 10.10 (Eutropius, *Eutropii Breviarium,* ed. Santini; and *The Breviarium,* trans. Bird); Festus, *Breviarium,* ed. and trans. Eadie, 26, 27; Jer. *Chron.* 344–45. Dagron, *Naissance,* 2nd ed., 49–51; Seeck, *Regesten,* 190–96; Matthews, *Roman Empire,* 33, 48–57.

even to members of his family and some close friends, and issued new coins to spread the message of a unified realm as quickly as possible. These coins signaled that while Constantius II was now Augustus of the entire realm, the East, where he had grown up and where he had ruled since 337/8, was to be the model. In the East Constantius had labored most to secure the *oikoumenē* against the aggressive Persians under Shapur II. Most of his trusted friends hailed from the East. He had, moreover, lavished much attention on monuments that showcased Constantinople as the new capital, and it was only appropriate that for him the New Rome now equaled the first Rome as the *gloria Romanorum* and *gloria rei publicae*.[53]

Constantius had paid dearly to suppress the rebellion of the Frankish officer Magnentius, and before him that of a certain Vetranio. While Magnentius's usurpation had not been the first attempt to seize the throne, it had been the most dangerous, not least because in 350 Magnentius had murdered the Western Augustus, who was Constantius's sole surviving brother, Constans. The situation had been further destabilized when the Danubian army elevated its commander, Vetranio, as Augustus on March 1, 350, a second usurpation in short sequence. Constantius learned of these events while in Edessa, engaged with the Persians under Shapur II, and moved west after entrusting the ongoing engagements to Lucilianus, who eventually defeated the Persians. On December 25, 350, the Danubian army, apparently after an eloquent display of diplomacy, joined Constantius's cause, and Vetranio elected to retire.[54] That left Magnentius and the Persians as the principal foci of Constantius's attention. To regulate matters in the East while engaged in the West, Constantius elevated his cousin Gallus, the son of his stepuncle Julius Constantius, as Caesar of the East on March 15, 351 (in the presence of bishop Theophilus the Indian). Constantius married him to his sister, Constantia, and dispatched Gallus to the imperial residence at Antioch. Magnentius reacted by also elevating one of his own relatives to the rank of Caesar and by withdrawing troops from the Rhine in order to march against Constantius. The ensuing battle at Mursa, in September 351, proved among the most costly of the time. Magnentius was finally beaten only in the summer of 353, and on October 10, 353, Constantius could at last celebrate his sole rule.[55]

The new *totius orbis dominus* took up residence in Arles, but he could not ignore the affairs of the East in favor of those preoccupying him in the West.[56] Gallus had

---

53. Kent, *Roman Imperial Coinage*, vol. 8, 451 no. 57, 459 no. 129, 517 nos. 69–74, first issued around 342, reissued about ten years later. Pietri, "Politique"; Dagron, *Naissance*, 51.

54. Eutr. 10.12; Aur. Vict. *Caes.* 42, praises Constantius's clemency for Vetranio. Pietri, "Politique," 146–48. According to Philostorgius, *HE* 3.22, Vetranio's election was a ploy hedged by Constantius's sister Constantina, who wanted to secure the Danubian provinces for her brother against Magnentius; Bleckmann, "Constantina," esp. 42–49; T. D. Barnes, *Athanasius*, 220; Barceló, *Constantius*, 92–101.

55. According to Amm. Marc. 14.5.1, the official celebration was held in Arles. The battle of Mursa took place on September 28, 351; Amm. Marc. 21.16.4.

56. Amm. Marc. 15.1.3.

not proved a felicitous choice. A food crisis that affected Antioch in particular—an economic and social challenge notoriously difficult to handle—had evidently overtaxed Gallus's leadership abilities. According to Ammianus, who was, however, ill disposed toward him, Gallus had fatally alienated the local *curiales* by accusing them (apparently with good cause) of speculative hoarding and had further instigated the populace to murder the *consularis Syriae,* activities Constantius could not ignore. Toward the end of 354, Gallus was executed.[57]

In the meantime, Constantius had to move further west in early 354 to restore order on the weakened Rhine frontier, managing to do so again by means of diplomacy. He spent the winter of 354 in Milan, henceforth his residence and staging ground for his Western campaigns along the Rhine until he moved east, first to Sirmium and then to Constantinople in 357/8.[58] While in Milan, Constantius entrusted Silvanus, master of infantry and a Frank, with the command of the Rhine army. Alas, Silvanus, evidently the victim of an intrigue, found himself forced to revolt in August 355 and was executed soon thereafter. Now Constantius requested that his sole surviving male relative, Flavius Claudius Julianus, his cousin and Gallus's half-brother, at that moment engaged in advanced studies in Athens, come to Milan and accept the mantle of Caesar. Julian was appointed Caesar on November 6, 355. He presented his Augustus and cousin with a panegyric that reflects his awareness of the enormous responsibility now placed on his shoulders as the second most powerful person on earth. To be a scion of the house of Constantine was a natural advantage, Julian conceded, but did not suffice to ensure the qualities of a ruler. (See Gallus's example.) That a natural aptitude had to be combined with strict discipline the excellent example of the Augustus demonstrated and the new Caesar understood perfectly well, as indicated by his inaugural speech.[59] Newly married to another of Constantius's sisters, Helena, Julian left for Gaul soon after his acclamation. Constantius remained in Milan until he concluded new treaties with the Alemanni in 356, whereupon he proceeded east to Sirmium in early 357.[60]

---

57. For the background, Bleckmann, "Constantina," 29–68; Vogler, *Constance,* 42 and 83–84; and Barceló, *Constantius,* 102–11. The principal sources, Ammianus and Julian's writings, are tendentious and represent the events from Julian's perspective and from that of the Antiochene curia. Even Barceló's excellent and judicious reconstruction echoes Julianic tendencies when he highlights Constantius's suspicions, which he then nuances by pointing out that almost none of the leading men supported Gallus, who appears to have been a bad ruler rather than someone who sought systematically to form an independent powerbase.

58. Pietri, "Politique," 150–51; Barceló, *Constantius,* 113–19, discussed the failed usurpation of Silvanus.

59. Jul. *Or.* 1. Most scholars interpret Julian's first orations, his relation to Constantius, and Constantius's attitude toward him through the lens of Julian's later *Epistle to the Athenians.* Even Barceló's revisionist account of Constantius characterizes his decision to appoint Julian as a reflection of Constantius's negative attitude to Julian, based on Julian's later descriptions: *Constantius,* 120.

60. Amm. Marc. 15.8; Matthews, *Roman Empire,* 33–39.

The actions briefly outlined above provide a framework for Constantius's principal duties as sole ruler and scion of the second Flavian dynasty: the defense and consolidation of the inheritance of the *divus Constantinus*.[61] Unification of the realm and the securing of its frontiers were paramount in these endeavors. To do justice to Constantius II, the man and his rule, is, however, no easy undertaking: our chief narrative sources present sharply divergent pictures.[62] Constantius is praised as erudite and just or condemned as boorish and cruel; characterized as generous, courageous, capable, and moral, or as feebly aping Constantine, a mere plaything of his eunuchs, wives, and courtiers. Two general tendencies account for such starkly opposing variations of the panegyric themes. One is the Julianic strand of contemporary writings, including Ammianus's work, in which Constantius becomes the negative foil for his successor Julian, representing the polar opposite of all Julian's outstanding qualities. The other strand—or, better, strands, both positive and negative, are represented by persons directly affected by Constantius's own rule and his imperial wish to consolidate his realm, namely leading Christians.

Phrased differently, as in the case of every new emperor, Constantius's accession and his efforts to consolidate the empire meant realignments among those with access to the ruler. Loyal men, mostly Easterners, were honored with favors and signs of imperial benevolence (*philanthrōpia*), while others suffered the consequences of his displeasure: execution, exile, removal to their homes, and more or less voluntary retirement. In both groups, those with access and favor as well as those demoted and removed, were Christian bishops and their advisors, some of whom wrote their Constantius for posterity according to the treatment they and their friends received at his hands. Here, an important historiographic strand clustered around Athanasius, bishop of Alexandria, and his supporters, who had been among those removed, and whose portrayal of the emperor was correspondingly unfavorable, to put it mildly.[63] The combined balance of the Julianic and Athanasian historiography was, hence, negative. Moreover, the Christian historiographic tradition that was positively inclined toward Constantius and opposed to Athanasius was declared heretical after 381, and survives only in fragments. Not surprisingly, this overwhelmingly negative portrayal of Constantius in the surviving and easily accessible narrative sources has dominated his modern scholarly assessment as well.[64] Recent research, however, is redressing this picture, and the chapters that

---

61. For a lucid analysis of Constantius's close relation to his father, Humphries, "*In Nomine Patris.*"
62. Vogler's discussion of the sources (*Constance*, 5–81) remains foundational.
63. Pietri, "Politique," 113–16; R. Klein, *Constantius*, 1–15.
64. Because of the bias of the narrative sources, much of Constantius's administrative and other activities have to be reconstructed from documentary and legislative sources, such as papyri, coins, laws, edicts, and imperial letters such as the one to the prefect Flavius Philippus: Cuneo, *Legislazione*, ciii–cxviii; Vogler, *Constance*, 12–29, 73–76; Swift and Oliver, "Constantius," esp. 248; Ruggini, "'*Felix temporum repartio.*'" For a discussion of the panegyrics, Rees, "Private Lives."

follow seek to contribute to that redress.[65] Nevertheless it is possible to reconstruct, with fair accuracy, Constantius's policies vis-à-vis the new religion in his realm, especially those policies that affected persons such as Gregory the Elder of Nazianzus and his son, Gregory the Younger.

Constantius and the Bishops, 337–358

Among those attending the emperor Constantine the Great during his final moments in Bithynia, in Nicomedia in May 337, was a man who had played an increasingly important role as friend and advisor during the emperor's final years. His name was Eusebius; he was then bishop of Nicomedia, the tetrarchic imperial residence adjacent to Constantinople, and he could draw upon a substantial network of friends, *hoi peri tou Eusebiou*, who profited as much from his closeness to the emperor as he did from their support. Eusebius is said not only to have been at the emperor's bedside at his death but also to have baptized Constantine just before. More important, if we are to trust the historian Philostorgius, the dying emperor entrusted Eusebius to relate his last wishes to his eldest son, Constantius II, who "alone among his sons . . . rushed [from Antioch] to be near him" as soon as he learned of his father's illness—alas, too late to reach him alive.[66]

Philostorgius, born in 368 in Borissa, Cappadocia, and writing about a hundred years after these events, has to be counted among Eusebius's friends; he related a version of the events sympathetic to Eusebius, and he belongs to the fragmentary pro-Constantius historiographic tradition.[67] Sympathy was required, because Constantine's succession—the real theme of the incident Philostorgius related—was a famously messy affair very much in need of subsequent interpretation. The details will probably never be untangled. The various interpretations will occupy us in subsequent chapters, but these are the salient facts: Constantine died on May 22, 337, intestate and in the midst of preparing a Persian campaign. In the preceding years, he had devolved increasingly important positions and functions to his sons Constantine II, Constantius II, and Constans, and in addition on his half-brothers and

---

65. For a summary of scholarly assessments and revisions, Barceló, *Constantius*, 15–17; Henck, "Constantius' *paideia*"; and Cuneo, *Legislazione*, ciii–cix; Whitby, "Images"; Tougher, "In Praise of an Empress"; Leppin, *Von Constantin*, 60–71; Humphries, "*In Nomine Patris*," 452–64; Pietri, "Politique," 148–49; Migl, *Ordnung*, 124–51, 176–208; Noethlichs, "Kirche." T. D. Barnes, *Athanasius*, remains an indispensable classic.

66. Philost. *HE* 1.8, 2.4.18, 2.16; Jul. *Or.* 1.16; Eus. *VC* 4.61–69, with the date of Constantine's death; Ath. *Syn.* 31.2 (Athanasius, *Werke*, ed. Opitz, vol. 2, part 1); Julius of Rome, *Ep. ad Orient.* 2, dating to 341, echoes Athanasius's claim that "those around Eusebius" formed a veritable cabal. Klein, *Constantius*, 29–45, esp. 40 n. 92; Hanson, *Search*, 276–79. For Philostorgius's praise of Eusebius, Marasco, *Filostorgio*, 138–42 (191–93 discusses further variations of the story); Fowden, "Last Days," with discussion of Constantine's baptism; Just, *Imperator*, 41–48.

67. For the chronology, Philostorgius, *Kirchengeschichte*, ed. Bidez and Winkelmann, 2nd ed., cxxxii. Philostorgius wrote his *Historia Ecclesiastica* between 430 and 440.

their sons, presumably intending to install a collegiate rule in the tetrarchic fashion, albeit on a dynastic basis.[68] On September 9, 337, however, nearly four months after his death, only his three sons were acclaimed as rulers—Constantine II of most of the West; Constantius of the East; and Constans of Italy, Africa, Illyricum, and Moesia. As a result of, or in the context of, a military revolt in Constantinople and its environs, Constantine's half-brothers and most of their male relatives were dead, among them Julius Constantius, Gallus's and Julian's father.[69]

Philostorgius's account reflects the troubles surrounding the succession by relating that Constantine's last wish entrusted to Eusebius was to deliver a letter to Constantius II, voicing the emperor's suspicion that he had been poisoned and urging his son, as his heir, to avenge his untimely death. Philostorgius's account, furthermore, reflects a reality not directly connected to the fateful months of 337: Constantius II as Augustus of the East acted as his father's heir at least insofar as he, too, retained Eusebius as friend and advisor. In characterizing Eusebius's role at this time (337), Philostorgius reflects this friend's subsequent influence at court and also exonerates and legitimizes Constantius II, the emperor who granted Eusebius access and accepted his advice.

Constantius II certainly could have used advice. Among the many things not in harmony in 337 were the affairs of Christianity, which at that point had been a legitimate religion in the East for barely twelve years (since the death of Licinius), though longer in the West. The situations at Constantinople, Alexandria, and Antioch are instructive. The first of these cities was just emerging as an imperial residence; the second lacked an imperial residence but was one of the most important cities of the East, and the third was both an imperial residence and an important city. In all three, prominent Christians and their supporters had spent years vying for influence and for the recognition of their interpretation of Christianity as the true one; such recognition would gain for them a commensurate devolvement of imperial assets. By 337 in Constantinople, the position of a certain Paul as bishop had been challenged by Macedonius; in Alexandria, Athanasius had been in conflict with a number of different contenders; and in Antioch the Christian leadership had been in flux after the deposition of Eustathius as bishop in 331.[70] By 338, Constantius, with the advice of Eusebius of Nicomedia, had begun to take things in

---

68. Tougher, *Julian*, 12–14.

69. Those murdered were the sons of Theodora and their children. Theodora, unlike Helena, was already imperial consort when her sons were born. Theodora's sons, now murdered, include Julian's uncle Flavius Julius Dalmatius and his cousins Dalmatius and Hannibalianus. For the circumstances of Constantine's death and succession, Amm. Marc. 21.16.8; Aur. Vict. *Caes.* 41.22; Eutr. 10.9; T. D. Barnes, *Athanasius*, 34–35; Klein, "Kämpfe"; Pietri, "Politique," 120–25; Barceló, *Constantius*, 46–48; Matthews, *Roman Empire*, 84.

70. See also the introduction to Eustathius, *Eustathii Antiocheni, Patris Nicaeni, opera*, ed. Declerck, xxvii.

hand. Eusebius had been ordained bishop of Constantinople, and one of his supporters, the Cappadocian Gregory, had been named bishop of Alexandria, while Athanasius was invited to go into exile at Rome.[71] Constantius's imperial authority enforced the decisions, but he acted with consensus established with the help of Eusebius and his supporters. These men included Flacillus, the new bishop of Antioch;[72] the bishops Dianius, now of Caesarea in Cappadocia; Maris of Chalcedon, on the shore opposite Constantinople; Theodore of Heraclea, in whose sphere of influence Constantinople belonged; and Theognis of Nicaea, another city close to Constantinople. All these men supported Constantius's and Eusebius's choices.

The efforts of Eusebius and Constantius were thus carefully orchestrated to achieve a consensus among important Eastern bishops by 339/40. However, Constantius did not rule alone. While the regents, Constantius's brothers Constantine II and Constans, made attempts to coordinate acts of governance, each had his own priorities and viewpoints, so that consensus between them was rare. More to the point, unanimity among his Christian subjects proved elusive even in Constantius's part of the empire, because those who opposed Eusebius, and thus Constantius, often found support in the parts of the realm to which they had been exiled, ruled by brothers of Constantius, who themselves often disagreed with him. Further, the emperor was almost always on the move and engaged in military operations, occasionally against his own brothers. Therefore, Constantius actively formulated and implemented religious policies in concert and dialogue with his bishops and their advisors, but he was also forced to respond and react to continuously changing circumstances over which he had only limited control.

For example, Paul of Constantinople and Athanasius of Alexandria both went into exile in parts of the empire controlled by Constantine II and, after his death in 340, by Constans alone, where each of them found support for his opposition to Eusebius and Constantius.[73] Thus, the fifth-century church historian Socrates quotes from a letter alleged to be from Constans to Constantius, requesting that Paul and Athanasius be reinstated. On firmer historical ground is a letter sent to Antioch around 340 by Julius, bishop of Rome, in which city Athanasius and a certain Marcellus, deposed from his see in Ancyra, had made common cause. Julius asked to meet with Eusebius and his supporters in Rome to discuss the cases of Athanasius and Marcellus. Eusebius rejected such interference, and Julius re-

---

71. Dagron, *Naissance*, 423–33; T. D. Barnes, *Athanasius*, 19–33; Hanson, *Search*, 172–78, reflecting Simonetti, *Crisi*, 99–134; Ayres, *Nicaea*, 100–104.

72. There a council further supported the emperor's decision by officially deposing Athanasius. Gregory was installed bishop of Alexandria only on March 2, 339, after a military command expelled the recalcitrant Athanasius: A. Martin, *Athanase*, 403–9; T. D. Barnes, *Athanasius*, 36–46.

73. Brennecke, *Hilarius*, 3–6; A. Martin, *Athanase*, 410–19.

sponded in 341 by sending a letter of protest to Antioch, where Constantius was in residence, accusing "those around Eusebius" and opposed to Athanasius of championing heretical views.[74]

Such accusations did not help matters either between East and West or among the Eastern bishops, because even the consensus reached by 339/40 on the basis of Eusebius's and Constantius's actions rested on unstable foundations. Reaching agreement among the leading Christians on the foundations of the new religion, to which the fate of the realm had now been entrusted, proved tension-filled and difficult, as the events of the subsequent years reveal. This comes as no surprise. After all, if the ruler and his advisors did not accurately comprehend the divinity now safeguarding the *oikoumenē*, they could not guide the *oikoumenē* according to the will of that divinity, and the consequences for the well-being of all were potentially disastrous. Hence both Constantius and his advisors needed to achieve harmony and unanimity on the foundational tenets of the new imperial religion and fought intensely to gain (imperial) acceptance of the superiority of their concepts. If it was almost impossible for Constantius and his advisors to create harmony in the East, his task as sole ruler of the *oikoumenē* after 353 was near monumental in magnitude.

Patristic scholars and church historians have discussed the reasons for the tensions that beset the Eastern bishops and their advisors and that jeopardized Constantius's efforts to establish harmonious unity in the context of the council of Nicaea and its legacy. I will refrain from using the standard terminology that labels these tensions as the struggle between heretical Arianism and Nicene orthodoxy, headings that anticipate the eventual outcome of the struggle in favor of the Nicene orthodox group.[75] My aim is to trace and analyze the evolution of that conflict and the mechanisms at play in the larger context of the empire, rather than in Christian circles alone, without anachronistically anticipating its outcome, implicit in the majority of our surviving Nicene orthodox sources, by employing the labels that these contemporaries used in a decidedly polemical manner.[76] To trace the evolution of what are known as Arianism and Nicene orthodoxy, I structure the account that follows around the persons involved and the technical terminology discussed explicitly by all the participants rather than around the two camps—even though this structure may make for a more difficult reading.

After all, bishops and their supporters were divided and united according to personal rivalries that often involved competing claims to leadership in important cities, exacerbated by the rivalry between emperors such as Constans and Constantius.

---

74. Socr. *HE* 2.22 (Socrates, *Kirchengeschichte*, ed. Hansen); Brennecke, *Hilarius*, 3–13.

75. Hanson, *Search*, and Simonetti, *Crisi*, remain fundamental, as are Brennecke, *Studien*, and Vaggione, *Eunomius*. Recent scholarship is now revising the role of Marcellus.

76. Lyman, "Topography"; S. Elm, "Polemical Use."

These personal rivalries were heightened by these Christian leaders' different interpretations of the divine, resulting in no small measure from their approach to the Christian scriptures and to the question of how they should read and explicate them as influenced by their own views of advanced Greek learning—namely philosophy. For now it suffices to point out that all those involved in these debates brought to bear on their interpretations of the scriptures their own understanding of the advanced techniques of grammar, rhetoric, and philosophy, and of the fundamental philosophical concepts of cosmology, anthropology, epistemology, language theory, and ethics.

At stake was precisely how the teachings of these scriptures, in particular those addressing the relationship between the Father and the Son, ought to be integrated into the matrices provided by the vocabulary, presuppositions, and assumptions of *paideia*—of Greek (and also Latin) learning and all that it stood for—assumptions shaped in turn by each person's access to *paideia* and hence each person's own social status. In short, most of the participants in these debates were driven by multiple personal viewpoints and concerns, though expressed in the common framework offered by their shared *paideia*. Hence, the difficulty of achieving consensus on any aspect of this complex process should come as no surprise. Alliances shifted constantly, often involving personal loyalties, so that common political exigencies—access to the emperor and his court—might well trump differences in approach to questions of philosophy or faith. At other times these philosophical differences proved too profound to be overcome even by friendship and advantageous political constellations.[77]

In the relationship between the Father and the Son, the most vexing question in all the attempts to illuminate their respective natures as based on the scriptures was causality. This question was of fundamental importance. If there was only one God, the creator of everything, then how should one conceive of the divinity of his Son? Given that the Father as the creator of all could himself not have been created, to what degree was the divinity of his Son as his creation equal in essence? How had the Son, the Word, been caused? And how could the process of the Son's causation or creation be explicated in human speech, using human grammar? Father and Son had to be closely related to remain one God, but they were also distinct. How ought one, then, conceptualize and phrase that distinction: ontological, or relational, or

---

77. The primary sources for much of the following—the history of Arianism, semi-Arianism, and neo-Arianism, and the rise of neo-Nicene orthodoxy—express partisan views, with the position of Athanasius and his supporters (the Nicenes, or orthodox) dominating the record. Many of the sources relating to or written by Eusebius and his followers, including the representatives of the different evolutions of his basic position, are highly fragmentary, because they came to be considered heretical by the pro-Nicene writers, especially after Theodosius I (after 381). The fragmentary nature of the non-Nicene sources also accounts (at least in part) for modern scholars' differences in dating and interpretation; Brennecke, *Studien*.

some combination of the two? Should their relation be expressed as a source and its product, or as the one that exists (for example) between the thought or intellect and its expression through the word? What were the consequences of such considerations for human salvation? How one defined the essence (*ousia*) of the divine and of all that it had created or caused affected the relationship between the creator and its creation, whether understood as the Divine Intellect (*Nous*) and its Word or as the Father and the Son. Since that creation did not cease with the Son, but encompassed the world (i.e., the cosmos and the human beings populating it), these questions were fundamental to understanding the relationship between man and his creator. That is, they also had immediate repercussions for human salvation. The correct understanding of the grammar of the divine was crucial, because faulty definitions and incorrect readings precluded the salvation of everyone and everything. And that divine mandate, after all, had always been given to those divinely chosen to lead, persons such as the emperor and his advisors, bishops prominent among them: to safeguard those in their care and to ensure that they guided them toward the divine that had caused them.

By 337—in our context, more accurately, by the late 330s and early 340s—two main tendencies in such matters predominated among the Eastern Christian leaders and some of their Western contemporaries: one that stressed the sameness between the Father and the Son and used language emphasizing their shared characteristics and qualities, including a shared essence, and one that stressed the difference between them, emphasizing as a result the unique character of the Father as prior cause. Those holding the latter position, though differing among themselves in numerous details, expressed that difference in relational terms, stressing that the Son is independent and hierarchically lower because "produced as altogether different in his nature and in his power, being in complete likeness of disposition and power to him who made him . . . , called into being by his will," to cite Eusebius of Nicomedia.[78] He and Eusebius of Caesarea, the church historian, prominently favored the position maintaining a difference between Father and Son, while Athanasius of Alexandria most prominently exemplified the position of their sameness. There was an additional strand within the sameness group, distinct from Athanasius and significant in the decades that followed. Marcellus of Ancyra represented that strand.[79] Controversies between those groups, in particular between bishops from the East and those exiled to the West and their supporters, date back to the council of Nicaea

---

78. Eus. Nic. *Ep. Paulin.* 3: γεγονὸς ὁλοσχερῶς ἕτερον τῇ φύσει καὶ τῇ δυνάμει, πρὸς τελείαν ὁμοιότητα διαθέσεώς τε καὶ δυνάμεως τοῦ πεποιηκότος γενόμενον. The full text is in Athanasius, *Werke*, ed. Opitz, vol. 3, part 1, Urk. 8.

79. "Begotten not made, consubstantial [ὁμοούσιον] with the father"; Dossetti, *Simbolo*, 226. Hanson, *Search*, 129–72; M. R. Barnes, "Fourth Century." For Marcellus, see especially *Markell von Ancyra*, ed. and trans. Vinzent; Seibt, *Theologie*.

in 325, and in fact predate that council but erupted in earnest as soon as that council, convened by Constantine, had been concluded.[80] At Nicaea, those who favored the sameness position had prevailed. All their underlying assumptions, however, were immediately questioned, especially their definition and use of terms that had played a significant role, such as *ousia* and *hypostasis* but also "begotten," "unbegotten," "made" (*gennētos, agennētos, genētos*). The ensuing debates revealed that the majority of the leaders in the East favored in effect the difference position, represented by Eusebius of Nicomedia and his friends, including Eusebius of Caesarea, even though they disagreed on philosophical specifics of their position.

Many of their disagreements resulted from divergent emphases of the philosophical underpinnings of the matters under debate. For example, if one preferred a more Aristotelian definition of *ousia*, or "essence," when applied to the divine Father, namely that essence does not permit of degree (*Categories* 3b34), a transfer of the Father's essence as first cause to the Son as product was not permissible. If, on the other hand, one saw essence more Platonically, as something capable of emanating or proceeding from something else, then an essential connection between a cause and its product was not inconceivable. Platonic language as used at the time also underscored divine transcendence, however, which in turn could favor a position of the Father as unique and hence essentially different from the Son, as Eusebius of Nicomedia argued. Such a unique, transcendent position of the Father could, however, also imply an understanding of the Son, as Word, as indistinct (in essence) from the speaker—that is, the Father.[81] In short, much remained to be clarified, requiring intense debate and inquiry along lines divided by philosophical school, technique, and methodology, and therefore by the different teachers, disciples, groups of friends, and regional alliances in each.[82]

In 341, ninety Christian leaders in the East were summoned to Antioch to dedicate a church built by Constantius but also to achieve a consensus on the matters concerning the correct relation of Father and Son adumbrated above in the presence of the emperor, who was then in residence.[83] Under the leadership of Eusebius

80. Dagron, *Naissance*, 410–16.

81. Describing this relationship in his commentary on John 1:1, Marcellus used language of power (*dynamis*) and activity (*energeia*) to define the link between thought and Word: the "Word was in the Father as a power . . . or as an energy"; Marcell. fr. 70 (52 ed. Vinzent): ἵν' ἐν μὲν τῷ φῆσαι "ἐν ἀρχῇ ἦν ὁ λόγος" δείξῃ δυνάμει ἐν τῷ πατρὶ εἶναι τὸν λόγον ἀρχὴ γὰρ ἁπάντων τῶν γεγονότων ὁ θεὸς "ἐξ οὗ τὰ πάντα," ἐν δὲ τῷ "καὶ ὁ λόγος ἦν πρὸς τὸν θεὸν" ἐνεργείᾳ πρὸς τὸν θεὸν εἶναι τὸν λόγον: *Markell*, ed. and trans. Vinzent. That is, the Word was in the Father (as mind) before coming forth actively as incarnate Son and would return there once his task was completed, which Marcellus understood to mean that, first, there cannot have been any division between them, and second, that the time in which the Son was active as Word was circumscribed.

82. Stead, *Divine Substance*, 133–56; R. Williams, *Arius*; Hanson, *Search*, 181–273; , and Lyman, "Heresiology."

83. See especially Hanson, *Search*, 284–91; and Dagron, *Naissance*, 417–25; Pietri, "Politique," 139–45.

of Nicomedia, now bishop of Constantinople, and Flacillus, bishop of Antioch, the bishops—including Acacius of Caesarea in Palestine, Eusebius's successor; Dianius of Caesarea in Cappadocia, with his advisor Asterius; Macedonius of Mopsuestia; Gregory of Alexandria; Eudoxius of Germanicia; and Theodore of Heraclea— proceeded to do so by elimination. They produced four documents, of which the second and fourth were to assume particular relevance.[84] The second one, also known as the "dedication creed," appears to have been the result of a real compromise, in part because it omitted several controversial expressions that had been used at Nicaea. For example, it does not say that the Son is "from the *ousia* of the Father," or that he is "begotten not made," pointing out instead that he is not to be considered "like one of the creatures" but rather as an "exact image" of the Father, generated by his will. At the same time, the Christian leaders also clarified other terminology further, for example that names such as "son" or "holy spirit" "are not given lightly or idly, but signify exactly the particular *hypostasis* and order and glory of each of those who are named, so that there are three *hypostaseis*, but one in agreement [*symphōnia*]"—that last, *symphōnia*, a neutral term well suited to unify moderately disparate views.[85]

The fourth document summarized the second for Emperor Constans in Trier and hence the West. It went even further toward reconciliation, omitting all language referring to image or essence, but it contained nevertheless a strike against Marcellus by stating that the Son's kingdom has no end, because Marcellus had argued that the reign of Christ had begun exactly four hundred years prior, when he was "created at the conception of the body of Christ," and that it would end once his task was accomplished. That is, the document oscillates between expressing the views of the difference position and extending a hand to those in the West favoring sameness, all, however, in a context where the actions of Constantius and Eusebius against Athanasius and Marcellus were defended as appropriate. Unfortunately, Constans did not receive the brotherly gesture favorably.[86] But Constantius, because he continued to struggle against the Persians, remained interested in reaching a compromise with his brother in the West. Thus, despite the negative outcome of this gesture, a follow-up meeting was envisaged for 343 in Serdica (modern Sofia), on the border between the brothers' spheres of interest.[87]

---

84. Socr. *HE* 2.18; Ath. *Syn.* 25.1–5; Hil. *De syn.* 36–37. A. Martin, *Athanase*, 419–22.
85. The full text is in Hanson, *Search*, 286–87; Socr. *HE* 2.10; Ath. *Syn.* 23; Hil. *De syn.* 29–30. Whether this text sought to supplant Nicaea is not clear. It did, however, rephrase and clarify much that had been said there, using aspects of Origen's thinking. Socrates stressed that the council spoke respectfully of Nicaea; Brennecke, *Hilarius*, 13–16; Ayres, *Nicaea*, 117–22; McLynn, "Use."
86. Socr. *HE* 2.8; Soz. *HE* 3.5.3; Brennecke, *Hilarius*, 17–25; Klein, *Constantius*, 42–43; Seibt, *Theologie*, 460–521.
87. T. D. Barnes, *Athanasius*, 71–81; Hanson, *Search*, 293–306.

From Serdica to Constantinople

In the interim, Eusebius of Nicomedia died, prompting Paul to return to Constantinople and to reclaim the position of bishop—by now, however, occupied by a Constantinopolitan presbyter called Macedonius.[88] Constantius did not wish to see someone supported by Constans as religious leader in Constantinople and dispatched the *magister equitum* Hermogenes to Constantinople to remove Paul. In the riots that ensued between supporters of Paul and those of Macedonius, Hermogenes was killed. To kill an imperial envoy was an unforgivable outrage, for which Constantius held Paul responsible. To restore order, the emperor in person went to Constantinople.[89] Paul was again removed and Macedonius installed as bishop a few years later.[90]

The events at Constantinople demonstrated that conciliatory gestures went only so far. Foreshadowing Serdica, they make it evident that neither emperor was willing to tolerate interference in matters of personnel, the friends and advisors he selected and whom he wished to see in charge as bishops of major cities in his realm. Indeed, even though Emperor Constans and about ninety-five bishops from his sphere of influence went to Serdica in late 343, and even though Constantius dispatched two high-ranking court officials together with an almost equal number of bishops, the meeting was a debacle. In effect, the sides never actually met, convening in separate venues.[91] Constans and his side wished to see Athanasius, Marcellus, and several other deposed bishops reinstated in their sees located in the sphere of Constantius, who together with his bishops rejected such interference.

Such heightened tensions were reflected in the documents produced: each side accused the other of endorsing an unacceptably extreme position. Thus, the representatives of the sameness position accused their Eusebian opponents of pushing their difference position, propelled by their desire to maintain God's transcendence, so far as to deny the Son full divinity, just as the heretic Arius had done.[92] Their opponents retaliated by claiming that the Westerners (including Athanasius, but in particular Marcellus, who argued that the Son was mere word) merged Father and Son into an undifferentiated one, thus creating a new Judaism (associated with teach-

---

88. Socr. *HE* 2.6–7, 12–13; Soz. *HE* 3.3–4, 7.4–7; Dagron, *Naissance*, 422–39.

89. Amm. Marc. 14.10.2; Lib. *Or.* 59.94. T. D. Barnes, *Athanasius*, 68–69.

90. Among other measures, Constantius reduced the grain rations for Constantinople. Hanson, *Search*, 278–84; Dagron, *Naissance*, 428–31; Brennecke, *Hilarius*, 46–50; Klein, *Constantius*, 71–77, 166–69, 205–6.

91. Hanson, *Search*, 295; Brennecke, *Hilarius*, 29–46. Barceló (*Constantius*, 84–90) argues that Constantius II repulsed Constans's interference, so that the Eastern theological concerns reacted to a firmly established Western status quo, an assessment that I do not share, following Ulrich, "Nicaea," esp. 17–19.

92. Extant in Theod. *HE* 2.8.37–52; Hil. *Frag. Hist. Coll. antiar.* B II(2) 1–4 (Hilary, *Collectanea*, ed. Feder, 43–196).

ings earlier proposed by a certain Sabellius), because such teachings suggested a single divinity.[93]

Serdica and its aftermath proved decisive for Constantius. It had been a nadir, a failure compounded by the difficulties of the battle against the Persians near Singara in 344, where the Roman army sustained significant losses.[94] In the six years between 344 and Constans's death in 350, Constantius made only a few attempts at rapprochement. The theological positions remained divided between those who followed Eusebian lines (emphasizing difference) and those who embraced the positions of Athanasius and Marcellus (on sameness) as reformulated at Serdica. The persons representing these positions were also divided by the spheres of influence of the competing emperors: theology and politics went hand in hand. Indeed, each emperor, but Constans in particular, appears to have employed his bishops to influence decisions in the realm of the other ruler, only to be rejected by a consensus of the bishops there as well as by the opposing emperor in question—whatever the theological justifications, it appears that no one could become bishop of an important see without imperial approval. Conversely, imperial approval often went hand in hand with the thinking of a majority of bishops and their advisors. Furthermore, as Marcellus and Athanasius demonstrate, the other emperor was the one to appeal to when deposed by a council of bishops. That emperor then acted often in concert with a council of his own advisors on behalf of the appellant, provided the appellant's influence—the city of his see—was sufficiently important.

Such developments did not produce unity and harmony, particularly not throughout the empire. Thus when Constans was murdered in 350, Constantius was well aware of the fact that many Christian leaders in the part of the realm he now had to bring under his control were not positively disposed toward him. To unite the empire based on the model of the East was going to be a hard sell indeed.[95] Time, however, was on Constantius's side—time and his insistence that a Christian leadership in unanimous agreement on the fundamentals of the faith was indispensable, because, in his words, "our commonwealth is sustained more by religion than through offices, physical labor, and sweat."[96] And indeed, about five years after the suicide of Magnentius in 353, Constantius as sole ruler seemed finally, between 358 and 360, to have achieved this goal: agreement among his Christian leaders on the essential characteristics of the supreme divinity, based on the majority opinion of

---

93. The synodal letter of the Easterners is extant in Latin in Hil. *Frag. Hist. Coll. antiar.* A.4.1–3, CSEL 65, 48–67; Klein, *Constantius*, 47–49. Seibt, *Theologie*, 460–521; Lienhard, "Did Athanasius Reject Marcellus?" esp. 71–73.

94. Portmann, "Politische Krise"; Brennecke, *Hilarius*, 46–64; Ayres, *Nicaea*, 126–30.

95. Ammianus Marcellinus (21.18) states, in essence, that the harder Constantius tried to unite the Christians, the more splintered they became.

96. *CTh* 16.2.16.36, "Magis religionibus quam officiis et labore corporis vel sudore nostram rem publicam contineri" (*Theodosian Code*, trans. Pharr, 443); Brennecke, *Studien*, 82.

those resident in the East. Among these Christian leaders and their advisors were Gregory the Elder, bishop of Nazianzus, and his son, the rhetor.

CONSTANTIUS'S TRIUMPH: UNITY AND HARMONY, 358–360

By January 360, what must on occasion have felt like "that state which is always receding, like full employment or a life without weeds,"[97] had finally become reality: consensus in the empire on the nature of the divinity. Two factors had been instrumental in achieving it. First, Constantius was sole ruler, and there was no other emperor to play off against him; and second, a new generation had succeeded many of the participants in the earlier disputes. Even though the newcomers had philosophical and theological concerns that fell within the broad categories of sameness and difference, the new generation nevertheless moved the debates forward, eventually creating an intellectual platform acceptable to most (at least briefly).

Constantius's steps along the road toward that momentous event of 360 began after Constans's death, in Sirmium, Arles, and Milan, because, as has become evident, he had to settle matters first in the West, and that involved not just dealing with usurpers but also pacifying the Christian leaders there. By 350 Photinus, bishop of the imperial residence Sirmium, in Pannonia, had become a prominent representative of the position of Marcellus of Ancyra, whose arguments aimed to preserve God's wholeness and transcendence in notions of the Son as Word circumscribed by time rather than eternal.[98] For those embracing difference—that is, most of the Easterners—such concepts became increasingly untenable. Basil, Marcellus's successor at Ancyra, among the most vocal opponents of Photinus, removed the latter from his see in 351 with the support of several bishops convened in Sirmium. Constantius, then in residence, approved.[99]

When Constantius had moved to Arles, in 353, after Magnentius's suicide, and then to Milan in 355, he used the opportunity to convene Western bishops, inviting them to stop supporting Athanasius and to agree to the formulations Basil and the other bishops had employed at Sirmium to remove Photinus, formulations largely identical to the fourth conciliatory document put together in Antioch in 341. Most were willing, but not all Western bishops agreed to renounce Athanasius and Photinus and thereby presumably also their support of the sameness position. As

---

97. Lane Fox, *Pagans*, 21.

98. Marcellus had argued that the title Son could become active only with his birth by Mary and that his kingdom, his role" as redeemer, would come to an end with the redemption; Marcell. fr. 107 (119 ed. Vinzent).

99. This was achieved with a document essentially identical to the fourth creed of Antioch, of 341; Hanson, *Search*, 326–28, has the full text. For Basil of Ancyra's role, see the editor's comments on Epiph. *Haer.* 71.1.5 (p. 250), 71.3 (p. 252), 71.5 (p. 254) (Epiphanius, *Ancoratus*, vol. 3, 2nd ed., ed. Dummer).

a result, bishops such as Hilary of Poitiers, Eusebius of Vercelli, and Lucifer of Calaris (modern Cagliari) were sent east into exile.[100]

In 357, with Julian firmly ensconced as Caesar and the Western frontiers largely in hand, Constantius turned east and once more sojourned in Sirmium en route to Constantinople. Again he used the opportunity to convene a small group of his advisors, including Valens, bishop of Mursa, and Ursacius of Singidunum, in Illyria, protégés of Eusebius of Nicomedia who had distinguished themselves in Serdica. Also present were Photinus's successor Germinius and perhaps George, formerly of Caesarea in Cappadocia and by now bishop of Alexandria. Their task was to adjust and clarify the language of the fourth document of 341 from Antioch, especially with regard to the meaning of *ousia* (essence).[101] To be precise, now the term *ousia*, used prominently at Nicaea, was not only left out, as had been the case in the Antiochene "dedication creed," but was denounced outright: "substance [*substantia*], which is called *ousia* in Greek—that is, to speak more explicitly, *homoousion* or *homoiousion*, as it is called—there should be no mention of it whatever, nor should anyone preach it."[102] These terms, after all, were found nowhere in scripture. Further, the revised document used a remarkable number of scriptural passages to emphasize the uniqueness of the Father and his difference from the Son, and to stress that both were beyond doubt God.

Two points are worth observing: matters of personnel (in particular, the role of Athanasius) were no longer of concern, and the formulations were aimed at those in the West, whom they largely convinced. They opened the way for an alternative qualification of the relation between Father and Son among those speaking Greek, in which communality could be expressed in ways other than in notions of sameness of essence, tainted by Marcellus and Athanasius. The explicit rejection of the *ousia* language at Sirmium, however, had the predictable though unintentional result of attracting the attention of the Westerners: previously not concerned with the implications of these terms, they now became attentive to ensuing Eastern debates of these matters, something further facilitated by the total immersion of men like Hilary in the Greek language and its concepts, exiled in the East and present at subsequent meetings there.[103]

---

100. Hanson, *Search*, 329–34; see Brennecke, *Hilarius*, 133–92, and 184–92 for suggestions regarding the relation between an imperial edict exiling uncooperative bishops and their refusal to agree to a theological document for which the sources offer no evidence; Ayres, *Nicaea*, 132–37, argues convincingly that Constantius's presence made such an agreement very plausible.

101. The later sources commingle Sirmium I and II, so that it is not clear who was present. All agree that the number was small; Brennecke, *Hilarius*, 312–13.

102. "De substantia, quae graece usia appellatur, id est (ut expressius intelligatur), homousion, aut quod dicitur homoeusion, nullam omnino fieri oportere mentionem," Hil. *Synod.* 11 (trans. Hanson, *Search*, 344–45; for a Greek translation, Ath. *Syn.* 28); Socr. *HE* 2.30.31–41.

103. Hanson, *Search*, 315–43; Pietri, "Politique," 144–63.

The Formulation of Constantinople

Constantius's moves to achieve unity among the Christian bishops in his realm progressed apace with his return to Constantinople from the West. While still in Sirmium in 359, he convened another small gathering to prepare a position paper for discussion at large assemblies of bishops to be convened at Rimini and at Seleucia in Isauria later that year. The man principally responsible for that draft (also known as the "dated creed") had been Basil of Ancyra. Several months earlier, in 357 and 358, Basil had once more been propelled into action, this time apparently by the deeds of the new bishop of Antioch, a certain Eudoxius, a "friend of Eusebius" who had already been present in Antioch in 341 as bishop of Germanicia. Eudoxius, who had supported the Sirmium document of 357, the year he became bishop of Antioch, had subsequently embraced a position that took the degree of difference between Father and Son too far, at least according to Basil. Though Basil in principle shared the difference position, he believed that notions propagated by a certain Aetius, who had moved to Antioch when Eudoxius came there and whom Eudoxius had subsequently sponsored, were too different, pushing the avoidance of *ousia* or essence language to an extreme and denying all essential links between Father and Son. While such a position was a useful corrective to the views of Marcellus and Photinus, whom Basil had just recently denounced, to deny all notions of shared essence, after all implicit in Father/Son language, in his view went too far.

In 358, Basil invited a few friends to Ancyra to discuss these ideas and subsequently wrote a letter to the emperor containing their views.[104] Differentiating between creator/created language and Father/Son language as concepts (*epinoiai* or *ennoiai*) that required different contextual readings, Basil of Ancyra developed a sophisticated statement according to which the Son is like the Father in essence, or *ousia* (*homoios kat' ousian*), to be understood not as material fatherhood but as indicating shared divinity: the Son's *ousia* flows out of the Father's energy, or *energeia* (but truly exists as separate, unlike the relation between mind and word posited by Marcellus). To deny the shared essence indicated by the Father/Son language, he argued, grants too much weight to the creator-created relationship: a father is more than a mere creator, and a son more than a creature. Basil, accompanied by a certain Eustathius of Sebaste and Eleusius, bishop of Cyzicus, went to Sirmium with this letter and presented it to the emperor. Constantius was immediately convinced by Basil's emphasis on the dual nature of the divinity as Father and Son as well as creator and created. He issued a statement to the effect that "when we first made a declaration of our belief . . . , we confessed that our Savior is the Son of God and of like substance [*kat' ousian homoios*]": that is, more than a mere creature. He then expressed his displeasure with those who had advised him badly, including George

---

104. Epiph. *Haer.* 73.2.1–11.11; trans. in Hanson, *Search*, 350–57.

of Alexandria, who had promoted Aetius there; and sent into exile Eudoxius, Aetius, and his advisor, a deacon by the name of Eunomius: Eudoxius to his family's estate in Armenia (Arbissus), Eunomius and Aetius to two different towns in Phrygia.[105]

In 359, encouraged by Basil's new middle road, Constantius (who in the interim had recalled Eudoxius, but not Aetius and Eunomius) appears to have felt that the time had come for a general assembly. He convened a small group of advisors, including Valens and Ursacius and a certain Marc of Arethusa in addition to Basil, to develop a compromise formulation (*ekthesis pisteōs*) as the basis for discussion at Rimini and Seleucia. The resulting position paper (or "dated creed," mentioned above) was probably written by Marc. Like a true compromise, it was a stripped-down document, avoiding mention of the three *hypostaseis,* because this difficult concept was hard to translate into Latin, as well as of language describing the relation between Father and Son as image (a concept that had caused difficulties in the West before). And it emphasized the difference position more than Basil's letter had done, stressing that *ousia* language should be avoided, since it was not familiar to the masses and caused disturbances. It emphasized (against Aetius), however, that "the Son is like the Father in respect to everything [*homoios kata panta*], as the holy scriptures also declare and teach."[106] Constantius now proceeded to Constantinople, halfway between Rimini and Seleucia, near Antioch, while his advisors and representatives went to Rimini and to Seleucia with this formulation and an imperial letter in hand, urging all to limit debates "to the faith and to unity [*de fide atque de unitate*]," and not to meddle in each other's matters of personnel.[107]

Although the eventual result accorded with Constantius's wishes, the path to unity proved more circuitous than Constantius and his advisors at Sirmium had anticipated. When presented with the statement from Sirmium in late May 359, the approximately four hundred bishops assembled in Rimini declared it perverse (*multae peruersae doctrinae*) and superfluous; the documents from the meeting in Nicaea in 325 sufficed, and they requested permission to return home, since their mission was evidently accomplished. Upon receiving notice that a delegation of those in Rimini had arrived in Adrianople, Constantius asked them to wait. He was at that

---

105. Soz. *HE* 4.14.1–7, quotes Constantius's letter in full on the basis of Sabinus of Heraclea's lost *Synagogue;* Epiph. *Haer.* 73.9.1–7; McLynn, "Use," 72–80, details Basil's influence on Constantius's action. George had to flee Alexandria after troubles on August 29, 358, and returned in 361; Ath. *H. Ar.* 2.3.7. Hanson, *Search,* 348–54; Brennecke, *Studien,* 9–16; Ayres, *Nicaea,* 149–53.

106. Drawn up by Marc of Arethusa in agreement with all present; Hil. *Coll. antiar. Paris.* B VI 3. Text in Ath. *Syn.* 8 and Socr. *HE* 2.37; trans. Hanson, *Search,* 363–64; also Brennecke, *Studien,* Anhang 1, 243, ll. 25–30, and ibid., 16–22; Hanson, *Search,* 364–70.

107. Valens, Ursacius, and Germinius of Sirmium, and the prefect Taurus (who may have been promised a consulship if all went well), went to Rimini, where some four hundred Western bishops had already assembled, brought there at the emperor's expense. *Ep. Const. ad syn. Arim.*; Hil. *Coll. antiar. Paris.* A VIII; Sulp. 2.41–45. Brennecke, *Studien,* 23–25.

moment otherwise engaged (fighting the Persians) and could not receive them; furthermore, their colleagues in Seleucia had not even met. During this wait in the summer heat, with the majority stranded in Rimini and their delegates waiting in Nike in Thrace, it emerged that the Westerners had not been quite so firm in rejecting the imperial document as it had appeared. By October those waiting in Thrace changed their minds and now accepted the document with some modifications, and, upon their return, eventually also persuaded most of those remaining in Rimini to agree. By late November or early December 359, the bishops returned home (just before the end of the traveling season), having sent a delegation to Constantinople to report their agreement.[108]

In the meantime, in September 359, between 150 and 160 Eastern bishops, high-ranking court officials, and the military leaders of the region (the *comes* Leonas and the *comes et praeses Isauriae* Bassidius Lauricius) had gathered in Seleucia. These men proved as unpredictable as their Western counterparts, at that time sweltering in Rimini and Nike. The gathering at Seleucia, however, unlike that in Rimini, was plagued from the start by personnel issues, to the point that matters of content lost out almost entirely. In essence, the bishops were divided into two groups, those sympathetic to Basil of Ancyra and his modified difference position (as formulated in the Sirmian position paper) and others—according to the later pro-Basilian sources, the minority—who favored a formulation of the difference position clearer than Basil's. This group was represented by Eudoxius of Antioch and Acacius of Caesarea in Palestine. Interestingly, Basil himself was not present. Along with Macedonius of Constantinople, Eustathius of Sebaste, and Cyril of Jerusalem (who had appealed to the majority to reverse his removal from his position at the hands of Acacius)—that is, with most of the key *homoios kat' ousian* players—Basil had been detained and excluded from the initial meetings because of alleged misdemeanors.[109]

Cyril's conflict with Acacius appears to have dominated the discussion and seems to have led to a hardening of the two camps' positions, even though they disagreed little on matters of importance. After some deliberation, Acacius of Caesarea presented a formulation that echoed the fourth document of Antioch in 341, in its turn similar to that of Sirmium; this formulation was accepted by the second, majority

---

108. In effect, two delegations arrived from Rimini, the earlier one waiting in Thrace, and the later one, charged with inquiring what had happened to the earlier one, proceeding to Constantinople. The reasons prompting those in Thrace (that is, Valens and his companions) to change their mind has caused much debate, then and now; Brennecke, *Studien*, 24–40, plausibly argues that the wait had the possibly intended consequence of permitting Valens and the others to clarify the meaning of the document and to allay fears that its formulations were too subordinate, too much of the difference or Arian position; *Ep. syn. Arim.*, Hil. *Coll. antiar. Paris.* A V 1, 2; Hanson, *Search*, 376–77; Ayres, *Nicaea*, 160–61, maintains that Valens's position was a fraud.

109. Socr. *HE* 2.39.11–15; Soz. *HE* 4.22.4; Theod. *HE* 2.26; Brennecke, *Studien*, 40–42.

camp, now also including Basil and Macedonius.[110] The second group did so in a closed session, with the minority around Acacius and Eudoxius absent, and as a result the minority rejected the agreement. In the end, despite the efforts of Leonas, the camps remained divided; each eventually sent a separate delegation to Constantinople.[111] That of Acacius, Eudoxius, and George of Alexandria arrived first and agreed to the modified version of the document of Sirmium (the "dated creed"), to which the Westerners had also just communicated their assent. Representatives of the *homoios kat' ousian* position arrived later, by the end of December. They included Basil of Ancyra, Macedonius of Constantinople, Eustathius of Sebaste, and Dianius of Caesarea, accompanied by his advisor, his newly appointed reader Basil, who had left Annesi at Dianius's request to accompany him to Constantinople.[112] Though they (at least according to later neo-Nicene sources) ostensibly represented the majority position in the East, they were presented with a fait accompli, to which in the end they also agreed.[113]

Basil of Ancyra, in other words, had not remained a favorite of Constantius for long. The events at Seleucia and their reception at Constantinople in December 359 had reversed his fortunes; he himself may have contributed to that reversal by overzealously exploiting his success in 358, when he had used his position as favorite to remove from their sees several bishops of the Eusebian mold. At any rate, despite Constantius's initial support of Basil's *homoios kat' ousian* and then *kata panta* positions, by the end of December 359 the new Eusebians Eudoxius of Antioch and Acacius of Caesarea, though they did not agree on all specifics, had carried the day, in accord with the delegates from the West and after protracted negotiations.[114] An-

---

110. Acacius's formula (Epiph. *Haer.* 72.9.6–8, 10.1) agreed largely with that of Basil of Ancyra and the fourth Antiochene formula: Acacius proposed that the Son was "like" the Father, *homoios*. In his interpretation, however, this similarity was best expressed with the language of "imprints" or "characters" (χαρακτῆρες); the imprints of the Father were impressed upon the being of the Son. Acacius also rejected the addendum proffered by the emperor, as requested by Basil, that the Son was "like [the Father] in all respects" (ὅμοιος κατὰ πάντα). The *homoios kat' ousian* majority initially rejected his version, though it agreed with their notions, only to accept it later, at which point Eudoxius, too, signaled his support; Ath. *Syn.* 25.2–5; Epiph. *Haer.* 73.25–26 (Brennecke, *Studien,* Anhang 2 and 3, 244–46). I follow Brennecke (*Studien,* 42–48), who argues convincingly that personnel issues were more important than those of doctrine. Hanson emphasizes doctrinal differences more (*Search,* 372–80, 584).

111. Socr. *HE* 2.40–41; Soz. *HE* 4.22.25. V. H. Drecoll, *Entwicklung,* 8–9.

112. Rousseau, *Basil,* 98–99; S. Elm, *Virgins,* 128–29, 132.

113. Theod. *HE* 21.3–7; Jer. *Adv. Luc.* 17 (Brennecke, *Studien,* Anhang 4 and 5, 246–47). Brennecke, *Studien,* 31–35; Hanson, *Search,* 376–80. As Brennecke points out (*Studien,* 48–53), the sources discussing the events of December 359 are so contradictory that a reconstruction is nearly impossible; Hanson, *Search,* 376; Vaggione, *Eunomius,* 209–11; Urbainczyk, *Socrates,* 154–56, 160–67.

114. Eudoxius, for example, maintained that the Son could not comprehend the Father's essence and thus could be only like him, even though this was the argument of the document he signed; Hil. *Contra Const.* 13 (Hilary, *Contre Constance,* ed. and trans. Rocher);Hanson, *Search,* 584.

other casualty of the accord now within reach was Aetius (whose extreme difference position mirrored Photinus's extreme sameness stance on opposite ends of the spectrum), from whom Eudoxius withdrew his support, whereupon Aetius's advisor Eunomius also chose to distance himself.[115] On December 31, 359, to reiterate, all Eastern bishops, including Basil's supporters, signed the formula to which the Westerners had already given their assent.[116] It stated, among other things, that the term *hypostasis* could not be employed to speak of the Father, the Son, and the Holy Spirit; that the relationship between Father and Son was *homoios*, "similar"; and that the term *ousia* was not to be used to define their relationship further.[117]

When Constantius celebrated the beginning of his tenth consulship on January 1, 360, he could also celebrate a feat never before accomplished, even by Constantine: the unity of Christian belief throughout the empire based on a formulation of the divine and its incarnation as similar—that is, different—accepted by bishops from both West and East as expressed in the Constantinopolitan document or creed.[118] As the preceding discussion has shown, to reach such a consensus had involved numerous debates with a cast of characters that, although it did not change dramatically, shifted its allegiances significantly over the decades in question. Nearly all debates had, at their crucial stages, involved the emperor in person. He had been not only present but a participant in these debates, themselves carried out at a high level of technical expertise, requiring an advanced level of philosophical training that Constantius appears to have been able to follow. To participate in these debates, in other words, and even more to be noted and noticed and hence gain access to the emperor, required thorough mastery of the philosophical underpinnings; only one well versed in advanced Greek learning could hope to have a significant voice. As far as Constantius is concerned, the preceding discussion suggests that the picture of him in Julianic historiography as an uneducated bore requires revision. It remains true, however, that he was the Arian of the Athanasian strand of historiography: the accord achieved in 360 emphasizing the difference between Father and Son certainly qualified as Arian, something worth keeping in mind in the following chapters.

The final accord of 360 was a felicitous outcome, all the more welcome to Constantius because in the summer of 359 Shapur had begun a major campaign after diplomatic efforts, initiated in 358 by the Roman *praefectus praetorio Orientis,* had failed. Constantius, responding with his proven defensive tactics while waiting for

---

115. Philost. *HE* 4.12; McLynn, "Use," 85–87.
116. Soz. *HE* 4.23.7.
117. Ath. *Syn.* 30.8; this was a greater restriction of *hypostasis,* because hitherto only the use of "one *hypostasis*" had been rejected; Brennecke, *Studien,* 52–53, and Anhang 4, 248; Klein, *Constantius,* 64–65.
118. Seeck, *Regesten,* 207.

troops from the West, had lost, however, the city of Amida.[119] In short, in 360, because another summer campaign against Shapur was imminent, to achieve harmony and at last unity in matters divine was all to the good. The prevailing group, for its part, wasted no time settling matters once and for all while Constantius was still in Constantinople. In January, Acacius assembled a small gathering consisting mostly of bishops from Bithynia, presided over by Maris of Chalcedon, who removed Basil of Ancyra, Eustathius of Sebaste, Macedonius of Constantinople, Eleusius of Cyzicus, and others who had supported them, from their sees, despite their all having just signed the new formula. An imperial order sent Aetius into exile again. Eudoxius became the new bishop of Constantinople, and Meletius, previously bishop in Beroea and then Sebaste, was poised to assume his position as bishop in Antioch. Eunomius replaced Eleusius as bishop in Cyzicus.[120]

On February 15, 360, Eudoxius, in the presence of Constantius and the assembled bishops, inaugurated the new imperial church dedicated to Holy Wisdom (*Hagia Sophia*), begun by Constantine himself. Eudoxius used the occasion, so it is said, to crack a joke about the Father at the expense of his own difference position.[121] Also in February, in Paris, Flavius Claudius Julianus was hailed as Augustus by his troops, who had been called east to assist Constantius in the defense against Shapur but had been reluctant to leave. Julian accepted his troops' acclamation of him as Augustus and considered himself equal to Constantius and no longer under his command: the specter of civil war appeared on the Western horizon.[122] In the spring the emperor left Constantinople to move east against Shapur, who had entered Mesopotamia in February. Constantius was in residence in Caesarea in Cappadocia when he received news of Julian's usurpation.[123]

At the same time, throughout the West and the East, a drive for signatures under the (Arian) Constantinopolitan formula of the *homoios* began that lasted until 361. Like their peers at Constantinople, almost all Eastern bishops signed the formula. Among the signatories was Dianius of Caesarea, who had probably signed already while in Constantinople.[124] In Nazianzus, meanwhile, Gregory the Younger, as his correspondence with Basil of Caesarea (between 359 and 360/1) attests, de-

---

119. Amm. Marc. 17.5.2–11, 18.4–10, 19.1–10.
120. Socr. *HE* 2.42–45; Soz. *HE* 4.24; Philost. *HE* 5.1–3; Theod. *HE* 2.27.21; McLynn, "Use," 82–85; Dagron, *Naissance*, 436; Vaggione, *Eunomius*, 229; Brennecke, *Studien*, 54–58, 192–94; Hanson, *Search*, 380–82. For the complex Antiochene situation, Spoerl, "Schism."
121. Soz. *HE* 4.26.1; Socr. *HE* 2.43.11.
122. For the ecclesiastical consequences in the West, Brennecke, *Hilarius*, 360–67.
123. Amm. Marc. 20.11.1–3; Barceló, *Constantius*, 164.
124. Bas. *Ep.* 51; Le Nain de Tillemont (*Mémoires* 9, 347) first identified the elder Gregory as a signer of Rimini/Constantinople. Calvet-Sébasti (*Grégoire de Nazianze: Discours 6–12*, 29 n. 1), following Bernardi (ed. and trans., *Grégoire de Nazianze: Discours 4–5*, 26–30), argues instead that he signed a less compromising document composed at Antioch in 363. Brennecke's analysis (*Studien*, 23–86, esp. 56–

cided after much deliberation that he could not, after all, at that time devote himself to the philosophical life, despite the wishes of his dear friend (who by then was advising Dianius of Caesarea, whom he accompanied to Constantinople). Gregory's sense of duty and obligation to his father demanded that he remain at Nazianzus to support and advise his father, Gregory, the bishop.

Nazianzus: Gregory the Elder

Gregory the Elder of Nazianzus, like the majority of Eastern bishops, signed the Arian accord of Constantinople, declaring Father and Son to be like but not the same in essence, sometime in 360. Dianius, the bishop of Caesarea, where the emperor resided in the spring of 360, had done the same. Both Gregory the Elder of Nazianzus and Dianius of Caesarea had by then been bishops for several decades. Dianius, as already noted, had first been mentioned as bishop of Caesarea and as one of Eusebius of Nicomedia's friends in 341, when he attended the meeting that Eusebius, by then bishop of Constantinople, and the emperor Constantius had called to dedicate the new church in Antioch, the same meeting that produced the fourth document foundational for the one signed in Constantinople twenty years later.[125]

Gregory the Elder's appointment as bishop appears to date back even further, to the time following Constantine's victory over Licinius. According to our primary source, the funeral eulogy that his son delivered in 374, Gregory the Elder assumed the mantle of bishop between 328 and 330, just after his marriage to Nonna and around the time of Gregory's birth. In his son's later elaboration, his ordination had been preceded by a momentous conversion, initiated by Gregory the Younger's Christian mother.[126] Previously, according to his son, Gregory the Elder had been a worshipper of *Theos Hypsistos*.[127] According to Stephen Mitchell, by the end of the third and the beginning of the fourth century, "Hypsistos was one of the most widely worshipped gods of the eastern Mediterranean world," especially in Asia Minor.[128] Inscriptions, votive offerings, and other material remains suggest that for his wor-

---

60) of the Eastern bishops' reaction in 360/61 supports the traditional view that he signed this document. See Zachhuber, "Antiochene Synod."

125. Ath. *Apol. Sec.* 21.1; Hanson, *Search*, 269–70.

126. Gr. Naz. *Or.* 18.11–12, *PG* 35.1000B (Gregory of Nazianzus, *Funeral Orations*, trans. McCauley, 119–56). The elder Gregory's birth is dated between the late 270s and early 280s, because when he died in 374 he was supposedly almost a hundred years old; Gallay, *Vie*, 22–24; Mitchell, *Anatolia* 2, 51, 68; Hauser-Meury, *Prosopographie*, s.v. "Gregor der Ältere," 88–90; *Gregor von Nazianz: Briefe*, ed. and trans. Wittig, 3–4. With the exception of Mitchell, all scholars attribute Gregory's conversion to Nonna, following his son's version of the event in *Or.* 18.11, *PG* 35.997b.

127. Gr. Naz. *Or.* 18.5, *PG* 35.990; Ruether, *Gregory*, 112–14, and J. Martin, *Antike Rhetorik*, 200–208, for the carefully constructed *epitaphios logos*.

128. Mitchell, "Cult," 99, *pace* McGuckin, *St. Gregory*, 3, who calls it "an obscure sect."

shippers *Theos Hypsistos* was the "highest God," the "Pantokrator," "the only God they worship," a divinity associated with the sun and the upper air of heaven to whom all other divinities (such as Apollo) were subordinate, acting as his divine messengers or angels.[129] These other sources corroborate Gregory the Younger's description of his father's prior religion as a mixture of "Hellenic error and adherence to Jewish law" (Gr. Naz. Or. 18.5).[130] The material evidence reflects such close interaction and mutual influence between Jewish and non-Jewish inhabitants, united in their worship of one all-powerful God. Indeed, Gregory of Nyssa observed that those who worshipped *Theos Hypsistos Pantokratōr* were distinct from Christians only because the former denied God the name of Father.[131]

Thus, at least as far as his prior religion was concerned, Gregory the Elder, aged about forty in 328, may not have struggled quite so hard as his son later would have had his audience believe. Further, in his funeral oration Gregory the Younger leaves no doubt that his father had received the mantle of the bishop as a matter of course: he was one of the most prominent citizens of Nazianzus (*politeias ou ta deutera eschēkōs*), if not indeed the most prominent.[132] Indeed, even if it was not a foregone conclusion that members of the curial elite such as Gregory the Elder would become Christian once Licinius was defeated, it was evidently assumed that if they wished they would be the bishops or at least Christian leading figures—their social status overrode most other criteria.[133] It followed as a matter of course that when Gregory the Elder, a prominent local citizen, adopted the sole emperor's new religion about 328, he also assumed the correspondingly prominent position of bishop of his city, presumably at the recommendation of one of his peers, Leontius, bishop of Caesarea. Gregory the Elder, in sum, belonged to the original generation of post-Constantinian bishops who had (to cite Peter Brown) "drift[ed] into a respectable

---

129. *Theos Hypsistos* and *Hēlios* were frequently conflated. Lamps and torches as symbols of the divinity's powers of illumination played a central part in the hypsistarian rituals. For the documentary evidence, Mitchell, "Cult," 128–47; Wischmeyer, "Theos," with extensive bibliography; R. Smith, *Julian's Gods*, 96–102.

130. *Pantokratōr* and *hypsistos* were terms also often used for the Jewish God: e.g., Philo *Leg*. 278, *In Flacc*. 46; Joseph. *AJ* 16.163. Mitchell, "Cult," 110–21; Ameling, "Jüdischen Gemeinden."

131. Gr. Nyss. *Eun*. 38 (Gregory of Nyssa, *Opera*, ed. Jaeger, vol. 2, 327). Inscriptions from Asia Minor attest to several hypsistarians who became Christian priests: Mitchell, "Cult," 122–23.

132. Gr. Naz. Or. 18.6. Kopecek, "Social Class," 455; Coulie, *Richesses*, 23–28, who also discusses earlier suggestions of senatorial class (e.g., Treucker, *Politische und sozialgeschichtliche Studien*, 10–13); Drake, *Constantine*, 235–38.

133. Eck, "Einfluss"; Rapp, "Elite Status," 387–88. Liebeschuetz (*Decline*, 2–15, 29–74, 104–24) is instructive, though focusing on the fifth to seventh centuries; Rouché, "Functions"; Carrié, "Gouverneur"; Van Dam, "Emperor," esp. 60–62; Heather, "New Men," 21–33; Garnsey and Humfress, *Evolution*, 81–83, 89–93. For a comprehensive overview, Rapp, *Holy Bishops*.

Christianity" almost by default rather than as the result of heroic transgressions or dramatic conversions.[134]

Gregory's later presentation of his father's conversion from the worship of *Theos Hypsistos* to Christianity as a dramatic rupture initiated by his new wife, Nonna—so dramatic that his own mother had threatened to withhold moneys from him, a threat that led to a period of rupture between them—has been taken at face value by nearly all scholars. That Gregory shifted religious allegiance need not be doubted, but the intense drama of the conversion from the old to the new nurtured by Nonna owes more to Gregory the Younger's rhetorical prowess and the exigencies of 374 than to Gregory the Elder's assumption of Christianity and the mantle of bishop in the late 320s.[135] By 374 another emperor ruled, embracing a Christianity very much in the mold of Constantius II—that is, highlighting the difference between Father and Son. By then, however, Gregory the Younger had come to think that such a stance was to be considered heretical, something neither he nor his father had believed in 360, when Gregory the Elder had signed the formula of Constantinople. Thus, in praising his father in 374, Gregory the Younger had some explaining to do, and a dramatic narrative of Gregory the Elder's deep struggle to become a committed Christian served both son and father well.

But in 360, things had not yet proceeded to where they stood fourteen years later. Then, most Eastern bishops had signed the Constantinopolitan document, which stipulated that the Father was the one supreme divinity, his transcendent position of monarch within the Trinity intact, while his Son occupied a subordinate, though like, position. It stands to reason that a man who had spent his formative years worshipping a *Pantokratōr* of very similar attributes should find it easy to subscribe to such an understanding of the (Christian) *Pantokratōr*.[136] This is all the more plausible if we take into consideration Gregory the Younger's finely calibrated (though at first glance somewhat underhanded) compliment, that his father was "more pious than those who possessed rhetorical power . . . , or rather, while taking second place as an orator, he surpassed all in piety."[137] Indeed, it is possible that neither Gregory the Elder nor a significant number of his peers who had drifted into a respectable Christianity some years earlier fully grasped the complexities of essential and causal language and their philosophical underpinnings. For that reason, as I have already observed in the summary of the events leading up to 360, many of them, including Dianius and Gregory the Elder, availed themselves of expert advi-

---

134. Brown, "Aspects," 9; idem, *Authority,* 47; idem, "Christianization"; Winkelmann, "Konstantins Religionspolitik"; S. Elm, "Inscriptions."
135. Gr. Naz. *Or.* 18.5, *PG* 35.992A.
136. See also Gr. Naz. *Or.* 6.
137. Gr. Naz. *Or.* 18.16. For different views, see McGuckin, *St. Gregory,* 2–4; Van Dam, *Families,* 41–42.

sors of a younger generation who had received advanced training in rhetoric and philosophy. These men included Asterius, Eunomius, Marc of Arethusa, and a number of others mentioned above, who were advisors to their bishops, as well as Basil of Caesarea and Gregory of Nazianzus—expertly trained younger men who in 360 and 361 could ill afford a prolonged period of retreat and withdrawal but needed to be actively involved in the debates of the day. For, as would soon become apparent, the accord reached in Constantinople in 360 and signed by most Eastern Christian leaders in the course of 360 and 361 was to prove of short duration.

REVERSAL: CONSTANTIUS AND JULIAN AUGUSTUS, 360-361

On January 27, 360, Eudoxius, formerly bishop of Germanicia and then of Antioch, was ordained bishop of Constantinople. When he dedicated the Hagia Sophia on February 15 in the presence of Constantius, the emperor and his advisor Eudoxius could celebrate much more than the completion of a major public monument inaugurated by Constantine the Great: for the first time since Nicaea in 325, the realm was united, and even the Christians within it were unanimous in their formulation of the fundamental nature of their divinity—a truly auspicious state of affairs (destined to last, alas, only a Constantinopolitan second).[138] When Constantius left Constantinople in March to campaign once more against Shapur II his house was in order.

But the very next month, the emperor, in Caesarea, learned of the events that had taken place in Paris in February and March. In late 359, after the loss of Amida, Constantius had requested that his Caesar, Julian, transfer troops east in preparation for the coming Persian campaign.[139] Many of these troops were native Germans, not pleased to be sent east against Shapur. In February they made their displeasure known by acclaiming their commander Julian as Augustus, and he had accepted.[140] (I discuss these events and those leading up to them, Julian's rise, the relation between the Caesar and his Augustus, and their interpretation in scholarship, in the chapter that follows.) By March Julian had sent envoys to inform Constantius of his elevation to Augustus and to offer to share power. It was not, after

---

138. *Chron. Pasch.* s.a. 360, *PG* 92.736-37. For the chronicle's use of reliable sources, see *Chronicon Paschale,* ed. and trans. Whitby and Whitby, xvi; Socr. *HE* 2.43.11; Soz. *HE* 4.26.1. Dagron, *Naissance,* 436-37; T. D. Barnes, *Athanasius,* 148-50.

139. In addition to three hundred men from each of his units, he was asked to send his auxiliaries also—i.e., Heruli, Batavi, Celts, and Petulantes—hence he described them as barbarian troops in Jul. *Ep. Ath.* 282b-d (Julian, *Oeuvres,* ed. and trans. Bidez, Rochefort, and Lacombrade; and *Works,* 2nd ed., ed. and trans. Wright; and *Imperatoris Caesaris Flavii Clavdii Ivliani epistvlae,* ed. Bidez and Cumont).

140. Amm. Marc. 20.4.1-3; Lib. *Or.* 12.58-61, 18.90-102; Zos. 13.10.11-16. Matthews, *Roman Empire,* 93-100, and chart, 102-3; Szidat, *Historischer Kommentar,* part 1.

the Tetrarchy, unheard of to have two Augusti from the same family ruling the empire, but Constantius, who had long competed with his brothers as regents and had suppressed a series of usurpers, was disinclined to share supreme power. He informed Julian's envoys that the Caesar ought to be content with his status; coins minted by Julian during this period featuring him as Augustus suggest that he did not concur.[141] Nevertheless, the external threats to their realm commanded, for the moment, the full attention of both rulers. Constantius moved toward the Tigris and then, for the winter, to Antioch, and Julian moved west against the Franks, returning to winter at Vienne, where he celebrated the fifth year of his rule in October 360.[142]

The Christian Leaders in the West in 360 and 361

Even as Constantius traveled east and his Eastern bishops were signing the formula of Constantinople, opposition against that formula gathered momentum in the West, and was encouraged by a new, autonomous Western Augustus, however questionable his legitimacy. The opposition was led by a Westerner who had been in Seleucia and Constantinople as an exile, and who therefore had had occasion to observe the debates in the East from up close, which prompted concerns regarding the philosophical underpinnings of what he and others had just signed: Hilary of Poitiers, who appears to have left Constantinople without Constantius's consent in early 360, when he learned of Julian's acclamation.[143] Upon his return to the West Hilary lobbied against the accord of Constantinople and for a return to the positions that those from the West had originally held at Rimini and Nike, before the long wait that had seemingly induced them to change their minds. By late 360 or early 361, bishops from Gaul (presumably including Hilary) gathered with the approval of the Western ruler, Julian, in the imperial residence at Paris and wrote a letter deploring that many "bishops in the East . . . eschewed the use of the word *ousia*, because it is essential to combatting Arianism. . . . They allow the word *similitudo*, 'likeness' [*homoios*]. . . . But we must realize not a union but a unity of Godhead." That is, they accepted the *homoios kat' ousian* position while rejecting the notions of Marcellus and Photinus, and declared the "like" (*homoios*) formulation of Constantinople heretical.[144]

---

141. Amm. Marc. 20.9.1; Kent, *Roman Imperial Coinage*, vol. 8, 226, no. 284; idem, "Introduction," 110–12.

142. Amm. Marc. 21.1.4.

143. Hil. *De syn.* 91; Bas. *Ep.* 51.1–2. Brennecke, *Hilarius*, 360–66; Hanson, *Search*, 459–64; D. H. Williams, *Ambrose*, 41–43; Ulrich, "Nicaea," esp. 20; idem, *Anfänge*, 195–216; Brennecke, *Studien*, 56–58.

144. Hil. *Coll. antiar. Paris.* A I 1–4, trans. Hanson, *Search*, 465–66. For a discussion of Hilary's doctrine after 360, Ayres, *Nicaea*, 180–86. For Julian, Hil. *Ad Const.* 2.2.1; D. H. Williams, *Ambrose*, 43; Brennecke, *Hilarius*, 366.

The Christian Leaders in the East

In the East, meanwhile, things did not go smoothly either. In late fall 360, Constantius arrived in Antioch for the winter. In early 361 he gathered George of Alexandria, Acacius of Caesarea in Palestine, and several others, in part, it seems, to get to know those now dominating Christian affairs in his residence. Eudoxius, as mentioned above, had suggested Meletius, at that point bishop of Sebaste, as his successor, and Meletius was duly ordained bishop of Antioch by early 361.[145] When the emperor invited him, together with George and Acacius, to give a public demonstration of their rhetorical brilliance, Meletius delivered a star performance with a homoian exegesis of the selected text, Proverbs 8:22. Deftly skirting the terminology banned at Constantinople and incorporating the *homoios kat' ousian* as well as the homoian position, Meletius suggested that the Son was "the inscrutable interpreter of the Inscrutable..., a product like the Father and accurately reproducing the *charaktēr* [imprint] of the Father... as the offspring of him who begot him."[146]

Within one month of that performance, however, Meletius was sent into exile and replaced by the Alexandrian Euzoius, one of George's presbyters. The reasons for this sudden reversal of fortune remain unclear, but subsequent events suggest that Meletius might already then have countenanced a far more *homoios kat' ousian* position than had at first appeared, one that Acacius and George could not accept.[147] Their reaction (and perhaps Meletius's removal) may be further explained by the disposition of another sizable group in Antioch in favor of a sameness position. Though this group, led by a certain Paulinus, was not in agreement with the supporters of Meletius, both combined could well threaten Constantius's accord. In 361 (probably after Constantius had left again for Persia) Lucifer of Calaris, a strident opponent of Constantius and fervent supporter of a strong sameness position, consecrated Paulinus bishop of (or in) Antioch.[148]

In late 360 and early 361, others revoked their signing of the Constantinopolitan document or broke ranks with those who had signed it. Among them was Basil of Caesarea. He had been in contact with Eustathius of Sebaste since returning from Athens, and in 361, motivated perhaps by his regard for Eustathius, who had suffered at the hands of the homoians, Basil broke with his bishop Dianius, who had

---

145. Theod. *HE* 2.31.2; Ruf. *HE* 10.25; Epiph. *Haer.* 73.23; Soz. *HE* 4.28.3–5; Socr. *HE* 2.44.2. Brennecke, *Studien*, 66–71.

146. Meletius in Epiph. *Haer.* 73.29–33: τοῦ ἀδιηγήτου ἑρμηνεὺς ἀδιήγητος ... γέννημα ὅμοιόν τε τοῦ πατρὸς καὶ τὸν χαρακτῆρα τοῦ πατρὸς ἀκριβοῦν ... γέννημα τοῦ γεννήσαντος. Dünzl, "Absetzung." When Meletius moved away from the *homoios* is unclear. Hanson, *Search*, 382–84, thinks as early as 361; but Brennecke, *Studien*, 74, V.H. Drecoll, *Entwicklung*, 10–15, and Dünzl argue that he became more antihomoian because of his removal rather than the reverse.

147. J. Chrys. *In Sanct. Meletium*, PG 50.516; Jer. *Chron.* 26 (Helm), 241.

148. Hanson, *Search*, 642–44.

signed the Constantinopolitan formula, and retired once more to his family's estate at Annesi.[149] In Nazianzus others reacted similarly. At some point during 361, men whom Gregory the Younger later described as "overzealous brothers" began to voice their disagreement with Gregory the Elder's signing the formulation declaring Father and Son like. During the months that followed, relations deteriorated to such an extent that some of their leaders were ordained by "foreign hands" (*chersin allotriais*)—that is, by a bishop other than Gregory the Elder. Neil McLynn has plausibly suggested that Lucifer of Calaris, en route from Antioch to Constantinople via Nazianzus, may have been the ordainer of the opposition to Gregory the Elder in Nazianzus as well.[150] In sum, toward the end of 361 and during 362, Nazianzus experienced a schism that was to last until 364.

The situation at Nazianzus mirrored the state of the Eastern bishops: most of them had signed a formula that began to be dissected and denounced as heretical in both the East and in the West—seemingly before their signatures had dried. Constantius on February 14, 361, shortly before he moved again toward the Eastern frontier, issued an edict reaffirming that members of the clergy were immune from taxation. His introductory words, expressing his joy at having created the unity and concord in matters of religion so much more vital to the prosperity of his realm than his own labors, were little more than wishful thinking.[151] By May 361, Constantius had declared Julian a public enemy (*hostis publicus*), and had returned from the eastern front to Antioch to prepare for an encounter with him.[152] He was traveling to Constantinople—Julian was moving against him there as well—when he fell ill in Mopsucrena, the first *mansio* after Tarsus. Euzoius rushed to his bedside from Antioch to baptize him. Constantius died on November 3, 361, having on his deathbed declared Julian his legitimate heir.[153]

---

149. Bas. *Ep.* 51; Rousseau, *Basil,* 62 n. 7, 66–68, 84–85, 98; S. Elm, *Virgins,* 63, 78–81; Gautier, *Retraite,* 284.

150. Gr. Naz. *Or.* 18.18, "a revolt was raised against us by the more zealous part of the church, when we had been tricked by a piece of writing and by technical words into a wicked fellowship"; Gr. Naz. *Or.* 6.11; *Or.* 4.10. McLynn, "Gregory the Peacemaker," 208–9. See also *Grégoire de Nazianze: Discours 4–5,* ed. and trans. Bernardi, 23–37; *Grégoire de Nazianze: Discours 6–12,* ed. and trans. Calvet-Sébasti, 11–36; Bernardi, *Prédication,* 97.

151. *CTh* 16.2.16, "gaudere enim et gloriari ex fide semper volumus, scientes magis religionibus quam officiis et labore corporis vel sudore nostram rem publicam contineri"; Klein, *Constantius,* 294–95; Barceló, *Constantius,* 168–77, 187.

152. Szidat, in *Historischer Kommentar,* part 3, 33, argues that Julian had not been declared *hostis publicus*.

153. Jul. *Ep. Ath.* 269d, 281b; *Ep.* 26 (Wright 8), *To Maximus; Ep.* 28 (Wright 9); Amm. Marc. 20.8.18–9.1, 21.7–15.2, 22.2.1. Socr. *HE* 11.2–3; Philost. *HE* 6.5; Seeck, *Regesten,* 208–9; Matthews, *Roman Empire,* 104–10; T.D. Barnes, *Ammianus,* 143–62; R. Smith, *Julian's Gods,* 4; Bouffartigue, *Empereur;* Athanassiadi-Fowden, *Julian,* 82–86; Bowersock, *Julian,* 18, 58–65; Klein, ed., *Julian,* 509–617, for a bibliographical summary up to 1978; Browning, *Emperor*.

Julian entered Constantinople as sole Augustus on December 11, 361. Among his first official acts were edicts and letters designed to reverse Constantius's religious policies. For example, in January 362 Julian issued an edict that restituted all temples and their properties and permitted all clergy exiled as a result of Rimini and Constantinople to return to their cities (but not necessarily to their sees).[154] All opponents of Constantius—that is, all who held grievances against Eudoxius, Acacius, George of Alexandria, and other close Christian advisors of the former emperor—profited from the sea change.[155] Among the new Christian men (*novi homines*) now invited to court at the pleasure of the emperor Julian were Aetius, Eunomius, a certain Novatus, and Basil of Caesarea.[156]

Constantinople and Nazianzus: Caesarius

Already present at Julian's court was someone else from Cappadocia with far closer ties to Nazianzus than Basil: Caesarius, Gregory's younger brother. We left Caesarius in Alexandria toward the end of 348 as he embarked on his advanced training in medicine, to follow his older brother to Athens and then back to Nazianzus. In the interim, Caesarius had completed his studies and moved to Constantinople, where he embarked on a successful career as a physician, which garnered him an advantageous engagement, though in the end he did not marry. In 358 or 359, when Gregory passed through Constantinople on his return to Nazianzus from Athens, Caesarius accompanied him to spend a few months at home, but he returned to Constantinople shortly thereafter. There, he was invited to hold a seat in the new senate, and he advanced his career as public physician (or *archiatros*), establishing close ties to Constantius's court. His connections to that court were well chosen. For, when Julian assembled his friends and advisors, Caesarius was among them, despite his ties to Constantius's court. In Gregory's words, Julian advanced Caesarius "to the first rank among the physicians . . . , and belonging to the friends of the emperor, he garnered the highest honors."[157] The position was probably that of an *archiater sacri palatii*, further enhanced by the "rank" of Friend of the Emperor, a truly

---

154. According to the homoian historiographer in *Chron. Pasch., PG* 92.740A; differently Ath. *Ep. fest.* 33 (Athanasius of Alexandria, *Histoire "acephale,"* ed. and trans. Martin and Albert, 263).

155. Jul. *Epp.* 46 (Wright 15), 110 (Wright 24). The edict arrived in Alexandria on February 9, 362. *Hist. Ath.* 3.1–2; Amm. Marc. 22.2.4. *Imperatoris Caesaris Flavii Clavdii Ivliani epistvlae,* ed. Bidez and Cumont, 42, 45. Brennecke, *Studien,* 87–88, 96–100. R. Smith, *Julian's Gods,* 208–12; Athanassiadi-Fowden, *Julian,* 44–45; Andreotti, "Kaiser Julians Gesetzgebung," esp. 152–65.

156. Jul. *Epp.* 46 and 32 (*Epp.* 26 and 15 in Wright). Knorr's arguments against Basil as recipient of *Ep.* 32 are not sufficient (*Basilius,* 53–62); nevertheless, it remains uncertain whether Basil actually went. For Aetius, see also Philost. *HE* 3.27; Soz. *HE* 5.15.5; Socr. *HE* 2.38.23. Vaggione, *Eunomius,* 148–63, 269–71.

157. Gregory's funeral oration for his brother is our principal source. Gr. Naz. *Or.* 7.9–10. Coulie, *Richesses,* 139–47; Van Dam, *Families,* 60–61.

honored position (albeit shared by many) that implied privileged access (and may have resulted from contacts that Caesarius had made at Alexandria, a prominent center for medical studies, where a student of Oribasius, one of Julian's closest personal friends, had taught in the early 350s).[158]

This, then, was the situation that Gregory the Elder faced when he ordained his elder son, Gregory, as presbyter or priest sometime toward the end of 361 or the beginning of 362.[159] A number of persons at Nazianzus challenged openly his signature under the formulation sponsored by Constantius and his advisors. Because the emperor who had sponsored that formulation was dead, and opposition against the formula on the rise, these persons were not inclined to modify their challenge.[160] Julian, on succeeding Constantius under hostile circumstances, had immediately begun to reverse Constantius's religious policies. Gregory's younger son, Caesarius, occupied an important position at Julian's court. Although some of those opposing Gregory the Elder's signature may have had reason to celebrate Julian's reestablishment of prominent bishops who had opposed the formulation of Constantinople and had been removed from their sees as a result, some signs of the new emperor's religious policies were troubling: he had also ordered the resumption of sacrifices in the temples. Under these circumstances, Gregory the Elder, wishing to avail himself formally and publicly of the advice of an Athens-trained rhetorician with advanced knowledge of philosophy, ordained Gregory the Younger as his presbyter or priest—as his official advisor.

Gregory the Younger reacted much like Basil of Caesarea. Sometime after his ordination, perhaps by the summer of 362, he left Nazianzus to join Basil at Annesi, where Basil had gone as a result of his disagreements with Dianius. When Gregory returned to Nazianzus, by Easter of 362 or 363 (I favor the later date, but the former is more commonly accepted), he came with his inaugural oration in hand, *Oration* 2, also known as *Apologia de fuga sua,* ready to assume his position beside his father on the terms laid out in that oration.[161]

As this chapter's discussion has shown, the emperor, in this case Constantius II, played a key role in establishing the intellectual foundations of the new imperial Christian religion. Constantius, neither a heretical tyrant who merely dictated nor a brute without deeper understanding—these are the portraits painted by the Athanasian and Julianic strands of the ancient historiography, still relevant for modern scholarship—acted as emperor in concert and dialogue with his close Christian advisors. With consensus the aim, the emperor both acted and reacted in an informed manner; he knew and understood the philosophical concerns under de-

---

158. The prominent Friends include Salutius; Guido, "Nozione," esp. 115–26.
159. For the date, Gautier, *Retraite,* 302–3.
160. Gr. Naz. *Ep.* 7.
161. *Grégoire de Nazianze: Discours 1–3,* ed. and trans. Bernardi, 84 n. 1.

bate. For example, when Basil of Ancyra pointed to some positions that could be considered extreme, the emperor reversed those positions (and removed those who had advised him badly), but he also tempered Basil's excesses in subsequently exploiting his new position as advisor by removing him. That is, the emperor was flexible and proactive while also seeking to react and harmonize; he was current with the debates and adjusted his views accordingly.

His advisors, the bishops and their own advisors, for their part, were eminently aware of the imperial voice. They needed access to court if they were to advocate for the acceptance and implementation of their positions. Access was granted because of friendships and personal ability. Thus, an advisor's prestige and access to court depended on his connections but also on his intellectual capacities (or those of his own advisor). These observations suggest two conclusions: first, successful bishops were on the move; to be a bishop did not imply being wedded to one see. Rather, successful bishops moved from lesser sees in peripheral cities to those where the emperor resided—in the East, Antioch and Constantinople—unless they already occupied sees in important cities: for example, a metropolis such as Caesarea in Cappadocia. Second, successful advisors often followed in their bishops' footsteps (for example by occupying sees that they had vacated) but were flexible enough to disagree and chart their own courses, if their situations demanded. Ordination as bishop was not required for access to the emperor; this could be achieved by prestige alone (though this might then result in ordination to a see).

The emperor's will was crucial in establishing the foundations of the new religion and those who would be its leaders; those who might influence that will had to be near the emperor. Because the emperor moved, gaining access to him also required movement, and so the bishops who wished to be influential moved (either temporarily to court, or to the synods or meetings, or, more permanently, from see to see). Advisors who lost favor and hence access also moved, in the opposite direction: home or into exile. Thus, people were in constant motion around the moving emperor and his court; and this did not change once the emperor's name was Julian or if the person seeking to write himself prestige to gain access, beginning with his second oration, was the young Gregory of Nazianzus. Part II of this book focuses on that oration, but to grasp fully the significance of Gregory's moves in the oration requires attention first to the person who played the central role in the empire for all its subjects in the years 361 and 362: Julian.

2

Julian, from Caesar to Augustus

Paris to Constantinople, 355–362

I swear to you by him who is the giver and preserver of all my good fortune that I desire to live only that I may in some degree be of use to you. When I say "you," I mean the true philosophers, and convinced as I am that you are one of these, how much have I loved and love you, you well know.

—JULIAN, EPISTLE 13 (WRIGHT 1), TO PRISCUS

Nazianzus, the *mansio* on the route linking Constantinople and Antioch, though a comparatively insignificant city when it appeared on the historical map in 362 or 363, had not remained unscathed by the seismic shifts accompanying the end of Constantius's reign and the beginning of Julian's. Indeed, Nazianzus owed its appearance on that map in no small measure to Julian's reign and his effect on both the emerging formulations of Christianity and their relevance within the Roman Empire. In other words, as the chapters that follow demonstrate, Gregory the Younger in his inaugural *Oration* 2 and in the subsequent ones—*Orations* 1 through 6 in particular—engaged and responded to the challenges that Julian's assumption of sole rule posed to the Christian elites. Julian's actions and pronouncements in his writings, coinage, edicts, laws, and imperial letters, and the concepts and notions regarding the divine and the philosophical life he expressed in these, were the catalyst that impelled Gregory and his peers to clarify their own thinking on these matters in direct engagement with Julian.

Furthermore, for Gregory at least, engaging Julian meant joining directly in the debates then of greatest moment to the Christian leaders and advisors. Because Julian directed some of his acts and pronouncements also at the tenets of the debates in the late 350s and up to 360/1 about the nature of the supreme Christian divinity, Gregory's response to Julian perforce participated in these debates as well. As a result Gregory the Younger emerged as a leading voice of the new generation of Christian thinkers and advisors who came into their own during the reigns of Julian and his immediate successors. Why did Julian have such an effect on Gregory, and on the majority of educated Christians for whom Gregory stands paradigmatic? To answer this question requires that I reconstruct what Julian argued and whom and what he argued against. The two chapters that follow trace Julian's rise to Caesar and then sole Augustus in the context of the dynastic and intellectual challenges he encountered. His acts and writings represent his response to those challenges. Gregory, however, remains the red thread throughout. Though I place Julian more fully in a broader historical and intellectual milieu than has been customary in scholarship, Gregory's knowledge of Julian's thoughts and actions prior to writing *Oration* 2 (that is, prior to Julian's departure from Constantinople and arrival in Antioch in the late summer of 362) is my principal concern. But while I try to make Julian stand on his own in the pages that follow, Gregory frames him as I demonstrate how deeply Gregory was formed by Julian.

TOWARD CONSTANTINOPLE: FROM CAESAR TO AUGUSTUS, 360–361

Julian as man and ruler has engaged the imagination of writers and scholars almost continuously since he first emerged as Augustus. The work of particularly profound importance characterizing the man and his rule, as well as his precursor Constantius as man and regent, is Julian's inaugural oration as newly acclaimed Augustus, the *Epistle to the Athenians*.[1] As Gregory's *Oration* 2 assumed extraordinary significance, so did Julian's *Epistle to the Athenians*. It did not mark Julian's first entry into the public arena of "letters" (nor was Gregory's *Oration* his de facto debut): earlier, Julian upon his accession to the purple as Caesar, had addressed his cousin, the emperor Constantius, in a panegyric, and had followed this with a speech of thanks to the empress Eusebia and another panegyric when his Augustus had won a series of decisive victories.[2] But much of the ancient historiography and nearly all modern historians have read these speeches and Julian's entire youth ex post facto, by way of Julian's *Epistle to the Athenians* and his shaping in this letter of his own life in deliberate contrast to that of Constantius.

According to the letter, a pivotal moment in Julian's life determined all that followed: the massacre after Constantine's death in 337. "That on the father's side I am

---

1. In what follows I use the editions published in Julian, *Oeuvres*, ed. and trans. Bidez, Rochefort, and Lacombrade; and in *Giuliano l'Apostata*, ed. and trans. I. Labriola (English translation: Julian, *Works*, ed. and trans. Wright). Labriola (p. 18) argues that the letter in its current form (with added prescript, proemium, and closing words) was published in Antioch between January and March 363 but that earlier versions circulated, to which Libanius, for example, had access.

2. Scholars debate whether Julian actually delivered these panegyrics in front of Constantius and Eusebia; Tougher, "In Praise of an Empress." I follow F. Curta, "Atticism," who assumes that Julian's circle and the emperor and his court heard or read them, or both. For a judicious assessment of this period, Tougher, *Julian*, 19–21, 31–43. I follow his dating.

descended from the same family as Constantius on his father's side is evident. For our fathers were brothers, having the same father. And although we were thus close relatives, this most philanthropic emperor treated us in such a way: six of my cousins and his, and my own father, who was his uncle, and another uncle we shared on the father's side, and my eldest brother, he killed without trial. And as for me and my other brother, he wanted to kill us, but in the end he imposed exile."[3] The *Epistle to the Athenians* presents a picture of Constantius's behavior toward Julian and Gallus that was consistent with a murderous character in its cruelty and amorality, indicating clearly that the emperor lacked all virtues. Constantius, Julian argued, was not fit to rule and did not legitimately represent the Flavian dynasty, or rather, represented only the degenerate branch of that dynasty. His every action, from the massacre of his siblings and relatives (whom Julian listed so as to emphasize precise family relations), to the shameful manner in which he exiled Julian and Gallus and kept them in solitary confinement throughout their youth and adolescence, to what Julian described as Constantius's murder of Gallus in 354, showed a man who embodied the opposite of every virtue, especially every imperial virtue. The gods, thus, had had no choice but to select Julian as their emissary and command him to reverse course and restore the ethical order of the realm and of its ruling dynasty.

Julian wrote that letter in the late summer or early fall of 361 while in Naissus, his last resting point on his progress toward the plain of Thrace and his descent into territory formally controlled by Constantius. Julian, that is, wrote the letter as a *hostis publicus* just before engaging the reigning Augustus, his cousin, in a civil war.[4] The letter is thus an *apologētikos logos,* Julian's justification of what could easily be seen as outright disloyalty and disobedience.[5] Without a doubt, the death of his father must have been a defining moment, but in 361 the sole survivor and thus the only person to blame for the events of 337 was Constantius, whatever his role at that earlier moment, and it was he against whom Julian was now about to march. In short, although the dramatic and dangerous events of 337 had an incalculable effect on Julian, then

---

3. Jul. *Ep. Ath.* 270c–271a[o]; quotation 270c–d: Καὶ ὅτι μὲν τὰ πρὸς πατρὸς ἡμῖν ἐντεῦθεν ὅθενπερ καὶ Κωνσταντίῳ τὰ πρὸς πατρὸς ὥρμηται φανερόν. τὼ γὰρ ἡμετέρω πατέρε γεγόνατον ἀδελφὼ πατρόθεν. οὕτω δὲ πλησίον ἡμᾶς ὄντας συγγενεῖς ὁ φιλανθρωπότατος οὗτος βασιλεὺς οἷα εἰργάσατο, ἓξ μὲν ἀνεψιοὺς ἐμοῦ τε καὶ ἑαυτοῦ, πατέρα δὲ τὸν ἐμόν, ἑαυτοῦ δὲ θεῖον, καὶ προσέτι κοινὸν ἕτερον τὸν πρὸς πατρὸς θεῖον ἀδελφόν τε ἐμὸν τὸν πρεσβύτατον ἀκρίτους κτείνας, ἐμὲ δὲ καὶ ἕτερον ἀδελφὸν ἐμὸν ἐθελήσας μὲν κτεῖναι, τέλος δὲ ἐπιβαλὼν φυγήν. The translations are Wright's (in Julian, *Works*), with my own and Tougher's (*Julian*, 80–85) modifications.

4. Szidat's argument ("Usurpation," 70, and *Historischer Kommentar*, part 3, 33) that Constantius did not declare Julian *hostis publicus* and that this reflects Ammianus's view has not found wide acceptance.

5. Amm. Marc. 21.5.1; Jul. *Ep.* 28 (Wright 9). Zos. 3.10.3 dates *Ep. Ath.* to Sirmium; Amm. Marc. 21.12.22, 22.2.1, 21.12.23–25; Lib. *Or.* 12.64, 14.29; Matthews, *Roman Empire*, 105–6; Bowersock, *Julian*, 60; Szidat, *Historischer Kommentar*, part 3, 17–19, 106–8. Ammianus dates this letter and the other ones addressed to Western cities after Constantius's death, thus highlighting Julian's legitimacy. For Naissus, Szidat, "Zur Ankunft."

merely six or seven years old, his views of 361 were not history but propaganda. His life up to 361, as he portrayed it in this letter, reflects the context of the summer and fall of 361 rather than what Julian thought in earlier years, before and immediately following his acclamation as Caesar, the second most important man of the realm.

To recapitulate, in February 360 troops under Julian's command had acclaimed Julian, the Caesar, as Augustus.[6] Constantius may not have been surprised in April 360, when he received the news in Caesarea in Cappadocia. Julian's second panegyric, delivered in the afterglow of a stunning victory near Strasbourg, had already suggested that he considered himself Achilles to Constantius's Agamemnon, inferior perhaps in rank but not in valor and importance.[7] Joint rule, at that time, was no exception, so that Ammianus's claim that Julian in 360 urged Constantius to accept an arrangement similar to the one he had had with Constans appears plausible.[8] As Clifford Ando has shown, Julian's envoys proceeded east deliberately, proclaiming Julian's Gallic victories as well as this conciliatory stance in all major cities, intending to force Constantius's hand by declaring Julian a legitimate contender.[9] Constantius, recently remarried and clearly hoping for a son, rejected Julian's requests to be recognized as Augustus. Instead, he began to suggest publicly that Julian retire to a private life; that is, he appears to have contemplated stripping him of his rank as Caesar.[10]

Early in 361, the bishops meeting in Paris under Julian's tutelage condemned Constantius's religious accord of 360 as heretical.[11] In April, Julian officially broke with the emperor (an act of *defectio* or *apostasia*), asked his soldiers to choose sides, and advanced with great speed toward Constantinople. While he consolidated his

---

6. Chapter 1, "Reversal: Constantius and Julian Augustus, 360–361." Jul. *Ep. Ath.* 282b–d; Lib. *Or.* 12.58–61, 18.90–102; Amm. Marc. 20.4.1–3; Zos. 13.10.11–16. The degree of Julian's involvement is much debated, ranging from claims that he was an innocent faced with Constantius's hostility (Athanassiadi-Fowden, *Julian*, 70–75) to his direct complicity; Bowersock, *Julian*, 46–52; Matthews, *Roman Empire*, 93–99; Drinkwater, "'Pagan Underground,'" esp. 370–83. See also Wiemer, *Libanios*, 28–32; and Lieu, ed., *Emperor Julian*, xii–xiv.

7. Some members of his army are said to have hailed him already then as Augustus; Amm. Marc. 16.12.64. Jul. *Or.* 2, ca. 358; *Ep.* 14 (Wright 4), *To Oribasius*. The battle took place in 357; Rosen, *Julian*, 150–51; Bouffartigue, *Empereur Julien*, 152–53. In comparison with the *Epistle to the Athenians*, Julian's earlier orations have received little attention, as I. Tantillo notes (Julian, *Prima Orazione*, ed. Tantillo, 12–16), in part because the adulatory genre reflects badly on the later emperor, who must have hidden his true feelings to flatter his cousin. Bowersock, *Julian*, 37, considers *Or.* 2 an act of diplomacy though Julian is beginning to demonstrate his independence; also Athanassiadi-Fowden, *Julian*, 63–66.

8. Rosen, "Beobachtungen."

9. Amm. Marc. 20.9.1. Ando, *Imperial Ideology*, 195–200, *pace* Szidat, *Historischer Kommentar*, part 2, *Die Verhandlungsphase*, 35–39; but see idem, "Usurpation."

10. Constantius's second wife, Eusebia, died in early 360, and he married Faustina during the period of negotiation; Amm. Marc. 21.6.4; Szidat, *Historischer Kommentar*, part 3, 54–55.

11. Brennecke, *Hilarius*, 360–67.

troops at Naissus prior to engaging Constantius, now also on the march, he began his public-relations campaign in earnest.[12] Julian's *Epistle to the Athenians* was part of a letter campaign addressing the citizens of Rome, Athens, Corinth, and Constantinople—cities that were in his part of the realm, with the exception of Constantinople—to demonstrate why and how he, the de facto usurper, a scion of the very same dynasty, differed from his cousin so that he, and not his cousin, truly represented the divine mandate imparted to the house of the Flavians.[13] As we know, Constantius died en route from the Persian frontier to Constantinople.[14] Julian was still in Naissus when he received the news of Constantius's death and the declarations of loyalty of high-ranking Eastern officials. On December 11, 361, he entered Constantinople as sole Augustus. Shortly afterwards, Julian accompanied Constantius's corpse to its final resting place in the Church of the Apostles, begun by Constantine but completed by Constantius—a gesture emphasizing the dynastic lineage they shared and hence his own legitimacy.[15]

At the same time, however, Julian made it clear that his profound differences with the deceased emperor had not been dictated merely by the circumstances. Among his first acts was a reorganization of the top echelon of leadership. It began, still in 361, with trials at Chalcedon conducted by Saturninius Secundus Salutius, praetorian prefect of the East, resulting in the execution of some of Constantius's staunchest supporters, especially among the high civil administration; the civilian palace administration was also reorganized.[16] Such measures were common after a change in leadership, but according to a number of sources Julian's reorganization sought not only to secure the loyalty of the army (which had provided the majority of the judges at Chalcedon) and the high administrators, but also to usher in a new style of imperial rule: a more modest form of imperial representation, less

---

12. Amm. Marc. 21.5.1; Jul. *Ep.* 28 (Wright 9). Naissus controlled access to Thrace via the pass of the Succi; Szidat, "Zur Ankunft," 375–78.

13. Amm. Marc. 21.10.7–8. Rosen, *Julian*, 217, emphasizes that these letters were addressed solely to cities in the West; he prefers an earlier date for the letter to Themistius; ibid., 220.

14. Jul. *Ep. Ath.* 269d, 281b; *Ep.* 28 (Wright 9); Amm. Marc. 20.8.18–19.1, 21.7.1–15.2, 22.2.1. Socr. *HE* 11.2–3; Philost. *HE* 6.5; Seeck, *Regesten*, 208–9; Kent, "Introduction," 109–17; Bowersock, *Julian*, 18, 58–65; Matthews, *Roman Empire*, 104–10; R. Smith, *Julian's Gods*, 4; Athanassiadi-Fowden, *Julian*, 82–86; Szidat, *Historischer Kommentar*, part 3, 181–92.

15. Amm. Marc. 21.16.20; den Boeft, den Hengst, and Teitler, eds., *Philological and Historical Commentary*, 275–77; Szidat, *Historischer Kommentar*, part 3, 235–39. In "Usurpation," 69, Szidat mentions that Julian walked ahead of Constantius's corpse, following (I presume) Gr. Naz.'s description in *Or.* 5.16–17; according to Philost. *HE* 6.6.6a–7a he walked behind the bier.

16. Claudius Mamertinus, who soon thereafter delivered a panegyric honoring Julian's consulship, and a certain Jovian assisted; among those executed were Constantius's powerful *praepositus sacri cubiculi* Eusebius and an infamous notary called Paul the Chain; Amm. Marc. 22.3.1–9; den Boeft, Drijvers, et al., eds., *Philological and Historical Commentary*, 17–35; Bowersock, *Julian*, 66–70; Matthews, *Roman Empire*, 251–52. For Saturninius Secundus Salutius, *PLRE*, vol. 1, 814, Secundus 3.

tolerant of corruption and ostentatious luxury, which made the ruler more accessible, in contrast to Constantius's style.[17]

This was not the sole contrast Julian intended. After being acclaimed as Augustus in Paris, Julian had begun to publicize his allegiance to the (pagan) gods while maintaining his adherence to the Christian religion. He had issued coins with a Christogram after 360; had celebrated the feast of the Epiphany in the church in Vienne on January 6, 361; presumably sponsored the council in Paris shortly thereafter; and, last but not least, presided over Constantius's Christian burial. But Julian also upon his acclamation appears to have sacrificed to the goddess Bellona, had begun issuing coins showing him with a philosopher's beard, had written to friends about worshipping the gods openly, and had declared the gods his saviors in the *Epistle to the Athenians* (*Ep. Ath.* 280d, 282d, 284b–c).[18]

As soon as he became sole ruler, he intensified his public displays of allegiance to the gods, without, however, neglecting the Christian religion. Such moves expressed a fundamental inclusiveness in matters religious, befitting a Roman emperor, responsible *tout court* for the *ius in sacris*. This openness or inclusiveness—evident also in Claudius Mamertinus's *gratiarum actio* delivered on January 1, 362, on the occasion of his consulate—is a topic that will concern us again.[19] According to Ammianus, Julian began to sacrifice openly almost immediately (something he and Constantius had forbidden in an edict issued in 356), and in January 362, after Constantius's burial, he issued an edict restituting all temple properties. But he also issued the edict, already mentioned, that recalled all those Christian leaders who had been sent into exile because they opposed the formulations of 359 and 360 and permitted them to return to their cities but not necessarily to their sees. Ammianus mentions, further, that Julian "summoned to the palace the bishops of the Christians, who were of conflicting opinions, and the people, who were also at variance, and advised them to lay aside their differences."[20]

---

17. Claud. Mam. *Pan. Lat.* 28.1–30.1 (Claudius Mamertinus, *Panegírico,* ed. and trans. García Ruiz); Dagron, *Empire romain,* 234; Bowersock, *Julian,* 70–78.

18. Kent, *Roman Imperial Coinage,* vol. 8, 45 n. 29, 192 no. 204, 422–23 nos. 217, 218, 220 for the beard; Claud. Mam. *Pan. Lat.* 11.6.4. Rosen, *Julian,* 231, dates Jul. *Ep.* 8, in which Julian mentions open pagan worship, after Constantius's death. Lib. *Or.* 18.114–15 mentions measures to restore temples in Macedonia and Greece. Hilary, however (*Lib. Const.* 2, ed. Feder, CSEL 65.198.5–7). called him "dominum meum religiosum Caesarem tuum Iulianum" in 359. Most scholars offer suggestions on when Julian shed his Christian mask and when he truly converted to paganism: e.g., Rosen, "Kaiser Julian"; Prostmeier, "'Wolke'"; Bleckmann, *Reichskrise,* 347–74, esp. 358–66.

19. Claud. Mam. *Pan. Lat.* refers to Julian's communication with the divine in a neutral manner with terms such as *deus,* 23.2, 28.5; *numen,* 3.2; *divinitas* and *divinus,* 15.2, 21.3. He makes no overt reference to Julian's religious actions, a telling silence, as Blockley remarks, "Panegyric," 447.

20. The text of the edict restituting temple properties has not been preserved; Amm. Marc. 22.5.2 refers to it as well as to public sacrifice. Inscriptions attest to temple rebuilding; Arce, "Reconstruc-

A similar equal-opportunity approach prevailed in the emperor's personal circle. In the process of reorganizing the court, Julian invited a number of persons he considered his friends to join him: pagan philosophers and rhetoricians such as Himerius, Libanius, Maximus of Ephesus, Chrysanthius, Priscus, Eustathius the Philosopher, and the Cynic Heraclius, but also Christian philosophers and rhetoricians such as Aetius and Basil.[21] Caesarius was already in Constantinople when Julian promoted him to the position of *archiater sacri palatii* and Friend of the Emperor.[22]

The Augustus of the Romans wished to differentiate his governance from that of his relative and precursor: so much was evident by late 361 and early 362. A change in imperial rule brought about tense times and always led to the realignment of high-ranking personnel, as the ascension of Constantius and his brothers also demonstrated. Julian's messages to his subjects, however, indicated that even though the transfer of rule had, in the end, proceeded without major bloodshed, he intended to alter some of the central tenets of previous Flavian rule. One of his fundamental alterations was his open proclamation of allegiance to the old gods, an implied consequence of which was a shift in the relevance of the Christian God as far as the emperor was concerned. A second alteration concerned Julian's imperial self-presentation, his demonstrative self-fashioning as a philosopher on the throne, proclaimed on his coins as early as 360. Not all the implications of these shifts for the status of Christians were evident in late 361 and early 362; grasping the implications, however, concerned many—in particular, members of the elite in Constantinople and elsewhere. They all had to chart the new territory represented by this emperor: Who would advise him, and what would their advice be, with what consequences? How was one to gain access to Julian and to those close to him? What would the new emperor's style of leadership be, and how would it affect his close circle and, through them and their intermediaries, the inhabitants of the *oikoumenē*?

Before engaging Julian's own proclamations on his rule as divinely authorized leader of the Romans and as a philosopher pledging allegiance to the old gods—concepts he elaborated in 361 in the *Epistle to the Athenians;* in a subsequent letter to the philosopher Themistius and through him addressing the senate of Constan-

---

ciones." *CTh* 16.10.6, Feb. 20, 356, punishes sacrifice as a capital offense. For the recall of the bishops, Amm. Marc. 22.5.3 and *Chron. Pasch.*, PG 92.740A; Ath. *Ep. fest.* 33; Philost. *HE* 3.27; Soz. *HE* 5.15.5; Socr. *HE* 2.38.23. Vaggione, *Eunomius*, 148–63, 269–72.

21. Not all came. For example, Chrysanthius remained in Lydia and became the high priest of the province. Jul. *Epp.* 32 (Basil), 34 (Eustathius), 46 (Aetius) (Wright 26, 43, and 15); Eun. *VS* 476, 477, 494, 497, and 501. Whether the Basil of *Ep.* 32 is Basil of Caesarea has caused much debate; Wiemer, *Libanios*, 32–48 and n. 98, often prompted by the wish to distance the later bishop from the Apostate. Basil's responding letters are spurious (*Epp.* 39–41 Courtonne); Smith, *Julian's Gods*, 41; Schlange-Schöningen, *Kaisertum*, 77–84; Matthews, *Roman Empire*, 122–29; Billerbeck, "Ideal Cynic."

22. Gr. Naz. *Or.* 7.9. Coulie, *Richesses*, 144–47.

tinople; and, in early 362, in two orations addressed to Cynics as well as in a hymn to the Mother of the Gods—it is worthwhile to consider how members of the elites not at court might have grasped the changes now upon them. What could someone like Gregory in Nazianzus have known? The answer, as we have seen in the preceding chapter, lies in the depth and density of individual members' connections to persons at court or in the residences at Constantinople and Antioch. As has already become apparent, those connections in Gregory's case were good.

The Emperor Speaks: But What Do His Subjects Hear?

When the news of Julian's acclamation reached the inhabitants of the Eastern Empire in the late spring and early summer of 360, most seem to have held their breath, realizing that a tense period lay ahead that would most likely be resolved in favor of the ruling emperor. Constantius, who controlled the majority of the troops, had dealt swiftly with past usurpers, and the fate of Gallus was also well known. Even though many of our sources were composed in hindsight, they report that many at the time adopted a stance similar in sentiment to, if more reserved than, that of the *honoratus* from Hierapolis mentioned by Ammianus who had openly asked for Julian's head, for Julian was no better than the usurper Magnentius.[23] Thus, a delegation from Rome arrived in the early summer of 361 in Antioch, led by the *senator conspicuus* Symmachus, to inform Constantius that the Roman senate did not approve of Julian's actions.[24] These activities were well known to Libanius, the prominent rhetor in Antioch, who befriended Symmachus and cultivated an extensive network, consisting mostly of former students (including Christian students); he also had relatives at court and in Constantinople. Libanius, too, continued to praise the reigning emperor—resident in Antioch, after all—but seems to have followed Julian's progress closely. Libanius, who counted Julian among his pupils and had exchanged letters with him at least until 358, functioned as a veritable clearinghouse for information.[25] Still, there was never enough news, especially once Julian began to move. As Libanius lamented: "Though many proclaim that they know things, in fact they know nothing."[26]

Gregory was less well connected than Libanius, but he knew persons (Basil, for

---

23. Amm. Marc. 22.14.4–5. Szidat, "Usurpation," 67–68; Bleckmann, "Constantina."
24. For Julian's attempts to win over the Roman senate, Ehling, "Kaiser."
25. Wiemer, *Libanios*, 13–17, 24–28, 38–39; Wintjes, *Leben*; Libanius, *Selected Letters*, trans. Bradbury, 6–7; Cribiore, *School*, 60–66.
26. Amm. Marc. 21.12.23; Lib. *Ep.* 1004.7 (Foerster); *Or.* 46.76–78 (*On Behalf of the Dancers*), *Epp.* 656.2 (Foerster), 661.3–4; quotation *Ep.* 677.2. Wiemer, *Libanios*, 30–31, 69–72; Szidat, *Historischer Kommentar*, part 3, 142–44. For the speed and dissemination of information, including private information, Ando, *Imperial Ideology*, 117–30. News of Constantius's illness, for example, reached Antioch within days; Euzoius was able to reach the emperor before he died. It reached Julian in Naissus, presumably via Nazianzus, five weeks later. Amm. Marc. 21.15.2; Lib. *Or.* 15.46; *Chron. Pasch.* 1.545.9–11; and *Art. Pass.* 20 for the call for Euzoius. Szidat, *Historischer Kommentar*, part 3, 184–85.

example) who in turn knew the rhetor and later on exchanged letters with him also. Moreover, he had ways and means of his own to gather information, primarily because of the location of Nazianzus along a principal route between Constantinople and Antioch. Constantius had been in residence in Caesarea, where the imperial household owned large estates, when he received the news of Julian's acclamation in 360, and he was there while deliberating his initial response.[27] The emperor in residence, as we noted in the preceding chapter, customarily received local notables, including bishops. The local bishop was Gregory the Elder's peer and friend Dianius; Basil, his reader, was in contact with Gregory the Younger. Furthermore, this was also the time when messengers spread out to collect signatures under the formulation of 360, and they would have spread news as well.

In addition, Caesarius was at Constantinople, had been close to Constantius's court since the late 350s, and was a member of Julian's court in late 361 and early 362. Gregory's access to news was thus at least as good as that of Libanius and conceivably even better; Libanius, as we shall see, soon complained that he was not as close to Julian as he felt he ought to have been. Gregory's circle of Constantinopolitan sources was in fact fairly wide. As later letters attest, Gregory knew the philosopher Themistius, whom Julian addressed in his official letter intended for a wider Constantinopolitan audience.[28] Himerius, whom Gregory had known since Athens, and who is said to have been one of his teachers, was among those Julian had invited to his court in early 362. Basil may also have received such an invitation. Whether Gregory and Basil knew the Cappadocian philosopher Eustathius, another recipient of an imperial invitation, is uncertain.[29] Gregory (and Basil), however, kept in touch with Cappadocians in imperial service and at the capital, men such as Candidianus, a judge (*archōn*) under Julian; Sophronius, Caesarius's friend, and Aburgius, both notaries in Constantinople; a certain Martianus; and Julian's military officers Arinthaeus, Jovinus, and Victor.[30] In short, Gregory was as well informed as anyone could have hoped to be. He had contacts with a number of persons with access to the court, especially his brother, and those persons could easily

---

27. Van Dam, *Kingdom*, 96.
28. For Gregory and Themistius, see Chapter 6, "Themistius as a Philosophical Model." Julian's original letter was written in the 350s, and revised, with an added ending, in 360 or 361. Vanderspoel, *Themistius*, 27–29, concurs.
29. Basil's *Ep.* 1, *To Eustathius the Philosopher*, is most likely addressed to Eustathius of Sebaste. For the debate, S. Elm, *Virgins*, 61 n. 3; Bouffartigue, *Julien*, 105 n. 388, thinks the addressee was Eustathius the Philosopher but seems unaware of other possibilities.
30. Candidianus: Gr. Naz. *Ep.* 10; Bas. *Ep.* 3. Sophronius: Gr. Naz. *Epp.* 21, 22, 29, 37; Bas. *Epp.* 75, 76; Amm. Marc. 26.7.2, notary in 365; Aburgius, too, was probably a notary. For Victor, Jovinus, and Arinthaeus, Amm. Marc. 26.1.2, 25.5.2, 25.10.9. Hauser-Meury, *Prosopographie*, s.vv.; Treucker, *Politische und sozialgeschichtliche Studien*, 43–61. For Victor's later stature and his Arab connections, Shahîd, *Byzantium*, 164–68. For Gregory's Constantinopolitan connections, McLynn, "The Other Olympias."

have furnished him with extensive notes and summaries of Julian's pronouncements, if not indeed actual copies of the emperor's writings.[31] To reiterate Leonardo Lugaresi's assessment,[32] Gregory knew well what Julian was doing and saying from an early stage, and was also aware of the reaction of others in Constantinople and Antioch to the events of 360, 361, and 362.

Gregory and Basil had been aware of Julian, member of the ruling dynasty, for some time. Julian had spent the years from 342 to 347/8 at the imperial estate of Macellum, a beautiful palace with gardens, pools, and perpetual fountains just outside Caesarea, where one of his teachers had been George, Dianius's predecessor as bishop of Caesarea, who moved to Alexandria to replace Athanasius. Julian, according to his letters, had made extensive use of George's library while at Macellum.[33] Furthermore, he had been a reader in the church at Caesarea, and both he and Gallus had sponsored the erection of a shrine there devoted to the martyr Menas.[34] Finally, Julian had spent some time at Athens in 355—while both Gregory and Basil were students there—studying for his part with Himerius and Prohaeresius as well as a certain Priscus, who became one of his most trusted advisors, accompanying him all the way to Persia. Thus, even though one can harbor the suspicion that Julian's letter inviting Basil to court is spurious, it is, if not true, then very well invented: Gregory and Basil had known Julian from a time long before his accession as Caesar, and he may well have known them also, as Gregory would later claim. (After all, Julian certainly knew Gregory's brother!)[35]

Once Julian was sole emperor—as he himself knew—his words and pronouncements took on a different character entirely, and their circulation had a different effect. "Letters from the emperor," Julian wrote to his friend Philip in early 362, "even to private persons, might well lead to their display for bragging and making false pretenses when they come into the hands of persons with no sense of propriety, who carry them about like seal rings and show them to the inexperienced."[36] Julian's proclamations, edicts, and imperial letters (even some private letters) now had

---

31. Any reconstruction of Gregory's access to Julian's pronouncements is circumstantial, because he never cites a work of Julian verbatim, as befitting the stylistic demands of the Second Sophistic, though he does cite the title of the *Misopogon;* see Chapter 10, "Procopius versus Valens" and "*Misopogon* and *Oration 5.*"

32. Gregory of Nazianzus, *Contro Giuliano,* trans. and comm. Lugaresi, 15.

33. Earlier, he had been educated by Constantius's counselor Eusebius, bishop of Constantinople, Amm. Marc. 22.9.4. N. Henck, "From Macellum." Interesting though criticized for its psychologizing is Festugière, "Julian."

34. Soz. *HE* 5.2 for the description of Macellum and Julian as reader; also Gr. Naz. *Or.* 4.24–26, 52, 97.

35. Gr. Naz. *Or.* 5.23. For Prohaeresius, Jer. *Chron.* at 363 (Helm); Watts, *City,* 64–67. Priscus will be discussed below; Bouffartigue, *Empereur Julien,* 45–46. On late-antique Athens in this context, Blázquez, "Academia."

36. Jul. *Ep.* 40 (Wright 30).

the force of law, and their publication was an awe-inspiring act. As John Matthews has illustrated, imperial letters and edicts, "imperial writings" (*basilika grammata*) inscribed in "celestial letters" onto stone or bronze tablets,[37] or, more commonly, on papyrus, linen sheets, or wooden tablets coated with wax and stamped with the royal seal, embodied the emperor's sacred person.[38] When they arrived at a destination, they were embraced and kissed, and when they were read out loud, it was the emperor himself who spoke, lectured, responded, exhorted, and ordered. To interrupt a reading, modify, or destroy an imperial writing was to attack the emperor, a near-unthinkable sacrilege.[39] Thus, whenever an imperial letter was read out, profound silence reigned.[40] Further, imperial letters and edicts were "posted in the usual fashion" on designated walls within easy reach of all, so that no one could claim ignorance.[41] Julian himself referred repeatedly to such publication methods by stressing that he addressed "all communities of citizens . . . to make known to all" his wishes, leaving no doubt, for example, that his instructions "should be displayed to my citizens of Alexandria."[42] Julian rightly assumed that his proclamations as Augustus would be inscribed and pronounced everywhere he wished them to be, and would affect everyone in the manner he intended.

Thus even those who had no access to privileged information, who did not live in imperial residences or along the well-traveled routes that provided occasions for sharing information, were aware of Julian's major announcements, which the emperor also communicated in shorthand in his statues, images, and coins—for example, by having himself portrayed as bearded like a philosopher.[43] That his subjects also heard him is attested by inscriptions. One from Asia, for example, was dedi-

---

37. "Celestial letters" as a distinctive type of writing; Matthews, *Laying Down*, 188. C. Williamson, "Monuments," esp. 180–81. For the terminology of tablets, A. Wilhelm, *Beiträge*, 239–49.

38. On imperial letters from Diocletian to Constantine, Corcoran, *Empire*, 123–69, 170–71; 198–203 for the general characteristics of edicts.

39. Matthews, *Laying Down*, 186–99; Ando, *Imperial Ideology*, 73–117; Price, *Rituals*, 87–100, and 170–206 on the identity of the imperial image and person. Interesting, though concerned with the early empire only, Benner, *Emperor*.

40. Amm. Marc. 28.2.11; J. Chrys. *Hom. on Genesis, PG* 53.112: "There is not the slightest noise; everyone listens most attentively to the orders contained in them. Whoever makes the slightest noise, thereby interrupting the reading, runs the greatest danger." Similarly, from Rabbi Isaac, in the time of Diocletian: "A king sent out his order to a city. What did the people in the city do? They rose to their feet, uncovered their heads, and read it in awe, fear, trembling, and trepidation." Lieberman, "Roman Legal Institutions," esp. 6–10; Matthews, *Roman Empire*, 264–65.

41. *CTh* 16.5.37; *Sirm. Const.* 9, 12, 14, 16; Ulp. *Digest*. 14.3.11; Matthews, *Laying Down*, 186.

42. Jul. *Epp.* 60, 114, 115 (Wright 21, 40, 41). For an indication of the wide and thorough spread of such information, A. H. M. Jones, "Notes."

43. Ando, *Imperial Ideology*, 206–28 on imperial control of the mints; for the impact of the imperial message (through coins) in general, see Noreña, "Communication"; S. Elm, "Gregory's Women," esp. 179–82 with bibliography on imperial images.

cated to Julian FILOSOFI[AE] MAGISTRO ... PRINCIPI PIISIMO [IMP]ERATORI; another, from Caria, "to Julian, the philosopher and emperor."[44]

JULIAN'S CONCEPTS OF LEADERSHIP: PHILOSOPHER AND KING

The True Philosophical Life: The Classical Matrix of a Continuing Debate

"If anyone has persuaded you that there is anything more delightful or more profitable for humankind than to philosophize free from cares, in leisure [*philosophein epi scholēs apragmonōs*], he is a deluded man trying to delude you."[45] Thus Julian wrote in 358 or 359 as Caesar in Gaul to two fellow students whom he "loved like brothers." The same sentiments pervade his letters to Priscus, probably the most influential of his Athenian teachers of philosophy, who had come to visit him in Gaul and to whom Julian wrote about the same time, as follows: "I swear to you by him who is the giver and preserver of all my good fortune that I desire to live only that I may in some degree be of use to you. When I say 'you,' I mean the true philosophers."[46] For Julian as Caesar, actively engaged in a series of highly successful military campaigns and, at least according to some sources (including perhaps his second panegyric), already preparing to become Augustus, the greatest human delight was to pursue the true philosophical life at leisure.[47] Julian expressed those sentiments in private to men who shared his preference for the ancient gods, already evident by then. The subject of philosophical leisure as ideal and its relation to active engagement in the affairs of the community, or *politeia*, was, however, at least at first glance, nothing the Caesar necessarily needed to keep private. Plato's and Aristotle's seminal pronouncements on the topic were, on the contrary, evoked and discussed regularly by many members of the educated elites holding public office.

At the heart of the debate was a question as old as Athens itself: Who was the ideal ruler? The man who favored a life of active involvement in the politics of the city, or one who lived mostly in retreat, contemplating divine justice, and intervened in the affairs of the *politeia* only when necessity demanded that he do so?[48] What should one value more, the "practical life" (*bios praktikos*) or the "theoretical life"

---

44. Arce, *Estudios*, 110, 156–58, 161; τὸν ἐκ φιλοσοφίας βασιλεύοντα καὶ δικαιοσύνῃ ... Ἰουλιανόν.
45. Jul. *Ep.* 8 (Wright 3), *To Eumenius and Pharianus*.
46. Jul. *Ep.* 13 (Wright 1): ἐγώ δὲ ὄμνυμί σοι τὸν πάντων ἀγαθῶν αἴτιον ἐμοὶ καὶ Σωτῆρα ὅτι διὰ τοῦτο ζῆν εὔχομαι, ἵν' ὑμῖν τι χρήσιμος γένωμαι· τὸ δὲ "ὑμῖν" ὅταν εἴπω, τοὺς ἀληθινούς φημι φιλοσόφους. For the date, Julian, *Epistolario*, trans. and comm. Caltabiano, 80–81.
47. Matthews, *Roman Empire*, 82; for Julian's early preparations, Bleckmann, *Reichskrise*, 345–52.
48. The bibliography on the subject is vast. In what follows I am relying primarily on Scholz, *Philosoph*; Allen, *World*, 182–96, 245–91; Saïd, *Sophiste*; Mayhew, *Aristotle's Criticism*; Laks, "Legislation"; Lanza, "Critica."

(*bios theōrētikos*)? The debate originated with the notion that leisure, freedom from care and ignoble labor, was the ideal state, the essential privilege of divine beings. Humans were condemned to work the earth. But if they undertook labor by choice rather than out of necessity or under duress, that labor was an excellent means to improve themselves. Even more, labor was an essential precondition for humans who sought to approach the divine.[49] Thus, though freedom from care and retreat from worldly concerns approximated the divine state, leisure must not be mistaken for inactivity or laziness (*argia*). For that reason, even rulers—or especially rulers—were obliged to work. Their work consisted in extensive study of the laws and guiding principles conveyed by the supreme lawgiver, Zeus, and consequently in the search for and dispensation of justice.[50] The ideal life for a freeborn, elite man combined the obligation to work for the benefit of his city and his fellow citizens and the freedom to contemplate the divine laws of justice and to acquire, in tranquility, a deep understanding of the meaning of the divine and its words. The person embodying this ideal most perfectly was the philosopher, who was therefore also the ideal ruler, because, to cite Plato's formulation in the *Theaetetus,* "he could assimilate himself to the divine in the highest possible degree."[51]

That was just the beginning of the debate, however. In Aristotle's formulation, those predisposed by virtue of their birth, wealth, and education to the nobler life could choose between two equally virtuous, equally rational, and equally good forms of "retreat" (*apragmosynē*): the retreat of the "practical life" (*bios praktikos*) and that of the "theoretical life" (*bios theōrētikos*). Although the concept of retreat as a form of engagement in practical life may appear self-contradictory, the debate refers in fact to complementary notions. According to Aristotle, to prepare for the practical life of involvement in the affairs of the *politeia* required retreat as preparation, whereas to live the theoretical life required a retreat fully devoted to rigorous intellectual pursuits, which, once achieved at a high level, had to be tested in practice. Both forms of retreat, which could be practiced sequentially, sought to approximate, to differing degrees, the divine state of freedom from care.[52] At issue, thus, was how to assess and practice an appropriate relationship between the two forms of good leisure. What kind of philosophical life was ideal for governance? What was the correct mixture of practical and theoretical life? In other words, what were the relative merits of utter dedication to intellectual training in tranquility, which incurred the risk of laxity and uselessness, and a life that combined retreat

---

49. Demont, *Cité*, 33–113; idem, "Problèmes."
50. J. Jouanna, "Réflexions"; von Staden, "Idéal."
51. Pl. *Tht.* 174a, 176a3–b3, and passim; Demont, "Problèmes," 34; Scholz, *Philosoph*, 75–121; and Goulet, "Vies."
52. Arist. *EN*, esp. book 1; Demont, *Cité*, 343–63; G. Huber, "*Bios*"; Kullmann, "Aristote"; Scholz, *Philosoph*, 125–81; and Kenny, *Aristotle*.

with active involvement and governance, certainly good and useful, but exposing the practitioner to improvisation, diminished time for theoretical reflection and training, and, almost inevitably, corruption through power?[53]

Plato and Aristotle's discussions of the proper disposition, preparation, and conduct of those who govern and their debate about the relative merits of various forms of retreat continued to elicit responses through successive generations, in particular when the importance of rhetorical training or *paideia* increased as markers of status. Later generations revisited the normative texts and reiterated these fundamental topoi, with subtle variations and nuanced differences between forms of leisure and activity.[54] It was essential that a leader declare his own choice (*prohairesis*) of the appropriate mixture of retreat and active participation. As the following section illustrates further, such a declaration was evidently required as part of an inaugural moment marking the acceptance of office. To display publicly one's mastery of the finer points of the debate demonstrated one's capacity to govern and permitted others to gauge it, for such a demonstration showed to best advantage the excellence of the man's education and thus of his status, while permitting his audience to give evidence of theirs as well by their own appreciation of the finer points on display. In other words, rhetorical sophistication in showcasing one's devotion to philosophical leisure and retreat was a skill especially valuable for those most engaged in active governance, including the emperor and the Caesars.[55]

Julian's letters to his confidants, praising the joys of leisure and tranquility, expressed these sentiments at an appropriate moment: right in the thick of a period of forceful leadership and valiant action. In his second panegyric of Constantius, Julian had hinted (and, later on, emphasized, in the *Epistle to the Athenians*) that the conditions along the Rhine frontier were terrible and that the troops at his disposal were so inadequate that he achieved his victories nearly miraculously, but also that those victories proved his considerable military acumen and leadership abilities. He made it clear in so many words that he considered it an opportune moment to receive (so that he would not be forced to seize) a position as leader on equal

---

53. Cicero, for example, favored greater practical involvement, and Theophrastus more theory; whereas Demetrius of Phalerum proposed a mixed life: Gottschalk, "Demetrius"; Gehrke, "Verhältnis"; School of Aristotle, *Schule*, ed. Wehrli, 2nd ed., 44; André, *Otium*, 168–69; Scholz, *Philosoph*, 185–249.

54. The subtleties of such elaborations are easily overlooked today, since a modern scholar is inevitably less aware of the nuanced code used by the highly trained men of the time. Demont, *Cité*, 14–30; von Staden, "Idéal," 156–60.

55. The emperors did so, on the whole, through others speaking on their behalf, but not Julian. Wallace-Hadrill, "*Civilis Princeps*"; Béranger, "Réfus"; André, *Otium*, 531–41; Brown, *Power*, 21–60; Henck, "Constantius' *paideia*"; Alexandre, "Clément"; Garzya, "Sur l'idée"; idem, "Sul rapporto" and "Ideali"; Hahn, *Philosoph*, 161–63, 192–208; and idem, "Philosophen," esp. 401–12; I do not concur with some of Hahn's conclusions on p. 412. For the influence of rhetoric, also Heath, *Menander*, esp. 52–89. C. P. Jones, *Roman World*; Jouan, "Loisir."

terms with the Augustus.⁵⁶ To emphasize one's desire for philosophical retreat and one's devotion to leisure at a moment of intense action (and a hoped-for, if not indeed demanded, acclamation as Augustus) corresponded precisely to a quality Plato had considered essential for the ideal ruler: that he had to be sought out and persuaded to accept office against his express wishes. Julian, correspondingly, loved only philosophy and could not imagine a higher calling than philosophical retreat and tranquility.⁵⁷ Only those least qualified sought out leadership roles, their very hunger for power (*philarchia*) revealing their incompetence. Julian was not such a person.⁵⁸ The greater the reluctance to accept public office, the higher the leadership potential; Julian's letters to his philosophical friends, cited above, thus express sentiments very much in line with his second panegyric of Constantius, written at about the same time, after recent victories. Those privy to these musings would have understood the message.⁵⁹

Julian's declaration to his friends and confidants of his desire for the philosophical life thus complemented rather than contradicted his activities as Caesar and military commander. Indeed, because they were in effect pronouncements of his intention to act as a leader and would have been understood as such, he was well

---

56. Jul. *Or.* 2.71c–73d, 85d–92d, 97b–101b—really the entire oration, which has been less studied than one would think; Jul. *Ep. Ath.* 277d–280d, echoed by Amm. Marc. 16.2, 16.11–12, 17.1–2, 17.8, 17.10.

57. These pronouncements praising philosophy cause scholars to question whether Julian was an innocent bystander in his acclamation by the army; my interpretation suggests the opposite; Athanassiadi-Fowden, *Julian*, 70–75; Buck, "Eunapius." Matthews (*Roman Empire*, 93–99) and Drinkwater ("'Pagan Underground,'" 370–83) see high-ranking army members responsible as the actors behind the scene of the acclamation.

58. In Plato's words: "The true nature of things is that . . . everyone who needs to be governed must go to the door of the man who knows how to govern, and not that the ruler should implore his natural subjects to let themselves be ruled, if he is really good for anything" (τὸ δὲ ἀληθὲς πέφυκεν . . . ἀναγκαῖον εἶναι [ἐπὶ ἰατρῶν θύρας] ἰέναι καὶ πάντα τὸν ἄρχεσθαι δεόμενον ἐπὶ τὰς ‹θύρας› τοῦ ἄρχειν δυναμένου, οὐ τὸν ἄρχοντα δεῖσθαι τῶν ἀρχομένων ἄρχεσθαι, οὗ ἂν τῇ ἀληθείᾳ τι ὄφελος ᾖ), Pl. *R.* 6.489c (*Platonis Opera*, ed. Burnet, vol. 4).

59. Debates about the relation between retreat and involvement also occurred in the West. For the Latins, too, *otium* was the ideal, and office an unwelcome and unsought distraction that the true leader eventually accepted to gain, in Cicero's classic formulation, "otium cum dignitate" (*De orat.* 1.1); *Sest.* 45.98, "neque enim rerum gerendarum dignitate homines efferi ita convenit, ut otio non prospiciant, neque ullum amplexari otium, quod abhorreat a dignitate"; and *Rep.* 2.42.69, "se ipso instituendo contemplandoque discedat, ut ad imitationem sui vocet alios, ut sese splendore animi et vitae suae sicut speculum praebeat civibus"; see also D.C. 36.24.5–6, 27.2; Plin. *Pan.* 5.5. When Sextus Petronius Probus was recalled to the praetorian prefecture in 383, Symmachus wrote to console him (*Ep.* 1.58): "Put aside your nostalgic thoughts of leisure [*otium*], . . . be tolerant, as you are, of all duties, and perform this obligation that you owe to the emperors; for in exacting it, they have considered more your abilities than your desires"—words addressed to a man who was, according to Amm. Marc. 27.11.3, like a fish out of water when not holding a prefecture; Matthews, *Western Aristocracies*, 1–12, quotation at 11; idem, "Letters"; Roda, "Fuga."

advised to express them initially in private letters to close friends, most likely also the test group for his panegyrics. Such deliberations gained far greater currency, however, once Julian had been acclaimed Augustus and after the open *defectio* or *apostasia* from Constantius in April 361. Further, once he became sole ruler, his own choice of the true philosophical life had real and profound consequences: as emperor, his thoughts became sacred imperial pronouncements with the force of law. Therefore, Emperor Julian's choices in combining labor and leisure—that is, his personal views of the true philosophical life—concerned all members of the elite, themselves formed by *paideia,* since these views would be the principles guiding his rule.[60] The two public letters that have survived among those that Julian sent from Naissus—the *Epistle to the Athenians* and the *Epistle to Themistius*—address precisely the issues just raised: the divinely authorized legitimacy of Julian's claims to sole rule, the main topic of the *Epistle to the Athenians,* and his understanding of true philosophy, addressed in the *Epistle to Themistius* and further elaborated in the orations that Julian pronounced in the spring of 361 in Constantinople, discussed in the chapter that follows.[61]

The Epistle to the Athenians: *Saved by the Gods through Philosophy*

Julian's *Epistle to the Athenians* was among his first public pronouncements after the breakdown of negotiations with Constantius and his swift move down the Danube to Naissus and then Constantinople. Julian had now challenged the ruling emperor openly; he was no longer content to share governance but wished to rule alone. Thus, the letters he wrote from Naissus to the inhabitants of Illyricum and Italy, to the Greek cities Sparta, Corinth, and Athens, and to the senates at Rome and Constantinople were justifications but also declarations of imperial intent, constituting his inaugural address as the presumptive emperor (who had, of course, Fate on his side). As many scholars have pointed out, Julian's choice of cities was not accidental. While Rome and Constantinople were the chief centers of Roman power, Sparta, Corinth, and Athens resonated differently, evoking particular ways of life and a special concern for philosophy, justice, and other virtues intrinsic to being Greek as a result of proper intellectual formation through *paideia.*[62]

As I have noted, Julian's *Epistle to the Athenians* was an *apologētikos logos* in the form of an autobiography: Julian sought to justify his actions and the impending civil war by recounting his fate as a youth under Constantius's thumb and by re-

---

60. See the contributions in A. Smith, ed., *Philosopher.*
61. Julian, *Epistolario,* trans. and comm. Caltabiano, 55–60.
62. Zos. 3.10.3 (Sirmium); Amm. Marc. 21.12.22, 22.2.1, 21.12.23–25; Lib. *Or.* 12.64, 14.29; Matthews, *Roman Empire,* 105–6; Bowersock, *Julian,* 60; Szidat, *Historischer Kommentar,* part 3, 17–19, 106–8.

porting his recent "conduct, . . . so that if there is anything you do not know . . . , it may become known to you and through you to the rest of the Greeks" (270b). As a genre, the *apologētikos logos* owed its popularity among rhetors and forensic advocates to its purpose: to persuade the audience, considered the judges in an imaginary or indeed real trial, that the speaker's position in defense of the accused was just, right, and virtuous.[63] The genre followed set rules, encoded like all other forms of forensic and epideictic rhetoric in a long teaching tradition.[64] The speaker, beginning with an evocation of the appropriate divine powers, proceeded in two steps: the first a detailed account of events, illustrating how the defendant's character and behavior refuted the accusation, and the second the defense proper, which highlighted the defendant's virtues. These steps involved the use of a number of stylistic elements, most prominently the *dialektikon*, or refutation of the adversary's position, and the *synkrisis*, or comparison of the protagonist with the appropriate heroes of the past.[65]

In the *Epistle to the Athenians*, Julian acted as his own advocate and consequently presented events to justify his behavior (the *dialektikon*) autobiographically: Julian had been forced by the circumstances of his life up to 361 to act as he had done. The judges called upon in the opening lines of this letter were the Athenians, whom Julian had chosen explicitly because of their city's "reputation for justice," which had been "assigned to [Athens] by ancient tradition" and had singled it out among all Greek cities (*Ep. Ath.* 268a–270a). The Athenians can best judge whether "one has accomplished [a] feat by just means, and then if he seems to act with justice." Hence the Athenians' (undoubtedly positive) judgment of Julian's case, once "it may become known to you and through you to the rest of the Greeks" (270b), was decisive. If they were "to praise [Julian] both in public and private" as having acted justifiably, who could then doubt his legitimacy (269d–270a)?

The essence of Julian's justification was straightforward. Julian was no tyrant, no usurper, but the legitimate ruler, because the current one was an illegitimate criminal, embodying the worst of their shared ancestry. Julian had thus been saved by "the gods through the means of philosophy" (272a) to restore legitimate rule; he, not his cousin, represented the divinely authorized, therefore true, heritage of the Flavian dynasty.[66] His recent military victories against all odds and his recognition of the true gods through philosophy manifested this divine authorization.

---

63. Men. Rh. *Treatise* 1.1 (*Menander Rhetor*, ed. and trans. Russell and Wilson, 2; *Peri epideiktikōn*, ed. Spengel, 331–32). Humfress, *Orthodoxy*, 9–21, 51–55, discusses the relation between rhetorical training and forensic advocacy in late antiquity; Volkmann, *Rhetorik*, 2nd ed., 148–64; J. Martin, *Antike Rhetorik*, 75–89; von Lingenthal, *Geschichte*, 3rd ed., 35–83.

64. An *invocatio* of the god (or gods) was a standard part of forensic speech; Ruether, *Gregory*, 75; Neumeister, *Grundsätze*, 17–31.

65. Ruether, *Gregory*, 76–80, 106–7.

66. Dagron, *Empire romaine*, 67–68, esp. 67 n. 189.

Military success and true philosophy were the cornerstones of his imperial endeavor. As far as the *Epistle to the Athenians* was concerned, Julian's recognition of the true gods and their choice of him as their divine emissary, saved through philosophy, were essential to his success in performing the high-wire act at the heart of the letter, namely to claim dynastic legitimacy while seeking to destroy the most exalted member of that dynasty in every way possible: by force and by destruction of his reputation.

Julian, effectively using the rules of the genre, began his *Epistle to the Athenians* and thus his assassination of Constantius's character with the vivid account of the murder of his family cited above (270c–d). His massing of terms denoting family relations leaves no doubt that Constantius's murder of Julian's family was also the slaughter of Constantius's own family, the most abhorrent of crimes. That a man who could perform such deeds could not be a legitimate ruler was borne out by his subsequent conduct. In every way possible Constantius acted vis-à-vis Julian as only a tyrant and murderer of his own family would and in the process revealed himself to be driven by deception, submissive to an undisciplined army, and beholden to "an androgyne, his chamberlain, who was in addition the steward of his cooks" (i.e., the eunuch Eusebius, 272d, 271b). Thus, he had "imprisoned" Julian throughout his youth "on a certain farm of those in Cappadocia, allowing no one to approach. . . . How should I describe the six years spent there? For [Gallus and I] lived as though on a stranger's property, closely observed as though we were in some Persian garrison: no stranger approached us, nor was any of our old intimates permitted to visit us; we lived cut off from all serious learning and from free converse, reared in magnificent servitude [*en tais lamprais oiketeiais*] and exercising with our own slaves as if they were comrades [*doulois hōsper hetairois*]" (271c).

The degradations and humiliations only increased when Constantius had made Julian Caesar. Now such treatment had even more deleterious consequences, since it no longer affected a merely private person, though a member of the imperial family, but a ruling Caesar, hence a man who carried the weight of the second-highest office in the realm.[67] Yet, just prior to granting Julian "that august title," Constantius had denied him access to his presence, though they spent six months in the same city, Milan, and had even asked Julian to retire to Greece, an outrage of near unprecedented proportions, topped only, when he in his turn refused to communicate with the palace, by Constantius's men grabbing him and forcing him to shave his philosopher's beard (273d–274d); thus he became Caesar.[68]

---

67. As Julian pointed out (*Ep. Ath.* 270d), he was a private man, but after Gallus's death he and Constantius, who was childless, were the only remaining male members of the dynasty.

68. Julian's stay at Athens, according to Matthews (*Roman Empire,* 85) and Drinkwater ("'Pagan Underground,'" 368), was de facto an exile, as Julian suggests in *Ep. Ath.* 273d, or at least a measure to prevent him from proceeding to Bithynia and his mother's estate (i.e., close to Constantinople) while

The purpose of all these accusations was to prove Constantius's inability to rule, made evident by such shameful treatment of his own family members. But why should Julian be different? After all, as everyone knew and he had stressed, "on the father's side [Julian was] descended from the same family as Constantius on his father's side" (270c). Furthermore, according to his own earlier panegyrics, as contemporaries presumably knew, especially those whose opinion mattered to Julian, Constantius had behaved appropriately vis-à-vis Julian and Gallus. He had let them live, had acted in their father's stead, had permitted Julian to inherit his mother's estate and Gallus some of his father's (273b), had accorded them an appropriate education, and had granted both of them leadership roles as Caesars. Gallus, as Julian was forced to admit, had been a failure. Given the responsibilities of the position, it was only prudent that Constantius (who was then fighting off usurpers) exercise a certain caution, at least until the new Caesar had proved himself. Conversely, if Constantius's behavior had indeed been as degenerate as Julian took pains to point out, then why should Julian be so much better, especially if his brother Gallus had fallen short (272a)?[69] Why should the Athenians, and with them all the Greeks, trust his protestations of legitimacy, and cast their lot with him?

Julian's answer was, because the gods had saved him explicitly to save the realm and thus also his dynasty. They had been his protectors during a youth marred by Constantius's brutality; they had kept him "pure and untouched"; indeed, by forcing him to live such a life they had tested his mettle and made it possible for him "to submit and consent to live under the same roof with those whom I knew to have ruined my family" (275a). His unfortunate brother's lack of such divine succor had rendered him almost as "unfit to govern" as their cousin (272a). Thus the gods, not Constantius or Gallus, were his true family.[70]

Constantius was engaged against Silvanius. However, Julian also claimed that he had very much wished to go to Athens as part of his philosophical quest; Tougher, "In Praise of an Empress," 120–21.

69. When discussing Gallus, Julian once again amasses terminology stressing their close family relation as *adelphoi;* the letter serves to rehabilitate Gallus (esp. *Ep. Ath.* 271a) as much as possible, given his "savage and rude" nature (271d, 272b–c). Ironically, the actual circumstances of Gallus's downfall, his mishandling of a grain shortage in Antioch, later posed similar difficulties for Julian; Matthews, *Roman Empire,* 406–8. Bleckmann, "Constantina," argues that Gallus's mistake may have been a similarly Tetrarchic (i.e., collegial) understanding of his role as Caesar such as Julian tried to implement and Constantius wished to curb. Malosse's "Enquête," a recent reconstruction of Julian and Gallus's early years, indicates that they hardly knew each other before their time at Macellum, between ca. 342 and 347/8; Gallus, six to eight years older, may have been entrusted with supervising Julian, which may have caused tensions. Julian's closeness to Gallus as evoked in the letter is largely a literary move to show how they were both mistreated by Constantius.

70. Julian's apparent reluctance to rely on dynastic succession alone rather than on merit (thematized, for example, in his panegyrics of Constantius, where he stresses Constantius's merit as the true source of his greatness, implying the same for himself) has frequently been noted. After 361, however, such reluctance arose from his need to disparage Constantius and does not imply a principled stance

To prove his point, Julian recounted the period just before he was elevated as Caesar as an elaborate *recusatio,* demonstrating his utter refusal even to consider the honor of becoming the second most important person in the known world. He had been in Athens at the moment when Constantius had requested that he accept the yoke of office, and as Athenian eyewitnesses could attest, his first inclination had been to take his own life rather than leave Athens to "journey to the emperor" (275a–b).[71] Julian, begging Athena not to abandon him, was granted favors similar to those given to Odysseus: constant and concrete guidance from Athena, "bringing guardian angels from Helios and Selene" (275b). Nevertheless Julian, upon returning to Milan, was still adamant that he ought to defy the gods' explicit wishes. Only after lengthy reflections echoing Plato's *Phaedo* (62c) did he conclude that he must not disobey the gods, his masters, "neglect his proper duties toward the gods," and "deprive the gods of his services," behavior he would not, after all, tolerate from his own animals (276a–d). Thus, he reasoned that he would "seek to possess nothing, seize nothing, but accept simply what is vouchsafed ... by [the gods]." So he "submitted to yield (*eixai kai hupēkousa*)": submitted nobly to the gods and consented to yield to Constantius's wishes.[72] "And immediately I was invested with the title and the robe of Caesar" (276d–277a). Who could be a better Caesar than a man on the verge of noble suicide who had submitted to the will of the gods fully aware of the "slavery" (*douleia*) of his office, subordinate to the criminal Constantius?[73]

Julian's strategy of legitimating was based on two arguments: first, because his cousin, the Augustus, was a criminal and hence an unfit ruler, the gods had to choose Julian, scion of the same dynasty, to replace him. His proof of this divine calling lay in his military victories (277d–280d), in Zeus's intervention at the crucial moment of his acclamation, showing him, as he had Odysseus, a sign (284c, *Od.* 3.173), and in the intensity of his *recusatio* and of his love of philosophical retirement, both manifesting the gods' gift to him of eminent ability to rule. (See also, e.g., 283a.) Second, these gods were not the God of Constantine, Constantius, and, alas, Gallus. Gallus, a Christian, had gone "straight from the country to the court" without understand-

---

against dynastic succession; *pace* MacCormack, *Art,* 45–50, 192–96, Julian was aware of his dynastic privileges; Malosse, "Noblesse"; Wiemer, *Libanios,* 113–16. For earlier examples of the debate weighing the dynastic factor versus individual merit and its reception, Rowe, *Princes,* 124–53, 173–75.

71. Julian evokes Pl. *Phd.* 62b–c, where Plato condemns suicide because the gods look after us; Julian's entire subsequent passage echoes that text.

72. All Julian's actions accorded with what the gods had ordered him to do "in precise terms, announcing salvation if I obeyed" but a horrendous fate otherwise; Jul. *Ep.* 28 (Wright 5), *To His Uncle Julian.*

73. Jul. *Ep. Ath.* 277b: "The slavery that ensued and the fear for my own life that hung over me every day—Heracles! How great it was, and how terrible! My doors locked; warders to guard them; the hands of my servants searched lest one of them should convey to me the most trifling letter from my friends; strange servants to wait on me!"

ing philosophy truly, and this was the reason why his character had remained tainted by a savagery and rudeness similar to that of Constantius, if less severe (272a).

Though not made explicit at this stage, the *Epistle to the Athenians* indicates that misapprehension of the true gods was to blame, at least in part, for the murderousness and the deviance of Constantine's dynasty, and that Julian's task, therefore, as the sole exception and sole remaining Flavian properly initiated into the true philosophy and its gods, was to reverse that course (272d). Julian, who submitted to the gods of the Greeks, was alive, victorious, and ethically sound, as demonstrated by his constant and complete loyalty to Constantius, toward whom he had behaved as he wished his "own son should behave toward me" (280d), until the gods and the army left him no alternative.[74] Thus, the struggle pitted two ethical spheres against each other: that of Constantius, the murderous plaything of his eunuchs corrupted by his God—this is implicit but not yet stated outright—and that of the divinely chosen philosopher, averse to power, submitting reluctantly to his duty. It was self-evident who acted justly and who would therefore prevail.[75] Julian's message was clear. Writing from Naissus after his rupture with Constantius, he cast his lot with the gods of Greece. He did so because these gods had saved him by means of philosophy. What that philosophy signified to him, the outline of his philosophy of leadership, Julian reserved for another inaugural speech, addressed to the philosopher Themistius and, through him, to the senate of Constantinople.

The Epistle to Themistius: *The Emperor (*Basileus*) as Philosopher versus the Philosopher as Ruler (*Stratēgos*)*

Themistius's moment in history began on September 1, 355. On that day, the proconsul of Constantinople presented to the Constantinopolitan senate a letter from Constantius containing the *adlectio* of the philosopher Themistius to its ranks. *Adlectio*, a procedure by which an emperor could promote to the senate a man not of senatorial background, was based on merit, and Constantius's letter was extravagant in its praise.[76] Themistius's *adlectio* was the emperor's gift to the "illustrious fathers" enrolled in the senate as well as to the people of Constantinople, because they were "worthy to share the gift that is characteristic of philosophy."[77] Philoso-

---

74. The entire acclamation as Augustus is cast as a surprise and in terms of Julian's continuing loyalty to Constantius, which he reluctantly disregarded as divinely commanded (*Ep. Ath.* 281a–286d).

75. For the extent to which Julian's characterization of Constantius still governs the historiographical assessment, see Chapter 1, "Constantius II as Sole Ruler, 352–358"; Pietri, "Politique," 113–16; Henck, "Constantius' *paideia*," 182–87.

76. For the *adlectio*, A. H. M. Jones, *Later Roman Empire*, 2nd ed., 530–42; Millar, *Emperor*, 277. Dagron, *Empire romaine*, 60–62. For the development of the senatorial order in the fourth century, Schlinkert, *Ordo*; Näf, *Senatorisches Standesbewußtsein*, has a Western emphasis.

77. *Ep. Const.* 19b: οὐ γὰρ μόνον Θεμίστιον τιμᾶν οἴομαι διὰ τῆς χάριτος, ἀλλ' οὐδὲν ἧττον καὶ τὴν γερουσίαν, ἣν τὸ μετασχεῖν δωρεᾶς ἄξιον νενόμικα φιλοσοφίᾳ πρεπούσης (Greek text: Themistius, *Themistii Orationes*, ed. Schenkl, Downey, and Norman, vol. 3, 123).

phy, according to Constantius, gave a city more splendors than its walls and buildings (of which the emperor had contributed many), and by giving Themistius to Constantinople, the emperor granted it the highest token of his friendship (*Ep. Const.* 21b–c).

For Constantius, philosophy was the foremost civic honor; to give Constantinople its philosopher superseded all else. And of the many philosophers he could have chosen, Constantius selected Themistius because of the philosophy his life made manifest: Themistius "does not practice a solitary philosophy, but he shares out the benefit that he has painstakingly assembled with ever greater pains among those who are willing [to hear], having established himself both as a spokesman [*prophētēs*] for the sages of the past and as an initiating priest [*hierophantēs*] at philosophy's inner sanctuaries and shrines. He does not allow the ancient teachings to wither away, but [ensures] that they always flourish and are renewed" (*Ep. Const.* 20a–b).[78] Themistius interpreted the mixing of the *bios theōrētikos* and the *bios praktikos* so as to favor the philosopher's active involvement for the benefit of the *politeia* over retreat, though such involvement, in his view, required extensive periods of retreat and scrupulous training. In short, Themistius's ideal philosophical life tended toward an Aristotelian interpretation of the interrelation between leisure and labor.[79] Indeed, it was not Themistius's training alone—not his "system of education" (*paideusis*) only—that Constantius considered worthy of the highest honor, but his conviction that philosophers ought to demonstrate rhetorical prowess, and that both, philosophy and rhetoric, ought to be made available for the greater good of the community, or *koinon*.

Themistius's *adlectio* to the Constantinopolitan senate, a highly public and widely publicized act, represented Constantius's endorsement of Themistius's philosophical concepts. In other words, Themistius's views and his philosophical life stood for Constantius's interpretation of the philosophical life as governance. Accordingly, Constantius made him senator at Constantinople when he began his rule as sole emperor, within a few years of his victory over the usurper Magnentius at Arles, in November 353. Constantius, as discussed in Chapter 1, understood that his role as *totius orbis dominus* was to consolidate the inheritance of the *divus Constantinus* into one empire under the tutelage of the New Rome.[80] He now sought to combine East and West in a perfect mixture based on the principles he had established dur-

---

78. I follow the translations published in Themistius, *Private Orations*, ed. and trans. Penella; and in Themistius, *Politics*, ed. and trans. Moncur, with modifications. See also Brown, *Power*, 68–70.

79. This elaborates earlier models developed by Dio Chrysostom and Aelius Aristides, though Themistius (*Or.* 26.330c) is critical of Aristides because of the latter's perceived criticism of Plato. This is further exemplified by Themistius's silence in *Or.* 25 regarding Aristides' precedent in rejecting extempore speeches as reported by Philost. *V. Soph.* 582–85; C. P. Jones, "Themistius"; Themistius, *Private Orations*, ed. and trans. Penella, 27–28.

80. Amm. Marc. 15.1.3

ing his rule of the East, a program he also emphasized by issuing coins representing the New and the Old Rome in harmony, but with greater emphasis on Constantinople.[81] As his letter to the Constantinopolitan senate shows, Constantius regarded Themistius and his philosophical life calling for public involvement as another expression of his own concept of an empire unified according to Constantine's precedent:[82] "in receiving from us a Roman honor [and rank, *axiōma*], [Themistius] offers Greek wisdom [*sophia*] in return, so that in this way, our city is revealed as the summit both of fortune and of virtue" (*Ep. Const.* 21a).[83] Themistius the philosopher and senator was "a singular citizen of our city, whom one might address with good reason as a citizen of the world" (*Ep. Const.* 22c). He embodied what Constantius sought to achieve: the correct mixture of Rome and Constantinople, West and East, in one universal *oikoumenē*. Themistius's dual citizenship perfectly combined loyalty to one's native polis with that to the cosmopolis, and thus the community or *politeia* of the empire.

Constantius's belief that Themistius and his active philosophical life represented the ideal Constantinopolitan senator was not mere theory (*Ep. Const.* 23d). In 358 and 359, Constantius dispatched Themistius on a campaign throughout the eastern Mediterranean that successfully recruited new members to the senate, in particular wealthier members of the curial class. These men of means and education, interested in geographic and social mobility, reflected elements of Themistius's own life.[84] On May 3, 361, a month after Julian's *defectio,* Constantius issued a law requiring that Themistius be present to designate new praetors, thus reemphasizing that Themistius represented Constantius's principles when choosing new members of the senate, of which he may have been by then the president.[85]

This, then, was the man to whom Julian addressed one of his inaugural letters from Naissus: Constantius's official voice and a figure representative of the Constantinopolitan senate as conceived by Constantius.[86] Because Julian required the support of that illustrious body for a smooth transition of rule, he addressed an au-

---

81. Cuneo, *Legislazione,* ciii–cix; Migl, *Ordnung,* 124–51, 176–208; Dagron, *Naissance,* 50–52.

82. Dagron, *Empire romaine,* 83–95; Ruggini, *Simboli,* 11–28; and now Elia, "Sui *privilegia,*" esp. 78–96.

83. Lendon, *Empire,* 277–79 for the vocabulary.

84. Petit, *Étudiants,* 154–55; Dagron, *Naissance,* 129; Heather, "New Men," 13; Henck, "Constantius' *paideia,*" 176.

85. *CTh* 6.4.12; and Henck, "Constantius' *paideia,*" 179–80. Themistius's official position in 361 will be discussed in Chapter 3, "Philosophy in the Shade versus Philosophy in the Open: Themistius and His Opponents."

86. The dating of the letter is controversial. Since Bradbury, "Date," it has been accepted (but not in *Giuliano imperatore: Epistola a Temistio,* ed. Prato and Fornaro, viii—the edition I use) that the letter in its existing form is a revision of an earlier version that already responded to Themistius. When the revised work was sent to Themistius remains debated. Vanderspoel, *Themistius,* 117–19, argues for publication in 360 but still considers it part of the "Greek city" dossier, whereas R. Smith (*Julian's Gods,* 27),

dience of real significance (unlike the mostly symbolic Athenians), which he could ill afford to alienate.[87] In writing to Themistius, however, the newly acclaimed Augustus also wrote to a former teacher—Themistius had been among the philosophers who had taught him Plato and Aristotle (*Ep. Them.* 257d)—and hence his words, though official, had a private quality; Julian maintained the tone of respect of a former disciple.[88] Nonetheless, his message was unmistakable: Julian begged to differ on the true philosophical life, and because he disagreed with Themistius's idea of the philosophical life, he therefore also disagreed with Constantius's.

Parts of Julian's *Epistle to Themistius* respond to an earlier letter Themistius had addressed to Julian, most likely a now lost *protreptikos* congratulating Julian on his accession as Caesar.[89] In it, to judge from Julian's response, Themistius had expressed the hope that Julian would intend "to rival men like Alexander and Marcus [Aurelius]," because "God has placed [him] in the same position as Heracles and Dionysus of old, who, being at once philosophers and kings [*philosophountes homou kai basileuontes*], purged almost the whole earth and sea of the evils that infested them." Thus Julian ought to "shake off all thought of leisure and inactivity" to be a good soldier and lawgiver, like "Solon, Pittacus, and Lycurgus."

Julian professed amazement at reading those words. He was fully aware "that by nature there is nothing remarkable about me ... except for falling in love with philosophy [*philosophias de erasthenti monon*]." Thus, when faced with hopes such as those Themistius expressed, Julian's soul recoiled and shivered in fear at the magnitude of the expectations and responsibilities they entailed. He had rushed to consult once again the normative texts, including those adduced by Themistius, to investigate whether they indeed argued that a life of greater action best befitted a

---

Bouffartigue (*Empereur Julien,* 198, esp. n. 283), and Prato and Fornaro (*Giuliano imperatore: Epistola a Temistio,* viii–ix), following Dagron (*Empire romaine,* 220), propose late 361. I follow their dating.

87. Several sources indicate the precariousness of the situation in the East. For example, the *praepositus sacri cubiculi* Eusebius sponsored others (including perhaps Jovian), as Constantius's successor; Amm. Marc. 21.15.4. Julian responded with the condemnations at Chalcedon; Szidat, *Historischer Kommentar,* part 3, 189–91; Matthews, *Roman Empire,* 66, 88, 106, also 215–16.

88. Bouffartigue, *Empereur Julien,* 22, 299–300, excludes the possibility that Julian ever studied with Themistius, for reasons that remain unclear; Prato and Fornaro (*Giuliano imperatore: Epistola a Temistio,* 47) argue that the passage in *Ep. Them.* 259c, "the beginning of my instruction with you," refers to Julian's time at Constantinople rather than to time spent with Themistius; Daly, "'In a Borderland'"; Vanderspoel, *Themistius,* 118 n. 17; Henck, "Constantius' *paideia,*" 175. Julian's references to Themistius as his teacher and correspondent are *Ep. Them.* 253c, 257d, 259c, 260a, and 263c. The most likely date would be 348/9, during Julian's brief stay at Constantinople after Macellum.

89. Scholars also debate whether Themistius's lost earlier letter is the Arabic *Risâlat* (Themistius, *Risâlat: Epistula Themisti,* ed. and trans. Shahîd). Internal evidence of Julian's letter suggests a protreptic rather than a panegyric: i.e., not the *Risâlat.* Shahîd (pp. 77–80) and Dagron (*Empire romaine,* 221–25) argue that the *Risâlat* was addressed to Theodosius, but Vanderspoel (*Themistius,* 127–34, 241–49) argues for Julian; in general, see Criscuolo, "Sull'epistola di Giuliano," and Brauch, "Themistius."

person such as Julian (253a–253c). From these renewed readings, Julian, the Caesar and now Augustus, gained the conviction that a philosophical life of intense retreat had far greater value than Themistius the philosopher claimed. Julian conceded Themistius's point that Epicurus had been mistaken in demanding that one "live in obscurity" (*lathein biōsanta*): Epicurus's views of *apragmosynē*, retreat and leisure, were those of an idle man. Nonetheless, "whether it is proper to urge into political life any and every man, both him who lacks natural abilities and him who is not yet completely equipped, is a point that deserves the most careful consideration" (255c).

Citing everyone from Plato's Socrates, by way of the Stoics, to the Cynic Diogenes, Julian pointed out that virtue alone (and thus even the philosophical life per se) did not guarantee good governance, since Fortune held great sway in the matter (255d–257d). To demonstrate what then constituted good leadership, Julian cited a passage from Plato's *Laws* that Themistius himself had taught him.[90] According to Julian's synthesis, Plato's requirements for good governance were so stringent that anyone of sound mind and virtuous character had to reject such a responsibility. "You hear what he says, that even though the chosen ruler is by nature human, his conduct must be divine and that of a demigod, and he must banish completely from his soul all that is mortal and beastly, except what must be retained to safeguard the body"; the Greek implies an anthropological hierarchy of god-man-beast that was evidently relevant to Julian's point.[91] When faced with such expectations, to conduct oneself like the gods, anyone would choose the philosophical life of freedom from care (*apragmosynē*), now positively understood: the gardens of Athens and the little house of Socrates. Such admiration of Athens's tranquility had nothing in common with Epicurus's lazy *apragmosynē*; to the contrary, Julian reveled in the quintessential toils (*tōn ponōn*) of philosophical leisure and, as he delineated in great detail, had dedicated his life to the rigors of learning despite the most adverse circumstances, and had resisted all kinds of injustices that tyrannical persons had wished to commit against him. Idleness versus labor (*apraxia kai praxis*) was not the issue (257d–260c).

It was, rather, Themistius's view of the more active philosophical life. According to Julian, Themistius misread Plato and Aristotle's key texts. Of course, Julian knew full well Themistius's mastery of Aristotle's *Politics;* citing Aristotle when writing to Themistius was like bringing owls to the Athenians. (Themistius had published commentaries on Aristotle and was known as a true exegete of Aristotle's concepts.)[92]

---

90. Pl. *Lg.* 709b—714e.

91. Jul. *Ep. Them.* 259a: Ἀκούεις ὅτι, κἂν ἄνθρωπός τις ᾖ τῇ φύσει, θεῖον εἶναι χρὴ τῇ προαιρέσει καὶ δαίμονα, πᾶν ἁπλῶς ἐκβαλόντα τὸ θνητὸν καὶ θηριῶδες τῆς ψυχῆς, πλὴν ὅσα ἀνάγκη διὰ τὴν τοῦ σώματος παραμένειν σωτηρίαν.

92. Arist. *Pol.* 3.15.1286b, 16.1287a, 7.3.1325b22–23. Bouffartigue, *Empereur Julien*, 198–200, thinks that Julian had no direct access to Aristotle's text and cited Themistius; R. Smith, *Julian's Gods,* 27–28.

Even so, as Julian pointed out, Themistius's notions of the philosophical life falsified Aristotle. For example, Aristotle had rejected dynastic succession: "Even if one maintains the principle that it is best for cities to be governed by a king, how will it be about his children? Ought his children to succeed him?" Julian, following Aristotle, thought not; Constantius was a case in point (as Julian had already intimated in his earlier panegyrics when emphasizing the power of merit). Furthermore, Aristotle thought humans by their nature incapable of ruling well alone, so that no good leader is ever called a king (in the sense "emperor," *basileus*). Moreover, both Aristotle and Plato stipulated that a true leader had to be more capable than others by nature and must furthermore have purified his mind and soul (and hence cannot have murdered his own family; 263a).[93]

In other words, men such as Themistius, who support a *basileus* who stands for absolute monarchy and dynastic rule, have failed to grasp what Aristotle meant. "You said that you approve a life of action rather than the philosophical life, and you call to witness the wise Aristotle, who defines happiness as virtuous activity, and, in discussing the difference between the political life and that of theory, shows a certain hesitation. . . . Though in other writings he prefers the theoretical life, in this place, you say, he approves the architect of actions." True, but when speaking of such architects of action, Julian argued, Aristotle, unlike Themistius, did not mean kings and emperors.[94] Rather, he spoke of "lawgivers and political philosophers [*nomothetas kai tous politikous philosophous*] and all those whose activity consists in the use of intelligence and reason," so that, according to Julian, Socrates, "the son of Sophroniscus, performed greater tasks than Alexander" (263b–264a). "To conceive true opinions about God [*alētheis de huper tou theou doxas analabein*] is a labor that requires virtue, and one may well hesitate whether to call the one who attains this [goal] man or god" (265a–b). To attain true opinions about God is the highest form of achievement, the true meaning of action and therefore also of philosophy. In contrast to Themistius's expectations of an active political philosophical life, Julian's (lower) expectations were premised on his possessing "neither sufficient training nor natural talents above the ordinary," and his realization that he had not yet attained his beloved philosophy (*hēs erōn ouk ephikomēn*), "which furthermore does not have a good name among the men of our day" (266c–267b). This philosophy, Julian's, differed fundamentally from that of Themistius and hence Constantius.

Julian's criticism of Themistius's and Constantius's conception of the philosophical life, and thus their theory of governance, focused on three points. Themistius's advice "to quit the shades of philosophy for the open air" (263a), his ideal of a more active philosophical life, was based on a faulty reading of the normative texts, which

---

93. E.g., Pl. *Tht.* 153b–c.

94. Unlike Themistius, who had, for example, called Constantius "a philosopher who had chosen a philosopher as collaborator in the exercise of power" (Them. *Or.* 2.40a–b).

also caused his mistaken identification of Plato's and Aristotle's ideal ruler, the "political philosopher," with the *basileus,* the emperor. Julian's preference for philosophical retreat and freedom from care, far from indicating a lack of capacity to govern or to participate in political life, demonstrated instead that he understood the prerequisites for good governance; he did not mistake a monarch for a just lawgiver and hence good ruler. His recognition that he was less fully prepared than the true philosophical life demanded underscored that point: Constantius had been a mere *basileus,* whereas Julian would guide the *politeia* as a true "leader and champion" of philosophers (267a).[95]

Julian's Constantinopolitan audience, from Themistius to the senate and anyone else familiar with philosophy, understood the nuances of his message more clearly than I can ever hope to do—though in the chapter that follows I look in greater detail at the debates about the correct philosophical life and its implications that had embroiled Themistius and other philosophers since the 350s, and in which Julian evidently took a position with this letter: against Themistius's philosophy of the open air and in favor of those advocating a philosophy in the shade. But even those among Julian's intended audience unfamiliar with the nuances of the philosophical debates and the persons alluded to would have realized that Julian directed his criticism of Themistius against Constantius, whom no one conversant with philosophy could consider a just ruler. Anyone in the senate who valued *paideia,* philosophy, and justice (that is, everyone) had to support Julian if for no other reason than to ensure that true philosophy would reign and laws be issued "that have a general application to all citizens without regard to friend or foe, neighbor or kinsman . . . , [and that would remain just] not only for contemporaries, but for posterity also" (262c).

These were but the first intimations of what was to come. Once in Constantinople, Julian laid out in far greater detail what he considered the true philosophy and what implications he derived from that understanding for governing and safeguarding the community of the Romans. This was the task the gods had entrusted to him. It was an awesome responsibility, to be sure, but the gods of the Greeks and the Romans had given it to a man whom they had chosen and who therefore was close to the divine in conduct (though in the things he required to sustain his body, he belonged to the sphere of man and beast).

By early 362, the shape of the new emperor and his governance had begun to emerge. Julian was no Constantius. Although he did not intend to reverse every act of the former Augustus of the Romans, to whose dynasty he after all belonged, Julian nevertheless made clear that significant changes were imminent. Among these changes was a return to the worship of the old, time-honored gods of the Greeks and the Romans, championed by an emperor who embodied the true philosophi-

---

95. Marcone, "Giuliano."

cal life pleasing to these gods. This did not spell the end of the Christian God, but it implied new rules for the members of the Christian elites, including those who wished to become Julian's advisors. All seeking access to the new emperor, in fact, Christian or not, knew that they must identify the tenets of that true philosophical life. How did Julian present his understanding of the true philosophical life and of the gods at its center?

3

Philosopher, Leader, Priest
Julian in Constantinople, Spring 362

> *But must we really speak of this also? And write about the ineffable mysteries and divulge what must not be revealed nor divulged? Who is Attis or Gallus? Who is the Mother of the Gods? And of what does this rite of purification consist? And further: Why was it taught to us like that from the beginning, transmitted from the most ancient Phrygians, but then first adopted by the Greeks? . . . And after the Greeks, this cult was adopted by the Romans.*
> —JULIAN, ORATION 5, HYMN TO THE MOTHER OF THE GODS 158D–159C

Julian entered Constantinople, the city of his birth, on December 11, 361, surrounded by troops of soldiers. As Sabine MacCormack has emphasized, the choreography of his *adventus* into Constantinople crystallized and projected the central tenets of his inaugural letters to the Athenians and to Themistius and thus to the Constantinopolitan senate: as his military victories demonstrated, Julian came as one chosen by the gods to alter Constantius's legacy. The new emperor, though acknowledging his dynastic connections to the mighty house of Constantine, entered the city as victorious military leader and independent man.[1] The citizens of Constantinople approved. They, too, "all ages and sexes, poured forth as though they were going to see someone sent down from heaven," just as the citizens of Sirmium before them had done, acclaiming Julian "as an epiphany, the appearance of one sent by the gods, as one coming into the world as a health-giving star."[2]

As soon as the Augustus "sent down from heaven" arrived in the city, he went

---

1. Amm. Marc. 15.9.8, 21.10.1–2, 22.2.3–5; Claud. Mam. *Pan. Lat.* 11.6.2–5, 11.2.3; MacCormack, *Art*, 46–50; den Boeft, Drijvers, et al., *Philological and Historical Commentary on Ammianus Marcellinus 22*, 14–15. According to Caltabiano ("Giuliano," esp. 344–53), Julian's *adventus* consciously evoked traditional Roman military virtues, and Ammianus used the *adventus* to legitimize Julian within a Roman imperial and religious context. Béranger, "Julien"; F. Kolb, *Herrscherideologie*, 91–100.

2. Amm. Marc. 21.10.2, 22.2.4; Ando, *Imperial Ideology*, 199.

to work at high speed—with his public sacrifices; measures to restore the temples; his gathering of his Friends, including the recall of those bishops exiled under Constantius; the trials at Chalcedon; and the removal of Constantius's staunchest supporters (including patrons of Themistius), ostensibly to eliminate corruption, ostentatious luxury, and other grave misdeeds.[3] As this chapter shows, however, in reorganizing the top court personnel, the new emperor also took the opportunity to showcase the philosophical life he considered true, hence the one he wished his Friends to adopt and propagate. At stake for the emperor was what being Roman actually entailed. How and according to what guidelines did Julian intend to govern the empire of the Romans? How would he meld Greek wisdom and Roman honor, the two key principles to which Constantius had referred in praising Themistius? Who embodied their melding most appropriately? What divinity or divinities had truly created Rome's universal greatness and hence guaranteed its security and longevity? What philosophical life would, therefore, ensure that the divine was properly heard and obeyed?

As the reaction of Libanius and Ammianus to Julian's purges of the court personnel demonstrates, Julian's empirewide audience well understood the philosophical component of his reorganization. Thus, both Libanius and Ammianus (no doubt echoing the views of many others) praised Julian's measures to reform Constantius's luxurious court, although they considered some of them too harsh, too philosophical, and thus damaging to the emperor. Ammianus, for example, felt compelled to explain that the thoroughness of Julian's purges was a personal lapse rather than behavior befitting "a philosopher claiming to search for the truth."[4]

Julian's perceived harshness in purging the court contrasted with his mild reaction to the riots that had erupted on December 24, 361, in Alexandria, which had cost the lives of Bishop George and two imperial officials. Julian's imperial letter of response, posted in Alexandria in January 362, began by recalling Alexandria's importance as a place where Serapis (a god who shared many traits with Helios, whose special favor Julian had emphasized in his *Epistle to the Athenians*) and Isis had long been worshipped. Further, the Alexandrians had been "Greeks since ancient times [*to . . . archaion Hellēnes*]" (*Ep.* 60.380d). Consequently, in Julian's view, they shared—at least in principle—the emperor's interest in the public good, humanity, and decorum (*to prepon*), attributes that induced Julian to act more mildly in response to their misconduct than he would have otherwise. Ordinarily, vigilante justice, particularly when it involved the murder of public officials, was unacceptable. But given Alexandria's Hellenic history and its importance to all those united by

---

3. Dagron, *Empire*, 234; Bowersock, *Julian*, 66–78.

4. Amm. Marc. 22.3–4, and compare 22.7.1, den Boeft, Drijvers, et al., *Philological and Historical Commentary on Ammianus Marcellinus 22*, 17–37; Lib. *Or.* 18.130; Socr. *HE* 3.1.53–58, φιλοσόφου ἔργον, οὐ μὴν βασιλέως; Zon. 13.12.15, uses "philosopher" negatively; Matthews, *Roman Empire*, 251–52.

paideia, Julian was willing to display a fraternal benevolence; as everyone knew, and as Julian pointed out, other cities in which similar crimes had been committed had been severely punished. That the very emperor who had judged Constantius's high officials at Chalcedon so harshly now displayed mildness at the murder of the bishop of Alexandria signaled that Julian might tolerate unrest that harmed prominent Christians who had been homoian supporters of Constantius. His leniency in Alexandria thus accorded with his measures to punish Constantius's men. Edicts posted in Alexandria on February 4 added another dimension: the emperor ordered the reopening of the very temples that George had closed and permitted to be desecrated.[5] Thus, Julian's early judicial measures already revealed to his subjects aspects of his philosophical life, his imperial intent.

THE CONTEXT OF JULIAN'S CONCEPTS OF THE TRUE PHILOSOPHICAL LIFE

Maximus of Ephesus and Julian's Philosophical Circles

At Constantinople, meanwhile, Julian organized his court and gathered his Friends, offering those not in Constantinople access to the *cursus publicus*.[6] Among those invited were most of Julian's teachers, a group less easily identifiable than one might think. Julian, for example, never mentioned explicitly who taught him at Athens, nor do all scholars agree that Themistius had been his teacher.[7] Nevertheless, there is scholarly agreement on many among that illustrious group. Prior to Macellum Julian had been educated by Eusebius of Nicomedia, later bishop of Constantinople, and one of Constantius's closest advisors at that time. While Julian was at Macellum, between 342 and 347/8, the eunuch Mardonius, who had already educated his mother, had been his principal tutor, but he had also been taught by the same George of Caesarea in Cappadocia, whose murder as bishop of Alexandria he had treated so leniently.[8] After leaving Macellum, he studied in Constantinople with the grammarian Nicocles (pagan), and the rhetor Hecebolius (Christian) and had attended the lectures of Themistius (pagan) before moving on to Nicomedia, where he either studied with Libanius (pagan) or gathered notes from others who did. From there Julian proceeded to Pergamon to further his education with other philosophers. These included Aedesius, Chrysanthius of Sardis, Eusebius of Myndus, and,

---

5. Jul. *Ep.* 60 (Wright 21); he also recalled a physician, Zeno, whom George had exiled, *Ep.* 58 (Wright 17); Julian, *Epistolario*, trans. and comm. Caltabiano, 105 n. 45, 251–52; A. Martin, *Athanase*, 538–40; Bowersock, *Julian*, 81.

6. Jul. *Ep.* 34, 35 (Wright 43, 44), *To Eustathius*; A. Kolb, "Kaiser Julians Innenpolitik," 352–58; Schlange-Schöningen, *Kaisertum*, 77–80.

7. Henck, "From Macellum to Milan," 106.

8. Amm. Marc. 22.9.4.

most important, Maximus of Ephesus, where Julian went next.[9] While in Ephesus in late 354, he was ordered to northern Italy, whence he went briefly to Athens in the spring of 355.[10] There he may have attended the lectures of Prohaeresius and Himerius, and he befriended Priscus, one of Aedesius's disciples, who lectured on Plato and became one of Julian's most trusted friends and advisors, accompanying him to Persia.[11]

Prohaeresius and Libanius were among Julian's teachers who received no invitation, nor did all who received one come to court.[12] Chrysanthius of Sardis remained in Lydia, prevented from coming by philosophical reticence, according to Eunapius, though such reticence did not interfere with his subsequent appointment as high priest of the province.[13] Others, especially Julian's favorite teacher, Maximus of Ephesus, were welcomed ecstatically, a welcome that prompted Ammianus again to criticize Julian's behavior as too philosophical and thus lacking imperial decorum. As his *Res gestae* makes clear, Ammianus blamed what he considered Julian's misinterpretations of the divine will on aspects of Julian's philosophical life, especially those represented by Maximus, which led to the loss of Julian's life and to Rome's defeat by the Persians. Ammianus orchestrated his criticism of Julian's philosophy carefully, so that his informed audience would readily recognize on whom he laid most of the blame. He framed Maximus's arrival in Constantinople so as to link the man to Julian's momentary loss of reason. When Maximus was announced, Julian, seated in the senate, "started up in an undignified manner, so far forgetting himself that he ran at full speed the distance from the vestibule, and, having kissed the philosopher and received him with reverence, brought him back with him." That this philosopher, in Julian's estimation, surpassed in dignity the senators and even his own imperial person could, Ammianus implied, only bode ill for the future.[14]

Ammianus's account of that event, though biased, corroborates Julian's own testimony to the influence of Maximus of Ephesus.[15] Maximus and his philosophical life—as Julian's embrace would have made clear to all who witnessed it—represented

---

9. Jul. *Ep. ad Ath.* 271b, *Or.* 3, *In Praise of Eusebia;* Eun. *VS* 473–74; Lib. *Or.* 15.27; 18.12–13; Amm. Marc. 15.2.7; Socr. *HE* 3.1; Bouffartigue, *Empereur Julien,* 29–39. Renucci, *Idées,* 40–60, combines his account of Julian's teachers with a detailed discussion of his religious evolution.

10. Jul. *Ep. ad Ath.* 272d–273d; Amm. Marc. 15.2.7–8.

11. Gregory later wrote that he and Julian had been fellow students under Himerius and Prohaeresius; Julian does not say that; Gr. Naz. *Or.* 5.23; Jer. *Chron.* at 363 mentions Prohaeresius. Priscus visited Julian while he was Caesar in Gaul; Bouffartigue, *Empereur Julien,* 45–46.

12. Jul. *Ep.* 31 (Wright 14), *To Prohaeresius,* is difficult to interpret. Watts, *City,* 64–67, argues convincingly that the letter was a sarcastic invitation to a Christian protégé of Constantius to write the history of Julian's rise, intended to call for a negative reply; for Libanius: Wiemer, *Libanios,* 35–39.

13. Eun. *VS* 501.

14. Amm. Marc. 22.7.3–4; Eun. *VS* 477; Matthews, *Roman Empire,* 23.

15. See, e.g., Jul. *Epp.* 26, 190 (Wright 8, 12); the second letter is probably spurious, as is *Ep.* 191, *To Maximus;* see Julian, *Epistolario,* trans. and comm. Caltabiano, 50.

the life the new emperor espoused and would sponsor (much as Constantius had endorsed Themistius and his philosophical life). What were the contours of Maximus of Ephesus's philosophical life, and how did they differ from those of Themistius? The answers were of consequence for all members of the elite formed by *paideia*, whether near or far from the imperial residences and the court, and whether Christian or not.

To answer the questions about Julian's and Maximus's philosophical life I go back to the years from 349 to 351, when Julian sojourned in Nicomedia, Pergamon, and Ephesus. According to Libanius, Julian then recognized in himself "a hidden spark of divination [*spinthēr mantikēs*] that had barely escaped the hands of the impious," inspiring him "to track down hidden lore, . . . to check [his] violent hatred against the gods," namely Christianity, and to "gaze . . . upon the beauty of philosophy."[16] In the narrative of Libanius, Julian became acquainted with the local philosophical circles of Nicomedia (partly, Libanius suggests, because of his own influence) that practiced a divinely inspired form of philosophy. The most respected representatives of that philosophy taught at Pergamon, where Julian received training at their hands.[17] These men were Aedesius, himself a student of Iamblichus (who had studied with Porphyry), and his pupils Chrysanthius of Sardis and Eusebius of Myndus. After Julian received instruction at Pergamon, the fame of another of Aedesius's disciples, Maximus, drew him to Ephesus. Maximus must have been an impressive man, for even Ammianus, not a fan, described him as "an illustrious philosopher, a man of great reputation for learning, who communicated to the emperor Julian outstanding knowledge through his rich discourses."[18]

These philosophers taught a form of Platonism, commonly described as Neoplatonism, that went back to Iamblichus, Porphyry, and Plotinus. This mid-fourth-century (Neo-)Platonism cannot easily be reconstructed, because the sources available are not the writings of the principals themselves. In addition to the writings of Plotinus, Porphyry, and Iamblichus, and of the fifth-century philosopher Proclus, who systematized earlier teachings, we have to rely on remarks by Julian, Libanius, and Themistius; on the late fourth-century account of Ammianus, the *Res gestae*; and on Eunapius of Sardis's *Lives of Philosophers and Sophists*, our primary narrative source. Eunapius wrote his *Lives* in 399, toward the end of his life and in the

---

16. Lib. *Or.* 13.11.

17. Athanassiadi-Fowden, *Julian*, 30–34, argues for contact with pagan philosophers already in Nicomedia, following Libanius; Bouffartigue, *Empereur Julien*, 42–43; Matthews, *Roman Empire*, 116–25. These contacts are the basis for scholars' debates of Julian's initiation into paganism and his conversion to philosophy, and thus how authentic his Christianity was. R. Smith, *Julian's Gods*, 180–89 (with bibliography, 182–83), cites testimonies (182–83) that Julian had been a committed Christian prior to his acquaintance with these philosophers; Rosen ("Kaiser Julian," 126–46, and *Julian*, 94–103) argues against a true conversion.

18. Amm. Marc. 29.1.42, on the occasion of Maximus's execution under Valens.

context of his debates and controversies with the intellectuals, both non-Christian and Christian, who were his contemporaries. The work is propaganda, intended to demonstrate the uninterrupted genealogical line of perfect discipleship leading from Plotinus to Iamblichus to Eunapius himself, who had been a student of Chrysanthius. Although Eunapius did not reconstruct the mid-fourth-century philosophical scene in all its complexity, he nevertheless made it clear that debates about the true philosophical life were central.[19] His *Lives,* especially when read in the context of the other sources, permits us to reconstruct opinions on the true philosophical life prevalent among the star students of Iamblichus and their circles.

Julian's Iamblichan teachers (*hoi hetairoi*) agreed with their master that "all forms of knowledge that passed from the gods to men . . . having commingled with much that is mortal, began to lose the divine character of knowledge."[20] Hence, any active involvement in the *politeia* was an issue for intense debate as prima facie antithetical to the true philosophical life, which consisted solely in contemplating and thus approaching the divine mysteries. Without the utmost purity, achieved by rigorously avoiding worldly matters, no such contemplation was possible.[21] In principle, therefore, following Plotinus, these philosophers relegated the active elements of Plato's concept of the philosophical life to the sidelines—or so at least their detractors claimed.[22]

Plotinus's most famous disciple, Porphyry, advocated near-absolute withdrawal from public life, while Porphyry's own most distinguished pupil, Iamblichus, interpreted Plotinus's teachings on philosophical withdrawal more moderately.[23] For Iamblichus, strict asceticism and retreat remained compatible with participation in a city's religious and political life, including marriage; he "interpreted Platonism as teaching the presence of gods in the material world. It followed that the embodied soul must not seek only to escape, but must do its share in establishing order and harmony."[24] Following Plotinus, Iamblichus argued in effect for two sets of ethical norms, for two different classes of persons: philosophers and all others. Once a

19. Born in 348/9, Eunapius returned to Sardis after his studies and remained there for the rest of his life; Penella, *Greek Philosophers,* 1–9; Miller, "Strategies."

20. Iamblichus *Myst.* 9.4.277.1–18; Eun. *VS* 459.

21. This has led scholars to dismiss political aspects of that philosophy, a view now revised by D. O'Meara, *Platonopolis,* and the articles in A. Smith, *Philosopher.* Ruggini, "Sofisti," 410–15, and *Simboli,* 28–45; Dagron, *Empire,* 42–44; cf. Fowden, "Pagan Holy Man," esp. 35–38, 40–44; Goulet, "Vies," 163–76; Lim, *Public Disputation,* 47–67; Vanderspoel, *Themistius,* 108–10.

22. Blumenthal, *Aristotle,* 23.

23. It is not clear when and where Iamblichus studied with Porphyry. Porphyry dedicated his *On the Maxim "Know Thyself"* to Iamblichus, and the latter claimed he heard Porphyry, though he is often critical of his precursor. *Jamblique: Vie de Pythagore,* ed. Brisson and Segonds; and *Iamblichus: On the Pythagorean Life,* trans. Clark; and also *Iamblichus: On the Pythagorean Way of Life,* ed. and trans. Dillon and Hershbell, esp. 17–22.

24. G. Clark, "Philosophic Lives," 41; Goulet, "Vies," 184–88.

philosopher had been thoroughly purified, his duty was to testify to all others by his example that a divine realm existed and that men of virtue could approach it, and thus also lead ordinary men toward "the dear country," the divine.[25]

Porphyry, in contrast, counseled that because the material world contaminated a pure philosopher, it had to be avoided at all costs; he was convinced that harmful *daimones* threatened human beings at every turn.[26] By the time of Aedesius, many of Iamblichus's disciples, too, seem to have adopted a more rigorous stance, closer to that of Porphyry, at least if we believe one of their opponents, Themistius. Though he never mentions anyone by name, Themistius clearly referred to Aedesius and his circle when contrasting his own philosophy of the open air with their philosophy of the shade, which he invited Julian to leave. Aedesius and his students, including Julian, advocated a philosophical life of retreat with little direct involvement in the *politeia*. But even this life of retreat had an active dimension, for it aimed to contribute to the public good by attesting exemplarily to the existence of higher spheres to which the virtuous man's soul could progress.

This is only one aspect of Plato's legacy as interpreted by fourth-century Neoplatonists. Another is its tenet that a philosopher in retreat could contemplate and thus approach the divine mysteries. One interpretation, which I call "revelatory"— usually linked to Iamblichus's school—held that philosophers could achieve enlightenment, elevation of the soul, and indeed a mystical union with the divine principle, the One, through "rites known to them alone."[27] Symbols and sacred ritual acts could bring the select human soul into contact with the divine through the personal guidance of a god (rather than a *daimōn*), so that such a person could "work gods" (that is, practice theurgy). In Iamblichus's words, through "these divine symbols, theurgy ascends to the superior beings to which it is united," permitting certain enlightened individuals to gain knowledge of the divine will through oracles and similar means.[28] In the fifth century, Proclus defined such theurgy as "greater than all human wisdom and knowledge, comprising the benefits of divinatory prophecy [*mantikē*] and the purifying powers of initiation; in a word, all the operative functions [*energēmata*] of divine inspiration."[29]

---

25. Plot. *Enn.* 1.6[1].8.16–17, using Homeric language. See Schniewind, "Social Concern"; D. O'Meara, *Platonopolis*, 46–49, 87–105.

26. In particular if sacrificial blood was concerned. Philosophers should thus abstain from sacrifices, even if they remain necessary for the public good; Porphyry: *On Abstinence*, trans. Clark; and *Porphyre: La vie de Plotin*, ed. and trans. Brisson; also *Porphyre: Vie de Pythagore*, ed. and trans. des Places; Rist, "Mysticism."

27. Eun. *VS* 476.

28. Iamb. *Myst.* 4.2; J. Dillon, "Image."

29. Marinus *V. Procl.* 28; a passage from Proclus's *Platonic Theology* cited in Proclus, *Proclus: The Elements of Theology*, ed. and trans. Dodds, xxii–xxiii; G. Shaw, *Theurgy*; Clarke, *Iamblichus' "De mys-*

One of the great theurgists of Julian's day was Maximus of Ephesus, who had initiated Julian into the first stages of this highly evolved philosophical method, which had had an enormous impact on the young man.[30] However, not all disciples of Aedesius followed the theurgic, or revelatory, method of acquiring knowledge of the divine. Whereas, according to Eunapius, Chrysanthius believed firmly in theurgic means of divination, Julian's teacher Eusebius of Myndus insisted that only the *logos,* only precise dialectical reasoning "can lead to the discovery of true realities."[31] The differences between these approaches, however, were less stark than they may appear. Thus Maximus of Ephesus, the great theurgist, wrote a commentary on Aristotle, the master of dialectic, that later Neoplatonists continued to use.[32]

These, then, were the men who had taught Julian and shaped his philosophical ideals. What position did they occupy in contemporary philosophical debates, and what was their standing before Julian's imperial patronage exalted them? Much modern scholarship—influenced in part by Ammianus's criticism of Maximus of Ephesus and his circle—has considered Julian's philosophy representative of a marginal group that would have had little influence had it not been for Julian's patronage, itself fostered by his idiosyncratic attraction to theurgist notions.[33] These modern assumptions are enhanced by Eunapius's authorial intentions, especially his emphasis on the sacred remoteness and extreme retreat of his exemplars, essentially Chrysanthius and his forerunners, "divine masters" whom he considered ideal archetypes of human wisdom.[34] Eunapius's *Lives,* as Robert Penella has pointed out, consequently omits philosophers like Themistius and all those who, like him, accepted public positions in the imperial administration, as well as those followers of Plotinus and Iamblichus who were less theurgic and leaned more toward Aristotelian dialectic: for example, Eusebius, Euphrasius, and Theodorus of Asine.[35] However, even Eunapius indicated by his omissions that the reality differed from his ideal reconstruction. Prior to Julian's sponsorship, fourth-century Neoplatonists partici-

---

teriis," esp. the introduction and chap. 1 for the historiographic assessment of Iamblichus's work and Julian's misapprehensions of some of Iamblichus's concepts; and Liefferinge, *Théurgie,* 23–126, 224–43.

30. Praechter, "Maximus (40)." How evolved this was becomes apparent when considering that Iamblichus devoted a whole book of his work *De mysteriis* solely to the issue of *mantikē!*

31. Eun. *VS* 474–75, quote p. 432: τὴν ἀκρίβειαν τὴν ἐν τοῖς μέρεσι τοῦ λόγου καὶ τὰς διαλεκτικὰς μηχανὰς καὶ πλοκὰς.

32. Bouffartigue, *Empereur Julien,* 43, 319–20. The Neoplatonic project of harmonizing Aristotle and Plato began, according to Hierocles, with Plotinus's teacher Ammonius Sacchas; Gerson, *Aristotle.*

33. J. Geffcken, *Kaiser Julianus,* 86, is an exception. Foussard, "Julien philosophe," summarizes the *communis opinio;* see also Raeder, "Kaiser Julian"; and A. Smith, *Philosopher;* despite Hahn, "Philosophen," 411–12.

34. Goulet, "Vies," 162–68; Penella, *Greek Philosophers,* 1–9; Miller, "Strategies."

35. Jul. *Ep.* 12 (Wright 2); Penella, *Greek Philosophers,* 134–39.

pated in public life and were deeply enmeshed—particularly those living in or near Constantinople or with ties to the (continuously moving) court—in debates regarding the true philosophical life and the philosopher's appropriate involvement in the affairs of the *politeia*.

Philosophy in the Shade versus Philosophy in the Open: Themistius and His Opponents

On September 1, 355, the emperor Constantius expressed his wish to adorn his father's city, Constantinople, with splendid buildings and with "the noblest of sciences, I mean philosophy, [and to make it] shine forth everywhere and among all men" by elevating Themistius to senatorial status (*Ep. Const.* 23c–d). Themistius was not the only cultural treasure he presented to his city. In the preceding decades Constantius had done much to ensure that Constantinople would become a center of *paideia* befitting himself and his father, its founder, whose mind, as historians like Aurelius Victor and panegyrists like Libanius and the later emperor Julian attest, was "adorned with literary studies . . . trained by practice in public speaking" and "versed in literature to the point of elegance" (*litterarum ad elegantiam prudens*).[36] Constantius's interest in *paideia*, evidenced by his involvement in Christian debates, had found expression in the care he devoted to Julian's education, and even more in the measures he took to "give literature, before anything else, the dignity that befits it" at Constantinople (*Ep. Const.* 23c). Thus between 343 and 352, before moving to Athens, the rhetor Himerius had taught at Constantinople, where Constantius had received him in an audience. He had also received Libanius, whom he had compelled to move to the city in 349 by an imperial letter (*basileiois grammasin*).[37] Other rhetors then teaching in Constantinople included Nicocles and Heceboulius.

Themistius's preferred status, especially after 355, gave further prominence to philosophy at court and in the city. Themistius not only held an official teaching chair, but was also invited to dine with the emperor.[38] In May 357—in good philosophical tradition—he led a formal delegation of the Constantinopolitan senate to Rome (where he gave his third oration); a year later, another philosopher, Eustathius, conducted an embassy to King Shapur. In 357 Themistius donated his collected speeches (*Orations* 1–4; Constantius's *Epistle to the Senate*; and *Orations* 20, *On His Father*; 21, *The Touchstone; or, The Philosopher*; 24, 27, 30, 32, and 33) and his work on Aristotle to the library in Constantinople, founded by Constantius in order that

---

36. Lib. *Or.* 59.34. Wiemer, "Libanius," argues for Libanius's dependence on Eus. *VC*; Jul. *Or.* 1.10d–11c; Aur. Vict. *Caes.* 42.23. Recent studies have done much to revise Ammianus's assessment of Constantius as a mere pretender: e.g., Henck, "Constantius' *paideia*," 173–75; Leppin, "Constantius II.," 457–58.

37. T. D. Barnes, "Himerius," 209, 212, 224; Lib. *Or.* 1.74, 2.17; *Libanius: Autobiography*, ed. and trans. Norman, 167–68.

38. Lib. *Ep.* 52.2 (Norman); Them. *Or.* 34.353a.

it could acquire the works of the great writers of the past.³⁹ As part of his recruitment drive for the Constantinopolitan senate in 358/9, Themistius managed to attract the philosopher Hierius of Sikyon, a former pupil of Iamblichus, and his entire school to Constantinople.⁴⁰ At the same time, in 359, the philosopher Celsus, one of Hierius's former students, moved to the city explicitly to enroll in the senate and to study under Themistius, as did the philosopher Iamblichus (not the famous one!) and the Egyptian poet-rhetoricians Harpocration and Andronicus.⁴¹

In short, even our somewhat sketchy sources on non-Christian philosophers and rhetoricians reveal a lively intellectual scene at Constantinople, fostered by the emperor Constantius.⁴² The ire evoked by the advancement of philosophy through Themistius attests most eloquently to the intensity of philosophical debates at Constantinople and throughout the East, and to the diverse opinions represented. Unfortunately, the main sources for these debates are again not the writings of the participants but their rebuke by Themistius, the target of the attacks. Indeed, nearly all of Themistius's orations delivered and published between 355 and 361 vigorously attack his detractors as well as propagate his own ideas on the true philosophical life.⁴³

No sooner had Themistius become a senator, in 355, than his competitors began to criticize his actions. Even his friendship with Libanius began to cool just after Themistius's *adlectio* and subsequent sojourn in Antioch in 356/7, as Gilbert Dagron has pointed out.⁴⁴ Libanius and Themistius had known each other for years and would continue an intense correspondence until 365 and a more sporadic one until 388, but their relationship changed with Themistius's acceptance of an official role.⁴⁵ Libanius, after all a rhetor and thus at least in theory more inclined to active

---

39. Amm. Marc. 17.5.15, 17.14.1; Them. *Or.* 4.60c, 61c–d; Dagron, *Empire,* 205–12; Vanderspoel, *Themistius,* 100–102, 164, 250. According Themistius, his words had grown feathers and flown to the emperor and from him to the empire; *Or.* 31.354d.

40. Vanderspoel, *Themistius,* 83–84, argues that Hierius and not Celsus is the "philosopher from Sikyon"; Them. *Or.* 23.296.

41. Lib. *Epp.* 368.1, 86.3 (Foerster); Alan Cameron, "Wandering Poets," esp. 487–88; Heather, "New Men," 13, 17–18.

42. Constantius's sponsoring of *paideia* included the Latin-speaking part of his realm; Henck, "Constantius' *paideia,*" 180–86.

43. I.e., *Or.* 2–4, 20–23, 26, 27, 29, 33, and many of his later ones, esp. 31; Themistius, *Private Orations,* ed. and trans. Penella, xiii; Vanderspoel, *Themistius,* 250.

44. They were near-contemporaries: Libanius was born in 314, and Themistius in 317.

45. Their friendship shows how the classic rivalry between rhetoric and philosophy had lessened by the middle of the fourth century: Themistius, the philosopher, following the example of Dio Chrysostom and of his own father, Eugenius, pronounced rhetoric indispensable for philosophy, while Libanius, the rhetor, frequently praised Themistius and was his guest in Constantinople before their friendship cooled. Fiscally, some rhetoricians were (badly remunerated) assistant teachers at municipally endowed rhetorical schools, headed by a "sophist," while others were better-paid forensic advocates or

involvement (and thus also keenly aware of competition), criticized Themistius increasingly after 355 because he now represented the political philosopher actively involved in the *politeia* of Constantius's New Rome.⁴⁶

Themistius's defense and his counterattacks against Libanius and other critics began with the funeral oration in praise of his father, Eugenius (*Or.* 20) and the oration defining the touchstones of the correct philosophical life (*Or.* 21), delivered in 355 and 356.⁴⁷ Later orations such as *Oration* 22 (*On Friendship*), *Oration* 23 (*The Sophist*), *Oration* 29 (*To Those Who Misunderstood the Sophist*), and *Oration* 26 (*On Speaking*), all from 359 and 360, responding to specific criticisms, clarify the nature of the attacks on Themistius and his philosophical concepts.⁴⁸

Themistius's *epitaphios logos* on his father, Eugenius, "a true-born and genuine philosopher," emphasized that philosophy was "sacred" and that only a philosopher descended from a sacred marriage (*gamos hieros*) could hope for union with the divine.⁴⁹ According to Themistius, however, such union was impossible without correct instruction in the teachings of the undisputed masters, Socrates, Plato, and Aristotle, which a grateful Themistius had received from his father (*Or.* 20.234, 240). "The divine Aristotle" took pride of place, for Eugenius, as his "lucid" interpreter, "would open the gateway of the temple" of Aristotle's wisdom "to the initiate, . . . clothe the god's statue [*agalma*] and make it beautiful and clean on all sides," thus presenting the philosopher's work to all those worthy of it (235).⁵⁰

Eugenius, however, though he "impress[ed] upon these sacred mysteries . . . the face and shape" of Aristotle, was in essence a Neoplatonist and hence eclectic. According to Themistius, he "helped to open up all the shrines to all the sages," but in

---

private teachers. Lib. *Or.* 31; Wolf, *Vom Schulwesen*, 12–24, 60–66. For Libanius's life, see Wintjes, *Leben*; for the relationship with Themistius, 135–50.

46. Themistius's letters have been lost, with the exception of a few marginalia in Libanius's corpus, specifically his *Ep.* 241 (Norman *Ep.* 42, codex Berolinensis). Dagron, *Empire*, 18, 36–42.

47. Themistius's father was still alive at the time of the *adlectio* but had died by *Or.* 2—i.e., by November 355. (*Or.* 2.28d refers to recently acquired property.) There is no evidence that Themistius delivered the funeral oration in Paphlagonia, as has often been asserted; Vanderspoel, *Themistius*, 87–91, 95–104; Themistius, *Private Orations*, ed. and trans. Penella, 10–22. Unless otherwise noted, I follow Penella's dating (Themistius, *Private Orations*, xiii), and Themistius, *Politics*, ed. and trans. Heather and Moncur, 43–44.

48. One effect of Eunapius's *Lives* and their emphasis on Neoplatonist philosophers has been that scholars relegate Themistius's philosophical ideas to the sidelines. Though his work on Aristotle has been studied, the scholarly focus on Neoplatonists, among whom scholars do not count him, has led to a neglect of his philosophical ideas. In *Platonopolis*, D. O'Meara's focus on the political aspects of Neoplatonism should aid Themistius's reception, especially once he is rescued from earlier scholarly assessments as mere flatterer and careerist; Vanderspoel, *Themistius*, 2–14; Themistius, *Politics*, ed. and trans. Heather and Moncur, xii–xiv, 12–29, 38–42, 98–103; Dagron, *Empire*, 44 n. 51.

49. Them. *Or.* 21.248; Pl. *R.* 5.48e. Fowden, "Pagan Holy Man," 33–34.

50. Them. *Or.* 23.298c-d, for the opening of a temple that reveals the cult statue as metaphor for philosophical truth; Themistius, *Private Orations*, ed. and trans. Penella, 54 n. 7.

particular to Plato, whom he considered second only to Aristotle; indeed, "he always got angry at those who actually tried to build a dividing wall between the two."[51] In Eugenius's view (and that means in Themistius's), Plato came second only because he required the fortification of Aristotle, without whose rigor Plato could become accessible to persons who were lazy and lax. Eugenius considered the study of Aristotle's dialectic logic a prerequisite for tackling Plato; it represented "an excellent preliminary rite to Plato's frenzy and at the same time a defensive wall and safeguard to it" (235).[52] On this sequence of study, with Aristotle essential for comprehending Plato, Themistius founded his own model of a philosophical life of active involvement. Like his father, and like Socrates, Themistius "showed the world that he had many public struggles in the civic arena and, no less, domestic ones in his own household, and that he was enduring and holding up against all these struggles easily, because one must elect to be a philosopher in deed, not in word" (239).

Themistius's targets were those who were lax and philosophers in word only. A most critical issue at stake for Themistius both in *Oration* 21, on the characteristics of a true philosopher, and in *Oration* 22, *On Friendship,* was the difference between a "social and gentle" soul and an "unsocial and savage" one (Pl. *R.* 6.486b, Them. *Or.* 21.254). A true philosopher, according to Themistius, had to delight in company and involvement, rather than "whisper [his] words to the young in some isolated corner.... [and] avoid the center of the city and those gathering places wherein the poet [Homer] says that men gain distinction." Themistius was content to leave such a "counterfeit" philosopher "on a couch in his room" (*Or.* 21.255). As for himself, "it will be my duty to bring speech [*logos*] out into the light and to accustom it to tolerate the crowd and to put up with noise and with the clamor of the seated assembly. If it is capable of benefiting people individually, it certainly will be able to benefit many individuals at once" (*Or.* 22.265).[53]

Those whisperers in corners, for their part, accused Themistius of false philosophy, precisely because he sought to "unveil the statues" and reveal at least some of the mysteries of philosophy to the populace instead of reserving it for full ini-

---

51. Themistius, like most of his contemporaries, professed devotion to other philosophical masters and had harmonized their thoughts, especially Pythagoras, the Stoic Zeno, and even Epicurus. He too held the belief that "philosophy is one, and virtually all philosophers have sought a single goal, though reaching it by diverse roads" (*Or.* 9.186a).

52. Scholars continue to discuss how much weight Themistius attributed to Aristotle as opposed to Plato. Schroeder and Todd (*Two Greek Aristotelian Commentators,* 33–39, 90) and Todd (*Themistius: On Aristotle's "On the Soul,"* trans. Todd, 2, 10) place more weight on Themistius's exposure to (Neo-)Platonism than, for example, Blumenthal (*Aristotle,* 8–10, 22–24), who considers Themistius a pure Peripatetic. All agree that Themistius's knowledge of Plato's writings was extensive and that he was conversant with Plotinian and Neoplatonic thinking. Balleriaux, "Thémistius"; Colpi, *Paideia,* 85–110; Wallis, *Neoplatonism,* 23–25.

53. D. Chr. *Or.* 32, *To the Alexandrians.* The reference is to Plato's *Grg.* 485d–e, a passage with many exegetes from Cicero to Aelius Aristides. The Homer reference is *Il.* 9.441. Dagron, *Empire,* 43 n. 43 *bis.*

tiates.⁵⁴ Such criticisms sharpened with Themistius's increasing involvement in public affairs, as a holder of public office. He responded to them in 359 with *Oration* 23. Taking his cue from Plato's enumeration of the characteristics of a sophist, Themistius refuted their applicability to him one by one, with particular umbrage at the accusation that he abused his position to attract students by offering them material benefits.⁵⁵ He pointed out how he had consistently refused to avail himself of the privileges and benefits associated with "the hammered tablets" of office.⁵⁶

Scholars have debated the specific office he referred to, their suggestions ranging from the proconsulate and the prefecture to the largely honorary presidency of the senate.⁵⁷ Undeniably, Themistius held a public position of some prestige (which he called *leitourgia* and *prostasia*) and of greater public involvement than was customarily associated with the chair of philosophy that he certainly occupied.⁵⁸ Equally undeniable, this exposure—his holding an office other than a chair of philosophy—elicited severe criticism from his opponents, who charged that the responsibilities of active involvement led to personal and material benefits unbecoming to a philosopher. In refuting these accusations Themistius mixed active involvement and philosophical reticence inextricably: "Whatever would have filled my wallet instead of relieving my slaves' hunger, whatever would have unfailingly

---

54. Them. *Or.* 22.255–56.

55. That is, that he had distributed wheat from the *annona* to his students. Themistius argued in *Or.* 23.292a that he had not profited personally, for example, by converting food he received for their support into cash.

56. "I was allowed to avail myself not only of grain but also of the long list [of items] of luxury and comfort that go hand in hand with the hammered tablets [ταῖς δέλτοις ... σφυρηλάτοις].... Nevertheless, though I was permitted to enjoy these prerogatives, I did not agree or consent to them despite the fact that the emperor was very eager that I should do so." "Hammered tablets" received upon the acceptance of office contained and displayed the specific honors and benefits associated with the office conferred and were thus virtually synonymous with imperial office as such—e.g., the proconsulate or the urban prefecture and lesser positions within the imperial administration. Themistius's term στρατεύεσθαι refers to the imperial administration. Referring to the prefecture and proconsulate, Themistius used τὰς δέλτους ... τὰς πολυθρυλήτους and πινακίδες in *Or.* 31.353b and 34.16. Dagron, *Empire*, 48; Lendon, *Empire of Honour*, 191–201.

57. See Dagron, *Naissance*, 215–39, on Constantinopolitan proconsuls and urban prefects. Themistius (*Or.* 34.13) accepted the position of proconsul under Theodosius but had rejected it once before, perhaps under Valens. It is possible that *Or.* 23.292 refers to this rejection. I follow Dagron (*Empire*, 213–17), who argues against the urban prefecture and for the position of *princeps senatus*, followed by Vanderspoel, *Themistius*, 104–8. Daly, "Themistius' Refusal," esp. 179, argues for proconsulship, followed by Penella (Themistius, *Private Orations*, ed. and trans. Penella, 1–2). Vanderspoel's argument, *Themistius*, 102, that Themistius simply rejected benefits associated with the chair of philosophy is too minimalist; such an appointment could not have caused such animosity in 358; *Themistios: Staatsreden*, ed. Leppin and Portmann, 3.

58. For a detailed analysis of Themistius's vocabulary denoting office, see Dagron, *Empire*, 52; and Karamboula, *Staatsbegriffe*, 53–73.

caused an unfitting name to cling to my philosopher's cloak, ... this I firmly refused. I did not dishonor my forbears, for I thought of the king and the philosopher in identical terms [*peri basileōs kai philosophou* ... *homoiōs*] and believed that both alike dwell on the summits of human happiness and can go no further.... You cannot be conveyed to those summits on a tablet made of gold; you can get there only if you master and profit from the tablet on which Plato and Pythagoras wrote, an ancient tablet and one that has not been eaten away by worms" (*Or.* 23.292–93).

Whatever office Themistius held (it may simply have been his *adlectio* to the senate combined with the mandate to expand it), by 360 his level of involvement in the *politeia* was causing considerable unease among his fellow philosophers and rhetors, who charged him with worldliness. Even graver, however, was the second accusation that Themistius's active philosophical life represented an innovation. He responded that those "who appoint themselves lawgivers to philosophers and advise them to be silent, to keep what they know to themselves," lodged "as in a court of law ... sworn statement[s] of accusation ... against me. 'He is committing an injustice,' they say in reference to me, 'through his philosophical innovation and his 'introduction of new deities.'"[59]

For those philosophers who regarded the *bios theōrētikos* as the highest calling, Themistius's philosophical life was no longer the correctly mixed life, because it went beyond what was considered fitting for the philosopher. It thus represented an assault on the foundations of the philosophical life itself. Themistius pointed to the original masters in responding to such charges of innovation. He argued that his philosophy not only did not innovate but interpreted the divine masters correctly and lucidly, that he tried "to clarify what Aristotle means and to draw that meaning out of the words in which he constricted and confined it, so that it would be intelligible to the utterly uninitiated" (*Or.* 23.294). It was not he who had committed an injustice but those who had so misread the ancients that for them the philosophical life consisted merely of whispering in corners and conversing with their disciples.[60]

In leading the life of a *politikos philosophos*, Themistius thought he was imitating Socrates, Plato, and above all Aristotle to the fullest degree possible: "Tell me, who was as active or innovative as Plato?"[61] If his philosophical life was an inno-

---

59. Them. *Or.* 26.312–13: οἱ ὀλίγοι οὗτοι ... χειροτονοῦσιν ἑαυτοὺς νομοθέτας τοῖς φιλοσόφοις, καὶ ἀποφαίνονται ἀφώνους εἶναι καὶ στέγειν ἅττα ἂν εἰδῶσιν ἐν τῇ καρδίᾳ καὶ μὴ ἐξαγγέλειν μηδὲ κοινωνεῖν.... [313] ὥσπερ ἐν δικαστηρίῳ τὴν ἀντωμοσίαν ὑμῖν ἀναγνωστέον, ἣν ὑπογράφονται καθ᾽ ἡμῶν οἱ κομψοὶ κατήγοροι οὗτοι καὶ τεχνῖται τῆς σιωπῆς. ἀδικεῖ, φασὶν ἐμὲ λέγοντες, νεωτερίζων εἰς φιλοσοφίαν, καινὰ εἰσάγων δαιμόνια (alluding to the accusations leveled against Socrates, Pl. *Ap.* 17a, 19b, 24b). Dagron, *Empire*, 48, 144–46; Ruggini, "Sofisti," 406–8.

60. *Or.* 26.314, 318b, 319, 325.

61. Them. *Or.* 26.318: καὶ τίς οὕτω πολυπράγμων ἢ καινοτόμος; Them. *Or.* 4; Dagron, *Empire*, 225–29.

vation, such innovation, like that of Plato, was good and necessary, because correct and appropriate innovation advanced the arts and sciences (*Or.* 26.315–20). Themistius, furthermore, had been asked by imperial mandate "to make new the ancient teachings."[62] His innovations thus represented an improved mimesis of the teachings of the ancients, a restoration of philosophy to its rightful place as medicine for the soul of both individual and community (*Or.* 26.318–23).

Themistius's supporters included the emperor, a number of philosophers, including those already mentioned, and in all likelihood a Cynic philosopher named Heraclius, who went all the way to Milan to be received by Constantius, where he may have encountered Julian.[63] They may have included even someone like the Alexandrian physician Aetius, the teacher of Eunomius (also known for his commentary on Aristotle's *Categories*), who went afoul of Constantius and was sent by him into exile because of his Aristotelian views of the relationship between Father and Son.[64] And presumably Themistius's supporters also included many of the new men whom he had recruited to the senate. Themistius noted in the 380s that of the more than two thousand men who by then constituted the Constantinopolitan senate, he had personally recruited most between 358 and 361; prior to his drive, the senate had numbered only about three hundred.[65] Julian knew that well when addressing his letter to Themistius.

For Themistius's opponents, whom he never mentions by name (following literary convention), the true philosophical life preserved an absolute purity in the circumscribed space of the *erēmia*;[66] the philosopher had to flee the world to become as far as possible like a god—as men such as Aedesius, Chrysanthius, Eusebius of Myndus, Maximus of Ephesus, and Priscus of Epirus and later of Athens had done.[67] But they did not completely agree among themselves about the correct interpreta-

---

62. *Ep. Const.* 20a: τὰς ἀρχαίας δόξας . . . γίνεσθαι νέας. According to John Lydus (*De magist.* 2.19), innovation was characteristic of tyrants (ἴδιον δὲ τυράννων)—one indication of its negative associations in a society predicated upon stability.

63. Later, Julian (*Or.* 7.233d) asked Heraclius accusingly, "Why is it that you visited the late emperor Constantius in Italy but could not travel as far as Gaul?" Eun. *Hist.* 4.25.2 (*Excerpt. de sent.* 19; Blockley, *Fragmentary Classicising Historians,* vol. 2, 36).

64. Aetius's Christian opponents accused him of abusing Aristotle's *Categories;* Gr. Nyss. *Eun.* 1.181 (*GNO*, vol. 1, 80) . L. R. Wickham, "*Syntagmation.*"

65. Petit, *Étudiants,* 154–55; Dagron, *Naissance,* 129, follows Themistius. Others, including Heather, "New Men," 13, judge Themistius's success more conservatively; but see Themistius, *Politics,* ed. and trans. Heather and Moncur, 14. Many high-ranking members of Constantius's administration were famous for their *paideia,* such as Strategius, PPO from 354 until 358, surnamed Musonianus because of his fluency in both Latin and Greek; Anatolius, praetorian prefect of Illyricum in 357–360, known for his keen intellect; and Alypius, the *vicarius Brittaniarum* in 358, a poet; Amm. Marc. 15.13.1–2, 16.9.2, 10.21; Lib. *Ep.* 40.10–11 and 4.5 (Norman); Jul. *Ep.* 10 (Bidez); and *PLRE,* vol. 1, s.vv.

66. Only Them. *Or.* 21.262d attacks a specific person.

67. Penella, *Greek Philosophers,* 49–50, 53, 57, 109–17; Bowersock, *Greek Sophists,* 66–69.

tion of the more theoretical and mystic aspects of this life, nor were they truly as opposed to public involvement and active participation in the *politeia* as Themistius's defense and counterattack make it seem.[68]

From what we can reconstruct, many of these men, Maximus included, belonged to extended families of great wealth and influence, and their siblings held public office as a matter of course. Indeed, holding public office did not prevent them from living the philosophical life, to judge from a letter written by Sopater (the son of one of Iamblichus's leading students, also called Sopater), himself a philosopher and decurion of Apamea in 361, to his brother Himerius, holder of a significant public office prior to 357. Rather, holding public office represented a second level of philosophical virtues, corresponding to the arrangement of the city in Plato's *Laws*. In this understanding, even if a philosopher's virtues had not reached the (unattainable) height of the perfect philosopher-king as posited in Plato's *Republic*, they nevertheless reached high enough to be actively employed for the public good (what is *kalos*, or noble) by "sanctioning the best of what is given rather than what is first absolutely." In short, what is perfect was not considered the enemy of the good.

In practice, according to Sopater, the philosopher's civic involvement created civic harmony by weaving together different strands of society, especially rulers and those ruled, which in turn required the philosophical virtues of steadfastness, freedom of thought and speech, and hence courage: a philosopher should assume the mantle of public official for the good of all.[69]

Indeed, for Themistius's opponents, public office, especially the role of the philosopher as advisor to those who ruled, provided a way out of the conundrum of tension between active involvement and withdrawal from public life. The theoretical argument ran as follows: granted the usefulness of the holder of public office as representing a second level of the philosophical life adumbrated in Sopater's letter, true philosophers still ought to strive for the perfect life of the true philosopher as king described in Plato's *Republic*. This role, however, inevitably courted the ever present danger already described: to be active and to hold office (as Themistius did) exposed one, as Plato had indicated, to the dangers of ambition and lust for honors, whereas the true philosophical life demanded that one flee the world to achieve maximal purity and closeness to the divine. To phrase it more simply, it posed the conundrum of being politically active without at the same time being deflected from doing philosophy.

As Dominic O'Meara has shown, fourth-century Platonists found a way out of the conundrum, not by withdrawing completely, as scholars have long suggested—

---

68. Blumenthal, *Aristotle*, 23.
69. The text is in Stobaeus *Anth.* 4.212.1–218.9; *PLRE*, vol. 1, Sopater 2, Himerius 3. D. O'Meara, "Neoplatonist Ethics," 93. For Gregory's nearly identical description of the "second philosophy" of his brother, Caesarius, S. Elm, "Gregory's Women," 185–90.

such a pursuit of philosophical life would have left them open to the charge of neglecting their duties to society and of practicing the unpopular Epicurean maxim of living unnoticed. That is, they did not seek to model themselves absolutely on the philosopher-king of Plato's *Republic*. Instead they read that philosopher-king as analogous to the Demiurge in Plato's *Timaeus;* something they could do because the highest divine principle in Neoplatonism, the One, which the philosopher sought to emulate and to which he wished his soul to return, was also the Good. As the highest Good, the One bestowed good on all else. Other divine entities that proceeded out of the transcendent One and highest Good extend that good to entities below them, including human beings and their social order, to make what was inferior to them good like themselves. As a consequence, the human soul, especially once it experienced closeness, if not union, with the divine, also wants to do good to those below it: the philosopher wants to do good altruistically to all others, like the wise man in Plato's *Timaeus* who desired to do good after his vision of the Good in the form of the Demiurge.

According to Plato's *Timaeus,* the Demiurge is the creative, active deity who actually made the universe. Because he himself is good, he wishes this universe to be as good as possible as well (Pl. *Ti.* 29c). To that end, the Demiurge contemplates what he has created, thus linking contemplation and action (in this case the act of creation). As a result, as Proclus pointed out, a philosopher's soul participates in the heavenly good through contemplation, and thus participates in an activity linked to goodness, which induces him to do good so as to benefit those inferior to him. And this applies not only to the philosopher's private realm, but also to the broader domain of politics. Here, the philosopher acted primarily in the sphere of jurisdiction and legislation—he acted in his capacity of philosopher as lawgiver and judge, ascertaining justice, and thus embodying the philosopher-leader.[70]

However, even in conceiving the role of the philosopher-king according to Plato's prescription, philosophers born of divine lineage, as Robbert van den Berg has noted, remained hampered by not being actual gods but human, entangled in this world, so that any connection with it had to deflect them from their contemplation of the intelligible heavenly world of the transcendent divine. Unlike Plato's Demiurge, they cannot both contemplate and be active, especially with regard to what is inferior in the wider world, without impairing the purity of their contemplation. Porphyry was justified to say that "as much as we can, we should detach ourselves from those places in which even an unwilling person can fall in with the crowd

---

70. D. O'Meara, *Platonopolis*, 40–115, and "Neoplatonist Conceptions." A late Roman Neoplatonic philosophical school excavated at Aphrodisias contains a central apse in which portraits of political leaders are paired with their philosopher-teachers: Socrates and Alcibiades, Aristotle and Alexander; Pythagoras and another Neoplatonic "holy man," Apollonius of Tyana, are also represented; R. R. R. Smith, "Late Roman Philosopher Portraits."

[*plēthos*]." A philosopher thus ought to stay away from the agora, the law courts, and the councils.[71]

Porphyry represented the most radical concept of such self-endangerment through active participation. Others argued that the philosopher-king, who promoted justice, practiced a cardinal virtue, whether he did so theoretically by writing, or practically and actively as a teacher. A philosopher could actively teach and promote justice by advising a person far more active than himself, such as a public official or even an emperor. In fact, to advise public officials or an emperor— the quintessential labor of the true philosopher as leader—did not require taking office oneself.[72] The true philosopher could retreat to his own heights like Plato's Demiurge, but from there he could advise, teach, and influence others more fully engaged in the active life by promoting justice and just legislation, thus acting for the common good without compromising his contemplative purity.[73]

Themistius and his detractors debated not active involvement versus contemplative retreat per se, but Themistius's level of active involvement, namely his own assumption of public office as (an essentially Neoplatonic) philosopher. He had justified his public position in an Aristotelian reading of the true philosophical life as one of open activity in holding office rather than limiting the philosopher's activity to that of indirect, or hidden, advisor. A philosopher as emperor could be such a philosopher-king, and that is what Themistius had urged Julian to become. Julian's *Epistle to Themistius,* in response, indicated his wish to remain on the second level of the philosophy as Sopater's letter described it: promoting justice and just legislation while holding office but making no claim to be a true philosopher-king. Julian was advised in this capacity by a true philosopher such as Maximus. For Julian, Themistius's intimation that an emperor, and a dynastically chosen one at that, could act as a true philosopher-king indicated his misreading of the normative texts. For that reason, Themistius's advice to Constantius cannot have been good, as was indeed borne out by that emperor's conduct.

Granted—such finely nuanced differences may seem to the modern reader to split hairs, much as the Christian musings on the relation between the Father and the Son in Chapter 1 may seem to be abstract deliberations with little relevance for governance. To the men engaged in these debates, however, these differences mattered, because of the underlying issue at stake in these debates: What was the divine and how could one approach it? For all concerned, to approach the divine required that one understand correctly the relation between the human and the divine and the means by which humans could communicate with the divine. These issues were highly relevant for those in leadership positions. Good leaders, who could safeguard those

---

71. Porph. *Abst.* 1.35–36 (*Porphry: On Abstinence,* trans. Clark); R. van den Berg, "Live Unnoticed!"
72. As thematized by Proclus, *Theol. Plat.* 5.18, quoting Pl. *Plt.* 272e5.
73. See also Dillon, "Philosophy"; and Lane Fox, "Movers and Shakers."

in their care, had to know how to read divine intention. A mistake in interpreting the divine will spelled disaster for all. These debates were true debates, with definitions and approaches, even though they revolved around essentially static normative texts, not static at all themselves. As a consequence, such discussions proved an ideal platform for showcasing leadership and gaining prestige: to demonstrate one's capacity to lead or to gain access to those who led was after all the name of the game.

Julian's views on the true philosophical life evolved between the *Epistle to Themistius* and his next pronouncements on the topic. When Julian wrote the core of that letter, he was still Caesar, so that he too had to negotiate between being ruled and ruling. Furthermore, in 361, when he revised the letter to address the Constantinopolitan senate, consisting largely of men chosen by Constantius and Themistius, he wanted to differentiate himself from Constantius without alienating that important body; he had not yet entered the capital as sole ruler. In the spring of 362 the situation was different. Then, Julian wrote three further orations on his philosophical life, two orations against Cynic philosophers, and a hymn to the Mother of the Gods. By then he had purged the court and the high echelons of the administration of Constantius's supporters and close friends, including Themistius and his patrons.[74] He was now the sole ruler; a divinely chosen Roman emperor—hence closer to the gods than most of his subjects, with the possible exception of Maximus. If anyone could live as a true philosopher and leader analogous to the Demiurge, and act without compromising the purity of his contemplation, it could only have been someone like Julian.

A PHILOSOPHER AS LEADER, IN JULIAN'S OWN WORDS: *AGAINST THE CYNIC HERACLIUS*

Julian's *Epistle to Themistius* announced his position in a debate on the philosophical life that had gripped the intellectual circles of Constantinople for some time. By correcting Themistius's views, Julian countered concepts of the philosophical life as decidedly active that persons of considerable political influence had supported in significant numbers, beginning with Constantius and counting many of those involved in his administration and the senate. Julian's resistance to such concepts did not imply that as emperor he would simply reverse course and henceforth allow himself to be advised only by the philosophers who had so evidently formed him. Just as he had invited Christian intellectuals and advisors to court, permitted others to return from exile, and removed yet others, Julian also gathered around him philosophers representing a range of positions.

For example, he invited to court the Iamblichan philosopher Eustathius, mar-

---

74. According to Dagron, *Empire*, 234 n. 26, these patrons were Saturninus, Clearchus (perhaps prosecuted), Datianus, Florentinus II, and Spectatus.

ried to another Iamblichan philosopher, Sosipatra, even though Eustathius was the philosopher Constantius had sent on an embassy to Shapur, entrusting him with an active political mission as Themistius advocated. Julian had also invited the Aristotelian Aetius, who was, like Basil, a Christian, and the Cynic Heraclius, who had traveled all the way to Milan to meet Constantius. We know little of other Cynics present at Julian's court, namely Chytron, Serenianus, and Asclepiades.[75] Julian did not relegate Themistius entirely to the sidelines either, allowing him to continue as a highly successful teacher at Constantinople; the emperor in person arbitrated a dispute between Themistius and Maximus, who had both published commentaries on the master's works, about the classification of Aristotle's syllogisms.[76] The gesture was important even if Julian, predictably, took Maximus's side.[77]

Such (relative) open-mindedness was not a trait specific to Julian. It permitted him, as it had other emperors shaped by *paideia* before him, to display the degree to which he practiced one of the essential imperial virtues: friendship, or *philia*.[78] Close friendships with other *philologoi*, lovers of culture or learning, were preeminent traits of emperors as well as philosophers, not least because only such friendships, particularly with men of differing opinions, provided the essential platform for the philosopher and the emperor to showcase how they handled the vital interaction of friendship and *parrhēsia,* or frank speech.[79] In voicing their differences to emperors and each other, the philosophers as advisors could display their frankness (and courage) as well as their powers of persuasion. Their fellow-philosophers, especially the emperors among them, could demonstrate their mildness and their ability to forgive (in particular if they were not persuaded). Or they could refuse to be mild and forgiving, as in the debate, similar to that between Themistius and Max-

---

75. For Eustathius, recipient of Jul. *Epp.* 34 and 35 (Wright 43 and 44), Julian, *Epistolario,* trans. and comm. Caltabiano, 46. Julian *Or.* 7.224d mentioned that these Cynics and another one, who was blond, were recent arrivals; *Giuliano Imperatore: Al Cinico Eraclio,* ed. and trans. Guido, 148–49, the edition used in what follows; Wiemer, *Libanios,* 33–34; Schlange-Schöningen, *Kaisertum,* 77–84.

76. Lib. *Ep.* 793. In *Or.* 7.99d Themistius called Julian the most philosophical of emperors. Scholars differ on the extent of Themistius's marginality under Julian. Brauch ("Themistius" and "Prefect") follows the *Suda* in thinking that he receded into obscurity, his role now taken by Maximus, Priscus, and others (Themistius, *Politics,* ed. and trans. Heather and Moncur, 141–42), but Dagron (*Empire,* 232–35) argues that he maintained his position as influential philosopher and teacher.

77. For the debate, Ammonius *In APr.* 1.1.24b, 18; Lee, *Griechische Tradition,* 11, 126–30; Dagron, *Empire,* 44 n. 51. The Maximus in question is usually identified as the one of Ephesus, though Vanderspoel, "Fourth-Century Philosopher," argues for Maximus of Byzantium, Themistius's father-in-law. Bouffartigue, *Empereur Julien,* 567–68, suggests that this dispute was not a life event; Dagron, *Empire,* 235.

78. Guido, "Nozione"; Konstan, *Friendship,* 53–121; I have not been able to access Henck, "Images."

79. Jul. *Or.* 8.241c–d, 242c, 243b, 245, based on the precepts of Arist. *EN* 1155a4, 1159b3–4; R. Smith, *Julian's Gods,* 40–43. For Aristotle on friendship, see also Cooper, *Reason,* 312–55. Themistius, too, wrote on friendship and frequently evoked *parrhēsia.* Vanderspoerl, *Themistius,* 13–23; Brown, *Power and Persuasion,* 61–70.

108   PART ONE

imus, that had taken place in Antioch between Meletius, George, and Acacius on the exegesis of Proverbs 8:22 in the presence of Constantius just a year earlier. Such public displays of *parrhēsia* required courage because the consequences could be real. After debating George of Alexandria and Acacius, Meletius was sent into exile.[80]

Julian, as philosopher and leader, seems to have taken care to provide many occasions to debate philosophy both in public and in private as soon as he had settled in Constantinople. In one of these debates, held in the spring of 362, the Cynic Heraclius engaged in *parrhēsia* to lasting effect. Heraclius's speech has not been preserved, but it so incensed the emperor that he stayed awake all night to compose his response, *Oration 7, Against the Cynic Heraclius*. In it, Julian demonstrated in detail what being a true philosopher entailed.[81] His prompt response, in which he demolished Heraclius's arguments, appropriately displayed his *philia* and mildness by not sending Heraclius into exile or worse. (I assume; Heraclius's subsequent fate is not known.) It certainly showcased Julian's capacity to speak frankly on the true philosopher and his involvement in the affairs of the *politeia*.

Against Heraclius   "'Truly with the lapse of time many things come to pass!' This verse I heard in a comedy and the other day I was tempted to proclaim it aloud, when by invitation we attended a lecture of a dog [i.e., a Cynic] who barked nothing either distinct or noble; but he was crooning myths as nurses do, and even these he did not compose as would a person of sound mind [*hygiōs*]" (204a). Frank speech, Julian continued, was well and good and a virtue Diogenes and the Cynics praised above all else, but to exercise it with the directness of the Cynics, one first had to be a true Cynic and a true philosopher. In Julian's eyes Heraclius was neither: his philosophy, an improper innovation, falsified the true Cynic philosophy. Julian, in *Oration 7*, pointed out how Heraclius fell short and defined what he considered the characteristics of a true Cynic philosopher.[82]

Apparently, Heraclius (already under a cloud, having demonstrated bad judgment by traveling all the way to Constantius's court in Milan without bothering to continue on to Gaul and to Julian, 224a), had centered his speech on an analogy Julian considered highly infelicitous. According to Julian's response Heraclius had

---

80. Chapter 1 above; Epiph. *Haer*. 73.29.4–7, 31.5–6; J. Chrys. *In Meletium*, PG 50.516; Jer. *Chron*. 241, p. 26 ed. Helm; Hanson, *Search*, 382–84; Brennecke, *Studien*, 74.

81. I maintain Wright's numbering of the orations, which does not follow chronology: *Or*. 7 predates *Or*. 5—i.e., the *Hymn to the Mother of the Gods* (*MoG*), also written overnight according to Lib. *Or*. 18.157, 17.16–17—and *Or*. 6, *Against the Uneducated Cynics*. R. Smith, *Julian's Gods*, 8, 49–50; Billerbeck, "Ideal Cynic," 216–20; Bouffartigue, *Empereur Julien*, 308–9, 359–79; idem, "Cynisme." For Julian's philosophical concepts, see now the contributions in Schäfer, ed., *Kaiser Julian*.

82. Based on Julian's interpretation of the most famous sayings (*chreiai*) of Diogenes and on the classic definitions of true and false Cynic behavior as given, for example, by Dio Chrysostom; Bouffartigue, *Empereur Julien*, 237–39; Döring, "Kaiser Julians Plädoyer."

told a myth in which he compared himself to Zeus and Julian to Pan.[83] Such an analogy, implying a reversal of hierarchy, might have been permissible had an established philosophical master (like Heraclius) addressed a student who was not yet a fully trained philosopher; Julian, after all, had claimed to be not fully trained when he addressed the Constantinopolitan senate. Julian's claim, however, had been a political stratagem, functioning much like his *recusatio,* his claim as Caesar to prefer philosophical retreat to all action. Julian's point to Themistius had, in fact, been that he knew better than the philosopher Themistius what Aristotle had really said regarding philosophers as leaders. Heraclius's pretense to take that *recusatio* at face value was a dangerous move.[84]

Heraclius, however, by comparing Julian to Pan (both were bearded), seems truly to have hit below the belt. Pan's love for the ever elusive Echo earned him fame as the inventor of masturbation and this—as Julian, Heraclius, and their audience well knew—made Pan a choice theme for Cynic philosophers and for those who wanted to debate Cynic sexual ethics. Dio Chrysostom, for example, in his oration *On Tyranny* had famously discussed Pan and masturbation in the context of Diogenes' philosophy: Diogenes' autarky, his self-reliance, led him to renounce what most others considered necessary, including sexual intercourse, by emulating Pan. Dio Chrysostom then used this to demonstrate that the Cynic's life was far happier than that of tyrannical rulers, because Diogenes' restraint, or *enkrateia,* afforded him greater joy than all the tyrants' indulgences.[85] Julian had not remarried after his wife,

---

83. Jul. *Or.* 7.233d; Bouffartigue, *Empereur Julien,* 126 n. 69. Rochefort (*L'empereur Julien: Œuvres complètes,* ed. and trans. Bidez, Rochefort, and Lacombrade, vol. 2, part 1, *Discours de Julien empereur* [Paris 1963], 34–90, esp. 34–42) gives biographical data and reconstructs Heraclius's speech.

84. Like R. van den Berg ("Live Unnoticed!" 109), modern philosophers tend to point out that Julian was not a real philosopher, citing the *Epistle to Themistius* as proof that Julian was aware of that shortcoming. Julian, however, early on declared himself a philosopher; portrayed himself as such on his coins; and was considered thus by his contemporaries. A second scholarly argument against his being a real philosopher focuses on his supposed lack of originality, that he did not develop his own philosophical system (R. Smith, *Julian's Gods,* 62–84, though he often writes against Athanassiadi's too-positive view of Julian). I argue that Julian used classic pro- and anti-Cynic topoi to make specific points tailored to his unique position, and that he was thus original. For Julian's sources, Bouffartigue, *Empereur Julien,* 237–44, 263–65, 272–75, 293–94; and Hammerstaedt, "Kyniker Oenomaus," and "Cynisme," esp. 412–18. Further, as with the writings of Gregory of Nazianzus and other contemporaries, systematic treatises were not the only method to develop original philosophical notions; rather, this occurred often in recourse and counter to other existing ideas. A further reason for scholars' dismissal of Julian as philosopher is his scant reception by later Platonists, even though the Academy in Athens began a new counting of years with his reign; Bouffartigue, *Empereur Julien,* 629; Raeder, "Kaiser Julian," 206–40.

85. Jul. *Or.* 7.212d; D. Chr. *Or. 6, On Tyranny,* 17–20, for Pan and masturbation; *Dion Chrysostomos Oratio 6,* ed. and trans. Krapinger; this oration forms part of a series on Diogenes. Branham, "Defacing the Currency," esp. 101; Jouan, "Diogène"; *Giuliano Imperatore: Contro i Cinici ignoranti,* ed. and trans. Prato and Micalella, xvi, and xxv–xxvii for Julian's reliance on D. Chr. *Or.* 4, *On Kingship,* especially for Jul. *Or.* 6.

Helena, had died in 360, and in his *Epistle to the Athenians* he had proclaimed his *enkrateia*. He had, thus, styled himself as a heroic (Cynic) wise man, able to overcome nature's dictate to marry and procreate by remaining alone to devote himself solely to the public good; Heraclius tested the emperor's equanimity by alluding to some of these elements of Julian's self-portrait in what appears to have been an entirely too favorable manner.[86]

Heraclius's analogy between Julian and Pan, used by Dio Chrysostom in his famous criticism of tyranny, succeeded in severely taxing the emperor's philosophical capacity to esteem frank speech. In Julian's view, a true Cynic philosopher gave meaning to the Cynic maxim "Restamp the common currency"—a Delphic oracle uttered by Apollo—by innovating correctly (208d).[87] That meant such a philosopher contributed to the common good by example, his own poverty and stringent asceticism showing his disregard for the opinions of the masses (214a–215a). Such ascetic rigor and aloofness, however, never meant abandoning the gods and the laws of society, including proper *paideia* (204c–205a). Rather, true Cynics emulated the true philosopher Diogenes, who by enacting Apollo's universal command Know Thyself by advocating for the gods among men, had contributed to a just society—actual practice entirely worthy of a man who wishes to "lead and philosophize" (*stratēgein kai philosophein*, 211a–214a).

To reject the gods and society's laws willfully (as Heraclius presumably implied in his infelicitous analogy) was thus a hallmark of false and shameless Cynics, an exhibitionism of pseudo-philosophers. False Cynics violated philosophy's fundamental axiom that all men are political animals. In disregarding the *politeia* they were worse than the "*apotaktitai* [renunciators], as the impious Galileans [i.e., Christians] call some persons among them" (224b), since they had the wherewithal to know better.[88] False Cynics and Christian renunciators were guilty of a similar mistake, indeed crime: their rejection of the gods and of the laws of society was a willful innovation. It posed a grave danger to the *politeia*, threatening its very foundations, and could not, for that reason, be considered philosophical in the least.

The issue, again, was the philosopher's appropriate involvement in the affairs of

---

86. On Julian's sex life, Cosi, *Casta mater*, 60–75; on Helena, Malosse, "Noblesse," 45–46. For Cynic and Stoic notions on sexual ethics, Gaca, *Making of Fornication*, 87–93.

87. Wright translates "to give a new stamp" (Julian, *Works*, ed. and trans. Wright, vol. 2, 83); Branham, "to deface." The original, παραχαράττειν τὸ νόμισμα, has echoes of false coinage and can mean either "to debase" or "to set a new standard"; Bouffartigue, *Empereur Julien*, 239–40; Courcelle, "Connais-toi toi-même," vol. 1, 93.

88. Epictetus *Diss.* 4.7.6 is the earliest use of "Galilean" as a derogatory term for Christians; it also appears in the martyrdom of Theodotus of Ancyra 31 (Franchi de' Cavalieri, *Martirii*, 80); S. Elm, *Virgins*, 52–56. Julian needed no direct model because to identify someone as originating from a remote region was a familiar insult: e.g., "Cappadocian" or "Phrygian"; Scicolone, "Accezioni." For the use of "renunciators" in contemporary sources, *Giuliano Imperatore: Al Cinico Eraclio*, ed. and trans. Guido, 148.

the *politeia*. Julian, prompted by Heraclius, now outlined a proper withdrawal rather than the proper active involvement he had described when addressing Themistius. The criticism of Epicurus has already indicated that there were correct and incorrect ways to withdraw, and the withdrawal Heraclius appears to have advocated went too far in equating withdrawal with a rejection of society's norms and of the gods who had provided them (as Julian suggests in his rebuttal). Such excessive rejection marked false Cynics and certain Christians (by using "Galileans," a label denoting a small ethnic group, Julian accused all Christians of marginal status, which the renunciators then pushed to extreme). Julian did not wish to be associated with such a philosophical withdrawal, notwithstanding his marital status as (masturbating?) widower.

Sacred Myths and Divine Revelations

Heraclius's rejection of the gods (and hence the norms of society) derived—according to Julian's response—from his fundamental misunderstanding of myth.[89] As his improper analogy between himself, Zeus, Julian, and Pan had indicated, Heraclius had shown himself unable to interpret myths in the correct allegorical fashion. Instead, he "was crooning myths as nurses do," telling stories suited at best to the simple minds of children. Julian's rejoinder thus discussed myth, its correct interpretation, and its place within philosophical progress towards the divine—how and by what means to interpret myths so as to grasp what they revealed about the true nature of the gods. Heraclius, as false Cynic, advocated a withdrawal that rejected both society and the gods, basing it on his misreading and misuse of myth; Christians, especially *apotaktitai,* erred in a similar manner. They too, by analogy, confused myths with nursery stories, since they were "barbarians attached to incredible myths and absurd miracles" (*Cons. Sal.* 252b).[90] Julian in responding to Heraclius and in describing his own notions of philosophical withdrawal offered his first explicit criticism of Christian teachings and Christian behavior; at least that of the renunciators (224b–c).

Listening to Heraclius, Julian had had to summon all his powers of self-control not to leap up and leave. "Endure," he said to himself, "for the brief fraction of the day even a babbling dog! It is not the first time that you had to hear the gods blasphemed! . . . But come, let me in your presence try to teach him the lesson that, first, it is more becoming for a dog [i.e., a Cynic] to write discourses than myths;[91]

---

89. Socr. *HE* 3.23.444 described *Or. 7* as "the discourse in which Julian teaches how to compose a sacred myth," an assessment that found its way into the subtitle of several manuscripts.

90. Thus Julian in his *Or.* 8 (Wright), *Consolation to Himself on the Departure of the Excellent Sallustius,* which he wrote ca. 358 from Gaul; this was a subject of grave concern.

91. ‹λόγους μᾶλλον› ἢ μύθους. Spanheim's supplement λόγους μᾶλλον has been accepted by subsequent editors; *Giuliano Imperatore: Al Cinico Eraclio,* ed. and trans. Guido, 4, 111.

then, how and in which form one must elaborate myth if philosophy requires the writing of myth at all; and finally I shall say a few words about reverence for the gods" (204d–205b). In clarifying the relationship between discourse and myth, Julian engaged in a long-standing debate about myth and its relevance to philosophy, going back once again to Plato.[92] How should one interpret the many scandalous and amoral myths about the gods? Were they a means to create poetic pleasure? Were they ancient absurdities, or did they have continuing ethical relevance, particularly with regard to the true philosophical life? Following Iamblichus, Julian posited in his oration that myths, properly narrated and understood, revealed both ethical maxims for the ordinary individual and mystic heights to the initiate.[93]

To achieve his pedagogical aim to demonstrate the correct form of myths and their interpretation, Julian began with a short, Plato-inspired genealogy of myth. It was, like the flute and the lyre, invented by pastoral peoples for pleasure and entertainment; such myths were for "childish souls" since they did not require further "learning, research and study, . . . labors most congenial" to the human race (206a–d).[94] When such myths reached the Greeks, whose desire for knowledge (in principle common to all men) had been enhanced by the inspiration of "a kindly god," the poets developed them into fables (*ainoi*), designed for men rather than children because they added "moral exhortation," or *parainesis,* even if it was concealed "for fear of alienating the hearers" (207a–b). Such concealment had been necessary at the time—according to Julian—because Aesop, the foremost author of such fables, had been a slave, prevented by law from practicing *parrhēsia* (207d). For that reason alone Heraclius, as a free man and supposed Cynic philosopher practicing frank speech, ought to have spoken openly rather than through myth: he had no need to use the disguise of myth for fear of alienating his audience: that is, Julian (207d–208c).

---

92. For Plato, myth had been a way to teach the masses ethics by eliciting fears and enjoyment. For Cynics and especially Stoics the true value of myth was its allegorical interpretation in the form of ethical and historical maxims, a concept of myth intensely debated during the Second Sophistic. Several modern studies address, for example, Dio Chrysostom's use of myth in constructing his perfect philosophical life: e.g., Gangloff, *Dion,* esp. 255–309, with further bibliography. Julian and Heraclius thus engaged an existing debate.

93. The loci classici for the identification of right and the condemnation of wrong myths are Plato, *Republic,* esp. 376c–377d; *Timaeus* 22c–d; *Phaedrus* 229c–230a. Fables and myths formed part of the *progymnasmata;* Hermog. *Prog.* 1.2.11–12; Theon, *Prog.* 3.2.74.4–5; Gangloff, *Dion,* 17–45.

94. Pl. *Phdr.* 251c–e. For Julian, even myths for children occasionally failed to educate, especially persons without true divine inspiration, because these are fooled by "mere shadows of true teaching . . . [to] profess a pseudoscience rather than the truth, and are very eager to learn and to teach such falsehoods as though they were something useful and wonderful" (*Or.* 7.206d): "Galileans." Comparing Christians to children was an anti-Christian topos Minucius Felix had already used in the *Contra Celsum* and Porphyry in the (highly fragmentary) *Against the Christians;* Bouffartigue, *Empereur Julien,* 380–88, 685–86, 113–19.

Although it was demonstrably a mistake, especially for a self-proclaimed Cynic, bound by tradition to frank speech, to use myth out of a cowardly fear to speak plainly, there was nonetheless a correct way for a philosopher to use myth (as Orpheus had). Julian proceeds to illustrate. He does so by delineating "the divisions and forms of philosophy," assigning myth its appropriate place in that structure (215b).[95] According to Julian's schema, itself reflecting an Iamblichan curriculum, philosophy consists of three parts: physics, or natural philosophy (*to physikon*), practical philosophy (*to praktikon*), and logic (*to logikon*), each with its own subdivisions. Physics is divided into theology, mathematics, and cosmology; practical philosophy addresses ethics, especially regarding the individual, economics of the household, and all that involves the *politeia;* and logic is concerned with language theory: that is, the demonstration (*apodeiktikos*) of the truth, the probable, and of false conclusions, based on what is probable—principles and probabilities.[96] Of these subdivisions only ethics and theology have any relation to myth—theology only insofar as "nature likes to hide itself." Here Julian is citing Heraclitus (215c–216d).[97]

Julian, influenced perhaps, as Jean Bouffartigue points out, by Porphyry as well as his principal source, Iamblichus, whom he held equal to Plato and Aristotle (217c), argued that theology, insofar as it addressed the divine mysteries, required myth because "what is hidden about the essential nature of the gods [cannot] be flung in naked words into impure ears" (216c).[98] Therefore, the very extremes of some mythical *paradoxa* and their "mysterious and even unknown nature" act as divine or sacred signs or symbols (the technical term that Julian uses is *charaktēr*), intended to be of use for men, because "they heal not only the souls, but also the bodies, and bring about the presence of the gods."[99] Therefore, "the absurd in the myths itself prepares the path to the truth. The more improbable (*paradoxon*) and wondrous the riddle, the more it seems to implore [us] not merely to believe what is being said, but to strive for the hidden and not to desist until, revealed with the

---

95. Julian was aware that Diogenes and Crates had used myth but that Heraclius differed from them because he mistakenly followed Oenomaus rather than Diogenes (*Or.* 7.208d–210c).

96. Logic is the foundation of all other forms of philosophy; Lloyd, *Anatomy of Neoplatonism*, 4–11; D. O'Meara, *Platonopolis*, 50–65.

97. Heraclit. fr. B 123 D-K (vol. 1, 178); see also Them. *Or.* 5.69 and Salut. *De diis* 4.1–3; *Saloustios: Des dieux et du monde,* ed. and trans. Rochefort.

98. Bouffartigue, *Empereur Julien,* 337–45, uses Macrobius's commentary on the *Somnium Scipionis* 1.2.7–12 to show that Porphyry may have been an additional source for Julian's discussion where it diverges from Iamblichus, but here the emperor developed his own concepts. Plato (*R.* 414b-c) argued that leaders of the *politeia* were permitted, indeed required, to engage myths for the benefit of the community, a point Aristotle *Metaph.* 1074b1 also made.

99. Jul. *Or.* 7.216c: ὅπερ δὲ δὴ τῶν χαρακτήρων ἡ ἀπόρρητος φύσις ὠφελεῖν πέφυκε καὶ ἀγνοουμένη· θεραπεύει γοῦν οὐ ψυχὰς μόνον, ἀλλὰ καὶ σώματα, καὶ θεῶν ποιεῖ παρουσίας; Iamb. *Myst. Aeg.* 3.13.131.4, 7.4.255.10–11; Proclus, *In R.* 1.78.18–79.4 and *In Ti.* 1.29.31 on Plato, *Ti.* 17b-c; Salut. *De diis* 15.2.6; Dillon, "Image," 248–53.

guidance of the gods, it fills us with reason, or rather fulfills reason."[100] In short, for the select, the very *paradoxa* of myth serve as revelatory or theurgic devices, granting the knowledge of the gods that Julian considers "more precious than to rule over the whole world, Roman and barbarian together"(222c).

The Myth of Julian's Origin as Son of Zeus and Helios

To comprehend the true meaning of the *paradoxa* essential to myth required differentiating between the literal myth (*lexis*) and its true meaning (*dianoia,* 218a). In Julian's view—contrary, presumably, to what Heraclius had said—when speaking of the gods, one had to use dignified and appropriate words (*lexis*), while whatever was absurd in meaning (*dianoia*) prompted a deeper search for the truth. As an example of appropriate myth, Julian elaborated the story of Dionysus. His complicated birth was full of absurdities, but its true meaning was the revelation that (Greek) culture was of divine origin. Dionysus, if read and understood allegorically, represented a hero who purified and civilized the world and as such was an exemplary ruler. Furthermore, his birth or creation, an eternal process, demonstrated how he and what he represented (i.e., his Greekness) belonged to the cosmic realm and was thus universal (219b–222c).[101]

Julian proceeded to contrast such a myth, which speaks to the true nature of the divine, with other myths more appropriately addressed to children, which seek primarily to teach ethical behavior (226c–d). The content of such myths must be controlled, so that they do not speak against the gods, as had recently been done. Heraclius's myth was so badly invented that it did not even fit the requirements of such a myth. To show how one ought to invent a myth, Julian now acted as a mythmaker, recounting the myth of his own origins.

What Julian had only hinted at in his *Epistle to the Athenians,* he now recounted openly in a myth thinly veiled; while he was literally (*lexei*) the scion of the Flavian dynasty, he was in truth (*dianoiai*) the offspring of Zeus and his son Helios (227c–234c). "A certain wealthy man had many flocks of sheep, . . . and he had many wives,

---

100. Jul. *Or.* 7.217c-d: τὸ γὰρ ἐν τοῖς μύθοις ἀπεμφαῖνον αὐτῷ τούτῳ προοδοποιεῖ πρὸς τὴν ἀλήθειαν· ὅσῳ γὰρ μᾶλλον παράδοξόν ἐστι καὶ τερατῶδες τὸ αἴνιγμα, τοσούτῳ μᾶλλον ἔοικε διαμαρτύρεσθαι μὴ τοῖς αὐτόθεν λεγομένοις πιστεύειν, ἀλλὰ τὰ λεληθότα περιεργάζεσθαι καὶ μὴ πρότερον ἀφίστασθαι, πρὶν ἂν ὑπὸ θεοῖς ἡγεμόσιν ἐκφανῆ γενόμενα τὸν ἐν ἡμῖν τελέσῃ, μᾶλλον δὲ τελειώσῃ.

101. Julian used the first person, "I heard," "I learned," several times (*Or.* 7.219a, 219b, 221a), indicating that this was his reading of that myth; he also combined it with that of Hercules (219c–220a), another philosopher-king. Dio (Gangloff, *Dion*, 310–11) also interpreted Hercules as purifying and civilizing the world. For Bouffartigue, *Empereur Julien,* 166–67, Julian's recounting of the Hercules myth alludes to Lk 2:40, 4:1–2. Hercules, as the supposed model for Alexander and his Persian campaign, resonated strongly with Julian: e.g., *Caes.* 325a; Them. *Or.* 1.253d. Gregory ridiculed Hercules in *Or.* 5; see below, Chapters 9 and 10. Döring, "Kaiser Julians Plädoyer," emphasizes the parallels Julian drew between himself and Diogenes.

and sons and daughters by them, among whom that man divided his wealth [and] then died. But he did not instruct them how to administer it . . . ," which led to "a widespread glut of slaughter, . . . and the sons demolished the ancestral temples that had been despised by their father, who had earlier despoiled them of their votive offerings, which had been dedicated by many worshippers, but not least by his own ancestors" (227c–228c). When Zeus observed the pitiful state of things, "all in confusion and . . . the laws of mankind profaned together with those of the gods," he felt pity and consulted Helios to see whether the course of events could be reversed.

Zeus noticed Julian and pointed him out to Helios: "Regard this child there . . . : this child . . . is your offspring. So swear by my scepter and yours, that you will take special care of him and cherish him and cure him of the disease," Christianity. Helios, aided by Athena, assumed the rearing of that child, saving him from despair and thoughts of suicide, and thus ensuring that Julian, guided by Hermes, the god of persuasion, "returned to [his] people so that [he] could be initiated and live there safely" as true philosopher and steward of all, endowed with the task of restoring the realm once again to "his father, Helios," Zeus, and Athena (231b–234c). "Know that a mortal frame was given to you that you might discharge these duties [*leitourgias*]. For we desire, out of respect for your ancestors"—Julian alludes here to the mythical founder of the dynasty, Claudius II Gothicus[102]—"to purify your ancestral house. Remember, therefore, that you have an immortal soul that is our offspring [*ekgonon*], and that if you follow us you shall be a god and with us behold our father" (234c).

In this famous myth of his origins, Julian thus laid claim to the "holy race" (*hiera genea*) of the true philosopher, equally prized by Iamblichus and his disciples and by Themistius. Though his earlier Christian affiliation had prevented him from practicing true philosophy from his earliest days (as other divine philosophers had done), as the true son of Zeus and Helios, he had nonetheless carried "the hidden spark" within him, so that he had always been divinely prepared to follow the path "to the door of philosophy to be perfected with that man whom I hold to surpass all men of [his] own time," Maximus.[103] As son of the gods, Julian owed allegiance to his literal family that need not exceed what decorum demanded. His true loyalty belonged to the gods and to the founder of the dynasty whom they had chosen, Claudius Gothicus, a devotee of the sun god, Helios. Julian's loyalty to them

---

102. Julian compared him to Pelops in his panegyrics to Constantius; *Or*. 2.51c–52a, 1.6d–7a; *Caes*. 313d, 336b.

103. Divine parentage permitted the philosopher to be filled with enthusiasm and to be "divinely possessed [ἐνθουσιάσας] with longing for the true goal of philosophy," the language Julian also employed; Hierocl. *apud* Phot. *Bibl*. 251.461a; cf. also Jul. *Or*. 11.136b–c; Fowden, "Pagan Holy Man," 34–35; Goulet, "Vies," 167–72. See Rosen, "Kaiser Julian," 127–29, for an assessment of this myth for Julian's conversion. Rosen argues that Julian's political and religious *apostasia* occurred at the same time in 360. Malosse, "Noblesse," 46–47, 50–52, opts for a more psychological reading.

had to supersede any loyalty to his literal family (227c–228d). The death of Julian's own, mortal, father verified his divine origin by removing the potential for a conflict of loyalty between an earthly (Christian) father and Julian's divine father, Zeus-Helios, whose mandate was revealed to him through philosophy.[104]

Sacred Symbols and Divine Pronouncements: Theurgy and Oracles

Myth properly understood and allegorically interpreted revealed the true nature of the divine, as Julian's myth of his origin demonstrated. His literal association with Constantius and Christianity cast a thin veil over Julian's true nature as divinely chosen (in fact, divinely generated) philosopher entrusted with the mandate to lead the *oikoumenē* back to its divine creator. As in any true myth, the *paradoxon* of his association with the dynasty of Constantine was a sacred symbol, or character, intended to activate the divine powers, to motivate the assiduous search for the truth, to heal men in body as well as soul, and "to bring about the presence of the gods" (*theōn poiei parousias,* 216c) through Julian.

As Julian's explicit reference to Maximus and other allusions to theurgy indicate, the theurgic aspects of gaining knowledge of the divine mysteries formed another central element of Julian's *Oration 7.*[105] Theurgic approaches to the divine, Julian made clear, were the foundation of his philosophical life and hence his rule. Whatever the content of Heraclius's oration, Julian, in his response, chastised him (and those like him, such as the *apotaktitai*) for rejecting explicitly such approaches to the divine, by associating Heraclius's stance vis-à-vis philosophy with that of the second-century Cynic Oenomaus of Gadara. For Julian, Oenomaus's philosophy, and by implication Heraclius's (and that of the Christians), was "a sort of madness, a method of life not suitable for a human being, but rather a bestial disposition of mind that considers the fine [*kalos*], the honorable, and the good nothing.... This, then, is his aim: to do away with all reverence for the gods, ... to trample on those laws that have been written into our souls as it were by the gods" (209a–b).

In the two works that Julian cited, preserved by Eusebius of Caesarea, Oenomaus (and by association Heraclius) had denied the existence of divine inspiration and foresight (*promētheia*) and had declared divination, oracles (including Apollo's Delphic oracles), and theurgic revelations absurd and fraudulent.[106] For Julian, such

---

104. Julian was neither the first nor the last to claim a divine substitute father; Basil of Caesarea, John Chrysostom, and Augustine did likewise; J. Chrys. *Sac.* 1.1–7; *Jean Chrysostome, Sur le sacerdoce,* ed. and trans. Malingrey. E. A. Clark, "Rewriting Early Christian History," esp. 10–19.

105. Julian altered the common notion that Dionysus had become divine through theurgy by asserting that as son of Zeus he had always been divine (*Or.* 7.219b).

106. One treatise in the form of a fictive dialogue with Apollo was entitled *The Charlatans Exposed.* Eusebius preserved the surviving fragments in *PE* 5.18.1, which Julian had read; Hammerstaedt, *Orakelkritik,* 71–108 for the text, 11–19 for dating, 53–60 for Eusebius's reception, and 441–42 for the

rejection of the gods, their laws, and their revelations to the initiated in sacred myths and their theurgic powers was a sure sign of utter incomprehension of the true nature of philosophy. Persons so misguided were like bandits and other criminals, and should be expelled from human converse. Philosophers, to be sure, they were not. After all, Diogenes and Crates themselves had been initiated into philosophy through Apollo's oracle: "He says himself that at home and in private he received the commands of the Pythian god, and hence came his impulse to philosophy" (239a, 238b; and see 211b, 212d).

As Julian in the myth of his origins and his path to philosophy demonstrated, true philosophers were called through divine oracles and revelations. Only such divinely called philosophers properly revered the gods and their laws and commandments, and derived ethical conduct from them, manifesting it by pious deeds, the refusal to speak ill even of an enemy, the pedagogical impulse to "expel from the lives of other men theatrical display and arrogance," themselves requiring "nothing or very little" so as not to be "hampered by [the] body" (214a–d). In addition to divine initiation, such a life required lengthy training: to "travel the short and ready road to virtue" (225b) led, as Heraclius and others made evident, to false teachings, improper myths, and the utter rejection of society. Imperial *philia* and *parrhēsia* notwithstanding, neither the philosophy of Constantius and his court as advocated by Themistius nor that of Heraclius and other pseudo-Cynics, including the Galilean *apotaktitai*, was that of Julian.

Julian's preoccupation with the twin themes of *Oration 7*—how to identify the true philosopher and how to prepare oneself for the true philosophical life by maintaining the proper boundaries of involvement and withdrawal—and with the meaning and function of myth continued. In May or early June 362, he gave himself two days "to set down for the benefit of the public what I learned from my teachers about the Cynics, so that all who are entering that life may consider" (181d) how to prepare correctly for the true philosophical life: his *Oration 6, Against the Uneducated Cynics*.[107]

Before that, however, in March of that year, Julian once more considered proper allegorical interpretation and how it revealed the true theurgic value of a sacred

---

city of Gadara, which the *Anth. Pal.* 7.417, 419, describes as an Attic city surrounded by Assyrians. Bouffartigue, *Empereur Julien*, 120–25; Anderson, *Sage*, 68–72.

107. Lib. *Or.* 18.157; Jul. *Or.* 6.203c. How much time Julian set aside is significant, given that he was also preparing his departure to Antioch and the Persian frontier; see *Or.* 6.181a for the June date. Julian's haste in composing *Or.* 7, in contrast, may explain why scholars frequently criticize it for what Bouffartigue, "Cynisme," 341, calls its "bariolage des thèmes"; *pace* Bouffartigue, I see a clear argumentative trajectory, using the conventions of upper-class criticism of lower-class Cynics; R. Smith, *Julian's Gods*, 58–62. Chapter 4, "Uneducated Philosophers," discusses Gregory's use of these anti-Cynic topoi.

myth for comprehending the divine in his *Hymn to the Mother of the Gods*.[108] In this hymn the emperor, no longer content with the myth of his origin and birth, connected the myth of the Mother of the Gods directly with his rule as emperor of the *oikoumenē* of the Romans.

A UNIVERSAL DIVINITY FOR A UNIVERSAL EMPIRE; OR, HOW TO INTERPRET MYTH: *HYMN TO THE MOTHER OF THE GODS*

Between March 22 and 25, 362, the spring equinox and the time of the festival of the Mother of the Gods, the emperor worshipped her by devoting an entire night to composing a philosophical discourse that was also a hymn celebrating the great goddess.[109] The choice of genre was indicative. Julian composed an innovative mixture of philosophical discourse and hymn that defied strict rhetorical definitions.[110] Indeed, as Julian emphasized, the true meaning of the myth of Cybele and Attis that he was about to reveal to his audience was his "personal interpretation" (*oikothen epinoō*, 161c). More important, however, by proclaiming this hymn on the occasion of a sacred festival, the emperor signaled that he spoke not only as philosopher and leader but also as *pontifex maximus*, the highest priest. The move was bold. Even though Rome's *sacra publica* had long included worship of the Mother of the Gods, the story of Cybele and Attis, already controversial, had also come under intense Christian criticism. Attis was the chaste lover who eventually betrayed Cybele with a nymph, whereupon he was castrated or castrated himself as punishment, bled to death, and was resurrected by the (his) Mother.[111] To make

---

108. In what follows, I use *Giuliano Imperatore: Alla Madre degli dèi e altri discorsi,* intro. Fontaine, ed. Prato, trans. Marcone, 46–93; and *Giuliano Imperatore: Alla Madre degli dèi,* ed. and trans. Ugenti, ix–xi for the dating.

109. Lib. *Or.* 18.157. In *Or.* 17.16–17, Libanius notes that *Or.* 6 and the hymn were written against "an opponent of Antisthenes," without further detail; Bouffartigue, *Empereur Julien,* 308. Composing a philosophical text overnight or in a very short time was a well-known topos that excuses potential shortcomings and was intended for the cognoscenti in the audience; thus, it need not reflect Julian's actual writing practice; Ker, "Nocturnal Writers."

110. Men. Rh. *Treatise* 1.1 (*Menander Rhetor,* ed. and trans. Russell and Wilson, 12–14; *Peri epideiktikōn,* ed. Spengel, 336.25–337.34) gave compositional guidelines for hymns: in a hymn "to Apollo, [one must say] that he is the Sun, and then one begins to talk about the nature of the Sun"—a dual path of reasoning that Julian followed. Menander forbade prayers in such a hymn, and Julian's final prayer is short. Bouffartigue (*Empereur Julien,* 541, 569–71) points out that the *MoG* is not a hymn in the rhetorical sense but a philosophical treatise with a final hymn, thus an inventive use of genre. For the significance of genre, D. A. Russell, *Criticism in Antiquity,* 112; Bowersock, *Julian,* 82–83.

111. Julian used the version of the myth reported by Ovid, *Fast.* 4.223–348, and Arnob. *Adv. Nat.* 5.5–7, rather than by Livy 29.10–15; F. Thome, *Historia,* 51, 223; Bouffartigue, *Empereur Julien,* 372–74. For other versions, see Sanders, "Kybele," 270–72. For the intense Christian criticism of Attis and

this myth the showpiece of Roman imperial political and religious philosophy was a daring enterprise.[112]

"But must we really speak . . . and write about the ineffable mysteries and divulge what must not be revealed or divulged? Who is Attis or Gallus? Who is the Mother of the Gods? And of what does this rite of purification consist [*ho tēs agneias tautēsi tropos hopoios*]?" (158d–159a).[113] Julian here, as in writing *Against Heraclius*, began by presenting a historical overview of the cult of the goddess, tracing its spread from Phrygia via Athens and Rome to Constantinople, a path that set the agenda for his *Romanitas*. The emperor's Mother of the Gods was a universal divinity, who subsumed in her divine person the expanse of the *oikoumenē* and the hierarchy of its ethnic composition. Though she had originally revealed herself in Phrygian Asia Minor, the Great Goddess truly came into her own as a Greek goddess in Athens. From there, she moved to Rome, before reaching her apogee in Constantinople through the proper worship that the emperor Julian now (finally) granted her.

Three themes provide the structure of *Oration* 5 and order my discussion. In explicating the path, or rise, of the goddess, Julian presented, first, his personal understanding of *Romanitas* as the perfect mixture of divinely inspired, universal Greek and Roman wisdom. (This subsumed barbarian wisdom and brought it to a higher plane, a theme already evoked briefly in the *Epistle to the Athenians*). Second, moving beyond that (literal) path, the emperor explicated how in the myth of Attis and the Mother of the Gods his inclusive and universal conception of *Romanitas* had been prefigured in cosmology, was hence divinely authorized, and as such presumably universal and eternal. Third, he elucidated the true meaning of the sacred signs and *charaktēres*, or symbols, in the myth (signs that included the goddess's statues), and the ethical norms deriving from those divine signs.

At the heart of all three themes was the interplay between transcendent and phys-

---

Cybele, see Firm. Mat. *De err.* 18.1; S. Elm, " 'Pierced by Bronze Needles,' " esp. 422–24. It would be worthwhile to examine whether the increase of Christian hostility against the cult of Attis and Cybele in the later fourth century reflects an increase in surviving sources or a response to Julian. Among those writing against the cult after Julian were Prudentius and Rufinus. Curran, *Pagan City,* 264–68, argues that the cult of Magna Mater among the fourth-century Roman aristocracy primed some of them for the intense Christian asceticism à la Jerome. Citing Vermaseren, Curran (p. 266) points to twenty-two Roman senatorial inscriptions dedicated to Magna Mater between 305 and 390.

112. To cite Foussard, "Julien philosophe," 208: "Peut-on concevoir exégèse plus 'hellène' d'un myth plus barbare?" Foussard's positive judgment is echoed by Bouffartigue, *Empereur Julien,* 379, who grants Julian's handling of the material something "que nous sommes prêt à appeler intelligente," and by Renucci, *Idées,* 141. The text has not received unanimous praise. Ugenti (*Giuliano Imperatore: Alla Madre degli dèi,* ed. and trans. Ugenti, xvii) considers the hymn so nebulous and obscure that it prevented even those of "buona volontà" from reading it, a judgment that he shares with, e.g., Klein, *Julian Apostata,* 286.

113. Bouffartigue, *Empereur Julien,* 360, lists the structure of *Or.* 5, which follows the tripartite scheme Julian here presents.

ical realities, and how—and through which epistemological tools, such as names, statues, rites—it ought to be read. How should one conceive the relationship between divine essence, its power (*dynamis*), activity (*energeia*), and product or works (*erga*)? What are the first principles (*archai*) of reality? What is the relation between a divine being, or essence, and its prior cause (*aition*); and should the latter be understood as having been begotten (*gennētos*) or not (*agenētos*)? Given that divine beings could be both begotten and creative (i.e., begetting), how must one conceive such a relation, in particular if the product of that generation is material in essence? These concerns and themes echo those mentioned in Chapter 1, in the debates that had preoccupied Constantius, his advisors, and so many other men of *paideia* throughout his reign, Christian and not.[114] Such questions deployed the highly sophisticated technical apparatus of philosophy. This apparatus and the philosophy were Greek, linguistically as well as conceptually. Julian's account of the goddess's progress corresponds to a deeply ingrained hierarchy of cultural achievement: being Greek—speaking Greek as a language and as a series of concepts verbalized by that language—was essential to understanding the true nature of the divine, because the divine had revealed its essence in the best (albeit not the only) way in the Greek language. This Greekness was combined with Romanness into a universal force of eternal relevance, represented by the Mother of the Gods. Julian never calls the goddess by her non-Greek name, Cybele.

A Universal Divinity

*And again: Why was [the myth of the Mother of the Gods and its rite] taught to us like that from the beginning, transmitted by the very ancient Phrygians, but adopted first by the Greeks? And not by any Greeks, but by the Athenians, who had learned at their cost that they did wrong when jeering at those celebrating the Mysteries of the Mother. For it is said that they insulted Gallus and drove him away with the accusation that he innovated in divine matters [*ta theia kainotomounta*], not comprehending what goddess she is and that she is the very same they already worshipped under the names Deo, Rhea, and Demeter. Hence the wrath of the goddess and the need to propitiate it; indeed, she who has guided the Greeks in all things noble, the prophesying priestess of the Pythian god [Apollo], ordered them to placate the wrath of the Mother of the Gods; and because of that they built, they say, the Mētrōon [or Motherhouse], in which the Athenians keep all the documents relating to the state. After the Greeks, the Romans adopted the cult, because the Pythian god advised them also to fetch the goddess from Phrygia as an ally in the war against the Carthaginians. . . . As soon as they had become aware of that oracle, the*

---

114. E.g., Lloyd, "Neoplatonic Logic," esp. 146–55. Dillon, "Looking on the Light," has a lucid discussion on first principles, *energeia*, and *dynamis*. Stead, *Divine Substance*, 125–80, provides an overview of the meaning of *ousia* in late antiquity, based, however, exclusively on Christian authors and Philo. Excellent is M. R. Barnes, "Background," esp. 233–36, though I disagree with his reading of Julian.

> *inhabitants of Rome, city beloved by the gods, sent an embassy to request from the kings of Pergamon, who then ruled over Phrygia, and from the Phrygians, the most holy statue of the goddess.*
> —JULIAN, HYMN TO THE MOTHER OF THE GODS, 158D-159C

This brief summary of the spread of the cult of the Mother of the Gods explains succinctly Julian's interpretation of the relationship of Greece, Rome, and the gods, and contrasts it with Constantius's conception.[115] Constantius, as will be recalled from Chapter 2, had privileged the philosophical views of Themistius—which sought to share philosophy's benefits with "those who are willing [to hear]," in contrast to more antisocial philosophical positions (*philosophian akoinōnēton*)—because they embodied the ideal combination of Roman honor and Greek wisdom.[116] As Constantius had emphasized in his letter to the Constantinopolitan senate, Themistius's philosophical life represented to the emperor the perfect combination of Rome and Greece, because the philosopher functioned "both as a spokesman [lit. "prophet"] of the sages of the past and as an initiating priest [*hierophantēs*] at philosophy's inner sanctuaries and shrines," so that through him "the ancient teachings [*tas archaias doxas*] . . . always flourish and are renewed [*akmazein aei kai ginesthai neas*]" (*Ep. Const.* 20a).

Constantius, like Julian, conceived of his reign as perfectly combining Greece and Rome, the old and the new, as a *politeia* in which ancient teachings are renewed through practical, active, and lucid instruction, thus combining the (old) strength of Greece with the (new) active power of Rome, as represented in "our city [Constantinople], . . . the summit both of fortune and of virtue" (*Ep. Const.* 21b). Constantinople had been founded by Constantius's father, Constantine, as a Christian city—and it is no leap of imagination reading the fierce debates about innovation and the old that have run through these chapters like a leitmotif as a debate about the validity of Christianity. Christianity as a legitimate religion was an innovation. Moreover, Christianity was an innovation in matters of the divine and therefore

---

115. Julian was probably an initiate in this and other Mystery cults, especially that of Mithras. Questions concerning his potential initiation occupy the majority of the scholarly work on the hymn, rarely discussed in its own right; exceptions are Cosi, *Casta mater*, and Näsström, "O Mother of the Gods and Men." Julian had ample opportunity to become an initiate. The goddess had cultic centers in Athens, Gaul, and Asia Minor, most famously in Pessinus; in Nicomedia and Ephesus, the Great Mother Goddess was amalgamated with Artemis; R. Smith, *Julian's Gods*, 114–17, 124–38; Bouffartigue, *Empereur Julien*, 367–72.

116. Literally, "antisocial," or rather, "antipolitical," an important nuance given that *politeia* and *koinōnia* were synonyms, as Julian's use of *koinōnikos* rather than *politikos* in the quote regarding humans as political animals shows; Jul. *Epistle to the Priest* Theodorus 292d, and 288b, where he uses *politikos*. The Greek for "Roman honor" is μεταλαβὼν γὰρ παρ' ἡμῶν ἀξιώματος Ῥωμαϊκοῦ ἀντεισφέρει σοφίαν Ἑλληνικὴν.

touched everything divinely ordered. It was a universal innovation that affected everything of universal character, not least the empire itself.

Hence, in praising Themistius—*nota bene* not a Christian!—as "a singular citizen of our city, whom one might address with good reason as a citizen of the world," Constantius promoted his universal vision of the New Rome in Greek Asia Minor as a correct innovation, renewing the ancient teachings that melded Greek and Roman supremacy with Christianity.[117] As the preceding discussions of innovation have shown, the debate was not simply between the old and the new; certainly not between the old pagans and the new Christians. What was at stake, instead, was how to innovate correctly, how to conceptualize and implement change in a society that always valued the old more than the new. At stake, then, was the proper integration of what was appropriately new into what had proved itself supremely valuable as old without jeopardizing that heritage. Or, as Themistius had asked when he defended himself against those "who appoint themselves lawgivers to philosophers," charging him with "committing an injustice ... through his philosophical innovation and by his introduction of new deities": "Who was as active or innovative as Plato?"[118]

The debates about correct and incorrect innovation, and thus about the significance of Christianity, were fierce, but the disagreements, fundamental as they were, could be debated fully only because of the participants' enormous reservoir of shared notions and values. All men engaged in these debates, Christian and not, were members of the elite bound by their common interest in preserving Rome's honor and *imperium* and their own honor and prestige. That honor and its manifestation in Rome's power relied on Greek wisdom, itself essential for understanding the God or the gods who had created Rome's greatness. Greek wisdom and Roman power were, further, distinct, in that each represented universality, understood as the proper inclusion, adaptation, and improvement of peoples, customs, divinities, and their teachings that were originally not Roman or Greek. That is, Greek wisdom and Roman dominance both embodied correctly integrated wisdom and knowledge (including knowledge of things divine) of barbarian origin; on that, all were

---

117. *Ep. Const.* 21d; quote 22c: πολίτην ἐξαίρετον τῆς πόλεως τῆς ἡμετέρας, ὃν τοῦ κόσμου πολίτην εὐλόγως ἄν τις προσείποι. For an excellent discussion of creating a Christian identity as citizens of Rome, see Rizzi, "Cittadinanza," esp. 226–28. See also Dagron, *Empire*, 36–42, 44–48, 61–68, and 83–95, regarding the universalism represented by Constantius, Themistius, and Eusebius as opposed to that represented by Libanius, Synesius, and Julian; for a discussion of *Romanitas*, 112–19; also idem, *Naissance*, 52–76. Ruggini, *Simboli*, 1–45, eadem, "Sofisti," 405–10; Averil Cameron, *Christianity and the Rhetoric of Empire*, 131–35; Pietri, "Politique," 113–78; Heather, "Themistius," 145–47; in general, Ando, *Imperial Ideology*, 373–98. Scholars have debated Julian's *Romanitas* and his Hellenism intensely, but not on the basis of this text. Bouffartigue, *Empereur Julien*, 658–65, 669–73; R. Smith, *Julian's Gods*, 163–78; Athanassiadi-Fowden, *Julian*, 141–43; Weiss, "Julien," esp. 129–30.

118. Them. *Or.* 26.312–13, 318.

in agreement. But such integration, especially of things divine, was dangerous, since false teachings of false gods—wrong innovations—threatened the security and longevity of the *oikoumenē*. Greek and Roman history provided sufficient examples of the divine wrath called forth by such mistakes. Who, then, was innovating correctly?

In Julian's eyes, the answer was evident. Divine judgment, as manifested in his victories and in Constantius's death just prior to their military encounter, as well as the deep amorality of Constantius's branch of the Flavian dynasty, proved him right.[119] Now, during the festival of the Mother Goddess in Constantinople, Julian presented his audience with the implications of his conviction. "The Mother of the Gods and of men, the companion of Zeus with whom she divides the throne" was the divine creator and hence symbol of universal *Romanitas*. She it was who manifested the correct mixture of Rome, Greece, and Phrygia, or what at the beginning had been foreign. Her worship, therefore, would remove the effects of false innovation, the "pestilence of atheism" (*tēs atheotētos tēn kēlida*), from "the community of the Roman people" (*koinēi . . . tōi Rhōmaiōn dēmōi*), and would "grant it Fortune's benevolence, with which it may rule the fate of the empire for many thousands of years" (180b). The emperor's hymn displayed him as priest and initiate, explicating the allegorical meaning of the myth's *paradoxa* to his audience. Read properly, the deeply shocking *paradoxa* of the literal myth revealed the cosmic dimension of Rome's universal power: Cybele and Attis themselves were the divine signs and symbols through which each individual as well as the entire community of the Romans would be healed, body and soul, and brought to the presence of the divine, guided by their highest priest, prophet, and hierophant: Julian.

The Symbolic Power of Statues: Cosmology and Theurgy

Julian began his *demonstratio*, or proof, of the intrinsic link between the Mother of the Gods, Rome's power, and its cosmological prefiguration by explicating the true meaning (*dianoia*) of her statue's arrival in Rome. Roman citizens, prompted by Apollo's oracle, had approached "the kings of Pergamon, who then ruled over Phrygia," and the Phrygians themselves to acquire "the most holy statue of the goddess" to help them fight the Carthaginians (159c).[120] The arrival of the goddess, on the

---

119. Julian's coins are instructive in this context, featuring only the *virtus exercitus Romanorum* type; Kent, "Introduction"; Arce, *Estudios,* 184–92. Still valuable and insufficiently received is Andreotti, "Opera."

120. Julian may well have considered it relevant that the statue was in the custody of the Attalid dynasty at Pergamon. Attalus I had won a decisive victory over the barbarian Gauls, or Celts, that the famous friezes celebrate as equivalent to the Athenian victory over Persia. The Pergamene altar defined the image of the Celt for generations and connected the Attalids to Hercules and Dionysus. Mitchell, *Anatolia,* vol. 1, 21–22; Robert, "Héracles." In Pergamon Julian had been initiated into theurgic philosophy, the beginning of his divine mandate to remove atheism from the *oikoumenē*. Thus, Julian came to Rome's aid as Pergamon's Cybele had done, at a moment of great peril through barbarian (Christian) aggression.

literal level (*lexei*), had not been smooth. After sailing from Asia Minor all the way to Ostia without incident, the ship carrying her statue "stopped as though it had suddenly planted roots in midstream" when it touched the Tiber (160a–b). Nothing could move the ship, and the purity of Claudia, the virgin entrusted with her image, became suspect. When Claudia entreated the goddess to prove her innocent, the Great Mother permitted her to draw the ship upstream all by herself with her belt.[121]

Julian read the episode as the goddess's showing "to the Roman people that they were not bringing an inanimate statue [*xoanon . . . apsychon*] from Phrygia, but that what they had taken from the Phrygians and were now bringing home was of higher and more divine power [*dynamin . . . theioteran*]" (160a). By first blocking and then freeing the ship, the goddess demonstrated to the Romans "that the load they brought from Phrygia was not cheap but of inestimable value, not made by human hands but truly divine, not inanimate clay but something that possessed life and divine powers. This is the first teaching. The second [teaching] is that it will not escape her notice whether the innermost [thought] of even one of the citizens is good or bad" (160d–161a).

The words indicated that Julian was about to engage a central issue in the relation between theurgy, myth, and philosophy: What did the statues of gods really represent? In the emperor's view, two positions on statues prevailed. To some, statues of the gods were merely inanimate clay, and to attribute divine powers to such images was an exercise "of little credibility and unworthy of a philosopher or a theologian"; some "know-it-alls" would even consider accounts such as that of the Great Mother's arrival in Rome nothing but "intolerable old wives' tales" (161b). Others, as Julian conceded in a later letter addressed to the priest Theodorus (*Ep.* 89b.293c), considered statues to be signposts of divine power, without themselves containing that power. But Julian himself, trusting the ancient traditions of the city, considered the statue itself "truly divine, . . . something that possessed life and divine powers."[122]

In addressing the relationship between the divine and its representation in statues, Julian once again entered a long-running philosophical debate, intrinsically connected to the debates about myth and philosophy. At stake was the relation between the gods as entirely immaterial entities and their material representation in statues. To comprehend that link was crucial, because the gods were related to their statues (or symbols) as the highest realm of the divine, where the creative forces reside, was related to the lower spheres, including the lowest material realm inhab-

---

121. For the Magna Mater's arrival at Rome, Bouffartigue, *Empereur Julien,* 361–64, 366–73; *Giuliano Imperatore: Alla Madre degli dèi,* intro. Fontaine, xlv–l; and *Giuliano Imperatore: Alla Madre degli dèi,* ed. and trans. Ugenti, 58–61; Burton, "Summoning"; Gasparro, *Soteriology,* 49–63.

122. As *Ep.* 89a–b shows, Julian's views on statues were in flux; I will discuss this further in Chapter 7 below and in the context of Gregory's *Or.* 4 and 5; U. Criscuolo, "A proposito di Gregorio."

ited by human beings. How do the immaterial gods communicate with humans? And how can human beings communicate with the transcendent divine?

Julian emphasized that he expressed in the hymn his own views of the relation between the divine and the material realms, and the means by which the gods communicate with men as represented by the myth of the Mother of the Gods: "I for my part maintain that this Gallus, or Attis, is the substance of the generative and creative Intellect that creates everything down to the lowest [level of] matter, and that contains in itself all the concepts and prior causes of the material forms."[123] Iamblichus's theology, especially his commentary on the so-called *Chaldean Oracles,* supported Julian's understanding of the crucial connection between humans and the divine.[124]

Cosmological Structures

The views Julian presented, and the debates about them, arose from the Platonists' assumption of an ontological incompatibility of the divine and the material realms,

---

123. Jul. *Or.* 5.161c: τοῦ γονίμου καὶ δημιουργικοῦ νοῦ τὴν ἄχρι τῆς ἐσχάτης ὕλης ἅπαντα γεννῶσαν οὐσίαν ... ἐν ἑαυτῇ πάντας τοὺς λόγους καὶ τὰς αἰτίας τῶν ἐνύλων εἰδῶν. Julian was aware of Porphyry's writings on the divine powers of statues and the cosmic realities they reveal, but says (*Or.* 5.161c) that he had not read Porphyry's *On the Statues*. Cosi (*Casta mater,* 87–98, supported by Bouffartigue, *Empereur Julien,* 337, 346–48) plausibly argues for Julian's indirect knowledge of Porphyry, gained through Eusebius's *PE*. For details regarding the debate between Porphyry and Iamblichus on theurgy, (e.g.) Taormina, *Jamblique,* esp. 133–58; Clarke, *Iamblichus' "De mysteriis,"* 39–57, and, though on a slightly different subject, 100–118; and G. Shaw, *Theurgy,* 96–113. The emperor's views reflect those of his friends: as Bouffartigue shows (*Empereur Julien,* 319, 357–59), Oribasius's summary of Galen (esp. *Nat. Fac.* 1.2.7) makes similar points; Staden, "Body," esp. 104–8.

124. In 359 in a letter to Priscus, *Ep.* 12 (Wright 2), Julian requested all of Iamblichus's writings, including those on the *Chaldean Oracles* composed by Julian the Theurgist (Bouffartigue, *Empereur Julien,* 345), though Bouffartigue (pp. 357–59) is not sure that Julian had the texts present when composing the hymn. Iamblichus's commentary on the oracles, the *Chaldean Theology* (the title cited by Damascius, *Pr.* 2.1.7–8 ed. Westerink), which consisted according to Damascius of twenty-eight books, is lost, as is another of Julian's likely sources, Iamblichus's *On the Gods,* in Damasc. *Pr.* 2.71.25–72 ed. Westerink. For a reconstruction of Julian's use of the commentary, Bouffartigue, *Empereur Julien,* 306–9, 331–48. Bouffartigue notes (pp. 348–52) that it is not clear whether Julian also used Iamblichus's *Commentary on Alcibiades* or his *On the Mysteries of the Egyptians,* nowithstanding earlier opinions. This is of interest because the terminology and associated concepts go back to Plato, especially his *Alcibiades I,* on which both Iamblichus and later Proclus wrote commentaries. Julian was familiar with Iamblichus's exegesis of *Alcibiades,* which he used in his *Or.* 6; *Giuliano Imperatore: Contro i Cinici ignoranti,* ed. and trans. Prato and Micalella, xv–xvi; Bouffartigue, *Empereur Julien,* 348–55. Excerpts of Iamblichus's commentary survive in Proclus, Iamb. *Comm. Alc.* frs. 12–16, *Iamblichi Chalcidensis in Platonis dialogos commentariorum fragmenta,* ed. and trans. Dillon; Proclus *In Alc.* 84.1–5 = Iamb. frs. 4, 6–7 Dillon; *Iamblichus: Exhortation to Philosophy,* trans. Johnson. For discussions, Nasemann, *Theurgie,* 41–67; Blumenthal, *Aristotle,* 36–37; Hadot, "Théologie"; Festugière, *Révélation,* vol. 3, 190. For the impact of Iamblichus on Julian's views in *Or.* 5, also Witt, "Jamblichus," esp. 62; Dillon, "Magical Power"; Lewy, *Chaldean Oracles,* 449–56.

according to which the universe consisted of two separate realms: the generative and creative realm of "the highest and first causes,"[125] and the material one, "the lowest and the last, after which there is nothing save privation that can be intuited only dimly" (161d).[126] Plotinus, though maintaining a separation between what he called intelligible and sensible matter, had already modified the dual construct by introducing into the divine realm additional layers or gradations that emanate from the entirely transcendent One, flowing downward. The supreme, divine realm itself, known as the noetic realm (*noētikon*) of pure ideas, consists of three gradations, or *hypostaseis,* the One (*Hen*), the Intellect (*Nous*), and the Soul (*Psychē*). These layers or gradations are dynamic; that is, the lower levels flow out of and are oriented toward the higher ones, but as their hierarchical structure implies, greater distance from the One diminishes the intensity of the divine essence and hence its perfection.[127]

Iamblichus, further lessening the ontological divide between the divine and the material realm by positing continuity between divine and sensible matter, declared matter essentially good. Moreover, he divided the divine Intellect, or *Nous,* itself into three parts, with the highest part of the Intellect identical with the One, the highest principle; the middle part the same as the noetic Helios, or Sun; and the third, lowest part of the Intellect, or *noeron,* identical with the visible sun, which had created the cosmos, belonging already to a lower intellectual realm.[128] This third level of the divine Intellect thus mediated between the heavenly realm of pure thought and the lower realm of matter, as the rays of the actual sun carry light to the earth. According to Julian, Attis represented the creative force of that third divine power: he "is the substance [or "essence," *ousia*] of the generative and creative Intellect [demiurgic *Nous*]" (161c), who "through his excessive fecundity [or generative power] descends from the highest spheres past the stars down to our earth" (162a).

Thus Attis (Julian also called him Attis-*Logos*), read allegorically as an abstract divine Idea, represented the creative power of the third, visible sun whose light originated in the higher realm of the noetic Sun and poured into the material world. Attis, as light, carried the creative force of the sun down toward matter, the earth, which he brought to life and made fecund.[129] By relating Attis up to the layer or *hypostasis* of the highest being, the One (i.e., the Mother of the Gods), and down to

---

125. τοῖς ἀνωτάτω καὶ πρώτοις αἰτίοις.

126. G. Shaw, *Theurgy,* 28–30.

127. Plot. *Enn.* 5.1.7.49; also 1.8 for the divinity or goodness of the heavenly bodies—i.e., the visible gods.

128. Iamb. *Myst.* 8.3 (*Iamblichus: De mysteriis,* trans. Clarke, Dillon, and Hershbell); Mau, *Religionsphilosophie,* 92–93.

129. In Porphyry's interpretation of the myth, Attis represents spring; this passage is in Eus. *PE* 3.11.12; Mau, *Religionsphilosophie,* 94–95.

matter and thus mankind, Julian revealed to his audience how the human soul could be transported back to its divine origin. The literal *paradoxa* of the myth of the Mother of the Gods and of Attis, along with their statues, and the rites and rituals associated with their myth, demonstrated the extension of the divine powers toward matter as well as the cause of their activity. Thus, they also demonstrated the presence of those divine powers in man, which saved mankind by making possible his ascent toward the divine.

Who is Attis, and who is the Mother of the Gods? The crux of Julian's hymn was to demonstrate how Attis-*Logos* participated in the essence or substance (*ousia*) of the Highest One, the first cause or first principle, and how he could diminish himself by descending toward matter without losing his full divinity, his divine power and active force, which alone enabled him to save man's soul by leading it back up toward the divine. The problems are familiar from Chapter 1 in the context of another *Logos*, called Christ. Julian, the student of Eusebius of Nicomedia as well as of George of Alexandria, devoted the greater part of his hymn to that question, "the nature, in sum, of Attis," and proceeded "to clarify further [his] thinking" about Attis-*Logos* (162a).

Attis Is a Creative God: Julian's Causal Language of Essence, Power, Activity, and Product

Such clarification required two related moves: first, Julian had to explain how Attis retained his full divine essence, which he had so significantly diminished by descending to matter and mankind. To do so required, second, that Julian clarify his views on how the transcendent layers, or *hypostaseis,* of the divine realm connected to the cosmos and the material realm, since Attis formed part of all of them. Julian began his exegesis of Attis's myth by elaborating how the "creative god Attis" (*theos gonimos,* 165b) remained divine (a *noeros theos* or intellectual god) throughout his descent. Julian explained how, read allegorically, the celestial sphere contained abstract and immaterial causes, which were necessary to produce or create material forms, and how that creation occurred (162d). Literally, Attis had been a human child exposed near the river Gallus, where, once he became a beautiful youth, the Mother of the Gods had fallen in love with him. Attis, however, eventually fell in love with a nymph (an almost but not quite human being). The Mother of the Gods retaliated by having him castrate himself, but resurrected him or saved him before he died, and allowed him to return to the divine realm (165b–168c).[130] How did Julian make this myth work to explain his views about the interaction of divine essence, activity, and power with matter and mankind?

To answer that question, Julian set out the cosmological hierarchies that structured his allegorical reading of the literal *paradoxa* of the myth. His move was im-

---

130. Salut. *De diis* 4.7–11 has a similar structure of the myth.

portant, because it involved questions of epistemology. How can human beings know anything at all about the divine sphere? How can they, with their human faculties, make any deductions about the transcendent, divine realm, and how, given the limitations of human language, can man speak about that divine realm? One obvious choice is to speak about the divine only via the negative, what god is not. But to speak affirmatively, to say in human language what the transcendent divine is rather than is not, is more difficult. To do so presupposes a connection between the transcendent, divine realm and that of humans, based on which affirmative deductions regarding the former are possible (162a–165a).[131] Julian followed Aristotle, who had argued that what he called "ether," or the fifth element, represents in fact that link, because ether carries "the incorporeal prior causes of the forms embodied in matter" (163a). Such immaterial or incorporeal prior causes are necessary for everything created (*gignomena*); because these prior causes are not just the One, but come in different layers or gradations, creation too is varied and multiform.[132] Moreover, it is precisely the hierarchical gradation of the divine realm, with the actions of its *hypostaseis* moving up and down as the rays of the sun, that grants humans knowledge of the existence of that transcendent realm of higher and prior causes (though man's perception of things immaterial remains clouded by his physicality). For Julian, this knowledge was no game of names or pure abstractions.[133] Those who purified "the eyes of the soul" through retreat and "turn [their] eyes inward" could, with divine guidance, discern these (transcendent) prior causes in their own souls, "not actually [*energeiai*], but potentially [*dynamei*]."[134] The human soul, though residing in the physical body, is sufficiently immaterial to reflect as in a mirror the transcendent, immaterial prototypes (residing, say, in ether) of what is actually created; those who purify their souls through retreat can discern these pro-

---

131. Marcone (in *Giuliano Imperatore: Alla Madre degli dèi,* intro. Fontaine, 275 n. 6) considers Julian's establishment of the cosmological fundaments "sostanzialmente estranea al tema del discorso," but they form the structure of Julian's reading of the myth. Julian here challenges views of persons he called Epicureans and specific Aristotelian readings of the relation between preexisting immaterial forms and matter.

132. At stake is the relation between the One as creator and the resulting variety of material forms, which must point to a plurality of divine archetypes, to be reconciled with the One; Plot. *Enn.* 5.7.

133. Julian argues against the first-century Aristotelian commentator Xenarchus of Seleucia, who posits in the surviving fragments of his work on ether, or the fifth element, that the divine is a pure abstract, a name, or verbal sign of the human mind without actual content; *Giuliano Imperatore: Alla Madre degli dèi,* ed. and trans. Ugenti, 65–66.

134. Julian argued that the human soul and mind are a sort of mold carrying the forms of embodied matter within them. This is why Aristotle called the soul " 'the place of the Forms,' except that the forms are there not actually [ἐνεργείᾳ], but potentially [δυνάμει]." This is so because the embodied nature of the human soul "allies it with matter" and thus clouds its vision. Were the soul "unmixed" (ἀμιγής)—i.e., free from its material embodiment—it would "actually [ἐνεργείᾳ] contain all these Forms." Julian, *Or.* 5.163b, citing Arist. *De anima* 3.4.429a.

totypes more clearly, because the mirror of their souls has been more thoroughly polished.[135] By analogy, for Julian, purified philosophers, turning inward, can see in their souls the true, divine meaning, or *dianoia,* of what is created, or literal, including the *paradoxa* of myth (because their souls reflect the divine intention). Thus, they can teach the deeper meaning symbolized by these *paradoxa* correctly to the less purified, as appropriate to them.

Attis   Julian, in sum, posited an immaterial prior cause or higher creative principle for all material forms. The act itself of creating the material forms belonged, according to Julian, to the Third Creator or Demiurge, the visible sun, Helios.[136] This Third Creator also created the stars, the galaxy, the visible fifth body, or ether, represented in the myth by Gallus, the river beside which Attis grew up, equated by Julian with Attis and with the Milky Way, or *Galaxias Kyklos.*[137] For Julian, Attis, representing the active rays of the Third Creator, Helios, Sun, descended toward that galaxy when falling in love with the nymph. This realm of the visible stars was

---

135. Julian uses Plato's analogy, Pl. *Sph.* 233b–236c: a mirror reflects the appearance of reality, but its reflection is not the actual thing. That "would be troublesome and difficult, and, by Zeus, borders on the impossible," just as an actor (*mimos*) can never so imitate (*mimeisthai*) that he becomes the persons he represents (*Or.* 5.163d). Similarly, the human soul reflects the divine realm without being actually divine; neither mirror nor actor can, however, reproduce or imitate things that do not actually exist, so that the human soul, too, can contain only the potential or power (*dynamis*) of prior causes, because they have an actual existence (*energeia*) and are, further, actually connected to that cause. Thus, though embodied, the human soul can discern incorporeal prior causes and can imitate or mirror them, because there is a connection between original and representation. That connection is the human soul's prior existence as nonmaterial (before birth), so that in humans matter and form are not completely separated, since "in our intelligence [ἐπινοία] the forms must have prior existence and be regarded as of a higher order" (*Or.* 5.165a). Though using Plato's analogy in a straightforward way, Julian followed Plotinus and Porphyry in granting the human soul a greater divine component than Iamblichus does; see also *Or.* 6.183a–d; Bouffartigue, *Empereur Julien,* 349–50.

136. For Epicurus, the cosmos and matter were created by chance and spontaneous motion; Julian disagreed. Xenarchus argued that the prior cause operative in creating matter and material forms was ether, "the fifth or cyclic substance" (*Or.* 5.162b–c). Julian's point here is that the prior cause resides above ether, though it extends down to incorporate it. Furthermore, Julian wanted to prove that Aristotle's thoughts on the relation between divine Ideas and matter were "insufficient unless they are brought in harmony with those of Plato, and even further, when even those are brought in harmony with the prophesies given by the gods" (162d). For Julian, neither physics nor logic alone could aid a philosopher's comprehension of the prior cause; such comprehension was possible only if divinely revealed through prophetic oracles, which only those initiated into the highest form of mystagogical theology could understand. Nasemann, *Theurgie,* 69–104, on ether as divine substance and Iamblichus's use of Aristotle and Plato in his own definition of that fifth substance; R. Smith, *Julian's Gods,* 98–99.

137. This merging of Attis and Gallus—i.e., the Milky Way—was Julian's own construct, and he insisted on it: *Or.* 5.159a, 161c, 165d, 168d, 169a. Cf. Prudent. *Peristeph.* 10.197; Arnob. *Adv. Nat.* 5.16.7–8; but most of all Salut. *De diis* 4.3.7–11, inspired directly by Julian's *Or.* 5; Bouffartigue, *Empereur Julien,* 373–74.

the border separating the heavenly realm and that of perishable matter, the realm inhabited by man. The Mother of the Gods had allowed Attis, the intelligent or noeric god, "to leap and dance" down to that border (165c). However, in loving the nymph, he had crossed it and had begun to move so far down toward matter that he risked diminishing his divine essence to the point of no return.[138] Therefore, the Mother intervened by allowing the castration to occur, preventing Attis from merging further with material form through intercourse with the nymph, which would have resulted in the unbridled creation of further material beings.[139] His mutilation, thus, marked both the lowest point of his diminishing and the point of his ascent back to a more intense divinity. It occurred at that precise point on the graded scale of descent and ascent, because "here the body capable of passion is intermingled with the cyclical motion of the fifth body without passion" (165c); here the divine and the human realms intersect.

Attis's transgression and intercourse with the nymph was a crisis. His descent had to be stopped, and he could not be permitted to create more material things through his intercourse with the nymph. The Mother of the Gods "exhorted Attis to serve her and not to leave her and love another" (167a), and so Attis castrated himself and returned to her. "What is this castration? The halting of the rush toward infinity [*Hē de ektomē tis? Epochē tēs apeirias*], the interruption of the generative process" (167c). For Julian, Attis's cruel mutilation was the turning point, reversing his descent so that he ascended toward the realm of the divine, to the Mother of the Gods.[140] Julian was, however, far more concerned with Attis's descent than with

---

138. Julian addresses once more the tension between the One as creative cause of all and the multiplicity of creation, and the relation between a transcendent cause and materially created things. For Julian, the nymph represented water, commonly understood as the substance out of which matter was formed. By loving a nymph, the intelligent god Attis (ὁ νοερὸς θεός), who contained in him material and sublunar forms, merged with water as matter's prior step, so that he came perilously close to activating the material forms that he contained: thus, he closely approached the impermanence and privations of physical matter out of which the human body, too, was formed. Further, even though the nymph belonged to the divine realm of immaterial causes, Attis's love for her was against the will and below the limit set by his mother and lover: he almost crossed the line and went below the celestial region sealed off by the moon, Hecate-Semele. For Hecate-Semele and her central role within theurgic cosmologies, Johnston, *Hekate,* 49–75, 143–63. For continuations of the debate, Wildberg, "Three Neoplatonic Introductions."

139. She asked Helios to send her lion (allegorically interpreted as fire) after Attis to "fight against the nymph and to be jealous of her union with Attis" (*Or.* 5.167c).

140. Cosi, *Casta mater,* 13–47, 106–13; Bouffartigue, *Empereur Julien,* 374–79, discusses literary and theological models for Julian's unusual interpretation of Attis-Gallus's castration, following the suggestion of Bogner ("Kaiser Julians 5. Rede," 292) that Julian's view echoes anti-Naassene (gnostic) passages of the *Refutation of All Heresies* attributed to Hippolytus of Rome, which Bogner (376, esp. n. 310) links to a source written by priests of Cybele. For the context, Gasparro, "Interpretazioni," esp. 399–408.

his return. The descent, in any event, occupies the larger share of his hymn. As a consequence, for Julian, Attis's position in the intelligible realm of the One was significant only insofar as it determined the intensity with which he preserved his divine essence on the way down, because that intensity was correlated with Attis's mediating force. For Julian, "Gallus or Attis [is] the essence [*ousia*] of the generating and creative Intellect [demiurgic *Nous*]." But since this creative realm contains "many essences [*ousiai*] and many creators [*dēmiourgoi*]"—what I have also called "gradations"—Julian more specifically defines Attis as "the nature [*physis*] of the Third Creator, ... [located] at the end, and who descends because of [his] excess of fecundity from the highest spheres past the stars down to our earth": that is, he merges him with the visible sun.[141] As such, he was close enough to the One to be able to send his rays to the material earth, but distant enough never to mingle with what his rays brought actually forth. Thus, Attis-*Logos* or Attis-Gallus could descend toward the earth, could touch changeable and perishable matter, but remained divine, "a demigod, or rather, as indicated by the myth, a god in all aspects, since he in fact proceeds from the Third Creator and, after his castration, returns to the Mother of the Gods" (168a): not so human that he could no longer, as god, save mankind, but not so transcendently divine that humanity remained outside his saving reach—a conundrum familiar from the concerns with Christ's divine nature. But how did Julian relate Attis to the transcendent One? How did he conceive of the Highest One?

The Mother of the Gods

"Who, then, is the Mother of the Gods? ... The source of the intellectual and creative gods [*tōn noerōn kai dēmiourgikōn theōn*], who govern the visible gods, the one who has borne the great Zeus and who dwells with him, the great goddess who came into being [*hypostasa*] after and together with the great creator" (166a). The Mother is the "companion of God [Zeus]" and the source of all intelligible [*noētoi*] gods, and, below them, the intellectual [*noeroi*] ones: "in very truth the Mother of the Gods"—*theotokos*. As mistress (*kyria*) of all life and cause of all generation she "gives birth [*gennōsa*] without pain," and her love for her son Attis, like his for the nymph, is without passion and does not resemble the mingling of male and female. It does not represent the mingling of two distinct essences but must be understood as two beings of like essence moving toward each other; this removes the sting, presumably, from the story of a mother's mutilation of her son and lover (165d). The Mother of the Gods, furthermore, is herself not created, because "her being is with the Father." Though mother, she is a "virgin without a mother" (*parthenos amētōr*)

---

141. Jul. *Or.* 5.161c–162a: Τὸν Γάλλον δὲ ἐγὼ τουτονὶ καὶ τὸν Ἄττιν αὐτὸς οἴκοθεν ἐπινοῶ τοῦ γονίμου καὶ δημιουργικοῦ νοῦ ... οὐσίαν εἶναι. ... Οὐσῶν δὴ πολλῶν οὐσιῶν καὶ πολλῶν πάνυ δημιουργῶν, τοῦ τρίτου δημιουργοῦ ... ἡ τελευταία καὶ μέχρι γῆς ὑπὸ περιουσίας τοῦ γονίμου διὰ τῶν ἄνωθεν παρὰ τῶν ἄστρων καθήκουσα, "φύσις" ὁ ζητούμενος ἐστιν Ἄττις.

(166a–b), just as Athena was in Zeus as well as created by him (or as the *Logos,* or Word, was God and created by him).

Julian's focus, to reiterate, is Attis's mediating function, his divine nature and descent, so that as a consequence the highest gradation of the transcendent realm, the One (or the Mother of the Gods) receives less attention and is not clearly defined; Julian is less concerned with the specifics of the transcendent One than with its presence in each layer, or *hypostasis.* He defines the Mother of the Gods as an intelligible, "hypercosmic" (*hyprakosmiōn*)[142] god without prior cause and as the source of the second layer of the intelligent gods.[143] This (highest) layer of the divine fell in love with (its own) creative and generative force (Attis), demanding that it turn its power upward to its intelligible source rather than toward its (own) lowest expression, matter, "since turning to the better is always preferable to turning to the worse" (166d); that way, the Mother belongs both to the noetic and to the noeric layer. Helios occupies the same hypercosmic layers, because Julian sees him as equal to yet different from Zeus, or the One (167c, 179d). Zeus, the Mother of the Gods, and Helios occupy the same layer, are of the same divine intensity or essence (*ousia*), but they are also, at the same time, different persons, representing different layers, or *hypostaseis,* of the transcendental realm. Thus, Helios, or the Third Creator, and the Mother of the Gods share the "throne and co-created all," including ether, or the realm of the stars.[144] Therefore, for Julian the "Third Creator [*ton triton dēmiourgon*] is ... Father and Lord [*patēr kai despotēs*]." But he distinguishes the visible sun,

---

142. A neologism of the *Chaldaean Oracles;* Lewy, *Chaldean Oracles,* 458.

143. Bogner, "Kaiser Julians 5. Rede," 279, refers to John Lydus's citation of Iamb. *Theol. Chald.,* which Julian's *Or.* 5.170c echoes. Though Julian's thoughts on Attis were often his own, his cosmology reflects the tripartite structure of Plotinus and of Iamblichus's commentary on the *Chaldaean Oracles,* the *Chaldaean Theology.* Näsström ("*O Mother of the Gods and Men,*" 52–54) considers the Mother a personification of the Plotinian Soul. Iamblichus had in fact remarked in his *Commentary on Alcibiades* that we perceive the *daimones* (i.e., divine beings, essences) through the energies of their powers (i.e., their "mothers"), explaining that "a power is a median between an essence and an activity, put forth from the essence on the one hand, and itself generating the activity on the other." Iamblichus concludes that since it is extremely difficult for humans to know the essence of the superior beings, the object of human knowledge ought to be the power (i.e., the intermediary cause rather than the prior); Iamb. *Comm. Alc.* frs. 4.12–16 Dillon; Bouffartigue, *Empereur Julien,* 351. Hence the importance Julian attributes to Attis as a vehicle of such recognition, an argument that involves also distinctions between generative (γόνιμοι) and creative (δημιουργικοί) powers or essences: that is, between begotten and made; Iamb. *Myst.* 203.9 and Nasemann, *Theurgie,* 93–94 on *aggenētos.* For Julian's views on the preexisting soul, *Or.* 6.183a–d; Bouffartigue, *Empereur Julien,* 349–50; G. Shaw, *Theurgy,* 28–36.

144. Julian often calls the creative act of noetic gods "genesis" (γένεσις), because it involved creation by gods who had themselves been begotten. The prior cause causes everything and therefore creates as well as generates; but causes belonging to the intellectual layer generate, because they have been caused. The third layer includes the stars and the moon, or Hecate-Semele. Here divine beings suffer a certain amount of change, a characteristic usually reserved for material beings. Such waxing and waning signified that this layer reached farther downward; indeed it is the only one visible to humans. For

or "the generative god Attis, the cause that descends toward matter," from this—transcendent—Helios, Sun, though they are one.¹⁴⁵ Thus, Julian differentiates the divinities in the highest grade of the One according to their different characteristics or creative powers, while attributing to them the same divine essence, or intensity, as being the first or prior cause of all creation (which makes them unbegotten and not created, or *agennētos*); but he also orders them hierarchically, because Helios's alter ego, Attis, is created, or begotten, and subordinate to Zeus, the Mother, and the highest Helios, and can thus descend while retaining his supreme divine essence undiminished.¹⁴⁶

The love of the Mother of the Gods for Attis, in Julian's interpretation, signifies the wish of the highest divine layer to draw into itself and unify all lower ones. Because the cause of all creation is the divine will to create, the first cause—that is, God the Father and the Mother—loves the offspring and wants to be united with it. As a result, the first cause inspires the lower layers, or *hypostaseis*, such as Attis, to seek "saving union" with the supreme divinity and to resist the attractions of lower, material forms. Thus, the myth's assertion that Attis descended against the will of the Mother below the limit she had set is ultimately not true: she loves all that she has created and therefore wishes it to return to her (171b). After all, the actions of the Mother of the Gods in the myth exemplify how love for "the highest sphere" and "conversion to higher things" is always preferable to conversion to lower things such as matter (166c–d). Attis's descent resulted in his "mixing" (*symmixis*) with the nymph, who stands for water, the substance prior or just above matter, so that he became distinct from the unchangeable gods, and in that sense a demigod (168a).¹⁴⁷ Because his castration limited the extent of that mixture and prevented any actual contact with matter, however, he remained fully a god. (The paradox has already been alluded to in Chapter 1: To what degree can a god who is created as man and becomes [almost] human remain fully god?) Because Attis remains god, his mother, the virgin Mother of the Gods, is a real bearer of gods, *theotokos*—in contrast to the mother of Jesus. For Julian, to call Mary *theotokos* was nonsense, because a human woman can never create a god (167b–d, 168a–c; and see *CG* 262c–e, 276e, 277a).

The rites and rituals associated with the myth of Attis that reenacted the central themes of his descent, mutilation, and ascent also expressed the link between the lit-

---

the association of Attis and Cybele with the lunar sphere, R. Smith, *Julian's Gods*, 100–102, 138; Johnston, *Hekate*, 49–75, 143–63.

145. Jul. *Or.* 5.165a–b: τῆς ὕλης καταβαίνουσαν αἰτίαν, καὶ θεὸν γόνιμον Ἄττιν εἶναι. Note the present tense. This is an ongoing act of descent, a historical moment that continues in the here and now.

146. According to Iamblichus's introduction to *The Arithmetic of Nicomachus* 79.5–8, "the god [*dēmiourgos*] is not the creator of matter, but when he receives it, as eternal, he molds it into forms and organizes it according to numerical ratio."

147. On mixture, Iamb. *Myst.* 202.4; Nasemann, *Theurgie*, 71–75.

eral *paradoxa* and their true cosmological meaning. After his long exposé of the cosmological implications of the myth, which he summarized again succinctly (170d–171d), the emperor delineated the rites and rituals associated with Attis and the Mother of the Gods as divine symbols whose power can activate the presence of the divine in our souls—even in the souls of those less purified than the initiated.[148]

Theōn Poiein Parousias: *Rituals as Sacred Symbols of the Divine*

> *In reality, the ancients . . . searched [themselves] for the cause of all eternal beings . . . with the gods as their guides. And when they had found them, they disclosed those meanings with paradoxical myths, so that the discovery of the mythic fiction, thanks precisely to the paradoxical and absurd, might prompt us to search for the truth.*
>
> —JULIAN, HYMN TO THE MOTHER OF THE GODS, 170A

The gods had created the analogous *paradoxa* of myth and sacred rituals to induce humans to search out the truth by connecting them and their cosmological implications by their own efforts. However, the gods provided a dual structure (170b).[149] For common people the literal level of the simple, *a-logos* symbol was beneficial enough, whereas those with higher logical power and greater purity had to proceed, under the guidance of the gods and with the help of their speculative capabilities, "to the end and, so to say, to the heart of the problem." They in turn could then enlighten the common people about the deeper meaning of the symbols (170b–c), "to break the rush toward the infinite [i.e., the disorder of matter] in ourselves and to imitate the gods, our guides, and return back to the defined and uniform, and, if it be possible, to the One" (169c).[150]

To do just that was Julian's supreme duty as one striving for "perfection in theurgy" (*en theourgiai teleiotēta*, 179d) as mystagogue, philosopher, *pontifex maximus*, and emperor. This was the intent of his *Hymn to the Mother of the Gods*: to explicate her myths so that "very many souls [are] lifted up" (172d). Hence he proclaimed his hymn on the occasion of the Mother's festival during the vernal equinox. Even if only those at court heard or read it at that moment, Julian as emperor could expect his proclamations to become widely known and—presumably—followed. He had then been in power only a short time and was probably still optimistic about the effectiveness of his actions: with this hymn, Julian would save the community of the Romans.

---

148. Bouffartigue, *Empereur Julien*, 161–66, 341, for New Testament allusions; Gasparro, *Soteriology*, 26–49, 84–106.

149. Echoing Iambl. *De mysteriis* 65.3–7 on the purpose of ritual: "Is not every sacred ritual legislated intellectually from the first principles according to the laws of the gods? For each rite imitates the order of the gods, both the intelligible and the celestial, and each possesses the eternal measure of beings and the wondrous symbols that have been sent here by the Demiurge, the Father of all things."

150. G. Shaw, *Theurgy*, 143–61.

Julian's hymn laid out how the sacred rites associated with the myth actualized "straightaway the divine light [that] illumines [*ellampei to theion phōs*] our souls" (178b), even if only "the blessed theurgists" (*theourgois tois makariois,* 173a) can penetrate fully the depth of the *mysterium* (172d). The rites and festivals associated with the cult of Cybele have been discussed frequently in scholarship, but we are not well informed about their celebration in Constantinople at that time.[151] According to Zosimus, Constantine had acquired a statue of Cybele from Mount Dindymon for which he had constructed a temple, but he seems to have intended that statue to represent the Tyche of Constantinople rather than Cybele.[152] Nevertheless, as Jean Bouffartigue suggests, the rites of Cybele were performed in Constantinople, even if in composing his hymn Julian did not have them in mind but relied, in accordance with literary practice, on the so-called Calendar of Philocalus of 354. There is no need to assume that Julian had been an initiate, either.[153] After all, the issue in the hymn was the function of such rites and rituals as symbols, or *charaktēres,* in a theurgic context, and not the actual performance of the rites in Constantinople; the audience, in the final analysis, was the entire *oikoumenē*.

As Julian had intimated at the beginning of the hymn, the statue of the goddess was for him not simply a construct of plaster, "not a human work but truly divine, not inanimate earth but something alive and superhuman"; the same was true of the rites associated with her festival.[154] Correspondingly, Julian illuminated the cosmological significance of every aspect of the ritual. Each practice activated the divine power immanent in it as symbol, so that those practicing the rites participated through them in the core cosmological drama of descent, mutilation, and resurrection (168c–169d). For example, the ritual cutting of a pine tree (March 22–24: *arbor intrat,* according to Philocalus) symbolized Attis's castration and death but also indicated his impending resurrection. It coincided with the spring equinox because this marks the high point and at the same time limit of the sun's cycle. Night and day are equal; "what is born interrupts its birth, and the day becomes longer than the night, which creates a close relation between the souls on their ascent."[155]

Similarly, other rituals addressed physical and mental purification. Since the rituals aid the ascent of the human souls, the celebrants should avoid fruits and vegetables "that grow downward into the earth." However, they may eat meat (except

---

151. Bouffartigue, *Empereur Julien,* 367–70; R. Smith, *Julian's Gods,* 114–38; Vermaseren, *Cybele and Attis,* 114–16.

152. Zos. 2.31.2–3; Dagron, *Naissance,* 373–74.

153. Philocalus ed. T. Mommsen, *CIL* 1:1, p. 260; Divjak, "Sogenannte Kalender." Bouffartigue, *Empereur Julien,* 368–69.

154. Jul. *Or.* 5.161a: οὔτε ὡς ἀνθρώπινον τοῦτον, ἀλλὰ ὄντως θεῖον, οὔτε ἄψυχον γῆν, ἀλλὰ ἔμπνουν τι χρῆμα καὶ δαιμόνιον.

155. Salut. *De diis* 4.11: περὶ γὰρ τὸ ἔαρ καὶ τὴν ἰσημερίαν δρᾶται τὰ δρώμενα, ὅτε τοῦ μὲν γίνεσθαι παύεται τὰ γινόμενα ἡμέρα δὲ μείζων γίνεται τῆς νυκτός, ὅπερ οἰκεῖον ἀναγομέναις ψυχαῖς.

pork: 177c), even though this presents another paradox: animals are animated beings, and to kill them causes pain, so that many considered eating meat not conducive to attaining purity (174a–c, 175b–176b).[156] Another important element of purification was sexual abstinence. Taken together, as the emperor points out, all measures that support the purification of the soul also heal the body, because the soul divinized (*theōtheisa,* 178c) by purifying rituals cleanses the body: even bitter mortal matter will be saved, as the gods promise the purest theurgists (175b–178d). Thus Julian, by explicating the *paradoxa* of the myth and rites of Attis and the Mother of the Gods, and by exhorting others to follow the practices prescribed by the "sacred law" (*ho hieros nomos,* 174a), was doing for all in his care what the gods had done for him, as he had intimated in his myth of origin in *Against Heraclius*: he showed how myth and rites "heal not only the souls, but also the bodies, and bring about the presence of the gods [*theōn poiei parousias*]" (*Or.* 7.216c).

In his concluding prayer to the Mother of Gods and Men, the emperor asked for such salvation for himself and for those who had reached advanced purification, and also for the entire *koinon* of the Roman people, so that by participating in the descent, mutilation, and resurrection of Attis, they might all be granted knowledge of the gods and be cured of the pestilence of atheism (180a–b).

HOW TO ACHIEVE TRUE PHILOSOPHY: *AGAINST THE UNEDUCATED CYNICS*

Julian did not rest with this explication of a true myth and its saving power. In June 362, about two months after his spontaneous response to Heraclius, which had contained the true myth of his origins, and after his near-contemporaneous proclamations about the Mother of the Gods, Julian took up the stylus (or dictation) once more. He allotted himself two days to provide some of his subjects with yet another instructional treatise on how to lead a life pleasing to the gods, this time by pointing out how one ought to prepare for the true philosophical life, in contrast to that led by uneducated Cynics.[157]

The topic mattered to the emperor. By June 362, Julian was either on the eve of his departure or already on his way from Constantinople to Antioch, where he intended to winter in preparation for a major military campaign against the Per-

---

156. Pl. *Tht.* 176a; Porph. *Abst.* 3.5; Mau, *Religionsphilosophie,* 108–13; Näsström, "O Mother of the Gods and Men," 57–101; Renucci, *Idées,* 140–52.

157. Lib. *Or.* 18.157; Jul. *Or.* 6.203c, and 181a for the June date. I am using *Giuliano Imperatore: Contro i Cinici ignoranti,* ed. and trans. Prato and Micalella, who argue convincingly (pp. xxix–xxxiii) that this oration was intended as a written circular for those who wanted to enter the philosophical life. R. Smith, *Julian's Gods,* 8, 49–50; Billerbeck, "Ideal Cynic," 216–20; Bouffartigue, *Empereur Julien,* 308–9, 359–79, and "Cynisme," 339–58.

sians.[158] That Julian set aside two days to compose a treatise just as he was about to depart, or was already en route, to Antioch—perhaps during his stay at Ancyra or Caesarea—should not, however, surprise us. The impending Persian campaign increased the pressure on the emperor as philosopher and *pontifex* to ensure that all matters pertaining to the divine were in order; after all, the favor of the gods would determine the outcome of the military campaign. As he wrote at that time to his uncle Julian (Iulianus Constantius), "I pray little even though at this moment I am more than ever in need of many and potent prayers."[159] As his own letters as well as other sources inform us, the emperor on his progress to Antioch took detours to visit sacred sites—for example, the sanctuary of the Mother of the Gods at Pessinus— and to attend to other matters pertaining to the gods.[160]

In chastising those he called "uneducated" (*apaideutoi*) Cynics, the emperor contended that philosophy is intrinsically linked to the belief in and worship of the gods who inspired it. This is true for all schools of philosophy, however diverse. "We need only say that whether one regards philosophy, as some people do, as the art of arts and the science of sciences, or as 'becoming like god as far as humanly possible,' or whether it means Know Thyself, as the Pythian god [Apollo] says, will make no difference to my argument. All these definitions are in fact interchangeable and closely related to one another."[161] As Julian had already pointed out in *Against Heraclius*, philosophy unites the plurality of life and guides it to "the One and the Good," to "the unmixed, uniform, indivisible being [*ousia*]" (*Or.* 7.217d, 222a). Philosophy was the path to the divine, and therefore philosophers were priests.[162] In fact, all priests ought ideally to be philosophers, and as philosophers they were entrusted with the duty to guide their "fellow citizens, not only through deeds but through words as well," devising regulations according to which the city can organize itself, from its economy to the relations between man and woman (*Or.* 6.185d), recognizing that "man is by nature a social and political animal" (201c).

---

158. Amm. Marc. 22.9.2–17 has Julian's itinerary, 8–12 for Ancyra; and Seeck, *Regesten*, 210–13.
159. Jul. *Ep.* 80 (Wright 29).
160. Amm. Marc. 22.9.5; Lib. *Or.* 12.87, 17.17, 18.161; Jul. *Ep.* 84 (Wright 22), *To Arsacius*, mentions Pessinus; *Ep.* 81 (Wright 42), written either June or July 362, addresses the priestess of Cybele at Pessinus. Soz. *HE* 5.4.1 refers to Julian's stay at Caesarea; all three sources mention the emperor's attempts to revive ancient religious customs.
161. Jul. *Or.* 6.183a: τὴν φιλοσοφίαν εἴθ', ὥσπερ τινὲς ὑπολαμβάνουσι, τέχνην τεχνῶν καὶ ἐπιστήμην ἐπιστημῶν, εἴτε "ὁμοίωσιν θεῶν κατὰ τὸ δυνατόν," εἴθ', ὅπερ ὁ Πύθιος ἔφη, τὸ "Γνῶθι σαυτὸν" ὑπολάβοι τις, οὐδὲν διοίσει πρὸς τὸν λόγον· ἅπαντα γὰρ ταῦτα φαίνεται προσάλληλα καὶ μάλα οἰκείως ἔχοντα.
162. Compare Jul. *Ep.* 89a (Wright 20), *To the Priest Theodorus*, where the emperor provided guidelines for the conduct of priests as philosophers. Bouffartigue (*Empereur Julien*, 634–36) notes, *pace* R. Smith (*Julian's Gods*, 36–38), that priests and philosophers are not the same, but for Julian the perfect priest combined the philosopher's ethical conduct with his priestly functions.

But to be able to fulfill that duty, all philosophers, Cynics and anyone else zealous to lead a truly ethical life, had to be properly trained. For that reason, the emperor wished to provide his audience, the public (181d), but in particular all who desired to lead such a life (201d), with a summary guide (*kephalaia*, 182b) for the proper way to the true philosophical life and an exemplar to imitate: Diogenes as portrayed by Julian. Having emphasized the unity of philosophy (182c–186b), Julian presented an analysis of Cynicism as he saw it (186b–188c), focusing first on the deeds, or *erga*, of Diogenes as the epitome of ideal Cynic comportment (189b–191c), and then criticized the uneducated Cynics (197d–198d) who had misunderstood Diogenes' true teaching (199a–200b), how "to sanctify one's soul through [divine] ideas" (199c). Julian concluded by presenting the proper *enkyklia paideia* or *cursus*—similar to what he outlined in *Against Heraclius*[163]—necessary for becoming a true Cynic: that is, for becoming a Platonic philosopher according to Julian. Only philosophers who had received the highest training combined with supreme purification were able to dig deep to the truth about the gods and hence instruct others and guide them.[164] Such training would lead to assimilation with the divine (*homoiōsis theōn*, 183a, 184a, 185b), its ultimate purpose, as the gods themselves had ensured. Thus, Diogenes "had chosen god and not a human being as first guide [or founder] of his philosophy" (191c). Conversely, no one who separated philosophy from the gods who had founded it could understand the divine truths and even less instruct others in them, for they were intrinsically linked: "The truth is one, and philosophy is one. Of that all those whom I have mentioned [i.e., all true philosophers] are lovers," even if they attain that Oneness by different means; only those who deny the value of education, and hence that of social order—that is, uneducated Cynics and the Galileans—depart from that common mold (185c–186b).

Julian's criticism of the uneducated Cynics echoes, once more, Dio Chrysostom's *Oration 4 On Kingship*, as well as Lucian's and Aelius Aristides' critical portrayal of the Cynic. Such Cynics simply don the philosopher's cloak and sport staff, pouch, and long hair, walking about like beggars, as if that conduct were sufficient to qualify them as philosophers (201a).[165] They commit outrageous acts supposedly to

---

163. Prato and Micalella (*Giuliano Imperatore: Contro i Cinici ignoranti*, xxix–xxxii) discuss the differences between the two programs; *Or.* 7.225c, 235d.

164. Prato and Micalella (*Giuliano Imperatore: Contro i Cinici ignoranti*, xii) for the structure of *Or.* 6. For Julian's *enkyklia paideia*, Bouffartigue, "Cynisme," 340–56, and *Empereur Julien*, 504–10.

165. D. Chr. *Or.* 4.16; Jul. *Ep.* 89b, *Epistle to the Priest Theodorus*, 292d; Amm. Marc. 25.4.9. Athanassiadi-Fowden (*Julian*, 128–31, 136–41) and Prato and Micalella (*Giuliano Imperatore: Contro i Cinici ignoranti*, xviii–xxxiii) further discuss Julian's sources. The issue of vanity was a stock theme. Diogenes had caused his own death by eating raw octopus. What to make of this? Some argued that it was the height of mere spectacle, but Julian defended the point that Diogenes had wanted to investigate whether to cook meat was "in accordance with nature," or merely customary, and had not intended to die and cause a

demonstrate their freedom, frank speech, and disregard of public opinion, but instead such actions are signs of vanity and vainglory (*kenodoxia*, 190c), pure show, and a hallmark of the uneducated Cynics, who flout society's norms and damage its harmonious order (*eutaxia*), disregard the gods, and are in truth slaves of their base desires (197b–199b).

True philosophers, including Cynics, possessed a natural aptitude and the ability to learn (*eumatheia*) and devoted themselves to acquiring, first, self-control, over both physical desires and mental dangers—for example, the wish to attain glory. Next, an aspiring philosopher practiced such self-control not only in retreat, but in the city, surrounded by others (200c): only there could he practice frank speech (201a). As far as intellectual training was concerned, Julian reiterated the indispensable preconditions as he had in *Against Heraclius*: sound knowledge of the Greek language (in the style of Isocrates: that is, pure Atticism), rhetoric, and literary genres,[166] and then, according to the canon of the *enkyklia paideia*, fluency in the epistemologies of Aristotle, Plato, and Pythagoras, linked to the daily practice of the correct philosophical life.[167] Such a life as embodied by Diogenes required subjection of the body through rigorous discipline (*askēsis*) and hardships (*ponoi*), self-sufficiency, freedom from emotion, disregard of the opinions of the masses, moderation, reverence toward the gods and the common good (*autarkeia, eleutheria, dikaiosynē, sōphrosynē, eulabeia, charis*: 194d–195b, 202a): virtues eminently displayed by the emperor, himself a *politikos* and *polypragmatos* philosopher as leader (203b).[168]

THE LAW REGARDING TEACHERS

All who profess to teach anything whatever [didaskein epangellomenous] must be men of suitable character, and must not carry in their souls opinions [doxasmata] opposed to what they profess in public . . . , above all . . . rhetori-

---

spectacle; Billerbeck, "Ideal Cynic," 219. See Vaggione, "Of Monks and Lounge Lizards," esp. 183–88, 210–12, for the use of anti-Cynic language in Christian ascetic rivalries, where Job was the positive model; Hagedorn, *Hiobkommentar*.

166. Jul. *Or*. 7.236a–b; Arist. *Rh*. 3.8.1408b21–31.

167. According to Julian, the Cynics "thought that there were two branches of philosophy, the theoretical and the practical [θεωρηματικήν τε καὶ πρακτικήν]" (*Or*. 6.190a).

168. Prato and Micalella (*Giuliano Imperatore: Contro i Cinici ignoranti*, 95–96) discuss the second term: though active as statesman and leader, Julian still studies and devotes himself to learning; indeed, despite his worldly advantages he had subjected himself to his teachers as leaders, reading everything they had instructed him to read. Because Julian was not uneducated, he had found the shortcut to philosophy: "A man must completely come out of himself and recognize that he is divine and keep his mind untiringly and steadfastly fixed on divine thoughts, which are stainless and pure. He must also utterly despise his body and regard it, in the words of Heraclitus, 'as more deserving to be thrown out than dung'" (*Or*. 7.226c); Billerbeck, "Ideal Cynic," 216.

cians, grammarians, and even more so sophists. For they claim . . . also to teach ethical conduct, and they assert that political philosophy [tēn politikēn philosophian] is their prerogative. . . . If they believe that those whose exegetes they are, and for whom they sit, so to speak, in the prophets' chair, were wise men, let them in the first place [prōton] emulate their piety toward the gods.[169]

On June 17, 362, about the time he composed the treatise *Against the Uneducated Cynics* and en route to Antioch via Cappadocia, the emperor issued an edict stipulating that "masters of studies and teachers must excel first in their character, and then in their skills."[170] The principal concern of this law, as adopted by the compilers of the Theodosian Code, was a reform of the *munus docendi*. Julian instructed city councilors to establish a register of teachers of higher education, both public and private [*quisque docere vult*], which should then be presented to the emperor in person so that he could vet their *mores* as well as their *facundia*; official teachers were exempt from liturgies.[171] This edict as preserved is innocuous; religious affiliation is nowhere mentioned. A subsequent edict issued on June 29 facilitating the construction of new (pagan) temples, however, may have given away the game.[172] Further, the compilers of the code may have left out entirely another edict regarding teachers that Julian described as *koinos nomos* or *lex generalis*, or the law as we

---

169. Jul. *Ep.* 61 (Wright 36); I am following the tradition of the manuscripts, all of which have *prōton*; Hertlein, followed by Wright, emended this to *prōtoi*, probably to improve the meaning of the sentence. This seems a random emendation that may give a wrong intonation to Julian's message. "If they believe . . . were wise men, let them be the first [*prōtoi*] to emulate their piety toward the gods" makes no better sense than the manuscripts' version: Julian need not wish that Christian teachers be the first in Hellenic piety but rather that they begin (their road to recovery) by emulating that piety.

170. *CTh* 13.3.5: "magistros studiorum doctoresque excellere oportet moribus primum, deinde facundia. . . . sed quia singulis civitatibus adesse ipse non possum, iubeo, quisque docere vult, non repente nec temere prosiliat ad hoc munus, sed iudicio ordinis probatus decretum curialium mereatur optimorum conspirante consensu. Hoc enim decretum ad me tractatum referetur, ut altiore quodam honore nostro iudicio studiis civitatum accedant" ("Masters of studies and teachers must excel first in character, then in eloquence. . . . But since I myself am not able to be present in all the cities, I order that if anyone wishes to teach he shall not leap forth rashly and suddenly to this office, but he shall be approved by the judgment of the municipal councils and shall obtain the decree of the decurions with the consent and agreement of the best citizens. For this decree shall be referred to me for consideration so that such teachers may enter into their studies in the cities with a certain higher honor because of our judgment"). Only the first part of this edict became part of the Justinian Code, *CJ* 10.53[52].7, ed. Krüger (1954), 1.2:741; trans. Pharr, with my modifications. See also Schol. Vat. *CTh, ad loc.* The edict reached Spoletium on August 29, 362; Lib. *Or.* 18.157–60; Kaster, *Guardians,* 66.

171. Without a centralized and comprehensive register of teachers it was difficult to assess the extent of their tax exemptions. Local records had existed since Antoninus Pius; Nutton, "Two Notes." Constantine's edict *CTh* 13.3.1 had extended tax exemptions to all teachers empirewide, thus requiring even better local record keeping; C. Drecoll, *Liturgien,* 64, 72–73. The scholarship on this law and the subsequent imperial letter is immense; Germino, *Scuola,* 24–49, 167–91; Watts, *City,* 68–71.

172. *CTh* 15.1.3.

have it may represent only a portion of that general law.¹⁷³ At any rate, the Christian compilers of the code ignored the emperor's next move. Shortly after arriving at Antioch, Julian issued an imperial letter (with the force of law) specifying that teachers may teach only matters in which they also believe; this letter, preserved in fragments, was not included in the code.¹⁷⁴

In this imperial letter Julian declared that "right *paideia* [*paideia orthē*] is not the magnificent harmony of phrases and language, but a healthy condition of mind that has understanding and true opinions about good and bad things,¹⁷⁵ honorable and base things. Whoever then thinks one thing and teaches another to his pupils, is, in my opinion, as far removed from being a good teacher as he is from being an honest man," especially when things of the highest importance were at stake. Only hucksters act in such a way. No one who held opinions in private that contradicted those he professed in public should therefore "associate with the young and teach them rhetoric by commenting on the ancient writings, rhetoricians, grammarians, and still more sophists, who claim ... to teach ethical comportment as well and assert that political philosophy is their prerogative."

To teach ethical comportment as well as eloquence Julian considered all for the good, but only if the teachers believed what they taught. For "the gods were guides of all learning for Homer and Hesiod and Demosthenes and Herodotus and Thucydides and Isocrates and Lysias.... I think it is absurd that men who interpret the works of these writers should dishonor the gods who were honored by them. Yet ... I do not say that they ought to change their opinions [*metathemenous*] in order to instruct the young. But I give them a choice, either not to teach what they do not think is excellent, or if they wish to teach, first they must persuade their pupils that neither Homer nor Hesiod nor any of these men whom they have ... declared to be guilty of impiety ... is such.... If they suppose that those writers went astray with respect to the most honored gods, then let them go to the churches of the Galileans to expound Matthew and Luke."¹⁷⁶

---

173. Jul. *Ep.* 61c.424a (Wright 36). Amm. Marc. 22.10.7 refers to a law issued in Antioch, which might be the general law mentioned in 424a.

174. Jul. *Ep.* 42 (61c Bidez, 36 Wright). Banchich, "Julian's School Laws," dates the letter between July 18 and early September and, following him, Matthews, *Laying Down*, 274–77, argues that the law regarding public instruction and the letter are two separate pieces of legislation—i.e., the second is not an interpretive tool for the first, as has often been assumed, though both are linked by the wish to regulate instruction. Germino (*Scuola*, 48–49, 135–66) considers the letter private and accessible to a limited circle (164–66); Brennecke, *Studien*, 105–7; Bouffartigue, *Empereur Julien*, 600–603; Colpe, "*Civilitas graeca*"; Klein, "Julians Rhetoren- und Unterrichtsgesetz"; Pack, *Städte*, 261–300; R. Smith, *Julian's Gods*, 18–19, 199; Hardy, "Emperor Julian."

175. ὑγιῆ νοῦν ἐχούσης διανοίας καὶ ἀληθεῖς δόξας.

176. ἄτοπον μὲν οὖν οἶμαι τοὺς ἐξηγουμένους τὰ τούτων ἀτιμάζειν τοὺς ὑπ' αὐτῶν τιμηθέντας θεούς. After all, these teachers "make a livelihood and receive pay from the works of those writers."

The emperor stated that this general law was imposed on preceptors and teachers, but did not affect any youths who wished to go to school.[177] He considered it ill advised to preclude the best path for boys still "too ignorant to know which way to turn," or to force them "through fear against their will to the beliefs of their ancestors [*epi ta patria*]." And in concluding this imperial letter the emperor summarized his religious policies, as "a man who commands and philosophizes":[178] "Although it might be just to cure these, even against their will, as one cures the mad, we, however, concede indulgence to all for this sort of disease. For one must, I think, teach, but not punish the insane."[179]

Both edict and letter appear to have sent shock waves through the ranks of the teachers in higher education who were Christian: grammarians, rhetoricians, and philosophers. Indeed, it affected all Christians who were men of *paideia,* which means all Christians who mattered as public men: all those whom we encountered in Chapter 1.[180] Though the emperor had not asked them to change their minds, his words were clear enough: whoever believed in the God of the Galileans could no longer lay claim to the foundational writings of the *oikoumenē*'s common Greekness and Romanness, the universal foundation of Rome's greatness.

What had been apparent ever since Julian had become sole emperor was now unmistakably manifest. The emperor as philosopher and priest, as almost perfect theurgist and son of Zeus-Helios, took his divine mandate, or *leitourgia,* very seriously. While arguing against Themistius, he may have stressed both that he did not consider himself a philosopher-king and that he praised retreat over action, but that stance owed more to his pointed opposition to Constantius than to the manner in which he put his own divine mandate into practice. He may not have been a perfect Platonic philosopher on the throne, but he was of sufficient philosophical merit to see that his divinely entrusted duty was to reveal to his subjects the deeper truth about the myths as well as the correct practice of the true philosophical life so that he would guide all in his care, as far as was humanly possible, to the divine. In doing so he obeyed his divine father, and fulfilling the divine commandments was re-

---

177. This is the *koinos nomos* mentioned by Amm. Marc. 22.10.7, 25.4.20, of which *CTh* 13.3.5 may have been a portion.

178. Jul. *Or.* 7.211b: ἀνδρὶ καὶ στρατηγεῖν καὶ φιλοσοφεῖν ἐθέλοντι. The verb στρατηγεῖν emphasizes the military function of the ruler, a conscious choice as Julian's *adventus* also indicates; MacCormack, *Art,* 192–96.

179. Prostmeier, "'Wolke,'" 39–41. This is a traditional sentiment of imperial edicts, based on Platonic notions of the consensus between the good ruler and the ruled, and of the emperor as father. Laws should, thus, teach, persuade, and heal rather than punish; Benner, *The Emperor Says,* 1–30; Corcoran, *Empire of the Tetrarchs,* 207–13.

180. Prohaeresius's case was famous. Hecebolius (Lib. *Or.* 18.12; Socr. *HE* 3.1.10, 3.13.5, 3.23.5) and Pegasius (Jul. *Ep.* 79 [Wright 19]) may also have been affected.

quired for the safety and prosperity of the realm. The emperor had to teach all how to purify their souls and to heal their bodies, even those uneducated Cynics and above all Galileans who had voluntarily deserted the divinely founded community of all. He wished to cure them by persuasion as well as by force of law, so as to reunite them with the community of the Romans. Among those whom the emperor either intended to cure or else invited to "go to the churches of the Galileans to expound Matthew and Luke" was Gregory of Nazianzus.

PART TWO

4

On the True Philosophical Life and Ideal Christian Leadership

Gregory's Inaugural Address, Oration 2

> *One has to begin by purifying oneself before purifying others; one has to be instructed before instructing; one has to become light prior to enlightening others, approach God before leading others toward him.*
> —GREGORY OF NAZIANZUS, ORATION 2.71

> *There are no codes of aptitude . . . ; [we think ourselves philosophers] if we know how to drape ourselves well in our cloak [tribōn], if we have become philosophers just to the level of our belts. . . . Bah! What sort of eminence and effrontery this is!*
> —GREGORY OF NAZIANZUS, ORATION 2.49

> *One requires . . . instruction and training in the arts of dance and of flute playing, and one must devote time to it, continuous pain, and sweat. Occasional honoraria must be paid, instructors hired, long voyages undertaken, not to mention a host of other things one must do or suffer to acquire the experience. But for the wisdom that presides over all others: . . . Do we believe it is sufficient to wish that one were wise to be so?*
> —GREGORY OF NAZIANZUS, ORATION 2.50[1]

During the summer of 362 Julian crossed Cappadocia en route from Constantinople to Antioch. The journey was the first phase of a daunting military campaign against the Persians under Shapur, the archenemy of the Romans. Thus the emperor, as part of his preparation, intensified his efforts, his *erga* as philosopher, priest, and leader, to guide those in his care to the divine by all imperial means at his disposal, for the favor of the gods was essential for the success of his military campaign. Nazianzus was on the emperor's route, and one of its prominent citizens was in his

---

1. Pl. *Prt.* 332a for the dialogue structure; *Phd.* 103c, *Cra.* 390c.

entourage: Caesarius, Gregory of Nazianzus's brother.[2] Gregory was probably in Nazianzus when the emperor passed through, just after issuing his edict on teachers in Ancyra. Soon thereafter, however, Gregory left Nazianzus once again, propelled this time, at least in part, by Julian's recent pronouncements and measures.[3]

To recapitulate: at some point between December 361 and early 362, after Julian's accession and before he passed through Cappadocia, Gregory the Elder had ordained his elder son, Gregory, as presbyter or priest.[4] By then, Gregory the Elder, Dianius of Caesarea, and the majority of bishops in the East had signed a document sponsored by the emperor Constantius that had defined the relationship between Father and Son as *homoios*, "similar," stipulating that in referring to that similarity the term "essence," or *ousia*, as well as the expression "one *hypostasis*" ought to be avoided.[5] The document was the first empirewide agreement among Christian leaders regarding the relationship between Father and Son, but the accord was short-lived, as noted in Chapter 1. Those who had lost out and had been removed from their sees as a result of the accord were first to voice their opposition. Most prominent among them were the followers of Eustathius of Sebaste and Basil of Ancyra, also called homoiousians because they argued that Father and Son were "similar according to essence [*ousia*]" and "similar according to everything [*homoios kata panta*]."[6] Constantius's demise in late 361 had strengthened their case, as had Julian's edict from January 362, which had recalled those exiled to their cities (but not their sees). In Ammianus's view this edict had been the emperor's clever device to increase inter-Christian tensions, knowing that "this freedom [to observe each

---

2. Jul. *Ep.* 40 (Wright 30); Amm. Marc. 22.12.1–2; Lib. *Or.* 18.163; Soz. *HE* 4.4.1; edict = *CIL* III 247 = *ILS* 754. Ammianus does not mention that Julian passed Nazianzus—there was no reason why he should have done so—but Gregory said twelve years later in *Or.* 18.32 that a troop of imperial archers on their way through town during Julian's reign had demanded shelter in the churches; Gregory the Elder had refused. Pack, *Städte*, 308–10; McGuckin, *St. Gregory*, 129–30. According to the *Artemii Passio* 24 (*apud* Philost. 7.4c.82.11–17), Julian stopped in Issus to honor Alexander the Great; *Artemii Passio* (*The Ordeal of Artemius*, BHG 170–171c CPG 8082 = Philost. *HE* 151.5–152.11, app. Bidez), in *From Constantine to Julian*, ed. Lieu and Montserrat, 235–36; Browning, *Emperor Julian*, 144.

3. He probably left after August 1, 362, when he had delivered *Or.* 15. It is difficult to reconstruct this phase of Gregory's life, because we have little external information and must rely on Gregory's own writings, principally the first six orations, the later autobiographical poems, *Or.* 43, *Or.* 18, *Epp.* 3, 7, and 10, and Basil's *Ep.* 51 to Bishop Bosporius. I consider the chronology that follows most probable, but others are equally feasible.

4. Gr. Naz. *Or.* 18.32–34.

5. Ath. *Syn.* 30.8; Soz. *HE* 4.23.7; Bas. *Ep.* 51; Le Nain de Tillemont, *Mémoires*, vol. 9, 347; Brennecke, *Studien*, 23–86, esp. 52–53, 56–60, and Anhang 4, 248; Klein, *Constantius II.*, 64–65; McLynn, "Gregory the Peacemaker," 204–16.

6. Socr. *HE* 2.42–45; Soz. *HE* 4.24; Philost. *HE* 5.1–3; Theod. *HE* 2.27.21; Brennecke, *Studien*, 54–58, 63, 192–94; McLynn, "Use and Abuse," 82–85; Dagron, *Naissance*, 436; Hanson, *Search*, 380–82.

their own beliefs] increased their dissent"—one is hard pressed to characterize the situation in Caesarea and Nazianzus in early 362 more succinctly.[7]

In Caesarea, Basil had joined forces with the mounting homoiousian opposition and broken rank with his bishop, Dianius, whom he had advised in Constantinople while the accord had been brokered, and who had ordained him as reader. As Basil would later assert, his continuing loyalty to Eustathius of Sebaste between 360 and 362 had caused him "intolerable grief, together with many people of our city who feared God," because Dianius "had subscribed to the creed brought from Constantinople by those around George [of Alexandria]."[8] In the early summer of 362, Basil's grief only increased, when a certain Eusebius, a member of the *curia*, succeeded Dianius as bishop of Caesarea after a highly contested election.[9] Eusebius, like Dianius before him, was a homoian: that is, a staunch supporter of the Constantinopolitan document. Among the bishops who supported his election was Gregory the Elder of Nazianzus.[10] Many of those who feared God in Caesarea, including Basil, opposed Eusebius, however, and questioned the regularity of his ordination. Basil, though Eusebius had ordained him as priest, reacted to the discord by retiring once more to his estate Annesi, in Pontus.[11] Julian too, then in residence in Caesarea, was highly critical of the election of Eusebius to the metropolitan see, as a homoian allied with those whom Constantius had sponsored. According to Gregory, Julian became enraged with the citizens of Caesarea because they razed a temple to the Tyche of the city; the election of Eusebius added further fuel to the fire, so that the city was close to facing serious retributions (*Or.* 18.34).[12]

---

7. Amm. Marc. 22.5.4: "Quod agebat ideo obstinate, ut dissensiones augente licentia"; Jul. *Ep.* 46 (Wright 15), *To Aetius,* Feb. 362; the edict reached Alexandria on February 9, 362. The homoian historiography followed Ammianus's view, whereas the homoiousian Neo-Nicene historians consider Julian's edict an attempt to flatter Constantius's Christian opponents; Brennecke, *Studien,* 98–100.

8. Bas. *Ep.* 51, dating to 370. George was probably en route to Antioch to debate the Psalms in the presence of Constantius; Brennecke, *Studien,* 59 n. 23, 66–77; Rousseau, *Basil,* 66–68, 84–85, 98; S. Elm, *Virgins,* 63, 78–81.

9. Gautier, *Retraite,* 292–317; S. Elm, "Diagnostic Gaze"; McLynn, "Gregory the Peacemaker," independently supports Gautier's points.

10. Gr. Naz. *Or.* 18.33–34. Eusebius had been ordained bishop in early 362, but this was immediately contested: according to Gregory, well into early summer. Gregory also reports that Gregory the Elder resisted attempts to invalidate Eusebius's ordination because he had not been baptized when ordained. The affair also involved the provincial governor, who petitioned Julian to remove Eusebius.

11. Rousseau, *Basil,* 66–67, 87–88, 135; Gautier, *Retraite,* 303–5.

12. Soz. *HE* 5.3–4, perhaps following Gr. Naz. *Or.* 18.34, reports that Julian punished the Caesareans by removing the city's rank and title as imperial because they had destroyed a temple to Tyche the previous winter. I am not as convinced as Van Dam (*Kingdom,* 99–100, 173–75) that the measures to rebuild the temple in Daphne referred to in Julian's *Ep.* 80 (Wright 29), written from Ancyra in July 362 (Julian, *Epistolario,* trans. and comm. Caltabiano, 172), were meant to include the one to Tyche in Caesarea.

The God-fearing at Nazianzus were similarly divided. As soon as Gregory the Elder had signed the document of Constantinople, persons whom Gregory the Younger later described as "overzealous brothers" began to voice their disagreement.[13] By the summer of 362, the situation in Nazianzus, like that in Caesarea, had worsened. "Foreign hands [*chersin allotriais*]," bishops other than Gregory the Elder, had formally ordained the leaders of those who had opposed him since his signing of the homoian (or Arian) creed—a signature he never retracted.[14] This was a serious affront, because it implied schism. Gregory does not specify who these foreigners were and when exactly these ordinations took place, but he noted in *Oration* 43.28–29 that "high priests of the Westerners" were in Nazianzus at that time. As Neil McLynn has plausibly argued, these men may well have been the avowed antihomoians Lucifer of Calaris and Eusebius of Vercelli (or persons in their entourage), who passed through Cappadocia in the summer of 362 on their return west from Antioch, where Lucifer had already ordained Paulinus as bishop of a group of followers of Eustathius of Sebaste.[15]

Gregory the Younger was not just any priest or presbyter in Nazianzus at that moment of intense crisis. His ordination, in late 361 or, more probably, early 362, had made official his role as the close advisor of his father, the bishop. He was, in any event, a prominent citizen of his native city. Gregory had taught rhetoric, probably at his uncle Amphilochius's school, ever since his return from Athens. In this capacity he had "shown off *logoi*," "danced for friends," instructed students "in the Attic training," and presumably enjoyed the welcome immunity from curial duties such a position granted.[16] Although Gregory may have relinquished his career as a

---

13. Le Nain de Tillemont, *Mémoires*, vol. 9, 347; the argument of Calvet-Sébasti (*Grégoire de Nazianze: Discours 6–12*, ed. and trans. Calvet-Sébasti, 11–36) and Bernardi (ed. and trans., *Grégoire de Nazianze: Discours 4–5, 23–37*, and *Prédication*, 97–103) for a less compromising document composed at Antioch in 363 have not been accepted; Brennecke (*Studien*, 23–86, esp. 56–60), McLynn ("Gregory the Peacemaker," 208–9), Gautier (*Retraite*, 292–305), and S. Elm ("Diagnostic Gaze," 88–91) all support the traditional view that the schism began in late 361 and ended 364/5.

14. Gr. Naz. *Or.* 6.11, 4.10, 18.18, "a revolt was raised against us by the more zealous part of the church, when we had been tricked by a piece of writing and by technical words into a wicked fellowship"; McLynn, "Gregory the Peacemaker," 202–3; S. Elm, "Diagnostic Gaze," 90–91.

15. McLynn, "Gregory the Peacemaker," 208–9. For Lucifer of Calaris's (modern Cagliari's) meddling, Socr. *HE* 3.6.9; at Antioch, Lucifer and Eusebius of Vercelli had presented the *Tomus ad Antiochenos*. Apollinaris of Laodicaea, also en route through Cappadocia, may also have been an ordainer: Soz. *HE* 5.13; Theod. *HE* 3.5. McGuckin, *St. Gregory*, 111 n. 83, suggests Eustathius of Sebaste, assuming that the opponents were ascetics. For irregular ordinations, Bas. *Ep.* 237; Brennecke, *Studien*, 108–12, 169–71, 176–78; Gautier, *Retraite*, 301 n. 3, 304 n. 10. Just, *Imperator et Episcopus*, 94–96, for Lucifer's stance in opposition to Constantius. For the complex Antiochene situation in 360/61, Spoerl, "Schism," and Zachhuber, "Antiochene Synod."

16. Gr. Naz. *DVS* 265, 274; *Ep.* 3, *To Evagrius*; *Ep.* 188.1 for Stagirius's and Gregory's Attic training. Gregory was almost certainly an unpaid teacher; Wolf, *Vom Schulwesen*, 12–24, 60–66; Kaster, *Guardians*,

rhetorician before his ordination in 362, that is by no means certain or, indeed, the foregone conclusion that scholars have often asserted; he may have continued teaching until the summer of 362.[17] Gregory never ceased corresponding with other professional rhetoricians such as Eustochius and Stagirius. In sum, he understood himself as a man of *logoi* par excellence for the rest of his life.[18]

Gregory's entire body of work testifies eloquently to how deeply he was affected by Julian's edict of June 17 on the *mores* of teachers and by his imperial letter of July 18, declaring that those who did not believe in the gods of Homer, Hesiod, and so on were unfit to teach and interpret their writings and should "go to the churches of the Galileans to expound Matthew and Luke."[19] Julian's imperial laws forced Gregory and other Christian men of letters like him to choose between the *Logos* and *logoi*. If Gregory had not left his teaching position as a result of his ordination, he now had no choice but to leave. Furthermore, ever since Athens Gregory had intended one day to devote himself to the true philosophical life, which the emperor's edict and earlier pronouncements claimed exclusively for those devoted to the gods of the Greeks and the Romans. Writing to the (pagan) governor Candidianus, Gregory lamented—in high literary style and with all the virtuosity of his Attic training—his recent premature decision to give up *logoi* so that he was unable to laud Candidianus as he deserved. Gregory as rhetorician would otherwise publicly have sung his praises.[20] His words in *Oration* 2 express his feelings clearly: "I am not afraid of the war now fought against us from the outside nor of the fero-

---

221–26; Cribiore, *Gymnastics,* 56–65; C. Drecoll, *Liturgien,* 35–43, 45, 47, 55–58, 72–73; Lizzi Testa, "Bishop."

17. Gautier (*Retraite,* 304, 314–17) plausibly suggests that Gregory's ordination as presbyter occurred after Eusebius's contested election, which would bring his relinquishing of the teaching post even closer to Julian's edict, assuming that ordination precluded teaching. (This is one way to read his *Ep.* 10.2, *To Candidianus:* he had to give up *logoi* not because of Julian's edict but because he had been ordained.) However, no texts that I know of, including synodal decrees, explicitly prohibit ordained priests from acting as rhetoricians. The mid-third-century Syrian *Didascalia Apost.* 1.6 prohibits all Christians from acting as teachers, but in its present form it was revised as the first part of the *Apostolic Constitutions,* dating to about 380, and thus postdates Gregory. The legislation regarding clerical immunities may make holding two positions at once impossible, which would have required differentiation between paid and unpaid rhetoricians (Gregory being the latter). Augustine, *Conf.* 9.5.13, relinquished his position once ordained, but he, unlike Gregory, taught to earn a living. Gautier (*Retraite,* 282, 166), based on the assumption that Gregory was baptized in 360 and that this precluded teaching, as implied in the *Didascalia,* assumes that Gregory gave up his chair then. McGuckin (*St. Gregory,* 55, 86–87, and "Autobiography," 162–63, 165) makes no explicit comment, but since he dates Gregory's baptism to Athens, he sees no conflict between baptism and teaching. Baptism did not preclude rhetorical function, as Prohaeresius and Marius Victorinus attest; Aug. *Conf.* 8.2.3–5.

18. Gr. Naz. *Epp.* 189, 191, 192; *Or.* 4.100, 6.5, 7.1. For Gregory's contacts with men of letters, McLynn, "Among the Hellenists," 220–26.

19. *CTh* 13.3.5 and *Ep.* 61c (Wright 36).

20. Gallay dates Gr. Naz. *Ep.* 10.2 to either 362 or 363; 362 seems more plausible.

cious beast now attacking the church, this incarnation of evil, even if he threatens fire, swords, wild beasts, steep cliffs, and deep ravines" (*Or.* 2.87).

This was the situation Gregory faced in the summer of 362. His father, the bishop, confronted a schism. The emperor had banned persons of high Attic training who believed in the Christian God from teaching *paideia* and de facto denied them the right to live the true philosophical life, as he pronounced his own desire as philosopher and priest to guide all back to the old gods of the Greeks and the Romans. Gregory's brother, Caesarius, held a high-ranking position at the court of that emperor and had just passed through Nazianzus with him. Probably before Caesarius left Constantinople, Gregory had written to report the alarming news that in Nazianzus his career at the imperial court had become the stuff of schoolroom exercises:[21] for example, "now the bishop's son is making a public career at court; now he aspires to power and glory among those on the outside; now he has been won over by riches. . . . How can our bishop prevent others from being swayed by the circumstances and from worshipping idols? How can he rebuke others who commit mistakes if he cannot speak frankly at home?" Gregory professed embarrassment at the situation, which had given rise to rumors and slanders on everyone's part, "since people prefer by far to philosophize about others than about their own affairs," a situation that could not have helped the embattled bishop.

For August 1, the festival of the Maccabean martyrs, Gregory composed an oration to celebrate them and their resistance against Antiochus IV Epiphanes.[22] It was also the first formulation of his own resistance. Gregory made the Maccabees into Christian martyrs *avant la lettre*. Even though they had not been able to "imitate the death [of Christ] incurred for our salvation" (*Or.* 15.1), Eleazar, an "old priest," his seven sons, and their mother, confronting Antiochus IV Epiphanes, were filled with "manly courage" and "demonstrated their perseverance in defense of the laws they had received from their fathers" to the point of suffering death (*Or.* 15.2–4).[23] The analogy was evident to Gregory's audience. Taking a Stoic diatribe as his model

---

21. Gr. Naz. *Ep.* 7, *To Caesarius*; Gautier, *Retraite*, 321–22; McGuckin, *St. Gregory*, 115–17; Van Dam, *Families*, 61–62; Coulie, *Richesses*, 139–41.

22. Gr. Naz. *Ep.* 10, dated to July or August 362.

23. Gr. Naz. *Or.* 15, PG 35.912-33 (*Gregorio di Nazianzo: Tutte le orazioni*, ed. Moreschini, trans. Sani and Vincelli, 374–91). Moreschini argues (1262 n. 1) that the oration circulated only in written form. Gregory refers to the spurious fourth Book of Maccabees (*Or.* 15.2), in antiquity often attributed to Flavius Josephus; see also 2 Mac 6:18; Wright, "Ancient Syrian Martyrology," for the inclusion of the Maccabees into the liturgical calendar on August 1. For Gregory's conflation of traditions as well as his Homeric allusions, Vinson, "Gregory Nazianzen's Homily 15." She suggests a date of December 1, 362. The classic discussion remains Sinko, "De Gregorii Nazianzeni laudibus Macchabaeorum"; Moreschini, *Filosofia*, 232; McGuckin, *St. Gregory*, 126–28; Bernardi, ed. and trans., *Grégoire de Nazianze: Discours 4–5*, 13, and *Prédication*, 101–2. Alternative dates for *Or.* 15 are August 1, 363, or 364, against Valens; McGuckin, *loc. cit.;* Ziadé, *Martyrs*. Criscuolo, "Gregorio di Nazianzo e Giuliano," 171, thinks Gregory addressed Antioch's Christians. As Vinson notes ("Gregory Nazianzen's Homily 15," 177–92), the ora-

and combining motifs from the *Iliad* with Jewish traditions, Gregory reworked the story of the Maccabees to make Julian the Antiochus "of our day" (*Or.* 15.12). In praising the Maccabees as paragons of virtue, he announced his own willingness as well as that of his father, mother, and friends to defend to the death their "divine law . . . , the tablets divinely engraved" (*Or.* 15.6).[24] Moreover, Gregory left no doubt that for him the mere words that the Maccabees had spoken to their persecutor were weapons of resistance as powerful as their physical suffering.

Shortly after completing the oration on August 1, 362, Gregory left Nazianzus, his father, and his public role, to retire with Basil to Annesi, to deliberate how he wished to lead the philosophical life, to ponder how one ought to lead the community of those devoted to the *Logos,* and to formulate his response to the events at home and "on the outside."[25] He returned to Nazianzus at Easter 363 with the result of his deliberations in hand: *Oration* 2, also known as the *Apology for His Flight to Pontus* and *On the Priesthood*.[26]

A HIGH-WIRE ACT: THE TRUE PHILOSOPHICAL LIFE AS THE MODEL OF PRIESTHOOD IN LATE ANTIQUITY

The events and pressures to which Gregory in *Oration* 2 responds increase one's appreciation of his rhetorical mastery in navigating such troubled waters—or, to use Gregory's own metaphor, how "those who balance on a wire strung high in the air cannot without danger veer in either direction" (*Or.* 2.34). The sequence of events I have outlined, placing Gregory's flight and return later than the customary dating between Epiphany and Easter 362, helps to clarify why Gregory left Nazianzus and why he apologized for his absence or flight: he could not have left his father and Nazianzus at a more tension-filled time.[27] For Gregory to leave the city, partic-

---

tion became instrumental in transforming the Maccabees into Christian heroes, making Antiochus IV Epiphanes Julian's precursor. It is also Gregory's earliest attempt to sanctify his family.

24. Gr. Naz. *DVS* 277–79, McLynn, "Among the Hellenists," 224–33. McGuckin, *St. Gregory*, 127, identifies the seven as Gregory, Caesarius, Amphilochius, and the brothers Basil of Caesarea, Gregory of Nyssa, Peter, and Naucratius; but see my discussion below in Chapter 5. Van Dam (*Families*, 46–47, and *Kingdom*, 100–101, 191–92) points to a connection between *Or.* 15 and Gregory the Elder's intervention with Julian on behalf of Bishop Eusebius of Caesarea, mentioned in Gr. Naz. *Or.* 18.34.

25. According to *Or.* 43.29.8, Gregory and Basil went to Annesi together: φυγὰς ἐνθένδε σὺν ἡμῖν πρὸς τὸν Πόντον.

26. For the manuscript titles of *Or.* 2, Somers, *Histoire*, 130–38; Bernardi, ed. and trans., *Grégoire de Nazianze: Discours 1–3, 14–17, 24–28*, 30.

27. Gautier, *Retraite*, 302–17. Most scholars associate Gregory's move to Annesi with his ordination and date his return and delivery of *Orations* 1–3 to Easter 362 (and the publication of his revised orations to late 362 or early 363); McGuckin, *St. Gregory*, 90–111; Daley, *Gregory*, 9–10; Beeley, *Gregory*, 11–12; S. Elm, "Orthodoxy." Mossay, "Date," suggests 364. Absence from the summer of 362 to Easter 363 appears more plausible both for the composition of the oration and as reason to apologize for a flight.

ularly if he sympathized doctrinally with those who opposed his father's signing of a homoian document, as Basil had sympathized with Eusebius's opponents, was a far more serious act of disobedience than it had been in Basil's case, for unlike Basil, Gregory left not only the bishop who had ordained him, but his very own father. That he left while his own brother was at the court of Julian did not help matters at a time when Julian's intentions vis-à-vis Christians, published as imperial edicts, were plain for all to see.

Gregory responded to the enormous pressures of that time, not surprisingly, by leaving to reflect and ponder his moves. How should an educated Christian, born to lead, react to the challenges posed by the new emperor, who was young and might rule for a long time? Gregory took almost a year to compose his answers in what would in effect be his inaugural oration. It was his first official announcement of what he considered essential for Christian leadership. Although those at Nazianzus were his most immediate audience, he evidently intended his announcement for all: addressing his household (*oikos*) and his city (polis), Gregory wished to be heard by the entire *oikoumenē,* indeed by the entire cosmos.[28]

Oration 2, or the *Apology for His Flight to Pontus,* is the central piece of the triptych formed by *Orations* 1, 2, and 3.[29] Originally circulated in a form much like that of today's edition by Jean Bernardi, *Oration* 2 resonated most with later writers.[30]

---

28. Somers (*Histoire,* 82–86, 121, 189–90, 303–11) argues for the circulation of Gregory's orations early and in small sets destined for groups of friends. It is difficult to reconstruct where these friends were, especially once we leave Nazianzus. Prosopography suggests that they were more likely to reside in Caesarea and Constantinople than in Antioch; see Chapter 1 above. Caesarius and (e.g.) Sophronius, later *magister militum* and prefect of Constantinople, and Julian, *praeses* of Phrygia (Hauser-Meury, *Prosopographie,* 110, 156–57), speak for Constantinopolitan connections, though McLynn ("Other Olympias") has weakened Bernardi's thesis ("Nouvelles perspectives") that Gregory was related to Constantinopolitan nobility. Constantinople was then less important than Antioch; by 381 Constantinople's bishop was still nominally subordinate to the metropolitan at Heraclea; Dagron, *Naissance,* 410–73 (esp. 446, 459), 518–44; Liebeschuetz, *Antioch,* 40–51, 105–18.

29. Gr. Naz. *Or.* 2 is framed by Gregory's call to peace on the Day of Resurrection (*Or.* 1), and by *Or.* 3, held eight days later, chastising those who had failed to attend the occasion of *Or.* 1. McLynn, "Gregory the Peacemaker," 191 n. 36, lists verbatim repetitions that show the cohesiveness of *Or.* 1–3. *Or.* 2 in its existing form was not intended for oral performance.

30. In contrast to Jerome (Rebenich, *Hieronymus,* 132–33), Gregory tells us little about his way of writing and publishing. In *Or.* 42.26 he mentions tachygraphs, who copied his words as he spoke. We know also that he revised and edited his letters, poems, and orations for publication in the 380s: *Epp.* 52, 53, 51, 54 (*Saint Grégoire de Nazianze: Lettres,* ed. Gallay, xxi–xxii, for this order); McGuckin, "Gregory of Nazianzus," 201–5. This prompts McGuckin, *St. Gregory,* 106–7, to assume that passages in *Or.* 2 critical of the clergy reflect Gregory's feelings after 382 rather than in 362/3, without any indications of the manuscripts. C. Macé, "À propos d'une édition," suggests, however, that Gregory's systematic revisions, *pace* Somers (*Histoire,* 82–86, 121, 189–90, 303–11), mean that he circulated all his orations in one batch after he had revised them; she is not certain that he had circulated them earlier in groups, as all scholars who discuss the orations in chronological sequence do. Sinko (*De traditione orationum,* vol. 1), who laid the foundation for the modern editions, distinguished two principal manuscript families, M and N; all

It is the earliest systematic discussion of the theoretical and practical foundations of Christian leadership; several ancient copyists for that reason added *On the Priesthood* to the title.[31] Priesthood as leadership, however, has rarely been the focus of scholarly attention; in fact, until recently *Oration* 2 has rarely been discussed extensively in its own right. Scholars have read it primarily as an apology for the flight as suggested by the main title added later by the scribes. The scholarly analysis has focused principally on Gregory's shock and revulsion at his tyrannical father's forcing him into the despised office of a priest when he himself yearned so demonstrably for the ascetic, contemplative retreat of the monk—that is, the philosophical life. Shock prompted his heedless flight and necessitated the apology composed shortly thereafter.[32] Read as such, elements of the oration that deal with leadership take on a particular, exclusively Christian, meaning. If scholars discuss them at all (they form the bulk of the oration; only about fifteen of the 117 chapters are devoted to the flight), they interpret them strictly as pertaining to the relationship between a reluctant priest, offended by other, less qualified priests, and his congregation: that is, as what Christopher Beeley in his discussion of *Oration* 2 calls "Pastoral Ministry."[33] Gregory's text offers a sound basis for such readings, but the debate about the philosophical life and its ramifications at that time far exceeded the Christian context presupposed by those readings. They represent only a part of the broad canvas into which Gregory inserted himself.

The philosophical life was indeed central to Gregory's apology. But while it helped to justify his flight, his oration was more concerned to prove that the true philo-

---

manuscripts of the M family, which Sinko considered superior, number *Or.* 2 first. Sinko ordered the early orations 4-5-1-3-6-2, etc., placing the anti-Julianic orations first. In 398 or 399, Rufinus translated the orations in the sequence *Or.* 2-38-39-41-26-17-6-16-27 (*Tyrannii Rufini orationum Gregorii Nazianzeni novem interpretatio*, ed. Engelbrecht). Bernardi's edition and translation retains Sinko's order, but he gives preference to the N family: *Grégoire de Nazianze: Discours 1–3*, 56–59. Sinko and most of the Sources Chrétiennes editors do not take into consideration the partial collections that group the orations liturgically, according to rhetorical genre (apologetic, panegyric, invective, etc.), and geographically; Somers (*Histoire*, 1–34, 40–41, 44–51, with greater details in 69–100) argues that new editions ought to do so, because the division into two families is obsolete.

31. Somers, *Histoire*, 130–38. For the impact of *Or.* 2 as translated by Rufinus on Gregory the Great's pastoral rules, see *Grégoire le Grand: Règle pastorale*, intro. Judic, ed. Rommel, trans. Morel, vol. 1, 27–32. Almost all sources specifying the duties of a bishop date to the fourth century; many postdate Gregory, such as the *Apostolic Constitutions* or the *Lives* of bishops, a major tool for discussions of the office, E. Elm, *Macht*, 9–12, 16–63. Efthymiadis, "Two Gregories"; Gautier, *Retraite*, 292–317; Beeley, *Gregory*, 237–70.

32. Bernardi, ed. and trans., *Grégoire de Nazianze: Discours 1–3*, 20–50; Daley, *Gregory*, 34–60, differentiates Gregory the philosopher, the theologian, and the priest, a division that counters Gregory's point that all three are one; Daley (p. 59) notes that "Gregory hoped in his own time to participate as an opinionated bystander, a 'philosopher' standing at a critical and ascetical distance from the fray," but also that he came to realize over time that leadership is a form of philosophical life. McGuckin, *St. Gregory*, 95–110, does not discuss *Or.* 2, because he considers it too redacted to yield much information for 362.

33. Beeley, *Gregory*, 235–70 (quotation p. 235).

sophical life was the indispensable precondition for priestly office as leadership of the *oikoumenē* and to delineate his personal definition of that life. As Julian had said, for Gregory, too, only a philosopher could be a priest, because only he would lead his community appropriately and guide it to God and salvation. This was so because only the philosophical life of ascetic self-control and retreat purified its practitioner so that he could comprehend the divine as far as humanly possible, and as a result intervene actively in the affairs of the *politeia* and guide others, less purified, toward God with "the words dedicated to the service of the Word" (*Or.* 4.3). The inaugural address with which Gregory resumed his public office aimed squarely at the debates about the true philosophical life, with its cosmic and political implications, then gripping the elites of the empire, including the emperor. Gregory conceived the philosophical life along the lines represented by Themistius and hence Constantius, in clear opposition to Julian. But he did more. He integrated scripture into the classic matrix of the true philosophical life. This was an innovation and, as such, inherently dangerous. Unlike Julian's innovations, however, which Gregory considered wrong, Gregory's were correct: his innovation revealed the will of the only true God. Therefore, only persons such as Gregory could guide (those who guided) the community of all (Romans) toward God and achieve salvation for themselves and for the *oikoumenē*.

Gregory's concept of Christian leadership in his second oration, the model of the bishop in late antiquity, originated in a specific historic moment and responded to specific historical configurations.[34] It was meant, however, to have universal significance and hence to transcend that moment. The scope of his undertaking was such that Gregory continued to elaborate his concepts in a series of orations, especially once Julian's death had again altered the landscape and the schism at Nazianzus had ended. Thus Gregory fine-tuned his prescriptions for the philosophical life as the precondition for the office of priesthood in his two orations *Against Julian* (*Or.* 4 and 5), written after the emperor's death, and in *Oration* 6, with which he celebrated the peace at Nazianzus. The fundaments laid here became the blueprint for his own later discussions of the topic, in which it is evident that his concepts applied equally to priests and bishops; the difference between the two was of no evident concern to him. In his subsequent work as public speaker, preacher, and writer for whom "eloquence is life" (*Or.* 43.1), Gregory reiterated again and again, at times verbatim, the ideas about Christian leadership he first articulated in 362, 363, and 364.[35] He was fully aware of his penchant for repetition, but also of his reasons: "I

---

34. Beeley, *Gregory*, 241 n. 19, notes that Gregory refers about a hundred times each to bishops and priests and about half as much to presbyters.

35. Mossay (*Grégoire de Nazianze: Discours 20–23*, ed. and trans. Mossay, 42–45) discussed these repetitions and their reasons. Olivar, *Predicación*, 596–99 and n. 22, following Rufinus, thinks that Gregory improvised but wrote his orations before he delivered them.

repeat the same words often, because I mistrust [our] weak, material thought processes" (*Or.* 20.10). In proclaiming the nature of true Christian leadership, Gregory could not risk being misunderstood, much less ignored.

Thus when Basil, by then bishop of Caesarea, consecrated Gregory as bishop of Sasima in 372, his *Orations* 9–12 again elaborated his concepts. This time, he stressed even more than in 363 the qualities of the priest, or rather bishop, as *mystagōgos* and one who speaks frankly to power (*parrhēsia*). Significantly, flight here played a central role as well. Gregory considered the position as bishop of Sasima—the next station beyond Nazianzus on the road to Antioch and still within Nazianzus's territory, where his father was the bishop—beneath contempt. It reduced him "from a lion to an ape," and he never accepted the charge, in fact accusing Basil of using him as a mere pawn in his own power plays; if he was to be used, according to the tenor of his orations, then he wanted to play a role other than that of bishop of a hole-in-the-wall.[36]

Constantinople was more what he had in mind, and his wish was granted. Gregory spent the years from 379 to 381 in the capital and returned to the themes of leadership, first as a priest and then as the city's bishop. Before his consecration as bishop on November 27, 380, on the initiative of Emperor Theodosius, Gregory delivered a series of orations on Christian episcopal leadership, reiterating the themes elaborated in 363. The series begins with *Oration* 20, which the ancient copyists have aptly titled *On Theology and the Installation of Bishops*. There follow his orations in praise of Athanasius of Alexandria (*Or.* 21) and of Cyprian of Carthage (*Or.* 24). In them he gave his concepts concrete form: both exemplars embody leadership as Gregory conceived it. His two orations first praising and then condemning the Cynic philosopher Maximus (*Or.* 25 and 26) also belong to that series, since here too Gregory used the occasion to showcase his version of the true philosopher active in the *politeia* and for the common good. Gregory's retirement from the office of bishop in 381 offered another occasion to summarize his notions for those who had not fully grasped them: *Oration* 42, which I have identified as following the model of a letter of discharge from office. The funeral oration for Basil of Caesarea, *Oration* 43, given in 382, praised the man who was for Gregory the greatest exemplar of a Christian leader—but again, as Gregory conceived that role. Many of his poems, in particular those that are autobiographical, served the same purpose. Gregory's stance on Christian leadership as true philosophical life, formulated in 363

---

36. Gr. Naz. *Carm.* 2.1.11, *DVS* 408–9. Basil consecrated Gregory after Valens had passed through Cappadocia in 371/2. Though both considered Valens a Julian redivivus, Gregory refused to aid Basil at that politically charged moment and never went to Sasima; he did not wish to be a bishop in his own father's territory, nor of a place without significance other than that it augmented the number of bishops associated with Basil. McLynn, "Gregory Nazianzen's Basil," 178–83, adds *Or.* 13 to the Sasima series. McGuckin, *St. Gregory*, 192–206; Calvet-Sébasti (*Grégoire de Nazianze: Discours 6–12*, ed. and trans. Calvet-Sébasti), 88–103; Gautier, *Retraite*, 332–48; Van Dam, *Families*, 159–72, 44–52.

and 364, wound itself like a red thread through his later works. The principal themes remained the same, though Gregory revised and adjusted them to fit occasion and context. For Gregory the nature and requirements of priestly office, including that of the bishop, were those first formulated in *Oration 2*.[37]

Refusal of Office

"Let us pardon each other; I for the beautiful tyranny that has tyrannized me—for so I can now call it—and you who have tyrannized me beautifully, if you have reason to reproach my tardiness, though my tardiness might be better and more honorable before God than the quickness of others."[38] The opening theme of Gregory's first three orations is the tyranny of public life imposed upon Gregory by his father and the people of Nazianzus: "I have been vanquished, and I acknowledge my defeat."[39] Such tyranny and Gregory's recoiling at his subjection to it, expressed in *Orations* 1–3 and reiterated in his later autobiographical poems, have contributed much to the historiographic iconography of Gregory as a man torn by a lion and a bear;[40] as a reclusive intellectual whose desire for retreat was brought harshly to an end by a father's heavy-handed demand for service (to which injury Basil later added insult: Sasima is the word), an act that rendered an emotionally labile man conflicted for the rest of his life.[41] Since the a priori equation of Gregory's retreat with Christian asceticism and indeed monasticism is central to that scholarly representation, everything Gregory says about the philosophical life is read as defining Christian asceticism. The origins of the Christian philosophical life as asceticism are then inserted into a well-established historiographic genealogy, tracing the debate back through Origen and Clement to Philo. In this reconstruction, scholars omit entirely the debates about the philosophical life as leadership during Gregory's own time and their classical antecedents.[42] No doubt, Gregory wished to create and sought to embody the true Christian philosophical life—these aims are what made him famous. But to equate the philosophical life he advocated in 362 and 363, without further ado, with a (presumably fully formed) Christian asceticism in conflict with

---

37. *Grégoire de Nazianze: Discours 20–23*, ed. and trans. Mossay, 45–53; *Grégoire de Nazianze: Discours 24–26*, ed. and trans. Mossay, 9–31; Rebillard, "Speaking for Salvation"; S. Elm, "Programmatic Life," 421–27; McGuckin, *St. Gregory*, 251–54, 243–48 on *Or.* 20, 266–69 on *Or.* 21 (*On Athanasius*), 372–75; McLynn, "Voice."

38. Gr. Naz. *Or.* 1.1: Δῶμεν συγγνώμην ἀλλήλοις, ἐγώ τε ὁ τυραννηθεὶς τὴν καλὴν τυραννίδα—τοῦτο γὰρ νῦν προστίθημι—καὶ ὑμεῖς οἱ καλῶς τυραννήσαντες, εἴ τί μοι μέμφοισθε τῆς βραδυτῆτος.

39. Gr. Naz. *Or.* 1.1, 2.1, 3.1.

40. Gr. Naz. *DVS* 408–9.

41. Van Dam, *Families*, 43–49; Gautier, *Retraite*, 113–34, 220–27, 292–317; McGuckin, *St. Gregory*, 106–13; Bernardi, ed. and trans., *Grégoire de Nazianze: Discours 1–3*, 8–10.

42. Fundamental for the philosophy as Christian asceticism, Malingrey, *Philosophia*, 207–26. Gautier reiterates this stance, *Retraite*, 7–112; exceptions are Lizzi Testa, *Potere*, 22–31; Rousseau, *Basil*, 70–72; McGuckin, *St. Gregory*, 85–113; and McLynn in all his published papers on Gregory.

priesthood does not do Gregory justice.[43] In other words, my analysis does not emphasize Gregory's use of scripture and the Christian antecedents of his notions, especially in Origen's work—others have stressed these, though less systematically than one might imagine—but considers the classical matrix into which Gregory inserted his scriptural citations and exemplars: the classical notions are the basis for the Christian concepts, and not the other way round.[44]

"I have been beaten, and I recognize my defeat: I have submitted myself to the Lord, and I have come to supplicate him."[45] The opening words of Gregory's *Oration* 2 begin a rhetorical tour de force in a now familiar genre, the *apologētikos logos* with autobiographical content.[46] As Julian had demonstrated in his *Epistle to the Athenians,* the *apologētikos logos* of the accused was the genre forensic advocates favored for persuading a judging audience of the correctness of their views. Like Julian, Gregory acted as his own advocate, but also as his own accuser and, in the final analysis, as his own judge: "I will practice an equal mediation between the two parties, those who accuse me and those who rush to my defense. I will do so by accusing myself on the one hand and by presenting my defense on the other" (*Or.* 2.1), always employing and playing with the formal requirements of the genre.[47] Accordingly, "so that my speech may progress with method," Gregory describes "what has happened to me," why he was accused, before launching into his defense, refuting his adversaries through the *dialektikon* and enhancing his points in the *synkrisis,* or comparison, with great heroes: his "flight" to Basil at Annesi, the "slowness" of his return, and the depth of his "submission" to the "yoke" of office (*Or.* 2.1–2).[48]

Gregory admitted that his flight had been an act of dissent (*stasis*) and disobedience (*apeitheia*), and that its length could be seen as a sign of "faint-heartedness" that undercut both others' estimation of him and the well-being of the community. For those at Nazianzus "who love nothing as much as to talk about the affairs of others" (as he had also said to Caesarius), Gregory so faint-hearted, resisting beyond the bounds of decorum, was a man unrecognizable either to those who sympathized with him or those who opposed him (*Or.* 2.1, 6).

Gregory had not acted out of ignorance or, rather, lack of *paideia* and under-

---

43. McGuckin, *St. Gregory,* 100, considers Gregory's reaction to ordination "little short of hysterical."
44. Beeley, *Gregory,* 235–70.
45. Gr. Naz. *Or.* 2.1: "Ἥττημαι καὶ τὴν ἧτταν ὁμολογῶ· ὑπετάγην τῷ Κυρίῳ καὶ ἱκέτευσα αὐτόν.
46. Gregory's opening words call upon David as a heavenly being to sustain him, following the genre's standard *invocatio* of the god(s); Ruether, *Gregory,* 75; and Neumeister, *Grundsätze,* 17–31. For Bernardi (ed. and trans., *Grégoire de Nazianze: Discours 1–3,* 30), Gregory's formal adherence to the genre did not affect the content.
47. Men. Rh. *Treatise* 1.1 (*Menander Rhetor,* ed. Russell and Wilson, 2–6; *Peri epideiktikōn,* ed. Spengel, 331–32). M. Guignet, *Saint Grégoire,* 231–65, 158–86, but also 187–210.
48. Ruether, *Gregory,* 76–80, 106–7.

standing, however. He knew the divine laws and prescripts stating that "the body contains one element that rules and presides [*archon . . . kai . . . prokathezomenon*], and another that is ruled and guided. In the same manner . . . God has determined that some in the churches are brought to the pastures and ruled . . . while others are shepherds and teachers [*poimenas kai didaskalous*] for the suturing together of the church [Eph 4:11–12]."[49] Order and hierarchy (*taxis kai archē*) must always supersede anarchy and disorder (*anarchia kai ataxia*). Indeed, "if everyone were to flee what one could call service as well as leadership"[50]—that is, carrying out the office of priest—then "the beautiful arrangement of the church [*tēs ekklēsias plērōma*] would be very much altered, and it would no longer be beautiful" (*Or.* 2.3–4). Nor, "as some might want to suggest," was Gregory's dissent a mere ploy to accede immediately to "a higher bench." He did not blush at the thought of being a mere presbyter. To obey before beginning to command "by no means transgress[ed] the rules of philosophy." All commanders, military or naval, must learn to obey before rising to the highest positions (*Or.* 2.5). Rather, as Gregory explained, his act of disobedience and the loss of control over his thoughts and his usually well-moderated behavior resulted from his sudden, overwhelming erotic "desire for the beauty of tranquility and retreat," for which he yearned far more intensely than "anyone else passionate about *logoi*"—for example, Julian.[51]

By this point, most members of Gregory's audience would have recognized the trope: refusal of office, the essential precondition for good governance professed by those ready to assume public position or already actively engaged in the life of the *politeia*, and the first and principal reason for Gregory's flight. Everything Gregory had done—his flight from authority (that of his father and implicitly that of God, into whose service he had been called) and the slowness of his return and submission to the yoke of office—corresponds precisely to Plato's qualifications for the ideal ruler, as Rita Lizzi's groundbreaking study has already pointed out.[52] Julian had used the same arguments. His first instinct on becoming Caesar, according to his *Epistle to the Athenians,* had also been to flee, to resist Constantius and even the will of the gods, and to pursue his desire for retreat and tranquility. Thus, both Gregory and Julian in their inaugural speeches set out the time-honored Platonic premise that those best suited to lead had to be sought out and persuaded to accept office

---

49. Gr. Naz. *Or.* 2.3.3–10. Cf. *Or.* 32.7–12.

50. λειτουργίαν χρὴ λέγειν εἴτε ἡγεμονίαν.

51. Gr. Naz. *Or.* 2.6: ἔρως τοῦ καλοῦ τῆς ἡσυχίας καὶ τῆς ἀναχωρήσεως . . . τῶν περὶ λόγους ἐσπουδακότων. The term *espoudakotes* evokes the zeal (*spoudē*) associated with those who transgress the boundaries of right (i.e., orthodox) behavior, and became a characterization of heretics; Le Boulluec, *Notion,* vol. 1, 22, 26–27. The main manuscript tradition omits ἐσπουδακότων, though it is required for the syntax; McLynn, "Among the Hellenists," 226 n. 45. For its use in the context of *logoi,* Basil *Ep.* 24.2; Lucian, *True History,* 1.1.5, uses it to refer to full-time students of literature.

52. Lizzi Testa, *Potere,* 33–41; Béranger, "Étude."

against their express wish, whereas those least qualified rushed to leadership, their very hunger for power (*philarchia*) revealing their incompetence.

Indeed, the first six chapters of *Oration* 2, read beneath their Christian references, are a synopsis of classical political theory.[53] Though Gregory had yet to cite the example from Plato about the training of dancers and flute players that serves as an epigraph to this chapter, he had used every one of the technical terms indicating that he would interpret the classic Platonic and Aristotelian texts on the principles and foundations of governance:[54] leadership in its various forms—*hēgemonia, archē, epistasia, prostasia, didaskalia, nomothesia* (lawgiving), good order (*taxis*), and appropriate service (*leitourgia*), and their opposites: anarchy, disorder, and tyranny (*tyrannis*).[55] All those in the audience and his eventual readers trained according to the rules of *paideia* would have recognized the classic leitmotifs and Gregory's variations on them. As has become apparent in my discussion of Constantius, Themistius, and Julian, a quintessential part of the classic debates about appropriate governance was the correct combination of retreat from and involvement in the *koina* that the true philosophical life entailed—the very theme Gregory introduced by stressing his deep "desire for the beauty of tranquility and retreat" at the moment when he officially resumed his office.

Thus, the opening lines of *Orations* 1, 2, and 3 announced for Gregory's audience the theme they expected to hear from one new to his office: how he, as "leader of souls," defined the appropriate interplay of retreat and involvement. They were not to be disappointed, because indeed Gregory proceeded to present his "canon of aptitude" (*kanōn tōn hexeōn*), his definition of the philosophical life and the role of retreat and preparation as required for good governance. No one doubted that it was Gregory's duty, his *leitourgia*, to lead the *koina* toward salvation: he had been commanded to do so by his Lord and God.[56] The length of his absence already proved that he could fulfill this duty well. In other words, Gregory's contemporaries, unlike modern scholars, would have heard no hesitancy in his orations about the demands of the public office that his ordination entailed: to the contrary.

What was in question for Gregory, and for everyone else, was his position on the correct mixture of retreat and involvement—the *bios praktikos* and the *bios theōrētikos*—and the more Aristotelian versus the more Platonic interpretation of

---

53. Principally Plato's *Laws, Republic,* and *Phaedo,* and Aristotle's *Politics;* e.g., Plato, *Laws* 12.942c, *Phaedo* 80a; Arist. *Politics* 1.5.4–6, 6.2.4–12. See also D. Chr. *Or.* 49, *Refusal of Office before the Council.*

54. Gr. Naz. *Or.* 2.50; Plato, *Protagoras* 332a, *Phaedo* 103c, *Cratylus* 390c.

55. Bernardi, ed. and trans., *Grégoire de Nazianze: Discours 1–3,* 45, and index s.vv.; Karamboula, *Staatsbegriffe,* 11–15.

56. *Koinōnia* had become largely a synonym of the *politeia* of the empire. Julian used *koinōnia* or *to koinon, ta koina,* and *politeia* indiscriminately: e.g., *Or.* 5, *MoG* 180c. Gregory, like Themistius, also used *oikoumenē*; Karamboula, *Staatsbegriffe,* 57–61, 68–73, and 96–99, 46–52 for Synesius's use of these terms.

the philosophical life that that mixture represented. Julian's stance, at least in theory, argued for greater retreat and against active involvement, because he considered the true philosopher-king an unattainable goal: he opposed the stance of Constantius and Themistius that an emperor could be such a ruler. All three (really four, if we include Constantius) agreed that retreat, or tranquil freedom from care (not to be confused with laziness), was indispensable. Without it, one could not immerse oneself in study, or achieve the purification required to Know Oneself and to approach the divine as closely as was humanly possible.[57] How such a philosopher should then become involved and promote actively the common good, as advisor and teacher or as an officeholder himself, was under intense debate.[58] Julian's proclamations had made his evolving positions clear; more important, his edict and imperial letter on teachers had left no doubt that for him the philosophical life per se was the privilege of those devoted to the gods of the Greeks and the Romans, whose divine utterances had inspired Plato and Aristotle. Those who did not believe in these gods were excluded from philosophy, from public discussions of the philosophical life, and thus from public office. By adopting the teachings of the Galilean, according to the emperor, such persons had deserted and abandoned the common foundations of *paideia* and of the community, or *ta koina,* of the Romans.

In claiming the true philosophical life for himself, Gregory thus demanded all that the emperor had just denied to Christians. By adding scripture into the matrix, he did even more: he maintained that the Christian God was the originator as well as the *telos* of the philosophical life. The *Logos* had created *logoi,* and it was to the *Logos* that *logoi,* under the leadership of the true philosopher, would guide the *oikoumenē*. The true universality of Rome was the correct mixture of *Hellēnismos* and *Romanitas* not as embodied by the old gods of the Greeks and the Romans but as manifest in the proper adherence to the words of the Word, exemplified by those who understood what Greekness truly meant: men such as Gregory, whose desire for *logoi* superseded that of all others, the emperor above all.

Hence Gregory's display—made even more obvious in his *Orations* 4 and 5, *Against Julian*—of his mastery of the normative texts.[59] In Athens, he too had stud-

---

57. Jouanna, "Réflexions"; Staden, "Idéal"; Demont, *Cité,* 33–113, and "Problèmes"; Garzya, "Sur l'idée de *scholè*," 211–17; Hahn, *Philosoph,* 192–208; Jouan, "Loisir chez Dion Chrysostome."

58. Demont, "Problèmes," 34; Scholz, *Philosoph,* 75–121; Laks, "Legislation and Demiurgy"; Goulet, "Vies"; Kullmann, "Aristote et le loisir"; Huber, "*Bios theoretikos.*"

59. Including Homer, Hesiod, Empedocles, Demosthenes, Herodotus, Thucydides, Aelius Aristides, Plutarch, Dio Chrysostom, and Galen, in addition to Plato and Aristotle. Gregory's *Ep.* 31, *To Philagrius,* refers to his library, mentioning Demosthenes and the *Iliad;* Demoen, *Pagan and Biblical Exempla,* 361–65; McGuckin, *St. Gregory,* 57–58. On the Second Sophistic, Swain, *Hellenism,* passim; Whitmarsh, *Greek Literature;* Francis, *Subversive Virtue;* Gleason, *Making Men;* Anderson, *Sage;* Bowersock, *Greek Sophists.*

ied with the likes of Prohaeresius and Himerius for nearly a decade (and not just a few months).[60] Athens was his golden city; there he and Basil had initiated their path toward the true philosophical life.[61] Now he had further purified himself by an extended period of retreat. So who was better able to comprehend *logoi* and the meaning of the true philosophical life than Gregory?

> Nothing has seemed as important to me as to close off all senses, as stepping out of my body and the world, as drawing myself upon myself and not attaching myself to anything of human concern other than those things that are absolutely necessary, to talk with myself and to God, to live above the visible realities, and to receive in me the divine reflections that are always pure, without any imprints mingled in of those things that roam about down here; to be and to become continually the immaculate mirror of God and the divine realities, to add light to light, namely a light that is more clear to a light that is more obscure.[62]

Julian could not have said it better. Gregory, by now a true philosopher (though perfection was a continuing process), knew that only a select few would fully comprehend his words and their true meaning—those in his audience who, like him, were "possessed by such a burning desire." "My words will probably not convince the common people [*hoi polloi*], those who will find such an attitude ridiculous because they are badly disposed toward it, whether because of their own stupidity or because of those who are unworthy of what they profess and who have given a beautiful thing a bad name, [calling] philosophy vanity [*tēi philosophiai tēn kenodoxian*], aided by the collaboration of envy and the ill will of the common people, always more eager to see the bad in everything, so that they themselves are bound to be wrong because they either do something bad or fail to recognize something good" (*Or.* 2.7).

---

60. Socr. *HE* 4.26; Soz. *HE* 6.17; Hahn (*Philosoph,* 46–60, 86–99) discusses rhetoricians and philosophers; Penella, *Greek Philosophers,* 79–83, and 97–98 for Himerius, who argued that devotion to *logoi* was impossible without periods of retreat and intense concentration. Such alternation between retreat and involvement was as natural to the philosophical life as a robin's alternation between song and silence. Himerius also used Platonic analogies, (e.g.) to compare retreat to the prolonged training of a ship's pilot; an athlete's training for Olympia; a musician practicing for the stage. Him. *Disc.* 63.15, 74.33 (*Himerii Declamationes et orationes,* ed. Colonna); Schouler, "Loisir et travail," esp. 204–5. Libanius agreed. He praised a certain Hierius for "joining the practice of philosophy to the exercise of commandment," Olympius for "having spent more effort in fleeing office than others have in attaining it," and Julian's uncle Julian, by then *comes* of the Orient, for finding joy in the leisure of his sword: Lib. *Epp.* 195, 70, 1261.4, and 1257, 350, 336 (*Libanii opera,* ed. Foerster).

61. Rousseau, *Basil,* 27–60; McGuckin, *St. Gregory,* 48–83; Rubenson, "Cappadocians," 122–27; Van Dam, *Families,* 156–59; Demont, *Cité,* 14–30; Staden, "Idéal," 156–60.

62. Gr. Naz. *Or.* 2.7: Οὐδὲν γὰρ ἐδόκει μοι τοιοῦτον οἷον μύσαντα τὰς αἰσθήσεις, ἔξω σαρκὸς καὶ κόσμου γενόμενον, εἰς ἑαυτὸν συστραφέντα, μηδενὸς τῶν ἀνθρωπίνων προσαπτόμενον, ὅτι μὴ πᾶσα ἀνάγκη, ἑαυτῷ προσλαλοῦντα καὶ τῷ Θεῷ, ζῆν ὑπὲρ τὰ ὁρώμενα καὶ τὰς θείας ἐμφάσεις ἀεὶ καθαρὰς ἐν ἑαυτῷ φέρειν ἀμιγεῖς τῶν κάτω χαρακτήρων καὶ πλανωμένων, ὄντως ἔσοπτρον ἀκηλίδωτον Θεοῦ καὶ τῶν θείων καὶ ὂν καὶ ἀεὶ γινόμενον, φωτὶ προσλαμβάνοντα φῶς καὶ ἀμαυροτέρῳ τρανότερον.

Uneducated Philosophers

Mounting his attack, Gregory now announced the second reason for his flight: the sight of others who rushed to the altars and hastily assumed office without suitable preparation. To witness persons who were "in no way superior to common people" approach the holy and perform sacrifices with "unwashed hands,"[63] crowding the sacred table like animals looking for feed, filled Gregory with deep shame. Such were their numbers, rushing to the altar only because it provided a living and permitted them to exercise power without control, that "with time and the progress of evil" there would soon be no one to lord it over, for no one wanted to be taught by God any more, but everyone wanted to teach and to prophesy. "To halt all this is beyond our capabilities, but it is not an insignificant aspect of our piety [*eusebeia*] to detest it and to be ashamed" (*Or.* 2.8). Indeed, the sight of such persons and their behavior had prompted Gregory to flee. To bring this to a stop insofar as he could was a principal reason for his return.[64]

First, there were those who resisted Gregory the Elder "like thieves who steal flocks of sheep and disperse them in the mountains" (*Or.* 1.7). But Gregory may have had a broader constituency in mind. In the passage I have just cited, *Oration* 2.7, Gregory used the vocabulary of the anti-Cynic discourses (*Peri Kynismou*) that Julian had also employed in his criticism of the uneducated Cynics. Such Cynics pretended to live the philosophical life but lacked the necessary training and preparation. They took shortcuts, like those Gregory accused of rushing to the altar with unwashed hands. Indeed, Gregory deplores that "there are no codes [*kanōn*] of aptitude.... [We think ourselves philosophers] if we know how to drape ourselves well in our cloak [*tribōn*], if we have become philosophers just to the level of our belts" (*Or.* 2.49). And these uneducated persons rushing to the altar added further insult to injury by criticizing the true philosophical life as being mere "vanity" (*kenodoxia*)—the classic anti-Cynic slur—as if Gregory, and not any of them, was an uneducated Cynic.[65]

Gregory had returned and had composed this oration to set out such codes of aptitude. In addition to criticizing certain persons (whom I will identify more

---

63. Hom. *Il.* 6.266; Hesiod, *Works and Days* 725.

64. McGuckin, *St. Gregory*, 106–7, interprets this and similar passages as insertions Gregory made while revising his orations in the 380s, after he had retired from the see of Constantinople, forced out by some of his colleagues. Indeed, Gregory in the 380s carried grudges, but he had worthy opponents already in 362/3.

65. Cynics were criticized for κενοδοξία and τῦφος because of Diogenes' self-inflicted death by eating raw octopus, which had given rise to debates over whether or not this was a dramatically performed public suicide or merely an experiment gone wrong, as Julian argued when stressing that Diogenes wanted to investigate why we cook meat; Billerbeck, "Ideal Cynic," 219.

specifically in the chapters that follow), Gregory defined the prerequisites for all who currently led or wished to lead Christians; whoever did not correspond with the exemplar that he delineated for the leader and true philosopher ought not to be permitted to approach the altar and lead others to God. Otherwise, in their complete ignorance of the magnitude of the task they assumed so frivolously, they would be persons for whom "to guide a flock of sheep or herd of cattle is the same as to govern the souls of men" (*Or.* 2.9).[66] Evoking the bucolic imagery of Alexandrian poetry rather than scriptural language, Gregory noted that a shepherd or cowherd need only ensure that his sheep and cattle are fed and protected; once in shady pastures, the shepherd may safely rest "on beautiful grass, besides cool waters," playing his flute and every once in a while singing a love song.[67]

Gregory's recognition that to guide men is an entirely different affair was the third reason for his flight. "It is difficult for a man to know how to obey, but . . . it may be much more difficult to know how to command men, most of all [when assuming] a position of command like ours, which is based on God's law and guides [others] toward God"—so Gregory paraphrases Aristotle's *Politics* 1.5.2.[68] The enormous danger posed by the exalted responsibility to guide men to virtue and the divine preoccupied Gregory most: "The magnitude and importance of this [command] are as great as are its dangers, at least for him who can discern them" (*Or.* 2.10). Gregory devoted the remainder of his long oration to the fear of the responsibilities inherent in the office to which God had called him and to the danger of failing to administer that office according to God's commandments.[69] The extraordinary responsibility required the extended and lengthy preparation that Gregory now delineated. Thus, Gregory's desire for philosophical retreat, combined with his recognition of the magnitude of the office and shame at the sight of uneducated and unprepared pretenders, had propelled him both to flee and to return to his office: his actions thus exemplified the very core of the Platonic topos of the refusal of office that so ideally defined the philosopher as leader.

---

66. Pl. *Ap.* 20a-b.
67. Ruether, *Gregory*, 97-98.
68. Gr. Naz. *Or.* 2.10: Ἀνθρώπῳ δὲ χαλεποῦ ὄντος τοῦ εἰδέναι ἄρχεσθαι, κινδυνεύει πολλῷ χαλεπώτερον εἶναι τὸ εἰδέναι ἄρξειν ἀνθρώπων, καὶ μάλιστα δὴ ἀρχὴν ταύτην τήν ἡμετέραν, τὴν ἐν νόμῳ θείῳ καὶ πρὸς Θεὸν ἄγουσαν.
69. The structure of *Or.* 2 is as follows: chapters 11-116 detail the abilities and virtues of the ideal leader, with particular emphasis on the philosopher as physician of the soul (chapters 14-56); chapters 36-44 and 78-93 address the ideal leader's grasp of the Trinity and its commandments (44-68 is a *synkrisis* with biblical exemplars like Paul, providing touchstones to identify right and wrong leaders); in 11-13 and 69-86 Gregory attacks his opponents and underscores his qualifications, especially considering the current "war from the outside" (87-102). He then returns to why he had to accept the office, including his duty to serve those at Nazianzus and his father (94-102 and 103-17).

THE CODES OF APTITUDE

To be a leader, according to Gregory, was a supremely difficult task, requiring natural aptitude, but for which such aptitude alone was insufficient: How much nature, how much nurture was required?[70] In Gregory's view, natural aptitude was essential, because the vast majority of men are drawn to the bad like moths to the flame but have to fight hard to attain the Good. They would rather practice even the smallest vice to perfection than attain a fraction of any virtue (*Or.* 2.11–14). Those who wish "to form others to virtue"[71] must have sufficient strength of character to begin with but must then undertake the arduous task of purifying themselves thoroughly: "One cannot cure others if one is covered in sores" (*Or.* 2.13)—physician, heal thyself.[72] To be oneself without vice, however, is but the first step. He who wishes to lead must not only "eradicate the bad imprints from his soul, but must then inscribe the better ones, so that he may surpass all others as much in virtue as in rank" (*Or.* 2.14).[73]

Vain display, self-aggrandizement, and self-enrichment were among the cardinal sins of those who rushed to the altar unprepared, pretending to be philosophers "just to the level of [their] belts." To be accused of kinship with such persons was abhorrent to Gregory. He aimed to provide his audience with "touchstones," to cite Themistius's term, to help them differentiate between the true and the false philosopher, so that all may be guided by those who have mastered "the art of arts and the science of sciences:[74] to lead the human being, the most versatile [*polytropōtatos*, "most tacked"] and most changeable [*poikilōtatos*, "most spotted"] of animals" (*Or.* 2.16; *Od.* 1.1). Such leaders are "legitimate and enduring, because [their rule] is secured by the chain of good will [*eunoia*]" and by free choice (*prohairesis*), whereas bad leaders, because they rule by inciting fear and exercising tyranny, cannot last (*Or.* 2.15).

The Philosopher as Physician of the Soul

Two foundational elements emerge at this stage in Gregory's concept of true Christian leadership. First, philosophers must engage actively in the life of the commu-

---

70. For Julian, the contrast had been between dynastic legitimacy (nature) versus philosophical purity as legitimacy (nurture).

71. Gr. Naz. *Or.* 2.14: τοὺς ἄλλους παιδεύειν πρὸς ἀρετήν.

72. Eurip. fr. 1086; Plu. *Quomodo adulator* (*Moralia* 1); Bernardi, ed. and trans., *Grégoire de Nazianze: Discours 1–3*, 107 n. 3. For philosophers, including emperors (as Julian had also said in his panegyrics for Constantius and in his *Epistle to the Athenians*), qualities achieved through persistent efforts were more valuable than those nature had provided; Kertsch, "Zur unterschiedlichen ethischen Bewertung."

73. Gr. Naz. *Or.* 2.14: οὐδὲ τοὺς φαύλους ἐξαλεῖψαι τῆς ψυχῆς τύπους μόνον, ἀλλὰ καὶ τοὺς ἀμείνους ἐγγράψασθαι. *Phauloi* were evil persons who opposed philosophers, themselves nonplussed when faced with their shenanigans: e.g., Pl. *R.* 489a–500c, *Tht.* 172c–176a, *Ap.* 18b–24c.

74. τέχνη τις εἶναι τεχνῶν καὶ ἐπιστήμη ἐπιστημῶν.

nity for the common good. Their leadership presupposes the ideal of "dual ethics," a phrase coined by Norman H. Baynes, to separate the stringent requirements for those who wished to lead from what was demanded of those being led.[75] As true philosopher, the leader was to embody an ideal life and represent a perfect canon of ethical conduct; those he formed to virtue were not expected to aspire to the same level of perfection. That was not their duty; the perfection of the true philosopher as leader, moreover, would make superfluous, if not outright dangerous, attempts by followers to achieve a similar perfection.[76] Second, kinship between the divine and its creation, including humanity, underlay Gregory's belief that differing ethical requirements for leaders and followers did not preclude salvation for the latter: that is, that they too could approach God as far as possible for human beings. The philosopher's duty to guide those less purified toward the divine in the service of the common good rested on the assumption that the created world was in principle good and benign: the well-ordered cosmos reflected the good will of its divine creator, with whom it was connected in kinship, *oikeiōsis,* or *syngeneia.*

Because it was divinely created and good, the philosopher could be active in the world without complete loss of purity; indeed, the philosopher was called upon to act for the common good. Further, each person in that good order could achieve the virtue proper (*oikeios*) to that person, and hence salvation. To expect too much or too little of each was the hallmark of inadequate leadership. According to Gregory, as leader it was the philosopher's duty to strengthen in everyone what was proper to each and at the same time God's own: the link between the individual and the divine according to each person's ability and measure. "One should not think that the same things are appropriate for all, in the same way that not all men have the same height or the same facial characteristics; nor are all animals of the same nature, all lands of the same quality, or all stars of the same size and splendor" (*Or.* 2.15). The philosopher-as-leader's centrality in strengthening the kinship nexus between, on the one hand, each and every one, and on the other God, accounts for Gregory's vehemence in attacking those false philosophers who acted out of self-interest. "For us, quick comprehension combined with self-love represents the greatest obstacle to virtue" (*Or.* 2.19)—precisely because those engaged in such behavior disregard the altruistic demand embedded in attending to the kinship between others and the divine rather than to the self.

Gregory adapted the analogy between the philosopher and the physician already

---

75. Baynes, "Thought-World," 26.

76. For Sterk, *Renouncing the World,* 75, Basil "encouraged ascetic living for the laity as a whole," and she suggests (p. 123) that the same was true for Gregory because of Basil's influence. Ascetic withdrawal from the world, ideally of all Christians, has become a commonplace when speaking of Eastern Christianity; see Kazhdan and Constable, *People and Power in Byzantium,* 33: "The final aim of *homo Byzantinus* was, in principle, a solitary, eremitical life, free from any form of social relationship."

employed by Plato to express these thoughts in *Oration* 2.16–36 and returned frequently to that analogy in the subsequent chapters. The details he evoked suggest his familiarity with medical literature. Though some writings by Hippocrates and Galen were part of the general educational *cursus,* particularly for those advancing in philosophy, Gregory's knowledge exceeded the norm, possibly because of his brother Caesarius's profession.[77] Gregory used the figure of the philosopher as physician of the soul to impress on his audience that during his time in retreat he had acquired the essential advanced training, that such retreats had to recur to renew his purification and perfect his training in a process never to be completed, and that the art and technique of leading men consisted in knowing each individual, discerning his innermost measure, and adapting one's guidance accordingly. Conversely, a man who led badly had the same adverse effect as a bad physician; each remedy is, after all, also a poison. Finally, only a trained physician ought to attempt to cure himself.

Physicians of the body can diagnose maladies in different people—old, young, weak, strong—often despite their attempts to disguise their true condition. To diagnose an illness, the physician must consider such details as a patient's age, his habits, his lifestyle, and his general disposition. Further, to heal the patient, physicians prescribe a regimen to remove all noxious influences. The patient must follow it, whether she likes it or not. And doctors resort on occasion to cauterization, lancing, and other cruel and painful remedies, all for the patient's good. Nevertheless, most patients follow the prescribed regime willingly or can be coerced into obedience to benefit eventually from even harsh measures; health is an easy concept to comprehend, and as Gregory notes, illness does not lie. Still, to practice medicine correctly requires years of training (*Or.* 2.16–19).

As difficult as it may be for the physician to acquire and practice the medical science, his labors and skills pale in comparison with those required of the philosopher. Whereas physicians treat primarily the material, physical body, which will ultimately perish, the philosopher's medical art cares for the soul (*peri psychēn hē spoudē*), "which originated with God and is divine, partaking of and striving toward the nobility that stems from above, even though [it is] itself bound to what is inferior" (*Or.* 2.17).[78] The philosopher's care affects something of infinitely greater value than the body, on which physicians lavish so much attention. In addition, those entrusted with leading the divinely created soul to the Good and the just face ex-

---

77. Following Plato, Gregory used the analogy for the ethical well-being of the *politeia.* Pl. *Grg.* 463a–465e, 477a–479c; *Cra.* 440c; *Lg.* 646b–d, 728c, 731c–d; *R.* 444c–d, 556e, 564b–c; D. Chr. *Or.* 32.11. For its widespread use, Cordes, *Iatros,* 138–69; and Dörnemann, *Krankheit,* 219–47; McGuckin, *St. Gregory,* 46–47.

78. Gr. Naz. *Or.* 2.21: "I judge the medicine [ἰατρική] that we practice to be more laborious by far than what is exercised upon the body, which gives it a higher virtue."

traordinary resistance in their patients. Their intellectual capacity, pride, and inability to admit ignorance or defeat are among the many obstacles the philosopher as physician must overcome: since the human soul is compelled far more to the bad than the good, the philosopher as physician must engage his patients in a continuing battle against themselves, and their resistance is ferocious (*Or.* 2.19). Man finds numerous disguises to prevent a diagnosis of the maladies affecting his soul, according to Gregory, and most act like sneaky slaves hiding from their masters and bury their errors deep, as if they were infected ulcers, though they know that they cannot hide them from God's penetrating eye. They plug their ears so as not to hear the "remedies," or *pharmaka*, that wisdom offers. Or else—"and this is the case among the more ardent and the better among us—we openly show no shame for our errors in front of those who wish to heal them, marching, as the saying goes, with head uncovered [i.e., without respect][79] toward all kinds of misdeeds.... And we repel those whom we ought to love as benefactors [*hōs euergetas*] as if they were enemies, hating those who accuse us at the city gates and loathing their saintly word" (*Or.* 2.20), an attitude that above all harms the patients or perpetrators.

The philosopher's diagnostic eye must penetrate such barriers, and the physician of the soul must therefore possess extraordinary powers of discernment. His eye must see into the very depth of the human heart through a mesh of dissimulation, and he must compel others even against their will to the Good—not as a tyrant, by force, but through the persuasion of their free will (*Or.* 2.21), because the Good "is not merely sown by nature, but is also cultivated by choice [*prohairesis*] and by the back-and-forth motions of the free will [*autexousios*]" (*Or.* 2.17).[80]

No wonder, then, that the labors of the physician of the soul are so much greater than those of the physician of the body. Yet "physicians of the body endure labors, vigils, and cares that we know, and the suffering of others causes them too a good measure of grief, as one of their wise men says" (*Or.* 2.27).[81] They conduct experiments on their own persons and collect like elements (i.e., practice homeopathy) to assist others better. Even the smallest observation and detail command their attention—all this for persons who may not even lead an honorable life and for a body destined to perish (*Or.* 2.27). How much greater care must the physician of the soul apply? Should he not be conscious of "how to measure the science [*epistēmē*] necessary to cure and to be cured, to change life radically, to restore to the soul [those parts] that belongs to the dust?" After all, "desires and impulses" (*hai epithymiai kai hormai*) affect each human being differently, depending on gender, age, intellectual faculties, disposition, whether one is irascible or mild, happy, or melancholy; and

---

79. Pl. *Phdr.* 243b.
80. Gr. Naz. *Or.* 2.30–32.
81. Ps.-Hipp. *De flatibus*, ed. Jones, vol. 2, 226; Bernardi, ed. and trans., *Grégoire de Nazianze: Discours 1–3*, 125 n. 3.

on social conditions such as wealth or poverty, on whether one leads or obeys, lives in the city or the countryside, is married or not; "and among the latter, whether one lives in *erēmia* or in communities and mixed,⁸² . . . proven and advanced in the theory, or simply moving in the right direction"; or on whether one leads the active life or is in retreat (*hēsychazōn*): all depends on the specifics of "the mixture and the combination of the elements out of which we are constituted" (*Or.* 2.28 and 29).

"As one does not give to all bodies the same medications [*pharmakeia*] and the same nourishment, but to some one kind and to others a different one, depending on whether they are healthy or ill, so too the souls must be healed according to different words and methods. The patients themselves bear witness to the cure: the word [*logos*] guides some; others are led by example [*paradeigma*]; some require incentives; others, restraints" (*Or.* 2.30). The philosopher as leader heals and guides the souls in his care by virtuously dispensing the right word at the right time, appropriate to each in his audience and adapted to the opportune moment, to achieve the ultimate goal: man's affiliation with the divine, or *oikeiōsis pros theon*.

> The zeal of the soul—which originated with God and is divine, partaking of and striving toward the nobility that stems from above, even though [it is] itself bound to what is inferior—exists (as far as I myself and those who are in agreement with me are able to recognize) for two reasons (aside perhaps from other reasons that God, who has bound [all] together, alone knows of, and whoever has received instruction from God in such mysteries). One is that the soul may inherit its share of the glory above through contest and struggle with the things below, having been tested by this life as gold by fire, and receive the things hoped for as a prize for virtue and not just as a gift of God—and this is indeed [a mark] of extreme goodness, to make what is good our own, as something not merely sown by nature but also cultivated by choice and . . . free will. The other reason is that it may pull to itself what is worse [i.e., the physical body] and install it above little by little, releasing it of its [material] thickness, so that the soul may become for the body what God is for the soul, so that it may educate the subservient [bodily] matter through her agency and affiliate it to God as her fellow slave.⁸³

---

82. Gr. Naz. *Or.* 2.29: τῶν τῆς ἐρημίας πρὸς τοὺς κοινωνικοὺς καὶ μιγάδας.
83. Gr. Naz. *Or.* 2.17: Τῇ δὲ περὶ ψυχὴν ἡ σπουδή, τὴν ἐκ Θεοῦ καὶ θείαν καὶ τῆς ἄνωθεν εὐγενείας μετέχουσαν καὶ πρὸς ἐκείνην ἐπειγομένην, εἰ καὶ τῷ χείρονι συνεδέθη—τάχα μὲν καὶ δι' ἄλλας αἰτίας ἃς μόνος οἶδεν ὁ συνδήσας Θεὸς καὶ εἴ τις ἐκ Θεοῦ τὰ τοιαῦτα ἐσοφίσθη μυστήρια, ὅσον δ' οὖν ἐμὲ γινώσκειν καὶ τοὺς κατ' ἐμὲ δυοῖν ἕνεκεν· ἑνὸς μέν, ἵνα δι' ἀγῶνος καὶ πάλης τῆς πρὸς τὰ κάτω τῆς ἄνω δόξης κληρονομήσειεν ὥσπερ χρυσὸς πυρὶ τοῖς τῇδε βασανισθεῖσα, καὶ ἀρετῆς ἆθλον, ἀλλὰ μὴ Θεοῦ δῶρον μόνον, ἔχῃ τὰ ἐλπιζόμενα, καὶ τοῦτο δὲ ἦν ἄρα τῆς ἄκρας ἀγαθότητος, ποιῆσαι τὸ ἀγαθὸν καὶ ἡμέτερον, οὐ φύσει μόνον κατασπειρόμενον, ἀλλὰ καὶ προαιρέσει γεωργούμενον καὶ τοῖς ἐπ' ἄμφω τοῦ αὐτεξουσίου κινήμασιν· ἑτέρου δὲ ὡς ἂν καὶ τὸ χεῖρον ἑλκύσειε πρὸς ἑαυτὴν καὶ ἄνω θείη λύσασα κατὰ μικρὸν τῆς παχύτητος, ἵν' ὅπερ ἐστὶ Θεὸς ψυχῇ, τοῦτο ψυχὴ σώματι γένηται παιδαγωγήσασα δι' ἑαυτῆς τὴν ὑπηρέτιν ὕλην καὶ οἰκειώσασα Θεῷ τὸ ὁμόδουλον.

Before addressing further Gregory's summary of the art of persuasion—the well-honed technique of finding the right words to cure each soul of its false beliefs and imprint it with the right ones (*Or.* 2.31–33)—and its purpose, *oikeiōsis pros theon*, I want to discuss briefly some aspects of the classic matrix underlying the concepts I have just presented. Gregory's delineation of the qualities of a true leader proceeded along the well-laid paths of Platonic and Aristotelian models, which were also important for Origen's emphasis on the analogy between Christ and the physician.[84] Plato had emphasized the philosopher's duty to act as if he were a physician in charge of the ethical well-being of the *politeia*.[85] Like physicians, those who lead and legislate must sometimes adopt harsh measures and punish the community for its own good, even though the uninitiated may not always comprehend such measures. For Plato too, however, persuasion rather than force is preferable in all cases, since free will best guarantees compliance and obedience.[86] Aristotle likewise used the analogy between the philosopher and the physician, in particular in his *Nicomachean Ethics*, where he argued that a philosopher's *erga*, or works, include not only the practice of a life formed by high ethical principles but the practice of medicine as well, because ethics are the medicine of the soul whereas the medical art heals the body, and both must be healthy for the individual and the community to prosper. The philosopher facing ethical shortcomings, like the physician facing illness, considers not whether to heal but how best to do so. For Aristotle, further, the training of those who wished to lead and form others ethically required the same scientific rigor as that of the physician.[87] The physicians discussed here belonged to the social elites; men such as Caesarius (or Galen) are the real-life examples Gregory (and his precursors) had in mind.[88]

---

84. The notion of Christ as physician is in scripture but was developed fully by Origen; Fernández, *Cristo médico*, 75–175, 179–215. H. Lutterbach, "*Christus medicus*," esp. 241–45. Wells, *Greek Language of Healing*, 120–78, 219–29, notes the confluence of Asclepius and Christ; Mathews, *Clash of Gods*, 70–78.

85. Pl. *Grg.* 463a–465e, 477a–479c; *Cra.* 440c; *Lg.* 646b–d, 728c, 731c–d; *R.* 444c–d, 556e, 564b–c; and then D. Chr. *Or.* 32.11. While a rhetor serves the community like a cook his master, the philosopher's responsibility is that of the physician; Plato's physicians were freeborn; Fernández, *Cristo médico*, 18–21; Jouanna, "Médecin"; Berg, *Metaphor*, 19–20; Wehrli, "Arztvergleich."

86. Pl. *Grg.* 478, *Lg.* 720d–e, 862, *Prt.* 324; Allen, *World of Prometheus*, 77–86.

87. Arist. *EN* 1104a14–27, 1104b19, 1105b5–18, 1112b11–15. Kenny, *Aristotle*, 97–98; Cordes, *Iatros*, 170–84; Fiedler, *Analogiemodelle*, 1–7, 21–46, 180–229, 251–59.

88. For most of Gregory's intellectual precursors, especially of the Second Sophistic, philosophy and medicine were nearly equivalent. But whereas a philosopher need not have been a physician, no physician could excel without being also a philosopher, trained both in theoretical knowledge and in its practical application. For Plutarch, "medicine and philosophy are indeed one, since both are concerned with human happiness, health, and a proper regimen in daily life": *Advice about Keeping Well* 122c–e (Plutarch, *Moralia*, ed. and trans. Babbitt, vol. 2, 216–18). For Galen, "clearly, all true physicians must also be philosophers. Philosophy is necessary for all physicians, regarding both preliminary learning

Words as Pharmakeia

The philosopher's *pharmakeia*, the remedies he employed to cure the souls of those in his care, were words. How did words act? By what means, according to which anthropological ideas were words considered therapy, effective agents of change and transformation? In late antiquity, Stoic and Epicurean teachings, especially those concerning passions and emotions and the means by which they are aroused and modified, elaborated on the Platonic and Aristotelian analogy between physician and philosopher as physician of the soul.[89] Passions and emotions were understood as natural elements of those parts of the soul under the control of reason (*logos*). As natural parts of the soul, emotions aided the soul's rational faculty insofar as they too were considered to have cognitive functions.[90] As a consequence, any disorder of these emotions caused errors in judgment or belief (*doxa*). This—according to the Stoics—called for their eradication or at least rigorous control, because in Galen's interpretation, the Stoic Zeno considered ignorance (*agnoia*) the cause of passions, and passions the maladies of the soul. Passions therefore had to be eradicated or strictly modified, because they counteracted nature, itself the equivalent of reason and knowledge.[91] Disorders of the emotions or an imbalance between emotions, passions, and desires could have a number of causes. Theories posing an intrinsic unity of the cosmos placed the human being too on a continuum between the inner and the outer man, between mind, soul, and the surrounding world: the boundaries separating the inner man, or the soul, from the external or physical man were porous, so that external stimuli could imprint themselves, if unchecked, directly on the soul.[92]

In anthropology, such concepts of an essential unity between inner and outer were reflected, for example, in the medical discovery of passageways, or *poroi,* which

---

and all subsequent training": *On Examinations by Which the Best Physicians Are Recognized* 5.5, 9.3 (ed. and trans. Iskandar, 71, 103); Staden, "Character and Competence"; Deichgräber, *Medicus gratiosus,* 13–22, 52–83, 105–7.

89. The discussion that follows expands the frame of reference in which to read Gregory's remarks; it is not intended as an overview of the evolution of philosophy and anthropology from Plato to Gregory. Recent works emphasize the centrality of emotions in ancient Greek philosophy: e.g., Nussbaum, *Therapy of Desire* and *Upheavals of Thought,* also "Therapeutic Arguments"; Sorabji, *Emotion and Peace of Mind;* and the exchange between Sorabji, Nussbaum, and Bernard Williams in Sorabji, ed., *Aristotle and After,* 197–213.

90. In Martha Nussbaum's words (*Therapy of Desire,* 369): "They embody ways of interpreting the world. The feelings that go with the experience of emotion . . . rest upon beliefs or judgments that are their basis." Cooper, *Reason,* 406–23.

91. Galen, *De placitis Hipp. et Platonis* 4.1.4 (*On the Doctrines of Hippocrates and Plato,* ed. and trans. De Lacy). D.L. *Lives* 7.110 (*SVF,* vol. 1, fr. 205). Rabel, "Diseases of the Soul"; Siegel, *Galen,* 138–51.

92. Plato's *Timaeus* constructs the cosmos as a single living thing (69c) and a single living God (92c); Arist. *On the Soul* 473b. D. B. Martin, *Corinthian Body,* 9–17.

(according to some authors of the Hippocratic Corpus and to Galen)[93] permitted ether, the immaterial, celestial substance out of which soul and mind were formed; air, or *pneuma,* understood as tangible, life-sustaining substance; and blood to circulate continuously.[94] These passageways connected cosmic substances such as ether and the human soul and mind with the physical body and the world around it. Consequently, the conditions of that world, but also the thought processes of the mind and the state of the soul, continually affected each other, so that physicians in their diagnosis always had to be cognizant—in Gregory's words that evoke the classic Hippocratic treatise—of "the places, the circumstances, the age, the seasons, and all aspects of that nature" (*Or.* 2.18).[95]

The concept noted in some of the citations of Gregory above (e.g., *Or.* 2.17), that the soul was a mixture of elements constituting the heavenly sphere (ether and fiery air, or *pneuma*) and those constitutive of (thick) matter (water and earth, which also formed the human body), underlay the notion that external, physical factors could tangibly affect both mind (reason, *logos*) and soul. Water and earth were imagined to be present or mixed in with the soul and mind in a form so light as to be virtually incorporeal.[96] These incorporeal material elements nonetheless rendered the soul so dense that it occupied space and so tangible that forces could leave their imprints on it. These forces originated from either the surrounding external matter or the soul's governing principle, namely reason (*logos*), which originated with the divine or God—two force fields that pulled the soul in opposing directions.[97]

If the logical part governing the soul was too weak to provide an effective shield, external stimuli could easily imprint their representations (*phantasiai*) directly onto the soul. Such imprints then emitted desires and impulses, or *hormai,* that coun-

---

93. Empedocles established the notion of πόροι, channels and passageways linking the inner with the outer. See Hp. *Humors*, 13–16, on the effects of bad weather and diseases; Plutarch, *Advice About Keeping Well* 129a–b (*Moralia,* ed. and trans. Babbitt, vol. 2, 250–52); Longrigg, *Greek Rational Medicine,* 46.

94. Teachings on *pneuma* are central to the Hippocratics, Galen, and Aristotelian and Stoic concepts of cognition and perception. *Pneuma* is life-sustaining air but also a fragile substance easily impacted by pain, stress, and excessive movement; Siegel, *Galen,* 151–64; Staden, "Stoic Theory," 97–105. Gottschalk, "Aristotelian Philosophy," 1167–72.

95. *Hippocrate: Airs, Eaux, Lieux,* ed. and trans. Jouanna.

96. Aristotle concluded that "all [philosophers] distinguish the soul by three of its attributes, movement, perception, and incorporeality": *On the Soul* 1.2.405b. For him, the soul was the form to the body's content or matter, and he described it as composed of very light parts, ibid. 1.5.409b20; Galen, *On the Elements According to Hippocrates,* ed. and trans. De Lacy.

97. E.g., Hierocles *El. Eth.* 4.38–48. According to D.L. *Lives* 7.134, the Stoics taught that two principles guide the universe, "the one that acts and the one that is acted upon." "The one that is acted upon is unqualified substance (that is, matter [ὕλη]); the one that acts is the reason [*logos*] within it (that is, god)." Stoic notions of matter and soul are elaborations of Aristotelian concepts, all of which are difficult to understand in a post-Cartesian frame of reference, since translations such as "matter," "soul," and "body" today imply separations that were unknown before Descartes.

teracted the positive actions of the *logos* and caused maladies of the soul, or passions, upsetting its harmony.[98] Conversely, the balancing and harmonizing faculty of the *logos* could prevent such disorders and indeed cure them when they occurred by literally overwriting the negative or disturbing imprints with positive ones. The therapeutic faculty of the *logos* was, of course, nothing other than the word.[99]

Thus, a philosopher's principal work as physician of the soul was to use the therapeutic power of words to aid the *logos,* word or reason, in maintaining a harmonious balance of the soul: that is, to cure it of the maladies resulting from a disturbed affect caused by ignorance and falsehoods. Philosophers must remove the imprints of erroneous words or teachings and overwrite them and the beliefs they express with good ones. Further, they must impose a daily regimen that minimizes exposure to physical impulses able to leave disturbing imprints leading to wrong opinions.

A philosopher could apply such a therapy effectively only if he himself had put his own passions and emotions in order and had achieved a sound balance in his own mental faculty, a state also known as temperance, *sōphrosynē*. To have achieved *sōphrosynē* was crucial, because the philosopher as physician of the soul collaborated with the divine force active in humans: he cared for the soul, which originated with God. In Gregory's words: "We, since we are seated above the others, are the servants and collaborators of this [divinely originated] cure, we who have already so much to do to recognize and cure our own passions and shortcomings" (*Or.* 2.26). Because the philosopher's words aided the soul's *logos*, or reason, they also guided that soul to the one from whom it had originated: *oikeiōsis pros theon*.

To lead souls toward the divine is supremely difficult. Each requires the appropriate healing word, measured precisely (*akribōs*), and any false word is immensely deleterious (*Or.* 2.30). Hence Gregory's brief overview of the art of persuasion: some must be praised, others exhorted; some publicly shamed, and others admonished in a private colloquy; but in all cases the philosopher must speak at the opportune moment (*kairos*) so as to avoid damage. Some persons must be observed attentively, even to the level of what we today know as micromanagement; others may respond well to a certain laissez-faire; here it is best to observe while pretending not to see and to listen while pretending not to hear (*Or.* 2.31–32).[100] Most important, no single cure is appropriate to all and sundry; no set words, harsh or mild, are applica-

---

98. Gregory used both terms (e.g.) in *Or.* 2.29, ταῖς ἐπιθυμίαις καὶ ταῖς ὁρμαῖς. Staden, "Stoic Theory," 97–105; Pigeaud, *Maladie*, 355–71; Hadot, *Exercices*, 119–33. Also Erler, "*Philologia medicans*."

99. See *Galen on the Passions and Errors of the Soul*, trans. Harkins. As Fortenbaugh observed (*Aristotle on Emotions*, 16–18), Aristotle conceived emotional response as "intelligent behaviour open to reasoned persuasion" and thus of comparable status to logical demonstration. The scholarly literature on the therapeutic quality of words is vast: e.g., J. Thome, *Psychotherapeutische Aspekte in der Philosophie Platons*; Voelke, *Philosophie comme thérapie*, esp. chaps. 3, 7; Entralgo, *Therapy of the Word*, 32–107, 138–239.

100. Gregory alludes to Aesch. *Agam.* 1623 and to Demosth. *C. Aristog.* 1.89.

ble always and to all persons. Nor may physicians of body and of soul depend on their comprehension of the science alone; even to reach the summit of that science would be insufficient. No single treatise or *logos,* and no series of *kephalaia,* or short summary prescriptions, expresses this therapy succinctly—the philosopher's and physician's experience, combined with the facts, brings all these elements to light and permits diagnosis and cure (*Or.* 2.33).

Hence Gregory's discursive style—shared by Julian and most of their learned contemporaries—for which both Julian and Gregory are chided by modern scholars intent on finding a systematic development: a style where "la struttura dell'orazione non è facile a delinearsi a causa . . . [dell']intreccio di molteplici temi e da un costante andirivieni su argomenti già trattati o comunque precedentemente accennati. Faceva parte della precettistica antica il non precipitare la narrazione perché l'animo umano ha bisogno di gradualità nel recepire." As Gregory said, "I repeat the same words often, because I mistrust [our] weak, material thought processes" (*Or.* 20.10).[101]

Thus to dispense the right word at the right moment (*kairos*) was, for Gregory, a task unsuited to the *phauloi* and those of little *pneuma,* or spirit, the common, uneducated, or unprepared. To dispense the divine and sublime word is like walking "on a wire strung high in the air," where to veer in either direction and to lose one's equilibrium because of evil or ignorance causes extreme danger (*Or.* 2.34).[102] "Therefore one must observe and walk carefully on the truly royal road [*hodōi basilikēi*], without deviating to either the right or left, as the Proverbs say [Prov 4:27]. Such must be [the state of] our passions, such the labors of the good shepherd, called to know the souls of his flock with true understanding and to lead them according to the rule of pastoral art [*logos poimantikēs*], the right and just [art] worthy of our true Shepherd. To dispense the Word [*Logos*] itself, to mention last what is first, I speak of the divine and the sublime [Word], about which today everyone philosophizes;[103] if someone else has the courage to comprehend it with all his intellect [*dianoia*], I admire his quick comprehension or better, his simple-minded foolishness" (*Or.* 2.34–35).

Because it is impossible to dispense the truth about the *Logos,* the Word, without true philosophical formation in the technical sense, Gregory concludes this argument by briefly summarizing his *enkyklia paideia*. To comprehend and then teach the Word requires knowledge of "what philosophy has stated about the cosmic spheres and the one cosmos; about matter [*hylē*], the soul [*psychē*], the intellect [*nous*], and the intellectual [*noeroi*] natures, both better and worse [i.e., one higher

---

101. *Gregorio Nazianzeno: Fuga e Autobiografia,* ed. and trans. Viscanti, 17; Bernardi, ed. and trans., *Grégoire de Nazianze: Discours 1–3,* 34; Webb, *Ekphrasis,* 131–65.

102. Cf. Lucian, *Rhetorum praeceptor* 9.

103. For Bernardi (ed. and trans., *Grégoire de Nazianze: Discours 1–3,* 134 n. 2), this refers to the diffusion of Christianity; I think it is a barb against uneducated persons presuming to philosophize about the *Logos.*

and the other lower]; about the providence [*pronoia*] that unites and governs everything; and about what appears to accord with the whole of reason [*logos*], and what accords with human reason here below" (*Or.* 2.35). Gregory's synopsis differs little from the standard curriculum of philosophical instruction, prescribed, for example, by Julian in his *Oration 6, Against the Uneducated Cynics*.[104] Like Julian, Gregory availed himself of the topos of modesty appropriate to true philosophers: neither had reached the summit of his philosophical preparation; neither was as yet a true philosopher, truly purified and as close to the divine as humanly possible. As Gregory put it: "I had tasted only a little, remaining in the vestibule [of philosophy], such that my desire [for the beauty of retreat] was only all the more aroused," when the tyranny of necessity had called him away and into action (*Or.* 2.6).

Such professed unpreparedness actually signaled that Gregory (like Julian) was far more prepared than most to guide those in his care to the *telos* of his endeavor. His undertaking was "to give the soul wings, to separate from the world and to give it to God, to preserve what is made in the divine image, to take by the hand what is at risk [in it], to restore what had been rendered, to bring Christ home into the [human] hearts through the Spirit: in sum, to make the God [*theon poiēsai*] of the heavenly bliss also the God of the heavenly order."[105]

Oikeiōsis pros Theon: *To Affiliate Man with God*

To bring Christ home into the human heart, to affiliate man with God—that is the *telos* of Gregory's divine mandate as philosopher and physician of the soul. Julian too saw man's assimilation to the divine to the greatest degree possible as his principal *ergon*. As he stated in his oration *Against the Uneducated Cynics*, the philoso-

---

104. D. O'Meara, *Platonopolis*, 50–65. To recall, philosophy consisted of three parts, natural philosophy (φυσικόν), moral philosophy (i.e., ethics, ἠθικόν), and logic (λογικόν). These divisions had then been integrated as theoretical (i.e., natural philosophy), practical (ethics), and dialectical learning (logic: θεωρητική, πρακτική, διαλεκτική). They were all preparation for the highest level of philosophy, the summit of *theōrētikē*, theology; Jul. *Or.* 7.215c–216a.

105. The full text is *Or.* 2.22: Τῇ δὲ τὸ προκείμενον πτερῶσαι ψυχήν, ἁρπάσαι κόσμου καὶ δοῦναι Θεῷ καὶ τὸ κατ' εἰκόνα ἢ μένον τηρῆσαι ἢ κινδυνεῦον χειραγωγῆσαι ἢ διαρρυὲν ἀνασώσασθαι, εἰσοικίσαι τε τὸν Χριστὸν ἐν ταῖς καρδίαις διὰ τοῦ Πνεύματος καί, τὸ κεφάλαιον, Θεὸν ποιῆσαι καὶ τῆς ἄνω μακαριότητος τὸν τῆς ἄνω συντάξεως; Pl. *Phdr.* 246b; Greg. Mag. *Regulae pastor.* 1.1. Bernardi (ed. and trans., *Grégoire de Nazianze: Discours 1–3*, 120 n.1) reads the last line as a baptismal formula implying renunciation of Satan and adhesion to Christ, which would be Gregory's only allusion to a priest's sacramental role in *Or.* 2, except for the remark about persons approaching the altar with unwashed hands; Ysebaert, *Greek Baptismal Terminology*, has no baptismal formula that would correspond to this passage. Though grammatically difficult, Gregory uses the construct elsewhere. Bernardi translates *poiēsai* twice to achieve his sense, but the text works as it stands. The emphatic word order alludes to *theopoiein*, the issue at hand; see also the discussion of *theon poiein* above in Chapter 3. For the meanings associated with ποιεῖν and ποίησις in Plotinus, particularly regarding divine activities such as creation, Špidlík, *Grégoire*, 51–53; and Delatte et al., *Index*, 157–58, 174; Festugière, *Révélation* vol. 2, 51–61; Folliet, "'Deificari in otio.'"

pher's Know Thyself encapsulated the surest route to this highest of human goals—this maxim and the teachings and rituals of the divinely sent *paradoxa* of myth properly understood. For Julian, too, philosophical labor consisted of two parts: first, to achieve a purity that would permit true comprehension of the divine signs and greatest assimilation with the divine; and second, to impart the saving powers attained through purification and assimilation to others, who were not philosophers and could therefore not be expected to achieve their purity. For both Gregory and Julian, even the philosophers' purity (and closeness to the divine), which permitted them to act as mediators, was one of degrees: those of a lesser degree of purity could still be saved, but according to the "dual ethics" discussed above, they needed the help and guidance of the true philosopher as leader. Despite the fundamentally similar concepts of Julian and Gregory on divinization, however, the two men sought to achieve their respective aims by significantly different means—leaving aside that they differed in their understanding of the divine to which they sought to ascend.

Deification or divinization was a staple of Eastern Christianity that scholars have identified as a "recognizable conflation of two views, the biblical and the Platonic."[106] The term commonly associated with this phenomenon is *theōsis*, recognized only recently as a neologism consciously created by none other than Gregory himself, in his *Oration 4, Against Julian*.[107] The idea of deification, of making humans divine in a Christian context, sits uneasily with many scholars and may have been controversial in Gregory's time, as Donald Winslow indicates when remarking that "Gregory himself was well aware that the constant use he made of the doctrine of 'deification' . . . must have been somewhat startling to his congregation."[108] Leaving the putative reaction of Gregory's audience aside, scholars find it startling that Gregory could have intended this as "the reassertion of any divine element within created nature" rather than solely as "a gift of God the creator," according to John McGuckin, who nevertheless notes the presence of a language of kinship with the divine nature. Norman Russell solves this conundrum by proposing that Gregory must have intended deifi-

---

106. Maslov, "*Oikeiosis*," forthcoming. The quotation (Winslow, *Dynamics of Salvation*, 173) refers to Gregory. Winslow's discussion of Gregory (pp. 171–99) remains foundational; his argument that Gregory merged Plato and scripture is accepted by N. Russell, *Doctrine of Deification*, 224–25, with the vocabulary of deification at pp. 121–54, 333–44. Wittung, "Resources on *Theosis*," has an extensive bibliography. Moreschini, *Filosofia*, 33–36, engages Gregory's vocabulary; Tollefsen, "*Theosis*," discusses the biblical precedents of the Platonic concept he sees in Gregory, who never quotes 2 Peter 1:4, the one New Testament passage alluding to divinization; Ps 82:6 is the second scriptural passage. Merki, *ΟΜΟΙΩΣΙΣ ΘΕΩΙ*, focuses only on Gregory of Nyssa, but his work is foundational. Molac, *Douleur*, 31–78, 104–61, discusses Gregory's concept of man as God's *eikōn*, of which he considered *theōsis* a part. Gr. Naz. *Or*. 4 plays no role in these discussions other than for the two occurrences of the term *theōsis*.

107. Winslow, *Dynamics of Salvation*, 179, on Gregory's neologism; N. Russell, *Doctrine of Deification*, 213–25, notes Gregory's distinctiveness but flattens his impact by labeling it "the Cappadocian thought." Thus, he misses Gregory's impact on Maximus the Confessor, 233–37.

108. Winslow, *Dynamics of Salvation*, 180.

cation as a metaphor only, because he cannot have meant to imply that a creature can "become God in the proper sense of the word."[109] In other words, the idea that startles scholars is that Gregory could have applied the notion of deification to individual persons (rather than to humanity as a whole, deified through Christ's incarnation), because that idea comes perilously close to pagan notions such as *apotheōsis,* and the theurgic operations that "make god" (*theon poiein*) present in the souls of men propagated by persons such as Julian, the emperor and theurgist.[110]

Such scholarly hesitations are well founded if the conflation, as posited, occurred indeed between Platonism and the Bible. Gregory, however—in contrast to Julian in the oration *Against the Uneducated Cynics*—never used the phrase *homoiōsis theōi,* commonly associated with the Platonic concept of assimilation to the divine. Instead, in *Oration* 2 he speaks exclusively of *oikeiōsis pros theon;* note that *theōsis* is a conceptual continuation of his understanding of *oikeiōsis pros theon,* and neither concept is prima facie Platonic.[111] That *oikeiōsis* is a well-known Stoic concept is significant, as Boris Maslov has stressed in "*Oikeiosis pros theon,*" to understanding Gregory's use of the terminology of deification. The verb *oikeioō,* from which the nearly untranslatable noun derives, means first, "to grow used to," "to treat [someone] as," or "to make [someone] one's own"; second, "to feel endearment for"; and third, "to assert kinship with [someone]," a semantic range that permitted the term *oikeiōsis* to travel beyond its technical Stoic usage.[112]

In Stoicism, especially as part of Stoic ethics, the term denoted a concept of the self in its relation with the external world; the natural impulse to love oneself that guarantees the individual's well-being was expanded to include the other: you love yourself best if you love others as if they were you. Parental love expresses the concept, but the expansion of that love outward—in widening circles, according to the famous image of the second-century-C.E. Stoic Hierocles, to more and more distant persons, including eventually not only humanity but the entire cosmos—was the principal point. Such a cosmic dimension of the power of self-love is easily explainable.[113] According to Epictetus, all men are brothers because they are Zeus's progeny, so that all humans form one *koinōnia;* both concepts formed part of Julian's

---

109. McGuckin, "Strategic Adaptation," 101–2; N. Russell, *Doctrine of Deification,* 222–23, makes much of Gr. Naz. *Or.* 42.17, the only time Gregory states that a created being cannot become God, which for Russell implies that, for Gregory, following Athanasius, man can become God only by analogy. Beeley, *Gregory,* 277–93, shows no connection between Athanasius and Gregory.

110. N. Russell's appendix (*Doctrine of Deification,* 333–44) demonstrates that Christian writers were at pains to develop a vocabulary that distanced their concepts from such associations.

111. Merki, in his conclusion to *ΟΜΟΙΩΣΙΣ ΘΕΩΙ,* observed that by the fourth century all philosophical schools used that phrase. Indeed, Gregory of Nyssa did so, but not Gregory of Nazianzus.

112. The point is not whether Gregory was conscious of the Stoic history of the term. Kerferd, "Search," 178–79, discusses the meaning and translations of the term. Bees, *Oikeiosislehre,* 248–49. Pohlenz, *Grundfragen,* 1–47, esp. 11, addresses the origins of *oikeiōsis* as foundational for Stoic ethics.

113. Reydams-Schils, *Roman Stoics,* 35–79, 115–34.

arsenal as well. All altruistic acts benefited both the self and the other; to recognize this provides all impulses for ethical behavior—especially since the altruistic act presupposes a choice (*prohairesis*) and results from free will (*autoexousios;* cf. *Or.* 2.17).[114]

Thus, care of the self, in contrast to Platonic notions, denotes not a retreat from the world into oneself but the expansion of the self in a voluntary, altruistic gesture benefiting all others. The demand that a Stoic philosopher prove his worth by engaging fully in life's activities directly challenges the distinction between the contemplative life and practical engagement.[115] Through such participation the Stoic philosopher who attained perfect *oikeiōsis* identified his self with the entire cosmos, including humanity, because he understood that all was justified by divine Reason (*Logos*), itself identical with Nature (*Physis*), which it also governs: hence the philosopher's *apatheia*, or absence of passion—that is, indifference to good and evil—which makes him the perfect mediator between divine Reason and man, and between human beings.[116] *Oikeiōsis*, the individual's linking his self to nature, was also expressed as the philosopher's *sympatheia* with the entire cosmos. This provided the cosmological dimension by which *oikeiōsis* entered the thought world of Platonism, especially in Plotinus, as Gary M. Gurtler has shown. Here the important point is that such a concept presupposes an understanding of the created cosmos, including man and his physical body, as essentially good because divinely created and shared by all.[117] By late antiquity (by way of Plotinus) such views resulted in the (un-Platonic) rehabilitation of the physical world as a well-ordered divine economy, in which all things and persons found their proper place.[118]

Gregory's second oration stood firmly in this tradition, to which Clement and Origen also contributed.[119] For Clement, a sense of intimacy with the divine was essential to *oikeiōsis;* Origen added an emphasis on the agency of God in establishing that intimacy between himself and the believer, and on the Christian's enthusiastic

---

114. Hierocles *apud* Stobaeus 4.671.7–673.11; see also Epict. *Diss.* 1.13.3; A. A. Long, *Hellenistic Philosophy,* 172, glosses the Stoic notion of *oikeiōsis* as follows: "All creatures are so constituted by Nature that they are 'well-disposed towards themselves.' The word translated 'well-disposed' (*oikeios*) is commonly used in Greek to mean 'related/akin/belonging to'; but the Stoics are expressing a technical concept.... *Oikeiōsis* determines an animal's relationship to its environment, but that to which it is primarily well disposed is itself (D.L. *Lives* 7. 85). Its self-awareness is an affective relationship, and all behaviour can be interpreted as an extension or manifestation of the same principle."

115. Epict. *Diss.* 3.1.4–6; Reydams-Schils, *Roman Stoics,* 74; Bees, *Oikeiosislehre,* 248–49, 285.

116. E.g., Chrysippus in D.L. *Lives* 7.87–88; A. A. Long, *Hellenistic Philosophy,* 165; also Reydams-Schils, *Roman Stoics,* 37. In Long's words ("Soul and Body," 37): "There is in Stoicism a great chain of being which tolerates no discontinuity or introduction of principles which operate at one level but not at another. The entire universe is a combination of god and matter, and what applies to the whole applies to any one of its identifiable parts."

117. Gurtler, "Sympathy."

118. Hadot, "Apport," 118–21.

119. Maslov, "*Oikeiosis,*" with full analysis.

embrace of that kinship: Origen, to recall, lived in a time of persecution.[120] In Gregory, that sense of intimacy with the divine remains, voluntarily offered by God and enthusiastically accepted: he too, as his oration *In Praise of the Maccabees* shows (*Or.* 15), considered Julian a persecutor. For him too, then, it is crucial to strengthen this link of kinship in everyone; each Christian person is a member of the body of the church, a single, well-ordered organism affiliated with God. Gregory's philosopher as leader was called to act altruistically on behalf of others, and he accepted that duty voluntarily (a choice enhanced, in a seeming paradox, by Gregory's laments about the tyranny that had forced him into service).

The philosopher as physician of the soul and as leader reinforced the individual soul's affiliation to, or kinship with, the divine, the *Logos,* by adhering to ethical demands that also affected the body: the physician of the soul must prescribe means that heal both, because "the soul is to the body what God is to the soul": the soul must educate the body so that it will become her "fellow slave, affiliated to God" (*Or.* 2.17). *Oikeiōsis* to God affects soul and body both; the link between soul and God is real and not a metaphor, as also are the ethical demands strengthening that link. Again, Gregory shares with others the notion of the physical body as essentially good and worthy of salvation. The idea of the cosmos as good was held widely by Christians and non-Christians alike; Julian expressed it when he stressed that the soul, deified through the purifying rites and the ethical conduct required by the myth of the Great Mother, also healed the body.[121] After all, Julian and Gregory both knew that the well-ordered cosmos and its manifestation, the *oikoumenē* of the Romans, was theirs (to lead); there was no reason to consider it anything but in essence good, even if it needed improvement (something Origen may have been less certain about).

Such were the central tenets of Gregory's definition of the philosopher as physician of the soul, which he continues to elaborate in *Oration* 2. Because as philosopher and physician Gregory had progressed "higher than the multitude in [his] virtue and *oikeiōsis pros theon,*" he now had to become active and show his mettle by

---

120. *Apatheia* as an aspect of *oikeiōsis* was particularly important for Clement *Str.* 4.23.148, 6.9.73; *Q.d.s.* 7, 33.1. Spanneut, *Stoïcisme,* 249–50, 377. For Origen, see, for example, *Cels.* 4.6.

121. In Brown's words (*Body,* 27): "An unaffected symbiosis of body and soul was the aim both of medicine and philosophical exhortation.... The body had its rightful place in the great chain of being that linked man both to the gods and to the beasts." Jul. *Or.* 7.178b–c uses the verb *theoō* for the deified state of the soul (θεωθεῖσαι). Note also that Julian's *Ep.* 61 (Wright 36), the imperial letter excluding Christians from public teaching, declared that right education resulted "in a healthy condition of the mind: that is, one that has understanding and true beliefs," and that those who believed mistakenly in Christianity suffered from a disease of the mind and soul, of which they ought "to be cured, even against their will, as one cures the insane.... For we ought, I think, to teach, but not to punish the demented" (Καίτοι δίκαιον ἦν, ὥσπερ τοὺς φρεντίζοντας, οὕτω καὶ τούτους ἄκοντας ἰᾶσθαι πλὴν ἀλλὰ συγγνώμην ὑπάρχειν ἅπασι τῆς τοιαύτης νόσου. καὶ γάρ, οἶμαι, διδάσκειν, ἀλλ' οὐχὶ κολάζειν χρὴ τοὺς ἀνοήτους).

altruistically taking on the yoke of servitude: to guide others to greater kinship with the divine also, body and soul. His means to do so were his words (*Or.* 2.3 and 91). His most powerful *pharmakon,* the words with the greatest healing effect but also, if misused, the greatest potential to cause infinite harm, were the words that encompassed the Trinity: the *Logos.*

To bring home (*eisoikisai*) Christ in the hearts of men (*Or.* 2.22) "is what the law, our teacher [*ho paidagōgos nomos*], intends for us; this the prophets intend who mediate between the law and Christ; this Christ intends, the fulfillment and the end of the spiritual law;[122] this is the intent of the divine that has emptied, of the flesh taken on. This is the intention of the new mixture [*mixis*], God and man, one thing out of two and both present in one. This is why God has been mixed with the flesh through the soul as mediator and why two separate realities,"[123] the divine and matter, "have been joined, because the soul, acting as intermediary, is affiliated with both," so that everything, because it has only one source, one Father, "strives toward the One."[124] Christ's birth, passion, and resurrection—the Christian myth (*Or.* 2.24–25)—are the means God, our teacher, devised for our "formation . . . and as a healing cure for our weakness."[125] Gregory is the servant of this healing cure: this is the "medicine that we serve, who sit above others, and of which we are fellow workers" (*Or.* 2.26).

Gregory actively administered this medicine on the Day of Resurrection, Easter 363, the traditional day for baptism (*Or.* 1.1 and 2–5), when together with his father, the bishop, he inscribed in the souls and on the foreheads of the newly initiated "not just words that remain in the open, fly through the air, and reach no further than the ear, but words written by the Spirit and engraved by him into tablets of stone, namely of your body, words not just traced onto the surface and thus not easy to erase, . . . words written deeply not with ink but with grace."[126] The purpose of *Oration 2* was to ensure that these words would unfold their transforming and saving power everywhere: Gregory would clarify for all what the words "in the name of the Father, the Son, and the Spirit" really meant.

---

122. ὁ τοῦ πνευματικοῦ νόμου τελειωτὴς καὶ τὸ τέλος.

123. διὰ τοῦτο Θεὸς σαρκὶ διὰ μέσης ψυχῆς ἀνεκράθη. The verb ἀνεκράθη, aorist passive of *anakerannymi*, means "dilute," used mainly for water and wine, which gives the passage a eucharistic tone. For the centrality in Iamblichus, Porphyry, and Plotinus of the soul as mean between two extremes, divine intellect and material (human) body, Iamblichus, *De anima*, ed. Finamore and Dillon, 14–17, 30–31.

124. Gr. Naz. *Or.* 2.23: Χριστός, τοῦτο ἡ κενωθεῖσα θεότης, τοῦτο ἡ προσληφθεῖσα σάρξ, τοῦτο ἡ καινὴ μίξις, Θεὸς καὶ ἄνθρωπος, ἓν ἐξ ἀμφοῖν καὶ δι' ἑνὸς ἀμφότερα.

125. Gr. Naz. *Or.* 2.25: παιδαγωγία τις ἦν περὶ ἡμᾶς τοῦ Θεοῦ καὶ τῆς ἀσθενείας ἰατρεία.

126. Gr. Naz. *Or.* 1.6: καὶ τούτων οὐ τοὺς εἰκῇ καὶ εἰς ἀέρα ῥέοντας καὶ μέχρι τῆς ἀκοῆς ἱσταμένους, ἀλλ' οὓς γράφει τὸ πνεῦμα καὶ πλαξὶν ἐντυποῖ λιθίναις, εἴτουν σαρκίναις . . . ἀλλ' εἰς βάθος ἐνσημαινομένους οὐ μέλανι, ἀλλὰ χάριτι. Gautier, *Retraite*, 307, considers this an allusion to the creed signed by Gregory the Elder. S. Elm, "Inscriptions and Conversions," 14–20.

5

The Most Potent *Pharmakon*

Gregory the Elder and Nazianzus

To comprehend all that [pertains to the Trinity] and to present it in a manner appropriate to the height of the subject requires an exposé well beyond the present circumstances; it indeed requires an entire life. Most important, . . . it requires the intervention of the Spirit. . . . Therefore, we have now addressed the subject in a few words only to demonstrate the difficulty of finding the word that has the power to put everybody on the right track and to illuminate them with the light of knowledge, especially because we are addressing a crowd composed of different people, . . . like an instrument of many chords, each of which must be struck in a different way.

—GREGORY OF NAZIANZUS, ORATION 2.39

In 362 and 363, as Gregory was writing his first three orations, the philosopher's principal duty as physician of the soul—to comprehend the *Logos* as fully as humanly possible, to imprint its healing words on the souls in his care, and to strengthen his own and their kinship (*oikeiōsis*) with God—had assumed particular urgency. The *koinōnia* of those affiliated with God was in deep crisis, indeed engaged in a veritable civil war (*Or.* 2.85). Incapable and insufficiently trained persons had assumed leading positions out of base motives: selfishness, vanity, hunger for money and power. Their words, rather than heal, had poisoned and weakened the body of the church so that it was open to great threat, the "war from the outside" waged by Julian (*Or.* 2.87).

In Gregory's view, the only *pharmakon* that could remedy the dire situation was the correct understanding of "everything one must profess about the Trinity, which rules and is blessed." But because sham philosophers who had shunned the "great effort" required to comprehend the Trinity (*Or.* 2.91) mixed and dispensed this *pharmakon* incorrectly, they destroyed souls and annihilated all hope of salvation (*Or.* 2.36). Hence, it was incumbent on Gregory as true philosopher to provide the touchstones for identifying true and false philosophers and tainted mixtures of the Trinity, and "to give to each at the right moment the right ration of the Word, and to dispense judiciously the truth of our doctrines."[1] As for the true philosopher, Gregory wrote himself as the paradigm. His refusal of office demonstrated his purity and affiliation with the divine, which predestined him to lead others toward God, healing them with the well-chosen words he now pronounced: in his hands (and only his) the mixture of the Trinity would protect, heal, and save.

Though Gregory diagnosed "three theological maladies"—three false mixtures of the Trinity threatening the health of the *politeia,* "atheism and Judaism and polytheism" (*Or.* 2.37)—the false philosophers and other persons he targeted are not easy to identify. Following rhetorical convention, Gregory never named names; thus we must deduce the identity of his opponents from his allusive remarks—much as had been the case with Themistius and his detractors, discussed in Chapter 3. Gregory's remarks indicate and the historical circumstances in the years 362 and 363 suggest he engaged homoiousians and homoians active in Nazianzus and in the empire at large (that is, as far as Gregory was concerned, in Antioch and Constantinople). Two men, Aetius and Eunomius, were already then prominent homoians; the most important person in this chapter, however, will be a prominent homoian (or Arian) at Nazianzus: Gregory the Elder. I turn now to him and to Gregory the Younger's shaping of him, as father and bishop, and of his relation to those at Nazianzus in the second oration.

Though Gregory's understanding of the Trinity—as he formulates and defends it against detractors in *Oration* 2—indicates his intention to enter the tumultuous debates that preoccupied Christian leaders in the East during the early 360s, his first three orations leave no doubt that for him in 363 the situation at Nazianzus was paramount. After all, Gregory had left his father, the bishop, in 362 at a moment of high tension, enmeshed in a full-fledged schism that had not been resolved when he returned at Easter 363. Gregory's *Apology for His Flight* and the presentation of his model of Christian leadership directly concerned Gregory the Elder, and the audience at Nazianzus was, presumably, very interested to hear how Gregory the Younger framed Gregory the Elder's role as father and as bishop.

THE OTHER HIGH-WIRE ACT: FATHERS AND SONS

> *This is what this venerable Abraham here present shows you, the patriarch, this precious and respectable man, this abode of all that is good, this [living] code [kanōn] of virtue, this perfect realization of priesthood, this man who today offers to the Lord his willing sacrifice, his only son, [born] of the promise.*
> —GREGORY OF NAZIANZUS, ORATION 1.7

When Gregory the Younger returned to Nazianzus at Easter 363 to resume his duties after spending nearly a year in retreat with Basil of Caesarea at Annesi, he had

---

1. Gr. Naz. *Or.* 2.35: διδόναι κατὰ καιρὸν ἑκάστῳ τοῦ λόγου τὸ σιτομέτριον καὶ οἰκονομεῖν ἐν κρίσει τὴν ἀλήθειαν τῶν ἡμετέρων δογμάτων. Lk 12:42.

to clarify his relationship to his father and bishop on several points. First, he had to confront his disobedience and explain his flight to Pontus; we have already seen how he tackled these. Second, he had to clarify his stance toward those who openly criticized his father's position on the Trinity: those, that is, who had criticized his signing of the homoian document of 360. Third, he had to clarify his own views on the Trinity, thereby taking a position on the views of his father. Gregory the Younger's interpretation of the Trinity was not identical to that of his father, but as a son he could not side openly with those in opposition; he could not even appear to do so if he did not simultaneously support his father. Gregory as son and presbyter could claim neither authority nor honor if he did not also safeguard, indeed enhance, the authority and honor of his father and bishop. Thus, he had to formulate his views on the Father and the Son so that they were not seen as criticism and did not weaken the link between father and son, while proclaiming the truth as he saw it—at all costs, given the intensity of the present crisis—even if that meant differing with the publicly stated position of his father, the bishop. The challenges facing Gregory were formidable—those, indeed, of a high-wire act.

To begin with Gregory's words in *Oration* 2.36, the greatest dangers to the correct conception of the Trinity were to reduce it to one *hypostasis* for fear of polytheism, "leaving us with mere names" without meaning, because Father, Son, and Spirit become interchangeable; or, equally mistaken, to take the opposite tack, and "to divide the *logos* into three separate *hypostaseis*," "estranged" (*allotrioi*) from one another—the term *allotrios* denotes the polar opposite of *oikeios*—and without hierarchy or order, as if one were dealing with rival divinities. Such beliefs are like bending a plant forcibly in the direction opposite to that into which it grows naturally.[2] In fact, "there are now three theological maladies: atheism and Judaism and polytheism. The Libyan Sabellius has led the first; Arius the Alexandrian, the second; and the third is led by some among us who are too orthodox" (*Or.* 2.37).[3] The response to such aberrations that Gregory advocates is to avoid the excess of each position, "to flee what is noxious," and to remain "within the strict limits set by piety" (*en horois menein tēs eusebeias*). The excess of Sabellius and his followers led them to atheism because their love of the Son made them consider him the same as the

---

2. Gregory returned to this image in *Or.* 6.8, which celebrates the end of the schism, to praise the healing effect of truth: once released from that force, such plants immediately spring back to the form *oikeios*, or proper, to them.

3. Numerous excellent studies discuss Gregory's theology. Most recently, Beeley (*Gregory,* ix) used all of Gregory's work, rather than focusing on the *Theological Orations* and Christological epistles, for his discussion of Gregory's doctrine of the Trinity. Brennecke, *Studien,* 107–14, 134–35; V. H. Drecoll, *Entwicklung,* 17–111; Hanson, *Search,* 639–53, 676–737; Kopecek, *History,* vol. 2, 299–440; Gregory of Nazianzus, *Faith,* intro. Norris, 12–71; Plagnieux, *Saint Grégoire;* Vaggione, *Eunomius,* passim; M. R. Barnes, "Fourth Century"; Beatrice, "The Word 'Homoousios'"; Löhr, "Sense of Tradition"; Zachhuber, "Basil."

Father, a "new analysis and synthesis, which no longer defines the one as all [*hen ta panta*]." That innovation had the consequence of erasing what is essential in each *hypostasis,* "making each being nothing," because (as Gregory continues) a being that changes its essential nature ceases to be what it is—an allusion to Aristotle, according to whom "essence does not admit of degree."[4] To love the Son so much as to make him indistinct from the Father robs him of his distinctiveness as son (and thus reduces all three to one). But one must not "paint and fabricate in one's mind a composite and absurd god similar to those mythic animals" of old,[5] either—an evocative aligning of this new (hence suspect) synthesis and old "mythic animals" (*Or.* 2.36).[6] The followers of the "madness [*mania*] of Arius" in contrast, revert to "the poverty of Judaism." By arguing that only the unbegotten (*agennētos*) Father is fully divine, they deprive both Father and Son, since they seem "afraid that God, by being Father of a true God of equal dignity in his nature [*homotimou tēn physin*], might be lost to us." Yet others, presumably those affected by the third malady, set the three persons or powers of the divinity against one another like rivals and thus reintroduce "the multiple [divine] powers of the Greeks that we have left behind" (*Or.* 2.37)—these were persons, I take it, who gave too much power to each *hypostasis* without respecting the proper internal hierarchy of Father, Son, and Spirit in the one Trinity.

To illustrate, Gregory explains that those he calls (sarcastically) "father-lovers" (*philopatores*) extend their love for the Father so that they deprive him of fatherhood by denying him a true son. "Of whom, in fact, could he be the Father, if the nature of the Son were to be separated from his and linked together with creation (in fact, what is estranged [*allotrios*] cannot be his Son), or if [the Son] were united and absorbed by him, or, what results in the same thing, if [the Father] were to absorb him?" In contrast, to love Christ too much, to be *philochristos,* besides reducing the power of the Father, threatens to deprive the Son of his essence as Son: "Of whom would he in effect be the Son if he would not refer to his Father as his cause [*archē*]—and not grant the Father the dignity of being the cause that is his [due], both as Father and as begetter [*gennētōr*]?" (*Or.* 2.38).

Gregory's definition of the limits of piety yields a few observations even before we address in detail the various positions and the persons representing them that Gregory opposed. Using the names Sabellius and Arius as code,[7] Gregory delin-

---

4. Arist. *Cat.* 5.3.33–37.

5. Where my translation offers "paint," Gregory uses *skiagraphon,* "written in shadows," a classic Platonic term.

6. Pl. *Phdr.* 229c–e considered the chimera and similar mythic animals examples of simple, or wrong, forms of myth; Ginzburg, "Myth," esp. 25–35; Koziol, "Truth"; and Chapter 9 below, "Myth and Allegory."

7. Gregory aligned two of the three theological maladies of his day with historic founding figures, or heresiarchs, the Libyan Sabellius and the Alexandrian Arius. This is reminiscent of Diogenes Laertius's association of philosophical ideas with (mythic) founders of schools, a technique Justin Martyr

eates what he considers extreme positions, as differentiating the three persons (*hypostaseis*, or "gradations," as I translated the term in Julian's writings) either too much or not enough, and failing to respect the proper weight or hierarchical position of each person within the whole, so that either the oneness of the Trinity is weakened, or its individual participants are. By stressing that he will avoid these excesses, Gregory suggests that he will set out a middle course: the "royal road" that deviates neither left nor right (*Or*. 2.34, 3.8). This will not be the equivalent of the easiest path either, a criticism that could be applied to the homoian formulation of 360. As Gregory's own formulation—to align the Son with creation and to separate him from the Father diminishes the Son and denies the Father his true role—indicates, he does not support the homoian move to reduce the relation between Father and Son to the lowest common denominator so as to defend the Father's role.[8] But while this formulation differs from the document his father had signed, we cannot equate that difference with criticism of his father, much less suggest that Gregory will embrace the opposing view. The "royal road," the middle ground that Gregory will present, will be, we may infer, something new and innovative—his own view of the Trinity: "The Father is the cause of the divinity and goodness that is contemplated in the Son and the Spirit, in the one as Son and Word [*Logos*], and in the other as procession and undiluted Spirit. Because of that the God who is one must be preserved and three *hypostaseis* professed, each with its own specific properties."[9]

These words are Gregory's first recorded response to the theological debates dividing the community at Nazianzus as well as the Eastern Christian advisors and bishops, much intensified now that Julian had rearranged the landscape. As true philosopher, Gregory could innovate without jeopardizing the good order of the *koina*. Since he was more closely affiliated with the divine than most, he comprehended the divine better—better even than his father. Though linked to his father in kinship, Gregory's closer kinship with the divine, his *hiera genea* as philosopher,

---

also used. Gregory used these names as labels, or code, to criticize his adversaries rather than teachings promulgated by either Sabellius or Arius. Sabellius, excommunicated by Callistus (217–22) in Rome, stands for teachings privileging the supremacy of the Father, including those of Marcellus of Ancyra and Photinus. Gregory's accusation "Christ-loving" is ironic or sarcastic: these men love the Son to the degree that they assimilate him so much to the Father as to be absorbed by him, so that the Father rules supreme. Le Boulluec, *Notion*, vol. 1, 79–91; Lyman, "Topography," 46, 61–62; S. Elm, "Polemical Use"; Bienert, "Sabellius"; Vinzent, *Pseudo-Athanasius*, 57–88, 135–67; Lyman, "Arians."

8. Gregory continues (*Or*. 2.38): to reduce the divinity of the Son makes the Father either into a small and insignificant first cause or into the cause of small and insignificant things, both unacceptable.

9. Gr. Naz. *Or*. 2.38: θεότητος ὢν ἀρχὴ καὶ ἀγαθότητος, τῆς ἐν Υἱῷ καὶ Πνεύματι θεωρουμένης, τῷ μὲν ὡς Υἱῷ καὶ Λόγῳ, τῷ δὲ ὡς προόδῳ καὶ οὐ διαλύτῳ Πνεύματι· ἐπειδή γε ἀναγκαῖον καὶ τὸν ἕνα Θεὸν τηρεῖν καὶ τὰς τρεῖς ὑποστάσεις ὁμολογεῖν, καὶ ἑκάστην μετὰ τῆς ἰδιότητος. Gr. Naz. *Or*. 20.6 and 31.9 are nearly identical. Athanasius in *Contra Arian*. 1.58 also uses ἰδιότης, arguing for the equal divinity of both Father and Son, based on Jn 14:28.

permitted him to heal and guide even the one who had generated him, without undermining his father's position and honor: Gregory the Elder became the father of a true philosopher, and as such he too was more akin to God than most. Gregory the Elder was—before Gregory came along—the venerable Abraham and the perfect embodiment of true priesthood, and he remained so. More than a successful balancing act, Gregory's *Oration* 2 presented a new model of priesthood without jeopardizing the old and offered a new formulation of the Trinity able to embrace most other formulations: a compromise aimed at consolidation.[10] To appreciate his achievement fully requires that I examine briefly Gregory's relationship with his father and bishop, as seen both in modern scholarship and in their late-antique context.

Father and Son: The Beautiful Tyranny

Gregory described his return to Nazianzus and to his official duties as an ordained member of Gregory the Elder's clergy as a defeat and submission to a "beautiful tyranny" (*Or.* 1.1). The ultimate perpetrator of this tyranny was Gregory's true master, whom he obeyed when accepting his yoke of servitude: God.[11] The community at Nazianzus, his "brothers and friends," also tyrannized him into surrender—he repeats the theme in the opening sentences of all three of his first orations. The crisis of that community had forced him to return and intervene to safeguard all, a process that would take time to complete, as the opening of *Oration* 3 implies: "Why this tardiness when coming to hear my word, friends and brothers, you who have been so quick and prompt to tyrannize me?"[12]

The third master was Gregory the Elder, who had ordained him, though Gregory never explicitly associates him with tyranny in his first three orations. In his later works on his ordination and subsequent flight, Gregory chose his words less carefully than in his first three orations, calling his father's act of ordaining him outright tyranny.[13] "My father was well aware of my thinking; nevertheless he exerted pressure to raise me to the auxiliary throne.... Why he did so I cannot say. Perhaps he was moved by fatherly affection, which when combined with power is a force to be reckoned with. Tyranny of this kind (I cannot find another word for it, and may the Holy Spirit forgive me for feeling this way) so distressed me that I suddenly shook myself free of everyone—friends, parents, fatherland, and kin."[14]

These words, written after his father's death in 374 and under the much-changed circumstances of the 380s, are the basis of most scholarly portrayals of Gregory's

---

10. Beeley, *Gregory*, 218.
11. Gr. Naz. *Ep.* 7, *To Caesarius*, described his new position as priest as τῷ θεῷ ... δουλεύειν.
12. Gr. Naz. *Or.* 1.1.5 and 6, 2.6.15, 3.1, 6.8.
13. Gr. Naz. *DVS* 2.1.11.345; *Or.* 10.5, 18.40, 36.2, 43.59.
14. Gr. Naz. *DVS* 337–49; trans. McGuckin, *St. Gregory*, 21.

father, of Gregory's relation to his father, and of the psychological consequences.[15] These different and nuanced scholarly assessments all attribute what they consider the sensitive character of Gregory the Younger that made public office so burdensome to him to his dependence on a tyrannical albeit beloved father.[16] Such chafing dependence encouraged an overidentification with his mother, Nonna. According to Raymond van Dam, Gregory saw himself "not so much as a junior cleric . . . but as a devoted son" whose "one true love had always been his mother," "constantly torn between his devotion to his father and his resentment at his father's meddling."[17] Such pressures made Gregory, in John McGuckin's words,[18]

> peculiarly vulnerable throughout his life to the demands or expectations of others. His power of introspection and innate sensitivity came at the price of a plasticity of character, insecure anxiety and vacillation, and also an explosive stubbornness that blew over quickly but often left him with troubles in a long following wake. All these things were to mark his mind and his church career decisively.

Leading scholars of Gregory and his writing thus consider his relationship with his father (and consequently also with his mother) essential to understanding his approach to public office and philosophical retreat throughout his life.[19] This chapter, therefore, examines how Gregory expressed and shaped the relation to his father in *Orations* 1–3 and the context of the early 360s. In light of the classic uses of the topoi of retreat and flight when he assumed office, I posited, with Rita Lizzi, that such a *recusatio* denoted Gregory's readiness to accede to office rather than the resentment and revulsion most scholars have seen. The question, then, is what framework other than modern psychology may illuminate Gregory's claim to have subjected himself to a beautiful tyranny (the Greek word *kalos* that Gregory used means "beautiful" but also "noble"), exercised by his father.[20]

A central theme of Gregory's *Oration* 2 is good governance of the *politeia*, "the

---

15. Bernardi, ed. and trans., *Grégoire de Nazianze: Discours 1–3*, 40–43; McGuckin, *St. Gregory*, 100–102; Rousseau, *Basil*, 85–90; Van Dam, *Kingdom*, 137–42, and *Families*, 75–76, 91; Gregory of Nazianzus, *Tutte le orazioni*, ed. Moreschini, xvii–xx; Gautier, *Retraite*, 69–82; and, for a different view, McLynn, "Self-Made Holy Man," 465.

16. McGuckin, *St. Gregory*, 1–34; on p. 8 he notes Gregory "depended on his father more than he cared to admit, and wanted his father's strong and commanding personality to remove all the obstacles from his own life's path, yet he fretted constantly at the imposition of that authority. He wanted to live in a safe dependence, but not in the shadow, and was thus like the eternal dependent; but he could not understand why that relationship exasperated his father so much and at times made the latter determined to interfere in his son's life to the extent of providing him with gainful employment."

17. Van Dam, *Families*, 6, 44–58, 76–78, 87–93; citations on pp. 6, 46, and 93.

18. McGuckin, *St. Gregory*, 34. Note also Rousseau's observation (*Basil*, 236) that Gregory had a remarkably subservient attitude toward his father.

19. This is Van Dam's principal point in *Families*.

20. Bernardi, ed. and trans., *Grégoire de Nazianze: Discours 1–3*, 42, 45.

philosophy ... of leading and governing souls" (*Or.* 2.78). One way of explaining good governance is to define *tyrannis,* its opposite (as in Plato and Aristotle's normative texts: e.g., Arist. *Pol.* 4.8.1–3, 5.9, 2–21, 5.10.1–6; Pl. *R.* 545a–c, 562a–564e). Gregory, as the preceding chapter has shown, did not spare those engaged in bad governance in *Oration* 2, even though he used the actual noun, "tyranny," only once: "A [sound] rule of short duration [is better than] a long tyranny" (*Or.* 2.72). The immediate context yields more. This short reference concludes a long *synkrisis* in which Gregory calls on a series of biblical figures to chastise those who have assumed leadership positions out of base motives and without sufficient—long— preparation. Only true leaders appreciate why such preparation must be so long and is so crucial, because only they grasp the magnitude of the task at hand (*Or.* 2.71)—all others are incredulous and suspicious, asking impatiently, "when will this [preparation] be sufficient?" Gregory responds: "The greatest old age would not be too distant a time: ... better an old age with circumspection than uneducated youth, better a considerate slowness than inconsiderate haste, better a short [sound] rule than a long tyranny" (*Or.* 2.72; cf. 2.15).

Those who rush to leadership without such preparation must be feared and mistrusted (*Or.* 2.73), for such leaders have caused the present state of "disorder and confusion" (which only the lucky can flee): indeed, a "war between the members" of the community, the worst of all fates (*Or.* 2.78). Impudence rules among such persons; they express piety by accusing others of impiety; and they throw the pearls of God's mysterious wisdom into profane ears and souls, thus fulfilling the wishes of "our enemies": priesthood is an empty word. They have reverted the well-ordered cosmos to its primordial chaos, a state of darkness in which we kill our friends, no longer able to distinguish them from our enemies (*Or.* 2.79–81). Haste, vanity, and pride cause disorder, confusion, and, worst of all, civil war (*ho pros allēlous polemos, Or.* 2.85), where all fight each other and all ties of kinship are severed (also *Or.* 2.111, *Or.* 2.44). While Gregory does not oppose those who fight for the right reason—the truth about God (*Or.* 2.82)—he soundly rejects those who transgress the rules of combat and exceed the limits of propriety. They forfeit victory and are dishonored: nothing justifies such conduct (*Or.* 2.85); only he who submits to the "law of obedience"—like Gregory—can serve God well (*Or.* 2.113).

Those who blithely follow "the stranger [*allotrios*] who enters the courtyard like a bandit and a schemer" and listen to him "who steals and disperses the flock and leads it away from the truth, conducting it to the mountains and into the deserts, into the pits, and the places that the Lord does not oversee [*episkopei*]" (*Or.* 1.7), are guilty of such a transgression. They, too, must follow Gregory's example and submit, obeying the good shepherd chosen for them by God, "the venerable Abraham here present." To him, to Gregory the Elder, and to his son as presbyter, they owe the obedience that preserves the divinely instituted good order. "You ought to ... allow yourself to be well shepherded. ... You know your pastor well, and he knows you; follow him when he, as a good shepherd and a free man, calls you" (*Or.* 1.6 and 7). To obey Gregory the Elder as Gregory the Younger obeyed him is to obey God and to preserve the divinely created *eutaxia* of the entire cosmos, including the well-ordered body of the church; to do otherwise is to destroy all. To submit to the tyranny of a good master, who rules by law, is right and just—an exemplary act, reifying good order and virtue, that guarantees lasting well-being and the salvation of all.

In other words, whatever their rationale, those at Nazianzus who violated the rules of the game and followed other leaders, who led them away from Bishop Gregory, leaders ordained by "foreign" or "strange hands" (*chersin allotriais, Or.* 6.11: again, the functional opposite of *oikeios*), should desist, follow the younger Gregory's example, and obey the laws. The good order of everything is more important than their faith, which, though laudable, has exceeded the limits of piety; they have become overzealous and have overreached, albeit motivated by their respect (*eulabeia*) for the divine. Some of these persons had become "hostile to the Word" because they resisted new insights, preferring to "abandon all else [rather] than those teachings that walk with them since their birth and the habit of the doctrines with which they have always lived." Excessive zeal for the truth had "deprived [them] of the light of knowledge";[21] their good intentions led them astray. Now was the time to return to the master like an obedient son and servant: out of choice and free will, like Gregory, as Isaac to his Abraham, Gregory the Elder.

To submit himself voluntarily to his father's "noble tyranny"—to act as a son must vis-à-vis his father—was a sign not of weakness and psychological overdependence but of the "art of authority"[22] signifying the good order of the cosmos intended by its creator, God, and the perfect implementation of a naturalizing metaphor that reflected reality precisely.[23] As such, this exemplary act must be imitated by all the bishop's children for the common good. "For this especially we consider a prime duty and one surpassing all others: the law of nature teaches us to care and take thought for no other person more than for a good father. From that derives also an unchallenged repute to the city, together with the ability to disdain those who are otherwise minded."[24]

Sons like Fathers

"I must confess it. I have gone back on my promise to be with you and live the philosophical life with you, as I promised as far back as our Athenian days. . . . One law has won out over another, the one that prescribes the care for one's parents [over]

---

21. Gr. Naz. *Or.* 2.40: δι' εὐλάβειαν τοῦτο πάσχειν καὶ ζῆλον . . . ἀλλ' οὐ κατ' ἐπίγνωσιν.
22. The phrase is K. McCarthy's: e.g., in the title of her *Slaves* and 29–34.
23. Bernardi (ed. and trans., *Grégoire de Nazianze: Discours 1–3,* 42) also cautions against too literal a reading of Gregory the Elder's tyranny.
24. P.Ryl. 624 = Moscadi, "Lettere," 111; Matthews, *Journey.*

that of loving friendship and togetherness."²⁵ The equation of care for a good father and the prosperity of the city at the end of the previous section is from a letter sent by two sons to their "lord and master," their father, Theophanes. It is preserved in an early fourth-century papyrus archive and, like Gregory's first letter to Basil, emphasizes a central tenet of late Roman life, especially among the elites, that certain laws govern the relationship of father and son.²⁶ Numerous sources confirm the significance of these laws for those participating in the *paideia* that shaped the norms and values of elite males across the Mediterranean: to honor one's parents and family assured the well-being of the *politeia*, a sentiment further manifested in Emperor Julian's high-wire act between condemning his cousin Constantius and maintaining dynastic legitimacy.

The honorary attributes that elite citizens in the late Roman East celebrated in inscriptions reflect "a world determined to admit no break in the easy flow of civilized life from generation to generation."²⁷ Expressing pride in the excellence of one's education, in offices well administered, euergetism liberally performed and made manifest in public works (*megalopsychia*), these celebratory attributes culminate in the praise of one's good birth, *eugeneia*—that is, the excellence of one's parents, manifested in oneself and handed down to one's progeny (*euteknia*)—which guaranteed the well-being of the city. Such emphasis on good birth included the entire family: mothers and fathers as well as siblings. Many funeral inscriptions address mothers, wives, and daughters, praising their own complement of civic and domestic virtues, immortalized in the figure of Penelope.²⁸ Gregory's epitaphs honoring his mother, Nonna, and his eulogies for his brother, Caesarius, and his sister, Gorgonia, belong to this context.²⁹

---

25. Gr. Naz. *Ep.* 1: νόμου νόμον νικήσαντος, τοῦ θεραπεύειν κελεύοντος τοὺς γεννήτορας. For the laws guiding friendship, White, *Christian Friendship;* Konstan, "How to Praise a Friend"; McLynn, "Gregory Nazianzen's Basil."

26. The classic studies are B. D. Shaw, "Latin Funerary Epigraphy"; Meyer, "Epigraphic Habit"; Saller, *Patriarchy,* 74–101. They focus on inscriptions from the Latin West but refer occasionally to the East. D. B. Martin, "Construction," emphasizes Asia Minor. Sironen, *Late Roman and Early Byzantine Inscriptions,* examines elite sentiments in Greek public inscriptions from the third to the sixth century; Roueché, *Aphrodisias,* chap. 3, inscrr. 20, 22, 24, 31; still foundational, Patlagean, *Pauvreté,* 113–55.

27. Brown, *Body,* 5–12 (quote p. 7), and *Power and Persuasion,* 35–41. Literary sources emphasize the same virtues. Thus, Men. Rh. *Treatise* 2 (*Menander Rhetor,* ed. and trans. Russell and Wilson, 174–76; *Peri epideiktikōn,* ed. Spengel, 420.10–31) prescribed that an encomium must include the honorand's family and good birth, his physical beauty and mental endowments, his education, conduct, actions, and fortune: his "wealth, happiness of children, love of friends, honor from emperors, honor from cities," in that order (*Menander Rhetor,* trans. Russell and Wilson, with modifications). Patrucco and Roda, "Crisi."

28. Jul. *Or.* 3 (Wright), *In Eusebiam,* 127c–d; Vérilhac, "Image." For late-antique women as civic benefactresses, Hemelrijk, "City Patronesses," using Western evidence; Vatsend, *Rede Julians,* 51–65, 97–98, 104–6, 108–10.

29. S. Elm, "Gregory's Women."

The laws of nature governing a son's care for his father, his lord and master, referred to by the sons of Theophanes and by Gregory, were more than a figure of speech. They were encapsulated in the Roman law of *patria potestas*. Gregory was bound by that law for much of his adult life: he was about forty-five years old when his father died, in 374. In *Oration* 2.116, he used the technical legal term when emphasizing once more his obedience: "You hold me in your power, O Father, utterly vanquished and subdued, even more by the laws of Christ than by those of the outside world." His dependence on his father was Roman law rather than a psychological trait.[30]

Patria potestas, a quintessentially Latin Roman legal construct, had made its way into the Greek East by the fourth century, though its extent and practice are difficult to assess.[31] In essence, it gave a father near-absolute legal and economic power over his dependents. According to Sextus Empiricus, "the Roman lawgivers also ordain that the children are subjects and slaves [*douloi*] to their fathers, and that power over the children's property belongs to the fathers and not to the children until the children have obtained their freedom like bought slaves; but this custom is rejected by others as being despotic."[32] Gregory's later writings corroborate Sextus's words. He criticized the custom as merely a (pagan) human law, detrimental to women and children—because, for example, it permitted adulterous husbands to go unpunished, whereas the divine law, scripture, granted no such immunity.[33] On the other hand, Gregory, discussing a father-son conflict in his poem *Ad Vitalianum*, written probably around 383, approved of the stricture of the law when he compared the father, who had disinherited his sons for disobedience, to God, who may condemn his children to wander around like pigs and share their meals with dogs if they displease him, yet commands that they obey him; in this instance, according to Gregory, human and divine law concurred.[34]

Still, the law that equates a son with a slave—though the son, as the father's heir, will one day become father and master—defines power abstractly and is not a so-

30. κατὰ τοὺς Χριστοῦ νόμους πλέον ἢ τοὺς ἔξωθεν ὑπεξούσιον; see, e.g., *POxy.* 2.237, 6.14, 7.41–42; and *CPR* 6.12–30.

31. *Inst.* 1.9 and 12 and imperial rescripts concerning *potestas* in the *CJ*, such as 2.2.3, 3.31.6, 4.19.16, 5.16.16, 6.9.4, etc.; Grubbs, *Law and Family*, 345–48, for a list of laws modifying *patria potestas* after Constantine; Arjava, "Paternal Power," esp. 147–48, and *Women and Law*, 28–52, 73–75; E. Eyben, "Fathers," esp. 112–16; B. D. Shaw, "Family."

32. Sextus Empiricus 3.211; Gaius = *Inst.* 1.55; Saller, *Patriarchy*, 102–32.

33. Gr. Naz. *Or.* 37.6, written in summer 381 in Constantinople, denounces that law: τοῖς πατράσιν ὑπ' ἐξουσίαν δεδώκασι τὰ τέκνα (*Grégoire de Nazianze: Discours 32–37*, ed. Moreschini and trans. Gallay)

34. Gr. Naz. *Carm.* 2.2.3, *Ad Vitalianum*, PG 37.1480A–1505C, esp. 6, 83, 189, 152, 341; McLynn, "Other Olympias," esp. 228–39: the father found the sons' rhetorical competence displeasing, either too brilliant or not brilliant enough; but more important, they had disobeyed him; Van Dam, *Families*, 21; Regali, "Carmen." See also *Gregorio Nazianzeno: Ad Olimpiade*, ed. and trans. Bacci. For the legal aspects of disinheritance as disciplinary tool, Arjava, "Paternal Power," 153–55.

ciological description of actual practice.[35] Fathers could emancipate their sons, granting them legal personhood, as encouraged in a law issued by Constantine.[36] Moreover, demographic data indicate that a sizable number of adult males had no living father, Basil among them.[37] Nonetheless, "a number of adult Romans . . . really did live under *potestas*"; Gregory and Caesarius are a case in point.[38]

To live in one's father's power had real consequences. For example, as Sextus Empiricus indicates, children under *potestas* could not formally own property. The law provided a practical solution in the form of the *peculium*, however, a revocable fund granted to those in *potestas* (including slaves) to conduct private and public business.[39] Though revocable and under paternal control, such funds were often substantial and de facto at the free disposal at least of the sons.[40] Such a fund must have paid for Gregory's and Caesarius's long education abroad, where Gregory was not among those students he described as "poor and without resources . . . to subsist for a single day."[41] Rather, as Gregory wrote to Basil, he was "fat, full, and without strict limits"; and Basil, whose father was already deceased, had money and walked about the agora. In sum, *patria potestas* notwithstanding, Gregory was well justified in writing to Caesarius that "our situation here is entirely sufficient to lead a life worthy of a free man."[42]

---

35. Thomas, "*Vitae necisque potestas*," esp. 545.

36. *CTh* 8.18.2; *Dig.* 1.7.31, 30.114.8, 36.1.23 pr.; *CJ* 8.48.3 (293), 8.48.4 (Diocl.); Lib. *Ep.* 87 (Norman) congratulates Hyperechius on being fully emancipated by his father, Maximus. This, so Libanius, was a case of exceptional *megalopsychia* on Maximus's part; though flattery, it implies that this was indeed a rare event. Advanced age did not suffice for emancipation: *CJ* 12.3.5.

37. Estimates of average life expectancy at birth vary, but most inhabitants of the later Roman Empire would have been fatherless by their late thirties; Basil's early loss of and longing for his father is one of Van Dam's main points (*Families*, 15–39). Saller, "Age"; Scheidel, "Progress"; Parkin, *Old Age*, 46–56; Arjava, "Paternal Power," 159–61.

38. Arjava, "Paternal Power," 148; Van Dam, "Self-Representation," 122–25, discusses the difficulties caused by Caesarius's intestate death in 368/9, when he was the highest-ranking imperial tax agent in Bithynia. His estate included properties in paternal *potestas* (as *peculium*), others he had earned and owned himself, and public moneys. Bas. *Epp.* 32 and 276 summarize *patria potestas* and its assumption by bishops.

39. Arjava, *Women and Law*, 41–47; Thomas, "Droit domestique." As Gregory's difficulties with Caesarius's estate indicate, it is hard to assess how privately earned income was handled; strictly speaking, it was under the father's *potestas*. Constantine's *CTh* 6.36.1 (cf. 6.35.3), however, used the model of the *peculium castrense*—i.e., property acquired as a result of military service and thus outside *patria potestas*—to exempt salaries earned as a member of the imperial administration (*palatini*); in the fifth century, this privilege was extended to public advocates and clerics: *CTh* 1.34.2, 2.10.6; *CJ* 1.3.33. Arjava, "Paternal Power," 149–52; Coulie, *Richesses*, 129–37.

40. Saller, *Patriarchy*, 123–25.

41. Gr. Naz. *Or.* 43.15.

42. Gr. Naz. *Ep.* 7.8. I am puzzled by McGuckin's frequent references to Gregory the Elder's procuring gainful employment for Gregory as priest (e.g., *St. Gregory*, 8), unless McGuckin is thinking of tax immunities. An alternative source of income for children in *potestas* was property inherited from the

To be in a father's power, furthermore, implied a reciprocal relation of honor between parents and children, and was not a one-sided affair, as inscriptions make clear. Gregory refers to such reciprocity when emphasizing, for example, that care for his parents included support as a "participant in his [father's] affairs, though not in his properties."[43] Gregory dealt publicly with tax collectors and handled Caesarius's complicated estate on his father's behalf, managed his father's estates, and oversaw the slaves.[44] As he stressed in *Oration 2*, among the principal reasons for his return was to fulfill the most important filial obligation, to aid his aging parents with all his faculties and to be "the staff supporting their old age" (*Or.* 2.103). More than twenty years later, in his autobiographical poem *De vita sua*, he reiterated the point: "It is the highest demand of reverence to grant the parents the highest honor after God."[45]

As Theophanes' sons also emphasized, the relationship between father and son, above and beyond *patria potestas*, ought to be characterized by reverence, *eusebeia* or *pietas*. Reverence or piety, *pietas*—as the Roman jurists knew—was not one-directional but reciprocal, with symmetrical obligations: a son was required to honor and obey his father, but the father too, especially if he wanted to be a good father, had to respect and honor his son.[46] According to the anonymous author of a text on education from the imperial period attributed to Plutarch, philosophy teaches that "one ought to revere the gods, honor one's parents," and "be affectionate with children."[47] Such mutual love and affection did not cancel parental power and authority, including strict discipline: Theophanes' sons speak of him as their lord and master; their Latin Roman contemporaries addressed their fathers as *Domine* (and denounced tyrannical rulers as *domini*); Gregory's beloved father exercised at times a beautiful tyranny.[48] Occasional harshness was part of a good father's duty; no good father was merely indulgent. To love and honor a son meant to discipline him (by

---

mother's side, the *bona materna*, which fathers could access only within the limits of a lifelong usufruct. This would not have affected Gregory, since his mother died a few months after his father. The *bona materna* appear in *Or.* 18.5, where Gregory alludes to his father's mother, who withheld her support for her son because of his marriage, causing him financial difficulties; Arjava, *Women and Law*, 85, 89–105; Coulie, *Richesses*, 178–79; Grubbs, *Law and Family*, 115–18.

43. Gr. Naz. *DVS* 380: κοινωνὸν ὄντα πραγμάτων, οὐ χρημάτων.

44. Gr. Naz. *De rebus suis, Carm.* 2.1.1.140–58; Kopecek, "Social Class," 454–56; McLynn, "Among the Hellenists," 220–28; Parkin, *Old Age*, 146–54, 168–72; Van Dam, "Self-Representation," 122–25.

45. Gr. Naz. *DVS* 312–21, esp. καὶ γὰρ εὐσεβέστατον / γονεῦσι πρώτην ἐκ θεοῦ τίμην νέμειν.

46. A notion shared by the second-century-C.E. jurist Sextus Pomponius: "[Ius gentium hominibus inter se commune est:] veluti erga deos religio: ut parentibus et patriae pereamus," *Dig.* 1.1.2; Saller, *Patriarchy*, 111–14; Parkin, *Old Age*, 203–16.

47. Ps.-Plutarch, *De liberis educandis* 10 (*Moralia*, ed. and trans. Babbitt, vol. 1, 4–69).

48. Dickey, *Latin Forms of Address*, 96–104.

flogging) and to enforce obedience, and a son's love and reverence for his father demanded that he obey, even occasionally against his will.[49] The key concept at stake was the right measure, the right degree of love and discipline at the right time, ensured by *sōphrosynē,* self-restraint, on the part of all concerned.[50] In dealing with one another, all members of the household, but the all-powerful father in particular, had to find the "royal road" of proper behavior.[51]

A good father's relationship with his son—bad fathers are not the theme here— was proper only if it combined affection, love, forbearance, support, and respect with (tyrannical) discipline; and a son reciprocated with love, respect, honor, support, and obedience. Such obedience was best offered voluntarily and did not have to be blind. After all, at some point, the son, legally speaking, would become the father: as heir he would assume his father's position as head of the household, himself called upon to make appropriate judgments on punishment and praise.[52] A son was (like) his father. Given the relevance of the hotly debated theme of generation and creation (albeit in relation to the Trinity), the anthropology of the father-son relationship, considered briefly, may sharpen our sense of how Gregory presented his relation to his father to his audience.

---

49. Platonic and Aristotelian texts equate the discipline of the well-run household to that of the well-run polis; thus, even if parental disciplinary measures, or those of a physician, can be harsh, they are ultimately for the good. For ancient debates of appropriate parental behavior, Sen. *Prov.* 1.6, 2.5; *Decl. min.* 377; *Ep.* 99.23; Jer. *Ep.* 68.1 (CSEL 54: 677); *Os.* 3.11.3–4 (CCL 76: 124); Plut. *Praec. Con.* 143b–c (*Moralia,* ed. and trans. Babbitt, vol. 2, 326); Bruyn, "Flogging a Son," esp. 262–63, 268–69 on Augustine, and 280–83 for the durability of such values; Eyben, "Fathers," 116–32; Harris, *Restraining Rage,* 71–79, 285–316. Most scholarly works on the late-antique father use Latin sources that stress different accents, as Scherberg has shown (*Vater-Sohn-Verhältnis,* 58–74, 185–88).

50. Men. Rh. *Treatise* 2 (*Menander Rhetor,* ed. and trans. Russell and Wilson, 90; *Peri epideiktikōn,* ed. Spengel, 376.2–13), advises how to praise imperial *sōphrosynē;* Jul. *Or.* 3.123a–c praised Eusebia as the embodiment, or statue, of the divine Sophrosyne. *Sōphrosynē* had an erotic component when used of men, reflected in the Latin translation *temperantia;* the Latin translation for women is *pudicitia.* The Greek word *enkrateia* is more narrowly concerned with sexual restraint; Vatsend, *Rede Julians,* 77–80. Rademaker, "*Sôphrosynê,*" though focused on the period up to Plato, analyzes the relation between self-restraint, demanded of each member of the household, and good governance (*eunomia*) of the city, superseding North, *Sophrosyne,* esp. 228, 243, 300–309, 320.

51. Gr. Naz. *Or.* 2.34 and 3.8; and *Or.* 7, 8, and 18; and Arist. *EN* 2.6.1–7.16; *EE* 2.3.1–18, 2.5.1–11; Sorabji, *Emotion,* 197.

52. Latin examples are Cic. *Pro Rosc.* 14.37; Sen. *Ben.* 3.38.2; Ovid *Ep. ex Ponto* 2.2.117–18. Barton, *Roman Honor,* 133–95, points out that a good father's disciplinary act was always tempered by affection, so that a son could submit to his father's will and obey his orders without compromising his honor, even if they contradicted his own wishes, whereas submission to an adversary was intolerable. This applied to the emperor also, not by coincidence the *pater patriae,* and to other father gods; Lendon, *Empire of Honour,* 78–95, 107–75; Ando, *Imperial Ideology,* 277–320, 385–405; Widdicombe, *Fatherhood,* 1–43.

Son as Father

For most philosophers and medical thinkers of the imperial period, fatherhood, the sacred power to beget legitimate sons and heirs, was, in the words of the fourth-century physician Aretaeus of Cappadocia, "what makes us men hot, well-braced in limbs, heavy, well-voiced, spirited, strong to think and act."[53] Such male heat and vital spirit began at conception, since only the strongest male semen produced sons; daughters came from weaker semen, further affected by a father's nonmasculine—irrational—thoughts at the crucial moment.[54] Sons embodied and represented what was most male in the father, from his strong limbs to his rational thoughts: that is, those that emanated from the most *logos*-like part of his mind-soul.[55] From a medical perspective, fathers and sons came from the same kind of seed and were in essence the same, even though they differed in manifestation: a father was not the son, and good fathers could generate bad sons, and vice versa. Masculinity was a fragile construct. An irrational thought at an inopportune moment could turn weak male semen into a female child; as Maud Gleason has shown, the difference between a man and a woman was one of degree rather than kind.[56] The heat that made a man male could cool off, and a man who did not cultivate his masculinity carefully and continually could slide toward effeminacy.[57] Hence, a son's maleness had to be

---

53. Aret. *On the Causes of Chronic Illness* 2.5 (*Extant Works of Aretaeus the Cappadocian*, ed. Adams, 346–47); Amm. Marc. 14.6.17. Thus, the collation to a law of 390 condemning transvestite male prostitutes to death explains "that all understand that those who are born as men must keep their gender sacred [*sacrosanctus*]"; *CTh* 9.7.6, collatio 5.3.2; Brown, *Body*, 10.

54. According to Aristotle (*GA* 728a, 737), whose premises Galen accepted and combined with Hippocratic teachings, men contributed the semen and women matter, because, since "the proximate motive cause, to which the *logos* and the form belong, is better and more divine in its nature than matter, it is better also that the superior one should be separated from the inferior one. That is why wherever possible the male is separated from the female, since it is something better and more divine in that it is the principle of movement for generated things, whereas the female serves as their matter. The male, however, comes together with the female and mingles with it for the purpose of generation," (737); Galen *On Semen* 1.16 (*Galen: On Semen*, ed. and trans. De Lacy); Galen *De usu partium corporis humani* 14.6 (*Claudii Galeni opera*, ed. Kühn, vol. 4, 158–65); Hp. *On Generation* 6.1–7.2. Following Iskander, "Attempted Reconstruction," 235, I assume that Gregory's medical knowledge derived mainly from Galen.

55. For Galen's use of the terminology "power," "activity," "product," see *On the Natural Facilities*, trans. Brock, 1.2.7, 1.4.9–10, 1.5.10, 1.7.16–18.

56. Gleason, *Making Men*, passim. Other medical writers thought that women produced weak semen, or that men and women could produce both weak and strong semen. Gaca, *Making of Fornication*, 94–116, draws attention to the distinctions between different ancient schools on reproduction; M. Boylan, "Galenic and Hippocratic Challenges"; King, *Hippocrates' Woman*, 7–12, 21–39, and 234–36 on later Greek uses. Harlow, "In the Name of the Father," esp. 156–61.

57. Brown, *Body*, 11: "No normal man might actually become a woman; but each man trembled forever on the brink of becoming 'womanish.'"

formed and nurtured from birth. Thus Galen's contemporary Soranus of Ephesus counseled Roman heads of households (who were in turn to impart such counsels to Greek wet nurses, who would feed infants Greek milk, thus creating the right mingling of Greece and Rome) how to swaddle a male infant and to exercise and mold his limbs to ensure that he would later walk, gesture, and comport himself as demanded by the decorum of the *paterfamilias*.[58]

Such formation required even greater attention to the inner man, the soul and intellect that would shape his external appearance to reflect proper civic values.[59] Words were the most powerful means of forming and shaping the inner self, expressed vocally and in writing. Therefore, the formation of the young man in his father's image—begun *in utero* and furthered in the infant's early months and years— went into high gear once a boy began his schooling. "The enduring legacy of Roman education is ... the insistence that texts and tests, through competitive displays of reading, writing and reciting, are essential to the socialization of the young," because a human being's sentient part was like a wax tablet into which social class and its corresponding ethics, morals, and codes of comportment were inscribed with each thought and word.[60]

To highlight one of these ideas, the schoolboy, in his memorization exercises, enacted the good order of the household and the city: he recited orders to slaves, greetings in hierarchical order, lists of the gods and of distinguished teachers and masters.[61] The farther a student advanced, the more he assumed his father's role.[62] Taking on his father's persona (*fictio personae, prosōpopoiïa*) as part of the *progymnasmata*, or rhetorical exercises, the son acted as if he were the father and thus became his father through imitation, *mimēsis*. Such exercises, in which the boy spoke in his father's voice when reading aloud, wrote the paternal persona and its social role into the son's soul as characters are written onto a wax tablet, forming both soul and son in the father's image.[63]

---

58. Sor. *Gyn.* 2.4–17 (*Soranos d'Ephèse: Maladies des femmes*, ed. and trans. Burguière, Gourevitch, and Malinas). See also the introduction to vol. 2, xii–xvi. For his (mostly lost) works, including *On Generation*, vol. 1, x–xxx.

59. Gleason, *Making Men*, 29–62.

60. Bloomer, "Schooling," 57; Webb, *Ekphrasis*, 16–17, discusses the lasting relevance of these practices. Small, *Wax Tablets*, 72–159, delineates technical aspects of writing and archiving in the context of ancient and modern theories of memory. For the Stoic origins of much of this, Staden, "Stoic Theory," 102; Atherton, *Stoics*, 39–130.

61. Dionisotti, "From Ausonius' Schooldays?"; Kaster, *Guardians*, 77–78, and "Controlling Reason."

62. The *progymnasmata* were elementary short set pieces, followed by the declamations, or full-length speeches, for more advanced students. Innes and Winterbottom, *Sopatros*; D. A. Russell, *Greek Declamation*, 4–9; Gleason, *Making Men*, 138–58; Kaster, "Controlling Reason," 320–26; Webb, "Progymnasmata," esp. 304–10.

63. Webb, *Ekphrasis*, 17–18. Bloomer, "Schooling," uses the misleading term "mimicry"; the point is to become the father rather than to impersonate him.

To become the father by acting as the father was also a means of addressing father-son conflicts, of which there were many. In the more advanced declamations, used in schooling between the ages of fifteen and eighteen, young men could act out both sides, tyrannical fathers and rebellious sons, in scenes often involving conflicts about money and the threat of disinheritance.[64] As D. A. Russell and M. Bloomer have stressed, however, such exercises aimed to do more than permit sons to negotiate their relationships with their fathers. Shaping sons into fathers meant enabling students as future citizens to participate in the complex power relations that formed and bound the community, not merely from the top down but also among peers and from the bottom up. Therefore, young men were taught to assume the role of peers and of social inferiors, to give voice to those dependent on their fathers.[65] A son thus learned to act in the voice of the dependents' advocate and the mediator, speaking both on behalf of his father as master and on behalf of those who were in his father's power: the more appropriate and evocative his representation of character (*ēthopoiïa*), the better his advocacy and mediation.[66]

In this perambulation through legal, medical-anthropological, and educational aspects of the father-son relationship I intend to make one principal point. Gregory may well have had a complex psychological relationship with his father that shaped profoundly his attitude toward life and priestly office. He was also a man of his time, however, and as far as I have been able to reconstruct, Gregory's first three orations reflect the norms and codes that informed the manner in which one spoke publicly about the relationship between father and son (whatever the individual may have felt).[67] A good father was entitled and indeed expected to act tyrannically on occasion; otherwise he did not fulfill his fatherly duty. Such tyranny was harsh but

---

64. Hermogenes 38, 41; Heath, *Hermogenes*; Quint. *Decl. Min.* 257; Lib. *Decl.* 26, 27, 33, 42 (*Libanius, Imaginary Speeches,* ed. and trans. Russell). According to the sixth-century rhetorician Choricius (*Decl.* 5), parent-child disputes were the central theme of declamations, such as: Was a father justified in killing his son, who had kidnapped his stepmother for ransom after being discovered by the enraged father in a lover's tryst with her? Can a disinherited son accuse his father of insanity after the father has forbidden him to marry the woman he has raped, because she has no dowry? Did the farmer rightly disown his son who has taken up philosophy? Tabacco, "Tiranno"; Sussman, "Sons"; D. A. Russell, "Panegyrists," esp. 28–33. For a critical overview of traditional scholarly assessments, Bloomer, "Schooling," 70–71; Kaster, "Controlling Reason," 318–23, 315; D. A. Russell, *Greek Declamation,* 4–9, 30–33, 40–73.

65. D. A. Russell, *Greek Declamation,* 1, 11; Bloomer, "Schooling," 58–61; examples include speaking on behalf of women, who were not persons *sui iuris*; of a soldier who had deserted; or a freedman wanting to marry a person above his status. Richlin, "Gender."

66. Hermog. *On Types of Style* 321.1–17, on *ēthopoiïa*; Quint. *Decl.* 1.11.1–2.

67. I do not wish to minimize the psychological pressures Gregory may have felt as a son under *patria potestas*, but I want to emphasize the difficulty of extracting psychological insight from highly constructed prescriptive and normative texts such as Gregory's. That a father's long life could give rise to impatience is evident, but what matters is how Gregory used that common knowledge; J. Chrys. (*Comm. in Epist. ad Coloss.* 1.1.3, *PG* 62.303) also remarks that sons get more impatient the longer their fathers live.

good. A son's first obligation was to revere and obey his father, even if occasionally he did so grudgingly. Occasions permitting disobedience were rare; to disobey a father, to deny him the reverence due, was the beginning of the end of all social order—the direct path to civil war. A father's harshness and a son's obedience, willing or unwilling, expressed familial affection—both preserved the good order essential to everyone's well-being. A good father respected his son's wishes, and a good son honored and supported the father in his affairs. Here the son's role as mediator was central. In speaking both to his father as a dependent on behalf of others (peers or dependents) and in his father's voice to them, the son aided in negotiating the many social constellations revolving around the father; as mediator he smoothed the path to harmony and unity.

At this juncture the intended audience of Gregory's first three orations comes to the fore. Those whom he addressed in the first three orations were those at Nazianzus who opposed Gregory the Elder. He exhorted these persons to act as his brothers (*Or.* 1.1), and therefore as his father's sons, by emulating his own relationship with his father: that of a good son who follows, above all, the law of obedience (*Or.* 2.113); but he also spoke, as son, on their behalf to his father, the bishop. With that, we return once more to the theme of *oikeiōsis*, kinship—including kinship with God—with which I concluded the preceding chapter.

On several occasions in *Orations* 1–3, Gregory denounced those who opposed his father as *allotrioi* while addressing his audience as friends and brothers, bound to him and to his father by kinship (e.g., *Or.* 1.1, 1.6; *Or.* 2.102; *Or.* 3.7). *Allotrioi* are the opposite of kin, *oikeioi,* and thus outside the vital nexus that I have already discussed in the preceding chapter. The orations leave no doubt that it is fatal to break the link of kinship when war threatens from the outside. To do so disrupts the good order of the cosmos, destroys the fabric of the community, and leads to civil war. Gregory's brothers as sons must remember the duty and obligation that binds them all together and affiliates them with God. Gregory is their example. His return was prompted by love and affection for his brothers at Nazianzus, his obligation to his parents, and the fear of disregarding the law of obedience, especially to God. There is "a right moment to be defeated," and a noble defeat, such as obeying a benevolent father, "is better than a dangerous and illegitimate victory." Gregory thus submitted himself voluntarily to the obligations imposed by his closest kin: his brothers, his father, God. This altruistic act of voluntary submission to the laws of kinship—submission to the yoke of leadership—was also his "first act as philosopher: to appear as if I had not chosen philosophy" (*Or.* 2.102–3, 2.110–13).[68]

Obedience to both Gregory the Elder and Gregory the Younger was also the duty

---

68. A psychological reading of Gregory's traumatic conflict between retreat and submission under parental tyranny also reflects contemporary Western notions of agency, where submission is rarely seen as a positive act; S. Elm, "Family Men."

of his brothers—especially if they, too, were philosophically inclined. Gregory was son and priest, and as such he spoke as his father's and master's voice: as father and son, Gregory the Elder and Gregory the Younger spoke as one (e.g., *Or.* 2.115–16).[69] "[My father] offers himself to you twice instead of once; transforming the staff of his old age into the staff of the Spirit, he adds a temple with a soul to that without one.[70] ... Everything he owns he offers to you! What magnificence [*megalopsychia*]! Or, to speak with even greater truth, what love for his children [*philoteknia*]! He offers you his white hair, his youth, the temple, the high priest, the testator, the heir, and the words you desire. Not those words that fly through the air ... but those the Spirit writes ... into the tablets of stone, or rather of the flesh, words not inscribed on the surface ... but written deep, not with black ink but with grace" (*Or.* 1.6; cf. *Or.* 3.6 and 7).

Gregory the Younger also spoke, however, on behalf of those who depended on his father, those now asked to submit and obey—as son and as philosopher. As son he mediated between his brothers and his father, and as philosopher he mediated between all in his care—including his father—and God. As philosopher, he "has progressed farther than others in [his] closeness to God," and is "higher than the multitude in [his] virtue and [his] *oikeiōsis pros theon*" (*Or.* 2.91, 2.3). As a philosopher who has prepared and purified himself more than others (in his audience), and not (merely) because he has been ordained (he had just argued at length that ordination without purification means nothing), he can now admonish all others, including his father, to accept his dispensation of the Word. He has observed silence; now he will speak (*Or.* 2.115). "You, who are my field, my vineyard, my entrails (or, rather, those of our common father here present ...), ought to respect us. ... Show your piety not by speaking often about God, but by silence. ... Keep present in your mind that to listen is less dangerous than to speak, so that to receive teachings about God is preferable to teaching. Leave the more precise [*akribesteron*] examination of this subject to those who dispense the word [*oikonomoi tou logou*]"—to the philosophers as physicians of the soul, who alone comprehend the correct measure of the Trinity (*Or.* 3.7). As son Gregory exhorted his brothers to obey their common father; as philosopher he offered a dispensation of the Trinity that would heal all in his care and unite those now estranged with his own father and the Father in *oikeiōsis pros theon*: it was an offer of conciliation and consolidation extended to all on the son's terms. The brothers in question delayed their acceptance for more than a year, however. I now turn to them and to the terms Gregory offered them as basis for the reconciliation.[71]

---

69. Van Dam, *Families*, 46–48, stresses that Gregory allowed his role as son to dominate his role as priest: indeed, there was little alternative while under *potestas*.

70. The church that Gregory the Elder had built, *Or.* 18.39 and *Ep.* 57.

71. S. Elm, "Diagnostic Gaze," 85–90, 94–97, 99–100.

THE ROYAL ROAD: GREGORY THE ELDER'S
OPPONENTS AT NAZIANZUS

In 374, Gregory pronounced the funeral oration for his father. By that time, he had rejected the position of bishop of Sasima to remain at Nazianzus (*Or.* 18.40), and it had become evident to him that the emperor Valens was a Julian redivivus, an apostate and hostile homoian or Arian. Thus, in Gregory's words, one of his father's principal virtues was staunch resistance against homoian heretics. Unlike others, neither father nor son had been enslaved by such an emperor (*Or.* 18.16, 18.37). Indeed, Gregory the Elder had opposed the homoian or Arian heresy even when he "had been tricked by a piece of writing and by technical words into a wicked fellowship" (*Or.* 18.18).[72] Admittedly, he too then had been drawn "into error and had not stood guard against the deceit." In his case, however, these writings remained on the surface and lost their power to penetrate his soul. He preserved his understanding (*dianoia*); the black ink did not contaminate him. Why? According to Gregory, his father's simplicity, which had allowed him to be tricked, had also shielded him against the effects of that trickery (*Or.* 18.18).

These words echo nearly verbatim those Gregory had used in 364 in his *Oration 6, On Peace*, when he celebrated the renewed unity of the *koina* at Nazianzus, his brothers' acceptance of his and his father's offer of reconciliation. Now they are reunited like "brothers with whom one has for some time quarreled over the paternal inheritance." As Neil McLynn has pointed out, these brothers include the shepherds who had been ordained by *allotrioi* (*Or.* 6.9).[73] "We have accepted with favor the heads this faction has given itself with the idea of innovating piety and defending the right [*orthos*] teaching now hard pressed, and we have not rebuffed them like enemies. . . . You have put to rest your suspicion regarding this writing and have run to the Spirit. You did not approve the simplicity that considered [only] the appearance of the words, but you did not consider [this simplicity] impiety."[74]

Suspicion of a document by persons intent on defending the *Logos* had caused the schism (*Or.* 6.20). In 363, Gregory had emphatically concluded *Oration* 1, echoing 2 Corinthians 3:1–3, with the promise that the words of baptism just spoken—Gregory the Elder's (and his own) gift to his metaphorical children—represented words not written superficially, but "written deep, not with black ink but with grace" (*Or.* 1.6). The document in question was the creed of Constantinople in 360.[75] The

---

72. Gr. Naz. *DVS* 53 (*Gregor von Nazianz: De vita sua*, ed. and trans. Jungck, 57).
73. For an excellent analysis of *Or.* 6, McLynn, "Gregory the Peacemaker," 194–203 (here p. 200).
74. Gr. Naz. *Or.* 6.11: τῆς . . . ἁπλότητος οὐκ ἐπαινέσαντες ἐπὶ τῷ φαινομένῳ τῶν ῥημάτων, ἀσέβειαν δὲ οὐκ ἐννοήσαντες.
75. *Pace* Calvet-Sébasti (*Grégoire de Nazianze: Discours 6–12*, ed. and trans. Calvet-Sébasti, 31–32); Gautier, *Retraite*, 302–5; McLynn, "Gregory the Peacemaker"; S. Elm, "Diagnostic Gaze"; Kurmann, *Gregor von Nazianz*, 6–11.

conclusion of *Oration* 1, already setting mere ink against the transformative powers of words written by the Spirit, might well be taken as the affirmation of the document's efficacy by Gregory the Younger, but it could more probably imply that he and his father had conceded the document's flaws and presented a different interpretation of the relation of Father, Son, and Spirit in whose name they baptized.[76] In any case, in 363 Gregory the Elder's continuing loyalty to the religious positions Constantius had favored was at stake. Given Julian's upheaval and the pressures exerted on all Christian leaders, Gregory the Younger was entirely justified in applauding his father's steadfastness. Further, although by 374 the doctrinal positions of the homoians had assumed clear enough contours to declare all homoians heretical, in 362, 363, and 364 things were far muddier. Nowhere (not even in *Oration* 18) does Gregory the Younger indicate that his father had altered his position or revoked his signature under the document; the others, he says, have put away their suspicions and have recognized piety (*eusebeia*) as the essential component of the simplicity (*haplotēs*) that had made him sign it.

As I have argued elsewhere, Gregory attributes his father's signature under the document to his simplicity—or better, simplemindedness—a characteristic also of his father's precursor, Leontius (*Or.* 18.12, 16), who possessed it in even greater measure. Such simplemindedness was good. It went hand in hand with "the venerable Abraham's" stellar qualities as shepherd and leader, his piety, his faith, his *megalopsychia* and *euteknia*.[77] But the times had changed. In the simpler times of Gregory the Elder's generation, guileless simplemindedness was all that was required; now strangers produced writings full of technical terms that deceived through trickery. Now, therefore, only men such as Gregory the Younger, the fully prepared philosopher in control of all the technical terms, could examine precisely (*akribōs*) and dispense the Word in right measure, because they knew the trickery hidden in words. But Gregory the Elder cannot be faulted and cannot be disobeyed; he is and remains the perfect representation of priesthood. But his son the philosopher as priest must advise him and speak in his voice. Only he can innovate regarding the *Logos*, and those in opposition must now consent to that innovation. *Oration* 6 closes

---

76. Gautier, *Retraite*, 307, also posits that Gregory proposed an altered understanding of the Trinity, but he thinks that Gregory the Elder had revoked his signature to the Constantinopolitan document.

77. The meaning of the term *haplos* oscillates between simplicity as frank directness and simpleminded naïveté. Simple directness was a hallmark of the true philosopher, as distinct from the artful sophist. One strives for simple truth; the other persuades in many guises. For Lucian, *Peregrinus* 13, Jesus was a sophist, and Christians simpleminded and gullible, *haploi*. By Gregory's time, *haplos* had assumed the sense "orthodox," because it separated the true Christian from the artful heretic, and became a leadership quality. Thus, Gregory the Elder acted as a true philosopher, albeit as one who was no longer able to master the new times. Le Boulluec, *Notion*, vol. 1, 148–53; Girardi, " 'Semplicità' "; Hahn, *Philosoph*, 46–53; Gleason, *Making Men*, 131–35; Francis, *Subversive Virtue*, 57–58.

with a definition of the Trinity that echoes the one Gregory had offered in *Oration* 2. Who were these opponents?

Overzealous Monks

The question is relevant for a number of reasons. Because we have no sources for the situation in Nazianzus other than Gregory's writings, we have to tease out who his opponents were and what they argued by reading Gregory's presentation of this opposition against the grain and by recourse to sources that talk about events outside Nazianzus. Yet we can comprehend what Gregory signaled to his intended audience, both those at Nazianzus and his peers in the East, only if we get a clearer sense of whom he opposed—a bit of a hermeneutical circle. Scholars have tended to downplay the local context of Gregory's first three orations, content with "romantic assumptions about his pastoral role, making him an assiduous shepherd of his small flock." But a more profitable starting point may be to remember that he was a "provincial notable, for whom [his] home town was principally an instrument" for self-presentation so as to gain prestige vis-à-vis his peers.[78] Gregory's presentation of his role as mediator between his father and those in opposition, as I have outlined, is central to his writing himself such prestige; it also resolves a conundrum that continues to trouble scholars, namely that his father, as the son tells us, signed a heretical creed because he was pious but simpleminded.[79] As far as the heretical aspect is concerned, Hanns Christof Brennecke's studies should have laid to rest any doubts. In the early 360s Gregory the Elder was in good company; revulsion against the homoians was a retrospective phenomenon.[80]

One reason that has prompted scholars to downplay the local context in favor of external developments is Rufinus's translation of *Oration* 6, entitled *De unitate monachorum*.[81] Reading it together with *Orations* 1–3, scholars have used this translation to posit that those whom Gregory addressed were monks. That monks opposed Gregory the Elder provides the next step in the scholarly argument according to which the three orations chronicle the transition of Christian leaders

78. McLynn, "Gregory the Peacemaker," 193.
79. McGuckin, *St. Gregory,* 111, comments on the "curious case that the only perceived way to defend his father's right to continue to rule over the church as bishop was to argue that he was theologically incompetent"; also ibid., 223–24. Jean Bernardi's suggestion of the Antiochene document of 363 offers a solution to that perceived conundrum (*Grégoire de Nazianze: Discours 4–5,* ed. and trans. Bernardi, 23–29); it also assumes (so Bernardi) that *Or.* 2 attacks bad clergy and not local schismatics, because they do not yet exist, a point McGuckin supports (*St. Gregory,* 106–7) when he considers those attacks to have been added in the revisions of the 380s or 390s. Van Dam, *Families,* 47–48, offers 360 and 364 as alternatives. Gautier, *Retraite,* 305–10, rejects Bernardi's suggestion.
80. Brennecke, *Studien,* 56–86, esp. 60.
81. Ruf. *Or. Gr. Naz. Interp.* 7 (Gregory of Nazianzus, *Tyrannii Rufini orationum Gregorii Nazianzeni novem interpretatio,* ed. Engelbrecht, 208–33). The full title is *De reconciliatione et unitate monachorum.*

from family men to monastics and the tension between the philosophical life as both asceticism and monasticism and the priesthood that monks now increasingly adopt.[82] Gregory, as philosopher, is seen as the model ascetic and monastic, reluctant to adopt priesthood, which creates the second conundrum: Why would Gregory, the orthodox champion of monasticism, oppose monks who fight against his father's signature of a heretical creed and pressure these monks to obey this tyrannical father?[83]

Gregory the Elder's opponents at Nazianzus have been identified specifically with the zealous ascetics who troubled Asia Minor on several occasions: persons loyal to Eustathius of Sebaste and devoted to the homoiousian position he had championed. Several arguments are adduced to provide this identification. Eustathius of Sebaste was Basil of Caesarea's mentor and the model of his philosophical life at Annesi. Zealous ascetics, condemned at Gangra in 343, are identified as Eustathius's followers. Because Basil is considered Gregory's mentor, especially of the philosophical life, Gregory's asceticism must thus also have been influenced by Eustathius (and his homoiousian stance). Eustathius's supporters, known since Gangra as zealous ascetics, also supported Basil against Dianius and then Eusebius of Caesarea. Because Gregory the Elder supported Eusebius and, before him, Dianius, and Gregory the Younger was Basil's friend and therefore a Eustathian ascetic, those who opposed Gregory the Elder at Nazianzus were also homoiousian Eustathian monks; moreover, Gregory the Younger characterized his father's opponents as zealous, indeed overzealous, and as his brothers, who had tyrannized him.[84]

Gregory's first biographer, Gregory the Presbyter, elaborated Rufinus's identification of the ascetics (at Annesi), described in a long passage in *Oration* 6, with Gregory the Elder's opponents.[85] Although it has been adopted by nearly all modern scholars (including myself), this identification hinges on a number of assumptions that focus more on the broader radius of Asia Minor and less on local pressures at Nazianzus. Eustathius's connection to the zealous ascetics condemned at Gangra for advocating radical poverty, begging, homelessness, freeing of slaves, and

---

82. Calvet-Sébasti (*Grégoire de Nazianze: Discours 6-12*, ed. and trans. Calvet-Sébasti), 11-13, 19-21. Van Dam, *Families*, 48; McGuckin, *St. Gregory*, 224; Rapp, *Holy Bishops*, 100-152; Sterk, *Renouncing the World*, 119-29.

83. Bernardi (ed. and trans., *Grégoire de Nazianze: Discours 4-5*, 25-26, 36-37) suggests that monks loyal to Basil used Gregory's visit to Basil in late 363 to instigate the schism, encouraged by bishops who passed through with the Antiochene document Gregory the Elder signed, and that Gregory returned with Basil so that Basil could reconcile Gregory the Elder and Basil's monastic followers.

84. Brennecke, *Studien*, 60-62; S. Elm, *Virgins*, 60-68, 102-12; Gallay, *Vie*, 80-84; Gautier, *Retraite*, 24-29, 302-15; McGuckin, *St. Gregory*, 100, 107. At pp. 106-13, McGuckin assumes that the more international monks collided with the locally minded Gregory the Elder; Rousseau, *Basil*, 72-76; and Calvet-Sébasti (*Grégoire de Nazianze: Discours 6-12*, ed. and trans. Calvet-Sébasti), 16-23 for yet another version.

85. Greg. Presb. *Vita S. Gregorii* 261c-264b.

equality of the sexes merits a second glance. The person mainly responsible for assembling the bishops at Gangra was Eusebius of Nicomedia, later of Constantinople, and an opponent of Eustathius, who was in 343 still a presbyter. To associate Eustathius (probably already a rising star) with the radical (or even not so radical) ascetic movements in the region, whose members resembled the *apotaktitai* criticized by Julian, may well have been Eusebius's assassination of Eustathius's character.[86] As Peter Brown has recently argued, Eustathius, a philosopher, certainly practiced an ascetic life, but he need not have been the leader of the overzealous ascetics condemned at Gangra.[87] Further, many specifics of the ascetic life associated with Eustathius derive from his appointment of a certain Aerius to head the local feeding place for the poor (*ptōchotropheion*) when Eustathius was elected bishop of Sebaste in 357. Aerius is known otherwise only through Epiphanius's attacks on him, which portray him as denouncing the church's and Eustathius's wealth, arguing for its distribution to the poor, and as abducting men and women to the mountains to roam about without shelter, actions condemned at Gangra. Though Aerius was part of Eustathius's staff at Sebaste, his ascetic activism need not reflect the philosophical life advocated by Eustathius and adopted, in 357/8, by Basil of Caesarea. Eustathius, in sum, need not be responsible for radical asceticism in Asia Minor, and the philosophical life Eustathius lived and Basil, following his example, adopted from 357/8 onward, was not that of the zealous ascetics condemned at Gangra.[88]

Eustathius certainly influenced Basil's ascetic and philosophical life. Their common homoiousian leanings are well documented, and it is plausible that those who supported Basil in his conflict with Eusebius at Caesarea also followed him and Eustathius in their way of life. Gregory the Elder clearly supported Eusebius, whereas Gregory the Younger was closely associated with Basil. Still, Gregory's philosophical life was not identical to Basil's, as already indicated in Chapter 1; nor is it obvious that absolutely all those who opposed Gregory the Elder at Nazianzus were aligned with Eustathius or Basil or even with Gregory the Younger. Nazianzus was not Caesarea, and Gregory was not Basil. Those opposing Gregory the Elder need not have formed a homogeneous group. Finally, Gregory the Younger and Basil, despite their support for Eustathius (which is not especially evident in Gregory's case) and their potential homoiousian leanings, were engaged from 362 to 364 in

---

86. Jul. *Or.* 7.224b–c on *apotaktitai*. For the radical ascetic experiments in Asia Minor, Caner, *Wandering, Begging Monks*, 83–117.

87. Brown, *Poverty*, 36–39; McLynn, "Gregory the Peacemaker," 212–13; Caner, *Wandering, Begging Monks*, 99–101.

88. Brown's argument rehabilitates Eustathius. The relation between Eustathius's and Basil's ascetic ideas has been intensively studied; Rousseau, *Basil*, 72–76; Sterk, *Renouncing the World*, 35–43. McGuckin (*St. Gregory*, 100, 190) describes Gregory's friends as practicing the radical form of asceticism evidenced in "local monks who took their lead from Armenia and Pontus" (i.e., Gangrian ascetics), concluding that his ordination was his father's attempt to remove him from their influence.

formulating their own ideas on the Nicene faith. What Gregory had done and pronounced since his return to Nazianzus in 358/9 may have caused opposition, whatever the situation at Caesarea and beyond.

Gregory, to recall, had identified three maladies afflicting the body of the church, one associated with Sabellius, the other with Arius, and a third that he attributed to the zealous, driven by excessive respect for the divine, who had resisted all innovation. This last group is the one at issue here. In my interpretation it is not a homogeneous group but encompasses those who opposed both Gregory the Elder and Gregory the Younger, for different reasons, with varying zeal, and perhaps at different times.[89] Some may have been motivated by opposition to the Constantinopolitan creed; others by their objection to Gregory the Elder's choice of his son as official advisor and obvious successor, as suggested by Gregory's rebuttal of those who accused him of rising above his rank (*Or.* 2.5);[90] and still others may have disapproved of either his philosophical life or his apparent renunciation of that philosophical life (*Or.* 2.7 and 103)—all motivations that gained increasing relevance given the war from the outside: Julian's reign and its consequences.

Friends and Brothers

When Bishop Gregory ordained his son in 362, Gregory the Younger had been back in Nazianzus for more than three years. During that time, after his return from Athens, Gregory had "shown off *logoi* [*logous edeixa*]" (*DVS* 265). However, rather than seeking public acclaim and the gold that came with it, according to his later poem *De vita sua*, he "danced for his friends. These [dances] were like warm-up exercises for battle or a preliminary initiation into higher mysteries." And because "there was then need for manly counsels, [Gregory had] establish[ed] at home a jury of friends, genuine encouragers of [his] reasonings." Among them, he continues, he debated which philosophical life to choose.[91] As I have indicated above, Neil McLynn has demonstrated convincingly that these and other remarks offer evidence that Gregory spent his early years after returning from Athens to Nazianzus as a professional rhetorician and emphasize his continuing involvement with *logoi* and with professional rhetoricians, underscoring the deep effect of Julian's edict and imperial letter.[92] Throughout his life Gregory "clung to *logoi* only"[93] while renouncing

---

89. In *Or.* 18.18 Gregory stated that those separated last were reunited first, suggesting that there was more than one group; see also *Or.* 6.10, and, in 380, *Or.* 21.22–25, esp. 21.24.11–12; Gautier, *Retraite*, 305–6.

90. McLynn, "Gregory the Peacemaker," 210.

91. Gr. Naz. *DVS* 274–79: τοῖς φίλοις ὠρχήσαμεν. ταῦτ' ἦν ἀγώνων ὥσπερ ἐγγυμνάσματα ἤ καὶ προτέλεια μειζόνων μυστηρίων... ἀνδρικῶν βουλευμάτων... τῶν φίλων κριτήριον; *Gregor von Nazianz: De vita sua*, ed. and trans. Jungck, 164–65; trans. McLynn, "Among the Hellenists," 224.

92. McLynn, "Among the Hellenists," 215, 220–26. Gregory's remark, after Julian's edict, that he prematurely had to give up *logoi* underscores the point; Gr. Naz. *Ep.* 10.2, *To Candidianus*. Candidianus is

"wealth, *eugeneia,* glory, power," and he reiterated that his desire for *logoi* surpassed that of any "who had devoted themselves to *logoi*" (*Or.* 2.6). This devotion did not lessen with his advancing years and greater clerical responsibilities. Gregory's life's work would be to give his *logoi* to the Logos.[94]

But who were the friends for whom he danced? Some were professional rhetors, men such as Eustochius and Stagirius, both at Caesarea. An analysis of several letters and poems, mostly later than 363 and 364, helps to identify others with whom Gregory shared a long-standing intimacy.[95] Evagrius, the father of a student, may well have been among them. Gregory wrote to him just after his return from Athens, claiming to have given the son only a few *logoi* but much "love for God and the disdain of the present things" (*Ep.* 3.2). The deacon Euthalius, who in 363 had to change his tax bracket (perhaps because he lost his clerical immunity under Julian), may also have been present when Gregory danced.[96] A famous letter of 372 or 373 to Basil, analyzed by McLynn, yields more.[97] In it, Gregory describes a symposium at his house, where "not a small number of [his] distinguished friends" had gathered to discuss philosophy, Athens, and Basil and Gregory's friendship there, "before the wine was brought in" (*Ep.* 58.4). Later letters and poems indicate, for example, that a certain Hellenius was present, who had been a classmate of Gregory's and Basil's at Athens, and now "equaliz[ed] the taxes at Nazianzus": that is, acted as *peraequator* (Bas. *Epp.* 98.1, 71.1). Hellenius, a wealthy Armenian, also received a poem from Gregory in 372 requesting tax exemptions for local friends (*Carm.* 2.2.1), including Gregory's cousin Eulalius (later bishop of Nazianzus), whom Gregory had described in an earlier letter as engaged in philosophy (while defending him in a property deal gone wrong: *Epp.* 14 and 15).[98] The local friends also included Cledonius, a retired imperial official, probably identical with the addressee of later letters encouraging him to fend off Apollinarists; Nicomedes, an-

---

also the addressee of Basil's *Ep.* 3, in which Basil describes his Pontian retreat (*apragmon*) as an elite household.

93. Gr. Naz. *Or.* 4.100 (and cf. 4.5, 6): τοῦ λόγου δὲ περιέχομαι μόνου.

94. E.g., Gr. Naz. *Or.* 6.5–6; *Carm.* 2.1.1.99–100; and see Camelot, "Amour des lettres"; Demoen, "Attitude," esp. 236–39, has different interpretations.

95. McLynn, "Among the Hellenists," 215–19. Others are the sophist Adamantius (*Ep.* 235, written probably in the 380s) and the aspiring rhetor Ablabius (*Ep.* 233), with whom he had "many conversations regarding the good." Hauser-Meury, *Prosopographie,* 22.

96. Gr. Naz. *Ep.* 3; in return he hoped to receive some fruits of Gregory's zeal (καρπὸν τῆς σπουδῆς); *Ep.* 9; Hauser-Meury, *Prosospographie,* 79 n. 148.

97. *Saint Grégoire de Nazianze: Lettres,* ed. Gallay, vol. 1, 73 for the dating; McGuckin, *St. Gregory,* 216–18, dates it to 373 and stresses only its doctrinal content, considering Hellenius a "priest monk" (p. 218).

98. Eulalius's brother Helladius was deceased by 372. Hauser-Meury, *Propospographie,* 97, is uncertain whether the addressees are identical; Pouchet, *Basile,* 622.

other one of Gregory's relatives, father of two children, who had exhausted his financial means funding the building of a church (in an epitaph Gregory called him "priest"); Rheginus, who eventually bequeathed some land to Gregory; and, finally, Carterius, in all likelihood the very same *paidagōgos,* now emancipated, who had accompanied Gregory to Athens.[99]

In *Epistle* 58 Gregory tells Basil that a visitor at the symposium "wearing the name and the garb of respect [*eulabeia*]"—an ascetic—criticized Basil's doctrine of the Spirit (*Ep.* 58.4). Basil and Gregory address Hellenius as "most reverend brother," which could, but need not, have had ascetic-monastic overtones. When requesting tax exemptions, Gregory makes it clear that those for whom he speaks are ascetics or monks. "The most economical inference would therefore be that the audience assembled at Gregory's party were the same monks who had received tax-benefits." Gregory's fellow ascetics, his friends and brothers, included thus "prosperous, propertied relatives and neighbors"; these were "his own disciples, who had (as it were) followed him into the hills."[100]

Those present at the party and others like them were the friends and brothers for whom Gregory had performed his warm-up exercises in the 360s, preparatory to initiation into the higher mysteries of the true philosophical life. They were men of his class, educational background, and corresponding prestige, and, like Gregory, "zealously devoted to *logoi*" and to the *Logos*.[101] These men of high social status, some his relatives, with property (or with parents who owned property) in Nazianzus, were his friends and brothers; with others he had shared long-standing intimacy since their student days in Athens. They were the friends and brothers of *Orations* 1–3 and 6, and a plausible audience for all of the first six orations. In defending his father and his own choice of the philosophical life, Gregory addressed a jury of his friends: those he invited to judge him were his peers; they knew him well enough to be astonished at his sudden lack of education (*Or.* 2.1, 2, 6).

In other words, his audience, those Gregory most needed to persuade, were educated, sophisticated, and fully appreciative of all the nuances of his performance. These were not persons easily swayed; and as it turned out, those among them who really opposed him and his father did not change their minds quickly. Furthermore, they had the education and discernment to perceive the trickery of technical terms in documents dealing with the philosophical underpinnings of the Trinity. In short, among such friends and brothers Gregory had to work hard to gain prestige; only if he really outperformed his competitors in the *agōn* of words could he sway such men. If he did persuade them, however, his efforts would be rewarded outside

---

99. Gr. Naz. *Carm.* 2.1.1.121–38, 143–170, 203; *Ep.* 182 for Eulalius's episcopy; *Epp.* 101 and 102 for Cledonius; for Rheginus, *Test. Gr., PG* 37.392a; and Hauser-Meury, *Prosopographie,* 52, for Carterius.
100. McLynn, "Among the Hellenists," 228–31 (quotation pp. 230, 231).
101. Gr. Naz. *Or.* 2.6: περὶ λόγους ἐσπουδακότων; and *DVS* 265, 274.

Nazianzus as well. These were men with connections. And they too, as Gregory pointed out, were inclined to the philosophical life. At least some combined philosophical life with public positions, much like the addressee of Sopater's letter, much like Caesarius, and, after all, much like Gregory himself. They could therefore criticize Gregory for having chosen a philosophical life they did not consider acceptable, either because he had overextended his retreat or because he had returned and accepted office at an inopportune moment: some may well have heeded Gregory's call for the true philosophical life as he had (originally) understood it in the early 360s and may have reacted strongly if he altered the philosophical life he had first embraced in response to the events of 362 and 363. The chapter that follows will return to Gregory's choice of philosophical life, and these are the men who have to remain in focus.

Gregory's brothers and friends, members of the wealthy, landowning, educated elite, were not thereby precluded from being Eustathian monks, though whether they were depends on how we interpret such monasticism. Eustathius, Basil, and Gregory all embarked on what they called "the philosophical life," an elite undertaking by men of means with connections. Whether Gregory's ascetic philosophical life was noticeably more elitist than that of Basil or Eustathius is a question that I cannot address here (though I do not think so).[102] It appears likely, however, that none of these men had much to do with the roaming, radical ascetics (condemned at Gangra), vividly brought to life by Daniel Caner and criticized by Julian, Libanius, and other (Christian) members of the elite.[103]

A Jury of His Friends

With that in mind, some of Gregory's remarks on his friends and brothers may give us further insight. That he addressed his relatives and peers may explain both the force of his criticism and his continuing wish to be conciliatory: Gregory directed his greatest vehemence against those who spread the first two maladies—loving Christ and the Father either too much or not enough (that is, Arians and Sabellians)—and his brothers and friends seem not to have belonged to those groups. They had permitted themselves to be guided by *allotrioi*, strangers not connected by kinship, but they had always remained brothers. Even at the height of dissent, they had been "brothers with whom one has for some time quarreled over the subject of paternal inheritance, brotherly and without malice" (*Or.* 6.11, 6.21). Absence

---

102. McGuckin [*St. Gregory*, 98] framed the issue thus: "those ... who have never known the rigorous demand of such a focused intellectual lifestyle [as Gregory's asceticism] might more readily regard Basil's form of communitarian simplicity as archetypal for monks, or Eustathios' social leveling as more authentic, but this would be to miss the chief point that Gregory was making despite all his aristocratic élitism. Such a life of dedicated reflection is not for all."

103. Gautier, *Retraite*, 83–154, stresses that Gregory's form of asceticism opposes the more "encratite," radical, form of the philosophical life; Caner, *Wandering, Begging Monks*, 1–18, 83–125.

of malice does not mean absence of ferocity, however—quarrels over inheritance are not generally known for consideration and restraint.

In fact "there was *stasis* among us," but in the end, like slender branches bent in the wrong direction, all fell—that is the paradox of healing—back into their natural (*oikeios*) place (*Or.* 6.1, 6.8).[104] *Oration* 3, of 363, particularly expressed Gregory's anger at his brothers' and friends' stubborn opposition. Why do they not reciprocate, now that he has abandoned the *erēmia*—"the aide and the mother of the divine ascent and of deification"—come back, and submitted himself?[105] Now that he has returned, they seem to want him less than while he was gone: "as if you wanted to triumph over our philosophy rather than profit from it" (*Or.* 3.1). They did not receive him as one should receive the stranger, thus violating the rules of hospitality; they did not offer guidance when he needed it, reassure him when he was afraid, or console him when he had suffered. "What do you want? That I appear before you to be judged, or to judge? That I pronounce the sentence, or be sentenced?" His verdict is clear: "You all want something from the old and the new pastor, [but] you do not respect the white hair [of the one] nor summon the youth [of the other]" (*Or.* 3.2–3).

Lest the language of affection scorned deceive us, let us restate Gregory's position. To continue opposing Gregory the Elder was unacceptable—after all, Julian was emperor, and Gregory the Elder, as homoian, stood by those now most under attack and was himself a target (*Or.* 6.8). In such a situation what counted was deep *eusebeia* and not the superficial ink of words that did not penetrate the soul. Moreover, his friends and brothers would do well to leave questions regarding the nature of the Trinity to him, because he was more purified than they and could thus examine such questions with greater precision. They ought to be silent rather than speak, learn rather than teach, and "hold fast to the faith you have received and in which you were brought up" (*Or.* 3.7): "Among us the Father is exalted; the Son his equal [*isazetai*], and the holy Spirit shares their glory" (*Or.* 3.6), a succinct summary of Gregory's explanation of the Trinity in *Oration* 2.37–39.

His friends and brothers had not always walked the "royal road, veering neither to the left nor to the right" (*Or.* 3.8); rather, as Gregory said in *Oration* 6.11, they had "given [themselves] new leaders with the idea of innovating piety [*eusebeia*] and defending the hard-pressed right word [*orthos logos*]." Gregory—at least by the time of *Oration* 6—understood their zeal, even if he disapproved of their hostile measures. After all, like his father, they had always carried within themselves the seeds of piety that had saved them from the "inundation of the entire world" (*Or.*

---

104. By then Julian was dead, and the period in which the "hand [revolted] against the eye and the eye against the hand, the head ... against the feet and the feet ... against the head," was over (*Or.* 6.8).

105. Gr. Naz. *Or.* 3.1: τῆς ἐρημίας ἣν ἐγὼ πάντων μάλιστα ἠσπασάμην καὶ ὡς συνεργὸν καὶ μητέρα τῆς θείας ἀναβάσεως καὶ θεοποιὸν διαφερόντως ἠγάσθην τε καὶ παντὸς τοῦ βίου προεστησάμην.

6.10). But as he said in *Oration* 2.39 (just after he had presented his true understanding of the Trinity, summarized in *Or.* 3.6), one of the difficulties of instructing all with the right words "comes from the fact that the very thing that makes reasoning easy and readily received . . . , [namely] the respect [*eulabeia*] of the audience, becomes [when abused by wrong teachers] a damage and a danger." Moreover, when God is at stake, "the greater the faith, the stronger the resistance to the word" (*Or.* 2.40). Those of the greatest faith often feel that "to yield to persuasion is a betrayal of the truth rather than piety [*eusebeia*]." They "would rather abandon everything [else] than the thinking that has walked with them from home [*oikothen*] and the habit of the teachings with which they have been brought up." Gregory does not consider such persons too bad, because even though they have not fully attained the truth, they have been prevented from so doing "out of [excessive] respect [*eulabeia*] and zeal [*zēlos*]." Thus, he cannot judge them too harshly and reprimand them too severely, because that same respect may cause them to change their minds more easily should the right word touch and penetrate them.

Gregory's brothers and friends opposed his father but were just like his father in their true, though misguided, piety—different indeed from the true enemies, who have abandoned the Lord out of evil malice (*Or.* 2.40). They remained "pure children of God . . . in the middle of a bent and perverted generation" (*Or.* 3.8), driven by excessive faith to be affected by "the third [malady] . . . , led by some among us who are too orthodox" (*Or.* 2.37). Both his brothers and his father required his therapy, because neither had quite attained the truth. Gregory presented that truth in his summary of the Trinity, in *Oration* 2.38, in *Oration* 1.7, and in *Oration* 3.6. Unlike the document of Constantinople that described the Son as "similar" (*homoios*) to the Father, Gregory stressed his full divinity, but he avoided the term *ousia* (essence), over which the homoiousians had fought, and used instead the term *theotēs* to describe the Son's divinity. Moreover, Gregory emphasized the hierarchy of the Trinity: though each *hypostasis* shares equally in the divinity of the Father, they are distinct entities observing an order that flows out of the Father as the first cause.[106]

Thus, Gregory's words were an innovation (acceptance of which was an act of piety), reflecting neither the homoian nor the homoiousian view, and they were not traditionally Nicene. "It is easiest to cut the truth freshly [*kainotomein*, "innovate"] into the soul, as if on a wax tablet onto which nothing has as yet been written, rather than to write over writings already there: that is to say, in this case, having to write the words of piety over lessons of pernicious doctrines and teachings, and to cause confusion between the first and the second text. . . . Otherwise, the calligrapher who serves God must accomplish two tasks [*erga*]: erase the earlier signs [*typoi*] and trace in their place those that are more acceptable and more worthy to endure. . . . These, then, are . . . the signs [*typoi*] and characters [*charaktēres*] of evil and derived from

---

106. Beeley, *Gregory*, 217–22.

evil; this [is] the task [*ergon*] of the one entrusted with this pedagogy and this stewardship of souls" (*Or.* 2.43).[107]

The chapter that follows will turn to these "signs of evil," to Gregory's true enemies. Gregory had been both firm and conciliatory in addressing his friends and brothers, who he considered in the middle, because they had acted wrongly for the right reasons. They were not his real enemies, and when addressing them he praised peace and unity on his conditions. "Let no one think I say that every peace is desirable," however (*Or.* 6.20). Without doubt "a laudable war is better than a peace that separates us from God, and therefore the Spirit arms even the mild man like a combatant [*hoplitēs*], so that he can battle nobly." Gregory was such a warrior, such a hoplite: "Could I only be one of those who fight for the truth and are [therefore] hated! In fact, I boast of being one" (*Or.* 2.82). Now, leaving Nazianzus behind, I reconsider Gregory's choice of the philosophical life in the context of the contemporary debates discussed in relation to Julian, and I then turn to Gregory's true enemies, those who dispensed theological maladies that incite civil war, and the enemy on the outside.

107. Pl. *Euthphr.* 3b: "innovation regarding the divine."

6

Armed like a Hoplite

*Gregory the Political Philosopher at War:
Eunomius, Photinus, and Julian*

> But to fight my war, I do not know who to become, what alliance, what word of wisdom, what charisma I should find, clad in what arms I should battle against the insidious methods of this evil one [ponēros]. Who is the Moses who will defeat him?
>
> —GREGORY OF NAZIANZUS, ORATION 2.88

> I am not yet speaking about the war within, the one inside us among our passions. We are battling them night and day because of our miserable body, at times in secret and at times openly, and because of the turmoil that sweeps over us like a wave from above and below, whirling us around through the sensations and pleasures of this life, . . . attempting to destroy the royal image in us and however much of that divine emanation may have been placed into us. Therefore, even a person who has educated himself through a great effort in philosophy . . . finds it difficult to master the matter that draws us downward. . . . But before having mastered it—to the extent possible—and before having sufficiently purified one's thinking [dianoia], and before one has progressed farther than others in one's closeness to God, I consider it unsafe to accept the commandment of souls and the mediation between God and men: for it is this, I guess, that a priest undertakes.
>
> —GREGORY OF NAZIANZUS, ORATION 2.91

Gregory faced a monumental task as philosopher–physician of the soul and as armed combatant, engaged in the war within himself as preparation for both the civil war that divided his kin inside and the attack of the enemy outside. Gregory's doubts and hesitations as he considered the dangers are poignant, even though they conform to the ritual of *recusatio*—the protestations expected from one chosen to lead. He must have found it excruciating to witness Christians tear each other apart while also under intense attack from outside. Thus, before he intervened, Gregory armed himself like a hoplite. He was Moses ready to deliver the chosen people, guiding them to safety. But he recognized "that I am too weak for the entire battle" (*Or.* 2.90): the *oikoumenē* of the Romans, the cosmos itself, was about to be submerged and destroyed.

No wonder that Gregory continued to doubt his own readiness for battle and to insist on thorough preparation on all fronts, given that for him the evil of the war brought by Julian was a lesser evil than the war of Christian against Christian. "I am not afraid of the war now brought against us from the outside nor of the ferocious beast that has now risen against the churches, that embodiment of all evil, even if it threatens fire. . . . I have one remedy [*pharmakon*] against all that, one path to victory: . . . to die for Christ" (*Or.* 2.87). Far more terrifying and dangerous because of the risks and consequences of failure was the command of souls (*psychōn prostasia*) in times of civil war. And far more challenging was combat against the evil imprints of those who dispensed the Trinity wrongly. After all, "civil war is more unnatural than war waged on foreigners, as the eating of one's own [*oikeios*] flesh is more to be shunned than the eating of the flesh of another [*allotrios*]" (*Or.* 4.109). To lead in such times, thus, truly required a near-unattainable perfection (the conundrum familiar from the Platonic philosopher-king).[1]

When Moses was called to the mountain, no one else, not even Aaron, had been permitted to follow; only Moses could approach God and comprehend his divinity (*Or.* 2.92). Unless perfect—entirely purified and flawless—no one is worthy to approach God as Moses did (*Or.* 2.94, 95). Indeed, no one, unless Christlike to the extent humanly possible, is worthy to lead souls and serve God as mediator.[2] "Who would [take on the mantle and the name of the priest] without the words of God . . . inscribed three times into the tablet of his soul, to have the spirit of Christ? . . . Who would present himself [for that office] without having passed with labor [*ergon*] and contemplation [*theōria*] through all the names and powers of Christ . . . ? Who would do so without retreat [*scholaios*]? . . . No one in my judgment and according to my counsel" (*Or.* 2.96–99). To guide others to the divine always demanded extraordinary readiness, and even more so in times of crisis. Purity and continuing purification were the hallmarks of that readiness; but crisis demanded action, which could be the very antithesis of purity. How to resolve that tension has been the leitmotif of the preceding chapters, which present an arsenal of ways to combine the two. Before leaving Nazianzus to insert Gregory into the broader debates of the philosophical life conducted in the Eastern empire at that time, it is worth asking whether Gregory, in response to Julian, changed the tenor of the philosophical life he had envisaged at Athens.

---

1. Compare Gr. Naz. *Or.* 2.78: "This is something that surpasses our strength, to be a philosopher to the degree of accepting the guidance and the leadership of souls."

2. In the New Testament, the term Gregory used for mediation (e.g., in *Or.* 2.91), *mesiteia*, is reserved for Christ as the sole true mediator; cf. Hebr 8:6, 9:15, 12:24. This language reappears in the *Apost. Const.* 2.25, 2.260, perhaps following *Or.* 2; and see Symeon the New Theologian *On Confess.* 11.

OIKEIŌSIS PROS THEON AS POLITICAL PHILOSOPHY

To lead souls and to mediate between men and God required proximity to the divine—expressed spatially and temporally—as a progressive purification acquired in retreat and contemplation of divine things: the *theologikē* of the philosophical *cursus*.[3] The true philosopher, therefore, had a head start. He was born into a sacred or holy family, closer already to the divine than most, so that the future philosopher would be closer to the divine *ab utero*. In addition, he should live in near-absolute retreat to safeguard and further his purity after proper initiation into the philosophical life. Yet Gregory returned to action. As I have argued, he insisted on retreat and contemplation not to turn inward, into himself, to flee the world, to "escape from here to there" (Pl. *Tht.* 176b), but to extend his purity to the world in order to bring it closer to the divine and hence to save it. Such was the tenor of Gregory's *oikeiōsis pros theon*; but this view of the philosophical life may well have been Gregory's response to the crisis threatening the community.

Gregory, following a more Aristotelian ideal of the *ergon* and *theōria* of the philosophical life, fully embraced the *ergon*, the practice of the office of priesthood.[4] Basil had done likewise. In a letter congratulating Basil on his new office as "presbyter" (*Ep.* 8), Gregory applauded him for taking this step, necessary "because of the present times, which excite against us many tongues of heretics," though neither Basil nor he himself had yearned for (*espoudazen*) office. Now they had to prove themselves worthy of philosophy and of the trust others placed in them, despite their love "for the pedestrian philosophy that remains below."[5] Now they had to fight, and *logoi* were their weapons.

But had Gregory always aspired to a more active philosophy in the open? Or had he first inclined to a philosophy in the shade, sheltered under a roof and behind a wall in near-absolute retreat, as he says in *Oration* 10.1? Gregory's *Epistle* 8, written after both he and Basil had been ordained, could imply that they had originally envisaged a different philosophical life—one that would fly high to what was above (and to which, of course, they still progressed). Can one find traces in Gregory's care-

---

3. Gr. Naz. *Or.* 2.75 expresses the spatial component, defining the cosmos as a continuum between what is closer to and farther removed from God. For *theologikē* as part of divinization, see D. O'Meara, *Platonopolis*, 31–131, and his definition of "political philosophy," ibid., 5–10.

4. Though emphasizing the practical, ethical implications of such engagement more than Aristotle; Sedley, "Idea." I am not arguing something entirely new. Gregory's mixed philosophical life—that is, his combination of monasticism and priestly office—has received much attention; Gautier, *Retraite*, 83–154, with bibliography. He stresses that Gregory's form of asceticism opposed the more "encratite" or radically retreating ascetics; Caner, *Wandering, Begging Monks*, 1–18, 83–125.

5. Gr. Naz. *Ep.* 8. Gautier, *Retraite*, 90, reads this remark as a sign of humility; I consider it ironic. See also Gr. Naz. *Ep.* 19. For the controversies regarding the date of Basil's ordination, either 362 or 364, Rousseau, *Basil*, 85, 88; Pouchet, *Basile*, 129–35; Gautier, *Retraite*, 304; I follow the 362 date.

fully controlled writings of a change in his philosophical aspirations in 362 and 363 that may have incited the criticism of some of his friends and brothers? No certainty can be expected; Gregory is a master of artful indirection. Nevertheless, some of his remarks, seen in the wider context of the debates relating to the true philosophical life engaging men such as Julian and Themistius, yield useful insights, since Gregory, in choosing the philosophical life, took a position in those debates. Boundaries between pagan and Christian were porous, with no neat line dividing them.

Born to a Holy Race

In chapter 6 of *Oration* 2 Gregory cites his preeminent motivation for his flight: a burning desire for "for the beauty of tranquility and retreat," which he had loved from the very beginning (*ex archēs*) far more "than any of the others who are passionate about *logoi*." Because of this intense yearning from the beginning, he had been thunderstruck by the blows that had tyrannized him into office when he had barely entered the vestibule of "the sacred asylum of this life" and had tasted but its first fruits.[6] Gregory found it hard to bear the tyranny of the present crisis that forced him into action, because in the middle of "the gravest and most terrifying dangers" he had promised God a life of *hēsychia* in *anachōrēsis,* tranquility in retreat (*Or.* 2.6). God had delivered him safely from the dangers, thus accepting his promise. Furthermore, God had chosen Gregory for such a life from the beginning: his mother, the "second Sarah," had borne him spiritually into the teachings of the faith (*Or.* 2.103). "I was called to this [contemplation of things above] from my youth, if I may tell something most people do not know; 'I was cast onto God from my birth' [Ps 22:10] and offered to him by my mother's vow. Later, I was confirmed in this at a time of danger. My longing grew, and my reason concurred; I brought everything and offered it all to the one who held my lot and saved me: properties, renown, physical well-being, and *logoi,* from which I drew only this benefit, namely to reject them and to have something to which to prefer Christ"(*Or.* 2.76–77; cf. *Or.* 4.5, 100).

Relying on Gregory's later poems, scholars have interpreted these remarks as a reference to a near-shipwreck Gregory endured en route from Alexandria to Athens: twenty days and nights of a storm at sea. This storm played a significant role as a time of transition in Gregory's later accounts of his life. He mentioned it at least three times, elaborating on his dangers and his promise by evoking Odysseus.[7]

---

6. I read this crisis as the situation of 362/3, and not, contrary to most scholars, as Gregory's ordination; Gallay, *Vie,* 72–74; Bernardi, *Prédication,* 96; idem, ed. and trans. *Grégoire de Nazianze: Discours 1–3,* 10; idem, *Saint Grégoire,* 122–25; McGuckin (*St. Gregory,* 100–102, 106–7) also considers the ordination as the greatest crisis but considers other factors, though (p. 117) for him Julian's effect on Gregory was slight. For Gautier too (*Retraite,* 294–95), Gregory did not want to avoid ordination.

7. Gr. Naz. *DVS* 124–210, esp. 164–65; *De rebus suis* 63–90, 307–21; and *Or.* 18.31.

Scholars have read his account of survival as a "'conversion' experience" that compelled him to adopt the philosophical life before Athens and Basil and to prepare himself for baptism.[8] According to John McGuckin, Gregory was baptized at Athens, still under the impression of the storm, while others date the baptism to his return to Cappadocia. Gregory never mentions his baptism explicitly, and we do not know for certain that he received it.[9]

In *Oration 2*, Gregory emphasized his mother's offering of him to God while he was *in utero*, "at the beginning"; his own affirmation of that vow when in danger; and his rescue as manifestation that God confirmed and accepted it. Gregory thus offered everything, including *logoi*, to God and Christ. As both Raymond Van Dam and John McGuckin emphasize, in the later elaborations Gregory's mother's role was again central. When he crafted the episode of the storm at sea in (the customary) Homeric language, Nonna acted as Pallas Athena, rescuing Gregory as Odysseus from mortal danger to guide him to philosophy—just as Athena rescued Julian from suicide to guide him to the philosophy of the imperial throne as Caesar (*Ep. ad Ath.* 275b–c).[10]

Full devotion to philosophy, to the greatest possible comprehension of divine things, divinely prepared and authorized, is the issue in *Oration* 2.77. That is, the storm at sea confirmed Gregory's initiation into the mysteries of philosophy, conveyed in the appropriate language of silence and reticence called for in alluding to unutterable matters, as John McGuckin's analysis of the retellings of the episode of great danger confirms. Indeed, McGuckin compares Gregory's experience explicitly to Julian's initiation into the Eleusinian Mysteries at Athens.[11] It is conceivable that Gregory considered baptism in fact an initiation into the mysteries of philosophy, because he employed the language of initiation common to describe access to such mysteries. A revelatory moment confirmed his choice of the philosophical

---

8. The storm at sea was a popular literary motif, customarily executed in the Homeric style; Kertsch, "Motiv." See Van Dam's (*Families*, 91–92) and McGuckin's (*St. Gregory*, 48–55, quotation 49) excellent analyses of Gregory's later fashioning of this event; McGuckin does not mention *Or.* 2.77.

9. McGuckin, *St. Gregory*, 55–76, for baptism at Athens. Breitenbach, "Unfreiwillige Hochzeitsgast," and Rubenson, "Cappadocians," 114 n. 4, with bibliography, both reject McGuckin's dating. Gautier, *Retraite*, 29–30, follows Gr. Presb. *V. Gr. Naz.* 74, PG 35.258 = *Gregorii Presbyteri Vita Sancti Gregorii Theologi* 5, Corpus Christianorum, Series Graeca (CCG), vol. 44, ed. and trans. Lequeux, 136, and Gallay, *Vie*, 67, in assuming baptism upon returning to Cappadocia, pointing to Syrian monastic parallels.

10. Hom. *Od.* 5.290–437. Nonna also received notice of her son's danger through a divine vision, as Athena informs Penelope of Telemachus's danger; *Od.* 4.790–840; Gr. Naz. *Or.* 18.31.

11. For Julian, see Eun. *VS* 7.3.1, 6–7; Athanassiadi-Fowden, *Julian*, 48. McGuckin's main point (*St. Gregory*, 58, 62–70) is the date of baptism, but his analysis (including Gregory's *Carmen lugubre*, *Carm.* 2.1.45; in *Gregorio Nazianzeno: Poesie*, vol. 2, ed. and trans. Crimi) describes precisely such philosophical initiations.

life that had begun *in utero*. By divine design his mother, a second Sarah and a second Athena, had offered him to God. Recurrent dreams in his youth strengthened the vow; Gregory reaffirmed it, and God confirmed it.[12] But Gregory, responding by offering God everything and having retreated into *anachōrēsis,* was stopped short by the now familiar tyranny. As I have argued elsewhere, baptism for him was an initial step in the gradual process of purification and conversion to the divine, a progression also emphasized in his definition of *oikeiōsis pros theon* as progressive purification and affiliation to God.[13] Thus, baptism itself, though relevant, is less important than the process it initiates; therefore Gregory does not mention it or provide a specific date.

Gregory, in sum, had been born spiritually to sacred parents. He belonged to the holy race (*hiera genea*) of true, divinely born philosophers.[14] As will be recalled from the discussion of the philosophical circles at Constantinople, late-antique philosophers, however intense their Platonism, considered philosophy a divine gift. "A trueborn and genuine philosopher" was descended from a sacred marriage (*gamos hieros*), the foundation for his progress toward and eventual (re-)union with the divine. Given the holy race to which he belonged, he was likely to be "divinely possessed with longing for the true goal of philosophy."[15] The path toward the divine, though determined *ab utero,* included experiences of initiation or conversion: Gregory's revelation and promise at a time of mortal danger or Julian's initiations at Athens and Ephesus, which demonstrated the philosopher's free will and agency in acquiring the necessary purity, for which divine election provided no shortcut.[16]

In *Oration* 2, Gregory established his divine calling, his membership in the sacred race of the true philosopher. While his claims to that divine calling and to sacred origin seem muted in this oration when compared with those of his later elaborations, they are fully in evidence. Gregory was a Moses and an Aaron; the Samuel but also the Isaac to his father's Abraham. His mother, Nonna (Sarah, Athena), offered him on God's altar—the phrasing of *Oration* 2.77 also echoes 1 Samuel 1:11. Having begun his divine ascent before birth, and thus from a privileged vantage point, Gregory was closer to God than those in his care and could better mediate between God and men (*Or.* 2.91). Sacred descent and divine calling were all the

---

12. Breitenbach, "Unfreiwillige Hochzeitsgast," 33–37, reads the *Carmen lugubre,* despite McGuckin (above, n. 11), as philosophical initiation (understood as monasticism) before Athens, dating Gregory's baptism to his return to Nazianzus and his ordination, following Gr. Presb. *Vita Sancti Gr.* 5, CCG vol. 44, 136.

13. S. Elm, "Inscriptions and Conversions."

14. Goulet, "Vies," 165–72, 175–90; Fowden, "Pagan Holy Man," 33–38; Francis, *Subversive Virtue,* 112–26; Lim, *Public Disputation,* 37–53. Gautier, *Retraite,* 84–94, points to the Platonic resonances of Gregory's notions of purification and divine ascent.

15. Hierocl. *apud* Phot. *Bibl.* 251.461a.32–34; cf. Jul. *Or.* 11.136b–c. R. R. R. Smith, "Late Roman Philosopher Portraits," 142–46; D. O'Meara, *Platonopolis,* 31–39.

16. Them. *Or.* 21.248; Plato, *R.* 548e. Fowden, "Pagan Holy Man," 33–34.

more necessary, of course, in times of mortal danger, such as the wars then threatening those on whose behalf Gregory had been called to mediate.

In his later funeral eulogies for his brother, sister, and father, Gregory explicitly wrote himself a sacred philosophical family, closely affiliated (through *oikeiōsis*) with the divine. His described his brother, Caesarius, as embodying the perfect philosopher as public official, "even in the *chlanis*," the public man's finely woven overcoat and the antithesis, traditionally, of the philosopher's rough cloak (*Or.* 7.11). His sister, Gorgonia, epitomized *sōphrosynē* as the philosopher as matriarch and mother of future philosophers (*Or.* 8.8, 15, 21). His parents, a second Odysseus and Penelope, like Moses, had been judged worthy to approach the divine, since they were closer (*oikeioteroi*) to God than others, having placed their love of God above that of their children (*Or.* 7.4, 9; *Or.* 8.4, 6, 11). Since Gregory issued from a sacred, philosophical, family, his closest kin were also more *oikeios* to God than most.[17] In the context of the deep crisis of 362 and 363—and throughout Gregory's life, a continued battle for the truth of the *orthos logos*—to have been divinely chosen to mediate as true philosopher between God and men was not only a good thing but *conditio sine qua non*. Only the divinely chosen philosopher could comprehend the divine will and guide others accordingly. Gregory thus met the precondition for right contemplation and the appropriate action in which he now engaged.

Furthermore, such philosophical descent from a sacred marriage (like Julian's from Zeus-Helios and Athena) cemented Gregory's role vis-à-vis his father, as discussed in the previous chapter. Because Gregory had been promised to God *in utero*, a promise divinely authorized and confirmed, he had been born closer to God—both spatially and in kinship—than his own father, whose *oikeiōsis*, though advanced farther than most, had begun later in his life, so that it remained farther down and removed from God than Gregory's. Gregory the Elder, though a second Abraham and Moses, could progress farther only with his more philosophical son's advice, guidance, and mediation. Nonetheless, as father of a divinely called philosopher brought forth in a sacred marriage of equals (*Or.* 7.4), he far exceeded all in his care except his son. As divine philosopher, the son could guide and even correct the father without endangering the good order of everything; the father's honor remained intact and was even enhanced.

Philosophy in the Shade or Philosophy in the Open

Gregory's insistence on his divine calling and participation in the holy race of the divine philosopher, his repeatedly voiced yearning for the beauty of tranquility and retreat, and his disdain for the tumult of this world—in sum, his "estrangement from this world" (*xeniteia tou kosmou*), discussed insightfully by Francis Gautier—could corroborate the dominant scholarly reading of Gregory as *weltfremder* man devoted

---

17. S. Elm, "Gregory's Women" and "Family Men."

to contemplation.[18] These might support a claim that Gregory favored the more Platonic interpretation of the philosophical life—albeit in a Christian form—also embraced by Julian and by those who attacked Themistius. Such passages in Gregory's writings seem more like a philosophy of strict seclusion than the Stoic *oikeiōsis* as engagement with the other I have outlined as essential for Gregory. Still, a close analysis of text and context leaves little doubt that Gregory called for engagement and involvement, preceded by and interspersed with retreat and contemplation; he inserted his reading of scripture into a more Aristotelian view of Platonic philosophical life, enhanced by Stoic ethical demands, thus Christianizing the matrix. It is possible, however—though to say so may strain the evidence—that Gregory had first advocated, or had wanted it known that he advocated, a deep commitment to an essentially Platonic ideal of the philosophical life as a complete withdrawal into the shade, and then adjusted that position under the pressure of necessity.[19] Perhaps Gregory and Basil, when debating their choice of philosophical life while at Athens, envisioned the Christian version of a life of more complete withdrawal, such as that advocated by Porphyry rather than by Iamblichus.[20] Basil's *Epistle* 33, written after the death of Caesarius, may suggest such a possibility: writing on Gregory's behalf, Basil laments that "one who so long ago determined to pass his life in tranquility [*hēsychia*]" should be dragged into the courts.[21]

Gregory himself framed his early letters to Basil to suggest that he, unlike Basil, had always chosen a philosophical life bound by ethical obligation to his kin. Gregory seems to emphasize that his view of the true philosophical life had always been more engaged than Basil's with the public good and the well-being of everyone (that is, more Aristotelian or Iamblichan or Stoic). Read polemically, although Basil, unencumbered by duties to his father and his city and not bound to his bishop as son as well as presbyter, could freely advocate a life of intense withdrawal—the fashion of the day, if we believe Themistius and Eunapius—Gregory all along combined his philosophical life with both his career as rhetor and active engagement in his father's affairs, and he embraced his duty as priest far more readily.[22] While initially Gregory may have committed himself to complete withdrawal as someone with a divine call stronger than Basil's (witness the storm at sea), he realized early on that such a life was the one Julian embraced and propagated, so that he, Gregory, divinely guided and hence prescient (though breaking the vow he made to a friend in Athens), opted

---

18. Gautier, *Retraite*, 29–82.
19. For example, Gregory uses the term *systraphēnai* (*Or.* 2.7, 12.4, 25.6, 28.3), a technical Platonic term, for conversion to the divine; Gottwald, *De Gregorio*, 44.
20. Gr. Naz. *Ep.* 1.
21. Bas. *Ep.* 223.5 stresses the same point, now in the context of Basil's break with Eustathius.
22. McLynn, "Among the Hellenists," 220–24, summarizes Basil's circumstances.

for the political philosophical life sponsored by the truly Christian Constantius and advocated, as early as the late 350s and early 360s, by Themistius.

Most scholars interpret the exchange of letters between Gregory and Basil when they returned from Greece to Pontus and Cappadocia as the attempt of Basil, already committed to the philosophical life, to persuade a vacillating Gregory to join him in retreat at Annesi.[23] But as Neil McLynn has emphasized, such a reconstruction fails to credit Gregory's own editorial skills in fashioning "one of the most longstanding, famous and stormy friendships in Christian history" in line with his intentions. Gregory's early correspondence with Basil concerning the philosophical life forms part of such self-fashioning.[24] Basil's *Epistle* 2, written in 359, responds to a request from Gregory for a more detailed description of the philosophical life Basil had in mind, "of [his] habits and mode of life" at Annesi.[25] Basil obliged, though he was "ashamed to write what I myself do night and day in this out-of-the-way place. For I have indeed left my life in the city, . . . but I have not yet been able to leave myself behind, [and I have as yet] derived no great benefit from our solitude [*erēmia*]." Still, Basil sought to avoid all worldly concerns in order that his soul might achieve the highest degree of purity,[26] and that he might "receive the impressions of divine instruction," predicated on the "unlearning of the teachings that already possess it, derived from evil habits. For it is no more possible to write in wax without first smoothing away the letters previously written thereon than it is to supply the soul with divine teachings without first removing preconceptions derived from habit."[27] Solitude [*erēmia*] was indispensable, because it "gives reason for leisure to sever [passions] from our soul."[28] The purpose of this leisure was to "nourish the

---

23. Rousseau, *Basil*, 24–26, 40–41, 57–82, 84–90; McGuckin, *St. Gregory*, 86–99; Gautier, *Retraite*, 284–91; Van Dam, *Families*, 156–61.

24. McGuckin, *St. Gregory*, 54–56, assigns Gregory the guiding force in the choice of philosophical life. McLynn, "Gregory Nazianzen's Basil," 185–86, highlights that Gregory edited his dossier of letters in the 380s to include epistolary dialogues that alternate a letter from Basil with a series of his own responses, to shape his persona in line with his autobiographical program. One such dialogue was Basil's *Ep*. 2, answered by Gregory's *Epp*. 1 and 8, also *Epp*. 47, 58. Foundational is Fedwick, *Bibliotheca Basiliana*, vol. 1, 139–43. As Wyss noted ("Gregor II," 807), Gregory was the first Christian Greek writer to collect his own letters; see Gr. Naz. *Ep*. 53.

25. Usually read together with Bas. *Ep*. 14; for the date, Rousseau, *Basil*, 62–68; Pouchet, *Basile*, 93–100. Translation Deferrari (*Saint Basil: The Letters*), with my modifications.

26. ὁ χωρισμὸς ἀπὸ τοῦ κόσμου παντός.

27. This does not necessitate physical removal, "but the severance of the soul from sympathy with the body to make it 'cityless'" (τῆς πρὸς τὸ σῶμα συμπαθείας τὴν ψυχὴν ἀπορρῆξαι καὶ γενέσθαι ἄπολιν).

28. σχολὴν διδοῦσα τῷ λόγῳ. Basil affirmed his determination to follow the one who said: "If any man will come after me, let him deny himself [ἀπαρνήσθω ἑαυτόν], take up his cross, and follow me" (Mt 16:24). "What we ought to do, however, and what would enable us to keep close to [his] footsteps, . . .

soul with divine thoughts,"[29] so that it might ascend "of its own accord to the thought of God."[30] Then, when it is illuminated without and within by that glory, "it becomes forgetful even of its own nature, [which is] no longer able to drag down the soul."

The philosophical life Basil describes here, uninterested in involvement in the *politeia*, devotes itself solely to solitude and purification to aid the soul's ascent to God.[31] Gregory's letters of response, as he later selected them, suggest his own advocacy of pursuing less retreat and greater involvement, in line with the one he promoted throughout his life.[32] Gregory's *Epistle* 1 invites Basil to share a life of partial withdrawal that would not only honor their friendship but also fulfill the commitment of the citizen to honor his kin. Gregory's *Epistle* 8, of 362, mentioned above, still answered Basil's second letter. In it, he congratulated Basil on his ordination, necessary at this moment of crisis though neither of them desired it, given their shared enthusiasm for "pedestrian" philosophy. As Gregory emphasized, the active involvement neither had desired—in line with the topos of *recusatio*—was demanded by "the times in which we find ourselves, which excite many tongues of heretics against us; therefore we should not be ashamed either of our life or of those who entrust to us their hope"; this was what they had been divinely called to do, as Gregory had argued all along, despite his earlier promise, at Athens, to join Basil's retreat.

In sum, Gregory emphasized, in the letters he later selected for posterity, that in his devotion to the philosophical life he always kept his responsibilities vis-à-vis his kin and the *koinon* in mind.[33] Thus, when the inner Christian civil war and Julian's attacks from the outside demanded engagement and action, Gregory the hoplite

---

is this: We must try to keep the mind in tranquility. For just as the eye that constantly shifts its gaze . . . cannot see distinctly what lies before it . . . so too man's mind when distracted by the concerns of the world [τῶν κατὰ τὸν κόσμον φροντίδων] cannot focus itself distinctly on the truth." These concerns are the family, marriage, and offspring, "management of household, oversight of his slaves [οἰκετῶν προστασίαι, stunningly translated by Deferrari as "protection of his servants' rights"!], losses on contracts, quarrels with neighbors, contests in the law courts, risks of business, or the labor of the farm"— in short, the duties and obligations of the elite citizen.

29. Which involved reading scriptures, prayer, avoidance of self-display and ostentation, observance of the rules of agreeable social intercourse, and appropriate teaching, which included humility and the occasional rebuke. The outer appearances should mirror the inner disposition, so that "the tunic [χιτών] should be drawn close to the body by a girdle; but let the belt not be above the flank, for that is effeminate, nor loose, so as to let the tunic slip through, for that is slovenly, . . . arguing for laxity of mind": a classic example of the gendered rhetoric Gleason, *Making Men,* 29–62, so vividly analyzed.

30. πρὸς ἑαυτόν, δι' ἑαυτοῦ δὲ πρὸς τὴν περὶ Θεοῦ ἔννοιαν ἀναβαίνει.

31. G. Clark, "Philosophic Lives," 38–47; D. O'Meara, *Platonopolis,* 44–49.

32. E.g., Gr. Naz. *Or.* 2.29, 14.4, 23.1, 25.4, 38.9; *Carm.* 1.2.30.15–16; 2.1.11.321–26. Gregory often aligned *praxis* and philanthropy as the essential virtue of the civilized human being, in contrast to the solitary beast. Cf. Pl. *Ep.* 8.334d; Arist. *EN* 10.8.1–13. Gautier, *Retraite,* 94–99; McGuckin, *St. Gregory,* 145–58.

33. Rousseau, *Basil,* 66–68.

was armed and had been training for some time; his preparations were well under way, combining action with purification to save those in his care. Gregory portrayed Basil here as one who had indulged more fully in retreat.[34]

As *Oration* 2 has made clear, and as his careful editing of the correspondence underlines, Gregory's choice in 362 and 363 had its critics. In the preceding chapter, I identified the group of those who criticized Gregory in Nazianzus as his friends and brothers, peers who had shared his love of *logoi* and the philosophical life since their days at Athens. Nazianzus was that chapter's focus, and I was concerned to position these persons clearly in the context of the wider Christian doctrinal struggles then affecting the city. But Gregory also had to defend himself against accusations of embracing a philosophical life that appeared not to be one (*Or.* 2.103), and of wishing to use his retreat to further his career—to grab more power than was his due. He had to emphasize, moreover, that assuming office and leading do not "exceed the limits of philosophy" and carry no blame (*Or.* 2.5; cf. *Ep.* 8). Indeed, *Oration* 2 above all advocates and defends the philosophical life of active intervention: the political philosophical life in the open.[35]

This was a defense against persons who advocated a philosophical life "in the shade," who considered an active political philosophical life no philosophical life at all (*Or.* 2.103). Scholars have long recognized as a major concern of Gregory's first three orations, especially *Oration* 2, that in them he defended himself against, indeed attacked, persons who advocated strict retreat. As noted in Chapter 5, this has been read in the context of monasticism and asceticism, in particular of the extreme forms of ascetic withdrawal associated with Eustathius and Egyptian and Syrian asceticism. Francis Gautier and John McGuckin stress that Gregory's emphasis on what he calls the "mixed life" criticizes such ascetic extremes, and McGuckin has suggested that Gregory's ordination may have been an attempt by his father to separate him from the ascetic life of extreme retreat he had previously embraced.[36]

I concur entirely, except that Eustathius's association with extreme ascetics can-

---

34. Rousseau, *Basil*, 66, notes a changing tone in Gregory's letters to Basil. In *Ep.* 4, Basil evoked Diogenes as a philosopher who disdained worldly things, especially the active life; cf., e.g., Max. Tyr. *Or.* 26.5; Krueger, "Diogenes."

35. As described by Hermias *In Pl. Phdr.* 221.10–15: "in general the philosopher, whenever he is turned toward ... the knowledge of ... god, ... is the [theoretical] philosopher; but when he turns from this to the care of the city and orders it according to that knowledge, then he becomes a political philosopher" (German translation: Hermias, *Kommentar*, trans. Bernard, 376); Pl. *Phdr.* 107d1–2, *Ti.* 90b–c6, *Lg.* 716c; Plotin. *Enn.* 176b8–c2; Sopat. *apud* Stobaeus 4.212.13–218.9.

36. McGuckin, *St. Gregory*, 87, 93–101, 145–52, 190, 204–6; Gautier, *Retraite*, 22–28, 54–69, 82, 89–112. Bibliography on the mixed life is extensive; Plagnieux, *Saint Grégoire*, 81–113, 141–59; Malingrey, *Philosophia*, 254; *Gregorio Nazianzeno: Poesie*, vol. 1, ed. and trans. Moreschini, 30; Moreschini, *Filosofia*, 28–35, 69–79; S. Elm, *Virgins*, 207–10; Brown, *Body*, 286; Špidlík, "Theoria," and especially *Grégoire*, 113–37 and passim.

not be sustained and that scholars' exclusive focus on Christian asceticism overlooks the elephant in the room: the contemporary non-Christian world.[37] As we have seen, in Gregory's time there was intense debate about how much retreat and how much action the philosophical life demanded, and no position was neutral—especially once Julian entered the fray in 361 and 362. In the late 350s, philosophers advocating obscurity attacked those who favored the open. Themistius's positions were widely known throughout the period, for he had been recruiting to the senate persons of similar disposition, including Gregory's brother, Caesarius, and men like his friends and brothers. Themistius's ideas, sponsored by Constantius, had elicited resistance among many who yearned deeply for the philosophical life, and there is no reason to assume that educated persons at Nazianzus, well trained and well informed, were immune to these debates and their implications. That is, Gregory, initially, and some of his friends and brothers, may well have embraced or wished to embrace a life of the greatest possible retreat. This is the implication of McGuckin's and Gautier's analyses if we put the issue in the philosophical terms then current rather than in exclusively Christian ones.[38] Those persons would then have had every reason to criticize what may well have been a volte-face by Gregory in 362 and 363: his advocacy of a more actively involved philosophical life.[39] Here timing becomes important. If Gregory, in 362 and 363, changed his view of a correct philosophical life from one more removed to one more involved, he did so because of Julian. What he advocated then, at any rate, conformed to the political philosophical life of Themistius and Constantius that Julian's more withdrawn philosophical life deliberately opposed. From the *homoios* to the political philosophical

---

37. Modern scholars of ancient philosophy likewise shy away from considering Christian writers. Thus, Rist, "Basil's 'Neoplatonism,'" esp. 205, discusses Basil's *Ep.* 2 in relation to Plotinus (*Enn.* 5.1.2.11–14, 5.1.12.12–20, 6.9.7.14) and Porphyry (*Abst.* 109.9), to exclude that Basil had been influenced by contemporary Neoplatonic philosophy; such philosophical references as there are, he argues, are either directly to Plato or to later Aristotelian epitomes. He certainly has a point when arguing that Basil's *Ep.* 2 referred to Plato rather than to Plotinus. This is not, however, proof that Basil remained unaware of contemporary philosophical debates. Rist (pp. 215–16) allows that Basil had read Eus. *PE*—a compilation of quotes from Porphyry. He maintains, however (pp. 219–20), that the Cappadocians' expressed hostility toward pagan culture equates with absence of any contemporary Neoplatonic influence, which he constructs as follows (p. 139): "to be influenced by a man's philosophy one has to read him directly or to have access to his work indirectly either through other written documents or through oral sources." Basil, after years of study at Athens (pp. 182–85), and as a reader of Porphyry in Eusebius, certainly fulfilled these criteria.

38. The pagan context of Athanasius's construct of the ascetic philosophical life of Antony might be worth examining; Rousseau, "Antony," esp. 91.

39. In his later editing of the correspondence (and in *Or.* 2), Gregory argued that he had not changed his mind but had always advocated the more open philosophical life. It is important to keep in mind, as D. O'Meara has stressed (*Platonopolis*, 5–10, 73–139, and passim) and as I noted above in Chapter 3, that most philosophers did not reject involvement "in the city"; at issue was the degree of involvement.

life in the open, Gregory embraced those whom Julian opposed; but as he did so he left room, as the preceding chapters have noted, for his own innovations.

Themistius as a Philosophical Model

Whether the philosophical life Gregory advocated in 363 represented a volte-face or was interpreted as such by some of his friends and brothers, the life of active political involvement as *oikeiōsis pros theon* was clearly not the one of complete retreat proclaimed by the philosopher as leader, Julian. The details of Julian's impact on Gregory will occupy us further in the chapters that follow. But before addressing my next topic, the civil war within Christianity and Gregory's Christian opponents, I would like to discuss Themistius as a possible model for Gregory's philosophical life. Just as no strict boundary lines divided pagan from Christian—the arguments Gregory used against his Christian opponents in the civil war were those he used against Julian and vice versa—likewise, such an exemplar as Themistius belonged to all, whatever their religious affiliation. Gregory was concerned to know who and what kind of argument was *oikeios,* ours, or *allotrios,* theirs; some, nominally Christian, were much farther from the Good than some of their pagan contemporaries, and the other way round.

When Gregory returned from Athens to Cappadocia in 358, he traveled overland, passing through Constantinople. Caesarius was already there, and the brothers spent some time together in the city before continuing on to Nazianzus. Caesarius's sojourn in Nazianzus was short. He returned to Constantinople almost immediately, because he had been offered a seat in the senate in addition to his position as public physician and his other public honors.[40] Themistius may well have been responsible for Caesarius's recruitment for the senate, for by imperial mandate he was then actively engaged in that task. In 358 Themistius's notion of the active life of the political philosopher was the talk of the town. As his writings indicate, that notion had excited intense criticism, because active involvement in the *politeia* and the power it conferred could prove a noxious influence on the philosopher, impairing his divine nature and destiny.[41] But as Constantius's letter appointing Themistius to the senate made clear, the emperor supported his philosophical life. The emperor also accepted Caesarius "as a physician and as a citizen" (*kai iatrōi kai oikētori*) by public decree, granting a petition that was conveyed to Constantius, in the West, by an embassy. It seems that Caesarius was aware of

---

40. Gr. Naz. *Or.* 7.8: τῆς συγκλήτου Βουλῆς μετουσίαν. Gallay, *Vie,* 33–35; Van Dam, "Self-representation," 120–21, and *Families,* 60–61. Caesarius seems to have rejected the seat in the senate, which did not impair his stellar career. A senate seat required some initial financial outlay, though it granted many immunities; Dagron, *Naissance,* 147–63.

41. Van Dam, *Families,* 60–61, suggests that Caesarius listened to Gregory's advice in *Ep.* 7 to reject the senate seat.

Themistius's political philosophical life in the *chlanis* and practiced it himself with the emperor's approval.[42]

In two later letters, Gregory praised Themistius as "king of *logoi*" (*basileus ... tōn logōn*): he had always been a philosopher who truly embodied the dictum of his "friend" Plato, "that the cities will not cease their evil ways unless power has been joined with philosophy" (*Ep.* 24). In the second of these letters to Themistius, Gregory stressed that *logoi* had united them "from the beginning" (*Ep.* 38). Furthermore, when recommending his cousin Amphilochius the Younger to Themistius's care in the 360s, Gregory reminded him that Amphilochius the Elder, at whose school Gregory taught before 362, had been Themistius's friend.[43] There is no need to assume that Gregory had met Themistius in person while in Constantinople. He would have had ample opportunity, in addition to Caesarius's connections, to become aware of Themistius's positions. Themistius's writings had been deposited and were publicly accessible in the newly founded Constantinopolitan library since 357, and he had traversed the country in his recruiting efforts for the senate between 358 and 361, addressing persons just like Caesarius, Gregory, and their friends of elevated status, formed by *paideia* to assume public administrative positions.[44] Between 358 and 363, the time of Gregory's early letters and his *Orations* 1–3, no one was more widely recognized as embodying a political philosophical life than Themistius.[45] Furthermore, Eustathius was present in Constantinople during the early 350s, also practicing a philosophical life of active involvement and care for the community through his feeding places for the poor. Until 360, Eustathius's friend Macedonius, too, was active through such *ptōchotropheia* as bishop of Constantinople: these men also combined demand for retreat with active involvement, and they too, at least between 358 and 360, were among Constantius's favorites.[46]

Although Gregory nowhere mentions Themistius in describing his true philosophical life,[47] it is difficult to imagine that he was unaware of him as a model for

---

42. Gr. Naz. *Or.* 7.8–9, 11; *Epigr.* 93, 94; Coulie, *Richesses,* 139–45.

43. Gr. Naz. *Ep.* 24 asks Themistius to intervene on behalf of Amphilochius the Younger; *Ep.* 37, *To Sophronius,* recommends to Themistius's patronage the son of Eudoxius, the rhetorician from Caesarea. The letter dates to the 380s. Themistius was probably one of the philosophers Gregory addressed directly in his speech to Emperor Theodosius: Gr. Naz. *Or.* 36.12.

44. According to the dating of Penella (Themistius, *Private Orations,* ed. and trans. Penella, xiii) and of Vanderspoel (*Themistius,* 250–51), Them. *Or.* 24, 30, 20, 21, 26 of the private orations and *Or.* 1, 2, 4, 3 would by then have been available in the library.

45. Vanderspoel, *Themistius,* 34–35, suggests that Themistius had been a student of Basil the Elder at Neocaesarea during the 320s and 330s, which would further strengthen the case for Gregory's awareness of him.

46. Soz. *HE* 4.2.3; Socr. *HE* 2.38; Macedonius had founded feeding places for the poor in Constantinople; S. Elm, *Virgins,* 111–12, 128–33.

47. I argue not that Gregory adhered strictly to all aspects of Themistius's political philosophy but that he knew both Themistius and Constantius advocated active engagement, which Julian opposed;

his eloquent proposal not to practice solitary philosophy but to share what the philosopher painstakingly gained with those willing to hear—the choice embodied by Themistius and supported by Constantius (*Ep. Const.* 20a–b).[48] Most of Gregory's audience in 362 and 363 knew of Themistius the political philosopher. And Julian, in his imperial letter of 362 excluding Christians from public teaching, singled out for scrutiny those who claimed to be political philosophers.[49] He had already, in his *Epistle to Themistius* intended for the Constantinopolitan senate in 361, distanced himself from Themistius, arguing that the political, active philosopher had misunderstood Aristotle's teachings on the matter. Julian professed his own support for solitary philosophers such as Maximus of Ephesus. Thus before 362 a person who wished to combine the duty to serve his parents with philosophy would have found support in Themistius's life. But by 362, a more active, Aristotelian political philosophical stance signaled support for Constantius and opposition to Julian.

As always, however, things were not quite so straightforward. For not only was Julian critical of the Themistian-Constantian political philosophy; he also attacked persons who practiced an extreme retreat he considered antisocial and contrary to the laws of man and nature like the Christian *apotaktitai,* renunciators, who gained "honor, crowds of attendants, and services" by making small sacrifices and by uttering divine revelations (*chrēmatizesthai:* Jul. *Or.* 6.201c–d, 7.224b–c). For Julian those on the outside who threatened the good order inside were the Christians, especially those who had chosen stark withdrawal. Like the uneducated Cynics, they were outside the common *politeia* of men as defined, for example, by Aristotle, who considered those too self-sufficient to belong either to the lower animals or to the gods.[50] Because Christian *apotaktitai* could not have been gods, Julian thought them closer to animals: that is, not fully part of mankind. Gregory was about to refute all such charges, especially once the emperor had issued his law and letter on teachers and political philosophers. But he found it all the more difficult to fend off Julian, the beast attacking him from the outside, while Christian fellow philosophers, unaware of the true philosophical life, aligned themselves with the opposition. Such men incited civil war and at the worst possible moment made Christianity "a new spectacle, not for angels and humans . . . but for nearly all evil persons [*ponēroi*] and in all circumstances and places, in public spaces, at drinking parties, at festi-

---

D. O'Meara, *Platonopolis,* 206–8. Themistius seems to share with Gregory the notion of the preexisting soul or intellect, in contrast to contemporary Aristotelians with whom Themistius is often aligned, such as Alexander of Aphrodisias; Ballériaux, "Thémistius."

48. For continued emphasis on active philosophy, see Gr. Naz. *Or.* 25.4, 6, *Eulogy for the Philosopher Maximus,* and *Or.* 26; also Gautier, *Retraite,* 63–66, 152; *Grégoire de Nazianze: Discours 24–26,* ed. and trans. Mossay, 106–7; Dagron, *Empire romain,* 43.

49. Saracino, "Politica culturale."

50. Arist. *Pol.* 1253a.

vals and funerals. Now we have jumped even onto the theatrical stage—I say it almost crying—and together with the most licentious we incite laughter: there is no subject of song or spectacle so agreeable as a Christian lampooned.... That is what this civil war has brought us" (*Or.* 2.84–85). Combatting the enemy was a tall order even for fully armed, divinely born philosophers in action.[51]

THE ENEMY ON THE INSIDE: PHOTINUS AND EUNOMIUS

Between 361 and 364 "the affairs of the Christians in the East were as a muddy pool and, as everyone sensed, far from settling, those waters were about to be deliberately raked again."[52] John McGuckin's vivid description of Christian affairs in the early 360s is certainly accurate. Much of the murkiness results from the rhetorical practice of our sources not to name opponents but to refer to them in allusions and codes, or by labels. (Gregory, for example, used the names of Arius and Sabellius.) Still, it is possible to discern something solid in the general murk and to describe more clearly the individuals whom Gregory attacked.[53] The older literature, prompted by Gregory's use of the name Arius, identified Gregory's opponents in *Oration* 2 as Arian, in part out of a desire to clear Gregory the Elder of Arian tendencies and also to emphasize Gregory's Nicene credentials; this reflects scholars' tendency to conceive the fourth-century Christian debates as between Nicenes and non-Nicenes.[54] Studies in the past ten to twenty years are more nuanced in assessing the theological context, recognizing the fluidity of the positions I outlined in Chapter 1, even while continuing to see two broad frameworks and excluding the tertium quid, paganism, almost completely.[55] Correspondingly, studies of Gregory's theology after Brennecke concur that Arians as such were not Gregory's target. As Brennecke has shown, in the 360s, the homoian or Arian signers of the Constantinopolitan creed were not a homogeneous group. The homoian umbrella covered most Eastern bishops, whose opinions differed and who formed fluid allegiances according to personal motives, changing constellations at court, and evolving doctrinal positions. In fact, the processes that differentiated the positions of homoians, anomoians or heterou-

---

51. Lugaresi considers Gregory's despair over Christians as spectacle (*Or.* 2. 84), "il vertice, l'espressione estrema della lotta anticristiana" ("Spettacoli," 446).

52. McGuckin, *St. Gregory*, 104; Abramowski, "Trinitarische und christologische Hypostasenformeln," esp. 41–47; Studer, "Personenbegriff."

53. Lyman, "Topography," 46, 61–62; Vinzent, *Pseudo-Athanasius*, 129–30.

54. Bernardi, *Prédication*, 96–108; Trisoglio, "Figura"; Loofs, "Gregor," esp. 142. Even Vaggione's excellent study reflects that binary view (e.g., *Eunomius*, 49–50), though less than Hanson, *Search*; see R. Williams's review of *Eunomius: The Extant Works*, ed. and trans. R. Vaggione, in *Scottish Journal of Theology* 45 (1992): 101–11.

55. Beeley, *Gregory*, 219–20; Gautier, *Retraite*, 302–15; McGuckin, *St. Gregory*, 131–33.

sians, homoiousians, and Neo-Nicenes or homoousians accelerated sharply during the reign of Julian. The very civil war Gregory had deplored led to the clarification and hence formation of more distinct and indeed new positions.[56]

Those whom Gregory targeted in 362 and 363 may have included leading homoians, such as Eudoxius or Acacius, and others then attacked directly by Julian. However, those who really mattered to Gregory were those representing positions on the Trinity that he considered extreme: Photinus and especially Eunomius. In using the names Arius and Sabellius, to reiterate, Gregory did not imply that he attributed to his opponents any real connection to the actual historical persons Arius and Sabellius or their positions. That Aetius and Eunomius subscribed to the Constantinopolitan "*homoios* according to the scriptures" did no more connect them than Gregory the Elder to Arius or Sabellius in any meaningful sense.[57]

Scholars have identified Eunomius and Photinus as Gregory's targets almost exclusively on the basis and in the context of the *Theological Orations*, which Gregory delivered in the summer and fall of 380 in Constantinople in his church, Anastasia.[58] In these orations Gregory most systematically attacked Photinus and in particular Eunomius and their followers, largely without mentioning names. By that year, the contours of their respective positions had sharpened.[59] Furthermore, most of the protagonists were in Constantinople, where Eunomius drew large audiences.[60]

The *Theological Orations* (*Or.* 27–31), which represent Gregory's summa, have been the preeminent source for scholarly reconstructions of his theology. As Christopher Beeley has pointed out, the reconstruction of Gregory's theological

---

56. Brennecke, *Studien*, 87–91, 100, with bibliography.

57. Eun. *Apol.* 12, 22; Philost. *HE* 6.1. For a long-overdue appreciation of Philostorgius as excerpted by (perhaps) Photius, Argov, "Giving," esp. 507–24. For Eunomius, M. R. Barnes, *Power*, 141; Cavalcanti, *Studi*, 24; *Basile de Césarée: Contre Eunome*, ed. and trans. Sesboüé vol. 1, 26–27; Vaggione, *Eunomius*, 204–5, 224–32. Kopecek, *History*, 133–53, argues for a distinct Neo-Arian party by 359.

58. Most scholars of Eunomius do not consult Gregory of Nazianzus's writings but rely on Basil, Gregory of Nyssa, and Philostorgius (in addition to Eunomius's fragments); M. R. Barnes, *Power*, 163, 216–17, 298–99; Lim, *Public Disputation*, 122–48; Vaggione, *Eunomius*, 143, 171. Those who do consult Gregory limit their inquiry to the *Theological Orations*, though Gautier (*Retraite*, 375–76) and McGuckin (*St. Gregory*, 38, 99, 104–6, 135, 144–45, 241) note Gregory's awareness of Eunomius in the early 360s; Gregory of Nazianzus, *Faith*, intro. Norris, 53–68.

59. Photinus is mentioned in Gr. Naz. *Or.* 33.16. Eunomius had begun to publish installments of his response to Basil's earlier attack between 378/9 and 383. Basil too continued to refine his arguments: e.g., in his *De Spiritu Sancto*, addressed, in 373, to Amphilochius; Rousseau, *Basil*, 260–69. For the date of Eun. *Apol.* and Gregory of Nyssa's *Contra Eunomium* (= *Eun.*), see Pottier, *Dieu*, 17–60, with a more general introduction; and *Eunomius: The Extant Works*, ed. and trans. Vaggione, 79–94. Gregory of Nyssa and Eunomius continued to exchange polemics between 380 and 383, such as Eunomius's *Expositio fidei* (*Eunomius: The Extant Works*, ed. and trans. Vaggione, 131–61), to which Gregory of Nyssa responded with the work Jaeger published as *Refutatio confessionis Eunomii* (*Gregorii Nysseni opera*, ed. Jaeger, vol. 2, 314–410).

60. Socr. *HE* 5.20.4; Soz. *HE* 7.6.2, 7.17.1.

thought has focused almost exclusively on these orations.[61] As a result, Gregory's early orations have rarely been considered in reconstructions of the Eunomian controversies, and even then only in passing; and these orations have figured much less in examinations of Photinus. Scholars concerned with Eunomius, Photinus, or any other aspect of Gregory's theological thought, moreover, have never examined his orations against Julian, in particular *Oration 4*. Because these orations are directed against a pagan emperor, they are prima facie excluded from any scholarly consideration of Gregory the Theologian (except for the short passages in them that mention the term *theōsis*).

It is possible that all the anti-Eunomian (and anti-Photinian) echoes I propose for the earlier orations reflect Gregory's editorial hand and hence his concerns in the 380s and 390s—a conundrum I have already mentioned in discussing *Oration 2*. Aside from the methodological difficulty of singling out specific phrases and passages as later without any basis in the manuscript tradition, several other factors speak for Gregory's active engagement with Eunomius—to privilege him for the moment—at an early stage.[62] In general, as Richard Vaggione and Michel R. Barnes have emphasized, Eunomius's "contemporaries . . . afforded him an eminence which the meagerness of the surviving fragments does little to suggest. Almost every major theological figure of Eunomius' own age undertook to refute him." Apollinarius, Didymus the Blind, Diodore of Tarsus, Theodore of Mopsuestia, Theodoret of Cyrrhus, and Sophronius are all said to have written full-scale treatises refuting Eunomius, even though only Basil of Caesarea's and Gregory of Nyssa's refutations are fully extant today (a dossier to which Gregory of Nazianzus's *Theological Orations* [*Or.* 27–31] are usually added).[63]

Basil of Caesarea prepared and composed his first attack against Eunomius's first *Apology* between 362 and 364 "in the company of his brother beloved by God, Gregory."[64] Basil went into high gear between 363 and 364, when he employed secretaries, or *tachygraphoi*, lent to him by Eustathius, to finish his *Contra Eunomium* in time for the council of Lampsacus, scheduled to take place in the late summer

---

61. Beeley, *Gregory,* ix; Beeley purposefully bases his inquiry on a far broader array of Gregory's writings (though the Constantinopolitan orations still form his main source).

62. Comparison with fragments of Aetius, Eunomius, and other anomoians, and with Gregory of Nyssa's *CE*, reveal that Gregory represented earlier Eunomian positions faithfully; Gregory of Nazianzus, *Faith,* intro. Norris, 81.

63. Philost. *HE* 8.12; Jer. *Vir. ill.* 109, 120. Citation: *Eunomius: The Extant Works,* ed. and trans. Vaggione, xiii. Translations are Vaggione's, with my modifications. M. R. Barnes, *Power,* 174 n. 1, adds Basil of Ancyra and John Chrysostom to the list of opponents and notes that Eunomius was known to Victorinus, Ambrose, and Augustine by name. Cavalcanti, *Studi,* 129–37; Anastos, "Basil's *Kata Eunomiou,*" esp. 72–73.

64. Bas. *Ep.* 223.5; Gr. Nyss. *Eun.* 1.82 (*GNO,* vol. 1, 50); Rousseau, *Basil,* 104 n. 30.

and fall of 364 under Eleusius of Cyzicus.[65] Gregory composed his *Orations* 1–3 in 362 and 363, as I have argued, and by 363 and 364 he was at work at his *Oration* 4, *Against Julian*, which he declared "a present of Basil and Gregory."[66] In short, Basil was formulating his response to Eunomius while Gregory worked on his first orations, intermittently staying with Basil at Annesi. It seems logical, then, that Gregory's counter to Eunomius, instead of springing fully formed from his mind in the 380s, had evolved since the early 360s and at least in part in concert with Basil. Furthermore, Gregory's arguments against Eunomius dovetail with those against Julian.

How to Falsify the Trinity The two principal misconceptions of the Trinity Gregory identified were those that reduced the Trinity to one being for fear that polytheism would "leave us with mere names" devoid of meaning, or those that would "divide the *Logos* into three separate *hypostaseis*," arranged in no set hierarchy and estranged (*allotrioi*) from each other and as if they were rival divinities (*Or.* 2.36). These two principal errors resulted in three theological maladies, affecting different groups (*Or.* 2.37). One of these groups consisted of overzealous persons, driven more by misplaced eagerness than real evil (*Or.* 2.40); they appear to be the friends and brothers discussed in the preceding chapter. Next are persons who arrogantly attack the Trinity out of vainglory and lust for power (*kenodoxia kai philarchia*). A third group, "without any education [*apaideusia*] and with the corresponding impertinence," resists the *logos* (or all instruction) and with the instinct of pigs defiles the pearls of truth (*Or.* 2.41). Then, fourth, there are those without firm opinions "at home" (*oikothen*), no firmly engraved "form of the *logoi* about God."[67] They adopt teachers and teachings indiscriminately, picking whatever they like best. Trusting only their own judgment, they bend in all directions because of the similarities of the arguments, and after throwing away many writings like dust in the wind, tired of thinking, "What folly!" (*alogia*), such persons finally "despise our entire faith because they judge it unstable and without healing sense [*hygieia*]," rejecting "our com-

---

65. For the council, Brennecke, *Studien*, 206–9; Hanson, *Search*, 760–72. Most scholars date Basil's redaction of the *CE* to 363/4, but Kopecek, *History*, 364–72, dates it to 360–62, even 360/61. Kopecek's date is supported by Hildebrand, "Reconsideration," who sees this as more consistent with the evolution of Basil's thought. In 364/5 Basil sent a copy to the "sophist" Leontius; Bas. *Epp.* 20 and 2; cf. also *Ep.* 35. For the period of preparation, Bas. *Ep.* 9, *To the Philosopher Maximus* (ca. 361/2), and *Ep.* 7; *Ep.* 25, *To Athanasius of Ancyra* (365/6); and *Ep.* 223.5, *To Eustathius of Sebaste* (375/6); Phot. *Bibl.* 137 refers to Basil's difficulties in obtaining a copy of Eunomius's *Apology*. Pouchet, *Basile*, 135–49; Rousseau, *Basil*, 101–6; *Basile de Césarée: Contre Eunome*, ed. and trans. Sesboüé, vol. 1, 30–34, 40–42; Vaggione, *Eunomius*, 226–34.

66. Gr. Naz. *Or.* 5.39.

67. Gr. Naz. *Or.* 2.42: τύπον τῶν περὶ Θεοῦ λόγων.

munity as if it were not one of pious persons" (*Or.* 2.42, 49). Hence Gregory's opinion that it is better to write new teachings onto blank wax tablets than have to remove first all that has been falsely engraved and his insistence on a high level of preparedness for whoever is entrusted to lead men (e.g., *Or.* 2.50), the most multiform and temperamental of all beings, in a manner appropriate to each and all in his care (*Or.* 2.43–45).

Instead, bad leaders and teachers abound. Who are they, and how can one identify such "traders of the word of truth, mixing water with wine and the word that gladdens the heart of men with cheap words . . . , so that they may . . . profit from this trade, speaking now in such a way and now in another, depending on who approaches and seeking to please all"? They are ventriloquists and empty talkers, "who serve their own pleasures with words that come from the earth and fall back to it" (*Or.* 2.46).[68] Such persons, furthermore, rush to lead and to teach without first learning anything (*Or.* 2.47). Ignorant of the need to be fully purified before progressing to the deeper meaning of scripture, they throw learning indiscriminately to all and sundry (*Or.* 2.48–49). Each considering himself a second Samuel, elected from birth (wrongly, as detailed in *Or.* 2.77), these bad leaders claim to be instant wise men and teachers (*sophoi kai didaskaloi*).[69] As soon as they know how to drape their philosopher's cloak (*tribōn*), having become philosophers "just to the level of their belts," they declare themselves fully formed authorities, spouting that "the letter counts nothing, all must be comprehended 'spiritually,' " and similar nonsense.[70] To deter such leaders and to prevent the maladies they spread is a labor worthy of Peter and especially of Paul, both of whom received the *charisma,* divine gift, to lead with words and deeds (*Or.* 2.51).[71]

Gregory—like Julian—used the standard vocabulary against uneducated and hence false Cynics in denouncing these persons. Their hallmarks were vanity, vainglory, rushing to virtue by a shortcut since they were born wise, supposedly of a sacred marriage, and hence needed to make no further effort to attain wisdom, seeking, like charlatans, to please the crowds for profit.[72] Their deceit was all the more dangerous because they aped the virtues of the true Cynic, Diogenes, and of the true Samuel: simplicity, ascetic strictness, and disregard for all worldly rewards.[73]

---

68. Jer 7:6, 22:3; Ps 105:38.
69. Gregory's main concern in *Or.* 2.71–73.
70. Gr. Naz. *Or.* 2.49: καὶ οὐδαμοῦ τὸ γράμμα, καὶ πάντα δεῖ νοηθῆναι πνευματικῶς.
71. For details of Gregory's understanding of Paul, S. Elm, "Paul as Seen by Gregory."
72. Sen. *Ep.* 5.2; D.L. *Lives* 7.121; D. Chr. *Or.* 34.2, 32.9; Epict. *Diss.* 3.12.16–17. Lucian evokes notoriety, δόξης ἕνεκα, at the beginning of *Peregr.* 1, and (e.g.) at 4, 8, 12, 14, 20, 22; Gal. *De pecc. dign.* 3.12–13 (Kühn 5); Branham and Goulet-Cazé, *Cynics,* 21–27, with bibliography; Francis, *Subversive Virtue,* 62–63.
73. Bas. *Ep.* 4 referred to Diogenes.

Anti-Cynic criticism, furthermore, had a real social agenda: evidently many of these "paragons of excellence and simplicity,"[74] "giving up their trades that they had before, dash off to don the wallet and cloak, tan their bodies in the sun the color of an Ethiopian, and go about as impromptu philosophers, come from cobblers and carpenters"—such uneducated Cynics and their Christian counterparts carried, in the eyes of their opponents, the traditional stigma of low(er) birth.[75]

Photinus

The men Gregory denounced in anti-Cynic language as responsible for the two principal misconceptions of the Trinity were Photinus and his followers, Aetius, and especially Eunomius. What did Photinus argue, and where was he in the early 360s? None of his writings are extant, and we know little of his whereabouts; much has to be reconstructed from what opponents such as Gregory say.[76] The intellectual heir of Marcellus of Ancyra, Photinus crossed our path in Chapter 1; he was condemned and dismissed as bishop of Sirmium in 351, having lost to Basil of Ancyra.

What happened to Photinus after 351 is not clear. He must have continued to advocate his positions, for they continued to be attacked. Apollinarius of Laodicea, for example, wrote the treatise *Contra Sabellianos* against him between 358 and 360, to which Basil had access when writing against Eunomius.[77] Photinus reappears, however, in 363: he was among those who profited from the reversal of Constantius's policies inaugurated by Julian in the spring of 362 and returned, probably to Sirmium. In February 363 he received a letter from Julian in which the emperor complimented him on having far better views on Christ than their common opponent Diodore of Tarsus, who seems to have written seven treatises against Photinus. According to Julian, Photinus did not believe that Mary had given birth to a fully divine being.[78] Julian mentioned Photinus again in his treatise *Against the Galileans,* by then, however, declaring that Photinus's position vis-à-vis the divinity of the *Logos*—Christ—was as irrelevant as the entire debate, since Christ was no divine being in any sense.[79] The continued significance of Photinus's positions is

---

74. Gr. Naz. *Or.* 2.49: οἱ χρηστότεροι καὶ ἀπλούστεροι.

75. Lucian, *Double Indictment* 6 (quotation); idem *Fugitives* 14–16 and *Philosophies for Sale* 11.

76. Scholars also use the surviving fragments of the theology of his teacher, Marcellus, to reconstruct Photinus's ideas; Seibt, *Theologie,* 241–459, 523–24. R. M. Hübner, *Schrift,* 163–96.

77. R. M. Hübner, *Schrift,* 197–251, identifies Apollinarius as the author of Ps.-Athanasius *Contra Sabellianos* (PG 28.96–121) and dates the text between 358 and 360. This has not been uniformly accepted in scholarship; see V. H. Drecoll, *Entwicklung,* 34–37.

78. See the *anathemata* against Photinus in Sirmium, 351; Vinzent, *Pseudo-Athanasius,* 313–16, 317–26.

79. Jul. *Ep.* 90 (Wright 55), excerpted in Latin by Facundius of Hermiane; Julian, *Epistolario,* trans. and comm. Caltabiano, 198, 267–68, for the date; and Jul. *CG* 262c. Photinus's position appears to have been more extreme than Marcellus's; Bouffartigue, *Empereur Julien,* 117–19.

apparent in the continuing attacks against so-called Sabellians, the label for Photinus and his followers. Basil of Caesarea composed an oration against Sabellians in the early 370s (*Hom.* 24); and homoians of all stripes opposed Photinus and his followers. Exiled again under Valentinian, Photinus died about 376.[80]

As Gregory had pointed out, the first extreme to avoid when conceiving the Trinity was the compression of the three persons into one for fear of polytheism, and the compounding of that mistake by overlooking any internal hierarchy or order, a mistake also made by those who separated the three persons unduly. Because the Father is the prior cause or source (*archē*) of the Son and the Spirit (*Or.* 2.38), the three persons cannot be understood simply as different names or manifestations of the Father. When begetting the Son and the Spirit, the Father endowed them fully with divinity, so that all three are one God, but this requires the Father to be the First Cause as Father: to deny him his first place in the Trinity—and therefore to reject its internal order and hierarchy—destroys the Trinity as both oneness and threeness, or triad (*Or.* 2.36–38). This must be understood to mean not that the Son and the Spirit are inferior in either nature or essence, but that the Father is higher than both through his generation of them. That is, polytheism results not from the higher position of the Father as prior cause but from a lack of strict ordering of the Son and Spirit he generated, compounded by a failure to appreciate the uniqueness of the Father, the Son, and the Spirit. As Gregory stressed, to deny the Son's full status as Son automatically diminishes the Father's position as Father as well, and ditto for the Spirit—thus diminishing the beauty of the Trinity.[81]

Photinus, together with Marcellus, appears to have argued that the term "Son" was akin to a name or title activated at the moment of his birth by Mary (prior to his incarnation he had been *Logos,* not Son), because the Son's kingdom, his role as redeemer, began with his incarnation and would end with the redemption.[82] The intent of such an argument was to preserve God's wholeness (in this, Photinus was close to Athanasius, with whom he was often linked) and transcendence by considering the Son as Word circumscribed by time rather than as eternal. Prominent among those who had attacked this stance was Basil of Ancyra, who formulated his own concept of the *homoios kat' ousian* in the context of the reaction to Photinus, to indicate how one must comprehend the closeness between the

---

80. Jer. *Vir. ill.* 107; Hübner, *Schrift,* 163–64. Vinzent (*Pseudo-Athanasius,* 35–42, 84–88, 307–16) notes that already *Contra Arianos IV,* written about 340, argued against Photinus. Vinzent argues for an Eastern *Sitz im Leben* and distinct early homoousian tendencies. An analysis of Ps. Athanasius *Contra Arianos IV* and Gregory's *Or.* 2, especially the identical formulas to describe the opponents (Vinzent, p. 91) and Christ's role as mediator (ibid., 204–10), may add further insights. For later works attacking Photinians—that is, Sabellians—ibid., 88 n. 125.

81. Beeley, *Gregory,* 201–17.

82. Vinzent, *Pseudo-Athanasius,* 61–83.

two without assuming material notions as implicit in the words "Father" and "Son"—indeed, many of the homoian formulations sought to counter Photinus's (and Marcellus's) positions.[83]

Gregory combined insistence on the distinctiveness and reality of the three persons with insistence on the superiority of the Father as a shield against potential critics who might have associated his position with that of Photinus. To claim full divinity of the Son and Spirit could easily be read as arguing that Son and Spirit were merely different human modes of comprehending the one Father: that is, humanly applied names to describe the Father's characteristics without denoting a reality of distinct divine persons. Arguing for three distinct divine persons was, after all, reminiscent of polytheism, which Gregory sought to avoid, without thereby falling prey to the error of Photinus. The continuing virulence of anti-Photinian or anti-Sabellian language during the second half of the fourth century signals the deep suspicion of any view that might diminish the distinctiveness of the Son, dissolving him, as mere name, into the supreme Father (*Or.* 2.37).[84] In that context, Gregory's insistent rejection of "the notion that the monarchy of the Father in any way conflicts with the equality of the three persons," to quote Christopher Beeley, assumes its contours.[85]

Aetius and Eunomius

Our position as far as Aetius and Eunomius are concerned is more fortunate. Although what we have of their writings is far from plentiful, and indeed often fragmentary, it is enough to give us, thanks largely to Richard Vaggione, a better sense of the men, their views, and their whereabouts in the early 360s. Aetius and Eunomius have made cameo appearances in the chapters preceding this one. Aetius, a physician and Christian Aristotelian philosopher, was among those Julian invited to court in early 362. Probably born around 315 in Antioch, Aetius soon became well known in "public contests of words," especially "logical studies" (Philost. *HE* 3.15, 3.16). After the death of his patron and teacher Paulinus, bishop of Antioch, Aetius left the city briefly but returned to study under Leontius. After 340, he went to Alexandria, where he studied medicine and Aristotelian dialectic. George of Alexandria, formerly of Caesarea in Cappadocia, may have made him a deacon in 346 or 348.[86] Around 350 Aetius returned to Antioch, where Leontius was now bishop. It seems likely that Leontius introduced him to the Caesar Gallus, who made him a Friend at court and a

---

83. Marcell. fr. 107 (119 ed. Vinzent). Ayres, *Nicaea*, 134–36.
84. Including Filast. *Haer.* 65, 91, 93; Epiph. *Haer.* 71 and *Anc.* 7.2; Hübner, *Schrift*, 165–96.
85. Beeley, *Gregory*, 210. He also discusses the lack of scholarly clarity regarding Gregory's monarchic notion he identifies as central: 209 nn. 67, 68. See also Vinzent, *Pseudo-Athanasius*, 192, citing Hübner.
86. Epiph. *Haer.* 4 (GCS vol. 3, 231.20–23); Kopecek, *History*, 96 n. 1.

teacher of sacred studies.[87] If we believe Philostorgius, Gallus even sent Aetius to visit Julian in Bithynia in 351, ostensibly to prevent his half-brother from delving further into pagan philosophical studies.[88] By then, Aetius had already become the sponsor of Eunomius, who considered him "his patron and guide of his life."[89]

Eunomius, born probably in the mid-320s in Oltiseris, a small village in northwestern Cappadocia on the Galatian border, had become Aetius's secretary, or *tachygraphos,* in Alexandria in the late 340s.[90] Aetius's father and Eunomius's grandfather had both supplied the troops at Antioch: the grandfather owned a tannery, a mill, and a farm, while Eunomius's father "engraved the alphabet": that is, instructed children taking their first steps in Greek education. In short, neither Aetius nor Eunomius was as well born as Gregory, Basil of Caesarea, and Gregory of Nyssa, though their origins were not so humble (or base) as the Gregories and Basil claimed. Eunomius had learned shorthand, a useful skill that virtually guaranteed him a position in the imperial administration as *notarius.* (Gregory later counseled his nephew Nicobulus to do the same.)[91] Apparently both talented and ambitious, Eunomius left for Constantinople, where he seems to have become *paidagōgos* in a prestigious household and to have used this position to further his own studies to a considerable degree. By 346 he moved to Antioch, where he too met Leontius. Visitors from Alexandria, in particular the Libyan Secundus of Ptolemaïs, then persuaded him to work for Aetius in Alexandria.[92] The year 350 found both Aetius and Eunomius again in Antioch. The emperor Constantius was in residence, preparing for yet another Persian campaign, when the murder of Constans in Gaul and Magnentius's usurpation forced him to move west and to establish Gallus as Caesar in 351. In the aftermath of Gallus's execution in 354, Aetius and his advisor and secretary returned to Alexandria, where they were now on the staff of Bishop George, formerly Julian's teacher in Cappadocia. In 357 Leontius died and was succeeded by Eudoxius, previously bishop of Germanicia. Aetius immediately returned to Antioch, where Eudoxius welcomed him and, in 358, also ordained Eunomius as a deacon.

By then, Aetius's and Eunomius's views had become well known beyond Anti-

---

87. Philost. *HE* 3.16, 27 (GCS vol. 21, 47, 52–53); Gr. Nyss. *Eun* 1.47 (*GNO*, vol. 1, 38); Kopecek, *History,* 106–13; Vaggione, *Eunomius,* 159–61.

88. Gr. Nyss. *Eun* 1.36–46 (*GNO*, vol. 1, 34-38); Philost. *HE* 3.15, 27; Soz. *HE* 5.15.5; Socr. *HE* 2.38.23; Vaggione, *Eunomius,* 148–63, 269–71; Lim, *Public Disputation,* 112–18, with some inconsistencies; Kopecek, *History,* 61–75.

89. Gr. Nyss. *Eun.* 1.36–37 (*GNO*, vol. 1, 34–35).

90. Gr. Nyss. *Eun.* 1.34 (*GNO*, vol. 1, 33); Socr. *HE* 2.35.14. Oltiseris was about equidistant between the Galatian city Tavium and the imperial spa Aquae Saravenae or Basilica Therma; Hild and Restle, *Kappadokien,* 156–57, 215; Vaggione, *Eunomius,* 2–3; and the excellent summary of Eunomius's career by Van Dam, *Becoming Christian,* 15–45.

91. Gr. Naz. *Epp.* 167, 174–77, 188.

92. Philost. *HE* 3.19, 20. Kopecek, *History,* 105–6; but see Vaggione, *Eunomius,* 27.

och and Alexandria. Despite his close association with Leontius, George of Alexandria, and then Eudoxius, Aetius considered their opinions on the relationship between Father and Son—the concept of homoios then current—imprecise, not sufficiently *akribēs*.[93] Constantius, in 357/8, moving east again, increased his efforts to find a universally valid definition of the divine nature. Aetius's teachings were not conducive to consensus. Though his only surviving writing, the *Syntagmation*, was not published before 359, it was evident nonetheless that he believed Father and Son unlike in essence—*an-[h]omoioi* or *heterousioi*.[94] His controversial stance became a liability in 358. At that point, the sophisticated positions of Basil of Ancyra and Eusebius of Sebaste, who argued that the Son is like the Father in essence or being (*homoios kat' ousian*), had convinced Constantius and instigated his criticism of the views of Eudoxius and George of Alexandria, which were less radical than those of Aetius, and his chastisement of them for supporting Aetius. Constantius ordered Eudoxius to go home to Armenia; he sent Aetius into exile to Pepuza, in Phrygia, and Eunomius into exile in a different Phrygian town.[95]

Within a year the winds of fortune changed. In 359 Basil of Ancyra and his supporters overplayed their hand and lost the emperor's support. In the context of Rimini and Seleucia, Eudoxius and his homoian supporters not only rehabilitated themselves but carried the day: in 360 Eudoxius became bishop of Constantinople. When he had arrived in the city, in December 359, for the council that signed the homoian accord, Aetius and Eunomius accompanied him. The success of the council, however, came at a price. Those sidelined included not only Basil of Ancyra and Eustathius of Sebaste and their homoiousian followers, but also Aetius, again sent into exile.

This time, Eunomius did not share his fate. In what must have been a command performance at the council, Eunomius modified Aetius's positions and distanced himself from his mentor. On January 2 or 3, 360, Eudoxius ordained him bishop of Cyzicus. The city lay across from Constantinople on the Sea of Marmara. Eunomius's precursor was Eleusius (a popular former government official associated with Macedonius of Constantinople and Basil of Ancyra), who had been exiled as a supporter of the *homoiousios* position.[96] Eunomius's elevation to the see of Cyzicus and his stance, evidently too precise for his audience, caused an uproar, especially among those loyal to Eleusius.[97] The protests were such that Constantius ordered Eunomius

---

93. Philost. *HE* 4.5, though Philostorgius here places these words into the mouth of Eunomius. For an insightful discussion of *akribeia,* see Caner, "Notions."

94. L. R. Wickham, "*Syntagmation.*"

95. Philost. *HE* 4.8.

96. I follow Vaggione's (*Eunomius,* 226–27) dating of Eunomius's ordination to early 360; L. R. Wickham, "Date," esp. 232–33.

97. Soz. *HE* 4.13.5, 4.20.1–2; Socr. *HE* 2.38.3–4; Thdt. *HE* 2.29.3–7; Hil. *Syn.* 63; Philost. *HE* 6.2–4, 9.13; Vaggione, *Eunomius,* 228–30.

to retire home to Cappadocia, an act neither exiling nor formally deposing him. Not until January or February 361 did the emperor, by then in winter quarters at Antioch, hear a formal case against Eunomius, brought by Acacius of Caesarea, one of Aetius's principal opponents. According to our main source, Philostorgius, Constantius remained unconvinced and postponed a decision. At the time of Constantius's death, in November 361, Eunomius was in limbo as a bishop sent home by the emperor.[98] While in retreat at Oltiseris, Eunomius composed a written version of his Constantinopolitan speech, the *Apology,* published by 361. In this work, he argued primarily against his foes of 360 and 361, most of whom were homoiousian.[99]

The death of Constantius and the arrival of Julian changed again the fate of Eunomius and Aetius. The spring of 362 found Eunomius in Constantinople; he had not made use of the permission Julian granted to exiled bishops to return to their sees. Eleusius, in fact, exiled as a homoiousian, preempted Eunomius and was already back as bishop in Cyzicus.[100] Aetius too was at Constantinople, recalled from exile by Julian, invited to court (as someone on the wrong side of Constantius), and subsequently presented with an estate on Lesbos. (Eunomius may also have received his villa in Chalcedon as an imperial present at that time.)[101] Even though Eunomius had distanced himself from Aetius in 360, their differences were now a thing of the past: for the next few years their stars rose together.[102] In early 362 Eudoxius, aware of Julian's favorable disposition toward Aetius (and according to Philostorgius, prompted by Eunomius) wrote to Euzoius of Antioch—then the more important see—asking him to exonerate Aetius formally. Euzoius complied, convening a synod of nine bishops for that purpose in Antioch in the fall of 362.[103]

Aetius, his official rehabilitation all but assured, began to gather his supporters for a council in Constantinople in the summer of 362. With the approval of Eudoxius, they began to consecrate a number of their own as bishops, including Aetius

---

98. Philostorgius (*HE* 6.3–4, 5.2) reports that Acacius complained Aetius received too mild a treatment. Socr. *HE* 2.45.9–10 mentions a small council that could have been gathered to deal with Eunomius. For an overview, *Basile de Césarée: Contre Eunome,* ed. and trans. Sesboüé, vol. 1, 18–34; Vaggione, *Eunomius,* 226–34 and n. 216; Kopecek, *History,* 407–10.

99. Vaggione, *Eunomius,* 228; see, e.g., Eun. *Apol.* 11.4–9, 18.9–13, 20.1–5, 21.4–5.

100. Philost. *HE* 7.6, 9.4. Julian quickly accused Eleusius for having destroyed a Novatian church and pagan temples in Cyzicus; Jul. *Ep.* 46 (Wright 15).

101. Philost. *HE* 9.4; Philostorgius mentions Eunomius's property but not that it was a gift. Malosse ("Enquête," 189–91, esp. 190 n. 47) questions Bidez's suggestion (*Vie,* 90–92) that Aetius tested Julian's Christian credentials.

102. Tensions between Aetius and Eunomius in 360 and 362 further complicate the reconstruction of the events: Eunomius was Philostorgius's hero, so that his fate dominates the *HE*. Philostorgius sought to exonerate Eunomius, whose behavior vis-à-vis Aetius in 360 could be perceived as disloyal, and thus cast Eudoxius of Constantinople as the villain, accusing him of vacillating in supporting Aetius as promised to Eunomius. Brennecke, *Studien,* 110, 111; McLynn, "Use and Abuse," 85–87.

103. Philostorgius (*HE* 7.6) had access to Eudoxius's correspondence.

himself.[104] Eunomius was already a bishop (though not at his see); Serras became bishop of Paraetonium; Heliodorus, of Sozusa in Libya; Leontius, of Tripolis; and Theodulus, of Chaeretapa in Phrygia. During the following year the number of Aetian or heterousian bishops rose to fourteen in addition to Aetius and Eunomius. They included bishops for Constantinople, first Poemenius and then Florentinus, and a bishop for Antioch, Theophilus the Indian. Regional bishops were also ordained: Euphronius was responsible for Pontus, Galatia, and Cappadocia; Julian, for Cilicia; Candidus and Arrian, for Lydia and Ionia; Thallus, for Lesbos; and another Theodulus, for Palestine.[105]

By the summer of 362 Eunomius had published his *Apology* and had been rehabilitated, and Aetius could reasonably expect that his rehabilitation was imminent. Both had close ties to Emperor Julian's court and began to consecrate their supporters as bishops in the imperial residences Antioch and Constantinople and for regions such as Cappadocia, Galatia, Pontus, Libya, and Palestine, activities condoned if not supported by Eudoxius and Euzoius, the powerful bishops of the imperial residences. In 360, Basil of Caesarea had been present at the council where Eunomius saved himself by presenting what became his *Apology*. Basil had witnessed firsthand the ascendancy of Eudoxius and other homoians, including Eunomius, and the demise of the homoiousians. By 362 and 363, he and his friend Gregory were intermittently in retreat and at odds with their bishops. And they too used their retreat: together with "his brother beloved by God, Gregory" and with Eunomius's written apology in hand, Basil pondered his response to Eunomius, and Gregory formulated his *Apology for His Flight*.[106] Both these works take on an additional dimension in relation to the leaders now ordained by Aetius and Eunomius both in the imperial residences and for the regions, one of which was Cappadocia.

Aetius's and Eunomius's Leadership as Philosophical Life

Scholars have interpreted the consecration of several of Aetius's and Eunomius's supporters as bishops as an attempt to found an Aetian or proto-Eunomian church, or

---

104. I follow McLynn's interpretation ["Use and Abuse," 88]: Eudoxius approved the ordinations in his capacity as bishop of Constantinople, which does not require or imply a doctrinal rapprochement; Brennecke, *Studien*, 110.

105. Philost. *HE* 7.6, 8.2; also 9.1, 9.4. Philostorgius stresses that all followed Aetius and Eunomius as their "common fathers and leaders." Brennecke, *Studien*, 110, and Vaggione, *Eunomius*, 276–78, place these events in the time of Julian, and I concur, though Philostorgius (*HE* 7.15, 8.1) dates them after Julian's death: he too wishes to downplay the positive effect of Julian's reign on Eunomius's career.

106. In *Ep.* 9.3, dated to 360 and addressed to a certain Maximus, Basil wrote: "I have definitively decided not to make public the opinions I have so far formed"; the quotation referring to Gregory is *Ep.* 223.5. See also Bas. *Epp.* 94, 244; Gr. Nyss. *Eun.* 1.82 (*GNO*, vol. 1, 50). Lim, *Public Disputation*, 120; Rousseau, *Basil*, 93–106, 226–35; *Basile de Césarée: Contre Eunome*, ed. and trans. Sesboüé, vol. 1, 40–45.

they have considered these bishops a philosophical coterie.[107] The question is relevant because, first, they were consecrated in imperial residences that already had bishops, and with the support of those bishops—that is, the anomoian or heterousian bishops were considered not schismatics but legitimate leaders—and because some were regional bishops, not tied to any see but presumably on the move throughout their regions.[108] Neither characteristic conforms to the notion of bishops as institutional figureheads tied to their sees, or to the idea of one bishop per city. Scholars who grant that these men were bishops keep them suitably marginalized as heretics by assigning them a separate Aetian or proto-Eunomian church. To call these men a "philosophical coterie" avoids such difficulties, because supposedly, pastoral care and institutional functions implicit in the commonly held understanding of a bishop do not apply: philosophical coteries, as the modern scholars concerned define them, consist of elite teachers and disciples not necessarily bound to cities or the (sacramental and social) duties of "normal" episcopal office; members of such coteries may roam at liberty without undermining common modern ideas about orthodox priesthood. As a coterie these men are, further, not part of the mainstream, however conceived.

Such modern notions of episcopal office level the actual diversity of late-antique bishops. We have already encountered bishops who moved from see to see (more concerned about their advisory role and their access to court than any pastoral function at home, if indeed they had one), and cities such as Antioch, Cyzicus, and Nazianzus with multiple bishops (though they were often not welcomed with open arms). Gregory's main point was that Christian leaders ought to be philosophers, and he was not alone in that demand—many successful and hence visible Christian leaders, from Eustathius, Basil of Caesarea, and Gregory of Nyssa to Eunomius and Aetius, considered themselves philosophers (and could also reasonably be called a philosophical coterie). The issue, given that bishops ought to lead a philosophical life, an essential marker of their status and a *conditio sine qua non* their (uneducated, low-status) opponents lacked, was which philosophical life was the true one. What did Aetius and Eunomius propose?

The question is difficult to answer, because on March 4, 398, the emperor Ar-

---

107. Brennecke, *Studien*, 63–64, 113–14; Vaggione, *Eunomius*, 277–80, describes Aetius's status as that of a general bishop, without specific geographical association; Lim, *Public Disputation*, 121, 129–30, speaks of a "philosophical coterie"; Rousseau, *Basil*, 117–32, esp. 124–25, reflecting Basil's counter, contrasts Eunomius the philosopher speaking for an elitist community with Basil as priest ministering to the "simple and unstudied faith of the majority" of the church (p. 124); see also idem, "Basil," esp. 94.

108. They are not so-called *chōrepiskopoi* (for whom see Rapp, *Holy Bishops*, 178 n. 38), local rural bishops supporting those in the cities.

cadius ordered that Eunomius's works be burned.[109] Only fragments remain of what must have been a prodigious output. Philostorgius, Socrates, and Photius indicate that Eunomius was a prolific letter writer, had composed a commentary on Paul's Epistle to the Romans, and had speculated about the population of the entire world, a salutary reminder of how limited a picture the remaining fragments represent.[110] Combining our remaining anti- and pro-Eunomian sources, which include the *Commentary on Job* composed by a certain Julian (perhaps the regional bishop of Cilicia) about the same time as Eunomius's highly fragmentary *Apology*, yields a few insights. Eunomius, Aetius, and the bishops they ordained were true philosophers, and considered such by their followers; they derived their episcopal authority from their divinely authorized "quest for the truth," made manifest by "divine signs" and conveyed through the "power of words."[111] Their opponents seem to take issue with what they consider their too active involvement as philosophers for the common good of the city.

The few surviving fragments of Theodore of Mopsuestia's counter to Eunomius (fragmentary because Theodore also went afoul of orthodoxy) contain a biting caricature of Aetius's philosophical Christian life, once again bearing the imprint of anti-Cynic rhetoric. In Theodore's description, Aetius was an uneducated Cynic whose theatrics included three types of flatulence (induced, it seems, by beans, lentils, and chickpeas), which he exhibited to demonstrate the unequal nature of the Trinity. Such antics, according to Theodore, were congruent with Aetius's self-serving behavior: he hung about the offices of physicians pretending to be one (a slander that alluded perhaps to Aetius's continuing professional engagement as a physician); scrounging everywhere for free meals, he was nothing but a greedy upstart.[112]

Gregory of Nyssa's characterization epitomizes those of all opponents whose writings have survived. He immortalized Aetius and particularly Eunomius as sophists. For him, Eunomius's literary style was that of a sexually ambiguous actor prancing about the stage while rapping his newfangled (innovated) syntax, using homonyms and alliterations like a percussionist, keeping the beat with his feet and snapping his fingers even while writing (he was dictating and thus speaking out loud), his pretense of zeal (*spoudē*) driving him to vainglory and hubris to im-

---

109. *CTh* 16.5.34; Philost. *HE* 11.5; Socr. *HE* 4.7; Photius *Bibl.* 138. Whereas Socrates claims that his works were burned under Arcadius (r. 395–408), Theodore of Mopsuestia, when writing his preface to his *Commentarius in Evangelium Johannis* (CSCO 115.3.7–13, trans. CSCO 116.1), between 400 and 410, knows of many who still read (lit. "heard") Eunomius's works with great delight.

110. Hagedorn, *Hiobkommentar*; whether this Julian was the bishop of Cilicia cannot be ascertained.

111. Philost. *HE* 4.12, 9.1; Eun. *Apol.* 27.

112. Thdr. Mops. *C. Eun.* fr. 3 Syr. 1–13, 13–54, 62–64; fr. 1 Gr. 1–17 "philosophical and Christian life"; fr. 3 Gr. 5–22, written against Eunomius's *Apology of the Apology*; cf. Thdt. *HE* 2.27.9; Vaggione, "Lounge Lizards," 183–84; and idem, "Some Neglected Fragments."

press his audience and to best his opponents (*philonikia*)—the anti-Cynic repertoire. Lack of taste (*apeirokalia*) and the inability to use rhetorical structures successfully in discourse were Eunomius's hallmarks; like Aetius, he was a low-class pretender pursuing wealth.[113]

Eunomius's *Apology* addressed (and anticipated) the classic anti-Cynic attacks and his critics' defamation of him as a mere sophist, a rhetorician of the Asianic style.[114] In a surviving fragment (that is, an excerpt worthy of preservation and comment), he declared (a few months before Julian's anti-Cynic orations, if the standard dating holds) that the philosophy of the Christians was far removed from that of the Cynics. True Christian philosophers shunned worldly concerns in their quest for truth, especially *philotimia* and *philonikia*, and were not compromised by undue favoritism of their kin.[115] Philostorgius's *Ecclesiastical History* and Eunomius's follower Julian's *Commentary on Job* provide further positive clues to Eunomius's philosophy.[116] Julian's *Commentary on Job*, an "image in writing" of its hero, presents Job as a man not well born but who nonetheless excels as a divinely inspired holy man engaged in public life. He administers his household with exemplary *eunoia*, understood as "an echo of the divine goodness" accessible only to the truly pious (*eusebēs*) and the right-minded, and he is in all respects a paragon of *sōphrosynē*. Julian enhances these qualities by comparing his hero to Moses.[117] In the Latin com-

---

113. Gr. Nyss. *Eun.* 1.11–18 (*GNO*, vol. 1, 25–27); English trans. of Gr. Nyss. *Eun.* 1 (following Jaeger's second edition, *Gregorii Nysseni opera* [= *GNO*], vol. 1) by Hall, "'Contra Eunomium I.'" As Burrus has emphasized (*Begotten, Not Made*, 98–106), there is no ambivalence in Gregory of Nyssa's estimation of Eunomius's philosophical masculinity: his literary output was an abortion, and he was neither a productive father nor a mother—in contrast to Gregory of Nazianzus's self-presentation as being both; S. Elm, "Family Men."

114. As for the Asianic style, this would have been that of Himerius and, at least according to Norden in *Antike Kunstprosa*, Gregory's own style. The distinction between Asianist and Atticist was more polemic than actual. Philostratus had already denounced the exaggerated rhythms of the so-called Asianic style: *VA* 8.6, *VS* 491–92, 589; D. Chr. *Or.* 32.68. Lucian *Nigrinus* 24, satirized itinerant philosophers, and in *Teacher of Rhetoric* 16–17 mocked stylistic inventions; Gleason, *Making Men*, 121–30. Favorinus, a champion of Asianic style, was a eunuch; Gregory of Nyssa's slander of Eunomius as nonreproductive male and foot-stamping sophist shares that gendered polemic. For the contrast between sophist, rhetor, and philosopher, Vaggione, "Lounge Lizards," 187–90, and *Eunomius*, 184–88; Lim, *Public Disputation*, 138–44.

115. Eun. *Apol.* 19.6, 2.7–8: πολὺ γὰρ κυνισμὸς κεχώρισται Χριστιανισμοῦ.

116. This dossier is augmented by the final version of the so-called *Apostolic Constitutions* (*CA*) and the long version of the *Ignatian Epistles* (*Ig. Ep.*), by the same author. For the relation between Julian's *Commentary on Job* (*Comm. Job*), the *CA*, and the *Ig. Ep.*, see Hagedorn, *Hiobkommentar*, xxxvii–lvii; the *CA* and the *Ig. Ep.* were in all likelihood composed after the *Comm.* The most recent translation of the *CA* is *Constitutions Apostoliques*, ed. M. Metzger; here esp. vol. 2, 10–39. To this should be added the Latin commentary on Job by an unknown author (Arian. Ign.) but ascribed to Origen, *PG* 17.371–522.

117. Julian, *Comm. Job* 3.16–4.14, 80.11, 96.10, 10.14–15; cf. *CA* 7.2; for a discussion of *eunoia*, see *Comm. Job* 6.4–8, 14.19–20, 228.8–9; Vaggione, "Lounge Lizards," 193.

mentary on the same text, Job is a "veri Dei servus verax" through exemplary leadership, a truly just "dux ac princeps provinciae suae."[118]

According to Philostorgius, both Aetius and Eunomius, neither of whom could lay claim to being as *eugenēs* as some of their opponents, were drawn to *paideia* and philosophy early on, and both were prodigies who dazzled with their mental acuity. Aetius soon became superior in logic, and Eunomius dreamed of becoming a new Demosthenes. Already on the path to philosophy, each received a divine call that converted him to true philosophy—Aetius in a vision, and Eunomius in a dream.[119] Both were thus divine or holy men (*entheoi*), a quality they shared with Theophilus the Indian (and with Wulfila, whom Philostorgius described as "the Moses of our day").[120] Theophilus, according to Philostorgius, had excellent connections to Constantius's court. Constantius consulted him when his wife was gravely ill, employed him as ambassador, showered him with public honors, and asked him to mediate between himself and Gallus as Caesar. Because Theophilus loyally accompanied Gallus on his last, fatal journey, he was exiled, only to be recalled to the bedside of Constantius's wife.[121] According to Philostorgius, all homoians, beginning with Eusebius of Nicomedia, had excellent connections to Constantius's court, but Aetius and Eunomius in particular; what matters here is Philostorgius's characterization of Theophilus as the typical political philosopher à la Themistius, but now in the Christian incarnation.[122]

If we are to believe Philostorgius's characterization, which the *Commentary on Job* corroborates, Aetius, Theophilus, and Eunomius were models of Themistius's new men and no different from other bishops at the time.[123] Though slightly less well born than those of the curial class, they had been sufficiently formed by *paideia* to permit them to associate with the court both in Antioch and in Constantinople. Highly trained, they had received a divine calling to philosophy, which they understood as active participation in the life of the *politeia* as ambassadors, physicians, teachers, and bishops. According to Photius's excerpts from Philostorgius's *Ecclesiastical History*—the only form in which that work survives—Aetius and his followers, originally on the side of Constantius and thus Themistius, fell afoul of Constantius over questions of Christology. This gained them, however, the favor of Julian—a point Philostorgius does not highlight—in part because Aetius and Theo-

---

118. Arian. Ign. (Ps.-Origen) *Job* 1, PG 17.379B–C, 380B; Julian, *Comm. Job* 247.16–248.20, 301.12–15; Vaggione, "Lounge Lizards," 192 (see also 197–202).

119. Philost. *HE* 3.15; Eun. *Apol. apol.* 1.30.1–2; Gr. Nyss. *Eun.* 3.10.50, 54 (*GNO*, vol. 2, 309–310).

120. Philost. *HE* 2.5; Gr. Nyss. *Eun.* 1.27 (*GNO*, vol. 1, 30) refers sarcastically to Eunomius's "divinely inspired [*entheos*] history" of himself.

121. Philost. *HE* 3.4–6; 4.1, 8.

122. Vaggione, "Lounge Lizards," 212–13.

123. Heather, "New Men," 11–33 (esp. 13, 21–33); Henck, "Constantius' *paideia*," 179–80; Petit, *Étudiants*, 154–55; Dagron, *Naissance*, 129; Themistius, *Politics*, ed. and trans. Heather and Moncur, 14.

philus had connections to Gallus Caesar, who had also suffered under Julian's principal foe.[124] Julian was aware of Aetius and Eunomius's philosophical life, of their doctrinal stance, and of their difficulties with Constantius (resulting in part from close ties to Gallus); he gave them sufficient support so that they and their followers flourished during his reign. That is, for Julian their manifest opposition to Constantius outweighed their pursuit of a more active philosophical life.

As Philostorgius reports, Eunomius's and Aetius's connections to the Flavian dynasty outlasted even its last emperor. When Procopius, Julian's maternal cousin, was contending against Valens for the throne, he reportedly spent time on Eunomius's estate in Chalcedon, both before his acclamation in the fall of 365 and after his defeat in the summer of 366.[125] Aetius died in the city in the spring of 366, during Procopius's brief reign, and was given a splendid burial by Eunomius. In sum, Philostorgius, though hostile to Julian as a pagan, nonetheless emphasized the strong and lasting connections between Aetius, Eunomius, Constantius, Julian, and Procopius. Procopius's defeat in 366 reversed Eunomius's fate once again, but between 362 and 366 Aetius's and Eunomius's philosophical life and their teachings were very successful, and they retained their appeal for many of the Constantinopolitan court elite, perhaps because many of the new men in the city and at court had similarly risen to power from relatively humble origins.[126]

Eunomius was a divinely inspired holy philosopher, actively engaged in the *koina* as bishop (though not at his see), with close ties to the imperial court. Though modern historians have not appreciated him for these characteristics, he and his fellow leaders were normal late-antique bishops of considerable influence.[127] Further, as

---

124. Philost. *HE* 3.27; see also Lib. *Or.* 12.29. Gallus had sent Aetius to Julian, and George of Cappadocia, later of Alexandria, the principal patron of Aetius there, had been Julian's teacher at Macellum. If we are to trust Gregory's later slander, George like Aetius was lower-class and uneducated (Gr. Naz. *Or.* 21.16); according to Ammianus 22.11.4, George was born in a fuller's shop.

125. Ammianus confirms Procopius's stay at Chalcedon, though he places him (more reasonably) with a certain Strategius, a member of the palace guard who rose to senatorial rank. Ammianus emphasizes the strategic importance of Chalcedon and Cyzicus for control of Constantinople, a fact that may have motivated Philostorgius's account of the Eunomian-Procopian connection. According to Philostorgius, on Lesbos one of Procopius's officials, as a favor to Eunomius, rescued Aetius from arrest as a supporter of Valens. Amm. Marc. 23.3.2, 25.9.12–13, 26.6.4–9 and 14; Philost. *HE* 9.5; Matthews, *Roman Empire*, 191–203; Lenski, *Failure of Empire*, 68–115. Socrates (*HE* 4.6.1–7.2) reports that Eunomius briefly returned to Cyzicus during Procopius's reign. He dates the council of Lampsacus one year later, to 365, and therefore dates Eunomius's resumption of control over Cyzicus before Procopius's usurpation; Vaggione, *Eunomius*, 292–94.

126. Eunomius was exiled to Naxos until about 379 (i.e., after Valens's death), when he returned to Chalcedon, attracted crowds, and became a favorite at parties: Soz. *HE* 7.6.2, 7.17.1; Socr. *HE* 5.20.4; Gr. Naz. *Or.* 27.2, 3, 6; Vaggione, *Eunomius*, 321, 342–44.

127. Thus, Claudia Rapp's excellent study *Holy Bishops* does not mention any Eunomians; Van Dam, *Becoming Christian*, 15–45, does not refer to this aspect of the rivalry among the contemporary Cappadocians either; he also excludes Gregory of Nazianzus from the competitors.

befitted a philosopher as leader, Eunomius sought to convince others of the correctness of his divinely inspired understanding of the divine *Logos* by the power of his words—as exemplified by the *Apology*, written in philosophical retreat from his duties as bishop and prior to his return to active duty under Julian. His understanding of the Trinity, like that of Aetius, was characterized by its precision, or *akribeia*, though the two men eventually went separate ways doctrinally. Julian saw no reason to exclude Aetius or Eunomius from his circle simply because they were Christian. Presumably, then, their views were acceptable to the emperor and many members of the Eastern elites, while also representing a formidable challenge to others (far more marginalized, at least while Julian ruled), among them Gregory.

WHAT DO WORDS MEAN?

How did Eunomius understand the nature of God and the Trinity, the Father's creative powers and their impact? To judge his ideas from the remaining fragments of the *Apology*, Eunomius aimed to demonstrate how the homoiousians' claim that Father and Son were similar in essence was antithetical to the very essence of God: to be without prior cause—that is, to be unbegotten. "God neither existed before himself nor did anything else exist before him.... What follows from this is the Unbegotten, or rather, that he is unbegotten essence."[128] Thus the sole logical conclusion was that "God is the only true and the only wise God, because only he is unbegotten" (*Apol.* 22.1), a conclusion Eunomius considered entirely in accord "both with innate knowledge and the teaching of the fathers" (7.1). Nevertheless, he realized that he might be suspected of innovation, because his stance differed from the one recognized by all, claiming that God the Father is without prior cause, since he insisted that precise logic demanded that to be unbegotten, *agennētos*, was itself the essence of the divine and not merely one of its characteristics (7.1–3). The necessary consequence of this insistence was to privilege the Father (Gregory's "father-loving"): the Son's divinity has to differ in essence, because he is generated or begotten.

Once again the sequence of essence, power, activity, and product was at stake (see above, Chapters 1 and 3): that is, the power (*dynamis*) or productive activity (*energeia*) of God as an immaterial cause of the creation or production of matter. The precise (*akribēs*) understanding of the relationship between the Father and his Son was crucial here, because it determined the subsequent sequence of productive activity—the creation of the cosmos and man—and by implication, therefore, the manner in which man might be saved. Eunomius employed formal and logical

---

128. Eun. *Apol.* 7.9–11: οὐκοῦν εἰ μήτε αὐτὸς ἑαυτοῦ μήθ' ἕτερόν τι αὐτοῦ προυπάρχειν δέδεικται ... ἀκολουθεῖ τούτῳ τὸ ἀγέννητον, μᾶλλον δὲ αὐτός ἐστιν οὐσία ἀγέννητος. Text and English translation are as in *Eunomius: The Extant Works*, ed. and trans. Vaggione.

methods to characterize the relationship of Father and Son, and thus the nature of God, pursuing two complementary heuristic strategies that also form the structure of the *Apology*: "There are two roads marked out for us for the discovery of what we seek: one is that by which we examine the actual essences and with clear and unadulterated reasoning about them make a judgment on each; the other is an inquiry by means of the actions, whereby we distinguish the essence on the basis of its products and completed works—and neither of the ways mentioned is able to bring out any apparent similarity of essence [in Father and Son]."[129]

The First Road: Divine Names

The first road, examining the actual essences,[130] required recourse to theories of language, because the issue was the relationship between an essence and its name—a topic of intense debate, as the controversies surrounding Marcellus and Photinus also reveal.[131] In Eunomius's words, "when we say 'Unbegotten,' then, we do not imagine that we ought to honor God only in name, in conformity with human invention; rather, in conformity with reality, we ought to repay him the debt that above all others is most due God: the acknowledgement that he is what he is" (*Apol.* 8.1). Eunomius argued (against Photinus, among others) that the name "unbegotten" itself originates in God rather than in human convention, and because it is synonymous with God, it cannot be applied to begotten entities such as the Son. "But birth has never been an inherent property of God! He was not first begotten and then deprived of that quality so as to become un-begotten!" (8.8–10).[132] If "the names are different, then the essences are different as well" (18.13–14): if "the Unbegotten" is the name of God, then " 'the Unbegotten' must be essence that is unbegotten [*ousia*]" (8.17–18).

Eunomius argued for unity of name and essence. There are specific names for God that are his alone because they characterize his essence, whereas other names might equally be applied to his Son—for example, attributes such as "just" and "good." As Raoul Mortley has pointed out, Eunomius's argument here engages with the concerns of contemporary Neoplatonic commentators on Aristotle's *Categories* about the distinction between negation and privation (*sterēsis*): by defining divine essence negatively, as un-begotten, Eunomius could be misunderstood to imply that

---

129. Eun. *Apol.* 20.5–10: δυεῖν γὰρ ἡμῖν τετμημένων ὁδῶν πρὸς τὴν τῶν ζητουμένων εὕρεσιν, μιᾶς μὲν καθ' ἣν τὰς οὐσίας αὐτὰς ἐπισκοπούμενοι, καθαρῷ τῷ περὶ αὐτῶν λόγῳ τὴν ἑκάστου ποιούμεθα κρίσιν, θατέρας δὲ τῆς διὰ τῶν ἐνεργειῶν ἐξετάσεως, ἣν ἐκ τῶν δημιουργημάτων καὶ τῶν ἀποτελεσμάτων διακρίνομεν, οὐδετέραν τῶν εἰρημένων εὑρεῖν ἐμφαινομένην τὴν τῆς οὐσίας ὁμοιότητα δυνατόν.

130. Eunomius in the first part, *Apol.* 7.1–19.23, analyzes the "actual essences" of the Father and then of the Son. The second part of the *Apology* focuses on the relation between the Son as product of the Father and the Spirit as product of the Son.

131. Pottier, *Dieu*, 150–57, with greater emphasis on Eunomius's *Apol. apol.*; see also pp. 193–220.

132. Referring to Arist. *Cat.* 12a26–34.

the divine was therefore deprived of the capacity to beget. But "to say that God has been deprived of anything at all is to be impious to the extreme, as being destructive of the true notion of God and of his perfection" (*Apol.* 8.10–11). Using the language of such Neoplatonic commentators on Aristotle as Alexander of Aphrodisias, Syrianus, and Dexippus, Eunomius stressed that he meant *agennētos* not as privation but as negation: "For if privatives are privatives with respect to the inherent properties of something, then they are secondary to their positives" (8.7–8).[133] His negation is simply negation: Eunomius took care to ensure that the essential unbegotten state of God cannot be seen as depriving the divine of a positive characteristic, having been born, since that was a characteristic it never had in the first place, and of which it therefore cannot be deprived.

A further and perhaps even more important argument concerns the origins of the name (or names) of god (or of the gods) and his (or their) distinctive powers, based on contemporary interpretations of Plato's *Cratylus*. Eunomius believed names are given by God and are not merely a result of human invention (*kat' epinoian*), so that God's name is indicative of his essence.[134] In *Cratylus* Plato uses names and their appellative and signifying function to define in detail the relationship between nature and the divine Mind-Soul, beginning with a discussion of synonyms.[135] He admits that "I may call a thing by one name, which I gave, and you by another, which you gave. And in the same way, I see that cities have their own different names for the same things, and Greeks differ from other Greeks and from barbarians in their use of names" (*Cra.* 384d–e). Even though different peoples use different names, however, the initiate easily recognizes that they denote one thing, namely the essential *dynamis* of a word, which remains the same whatever signifiers are applied to the signified. The names Hector, Astyanax, and Archeptolis all mean "king"; that is, they all denote the same distinct property or defining characteristic inherent in the thing thus named. The etymology of the names of the gods further illuminates the point: according to Plato, it denotes their distinctive powers. Apollo's

---

133. For example, Syrianus (*Commentaria in Aristotelem Graeca* [= *CAG*], 6 vols. [Berlin 1883–99; reprint 1956–60], mostly on Arist. *Metaph.*, here *CAG* 6.61.37–38, 61.10–12, 61.29–39, 61.57–64) and Alexander (*CAG* 1.327.20–27, commenting on Arist. *Cat.*) used the classic example of blindness as privation of the inherent property of sight; Dexippus (*CAG* 4:2.44.4–17, 33.10–18, also referring to *Cat.* 2a.11) asserted that negation reveals the truest essence of things; Mortley, *From Word to Silence*, vol. 2, 85–96, 137–43.

134. Eun. *Apol.* 8.1–6; Pl. *Cra.* 383a–385a for names reflecting convention. Daniélou, "Eunome," remains the classic study. Kobusch, "Name und Sein"; Stead, "Logic"; Vaggione, *Eunomius*, 239–66; Mortley, *From Word to Silence*, vol. 2, 147–53. For Plato's *Cratylus*, esp. Rijlaarsdam, *Platon über die Sprache*, 104–50, 156–90. Aristotle attributed a signifying function regarding the *dynamis* named only to simple and not to composite names (words); Charles, *Aristotle on Meaning*, 78–109.

135. M. R. Barnes, *Power*, 70–76. For the use of Plato's *Cratylus* in Stoic circles and the important notion of the material existence of words and, thus, their rational cause, A. A. Long, *Hellenistic Philosophy*, 131–47.

name, for example, is "admirably appropriate to the power [*dynamis*] of the god" because it "aptly indicates [his] four functions [*dynameis*], ... music, prophecy, archery, medicine" (404e–405a).

In other words, the *dynamis,* the defining characteristic, of an object named by a word remains constant even if the letters and syllables of the word obscure this for the uninitiated. As a result, a name refers to the *ousia* of an object, to its essential qualities (*stoicheia*), because "the elements of which names are composed exist in the first place and possess some kind of likeness to the things names imitate" (*Cra.* 434b1–7). Hestia is called this because her power or function is "essence," *ousia* or, as others may say, *essia.* (Socrates notes the shape of the related word *esti,* 401b–e.) Hera's name is *hēra* because her power or function is that of the air (*aera,* 404c).[136] Words and names are not random sounds, but imitate the essence of the object thus named, so that their correct and precise understanding is vital to the understanding of the object's essence.

Thus the relationship of the divine Mind-Soul and nature, on the one hand, and between the essence of the thing named and the name, on the other, takes shape as an analogy. "It would be appropriate to give to the power that carries and holds nature [*physis*] the name *physechē*; twisting it, it is also possible to say *psychē*."[137] The sounds of the name imitate both the function and the essence of the thing named (divine *Psychē* carries and holds *physis*), but they do so without actually being that thing, since imitation, *mimēsis,* indicates both communality and ontological difference. As Plato points out, a portrait of Cratylus with all his properties would be Cratylus himself; likewise, a word with all the properties of the object named would be the object. Neither is the case, and hence one merely imitates the other. Conversely, however, the names as imitations permit us to deduce the essence of the things named. Because the divine Intellect is the *dynamis* that carries and holds all nature (*Cra.* 399e–400b), it also produces names; naming is thus an essential *dynamis* of the Intellect. And names reflect communality between the divine Intellect and the names imitating it while maintaining the ontological difference inherent in *mimēsis*. In other words, the names of the gods, properly understood, indicate both their powers and their essential qualities, and they do not merely reflect human convention or invention.[138]

---

136. E.g., Pl. *Cra.* 404c, 423, 432e–433a; this is why mere vocal imitation or a bird call imitating a sound is not a name; cf. Arist. *Metaph.* 5.3.1014a25–b15 for the essential qualities of things (*stoicheia*).

137. Pl. *Cra.* 400b: τῇ δυνάμει ταύτῃ ἣ φύσιν ὀχεῖ καὶ ἔχει "φυσέχην" ἐπονομάζειν. ἔξεστι δὲ καὶ "ψυχὴν" κομψευόμενον λέγειν. This passage is part of a longer discussion of the two parts of *anthrōpos,* soul and body, so that Plato is speaking about the human rather than divine soul.

138. Proclus reaffirmed the link between the gods and their names. He used hymns because, based on his interpretation of *Cratylus,* he considered the words of the hymns to contain symbols of the divine; Erler, "Interpretieren," esp. 185–217.

Divine Names and the Statues of the Gods: Cratylus's *Implications; Porphyry, Iamblichus, Eusebius, Julian*   When Eunomius wrote his *Apology,* the relation of names to divine essence had been the object of fierce controversy for some time, and not only among Christian intellectuals. Plato's *Cratylus* and the question of interpreting that text to clarify the link between the gods, their powers, and their names had played a significant role when Porphyry and Iamblichus debated the purpose and efficacy of the statues of the gods in aiding the return of the soul to the divine, a debate in which the emperor Julian later declared his position. Julian proclaimed his *Hymn to the Mother of the Gods* in the spring of 362, shortly after Eunomius's *Apology* was published. The hymn opens with a summary of the goddess's multi-ethnic origins that culminates in the miraculous circumstances of the arrival of her statue (*agalma*) in Rome. Here, in Julian's words, the goddess demonstrated that her statue was not an inanimate, man-made object of plaster but was filled with divine power.[139]

Julian in formulating his arguments on the divine power inherent in the statues of the gods (later resumed in his *Epistle* 89) emphasized that he was setting forth his own insights and those of the divine Iamblichus without having read Porphyry's works on the topic. The remark, rather than listing Julian's sources, was polemical. It referred to Iamblichus's debate with Porphyry on the return to the divine of the souls of ordinary persons, as opposed to the souls of philosophers, and whether or not sacrifice was efficacious, and if so, for whom. Porphyry had argued that the purified philosopher did not have to make sacrifices or worship statues, since both belonged to the realm of matter. Though sacrifices and statues of the gods were of continuing benefit for ordinary persons as a way to approach the intelligible as emphasized by Plotinus (*Enn.* 1.6.4), they were not useful for the purified philosopher, because he began his ascent to the divine from a more advanced point, having left behind the material realm of statues and sacrifice. Iamblichus, however, insisted that sacrifice, rituals, and the worship of statues were first steps in the divine ascent, necessary and universal, a path to the divine for all.

Though both men (apparently) agreed that statues, rituals, and sacrifices could help ordinary persons achieve a form of union with the divine, even if at a level far below that of the purified philosopher, Iamblichus stressed their continuing relevance for everyone, including philosophers (a position built on the positive view of matter as essential to the process of salvation and approach to god). Porphyry responded by denouncing all systems that advocated only one path to the divine for all; he directed part of his attack against Christians. Eusebius of Caesarea, above all in his *Praeparatio Evangelica,* argued against Porphyry and in favor of one way

---

139. Jul. *Or.* 5.160a: δύναμίν τινα μείζω καὶ θειοτέραν, in contrast to Ovid's account of the event, *Fasti* 4.255–346.

to the divine, open to all peoples, though (much like Porphyry) he also considered sacrifices unnecessary, a practice belonging to the distant (Jewish) past. Julian had read the *Praeparatio*. Though he was, after his rejection of Christianity, no longer on the side of Eusebius, Julian too followed Iamblichus, against Porphyry, as far as rituals, sacrifice, statues, and the universal nature of religion was concerned.[140]

Eusebius's *Praeparatio Evangelica*, written between 313 and 324, is our only source attesting to the relevance of Plato's *Cratylus* to Porphyry's *On the Statues* (*Peri agalmatōn*) and the question of names as signifiers of divine essence, because Eusebius engaged and cited Porphyry on precisely this issue.[141] Against Porphyry's rejection of oracular revelations and their exegesis, Eusebius sought to demonstrate that Plato and Moses understood names correctly, citing Plato's *Cratylus* and paraphrasing it nearly in its entirety (the only Platonic dialogue Eusebius treated so extensively). Plato and Moses, according to Eusebius, knew that names were divinely created ("by nature") and not the result of human invention or convention (*kat' epinoian, PE* 11.6.9). Because of their imitative quality, they functioned heuristically to reveal the truth about the nature of the thing named.[142] Only advanced peoples, however, like the Hebrews or the Greeks, and persons capable of receiving divine revelation may know the true meaning of names and the essence to which they correspond. Because Moses and Plato received true revelations, the names chosen by Moses, the only barbarian capable of so doing, were of the same heuristic value as Plato's Greek ones; because it was a function of the (Greek) divine lawgiver and dialectician (*dialektikon . . . kai nomothetēn*), God, to establish "just"—that is, correct—names, Greek logic was essential to understand those names.[143] Eusebius's ethnic argument will concern us again in the context of Julian's *Against the Galileans*

---

140. Porph. *On the Statues* would have been an obvious text for Julian to have reacted to. Cosi (*Casta mater*, 87–98; followed by Bouffartigue, *Empereur Julien*, 334–38, 346–53, 366–67, 373–75) noted Julian's indirect knowledge of Porphyry. If Julian had indeed not read Porphyry's own writings, he would have seen Eusebius's excerpts in the *PE*. Julian may have had other ways of being aware of the debate. In addition to Iamblichus's *Chaldaean Theology*, he used Iamblichus's work *On the Statues of the Gods*; Bouffartigue, *Empereur Julien*, 365 n. 251, notes precise parallels. For the Neoplatonic debates on statues, sacrifice, and ritual, now Digeser, "Power."

141. Eus. *PE* 3.2.5, 9.14, 11.1–51, 11.6.1–8; *Eusèbe de Césarée: La préparation évangélique*, ed. and trans. des Places, Sirinelli, and Favrelle. For the date, see livre 1, pp. 8–15; for the relevance of Porphyry, livre 1, pp. 28–34, and livre 3, pp. 14–19; for Eusebius and Plato, livre 11, pp. 243–391, esp. 267–69, 282–93. The title of Porphyry's *Peri agalmatōn* is preserved by Stobaeus *Anth*. (ed. Wachsmuth, vol. 1, 31, 209); Bidez edited the fragments separately in his *Vie de Porphyre*, 1*–23*; but see now *Porphyrii philosophi fragmenta*, ed. Smith and Wasserstein. Van Liefferinge, *Théurgie*, 176–211, reconstructs Porphyry's entire theurgic method (of which the question of sacrifices and status forms only a part); she clarifies the difference between Iamblichus and Porphyry. Hirschle, *Sprachphilosophie*, 12–50, though based primarily on Proclus, provides a useful overview of the link between names and statues.

142. Eus. *PE* 11.6.1–8; Pl. *Cra*. 439b6–8, 386e, 440c.

143. Eus. *PE* 11.6.4, 8–11; cf. 11.5.1–9.

and of Gregory's *Against Julian*. What matters here is Eusebius's insistence on the divine origin of names and their revelatory function.[144]

Plato's *Cratylus* provided the foil for Eusebius's next move. Even though Porphyry claimed that the purified and the initiated had no need of statues and rituals, he had argued nonetheless for their usefulness for the less purified, *hoi polloi*. Eusebius denounced such noxious innovations (*PE* 3.7.5, 14.4.14), in particular Porphyry's mistaken deduction that the divine powers inherent in the visible celestial regions and even in the earth as a divinely created entity also reside in statues of the gods. As a result, Porphyry (whose *On the Statues* Eusebius cited extensively) perversely argued that for those properly initiated, visible representations of the gods, statues, perform the same heuristic function, indicating divine essence, as the names of the gods, so justly elaborated by Plato (*PE* 11.7.1).[145] "Since the divine is luminous, sojourns in fiery ether, and remains invisible to the senses preoccupied by mortal life," in Porphyry's words, crystal, ivory, or marble may evoke "the idea of [that] luminosity" (*PE* 3.7.2). Eusebius believed that if Porphyry had read Plato's *Cratylus* correctly, he would have been saved from such a mistaken concept; Plato had already pointed out that the first Greeks mistakenly worshipped "deities who are today those of many barbarians: the sun, the moon, the earth, the stars, the heavens" before they had advanced sufficiently in logic to be conscious of the intelligibility of the divine; true Greeks—like the Christian Eusebius—understood that the time of sacrifice and statues had passed.[146]

For Eusebius, however, Porphyry's true impiety had been "to identify the god and the world" as one continuum, an outrage that far surpasses quibbles such as "whether ether is conceived to be the intellect of the creator of all or [merely] the

---

144. Philo also asserted that names were given by God: e.g., *On the Creation* 4, 14; *On Exodus* 16.2; Mortley, *From Word to Silence*, vol. 1, 40–46, esp. 41. Gr. Nyss. *Eun*. 3.7.8 (*GNO*, vol. 2, 217), claimed that Eunomius borrowed from Philo his notion of names as divinely given.

145. Proclus (*Theol. Plat*. 1.29, ed. Saffrey–Westerink, 124) retained that concept when he claimed that divine names (*onomata*) perform a heuristic operation analogous to that of statues (*agalmata*); A. Smith, "Porphyry."

146. Pl. *Cra*. 397c–d; Eus. *PE* 3.2.5. Eusebius, therefore, criticized Porphyry's exegesis of an Orphic hymn, where he argued that Zeus, whose name indicates "the cosmic intellect and whose ideas have thus created the world," is also the divine body carrying within him everything down here: the heavens are his head and face, the stars his magnificent hair, "his infallible intellect the royal ether," "his sacred belly the earth, universal mother." "Zeus is thus the entirety of the cosmos, a living being formed out of the living beings, and god formed out of the gods" (Ζεὺς οὖν ὁ πᾶς κόσμος, ζῷον ἐκ ζῴων καὶ θεὸς ἐκ θεῶν, *PE* 3.9.3, 11). Therefore, "the theologians" have correctly "anthropomorphized the representation of Zeus" as an allegory of his divine powers imitating his true essence (*PE* 3.9.1–5). For Eusebius, such a conclusion is entirely mistaken, not least because Porphyry relied on "the Thracian Orpheus" without further investigating where Orpheus received this theology—Porphyry had not checked his source, a cardinal error. And as Plato had already said in *Cratylus* as cited by Eusebius, neither the very earliest, pre-Platonic Greeks nor the magic-obsessed Thracians knew anything about incorporeal essence.

intellect of the Demiurge."[147] To suppose a nature shared between the divine intellect and man's physical self (and thus the usefulness of statues for *hoi polloi*) was the fatal flaw at the heart of Porphyry's argument (at least as excerpted and commented upon by Eusebius): Porphyry justified the creation of anthropomorphic images "because it is according to the intellect that [Zeus] creates and according to the seminal reason that he executes all."[148] What the divine has created thus reflects its essence and may therefore be called on to evoke the supreme divine to aid human salvation through the divine powers inherent in the representations of the divine it had originally created, be they statues, sacrifices, or names.[149]

Eusebius counters that only "the *logikon* and immortal human soul, the intellect without passion," may be the guardian of the "image and resemblance of the divine," for only its essence was formed in like manner (*PE* 3.10.17). If a statue has all the properties of the soul (i.e., immateriality, incorporeality, intellect, reason), then it may reflect divine powers; but this is impossible. (Recall the discussion of the relation between Cratylus and his portrait.) Therefore, a statue of Zeus is nothing more than a theatrical mask. The representations of Zeus found among the Phoenicians, Egyptians, Cretans, and so on, are a mere human convention, "mere fiction of the philosopher" (*PE* 3.10.26); they neither have nor attest to the immanence of a universally recognized divine power.[150]

To place Eunomius's argument in the *Apology*—that names such as "unbegotten" indicate divine essence—in the broader context of debates about *Cratylus* on the relevance of the statues of gods and therefore also of sacrifice and ritual for human ascent to the divine (by Porphyry responding to Iamblichus, Eusebius responding to Porphyry, and later Julian supporting Iamblichus against Porphyry) reveals the true extent of the difficulties encountered by Eusebius, Eunomius, and all other Christians: the participants in these debates were more similar than different. The boundaries separating elite Christian philosophers from their non-Christian

---

147. Eus. *PE* 3.10.2–3: τοῦ τῶν ὅλων ποιητοῦ, ἢ τοῦ νοῦ τοῦ δημιουργικοῦ.

148. Eus. *PE* 3.10.13: ὅτι νοῦς ἦν, καθ' ὃν ἐνδημιούργει, καὶ λόγοις σπερματικοῖς ἀπετέλει τὰ πάντα.

149. "Many have also manifested the invisibility of their essence with a black stone. They represent the gods with human traits because the gods are reasoned [*logikoi*]."

150. Eusebius's denunciation of Porphyry's argument as fiction is also apparent when he claims Porphyry's deduction that "they made Hera the companion of Zeus by calling Hera the 'power' of ether or air"—Eusebius citing Porphyry citing Plato's *Cratylus*—was inconsistent with his theology: here, he said that Hera as the *dynamis* of ether was the creator of the sun, the moon, Apollo, and Artemis; elsewhere, that Zeus was the sole creative force. In the *Chaldean Oracles* (e.g., frs. 3, 4, 5, 51 ed. Majerick), Porphyry placed the creative *dynamis* "with the Father, but Intellect is from him" (i.e., Father and power produce Intellect), identifying Intellect with the goddess Rhea, a concept influential for Julian's trinity in the *Hymn to the Mother of the Gods* (= *MoG*); Bouffartigue, *Empereur Julien*, 365–67, 373–79; and above, Chapter 3, "A Universal Divinity: *Hymn to the Mother of the Gods*." Eusebius wanted to expose Porphyry's contradictions as a result of his failure to recognize the one true divine power; *PE* 3.11.1, 3.13.57; *DE* 4.5.

contemporaries were delineated clearly but remained porous. To argue that names reveal divine essence brought one remarkably close to arguing that sacrifice and statues do the same; the onus was indeed on those who had to separate the heuristic function of statues from that of names.

If one wanted to preserve, as Eusebius and Eunomius evidently did, Plato's assertion in *Cratylus* that names permitted deductions regarding the nature and essence of the divine, it was difficult, as shown by Eusebius's defensive arguments, to deny such deductive capacity to statues and sacrifice. If names were created divinely and revealed divine essence rather than invented by humans and assigned by convention (so that the name "Son" was not a title or a mode to represent the Father but a fully distinct person with its own essence, however related to the Father), then how and to what extent (in time? eternally? as historical artifacts? for all? only for the less purified?) did names differ from statues and sacrifices? How, as means to approach the divine, did the sacrifice of Jesus and the Eucharist or the ritual of baptism differ from the worship of statues and the rituals associated with the Mother of the Gods?

Arguments about the deductive power of names—in which Eunomius, Photinus, and all their opponents were engaged—belong to a broader debate of longer standing than that about Nicene and non-Nicene theology. Indeed, the debates about non-Nicene and Nicene theology, as has long been recognized, emerged out of the Alexandrian philosophical schools, including that of Ammonius Sacchas, and the school of Numenius in Rome, the same circles that produced the debates between Porphyry, Iamblichus, Origen, and later Eusebius.[151]

As far as Eunomius is concerned, though it is impossible to prove direct connections, the implications of his argument and that of Photinus regarding names could not have escaped Julian. He composed his treatises on the continuing relevance of hymns, rituals, and sacrifice, as well as the correct manner of reading myth (whose *enigmata* or *paradoxa,* just like the words of hymns, signify and activate the divine *dynamis* inherent in them)[152]—as a means for all to ascend to the divine according to their abilities—in 362, and then in early 363 he responded to Eusebius and others in *Against the Galileans,* influenced by Porphyry's *Against the Christians.*[153] Correspondingly, by 362 Julian's views would also have been apparent, especially to those in Constantinople and at court such as Aetius and Eunomius, philosophers guiding others toward the divine through the power of

---

151. Dawson, *Allegorical Readers,* 125–26; Edwards, *Origen against Plato,* 11–55, 123–33. Eusebius also cites Numenius in the *PE* (*Eusèbe de Césarée: La préparation évangélique,* ed. and trans. des Places, Sirinelli, and Favrelle, livre 11, 397, s.v.).

152. Eus. *PE* 4.1 attacks pagan oracles, a line he continues in Book 5, whereas the main part of Book 4 focuses on sacrifices.

153. Of Porphyry's treatise on divine names we only know the title; Erler, "Interpretieren," 185–217.

their "god-speaking" (*theologikē*)—or their "god-working" (*theurgikē*): *theōn poiein parousias.*[154]

Back to Eunomius   Eunomius's argument that God is in essence *agennētos* because of his name—"when we say 'Unbegotten,' then, we do not imagine that we ought to honor God only in name, in conformity with human invention; rather, in conformity with reality, we ought to repay him the debt that above all others is most due to God: the acknowledgment that he is what he is" (*Apol.* 8.1)—was thus highly charged with implications beyond Christological debates. Those implications may well account for the intensity of the debates about his (and Photinus's) views. Eunomius was aware of contemporary Aristotelian logic and language theory (e.g., regarding privation) and of contemporary debates about Plato's *Cratylus;* when discussing the productive activity of the Son in *Apology* 22.10, for example, he criticized as Greek sophists those who connect activity to essence too easily. His opponents were also aware of these criticisms. Thus Basil in his first response to Eunomius accused him of paraphrasing, wrongly and inversely, Aristotle's *Categories* on privation.[155] Gregory of Nyssa criticized him for relying excessively on Plato's *Cratylus*—Eunomius, "struck by the beauty of Plato's expression, . . . thinks it convenient to make his philosophy into the teaching of the church"—arguing that names were mostly human invention.[156] Eunomius, responding to his critics in the *Apology of the Apology*—insofar as we can discern from the fragments—elaborated his theory of names in greater detail, now taking pains to do so entirely in the context of an exegesis of Genesis, like Eusebius identifying Moses as the first source of just names.[157] Eunomius's first road toward a clearer understanding of the relationship

---

154. Bouffartigue, *Empereur Julien,* 300, 385–88. Mortley, *From Word to Silence,* vol. 2, 141–42, points to Eunomius's wide-ranging circle of interlocutors in the ongoing debates about privation and negation. In a fragment Gregory of Nyssa cited in *Eun.* 2.565 (*GNO,* vol. 1, 189), Eunomius appears to respond to ongoing Neoplatonic criticism of his language of negation.

155. Bas. *Eun.* 1.5.43–45; Pottier, *Dieu,* 134–39, 150–57. Mortley, *From Word to Silence,* vol. 2, 140, notes that Basil's argument cannot be traced back directly to Aristotle's *Categories* but suggests that Basil and Eunomius relied on fourth-century Neoplatonic commentaries on Aristotle. Basil's *Hexaemeron* proves that he knew his Aristotle. For a more detailed analysis of Basil's refutation of Eunomius's language theory, Pottier, *Dieu,* 158–66, esp. 150–57.

156. Gr. Nyss. *Eun.* 2.405 (*GNO,* vol. 1, 344); he too relied on *Cratylus,* but understood in a more Aristotelian manner, as I will discuss in the context of Gr. *Or.* 4. Gr. Nyss. *Eun.* 2.404 mentions *Cratylus* explicitly (*GNO,* vol. 1, 344); see also Gr. Nyss. *Eun.* 1.151–54 (*GNO,* vol. 1, 71–72). A significant part of the second book of Gregory of Nyssa's *Against Eunomius* (*Eun.* 2 = *GNO,* vol. 1, 305.23–24) refutes his language theory; M. R. Barnes, *Power,* 284–86. Basil's (Aristotelian) *Hexaemeron* also argued for names as human convention; Callahan, "Greek Philosophy," esp. 45–46. For the Platonic tradition common to all three, Daniélou, "Eunome," 412–32.

157. *Eun. Apol. apol.* 2 (*GNO,* vol. 1, 315.31–316.3); Aetius in L. R. Wickham, "*Syntagmation,*" 560; Pottier, *Dieu,* 167–70; M. R. Barnes, *Power,* 185–89, 202–6. Barnes (p. 203 n. 132) shows convincingly

between Father and Son—the a priori deduction of divine essence from a precise analysis of their names—thus had wide-ranging contemporary implications, evident to all involved in these debates, from Emperor Julian to Basil, Gregory of Nyssa, and Gregory of Nazianzus, especially in his *Oration 4, Against Julian*.

The Second Road

After he had made clear in the first part of his *Apology* that an a priori analysis of the divine names results inevitably in the understanding that God is unbegotten essence, Eunomius turned to the second road, the a posteriori analysis of the effects of divine creativity and what they reveal about the Father and the begotten Son. Eunomius had addressed the significance of the name, or attribute, "begotten" for the Son in the first part of his *Apology*. In chapter 9, he stressed that the Father, given his unbegotten essence, "could never undergo a generation that involved the sharing of his own distinctive nature [i.e., being unbegotten] with the offspring of that generation, and could never admit of any comparison or association with the thing begotten" (*Apol.* 9.1–3). Association (*koinōnia*, in Eunomius's text) would require shared essence—impossible, since the Son is clearly begotten. The same applies to comparison (*synkrisis*), which also requires at least some basic communality: communality of essence, then, would require "that the name ... be made common as well [*koinopoiēthēsetai*]" (9.8–12). If one takes names seriously as reflecting divine essence, however, then such communality is impossible: "After all, there is no one so ignorant or so zealous for impiety as to say that the Son is *equal* to the Father! The Lord himself has expressly stated that 'the Father who sent me is greater than I.' Nor is there anyone so rash as to try to yoke one name to the other [such as 'Son-who-was-not-begotten' or 'Father-who-did-not-beget,' 14.8–9]! Each name pulls in its own direction, and the other has no common meaning with it at all: if the one name is '[the] Unbegotten,' it cannot be 'Son'; and if 'Son,' it cannot be '[the] Unbegotten' " (11.9–14). Eunomius then elaborated these arguments in chapters 12–19.

Eunomius's conception of the Son as begotten did not imply a creative activity analogous to that of human fathers, which involves entirely undivine passion. "It is by no means necessary, when God is called 'Father,' to understand this activity as having the same meaning as it does with human beings. ... Rather, ... we preserve the proportionate relationship, so we are not at all disturbed to hear the Son called 'thing made' " (*Apol.* 17.4–9). In insisting on the genuine (though not human) nature of the act of begetting, Eunomius differentiated himself clearly from Marcellus and Photinus, the so-called Sabellians, accused of considering the Trinity a mere assembly of names or modes of speaking of the Father, and not persons: "The Son

---

that Eunomius derived his language theory primarily from Eusebius's *PE*, and not, as commonly argued, from Clement and Origen.

is the 'offspring' and 'thing made' of the Unbegotten and Unmade" (17.10). Such a statement also responded to homoiousian critics who argued that Eunomius's insistence on the Son's generation as an action (*energeia*) rather than an essence (*ousia*) diminished the scriptural metaphor of birth.[158]

For Eunomius the Son's essential *dynamis* is twofold. He is the only thing made directly by the Unbegotten, and as such he is the creative capacity through which the unbegotten Father created everything else. Because the Son is the Only-begotten, "the creative power [*tēs dēmiourgikēs dynameōs*] was begotten coexistentially in him from above; he is therefore the Only-begotten God [*einai theon monogenē*] of those things that came into existence after him and through him." Thus "he became the perfect servant of the whole creative activity and the purpose of the Father" (*Apol.* 15.12–16). The Son's primary essence is therefore that of the creator or Demiurge, because he himself is created. In Eunomius's interpretation this implies subordination, since the created Son is the servant on whom this divine *dynamis* has been bestowed. For him, such subordination also implies separation. Eunomius in fact posits separation between the essence (the Father's *dynamis* to create) and its productive capacity (delegated to the Son). In concluding his *Apology*, he makes the point in all clarity. The Son is the image of the Father but not his essential likeness. Their likeness resides in their shared creative power, or *dynamis,* of which the Son is the image, so that the creative power of God that produced the Son is also manifest in the Son, since through him all else is made (*Apol.* 24).

Eunomius's prior differentiation between *dynamis* (power) and *energeia* (activity) is central to his discussion of the essential dissimilarity of Father and Son.[159] Again, Eusebius's *Praeparatio Evangelica* illuminates the issue at hand, now in the context of the debate about creation and whether it occurred out of nothing. Eusebius argued for creation ex nihilo (a position he considered a stellar achievement of the Hebrews and hence of Christianity).[160] Matter is not coeternal with its creator and therefore cannot be unbegotten. (As Eunomius also argues in *Apol.* 7.4–11 and 15.8–9, "We do not, however, include the essence of the Only-begotten among things brought into existence out of nothing, for 'no-thing' is not an essence.") Although matter must be generated—created by prior cause—God has no prior cause; for if he did, he could not be creator of all. Eusebius cited a number of authors to support his case, among them Methodius of Olympus.[161] In the context of the argument

---

158. See also Eun. *Apol.* 6.12–13; Bas. *Eun.* 1.24.13–15; Epiph. *Haer.* 73.13.2; Vaggione, *Eunomius,* 243–44, 251.

159. For a detailed discussion of Eunomius's technical vocabulary, Vaggione, *Eunomius,* 130–47.

160. Eus. *PE* 7.18.11.

161. Eusebius cites Methodius but calls the author Maximus, *PE* 7.18–7.20; the identification of Methodius is by Patterson, "*De libero arbitrio.*"

demonstrating that God is ingenerate (in essence), Methodius, as cited by Eusebius, pointed to a difference between a name that denotes an essence and a name that describes a characteristic, an accident, an activity or action, *energeia* (*PE* 7.22.31–34; to paraphrase Methodius, a grammarian is not in essence a grammarian but is so called because he possesses the accident of grammar; grammar is his action: *PE* 7.22.30).

Eunomius also distinguished between what something is called and therefore is in essence, and something that is what it is and called thus by accident: that is, called by a term denoting its activity rather than its essence. Accidents or activities require the prior existence of something (there must be a preexisting agent causing the action), but this is not the case for essences. If something is an activity, it is the effect or work (*ergon;* cf. *PE* 7.22.29) of the agent or essence that brought it forth, but the activity is not the essence itself—a distinction Eunomius assumed as a given and maintained throughout. This distinction is, in fact, the basis for the structural division of his *Apology*, which examines first the essence or *ousia* of the divine and second its activities or *energeia* (*Apol.* 20.8), with the former corresponding to the Father and the latter to the Son, as activity and product. For Eunomius, it is impossible to "examine the nature of the universe, [or] make judgments about these things with clear minds" (20.3–5) without such an epistemological distinction.[162] Indeed, according to Eunomius, those who connect the action to the essence are led astray by Greek sophisms. If, for example, God's activity were essential to his nature, it would exist eternally, which would mean that matter and God, its creator, coexisted from the beginning; and to present the world as coeval with God is a Greek argument (22.10), because the Greeks "on the outside" (of Christianity) deny creation ex nihilo (23.8–12).[163] In contrast, Eunomius claims to "judge the action from its effects in accordance with the principles enunciated just a moment ago."[164]

Therefore, if he who studies things divine begins by deducing the nature of the divine "from the things that have been made [*ek tōn dēmiourgēmatōn*], he is led from them to the essences and discovers that the Son is the 'thing made' [*poiēma*] of the Unbegotten" (*Apol.* 20.15–17). The second road, the examination of the product, demonstrates that the Son is the *energeia* or the *ergon* of God and that his cre-

162. M. R. Barnes, *Power,* 185–89.
163. One example of such Greek thought would be Plato's notion that souls were without beginning (e.g., *Phdr.* 245c–246a) or Arist. *Cael.* 270a12–22, where the author claims that the universe is self-moving and hence also never came into existence. At stake here are two distinct notions: *agenetos,* "not coming into being," and *agennētos,* "not begotten." For Eunomius both are synonymous when applied to God, but for other contemporary Christians these terms and concepts were quite distinct; Vaggione, *Eunomius,* 248–49.
164. Eun. *Apol.* 23.4–5: τὴν ἐνέργειαν ἐκ τῶν ἔργων κρίνοντες.

ation was an action of the Father's will [*tēn boulēsin*, 23.14–17] but not of his essence; to cite Michel Barnes: "God's productive capacity is not an essential attribute, property, or quality."[165] As *Monogenēs* of God's will, the Son is unique among all created essences, but created he is and therefore, as God's work, subordinate to him. In other words, the existence of the activity is deduced from its products: "We ... judge the action [*energeia*] from the effects [*erga*]" (23.4–5). This relationship, created by divine design and purpose—for example, to refute those Greeks who propose, uniting activity and essence, that matter is coeternal with its creator—included a temporal dimension. Because the Son was created, he had a beginning (unlike God, the prior cause), and therefore also (at least in theory) an end (23.6–11).[166] In sum, Eunomius's "argument has demonstrated that God's will is an action [*energeia*] and that this action is not essence, but that the Only-begotten exists by virtue of the will of the Father." As a consequence, the Son is similar to the Father "not with respect to the essence but with respect to the action, which is what the will is" (24.1–4). To cite Richard Vaggione, to call God the Father, "described what God was doing, not who God is," and the Son demonstrates the effect of that activity but not the essential sameness of both.[167]

Neither a priori analysis of the divine names and their heuristic value for deducing divine essence nor a posteriori examination of the effect of divine activity—that is, creation—permitted the assertion that Father and Son are the same in essence. Close analysis of scripture demonstrates the same; after all, Paul said of the Son that "he is the image of the invisible God, the first-born of all creation, because in him all things were created" (*Apol.* 24.6–8). To argue otherwise denies that names have divine origin and hence denote divine essence. To declare that an essence, its activity, and its product are the same denies what makes the essence essential; in the case of God it also negates the fundamental Christian (Hebrew) cosmological insight that matter cannot be coeternal with its creator, as some Greeks claim.

This summary of Eunomius's central arguments does not do justice to his (not to mention Aetius's) theological positions in the early 360s. It should suffice, however, to indicate what Eunomius's opponents had to confront: a sophisticated and consistent argument that arose out of and engaged a wide range of existing debates, as made evident in the references to Eusebius and his intellectual challenges, represented by Porphyry, Iamblichus, and others. For us, the questions remain if and how Gregory of Nazianzus's second oration engaged with these debates. Did he have Eunomius in mind when he formulated *Oration* 2?

---

165. M. R. Barnes, *Power*, 190–91.

166. Eunomius leaves this point unaddressed in the fragments we possess, though in practice the activity of the Father exists as long as he does and is thus de facto without end.

167. Vaggione, *Eunomius*, 134.

OIKEIŌSIS PROS THEON:
ORATION 2 AGAINST EUNOMIUS

Circumstantial evidence, such as Gregory's intermittent presence at Annesi when Basil formulated his arguments against Eunomius (who had just spent time at home in Cappadocian Oltiseris, near Corniaspa, a station at the intersection of the east-west road linking Galatia and Armenia and the north-south road between Tavium and Caesarea, and about equidistant between Caesarea and Nyssa),[168] suggests that Gregory's second oration also responded to Eunomius. Gregory's use of anti-Cynic topoi to characterize persons falsely administering the Trinity, especially the second and third groups, those he described as excessively vain (*Or.* 2.8), shameless in their play to the masses, unseemly in their rush to power, full of pretended wisdom, and low-class in origin, anticipate the accusations leveled against Eunomius and Aetius by Basil of Caesarea, Gregory of Nyssa, and Theodore of Mopsuestia. As a historian I face here the conundrum inherent in any use of a topos: How much is topos, and how much describes historical circumstances? Anti-Cynic language—as Julian's example has also shown—targeted, after all, competing philosophers who shared with their attackers claims to divine origin, oracular insights (those, at least, who did not criticize oracles), and a strictly ascetic life.

Eunomius in the early 360s certainly fits the bill. If we take seriously his and Aetius's episcopal status, known to Gregory since Basil had witnessed the rushed elevation of Eunomius to the see of Cyzicus as the result of his vain, power-grabbing display of pretended wisdom at Constantinople (*Or.* 2.41), and his and Aetius's ordination of divinely inspired philosophers as bishops, including Euphronius for Pontus, Galatia, and Cappadocia, Gregory's vehemence could easily be directed against Eunomius and Aetius. False leaders are a predominant theme of *Oration* 2. Gregory attacks them directly in nearly a third of *Oration* 2, especially chapters 8, 40–51, and 57–93; and the theme of leadership dominates the entire oration, chapters 11–116, if we count those chapters opposing good and bad conduct. His virulence against those who rush to the altars unprepared, dispensing so-called wisdom before they have even mastered the most elementary steps, because they claim to be a second Samuel, saintly *ab utero* (1 Sam 1:19–28), ready to teach the spirit inspired by divine dreams, and rejecting the letter as superfluous (e.g., *Or.* 2.49), indicates that he attacked persons of substance and influence. For Gregory, these persons "engaged openly in war against priests" (*Or.* 2.82). If we add Julian's support of Aetius and Eunomius into the equation—both prospered, as we have seen, during his reign, whose length no one, including Gregory, would have known in 362 and 363—both men become even more plausible as leaders engaged in a civil war. Indeed, it may well have been with intent that Gregory placed the vain and un-

---

168. Hild and Restle, *Kappadokien,* 215.

educated leaders just before the persons he described as vacillating, lacking any firm notion of things divine at home, so that, having tried everything, they finally abandon Christianity as impious—persons, that is, like Julian, thus enhancing the link between him and the vain leaders (*Or.* 2.49).

The *eugenēs* Gregory, who chose retreat to learn what must be said and done before he said and did it, who never spoke in an uneducated manner, towered of course above such "paragons of excellence and simplicity [*hoi chrēstoteroi kai haplousteroi*]" (*Or.* 2.49). Nevertheless, he had returned to engage them in the *agōn* of *logoi* (*Or.* 2.85), and he was fully conscious that an enemy of such caliber—worse than Julian, the enemy on the outside! (*Or.* 2.85)—required a present-day Moses who prophesied and led (*Or.* 2.52), and fought as one ought to fight (*Or.* 2.82). A new Moses and a new Paul, in fact, who, together with Peter, received the *charisma* of the leadership of souls through *logoi* and *erga*. Paul indeed is Gregory's principal exemplar (*Or.* 2.51–56); he suffered hardship and was persecuted for speaking appropriately to each who heard him, to slaves and to masters, to those who command and to those who obey, to men and women, those who are married and those who are not, "becoming all things to all, in order to gain all" (*Or.* 2.51; Lk 8:6). Gregory acted as Paul had, and as Paul had described Christ acting in 1 Timothy 2.5:[169] "placed between God and humans, engaging in a contest on behalf of the latter while leading the chosen people toward—and affiliating them to [*oikeiōn*]—the former."[170]

Gregory's contest focused on the correct mixture of the most potent *pharmakon*, the Trinity, and its misuse by Eunomius: "to divide the *Logos* into three separate *hypostaseis*," estranged (*allotrioi*) from each other as if they were rival divinities (*Or.* 2.36). Gregory illustrated such misuse by noting that those he calls "father-lovers" (*philopatores*) so loved the Father that they deprived him of fatherhood by denying him a true son. "Of whom in fact could he be the Father if the nature of the Son were to be separated from his and linked with creation (in fact, what is estranged [*allotrios*] cannot be his Son), or if [the Son] were united to and absorbed by him, or, what yields the same result, if [the Father] were to absorb him?" To love Christ too much, to be *philochristos*, not only reduces the power of the Father but also deprives the Son of his essence as son: "Of whom would he in effect be the Son if he would not refer to his Father as his cause [*archē*]—and not grant the Father the dignity of being the cause that is his [due], both as father and as begetter [*gennētōr*]?"

---

169. Gr. Naz. *Ep.* 79.1 and *Or.* 30.14. S. Elm, "Paul as Seen by Gregory," 106–16.

170. Gr. Naz. *Or.* 2.53: μέσος Θεοῦ καὶ ἀνθρώπων ἱστάμενος, ὑπὲρ μὲν τῶν ἀγωνιζόμενος, τῷ δὲ προσάγων καὶ οἰκειῶν λαὸν περιούσιον. See S. Elm, "Gregory's Women," 185–91. Gregory, in his *synkrisis* to exemplify leadership, then lists Isaiah, Hosea, Micah, Joel, Habakkuk, Malachi, Zachary, Joshua, Daniel, Ezekiel, and Jeremiah. For the rhetorical aspects, Neumeister, *Grundsätze*, 8–9, 78–83; Guignet, *Saint Grégoire*, 278–82; Ruether, *Gregory*, 112–15.

(*Or.* 2.38). To deprive the Son of his divine essence as son is particularly prone to result in "the poverty of Judaism and introduce jealousy into the bosom of the divine nature by reserving divinity solely for the ingenerate [*agennētos*], as if we were afraid that by being Father of a true God of equal dignity with regard to his nature [*homotimou tēn physin*] God might be lost to us" (*Or.* 2.37).

Eunomius had proposed just that. For him, the Son was *allotrios* from the Father in that he could not have been essentially the same, since he shared with the Father only the activity of creation. As *Monogenēs* the Son was essentially created (from the beginning and irrespective of his incarnation) and because of that created everything else. For Gregory, such an argument deprived both Father and Son, suggesting that the Father was either a small and insignificant first cause or the cause of small and insignificant things. To deny that the Son as begotten is of the same essence as the Father reduces the fullness of the Trinity. "The Father is the cause of the divinity and goodness that is contemplated in the Son and the Spirit, in the one as Son and Word [*Logos*] and in the other as procession and undiluted Spirit. Because of that the God who is one must be preserved and three *hypostaseis* professed, each with its own specific properties [*idiotētos*]" (*Or.* 2.38)—an expression Gregory repeated nearly verbatim some twenty years later in his *Oration* 31.9 against Eunomius, who never used the controversial term *hypostasis*.[171]

Gregory argued rigorously for the divinity of the Son, having deduced it from the history of salvation as he summarized it in *Oration* 2.36, just before defining the two main falsifications of the Trinity (and again, in greater detail, in chapters 74–76 and 96–99) as turning away from letter to spirit, from the milk of infants to

---

171. See also Gr. Naz. *Or.* 20.6. Athanasius, too, used ἰδιότης (*Contra Arian.* 1.58) to argue for the equal divinity of Father and Son based on Jn 14:28. The council of Constantinople held on December 31, 359, banned *hypostasis* as too controversial a way to describe the Trinity. *Hypostasis* also played a part in the debates whether or not names denote divine reality or are constructs of human invention or convention. In Stoic debates the term was used in the context of defining reality as material, which created problems for certain categories of the real: geometrical shapes, for example, are real and can be discerned cognitively (*kat' epinoian*) without physical reality (*kath' hypostasin*). Here, *hypostasis* denotes a physical reality independent of human cognition. Gregory's argument, insisting that the three persons are distinct realities, echoes this move; Sext. Emp. *Adv. mathematicos* 8.453; Proclus *Hypotyposis astronom. pos.* 7.52. The Stoic usage of *hypostasis* also resembles Basil's use of the term against Eunomius, *Eun.* 1.5–6. Pottier, *Dieu*, 101–6 on *hypostasis*, and 85–86, 158–66. At issue was the operation of *epinoia*, or cognition, as an act of the human mind that recognized reality in immaterial things. Knowledge through acts of *epinoia*, however, could be construed as mere fiction: that is, names applied to the divine without relating to its essence, arguments brought to the fore in debating Marcellus and Photinus before 360. Arian insistence that names such as "power" or "wisdom," when applied to the Father, were *kat' epinoian* was also controversial; Athanasius, for example, saw this as mere fiction, *kata thesin*: Ath. *Decr.* 16.1 (*Athanasius: Werke*, ed. Opitz, vol. 2, 12.19–21), *Syn.* 15.3 (*Athanasius: Werke*, ed. Opitz, vol. 2, 243.5–7); Vaggione, *Eunomius*, 241–44; M. R. Barnes, *Power*, 127–28; Pottier, *Dieu*, 143–49, with reference to the use of *epinoia* in Origen.

the solid nourishment of those initiated into the knowledge that God is Word, the first born before creation, Father and Son (*Or.* 2.98). Responding to these falsifications, Gregory posited his understanding of the Trinity as Oneness, where the essential nature of the Father as the First Cause is made evident precisely through the existence of his Son as a distinct yet essentially divine person. Indeed, only as fully divine Son could the *Logos* be *oikeios,* affiliated to God (as opposed to *allotrios*).

The Son's full divinity, in fact, makes possible what Gregory emphasized in his first oration. "Let us become like Christ, because Christ has become like us. Let us become gods because of him, because he has become human because of us" (*Or.* 1.5).[172] If the Son was not *oikeios pros theon* as fully divine Son, then the entire concept of *oikeiōsis* with the divine was meaningless: Who or what could then be affiliated with the divine and therefore saved? Gregory's concept of *oikeiōsis* embracing all in concentric circles outward, originating in divine love for mankind (*philanthrōpia*), contrasted sharply with Eunomius's assertion that not even the Son as *Monogenēs* shared the Father's unbegotten essence.[173] As has become apparent in the preceding discussion, affiliation to the divine, *oikeiōsis,* was central to everything Gregory stood for, from his understanding of the role of the philosopher as leader to his concept of the Son and his function within the Trinity, and therefore that of the Trinity as one. For him, the language of begetting, of giving birth, of a procession out of something else, was more central, more appropriate to the divine than Eunomius's (equally scriptural) preference for the language of making and creating. This language of affiliation—of family, in effect—structured his understanding not only of the Trinity but also of the priesthood as active philosophy, a mediating between God and men because philosophers, divinely born—begotten, not made—and sufficiently purified, had "risen higher than the multitude in their virtue and their affiliation to God," so that they could lead others toward him (*Or.* 2.71).[174]

To deny the Son equal dignity with regard to his nature broke the chain of divine economy in which everything was linked from its very origin. If Christ was not fully divine, then his assumption of humanity could not redeem all mankind, for then the potent *pharmakon* of the Trinity did not heal all. To grant everyone, from *hoi polloi* to the purified philosopher, closeness to the divine, able to become gods (*genōmetha theoi, Or.* 1.5) and be saved, was after all the paramount Christian message, at least according to Gregory. Raymond Van Dam has a point when he states that "the formula eventually adopted as the orthodox doctrine to describe

---

172. See also Harrison, "Some Aspects," esp. 11.
173. A difference that also resulted in different baptismal rituals; S. Elm, "Inscriptions and Conversions," 20–24. For Gregory's use of *theōsis* in the later *Theological Orations* against Eunomius, see below, Chapter 9; Gregory of Nazianzus, *Faith,* intro. Norris, 66–68.
174. Gr. Naz. *Or.* 2.3: ὅσοι τῶν πολλῶν εἰσιν ἀνωτέρω κατ' ἀρετὴν καὶ τὴν πρὸς τὸν θεὸν οἰκείωσιν.

the Son could hence also serve as a reassertion of the normal [familial] source of prestige and influence in local provincial society: 'begotten [like Gregory,] not made [like Eunomius].'"[175] Gregory was the son and heir of his father, to whom he ascribed a sacred marriage to confirm his own sacred birth, so that he was Paul to his father's Moses, the fulfillment of what had been prefigured. But his understanding of the divine economy as *oikeiōsis* also solved a conundrum that had incited Porphyry and Iamblichus, and also preoccupied Julian just at that time: how to guide to the divine and to salvation, as true slaves of God, all those whom one has been divinely ordered to lead and safeguard.

Gregory's concept of *oikeiōsis pros theon*, of making men gods, so fundamental even in his earliest orations, countered two significant contemporary notions. One was Julian's way to achieve assimilation with the divine and *theōn poiein parousias*—which differed for persons of differing purity but finally included everyone—through sacrifices, rituals, and the power of the *paradoxa* of myth, properly understood and taught; the other was Eunomius's influential teaching that salvation was possible because the Son was of lesser divinity than the Father and therefore closer to man than the unbegotten essence, so that man could share essential characteristics of the Son through *mimēsis*.[176]

Gregory as divinely chosen political philosopher, born to a sacred family, was armed like a hoplite (*Or.* 2.82) to combat nobly both those who falsified the Trinity by overstepping the limits within which it ought to be comprehended—Eunomius and Photinus and their followers—and the emperor Julian, who represented what Gregory sarcastically called "the more spiritual and more elevated [*pneumatikoi mallon kai gennaioteroi*]," persons who "have condemned us whenever they considered this opportune, have put us to the test and judged us nothing:[177] and then they have left us, spitting upon the community as if it were not one of pious persons." These persons were really only one man, Julian, "the beast now risen against the church that is the fullness of evil" (*Or.* 2.49, 87).

As mediator chosen by God, Gregory had purified himself properly by living the true philosophical life so that he could lead others to the divine, as demanded by

---

175. Van Dam, *Becoming Christian*, 17.

176. Mimesis implies that one shares commonalities with but never fully becomes what one imitates, whereas both *oikeiōsis pros theon* and *theon poiein* or *theopoiein* denote a greater degree of merging. I think that this distinction reflects the central difference between Eunomius and Gregory: for Eunomius, as created, humans can never merge or approximate something essentially unbegotten, but they can imitate the *Monogenēs* to the greatest possible degree. See also Gregg and Groh's (*Early Arianism*) understanding of the Son as the primary carrier of salvation in non-Nicene thought, corroborated by Eunomian ritual practices; S. Elm, "Inscriptions and Conversions," 20–24; Vaggione, *Eunomius*, 332–44.

177. Where my translation offers "have put us to the test," Gregory literally says "put us to the touchstone," *basanisantes*, the term Themistius had also used to define the true philosophical life.

his understanding of philosophy as active engagement for the benefit of all—an entirely political choice because the *oikoumenē* of the Romans and of mankind as a whole was at stake. To do what he had been commanded to do required that Gregory write himself prestige, since only through his prestige and the authority derived from it could he persuade those in power (in Nazianzus and everywhere else) that his way to the divine and to salvation was the one and only true way for all, so that those who ruled and legislated must follow his philosophical advice: against Julian, against Eunomius.

Gregory's prestige and authority derived both from his father and from his philosophical life. That life permitted him to guide and even correct his father without diminishing his father's parental authority: by tyrannizing him into public office, his father had in fact reinforced a divine command for the sake of the *oikos* and the *politeia*. As true mediator, between those in opposition in Nazianzus and his father as well as between mankind and God, Gregory fought against the two most dangerous enemies while he was conciliatory vis-à-vis those he considered the lesser evil. His notion of the Trinity offered all those who were less extreme than (for example) Eunomius a way back into the fold as he defined it. He offered a "royal road" that was more than a mean between the two extreme ways of falsifying the Trinity, because that road represented a fuller understanding of the Trinity that aimed at integrating all—the entire *oikoumenē*—with the creator.

Gregory, to demonstrate that only the true Christian political philosopher actively engaged for the common good could be a true leader of the *oikoumenē* as Christian—in sum, a man just like him, the model priest and bishop—relied on the traditional model of the advisor to those in power: indeed, that of the true leader. He engaged the classic model of the true philosopher as leader as defined in the normative texts, by Plato and Aristotle and other fathers of Greek learning, as debated in his time. He considered contemporary debates before taking a position that aligned him with Christians and non-Christians, Themistius and therefore Constantius, and set him against others, Christian and non-Christian, most important among them Eunomius and Julian. Eunomius and his followers also used the model of the philosopher as advisor, and also aligned themselves with others, Christian and non-Christian, as did all the bishops and priests about whom we know most: those who gained access to court and, ideally, to the ruler. At stake here was how to use the purity gained in retreat and its corresponding social capital to influence the center by besting one's peers—both Christian and non-Christian—in the *agōn* to define the divine and to demonstrate the one true way toward it for the salvation of all.

Classical learning, Greekness, the social capital that accrued to those of true *paideia* and elevated status who ruled the *oikoumenē*, the technical expertise provided by advanced training, ideally at Athens—all these were essential for every move Gregory made. He yearned for *logoi* more than anyone, and in relinquishing them for the *Logos* he nonetheless placed them second, above all else. He was not going to allow Julian to condemn him and to judge him nothing—in particular since his vision for the New Rome and that of Julian were far more alike than different. As men representative of their time, each understood the other well. Before examining Gregory's direct response to Julian, his *Orations* 4 and 5, in which he engaged the emperor's claim to *logoi* and in so doing claimed for himself all they stood for—Greekness and Romanness in all its cultural and political might—I turn to Julian's progress, intellectual and geographical, from Constantinople to Antioch.

PART THREE

7

A Health-Giving Star Shining on the East
Julian in Antioch, July 362 to March 363

> *It is better for us to be persuaded to acknowledge the universal god . . . than to honor, in place of the creator of all things, a god to whom has been given the leadership of a very small part.*
> —JULIAN, AGAINST THE GALILEANS, FRAGMENT 28.148C

I left Julian, the beast threatening Gregory and his church from the outside, in early summer of 362 en route from Constantinople to Antioch. The emperor and his court, including Caesarius, passed Nazianzus shortly after Julian issued an imperial letter declaring those who denied the true gods' inspiration of men such as Homer, Hesiod, Plato, and Aristotle unfit to teach and comment on their writings. This and other, similar imperial pronouncements propelled Gregory of Nazianzus and other members of the Greek Christian elites into action. Gregory claimed only his own (Christian) reading of these writings, inspired by the *Logos,* granted the true philosophical life—the life that alone would ensure *oikeiōsis pros theon* for all in the realm, because it was the life the only true God, the Trinity, mandated. Therefore, even though the beast stood ready, for Gregory the most important battle at hand was not that against Julian, crucial though it was, but the civil war among Christians threatening the Trinity, which had erupted during Julian's reign and—though he does not say so explicitly—had been caused by that reign, which encouraged persons such as Eunomius and Photinus and other false Christian leaders. How Gregory used Julian to attack these enemies on the inside and, in so doing, to claim *logoi* for himself is the focus of the chapters that follow.

This chapter considers what Julian said and did in late 362 and early 363, before his departure for Persia—because despite his protestations that he did not fear the enemy on the outside and that civil war was worse, Gregory was deeply afraid. That he continued to write of Julian long after his death as a divine scourge, warning and reminding all Christians to use their power wisely, attests to his fear. Even once Julian died, after a mercifully short reign, Gregory never allowed Julian and what he stood for to slip from his mind or that of his audience: an emperor, the embodiment of evil, who considered himself close to the gods as a divinely chosen and divinely born philosopher and as a priest commanded to lead all to the old gods, and who could implement such innovation through the force of law. After all, Julian could justly claim not only the divine mandate and the personal purity of the true philosopher, but also the divine authorization manifest by centuries during which the power of the Romans (*Rhōmaiōn archē*), the *imperium Romanum,* embodied in his person, dominated the world (Gr. Naz. *Or.* 4.74).

The *oikoumenē*, Julian's subjects, recognized his mandate, and (many) considered him the epiphany of the gods, who had chosen him as theirs: above all, his father Zeus-Helios. As contemporary descriptions of Julian's *adventus* into the cities of the West and especially the East make vivid, the people believed in Julian's divine nature. In city after city "all ages and sexes poured forth as though they were going to see someone sent down from heaven [arisen] like some health-giving star for mankind."[1] Even during the early months of Julian's rise, when his fate was far from certain, as Ammianus points out, citizens like those of Vienne poured out to greet him with candles and flowers as the embodiment of a good omen.[2] Indeed, the momentum of Julian's acclamation by city after city ratified his progress (despite his usurpation) as divinely authorized and preordained. Once he had become Augustus, Julian's own pronouncements and writings conveyed an increasing confidence in the truth of his understanding of the divine will. The farther East Julian proceeded, the more the *oikoumenē* embraced him and his divine mandate to safeguard the entire *politeia* by merging once again the best of Greece and Rome according to the *palaion ēthos,* to reverse all ill effects of the recent misguided innovation, and to honor and revere the true gods through right *paideia,* philanthropy, euergetism, sacrifice, and the appropriate rituals. Yet each new *adventus* also raised the stakes, by bringing Julian closer to the ultimate test of his rule as truly divinely inspired: victory over the Persians.

From 355, when Julian was proclaimed Caesar, until autumn of 362, everything had gone right for him, and there was no reason to presume his good fortune would not last. Constantinople welcomed him enthusiastically in December 361, no doubt relieved by the narrow avoidance of civil war. Antioch (modern

---

1. Amm. Marc. 15.9.8, 22.2.3–5, 22.9.4 (Nicomedia); Claud. Mam. *Pan. Lat.* 11.2.3, 11.6.2–5; MacCormack, *Art,* 46–50.

2. Ammianus 21.10.1–2 indicates that Julian was fully aware that such a positive reception was not a foregone conclusion. Thus he says of the *adventus* into Sirmium that Julian was "glad of the outcome and the omen, with his hopes for the future confirmed, [and] thought that . . . he would be welcomed in other cities also as a health-giving star." Caltabiano, "Giuliano imperatore," 344–53, analyzes how Ammianus uses the *adventus* narratives to legitimize Julian within a specific Roman imperial context and its religious significance.

Antakya), where he arrived before July 28, 362, received him with even more enthusiasm, if we trust the words of Libanius. For him, Julian's divinely inspired powers of salvation were an acknowledged fact. "If all mankind had been afflicted with a common disease of the eyes and by the kindness of some divinity had suddenly recovered their eyesight, they could not have been more glad." "What they say Asclepius did for Hippolytus you performed for the body of our world. You raised the dead to life and the name of kingship has, as formerly, gained practical meaning [*ergon*]." According to Ammianus, "when [Julian] came near [Antioch], he was received like some divinity with public prayers and was surprised by the clamor of the multitude, which acclaimed him as a health-giving star shining on the East."[3] Yet, during Julian's brief stay—about nine months—at Antioch before he set out for Persia on March 5, 363, the emperor experienced his first real setbacks, a first bad omen. A temple he particularly wished to have restored was destroyed by fire, and the city was shaken by famine during the winter of 362/3, though Julian had come to the rescue. Antioch, thus, forced Julian to perform his own high-wire act: he felt particular affinity for the city but also experienced there his most serious crisis so far.

For Julian, Antioch was truly a Greek city, and its citizens true sons of Greeks. Indeed, the city and its wealthy suburb Daphne had become a center for philosophers, "à la fois véritable lieu de pèlerinage et centre philosophique grec," especially for those who, like Julian, followed the teachings of Iamblichus.[4] As such, Antioch represented a counterweight to Constantinople, the city of Julian's birth, now polluted as the official capital of the Christian Constantius. Because Julian considered himself "though . . . Thracian [by birth], a Greek in his habits," he "intended to make [Antioch] into a city of marble," transforming it as Augustus had transformed Rome.[5] Consequently, the emperor expected that he and the citizens of Antioch "should regard one another with the greatest possible affection" (*Mis.* 367c).

But his affection for Antioch's Greekness only partly explains his impatience to leave Constantinople and to rush east. Julian looked expectantly to Antioch also because it was the staging post for Persian campaigns. As he wrote to one Philip in the spring of 362, still from Constantinople: "The first signs of spring are here already. . . . The swallows, which are expected almost immediately, as soon as they come, drive our band of campaigners out of doors and remind us that we ought to

---

3. Lib. *Or.* 13.41 calls the entire world to celebrate, and ibid. 42. Amm. Marc. 22.9.14.
4. Soler, "D'Apollonios," 381.
5. Jul. *Mis.* 367c: ἐμαυτὸν δέ, εἰ καὶ γένος ἐστί μοι Θρᾴκιον, Ἕλληνα τοῖς ἐπιτηδεύμασιν, ὑπελάμβανον. Lib. *Or.* 15.52; Suet. *Aug.* 28; Bowersock, *Julian*, 96. Julian left Constantinople without declaring his intentions as to his return. He had used his short stay to leave his mark on the city, purging parts of the court of Constantius's influence, and, for example, building a shrine to Helios in the palace and adding a new harbor; Lib. *Or.* 18.127.

be over the border."⁶ His writings and those of his contemporaries suggest that Julian considered victory over Shapur II and the Persians the best and most certain testimony to his divine calling; such victory would have cemented once and for all his superiority over Constantius, whose engagements with the Persians had been unsuccessful (owing partly to Julian's own actions).⁷ Given his high expectations and even higher stakes, Julian's setbacks at Antioch took on particular significance: if success revealed divine favor, the opposite was also true.

No wonder, then, that the emperor acted and wrote at a frenetic pace. During his months at Antioch Julian composed some of his most influential works, most of them between December 362 and the first months of 363. In them, he explained the reasons for his impending Persian campaign (the *Caesars*); elaborated his special relationship with his father Zeus-Helios (the *Hymn to King Helios*); highlighted the mildness of his response to the Antiochene citizens' ire during the worsening famine and the degree to which such restraint revealed his qualities as a true Platonic leader (the *Misopogon* or *Antiochikos*); and systematized his views of the Galileans, whom he held responsible for the silence of Apollo's oracle and the burning of his temple, but whom he nevertheless wished to cure of their illness, as befitted the benevolent emperor as *pater patriae* (*Against the Galileans*). A discussion of these writings, together with Libanius's *Oration* 12, his *Hypaticus* in praise of the emperor's fourth consulate delivered on January 1, 363, forms the substance of this chapter.⁸ In keeping with my aim to narrow the focus to Gregory of Nazianzus's response to Julian rather than Julian per se, I consider other contemporary writings sparingly, because their authors, Christian or not, all wrote under the impression of Julian's fate after Ctesiphon, framing their accounts of the events at Antioch as a series of divine portents the emperor had either woefully misread or ignored out of the hubris characteristic of evil tyrants. Ammianus may stand as *pars pro toto:* in his view, the day Julian chose to enter Antioch was a gloomy omen, for it coincided with the festival of Adonis, and the mutilations accompanying it filled the city with "melancholy wailing . . . and cries of grief," in sharp contrast to the joyful acclamations.⁹

---

6. Jul. *Ep.* 30 (Bidez 40), *To Philip,* perhaps the addressee of Lib. *Ep.* 1190; Claud. Mam. *Pan. Lat.* 11.3.14–15.

7. Thanks to its port at Seleucia Pieria and its well-developed road system leading to Beroea (modern Aleppo) and farther east. For Antioch's traditional role as imperial headquarters, see (e.g.) Lib. *Or.* 11.177–79, 15.15–17, 19.54–55; *Exp. totius mundi* 23; Casana, "Archaeological Landscape"; Hahn, *Gewalt,* 123–30; Matthews, *Journey of Theophanes,* 77–88. For Julian's role in Constantius's Persian endeavors, Blockley, *East Roman Foreign Policy,* 22–23.

8. Salutius's *De diis et mundo,* written in December 362, is highly relevant. I will comment on the text only in passing, because a more thorough engagement would exceed the scope of this chapter.

9. Amm. Marc. 22.9.15, 23.2.6. Den Boeft, Drijvers, et al., *Philological and Historical Commentary on Ammianus Marcellinus 22,* 177–78, discuss the date of Julian's arrival in the city (before July 28) and the celebrations of Adonis.

For my purpose hindsight will be the privilege of Gregory of Nazianzus. To give due credit to his shaping of Julian as the Apostate after his death, I reconstruct as precisely as possible the emperor's concepts as they had evolved by late 362 and early 363.[10] During this period, Gregory wrote his first three orations and prepared his direct response in *Oration* 4. (*Oration* 5 belongs to a later period.) Caesarius too was still with the imperial court. Thus it is plausible that Gregory's first three orations may have echoed some of Julian's Antiochene writings, though Gregory engaged the emperor directly only in his so-called invectives *Against Julian*. These invectives elaborated on Gregory's earlier arguments and now triumphantly affirmed his claims: by Julian's providential destruction, God had manifestly assured Gregory that only his version of the philosophical life, by which he and men like him now guided the *koina* of the Romans, was divinely inspired and hence the only true one.

THE EMPEROR AS PRIEST

Famine and Fire

While at Antioch, Julian never lost sight of his immediate aim, which would best demonstrate his divine mandate: "He burned to add to the ornaments of his glorious victories the surname Parthicus." According to Libanius's later account, Julian wanted to follow the strategy he had employed so successfully against Constantius and press on with maximum speed to attack Shapur II as early as summer 362. The exhausted army, however, required a winter's rest.[11] As it happened, the delay occurred at the worst possible time for city and emperor. The crowd had good reasons for celebrating Julian's entry into their city, the Crown of the East (*orientem apicem pulchrum*), then in the grip of a severe food shortage, as the revival of a body close to death.[12] Insufficient rainfall during the winter of 361/2 had decreased the harvest in Antioch's hinterland, usually well watered by its many canals and rivers.[13]

---

10. Scholarly discussions of the events at Antioch are numerous. Historians focus mostly on the food shortage, because this particular one is especially well documented. Discussions also focus on the burning of the Apollo temple; the reconstruction of the Temple in Jerusalem; and the Christian reaction to both; while modern theologians and church historians address the complex relations of Antioch's Christians. Antioch's place in Julian's politics is also controversial. Did he have a particular Antiochene program, and if so, what were its characteristics? Athanassiadi-Fowden, *Julian*, 192–225; Bowersock, *Julian*, 94–105; Browning, *Emperor Julian*, 144–58; R. Smith, *Julian's Gods*, 207–24; Liebeschuetz, *Antioch*, 224–35; Matthews, *Roman Empire*, 108–14, 126–29; Pack, *Städte*, 301–77; Scholl, *Historische Beiträge*, 110–44; Wiemer, *Libanios*, 269–355.

11. Amm. Marc. 22.12.1–2 (quotation 12.2); Lib. *Or*. 18.163.

12. Amm. Marc. 22. 9.14; Lib. *Or*. 13.41–42; Claud. Mam. *Pan. Lat.* 11.2.3. Wiemer, *Libanios*, 269–355, discusses the food shortage and provides an overview of the relevant scholarship.

13. Amm. Marc. 14.7.2, 11.19–23; Lib. *Or*. 1.97–103, *Ep*. 391.9–10, and esp. *Or*. 11.260, *In Praise of Antioch* (*Libanios, Antiochikos*, trans. and comm. Fatouros and Krischer, 263); Casana, "Archaeological Landscape," 106–11.

Food prices had risen continuously, exacerbating a process set in motion in 360, when Constantius, by levying a supplementary tax (*supraindictio*) on agricultural products and on labor, had initiated a steady decrease in the amount of food available for sale.[14] Julian's arrival placed further pressure on food supplies with his court and additional parts of the army augmenting those stationed regularly at Antioch. Speculative hoarding, a customary response to impending food shortages, produced a situation in Antioch by late 362 in which prices were about 200 percent more than those following a normal harvest.[15] Not surprisingly, theatrical claques wasted no time in reminding the emperor of the situation: "Everything plentiful, [but] everything dear!"[16] Julian faced a rapidly escalating crisis, just like the one that Gallus had mishandled so utterly in 354 that it cost him his life.

Unfortunately, the emperor did not act with the swiftness he had displayed on other occasions. Perhaps trusting that the gods would provide autumn rains (which, however, would have ensured sufficient grain only for the following year), Julian waited until the end of October before taking measures.[17] Only when the rains failed did he issue an edict stipulating maximum prices and order the importation overland of 400,000 *metra* of additional grain from nearby regions less affected. He also provided for the sale at lower-than-market prices of 22,000 *modioi* from his imperial estates in Egypt. Julian, from his perspective—and with good reason—saw these measures as splendid in their generosity; Ammianus considered them excessive.[18]

As Hans-Ulrich Wiemer and others have pointed out, Julian's imports provided grain for four to eight weeks for the entire city—a major logistical and financial feat, not least because of the difficulties and costs of transporting grain overland.[19] The

---

14. Amm. Marc. 21.6.6.

15. According to Jul. *Mis.* 369a–d, the elevated price of the summer of 362 was 10 *metra* per *solidus*; his edict restricted it to 15 *metra* per *solidus*, one-third of the then-current market price of 5 *metra* per *solidus*. Such increases accord with Ammianus's prices (28.1.1), paid in Carthage in a similar crisis a few years later.

16. Amm. Marc. 22.13.4; Jul. *Mis.* 368c; Lib. *Or.* 18.195. Matthews, *Roman Empire*, 108–9; Wiemer, *Libanios*, 287–94; Pack, *Städte*, 366–67.

17. Amm. Marc. 22.13.4; Jul. *Mis.* 369c; Lib. *Or.* 15.21, in particular November and December rains.

18. Jul. *Mis.* 370d; Amm. Marc. 22.14.1–2; Lib. *Or.* 18.195. The text of the edict, in all likelihood proclaimed in the theater, has been lost. Lib. *Or.* 16.21–27 implies that the *curia* was responsible for enforcing the edict. Julian mentions a price of one *solidus* per 15 *metra*: Jul. *Mis.* 369a, 369c, 370c; *Ep.* 101 (Bidez). Downey, *History*, 382–91.

19. Wiemer, *Libanios*, 301–8, calculates the total amount of grain imported overland as about 3,600 metric tons (= 400,000 *metra*), to which 198 metric tons from the Egyptian domains must be added. Populations are notoriously difficult to estimate; for the number of Antiochenes, the estimates range from 150,000 to 300,000 (excluding the court and the additional soldiers): Wiemer, *Libanios*, 304. Wiemer discusses the causes of the worsening crisis and the debates regarding the calculations at pp. 305–15 and 326–41.

citizens of Antioch, however, had a different view, with at least as much cause. As Wiemer also points out, an emperor customarily supported a city in which he resided, and Antioch's citizens had every right to expect an imperial intervention, in particular given the presence of many additional members of the army.[20] More important, despite Julian's measures, food remained scarce, and grew scarcer as winter progressed; in June 363, Libanius still spoke of hunger in the city.[21] The Antiochenes, further exasperated, as Ammianus tells us, by the raucous behavior of some of Julian's soldiers, openly expressed their mounting displeasure with the emperor, prompting Julian to react with the satirical *Misopogon,* or *Beard Hater,* to which I shall return.[22]

Insufficient rainfall contributed to Julian's second bad omen in late 362, the burning of the Temple of Apollo at Daphne, a pleasant, wealthy suburb of Antioch. As early as June or July 362, Julian, on the road through Asia Minor to Antioch, the center of Greek (Iamblichan) philosophy, instructed his uncle and namesake Julian, then *comes Orientis* resident in the city, to restore the temple for his imminent arrival, reclaiming its missing pillars, now used in imperial buildings, and replacing others with pillars from recently confiscated houses.[23] Should the recovered *spolia* not suffice, the emperor encouraged the *comes* to use temporary replacements of brick and plaster encased in marble—what mattered, according to the emperor, was piety rather than luxury. Apparently Julian anticipated great celebrations during the traditional festival honoring Apollo. Customarily this took place in August, and Julian wished to contribute a restored temple; he had already sent ahead one

---

20. As Ammianus 14.7.5 noted, referring to Gallus. Only a small portion of the financial burden associated with these imports was assumed by the emperor. The landowners of the surrounding regions bore the lion's share, because Julian's edict capped their prices.

21. Lib. *Epp.* 813.2, 815.1 (Foerster). The situation worsened also because Julian's measures failed to prevent inhabitants of the surrounding countryside from purchasing the subsidized grain or bread (or both) intended for the city, or merchants in the city from diverting and reselling subsidized grain in the countryside. (It is hard to see how this could have been prevented.) Because the drought continued, hoarding of food (whether speculative or not) increased everywhere. Thus a good portion of the imported grain never reached the market and its intended beneficiaries, the inhabitants of Antioch. (Recall also that the municipalities en route carried most of the costs of overland transportation, a disincentive.) The discrepancy between the supply and demand continued to increase, rendering the maximum-price edict ineffective. By late 362 or early 363 Antioch suffered a full-fledged famine, which the Antiochene *curia* attributed in part to the price edict, because it blocked market forces; Lib. *Epp.* 777.1–3 (Foerster), 96.1, 98.5 (Norman); *Or.* 16 and 15; Wiemer, *Libanios,* 308–26, 336–41; Matthews, *Roman Empire,* 410–11; Pack, *Städte,* 373; Liebeschuetz, *Antioch,* 127–31; A. H. M. Jones, *Later Roman Empire,* 749, 830–34; Garnsey, *Famine,* 230.

22. Amm. Marc. 22.12.6–7.

23. As Libanius makes clear, the conversion of temple properties into private domains had been accepted and fairly frequent practice under Constantius and was now reversed. Jul. *Ep.* 29 (Bidez 80); Lieu, *Emperor Julian,* 47. Lib. *Epp.* 91, 103, 105 (Norman), 763 (Foerster). Fowden, "Bishops," esp. 62–69.

of his own priests, Pythiodorus, to supervise the religious proceedings. When Julian rushed to Daphne after visiting the Temple of Zeus on nearby Mount Casius, however, he found the Temple of Apollo still somewhat dilapidated and the celebrations lackluster at best.[24]

None of these disappointments deterred the emperor from his goal of restoring the temple to its former glory and of reviving Apollo's oracle. The oracle at Daphne was one of the major Apolline oracular sites, active until well into the fourth century and often associated with Roman emperors. Diocletian consulted it in 299 only to be told that the presence of Christians prevented accurate prophecies. According to Constantine that response was the catalyst for the Great Persecution. In 313, after Licinius's victory over Maximinus Daia, priests associated with the oracle were persecuted as frauds, but the oracle itself maintained its attraction at least until the Antiochene residency of Gallus.[25] In contrast to other Apolline oracles, where the god spoke through a priestess, Apollo at Daphne traditionally communicated through his magnificent statue, by the sculptor Bryaxis, so "gentle . . . of form" that its sight calmed the most turbulent soul, and through the murmurs of the Castalian spring, so called after the one in Delphi.[26] The emperor Hadrian had already silenced these murmurs by ordering the spring blocked off after it predicted his own accession (a notoriously dangerous portent, since the oracle might repeat it for a competitor). By the time of Julian, the statue, too, had ceased to speak.[27]

Julian wished to rectify this state of affairs. Unfortunately, the Castalian spring remained silent; the drought of 361 and 362 did not help.[28] The statue, however, resumed its activities, albeit briefly: a consultation with the god (according to Ammianus, or with the theurgist Eusebius according to Philostorgius's source) prompted Julian to move "the bodies, which had now been buried around the spring, . . . to another place, under the same ceremonial with which the Athenians . . . cleansed

---

24. Jul. *Mis.* 361d, *Ep.* 29 (Bidez 80); Lib. *Ep.* 80 (Norman); John Malalas, *Chronographia*, ed. Thurn, 12.284 (*The Chronicle of John Malalas*, trans. Jeffreys, Jeffreys, and Scott), mentions that Commodus ordered the Olympic festivals to be celebrated every fourth year for 45 days during the "festival of the offerings or Traditional Sacrifices; that is, the months of Panemos-July and Loos-August"; Lib. *Or.* 60.7–10 points out that Olympic Games honoring Apollo had been planned for 364; Hahn, *Gewalt*, 130–36.

25. See "To the Eastern Provincials" in Eus. *VC* 2.49–54; Eus. *HE* 9.11.6, *PE* 4.2. For the date and identification of the oracle, Digeser, "Apollo"; Löhr, "Some Observations," esp. 84–90; Carotenuto, "Six Constantinian Documents."

26. Lib. *Or.* 60.11 (*Monody on the Temple of Apollo at Daphne*), frag. in J. Chrys. *Hom. Bab.* 20.112, trans. Lieu, *Emperor Julian*, 80–81; Fontenrose, *Didyma*, 206–7, and *Delphic Oracle*, 425; Gregory, "Julian," esp. 357–58; Lane Fox, *Pagans*, 595; Potter, *Prophets*, 41–42.

27. Jul. *Mis.* 361d–362d; Lib. *Or.* 1.27, 30.7; *CTh* 15.10.4–6; Soz. *HE* 5.19.10–11; den Boeft, Drijvers, et al., *Philological and Historical Commentary on Ammianus Marcellinus 22*, 224–25; Bradbury, "Constantine," esp. 120–29.

28. Jul. *Mis.* 346b; John Malalas *Chron.* 11.278.2–6.

the Temple of Apollo at Delos."[29] In Julian's mind, the pollution of human remains buried nearby prevented the oracle from speaking, and so he had them removed.[30]

Then, on October 22, 362, the Temple of Apollo burned, destroying Bryaxis's famous statue of Apollo Musagetes. All our authors give tremendous significance to this event: a truly bad omen—recall Julian's notions about statues of the gods—with, for the Christian sources, positive implications. Julian, enraged, immediately ordered "stricter investigations even than usual and the closure of the Great Church." Libanius was on the committee of city officials in charge of these investigations. Arson was suspected, but Libanius's writings reveal that no one was ever identified as the culprit, torture of the priests (reported only by our Christian sources) notwithstanding. Ammianus corroborates Libanius's account, adding that some claimed the temple had burned, ironically, because the philosopher Asclepiades had left candles lit in it while he traveled to visit Julian (signaling again Ammianus's disapproval of Julian's reliance on certain philosophers).[31]

Julian immediately suspected Christians. As he later wrote in his *Misopogon*, "when I sent away the corpse [of Babylas] from Daphne, ... others [among you] hurled the terrible fire [against the sanctuary]" (361b–c). Indeed, both Julian and Libanius imply, and local Christian historiography corroborates, that one corpse had especially displeased the god: the remains of a certain Babylas, venerated as a martyr. John Chrysostom and Philostorgius's source, the so-called Arian (i.e., Homoian) Historiographer, also connected the oracle's silence and the burning of the temple with the presence and subsequent removal of that corpse. In retaliation, Julian closed the Great Church.[32]

The burning of Apollo's temple derives its significance, first, from its effect on Julian—and his perception of the interrelation between his religious activities, the preparation for the Persian campaign, and the role of Christian interference—

---

29. Amm. Marc. 22.12.8. Only Philost. *HE* 7.8 reports Eusebius's futile attempts to mobilize the statue's *energeia*. Marasco, *Filostorgio*, 150–54, suggests that Philostorgius conflated Eusebius of Myndus, who opposed theurgy as mentioned in Chapter 3 above, with Maximus of Ephesus.

30. Amm. Marc. 22.12.8, referring to Hdt. 1.64 and Thuc. 3.104.1–2, is rather vague, in particular "affatus ... transferri." Only John Chrysostom's later account in *De sanctu hieromartyre Babyla* 5–7 provides context for the removal of Babylas's bones; den Boeft, Drijvers, et al., *Philological and Historical Commentary on Ammianus Marcellinus 22*, 225–26; Gregory, "Julian," 358 and n. 16.

31. Amm. Marc. 22.13.2–3; Jul. *Or.* 7.224d; Lib. *Or.* 60.5.7–10 on the destruction of the temple, frag. in J. Chrys. *Hom. Bab.* 18.98, 19.104–6, 20.112, trans. Lieu, *Emperor Julian*, 80–81 and *ad loc.*; Lib. *Ep.* 107 (Norman); torture in J. Chrys. *Hom. Bab.* 19.107, *pace* Athanassiadi-Fowden, *Julian*, 206.

32. Amm. Marc. 22.13.2; Jul. *Mis.* 346b; Philost. *HE* 7.10; *Artem. Pass.* 57 = Philost. *HE* 7.8a; *Chron. Pasch.* s.a. 362, 548; Soz. *HE* 5.20.5; J. Chrys. *Hom. Bab.* 17.95, 19.107. The link between Babylas's remains and the oracle's silence echoes Diocletian's consultation of the oracle, where the presence of Christians was also blamed for oracular silence. Ammianus adds that Christians were propelled by envy, because Julian en route to Antioch had ordered a glorious peristyle to surround the temple, already under construction; Wiemer, *Libanios*, 193.

and, second, from its interpretation by contemporary authors and their impact on later scholarship. Later Christian sources continue to dominate modern scholarly interpretations of the episode: according to these sources, the predominantly Christian city erupted into open hostility against the pagan emperor when he removed the remains of the martyr Babylas. Such views prevail because scholars rely on John Chrysostom's and Philostorgius's accounts—more specifically, the versions of their accounts preserved in texts by the fifth-century church historians Rufinus, Socrates, Sozomen, and Theodoret. While the early fifth-century Christian historiographic traditions are valuable sources for Julian's actions vis-à-vis Christians in Antioch and the Christians' response, modern scholars' reliance on them results in the construction of a sharp divide along religious lines between the majority of Antioch's inhabitants, supposedly Christian, and the pagan emperor in residence. In so doing, scholars overlook the (Nicene) orthodox tendencies of these fifth-century sources and, furthermore, the degree to which the entire affair has been shaped by John Chrysostom and his concerns, to which Ammianus also responded.

Julian did order reprisals against Christians, and there was mounting disaffection between him and the Antiochenes, Christian and non-Christian alike, but it is not certain that the majority of Antiochenes were Christian at the time or that all Christians were affected equally by Julian's presence or responded uniformly to it.[33] In fact, Julian targeted the homoian Christians closely associated with Constantius, and as a result homoian Christians protested and suffered most, a fact the later orthodox sources corroborate by eliding it. Other Christians, both heretical and orthodox, fared quite well during Julian's stay. Christian sources written most closely to the events—John Chrysostom's *On Babylas* (over half of which consists of anti-Julianic polemic) and Philostorgius's account, as preserved in the ninth-century *Artemii Passio*, which draws on a local source dating to the reign of Theodosius, the Arian (i.e., Homoian) Historiographer—provide a far more complex picture of pagan-Christian relations at Antioch and hence of the immediate context of Julian's *Against the Galileans*.[34]

---

33. Lib. *Ep.* 1119.3–4 (Foerster) mentions 150,000 true believers in 363, and John Chrysostom, *Hom. in Matt.* 85(86).4, PG 58.762–63, 100,000 Christians, whom he considers 50 percent of the population (i.e., male citizens, without women, children, and slaves). Both describe the city as at best partially Christian. Hahn, *Gewalt*, 125–26, 148–52, points to stagnating Christian building activities.

34. Jul. *Mis.* 361b; Lib. *Or.* 60.5; J. Chrys. *Hom. Bab.* 11.64–17.97; *Artem. Pass.* 53–54 = Philost. *HE* 7.8a.88; Rufin. *HE* 10.36; Socr. *HE* 3.18; Soz. *HE* 5.19.4–19; Thdt. *HE* 3.10. John Chrysostom, *Discours sur Babylas*, ed. and trans. Schatkin, 15–19. For the relationship between Philostorgius, the *Artemii Passio*, and the so-called Homoian (or Arian) Historiographer (AH), *Philostorgius: Kirchengeschichte*, ed. Bidez and Winkelmann, xliv–lxviii, cvi–cix, cli–clxiii; Anhang 7. Lieu and Montserrat, eds., *From Constantine to Julian*, 210–62; Brennecke, *Studien*, 114–31; Lenski, "Were Valentinian, Valens and Jovian Confessors?" reconstructs the fifth-century historians' interdependence, though in a different context; Marasco, *Filostorgio*, 122–28, 153–54; Hahn, *Gewalt*, 148–52.

The figure of Babylas was pivotal to the entire story—explicitly according to our Christian and implicitly according to our non-Christian sources. We have scant information on him prior to John Chrysostom's homily, written in 379 or 380. According to Eusebius, Babylas was bishop of Antioch under Gordian and suffered martyrdom under Decius.[35] According to John Chrysostom, however, his true fame began when Gallus had his remains transferred from their resting place in the city to Daphne, to counterbalance the site's pagan significance: the bones of Babylas silenced the oracle. Consequently, John Chrysostom's and Philostorgius's sources dramatize the divine portents of Julian's transfer of Babylas's remains to their original resting place in a *koimētērion* in the city. John Chrysostom styled the transfer of Babylas's sarcophagus like the *adventus* of a victorious emperor, embedding the account into tales of the ills that befell the persecutors, including Julian's uncle. He thus created a series of portents of the fiery destruction of the temple. Philostorgius's source highlighted the actual transfer, recounting how the "urban mob, [which] poured out of the city as for an important cause," easily carried the heavy sarcophagus more than fifty stades, "as if by some superior force." None of the earliest sources contains the standard narrative of modern scholarship, which relies on the later church historians' description of the transfer as a triumphal act of resistance by Christians, united in opposition to the emperor and chanting Psalm 96:7: "Confounded be all they that worship graven images and who vaunt themselves in idols."[36]

Julian, having also seen a connection between the burning of the temple and the removal of Babylas's bones from Daphne, ordered the Great Church closed.[37] This church had been inaugurated on June 1, 341, by Constantius. (See Chapter 1.) In 362 it was the seat of the bishop Euzoius, leader of the homoian Christians at Antioch.[38] Euzoius had been a presbyter under George of Cappadocia, Julian's teacher and Constantius's choice as bishop of Alexandria, whose execution by an enraged mob in early 362 elicited only a lukewarm response from Julian. Euzoius became

---

35. Eus. *HE* 6.29.4, 6.39.4; John Chrysostom, *Discours sur Babylas*, ed. and trans. Schatkin, 15–18.

36. J. Chrys. *Hom. Bab.* 16.87, 90; Philost. *HE* 7.8 (p. 92) = *Artem. Pass.* 55; Rufin. *HE* 10.36; Thdt. *HE* 3.10.3; Soz. *HE* 5.19.17–19; Socr. *HE* 3.18.3–4. The significance of Chrysostom's account of this transfer still awaits assessment. Theodoret preserves traces of the AH and is also using Rufinus, who says that he spoke to eyewitnesses of the events, though there is no firm evidence that he ever was in Antioch; Brennecke, *Studien*, 138–39. Already Festugière, *Antioche*, 80–85, noted the complexity of the pagan-Christian relationship; Lieu, *Emperor Julian*, 50; *Libanios: Kaiserreden*, trans. and comm. Fatouros, Krischer, and Portmann, 126–27; Bowersock, *Julian*, 99. Athanassiadi-Fowden, *Julian*, 206–8, does not mention Babylas. R. Smith, *Julian's Gods*, 214–16, places Antioch in a wider context, for which see Hahn, *Gewalt*, 161–77. For a representative modern account of the event, Rosen, *Julian*, 293–97.

37. Amm. Marc. 22.13.2; Jul. *Mis.* 346b; Philost. *HE* 7.10; *Artem. Pass.* 57 = Philost. *HE* 7.8a; *Chron. Pasch.* s.a. 362, 548; Soz. *HE* 5.20.5; J. Chrys. *Hom. Bab.* 17.95, 19.107; Wiemer, *Libanios*, 193.

38. According to Theodoret (*HE* 3.12), who drew here on the Homoian Historiographer (AH).

bishop in 361 at the instigation of Constantius after the emperor exiled Meletius, who had displeased him in a series of orations. Later that same year Euzoius baptized Constantius on his deathbed.[39]

Euzoius, bishop of the Great Church closed by Julian, was a leading homoian and one of Constantius's men. He did not take things lying down. According to the Homoian Historiographer, Euzoius protested against Julian's order and suffered physically as a result, which made him a bona fide confessor—of whom there were few, something our orthodox sources do not seem eager to emphasize.[40] Babylas the martyr also had a homoian pedigree: Euzoius's precursor was Leontius, a leading homoian with close ties to Gallus, who had sponsored Aetius.[41] According to John Chrysostom, Gallus, not Bishop Leontius, instigated the transfer of Babylas's remains to Daphne (though the reverse is more probable). John Chrysostom, to argue from silence, by omitting Leontius entirely from his account, downplayed the homoian (that is, Arian) character of the veneration of the martyr Babylas.[42] Taken together, our orthodox sources claim a Christian Babylas for a united Antiochene Christianity, thus eliding the predominantly homoian (Arian) character of both martyr and opposition. Babylas, as Hanns-Christof Brennecke has emphasized, was a homoian martyr; the removal of his remains, and the reprisals following the burning of the temple, affected homoians: their church was closed, and their bishop punished.[43] Julian, at that point in residence at Antioch for several months, was aware of the prevailing homoian character of city's Christianity (and may have been aware of the transfer under Gallus). Homoian Christians were targeted in his retaliations because they were most closely associated with Constantius. Indeed, Julian hinted at the connection in emphasizing in his *Misopogon* how he took particular offense at a slogan then making the rounds, that in contrast to him "neither the Chi [i.e., Christ] nor the Kappa [i.e., Constantius] did us any harm."[44]

The impression conveyed by the majority of modern scholarly discussions that Julian targeted Christians uniformly and that Christians uniformly opposed his

---

39. Brennecke, *Studien*, 68–82.

40. Later orthodox (Nicene) sources played down Euzoius's fate to avoid highlighting that there were few good confessors on their side; Thdt. *HE* 3.12; *Philostorgius: Kirchengeschichte*, ed. Bidez and Winkelmann, 231 = AH 7.35; Brennecke, *Studien*, 140–41.

41. Between 344 and 358/9; Ath. *Hist. Ar.* 2.10; Thdt. *HE* 2.9.1–10.2; Hanson, *Search*, 307, 312, 348; Vaggione, *Eunomius*, 159–60. Leontius had been an early patron of Aetius, whom he is said to have introduced to Gallus; this resulted in such close relations that Gallus sent Aetius to restrain the paganism of his half-brother, Julian.

42. J. Chrys. *Hom. Bab.* 14.76.

43. Brennecke, *Studien*, 137. Babylas's heretical genealogy explains John Chrysostom's insistence that Gallus (and not the bishop) ordered his remains transferred and the scant orthodox information about him prior to Chrysostom, including the fact that Gregory of Nazianzus alludes to but never mentions Babylas in his orations *Against Julian*.

44. Jul. *Mis.* 357a: τὸ Χῖ, φασίν, οὐδὲν ἠδίκησε τὴν πόλιν οὐδὲ τὸ Κάππα.

presence in the city (and the emperor himself) derives from late fourth- and early fifth-century Nicene orthodox sources and reflects their views. Antioch had been a homoian stronghold, and the majority of Antioch's Christians probably opposed Julian as much as they had supported Constantius's version of Christianity. But there were other Christians in Antioch, and they fared quite well under Julian. The "Old Church" remained open, with its bishop, Meletius, reinstalled after he returned from exile, thanks to Julian's amnesty of early 362. The church of Paulinus, consecrated as bishop in 362 by Lucifer of Calaris (modern Cagliari), one of Constantius's staunchest opponents, likewise remained open for worship, and not only did not share the difficulties experienced by Euzoius and the homoians but may well have prospered.[45] Furthermore, according to Philostorgius, the synod set to rehabilitate Aetius and Eunomius convened at Antioch in the late summer or early autumn of 362, installing Aetius's supporter Theophilus the Indian as bishop responsible for Antioch.[46] Gregory of Nazianzus, who never mentions Babylas, would have known that some leading Christians in Antioch, such as Aetius, Eunomius, Meletius, and Paulinus, fared quite well under Julian. Further, there were reasons to criticize Julian other than Christian belief. After all, the emperor had ordered the theaters closed but sacrificed lavishly and permitted his soldiers to gorge themselves while the city remained in the grip of famine.[47]

The Persian Campaign

> You will find no pillar of stone, bronze, or copper, nor even of diamonds, to be more enduring than the fame that this noble institution [of the consulate] confirms for its recipient.[48]
> —LIBANIUS, ORATION 12.10.369

The intensifying food crisis and the destruction of Apollo's temple occurred while the emperor was preparing his Persian campaign, the apex of his burning ambitions. According to Ammianus, Julian wanted to erase the stigma inflicted upon the Roman Empire by Constantius's heavy losses against the Persians—a punishment for abandoning the religion of the true gods—and to add to his past military glories

---

45. Ath. *Tom.* 1.3, *PG* 26.796B–797A; Socr. *HE* 3.9.4; Soz. *HE* 5.13.1; see also Socr. *HE* 4.2.5; Soz. *HE* 6.7.10; Brennecke, *Studien*, 99, 108; Hanson, *Search*, 383–84, 509, 603, 643–44; Dünzl, "Absetzung," esp. 91–93; and above, Chapter 1.

46. Philost. *HE* 7.6, 8.2, also 9.1; Brennecke, *Studien*, 63–64, 113–14; Vaggione, *Eunomius*, 276–80; Lim, *Public Disputation*, 129–30.

47. Jul. *Mis.* 344a; *Exp. totius mundi* 32 for the lavishness of Antioch's games. For their reopening, Lib. *Ep.* 1399.4.

48. οὔτε λιθίνην οὔτε χαλκῆν οὔτε ὀρειχαλκίνην, ἀλλ' οὐδὲ ἐξ ἀδάμαντος στήλην εὑρήσεις μονιμωτέραν τῆς μνήμης ἣν τουτὶ τὸ καλὸν τῷ τυχόντι βεβαιοῖ.

the crowning agnomen Parthicus, "Victor over the Persians."[49] Ammianus, fortified by hindsight, saw a direct connection between Julian's preparations for war and his ever-increasing religious activities. In his view the emperor, losing sight of the just measure of the religious rituals, was no longer prudent in his conduct of the war and failed to read the gods' will correctly, misreading omen after omen with deplorable yet inevitable results.[50] Ammianus writes that the decrees of heaven had countermanded Julian's plans and splendid deeds, but "since his detractors alleged that he had stirred the tumults of war anew to the detriment of the common good, they should know clearly through the teachings of truth that it was not Julian but Constantine who kindled the Parthian fires."[51] Even Ammianus, however, narrating Julian's life as a quasi-panegyric, criticized the emperor's Persian endeavor, noting that at the time Julian's aggressive plans already encountered strong opposition, a fact Libanius corroborates.[52]

In Antioch, then, the emperor had to persuade his subjects, at least those who mattered, of the wisdom of an aggressive Persian campaign by declaring it preordained by divine will and his divine mandate. The celebrations of Julian's fourth consulate on January 1, 363, provided the first public opportunity for him to undertake such persuasion.[53] The occasion traditionally assembled the court in residence, local elites, and a number of important persons in the empire; on this occasion Julian himself seems to have ensured that the right persons were all assembled. Further, the emperor enlisted the most talented local to do his persuading for him, and Libanius's *Hypaticus on the Emperor as Consul* (*Or.* 12) proved a resounding success. Julian even "jumped up from the *sella curulis*" and waved his *trabea* (the triumphal purple of the consul) in excited approval. A written version of the oration was published widely soon thereafter, probably with imperial support, and it is plausible, as his *Oration* 5 suggests, though impossible to prove, that Gregory had access to a version.[54]

---

49. Amm. Marc. 22.12.1–2.

50. Even though he does not make the connection explicit here, Ammianus's construction of Book 22, chapter 12, speaks for itself by linking the two themes: §§ 1–5 treat the preparations for war, and §§ 6–8 his divinatory activities, in a rather critical light. Secondary literature on Julian's Persian campaign is enormous. For a detailed discussion, Wiemer, *Libanios*, 151–66; Martig, *Studi*, 11–50; Matthews, *Roman Empire*, 108–14, 130–79. R. Smith, "Telling Tales," 89–104 focuses on Books 23–25 but reflects Book 22, esp. at pp. 92–93; Caltabiano, "Giuliano," 335–55; den Boeft, Drijvers, et al., *Philological and Historical Commentary on Ammianus Marcellinus 22*, 213–14.

51. Amm. Marc. 25.4.23, 26.

52. Amm. Marc. 16.3.1: "ad laudativam paene materiam pertinebit." Photius also called Eunapius's treatment of Julian a quasi panegyric (*Bibl.* 77); Matthews, *Roman Empire*, 175.

53. The elaborate ceremonies celebrating the *Kalendae Ianuariae* are well documented; Lib. *Or.* 9, 1.127–29; Amm. Marc. 22.7.2, 23.1.1; Claud. Mam. *Grat. act.* = *Pan. Lat.* 3[11].28–30; J. Chrys. *Hom. in Kal.*, PG 48.953–62; Gleason, "Festive Satire," esp. 108–13. Wiemer, *Libanios*, 152–54, criticizes Gleason's mingling of Western and Eastern materials.

54. Lib. *Or.* 1.129.

Libanius composed the *Hypaticus* in close cooperation with Julian.⁵⁵ Reflecting the emperor's interests, he represented Julian as an exemplary ruler and legitimate bearer of the honorific "consul" (*Or.* 12.7–26), which gave Julian a more lasting honor than any stele of stone, bronze, copper, or even diamonds.⁵⁶ That very excellence guaranteed Julian a prosperous realm and military success abroad; it also affirmed his rule as divinely ordained and the impending Persian war as a just war, for it too had been preordained by the gods whose *pontifex maximus* the emperor was (*Or.* 12.33–68).⁵⁷

Libanius states unequivocally that the gods granted Julian imperial honor to ensure his military success; conversely, he would achieve that success because he revered the proper gods as one imbued with true *paideia*. In stark contrast to his unworthy precursor, Julian as "priest no less than emperor" safeguarded the *politeia* by unceasing worship of the gods with the appropriate sacrifices—the essential precondition for and guarantee of victory over the archenemy—in the circular logic of the Roman imperial tradition (*Or.* 12.80, 83, 88, 92).⁵⁸ Because the true gods had once again replaced Christ, the Persian defeat was assured, by "no infantry battle, no cavalry activity, no innovation in armament or invention of engines of war, but [by] the many sacrifices, the frequent blood offerings, the clouds of incense, the feasting of the gods and spirits."⁵⁹ The Persians, according to Libanius, knowing they would be defeated, sent an embassy offering to negotiate. This Julian rejected, "for he thought it a disgrace that anyone who deserved punishment should dare to speak of peace."⁶⁰

Given the magnitude of the endeavor, however, even Libanius, in his very same *Hypaticus* (*Or.* 12.77), expressed surprise at the emperor's cavalier rejection of diplomacy, reiterating his response later in his lamentations for the deceased Julian, where he stressed the court's surprise at Julian's rejection of Shapur's advances.

---

55. As demonstrated by the many references to the *Epistle to the Athenians*. This does not mean that Libanius and Julian thought alike about all aspects of *paideia* and religion—Libanius's concept of *paideia* appears far less religious or religiously motivated than Julian's—or that Libanius was fully aware of Julian's thoughts and notions, or of those of his circle of philosopher friends. Other works by Julian to which Libanius alludes are the *Epistle to Themistius* and *Or.* 6, *Against Heraclius*.

56. Lib. *Or.* 12.10; Wiemer, *Libanios*, 151–88.

57. For the part on the emperor's youth and ascendancy, required by the genre, Libanius relied on Julian's *Epistle to the Athenians;* Wiemer, *Libanios*, 162–66.

58. Lib. *Or.* 12.20–21. For an in-depth discussion of the early empire's "theology of Victory," see Blockley, *East Roman Foreign Policy*, 1, 24–26, 98–101, 109–27.

59. Lib. *Or.* 12.78: αἱ πυκναὶ θυσίαι καὶ τὸ αἷμα τὸ πολὺ καὶ οἱ τῶν ἀρωμάτων ἀτμοὶ καὶ θεῶν ἑστιάσεις καὶ δαιμόνων. Also ibid. 69, 70, 76, 78–83.

60. Lib. *Or.* 12.77: εἴ τις ὀφείλων δίκας περὶ σπονδῶν διαλέξεται, trans. Norman (Libanius, *Selected Orations*), and *Or.* 12.70–73, 74–77. Another sign of the Persians' fear was that a certain Antoninus, a former merchant and high-ranking Roman official who deserted to the Persians under Constantius and acted as their military counsel, now also advised diplomacy, *Or.* 12.74; for this story as told by Ammianus, Matthews, *Roman Empire*, 41–43, 68.

Other assessments, though colored by the negative outcome, further corroborate the existence of dissenting voices. Ammianus relates that members of Julian's court, including his close friend and coconsul Flavius Sallustius, actively opposed his Persian plans, because they considered Constantius's defensive policy a safer option, were concerned at Julian's haste, and feared the results of withdrawing soldiers from frontiers along the Rhine and the Danube and the diminished resources available against the Goths, an enemy Julian apparently considered beneath him.[61] Thus on the eve of his most important military campaign Julian encountered doubts even among his staunchest supporters. Adverse omens like the food crisis and the burning of Apollo's temple did little to mitigate such sentiments.[62]

Julian, feeling the tension, reacted on several levels.[63] First, he intensified his devotion in order to persuade the gods and to induce others to follow his example. No one at Antioch could fail to notice that Julian was a priest and philosopher at least as much as an emperor. Libanius's official, collaborative portrait in the *Hypaticus* emphasized that Julian had made a temple of his palace. "He greets the rising of the sun and sees it to its rest with offerings of blood, and also prepares the same for the spirits of the night, . . . [performing] the sacrifice in person; he busies himself with the preparations, gets the wood, wields the knife, opens the birds and inspects their entrails" (*Or.* 12.80–82). However, the citizens of Antioch did not embrace the imperial example; nor did all of Julian's supporters, including Ammianus—no surprise, given the debate since the time of Porphyry and Iamblichus on the efficacy of material sacrifices to immaterial gods, and the misconduct of Julian's soldiers, who gorged themselves on the sacrificial animals.[64]

But the emperor used all means at his disposal to persuade others that his convictions reflected divine will. He issued coins—for example, a series authorized in early 363 depicting a bull and two stars, and carrying the legend SECURITAS REI

---

61. Lib. *Or.* 17.19–20 and 18.164, used by Socr. *HE* 3.19; Amm. Marc. 22.7.7, 22.12.3–4, 23.1.6–7, 23.5.4; Wiemer, *Libanios*, 179–81, with further bibliography; Flavius Sallustius 5 in *PLRE*, vol. 1, 797.

62. Marcone, "Significato," focuses on Ammianus in stressing the unpopularity of the campaign; Benedetti, "Giuliano," also discusses opposition against the Persian campaign and the sacrifices.

63. Athanassiadi-Fowden, *Julian*, 200, suggests that Julian's frequent visits to the Tychaeum indicate the level of tension.

64. Ammianus emphasized the ire soldiers, in particular those who had secured Julian's Gallic victories, caused by feasting on sacrificial meat and passing out drunk in temples in times of hunger and the excessiveness of Julian's sacrifices as indications that he misread the divine will. For Ammianus, moreover, the emperor compromised his dignity by "improperly [taking] pleasure in carrying the sacred emblems in place of the priests, and in being attended by a company of little women [*mulierculis*]"; Amm. Marc. 22.12.6, 14.3; den Boeft, Drijvers, et al., *Philological and Historical Commentary on Ammianus Marcellinus 22*, 219–22; *CTh* 15.1.3 (362). Julian's "personal temple" and liturgical routines in the palace parallel the practices of Constantine and Constantius, both mobile emperors; Eus. *VC* 4.17, 4.29–32; McLynn, "Transformation," esp. 236–38; Arce, "Reconstrucción," 201–5; Bradbury, "Julian's Pagan Revival," esp. 340–47; Gregory, "Julian."

PUB(LICAE), shorthand for the military defense of the empire and its territory. The obverse represents the bearded and diademed emperor, with the legend DOMINUS NOSTER FLAVIUS CLAUDIUS IULIANUS PIUS FELIX AUGUSTUS. Whatever Julian's intention in choosing a bull—still under debate, with scholarly interpretations ranging from a representation of Sol (Helios) to astral signs—the coins were unusual enough to prompt the Antiochenes to ridicule them; later church historians linked the bull to Julian's sacrificial practices.[65]

And the emperor wrote. For the Kronia or Saturnalia, a festival devoted to joking celebrated in mid-December, the month during which Libanius prepared the *Hypaticus,* Julian composed his first full-length Antiochene treatise, the *Symposium* or *Kronia,* later also called the *Caesars.* As befitted the occasion, it was a satire, modeled after Lucian's *Council of the Gods* and dedicated either to Flavius Sallustius or to Julian's close friend and *praefectus praetorio Orientis* Salutius.[66] In it, the emperor identified the place he would hold among his precursors once he too joined them in their celestial dwelling: Julian was a new Hercules—Alexander, as he had already revealed in the myth of his divine origin in his *Oration 7, Against Heraclius* (see Chapter 2), a new Trajan, indeed the new Marcus Aurelius. Julian's models were those Roman emperors (Alexander *honoris causa*) who, as true philosopher-kings, had been successful against Persia. At the same time, he denounced the men of the wrong branch of his own dynasty, Constantine and Constantius, as floundering dunces. Constantine's deeds on earth had been as transitory and fleeting as a garden of Adonis, blossoming one day and gone the next (*Caes.* 329c). Worse, he had been duped by the man Jesus, who had spoken thus: "Whoever is a criminal or a murderer, cursed or infamous, let him come without fear. I will wash him with this water and

---

65. E.g., Kent, *Roman Imperial Coinage,* vol. 8, 46–47; Jul. *Mis.* 355d; Ephr. *Hymns c. Jul.* 1.16–17; Socr. *HE* 3.17.4–5; Soz. *HE* 5.19.2. The legend has precedents, but the stars and the bull are unusual; Scholl, *Historische Beiträge,* 154–62; Blockley, *East Roman Foreign Policy,* 106–7; den Boeft, Drijvers, et al., *Philological and Historical Commentary on Ammianus Marcellinus 22,* 220. Arce, "Algunos problemas," esp. 488–89, sees the legend as religious policy; Woods, "Julian," esp. 159–61, uses Gallienus's coin imagery to argue for Sol (Helios), whereas Tougher, "Julian's Bull Coinage," links it to Trajanic-Homeric ruler imagery, with echoes of Alexander; Berrens, *Sonnenkult,* 231–32, also argues against associations with Sol Invictus.

66. The identity of *Saloustios* is complicated, because the Greek is the same for both the coconsul Flavius Sallustius and Julian's close friend Saturninius Secundus Salutius (or Salustius; Jul. *Or.* 8.241d), and it is unclear who authored the treatise *On the Gods and the World.* While the first, Flavius Sallustius, was the coconsul of 363 as well as *praefectus praetorio* of the two Gauls between 361 and 363, the dedicatee may not have been he but rather, as argued by most scholars, Saturninius Secundus Salutius (or Salustius), *praefectus praetorio Orientis* until 367, and, also according to most scholars, responsible for the treatise *On the Gods,* composed probably during the late summer of 362; *PLRE,* vol. 1, 796–98, 814–17, s.vv. Sallustius 1 and 5, and Secundus 3; Amm. Marc. 21.8.1, 25.3.14, 21; *Saloustious: Des dieux,* ed. and trans. Rochefort, x–xxi; Bouffartigue, *Empereur Julien,* argues that Saturninius Secundus Salutius was the *Caesars'* interlocutor; cf. Étienne, "Flavius Sallustius."

make him clean immediately. And should he revert to the same sins a second time, I will have him tap his chest and pat his head and make him clean again."⁶⁷ Julian and his models, Hercules above all, are philosopher-kings; Constantius and Constantine, criminal fools—a leitmotif Libanius faithfully echoed in his *Hypaticus*.⁶⁸ Julian's audience got the message. Libanius, Gregory of Nazianzus, Ammianus, and the citizens of Antioch referred to Julian as a new Hercules, each with his own laudatory or satirical slant.⁶⁹

JULIAN'S DIVINE MANDATE
The Hymn to King Helios

> *This treatise [logos] concerns all 'that breathes and moves on earth,' . . . but more than anything it concerns myself, for I am a follower of King Helios. . . . For since my infancy I have been penetrated by a passionate love for the rays of the god.*
>
> —JULIAN, HYMN TO KING HELIOS 130B–C

Satirical levity notwithstanding, Julian's relationship with the gods of the Greeks and the Romans was no laughing matter. Within days of writing the *Caesars*, the

---

67. Jul. *Caes.* 336a–b: ὅστις φθορεύς . . . ἴτω θαρρῶν. ἀποφανῶ γὰρ αὐτὸν τουτῳὶ τῷ ὕδατι λούσας αὐτίκα καθαρόν, κἂν πάλιν ἔνοχος τοῖς αὐτοῖς γένηται, δώσω τὸ στῆθος πλήξαντι καὶ τὴν κεφαλὴν πατάξαντι καθαρῷ γενέσθαι.

68. I am using *Giuliano imperatore: Simposio i Cesari*, ed. and trans. Sardiello. The Kronia was originally held on December 17 but soon occupied an entire week. Julian's work is composed as a Menippean satire in the manner of Lucian's *Council of the Gods*, his *Dialogues of the Dead*, or his *Symposium*, his literary models. The text has been intensively studied as an essential source for the history of later Roman emperors, "de toutes les œuvres de Julien . . . la plus étudiée," Bouffartigue, *Empereur Julien*, 397–407 (quotation p. 397). Thus it forms (or ought to form) part of any discussion of the *SHA*, the works of Eutropius, Festus, Eunapius, Ammianus and the so-called (lost) *Kaisergeschichte*. For discussions, (e.g.) *Eutrope: Abrégé d'Histoire romaine*, ed. and trans. Hellegouarc'h, xii–xxi, xxiv–xxx; Kaegi, "Emperor Julian's Assessment"; den Boer, *Some Minor Roman Historians*, does not discuss the *Caesars*. Julian's selection of imperial models, in particular Marcus Aurelius and Alexander, and the severity of his denunciation of his Flavian ancestors have led scholars to differ regarding the *Caesars*' date, 361 or 362. I follow the majority opinion in dating it to mid-December 362; Müller, *Beiden Satiren*, 31, 37–39; Bidez, *Vie*, 300; Bowersock, *Julian*, 101–2; Martig, *Studi*, 27–28; Matthews, *Roman Empire*, 137–38; R. Smith, *Julian's Gods*, 8; and *Giuliano imperatore: Simposio*, ed. and trans. Sardiello, vii–ix. Bouffartigue, ("Du prétendu parti," esp. 71, and *Empereur Julien*, 401–4) argues for 361, because Aurelius Victor presented his *Caesars* that summer. Julian's use of Aurelius Victor forms part of the discussions about his command of Latin, which the communis opinio considers poor; Bouffartigue, *Empereur Julien*, 408–12.

69. Julian alluded earlier to the parallels between himself, Marcus Aurelius, Hercules, and Alexander: e.g., in his *Epistle to Themistius* 253a–b, 253c, 267b. Libanius compared Julian's actions in Gaul to the labors of Hercules (*Or.* 18.32) and compares him to Alexander regarding Persia (*Or.* 18.282). Ammianus 22.12.4 compared those who criticized Julian's Persian campaign to yapping dogs attacking Her-

emperor switched registers and composed an entirely different opus: the *Hymn to King Helios*.[70] The occasion was the *agōn Solis,* celebrated in Rome on December 25, the sun's "festival that the imperial city adorns with annual sacrifices," instituted by Aurelian, who succeeded Claudius II Gothicus.[71] Julian dedicated the hymn, like the *Caesars,* to Salutius (or Sallustius), the author of the treatise *On the Gods and the World,* the programmatic text complementing the emperor's earlier *Hymn to the Mother of the Gods*.[72] Indeed, the *Hymn to the Mother of the Gods* together with the *Hymn to King Helios* and the treatise *Against the Galileans* forms a triptych.[73] In these three pieces, each of a different literary genre, the emperor accented different aspects of the same essential idea: that the Roman *oikoumenē* was created in its universality by divine Providence and was not an inferior human invention. Thus, Julian's *eusebeia,* as divinely chosen emperor, demanded that he shield the *politeia* from faulty innovation, especially innovation regarding the gods, and that he guide his subjects to the truth and to the gods' philosophy revealed to him,

---

cules but criticized Julian's excessive sacrifices by observing that here he fell short of Marcus Aurelius (25.4.17), whom he rivaled in other aspects; for comparisons to Alexander, Lib. *Or.* 16.5.4, 25.4.15. Gr. Naz. *Or.* 4.77, 103, 122 gleefully reports that the Antiochenes ridiculed Julian as Hercules the Beefeater (or Beefslayer, Βουθοίνας) because of his sacrifices; den Boeft, Drijvers, et al., *Philological and Historical Commentary on Ammianus Marcellinus 22,* 213–14. Lane Fox, "Itinerary," 239–52, attributes less weight to Julian's comparison to Alexander. G. Kelly, "Constantius II."

70. Jul. *Or.* 11 (Bidez = *Or.* 4 Wright), *To King Helios; Empereur Julien: Œuvres completes,* vol. 2, *Discours,* ed. Lacombrade, 73–138 (for the date, p. 75); *Giuliano imperatore: Alla Madre degli dèi e altri discorsi,* intro. Fontaine, 95–169 (text with Italian trans.); Fauth, *Helios,* 121–64; Wallraff, *Christus,* 35–36; Berrens, *Sonnenkult,* 170–234; Bouffartigue, *Empereur Julien,* 331–59; R. Smith, *Julian's Gods,* 117–78; Athanassiadi-Fowden, *Julian,* 147–60; Bowersock, *Julian,* 102–3.

71. Quotation: Jul. *Hel. R.* 131d, 155b; Jer. *Chron.* 185, "primus agon Solis ab Aureliano institutus." An alternative date is October 19, but the communis opinio dates these celebrations to December 25, the *dies natalis* [*Solis*] *Invicti;* see *Hel. R.* 156c; Berrens, *Sonnenkult,* 108–9. Den Boeft, Drijvers, et al. (*Philological and Historical Commentary on Ammianus Marcellinus 22,* 153–54) emphasize the uncertain date of both the *Caesars* and the *Hymn to King Helios.* Though Claudius's brother, Quintillus, became Augustus in 270, Aurelian, Claudius's *dux equitum,* then fighting the Goths in Thrace, was acclaimed Augustus by his troops and succeeded. Quintillus died soon thereafter, either murdered or through suicide; Zos. 1.45–47; SHA *Claud.* 12.2.5.

72. The treatise *De diis* was composed shortly after Julian's *Hymn to the Mother of the Gods* (*MoG*) and before the *Hymn to King Helios* (*Hel. R.*), complementing Julian's thoughts (e.g.) by adding ritual detail; *Saloustios: Des dieux,* ed. and trans. Rochefort, xxii–xxv for the date; he dates the *Hymn to King Helios* to August 362. Den Boeft, Drijvers, et al. (*Philological and Historical Commentary on Ammianus Marcellinus 22,* 18–19); Étienne, "Flavius Sallustius," 104–13; Bowersock, *Julian,* 125; and Fontaine (*Giuliano imperatore: Alla Madre degli dèi e altri discorsi,* intro. Fontaine, 97) all see Salutius as dedicatee rather than Sallustius.

73. Fontaine (*Giuliano imperatore: Alla Madre degli dèi e altri discorsi,* intro. Fontaine, xlvii–lvi; "dittico" p. lv) suggests that Julian's two hymns are the component parts of a diptych; for the date of the *CG*, see Julian, *Contra Galilaeos,* ed. and trans. Masaracchia, 9.

by preserving and re-forming the correct mixture of Greekness and Romanness that the gods created and instituted through their *religio* and *cultus*.

As before, Julian composed his *Hymn to King Helios* in a short burst of activity during three nights when "others were more interested in the affairs of Aphrodite."[74] Central to the hymn was a theme that also preoccupied Julian's intellectual peers: the nature of the divine and its creative or productive capacity. Julian set out to speak "about the essence [*ousia*] of [the god], his origin, his powers [*dynameis*], his visible and invisible activities [*energeiai*], and about the benefits he dispenses to the entire universe."[75] The *Hymn to the Mother of the Gods* focused on the divinity of Attis-*Logos* and his relation to the Mother of the Gods and to Zeus-Helios—that is, on how Attis as a god creates, given that he belongs to the sphere where immaterial causes and material form meet. In the *Hymn to King Helios* (or to Zeus-Helios), Julian explained the focal point of that trinity: Zeus-Helios, "who rules over the fifth visible body [ether]" (*MoG* 165a), and his relation to the prior cause, "which existed unbegotten [*agennētos*] since eternity and will exist in eternity in the future."[76] For Julian, Helios is the mediator between transcendent realities and visible ones, since the noeric Sun, emanating from the Highest One, is the Demiurge of the universe and Father of all men (*Hel. R.* 131c). However, as a prelude to examining the intricacies of Julian's *physikos hymnos*, the genre the emperor chose for this particular opus, I want to highlight the dynastic and imperial significance of the central figure of the hymn, the Sun.[77]

---

74. Jul. *Hel. R.* 157b-c; Lib. *Or.* 18.178-79. Many modern scholars, usually those less than enthusiastic about Julian's qualities as an author, attribute the density of his arguments to this particular work habit.

75. Jul. *Hel. R.* 132b: περὶ τῆς οὐσίας αὐτοῦ καὶ ὅθεν προῆλθε καὶ τῶν δυνάμεων καὶ τῶν ἐνεργειῶν . . . ὁπόσαι φανεραὶ ὅσαι τ' ἀφανεῖς, καὶ περὶ τῆς τῶν ἀγαθῶν δόσεως, ἣν κατὰ πάντας ποιεῖται τοὺς κόσμους. This schema structures the hymn: 132b-142b deal with Helios's essence and origin; 142b-152a, his powers and activities in the visible and in the invisible world; 152a-157b, the benefits granted to the entire world; closing with a brief prayer. Mau's classic treatment (*Religionsphilosophie*, 4-5), on which many of the later works rely (e.g., *Giuliano imperatore: Alla Madre degli dèi e altri discorsi*, trans. Marcone, 294, with slight moderations), further subdivides the first two parts: the first part is divided into origins (132c-137c) followed by essence (137b-142c); the second, into activities in the invisible (143d-145d) and in the visible sphere (145d-152a).

76. Jul. *Hel. R.* 132c: ἐξ ἀϊδίου γέγονεν ἀγέννητως ἔς τε τὸν ἐπίλοιπον χρόνον ἀΐδιος.

77. Men. Rh. *Treatise* 1.1 (*Menander Rhetor*, ed. and trans. Russell and Wilson, 12-14; *Peri epideiktikōn*, ed. Spengel, 336.25-337.34) gives clear compositional guidelines for a *physikos hymnos*. If writing a hymn "to Apollo, [one must say] that he is the Sun, and then one begins to talk about the nature of the Sun"—a dual path not unlike the one adopted by Eunomius in his *Apology*. Menander forbids prayers in such a hymn, and indeed Julian's final prayer is brief. A second rhetorical genre Julian employed is the encomium; see 132b; Bouffartigue, *Empereur Julien*, 540-41; R. Smith, *Julian's Gods*, 144-45. As Bouffartigue points out (*Empereur Julien*, 537, 541, 569-71), the *MoG* was not a hymn in the strict rhetorical sense but a philosophical work with a final hymn, and the *CG* a philosophical-dialectic invective; Hadot, "Philosophie." For the genre, see also Hose, "Konstruktion."

Helios, Sol, and the Greek Origin of Roman Supremacy   Julian's concept of the Greekness of the Roman *oikoumenē* profoundly shaped his views of the Mother of the Gods and of Attis-*Logos*. (See Chapter 3.) As he emphasized, these divinities, in myth and ritual, signified the divinely ordered merging of Greece and Rome into one universal commonwealth, one *koina* or *imperium*. As symbol of empire and governance, however, the sun was far more potent and far easier to recognize, as Julian well knew.[78] After all, as he stressed in his opening sentence, the emperor wrote his hymn as "personal attendant of King Helios," as member of an imperial dynasty that had served this god as his slaves for at least three generations—longer, if one included the mythic founder, Claudius Gothicus.[79] The Greek term "personal attendant," *opados*, carried imperial and dynastic overtones. It alluded to an idea that particularly appealed to Constantine, that of the Invincible Sun as personal companion of the emperor ("sol invictus comes Augusti")—a fortuitous relationship initiated by the god.[80] Julian evoked and enhanced this link by claiming a dual relationship to the divinity, dynastic and individual. Though "born into the family that dominated over and ruled the world in [his] time," Julian also claimed to belong to the sacred race (*hiera genea*) of the true philosopher.[81] Zeus had entrusted him to Helios as his son, to be saved through philosophy (Jul. Or. 7.229c). As this hymn would demonstrate, Zeus and Helios were in essence one, so that the emperor had been chosen by Zeus the Invincible Sun as his own son. Thus Julian's "*logos* concerns . . . more than anything

---

78. This accounts for the far greater scholarly attention paid to this work compared with the *Hymn to the Mother of the Gods*. The scholarly treatments are concerned either with the text's philosophical ideas (e.g., Renucci, *Idées*, 109–39, with slender bibliography and based on Mau, *Religionsphilosophie*) or with its historical implications, such as (a) the dynastic references, (b) the cult of Sol Invictus and sun worship in all its aspects, (c) Julian's Mithraism, or (d) all or any of these together. For Julian's dynastic concerns, see Mazza, "Filosofia," esp. 76–90.

79. Beginning with his panegyrics to Constantius, Julian's allusions to Claudius Gothicus abound: e.g., *Or.* 2.51c–52a, *Or.* 1.6d–7a. Julian's *Epistle to the Athenians* demonstrates how conscious he was of his dynastic position and the legitimacy it afforded; in the exemplary myth of his origins (*Or.* 7.234c), to be Zeus's son meant correcting the mistaken innovations of his relatives; here as well as in the *Caesars* (313d, 336b), Julian's allusion to Hercules evokes Tetrarchic connections via Constantius Chlorus to the founder of the dynasty, the Illyrian Claudius II Gothicus (a Constantinian fiction); Berrens, *Sonnenkult*, 85–88, 139–69.

80. The relationship and its terminology carry notions of patronage and *clientela* and those of equal rulership. Though the concept has earlier antecedents, it gained particular currency under Constantine and was still in use under Constantine II; Berrens, *Sonnenkult*, 206–10; Nock, "The Emperor's Divine *comes*." For the notion of service to the gods, see also Jul. *Hel. R.* 131c: κάλλιστον μὲν οὖν, εἴ τῳ ξυνηνέχθη καὶ πρὸ τριγονίας ἀπὸ πολλῶν πάνυ προπατόρων ἐφεξῆς τῷ θεῷ δουλεῦσαι.

81. Julian (*Hel. R.* 131b) professed envy for "the good fortune of the man to whom the god has granted a body generated by a sacred and prophetic semen and who can thus discover the treasures of wisdom" (ζηλῶ μὲν οὖν ἔγωγε τῆς εὐποτμίας καὶ εἴ τῳ τὸ σῶμα παρέσχε θεὸς ἐξ ἱεροῦ καὶ προφητικοῦ συμπαγὲν σπέρματος ἀναλαβόντι σοφίας ἀνοῖξαι θησαυρούς); he nevertheless considered himself sufficiently divine.

[him]self, ... because since [his] infancy [he had] been penetrated by a passionate love for the rays of the god," his true father.[82]

All that Julian was about to say about the essential unity of Zeus and Helios and their focal place in the tripartite cosmos—made one by the highest power that had created, ordered, and ruled it—thus applied also, by analogy, to Julian the emperor, himself linked to the god by the triple allegiance of dynasty, philosophy, and sonship. All citizens of the *politeia* were united in his person as leader, just as Zeus's original creation of man and cosmos united all in common parentage (*Hel. R.* 131c), which in turn required service to the master (131d) in the proper order: to the gods, *daimones,* heroes, and parents.[83] The analogy between these two kings, Zeus-Helios and Julian, though never made explicit, runs through the hymn like a subtle leitmotif. It is present in Julian's citation of the passage in Plato's *Republic* (508b) where the philosopher declares the sun "the offspring of the Good, which the Good generated in analogy to itself, so that what the Good is in the intelligible world in relation to the intellect and the objects it conceives, the sun is in the visible world in relation to sight and what is seen" (*Hel. R.* 133a). Plato's passage became fundamental to political theories of kingship as analogous to the illuminating and life-giving presence of the sun. Significantly, Dio Chrysostom employed the analogy in his *Third Oration on Kingship* (68), a model for Julian's second panegyric of Constantius: Julian then had already used that same Platonic analogy (*Or.* 2.80c–81b).[84]

As Julian's allusions to the Constantinian Invincible Sun as *comes Augusti* indicate, Plato was not his sole reference. Rather, he repeatedly emphasized that Rome especially, since its inception, recognized the divinity of Sol Invictus and honored it in its various representations above all other gods. But Julian being Julian, this argument takes its starting point in things Greek. In detailing the benefits Helios gave mankind, Julian emphasized that Apollo, as his coruler, installed oracles to give men inspired wisdom and to order their cities by means of sacred and political laws, so that through him "the Greek colonies civilized the greater part of the *oikoumenē,* thus preparing it to submit more easily to the Romans. For not only are the Romans

---

82. Jul. *Hel. R.* 130b–c: Προσήκειν ὑπολαμβάνω τοῦ λόγου τοῦδε μάλιστα μὲν ἅπασιν, ὅσσα τε γαῖαν ἔπι πνείει τε καὶ ἕρπει, ... οὐχ ἥκιστα δὲ τῶν ἄλλων ἁπάντων ἐμαυτῷ· καὶ γάρ εἰμι τοῦ βασιλέως ὀπαδός Ἡλίου. ... ἐντέτηκέ μοι δεινὸς ἐκ παίδων τῶν αὐγῶν τοῦ θεοῦ πόθος," citing Hom. *Il.* 17.447 and *Od.* 18.130, and echoing Cleanth. *Hymn to Zeus* fr. 537.5.5.

83. Hierocl. *In CA* 7.23–28.16; Iamb. *Myst.* 5.21.230.9–10. Julian returned to this theme, fundamental for *oikeiōsis,* in his *Epistle to the Priest Theodorus.*

84. Pl. *R.* 540a–b makes the analogy explicit; Pl. *R.* 508e–509e informed much of Julian's thought. I am translating Julian's citation; see *Or.* 2.69a–70d, 79a–93d; D. Chr. *Or.* 3.1–3. For the analogy with kingship, also Plut. *Ad princ. inerud.* 3.780e–f; Them. *Or.* 27.4. The author of the *SHA Aur.* 4.2 claimed that Aurelian was born from the Sun in *heliogenesis.* According to Suet. *Aug.* 96.4, Octavian as a boy climbed a tower to be closer to the rays of the sun. For the spread of the concept, Eitrem, "Zur Apotheose"; Nock, "Emperor's Divine *comes,*" 672–74; Renucci, *Idées,* 110.

Greek by origin, but so also are their sacred laws and pious belief in the gods, which they have instituted and preserve.... Therefore I myself regard through my own insight our city as Greek both by origin and by constitution."[85] Romans were in essence Greek and therefore direct beneficiaries of the civilizing impact that Zeus-Helios dispensed in his persona as Apollo. Thus the expansion of Rome to include the Greek world was not conquest but a divinely ordered and hence natural unifying move within one family that had its common origin in Zeus's act of creation: the ideological power of Greekness as properly Roman cannot be expressed more succinctly and clearly.[86]

To be sure, while Julian reiterated that all creation in all its aspects benefited from the munificence of Zeus-Helios, the emperor also left no doubt that Rome ruled supreme, because the Sun had preordained its sovereignty. "Moreover, he is the founder of our city" (*Hel. R.* 153d). Helios in his various representations (as Jupiter, Apollo, or as Sol Invictus in the temple erected by Aurelian) ruled the Capitoline and the Palatine, and the offspring of his relative Aphrodite—Romulus and Aeneas— had founded the city.[87] Further, from the divine King Numa's rule onward "our forefathers paid greater reverence to the god Helios [than other peoples]." Numa had already appointed the Vestal Virgins to guard "the undying flame of the Sun at different hours in turn" and had altered the calendar to follow the turns of the sun more closely (154a–155d), thus initiating a new golden age for the city.[88]

Julian's *Hymn to King Helios* showcases how the emperor wanted the perfect mixture of Greece and Rome to be understood. Taking its starting point from Plato and above all from the "divine Iamblichus, ... from whose writings [he had] taken a few thoughts out of [their] great richness, just as they came into [his] mind" (*Hel. R.* 157d), Julian's hymn combined the cosmological, philosophical, and mythical aspects of the unifying force of Helios with all the imperial connotations implicit in the purportedly ancient Roman Sol Invictus.[89] On the eve of his Persian cam-

---

85. Jul. *Hel. R.* 152d–153a: Οὗτος ἡμέρωσε μὲν διὰ τῶν Ἑλληνικῶν ἀποικιῶν τὰ πλεῖστα τῆς οἰκουμένης, παρεσκεύασε δὲ ῥᾷον ὑπακοῦσαι Ῥωμαίοις ἔχουσι καὶ αὐτοῖς οὐ γένος μόνον Ἑλληνικόν, ἀλλὰ καὶ θεσμοὺς ἱερούς, καὶ τὴν περὶ τοὺς θεοὺς εὐπιστίαν ἐξ ἀρχῆς εἰς τέλος Ἑλληνικήν, ... ἀνθ' ὧν οἶμαι καὶ αὐτὸς ἔγνω τὴν πόλιν Ἑλληνίδα γένος τε καὶ πολιτείαν. Gregory shared Julian's concept of the greater antiquity and hence superiority of Greekness: e.g., *Carm.* 1.2.10.350–51. Dionysus of Halicarnassus, *Roman Antiquities* 1.89.4, had already emphasized that Rome's origins were Greek, not Trojan (as Vergil would have it).

86. Also Jul. *Caes.* 324a for the Greek origin of all things Roman.

87. Berrens, *Sonnenkult*, 104–9.

88. Julian thus predates a number of Aurelian measures to the mythical Numa. Aurelian had used Sol Invictus as symbol of a newly restored Roman Empire and hence a new Golden Age; Berrens, *Sonnenkult*, 99–102, 124–26.

89. As understood by Julian rather than modern historians of Roman religion; Athanassiadi-Fowden, *Julian*, 169–70, 175–81. This is also the context of Julian's Mithraism: most modern scholars discussing the *Hymn to King Helios* focus on whether Julian was an initiate and if so to what extent his ideas

paign, just prior to his fourth consulate, such a display of all the geopolitical and dynastic implications of Julian's intimate connection to Zeus-Helios, the Roman imperial deity Sol, made a powerful point. Further, the combination of Platonic concepts with Roman imperial ones exactly reflected Julian's view of his Iamblichan Platonic philosophical life as emperor. The *oikoumenē* of his vision was the perfectly merged Greece and Rome—Plato's notion of the philosopher as leader who guides those in his trust from darkness into light like the sun, and the Roman sense of the emperor's world rule as analogous to the one divine Sun, because Zeus-Helios was the origin of all creation and civilization, and its *telos*.[90] The sun, eternal, victorious, invincible, guaranteed the security of the *res publica*; endowed with providence, it was beneficent, bestowing felicitous times on all, illuminating everything with its light and wisdom, and uniting all into one—as did his *comes*, the Augustus Julian, Helios's son, the offspring of a dynasty that had served the Sun and stood under its particular protection.[91] Because Julian was both Iamblichan political philosopher and Flavian emperor, tracing his line back to Claudius II Gothicus, his concluding prayer to the invincible celestial ruler, the Sun, resonated profoundly:[92] "To endow my city, if possible, with eternal existence and protect her in his benevolence; may he grant me personally, as long as I live, success in my human and divine affairs

---

about the sun reflect Mithraic associations, even a Mithraic theology. Whereas earlier scholarship asserted Julian's close Mithraic connections, thus explaining his orientalizing of ancient Greek religion as manifest in his extreme reliance on oracles (following Cumont, *Textes,* vol. 1, [e.g.] 27; Bidez, *Vie,* 222; *Empereur Julien: Œuvres complètes,* vol. 2, *Discours,* ed. Lacombrade, 93–95; Athanassiadi-Fowden, "Contribution" and *Julian,* 38–41, 58, 117, 160), recent scholarship since R. Smith (*Julian's Gods,* 139–59) and Renucci (*Idées,* 122–39), influenced by Turcan (*Mithras,* esp. 105–28), rejects such influence, in my view rightly. Fauth, *Helios,* 150–54, takes a middle position. Julian worshipped Mithras, but merely as one god in his inclusive pantheon, and the theology of the *Hymn to King Helios* is based on the *Chaldaean Oracles* and Iamblichus.

90. As D. O'Meara points out (*Platonopolis,* 120–21) and the *Epistle to Themistius* suggests, Julian's concept of the philosopher as leader may well be the more modest, second best model of Plato's *Laws* rather than the full-fledged philosopher-king of the *Republic*. (See above, Chapter 3.) I think, however, that by the time of the *Hymn to King Helios,* Julian's views regarding his divinity and purity had evolved to resemble more those of Plato's *Republic,* which he cites explicitly.

91. The dynastic link remained paramount, so that even in *Caes.* 336b, Julian has Zeus preserve Constantine's dynasty "for the sake of Claudius and Constantius [Chlorus]"; Berrens, *Sonnenkult,* 146–204, 224–28. Soler, "D'Apollonios," 392–98, intriguingly suggests that Julian may have intended to make Antioch into a holy city devoted to the sun.

92. Modern authors who discuss this aspect of the *Hymn to King Helios*—e.g., Berrens, Fauth (*Helios,* 147–55), and R. Smith (*Julian's Gods,* 143–63)—distinguish Julian's view of the sun god sharply from Constantinian and pre-Constantinian imperial concepts (because they assume that Neoplatonic political philosophy did not exist, or because earlier concepts of the sun were more polytheistic), so that for Berrens (*Sonnenkult,* 231) "der julianische Sol/Helios . . . demnach vor diesem Hintergrund zu sehen und ein direkter Vergleich [with Constantinian notions] nicht möglich ist," though he contradicts that at pp. 224–28; Wallraff, *Christus,* 27–31; D. O'Meara, *Platonopolis,* 120–23.

and permit me to live and to serve the *politeia* with my life as long as it is pleasing to him, useful to me, and advantageous for the community of the Romans."[93]

Zeus-Helios the Mediator: Three in One

> *I flee innovation in all things, ... and in particular in those that concern the gods. I think one must hold on to the laws that our parents have had since the beginning and that are manifestly a gift of the gods. They would not be as good if they were merely human works.*[94]
>
> —JULIAN, EPISTLE 89A.453B-C

Modern scholars accuse Julian, in his *Hymn to King Helios,* of muddled thinking or at least obtuse sentence structure, presumably caused by work habits that deprived him of sleep.[95] Inscriptions demonstrate, however, that at least some local nobles grasped well the central message of the emperor's hymn and indeed of his rule when they proclaimed, "One God wins. One Julian, the Augustus. Eternally, you, Augustus Julian"; "Julian, the eternal victor and *triumphator,* born to benefit the state"; "Soli invicto Aug(usto) sac(rum)"; *ex philosophias basileuonta ... hyph' Hēliou ... Ioulianon ... theōtaton autokratora Augouston.*[96]

How, then, did Julian conceive of Zeus-Helios and the manner in which all good, power, and knowledge emanated from him? What thoughts had he taken from Iamblichus, whom he cited again from memory, and what did he add to the philosopher's thoughts about the origin, essence, and creative capacity of Helios, a subject that "Iamblichus, the beloved of the God," had treated "more perfectly" than anyone (*Hel. R.* 157d)?[97] To elaborate the philosophical foundation of his political

---

93. Jul. *Hel. R.* 157b: κοινῇ μὲν τῇ πόλει τὴν ἐνδεχομένην ἀϊδιότητα μετ' εὐνοίας χορηγῶν φυλάττοι, ... ζῆν δὲ καὶ ἐμπολιτεύεσθαι τῷ βίῳ ... ἡμῖν τε λῷον καὶ τοῖς κοινοῖς Ῥωμαίων συμφέρον πράγμασιν. See also Pl. *R.* 496c–e, 540b, for the role of the leader vis-à-vis the *koina*.

94. καὶ φεύγω τὴν καινοτομίαν ἐν ἅπασι μέν, ὡς ἔπος εἰπεῖν, ἰδίᾳ δὲ ἐν τοῖς πρὸς τοὺς θεούς, οἰόμενος χρῆναι τοὺς πατρίους ἐξ ἀρχῆς φυλάττεσθαι νόμους, οὓς ὅτι μὲν ἔδοσαν οἱ θεοί, φανερόν· οὐ γὰρ ἂν ἦσαν οὕτω καλοὶ παρὰ ἀνθρώπων ἁπλῶς γενόμενοι.

95. Fauth, *Helios,* 147, is representative. Dillon's remark ("Theology," 104) that "in the area of philosophy, Julian has no aspirations to originality," content to present to his audience "as faithfully as he can" the insights of Iamblichus, represents the second, widespread characterization. Dillon concludes that Julian's Helios combines the Iamblichan transcendent soul, not mentioned in the text, and the Demiurge.

96. Conti, *Inschriften,* 59–64; see especially inscription 34, from Iasus in Caria. Some of these inscriptions are officially authorized milestones from the diocese Arabia. For the panegyric inscriptions, Conti, ibid., 201–3; for religious values, 46–48. Julian did not consider himself a god and did not intend to reinstall emperor worship. For an analysis of nine milestones from Dalmatia bearing the address *totius orbis Augusto* (62 stones read *semper Augusto*), Wirbelauer and Fleer, "*Totius orbis Augustus.*"

97. Julian wrote the hymn as an encomium, translating Iamblichus's philosophical writings into a sacrificial offering. He again relied on his memory and to make his points adjusted what (we know)

thought, Julian proceeded via "two roads [to] discover what [he sought], one by which we examine the actual essences . . . ; the other is an inquiry by means of the actions whereby we distinguish the essence on the basis of its product and completed works." I quote Eunomius's *Apology* 20.5–10, but both Eunomius and the emperor deduced by analogy knowledge of what Julian calls "What Is beyond All Thought" (or "the Supra-Intelligible," *to epekeina tou nou*), "the Uncompounded Cause of the Whole" (*hē monoeidēs tōn holōn aitia*), "the King of the Whole Universe," "the One," on the basis of what the One has produced, "by virtue of the primal creative substance [*prōtourgon ousian*] that abides in it" (*Hel. R.* 132c–d). What interested Julian most was not the One but its product, through which by analogy deductions about the First Cause became possible. How did the First Cause, the incorporeal, transcendent One, interact with the layers or gradations below it, including the physical world, taking for granted the presence of the One in each of these gradations? The emperor, using Iamblichan structures, wished to delineate here how these lower layers proceeded from and would return to the One.[98] Specifically, he defined and described the mediating function of Helios as "the Middle of the Middle" between the One, the intellectual gods, and the visible, sublunar, physical world. The sun's light represented the continuity and hence mediation between the intelligible and intellectual realms and visible, physically manifest reality—between the divine and human.

Indeed, the question of the transcendental cause of everything forms the context for the passage from Plato (*R.* 508b–509b) that Julian cited in drawing the analogy between the role of the Good in the intelligible world and that of the sun in the visible. This passage became central in philosophical debates about creation and achieved particular significance among Julian's immediate precursors and contemporaries.[99] Plato's exposition of how (and by implication why) a First Cause that

---

Iamblichus argued. As Bouffartigue points out (*Empereur Julien*, 331–37, 356–59), we do not know what Iamblichan writings Julian had in mind; Bouffartigue finds little evidence of the *Chaldaean Oracles* in this hymn, whereas R. Smith (*Julian's Gods*, 92, 143–59) considers them fundamental. Renucci, *Idées*, 110–17, rightly emphasizes Iamblichan influence, irrespective of the specific work.

98. This explains the apparent contradictions, inconsistency, even confusion, in Julian's discussion of the relation between the Greatest Helios as Demiurge and its relation to Zeus, the Highest One, or both: he is not interested in that Highest One but uses the Iamblichan tripartite structure to discuss the mediating function of Helios—i.e., the One—in relation to the other layers. Thus there is no need to attribute Julian's cosmic scheme to Numenius or other Middle Platonists, *pace* Dillon, "Theology," 107: Julian made a particular point and tailored his hymn accordingly, based on the Iamblichan structure.

99. The full passage from Plato *R.* 509b reads: "Therefore, say that not only being known is present in the things known as a consequence of the Good, but also the 'to be' and being (their very existence and essence) are in them besides as a result of it, although the Good itself is not being [essence] but still transcends being [essence], exceeding it in dignity and power" (οὐκ οὐσίας ὄντος τοῦ ἀγαθοῦ, ἀλλ' ἔτι ἐπέκεινα τῆς οὐσίας πρεσβείᾳ καὶ δυνάμει ὑπερέχοντος), trans. Sallis, *Being*, 401–12, here 408; Whit-

is beyond being produces effects, or products, that "receive from 'the Good'— meaning of course God—not only the faculty of being known but also their very being and essence, even though the Good 'is not an essence but something that far transcends essence in dignity and power' " permitted a number of alternative accounts of this creative process, especially after Plotinus.[100] Eusebius, for example, who quoted Plato's analogy in full in his *Praeparatio Evangelica* and whose gloss of Plato's *Republic* 509b I have just cited, argued from the passage that neither the Son nor Ideas "are of the same essence [*homoousios*] as he," the Father, nor have they been generated (*agennētos*), since the Father alone, "whom the Hebraic sayings proclaim God," is "the First Cause of all things."[101] Eunomius, as we have seen, read this causal act as God's delegation of his "creative activity and intention" to his perfect servant, the Son, thereby preserving God's transcendence.[102]

To preserve transcendence while explaining production was the heart of the matter (though to Julian production mattered more). Plotinus, who influenced all later interpreters, read the passage to mean that Plato called "the Good . . . what is beyond Intellect and 'beyond being.'" This reading implies a differentiation Iamblichus then made explicit by positing three *hypostaseis*, or cosmic principles.[103] Whereas Plato proceeded by a dual analogy between the intelligible world (*kosmos noētos*) ruled by the Good and the sensible or visible one (*kosmos horatos*) illuminated by the sun, Iamblichus separated the former further into the intelligible (*kosmos noētos*) and the intelligent world (*kosmos noeros*) on the one hand and the sensible world (*kosmos horatos*) on the other. He thus separated the highest Thought (*Nous*) from its product or object, the thought, permitting the highest sphere to remain fully transcendent while affecting the material one through its powers, acting as intermediaries. Consequently, Iamblichus concluded that humans can know the essence of all superior beings only through their powers (*dynameis*), which themselves are known by their activities. "A power," he stated in his *Commentary on Alcibiades*, "is a mean between an essence and an activity, put forth from the

---

taker, "ΕΠΕΚΕΙΝΑ ΝΟΥ ΚΑΙ ΟΥΣΙΑΣ," 91–104, for the influence of the passage on Middle Platonic and pre-Neoplatonic thought.

100. Eus. *PE* 11.21.3–6: μὴ εἶναι οὐσίαν, ἀλλ' ἐπέκεινα τῆς οὐσίας, πρεσβείᾳ καὶ δυνάμει ὑπερέχον.

101. Eusebius used this passage to demonstrate that only one God was responsible for creation, and not many gods; see *PE* 3.6.6, 7.15.5; M. R. Barnes, *Power*, 87–89; for Eusebius's cosmology, Lyman, *Christology*, 82–123.

102. Eun. *Apol.* 15.14–16, 27.2–5; M. R. Barnes, *Power*, 212–14.

103. Plot. *Enn.* 1.8.5–7. *Enn.* 5.3.13 postulates that there is something beyond the Intelligence, "which has no name." Other relevant Plotinian passages with many implications, in particular for Gregory of Nazianzus but also for Gregory of Nyssa, are *Enn.* 1.7.1.19–21, 5.4.2.30–34, 36–39, and 5.6.4.19–20, where he emphasizes that the Highest Good, however transcendent, is still a cause and hence generates. For Iamblichus's differentiation, (e.g.) Mau, *Religionsphilosophie*, 28–29, 35–38.

essence on the one hand and itself generating the activity on the other."[104] For Julian, who adopted Iamblichus's tripartite cosmos as a matter of course, that crucial middle position, or mean, was occupied by Helios, the Sun.

> This divine and wholly beautiful universe, which extends from the highest vault of heaven down to the limits of the earth, held together by the continuous providence of the God, exists ungenerated since eternity and will exist in eternity in the future, and is directly preserved by nothing other than the fifth substance [ether], whose head [apex] is the ray of the sun; and on a second level, so to speak, it is sustained by the intelligible world [kosmos noētos], and higher still by the King of the World, the center of all that exists. This Highest One, however it is designated, . . . as 'What Is beyond Intellect' [to epekeina tou nou], 'the One,' . . . or the Good . . . , by virtue of the primal creative substance [prōtourgon ousian] that abides in it, has produced as mediator in the middle of the middle causes, which are the intelligent and demiurgic [creative] causes, Helios, the highest God, proceeding from [the highest principle, the Good,] and in everything similar [homoios] to it[self].[105]

Helios's very essence as "the Middle" (mesotēs) of the middle cosmos makes him according to Julian the nexus of "all the kosmoi" (Hel. R. 132b), extending above to the Highest One—whom Julian considers both identical with and above the kosmos noētos, as the quotation just above reveals—and down to the sensible and visible world, uniting all three hypostaseis into one. "I assert then that he is midway between the visible gods who surround the universe and the immaterial and intelligible gods who surround the Good" (138d).[106] Julian deduces Helios's "intermediary essence" (to meson tēs ousias, 139b) by analogy, as a function of his origin. Helios "in his totality, since he is the son of the Idea, the first and Highest Good, and exists [hypostas] since eternity in the region of its everlasting substance, has been given dominion over the intelligent gods (theoi noeroi) and dispenses to them what the Good produces for the intelligible ones [noētoi]."[107]

Julian, following Plato, begins his analogy by making a deduction from the visible world. "The third sun [is] the disc that we see, which is clearly the salvation of

---

104. Iamb. *Comm. on Alcibiades* fr. 4.84.14–16, which Julian does appear to have used here.
105. Jul. *Hel. R.* 132c-d: οὐχ ὑπ' ἄλλου του φρουρούμενος ἢ προσεχῶς μὲν ὑπὸ τοῦ πέμπτου σώματος, οὗ τὸ κεφαλαιόν ἐστιν ἀκτὶς ἀελίου, . . . μέσον ἐκ μέσων τῶν νοερῶν καὶ δημιουργικῶν αἰτίων Ἥλιον θεὸν μέγιστον ἀνέφηνεν ἐξ ἑαυτοῦ πάντα ὅμοιον ἑαυτῷ.
106. Jul. *Hel. R.* 138c–141b defines Helios's essence as *mesotēs*. First, Julian defined Helios's middleness "not as a mean between extremes"—see also Gregory's notion of the Trinity not as a mean between extremes but as fulfillment of the One—to discuss subsequently its various forms; Mau, *Religionsphilosophie*, 59–61; *Empereur Julien: Œuvres complètes*, vol. 2, *Discours*, ed. Lacombrade, 86; R. Smith, *Julian's Gods*, 148–51.
107. Jul. *Hel. R.* 133b: ἅτε δὴ τοῦ πρώτου καὶ μεγίστου τῆς ἰδέας τἀγαθοῦ γεγονὼς ἔκγονος . . . καὶ τὴν ἐν τοῖς νοεροῖς θεοῖς παρεδέξατο δυναστείαν, ὧν τἀγαθόν ἐστι τοῖς νοητοῖς αἴτιον, ταῦτα αὐτὸς τοῖς νοεροῖς νέμων. Mau, *Religionsphilosophie*, 45–47.

the visible beings; and this visible Helios is the cause for as many blessings to the visible gods as the highest Helios is to the intelligent ones" (*Hel. R.* 133c). As Julian reiterated (141b), Helios because of his centrally mediating position captures and unites in one the highest Forms (*ideai*), their *paradeigmata* in the intelligent world, and their *hypostaseis*, or realities, in the visible one.[108] By assuming into himself all three, Helios mediates between the original Idea, its exemplars in the immaterial world, and their existence in the material, sublunar world that begins with the sphere of the stars (134b–c, 148a).[109] In sum, just as the Highest One contains in itself abstract and transcendental Thought but also produces the whole beautiful cosmos in eternity and perpetuity, so the visible sun unites the visible and sensible world. The intelligent Sun unites all three; emanating as Son from the Highest Good, the Father (136d), he rules the middle as the second king, the Great Helios (139d–140b), and gives visibility and hence existence to the third as the disc of the sun (138c, 139b–d, 140a). To rule the middle and to be active in the heavenly and sublunar spheres is his threefold creative force (*hē triplē tou theou dēmiourgia*, 157b–c). Importantly, Helios unites and mediates between these worlds without mixing or intermingling them; each principle keeps its own distinct qualities (138d–139a; see Gregory's notion of the Trinity as three distinct *hypostaseis* as one God: e.g., *Or.* 2.38).

Light: Helios's Threefold Activity   Julian offered several explanations of how the Highest *Nous*, the Intelligent or Greatest Helios, and the visible sun were united into one. As Georg Mau has pointed out, though Julian differentiated between the intelligent and visible Helios as origin and product, he also considered them identical. Zeus and Helios, though father and son, are one god, active on different levels (*Hel. R.* 132d, 136a). Light, as both immaterial and active manifestation of divine nature, as product and activity proceeding from the highest Sun, the highest or unique principle (*monoeidēs*, 132d), unites all three. The visible sun is "the living, soul- and intelligence-filled beneficent statue [*agalma*] of the intelligible Father."[110] As product of the activity (*energeia*) of the Highest Good and the Great Helios, the visible sun permits man to deduce by analogy the operation of the intelligent and intelligible Sun from which it proceeded: "The culmination . . . of light, itself incorporeal, is the sun's rays. Now according to the teaching of the Phoenicians, . . .

---

108. ἐν παραδείγματι τὴν ἰδέαν καὶ τὴν ὑπόστασιν ἔχουσα.

109. For Julian, the stars, especially the planets circling around the sun as if around a king (*Hel. R.* 134c–135a), are the visible aspects of the intelligent gods. Julian uses *agalma*, "visible representation" or "statue," to describe the stars, thus signaling the analogous role of statues as visible aspects of the gods. Though Plato used *eikones* rather than *agalmata*, the notion had a long tradition; Pl. *Ti.* 39d–e, 40a, *Epin.* 984a; Porph. *Abst.* 2.36; Iamb. *Myst.* 1.19.58.1; Fauth, *Helios*, 152–53; Renucci, *Idées*, 113–17.

110. The quotation is Jul. *Ep.* 111, *To the Alexandrians* (Wright 47), 434d, written in October or November 362 and reaffirming Athanasius's exile. Mau, *Religionsphilosophie*, 51–52.

the splendor of light diffused everywhere is the immaculate activity [*achranton* . . . *energeian*] of the pure Mind [*tou katharou nou*]." Because light is incorporeal, its source must be too, as Julian continues to argue: "Therefore our theory is not at variance, namely that we consider the source of this light, without giving it a body, the immaculate activity of the Intellect, illuminating its own home, which is situated at the center of the entire heaven, whence it fills the circles of heaven with its own vigor and illuminates all with its divine and immaculate light."[111] This activity, illumination, perfects the visible things; it is creative, and it unites and preserves all in one[112]—beneficial activities Helios shares with the other gods over whom he rules: Zeus, but also Apollo, Hades, and Serapis (135d–136a).[113]

Central to Julian's concept is the unity and continuity of the creative process, eternal and everlasting in an uninterrupted sequence of activity proceeding from the highest ingenerate (*agennētos*) First Cause, the One, by way of the creative Middle to the earth (*Hel. R.* 141d–142b). This process was a consequence of the oneness of the god's essence, power, and activity, "for it cannot be that a god's essence is one thing, and his power another, and his activity . . . a third thing besides these" (142d). Thus, the creation of the Greatest Helios is as eternal and everlasting as the god himself; both his essence and his activity are eternal: creation did not come from nothing, nor could a god be generated in a single, discreet act, but it exists and is produced through generation without passion in everlasting Thought (144a, 136c). And Helios, though he is their ruler, shares his nature (*syngenēs, symphyēs*) and especially his beneficent activity in the visible realm with all other intelligent gods (*theoi noeroi*), who represent Helios's different aspects or works (*erga,* 143b, 144a, 144c, 145a–c).[114]

As Apollo Musagetes, Helios is "the interpreter for us of the purposes of our god" (*Hel. R.* 144b). As mentioned above, from him mankind "was born, and by him nourished"; he frees man's soul from the body and guides it toward the divine; through his oracles everywhere man was granted wisdom and the means to regulate the cities by religious and political ordinances. He civilized the *oikoumenē* by establishing Greek colonies (*apoikiai*), and thus prepared it for Roman supremacy. By begetting Asclepius, he granted all health and "gave the whole world a savior" (152b–153b). Dionysus was Apollo's partner on the throne, who "begat Asclepius in the world, though from the beginning of the world he had him by his side" (144a-b). Both Dionysus and Asclepius (as indicated by their myths of origin) are at once part of the noeric, transcendental creative realm and of the visible cosmos: both have a divine and a human parent. Dionysus, as creative god, supervises the cre-

---

111. Jul. *Hel. R.* 134a–b: τοῦ παντὸς οὐρανοῦ τὸ μέσον εἴληχεν, . . . πάντα δὲ περιλάμπει θείῳ καὶ ἀχράντῳ φωτί. Also 140a–d.

112. Jul. *Hel. R.* 135c: τὸ δὲ ἐν ἑνὶ πάντων συνεκτικόν.

113. See also Jul. *Hel. R.* 139c–d, τῆς ἐν τῷ νοητῷ πάντα ἐν ἑνὶ πάντων συνεχούσης, and 132c.

114. Macr. *Sat.* 1.17, 1.19.7; Festugière, *Révélation,* vol. 3, 158–60.

ation of man; Asclepius represents and guarantees man's ascent to the divine.[115] "And we recognize that Helios is their common lord, since he is celebrated as the father of Dionysus and the leader of the Muses.... Shall I now go on to tell you how Helios took thought for the health and safety of all men by begetting Asclepius to be the savior of the whole world?" (152d, 153a).[116] Both Dionysus and Asclepius, as subordinate yet consubstantial powers, are "blessings Helios has given to mankind" (152b) as distinct *hypostaseis,* distinct gods united as one to safeguard creation.

Julian's points, though complex, are straightforward. Helios as central, or middle, essence is three in one. As the son of the ingenerate First Cause, the One and the Good, he is, as the universal Demiurge, the carrier of the Father's creative force. Thus, he is in everything similar to the Father, but not the same, because created and creating. (The First Cause is not a Demiurge, having delegated this activity to Helios; see Eunomius, *Apol.* 15 and 24.) At the same time, he is an intellectual god, eternal as Thought, and identical with Zeus, identified in Plato's *Timaeus* as Demiurge. He is the perfect mediator, because he emanates from the One and is thus below the intelligible (noetic) sphere; he rules the intellectual (noeric) sphere and its gods, who are coeternal and consubstantial with him; and together with them he creates and rules the visible sphere (which is also eternal, and not created out of nothing). Therefore, again as in the *Timaeus,* he bestows particular benefit on man's soul, which he brought forth and guides back.[117] He is present in the visible world as the sun, which rules the celestial sphere as its center and apex, and unites everything harmoniously.[118] Through his helpers, especially Dionysus, he disperses his benefits everywhere; through Apollo, he makes his civilizing force manifest in each city. The universal, distinct, yet united power of Zeus-Helios-Apollo, originating with the Greeks (*genos Hellēnikon*), has found its best expression in the Roman *oikoumenē* as Helios's *agalma:* also distinct and dispersed, yet united as one in its emperor, the mediator between the celestial realm from which he springs and the physical realm he rules. Because this beautiful, divinely ordered harmony is made visible daily by the life-giving rays of the sun, "it is better for us to be persuaded to acknowledge the universal god than to honor, in place of the creator of all things, a god to whom has been given the leadership of a very small part."[119]

---

115. Mau, *Religionsphilosophie,* 64–66; R. Smith, *Julian's Gods,* 149–52, 158–60; Renucci, *Idées,* 117–21; Fauth, *Helios,* 155–59; Witt, "Jamblichus," 38–39.

116. In Jul. *CG* frs. 46,200a–b, 57.235b–c, Asclepius plays a role much like that of Christ.

117. Pl. *Ti* 41c6–d1, 41d4–42d5, 47a1–b2, 90c6–d7; *Epin.* 977a2–b8.

118. Eusebius wrote in *DE* 4.5: "There is one general, identical divine power governing the whole universe, creative of the heavens and of the stars, the living things in the earth and air and sea, the elements generally and individually and all natural things"; M. R. Barnes, "Background," 234–36.

119. Jul. *CG* fr. 28.148 b–c: ἄμεινον τὸν τῶν ὅλων θεὸν ἡμῖν πειθομένους ἐπιγνῶναι ... ἢ τὸν τοῦ ἐλαχίστου μέρους εἰληχότα τὴν ἡγεμονίαν ἀντὶ τοῦ πάντων τιμᾶν δημιουργοῦ. See also *Ep.* 111 (47 Wright), 433a–434b; Athanassiadi-Fowden, *Julian,* 167–69.

Against the Galileans

Julian's tripartite Helios as one, distinct from the *agennētos* First Cause as a creative force yet emanating from it—uniting in one the distinct creative *hypostaseis*, engaged in a continuous process of creation made visible through illumination (*phōs*)—forms part of and responds to contemporaneous Christian debates reflected in the writings of Eunomius and Gregory, but also Eusebius. As we have seen, everyone grappled with the central question, how a transcendent first cause, as father, generated or created—eventually—visible, material form, including man, and how such a creative process, deduced from its effect, the physical world and mankind, could assure salvation, understood as a return to the divine. The answers, though similar, differed in important nuances. Similar, because everyone relied on and interpreted the same classic normative texts—Plato's *Republic, Laws, Cratylus,* and *Timaeus,* augmented by other Platonic and Aristotelian texts as interpreted by Porphyry, Iamblichus and others. Different, because these texts permitted different readings, even more emphatically different when they served as the matrix for the reading of scripture—that is, for the formulation of Christianity. Julian responded to the reading of these texts as the formulation of Christianity in his conceptualization of Helios, Attis-*Logos,* and the Mother of the Gods as well as in his proclamation of imperial Roman rule as philosophy—which represents his creative expression of Iamblichan maxims. Julian, in his response, challenged Christians to answer his challenge that their God, if a god at all, was a latecomer, responsible for only a small part of the *oikoumenē,* Galilee. He called them to demonstrate that the Christian God was in fact the One in Three, the universal mediator between the first cause and creation, uniting all into one universal whole, and that their teachings were not an innovation, and thus false, but derived from the most ancient wisdom, from which everything else good and wise had emerged.[120]

Julian's work *Against the Galileans* (or *Against the Christians*) occupies a special place among his imperial pronouncements, orations, and letters.[121] In contrast to his other orations, written in short bursts of activity, often overnight and drawing on texts he knew by heart, the emperor wrote this work against, or as I will argue, for the sake of, the Christians by dedicating time and by preparing intensively to

---

120. Jul. *Ep.* 89b, *Epistle to the Priest Theodorus* (Wright 2, *Letter to a Priest*) 295d–296b.

121. Julian's own title might have differed; the scribes of the Greek manuscripts usually used titles to denote content. In 1898, Bidez and Cumont opted for *Against the Galileans;* a catalogue of Greek manuscripts from the sixteenth century in the Escorial edited by Charles Graux in 1880 also mentions a work *Against Galileans,* which reflects the first lines of Cyril's refutation, *Cyrille d'Alexandrie: Contre Julien,* vol. 1, livres 1 and 2, ed. and trans. Burguière and Évieux, 27–29. Prior to Bidez and Cumont, the most widely used title was *Against the Christians* (either *Kata* or *Pros*), based on Theodore of Mopsuestia's refutation; Julian, *Contra Galilaeos,* ed. and trans. Masaracchia, 12–13.

compose it. Writing (according to Libanius) in Antioch over the course of several months during the winter nights of 362 and 363, Julian appears to have planned the work as early as February or March 362 in Constantinople, immediately upon his accession as sole emperor.[122] He had already then publicly denounced renunciating Christians and uneducated Cynics as united by a misanthropic disregard for the common *politeia* of civilized persons and had characterized Christians as Galileans, a narrow ethnic group with no claim to universality.[123] And the emperor presented what he considered a true myth, that of Dionysus and of his own origin, in part to criticize the childish myths considered true by uneducated Galileans. In the same true myth (*Or.* 7.228c), he voiced his repugnance at the Christian practice of venerating the dead.[124] In his *Hymn to the Mother of the Gods,* he stressed that the Mother, Cybele, and no one else was truly god-bearing, *theotokos,* counting among her offspring Attis-*Logos,* a subordinated, mediating god created to give humans an approach to the divine through sacrifice, ritual, and the purifying effects of understanding mythical *paradoxa* reserved for the few rather than by belief in the material presence of a dubious divinity incarnate. In short, in Constantinople in the spring of 362 Julian had already begun to formulate and proclaim his principal criticisms of Christianity and his counterarguments. By the summer he had signaled to a wide public what he intended to do. As indicated already in the *Fürstenspiegel* he had addressed to Constantius as part of the second panegyric, imperial clemency and philanthropy demanded that Julian as emperor "teach and not punish the demented."[125] Writing on August 1 to the citizens of Bostra—an imperial letter also published in Antioch—he reiterated the sentiment of his letter regarding teachers just cited: "One must convince and educate [Christians] through reason, not through blows, insults, or physical torture."[126]

When Julian issued these imperial letters, he was already preparing *Against the Galileans.* In midsummer and again in late summer 362, he requested that the li-

---

122. For the date, Lib. *Or.* 18.178.

123. Julian used the term in two imperial letters, one inviting Aetius to court, the other revoking curial exemptions for Christian clergy; Jul. *Epp.* 46 (Wright 15), *To Aetius,* and 54 (Wright 39), *To the Byzacenians,* in conjunction with his law of March 13, 362, on the restoration of the *curia* (*CTh* 11.23.2). *Ep.* 54 was revoked by Valens and Valentinian (*CTh* 12.1.59, 12.2.17), reinforcing once again Constantius's provisions in *CTh* 12.1.49, revoked by Julian's letter; Julian, *Epistolario,* trans. and comm. Caltabiano, 248–49; Pack, *Städte,* 224–43; C. Drecoll, *Liturgien,* 55–58.

124. See Chapters 2 and 3 above.

125. Jul. *Ep.* 61c (Wright 36), *Or.* 2.79a–93d. The sentence could be read as applying only to children, as R. Smith, *Julian's Gods,* 208, reads it, but Julian's Platonic model and his other proclamations suggest that he had all Christians in mind.

126. Jul. *Ep.* 114 (Wright 41); in *Ep.* 61c (Wright 36) Julian said: "We ought, I think, to teach and not punish the demented."

brary of Bishop George of Alexandria, his former teacher murdered at the beginning of 362, be transferred to Antioch.[127] Julian, in the first extant letter about the transfer, exhorted Ecdicius, prefect of Egypt, to employ George's secretary to assure the conveyance of his deceased master's entire library, which the emperor knew very well, and threatened torture should volumes go missing. Porphyrius, Egypt's *katholikos*, or chief financial official, received the same order in another letter. Julian gave each recipient a short inventory: George's library contained many philosophical works of different schools, including commentaries; many rhetorical works; and most important, "many and varied works of the Galileans."[128] Julian's preparation and consultation of these works paid off. Libanius, in his *Epitaphius* for Julian, praises lavishly his three-volume work "attack[ing] the books in which that fellow from Palestine is claimed to be a god and son of a god," surpassing even the writings of "the old man from Tyre" on the same subject—none other than Porphyry. "And right pleased and happy may this Tyrian be to accept this statement, beaten, as it were, by his son."[129]

Most of the scholarly interest in Julian's *Against the Galileans* is *Quellenkritik*—writings on the relation of the work to its famous precursor, Porphyry's "against Christians." Ascertaining such a relationship or its absence is complicated by the fragmentary text of both works.[130] Porphyry's criticism was so effective that Constantine had already ordered the condemnation of his work at Nicaea. Methodius of Olympus, Eusebius of Caesarea, and Apollinarius of Laodicea composed long refutations, and later writers, most notably Jerome, Augustine, and Theodoret of Cyrrhus, also responded.[131] Eusebius composed two related refutations, the *Praeparatio Evangelica* (written prior to Nicaea) and the *Demonstratio Evangelica*. With their many citations, the *Praeparatio* and the *Demonstratio,* together with Jerome's response, offer the best means of reconstructing Porphyry's lost writings.[132]

---

127. Julian probably donated the library to the Traianaeum, the public library he completed in Antioch, before departing to Persia; Hahn, *Gewalt,* 179.

128. Jul. *Epp.* 106, 107 (Wright 38, 23); date: Julian, *Epistolario,* trans. and comm. Caltabiano, 204–5.

129. Lib. *Or.* 18.178, trans. Norman (Libanius, *Selected Orations*); for the number of volumes, *Cyrille d'Alexandrie: Contre Julien,* ed. and trans. Burguière and Évieux, 26–27.

130. *Iuliani Imperatoris librorum contra Christianos quae supersunt,* ed. Neumann, presented a text of most fragments of Julian's *Against the Galileans.* Celsus's work against the Christians is less relevant for Julian. It survives relatively intact, as excerpted in *Origen's Contra Celsum libri VIII,* ed. and trans. Marcovich.

131. For the condemnation, Socr. *HE* 1.9.30; Gel. Cyz. *HE* 2.36.

132. Harnack, *Porphyrius gegen die Christen,* is the principal edition of Porphyry's fragments against Christians, now translated into English, with additional fragments, by Berchman, *Porphyry against the Christians,* 118–225; he does not note Beatrice. See now *Porphyrii philosophi fragmenta,* ed. Smith. Scholars debate, however, whether Porphyry wrote a comprehensive work against the Christians (in 15 volumes), or whether his writings on that subject form part of other works, primarily the *Philosophy from Oracles,* so that there never was a distinct work against the Christians. Beatrice ("Towards a

A joint imperial edict by Theodosius II and Valentinian II in 448 condemned Porphyry's "madness" and consigned Julian's *Against the Galileans* to the flames.[133] Flames seem to have been necessary to refute Julian's three books. In 430, some seventy years after Julian's death, Cyril of Alexandria explained, in dedicating his refutation *Against Julian* to Emperor Theodosius II, that the work was necessary because "many adherents to the superstition" attacked Christians using Julian's works, "proclaiming [their] unparalleled efficacy, adding that there has never been a teacher among us [Christians] capable of refuting them."[134] Indeed, prior to Cyril, only Theodore of Mopsuestia and Philip of Side seem to have responded point by point to Julian's treatise, but their texts are almost entirely lost.[135] So, unfortunately, is Cyril's own refutation of Julian's three books. Only Cyril's ten books responding to Julian's first book are preserved in full; of his ten books refuting Julian's second volume only portions are extant, and no traces remain of either Julian's third book or Cyril's response to it.[136] Cyril of Alexandria's excerpts of Julian's treatise and a few quotations elsewhere are all that remains of *Against the Galileans*.[137]

Despite these limitations, we can gain a sense of Julian's opus because his introductory sentences present the plan of his work and his intentions: "It appears to me expedient to expose to all the reasons that have convinced me that the fabrication of the Galileans is a fiction men have composed out of malice. It has nothing divine, but acting on the irrational part of the soul that loves myths as children do, it has represented such marvelous tales to be trusted as truth. [I propose to write my

---

New Edition," esp. 355, and *Anonymi Monophysitae Theosophia*, xxvii) argues against one treatise, whereas Goulet, "Hypothèses," esp. 63-64, and Riedweg, "Porphyrios," defended the one-work thesis. Foundational for the traditional view is Meredith, "Porphyry." Other sources for the reconstruction of Porphyry's works against the Christians include Arnobius, and, in the 370s and 380s, Epiphanius's *Panarion* and Macarius Magnes's *Apokritikos*, or *The Monogenēs*. The latter represents a special case, because Macarius's paraphrases of the anti-Christian arguments may derive from Hierocles, who also wrote against Christians under Diocletian, or from Julian; the most recent editor, Goulet (*Macarios*, vol. 2), opts for Porphyry as the source; see vol. 1, p. 65, for the date and author, and pp. 66–149 for the source. For Hierocles, Digeser, *Making*, 91–114; and Meredith, "Porphyry," 1120–21.

133. Cyr. *Juln.* 1.1.3, with modifications by Justinian dating to 529 and 534. Neumann (*Iuliani imperatoris librorum contra Christianos quae supersunt*, ed. Neumann, 8–10) thinks the edict caused the destruction of Julian's writings.

134. Cyr. *Juln.* praef. 5; *Cyrille d'Alexandrie: Contre Julien*, ed. and trans. Burguière and Évieux, 10–20, for the date and Cyril's motivation. A final redaction occurred probably ca. 439–41.

135. *Cyrille d'Alexandrie: Contre Julien*, ed. and trans. Burguière and Évieux, 52–58. Guida, "Frammenti," has identified fragments cited by Theodore; idem, "Per un'edizione," and *Teodoro di Mopsuestia: Replica*, Guida, with new fragments from Julian's *CG*.

136. *Cyrille d'Alexandrie: Contre Julien*, ed. and trans. Burguière and Évieux, 29–30.

137. Julian, *Contra Galilaeos*, ed. and trans. Masaracchia, 12 n. 5 and 48, has added fragments identified since Neumann's edition, including some cited by Theodore, Jerome, Photius, and Arethas. In what follows I use her edition. A new edition of Cyril's work is in preparation and may result in further modifications; Huber-Rebenich and Chronz, "Cyrill."

treatise about all their teachings, but I wish to say first that if my readers intend to refute me, they must,] as in a court of law, not deviate from the task at hand, or, as they say, present counteraccusations until they have defended themselves against the first charges."[138]

In fragment 3.43a–b, Julian announced his four steps to expose the weaknesses of "all their teachings."[139] First, he will demonstrate where and how the idea of the gods originated; second, he will compare the religions of the Greeks and the Hebrews; third, he will "inquire of those who are neither Greeks nor Jews but belong to the sect [*hairesis*] of the Galileans why they have preferred the belief of the Jews to ours"; and then, in a further step, he will discuss "what can be the reason why they do not adhere even to the Jewish beliefs but have abandoned them also and followed a way of their own."[140] Such an inquiry is all the more pertinent since "refuting all that is good and valid, be it in us Greeks or the Hebrews of Moses, they in reality get from [both] what has been attached to both peoples like goddesses of doom: from the Jewish superficiality, atheism; and from our own indolence and vulgarity, a squalid [*phaulos*] and disorderly life; and they wish to call this the best form of religiosity [*theosebeia*]."[141]

Julian adduced arguments from philosophy, history, and textual exegesis to convince his Christian subjects that what they considered truth and universal revelation was an inferior myth that could be redeemed neither through allegorical nor by figurative reading (both forbidden by their own teaching, at any rate). This myth is devoid of reason (*alogos*) and dangerous, for it makes its believers outsiders, estranged from the common family of man and from the gods who created it. Julian was familiar with Porphyry's work and with anti-Christian polemic in general. But

---

138. Jul. *CG* frs. 1.39b and 2.42a: ἔχουσα μὲν οὐδὲν θεῖον, ἀποχρησαμένη δὲ τῷ φιλομύθῳ καὶ παιδαριώδει καὶ ἀνοήτῳ τῆς ψυχῆς μορίῳ, τὴν τερατολογίαν εἰς πίστιν ἤγαγεν ἀληθείας... ὥσπερ ἐν δικαστηρίῳ, μηδὲν ἔξωθεν πολυπραγμονεῖν μηδέ, τὸ λεγόμενον, ἀντικατηγορεῖν, ἕως ἂν ὑπὲρ τῶν πρώτων ἀπολογήσωνται. Jul. *CG* fr. 2.42a continues: "It is better and clearer [that they defend their idea] if they wish to refute any of our views; but when they are defending themselves against our charges, they may not respond with counteraccusation" (ἄμεινον μὲν γὰρ οὕτω, καὶ σαφέστερον ἰδίαν μὲν ἐνστήσασθαι πραγματείαν ὅταν τι τῶν παρ' ἡμῖν εὐθύνειν θέλωσιν, ἐν οἷς δὲ πρὸς τὰς παρ' ἡμῶν εὐθύνας ἀπολογοῦνται μηδὲ ἀντικατηγορεῖν). Julian and his opponents used a rhetorical technique known as *anaskeuē* and taught as part of the *progymnasmata*: how to entangle the adversary in his own contradictions; Bouffartigue, "Philosophie," 124–26.

139. I am following Riedweg, "Mit Stoa," 62, who identifies four steps rather than three.

140. ἀλλὰ κἀκείνων ἀποστάντες ἰδίαν ὁδὸν ἐτράποντο.

141. τὰς παραπεπηγυίας τοῖς ἔθνεσιν ὥσπερ τινὰς Κῆρας δρεπόμενοι... τοῦτο τὴν ἀρίστην θεοσέβειαν ὀνομάζεσθαι ἠθέλησαν." Neumann (*Iuliani imperatoris librorum contra Christianos quae supersunt*, ed. Neumann, 203) based his edition of the fragments on this outline, thus ordering the fragments thematically (and highlighting convergences with Porphyry and Celsus). Masaracchia's edition [Julian, *Contra Galilaeos*, ed. and trans. Masaracchia, 39–50] follows the order of Cyril's *Against Julian*. I cite according to Masaracchia's numbering but add Neumann's notations as used in Wright's translation.

as a follower of Iamblichus and, more important, a Roman emperor, in Jean Bouffartigue's words, Julian "avait à exprimer, face au christianisme, une autre position idéologique [than Porphyry's]."[142] Julian wished to educate and to cure his Christian subjects, admonishing them to return to the family of mankind, so that they no longer threatened the well-being of the *oikoumenē* through their desertion, or *apostasis.*

The emperor, rather than continue where Porphyry had left off, composed a work tailored to his concerns. Julian responded to Eusebius's *Praeparatio* and *Demonstratio Evangelica:* that is, to Christian responses to Porphyry.[143] George's library may well have included other treatises *Ad Graecos de vera religione,* such as one written (perhaps) by Marcellus of Ancyra that Cyril later used to respond to Julian. Julian's letter to Photinus, dated to January or February 363, suggests that he had read such works.[144] Julian praised Photinus because he "absolutely [did not] introduce into a maternal uterus him whom [he] thought a god," and Julian declared Photinus far closer "to the truth and salvation" than Diodore of Tarsus, then presbyter in Antioch, who had attacked Photinus's views of two *hypostaseis* of the *Logos,* one divine, one human (read polemically as considering Jesus a mere man).[145] Julian despised Diodore as a "sharp-witted sophist of a rustic religion" who had injured the common good by sailing to Athens to study philosophy, only "to use rhetorical techniques to arm his hateful tongue against the heavenly god." But with the help of the Muses and the Tyche (of Antioch), Julian continued in the same letter, he would demonstrate that the divinity Diodore had invented for Christ was false. Julian thus wrote in the context of contemporary Christian debates and responded to them specifically. He knew Photinus and Diodore's views, and was aware of and may have read what Diodore had written against "the mysteries of the Greeks" (perhaps the lost *Against Plato about God and the Gods*).[146]

---

142. Bouffartigue, *Empereur Julien,* 385. Moreover, Julian, unlike Porphyry and Celsus, did not write against Christianity while it was still considered an illegitimate superstition. Recent discussions concur that Julian knew both Porphyry's and Celsus's arguments but that he also engaged in standard anti-Christian polemic. Bouffartigue *Empereur Julien,* 380–95, and "Philosophie") sees a lesser degree of dependence on Celsus than Riedweg ("Mit Stoa," 62–63, 79–81) and Meredith ("Porphyry," 1147). Scholars agree, however, that Julian's work is derivative; Riedweg, "Mit Stoa," 68, and R. Smith, *Julian's Gods,* 92. The debate between R. Smith, *Julian's Gods,* and Bouffartigue, "Philosophie," on whether Julian's anti-Christianity was rooted in his philosophical convictions or in his polytheistic sentiments overlooks that for Julian all was one organic whole.

143. Julian knew Eus. *PE* and at least Book 1 of the *DE;* Bouffartigue, *Empereur Julien,* 300, 384–89.

144. Jul. *Ep.* 90 (Wright 55); Julian, *Epistolario,* trans. and comm. Caltabiano, 198, 267–68; Bouffartigue, *Empereur Julien,* 117–19. For Marcellus as author of the Ps.-Justin *Ad Graecos* and for Julian's potential knowledge of the text, or at least its arguments, Riedweg, *Ps.-Justin,* 28–53, 167–82, and "Mit Stoa," 69–70; critiqued by Parvis, *Marcellus,* 247.

145. For Photinus, see above, Chapter 6; Vinzent, "Gottes Wesen"; Parvis, *Marcellus,* 30–37.

146. Jul. *CG* frs. 62.253b–254b and 64.262c, mention Photinus again. Diodore and his disciple Theodore of Mopsuestia returned the favor and attacked Julian (posthumously). Further, as will be dis-

Furthermore, Julian did not intend to rebut a Eusebius or a Diodore point by point. Rather, as philosopher-king and Flavian emperor, he was most concerned to argue the illegitimacy of Christianity as the *religio* of the Roman ruler of the entire universal *oikoumenē* and the guarantor of the well-being of all. Eusebius, for example, had claimed the Christian God as the founder of Rome's greatness; for him Christ was the best possible guardian of the *oikoumenē*. Indeed, Eusebius had praised Constantine as a new Moses, the true exemplar of a divinely ordained Roman ruler as philosopher.[147] For Julian, this fatally incorrect innovation—an apostasy from the true origins of imperial power (of human existence, even)—had dramatic results. It had brought forth a criminal emperor who murdered his kin, and "through the folly of the Galileans almost everything was turned upside down; solely through the grace of the gods have we all been saved."[148]

Against the Galileans, though important, was but one tool in Julian's arsenal to save the *koina tōn Rhōmaiōn* from its recent deviations (Constantius's antipagan legislation was a mere ten years in the past); its integral role in Julian's imperial program mitigates, from a methodological perspective, the fragmentary nature of the treatise.[149] It was yet another manifestation of the emperor's exemplary qualities as Platonic ruler: motivated by his imperial clemency and *philanthrōpia*, he wished to enlighten those caught in the fog of darkness and to reintegrate them into the family of men created by Zeus-Helios as one universal community. The reaction of Christians attests that they too were aware of Julian's challenge as comprehensive, comprising but far exceeding *Against the Galileans*. Christians reacted by composing point-by-point rebuttals and, as Gregory of Nazianzus demonstrates, by announcing and defending their claim to the universality Rome embodied. And they did so equally comprehensively. From Christology, cosmology, and history to exegesis, all subsequent debates about Christian orthodoxy and orthopraxis responded to Julian's challenge to a degree modern scholars have not fully appreciated.[150]

---

cussed below in the chapters that follow, Diodore responded to Julian by developing a Christology that sought to emphasize Christ's divinity by downplaying his human characteristics. He was eventually considered heretical, as was Theodore. For Diodore's lost work, Bouffartigue, *Empereur Julien*, 119.

147. In his *Life of Constantine*, the last book of the *HE*, the *Tricennial Orations* 7.5, but also in his *Commentary on Isaiah*; see Rapp, "Imperial Ideology"; Hollerich, *Eusebius of Caesarea's "Commentary on Isaiah"*; Mazza, "Filosofia," 90–106; Drake, *In Praise of Constantine*, 65–68, 149–51. The interconnectedness of Roman imperial rule and Christianity was a topos already developed in earlier Christian apologetics, which gained new significance with Constantine. The bibliography on the subject is vast; see (e.g.) Rizzi, "Cittadinanza," and "Problematiche"; Bowersock, "From Emperor to Bishop."

148. Jul. *Ep.* 83 (Wright 37), *To Atarbius*: διὰ μὲν γὰρ τὴν . . . Γαλιλαίων μωρίαν ὀλίγου δεῖν ἅπαντα ἀνετράπη, διὰ δὲ τὴν τῶν θεῶν εὐμένειαν σωζόμεθα πάντες.

149. After Constantius's defeat of Magnentius in 353 his antipagan legislation increased; (e.g.) *CTh* 16.10.5 and 6, 11.16.4 and 5; Cuneo, *Legislazione*, xci–xcv, cix–cxi, 222, 288; T. D. Barnes, "Christians," esp. 332.

150. This is slowly changing; see F. Thome, *Historia*, 219–20, and García, *Homilias*, 177–228.

Barbarian Wisdom and Greek Universalism: Porphyry and Eusebius Before I discuss Julian's arguments in *Against the Galileans*, I want to return to Eusebius's rebuttal of Porphyry's attacks, which Julian knew and cited, as to do so will help to clarify some of the central points under debate.[151] As is apparent from the discussion of Greekness and Romanness, from the opening sentences of *Against the Galileans*, and from the very epithet the emperor chose for the Christians, the chief bone of contention was the claim to universality. Was there one way for all to approach the divine and salvation; and if so, which way, and who owned it? Assuming that Rome's greatness reflected divine Providence—as everyone agreed—which divinity's providence? And what did Rome stand for, as a consequence? As I mentioned in Chapter 6, Eusebius's response to Porphyry belongs to a debate among followers of Plotinus—including Christians like Origen—whether the soul could ascend to the divine by only one path or by several possible paths, and whether oracles, statues, sacrifices, and rituals were necessary to that ascent. If they were, then were they required of every soul, or only of those with souls less purified than the philosophers'? Eusebius's *Praeparatio* and *Demonstratio*, composed between 313 and 324, respond primarily to Porphyry; after Plato, he is the author cited most often in them.[152]

Porphyry claimed that many different approaches led to the divine, as indicated by those of different ethnic groups, and that all were efficacious in gaining for the lower parts of the soul and those less purified at least some access to the lower divine spheres. He wrote, however, that true ascent was reserved for very few, because it was immaterial and required the philosopher's purification, to which there was no sacrificial, oracular, or ritual shortcut.[153] Porphyry reached his conclusion by pursuing significant research according to a methodological principle common to later Platonists: strict textual exegesis to ascertain the authenticity of a given text, including divine sayings or oracles.[154] By this method Porphyry had identified, in Eusebius's words, a "'theosophy,' as he liked to call it," a universal philosophy that

---

151. Specifically, Eus. *PE* and Book 1 of the *DE*. Both are massive tomes, and the following summary by necessity simplifies. So far as I am aware, Bouffartigue, *Empereur Julien*, 385–88, is the only scholar to discuss the *PE*'s influence on the *CG* in some detail. Translations of Porphyry are Berchman's, with my modifications. I follow Goulet, "Hypothèses," 64–97, in assuming that Porphyry attacked Christians in at least two distinct texts: that is, his criticism of oracles comes from *Philosophy from Oracles*, and the textual criticism from *Against the Christians*. J. J. O'Meara, "Porphyry's *Philosophy from Oracles*," focuses on Augustine.

152. Eusebius's citations of Porphyry's works would have given Julian insight into his thinking, even if he knew Porphyry's arguments only through Iamblichus; Bouffartigue, *Empereur Julien*, 337–40, 361–63, 374–76, 382–85. Given Libanius's comment, Julian may well have had direct access to Porphyry's writings against Christians.

153. Saffrey, "Connaissance."

154. Dawson, *Allegorical Readers*.

allowed different, ethnically specific approaches—which, however, revealed but one truth once these approaches had been interpreted by the enlightened philosophers.[155] Thus a true philosopher—a Greek Platonist—could understand the cultic practices proper and appropriate to other peoples with ancient wisdom, like the Egyptians, Phoenicians, or Hebrews, so that they revealed to him "the way of the blessed" (*hodos makarōn, PE* 9.10.2), even if the uninitiated might recognize only the literal meaning of their local religious customs. Though different gods had been assigned to different local *politeiai,* with their own particular practices, only those few who knew how to reveal the true nature of the customs proper to the ethnic gods could find the true philosophy uniting all, for "the way of the blessed . . . is both steep and rough."[156]

Porphyry's teachings in *On Statues,* as preserved by Eusebius, present the paradigm of his figurative or revelatory reading.[157] "It is unremarkable that the uneducated believe that statues are nothing but wood and stone, just as the illiterate see stelae as stones, tablets as pieces of wood, and books as nothing but woven papyrus." Those properly schooled, however, know "how to read from statues, just as from books, the things written there concerning the gods" (*PE* 3.7.1). Thus, purified theologians can properly read Zeus's anthropomorphic representations. Since they dwell, like Zeus, in both the intelligible and the sensible world, they too can comprehend what is true in every image, ritual, and myth, even in barbarian icons and their myths, just as they comprehend Zeus's statue: for the theologians, "mind was that according to which [Zeus] wrought and by generative laws brought all things to perfection; and he is seated, indicating the steadfastness of his power; and he is naked on top because he is evident in the intellectual and heavenly parts of the cosmos" (*PE* 3.9.5).[158]

Crucial to such readings and essential to the way of the blessed, however, were Greek wisdom and Greek philosophy. Greek philosophers might discern paths to universal truth in the religious and civic practices of different peoples, but not the other way round. No barbarians, be they Egyptian, Phoenician, or Hebrew, could claim universality based on customs proper to their own sphere in the *oikoumenē*: that was the prerogative of the Greeks. Christians, therefore, erred in four major ways. First, their wisdom did not reflect ancient custom but was an innovation; oth-

---

155. Eus. *PE* 4.6.3–4: εἴς . . . προτροπὴν ἧς αὐτῷ φίλον ὀνομάζειν θεοσοφίας. Schott, "Founding Platonopolis," and "Porphyry."

156. See also Porph. *Phil. ex Orac.* fr. 303f = Eus. *PE* 4.7.2: the differing ethnic traditions offer "an account of many philosophical doctrines that the gods declared to be true."

157. Dawson (*Allegorical Readers,* 5, but also 2, 8–9) suggests the term "figurative" to describe exegetic readings that include allegorical, typological, and etymological interpretations, as exemplified by the citations of Porphyry in Eusebius's *PE*. For Porphyry's teachings about statues in the context of theurgy, see also Berchman, *Porphyry,* 47–56.

158. See Plot. *Enn.* 5.8.

erwise it would remain inexplicable "how ... a compassionate and merciful God [can] allow that from Adam to Moses, and from Moses to the appearance of Christ, all nations perish out of ignorance of the law and the community of God."[159] Second, their claim to universal truth was false, because in addition to being novel their revelations were limited in time and in place to a very small group under Roman control. "Why has the so-called savior made himself unavailable in all these centuries; what then should happen to Latin souls, who are deprived of Christ's grace, who had not appeared yet up to the time of Augustus? But they should not say that mankind has been cared for by the old Law of the Jews; the Law of the Jews appeared a long time afterwards and flourished in a tiny area of Syria only."[160] Third, unlike the Hebrews, who worship a local god well integrated into the hierarchy of ethnicities that structures access to the "way of the blessed" (*PE* 9.10.1–2), Christians worshipped as a god merely a wise human being. Finally, again unlike the Hebrews, Christians have abandoned their ancestral gods twice. They are "neither Greeks nor Jews" (*PE* 1.2.1–4), "and how can men not be in every way impious and atheistic who have abandoned [*apostantes*] ancestral customs by which every state and nation has been nurtured?" (*PE* 1.2.2).

Worse, Christians, who had twice rejected their ancestral traditions, had even abandoned superior Greekness, which alone permitted the reading of truth in ethnic diversity, for barbaric traditions novel to them. "To what kinds of punishments would they not be justly subjected, who deserting their ancestral customs have become zealots for the foreign [*othneiōn*] mythologies of the Jews, who are in ill repute among all men? And would it not be proof of extreme evil and lightheartedness to put aside the customs of their own peoples [*tōn oikeiōn*] and choose with unreasonable and unquestioning faith [*alogōi de kai anexetastōi pistei*] those of the impious adversaries of all people?" (*PE* 1.2.3–4). Jewish customs, including religious customs, were acceptable in the sphere proper to the Hebrews; but were they to claim that they alone possess universal truth, that would be intolerable. For Christians to make just such a claim based on their exceedingly limited teachings, read incorrectly, which they already abused "to carve out for themselves a new way in a pathless desert, that adheres to the ways neither of the Greeks nor the Jews" (*PE* 1.2.4), and above all not to that of the blessed, was an abomination meriting such imperial punishment as the Great Persecution.[161]

Eusebius reacted to Porphyry by using similar methods of textual exegesis (hence his citations) in order to demonstrate Christians had justly and reasonably abandoned the religion of their forefathers the Greeks, preferring "the oracles [*logia*] of the Hebrews" to the ideas of the (Greek) philosophers. And he justified their

---

159. Cited in Jer. *Ep.* 133.9, *Ad Ctesiph.* = fr. 82 Harnack; Berchman, *Porphyry*, 170.
160. Aug. *Ep.* 102.8 = fr. 81 Harnack; Berchman, *Porphyry*, 172.
161. Digeser, "Power."

decision not to follow the Law of the Hebrews, even though they used Hebrew writings and oracles (*PE* 15.62.16–18).[162] Eusebius, to make his points, presented a cosmogony, bringing the origin narratives of the Phoenicians, Egyptians, and Greeks into a unified narrative of descent (or, rather, decline), which he then contrasted with the Hebrews' narrative of origin. In the process, he showed how the treatment of humans as gods and the impiety of sacrifice, originating with the Phoenicians, was adopted subsequently by the Egyptians and Greeks. The *Preparatio Evangelica* thus proceeds as summarized by Eusebius in Book 1.6.5–7 and Book 15.1: six books refute polytheism—that is, the ancient wisdom of the Phoenicians, the Egyptians, and the Greeks and Romans. The first three of these six books criticize the cosmogonies taught by their theologians and the myths "staged by the children of their theologians and poets" (*PE* 15.1). In Book 3, Eusebius attacks the allegorical interpretations—that is, the figurative readings of the *paradoxa* of these myths, offered by theologians and philosophers—that integrated diverse myths into a single superior Greekness.[163] In Books 4–6, Eusebius used a tripartite scheme of theology (mythical, physical, and political: *PE* 4.1.2) to criticize political theology based on oracular practices, sacrifices, statues, and other rituals, all of which, he argued, evolved out of the impious practices he had just localized in the original impiety of the Phoenicians. Such practices are not efficacious and do not reveal truth, as demonstrated by the narrative of their descent and proved by the death of oracles at the advent of Christ, and the ambiguity and fatalism or the absence of free will evident in the political theologies derived from such oracles, foolishly accepted by misguided rulers. (At *PE* 5.23.4 and 5.27.5 he cites approvingly Oenomaus of Gadara's criticism of oracles, subsequently attacked by Julian in *Against Heraclius*: e.g., *Or*. 7.209b.)

Eusebius's counternarrative of descent demonstrated how Greeks came late to the game and took their practices from other, older, wiser barbarian nations that had worshipped astral beings before descending to the worship of statues and to animal sacrifice (*PE* 1.9.9–13); Rome was also a wiser nation because Numa, enlightened by Moses, had forbidden worship of statues and rejected Greek theories of the gods (*PE* 2.7.9, 9.6.3–4). Nonetheless, only Christ could truly save Rome, though Augustus had prepared a unified realm (*PE* 1.4.4).[164] The Greeks picked the

---

162. See Sirinelli's introduction in *Eusèbe de Césarée: La préparation évangélique*, ed. and trans. des Places, Sirinelli, and Favrelle, vol. 1, 8–15, 28–34, 38–47, 76–84; Eusebius of Caesarea, *The Preparation of the Gospel*, trans. Gifford. *Eusebio di Cesarea: Dimostrazione evangelica*, ed. and trans. Carrara. Johnson, *Ethnicity*, esp. 55–93.

163. To make his point, Eusebius emphasized the differences among the philosophers, citing Porphyry's criticism of ancient Egyptian allegories (*PE* 1.9.25) and Plato's *Cratylus*: for him, such variations invalidate these philosophers' readings (*PE* 3.3.12).

164. Johnson, *Ethnicity*, 174–78, emphasizes that Eusebius stressed Augustus's sole rule during a Tetrarchic emperor's reign, arguing that Eusebius thus made a subversive move.

wrong barbarian nations to steal from, for these nations too had degenerated into full-scale impieties. As Eusebius's account of the various cosmogonies revealed, the myths of origin contained no deeper truths, because even the philosophers who read them allegorically differed, giving "first one allegorical rendering [of the gods and goddesses] and afterwards another" (*PE* 3.3.12). The myths are thus mere stories of human beings subsequently divinized. Here the statues provide additional evidence: they are nothing but representations of human beings. To worship them is to prefer man-made effigies to the universal creator of everything (*PE* 3.3.13–15, 3.4.4). It was therefore necessary and good to depart from such practices (*PE* 1.6.7, 3.1.1–6.11.83).

In Books 7–15, Eusebius turned to the descent of the Jews, whom the Christians had also justly deserted. He separates Hebrews and Jews to demonstrate why among the ancient peoples the Hebrews, as "friends of God" and "royal priesthood" (*PE* 7.4.6), are most ancient and alone possess superior wisdom, but why some of them descended as Jews: during their exile in Egypt, the descendants of Joseph assimilated to the impious customs of the Egyptians. Not even Moses, their "leader and lawgiver," could re-form in their souls the ancient purity (*PE* 7.8.37). "Moses' polity," Aaron Johnson explains, "was meant to function as a remedial form of legislation until the coming of Christ.... Christ's 'customs and ordinances' were to replace those of Moses."[165] Book 10 is central to Eusebius's argument: even Greek historians agree, he avers, that Greek civilization is derivative, because all that was best and rational in its most important intellectual leader, Plato, had been garnered while he traveled in Palestine. In Books 11–13, on the congruencies between Plato and Moses, Eusebius shows that the best Greek philosopher was a translator of the principal lawgiver of the Hebrews. Books 14 and 15 highlight again the contradictions and disagreements within the various Greek philosophical schools, denying any claim on their part to lead to one universal truth: that path, proved in words and in deeds, belonged solely to the true offspring of the Hebrews, the Christians, who had turned away from both the degenerate Greeks and the Jews toward the sole universal creator—points Eusebius further elaborated in the *Demonstratio*.[166]

Not content to refute Porphyry, Eusebius also wished to persuade others through

---

165. Johnson, *Ethnicity*, 108, 94–125.

166. Eus. *PE* 1.3.7: "All words are superfluous when the works [*erga*] are more manifest and plainer than words, works that the divine and heavenly power of our Savior distinctly exhibits even now." According to Bouffartigue, *Empereur Julien*, 387–88, Julian knew Book 1 of the *DE*; but because Cyril's refutation of that part of the *CG* in which Julian engaged the New Testament is lost, we cannot be certain. In Book 1 of the *DE* Eusebius agreed with Porphyry and others that Mosaic Law was circumscribed by time and place. He concluded that it thus required a second Law to realize the universal truth contained in the first: Christianity (*DE* 1.2). Julian reversed that point to show that Moses had intended his Law to be eternal and universal, whereas the so-called second Law, Christianity, was limited in time and space (*CG* fr. 75.319d).

reason: his work ought to "play its role well, to serve as elementary formation and introduction and to adapt itself to those who will come to us from the nations [i.e., the Greeks]" (*PE* 1.1.12). To that effect, Eusebius was keen to demonstrate that Greek philosophy followed Hebrew wisdom; even Plato had come late and had only borrowed imperfectly. Thus, "we gladly welcome all that is noble and excellent in him, and bid a long farewell to what is not of such character" (*PE* 13.21.14). Plato was useful insofar as he preserved and transmitted Hebrew reason and wisdom to the Greeks, but true reason resided alone in "the precise knowledge of the essential notions of the mysterious economy relating to our Savior and Lord Jesus, Christ of God." This point was crucial, because certain persons among the Greeks, such as Porphyry, "imagine in effect that Christianity respects no logic [*logos*]" and that Christians "base their beliefs on an unreasonable and unquestioned faith [*alogōi de pistei kai anexetastōi*]" (*PE* 1.1.11).[167]

Julian's Response   Writing *Against the Galileans,* Julian both reacted as a follower of Iamblichus to certain assertions made by Porphyry and refuted persons such as Eusebius and his claims that Christians, as true followers of the most ancient and the only wise Hebrews, alone represented the way.[168] In the arrangement of the fragments quoted by Cyril of Alexandria, Julian too began his discourse with cosmogony and cosmology, with a narrative of descent: he compared the cosmogony of Plato's *Timaeus* with Moses' Genesis "so that it will become clear which one of the two is the greater and more worthy of God, Plato 'the idolater,' or the one about whom scripture says that God spoke to him mouth to mouth": Plato's sophisticated philosophical proof by far surpassed Moses' story of a limited creative god of a subordinate nature.[169]

Julian introduced his comparison with a brief statement about the Greek myths

---

167. *Eusèbe de Césarée: La préparation évangélique,* ed. and trans. Sirinelli, Favrelle, and des Places, 72, and 71–75; see also Eus. *PE* 1.2.4, 1.3.1. Johnson, *Ethnicity,* 128–52. For Eusebius's place in an apologetic tradition, Johnson, *Ethnicity,* passim, and Riedweg, "Mit Stoa," 62. For pre-Constantinian apologetics, Wlosok, *Apologétique;* Digeser, *Making;* Rizzi, "Cittadinanza," and "Problematiche"; Renucci, *Idées,* 244–53, and Fiedrowicz, *Apologie.*

168. Iamblichus argued that all rituals, from sacrifice to philosophical *askēsis,* performed *erga* the gods demanded of everyone; Liefferinge, *Théurgie,* 91; Camplani and Zambon, "Sacrificio."

169. Jul. *CG* fr. 6.49b: τίς ὁ κρείττων καὶ τίς ἄξιος τοῦ θεοῦ μᾶλλον, ἆρ' ὁ τοῖς εἰδώλοις λελατρευκὼς Πλάτων ἢ περὶ οὗ φησιν ἡ γραφὴ ὅτι στόμα κατὰ στόμα ἐλάλησεν ὁ θεὸς αὐτῷ. Julian cited Genesis 1–17 nearly in full. Eusebius spoke of Moses' relation to God as "mouth to mouth" in his *Prophetic Eclogues* 22.1064b; earlier he discussed who saw or did not see God, 22.1049b–1053a. He also compared Genesis and Plato's *Timaeus* in *PE* 11.29.1–4, 30.1–2, 31.1. Further, both Eusebius and Julian cite Pl. *Ti* 41a–b in *PE* 11.32.4 and 13.18.10 and at *CG* fr. 9.58b; Origen, *Cels.* 4.56, had also compared both. Bouffartigue, *Empereur Julien,* 386, suggests that the comparison originated in a Christian milieu, and Droge, *Homer or Moses?* 12–72 and passim, traces it back to Jewish texts. Greeks, the dominant cultural force, had little interest in such a comparison.

of the origin of the gods and the cosmos: "They are surely incredible and monstrous." Kronos ate and regurgitated his children; Zeus had intercourse with his mother and with their daughter, whom he married to another; Dionysus had been dismembered and reconstituted (*CG* fr. 4.44a). But as he had pointed out in his other writings, Julian like Iamblichus considered such literal monstrosities *paradoxa,* sacred signs and symbols that guided the initiated and allowed them "to heal the souls [of men] as well as their bodies, and to bring about the presence of the gods [*theōn poiei parousias*]." Christians instead followed a childish fable that had nothing divine and led nowhere (fr. 1.39b): Julian compared the religious traditions of the Greeks and the Hebrews to explain the inexplicable—why Christians, though Greeks, had deserted both their own ethnicity and that of the Hebrews, to become mere Galileans (fr. 3.43a).[170]

According to Plato and Julian, all human beings by nature have a sense of the divine, "whether individual persons or peoples. Each of us believes spontaneously in a divine entity even if all cannot attain precise knowledge about it; nor is it possible for him who has attained it to communicate it to all." All humans are by nature united to the heavens and to the gods that dwell in them (*CG* fr. 7.52b–d).[171] To recognize the divine is an innate and unteachable human ability, because, as Plato said: "The heaven or the cosmos ... was generated in truth through the Providence of the god" (fr. 8.57c–d; Pl. *Ti* 28b). Humans, that is, recognize the divine because they were created as the cosmos was. Julian's subsequent explication of Plato's *Timaeus* summarizes essential aspects of his *Hymn to King Helios*:[172] the true universal creator or Demiurge is that of Plato, who said that "the gods of the gods, of whose works I am the Creator [*dēmiourgos*] and Father, will be indissoluble because I want it to be so" (fr. 9.58b; Pl. *Ti* 41a–d). Moses' God, as the analysis of Genesis proves, was a local creative god. Furthermore, the true universal Creator or Demiurge emanates from but is not the same as the Highest One. Therefore, Moses' God, even if he were more than a local god, cannot be that Highest One. This Genesis admits, since proper reading ascertains that its God is "not a creator of beings without body but merely an organizer of matter already in existence."[173] That is, he stands on a par with the lower creative gods that create matter, such as those who aid Helios in his creative work (fr. 11.69c).

According to Plato, the sun, the moon, the stars, and the heavens are visible gods,

---

170. Jul. *Or.* 7.216c; cf. 7.205c–207d; F. Thome, *Historia,* 66–72. On the value of myths for approaching the divine, Iamb. *Myst. Aegypt.* 3.13.131.4, 7.4.255.10–1; Proclus *In R.* 1.78.18–79.4, and *In Ti.* 1.29.31 on Plato *Ti.* 17b–c; Salut. *De diis* 15.2.6; Dillon, "Image," 248–53.

171. Jul. *Ep.* 111 (Wright 47), *To the Alexandrians,* 434b–435a; Riedweg, "Mit Stoa," 69–70; Meredith, "Porphyry," 1140–41.

172. E.g., Jul. *Hel. R.* 131c, 151a–152a, 156c–157a.

173. Jul. *CG* frs. 6.49e, ἀσωμάτων μὲν οὐδενὸς ποιητήν, ὕλης δὲ ὑποκειμένης κοσμήτορα, and 18.96c–e.

but they are images (*eikones*) of the intelligible (noetic) and intellectual (noeric) gods, with which they are "coexistent and by whom they have been begotten and from whom they proceed" (*CG* fr. 10.65b–c).[174] One supreme divinity begat all creative powers in the intelligible and intellectual world as archetypes of the visible one, where the creative gods begat all else, "heavens, mankind, and animals too, . . . all the way down to the creeping things."[175] What the Demiurge has created, namely the cosmos as a whole and man's soul, is immortal, whereas the lower creative gods also created mortal components.[176] If there were no difference between heaven and earth, between immortal gods and mortal beings, then one creator god—as Moses seems to think—would suffice; Genesis, in contrast to *Timaeus,* does not account for the difference between immortal and mortal. "But since there is a great gulf fixed between immortals and mortals, which does not grow or diminish as it happens to beings subject to mortality and dissolution, it follows that one set of gods was the creative cause of the one [i.e., mortals], and a different set was that of the others [i.e., the immortal gods].[177] Moses' Genesis presents its creator God as the sole creator of everything. This is imprecise to an extreme, since it does not account for the gulf separating mortal and immortal. Thus, exacting exegesis proves Moses' God to belong to the lower creative gods (fr. 11.69c). As such, this god belongs to the well-ordered, harmonious whole of the cosmos, with clearly delineated powers. Since he has explicitly "chosen the Hebrew people" (fr. 19.99e), he is one of several subordinate gods in charge of particular ethnicities. "Our people say that the Demiurge is the common Father and King of All Things,[178] but that he has assigned the remaining affairs of the peoples to gods who rule over these peoples and hold cities; of those [gods], each governs his own part in the manner particular [*oikeios*] to him," acting like viceroys (*hyparchoi basileōs*) in the Roman Empire, each administering his own province in the interest of the supreme ruler (frs. 21.115d, 28.148b).

That each *ethnos* has its own presiding god also accounts for the differences between different ethnicities, their characteristic aspects, and the differences in the laws that govern them, "because the peoples over which the gods preside conform

---

174. γεννηθέντας καὶ προσελθόντας. The argument is based on Pl. *Ti.* 28b, 39b–c, 41a–d. Bouffartigue, "Philosophie," 126–27, points out that Julian presents two cosmogonies, one strictly Platonic, the other more Iamblichan.

175. *Pace* Julian, *Contra Galilaeos,* ed. and trans. Masaracchia, 51 n. 2, I read this as the Demiurge creating both the immaterial and the visible realms.

176. Salut. *De diis* 8.1; Jul. *Or.* 6.182d, 194d; Iamb. *Myst.* 269.1–5.

177. Jul. *CG* frs. 10.65e–66a, εἰ δὲ πολὺ τὸ μέσον ἐστὶν ἀθανάτων καὶ θνητῶν, οὐδεμιᾷ προσθήκῃ μεῖζον οὐδὲ ἀφαιρέσει μειούμενον πρὸς τὰ θνητὰ καὶ ἐπίκηρα αἴτιον εἶναι προσήκει τούτων μὲν ἄλλους, ἑτέρων δὲ ἑτέρους, and 11.69b–d.

178. For *koinon,* "common," omitted in Masaracchia's text, see Riedweg, "Mit Stoa," 72 n. 106.

each to the nature of their proper [*oikeioi*] gods."¹⁷⁹ This subdivision of labor reflects the ordering hand of the divine *Pronoia* (Providence, made visible in Roman imperial rule): if ethnic differences were merely accidental or human invention rather than divinely ordered, there would be no reason to assume—as all humans do—that the cosmos is governed by Providence. The common belief of all human beings in the divine noted above, however, reflects the existence of one universal divine Providence, one universal truth that governs the polymorphous community.¹⁸⁰

Moses' account of the differences between peoples in the myth of the Tower of Babel fittingly reflects his God's limited scope. He is concerned merely with "the confusion of language," with no thought of "the greater and more perfect things," such as peoples' "way of life, character, inclination, good laws, and political constitution."¹⁸¹ The universal Demiurge has assigned Moses' God a circumscribed domain because of his deficiencies, reflected in the history of the people proper (*oikeiōs*) to him (*CG* fr. 36.171e).¹⁸² Because this god is angry, jealous, vengeful, and selfishly centered on worship particular only to him and, as a lawgiver, gave his people a "harsh and stern, savage, and barbarous law" (fr. 47.202a; also frs. 16, 17, 30, 33, 36), he condemned his people to slavery and dispersion (fr. 49.209d). Compare his harshness to the benevolent clemency of the Romans (visible in emperors such as Julian) vis-à-vis those who have transgressed—*parcere subiectis* (Verg. *Aen.* 6.853; the *Misopogon* was also not far from Julian's mind: fr. 35.168c, *Ep.* 89b.289b–c). Who, asked to choose, would reasonably question whether "it is better to be free without interruption and to dominate the greater part of the land and the sea for a total of two thousand years or to be slaves and to live at the command of others"?¹⁸³

Julian cannot fathom why anyone would want to abandon the common, universal gods of the Greeks and Romans for the particular one of the Hebrews. Reason and stringent exegesis prove beyond doubt the superiority of the former. In accord with divine Providence the gods of the Greeks and the Romans have given their peoples good literature and arts, good laws, good customs, a good political system, and world dominion, "even though the impostor Eusebius alleges that even

---

179. Jul. *CG* frs. 21.115d–116c, καθ' ἑκάστην οὐσίαν τῶν οἰκείων θεῶν ἕπεται καὶ τὰ ἐπιτροπευόμενα παρὰ σφῶν ἔθνη, and 22.131c–d, 26.143a. One aspect of the idea of human assimilation to the divine, or *homoiōsis theōi*; Merki, ΟΜΟΙΩΣΙΣ ΘΕΩΙ, 1–35.

180. Jul. *CG* frs. 21.116b, 22.131c–d, 24.137e–138d, 26; Julian's discussion echoes the debate about the divine or human origins of the names of the gods, following Plato's *Cratylus*; see above, Chapter 6.

181. Jul. *CG* fr. 24.138b–c: οὔτε βίων οὔτε ἠθῶν οὔτε τρόπων οὔτε εὐνομίας οὔτε πολιτικῆς ἐμέλησε καταστάσεως.

182. Jul. *CG* fr. 36.171e: ἐξομοιούμεθα τῷ θεῷ. τίς δὲ ἡ παρ' Ἑβραίοις ὑμνουμένη τοῦ θεοῦ μίμησις;

183. Jul. *CG* fr. 51.218a–b: πότερον ἄμεινον τὸ διηνεκῶς μὲν εἶναι ἐλεύθερον, ἐν δισχιλίοις δὲ ὅλοις ἐνιαυτοῖς ἄρξαι τὸ πλεῖστον γῆς καὶ θαλάσσης, ἢ τὸ δουλεύειν καὶ πρὸς ἐπίταγμα ζῆν ἀλλότριον;

[the Hebrews] have poems in hexameter and pretends that the science of logic exists among the Hebrews" (*CG* fr. 53.222a; *PE* 11.5.5). The Hebrews were at least "of sacred and theurgic origin" (*genous hierou kai theourgikou*) and formed part of the universal community (fr. 86.354b). However ill conceived and limited, theirs was a demiurgic God with ancient traditions and laws and as such deserved reverence and the sacrifices due him (frs. 86.354b, 87.35c–d). Thus, in January 363 Julian had begun to rebuild "with all zeal the Temple of the Most High God." An earthquake and a fire interrupted the work, and Julian's death prevented resumption. As Ammianus pointed out, the restored Temple, had it been completed, would have been yet another of Julian's splendid "great works," preserving his memory; in the event it became another adverse omen.[184]

As far as the Galileans were concerned, matters differed entirely. Whereas the Jews had (merely) mistaken their particular God for the universal (Greek) creator of everything, the Galileans had abandoned all belief in the ancient true gods to worship "the corpse of the Jews."[185] Though most of Julian's arguments against the Christians specifically (as opposed to his comparison of the Greeks and the Hebrews) are lost, the outlines are recognizable. The emperor, arguing from his extensive knowledge of scripture, rejected as false and not confirmed by the Gospels the claim that Jesus Christ was the Son of God as foretold by the Hebrew prophets. Citing Numbers, Deuteronomy, and Exodus, he demonstrated that Moses spoke ever of only one God, "never of a second one, regardless of whether *homoios* or *anomoios* [*oute homoion oute anomoion*], as you have done" (*CG* frs. 62.253b–d, 64.261e–263a). Christians professed also to speak of one god only, but Julian counters that "the good John," contradicting Moses, the Apostles, Paul, and the other Evangelists, proclaimed two divinities "by calling Jesus God."

"He was the first to have the courage to make such an affirmation.... He turns to speak about the *Logos* he proclaimed: 'and the *Logos*,' he says, 'became flesh and encamped among us,' but how he did this he is ashamed to say. Nowhere does he call him either Jesus or Christ as long as he calls him God and *Logos*, ... [but he adduces John the Baptist to say] that it is he whom we must believe is truly God

---

184. Jul. *CG* frs. 47, 69, 72, 74, for further comparisons. The citation is Jul. *Ep.* 134, preserved by John Lydus, *Mens.* 4.53. See also Jul. *Ep.* 89b.295b–d; Gr. Naz. *Or.* 5.3–7; Amm. Marc. 23.1.2–3. The authenticity of Jul. *Ep.* 204 (Wright 51), *To the Community of the Jews*, is debated; Hahn, "Kaiser Julian," 247, 252, considers it authentic. The project would have reversed Hadrian's measures, which had made Jerusalem a no-go area for Jews; see Drijvers, "Ammianus." For Julian's attitude toward the Jews (he uses the terms "Jews" and "Hebrews" interchangeably) and its assessment by scholars, Hahn, "Kaiser Julian"; Bouffartigue, *Empereur Julien*, 390–97; R. Smith, *Julian's Gods*, 192–96; Gregory of Nazianzus, *La morte di Giuliano l'Apostata: Orazione 5*, trans. with comm. Lugaresi, 27–51; Renucci, *Idées*, 360–79.

185. Jul. *CG* frs. 43.194d, τοὺς αἰωνίους ἀφέντες θεοὺς ἐπὶ τῶν Ἰουδαίων μεταβῆναι νεκρόν, and 81, 82.

Logos. . . . That John says that about Jesus Christ I do not deny, even if some of the impious say that Jesus Christ is one and the *Logos* announced by John another.[186] But this is not how things stand. According to John, the one whom he calls God *Logos* John the Baptist had identified in Jesus Christ. . . . And then, quietly, without anyone noticing, he introduces into the drama the height of impiety . . . :[187] 'No one has ever seen God. The Only-begotten [*Monogenēs*] Son, who is in the lap of his Father, is he whom he has revealed.'[188] Is this perhaps the God *Logos* made flesh, the Only-begotten Son who is in the lap of his Father? And if he is, as I believe, then there is no doubt that you too have seen God [*etheasasthe dēpouthen kai hymeis theon*]. . . . How can you then say that no one has ever seen God? You have in fact seen if not God the Father then God *Logos*. If, however, the Only-begotten God is one and the God *Logos* another, as I have heard some of your heresy say, then evidently not even John dared to say it" (*CG* frs. 79.327a–c, 80.333b–d).

Julian's awareness of, and response to, the whole range of Christian debates is evident.[189] His distinction between the Highest One as unbegotten First Cause and Father, who delegates the creative activity to the Son, Helios, emanating from him, paralleled the argument of Eunomius, whose method of deduction by analogy from the (visible) product Julian also shared. Whether Father and Son were dissimilar (or not) was, of course, at the center of Christian debates: Julian finds the origin of the controversy in John, who unlike Moses (and indeed commenting on Genesis in his Gospel) had introduced a second god. Whether this second god "is the son of Mary or of someone else—to respond also to Photinus—makes for the moment no difference" (*CG* fr. 64.262d). We already know that Julian was well aware of the Sabellian controversy. The homoousian tenor of his argument (if you have seen the *Logos,* you saw God) is predicated on the Christian claim that the incarnate *Logos* was a true (second) God, without which Julian's entire attack would lose much of its foundation. If Christians had considered Jesus merely a wise man, as Porphyry had suggested they should, Julian's attack would have lost its sting. The emperor's arguments for the allegorical reading of myth versus history cited at the opening of this section would engage many others, from Diodore to Gregory. Also noteworthy is the emperor's emphasis on whether or not one has seen god: Can one comprehend the divine, or must it remain incomprehensible? Gregory, in his ar-

---

186. See above, Chapter 6, "Photinus."
187. ἠρέμα καὶ λεληθότως ἐπεισάγει τῷ δράματι τὸν κολοφῶνα τῆς ἀσεβείας.
188. θεὸν οὐδεὶς ἑώρακε πώποτε. ὁ μονογενὴς υἱός, ὁ ὢν ἐν τοῖς κόλποις τοῦ πατρός, ἐκεῖνος ἐξηγήσατο.
189. Pace R. Smith, *Julian's Gods,* 205, who thinks "that the Arian colour of [his] upbringing seems to have left no discernible trace in any of his writings"; similarly Bouffartigue, *Empereur Julien,* 389; Festugière, *Antioche,* 70; *Cyrille d'Alexandrie: Contre Julien,* ed. and trans. Burguière and Évieux, 14. I concur with Bouffartigue and with Renucci, *Idées,* 259, that Julian's work is sophisticated, *pace* R. Smith, *Julian's Gods,* 200, 205, who judges the *CG*'s "intellectual pitch" low.

guments against Eunomius (*Or.* 2.91–95), posited that no one has truly seen God, not even the thoroughly purified, divinely chosen philosopher Moses.

Julian's engagement with Christian controversies was direct, detailed, and au courant. That the emperor engaged his Christian contemporaries at all at this level is remarkable, though it should no longer surprise us. After all, in his eyes the true *skandalon* was that the impious had given god a "spurious son, whom he has never considered a son nor acknowledged as his":[190] Christians worshipped as God a mere human—in reality the entire argument regarding the divinity of the *Logos* was moot. In claiming divine status for a mere man, moreover, they argued for a historically specific moment as crucial for the salvation of mankind (implying that salvation was also limited and finite)—rejecting the eternal existence of the cosmos as a divinely created, living being, which therefore does not limit the salvation of souls to a moment. The Christian claim undercut the analogy between the eternal, immortal quality of the human soul and the Demiurge. Thus it is no surprise that even John is ashamed to explain how such blasphemy occurred, how a married human woman could be *theotokos* and give birth to a regional and historically circumscribed god (*CG* frs. 64.262c–d, 65.277a).

Julian's arguments were sophisticated. In keeping with his imperial mandate to cure and not to punish, he drew boundaries of different porosities. That between pious and impious, pagan and Christian, was stark and rigid. But on a different level, as already observed above, this seemingly firm boundary was porous. Julian did engage individual Christians and their positions at their own levels, preferring some interpretations to others. He supported Eunomius and Aetius, invited Basil of Caesarea, had positive things to say about Photinus, permitted those who had opposed Constantius to return, and definitively targeted persons loyal to his precursor, mostly homoians (but non-Christians too, in the context of his purges). Eusebius's and Gregory's approaches to what they thought of as pagan learning followed the same logic. Pagan learning was bad, with a boundary carved in stone dividing those on the inside from those on the outside. Yet pagan learning permeates the *Preparatio* as Eusebius makes important points about Christianity as Greek wisdom perfected through Hebrew.[191] Gregory also made claims to pagan learning that were far from simple repudiation. After all, the entire debate about inside and outside, *oikeios* and *allotrios,* circled around the common good and who owned it: Those who wished to preserve Rome's universality as Greek, or those who claimed Rome's Greek universality for the most ancient wisdom of the Hebrews?

Julian, as his imperial letter about teachers indicated, not only used such porous boundaries but was also fully aware that his opponents followed the same practice: that was what irked him to the point of rectifying matters with the force of law. "Why

---

190. Jul. *CG* fr. 31.159e: τὸν νόθον υἱὸν . . . ὃν ἐκεῖνος ἴδιον οὔτε ἐνόμισεν οὔτε ἡγήσατο πώποτε.
191. Lyman, *Christology,* 91–92.

do you gnaw at the learning [*mathēmatōn*] of the Greeks if the reading of your own scriptures is sufficient for you?[192] And yet it would be better to keep men away from that learning rather than from eating the meat of the sacrifices." This is so, because his audience, like him, is aware of the power of words, knowing "the very different effect on the intelligence of your writings as compared with ours; and [knowing also] that from studying yours no man could attain to excellence or even to ordinary goodness, whereas from studying ours every man would become better than before, even though he should be altogether without natural fitness." Greek learning has forced every "being that is noble among you to abandon the impiety immediately." For this, Julian is the best example. Indeed, the ultimate proof would be "to select children from among you and have them study the scriptures. If, once adults, they prove to be superior to slaves, consider me a mere chatterer" (*CG* fr. 55.230a).

For Julian, to follow a mere human made into a god led those *oikeioi* to such a *skandalon* to behave equally scandalously, because persons imitate the divinities *oikeioi* to them (*CG* fr. 58.238b–e). Take "the custom you have then invented to introduce the cult of many new corpses next to that of the old corpse. You have filled the world with tombs and sepulchers,[193] . . . and you have reached such a point of depravity that in this regard you no longer believe it necessary to obey the words of Jesus the Nazarene, . . . who said that sepulchers are full of pollution. How is it, then, that you evoke God at them?" (frs. 81.335c–d, 82.399e). Such worship of the divine at tombs has replaced true sacrifices, which alone effect the gods' *erga* (theurgy), the time-honored means to ascertain the benevolence of the gods, and universally embraced, even by the Hebrews.[194] Julian's discussion of Jewish or Hebrew sacrificial practices carries Iamblichan overtones. He uses biblical examples to point to material and immaterial sacrifices, both of which are valuable, though one is of lesser perfection than the other and God prefers the more perfect (as Julian explained to a very wise bishop when discussing Cain and Abel's offerings: fr. 84). The water of baptism alone, however, which cannot restore even physical impairments such as leprosy, pustules, and dysentery, cannot remove "all the disorders of the soul" (fr. 59.245b–e). Mere water as sole means of political theology—to resort to Eusebius's definition of oracles, sacrifices, statues, and rituals—consequently cannot offer a real political order. "Listen to a beautiful and civil [*politikos*] recommendation: 'Sell your goods, and give them to the poor; procure riches for yourselves that will not perish.' Who could pronounce an order more civil than that?[195] If indeed all were to listen to you, Jesus, who would be the buyer? Who could approve such a teach-

192. Jul. fr. 55.229c–d: αὐτάρκης ὑμῖν ἐστιν ἡ τῶν ὑμετέρων γραφῶν ἀνάγνωσις.
193. πάντα ἐπληρώσατε τάφων καὶ μνημάτων.
194. Jul. *CG* frs. 71.305b–c, 72.305e, 83.343c–d, 84.346e–347c, 87.356c–e.
195. ταύτης τίς εἰπεῖν ἔχει πολιτικωτέραν τῆς ἐντολῆς;

ing, which, once implemented, would not allow a people, a city, even a single family to exist?[196] How indeed could a family exist if all were to be sold?" (fr. 100). Jesus' innovations invite his adherents "to kill their father; many others, to kill their children." They incite war and conflict between those "wishing to defend the sacred customs of time-honored religion and those who embrace this novelty" (fr. 107).[197]

The sacred customs that Zeus-Helios, through his co-gods Apollo, Dionysus, and Asclepius, has given the Greeks and the Romans have united all into one family *oikeios* to its creator (*CG* frs. 42.193c–194c, 43.194b–e, 45.198b–d). Thus "when [Asclepius] descended from heaven to earth, he appeared . . . at Epidaurus in the form [*morphē*] of a man; later on, however, with the multiplication of his apparitions, he extended his saving right hand over the entire earth. He came to Pergamon, to Ionia, . . . and later on to Rome. . . . He visits none of us separately, and yet he raises souls that are in disorder and bodies that are sick" (fr. 46.200a–b). Zeus, through his philanthropic divinities, cures humans soul and body, and has given all an abundance of goods. Why would Christians abandon all that for "a man, or rather many wretched men," the martyrs (frs. 46.200a–47.201e, 57.235c–d)?[198] How can Julian help "detesting the more intelligent among you [while] pitying the more foolish, who by following you have sunk to such depth of ruin that they have abandoned the eternal gods and have gone over to the corpse of the Jews?"[199]

The fragmentary nature of Julian's *Against the Galileans* prevents sustained comparison with Eusebius's *Praeparatio Evangelica,* which it engaged. Still, Julian's points are evident when this text is read in the context of his nearly contemporary *Hymn to King Helios* and his other treatises. Christians (who as Greeks are by no means ignorant) have perverted man's natural inclination toward the true gods (who created the human soul and the eternal cosmos as one) by deserting the universal community *oikeios* to the Highest One—that of the Greeks and the Romans—for the novel teaching of a Galilean man. Why, as educated, sophisticated Greeks, they would do such a thing, Julian cannot fathom. Christianity was a boorish religion invented by uncultivated fishermen for the benefit of the simpleminded, and as such it is acceptable; those who are simple are welcome to teach Matthew and Luke in their churches.[200] That such a religion should be the one of Greek Rome, dominat-

---

196. ἐπαινεῖ ταύτην τίς τὴν διδασκαλίαν, ἧς κρατυνθείσης οὐκ ἔθνος, οὐ πόλις, οὐκ οἰκία μία συστήσεται;

197. Jul. *CG* fr. 107 = Areth. *Scripta minora* 24: ἀναγκαζομένων τῶν ἀνθρώπων ἢ τοῖς πατρίοις βοηθεῖν καὶ τῆς ἐξ αἰῶνος αὐτοῖς εὐσεβείας παραδεδομένης ἀντέχεσθαι ἢ τὴν καινοτομίαν ταύτην προσίεσθαι.

198. Julian explained Dionysus's, Hercules', and Asclepius's human birth as the gods' "stepping down" (*synkatabasis, MoG* 171b–c); see also Jul. *Ep.* 111 (Wright 47).

199. Jul. *Ep.* 62d Bidez (Julian, *Works,* ed. and trans. Wright, vol. 3, 299 fr. 7); *CG* fr. 43.194d.

200. E.g., Jul. *CG* frs. 43.194c–e, 48.206a–b; *Ep.* 90 (Wright 55), a common argument. Neri, "Ammianus' Definition."

ing and uniting the *oikoumenē*, was the true *skandalon* and portent of extraordinary danger. This the emperor had been divinely mandated to reverse, and on the eve of his Persian campaign he had to be certain that he was healing the demented though the power of his words. Thus I concur with the majority of scholars, who note that Julian's anti-Christian language became more strident as his departure for Persia approached.[201] As I hope my discussion of different levels of porosity in the boundary separating Christians and pagans has indicated, however, I do not think that the emperor became more anti-Christian. To the contrary—as Julian's *Epistle to the Priest Theodorus* shows—his duty to reintegrate Christians into the universal community of Zeus-Helios and Rome became increasingly urgent. Christian renitence to his benevolence merited less toleration as the date of the campaign approached and bad omens became more frequent.

Epistle to the Priest Theodorus;
or, Philanthrōpia and Oikeiōsis pros Theon

From the time Julian tackled the Antiochene food crisis in the fall of 362 to the spring of 363, he addressed several imperial letters to (pagan) priests.[202] Of these, the most significant is the one to the high priest Theodorus, dating to February or March 363 and thus to the time when the emperor completed *Against the Galileans*.[203] This fragmentary letter appoints Theodorus as "governor [*archieros*] of all temples in Asia" (*Ep.* 89a.452d); its theme is an ideal priesthood based on philosophy and philanthropy. That the letter coincides with *Against the Galileans* was no accident. As in his imperial letter banning Christians from teaching, issued in Ancyra about nine months earlier, here too Julian summarized and further publicized views he had previously elaborated in the *Hymn to King Helios* and in the *Against the Galileans*.[204]

What the philosopher-emperor as priest had outlined in his treatises he also wished to see implemented across his widespread *oikoumenē*: everyone ought to

---

201. For a summary of the debates and bibliography, Tougher, *Julian*, 55–62.

202. Jul. *Epp.* 81 (Wright 42), *To the Priestess Callissena;* 88 (Wright 18), to an unknown; 85–86, perhaps 87 (Wright 33, 32, 34), *To the Priestess Theodora;* in addition also *Ep.* 30 and perhaps 79 (Wright 16, 19), *To Theodorus*.

203. Jul. *Ep.* 89a (20 Wright) and Jul. *Ep.* 89b, separated from 89a by a lacuna (for the completion of *CG*, see 89b.288c); Julian, *Epistolario*, trans. and comm. Caltabiano, 263 n. 2. Wright (*Letter to a Priest:* Julian, *Works*, ed. and trans. Wright, vol. 2, 297–339), considers 89b a separate letter. I will follow Bidez and Caltabiano (Julian, *Epistolario*, trans. and comm. Caltabiano, 264 n.1) and consider both as fragments of one letter, 89a and 89b. Julian, *Epistolario*, trans. and comm. Caltabiano, 123–26, 180, and 261 n. 2, suggests a date in the fall or winter of 362/3; Wright (*op. cit.*, vol. 2, 67), a date in the summer of 362. Nuffelen, "Deux fausses lettres," esp. 136–50, also assumes one letter (p. 136) and argues for a date in February or March 363 (p. 143 n. 66), which I follow.

204. Jul. *Ep.* 61 (Bidez); Watts, *City*, 68–71.

receive the salvific benefits of his imperial *philanthrōpia*.[205] Therefore, the letter appointing Theodorus, "a task dear to [his] heart, while to all men everywhere . . . of the greatest benefit" (*Ep.* 89a.452c), summarized his notions of true priesthood (452d–454a). A true priest must avoid incorrect innovation and be pure in his personal life, and his religious fervor—which in practice was all too often muted by ignorance, apathy, wealth and luxury—must be freshly rekindled. Theodorus, as a fellow student of Maximus of Ephesus, who had vouched for him while Julian was still living in the West, had the emperor's full confidence (452a).

As a follower of Maximus of Ephesus, Theodorus embodied and was well prepared to represent Julian's ideas of priesthood, which required "above all else that one practice philanthropy."[206] Philanthropy was the priestly virtue par excellence, for it emanated from and thus activated the divine benevolence of the gods, who are philanthropic in essence.[207] Just as those slaves who show concern for their masters' likes and dislikes receive better treatment than their oblivious fellow slaves, so those who practice *philanthrōpia* please the gods most. Divine *philanthrōpia* gave men not only "tunics of skin," as Moses said (Gen 3:21), but the bounty of nature and of civilization. Thus Athena provided the Greeks with oil, wine, bread, and gold (289d). And man, "by nature a civilized and sociable being," must share his wealth; otherwise, by depriving out of greed those who are honest but poor, he deliberately rejects divine *philanthrōpia*.[208] As Julian's own fate demonstrates, generosity has its own rewards. When he was a private man, he gave away much while possessing (relatively) little, and the gods multiplied his rewards manifold.[209] That taught him to extend benevolence even to enemies and those incarcerated, because true *philanthrōpia* regards the person and not the condition (290b–291a; see also his allusion to Roman clemency in *CG* fr. 35.168c). In light of this, the emperor was deeply dismayed to observe that many people do not give a single drachma to a poor person and treat their parents worse than strangers, though they know full well that to extend love of self to those who are *oikeioi* is the basis of reverence toward the divine and of all worship. Philanthropy, hospitality to strangers and beggars, and protection of the family are Zeus's most cherished commandments and thus Julian's greatest concerns (291b–d).[210] This is so because philanthropy, the extension of self-

---

205. See Arist. *EN* 8.1.1–5, 9.7.6–7. For the long tradition of *philanthrōpia* as civic and imperial virtue and sign of *megalopsychia*, Schouler, *Tradition*, 979–97; Wiemer, *Libanios*, 232–36; Athanassiadi-Fowden, *Julian*, 187–89; Bouffartigue, *Empereur Julien*, 659; R. Smith, *Julian's Gods*, 211–15; Kabiersch, *Untersuchungen*; in general Kloft, *Liberalitas*, 166–77.

206. Jul. *Ep.* 89b.289b: ἀσκητέα τοίνυν πρὸ πάντων ἡ φιλανθρωπία.

207. Jul. *Ep.* 89b.289b–294d.

208. Jul. *Ep.* 89b.288b: ὄντος ἀνθρώπου φύσει πολιτικοῦ ζῴου καὶ ἡμέρου. Pl. *Phd.* 82a; cf. Arist. *Pol.* 1.1253a3; *EN* 1.1169b12; *EE* 7.1242a22; here Julian evokes his *Or.* 6.201c.

209. He is not comparing private beneficence with imperial largesse.

210. Citing Hom. *Od.* 14.57–58.

love outward to encompass others, permits humans to ascend toward the divine, since each human being is *oikeios,* affiliated to others and to the divine, in concentric circles outward: *oikeiōsis pros theon.*

"We are all born from the gods,"[211] and have received our "souls from the Demiurge from eternity" (292d), so that "all men ... are related [*syngeneis*] to all other men" (291d). The gods have created mankind either from a common pair of ancestors or from as many prototypes at the same primordial moment, already endowed with different customs, laws, and the "sacred sayings of the gods that have been handed down to us by the ancient theurgists, namely that when Zeus ordered all things, drops of sacred blood fell from heaven, out of which grew the human race. Therefore we are all related" (292a–b). Willfully to deprive those who are *oikeioi* thus acts against the gods, Greek civilization, mankind itself: the ancient writers have composed numerous exhortations to live in community with our neighbors.[212]

Philanthropy is the active expression of the *oikeiōsis* affiliating all men with each other and with the gods. Fundamental to all acts of piety (*eusebeia*) and worship, and as part of every human being's most natural inclination, philanthropy permits all to become more affiliated with god and with their neighbors (293a). Here the priest as guide is central; his philanthropy consists in instructing with plain speaking or punishing severely "whoever is unjust to men, profanes the gods, and is arrogant to all" (*Ep.* 89a.453a). Philosophers as priests perform their philanthropic work because their souls are prepared and purified (*hagneuein, Ep.* 89b.300c) through the *enkyklia mathēmata* (which distinguishes them from prophets not so prepared: 295d), a set of readings including "Pythagoras, Plato, Aristotle, and the school of Chrysippus and Zeno" and excluding frivolous poets, comedians, novelistic historians, the teachings of Epicurus, and above all "those fables that the prophets of the Jews take pains to invent and are admired for by those miserable men who have attached themselves to the Galileans" (300b–301a).

Julian's letter was an exercise in moral philosophy expressing the ethical demands of the Stoic ("the school of Chrysippus and Zeno") concept of *oikeiōsis pros theon,* discussed above in the context of Gregory's prescriptions for ideal priesthood as active philosophy. What the emperor had woven like a red thread through his treatise *Against the Galileans,* the contrast between what was *oikeios* to men and gods and what was *allotrios,* he now brought to a trenchant point.[213] Indeed, the theme had been present throughout his earlier writings. For example, when Julian pre-

---

211. Jul. *Ep.* 89b.292b: ἐκ τῶν θεῶν πάντες γεγονότες.
212. Jul. *Ep.* 89b.292d: περὶ τοῦ φύσει κοινωνικὸν εἶναι ζῷον τὸν ἄνθρωπον. Jul. *Or.* 7.219a–222d has another account of the origins of man and the interrelation between divine and human. D. Chr. (*Or.* 1.39, 12.75) called Zeus *Homognios,* he who created the community of men and gods. As in the *CG,* Julian here refers to Pl. *Ti* 41c (also discussed by Proclus, *In Ti* 4.288e).
213. As pointed out by Kabiersch, *Untersuchungen,* 64–73, and Nuffelen, "Deux fausse lettres," 143–45.

sented his interpretation of the maxim Know Thyself as a means to achieve *homoiōsis theōi,* assimilation with the divine in the more Platonic register, in his attack against the uneducated Cynic philosophers, the context—his chastisement of false Cynics and Christians, both of whom repudiated the community of men—already carried overtones of *oikeiōsis.* In every work discussed so far, Julian's foremost aim, as Iamblichan philosopher and ruler actively engaged for the common good as demanded by Stoic *oikeiōsis,* was to preserve and restore the unity of mankind created by Zeus and affiliated with him, by leading those in his care closer to him—*oikeiōsis pros theon.* This is also the context of Gregory's development of *oikeiōsis pros theon,* fundamental to his construction of the philosopher as priest and mediator. Thus, both the emperor and Gregory drew on several notions of the purified philosopher as mediator between the divine and man to shape their unifying visions. Once more, the similarities of their syntheses—designed to approach and proclaim the one ancient unifying truth—are striking, and the differences subtle yet profound.

Statues as Symbols of Divine Presence and Worship as Oikeiōsis   Imperial *philanthrōpia* required *liberalitas* and true *philanthrōpia,* integral to *oikeiōsis pros theon,* which for Julian required worship of the gods by all the sacrifices, rites, and rituals they had created and could therefore demand as their due: to give the master what he wishes to receive assures his benevolence.[214] It demanded, that is, the veneration of statues and temples as signposts for the "presence of the gods—not that we consider them gods but that we may worship the gods through them" (293c). *Epistle* 89b consequently delineates Julian's guidelines for the worship of statues (inspired by Iamblichus).[215] In the *Hymn to the Mother of the Gods* Julian called the statue of the goddess an object filled with divine power; now he specified that statues "have been established by our fathers as symbols of the presence of the gods."[216] Constructed by men out of stone, statues require reverence and inspire sacred fear, because through them the gods look at the worshipper "from the unseen world."[217] Like the visible gods or stars, statues reveal the presence of the immaterial gods. Since men are in the body, they need physical means to worship the immaterial gods, who for that reason revealed themselves through *agalmata,* statues that circle the heavens, from which statues of stone were invented on earth, "as living images of [the gods'] invisible nature," making human worship possible (293b-c).[218] Out of

---

214. Kabiersch, *Untersuchungen,* 26–49.
215. Bouffartigue, *Empereur Julien,* 361.
216. Jul. *Ep.* 89b.293a: σύμβολα ... τῆς παρουσίας τῶν θεῶν.
217. Jul. *Ep.* 89b.294d: φρίττων ἐξ ἀφανοῦς ὁρῶντας εἰς αὐτὸν τοὺς θεούς.
218. Jul. *Ep.* 89b.295a: ὑπὸ τῶν θεῶν ζῶντα ἀγάλματα κατασκευασθέντα τῆς ἀφανοῦς αὐτῶν οὐσίας. In keeping with the tripartite cosmology of both hymns, Julian evoked the three classes (*genē*) of the gods.

divine philanthropy, the gods created statues so that everyone who worshipped them as symbols of their divine presence could in turn come closer to that divine presence by purifying his soul by the act of veneration.[219] Christians, who argue that statues are merely man-made stone, simply missed the point (294d–295d).

Priests as "most precious possession of the gods" (297a) and as keepers of these visible symbols must be revered and must lead a life appropriate to "servants of the Gods" (*hōs leitourgous theōn*, 296b).[220] Theodorus knew (as the disciple of Maximus of Ephesus), and had to convey to all others by order of the emperor, that this life was the true philosophical life according to the maxims of the *enkyklia mathēmata* (298b–d, 300d–301c). Priests who prove to have fallen short of the demands of this life will be punished (296d–298a).[221] Like Julian in Antioch, philosophers as priests must pray three times daily, privately and in public, with hymns; they must sacrifice, retreat from public view into the temples, philosophize during festivals, wear sumptuous robes during sacred ceremonies but otherwise dress simply, visit the houses of magistrates and public officials rarely (and only if these are of good repute), and avoid all public ostentation, especially the theater and public spectacles. Priests must be the best in their cities—that is, those who love the gods and men most. Should they be obscure or even (relatively) poor, their love for gods and men, shown by active charity, ought to be paramount in their selection. This last element is particularly relevant, because Julian thought that the priests' neglect of the poor had driven many to the Galileans, "who practiced philanthropy" (299b–305d). In sum, "inasmuch as the priestly life ought to be more holy than the political life, [priests] must guide men toward [the gods] and instruct them, . . . displaying their own lives as examples of what they ought to preach to the people."[222]

Julian's imperial letter to Theodorus prescribed what he had elaborated in his

---

219. Julian also responded to the question of why gods, who require nothing, need reverence, sacrifice, or prayer, by emphasizing that the gods do not need but observe the reverence paid to their visible representations.

220. Julian entrusted Theodorus with "administering all manifestations of the cults"; "supervising [*episkopein*] all priests in each city" in his province; and "assigning to each what is proper" (*Ep.* 89a.452d). Read in conjunction with Julian's edict and imperial letter about teachers, *CTh* 13.3.5 and Jul. *Ep.* 61 (Bidez), *Epistle* 89a–b suggests that Julian wanted to regulate and perhaps centralize the priesthood, in a manner akin to establishing a centralized register of public teachers; Watts, *City*, 68–71. If so, he may have had in mind a tradition revitalized by Maximinus Daia; he "was not inventing anything offhand," *Ep.* 89b.298a; Merkelbach and Stauber, "'Unsterbliche Kaiserpriester'"; Nicholson, "'Pagan Churches.'" Originally, the title "archpriest" (*archiatros*) honored outstanding citizens who presided over (and financed) the imperial cult on the occasion of the festival of the province. Theodorus's mandate was broader, and it differed because emperor cult was not its objective. In addition, wealth was no longer *conditio sine qua non;* Nuffelen, "Deux fausses lettres," 148.

221. Compare Jul. *Ep.* 62.422d–423b.

222. Jul. *Ep.* 89b.288c, ἐπεὶ δὲ τὸν ἱερατικὸν βίον εἶναι χρὴ τοῦ πολιτικοῦ σεμνότερον, ἀκτέον ἐπὶ τοῦτον καὶ διδακτέον, . . . [299b] ὧν πρὸς τὰ πλήθη χρὴ λέγειν δεῖγμα τὸν ἑαυτῶν ἐκφέροντας βίον.

treatises. *Oikeiōsis pros theon,* with all its ethical connotations, was central, because Julian, like the ancient sages, considered Zeus-Helios "the common father of all men" (*Hel. R.* 131c).[223] To affiliate all—even enemies, even honest poor—with each other and with the gods was the driving motivation behind the treatise *Against the Galileans;* Julian as philosopher and emperor sought to cure those who were outside the community of men just as the gods bestowed benevolently the benefits of their divine *philanthrōpia.*[224] Acting much like his precursor and exemplar Trajan (for whom he had just built a temple with a library), Julian sought to teach and integrate and not to punish the demented.[225]

Julian's *Epistle* 89a–b and *Epistle* 84, *To Arsacius,* have often been read as reflecting Julian's attempt to establish a pagan church in counterpoint to and imitation of the Christian one.[226] That notion is Gregory of Nazianzus's polemical interpretation, and its continuing relevance testimony to his persuasive powers.[227] Granted, in *Epistle* 84 Julian alluded to a well-established network of Christian philanthropic institutions (reminiscent of those established and made famous by Basil at Caesarea after 370) that he wanted to emulate and outdo.[228] As Peter van Nuffelen has shown, however, *Epistle 84* is a fifth-century product, reflecting fifth-century Christian institutional charity and drawing on *Epistle* 89a–b, Basil's foundation, and on Greg-

---

223. Recall A. A. Long's gloss of the Stoic notion of *oikeiōsis* (*Hellenistic Philosophy,* 172), above, Chapter 4, n. 114.

224. Those who are indigent but honest deserve particular consideration, (ἄλλως τε ὅταν καὶ ἐπιεικεῖς τινες τύχωσι τὸν τρόπον, 290a; cf. 290d), but because of the common ancestry of all men, even enemies and those incarcerated require mildness (291a). Kabiersch, *Untersuchungen,* 64–65, suggests that Julian's expansive notion of *oikeiōsis* as precondition for true *philanthrōpia* derives from Theophrastus, as interpreted by Porphyry in *Abst.* 3.25–26, where *oikeiōsis* includes animals. Porphyry, however, argues that this prohibits sacrifice of animals and hence all sacrifice, and he does not discuss philanthropy; Dierlmeier, *Oikeiosis-Lehre,* 1–100, esp. 47–81, 88–92; and Guido, "Nozione."

225. See Trajan's famous rescript to Pliny the Younger's inquiry about the novel superstition Christianity, Plin. *Epp.* 10.96, 97 (Pliny, *Epistularum libri decem,* ed. Mynors, 338–40); Jul. *Epp.* 83 (Wright 37) and 115 (Wright 40), 425a. Bowersock, *Julian,* 84–85, argues that Julian sought to eradicate rather than integrate Christianity, which admittedly would have had the same results, but I think the difference in intent is important. For the temple and library, burned under Jovian, Eunapius fr. 29 (Blockley).

226. Jul. *Ep.* 84 (Wright 22); Bidez, *Vie,* 266–67. Koch ("Comment l'empereur Julien tâcha fonder une église païenne") first argued for Julian's intention to establish a pagan church. The bibliography on the subject is extensive; Nuffelen, "Deux fausses lettres," 136 n. 31, to which may be added Bouffartigue, *Empereur Julien,* 361, 379; and R. Smith, *Julian's Gods,* 110–11. Mazza, "Giuliano," argues against a counterchurch and highlights Julian's tolerant approach to Christians. Pope Benedict XVI recently referred to Julian's philanthropy as influenced by Christian charity in his encyclical *Deus Caritas Est,* 24 n. 16, based on *Ep.* 84. (The note cites *Ep.* 83, but that must be an oversight.) As Kabiersch notes, *Untersuchungen,* 15–49, *Ep.* 89b.290c echoes Mt 19:29 and Lk 18:30, but this does not mean that Julian wished to copy a Christian church, however conceived.

227. As suggested by Finn, *Almsgiving,* 87–88, Julian's philanthropy may have fostered Christian philanthropic acts; he considers *Ep.* 84 authentic.

228. Bas. *Ep.* 94; Gr. Naz. *Or.* 43.34–37; Rousseau, *Basil,* 139–44.

ory's presentation of Julian's measures as mere plagiarism of Christian practices.[229] Julian's notions of philanthropy had a different aim: true worship of the real gods with sacrifices initiating and enabling *oikeiōsis* with them. That aim does not minimize the ethical components of such affiliation, especially imperial benevolence, clemency, and juridical mildness, none of which required, however, a pagan church or a Christian precedent. Indeed, Ammianus, Libanius, Eutropius, and even Gregory and, following him, Sozomen praised what the author of an inscription from the Temple of Zeus in Magnesia also noted in addressing Julian as *philanthrōpotatos*, the most philanthropic emperor: Julian's imperial philanthropy.[230]

THE PLATONIC PHILOSOPHER-KING: THE *MISOPOGON* AND JULIAN'S UNIVERSAL VISION

> *But as for Christ, you love him, you say, and adopt him as the guardian of your city instead of Zeus and the god of Daphne and Calliope. . . . Before I came here, I used to praise you in the strongest possible terms, . . . since I thought that you were sons of Greeks; and I myself, though my family is Thracian, am a Greek in my habits, and I supposed that we should regard one another with the greatest possible affection.*[231]
>
> —JULIAN, MISOPOGON 357C, 367C

Imperial benevolence and juridical mildness were the key themes of Julian's last work, the *Antiochikos* (*logos*) or *Misopogon*. In February 363, "having put up with [Julian] for seven months" (*Mis.* 344a), the citizens of Antioch found on display "the speech he had delivered against them outside the palace in the city on what is known as the Tetrapylon of the Elephants, near the Regia," the royal street.[232] At

---

229. Nuffelen, "Deux fausses lettres," 136–50. Though Julian may well have known the precursors to Basil's establishment in Constantinople, these were not the network of *xenodocheia* in each city as suggested in *Ep.* 84, which were, however, widespread by the time of Justinian; Procop. *Anec.* 26.5; Nuffelen, 139–40. *Ep.* 84 mentions that Julian had promised 30,000 *modii* of grain and 60,000 *sextarii* of wine per annum as subsidies for Galatia's poor. This is very high when compared to the grain imported to Antioch in 362/3 (Wiemer, *Libanios*, 341) and could serve as an additional argument against the letter's authenticity.

230. Amm. Marc. 25.4.15; Eutr. *Brev.* 10.16; Lib. *Or.* 15.25, 27–29, 39, 43, 75; 16.23; 18.110; *Ep.* 153.4 (Norman); Arce, *Estudios*, no. 105, and comments, pp. 158–60. Gr. Naz. *Or.* 4.111; Soz. *HE* 5.16; Kabiersch, *Untersuchungen*, 6–15; R. Smith, *Julian's Gods*, 42–46. In general, see now Noreña, "Communication."

231. Χριστὸν δὲ ἀγαπῶντες ἔχετε πολιοῦχον ἀντὶ τοῦ Διὸς καὶ τοῦ Δαφναίου καὶ τῆς Καλλιόπης. . . . καὶ δὴ πρότερον ἐπῄνουν ὑμᾶς ὡς ἐνεδέχετό μοι φιλοτίμως, . . . νομίσας ὑμᾶς μὲν Ἑλλήνων παῖδας, ἐμαυτὸν δέ, εἰ καὶ γένος ἐστί μοι Θρᾴκιον,Ἕλληνα τοῖς ἐπιτηδεύμασιν ὑπελάμβανον, ὅτι μάλιστα ἀλλήλους ἀγαπήσομεν.

232. This was his last discourse, though later letters are extant. For the placement on the stele, see John Malal. *Chron.* 13.328.3–4. Amm. Marc. 22.14.2, Gr. Naz. *Or.* 5.41, and Socr. *HE* 3.17.9 all cite both titles. I am using the edition and commentary *Giuliano imperatore: Misopogon*, ed. and trans. Prato and

first glance, one sees no clemency or mildness in the *volumen* Ammianus characterized as *invectivum:* Julian "enumerated in a hostile spirit the faults of the city, including more than were justified."[233] As the dual title suggests, Julian turned the classic genre of praise of a city, such as Libanius's famous *Antiochikos* composed for the Olympic Games of 356 and Dio Chrysostom's panegyric to Alexandria, into a scathing attack, a "panegirico rovesciato."[234] Julian no longer loved the pearl of the East he had once considered his most congenial city. But rather than punish Antioch as he had punished Caesarea, stripping it of its metropolitan status and reducing it (legally) to a village, closing the hippodrome, baths, and theaters, and jailing the entire senate, the emperor merely wrote. Maud Gleason has called the *logos* an "edict of chastisement," and Julian's *Antiochikos* was indeed more than invective.[235] As the second title indicates, *Beard Hater,* the emperor compounded the effect by interweaving the *psogos* with another genre he had used in Constantinople, the anti-Cynic diatribe, this time directed at himself. The *Misopogon*'s satire praised the true Cynic wise man, Julian the philosopher, who knew how to rule justly but mildly in accord with divine and human law. The speech was thus a punishment (*timōria*), to cite Libanius, of the city that had failed to recognize the emperor's benevolent restraint, posted on the pillars of the royal street.[236]

The Kalends of January 363, the New Year festivities coinciding with those celebrating Julian's fourth consulate, appear to have brought matters to a head. During the festivities, which included a parade through the agora to the hippodrome with much joking and jesting (*Mis.* 364a, 366c), "the rowdy citizens of Antioch gave vent to their apprehensions and hostilities at what was commonly considered to be a season of ritual impunity." Gripped by famine, burdened by the presence of the army, confronted with Julian's sacrificial excess, the citizens seized the opportunity "for cathartic expressions of enthusiasm and hostility."[237] For Julian, the citizens' witticisms, even if customary on these festival days, went too far.[238] "But since you do not like the length of our beard, our unkempt hair, our refusal to attend the the-

---

Micalella; also *Giuliano imperatore: Alla madre degli dèi e altri discorsi,* intro. Fontaine, ed. Prato, trans. Marcone, 170–251, 321–51.

233. Amm. Marc. 22.14.2.

234. Lib. *Or.* 11 (*Libanios, Antiochikos,* trans. and comm. Fatouros and Krischer); Marcone, "Panegirico," for the two genres and their interweaving; J. Long, "Structures"; Rosen, *Julian,* 342–44.

235. Gleason, "Festive Satire," 116–18, for edicts of chastisement.

236. Libanius mentions other forms of severe imperial punishments of cities in his response to the *Misopogon;* Lib. *Or.* 16, *To the Antiochenes,* 4, 9, 13, 14, and indirectly in *Or.* 15, *Presbeuticus to Julian,* 25–43; for the *Misopogon* as punishment, see *Or.* 18.198; Wiemer, *Libanios,* 189–244.

237. For the New Year as the last straw, see Liebeschuetz, *Antioch,* 229; and Gleason, "Festive Satire," 108–13 (quotations pp. 113, 110). For burdensome soldiers, see also Lib. *Or.* 15.17–18.

238. It is possible that *Mis.* 337b refers to the *lex Iulia de maiestate,* which the emperor could have enforced but chose not to; Wiemer, *Libanios,* 197.

aters, that we require men to be dignified in the temples; and since more than all these things you dislike our constant occupation [*ascholia*] with judicial affairs and our efforts to banish greed from the marketplace, we willingly depart from your city" (365d). The common people hate him because they prefer godlessness (i.e., Christianity); the powerful and wealthy, because he suppressed their greedy profiteering; and everyone, "because [they adore] the dancers and the theater" that he hates profoundly and does not sponsor as Constantius, a "real" emperor, had done (357d, 340a).

With biting anapests, at which they evidently excelled (*Mis.* 345d), Antioch's citizens ridiculed everything Julian stood for. They despised his rule as an ascetic philosopher with Cynic disdain for personal appearance (340b-342a) and imperial ceremonial—above all, what surrounded emperors in the theater and the hippodrome (342d-344b). They laughed at his devotion to philosophical *erga* such as impartial justice (354d-355d),[239] philanthropy,[240] and reverence toward the gods.

Julian responded with a sophisticated *logos* in the ironic mode, in which he expressed what he meant by saying the opposite.[241] The *Antiochikos* (normally a panegyric) was in reality an invective, so that whatever the citizens applauded and criticized should be inverted, just as Julian's self-critical Beard Hater was the ideal philosopher on the throne, as his not-too-subtle allusion to Marcus Aurelius's writings about himself implies (*Mis.* 338b). In effect, Julian's inversion of the Antiochenes' criticism showcased imperial *sōphrosynē* at an exemplary level, as befitted a divinely chosen philosopher.[242] His satirical inversion of his imagined audience of Antioch's citizens embodies the obverse to each of Julian's exemplary characteristics as temperate ruler modeled after Plato (Julian sprinkled citations from the *Laws*, especially Book 5, and the *Republic* throughout the text). What the citizens considered freedom (*eleutheria*), granted even to women, children, donkeys, and camels (356a-d), he saw as lawlessness; his imperial and philosophical *sōphrosynē* was in their eyes the unkempt harshness of a boor (*agroikia*: e.g., 343a-d, 348c-d, but also 340d-342b). From childhood, Julian had been trained by his tutor, the

---

239. Thus, whereas he, the emperor, submitted himself like a private person to the laws that guide all, the citizens called their illegitimate licentiousness frank speech (*parrhēsia*): *Mis.* 344b-345c, 357, 364c, 355b-c, 356c, 343c.

240. Visible in his efforts to ameliorate the food crisis and the remission of taxes: *Mis.* 365b, 368c-369c.

241. For sophisticated analysis of Julian's literary construct, see J. Long, "Structures," 15-23, and especially Marcone, "Panegirico." I cannot follow Müller's (*Beiden Satiren*, 64) characterization of the *Misopogon* as "eine[n] Fehlgriff, eine[n] mißlungenen Versuch, wie ... [Julian's] Auftritt als Person in der Öffentlichkeit nur als fehlerhaft, als würdelos und geschmacklos zu bezeichnen ist." His assessment reflects the tenor common among scholars discussing the work, from puzzlement to downright dismissal of the text (and the mental state of its author), noticeable even in Wiemer's nuanced analysis, "Kaiser." For a summary of scholarly assessment, Wiemer, "Kaiser," 734.

242. Rademaker, "*Sōphrosynē*," 210-53, esp. 242-53, and the discussion above in Chapter 5.

Scythian eunuch Mardonius, to display the ("boorish") manliness (*andreia*) gained by "not submitting to desires [and] achieving happiness [*eudaimonia*] by that means" (351c). The same tutor had taught him to enjoy chariot races in Homer rather than the hippodrome (351c–d). Under his tutor's ("boorish") guidance Julian became persuaded by Plato, Aristotle, and Theophrastus (358a), men often ridiculed in comedy; and through him, even as a child, he had been overcome by "a strange and senseless delusion [that] persuaded me to war against my stomach, so that I do not fill it with a great quantity of food" (340c). By such misguided practices from his early youth on, Julian learned of "another of Plato's laws that has made me hateful in your eyes: I mean the law that says that those who govern ... ought to train themselves in respect for others and in self-restraint, so that the masses may look at them and rightly order their own lives" (354b).

Julian's biting *eirōneia* inverted the very Greekness of Antioch the emperor had so longed for and praised. Once he had thought that the Antiochenes' Greekness was his; but now, to demonstrate true Greekness to the Antiochenes, he referred (in time-honored manner; see Tacitus, *Germania*) to good—because uncivilized and therefore not yet degenerate—barbarians such as the rustic Celts, among whom he was greatly appreciated and who hated the theater as much as he did, Scythian eunuchs, rough Romans such as Cato, and his own Thracian origins (e.g., *Mis.* 348c–d).[243] The well-shaved, perfumed, indulgent, luxury-loving, theatergoing Antiochenes were a perversion of the Greekness they claimed so proudly, their degeneration foreshadowed in the story of the origin of the city Libanius had compared to Athens: Antiochus fell in love with his stepmother, whom the father gave up to him after discovering his passion (347a–348b).[244]

Realigning rather than inverting the hierarchy of ethnicities within the *oikoumenē*, Julian wrote his imagined citizens of Antioch to express and define what he had called the worst characteristics of the Greeks in *Against the Galileans* (fr. 3.43b) and to claim true Greekness, defined by the *paideia* of Homer, Hesiod, Plato, Aristotle, and Theophrastus, for himself as a Scythian-trained Thracian who had reached manhood in Celtic Gaul. The invective of the *Misopogon* personalized all that Julian considered wrong and wished to chastise in Greekness by attaching it to the citizens of Antioch, thus teaching everyone else what was right about Greekness as he himself exemplified it (*Mis.* 367c).

The fate of the Antiochenes, their degeneration, reflected their long association with Constantius (and Gallus), to whose vices their story of origin made them prone.

---

243. Marcone, "Panegirico," 233, discusses the *locus amoenus* motif in Julian's description of Lutetia (i.e., Paris).

244. Lib. *Or.* 11.47–54, 63, 68; for the importance of origin narratives in praising cities, see Men. Rh. *Treatise* 1 (*Menander Rhetor*, ed. and trans. Russell and Wilson, 32, 46–50; *Peri epideiktikōn*, ed. Spengel, 332, 336).

Constantius was Julian's counter in every respect. Constantius and Antioch thus deserved each other as kindred souls, and Julian with his habits and his friends was to them a stranger (*xenos*) about to leave, never to return to that city. "'The Chi,' they say, 'never wronged our city; nor did the Kappa'" (*Mis.* 357a, 360d–361a): Julian's relation to the criminal, licentious, indulgent Constantius, as elaborated in the *Epistle to the Athenians,* leaves no doubt that the degenerate Antiochenes found the morally inferior Christianity more congenial than Julian's demanding Greekness in the undiluted form practiced by simple (*haplos*), free-speaking Celts and Germans (359c). Because they now have Christ as their protector, Julian wished the Antiochenes the joy of many more Constantiuses, a double serving of the Kappa, saying to them that indeed "Constantius did wrong you only [in one thing], that when he made me Caesar he did not kill me" (357b).

The imperial chastisement of the *Antiochikos* was not all. Julian as good philosopher and ruler also acted. He ordered the transfer of the imperial residence to Tarsus, a move perhaps worse in its effect than the abrogation of city rights.[245] Further, he installed Alexander of Heliopolis, a pagan known for his harshness, as *consularis Syriae,* whose residence was Antioch. These were real punishments, and magistrates and large crowds of citizens came to plead with the emperor. Libanius appealed to his philanthropy, vowing that Antioch would amend its ways, reduce theater productions, and increase reverence for the gods—already in evidence in the numerous offerings for Julian's safe return to Antioch.[246] Indeed, on February 26, Julian declared in an edict that to preserve ancient *mores* was his guiding principle for the future; what the ancients had practiced should be maintained unchanged for the public good. Therefore temples should be restored and their revenues reinstalled (at the expense of churches and through the removal of immunities granted to Christian clergy), and daytime funerals should cease, for Helios ought not to face such pollution (as that practiced by martyr-worshipping Christians such as Constantius, who had revered martyrs even in his palace).[247] In early March the *pontifex max-*

---

245. After returning from Persia, Julian intended to winter in Tarsus and ordered the residence transferred there: *Mis.* 354c, 364d, 370b–c.

246. Amm. Marc. 23.2.2–5; Lib. *Or.* 16.53, 15.77, 86; *Epp.* 838, 811, 1256, 1368; Socr. *HE* 3.17.6; Wiemer, *Libanios,* 198–203 and 217–27 for Libanius's two orations (*Or.* 16 and 15) responding to the *Misopogon.*

247. *CTh* 5.20.1, 9.17.5; Jul. *Ep.* 136a, 136b (Wright 56); Julian, *Epistolario,* trans. and comm. Caltabiano, 275–76; Ath. *Hist. aceph.* 3.1 (Athanasius of Alexandria, *Histoire "acephale,"* ed. and trans. Martin and Albert, 148–50); Amm. Marc. 22.5.2; den Boeft, Drijvers, et al., *Philological and Historical Commentary on Ammianus Marcellinus 22,* 55–58. McLynn ("Transformation," esp. 240–42, 246–48) analyzes the pronounced veneration of saints under Constantius and Gallus. Constantius celebrated the success of the council of Constantinople (360) by transferring the remains of Luke and Andrew to the Church of the Holy Apostles, his father's resting place; and Gallus, those of Babylas. See also R. Smith, *Julian's Gods,* 207–18; Renucci, *Idées,* 282–323.

imus and emperor left Antioch in anticipation of another sign of the gods' approval of their chosen son, victory over the Persians and the new name Parthicus.[248]

Julian died during the night of June 25 to 26 about a hundred miles north of Ctesiphon, shocking the *oikoumenē,* Christian and not. The disaster and the crisis that inevitably followed colored all later accounts of the emperor. As has become apparent, my own reading of Julian does not reveal him as the impetuous, emotional, reactionary, romantically Greek, derivative philosopher on the throne, still reflected in scholarship. Julian was exceptional as emperor because he wrote more than any other Roman ruler, and he was exceptional as a writer because he was the emperor. Thus we know far more about his vision for a unified Roman *oikoumenē* than we do about other emperors, whose ideas we must cull from their laws, coins, buildings, inscriptions, military campaigns—and from what others say about them. How different Julian was from emperors who did not write, or whose personal writings are not preserved, is thus difficult to say.

It is certain, however, that Julian was a man of his time. He spoke the idiom of his time (and I do not mean merely his *attikizein*) to address the questions and issues he faced. That is, he is exceptional qua emperor, but not by any means because he stands outside the culture of his time—quite the opposite. As a follower of Iamblichus, Julian practiced and advocated a form of the true philosophical life whose aim was by *askēsis* to purify himself to the extent that he could become as close to the gods as possible for a human being. But as Caesar and then Augustus, he also knew that perhaps the less pure (or second) form of the philosophical life described in Plato's *Laws* (see above, Chap. 3, the section "Philosophy in the Shade versus Philosophy in the Open") was the one that he might have to practice (though the longer he ruled alone, the more kinship he felt with Plato's ideal philosopher-king). As emperor, his philosophical life demanded that he actively extend his self-love to all in his care, for the common good, and guide everyone closer toward the divine: *oikeiōsis pros theon*. This made him no less an Iamblichan Neoplatonic philosopher—just an active, political one, with Stoic leanings as his position demanded. This position of philosopher, emperor, and priest, for which he had been divinely chosen, obliged him to use all the means at his disposal, from laws to sacrifices, and the power of his words, to guide all to the one truth.

Herein lay Julian's innovative force. He may not have been so original and philosophically rigorous as Proclus, as modern scholars so often lament; but then, Proclus was not an emperor. As an emperor and a politically active Platonic philosopher, Julian created an internally consistent vision of great sophistication that achieved what he wished to achieve. Whether he would have been able to imple-

---

248. The emperors assumed the office and title of *pontifex maximus* until Gratian; Zos. 4.36.4 Paschoud. For Julian's connection between Persian victory and divine favor, Matthews, *Roman Empire*, 140.

ment it in practice had he ruled longer than twenty-two months is a question that cannot be answered. Julian's vision was dominated by (Iamblichan) notions of universality brought into Oneness; it arose from traditional Roman ideas of the emperor and his virtues, which Julian integrated fully and consistently into the Platonic visions of the cosmos as one benevolent and unified whole. Good rule and good rulers emanated, through divine intermediaries, from the Highest One that is Goodness itself, whose exemplary virtues—justice, benevolence, mildness, clemency, and self-control—rulers must imitate. This is why the best rulers are philosophers: because, closer to the divine, they are better able to practice those virtues and thus guide human souls back to their divine source, Zeus-Helios and the Highest One.

Much of what Julian said was not itself new, but was new and radical because of who he was, how he said it, and the historical moment in which he said it. In fact, he often referred back to Plato's writings because they gave him the answers he needed for his day and time and the issues he had to confront—answers that Iamblichus's political theory or that of other contemporary philosophers apparently could not provide. In nearly all the writings I have discussed, Julian pointed out that the thoughts he proclaimed were his own, though the divine Iamblichus had inspired them. The emperor innovated, and he knew it. But his innovation was good, because it returned to and in the process correctly reformed the wisdom of the ancients that more recent times had deformed. This is so because the very act of turning to oneself, to the soul, and therefore to the gods, was a turning back to the gods, from whom everything had sprung. To be able to progress to god in one's soul therefore required a turning back—historically—to the origins of philosophy or wisdom, first because the gods had revealed to the ancients (through oracles) the Oneness at the origin of everything, and second, because in the historical evolution and diversity of philosophy mankind could recognize that the One is eternal and unchanging, and so is man's soul. Such recognition takes place because the philosopher, who is (spatially) close to the divine and its Oneness, also dwells in matter and therefore in the diversity it represents (as spatially far removed from Oneness), so that he can discern in the diversity of philosophies (and other religious and social customs) the one truth. As mediator between the divine and matter, the philosopher can thus guide all along the "royal road" to the divine, each according to his capacity, and with the help of all the myths, sacrifices, and rituals proper to each *ethnos,* city, and person.

This is the art of arts and the science of sciences Julian the philosopher as emperor practiced. Ethnic diversity and the unity of the Highest One, manifest in Zeus-Helios, were both part of the divine Providence, emanating from the Father, ruler of the middle, visible creator of all visible things he illuminated through his light. Greeks are not the most ancient, but as true philosophers they recognized in the diverse customs of others the guiding, mediating, and unifying power of Zeus-Helios, aided by Apollo, who had laid the ground for the *oikoumenē,* brought to fruition in Rome's Sol Invictus, in the *oikoumenē* Julian ruled and guided as mediator, in analogy to Zeus-Helios (Sol), back and upward to that divine Oneness. Because Julian is their son, these divine mediators are truly his guides. Consequently, his political theological reflections focus on Helios, Attis, the Mother of the Gods, Apollo, and so on, and not on the Highest One (about whom one can say only very little, through negation, anyhow).

Julian wished to convey that Greek Rome manifested divine intent best by assimilating diversity into well-ordered, harmonious Oneness proper (*oikeios*) to the one divinity that had produced it, with which it was therefore affiliated, and whose essential unity in diversity, three in one, it reflected by analogy. Rome, like its emperor, as the visible expression of a benevolent creator, was itself benevolent (philanthropic): thus all Romans, all inhabitants of the *oikoumenē,* were able to return to the Oneness, albeit to differing degrees. Rome's divinely chosen philosopher as emperor was higher and closer to the divine and so had to guide those lower and farther away back to it. This was true even for those very low and very far removed: uneducated Cynics and Christians. Those who followed the Galilean had made their own everything that was as far removed from the Good at the center as Galilee was from Rome (or from the Greek Rome, Constantinople). Christianity was therefore vulgar, simple, uncivilized.

What was true of Christianity, however, did not necessarily apply to the Christians, at least not by nature, since they were, like Antioch, Greek in origin. Julian's audience included sophisticated Greek Christians and other members of the elite, all formed by the same *paideia,* all—more or less—learned and conversant in Aristotelian logic, Platonic language theory, the tripartite structure of the cosmos, and Iamblichan and Porphyrian debates regarding the efficacy of sacrifice and statues. For that reason, Julian used the classic normative texts to address contemporary debates in non-Christian as well as Christian philosophical circles—that is, among Christian leaders such as Aetius, Eunomius, Meletius, Eudoxius, Euzoius, Basil, Gregory, and so on, who used the same normative classical texts to address the same debates: Homer, Hesiod, Plato, Aristotle, Theophrastus, Dio Chrysostom, Porphyry, Iamblichus, and the Bible. They had long done so, as is made clear by Porphyry and especially Eusebius, whose texts were also used by those most engaged in these debates. The Christians Julian addressed were his peers; some he knew through their writings, many others personally, because they were leading men in the imperial residences and part of his court—some, like Caesarius, as one of his physicians.

Julian's comprehensive and unifying vision centered on the imperial power that he saw as a manifestation of divine Providence. Based on ancient (classical) precedents, his vision could account precisely for much of cosmology and causality. Some elements of these addressed the reasons for different levels of creation to account for the bridging of the ontological divide separating mortal and immortal, divine and human spheres—something Genesis failed to do. Such bridging also explains why the Highest One, as First Cause, was *agennētos* and gave his creative capacity to his emanation, his son, Helios, who became visible and thus active in the material world without himself becoming matter, and how a very low demiurge such as Attis could become almost incarnate and thus very close to man without depriving his mother of the title *theotokos* by becoming fully human. And why creation and procession were eternal and immutable, so that souls could be eternally saved and required no historical savior figure with a beginning, whose saving function would therefore, by necessity, come to an end.

Julian's vision for Rome was new, its details shaped by his need to confront the wrong innovation of Christianity. His vision was an attack but, much more than that, a consistent system that merged everything, from the Highest One to the selection of magistrates, from the issuing of laws to the celebration of festivals, from sacrifice and statues of the gods to the reduction of taxes and the conduct of war, into one well-ordered, harmonious whole (on the theoretical level) and in so doing engaged numerous elements of Christianity, which at that moment was establishing a comprehensive vision of its own. It was a vision, *nota bene,* that now had to account for the political reality of governing the Roman *oikoumenē* as well. The challenge was formidable for Julian, but even more so for those Christians who had to counter his vision with another as comprehensive, that also harmonized everything better than Julian, from the Highest One to the celebration of festivals and the selection of magistrates. They succeeded (with a little help from the divine Providence that made Julian's rule a short one), and that is why Gregory of Nazianzus was honored as Gregory the Theologian.

8

The Making of the Apostate
Gregory's Oration 4 against Julian

"Listen to these words, all people; lend your ears, all you inhabitants of the earth," I call you all. . . . Listen, . . . men of all kinds and ages, those who are alive today and those who will live in the future, . . . all you powers of the heavens, all angels whose work is the fall of the tyrant and who have beaten . . . the dragon, the Apostate, . . . the common adversary and enemy of all.

—GREGORY OF NAZIANZUS, ORATION 4.1; PSALM 48:2

"Rumor, the swiftest messenger of sad events, . . . flew through provinces and nations," bearing the news of Julian's death while the emperor was on the *katabasis* from Ctesiphon back to Roman territory.[1] Libanius knew only that "a cavalryman's spear struck him when he was without armor, . . . and the spear went through his arm and entered his side. . . . You are anxious to hear who killed him. I do not know his name."[2] By early August Jovian had been elected the new emperor by the army, still in Persian territory. To control the worst effects of the rumors, Jovian sent messengers to Illyricum and Gaul "to announce the death of Julian and [his own] elevation, after Julian's demise, to the rank of Augustus." The messengers, passing through Antioch by mid-August, also conveyed Jovian's instructions to the mints to issue new coins with his portrait and the legend VICTORIA AUGUSTI, VICTORIA RO-

---

1. Amm. Marc. 25.8.13: "fama . . . index tristiorum casuum velocissima per provincias volitabit et gentes." The exact location of Julian's final battle is unknown. Ammianus 25.3.9 relates that on Julian's inquiry as to where he was on that fatal day, he was told the place was called Phrygia, which accorded with an earlier oracle foretelling Julian's death, reminiscent of the death of Cambyses, Hdt. 3.64.3–5: the name has symbolic rather than geographical significance. The scholarly consensus locates the battle south of Samarra, about 50 miles north of Baghdad and 100 miles north of Ctesiphon, which the army reached a few days later, Amm. Marc. 25.6.4; den Boeft, Drijvers, et al., eds., *Philological and Historical Commentary on Ammianus Marcellinus 25*, 61, 75–76, 270; Rosen, *Julian*, 363; Matthews, *Roman Empire*, 181, 506.

2. Lib. *Or.* 18.272, 274 (Libanius, *Selected Orations*, trans. Norman).

MANORUM, SECURITAS REI PUBLICE.[3] Such coins fooled no one. Pamphlets plastered on Antioch's columns to welcome Jovian when he arrived there in October ridiculed the emperor with slogans such as YOU CAME BACK FROM THE WAR: YOU SHOULD HAVE COME TO GRIEF THERE! or ILL-OMENED PARIS, MOST HANDSOME TO LOOK UPON! Julian was not the only emperor to feel the sting of the Antiochenes' tongue. Indeed, Jovian, in terrible quandary after Julian's death, had to conclude "a necessary but humiliating peace treaty" with Shapur II to salvage the Roman army.[4]

Sometime that summer of 363 the rumors of Julian's death reached Gregory in Nazianzus. His reaction, as he recorded it, was exultation.[5] As his *Orations* 4 and 5 indicate, however, his initial elation soon gave way to a more nuanced assessment of Julian the man and emperor, and of the consequences of his life and death for the community of the Romans.[6] In these two orations, Gregory made Julian the Apostate, creating the Julian who would dominate posterity until the discovery of Ammianus Marcellinus's *Res gestae* by writers such as Jean Budin, Abbé de la Bléterie, Montaigne, and Montesquieu slowly changed Julian's image again, to that of Roman emperor rather than the Apostate par excellence.[7]

In Gregory's orations, Julian became God's divinely preordained teaching tool with which to instruct the *oikoumenē* and the world through his prophet Gregory on the true meaning of Greekness (to be *hellēnikos* and *hellēnizein*), by associating with Julian everything he considered the wrong way of being Greek, a *Hellēn* (a term that came to signify "pagan")—from the mistaken use of Aristotle's logic to define the Trinity to the misconduct of festivals, from the mismanagement of war to misconceived legislation. In this way Gregory could declare all the good ways of being

---

3. Amm. Marc. 25.7.5–14, 8.8, 8.12; den Boeft, Drijvers, et al., *Philological and Historical Commentary on Ammianus Marcellinus 25*, 228–29, 269; Ehling, "Ausgang."

4. Eutr. *Brev.* 10.17.1: "pacem cum Sapore necessariam quidem, sed ignobilem fecit"; Amm. Marc. 25.10.1. Eunapius fr. 29.1 (Blockley 46) mentions the pamphlets; see Matthews, *Laying Down*, 194–95. The treaty demanded that Nisibis and significant terrain on either bank of the Tigris, gained since 298, be ceded to Persia and that Rome refrain from involvement in Armenian affairs. For the date, den Boeft, Drijvers, et al., *Philological and Historical Commentary on Ammianus Marcellinus 25*, 316–17; for the treaty, Rosen, *Julian*, 370.

5. Gregory and Caesarius were both in Nazianzus in the summer of 363. Gregory had returned from his extended stay with Basil at Annesi, and Caesarius had returned as a "blessed exile" while the emperor was preparing the Persian campaign (Gr. Naz. *Or.* 7.13), which suggests that he may have remained with Julian in Antioch as late as February 363; McGuckin, *St. Gregory*, 115–17, dates Gr. Naz. *Ep.* 7 to late 362; Van Dam, *Families*, 61–62; Gautier, *Retraite*, 321–22; Coulie, *Richesses*, 139–47.

6. Bernardi, ed. and trans., *Grégoire de Nazianze: Discours 4–5*. In *Or.* 4.53.3 Gregory speaks of writing; these orations were not meant for oral delivery; Bernardi, ibid., 21. I am also using Gregory of Nazianzus, *Contro Giuliano*, trans. and comm. Lugaresi, and *La morte di Giuliano l'Apostata: Orazione 5*, trans. and comm. Lugaresi; and Kurmann's essential *Gregor von Nazianz*.

7. S. Elm, "Gregory of Nazianzus's *Life*," esp. 169–70; Braun and Richer, eds., *Empereur Julien*, vol. 2; Rosen, *Julian*, 396–413.

Greek as *logoi*, from the beginning associated with the *Logos* and therefore his property. Through Julian, as explicated by Gregory, God taught Christians how to govern the Roman Empire correctly, how to safeguard the *archē tōn Rhomaiōn*. Because they had not done this properly before, God sent Julian as punishment. In his divine *philanthrōpia*, however, God had shortened the punishment and combined it with instruction, to warn and to guide.

Addressing the *novi homines* governing the realm, men in public positions, including members of the clergy, Gregory now presented the foundations of Christian Roman rule—from prescribing the behavior of emperors vis-à-vis their bishops as advisors to describing the appropriate conduct of war, from outlining the proper arrangement of the agora and the theaters in the cities to detailing the means for selecting magistrates. Since the public officials addressed included bishops, the presbyters who advised them, and other members of the clergy, Gregory in these orations also presented his exegesis of the correct and incorrect ways of administering the *pharmakon* of the Trinity, associating incorrect (heretical) views with Julian. Gregory's principal aim was to demonstrate to all Christian leaders that they must administer wisely the power invested in them by divine will, and that failure to do so could at any moment call forth another Julian, another Apostate and Antichrist, to remind them that they displeased God at their peril (but also that they might, even so, receive his benevolent clemency). Most important, in these orations Gregory conveyed to all that Roman power was divinely (pre)ordained to be Christian. This was the unifying force that gathered Rome's diversity into one, since this God as One in Three had created everything, including Rome, and would bring it to completion in the fullness of time. Greek Rome's supremacy, based on and ordered into a harmonious whole through *logoi, paideia,* the *hiera,* and the poleis, was thus and had been from the beginning "ours," Christian. Everything and everyone else was *hellēnikos,* "theirs," belonging to persons outside the community of the civilized—that is, orthodox Christians.

Of all Gregory's works, *Orations* 4 and 5 are the best (and usually the only ones) known to scholars of ancient history, for they are a prominent source for the history of Julian. As these scholars reconstruct that history, Gregory, to cite Glen Bowersock, serves as "an intelligent recipient of facts and gossip that were current, so that ... as a witness, [he] is perceptive as well as passionately hostile."[8] Most historians today are more kindly disposed toward Gregory's orations as a source for Julian's life and career than Johannes Quasten, according to whom "hate and anger so predominate in them that their historical value is almost nil"—but not by much.[9] For Van Dam, Julian brought out the worst in Gregory, as exemplified in these orations, which he considers "predictably digressive and baggy, simultaneously hys-

---

8. Bowersock, *Julian,* 5; and Rosen, *Julian,* 8, 18–19, 31–33, and passim.
9. Quasten, *Patrology,* vol. 3, 242; Asmus, "Invektiven," 366.

terical and pedantic, fiercely caustic and pompously ponderous. . . . To read them is to cringe both from embarrassment at Gregory's petulance and from boredom with his long-windedness." As an "attempt at writing history," he concludes, Gregory's work "was not very successful."[10]

Scholars interested in Gregory's theology study these orations only as they relate to *theōsis,* a neologism Gregory used here first to define affiliation to the divine. Those concerned with church history generally read them as representing Gregory's most sustained repudiation of classical culture.[11] Jean Bernardi's assessment that "la lecture de cette polémique laisse au coeur de l'homme moderne un certain malaise" appears to strike a chord. Gregory's extravagant praise of Constantius and Marc of Arethusa (both Arian), and especially his tone, are disconcerting, so that "cette espèce de danse allègre du scalp sur le corps d'un ennemi mort de la veille a quelque chose de gênant." In fact, it is no small feat to integrate the image of Gregory as "esprit de haute culture, brillant et grâcieux; âme douce et tendre, mal armée, faute peut-être de sens pratique, pour soutenir les lutes dans lesquelles le hazard de la vie le jettera," so dear to much Gregorian scholarship, with the dancing Gregory happily swinging Julian's bloody scalp.[12] Though widely cited, these orations have, as a consequence, been comparatively little studied.[13]

Jean Bernardi's metaphor of the "danse allègre du scalp" is apt. Gregory's orations are a performance piece.[14] In presenting a person now absent, the dead em-

---

10. Van Dam, *Kingdom,* 100–102, 192–202, for an analysis of the orations; quotations 195, 194.

11. McGuckin (*St. Gregory,* 119–20 and n. 106) explains Gregory's positive portrayal of Constantius as resulting from the genre. Kaldellis's view of the orations is representative (*Hellenism in Byzantium,* 158–61). Following Van Dam's characterization of the orations as hysterics, he grants that Gregory separated Greek, or speaking it, *hellēnizein,* as a language from the religious association of its literature but charges him with "having no adequate philosophical solution for the quagmire of his own Hellenism," because even "a solid refutation of Julian . . . would not have been of much use to Christians, who would still have had to negotiate between their faith and an *alien* culture" (emphasis mine). Coulie, "Chaînes," demonstrates how Gregory's use of citations and allusions to classical texts gives the orations an internal cohesion that does not sit well with the common "reproches d'abus de procédés rhétoriques et d'omniprésence de la passion ou de la virulence" (pp. 137–38); still, for Coulie, Gregory's classical culture is a matter of form rather than content. Beeley, *Gregory,* 115–16, briefly refers to *Or. 4* in the context of *theōsis.*

12. Bernardi, "Réquisitoire," 91; and Godet as cited in Gregory of Nazianzus, *Contro Giuliano,* trans. and comm. Lugaresi, 13–14.

13. McGuckin, *St. Gregory,* 119–26. Daley, *Gregory,* 35, treats the orations in the context of Gregory's relation to philosophy; Gautier, *Retraite,* 176–78, presents a succinct analysis in the context of the *imperium.* For an overview of older scholarship, Gregory of Nazianzus, *Contro Giuliano,* trans. and comm. Lugaresi, 12–15; Kurmann, *Gregor von Nazianz,* 6, notes the scant scholarly engagement.

14. The following is indebted to Gregory of Nazianzus, *Contro Giuliano,* trans. and comm. Lugaresi, and to Kurmann's excellent commentary. For theoretical approaches to theatrical representation and performance, Goody, *Representations,* 1–34. Also informative is Martschukat and Patzold, eds., *Geschichtswissenschaft,* esp. 1–54.

peror, Gregory explicitly and emphatically intended not to write history but to perform a sacred rite (*Or.* 4.20). The orations are a *panēgyrismos* and an *epinikion* celebrating a victory: "a bloodless sacrifice of words," "more sacred and more pure than any sacrifice of mute animals."[15] Gregory's performance contrasted sharply with that of the emperor. Gregory chanted a sacred hymn and performed a sacred rite destined to last, whereas Julian's deeds and words had been nothing but theater (*skēnē*), make-believe, fleeting like "the grass of the fields that soon falls off" (*Or.* 4.3, 113–14; cf. Ps 36:2). Gregory's aim was to make Julian lose face, and he presented him masked as a mime, a *histrio*, a pantomime. The man and his rule had been histrionics, as transient as a theatrical performance. As it turned out, Gregory's performance of Julian as mime formed the emperor's future. Gregory's picture of Julian and his rule shaped historiography more than anything the emperor had done or written in the twenty-two months of his rule, though he had done and written quite a lot.[16]

By the summer of 363, Gregory, armed "like a hoplite," had spent almost as much time thinking and writing about the emperor's actions and words as the emperor had spent writing and acting. Now the emperor's death presented new questions and challenges. As a Roman, Gregory could not but lament the fate of the army struck by the loss of its commander in enemy territory, nor could he applaud the humiliating peace treaty.[17] As a Christian Roman, he had to explain why Jovian, also a Christian, had consented to such a shameful agreement. And as a Christian he had to explain why the first baptized Roman emperor, scion of Constantine's dynasty, had deserted and become the Apostate. That God had permitted such a disaster, including the end with all the perils it entailed for the Roman *oikoumenē*, could not be ignored. Furthermore, Gregory, as a member of the elite, had to demonstrate to his peers that he had the authority to explain by underscoring his distance from the bad emperor while showing his closeness to Julian's good precursor, which entitled him to advise his successors—or to write as if he had that privilege.[18] What did Julian's reign signify for Christians, for Rome's power, and for the relationship

---

15. Gr. Naz. *Or.* 4.3: πάσης ἀλόγου θυσίας ἱερώτερόν τε καὶ καθαρώτερον. *Or.* 4.7, 8, 12, 17; *Or.* 5.35; Kurmann, *Gregor von Nazianz*, 14.

16. Braun and Richer's collaborative effort *Empereur Julien* is invaluable for the Western reception of Julian; his reception in the Byzantine literature remains a desideratum. Gregory's impact on the presentation of Julian in early fifth-century Christian historiography, both Greek and Latin, has also not received scholarly attention. Philip of Side's refutation of Julian's *Against the Galileans*, mentioned above in Chapter 7 and referred to in Socr. *HE* 7.27, is lost. Socr. *HE* 3.23 cites Gr. Naz. *Or.* 5.23–24, and Philostorgius respected him; cf. Photius *Bibl.* 40. Julian's (spurious) *Epistle to Arsacius* (Nuffelen, "Deux fausses lettres," 136–50) further attests to Julian's impact on Christians. See also Gregory of Nazianzus, *Contro Giuliano*, trans. and comm. Lugaresi, 342–33.

17. Gr. Naz. *Or.* 4.1, 5.15.

18. Compare Sailor, *Writing and Empire*.

between emperor and priest? How should Julian be remembered? What lessons had God wished to impart to the faithful, now and in the future?[19]

Gregory's *Orations* 4 and 5 are modeled after Demosthenes' *Philippics* and are at least in part responsible for Gregory's later renown as the Christian Demosthenes. They are a tour de force of classical learning, demonstrating that Gregory the Christian, inspired by Christ the *Logos,* was more Greek in his *paideia* and a better philosopher than the *Hellēn* Julian, who had declared by edict that *logoi* belonged only to those who believed in the gods of the Greeks and the Romans.[20] Gregory's orations, following the structure of the invective, or *psogos* (though Gregory claimed not to consider these orations invective), countered every theme Julian had evoked and considered central to his rule—everything discussed in Chapters 3, 4, and 7. A second, underlying structural element of Gregory's *Oration* 4 is the philosopher as leader, as detailed in Plato's *Republic* and *Laws,* beginning with the emphasis on legislation, exemplified by Minos, and just jurisdiction, as evidence of the correct relation between knowledge (of the divine), action, and production, activated in administering the city—Julian had perverted all these to their opposite.[21] As Leonardo Lugaresi has remarked, "Gregorio, dunque, ci pare che abbia capito benissimo il suo avversario," a point of which most modern scholars are, however, not convinced.[22]

Gregory had in fact begun to respond to and thus prepare his orations against Julian in the summer of 362. As I have mentioned, in his *Epistle* 10, *To Candidianus,* he bemoaned that the new *nomos* prevented *logoi* from running freely and constrained him to silence.[23] On August 1, 362, Gregory celebrated the Maccabeans' resistance to Antiochus IV Epiphanes in a thinly veiled comparison between his family and friends and Julian, who had just passed Cappadocia on his way to

---

19. Julian's life, death, and afterlife preoccupied Gregory for the rest of his days. He evoked Julian's rule in his *Or.* 6, *On Peace;* in the funeral eulogies for Caesarius (*Or.* 7.11), his father (*Or.* 18.32), for Athanasius (*Or.* 21.32), and for Basil (*Or.* 43.11); in praising a Cynic philosopher (*Or.* 25.10); on his retirement from the episcopal see of Constantinople (*Or.* 42.3); and in his *poemata moralia, Carm.* 34.245–48, PG 37.963. Indeed, he eventually declared Valens a new Julian, a new apostate: see below, Chapter 10.

20. McGuckin, *St. Gregory,* 57, 125, notes Gregory's conscious emulation of Demosthenes. For a systematic overview of pagan exempla in *Or.* 4 and 5, see Demoen, *Pagan and Biblical Exempla,* 361–65, 23.

21. See Pl. *Lg.* 624a, the Platonic dialogue *Minos* 319b–320b, combined with Pl. *R.* 500c, 500e–501b; Plot. *Enn.* 4.35, 6.9.7.25–26; D. Chr. *Or.* 4.39–41; D. O'Meara, *Platonopolis,* 87–115.

22. Gregory of Nazianzus, *Contro Giuliano,* trans. and comm. Lugaresi, 15; Criscuolo, "Gregorio," 205, assumes that Gregory read Julian's most important texts. Bernardi, ed. and trans., *Grégoire de Nazianze: Discours 4–5,* 46–50, is representative of the majority view that Gregory had no knowledge of Julian's writings. McGuckin, *St. Gregory,* 116, 125, who does not comment on whether Gregory knew Julian's writings, considers Caesarius a good source, and thinks that Gregory had access to firsthand accounts for his discussion of the Persian campaign; Daley, *Gregory,* 32–34.

23. Gr. Naz. *Ep.* 10, dated July or August 362.

Antioch.[24] Julian, as mentioned in Chapter 4, was the Antiochus "of our day" (*Or.* 15.12), and Gregory, his family, and his brothers and friends were paragons of virtue like the Maccabeans, whose words were weapons of resistance as powerful as their physical suffering (*Or.* 15.6). Gregory again announced his willingness, indeed eagerness, to suffer martyrdom in *Oration* 2.87. The entire oration, as we saw, was written under the impact of Julian, though not with the same directness as *Orations* 4 and 5, and his bitter complaint in *Oration* 4.6 that Julian in his deviousness had taken care not to encourage martyrdom could reflect real disappointment. Still, Gregory had his words, as powerful as those he had placed in the mouth of the Maccabeans in extremis.[25]

Though Gregory had begun to prepare his orations *Against Julian* in 362, the final redaction of *Oration* 4, as Ugo Criscuolo has suggested, took place after Julian's demise, in late 364 or early 365.[26] He composed *Oration* 5 about a year later, in late 365 or early 366, so that chronologically *Oration* 5 follows *Oration* 6.[27] This

---

24. Gr. Naz. *Or.* 15, *PG* 35.912–33 (Italian trans. Moreschini in *Gregorio di Nazianzo: Tutte le orazioni*, 374–91); above, Chapter 4. For these friends, Gr. Naz. *DVS* 277–79. McGuckin, *St. Gregory*, 127, identified the seven as Gregory, Caesarius, Amphilochius, Basil, Gregory of Nyssa, Peter, and Naucratius. But see McLynn, "Among the Hellenists," 224–33; and above, Chapter 5.

25. Gr. Naz. *Or.* 4.57–58, 61–62, 68, 94.

26. Criscuolo, "Gregorio," 171. Between 362 and 363 Gregory spent time with Basil, with whom he cooperated in writing against Julian: see *Or.* 5.39.3; and Gregory of Nazianzus, *Contro Giuliano*, trans. and comm. Lugaresi, 45.

27. The dating of *Orations* 4 and 5 is significant, because their composition and completion covers Jovian's reign, the early months of Valens's rule, and Procopius's usurpation. The dating of these orations reflects (the respective scholars' interpretations of) Gregory's attitude toward these rulers in light of their orthodoxy and heterodoxy (i.e., Valens's Arianism). Two passages are crucial for dating *Or.* 4. In *Or.* 4.6.18, Gregory says that *logoi* have regained their freedom. Scholars have read this as referring to *CTh* 13.3.6, issued by Jovian on January 11, 364 (though the *inscriptio* has Valentinian I and Valens; see Germino, *Scuola*, 193–95, for Jovian's authorship), and addressed to the *praefectus praetorio* Claudius Mamertinus (of panegyric fame). Scholars have interpreted this edict as revoking Julian's edict about teachers. Thus January 11, 364, is considered the *terminus post quem* for *Or.* 4 (e.g.) by Bernardi, ed. and trans., *Grégoire de Nazianze: Discours 4-5*, 31; Kurmann, *Gregor von Nazianz*, 9–10; Gregory of Nazianzus, *Contro Giuliano*, trans. and comm. Lugaresi, 43, 231. However, as Germino, *Scuola*, 196–239, has pointed out, *CTh* 13.3.6 was more likely a rescript, addressing a specific case in 364 that required the emperor to vet a teacher, and not the general law that the *CTh*, compiled around 435, presents it as. The original law of 364 thus did not revoke Julian's school law, which remained in effect until Tribonian: i.e., *CJ* 10.53[52].7. (It is possible that the law of 364 revoked another law of Julian, now lost, concerning education, perhaps that criticized by Amm. Marc. 22.10.7; cf. 25.4.20.) *CTh* 13.3.6, in sum, does not bear on Gregory's *Or.* 4, so that Julian's death is the *terminus post quem*. In practice, imperial control of teachers may have ceased over time as impracticable, as implied by its context, namely greater autonomy of local organs, so that the specific law of 364 anticipated the status quo of 435; Matthews, *Laying Down*, 274–75. In the second quote relevant for the date, *Or.* 4.10, Gregory laments the unresolved schism in Nazianzus. *Or.* 6, dated to early 364, celebrates the end of that schism and is considered the *terminus ante quem* of *Or.* 4; McLynn, "Gregory the Peacemaker," 194; *Grégoire de Nazianze:*

dating of *Orations* 4, 6, and 5 presupposes that *Orations* 4 and 5 were not two parts of one work, as they are usually treated, but were both distinct yet related works, intended for their own occasions and addressing different though overlapping audiences.[28] Once we consider them independent of each other, as Criscuolo and Lugaresi have suggested, it becomes evident that *Oration* 5 entered a hotly contested debate about Julian's divinity, his death, and his sanctification, represented by Libanius's *Monody* and especially his *Epitaphius*. When writing *Oration* 5 Gregory was aware of Libanius's works commemorating the emperor. Thus, he directly engaged questions of Julian's afterlife and the manner in which he ought to be memorialized— his imperial legitimacy, in sum—at a time when these issues were particularly pressing for pagans and Christians, namely the usurpation of Julian's relative Procopius, the period during which I suggest Gregory composed *Oration* 5.[29]

Indeed, when considering each oration in its own right, we see the scope and complexity of Gregory's countervision in full relief. Such consideration gives proper

---

Discours 6–12, ed. and trans. Calvet-Sébasti, 31; McGuckin, *St. Gregory,* 109; Gautier, *Retraite,* 307. Indeed, several remarks concerning Jovian suggest that Gregory composed most of *Or.* 4 during his reign (he died February 17, 364) and completed it under Valentinian and Valens. Regali, "Intenti," supports that date, though his alignment of emperors and religious policy is too rigid: for example, when he proposes that Gr. Naz. *Or.* 5.15, 19, and 32 defend Valens (rather than support Jovian).

28. Criscuolo, "Gregorio," 173 (and see 194), remarks that "i due testi . . . appaiono diversamente motivati e la loro visione unitaria resulta solo *a posteriori,*" motivated by the fact that Julian connects both orations thematically, programmatically, and structurally, a point taken up by Lugaresi (Gregory of Nazianzus, *La morte di Giuliano l'Apostata: Orazione 5,* trans. and comm. Lugaresi, 9–27) that I am pushing further. The question of the date is connected to that of the unity of the work. On the assumption that both orations are essentially one, scholars have proposed dates from early 364 to late 368; Bernardi, ed. and trans., *Grégoire de Nazianze: Discours 4–5,* 11–37; Kurmann, *Gregor von Nazianz,* 6–12; Gregory of Nazianzus, *Contro Giuliano,* trans. and comm. Lugaresi, 39–48. Style and practicality (Asmus, "Invektiven," 326–27, felt that their sheer size required publication in two parts), rather than different occasions, are the common explanations for separating one big oration into two, albeit of very different lengths. For Bernardi (ed. and trans., *Grégoire de Nazianze: Discours 4–5,* 33–34), *Or.* 4 was devoted to Julian's life and *Or.* 5 to his death. Kurmann, *Gregor von Nazianz,* 12–14, proposes a tripartite division: *Or.* 4 covers two parts; *Or.* 5, one.

29. Asmus, "Invektiven," 327, 358–59, drawing mostly on *Or.* 4, first suggested that Gregory responded to Lib. *Or.* 18, the funeral eulogy for Julian. Bernardi (ed. and trans., *Grégoire de Nazianze: Discours 4–5,* 21–25) and others rejected this, based, however, on the consideration of *Or.* 4 and 5 as essentially one oration; Gregory of Nazianzus, *La morte di Giuliano l'Apostata: Orazione 5,* trans. and comm. Lugaresi, 15–20. The dating of Lib. *Or.* 18 is complicated. Most scholars assume that its completion predates the earthquake and tsunami of July 21, 365. According to Wiemer, *Libanios,* 260–68, the oration circulated outside Antioch only after Valens's death (which need not have prevented Gregory from being aware of it; Gregory of Nazianzus, *La morte di Giuliano l'Apostata: Orazione 5,* trans. and comm. Lugaresi, 14–27). Felgentreu, "Zur Datierung," argues for 365/6. G. Kelly, "Ammianus," focuses on the parallels between the tsunami and Julian's rule. Lib. *Or.* 17, *Monody for the Dead Emperor,* was composed soon after January 1, 364, predating *Or.* 18, and was presumably shared only with a restricted circle; Wiemer, *Libanios,* 251–58. These were the men whom Gregory's *Or.* 5 sought to engage.

due to the formidable range of themes he engaged and tailored to his audience. Both orations address the "new" and old men governing the empire, Christian public officials. But whereas *Oration* 5 is more weighted toward an audience involved in the secular administration of the empire, linked to the court residing in Caesarea and Antioch while Procopius held Constantinople, *Oration* 4, in addition to themes of public governance, elaborates arguments about the correct understanding of the Trinity, familiar from *Orations* 1–3 and brought to a close with *Oration* 6. *Oration* 4 thus addressed persons similar to those addressed in *Orations* 1–3 and 6: public officials and persons who advised others (at court and elsewhere) in doctrinal matters, bishops and presbyters.[30] At the same time, Gregory's true audience was again both local and universal: the *oikoumenē* and the cosmos, the angels and God.

THE PILLAR OF INFAMY: AN INVERTED *FÜRSTENSPIEGEL*

We, saying only a few things out of the many, will leave to posterity a writing on a pillar [stēlographia], so to speak.
—GREGORY OF NAZIANZUS, ORATION 4.20

[They found] the speech he had delivered against them outside the palace in the city on what is known as the Tetrapylon of the Elephants, near the Regia.[31]
—JOHN MALALAS, CHRONICLE 13.328.3–4

Gregory opened *Oration* 4.1–20 with a grandiose victory hymn (*tēn epinikion . . . ōidēn, Or.* 4.12), echoing Pindar, which set the scene: "'Listen to these words, all people, lend your ears, all you inhabitants of the earth,' I call you all, . . . all you powers of the heavens, all angels whose work is the fall of the tyrant, and who have beaten . . . the common adversary and enemy of all."[32] His oration was a triumphant counter to Julian's hymns to Zeus-Helios and to the Mother of the Gods. Gregory was the true priest, the true philosopher, the true prophet. Like a new Isaiah evoking the glories that have arisen once again (*Or.* 4.3), he gave voice to the community of everyone, past, present, and future, from the heavens, residence of the sanctified soul of the great Constantius, to the farthest reaches of the earth. "This is the right moment [*kairos*] for me to sound again the same accents as the most eloquent of the prophets," not to chastise Israel rebelling against God but to sing "against a tyrant who also rebelled and who has taken a fall worthy of his impiety."[33] Invit-

---

30. Bernardi's proposal (ed. and trans., *Grégoire de Nazianze: Discours 4–5*, 69, 73–80) that the manuscript tradition N originated in Constantinople is suggestive.

31. Gr. Naz. *Or.* 4.20: αὐτοὶ δὲ ὀλίγα ἐκ πολλῶν διελθόντες στηλογραφίαν ὥσπερ τινὰ τοῖς μεθ᾽ ἡμᾶς καταλείψομεν. John Malalas *Chron.* 13.328.3–4: καὶ προέθηκε τὸν κατ᾽ αὐτῶν ῥηθέντα παρ᾽ αὐτοῦ λόγον ἔξω τοῦ παλατίου τῆς αὐτῆς πόλεως εἰς τὸ λεγόμενον Τετράπυλον τῶν ἐλεφάντων πλησίον τῆς Ῥηγίας.

32. Gr. Naz. *Or.* 4.1, Ps 48:2: οἷς ἔργον ἡ τοῦ τυράννου κατάλυσις.

ing the entire universe to sing and dance with him in celebrating the common joy at the renewed freedom of *logoi,* Gregory announced his central themes. He will proclaim to all successive generations

> the wonders [*thaumata*] of the power of God. But because these cannot be illustrated without first presenting the magnitude of the danger, and this in turn cannot be done without first demonstrating the evil of [Julian's] character and examining the beginnings and seeds of this evil that made him fall into such [evil] madness [*kakodaimonian*], after which he developed bit by bit his impiety as serpents do their venom . . . , we will leave to the books and histories the task of representing with the appropriate emphasis [*ektragōidein*] all of his facts. We do not have the leisure [*scholē*] to extend our account beyond the limits of the subject we have proposed for ourselves but, rushing through a few facts among the many, we will leave posterity a writing on a stele [*stēlographia*], so to speak, limiting ourselves in our discourse to the most important and evident facts among those that concern him.[34]

That Gregory defined this oration, indeed both *Orations* 4 and 5, as writing on a stele rather than as history or invective was no accident. As Alois Kurmann has pointed out, the term *stēlographia* is a neologism deriving from the verb *stēliteuein,* which relates to the practice of inscribing the names of convicted criminals after their execution (or if they had absconded) on a *stēlē.* Persons thus inscribed (*stēliteuein*) were marked and shamed forever and for all to see, present in the community even though they were absent.[35] For Gregory, a history, in contrast, means the assembly and assessment of all facts relevant to an emperor's rule, and this he had no intention of providing, as he reemphasized in *Oration* 4.79: others were already engaged in filling "our ears . . . with the praise of his good administration of the public post, relaxation of taxes, good choice of magistrates, and punishment of robbery" (*Or.* 4.75). Gregory's opening *epinikion* inviting all to join the celebration hints at another reason for Gregory's assertion that he was not writing history. As Gregory had just pointed out, history as a genre required the enumeration of all rele-

---

33. Gr. Naz. *Or.* 4.2: ἐπὶ τυράννῳ καὶ ἀθετήσαντι καὶ πεσόντι πτῶμα τῆς ἀσεβείας ἄξιον. Julian set great store by his own *kairos*, especially in military affairs; Athanassiadi-Fowden, *Julian*, 76 n. 180, 176 n. 58, 222 n. 98.

34. Gr. Naz. *Or.* 4.20: Ἐπειδὴ οὐχ οἷόν τε ταῦτα δηλῶσαι μὴ τὸ τοῦ κινδύνου παραστήσαντας μέγεθος, τοῦτο δὲ οὐχ οἷόν τε μὴ τὸ τοῦ τρόπου κακόηθες διελέγξαντας καὶ ἐξ οἵων ἀρχῶν καὶ τῆς κακίας σπερμάτων ἐπὶ τὴν κακοδαιμονίαν ταύτην ἐξέπεσε, κατὰ μικρὸν τὴν ἀσέβειαν συναυξήσας ὥσπερ τὸν ἰὸν τῶν ἑρπετῶν καὶ τῶν θηρίων ὅσα πυκρότατα, πάντα μὲν οὖν ἐκτραγῳδεῖν τὰ ἐκείνου βίβλοις καὶ ἱστορίαις παρήσομεν, οὐ γὰρ ἡμῖν γε σχολὴ μακρότερα τῆς παρούσης ὑποθέσεως ῥαψῳδεῖν, αὐτοὶ δὲ ὀλίγα ἐκ πολλῶν διελθόντες στηλογραφίαν ὥσπερ τινὰ τοῖς μεθ' ἡμᾶς καταλείψομεν, ἐπὶ τὰ κυριώτατα καὶ περιφανέστατα τῶν κατ' ἐκείνον τῷ λόγῳ χωρήσαντες. Gr. Naz. *Or.* 4.79 and 116 stress again that he is not writing history; Kurmann, *Gregor von Nazianz*, 81, 269, 392. I have tried to retain some of Gregory's play with *kakos,* "evil."

35. Kurmann, *Gregor von Nazianz*, 19–20; for the inscribing of convicts, Isoc. 16.9; D. 9.45; Arist. *Rh.* 2.23.25.1400a; Ps.-Plut. *V. decem or.* 838b; Philo, *Quis rer. div. haer.* 30; Jos. *AJ* 16.6.2; Philochorus, *FGH* 328 F 134; Iambl. *VP* 35.252. According to Lampe s.v. 3, Athanasius used *stēlographia* to denounce heresy.

vant facts. Here that would have meant recounting the closeness to Julian of many (orthodox as well as heretical) Christians, such as Caesarius, and their advances during his reign. Gregory's invective was thus also an apology, excusing those he now invited explicitly to join the common choir of thanksgiving who, too "stupefied by the theater of this world," had been unable to resist Julian as fervently as the most stalwart (*Or.* 4.9). When Gregory defamed Julian as an actor, he also hinted that while Julian was in power Christians had been forced to act and only now dared speak the truth openly. A history would have had to note those persons and their actions, but invective could elide them (though Gregory's promise to forgo history, combined with the invitation to all to join, suggests that Gregory and his audience knew whom he meant): echoes of Pliny's panegyric to Trajan.[36]

Gregory also pointed out emphatically, however, that he did not intend to write a *psogos* either: no invective could do justice to Julian's depravity.[37] *Psogos* or *oratio invectiva* was a set genre, an inverse of the encomium in which the author publicly ridiculed, accused, prosecuted, and implicitly convicted a specific person. Structurally speaking, as I have mentioned, *Oration* 4 follows the rules of that genre. As Gregory indicated, he began with Julian's youth and education to highlight his *eugeneia,* all the better to contrast it with the evils particular to him (hence addressing the origin of that evil, a difficult task given Julian's good family of Christian emperors), which culminated in his *apostasia* (*Or.* 4.21–56). From that moment on, Gregory enumerated Julian's deeds (or rather, misdeeds) while in office as the direct result of his apostasy, moving outward from the purges of the court and the army via his nefarious actions in the cities to the effects on the entire empire, set in sharp relief by the *synkrisis,* or comparison, of Julian with truly worthy leaders such as Constantius (*Or.* 4.57–124).[38]

Gregory, by insisting that the genre of these orations was neither *psogos* nor history, despite their structure, consciously chose to forgo the role of the prosecutor arguing his case to elicit a conviction.[39] Rather, he wrote a *stēlographia,* evoking the

---

36. This could well be what Gregory implied when lamenting in *Or.* 2.84 that "we have become a new spectacle, not for angels and humans . . . but for nearly all evil persons [*ponēroi*] and in all circumstances and places, in public spaces, at drinking parties, at festivals and funerals. Now we have jumped even onto the theatrical scene—I say it almost crying—and together with the most licentious we incite laughter: there is no subject of song or spectacle so agreeable as a Christian lampooned." For Pliny, see (e.g.) *Pan.* 68.6–7; Bartsch, *Actors,* 148; S. Elm, "*Persona,*" with further bibliography.

37. Gr. Naz. *Or.* 4.79: οὗ μηδὲ ψόγον ἔστιν εὑρεῖν ἄξιον.

38. See Gr. Naz. *Or.* 4.66: "Having thus brought the situation around him under control according to his plan, he now applied himself in the same manner to the things that came next." For invective, see Arist. *Poet.* 4.1448a24–26a; Pl. *Lg.* 11.934d6–936b2; Men. Rh. *Treatise* 1.1 (*Menander Rhetor,* ed. and trans. Russell and Wilson, 2; *Peri epideiktikōn,* ed. Spengel, 331–32). Koster, *Invektive,* 7–17, 38–39, is valuable, though he does not address Christian writers.

39. *Pace,* e.g., Van Dam, *Kingdom,* 195; McGuckin, *St. Gregory,* 120–21; Bernardi, ed. and trans., *Grégoire de Nazianze: Discours 4–5,* 39.

public proclamation of the legal act *stēliteuein*.⁴⁰ Such public proclamations, on pillars in public places, were the domain of those who ruled. Julian's edict and imperial letters had been thus posted, including the *Antiochikos* or *Misopogon*, on the Tetrapylon of the Elephants near the royal street in Antioch. In these Julian presented himself as philanthropic Platonic philosopher-king displaying exemplary *sōphrosynē*. Stelae also displayed those decrees that had excluded Christians from *logoi* and by implication from the agora, the public domain. In his counterstele Gregory, as the voice of the *Logos*, overwrote—in a public, official, performative act of his own—Julian's edicts, deeds, and concepts, one by one. And whereas Julian's words, written on stone, would pass like dried grass, Gregory's, written on flimsy linen or on wax tablets, would last, as he reemphasized at the close of *Oration 5*: "Here is our stele for you, higher and more visible than the Stelae of Hercules.... This stele cannot but move about and make itself known to all; and it will be received even in the future, of that I am certain, to shame you and your works [*sa stēliteuousan*], and to teach everyone not to attempt such a rebellion against God, lest they may be punished in like manner for having committed similar crimes" (*Or.* 5.42).

That was Gregory's task: *damnatio memoriae* by representation rather than erasure, stripping Julian of honor by shaming his person and deeds.⁴¹ (*Oration 5* directly engages debates about Julian's afterlife, his *mémoire*.) Gregory did not need to prosecute to elicit conviction. By divine decree, Julian had been sentenced, convicted, and executed in the theater of war. God had been prosecutor, judge, and executioner (*Or.* 4.13–14). Gregory, as his prophet "filled with divine inspiration" (*enthous*) (*Or.* 4.17), merely proclaimed the sentence and explicated it to all in the present and in the future.⁴² Anticipating Augustine's observation in the *City of God* (5.21) that God grants earthly rule both to the pious and to the impious, but does so advisedly, Gregory provided a providential explanation for Julian's rule and the calamity it entailed for the community of the Romans.

By calling his writings an act of *stēliteuein*, Gregory also highlighted the antithetical themes of that providential explanation. Here, true legitimacy and hence true justice and just jurisdiction; there, injustice and hence the mere pretense of jurisdiction, without any legitimacy. Here, true and lasting deeds; there, fiction and

---

40. The relevance of this new genre was evident to the copyists of Gregory's orations. A significant number of manuscripts are entitled *logos stēliteutikos*, the title also chosen by Bernardi, ed. and trans., *Grégoire de Nazianze: Discours 4–5*, 86 app. crit. Asmus, "Invektiven," highlights Gregory's choice of *stēlographia* as countering Libanius's *Epitaphius*.

41. For a discussion of the theory and practice of *damnatio memoriae* in the empire, E. Elm, "Damnatio."

42. For the notion of the poet's divine inspiration, Pl. *Ion* 543b, *Phdr.* 241e; D. Chr. *Or.* 1.56, and Gr. Naz. *Or.* 24.5, 39.14; this comes after passages of biblical citations that are Gregory's source of divine inspiration; Kurmann, *Gregor von Nazianz*, 75.

dissimulation. Here, acts of true citizenship based on the real understanding of the *oikos,* the *politeia,* and *koinōnia* of the Romans; there, willful disregard of those values, a clinging to false idols, and the committing of misanthropic acts. The sites of Gregory's encounter with Julian the emperor were, as a consequence, precisely those where emperor and citizen met each other most directly, the theater and the agora.

The Theater

In the rhetorical fireworks Gregory unleashed against Julian, the theater played a central role. Gregory acted as *editor* on earth, explicating the divinely set scene by unmasking the emperor and revealing him as the dissimulator he was. His oration evokes "the *skēnē* of the cosmos and its great theater" (*Or.* 4.9), inviting all to sit in judgment of Gregory's own performance as he reveals Julian's bad acting, his histrionics, in order that all can appreciate more fully God's miracles.[43] Despite the undeniable importance of Gregory's unmasking of Julian, however, this was merely a tool to achieve his overarching aim to dismantle Julian's notions of *logoi* and *hiera,* and thereby establish and showcase the true nature of these notions as Christian.

Words, *logoi,* and their relation to the sacred, *hiera,* were at the heart of Gregory's response to Julian because they had been at the heart of Julian's endeavor.[44]

> I offer a discourse of thanks [*logos*] to God, more sacred and pure than any of his sacrifices of mute [*alogou*] animals, not like his impious and vain discourses and his even more impious sacrifices, the richness and power of which were a power of impiety, and of an unwise ... wisdom [*asophos ... sophia*], because all power and culture of this world walk in darkness and end far from the light of truth.... But for me, offering today a sacrifice of praise and presenting the bloodless offer of words, who will provide a theater adequate to my thanks, what language [*glōssa*] will provide an echo for me as great as I would wish? What ear will hear my words with as much passion [as I speak them]? Indeed, not only is an action of thanks through the word the most proper [offering] for the Word [*Logos*]—among the other names by which he is called, he enjoys this denomination most because of the power of the appellative[45]—but it is also fitting that Julian be condemned to punishment by a discourse for the lawlessness committed against words common to all logical beings, which he denied Christians as if [*logoi*] were his sole property, having elaborated the most illogical concepts regarding *logoi,* he who considered himself the most educated ["most logical," *logiōtatos*] of all.[46]

---

43. In Gr. Naz. *Or.* 4.114, he invited his audience to don the purple robe of those adjudicating the performances presented in an *agōn* or contest.

44. Indeed, Julian's attitude toward Greek *logoi* and Gregory's response so dominate *Or.* 4 that most manuscripts of the so-called family QJWVTX (where only B does not have it) added to the title *kai kata Hellēnōn,* "and against Hellenes," or "against Hellenes and against Julian"; Bernardi, ed. and trans., *Grégoire de Nazianze: Discours 4–5,* 51, 67–69. Somers, *Histoire,* addresses *Or.* 4 and 5 at pp. 28–29 and 36–37.

45. τῇ δυνάμει τῆς κλήσεως. See Pl. *Cra.* 400e.

46. Gr. Naz. *Or.* 4.3–4: Λόγον γὰρ ἀναθήσω τῷ Θεῷ χαριστήριον, πάσης ἀλόγου θυσίας ἱερώτερόν τε καὶ καθαρώτερον, οὐ κατὰ τοὺς ἐναγεῖς ἐκείνου λόγους . . . ἡ τοῦ αἰῶνος τούτου δύναμίς τε καὶ

Words and sacrifices: as their juxtaposition in this remarkable passage demonstrates, in an intricate play on the word *logos* and its multiple connotations, Gregory realized that the crux of the matter was to separate what Julian had considered inextricably linked, *logoi*—that is, the entire cultural and ideological apparatus of *paideia*—and the sacred.[47] Gregory strenuously objected throughout *Oration 4* not to the link between *logoi* and the sacred but to Julian's attachment of *logoi* to a sacred embodied by the gods of the Greeks and the Romans. Gregory countered: *logoi* were indeed linked to the sacred, but that sacred was the *Logos*. As a result *logoi* were not the patrimony of those worshipping the gods of the Greeks and the Romans but belonged in truth to those affiliated with the *Logos*. To claim such a link *ab origine* between *logoi* and the *Logos* was one thing; however, to demonstrate it, and to persuade his audience that it is so, was another. The *logoi* in question here were, after all, the entire classical tradition, Greekness, from Homer, Hesiod, and Herodotus by way of Plato, Aristotle, Zeno, and Theophrastus to Porphyry and Iamblichus.

Julian, in *Against the Galileans* (*CG* fr. 55.229c), mocked Christians for "gnawing at the learning of the Greeks" if they believed, as they posited, that the sole knowledge of the scriptures was sufficient. But Christian attitudes toward *paideia* were complex and ambivalent.[48] Gregory's engagement with his own father's simplicity demonstrated that the simple, literal word of scripture was insufficient to the full and correct comprehension of the Trinity, or at least it no longer sufficed now that others used sophisticated arguments and all the technical expertise of advanced philosophical training to promote their mistaken mixture of the most potent *pharmakon*, the Trinity. To reject all philosophical learning was not an option; to the contrary, according to Gregory, Greek learning, especially the technical expertise provided by philosophy, was essentially good, useful, and necessary to repudiate those Christians who had misused it and continued to misuse it to falsify the Trinity, and to achieve the closest possible affiliation with the divine that he sought for and wished to strengthen in the souls of all. Gregory the Elder's entanglements with the *homoios* and the injurious influence of Eunomius and those whose attitudes he represented exemplified the indispensability of Greek learning, *logoi*, and suggested that using it correctly in recognizing and truly understanding the Trinity was a difficult task, best left to fully prepared and purified philosophers (such as Greg-

---

παίδευσις... καὶ τὴν ἀναίμακτον τῶν λόγων τιμὴν ἀνάπτοντι... τῷ Λόγῳ μόνον ἡ διὰ τοῦ λόγου χάρις οἰκειοτάτη... λόγῳ κολάζεσθαι ὑπὲρ τῆς εἰς λόγους παρανομίας, ὧν κοινῶν ὄντων λογικοῖς ἅπασιν, ὡς ἰδίων αὐτοῦ χριστιανοῖς ἐφθόνησεν, ἀλογώτατα περὶ λόγων διανοηθεὶς ὁ πάντων, ὡς ᾤετο, λογιώτατος.

47. Lib. *Or.* 18.157 claims that Julian considered *logoi* and *hiera* brothers.

48. The literature on Christian engagement with *paideia* prior to Gregory is extensive. I am purposely limiting myself here to Gregory and his challenges. For an insightful discussion, Lyman, "Politics"; and Kaldellis's useful summary of Christian criticism of pagan learning, *Hellenism in Byzantium*, 11–172.

ory). God had sent Gregory the perfect teaching tool in the person of Julian, a negative touchstone by which all, according to their abilities and requirements, could differentiate between correct and incorrect use of Greek learning, from the administration of justice to the comprehension of Aristotle's logic, as illustrated in *Oration* 4 (and 5). Gregory's real targets were, thus, neither those who had lapsed and converted to the gods of the Greeks and the Romans under Julian, nor even the emperor himself, but those Christians who rejected the use of philosophy *tout court* (ostensibly, because a complete rejection had never been feasible) and those who used philosophy incorrectly to falsify the Trinity—persons such as Eunomius. Gregory fashioned Julian as the Apostate in *Oration* 4 precisely to counter these mistaken notions of *logoi* among his Christian audience.

> Let the theater be ready. . . . The heralds may raise their voices; the people come together. Those preside in the seats of honor who excel by their white hair, their age, their good conduct as citizens, or who attract attention to themselves by their birth, their fame, or their wisdom bound to the affairs of this world. . . . Let them appoint themselves judges sitting in the first ranks: they will be adorned in purple, with ribbons and beautiful crowns of flowers, because I have often observed how they aim for a more solemn appearance, superior to the common folks, . . . valuing only what is pompous and reserved for the few.[49]

The theater was crucial for the self-representation and self-constitution of a city (in fact, all games were), nowhere more than in Antioch, famous for its theaters and the sophistication of its actors and audience.[50] Here the elites of the polis were seated in hierarchical order and proportional overabundance, viewing (*theatai*) the results of their munificence and being seen doing so; here too the nonelites saw and heard them, voicing their approval and disapproval clearly. Thus the theater served as an "ideological map of the social structure of [the city and] the Roman state."[51] As Blake Leyerle has noted, the theater, in particular what Lucian calls "the dance," usually performed by mimes or pantomimes, also "served as a primary vehicle for the inculcation of classical culture."[52] At its center stood the visual representation of the

---

49. Gr. Naz. *Or.* 4.114:"Ἔστω τὸ θέατρον εὐτρεπές, . . . οἱ κήρυκες βοάτωσαν, ὁ λαὸς συνίτω, τὴν προεδρίαν ἐχέτωσαν εἴτε οἱ πολιᾷ καὶ χρόνῳ καὶ τῷ τῆς πολιτείας ἐξειλεγμένῳ προέχοντες εἴτε οἱ γένει καὶ δόξῃ περίβλεπτοι καὶ σοφίᾳ τῇ κάτω πλεκομένῃ . . . αὐτοὶ τοὺς ἑαυτῶν προέδρους γραψάτωσαν. Ἁλουργὶς αὐτοὺς κοσμήσει καὶ ταινία καὶ στεφάνων ἄνθος καὶ κάλλος, ἐπειδὴ πολλαχοῦ τὸ σεμνὸν ἔγνων αὐτοῖς σπουδαζόμενον καὶ τὸ ὑπεράνω τοῦ ἰδιώτου . . . τοῦ δὲ ὑπερόγκου καὶ δυσεφίκτου τὸ ἀξιόπιστον. *Halourgis*, "dressed in purple"; he uses the same word in *Or.* 4.108 to mock Julian's purple.

50. Leyerle, *Theatrical Shows*, 13–20. Lim, "Converting," esp. 85–86.

51. Lib. *Or.* 11.218, 61.7, 49.27; Gunderson, "Ideology," 125; for Gregory's use of the theater as metaphor, Gregory of Nazianzus, *Contro Giuliano*, trans. and comm. Lugaresi, 36–37, 400–406; also Lugaresi, "Tra evento e rappresentazione," and "Ambivalenze."

52. Leyerle, *Theatrical Shows*, 18.

classic comedies and tragedies, at least their dramatic highlights, and the essential myths about the gods, their origins, and their love lives—or rather, sex lives. By Gregory's time such representations had become elaborated and sophisticated to the extent that they exemplified what Lugaresi has called "hyperrealism." Moreover, they were so successful that the most succinct plot summaries sufficed to evoke Phoenix, Phaedra, Oedipus, or Clytemnestra: "One man loved his stepmother; another woman, her stepson, and in consequence hanged herself.... What else? Do you want to see a son married to his mother? The wife of a certain man fell passionately in love with another and slew her husband upon his return with the help of her adulterer."[53] Indeed, as both Lucian and Libanius emphasize, no one could enjoy the performance, let alone perform, unless he or she knew at least the whole of Homer, Hesiod, and the best poets, but above all the tragedians—in sum, the fundamentals of *logoi*.[54] The subject matter of the pantomimes linked them intrinsically to the *hiera*. Even the comic burlesques mocking the gods' more spectacular entanglements were unthinkable without the *hiera* at their foundation. As Libanius said when eulogizing his native Antioch, one praised the gods as much by constructing a theater or indeed an aqueduct as by building a temple or shrine—eloquent testimony to the strong ties between the gods, the theater, and the polis, between civic service and *eusebeia*.[55]

Julian had sought to reinvigorate these very *logoi* and the *hiera* at their center, albeit not their theatrical performance—because he hated it and indeed tried to curtail it, thus giving additional bite to Gregory's presentation of his reign as theater. It was a pointed defamation by someone like Gregory, who knew the *Misopogon*. In fact, Julian and Gregory shared the ambivalence, indeed revulsion, the theater evoked among many intellectuals, Christian or not.[56] This common ambivalence was influenced deeply by Plato's famous repudiation, in Books 3 and 10 of the *Republic*, of rhapsodic performances of Homer as infecting the audience, through their *mimēsis* of reality, with emotions that were real, though evoked by fiction.[57] By the time of Gregory and Julian, the hyperrealism of theater had reached such an extent of mimesis to elicit fears that the distinction between the representation of mimes and pantomimes and reality itself had been erased altogether—Plato's worst fears

---

53. J. Chrys. *Hom in Tit.* 5.4; Lugaresi, "Ambivalenze," 284–86, 294–95; Leyerle, *Theatrical Shows*, 20–21; Coleman, "Fatal Charades."

54. Lucian *Salt.* 37–61; Lib. *Or.* 64.112; Kokolakis, "Pantomimus," esp. 55–56; C. P. Jones, "Greek Drama," esp. 48.

55. Lib. *Or.* 11.124–25.

56. Games and the theater routinely elicited criticisms: for example, Amm. Marc. 14.6.1, 19; Sen. *QN* 7.32.3, *Ep.* 108.6–9; Marc. Aur. *Med.* 11.2; Plut. *Quaest. Conv.* 9.748d; Aristid. *Or.* 29; Lucian *Salt.* 2–3; Philostr. *VA* 4.21; Goody, *Representations*, 18–31, 99–152.

57. Esp. Pl. *R.* 10.605c–606c. Aristotle rejected this argument in *Poetics* 6.1–28, defending authentic mimesis as a method of learning congenial to man, especially if controlled by the rhetorician or poet.

come true.[58] That this erasure was the source of the theater's powerful attraction made matters even worse: mimes and pantomimes now evoked emotions not by imitating reality but by really performing certain acts in which the audience participated by watching. Yet despite the hyperrealism of the late-antique performances, they remained in the theater: that is, they remained performances and were not real deeds, calling forth precisely emotions that were false, as Plato had warned.[59]

That mimes and actors were *infames* in perpetuity and stood legally outside society only increased the ambivalence of many intellectuals to the interplay of the real and the fictional. After all, these intellectuals belonged to the class of persons who financed these theatrical performances and were expected to participate enthusiastically, as Julian's *Misopogon* made abundantly clear.[60] The status of the mimes and actors created a deep gulf between their personal celebrity and wealth, their exalted roles as kings, queens, or gods, and their despised social position. They were paragons of dissimulation and falsehood, because there was no one hiding behind their continuously changing masks imitating others, although a good actor was at least no liar, since he did not pretend to be anything but an actor.[61] Gregory, evoking the theater and associating it with Julian's rule, tapped into a theme that resonated with his audience, Christian and pagan. The theater was powerful; it evoked real emotions with the power to transform, but it did so through skillful mimesis of a reality that was not real but a transitory fiction, a dissimulation, and a lie.[62]

To call Julian's entire reign nothing but theater said all. It instantly juxtaposed imitation and reality, fiction and deed, dissimulation and truth, transience and durability. Moreover, it placed Julian firmly in the political register of the tyrant as master of deception and dissimulation. Indeed, it evoked the quintessential theatrical tyrant and supposed first persecutor, none other than Nero *scaenicus*.[63] Julian was

---

58. Some mime actors no longer used traditional masks but wore sumptuous contemporary clothing.

59. J. Chrys. *Hom in Mt.* 6.7; Lugaresi, "Ambivalenze," 284–87; see also Gombrich, *Meditations*, 1–29, 151–59.

60. Actresses were classified as prostitutes, and all actors were denied rights as citizens, also emphasized by Aug. *Civ. Dei.* 2.11. Lim, "Converting," 87–91; French, "Maintaining"; S. Elm, "Marking."

61. Gr. Naz. *Carm.* 2.2.8.94–97, *PG* 37.1583; Aug. *Civ. Dei* 2.11, 13. In *De ver. rel.* 33.61, Augustine argues that the actor, though false because of his roles, is real qua actor and not a liar, because he openly pretends. Webb, "Protean Performer"; Leyerle, *Theatrical Shows*, 22–29.

62. As Augustine pointed out, what was real in the temple was play in the theater. Yet, the fictional representation of the rite enacted in the theater clearly had transformative effects; actors, in reality despised, evoked real love and admiration, caused by transient fiction; Aug. *De ver. rel.* 49.94–95 and especially *Conf.* 3.2.2; Lugaresi, "Ambivalenze," 297–99. The list of theater critics is long and illustrious, with a particularly fruitful period in the Second Sophistic, including Aelius Aristides *Or.* 29 and Plutarch *Quaest. Conv.* 9.748d, but also Sen. *QN* 7.32.3 and Marc. Aur. *Med.* 11.2.

63. Arist. *Pol.* 5.1314a: "Such, then, is the nature of one method by which security is obtained for tyrannies. . . . For just as one mode of destroying royalty is to make its government more tyrannical, so a mode of securing tyranny is to make it more regal, protecting . . . its power, in order that the ruler may

worse. Convinced that he was a true, divinely sent ruler, he did not even realize that he acted the role of the tyrant badly, insisting that he believed his inept performance of imperial rule reality. Julian could not even act regal, as a proper tyrant would have done. Rather, "ashamed to use violence like a tyrant, hiding the fox under the skin of the lion, or if you like, the height of injustice under the mask of Minos, he committed violence—How to say it?—sweetly." Faced with such a monstrosity, Gregory could only leave to others the task of writing Julian's history, the full description of the "tragedy, or rather, comedy" of his rule (*Or.* 4.79).

The Agora

In the theater the emperor interacted directly with his subjects; here he performed imperial rule and was seen doing so. Here he could be petitioned in person and views on his rule were voiced directly, a prerogative the populace did not relinquish easily—as Julian learned in Antioch, where the citizens had not appreciated his absence. The theater was also one of the public places where imperial letters and decrees were read aloud and received with the solemnity due to the imperial person, "as if the emperor himself were present."[64] The emperor also performed empire in the agora. Here, too, imperial legislation was promulgated, "the culminating moment and the most dramatic" in the life of a law.[65] The marketplace and the pillars of the often splendid peristyle enclosing and leading to the agora displayed imperial laws, edicts, and letters, including those in which Julian ordered sacrifices and the reopening of temples. Here too Julian's theater, his histrionic performance of a sham rule, had its effect: the agora was the site, after all, where the ruler displayed the acts of injustice concealed behind his mask of Minos, the classic model of the ideal legislator, whom Julian himself evoked in *Against the Galileans* (fr. 40.184b).[66]

To underscore his point Gregory highlighted the agora as the place where emperors displayed their imperial images, symbols of their legitimate power (and the place where *damnatio memoriae* by erasures on statues and inscriptions was also enacted):[67]

---

govern not only with the consent of the subjects but even without it; for if he gives up this, he also gives up his position as tyrant. But while this must stand as a fundamental principle, all the other measures he may either adopt or pretend to adopt by cleverly acting the royal part." See Suet. *Nero;* D.C. 61–63, esp. 61.6, 62.17–18, and 62.20; Tacitus *Ann.* 13.25, 14.14–16 and 20–21, 15.33 and 39, 16.4–5; Sen. *Clem.;* D. Chr. *Or.* 6. For the theme of theatricality and tyranny, Bartsch, *Actors,* 1–97; and E. Elm, "Damnatio," 268–90, for the defamation of Nero and Caligula as actors.

64. J. Chrys. *Hom in Mt.* 19.9, PG 57.285; note his juxtaposition of the theater and the reading of imperial letters. See Matthews, *Laying Down,* 185–99.

65. Matthews, *Laying Down,* 187.

66. See also Jul. *Or.* 5.20; Pl. *Lg.* 624a–b; Plot. *Enn.* 6.9.7; Gregory of Nazianzus, *Contro Giuliano,* trans. and comm. Lugaresi, 342.

67. E. Elm, "Damnatio," 149–88.

It is an imperial rule that the emperors are honored through official images; I do not know whether among all peoples who have a monarchic regime, but among the Romans it is one of the most zealously observed. The crowns and diadems, the splendor of the purple, the numerous guards armed with lances and the throng of their subjects do not suffice to consolidate their imperial rule. To appear more venerated they also require *proskynēsis,* not only that directed to their persons but also that directed to their statues and painted images, so that they may be venerated more broadly and completely. The emperors enjoy writing on their images, the one this and the other that: some, the most famous cities bearing gifts [to them]; others, Victories placing the crown on their heads; others again, the magistrates prostrate before them.... In fact, they love not only the reality of the deeds of which they are proud but also their representation.[68]

The norms and practices of emperor worship here described—including the relation between the imperial image and person, mirroring that between a statue and the divinity it represented—accord with the representational practices of Christian emperors, as Julian himself pointed out in his *Epistle to the Athenians* (278a) when he said that Constantius sent him to Gaul only in order that he could carry around his image.[69] Gregory did not censure these practices per se, cognizant of their value for the consolidation of the empire, though his emphasis on the contrast between deeds and representation reveals a critical stance. But he took this opportunity to instruct future Christian emperors in how to employ this central aspect of imperial ceremonial correctly: not as Julian had done.[70]

Julian's use of imperial portraits was a key element of his dissimulation, revealing his deeply duplicitous character and hence the fundamental illegitimacy and injustice of his rule and legislation. Julian had "mixed impiety with the honors traditionally rendered the emperors by combining into one the laws of the Romans and the *proskynēsis* in front of the idols, just like those who mix poison into food," because he had affixed to his representations "the images of the demons" (*Or.* 4.81). This was an act of supreme duplicity, because to present his images together with those of his gods "to the eyes of the people, of the cities, and above all of the magistrates," made it impossible for all—particularly those in public office—to escape

---

68. Gr. Naz. *Or.* 4.80: Νόμος ἐστὶ βασιλικός.... Ῥωμαίοις δὲ καὶ τῶν λίαν σπουδαζομένων, εἰκόσι δημοσίαις τιμᾶσθαι τοὺς βασιλεύοντας. οὐ γὰρ ἐξαρκοῦσιν οἱ στέφανοι καὶ τὰ διαδήματα καὶ τὸ τῆς ἀλουργίδος ἄνθος... συγκροτεῖν τούτοις τὴν βασιλείαν,... οὐχ ἣν αὐτοὶ προσκυνοῦνται μόνον, ἀλλὰ καὶ τῆς ἐν πλάσμασί τε καὶ χρώμασιν.... φιλοῦσι γὰρ οὐ τὰς ἀληθείας τῶν πραγμάτων μόνον ἐφ' οἷς μέγα φρονοῦσιν, ἀλλὰ καὶ τὰ τούτων ἰνδάλματα.

69. Lib. *Or.* 21.30. Only the emperor could authorize the erecting of his statue; McCormack, *Art,* 67–73.

70. For an invaluable discussion of the topic and of the later evolution of imperial ceremonial, Dagron, *Empereur,* 35–44, 141–59, 303–22.

the evil.[71] All Christians frequenting the agora, and especially those in power, thus were again presented with the dilemma of either violating Christian commandments or refusing the sovereign the honor due him. Should they wish to remain Christian, they were effectively excluded from the agora and the power it signified, because they could not honor their emperor. If they wished to maintain power, they had to abjure their Christianity. That "ruse, such a trap of impiety devised with such sophistication" was characteristic of "a comportment that alone suffices to expose to public scorn [*stēliteuein*] the moral character of a ruler" (who dissimulated as if he were an infamous actor). In a private person, such comportment may be reprehensible, but a ruler who conceals "enterprises and projects behind such artifice" subverts utterly his dignity (*Or.* 4.81). The duplicitous emperor, without morals, also lacked the *ēthos* to comprehend justice, so that his jurisdiction was unjust—and ought to be transitory. Only a morally sound ruler anchors his rule in genuine—that is, just—legislation, which is lasting.

The Empire

Gregory's presentation of the dual theme of Julian's immorality and the theatrical fiction and artifice of his rule, which made his legislation illegitimate, occupies a significant portion of *Oration* 4. The point of this emphasis is apparent. It advised Julian's successors, both the emperors and the public officials ruling in their name and on their behalf, to revoke Julian's legislation in the knowledge that the effects of his rule would pass like dried grass. To give this admonition practical bite, Gregory's own *stēlographia* focused "on one or two things as an example," in order to highlight how a true Christian emperor ought to act by illuminating what a pseudo-emperor and lawgiver Julian had been. That is, Gregory demonstrated why all remnants of Julian's rule, especially his laws, ought to be erased, and why no invective he himself composed could do Julian justice, though he longed—his disclaimers notwithstanding—for the leisure (*scholē*) of a Herodotus or a Thucydides, and their power of language, so that his *stēlographia*, his column of shame, could achieve the longevity of their histories (*Or.* 4.79, 92).

The Law   Gregory singled out for particular condemnation Julian's claim to represent the ideal (Platonic) servant and guardian of the law, *nomophylax*, a concept that contrasted with that of Themistius, who conceived of the emperor as animate or

---

71. According to Soz. *HE* 5.17.3–4, Julian had himself depicted with Zeus, Ares, and Hermes, but no archaeological evidence remains. This need not be the result of *memoria damnata*, to which Julian had never been subjected; the documented erasures of his inscriptions occurred later, probably under Theodosius II; Arce, *Estudios*, 226; Conti, *Inschriften*, nos. 28, 32, 35, 136, 170, 174; Rosen, *Julian*, 391.

living law, *nomos empsychos*.⁷² Despite his pride in his just and equitable jurisdiction, Julian, according to Gregory, had been unable even to formulate his intentions in "clear letters": that is, in unambiguous laws and edicts, as other emperors before him had done. (The context is Julian's refusal to engage in open persecution.) Acting neither "imperially, nor as a tyrant would," but in a "slavish and ignoble manner," he left it to his subjects to act tyrannically on his behalf. "Announcing his wish as unwritten law," he encouraged peoples and cities to act rashly and spontaneously against Christians and their properties without "reprimanding their natural inclination toward violence."⁷³

Gregory referred here to imperial letters such as those to the citizens of Alexandria, Bostra, and Edessa, where Christians suffered violence. But he also engaged in a long-standing debate about the topos of the imperial will or, rather, the unwritten intentions of the legislator, their written expression, and the legality of both, going back to Plato, who had also considered the rulers' unwritten law binding.⁷⁴ Julian, according to Gregory, was no *nomophylax* (never mind the living law), because he was neither a true emperor nor even a true tyrant. Like all actors he too, once unmasked, was only infamous (*Or.* 4.62). His legislation therefore was likewise false, for he lacked the mental force to issue laws that truly corresponded to his intention, leaving it to his subjects to infer his unwritten wish. As a consequence of this argumentative strategy, Gregory could attribute every violent act against any Christian anywhere to Julian without the proof of a law or edict endorsing such violence, since Julian himself had granted his unwritten wish higher authority than his own written laws (*Or.* 4.61, 93).⁷⁵

Such attitudes toward the law had the expected result. Rather than protect the cities as his imperial mandate required, Julian harmed them by permitting public buildings to be despoiled (that is, churches), civic leaders to be attacked (bishops as well as those magistrates truly dedicated to justice), and citizens to erupt in violent outbursts against each other. All this he did under the pretense of maintain-

---

72. For Julian's self-representation as guardian of the law, *Or.* 1 and 3, praising Constantius, and *Epistle to Themistius* 261a and passim, countering Themistius's notions of the emperor as embodied law, for which see Them. *Or.* 5.64b, 16.212d, 19.228. The relevant Platonic passages are Pl. *Grg.* 447b–475e, 469c, 508b–c, 527b; *Lg.* 757b–c; and Arist. *Pol.* 1284a11–15. For Julian's reception as just lawgiver, Lib. *Or.* 12.64 and 18.176, and Amm. Marc. 22.7.2. Athanassiadi-Fowden, *Julian*, 114–20, highlights Julian's intention to administer the empire reasonably and honestly with magistrates of like mind (cf. Jul. *Ep.* 32 [Wright 26]) and to reform justice.

73. Gr. Naz. *Or.* 4.61: μὴ βασιλικῶς, τυραννικῶς γε . . . διὰ τὴν ἀλογίαν . . . ἄγραφον προθεὶς νόμον τὸ βούλεσθαι.

74. Pl. *Lg.* 793a, 838b; see also Gr. Naz. *Or.* 4.93. Mazza, "Filosofia," 58–60; and see Calderone, "Teologia," 228–30 for *nomos empsychos*; Ruggini, "Apoteosi," 455–60.

75. For cities in which Christians were attacked, see Jul. *Epp.* 60 (Wright 21), 114, 115; Julian, *Epistolario*, trans. and comm. Caltabiano, 55–70.

ing the public good (*Or.* 4.90) and by ostensibly proper legislative action, such as his edicts requisitioning the property of Christian churches to finance the reconstruction of temples and ordering the profanation of sacred objects and the incarceration and torture of priests and of magistrates who chose to act with true justice and "attempted to mediate between the circumstances of the moment and the laws" (*Or.* 4.92).[76]

Julian, to reiterate, was and remained a legitimate Roman emperor. In particular when Gregory wrote, all Julian's laws were in force, from forbidding public Christian teachers to comment on Homer to the interdiction of daytime funerals, and many of the magistrates and high public officials he had selected were still in office. Julian had not been condemned—and never would be in any official way—and his followers could reasonably expect him to be divinized. Jovian was on the move; things were in flux, even more so after his untimely death and the election of yet another new emperor, and how this emperor would act was utterly uncertain. Gregory's insistence on the illegitimacy of Julian's rule and legislation was not mere polemic. Julian's laws were in effect and could be enforced: hence Gregory's urgency, which to modern readers may seem mere repetition.

True emperors, Gregory continued, did not tolerate *stasis*, disorder and revolt in the cities that led citizens to murder their fellow citizens, like the rebellion leading to the murder of George in Alexandria and the rampages of the citizens of Gaza and Arethusa against Christians (*Or.* 4.88–91). Julian, neither emperor nor tyrant, tolerated such outrage while punishing Caesarea with the loss of city status when its citizens resisted him by destroying the Temple of Tyche.[77] Hiding like a slave (another character trait of tyrants) behind his unwritten laws, whose intentions an unrestrained mob carried out, Julian violated yet another cardinal requirement of the true legislator, namely consistency (*Or.* 4.93). "Those who venerate the acts of this man and represent him as a new god, sweet and philanthropic, absolve him [of responsibility for] the accusation of persecution because he did not officially decree 'the Christians be persecuted.'" They were misguided.[78] Julian presented himself as the guarantor of law and justice, but his deeds were unjust, contradicting his words, and such inconsistency made him injustice impersonated, holding absolute power. Therefore, the responsibility whenever and wherever Christians were mistreated was his, despite the absence of an official decree. Nothing exculpated Ju-

---

76. Gregory implies legislation reopening temples, a law like *CTh* 15.1.3, giving priority to the restoration of temples, and measures undertaken to refurbish the Temple of Apollo at Daphne. Julian (e.g., *Ep.* 60 [Wright 21]) accused Christians of having committed similar crimes against temples, such as the destruction of the Temple of Tyche in Caesarea: Gr. Naz. *Or.* 4.92, 86.

77. Libanius also mentions the punishment of Caesarea after this destruction as a cautionary example: *Or.* 16.14; Soz. *HE* 11.7–8.

78. Gr. Naz. *Or.* 4.94: Οὔ φασιν οἱ τὰ ἐκείνου σέβοντες καὶ τὸν νέον ἡμῖν θεὸν ἀναπλάττοντες, τὸν ἡδὺν καὶ φιλάνθρωπον, ἀλλ' ὅτι μὴ δημοσίᾳ διωκέσθωσαν χριστιανοὶ προὔθηκε.

lian, "our assassin as well as protector, transgressor of the law as well as legislator" (*Or.* 4.97).

The Army The contrast between adherence to explicit laws and to the emperor's unwritten wishes helped Gregory to denigrate yet another area where Julian had presented himself as a model emperor-philosopher and *stratēgos:* his relation to the army.[79] His closeness to the army, being *philostratiōtēs,* had been another facet of Julian's public imperial persona countering that of Constantius.[80] Evoking his Tetrarchic ancestry, wherein military demeanor had been an important imperial attribute, Julian stressed in his *Epistle to the Athenians* (274c–d) that he felt far more at home with the army than with the court, in particular Constantius's court.[81] Now Gregory read Julian's initial purges of that court at Chalcedon as an early sign of the dichotomy between written law and imperial intent. Julian found it easy to remove Constantius's men—that is, Christians—from the court because the simplicity (*haplotēs*) of military men and their democratic and opportunistic ("slave to the right moment," *tou kairou doulon*) attachment to an emperor predisposed them to "acknowledge the emperor's wish as the sole law" (*Or.* 4.64–65). In fact, the judges at Chalcedon, whom Ammianus criticized as harsh and partial, had been mostly high-ranking military officers, and the trial had taken place in the presence of generals and tribunes of the Joviani and Herculiani, all, in Gregory's account, doing the emperor's bidding uncritically when it came to removing (Christian) civilian officials. As Bowersock notes, the trials at Chalcedon may in fact have been Julian's move to win over Constantius's army.[82]

Julian practiced his artifice and dissimulation with the army, with its standards and banners, as he did in the agora, according to Gregory. Where once the terrible yet majestic sign of Christ, the labarum, had unfurled, ruling "over all other standards, even those bearing the imperial likeness," now "Baal [and] golden images" of the emperor and his gods required men to bow down in *proskynēsis.* As with Julian's mixing of his imperial images with those of the gods of the Greeks and the Romans in the agora, the result was to marginalize and disenfranchise Christians who occupied leading positions in the army or served as ordinary soldiers. The fighting power of an army that had been so terrifying under the protection of the Chris-

---

79. A delicate subject because of rumors that Christians in the army had killed Julian; see Gr. Naz. *Or.* 5.13.

80. Jul. *Or.* 1.21c–d, also *Or.* 3.86b–88b; Amm. Marc. 16.5.3, 21.9.2, 25.4.4–5 and 10–13; Lib. *Or.* 13.49. For the Tetrarchic connections, S. Elm, "Gregory's Women," 179–82, with further bibliography.

81. For the reorganization of the court and the purges of Chalcedon, Amm. Marc. 22.3.2, 7, and 22.4; Claud. Mam. *Grat. act.* 10–11; Lib. *Or.* 18.130–41, 152.

82. Amm. Marc. 22.3.1–9 is colored by his favorable view of the *comes sacri largitii* Ursulus, punished despite having served Julian loyally in Gaul; Lib. *Or.* 18.152. Bowersock, *Julian,* 66–70.

tian labarum was thus weakened, even though some heroic soldiers persevered and resisted (*Or.* 4.65).[83]

Gregory depicted Julian as corrupting the army to demonstrate that from the beginning of his rule as Augustus he was unfit as a lawgiver (because he issued partial and inconsistent legislation) and irresponsible as a commander in chief who, by disrupting his army's fighting power, inevitably led them into the Persian calamity. Gregory then attacked another imperial virtue of which Julian had been proud: his *philanthrōpia* vis-à-vis the army. According to Gregory, Julian again used virtue as a pretense or a mask for his evil when he made the burning of incense as sacrifice to his gods the precondition for soldiers to receive a special bonus called the *donativum*, exploiting the soldiers' need and greed.[84] Gregory's description of one of these events, which duped many soldiers who no longer recognized the religious significance of burning incense and its implication for Christians, once more instructed future emperors *ex negativo* in conducting such ceremonies the proper Christian way. A donative was essentially laudable, because it benefited ordinary soldiers; but it had to be distributed, according to Gregory, as homage to the emperor's achievement as a person, without reference to any divine attribute associated with him (*Or.* 4.82–84).[85]

True and False Enemies: Securitas Rei Publicae? According to Gregory's deconstruction of Julian's rule, the emperor abused the law and weakened the army. Because he was not a private person, his mistakes mattered. Although he was merely an actor badly acting the role of the tyrant, his rule, transient though it was, had lasting consequences for the *koina* of the Romans. Though his actions were a theatrical perversion, they shaped reality as much as those of a good emperor, but with disastrous results. "Two things preoccupied him: the Galileans—so he himself called us to insult us—and the Persians, who remained openly hostile. But our question

---

83. A similar description of the military banners in Them. *Or.* 1.2a and Amm. Marc. 16.10.7; further bibliography on army banners and their symbolism in Kurmann, *Gregor von Nazianz*, 212–16.

84. Occasions for such bonuses were the emperor's birthday or the anniversary of the beginning of his rule, but a donative could also be granted on special occasions such as extraordinary exertions during a march; its size was related to the military rank: A. H. M. Jones, *Later Roman Empire*, 623–30; Rosen, *Julian*, 288–89, 351, 355; at pp. 157–58, Rosen relates Martin of Tours's refusal of Julian's *donativum*; Renucci, *Idées*, 311–12; Banaji, *Agrarian Change*, 44, considers the actual value of Julian's donative about nine *solidi*.

85. According to Gregory, some soldiers demanded to be martyred as soon as they found out that burning incense meant denying Christ. Julian rather sent them into exile, allowing Gregory to reiterate his themes of Julian's deceptive mixing of poison and honey to remove Christians from the sites of imperial power and his refusal to allow martyrdom. Gr. Naz. *Or.* 4.83 resembles Lib. *Or.* 18.168, though their interpretations of the incident are diametrically opposed; Lib. *Or.* 18.199 also mentions soldiers resisting Julian, though it is unclear whether this is the same episode.

was so much more important and so much closer to his heart that he considered war against the Persians a nothing, a game."[86] So delusional was Julian in his mania that he could not differentiate between real and imagined enemies—that is, between a justified defensive or preemptive war and a war of the worst kind: civil war.[87] Gregory did approve a few of Julian's measures, such as his reform of the *cursus publicus*, tax reductions, greater care in selecting magistrates, and measures against corruption. But they all paled in light of his true success: his "security of the commonwealth," achieved at the cost of people and cities divided, families separated, and houses in dissent (*Or.* 4.75)—the very antithesis of *oikeiōsis*.[88]

Ordering that Christians officially be called Galileans, "an unknown and unused name," signified Julian's puerile and vain behavior, "unbecoming not only for a sovereign but for anyone of even minimally sound mind."[89] The real consequence of this imperially ordered name, however, was officially to marginalize Christians (*Or.* 4.76–77). By escalating his measures, Julian nearly succeeded in "depriving Christians of all free speech, excluding them from all assemblies, from the public places [*agorōn*], the festivals [*panēgyreōn*], from the tribunals [*dikastēriōn*]. Indeed, whoever had not burned incense on the altars erected there, thus paying a price too high for that condition, would not have been permitted to be active in these places."[90] Julian deprived Christians of justice and laws intended, by a universal (*koinē*) divine philanthropy, for all free men without discrimination, just like "the beauty of the sky and the light of the sun."[91] He wanted to make Christians foreigners and no citizens in their own homeland, "eliminated and almost forbidden to breathe,"[92] as if they and not "the Persians, Scythians, and all other barbarians" were the true enemy (*Or.* 4.86, 96).

---

86. Gr. Naz. *Or.* 4.74: Καὶ δύο μὲν ταῦτα ἦν αὐτῷ τὰ σπουδαζόμενα, Γαλιλαῖοί τε, ὡς αὐτὸς ἐφυδρίζων ἐκάλει, καὶ Πέρσαι τῷ πολέμῳ καρτερῶς παραμένοντες, οὕτω δὲ τὸ ἡμέτερον μεῖζον καὶ περισπουδαστότερον ὥστε λῆρον καὶ παιδιὰν αὐτῷ τὸ κατὰ Πέρσας νομίζεσθαι.

87. Here Gregory mirrors concerns voiced at court, see above, Chapter 7; Amm. Marc. 22.12.5, 23.5.4; Jul. *Mis.* 360d; Gr. Naz. *Or.* 5.8.2, 18.32. Kurmann, *Gregor von Nazianz*, 252–53, considers Gregory's sequence of the naming of Christians and the Persian war as a chronological sequence. I concur with Lugaresi (Gregory of Nazianzus, *Contro Giuliano*, trans. and comm. Lugaresi, 332–34) and read this as a value judgment.

88. τῷ κοινῷ πρὸς ἀσφάλειαν. Compare Ambrose on Valens, *De obitu Val.* 21; Kurmann, *Gregor von Nazianz*, 255–58. Julian's good administration was central for his admirers Libanius and Ammianus, and his later champions; see S. Elm, "Gregory of Nazianzus's *Life*," 169–71.

89. Gr. Naz. *Or.* 4.76: σφόδρα μειρακιώδες καὶ κοῦφον . . . οὐχ ὅπως βασιλέως ἀνδρός, ἀλλ' οὐδὲ ἄλλου τινὸς τῶν καὶ μετρίως στιβαρῶν τὴν διάνοιαν.

90. Gr. Naz. *Or.* 4.96: πάσης μὲν παρρησίας ἀποστερεῖσθαι . . . πάντων δὲ αὐτοὺς εἴργεσθαι συλλόγων . . . μισθὸν δοίη μέγαν οὕτω καὶ τοσούτου πράγματος. Compare Julian's juxtaposition of the Antiochenes' mistaken notions of free speech and freedom.

91. καθάπερ οὐρανοῦ κάλλος καὶ ἡλίου φῶς.

92. ἐξορίστους εἶναι καὶ ἀναιρεῖσθαι καὶ μικροῦ τῶν ἀναπνοῶν εἴργεσθαι.

Julian, this "most intelligent and this best of all governors of the commonwealth," failed to realize that to try to alter and disturb Christianity "now that the word of salvation has been poured out and rules as sovereign [among us] ... would be nothing less than to shake the power of the Romans to the foundations and endanger everything, and to suffer from our own hands things worse than even our enemies could wish against us—and all because of this newfangled and wonderful philosophy and rule, which has brought us happiness [*eudaimonia*] and led us back to the golden age and to that *politeia* that does not know rebellions and wars."[93]

In Gregory's ironic persiflage of Julian's political program and propaganda, the philosopher and military leader on the throne, who had promised the *felicitas temporum* (*eudaimonia*) and *securitas rei publicae* of an Augustan golden age, achieved the opposite.[94] By his apostasy and impiety Julian created disunity in the *politeia*, deeply endangering its well-being as only a true misanthrope could. The common body of the *oikoumenē* (a Platonic and Aristotelian theme already prominent in Gregory's *Oration* 2) can tolerate a few wayward members, but the derangement at its head, the most crucial part, puts the entire body politic at grave risk.[95] Julian, by deserting, disrupted the crucial link between God and the *oikoumenē* of the Greeks and the Romans, first established during the reign of Augustus (whom Julian's *Caesars* 309a–b, 332c–d, ridiculed as a chameleon), that had permitted Rome to prosper ever since. The Apostate had thus fatally endangered everyone and everything.

Following the rules of the *psogos* as genre, Gregory, in his deconstruction of Julian's rule, homed in on each aspect of his imperial program and propaganda. Gregory systematically dismantled Julian as philosopher-king and as the embodiment of the virtuous ruler of Plato's *Laws* and *Republic*. For Gregory, Julian became a perversion of justice as a lawgiver, subjecting himself to the law as if a private citizen (*Mis.* 343c, 344b–345c, 355b–c, 356c, 357, 364c) by his inconsistency, partiality, and duplicity. The reformer of Greek *paideia*, repelled by Antioch's decadent love for the theater that indicated the Christian deformation of its Greekness, became himself an infamous actor, playing the tyrant badly because he did so inadvertently. His philanthropy, the imperial expression of his analogy to the one, universal, benevolent sun as the visible representation of Zeus-Helios, not only failed to merge the *oikoumenē* into a harmonious one, but fomented civil war, dividing city and household. Julian's apostasy, his innovation, caused disaster because in his hubris the em-

---

93. Gr. Naz. *Or.* 4.74: νῦν δὲ ἤδη τοῦ σωτηρίου λόγου χεθέντος καὶ περὶ ἡμᾶς μάλιστα δυναστεύσαντος τὸ πειρᾶσθαι τὰ χριστιανῶν μετατιθέναι καὶ παρακινεῖν οὐδὲν ἕτερον ἦν ἢ τὴν Ῥωμαίων παρασαλεύειν ἀρχὴν καὶ τῷ κοινῷ παντὶ κινδυνεύειν ... τῆς νέας ταύτης καὶ θαυμαστῆς φιλοσοφίας καὶ βασιλείας.

94. Julian used classic terminology but emphasized specific aspects; Claud. Mam. *Grat. act.* 22–23; Guida, ed., *Anonimo panegirico*, 129–31; Noreña, "Communication."

95. Gr. Naz. *Or.* 2.3; Pl. *R.* 462c; Arist. *Pol.* 1.5.1254a–1255a; Eus. *VC* 2.191; Guida, *Anonimo panegirico*, 128.

peror thought he could by substituting his man-made inventions displace a divinely created order and preordained unity that truly represented the *oikeiōsis* between God and men as manifest in the power of the Romans. His presumption and the actions that followed upon it turned the world upside down, placing mere human invention above divinely ordained truth.

Had not the God of Christ, the source of all things, including Rome's power extending to the limits of the earth, intervened and punished the deserter with execution, only God knows what would have happened. Naming Christians "Galileans," seeking to marginalize them as if they were not the center, the very foundation of Rome's power and security, illuminated the depth of Julian's mania. He had presumed that a mere (humanly created) change of name could affect the majesty of "the creator and ruler of everything," who with one word could crush all his enemies. (That presumption showed, furthermore, that Julian, the great philosopher, was not au courant on the philosophical debates about the proper relationship between the divine origin of a name, the *dynamis* it expressed, and its transformative effect: *Or.* 4.76, 78.) Julian's attempt to rename the Christians only underscored his fear of the power residing in the name.[96] Julian's Christian adversaries had no such fears and no reason to rename Julian's gods: Pan, Hercules the Beefeater, and so on, were names so ridiculous that changing them made no difference. Allusions to Julian's favorite gods and to wordplay such as that of the citizens of Antioch, to which Julian's *Misopogon* reacted, indicate not only that Gregory was thoroughly familiar with Julian's public persona but also that his text operated on multiple levels. Like Julian, Gregory connected the political and the philosophical, which he too considered intrinsically related to each other and to the divine at their source (*Or.* 4.75–77).[97]

Sacrifice Julian's political, philosophical, and religious views had coalesced in statues of the gods, sacrifices, and their associated rituals. Just as in *Oration* 4 Gregory's opening words indicate that his *logos* was a sacrifice of words far more powerful than those of Julian's mute animals, so too did his attack. Julian's misconception about the power of his invented name, Galileans, to override the true divine appellation, Christians, had its analogue in his bloody sacrifices of *alogoi*, beasts, which he meant to replace the one and only true sacrifice. Only "stupidity, impiety, and ignorance of the truly great things" could make a mere mortal set himself against the Word: "You with your pollution [*miasma*] [stand] against the sacrifice of Christ? [You prefer] the blood of your sacrifice [to] the blood that purified the world?" "You [set yourself] against such a great inheritance, against [the church],

---

96. Gr. Naz. *Or.* 4.76: τὴν δύναμιν τῆς προσηγορίας.
97. E.g., Jul. *Mis.* 345d, 364c, 366b; Amm. Marc. 22.12.6, 22.14.3.

the harvest of the world that extends to the ends of the earth," prefigured and therefore both ancient and new? It was criminally absurd.[98]

So deluded had Julian been in admiring the suffering of Hercules, the mutilations of the Phrygians, the ritual beatings in the temples of Mithras, and the killing of strangers among the Taurians that this "most philosophical and most wellborn of men" failed to honor those who gave their lives so as not to change one word of the Word. Nor did he recognize the true philosophical life of the present times, led by thousands of men and women of manly virtue, and adopted by both the poor already habituated to privation and those of highly elevated rank, exceedingly wellborn and powerful, persons who might not discourse on philosophy but whose entire lives taught balance of reason and practice (*Or.* 4.73).

Their philosophical life was far worthier than that of Solon, Socrates, and Plato. After all, those philosophers' grave moral flaws indicted their ethics: love of boys, money, and pride (*Or.* 4.69–73). Such loves were examples of pure self-love, in contrast to a love of self that extended outward to include others. Julian set these men as his exemplars despite his reading of the scriptures, his membership in the clergy, the honor he had paid the martyrs: despite knowing better (*Or.* 4.97). Instead he used his knowledge to proclaim that his measures against Christians—at first hidden, then more evident, but cunningly never persecution openly declared—actually helped them lead the life prescribed in the Gospels, to be poor and exiled from this world, forced to show the other cheek, as if his human legislation could enforce the moral behavior demanded by divine decree (*Or.* 4.97–99). All this against Christians, who had never deprived anyone of frank speech, never divided a house and a city, forced anyone into mortal danger, or had them killed (*Or.* 4.98).

Gregory's description of Julian's actions against Christians as increasing in ferocity and as undeclared yet deliberate persecution anticipates the modern scholarly debates about Julian's anti-Christian policies, though modern scholars do not always acknowledge Gregory as their precursor.[99] In fact, the coincidence of modern scholarly assessments of Julian's anti-Christian policies and those of Gregory should occasion no surprise, given the common source of both in Julian's laws, edicts,

---

98. Gr. Naz. *Or.* 4.67–68: Σὺ κατὰ τοσούτου κλήρου καὶ τῆς οἰκουμενικῆς καρποφορίας, τῆς πάντα διαλαβούσης τὰ πέρατα. . . . Σὺ κατὰ τῆς Χριστοῦ θυσίας τοῖς σοῖς μιάσμασι; Σὺ κατὰ τοῦ τὸν κόσμον καθήραντος αἵματος τοῖς σοῖς αἵμασι;

99. Bidez, *Vie*, 261–62, first suggested that Julian intended to eliminate Christianity, and his view has maintained its force; see Tougher's excellent summary, *Julian*, 55–62. R. Smith (*Julian's Gods*, 207–18) and Rosen (*Julian*, 398–400, 416) offer nuances, emphasizing Julian's educational intentions; Renucci, *Idées*, 282–323, esp. 320–33, sees a tendency to ghettoize Christians so that apostasy would have been the sole way out, what Jerome called "blanda persecutio": *Chron.* 285 (362 C.E.: GCS Eusebius, vol. 7, part 1, 242.12–15 Helm). In these scholarly discussions Gregory's two orations appear but rarely.

imperial letters, and his other writings. As I have tried to convey, Gregory knew Julian well. His attacks, though corresponding to the generic demands of the *psogos,* reveal a great deal of precision in Gregory's engagement with Julian—as if he had indeed read the *Misopogon* or *Against the Galileans,* the *Epistle to the Athenians* or the *Hymn to Helios.* Because with one exception Gregory never cited Julian's writings, the scholarly *communis opinio* has been that he did not know them. Not to cite does not mean not to know, however. Gregory, in keeping with classic literary devices, claimed the closeness to the emperor and hence access to those in power that was the common currency of prestige, especially vis-à-vis one's peers.[100] On several occasions, he mentioned special sources and privileged access to those who knew the emperor's secrets; and his formulations ("Oh! to what level of discourse do I have to stoop!"), moreover, imply that he had not only Caesarius in mind. Gregory, in short, demonstrated an access to the court that allowed him to convey to his audience privileged information above and beyond what was publicly known (and written: *Or.* 4.52, 96). To do so was part of his authorial strategy. His nearness to this emperor, combined with his obvious resistance to the evil one, brought him into constant danger of martyrdom for his frank speech: he was the critical outsider on the inside. It was a strategy already used to good effect by historians in particular, and Gregory's wish that what he engraved on Julian's pillar of shame might last as long as the histories of a Herodotus and Thucydides is no accident. He achieved his aim. His *stēlographia* has indeed proved as long-lived, mutatis mutandis, as Herodotus's or Thucydides' histories (though classicists or ancient historians would be hard pressed to compare Gregory's *stēlographia* and the histories).[101]

To accuse Julian of encouraging persecution represents Gregory's perception and that of many other Christians, especially the elites most affected, as rhetoricians, magistrates, and military men. But the accusation also helped Gregory the author to establish his critical distance and authenticity by emphasizing that from the beginning he had sought martyrdom by using his words, his frank speech, as weapon. That such martyrdom was granted to very few was yet another sign of Julian's cunning. This aspect of Julian's duplicity galled Gregory, because it deprived him and other true Christians of the chance to resist and prevented them from making the ultimate sacrifice of their own lives for the sake of the Word.[102] From Gregory's perspective, Julian had thus been too tolerant: had he been a proper tyrant, at least, he would have been man enough to persecute for real, like his Tetrarchic precursors Diocletian, Galerius, Maximinianus, and Maximinus Daia, whose images, bearing

---

100. Griffin, "*De Beneficiis,*" esp. 98–102, 113.
101. Sailor, "Becoming Tacitus"; Marincola, *Authority,* 217–18.
102. See the brief direct attack against Julian in *Or.* 4.67–73 that Lugaresi (Gregory of Nazianzus, *Contro Giuliano l'Apostata: Orazione 4,* trans. with comm. Lugaresi, 129) characterizes as a mini-invective.

the marks of defacement (*stēliteuein*), could still be found in public places.[103] Given that God had structured Julian and his reign so that the true age of the martyrs did not return, what then had been his reason for Julian to exist in the first place? So far, Gregory had not explained why God had placed the *oikoumenē* in such danger by allowing Julian not only to live but to rule.

IMPERIAL DECREES AND DIVINE ENACTMENTS: JULIAN AND CONSTANTIUS

The extraordinarily similar concepts that Julian and Gregory—paradigmatic of others at their time—used against each other to argue diametrically opposed positions also include the conundrum of Julian's dynastic relation to Constantine the Great and his sons. Whereas Julian claimed the legitimacy of his dynastic forebears while denouncing them, especially Constantius but also Constantine, Gregory did the opposite to explain how and why the first Christian Roman imperial dynasty had produced Julian. Any providential explanation of God's punishing the *oikoumenē* through Julian thus had to exculpate Constantine and Constantius and in so doing justify both Christian imperial power and its proper execution and administration. To achieve these interrelated aims, Gregory provided a *Fürstenspiegel* in its inversion, in the person of Julian, and positively, in the *synkrisis* with Constantius, and combined both, the negative and the positive, with a theory of the correct Christian political philosophy.

A Christian Dynasty and Its Deserter

> Must our ears be filled with the praise of his good administration of the public post, relaxation of taxes, good choice of magistrates, and punishment of robbery?[104]
> —GREGORY OF NAZIANZUS, ORATION 4.75

Gregory's performative counterstele claimed the agora, jurisdiction, the army, and indeed the entire *imperium Romanum* for Christians. To do so required more than

---

103. Literally, "making public [Maximinus's] bodily disgrace" (στηλιτεύουσαι τὴν λώβην τοῦ σώματος). According to Gregory, *Or.* 4.96, had Julian lived, he would have been on a par with those persecutors, according to the testimonies of those privy to his secrets. Bernardi (ed. and trans., *Grégoire de Nazianze: Discours 4–5*, 240 n. 1) remarks that Gregory's reference to Diocletian as the first persecutor called into question his knowledge of historical date. But these persecutors were Tetrarchs, Julian's dynastic and ideological precursors he emulated in style and message; Rosen, *Julian*, 43–45. In addition, Criscuolo, "A proposito di Gregorio," 44, points out that Gregory referred to history recent enough to be in his audience's memory.

104. Gr. Naz. *Or.* 4.75: "Ἡ δρόμος μὲν ἀνεκτῶς διοικουμένος καὶ φόρων ἄνεσις καὶ ἀρχόντων ἐκλογὴ καὶ κλοπῶν ἐπιτίμησις . . . περιθρυλλεῖσθαι ἡμῶν ἔδει τὰ ὦτα τούτων ἐπαινουμένων;

removing the statues of the gods from the imperial images and replacing the labarum among the army's standards. Julian had made abundantly clear that to rule the empire was not a matter only of deeds and actions; those deeds and actions also had to represent an internally consistent theory of imperial rule that linked the *oikoumenē*, through the ruler, to the divine that had caused its existence and preserved it in safety and harmonious unity. Thus, Gregory had to do more than deconstruct Julian and unmask him as inept tyrant; he had to provide a countervision of his own Rome, a Christian philosophy of leadership as comprehensive and authoritative in its claim to the ancient, normative foundations as that of the emperor.

Gregory, like Julian, believed that the divine instilled virtues and ethical comportment proper (*oikeios*) to those affiliated (*oikeioi*) with that divine. The divinity was reflected in the character (*ēthos*) and comportment of those whom it had created and who followed its commandments. The amoral and antisocial behavior of a divinity's adherents, for Julian and for Gregory, reflected by analogy the deficiencies of the divinity at its roots. According to Gregory, Julian was unjust, deceptive, and divisive; therefore, his gods were also the polar opposite of the truly divine, the Good, the Truth, the One. Because goodness, justice, unifying harmony, and philanthropy are the essence of the divine, Julian's gods, revealed as unjust by his behavior, could not have been gods but were mere human invention, as proved by the statues erected in their honor. Julian, in his *Epistle to the Athenians* and *Against the Galileans*, made the same argument in reverse: his experience of Constantine and especially Constantius convinced him that whatever a murderous emperor claimed as his guiding principle was not a god, but a deficient, amoral human invention.

Julian's case was fairly straightforward. Those who had murdered his family were tyrants, and the God whom they served was, as a consequence, no god. Gregory's task was harder, given that human behavior reflects the divine to which it is *oikeios* and that Julian's *genea* and upbringing were Christian: he had to explain why God had permitted evil like "the poison of the snakes" (*Or.* 4.20) to take root in Julian. Why had Julian, the first baptized Roman emperor and scion of Constantine's philo-Christian dynasty, become the Deserter? The structural requirements of invective, the genre to which *Oration* 4 formally adheres, demanded that Gregory engage Julian's *eugeneia* and his *paideia*: now, however, inverted. The challenge was where to locate the root of the evil—the perennial question of theodicy, the origin of evil in light of divine goodness—since it could not be simply divinely caused, nor could *genea* be held responsible. What in Julian's family background and upbringing could account for his deviation? What did the comparison with Constantius reveal about God's providential will?

Oration 4 opens with the crucial juxtaposition. It exults in the death of the "dragon, the Apostate, the great mind, the Assyrian, the common adversary and enemy of all," and evokes the "soul of the great Constantius . . . and of all Christ-loving [*philochristoi*] emperors before him, but [Constantius] above all" (*Or.* 4.1,

3).[105] Then Gregory moves into *medias res*. "Grown together with the inheritance of Christ, after having made it grow further, as far as was possible, and having consolidated it in time, to become thus the most illustrious of all rulers of all times, [Constantius] committed—What disgrace!—an error absolutely unworthy of his own piety. Without knowing it, he nurtured the enemy of Christ for the Christians, and in this one case did he not use his philanthropy well, having saved [Julian] and made him rule." Constantius, the philo-Christian emperor great in *philanthrōpia* and above all *eusebeia*, made one grave error: he did not kill Julian. (Compare Julian's observation to the exact same effect in *Misopogon* 357b.) Why had Constantius's imperial philanthropy lapsed in this one instance?

In this opening passage, Gregory homes in on Julian's central argument in defense of his rebellion against the Augustus, that Constantius had murdered his entire family. Indeed, Gregory's praise of Constantius, his panegyric making that emperor rather than, say, Constantine the paragon of a Christian Roman ruler, responds to Julian's special animosity: Gregory praises Constantius because Julian rebelled against him and thus against God, in whose name he ruled. Gregory presents what was apparently the official version of Constantius's court (also evident in *Or.* 1 and 2, Julian's two panegyrics): Constantius saved Julian out of unusual benevolence and philanthropy.[106] "The army had taken up arms against the leaders," fearing *kainotomiai*, innovations, or change in the succession to the detriment of Constantius and his brothers (*Or.* 4.21). Constantius barely brought the situation under control, and to save Julian and Gallus, "in an incredible and paradoxical fashion," under such circumstances showed unusual *philanthrōpia* and *megalopsychia*; normal imperial behavior would have been to eliminate them with all other male members of their family. In this reading, the (malleable, democratic) army had forced Constantius into circumstances wherein he allowed philanthropy to overwrite imperial reasoning.[107]

Gregory's emphasis on Constantius's philanthropy was also designed to contrast with Julian's: in this case, for example, Constantius truly extended philanthropy to his enemies, as Julian claimed to have done. Indeed, "whether it was because Constantius considered this a defense [*apologia*] against accusations related to the upheavals at the beginning of his reign, demonstrating that they had not occurred at his orders, or because he wanted to display magnanimity by uniting [Julian and Gallus] to the common rule, or because he wanted to render the rule more secure by

---

105. Lugaresi (Gregory of Nazianzus, *Contro Giuliano*, trans. and comm. Lugaresi, 219) notes that Constantius's iconography included him subduing a dragon.

106. E.g., Jul. *Or.* 1.17a, 45c; Eutr. *Hist.* 10.9. Ammianus 21.16.8, following Julian, held Constantius fully responsible; den Boeft, den Hengst, and Teitler, *Philological and Historical Commentary on Ammianus Marcellinus 21*, 257–58; Gregory of Nazianzus, *Contro Giuliano*, trans. and comm. Lugaresi, 245–48.

107. Though Gregory blames the army, he nevertheless hints at Constantius's culpability: had he prevented such upheaval, Julian would have been too far down in the succession to cause harm; on the other hand, this was all God's plan.

adding them . . . , all fruits of thoughts more benevolent than wise" (*Or.* 4.22), he sent Julian and Gallus to a splendid imperial estate to be groomed for the throne. Responding to Julian's version of the events, as propagated in the *Epistle to the Athenians* (270c-d), Gregory pointed out that Constantius was not responsible for the murder of Julian's family, nor had he imprisoned him at Macellum but had offered him an excellent (Christian) education as befitted an imperial prince groomed to rule; again Gregory echoed Julian's own panegyrics (*Or.* 4.23). Because there had never been a legitimate reason for him to violate all laws of gratitude and proper behavior vis-à-vis his family (Constantius, after all, was family), he rebelled against cousin, emperor, and God out of sheer malevolence (*Or.* 4.21). What caused such depths of ingratitude?[108]

At a later stage Gregory elaborated what he had merely suggested: God, acting through Constantius, had saved Julian for reasons of his own. In fact, according to Gregory, Marc of Arethusa had actually done the saving. Marc, a homoian (Arian) Christian, had spirited Julian away during the tumultuous events, only to escape narrowly from being martyred himself by the inhabitants of Arethusa acting on Julian's unwritten will, and therefore actually by Julian, a sign of his philanthropy and ingratitude (*Or.* 4.89–91). Thus what to normal humans seems paradoxical and mistaken philanthropy could reveal God's deeper design when a purified philosopher such as Gregory explained it. God had saved Julian for a reason hidden from the uninitiated: "The God of the martyrs did not halt the impiety, . . . for reasons known only to him in his ineffable wisdom and governance."[109]

If we compare Julian and Gallus, we note another apparent paradox (given that both came from the same family), which further illuminates God's plan. Saved and educated the same way with *enkyklia paideia,* both had practiced "our philosophy," entered the clergy, and honored the martyrs. But without apparent reason one deserted and the other did not (*Or.* 4.23, 24).[110] Those closer to God, however, who could read his will better than others more removed, could see divine portents in the fate of a monument Gallus and Julian, while in residence at Macellum, jointly erected to honor the martyr Mamas near Caesarea. Gallus's portion of the monument rose in splendor, whereas Julian's collapsed in an earthquake. God refused his offering because he knew that Julian's intentions were impure and that he dissimu-

---

108. Jul. *Ep. ad Ath.* 270c for Macellum as prison. Julian's defense in the *Ep. ad Ath.* could imply that Constantius's propaganda accused Julian of being ungrateful; Zonaras 13.10. For the paradox of Julian's salvation, see also Socr. *HE* 3.1.6–8 and Soz. *HE* 5.2.8–9; both cite Gallus's health and Julian's youth as reasons; Lib. *Or.* 18.10; Amm. Marc. 21.10.7; den Boeft, den Hengst, and Teitler, *Philological and Historical Commentary on Ammianus Marcellinus 21,* 140–43.

109. Gr. Naz. *Or.* 4.28: οἷς αὐτὸς ἠπίστατο λόγοις, κατὰ τὴν ἄρρητον αὐτοῦ σοφίαν τε καὶ κυβέρνησιν.

110. Gregory mentions Gallus's rash temper but foregrounds his good piety; cf. Jul. *Ep. ad Ath.* 271d; Amm. Marc. 14.11.28; Aur. Vict. *Caes.* 42.12.

lated. Thus, in a "prophecy hidden from the others," the monument and its destruction foreshadowed Julian's deception and fate. God destroyed Julian's false temples (as Babylas's remains caused Apollo's temple to burn: *Or.* 4.25–27, 86). The martyrs, whose remains and memories Julian attacked so viciously, were the first to unmask the traitor and to defy his powers through forces greater than his will.[111]

Gregory phrased God's rejection of Julian's offer of the martyr shrine in language evoking pagan sacrifices, the abandonment of which Julian considered another crime committed by Constantius's legislation. Gregory also used the passage to argue that Christian sacrifice is not material and physical, but internal and immaterial as befitted a transcendent God. The virtues of Christian sacrifices penetrate deep below mere surface, in analogy to Christian rule, which is founded on deeds and is no theatrical fiction (*Or.* 4.29).[112] To confuse the efficacy of what is at the surface (pagan material sacrifice, human fiction) with the real power of what is rooted deep in divine truth (Christian immaterial sacrifice, true deeds) had been Julian's fatal mistake, caused by his incorrect understanding of philosophy, and his entire misapprehension, in consequence, of the divine will.

In a polemical rather than chronological sequence, Gregory discussed Julian and Gallus's advancement in *paideia* immediately after describing the divine reaction to Julian's duplicitous attempt to honor a martyr. Here, Julian's reaction to his initiation into philosophy was crucial.[113] Because Julian was already a deceptive and dissimulating person, outed as such to the initiated by the fate of his part of the *martyrium,* his advance in philosophy did not lead him to the higher truth of the purified, but instead deviated to the questionable practices of Maximus and other theurgists. "When the philanthropy of the *autokratōr* made his brother [Caesar] and assigned him a significant part of the *oikoumenē*" (again Gregory counters Ju-

---

111. The *figura* of the earth's rejection of the sanctuary, completed by fire, returns in *Oration* 5.4, when God similarly rejected the Temple in Jerusalem. Jul. *Mis.* 361b–362b for Babylas, whom Gregory does not mention; *CG* fr. 47.201e against martyr veneration; fr. 86.354b and Jul. *Ep.* 134 in John Lydus, *Mens.* 4.53 for the Jerusalem Temple. In *Or.* 21.33 Gregory alludes to another earthquake showing how the earth rejected Julian's corpse.

112. Jul. *CG* fr. 72.305d–306c; Eus. *PE* 4.10.6. Gr. Naz. *Or.* 29 engages the Presocratic critique of sacrifice—namely that God does not need it, or the gods do not; otherwise they would also accept unworthy offerings—and responds that the fact that the divine does not require sacrifice does not make it superfluous. Using again Greek rather than biblical language, Gregory maintains, however, that only the spiritual, immaterial sacrifice made with the right intention is worthy of God.

113. See above, Chapter 4; the date of Julian's conversion to paganism remains debated. According to Rosen, *Julian,* 83–89, Gregory's narrative sequence dates that conversion to Macellum, but in my view Gregory's structure is above all polemical, though that does not rule out a chronological sequence. The point is that Julian could not read divine symbols, because he followed magic rather than philosophy. Julian and Gallus left Macellum around 348, when Julian's studies truly began; Gallus was made Caesar in 351, so that Gregory is relatively accurate; R. Smith, *Julian's Gods,* 25–27.

lian's official account, in which Constantius acted out of ill will),[114] "he on his part could with much liberty and without fear frequent the most pernicious teachers and teachings. Asia became for him the school of that impiety that tells humbug about astronomy, horoscopes [*geneseis*], predictions of the future, and the magic that accompanies it."[115]

Rather than a divinely inspired philosopher, Julian became a charlatan, a *magos* and *goētēs*, a devotee of astronomy, horoscopes, and magic. "After [Julian] tasted of the philosophical teachings—Oh! if only [he] had never done it!—he went to acquire the power of words, which is a weapon of virtue for the good but for the bad the sting of evil." Philosophy falsely acquired by the wrong person resulted in false philosophy, that of the Hellenes, which taught dissimulation, ingratitude, injustice, desertion, and indeed magic such as theurgy.[116] "That is what the noble masters taught him, the defenders of the empire and the legislators he assembled around him, called forth from the three ways [where Hecate and other magical divinities were honored] and the depths [in which criminals were thrown]: people whose behavior he did not applaud but whose eloquence he admired, and perhaps not even that, but only their impiety as the right counsel and teacher of what deeds to perform and to omit" (*Or.* 4.43)—Gregory's attack on Julian's friends and advisors, such as Maximus.

---

114. In *Ep. ad Ath.* 270d, 271d–272a, Julian presents Gallus's advancement to Caesar as yet another hostile act of "the most philanthropic" Constantius.

115. Gr. Naz. *Or.* 4.31: Ἐπεὶ δὲ τὸν μὲν ἀδελφὸν ἡ φιλανθρωπία τοῦ αὐτοκράτορος ἀποδείκνυσι βασιλέα καὶ μέρος οὐκ ὀλίγον ἐγχειρίζει τῆς οἰκουμένης, τῷ δὲ ὑπῆρχε κατὰ πολλὴν ἐξουσίαν καὶ ἄδειαν καὶ λόγων καὶ διδασκάλων τοῖς ὀλεθριωτάτοις προσομιλεῖν, Ἀσία δὲ ἦν αὐτῷ τὸ τῆς ἀσεβείας διδασκαλεῖον, ὅση τε περὶ ἀστρονομίαν καὶ τὰς γενέσεις καὶ φαντασίαν προγνώσεως τερατεύεται καὶ τὴν ἐπομένην τούτοις γοητικήν. For *geneseis* as horoscopes at birth rather than as teachings about the origins of the world, Kurmann, *Gregor von Nazianz*, 113, referring to *Or.* 5.5, though Gregory may have had both in mind, given the centrality of *Timaeus* in Julian's writings. For Julian's secret conversion at the hands of Maximus, see also Lib. *Or.* 18.19, 21–22, 24; and *Or.* 13.13–14. Gregory was aware of further details of Julian's conversion (*Or.* 5.23) but streamlined the account here; the sequence echoes Julian's own description of his conversion in the *Hymn to King Helios* 130b–131a: Julian immersed himself in philosophy, already a dissimulator, though he kept his illness concealed from all but his closest friends. But the philosophy so deceptively acquired wanted only a little bit of air to burst into flame. For illness (*nosos*) when referring to Christianity, see Jul. *Ep.* 61.424a–b.

116. Gr. Naz. *Or.* 4.43 remarks sarcastically that such behavior is what "the Platos, the Chrysippuses, the illustrious Peripatetic, and the venerated Stoa, and those shouting out their ingenuities [οἱ τὰ κομψὰ λαρυγγίζοντες]; that is what the sense of proportions of geometry and the discourses regarding justice, regarding the obligation to choose to submit to injustice rather than to commit it [τὸ χρῆναι ἀδικεῖσθαι μᾶλλον αἱρεῖσθαι ἢ ἀδικεῖν] [taught him]." Gr. Naz. *Or.* 27.1 criticizes "shouters of ingenious discourses." Pl. *Grg.* 508a and 447b–475e debate the effects of geometry on ethics and the human mind. Coulie, "Chaînes," 139–43, analyzes Gregory's strategy of alternating between citations and allusions in *Or.* 4.42–43 and elsewhere: first Gregory names Plato, then he alludes to *Gorgias*, then to Plato's life in Sicily, and again to the *Republic*. Lugaresi (Gregory of Nazianzus, *Contro Giuliano*, trans. and comm. Lugaresi, 277–78) and Kurmann (*Gregor von Nazianz*, 146) discuss the philosophers listed further.

Philosophy per se was not the culprit. A person such as Eunomius went wrong because his inferior *genea* made him overambitious and led him to shortcuts, whereas Julian, in contrast, freely chose to desert his good *genea*. His choice (*prohairesis*) led him to dissimulate, and encountering philosophy only exacerbated that tendency, leading him to choose wrong teachers so that he deserted Christ and led the Christian Roman *oikoumenē* to disaster: "Now only one thing was missing—that to the impiety was added power" (*Or*. 4.31).

"Not long thereafter [God] also gave him that [power] against us, [for] the iniquity of the masses had grown and, one may say, the prosperity of the Christians had reached heights that required a reversal; power, honor, and satiety had made us arrogant."[117] God allowed Julian to survive and to choose deception, first to instruct all which philosophical maxims and practices turned philosophy into impiety and magic, and second to remind all who governed (as philosophers—i.e., bishops—and public officials) that "power, honor, and satiety" could corrupt them and indeed had done so. "In reality, it seems more difficult to conserve goods than to acquire them, and easier to recover lost felicity with an effort than to safeguard what one has at present; before ruin comes arrogance—as Proverbs [15:33] says so well—and before glory, humiliation; or to say it more clearly, ruin follows arrogance, and humiliation [is rewarded by] glory." Through Julian, God punished and taught. As long as Christians had been humble and oppressed, they had grown in strength (and numbers), but once they reached the summit of world rule they became fat and lazy, and "dispersed all the force they had gathered during the persecutions and the trials" (*Or*. 4.32).

In Praise of Constantius: To Advise Valens

Gregory's short panegyric, or *basilikos logos*, for Constantius (*Or*. 4.34–42, 45), was structured as a dialogue between Gregory and some in his imagined audience who had accused Constantius of having made Julian Caesar. In it, Gregory emphasized that Constantius (and not, of course, Julian) had been a true divinely inspired and Christ-loving emperor.[118] Being closest to God, he had, upon his death, exchanged earthly rule for a heavenly one, united to God, beside whom he is seated among the heroes.[119] As a description it entwines classical notions of *apotheōsis* with Christian appellations, assigning Constantius a place in the heavens different from that Julian had given him in *Caesars*.[120] Echoing Themistius's praise of Constantius, Greg-

---

117. Gr. Naz. *Or*. 4.31: ἡ πληνθυνθεῖσα τῶν πολλῶν ἀνομία καὶ ἡ ἐπ' ἄκρον, ὡς ἂν εἴποι τις, Χριστιανῶν εὐεξία, τὴν ἐναντίαν ζητοῦσα μεταβολήν.
118. θειότατε βασιλεῦ καὶ φιλοχριστότατε.
119. Ephraem *Hymns c. Jul*. 1–4 shared this positive view.
120. Via association with Constantine: e.g., Jul. *Caes*. 335c–336c. For emperors as *theiotatoi*, see Men. Rh. *Treatise* 2 (*Menander Rhetor*, ed. and trans. Russell and Wilson, 76; *Peri epideiktikōn*, ed. Spengel,

ory describes Constantius as far above all other Roman emperors in discernment and wisdom.[121] He proved that his virtues were divinely inspired by his many victories over internal and external enemies, above all the Persians, whom he subdued, "guided by God's hand," with force and diplomacy. Julian had neither Constantius's virtues nor his accomplishments. Given Constantius's excellence, it was hard to choose what to admire most: his military prowess, his wisdom, his philanthropy, or his *eusebeia;* but in the end Gregory declared *eusebeia* his most significant characteristic: it was divinely inspired, and it ensured that Constantius's deeds were real and lasting (*Or.* 4.34–36).[122]

Christian imperial panegyrics at the time Gregory wrote *Oration* 4 were a genre in the making. Though Eusebius's *In Praise of Constantine* is earlier, Gregory charted new territory. As Aaron Johnson has pointed out, Eusebius had an ambivalent relation to Rome.[123] On the one hand, he praised Constantine as a philosopher-king and "friend of God" and welcomed the imperial favor shown to Christianity. But even at that point, he considered Rome a city enmeshed in veneration of idols and hobbled by bad oracles that ensured its rule would be transitory.[124] The only durable, lasting thing in Rome was a burgeoning Christianity and its civilizing impact. For Eusebius, however, Christianity was not Rome, even though Augustus's peace gave Christianity the framework to rise (e.g., *PE* 1.4.8). This view of Rome, as bound to an oracular political philosophy that Christ had to destroy in order to save the world, remained dominant even in Eusebius's later works.[125]

For Gregory, the world was different. Though he too knew a Rome beholden to demons and their oracles, destined to be transient, he now aligned that Rome exclusively with Julian; in the Christian Rome of Constantius, Christianity and Rome

---

368.19); Gr. Naz. *Carm.* 1.2.5.296–97; Eus. *VC* 4.48; Gregory of Nazianzus, *Contro Giuliano,* trans. and comm. Lugaresi, 266–67. In general, Ruggini, "Apoteosi"; and Wallace-Hadrill, "Emperor," esp. 310–23.

121. Lugaresi (Gregory of Nazianzus, *Contro Giuliano,* trans. and comm. Lugaresi, 267) points out that Gregory here uses *synesis* rather than the more common *phronēsis,* the same term used by Libanius in his *Or.* 59 in praise of Constantius, suggesting that Gregory may have had that oration in mind.

122. Another model may well have been Them. *Or.* 1 in praise of Constantius's philanthropy, a virtue he considered central; see also *Or.* 6 and 19. Though *philanthrōpia* is a classic imperial virtue that Julian also mentioned, *Ep. ad Ath.* 349a, the nuances in emphasis are noteworthy: Julian's own emphasis on philanthropy may have responded to Constantius's, to which Gregory now returns. Wirth, "Themistius," demonstrates the convergences between Gregory's and Themistius's praise of Constantius, though he does not cite Gregory at all. See also Vanderspoel, *Themistius,* 87–104; Kurmann, *Gregor von Nazianz,* 125.

123. Johnson, *Ethnicity,* 153–97.

124. Eus. *LC* 1.6, 2.1–4, 5.1, 5.4; Johnson, *Ethnicity,* 183–84, based on *DE* 15 fr. 1; E. Elm, "'Du bist wie jener Gott.'"

125. The panegyric (*LC* [trans. Drake, *In Praise of Constantine,* 83–102]), *Vita Constantini* (*VC* [*Eusebius: Life of Constantine,* ed. and trans. Cameron and Hall]) and the *Oration on the Church of the Holy Sepulchre* (*SC* [trans. Drake, *In Praise of Constantine,* 103–27]).

since Augustus had risen together. Constantius is a truly Roman ruler, since Rome is truly Christian, and hence Constantius's deeds and the Rome he represents are (despite its flaws) lasting because rooted in divine will, manifest in (Constantius's good) deeds. For Gregory, as for Eusebius, the driving force was Christ the *Logos* and the God with whom he is one.[126] Gregory portrayed Constantius to reflect, subtly, an altered view of the relation between Roman imperial power and its representative. He was, after all writing for Constantius's and Julian's successors, hoping they would be orthodox Christians. For Gregory, Constantius's *eusebeia* had been his most glorious virtue. He concurred with Eusebius that *eusebeia* ranked highest among imperial virtues, though in Constantius's case, according to Gregory, that piety united Christians, rather than destroying demons.[127] That *eusebeia* outstripped all Constantius's other substantial imperial virtues and deeds, because Constantius realized in his piety that the greatest of all imperial accomplishments was to preserve Christianity's supremacy, harmony, and unity. "He knew well, because he reflected on these things in a more elevated and regal manner than many others, that Roman might had grown together with that of the Christians and that the empire had arrived together with the coming of Christ, whereas before it had not entirely constituted itself as a monarchy. Thus it seemed to me that he treated our side with greater favor, and he did well . . . so that we all might be one thing and in agreement, not lacerated and divided by schisms," and that "we through him and he through us would have glory before God and before men, and that his authority would remain forever indissoluble from us."[128]

Emperor and Priest

Roman imperial power was linked to the fortunes of Christianity, and prosperity rose and fell with the unity and harmony of the Christians.[129] Thus, piety (*eusebeia*) and care for the well-being of all Christians, especially their (doctrinal) unity and harmony, superseded all other imperial virtues. This addition to the canon of imperial virtues and accomplishments was essential, because intra-Christian strife had, in effect, caused Julian. Their schisms and arrogant lack of unanimity, exacerbated greatly under Julian, further proving Gregory's point, had called forth God's direct

---

126. Eusebius's Arian pedigree, presumably, has thus far prevented any sustained investigation of Gregory's relation to him; Origen remains the reference point.

127. See Eus. *LC* 5.8; see also his "abundance of piety," *LC* 7.12. Drake, "Eusebian Template," esp. 76–78.

128. Gr. Naz. *Or.* 4.37: Καὶ γὰρ πρὸς τοῖς ἄλλοις ἐκεῖνο ᾔδει σαφῶς, ὑψηλότερόν τε καὶ βασιλικώτερον ἢ κατὰ τοὺς πολλοὺς περὶ τούτων διανοούμενος, ὅτι τοῖς χριστιανῶν πράγμασι τὰ Ῥωμαίων συνηύξησε καὶ συνεισῆλθε τῇ ἐπιδημίᾳ Χριστοῦ τὸ κράτος . . . ὥστε πάντας ἓν εἶναι καὶ συμφρονεῖν . . . καὶ μὴ διακεκόφθαι μηδὲ διεστάναι τοῖς σχίσμασιν.

129. Eus. *DE* 3.7.30–35, 7.2.22; *VC* 2.19.2. For the notion of the synchronicity of Christianity and Augustus's empire, also Lk 2:1–7; Hippolytus *Dan.* 4.9.2–3; Orig. *Cels.* 2.30.20, 27.

punishment. Misguided Christians (those who disagreed with Gregory and who were therefore heterodox), had caused God's pedagogical punishment, of which Constantius's paradoxical philanthropy and Julian's choice of deception and desertion were merely the manifestation.

Consequently, a Christian emperor's first order of business was to preserve Christian unity, harmony, and concord: right teaching, or orthodoxy. An emperor could do this, however, only if advised by persons who truly understood Christian teaching and dispensed the Trinity correctly, persons such as Gregory (as Theodosius finally understood when making Gregory Constantinopolitan bishop). An emperor, if correctly advised, would discern the divine will—of which he was but the executor—preserve unity and harmony, and rule as long and successfully as Constantius. But the emperor was not a priest: he could rule in such a manner only if true philosophers-as-priests advised him.

Constantius was the ideal manifestation of this logic of governance in a Christian emperor. He had made his sole yet far-reaching error—to let Julian live—because of his simplicity, his *haplotēs*.[130] Being simple at heart, Constantius never suspected Julian, since "he who is free of evil does not suspect evil" (*Or.* 4.38). Constantius's *haplotēs* left him defenseless, unable to differentiate between artful dissimulation and truth, and Julian, who could not exceed him in goodness and philanthropy, bested him through the "reasonable" and "excellent" teachings of the Greeks. "In truth I would be ashamed if we, who received from [Constantius] so many honors and were convinced of his extraordinary piety, would not defend him justly" (*Or.* 4.39). The audience at Nazianzus, still in schism, no doubt understood. Gregory's explanation of Constantius's action evokes his defense of his own father, who had signed the deceiving document that he could not unmask as fiction, defenseless, like Constantius, against the excellence of the dissimulators. The elder Gregory had signed a homoian document that had achieved, under Constantius's auspices, unity after decades of strife. Those whom Gregory accused of having been the reason for God's punishment, manifest in Julian, were those who had opposed that homoian document and the unity it signified. Such an accusation was harsh, especially since a significant part of Gregory's intended audience in Nazianzus at the time of *Oration* 4 still opposed Gregory the Elder because he had signed that document. Here, Gregory's second, related argument comes into play: those who were or had been simple, like Constantius and the elder Gregory, needed Gregory the Younger, a man schooled in the true philosophical life who could penetrate the deception of those who proclaimed falsely understood philosophy. Otherwise, schism would continue to endanger the *oikoumenē*, even after Julian's death. Be-

---

130. For simplicity as imperial virtue, D. Chr. *Or.* 1.61; Gr. Naz. *Or.* 21.21, where Athanasius's counterpart George of Alexandria exploits Constantius's *haplotēs*; and the discussion of Gregory the Elder as *haplos* above in Chapter 5.

cause schism had brought Julian to power in the first place, however, Constantius, and Gregory the Elder, could be blamed only a little for their excess of philanthropy. "That is the defense of Constantius" (*Or.* 4.38).[131]

Gregory's presentation of Constantius as the ideal Christian philosopher and ruler has caused his Maurist editors and modern scholars considerable concern. Even John McGuckin's nuanced assessment stresses Gregory's otherwise "less-than-enthusiastic attitude to Constantius."[132] McGuckin explains Gregory's praise as resulting from the structural conventions of invective. Because one is bad, the other must be good. But even if this works for Constantius, it does not explain Gregory's praise of another well-known homoian (Arian), Marc of Arethusa, the man whom the citizens of Arethusa almost martyred even though he had been Julian's savior (*Or.* 4.88–91).[133] Explanations of Gregory's praise range from the startled Maurists' suggestion that Gregory mistook Marc's identity or, alternatively, that by Gregory's time the formerly prominent Arian Marc must have converted to orthodoxy, to modern views that doctrinal divisions paled in light of the danger Julian posed, in the face of which "even the chasm between Arian and Nicene could be overcome in a moment."[134] But Constantius and Marc of Arethusa play their important role in the economy of Gregory's *Oration* 4 precisely because they were homoian.

In Gregory's account, Marc of Arethusa converted many to Christianity while Constantius ruled. He also destroyed a temple in Arethusa, angering the city's pagan citizens. Thus, as soon as Julian came to power, Marc was attacked. His first response was to leave town to preserve peace and harmony. When he learned, however, that his supporters suffered, were imprisoned, and risked their lives, he returned and, as befitted a true philosopher, offered himself to appease the masses (*Or.* 4.88). Julian's pagan supporters—the majority of the citizens—tyrannized the old man, of eminently civilized comportment,[135] by parading him around the city, tormenting him by releasing bees that stung him, and lacerating him with knives (allegedly a custom among followers of Mithras). Worse, they transformed such tragedy into farce

---

131. In *Or.* 4.33, 34, 36, 37, Gregory also defends Constantius.

132. McGuckin, *St. Gregory*, 119. In *Or.* 21.26 and *Or.* 25.9, composed in entirely different circumstances, Gregory was more critical of Constantius.

133. Marc was a prominent homoian, which makes his presence at court, assumed by Gregory, likely. He had mediated at Sirmium in 351, had supported Acacius in Seleucia in 359, and presumably signed the formula of 360 the elder Gregory had also signed; Epiph. *Haer.* 73.26.1; Brennecke, *Studien*, 14–16, 83, 134–35, 198 n. 126.

134. PG 35.530, 616–20. For modern scholars' views of Gregory's praise of Constantius and Marc, McGuckin (*St. Gregory*, 120), who notes that Gregory here disregarded Marc's standing as leading homoian theologian, "and thus an enemy of all that Gregory stood for in his own religious understanding." Bernardi, ed. and trans., *Grégoire de Nazianze: Discours 4–5*, 30–33; Kurmann, *Gregor von Nazianz*, 24; Van Dam, *Kingdom*, 97, 193–94; Brennecke, *Studien*, 84–86.

135. Gr. Naz. *Or.* 4.89, τὴν πολιτείαν αἰδεσιμώτερος.

by asking him to pay symbolically for the damage his harassment had caused the temple (*Or.* 4.89). Marc remained firm and steadfast until the prefect (probably Saturninius Secundus Salutius) put an end to the spectacle, ashamed of the citizens' uncivilized behavior, which he immediately reported to Julian (*Or.* 4.91).[136]

The passage is self-explanatory, containing in a nutshell the dichotomy between Julian and Constantius, pagan and Christian. The homoian Marc, as the most philosophical bishop, remained the true citizen, alone preserving civic values, whereas the city, following its emperor, degenerated into tyrannical cruelty to behave more or less like wild animals—all in fulfillment of the unwritten law of the man whom Marc had saved in true philanthropy, emulating the homoian Constantius.[137] Indeed, both men had risked their lives to resist the evil tyrant, Marc by opposing the unchained rage of his followers, Constantius by preparing war to stop the usurper.[138] To these homoian confessors a third must be added: the elder Gregory. As Gregory makes clear in praising the Maccabeans in *Oration* 15, his own father, a venerated elder bishop and citizen par excellence, happily risked martyrdom by opposing Julian steadfastly—for example, when resisting the sequestration of his church, the monument of his *megalopsychia*, "on the order of the emperor" to house Julian's archers (*Or.* 18.32).[139] Three men who had been willing to oppose Julian nearly to the point of martyrdom, three embodiments of virtue who stood as exemplars for everything Julian opposed, all of them homoian Christians—who indeed were the Christians Julian attacked most, because of their support for Constantius—three men who stood for the civilized unity of Christianity that alone could oppose and prevent the likes of Julian.[140] In praising Constantius and Marc as homoians, Gregory could both denigrate Julian and those who followed his uncivilized—and therefore not Greek—behavior, and also chastise those who opposed his father, those whose stubborn resistance to unity and harmony rent the fabric of the polis just as Julian had done.

My analysis of Gregory's *Oration* 4, which so far has emphasized the political (in a modern sense) aspects of his presentation opposing Julian and Constantius, Hellenic and Roman Christian imperial rule, nevertheless already hints at the theological overtones. Gregory negated Julian's claims to be a Platonic philosopher-leader who respected the supremacy of law and justice, secured the realm, and acted in analogy to the Good and the Just as mediator here on earth through his philan-

---

136. Lib. *Ep.* 819.6–7 also mentions the event, noting that Marc was venerated as a god as a result of these tortures and pointing out that Julian had not executed him for the destruction of the temple.

137. *Pace* McGuckin (*St. Gregory*, 120), Marc of Arethusa died ca. 364. For his popularity, see also Thdt. *HE* 3.7.6–10; Soz. *HE* 5.10.8–14; Hauser-Meury, *Prosopographie*, 116–17.

138. Gregory even suggested that Julian had contributed to Constantius's sudden death: *Or.* 4.47–48.

139. McGuckin, *St. Gregory*, 129.

140. See Brennecke's discussion, *Studien*, 114–41, of the homoian martyrs, to which Babylas must be added.

thropy, guiding everyone in his care to unity and harmony as appropriate to the gods to which everyone and everything was affiliated (*oikeios*). For Gregory, rather, Julian's rule was transient theater, his legislation illegitimate and hence to be revoked; and each of his acts was designed to cause civil war, rend the fabric of the *politeia*, and threaten the security of the commonwealth. Julian was no legitimate Roman emperor (indeed no emperor), but merely acted the part badly, for he had no divine mandate: he had deserted God, as proved by his deeds and his end. Gregory did not rest with such negation, however. Constantius was the countermodel, a true Roman emperor, because he represented the unity of the realm, expressed in the unity of orthodox Christianity (orthodox, because good and right unified reflects divine harmony). Thus, Constantius's deeds had been good and plentiful, and his rule (including his antipagan legislation) was long and lasting. Gregory countered Julian's with his own philosophical construct, *theōsis*, which also cemented (at least for him) the relation between emperor and priest, such that the priest or bishop was the political philosopher active for the common good, guiding all in his care (including the emperor) and affiliating them with—indeed, making them—God.

9

A Bloodless Sacrifice of Words to the Word

Logoi *for the* Logos

Mine, then, and for those dear to me is the power of eloquence [logoi], which I have embraced first of all and continue to embrace first after what is truly the first: I will say the divine realm and our hope of what lies beyond the visible.[1]

—GREGORY OF NAZIANZUS, ORATION 4.100

The nexus between the gods and the philosophy proper to them, the appropriate way to venerate the Greek and Roman gods, and following god as instituted by the ancients stood at the center of Julian's imperial endeavor, because for him too piety had been the highest virtue. As Plato had demanded in his *Laws,* Julian as legislator served the gods at all times in their hierarchical order (down to *daimones* and heroes) and as proper to each cultic place, because venerating the sacred (*hiera*) and the *logoi* proper to them guaranteed the well-being of the *politeia*.[2] To strengthen again that crucial link between *logoi* and the sacred, philosophy and the gods that had caused everything, was thus central to Julian's aims. This link, in consequence, also formed the core of Gregory's response.

Logoi and philosophy as its apex were fundamental to Greek Rome's preeminence and dominance, culturally and militarily, for they were in essence one, ever since Herodotus praised the leadership of Athens against the Persians based on "our common Greekness [*to Hellēnikon*]": "We are one in blood and one in language; those shrines of the gods belong to us all in common, and there are our habits, bred of a common upbringing." Isocrates' view that "Athens has made it so that the name of the Greeks designates not a people [*genos*] but a mind-set, and those are called Greeks

---

1. Gr. Naz. *Or.* 4.100: Ἐμοὶ γοῦν εἴη καὶ ὅστις ἐμοὶ φίλος τὸ τῶν λόγων κράτος ὃ πρῶτον μετὰ τὸ πρῶτον ἠσπασάμην τε καὶ ἀσπάζομαι, τὰ θεῖα λέγω καὶ τὰς ἔξω τῶν ὁρωμένων ἐλπίδας.

2. Pl. *Lg.* 716a–718a (esp. 716b), 738b–c, 889b–e; the slightly different emphasis of religion in, e.g., Pl. *R.* 372b, 379b, 380c, 427b–c will occupy us below.

who share in our culture rather than our common stock [*physis*]," though altering some specifics, stated the same conviction that "whatever Greeks receive from the barbarians they elevate to a higher perfection."[3] An edict issued several hundred years later by Constantius together with Julian as Caesar succinctly expressed the practical implications of the premise: "No person shall obtain a post of the first rank unless it shall be proved that he excels in long practice of liberal studies and that he is so polished in literary matters that words flow faultlessly from his pen."[4]

Gregory agreed entirely. *Logoi* were the sine qua non for supremacy, and the divinity that had created man, with whom man was affiliated (*oikeios*), and whose virtues, morals, and comportment man mirrored, had given him these *logoi*, this culture. Julian and Gregory differed, however, on the divinity in question. Which God was truly ancient? Who in truth had caused *logoi* and therefore (Greek) Rome's supremacy? The *Logos*, or Zeus-Helios? A small but significant difference. Because, as Julian and Gregory also agreed, only correct service and reverence to the *hiera* could assure the well-ordered harmony and unity of the Roman *politeia*, the crucial question was: Which divine? Mistakes were fatal, as history had proved time and again. Thus, while proper attachment to the *hiera* and the predominance of *eusebeia* for the legislator, as demanded by Plato in the *Laws*, was also Gregory's matrix and foundation, he had to alter subtly the nature of the divine at its origin and to prove that his divinity represented what was ancient and hence truly foundational, altering all aspects of civic religion accordingly, philosophy most of all. Since the *Logos* was the origin of everything, *logoi* were proper to him, and to be *oikeios* to the *Logos* meant to understand *logoi* properly as Christian; thus, only those who understood *logoi* as proper to the *Logos* were truly *oikeioi* to him: that is, the true Greek citizens of his *oikoumenē*, that of the Romans. All others were *allotrioi*, or *Hellēnes*.

The task Gregory faced may seem straightforward, but it was not. He had to perform a translation, to alter a culture with that culture's own means, including its language. "Greek" has no Greek etymology; the word derives from the Latin *Graecus*. For Greeks everything Greek was *Hellēnikos*. And, as indicated by his subtle altering of the relation of Rome and Christianity posited by Eusebius, Gregory could no longer merely reject everything Greek or Roman as "theirs." It was now "ours" (his) to administer.[5] Rome had become Christian in everything it stood for, and to make it Christian, including the intellectual foundations of its imperial power, was

---

3. Quotations Hdt. 8.144.2; Isoc. 5; Ps.-Pl. *Epin*. 987d. For classical concepts of citizenship and participation in the sacred (both *hiera* and *hosia*), Blok, "Becoming Citizens"; Parker, "Law and Religion"; Cartledge, "Greek Political Thought."

4. *CTh* 14.1.1, trans. Pharr, issued on February 24 or 25 at Constantinople, received in Rome on May 15, 360. The edict goes on to declare eloquence the greatest virtue.

5. Gregory rephrased the rhetorical stance of rejecting pagan learning; S. Elm, "Translating Culture."

Gregory's task—and also that of all whom Gregory addressed: all members of the elites now Christian and entrusted with governing the *oikoumenē*. How to perform that translation, to claim specific, essential parts of one's own culture in one's own language and alter it by such means, slightly but significantly, is the theme of *Oration* 4: by declaring everything proper to Julian as to be rejected and naming it *Hellēnikos*, Gregory took everything else as *logoi* and his, Christian, and thus he reversed Julian's attempts to make Greek Roman Christians into Galileans.[6]

Gregory's central task, to dissociate *logoi* from the gods of the Greeks and the Romans and align them with the *Logos,* also demanded a definition of the *Logos:* an explication of the Trinity and the correct comprehension of the greatest *pharmakon* of all through philosophy, correctly understood. Gregory thus moved from the practical political implications of Julian's falsely understood philosophy to his technical misuse of philosophy in his methods of logical deduction, language theory, and so on. Once again, his audience included Christian leaders, public officials, and members of the clergy, the last most of all. For that reason, the incorrect philosophical techniques he detected in Julian's reasoning, a principal cause of his *asebeia* with its negative consequences for the *hiera* and the polis, Gregory also identified in—really imputed to—his Christian opponents. Julian's mistakes were their mistakes. His negative portrayal of Julian's philosophical methods served to demonstrate how to use *logoi,* more narrowly defined now as the *instrumenta* of Greek philosophy, for the right, true comprehension of the Trinity, and against Eunomius's and his followers' understanding of it. The theater and the relationship between fiction, imitation, reality, and truth presented a way to achieve this demonstration.

MYTH AND ALLEGORY

Julian's *asebeia* had led him to pursue all that was false in philosophy, and driven by fleeting theories about *politeia,* without any merit in practice, he had misruled the *oikoumenē*. Gregory could do "nothing better than to contemplate, as on the stage of a theater, their wonderful innovation or reconstruction . . . , so that we see, as Plato said with regard to his city constructed out of words, their 'concept in action.'"[7] To do so reveals, according to Gregory, that only Christians understand correctly the relation between active and theoretical philosophy. "Given that all philosophy is divided into these two parts, I mean theory and practice, and given that one is more elevated but harder, the other more humble but more useful, we appreciate both and each because of the merits of the other: we make theory the way

---

6. A point also made by Demoen, *Pagan and Biblical Exempla,* 23.
7. Gr. Naz. Or. 4.113: τὴν θαυμασίαν αὐτῶν ταύτην ἀνάπλασιν ἢ μετάπλασιν ὡς ἐπὶ σκηνῆς θεωρῆσαι . . . ἵν', ὅ φησι Πλάτων περὶ τῆς ἐν λόγῳ πόλεως, ἴδωμεν κινουμένην αὐτῶν τὴν ἐπίνοιαν. The reference is to Pl. *R.* 369c, combined with Pl. *Ti* 19b; also Pl. *R.* 374a, 410c, 466a.

of ascent toward heavenly things and action the means to approach that theory; in fact it is not possible to partake of wisdom without behaving wisely."[8] Julian's actions had been dissimulations, so that Gregory could not decide "which of the two [Julian's theory or practice] will seem more ridiculous and weaker . . . , given that [Julian and his followers] lack the force of a system that derives from divine inspiration, [so that their pagan concepts are] like roots brought to water without having been planted in soil. . . . So let us too laugh a bit with them who laugh and tell their myths in many works of theater. . . . The poets too know of laughter mixed with tears."[9]

Myths as Fictions

The stage was set for Gregory's presentation of these myths and of Julian's concepts in action. One of the concepts in action Gregory refers to was that Julian, under the cloak of imperial benevolence, deliberately plagiarized "our culture," "our" *logos*. Such an act represented the apex of Julian's deceptive manipulation, cleverly disguised by his persuasiveness. Inspired by the Assyrian Rapsaces, who had tried to persuade the inhabitants of Jerusalem to surrender by speaking to them in their own language, Julian planned to lure Christians to his *logoi* by aping their achievements (*Or.* 4.112).[10] Thus, Gregory charged, Julian had founded schools; organized the priesthood into higher and lower ranks; and written treatises explaining the Hellenic doctrines, illuminating their secret meanings, clarifying their initiation rites and those leading to perfection, and prescribing appropriate behavior. He had instituted regular prayers and hymns with alternating choirs and saw to it that the penance of sinners was commensurate with their sins. Julian, according to Gregory, had also established hospices and hostels for the general public as well as those associated with temples that were intended for ritual purification prior to sacrifice, and places for virgins and other women as well as houses to think in (*phrontistēria*);[11]

---

8. Gr. Naz. *Or.* 4.113: Εἰς δύο γὰρ ταῦτα διῃρημένης πάσης φιλοσοφίας, θεωρίαν τε λέγω καὶ πρᾶξιν, καὶ τῆς μὲν ὑψηλοτέρας οὔσης, δυστεκμάρτου δέ, τῆς δὲ ταπεινοτέρας, χρησιμωτέρας δέ, ἡμῖν μὲν ἀμφότερα δι' ἀλλήλων εὐδοκιμεῖ. Καὶ γὰρ θεωρίαν συνέκδημον πρὸς τὰ ἐκεῖθεν ποιούμεθα καὶ πρᾶξιν θεωρίας ἐπίβασιν. Pl. *R.* 511b. This is Gregory's mixed life, consisting of the contemplative and the active, scholars have discussed extensively in the context of asceticism and monasticism; Gautier, *Retraite*, 83–112.

9. Gr. Naz. *Or.* 4.113: οὐκ ἔχουσιν ἐκ θείας ἐπιπνεύσεως τὸ δυνατὸν τοῦ συστήματος, ὥσπερ τῶν ῥιζῶν αἳ καθ' ὕδατος ὀχοῦνται πῆξιν οὐκ ἔχουσαι. Lugaresi (Gregory of Nazianzus, *Contro Giuliano*, trans. and comm. Lugaresi, 401) suggests that this passage alludes to the famous last encounter of Hector and Andromache (*Il.* 6.484), probably by way of Callimachus (fr. 298 Pfeiffer, vol. 1, 274), whom Gregory knew well according to a scholiast, *PG* 36.1237C.

10. See 4 Kings 18:17–36.

11. Gregory used the same term for his and Basil's retreat; S. Elm, *Virgins*, 69, 97–98, and 97 n. 70; see Ar. *Nu.* 94, Philostr. *VA* 3.5. Gr. Presb. *PG* 35.269C glosses *phrontistērion* as asylum. Kurmann, *Gregor von Nazianz*, 374–76, discusses the terms and notes the social, nonreligious aspect of many of the

and he had instituted philanthropic measures that he had admired among the Christians (Or. 4.110–12): this is the passage, combined with Julian's *Epistle to the Priest Theodorus*, that has prompted scholars to posit that Julian had wished to establish a pagan church.

Gregory's enumeration of the practices Julian had aped, the new dogmatic and sophist, represents a valuable picture of Christian liturgical and philanthropic practices at the time; it also reflects concepts, measures, and regulations the emperor had sought to institute.[12] But it is important to keep in mind that Gregory is writing a polemic, and that his accusation that Julian invented a pagan church to counter the Christian one is part of his polemic logic. By the definition of that logic, every one of Julian's actions concerning the *hiera*—that is, everything Gregory listed in that passage—had to imitate true Christian acts, because Julian could only dissimulate and not truly act; at best, his actions were bad innovations. This is so because only Christian *logoi* are both old and new in correct proportion—"old in the predictions and the shining movements of the divinity, new in the definitive divine manifestation [of Christ]" and its resulting *thaumata*. This is so because the divine origin of the Christian system has been attested from above;[13] its *erga* are real, whereas all Julian's actions were imitations, ephemeral human concepts without the stability in time granted by divine power.[14] Gregory's declaration that Julian sought to implement a pagan church is polemics that tell us little if anything about Julian's intentions.

The context of Gregory's allegation that Julian plagiarized Christian practices to found a pagan church should only heighten our caution: the fictional character of Julian's gods as revealed in their myths. (In sum, Gregory's *Oration* 4 cannot be used as a source to argue for Julian's pagan church.) "The theater is well prepared—I do not know how else we want to describe the dwellings [of his gods]." Gregory now presented as if on a stage the originators of Julian's books of theology and ethics, his "interpreters of divinely inspired words [*theophorōn logiōn*]" (Or. 4.115),[15] tak-

---

institutions here mentioned, highlighting the difficulties associated with many translations into modern languages that presuppose Christian institutions.

12. Soz. *HE* 5.16.2–4 depends on this passage, *Or.* 4.110–11. For Julian's measures, see (e.g.) *Ep.* 89b.301d for the singing of hymns and 297a–b for penance; also Jul. *Ep.* 88 (Wright 18), 451b (cf. Aug. *Ep.* 91.5). For a special period of purification prior to the initiation of Christians converted to Greek religion, see Jul. *Ep.* 114 (Wright 41), 436c–d; and see Jul. *Or.* 5, *MoG* 173c; *Ep.* 26 (Wright 8). For the foundation of a choir school in Alexandria, *Ep.* 109 (Wright 49), and in general the *Epistle to the Priest Theodorus* (above, Chapter 8).

13. Gr. Naz. *Or.* 4.110: ταῖς ἄνωθεν μαρτυρίαις, τὸν αὐτὸν παλαιόν τε καὶ νέον, παλαιὸν μὲν ταῖς προρρήσεσι καὶ τοῖς ὑπαστράπτουσι κινήμασι τῆς θεότητος, νέον δὲ τῇ τελευταίᾳ θεοφανείᾳ.

14. Gr. Naz. *Or.* 4.112: ἀνθρωπίναις ἐπινοίας . . . θείᾳ δυνάμει.

15. Recall Gregory's lament at *Or.* 2.84 that under Julian Christianity had become a laughingstock, its truth turned into comedy; Lugaresi, "Tra evento e rappresentazione," 455, 458.

ing his cue directly from Plato's *Republic* and its discussion of the norms (*typoi*) according to which Homer's and Hesiod's myths of the gods should be explained to the young so that the gods exemplify the true virtues of the city.[16] Those who inspired Julian's theology (*Or.* 4.115–19) and his ethics (*Or.* 4.120–24) were "those who joke and tell myths in the theaters": Hesiod, Orpheus, and "the great comediograph, or better tragediograph, of your gods," Homer.[17] Hesiod appears first on the scene, presenting the tumultuous wars of the Titans and Giants, monsters with snakes' heads and dragons' feet. Orpheus follows to showcase Kronos, the father of all men and all gods who ate his children, and Zeus, who proved his virility by becoming entangled with sheep, goats, and horses (*Or.* 4.115).[18] Such are the scenes presented to "the admiring listeners to this theology," for whose benefit one must then search for fanciful allegorical interpretations that soon move further and further from what is actually said "toward the abyss and precipice of theory [*theōria*] without a solid base."[19]

Myths, rituals, and allegorical interpretations: Whose myths were childish stories told to the simple and the feebleminded, and whose myths reflected divine inspiration? What was fiction, and what reality? Julian's myths, or Gregory's? The divinely inspired poets of the Greeks, or those who revealed the *Logos*?[20] Julian's actual attitude to the theater was not at stake except as an acerbic polemical inversion of his well-known antipathy. But Julian's concept of myth as a divinely inspired tool for the initiated to approach the divine by evoking divine presence was very much at stake.[21] The emperor had argued in his orations that myths were meant to be paradoxical and unbelievable on the literal level (*lexis*) in order to force the educated, purified, and initiated to search for the hidden meaning (*dianoia*) in allegory (also

16. Pl. *R.* 379b, 380c, 382e, 390e, 392a, 395c–d. Plato's concern about the effects of Homer and Hesiod on malleable children, which he reiterated and expanded in the *Laws* by offering prescriptions for civic religion aimed at everyone, is the intertext of Julian's imperial letter *Ep.* 61 (Wright 36), limiting the teaching of these writers to non-Christians and likewise addressing the young. Scholars noting that this imperial letter concerned only children and was not a general measure—in Plato's sense—miss that parallel.

17. Gr. Naz. *Or.* 4.113, 116: παίζουσιν ... καὶ μυθολογοῦσιν ... τὸν μέγαν τῶν θεῶν σου κωμῳδιογράφον, εἴτ' οὖν τραγῳδοποιόν.

18. The myth of Kronos and its allegorical interpretation also features prominently in Salut. *De diis* 4.1–2.

19. Gr. Naz. *Or.* 4.115: ἀλληγορήματα καὶ τερατεύματα ... εἰς βάραθρα χωρείτω καὶ κρημνοὺς θεωρίας οὐκ ἐχούσης τὸ στάσιμον.

20. See also Aug. *Civ. Dei* 2.26.2 for the connection between theater and the allegorical interpretation of myths and religious rites. For Gregory's use of myth in his poetry, Demoen, *Pagan and Biblical Exempla*, 215–31.

21. Julian's polemic against the theater permeates the *Misopogon* (e.g., 339c, 340a, 343d–344a, 351c–352a, 354c) and is central to his point that Antioch's excessive love for the theater predicted its descent into Christianity; in *Ep.* 89b he forbade priests to attend the theater; Lib. *Or.* 16.41. Gregory responds to Julian's theory of myth as pronounced in *Or.* 7, *Against Heraclius*, esp. 221c–223a, and in *Or.* 5.161c–167b; F. Thome, *Historia*, 46–65.

called *theōria*).²² Once the initiated had discovered that hidden meaning and had properly communicated it to all, behind the seemingly scandalous literal a highly moral universe could be read properly in both the myths and the corresponding festivals and rituals celebrating the gods. Only the uneducated, such as certain Cynics and Christians, criticized those myths as unethical while themselves proclaiming as truth what was self-evidently fiction.²³ Even the Galileans fervently declaring their myth to be true and real depended on allegorical interpretation, as Julian was quick to point out, thus admitting that their myth too had a hidden meaning, albeit a thoroughly impious one. For Julian, the Christian myth had never been a proper myth such as those he had explicated in *Against Heraclius*, but was merely a fable as told to children with none of the revelatory *paradoxa*, recognizable to the initiated, that were so central to true divine myth.²⁴

Gregory countered these claims in *Oration* 4.113–24, using in essence the very arguments from Plato that the emperor himself had used against the theater-loving citizens of Antioch in his *Misopogon*. Gregory asked what Julian wished his myths to be: truth, or fiction? Reality, or theater? The answer is evident, because Julian conceded too readily that neither Hesiod nor Orpheus should be read straight; the same was true for Homer's stories regarding the gods, "so wise and artfully [*polytropōs*] composed and so entirely beyond the normal." Gregory, echoing Plato, cited standard Homeric passages criticized for their dubious morals ever since the Presocratics, sarcastically summarizing well-known allegorical interpretations of Homer's tales of Hera, Ares, and Aphrodite (*Or.* 4.116).²⁵

Given that the construction of the myths is extraordinarily artful (the Odyssean *polytropōs*), Gregory asked: "Who then among you is so elevated and great in his mind, and comparable to Zeus in his wisdom, to know how to bring them back to a decent significance with words of a *theōria* that float high above the clouds and above the limits of our comprehension?"²⁶ If these myths are allegories of the truth,

---

22. Jul. *Or.* 7.218a–219a; an argument Salutius also made in *De diis* 2–4.
23. Jul. *CG* fr. 4.44a–b, and frs. 13–17.75a–94a; F. Thome, *Historia*, 69.
24. Jul. *Or.* 7.226c–d; *CG* fr. 3.42e, 43a. To mistake theatrical representations (of myths) as reality was a topos indicating naïveté and lack of culture, which could be positive; see *Mis.* 359d–360b, where Julian shows that rustic Celts did not appreciate a lascivious Cappadocian dancer, thus demonstrating their plain morals. Likewise, Suetonius relates that a simple, honest soldier jumped onto the stage to protect Nero impersonating Hector from an attack (*Nero* 21). Philostratus *VA* 5.9 says that the customs of the people of Ipola in Spain were so primitive that they ran away when they first saw an actor on stage because they took him for a demon; Lugaresi, "Ambivalenze," 295–96.
25. Gregory repeated the criticism of wrong allegorical method in 380 in his poem for his friend Nemesius (the addressee of *Epp.* 198–200) in *Carm.* 2.2.7.91–102, 130–69, and 244, and in *Or.* 39.3. In the poem and in *Or.* 4 Gregory conceded that the myths may conceal some truth, which he had denied in *Or.* 2.104. Kurmann, *Gregor von Nazianz*, 392–95; Gregory of Nazianzus, *Contro Giuliano*, trans. and comm. Lugaresi, 405–10.
26. Gr. Naz. *Or.* 4.117: λόγοις θεωρίας ὑπερνεφοῦς καὶ ὑπὲρ τὰ ἡμέτερα τῆς καταλήψεως μέτρα;

why is that truth so deeply veiled that only the greatest minds can grasp it? Why not acknowledge that truth proudly and intelligibly to all, without recourse to allegory? If these myths, in other words, were true allegories of an existing truth, not mere theatrical fictions, then Julian and other "naked theologians" who have these insights ought to produce a correspondingly open and accessible theology that all may engage critically. Because there is no such theology, as Julian admitted, these myths are mere fictions, and false.[27]

But if they are fiction, then "let them next admit how silly it is to embellish, as if they were solid, what they then downplay as myths and expose them to the public eye (though these things could well stay hidden from the crowd, for education is not for everybody) in literary fictions,[28] theatrical presentations, and—most perversely—in temples, altars, statues, dedications, and sumptuous sacrifices involving great financial expenditure: Why choose to act impiously at great cost, when it is possible to be pious free of charge?" (Or. 4.117).[29] And if myths are indeed nothing but fictions and vain words of the poets used to sweeten the ear, then why are private persons who say something similarly blasphemous about these gods punished, whereas poets are revered (Or. 4.118)?[30] Because no theology exists that opens to all the truth concealed in these fictional myths, the mythical protagonists, represented by man-made statues, should not be honored at great cost in theaters, and in the temples with sacrifices, nor should those who transgress the literal tenets of these myths be punished by law—arguments similar to those Augustine later used in his *City of God*.

Christians too—"and it is right to make this argument—also have certain sayings whose meanings are hidden; I will not deny it. But what is the dual nature they signify?"[31] Their external, literal story is never scandalous, and their deeper, hidden significance is "magnificent to those who have penetrated the profundities" and

---

27. In Or. 4.44–45 and 50, Gregory had already attacked Julian's false reliance on Providence and divination, which Gregory defines as fatalistic belief in the determinism of astronomy; his mistaken claims that human reason can comprehend the divine (see also Gr. Naz. Or. 27.10) and that humans are not held accountable in the hereafter; Kurmann, *Gregor von Nazianz*, 146–54; Gregory of Nazianzus, *Contro Giuliano*, trans. and comm. Lugaresi, 279–83.

28. What my translation renders as "literary fictions" is *plasmata*, "things molded," in the Greek, a common term for literary fiction: e.g., Xenophanes 1.21, speaking of Homer.

29. Jul. Or. 7.218a–219a stressed that language had to be worthy of the god addressed before explaining in 221c–223a the meaning concealed in the myth of the birth of Dionysus. Gregory's reference to "naked theologians" sarcastically alludes to the concept of the naked truth as opposed to that concealed by myths and their *plasmata*; see Jul. Or. 5.38; Gr. Naz. Or. 28.14–15, 39.3–7; Pyykkö, *Griechischen Mythen*, 85–96.

30. Jul. Or. 7.207b, 8.170a–b; Gr. Naz. Carm. 2.2.7.130–36; Pl. Lg. 659e–660a, 800b–d, R. 381d–e; Plut. Per. 32.2.

31. Gr. Naz. Or. 4.118: εἰσὶ καὶ παρ' ἡμῖν κατ' ἐπίκρυψιν λόγοι τινές, οὐκ ἀρνήσομαι, ἀλλὰ τίς ὁ τρόπος αὐτῶν τῆς διπλόης καὶ τίς ἡ δύναμις;

has never been cloaked in ugly raiment. Christians, unlike Julian and his poets and philosophers, use allegory only to magnify divine beauty, never to conceal it: they have a corresponding theology that reveals its truth to all. Christian ("our") allegorical exegesis is true because the signifier corresponds to the signified (both worthy of the divine), so that it "delights the wiser ones without harming the masses." It is a single, cohesive narrative that connects seamlessly the literal (even the literal *paradoxa*), the historical, and the deepest truth, whereas "their" myths make no such connection, because what those myths signify, their so-called hidden truth, is unworthy of belief, and the external signifiers, those scandalous stories, are actively pernicious (*Or.* 4.118–19). These arguments played a central role in contemporaneous and later debates among leading Christians about the proper way to read and hence interpret scripture literally and figuratively, as I will discuss shortly.

Ethics That Are None

It is self-evident that a theology such as Julian's cannot produce ethics. "What can one say about their ethics?" How could one ever derive a system of civic virtues from such myths? "The best [and first ethical imperative] is concord and the reciprocal accord between cities, peoples, families, and those on their own, observing the law and the order of nature that separates and connects all things and creates from all this one cosmos out of a multiplicity."[32] Gregory gives the classic definition of *oikeiōsis*, represented by Christians, whose true civic virtues and ethics reflect their ordered and civilized theology.[33] They practice neighborly love, know when they have erred, are zealous in their wish to own nothing, consciously try to punish not merely the deed but also the intention, and willingly repay abuse with goodwill—that is, truly embrace their enemies. In sum, they embody the ethical and moral foundations of the virtuous republic. Christians, according to Gregory, rather than run in circles going nowhere (an allusion to Pl. *R.* 436d), continually advance, becoming new men, aspire to higher virtue and to that *theōsis*—becoming God—for which they have been born and toward which they hasten, lifting their spirit toward the divine in the hope their God will find them worthy of his magnanimity (*Or.* 4.123, 124).

The myths that the great Platonic philosopher and ruler Julian had championed as the foundation of his rule and his imperial policies were instead rife with discord and *stasis*, violent passion and frenetic free speech. Following such ethical guidelines, Julian could be only unjust and amoral, set on disrupting the harmo-

---

32. Gr. Naz. *Or.* 4.120: Ἄριστον ὁμόνοια καὶ τὸ συμφρονεῖν ἀλλήλοις πόλεις καὶ δήμους καὶ οἰκίας καὶ τοὺς καθ' ἕκαστον, νόμῳ καὶ τάξει φύσεως ἑπομένους ἢ πάντα διεῖλέ τε καὶ συνέδησε καὶ τὸ πᾶν τοῦτο κόσμον ἕνα ἐκ πλειόνων πεποίηκε.

33. Hierocles *apud* Stobaeus 4.671.7–673.11; Gr. Naz. *Or.* 6.14 (and 12 for disorder caused by *stasis*). Reydams-Schils, *Roman Stoics*, 35–79, 115–34; and above, Chapter 4.

nious, civilized *politeia* by inciting civil and external war (*Or*. 4.120). Under his rule, parents were not respected, greed was encouraged, and moderation (*sōphrosynē*) and continence (*enkrateia*), character traits of which Julian had been so proud, became foreign (*Or*. 4.121-22).[34] Nowhere did the negative results of such theology and such ethics find a clearer expression, however, than in Julian's attitude toward *logoi*, an attitude that crystallized all the evil he perpetrated.

LOGOI: THE THEOLOGICAL IMPLICATIONS

Gregory wrote his *stēlographia*, as he pointed out, to highlight elements of Julian's character and misrule he considered exemplary in their abomination. The blow Julian delivered against *logoi* held pride of place among his negative acts and explains why it was so fitting that Gregory now condemns Julian with a *logos*, a discourse, dedicated to the *Logos*. Julian, perverting the very idea of justice, had committed a crime against *logoi*. He had prohibited *logoi*, though common to all logical beings, by law for Christians as if they belonged to him alone, "having elaborated the most illogical concept of *logoi*, he who considered himself the most educated of all."[35] His crime consisted of several parts.[36]

"In the first instance [Julian had] maliciously changed the sense of the word to accord with his intent, as if the word 'Greek' belonged to religion and not to language, and thereby took from us the words as if we were robbers of a good belonging

---

34. Gregory emphasizes that in addition to Kronos eating his children, Hermes championed commerce and (illegal) gain, Dionysus was a roaring drunk, Zeus a sexual profligate, Ares in a constant fury, Artemis hated strangers, and Hercules, the Beefeater (*Bouthoinas*: *Or*. 4.77, 103), could not curb his appetite.

35. Gr. Naz. *Or*. 4.4: ὑπὲρ τῆς εἰς λόγους παρανομίας, ὧν κοινῶν ὄντων λογικοῖς ἅπασιν, ὡς ἰδίων αὐτοῦ Χριστιανοῖς ἐφθόνησεν, ἀλογώτατα περὶ λόγων διανοηθεὶς ... λογιώτατος.

36. As Criscuolo, "Gregorio," 182-84, and others have observed, Julian never sought to prevent Christians from speaking Greek, as Gregory argued polemically, an argument Ambrose (*Ep*. 72.4 [= 17 *PL*], "Petunt etiam, ut illis privilegia deferas, qui loquendi et docendi nostris communem usum Iuliani lege proxima denegarunt" [*Sancti Ambrosii opera*, ed. O. Faller, H. Schenkl, and M. Zelzer, vol. 3, *Epistulae*, 13]) and Augustine (*Conf*. 8.5.10, *Civ. Dei* 18.52.40-43) adopted. Socr. *HE* 3.12.7. Soz. *HE* 5.18.1 and Thdt. *HE* 3.8.1 imply that Christians had been prohibited from attending schools; Gregory of Nazianzus, *Contro Giuliano*, trans. and comm. Lugaresi, 225-28; Kurmann, *Gregor von Nazianz*, 51; Bernardi, ed. and trans., *Grégoire de Nazianze: Discours 4-5*, 13-14, 56-57. Julian's so-called school law systematized public and private teaching but combined that with requesting assurances about the character, or *mores*, of those who taught *logoi*. Given that Julian wished to vet these *mores*, and given his many pronouncements about *logoi*, the gods, and the *oikoumenē*, the law—as Gregory, the Apollinarii, Ammianus, and Libanius saw it—de facto excluded Christians from public teaching; Amm. Marc. 22.10.7, 25.4.20; Lib. *Or*. 18.126, 157; Gr. Naz. *Ep*. 10; Criscuolo, "Sull'epistola 10." Gregory's interpretation became standard in Christian historiography and dominated modern interpretations of Julian's school law; Pack, *Städte*, 261-300; Watts, *City*, 68-71; Bowersock, *Julian*, 84. For other Christian responses, Nesselrath, "Christen," esp. 81-83.

to another; he acted as if we were excluded from all the arts that have been invented by the Greeks, as if he thought that they belong to him because the words are homonyms."[37] Because the term for language and for culture is the same, *logos*, Julian, who did not understand how homonyms function, wrongly considered the Greek language his property by equating it with his religion. Second, Julian may have thought that the Christians would not understand his true motivation, even though they (that is, Gregory) understood him far better than he did himself: while Julian believed that he was depriving Christians of eloquence, the second highest good after the divine itself, he was in truth afraid that Christians, if permitted to employ the power of rhetoric freely, might refute his impiety, as if in their refutation they would have "found their power in elegance of expression rather than in the knowledge of truth or in arguments."[38] Thus, "having given this order, he deprived us of the [elegant] Attic idiom [*attikizein*] but not of truth" (*Or.* 4.5).

Christians, endowed with the language that is a common good freely accessible to all, may be prevented from praising God publicly in the Attic idiom, but that does not affect their possession of truth (*Or.* 4.5). Julian's laws merely revealed his weak faith in the power of his own words, because he had to disarm his opponent (Gregory) before engaging him in battle. With such actions "our wise ruler and lawgiver" announced his unreasonable nature at the very beginning of his rule, tyrannizing culture above all else.[39] His death restored the freedom of *logoi*, culture. Thus, nothing should be spared—not money, gifts, or especially words—in thanking the *Logos*. How great was the joy of Constantius's soul now that *logoi* once again held their rightful place, serving the *Logos*, whom Constantius had also served (*Or.* 4.3)!

Gregory's words in his discourse are an indictment but also a joyous panegyric inviting all to celebrate this victory in united praise. Those who were to participate now in the communal thanksgiving included those who had been unable to resist Julian as fervently as the most stalwart; Gregory here demonstrated the apologetic component of his invective (*Or.* 4.9; see above, Chapter 8). He also extended the invitation to those at Nazianzus who had not yet joined "our" celebratory choir, those separated from his father in schism as a result of his having signed Constantius's homoian creed (*Or.* 4.10).[40] Only one group was excluded from the celebration, ex-

---

37. Gr. Naz. *Or.* 4.5: Πρῶτον μὲν ὅτι κακούργως τὴν προσηγορίαν μετέθηκεν ἐπὶ τὸ δοκοῦν ... ὥσπερ ἂν εἰ καὶ τεχνῶν εἴρηξεν ἡμᾶς ὅσαι παρ' Ἕλλησιν εὕρηνται, καὶ τοῦτο διαφέρειν αὐτῷ διὰ τὴν ὁμωνυμίαν ἐνόμισεν.

38. Gregory qualifies the notion of *logoi* as highest good, adding that Christians did not consider it such, alluding to opposition to his view of *logoi*; *Or.* 4.100, 43.11.

39. Gr. Naz. *Or.* 4.6: ὁ σοφὸς ἡμῖν βασιλεύς τε καὶ νομοθέτης ... προκηρύξῃ τὴν ἀλογίαν ἐν ἀρχῇ τῆς ἑαυτοῦ βασιλείας, τυραννήσας πρὸ τῶν ἄλλων τοὺς λόγους.

40. Bernardi (ed. and trans., *Grégoire de Nazianze: Discours 4–5*, 23–37), Kurmann (*Gregor von Nazianz*, 6–12), and Lugaresi (Gregory of Nazianzus, *Contro Giuliano*, trans. and comm. Lugaresi, 39–44) discuss this remark only as it relates to the dating of *Or.* 4 and 5; above, Chapter 8, n. 27.

pelled from the common choir of all mankind: those who had given up their salvation and had joined Julian out of fear or, worse, because of ambition and the hope of ephemeral gains, apostates like the Apostate (*Or.* 4.10). To shame and expel in perpetuity such persons—those who were Greek (*Hellēnes*) in the same way Julian had been Greek—was part of Gregory's strategy in his *stēlographia*.

As is to be expected of an author of Gregory's caliber, his opening (Pindaric) *epinikion*, just summarized, contained every theme he elaborates in the chapters that follow. Gregory returned to the theme of words and their meaning, their signifying power, or *dynamis*, in *Oration* 4.100-109. At stake, exemplified by Julian's negative example, was the theory of language and its power to signify the divine through myth, allegory, and other exegetical techniques that reveal the appropriate relationship between words, their objects, and the capacity to comprehend, illuminate, and hence approach the divine.

Language Theory: Homonyms and Synonyms; Hellēnizein

At the time of Julian and Gregory, words and their signifying power in relation to the divine, including the words of the scriptures and what they reveal about the Trinity, were hotly contested (continuing the debates between Porphyry, Iamblichus, and Eusebius). As far as the Christian debates were concerned, the questions included whether appellations of God and the *Logos* that were not literally found in scripture could be used to define their relationship. Many noted that a term such as *homoousios* (which Gregory rarely used) was not scriptural.[41] Those who argued for strict adherence to the letter of the divine law as laid down in scripture were opposed by others, including Gregory and Basil, who argued that on occasion the divine legislator's unwritten intentions had to be deduced from his written laws. The literal sense of the scriptures contained a deeper, hidden meaning that could heighten the beauty of the literal but could be comprehended and deduced correctly only by truly purified philosophers. Thus those who read the scriptures too literally could go wrong either because, like the elder Gregory, they were too simple and lacked sufficient philosophical training to perceive the deeper meaning the literal signified, or because they had been wrongly trained and thus read the deeper meaning wrong. As Gregory argued at a later point, persons (such as Eunomius) who accused him of introducing a God who was unwritten (*agraphos*) and therefore not scriptural used the literal meaning to cloak their impiety.[42] Persons who claimed to comprehend the deeper meaning but in deducing it departed too far from the literal fell into the opposite error. They allegorized, as Julian had done. Gregory's

---

41. Bas. *Ep.* 9; Ayres, *Nicaea*, 93-98, provides a useful summary of the use of *homoousios*. Eunomius, for example, accused Basil of using nonscriptural terminology; Vaggione, *Eunomius*, 95; Gregory of Nazianzus, *Faith*, intro. Norris, 183-90, 203-4; Rousseau, *Basil*, 102-5; Brennecke, *Studien*, 216-28.

42. Gr. Naz. *Or.* 31.1, 3-5, 21 (*asebeia*); Pl. *Lg.* 793a, 838b.

accusations here evoke the twin themes of Julian's unwritten intentions and his mistaken allegories of myth.

How had Julian, so highly trained, revealed profound ignorance of the meaning of words, particularly of words denoting the divine? "It is necessary that I direct my discourse again toward the *logoi;* I cannot but return frequently to this argument, and I must seek to defend my cause with all my power. Even though there are many and great reasons why it is right to hate this person, there is none like this one, where he has shown himself [more clearly] a criminal. Together with me anyone must disdain this [act] who loves *logoi* and who dedicates himself to them as a choice of life, and I will not deny that I am one of them."[43] Gregory had left "all other things to those who want them: wealth, good birth [*eugeneia*], reputation, power." And having left such ephemera behind, he emphasized that "I cling solely to culture [*logoi*], and I do not lament the struggles traveling over land and sea that won these for me. To me, then, and to those dear to me belongs the power of eloquence [*logoi*], which I have embraced first of all and continue to embrace first after what is truly the first: . . . the divine realm and our hope of what lies beyond the visible."[44] *Logoi* are Gregory's sole possession, the only one he loves. They are his way of life, what he holds most dear next to the divine realm. He owns *logoi,* as this very discourse proves, "this word in favor of the words." Gregory, by correctly using the argumentative and hermeneutic techniques of *logoi,* of rhetoric and philosophy, dialectic and logic, shows that Julian had erred in his innovation regarding culture.[45] In so doing Gregory laid to rest Julian's notion that *logoi* were his possession rather than that of the Christians, a notion so *alogos* that one had to wonder "what eloquent Hermes, as you would say, has put this into your head" (*Or.* 4.101).[46]

When Julian sought to exclude Christians from *logoi,* the emperor, according to Gregory, used an old argument that denied Christians participation in reason because of their childish belief in faith. " 'We, who also revere the gods,' [Julian] says, 'own literature [*logoi*] and the Greek language [*hellēnizein*]; you instead [have only] unreason [*alogia*] and boorishness, and your wisdom does not go beyond *Believe!*' " (*Or.* 4.102).[47] The argument is familiar from Porphyry, Eusebius's response, and Julian's renewed attack against Christians; indeed it is one of the theoretical premises

---

43. Gr. Naz. *Or.* 4.100: πᾶς ὅστις λόγοις χαίρων καὶ τῇ μοίρᾳ ταύτῃ προσκείμενος, ὧν εἶναι καὶ αὐτὸς οὐκ ἀρνήσομαι.

44. Gr. Naz. *Or.* 4.100: τὸ τῶν λόγων κράτος ὃ πρῶτον μετὰ τὸ πρῶτον ἠσπασάμην τε καὶ ἀσπάζομαι, τὰ θεῖα λέγω καὶ τὰς ἔξω τῶν ὁρωμένων ἐλπίδας. In *Or.* 2.77 Gregory enumerates a nearly identical list of what he abandoned for the *Logos;* in *Or.* 6.5 he says that he clings solely to *logoi.*

45. Gr. Naz. *Or.* 4.101: τῆς περὶ λόγους καινοτομίας.

46. Gr. Naz. *Or.* 5.32; Jul. *CG* fr. 57.235b, *Caes.* 330a–336b, and the myth of Julian's origin, in which Hermes is central, *Or.* 7.

47. Gr. Naz. *Or.* 4.102: Ἡμέτεροι, φησίν, οἱ λόγοι καὶ τὸ ἑλληνίζειν, ὧν καὶ τὸ σέβειν θεούς, ὑμῶν δὲ ἡ ἀλογία καὶ ἡ ἀγροικία, καὶ οὐδὲν ὑπὲρ τὸ "Πίστευσον" τῆς ὑμετέρας ἐστὶ σοφίας.

of his calling Christians "Galileans": Greek sophistication versus barbarian uncouthness (*agroikia*), reason (*logos*) versus its lack (*alogia*), wisdom (*sophia*) versus unquestioning faith (*Pisteuson!*).⁴⁸ But, Gregory continues, this assertion alone revealed Julian's ignorance of the *logoi* he claimed to own, because the followers of Pythagoras, hardly uncouth barbarians, had already praised unquestioning faith and considered the maxims of their founder, the "'He said it,' the first and most important of their *dogmata*, higher even than the *Golden* (or, rather, leaden) *Verses*."⁴⁹ Disciplined silence and recourse to the teachings of Pythagoras without argument sufficed for them, so that both function just as the *Believe!* does for Christians. "It is not legitimate to doubt the words spoken by men inspired by God.... The proof ["demonstration," *apodeixis*] of their teaching is its truth, more powerful than logical argumentation and objection."⁵⁰

Unquestioning faith is thus no more proper to Christians (qua barbarians) than *sophia* about divine things is to *hellēnizein*. Here Gregory begins to separate what Julian had declared intrinsically linked, namely Greekness, *logoi,* and the sacred, defined as the gods of the Greeks and the Romans. Gregory's next step was to prove mistaken Julian's assertion that a particular link bound Greekness only to the divine as embodied in the gods of the Greeks and the Romans. Julian's mistake, Gregory argued, resulted from an insufficient grasp of basic rhetoric, Aristotelian logic, and Platonic language theory. Julian's claim to be a divinely inspired philosopher was baseless, because he failed to grasp even the elementary rules of grammar and rhetoric, with predictable results in his deduction of divine essence.

If one were momentarily to grant Julian that Greek religion and Greek language are one and the same (and with Christians qua Christians excluded from both), then "How do you demonstrate that *logoi* belong to you? And even if they were yours, why could we, according to your unreasonable [*a-logos*] legislation, not participate in them?" What, in other words, does the term *hellēnizein* signify, how should its meaning be defined? "To what 'Greekness' [*hellēnizein*] does literature [*logoi*] pertain, and what should it be called, and how understood? Let me show you"—now

---

48. For the low regard in which simple, unexamined faith was held, see Pl. *Ti.* 29c; Jul. *CG* frs. 4.44b, 55.229c; *Or.* 7.222c, regarding simple belief in myths; and Jul. *Mis.* 348d, 353a, for the Greek versus rustic or barbarian opposition.

49. The *Golden Verses*, part of the Neoplatonic curriculum, were a short second-century-C.E. poem containing elementary moral instructions that Iamblichus *Protr.* 3 attributed to Pythagoras. Hierocles *In CA* pp. 5.1–77 and 84.7–8 (*Hierokles: Kommentar,* ed. and trans. Köhler) considered it useful to teach "higher things"; his commentary on the *Golden Verses* also stresses piety and reverence toward god, demons, heroes, and parents as essential for the public good, as did Julian; D. O'Meara, *Platonopolis,* 65–66, 120. For the importance of silence, Gr. Naz. *Or.* 27.10; Diogenes Laertius *Lives* 8.10.

50. Gr. Naz. *Or.* 4.102: μὴ ἐξεῖναι διαπιστεῖν τοῖς τῶν θεοφόρων ἀνδρῶν εἰρημένοις, ἀλλ' ἀπόδειξιν εἶναι τοῦ λόγου τὸ ἐκείνων ἀξιόπιστον, πάσης δυνάμεως λογικῆς καὶ ἀντιλογικῆς. Eus. *DE* 3.5.74–96 argues that the lives of divinely inspired men (Pythagoras included) prove the truth of their words.

follows a quick lecture in rhetoric—"you who cling to the [level of] homonyms, the power," *dynamis,* or the semantic meanings, "of a name and of the expressions that denote either with one term different things," a true homonym, "or with different terms one and the same thing," a synonym, "or different terms for different things. Would you say, in fact, that [*hellēnizein*] refers to the religion or, and the evidence points that way, to the people and to those who first discovered the power of that language?"[51]

Analyzing only the literal level (*lexis*) of the homonym—the sameness of the term—Julian failed to investigate the true inner meaning, the *dynamis,* of the homonym. The same word can denote different, unconnected things. *Hellēnizein* may indicate a religion as well as the people who first discovered the language (and still use it). Now, even if his rhetorical training went no further than the basic recognition that one word may denote two things, Julian could have recognized the fallacy of his deduction by simple observation. Gregory knows of no case of religious observance where speaking Greek functioned like a rite. Among those who believe in Julian's gods various sacrificial practices are common—Gregory listed only extreme practices such as the flagellation and self-castration of the devotees of the Mother of the Gods or sacred prostitution—but none is predicated on speaking Greek, so that there is no indication that any of these gods ever chose speaking Greek in the way they chose their rituals: "Where has the speaking of Greek ever been chosen in that same way by one of the gods or demons [i.e., lesser gods]?" (*Or.* 4.103). Even if a religious rite were to demand speaking Greek as essential, it does not follow that only Greeks could worship that god, for many common goods may be used in a sacrifice to a specific god without thereby losing their quality as common property (*Or.* 4.103).[52] The flaws in Julian's logic are all too evident.

Julian was incapable of logical thinking, nor had he mastered syllogistic logic, as the next step in Gregory's argument reveals. If Greek were Julian's property, and Christians were excluded from Greek as if from an inheritance to which they have no claim, it nonetheless remains difficult to see, according to Gregory, how Julian, first, can make such a claim and, second, can link Greek to his demons. "Because that the same people use the Greek language who also profess Greek religion does not mean that the words [and the literature] thus belong to the religion, and that we are naturally excluded. That conclusion is not logical [*asyllogistikos*], and it disagrees with [what you learned from] your own teachers of [Aristotelian] logic [*technologoi*]" (*Or.* 4.104). If (1) some people believe in certain gods and (2) these people speak Greek, then it does not follow that (3) Greek belongs to these gods. "If two

---

51. Gr. Naz. *Or.* 4.103: ἢ γὰρ τῆς θρησκείας εἶναι τοῦτο φήσεις ἢ τοῦ ἔθνους δηλαδὴ καὶ τῶν πρώτων εὑρομένων τῆς διαλέκτου τὴν δύναμιν; Pl. *Cra.* 430a.

52. For example, prostitution is not limited to Aphrodite and her cult just because it belongs to that goddess.

terms address the same thing, that does not make the two identical." If it did, it would follow that if one person were both goldsmith and painter, these activities would also be identical—clearly a conclusion as nonsensical as the exclusion of Christians from *hellēnizein* Julian failed to understand Aristotelian syllogistic logic.[53]

Next, Gregory cannot help asking Julian, the great *philologos* and Philhellene,[54] what level of Greek he had in mind when he wished to exclude Christians from speaking Greek: the common Greek used by all, or the Attic attainable only by those who have received the *enkyklia paideia* (*Or.* 4.105)? With that question Gregory launches into a series of recherché Atticisms ridiculing the second suggestion. (Julian's own style, perhaps because of his sleep-deprived writing habits, is not considered stylish, a point that cannot have eluded Gregory.) Rather than merely deny Christians the literary language, Julian might as well have denied them all Greek, a ludicrous idea. In response, Gregory engaged now, in an elevated and complete style, the relationship between the divine and language that Julian had so utterly botched: Did language have a divine origin, or was it the result of human invention (*Or.* 4.106)? Did a divine being, God, create language, and could language thus, properly understood, reveal the essence of the divine that had created it, or was language a human invention, of lesser heuristic value? This question was at the heart of the debates about the Trinity and already familiar, not by coincidence, from Eusebius's engagement with Plato's *Cratylus* in his *Praeparatio Evangelica*.

Cratylus *Revisited:* Logos *as* Romanitas

According to Gregory, Homer had already posited that the gods used particular divine words, indicating that words had divine origin,[55] though Gregory did not wish to pursue the alternatives of Homer's suggestion—that divine sounds produced by divine vocal organs are diffused either through the air like human sound, albeit "better and richer in meaning than ours,"[56] or "through bare [soundless] thoughts

---

53. In *Ep.* 12 (Wright 2), *To Priscus,* Julian mentions a collection of Aristotle's writings with which he was familiar; D. O'Meara, *Platonopolis,* 53–55.

54. The title *philhellēn* was customarily given to foreign rulers with Greek affinities; Gregory of Nazianzus, *Contro Giuliano,* trans. and comm. Lugaresi, 385; Kurmann, *Gregor von Nazianz,* 347–48. Later, Gregory alludes to Julian's Thracian background, which the emperor stressed in the *Misopogon,* where he also claimed Mysian ancestry (*Mis.* 348d).

55. See Chapter 6. Hom. *Od.* 10.305, 12.61, and *Il.* 20.74, 14.291, and 1.403, 2.814 mention a different language of the gods; and see Pl. *Cra.* 391d–392b and 400d, where Plato refers to names the gods call each other; also *Phdr.* 255c, *Ti.* 36c. Gregory cites examples of "divine words" in both authors to ridicule the words but not the idea of the divine origin of language. Pl. *Cra.* 400d–401a further discusses the names of gods and their *dynamis,* appellative power, in part in connection with sacrifices: above, Chapter 6; Clem. *Str.* 1.143.1; Eus. *PE* 11.6.9. D. Chrys. *Or.* 11.23 thought that Homer understood this divine language; Hirschle, *Sprachphilosophie,* 21–28; M. R. Barnes, *Power,* 70–80.

56. For the levels of language, higher and better for gods, lower for humans, see Hirschle, *Sprachphilosophie,* 28–35, based on Proclus's commentaries on *Cratylus* and *Timaeus.*

and impressions"—though he signaled his awareness of them.[57] Gregory's point here is that "neither a word [*phōnē*], nor any art [*technē*], nor any activity one can imagine belongs solely to those who invented it; it belongs to all who participate in it." Greek *sophia* and Greek *logoi* are not limited to Hellenic (religious) purposes, but are common property, free to be borrowed by all who wish to use them. "As in an artful and musical harmony one sound originates from one string and another from another one, [depending on whether they are] drawn tight or relaxed, but all [sounds] come from one sole joiner and artist, tending toward one harmonious beauty, so also in these things the artist and creator who is the *Logos* [*ho technitēs kai dēmiourgos Logos*] brought forth an inventor for all the various activities and arts; but he made them all available to all who want them, binding our lives together and making them milder through community and philanthropy."[58]

God, the artful and creative *Logos,* brought forth an inventor for all arts, including language, but offered them freely to all (*Or.* 4.107–9). Depending on whose tradition one preferred, the Phoenicians, the Egyptians, or the Hebrews had invented the letters of the alphabet, but these letters were also used to write Greek.[59] Poetry had been invented by an old woman, Iambe.[60] Weapons were invented by the Cyclopes, and Julian's purple, symbol of his rule (Gregory's formulation, *halourgis,* alludes to the jury in the theater), came from Tyre. The Athenians invented agriculture, especially the cultivation of the olive and grain, and navigation (see Jul. *Ep.* 89b.289b–d), and even Julian's own exalted religiosity, his divinely inspired madness of *thrēskeuein,* originated in Thrace, the region of his birth. Even the sole in-

---

57. Proclus expanded the second argument on the basis of Pl. *Cra.* 392b, 400d, and *Ti.* 36c, to posit that the gods do not require an "external" language, since their thoughts are *typoi* or *typomata*, so that in thinking (*noein*) they form (*poiein*); their "naming" (*onomazein*) is not vocalized but is itself an act of creation (*noein = poiein*); Hirschle, *Sprachphilosophie,* 21–25.

58. Gr. Naz. *Or.* 4.106: πάντα δὲ εἰς μέσον προὔθηκε πᾶσι τοῖς βουλομένοις, τῷ κοινωνικῷ καὶ φιλανθρώπῳ συνδέων τὸν βίον ἡμῖν καὶ ποιῶν ἡμερώτερον. Pl. *Cra.* 401b discusses the appellative power of foreign names of the gods; *Cra.* 411–422a discusses the origins, including foreign ones, of concepts such as justice, art, music, and their semantic fields, and at 422b–426a treats the invention of language and how to judge the correctness of words as measured by their imitating the power and quality of the thing named; 426a–b considers the foreign origin of many Greek words. Isoc. *Nicocl.* 5–10 delineates the progress of civilization. For the harmonious-sounding whole, Pl. *Laws* 1.643c6–644e1.

59. Pl. *Cra.* 393e. Listing (foreign) inventions has a long tradition, going back to Herodotus; here Eus. *PE* 10.5–6, referring to Clem. *Str.* 1.74–79. Gregory's list differs; Kurmann (*Gregor von Nazianz*, 355) and Lugaresi (Gregory of Nazianzus, *Contro Giuliano*, trans. and comm. Lugaresi, 387–88) assume a slightly adapted common source for Eusebius and Gregory. Unlike Clement and Eusebius, Gregory is not interested in proving that pagans plagiarized Christians but seeks to demonstrate that the *Logos* is universal.

60. Rather than by the classic inventor of poetry, Orpheus, whom Gregory—eventually himself the author of a poetic oeuvre of some nineteen thousand verses in all meters—associated with Julian. Nonnus's scholion (*PG* 36.1017C–D) identifies the old woman as Sybilla, Phimone, or Philyra, but Iambe is most plausible; Kurmann, *Gregor von Nazianz,* 357–58. According to Arist. *Poet.* 4.1448b24–26b; 1449a32–34, the metric version of a *psogos* ought to be composed in iambic verse; Koster, *Invektive,* 7–13.

vention to which he could personally lay claim, to have been "the first among the Christians to have rebelled against the Master," had been anticipated in the realms of the Scythians, whose slaves had also rebelled (*Or.* 4.109; Hdt. 4.3–5). It would have been ideal had Julian and his ilk disbanded quickly like such bands of rebellious slaves, so that the Christians would have been free sooner and Roman rule would have returned to its old splendor earlier and without the threat of civil war (*Or.* 2.85; 4.75, 86, 120)—but all is well that ends well.[61]

Gregory's argument that all arts were, by divine intent, invented (by different human inventors) so that they could be used by all differs from Eusebius's essential point that the best of Greek learning had been borrowed from the Hebrews. Gregory argued instead that the universal *Logos* intended *logoi* to belong to all. He wished to counter Julian's point that *logoi* belonged exclusively to the gods of the Greeks and the Romans—Gregory's emphasis here reflecting his polemical narrowing of Julian's argument—but the implications are significant. As with Constantius's rule and the link between *Romanitas* and Christianity, Gregory's argument that *logoi* were intended as universal claimed them also as intrinsically Christian. The wish to oppose Christianity and Greek Rome's achievements, still present in Eusebius even after Constantine had become sole ruler, has given way to identifying Rome, *logoi*, and Christianity as one.

With that identification of the three the issue was now the proper administration and implementation of Roman imperial rule and *logoi*. Here, Gregory again used Julian's points against him to demonstrate how to achieve that identification. Julian had argued, (for example, in the *Hymn to King Helios:* 131c, 140a, 148c–150d) that Zeus-Helios as the highest creative divinity had created (Greek) language and civilization and, out of his divine philanthropy, gave them to man as the highest good through the demiurgic gods. Thus he created the human *politeia* or community held together through love of self extended outward to include those who were *oikeioi*, ensuring a better life for all. Because Rome assumed and improved the divinely instituted Greek civilization, participation in that community required reverence for its divine creator Zeus-Helios.[62] For Gregory, the *Logos* had fostered the invention of all arts and languages so that they could be freely borrowed. Therefore, he argued that the divine creator had seen to it that Rome prospered, so that the superior Greek language and culture could become freely accessible to all in the *oikoumenē*. Rome's supremacy reflected the true universal power of the *Logos*, uniting all ethnicities into one *Romanitas* in which all could borrow the best from one

---

61. The passage, referring also to Julian's rules and laws (κατὰ τοὺς κειμένους ὅρους), could comment on the emperor's attempt to consolidate *Romanitas* through laws excluding Christians; for Gregory the simplest prevention of strife and civil war would have been if Julian had died even sooner.

62. Jul. 89b.292d; *CG* frs. 21.115d–e, 22.131c–d, 24.137e–138d, 37.176a—c, and especially fr. 38.178b–c; *Hel. R.* 131c, 140a.

another for the greater good of Christian Rome. Greekness, community, and philanthropy were divinely created and accessible to all humans because the God creating them was the universal Christian one and not a god particular (*oikeios*) to the Greeks only. And, like Julian, Gregory used his argument to exclude. Julian, by mistakenly linking *hiera, logoi,* and Greekness, had claimed an exclusiveness, *hellēnizein,* that was in effect desertion of the common fold of all (Christians), which was universal *Romanitas.* Thus Gregory now excluded all who followed Julian's mistake, *Hellēnes,* as pagans.

The Divine Origin of Language: Eunomius

Gregory had made his point. Julian was neither philosopher nor sophist, since even the most elementary rules of grammar, rhetoric, and logic eluded him, and no divinity had chosen him, because his philosophy was his own invention. Gregory's long discussion of myth, fiction, allegory, and the difference between the simple, literal meaning and the truth hidden beneath indicates, however, that he had more to say on that topic to those in his audience who could understand his meaning. In *Oration* 4.106 he had commented on Homer's divine words, mentioning that he did not wish to engage the question whether these sounds worked like human sound or like bare thoughts and impressions. For him, all words, *phōnai,* and all arts, *technai,* had been created either directly by the artful and creative *Logos* or by divinely created inventors. In my view, this implies that Gregory thought language originated with God—that is, was of divine origin—but had been given to humans by means of *technē,* art, invented by (human) inventors.

Gregory had spent some time during his preparation and composition of *Oration* 4 with Basil at Annesi, while Basil was engaged in refuting Eunomius's *Apology.* Part of the debate about the *Apology* had focused on the heuristic process by which the definition of God's essence was connected to his name (or names). In his response to the *Apology,* Basil shifted from Eunomius's precise definition of God's name as indicating his essence as unbegotten to "the meaning of Biblical language itself and what it can and cannot tell us about God."[63] Briefly, Basil's broader methodological focus addressed the long-standing conundrum of what human language signified when addressing the divine. Basil drew attention to the difference in meaning of such words as "begotten," "shepherd," "king," "physician," "bridegroom," "father," and "son" when used in ordinary speech and when used as appellatives for God and the *Logos,* when such words, to cite Gregory, are "better and richer in meaning than ours": that is, they were not used only literally (*Or.* 4.106).[64] What did such

---

63. Above, Chapter 6; Vaggione, *Eunomius,* 232–39, quotation 235; Rousseau, *Basil,* 102; *Basile de Césarée: Contre Eunome,* ed. and trans. Sesboüé, vol. 1, 40–49, 65–97.

64. Orig. *Princ.* 1. praef. 8–9, 1.2.4; Bas. *Eun.* 1.4.16–56 (509c–513a), 1.20.12–19 (557a); Dawson, "Allegorical Reading."

terms mean when used in scripture to denote God and the *Logos*? What was such a term's *dynamis,* or signifying power, vis-à-vis the divine? To arrive at that *dynamis* required allegory and logical abstraction, the rhetorical wherewithal to use synonyms, homonyms, and syllogistic logic—that is, the hermeneutical tool kit provided by Greek *logoi.* As my earlier discussions of Plato's *Cratylus* have shown (see Chapter 6), how to use these tools was the crux of the matter. It was central to the fourth-century debates about heresy and orthodoxy.

For example, when moving from one level (the literal) to the other (the allegorical), the necessary abstractions required the removal of some ordinary content of words when applied to God; but which content? For some, "begetting," even if stripped of its sexual connotation, as it generally was when applied to the divine, still implied the transmission of essence. One cannot speak of the *Logos* as Son and "deny that he was 'from the essence'" of the Father. Others thought it nonsensical to speak of begetting without retaining the priority of the Father over the Son, and that as a consequence the *Logos* had to be essentially different, because at some point he did not yet exist.[65] To cite Richard Vaggione, "For Aetius and Eunomius, ... even when scripture uses the same word of both God and Christ, the ontological status of the being to which it refers is what determines the meaning, not the word itself." One word may denote two different entities or essences, as Gregory had pointed out in arguing against Julian's use of *hellēnizein.* To cite Eunomius: "But perhaps someone who has been goaded by all this into responding will say, 'Even granting the necessity of paying attention to the names and of being brought by them to the meanings of the underlying realities, still, by the same token that we say that the unbegotten is different from the begotten, we also say that "light" and "light" . . . are alike with respect to both.' . . . Our response, then, to such a person is to say that the one 'light' is unbegotten, and the other begotten."[66] For Eunomius the word "light," when applied to God and the *Logos,* was a homonym for the *Logos.* It applied to God as well as to the *Logos* without making them intrinsically or essentially the same.

Here the *dynamis* of homonyms and synonyms and what such words signified when applied to the divine was thus at issue—the same point Gregory had addressed against Julian's use of homonyms applied to the divine as Greek in *Oration* 4.103–4. Implicit in all these arguments about the *dynamis* of a word applied to the divine were the continuing debates about the relation between names and the objects (*pragmata*) or realities they signify, originally theorized by Plato in *Cratylus.* Plato had further complicated the question of the origins of names, or language, by questioning whether the realities (or things) signified by language had been invented (by humans, *thesei*) or whether they were natural (*physei,* given by the divine), or both,

---

65. Gr. Naz. *Or.* 2.37, 38.
66. Eun. *Apol.* 19.1–9; Vaggione, *Eunomius,* 236–37.

depending on what it was that was signified. Plato had considered names tools, intended to reveal what things are by differentiating between sounds made by words and the meaning or essence of which such sounds are carriers. Given that differentiation, what then is the relation between a name and the essence it designates? Are its sounds, that is, language, pure convention, created by a human inventor without a compelling link to the object or essence (*thesei*)? Or are they initially divinely inspired and thus connected to the essence in a real, universal way, accessible to all in any language (*physei*)? According to Plato the latter, in principle, was the case, because otherwise true knowledge of the divine would remain impossible.[67]

Yet for Plato, *thesei*, or artfulness, was also involved; he did not argue an either/or position.[68] As later Stoic contributors to the debate stressed, it is not human physical nature per se that forms names and words but the intellect (*dianoia*), which can create objects proper to it by thinking. These thoughts possess a different, nonmaterial reality, as opposed to the reality of physical objects.[69] For example, a triangle is not a material object but exists nonetheless as a concept (*kat' epinoian*) rather than as an object in physical reality (*kat' hypostasin*). Both are real, however, because the active power of the intellect really creates (*poiein*) the object of the thought.[70] Thus, it was possible to speak of one object with different names that reflected its different conceptual aspects (*epinoiai*)—and in such cases the different names did not imply a different *dynamis*, or underlying meaning (or essence).[71] Words denoting conceptual objects (*kat' epinoian*), such as triangles and their char-

---

67. Plato saw names as tools telling us what things are, so that the sounds of language refer to individual objects (*pragmata*) and to the nature (*physis*) of each object: names as sounds are different from names as carriers of meaning. Thus, even barbarian sounds can carry meaning, because it is the object that confers meaning, and not the sound. This begs the question of whether sounds are human inventions without an intrinsic link to the object named (*thesei*), or whether they are in some essential way connected to the essence of the object (*physei*). Plato thought the latter, because of the imitative nature of language: *Cra.* 388c, 389d–390a, 421c–423b, 428e; Aug. *Trin.* 14.7.48–51; above, Chapter 6.

68. Bas. *Ep.* 235 describes how we learn to read: first we learn the letters and their pronunciation; then, once we comprehend their composite, we begin to grasp their *dynamis*, or meaning. Modern linguistic theories are informative, such as Wörner, *Performatives und sprachliches Handeln*; Recanati, *Meaning*, esp. 1–27, 219–66.

69. Pl. *R.* 5.477c–478a, *Ti.* 29b, 51d; Sextus Empiricus *Adv. mathematicos* 8.453; M. R. Barnes, *Power*, 76–80; Dawson, "Allegorical Reading."

70. Pl. *Tht.* 182a–b, 156b–d, discusses the distinction between the active power of the sense and the passive power of the object perceived; and *R.* 507e, debating the corresponding powers of perception: one cannot see without also being seen; Bas. *Eun.* 1.6.1–26 (521b–524a); Vaggione, *Eunomius*, 241–43.

71. According to Sextus Empiricus *Adv. M.* 8.11, Stoic thinkers differentiated three levels of language: the sign (*sēmainon*), which signifies; the meaning (*sēmainomenon*), what is signified; and the object to which the user of the sign refers. The sign was *phōnē*, human speech, so that both sign and the object referred to were material, physical realities. A meaning, on the other hand, was a nonphysical reality, and its object, "what is said," was also called *pragma*, "thing" said, an interesting technical use of *pragma*, the word for material thing.

acteristics, had little to do with *physei,* because they are artfully created products of the mind-soul (*kata thesin*) that really exist as objects nonetheless.[72]

When Proclus commented on Plato's *Cratylus,* he stated without ado that names and words are artfully created (*thesei*) because they are products of *dianoia,* of knowledge (*epistēmē*) rather than of matter or nature (*physei*). Thus, by definition, words and names belong to a level of reality higher than the physical or material one. For that reason Proclus in his commentary focused only on the different higher levels of reality. His concern was how the higher levels proceed from the divine cause of everything down to real objects and the names associated with them. To explain this relationship Proclus used that between a god and his statue: he declared that words and names, *onomata,* signify the divine as statues, *agalmata,* do the god. On that premise, he argued that words, though immaterial, are *physei* as regards their meaning (*eidos,* "form"), or the essence signified (*to sēmainomenon*), for they imitate the *pragma* (object) named and its *dynamis* (meaning). They are *thesei,* artful, however, with respect to the actual sounds and syllables (*phōnai*). The *physei* aspect of words is especially pronounced when the things named are eternal (*ta aïdia*) or divine.[73] Transient things, in contrast, may well be denoted by words that are entirely artfully created. *Physei* defines the similarity between word and object, and *thesei* the knowledge of that relation, so that all words are both *physei,* because they imitate the essence of the object named, and *thesei,* because they are based on human knowledge, *epistēmē.* But human knowledge and hence the names to which it contributes *thesei* are always limited by their human origin and hence not fully capable of revealing the divine.[74] The names of the divine are *physei,* divine in origin or nature, to permit human (and thus essentially material) deductions about the divine (immaterial essence).[75]

---

72. Orig. *Hom. in Jer.* 8.2, *Comm. in Mt.* 17.6, *Princ.* 1.2.1, *Cels.* 2.64; Bas. *Eun.* 1.7.1–17 (524c–525a).

73. This is so because the gods, when thinking things, named and thus created them on the intellectual level of thought, so that on the divine level thinking, naming, and creating coexist. Human thought and naming operates on a lower yet connected level; *Ti.* 36c; Procl. *In Cra.* 33.7.

74. For example, Proclus thought a father who names his son Ambrosius or Athanasius (that is, "Immortal") demonstrates a mistaken comprehension of the human condition. Such names may name his hope for the child but not his human essence: an anti-Christian swipe that shows that the *physei-thesei* debate was still alive in Proclus's time; Procl. *In Cra.* 1.1, 4.6, 4.13, 4.15, 4.17, 8.5–11, 16.9, 17.17, 26.2; Hirschle, *Sprachphilosophie,* 4–11.

75. Origen stated in *Cels.* 1.25 that "it is not the meanings [*sēmainomena*] associated with the realities [*tōn pragmatōn*] that have a certain power to do this or that, but the qualities and characteristics of the sounds," a position counter to the one he adopted in *Jo.* 4.1, when saying that "the one who distinguishes for himself between the expression [*phōnē*], the meanings [*sēmainomena*], and the realities [*pragmata*] on which the meanings are based will not take offense at the incorrect use of expressions when he searches and finds that the realities [*pragmata*] whose expressions are used are sound. This is especially so when the holy writers confess that their words and message are 'not in persuasive words of wisdom, but in the demonstration of the Spirit and power' [1 Cor 2:4]"—except that Origen also upheld

Eunomius too assumed that words denoting the divine related to divine essence and were therefore to some degree divine in origin. He argued that God could be known solely *kat' ousian* (i.e., *physei*) and not *kat' epinoian,* and thus not *kata thesin,* countering others (whom he identified as Sabellius the Libyan, Marcellus the Galatian, Photinus) who argued or were said to argue that the Trinity consisted of names, understood as concepts describing qualities rather than distinct persons (implying, according to their opponents, that the persons of the Trinity were mere fictions).[76] Eunomius responded to Photinus that if the Trinity, and particularly the Father, were to be comprehended merely *kat' epinoian,* as a concept, the divine would exist only in name, in meaning, and not in any real, historical sense. To claim that the divine did not really exist, however, would be the height of impiety. If, as is given, the divine really exists, then the difference between designating the Father as "father" and the Son as "son" also had to be real (Eun. *Apol.* 18.13–14).[77] Further, if the Father were known through concepts (*kat' epinoian*) rather than *kat' ousian* or *kata physin,* that would mean attributing different levels of reality to the One, a notion of composition or even division ill sorted with the oneness and simplicity of God as the source of all things (Eun. *Apol.* 8.7–18). Therefore, at the very least names applied to the Father could not denote merely conceptual qualities (*kata thesin*), but had to be *kat' ousian* (or *physei,* in the more complex sense delineated above, a position akin to Proclus's later definition of the *physei* character of names for the divine), so as not to dissolve the Father's essence. And the essence of the Father as first cause of all existence is to be unbegotten, so that the Son as son is in essence different.[78]

In the context of such pressing contemporary debates, Gregory's discussion of myth, allegory, divine language, and the signifying power of homonyms and synonyms, when applied to the divine or to *ta aïdia,* assumes its full force. Language theory falsely applied, mistaken notions about *logoi* and their appellative power, and

---

the concept of imitation. Like Plato, Origen thought that the primary sounds of language imitate things, so that human words indicate divine realities; Dawson, "Allegorical Reading," 28–29.

76. Eun. *Apol.* 6.5, "Now if we could see that those who once accepted the sounds [*phōnas*] [that make up the profession of the Trinity] must of necessity keep their real meaning [*dianoia*] undistorted along with the words [*onomasi*]," and 6.12–13. As Vaggione points out (*Eunomius,* 172–74, 243), a common accusation hurled against homoians and others was that their characterizations of the Son as Word only *kata thesin* meant that they thought he possessed those qualities in name only, fictitiously, a polemical distortion to which Eunomius reacted.

77. Eun. *Apol.* 8.3–5; Bas. *Eun.* 1.5.127–29 (520c); Vaggione, *Eunomius,* 244–45.

78. Proclus, like others before him, also struggled to preserve divine oneness while accounting for the diversity of creation. He thus posited the existence of "henads," containing everything, as cogenerators and cocreators; the divine layer does not separate perception and the perceived, knowing and the object of knowing: i.e., there is no difference between perception and reality; Hirschle, *Sprachphilosophie,* 22–32.

faulty deductive and inductive logic could do immeasurable harm, in particular when applied falsely to the Trinity. Gregory, as he had in *Oration* 2, proposes a comprehensive view, a middle way that navigates between those of Photinus and Eunomius at either end of the spectrum. According to Gregory in *Oration* 4, words are divine in origin (*kat' ousian*), but are given to humans by way of inventors created by *Logos*, the *technitēs* who artfully (*kata thesin*) invented language, *phōnē*. That is, the *Logos* brought forth the inventors to invent language, so that language per se is humanly invented (*thesei*) even if divinely inspired and created (*physei*).

Gregory's remarks in *Oration* 4.104–6 are concise and address, in the first instance, Julian's *hellēnizein*. A more precise discussion of Gregory's position and its implication for scriptural exegesis, appropriate allegory, and the consequences for formulating the Trinity requires that I compare it with other texts, both Gregory's own and those of others then discussing the heuristic value of words and names to deduce divine essence by reading the scriptural texts allegorically. Prominent among others alarmed by the impact of Julian's notions of myth and allegory on the formulation of Christianity was Diodore of Tarsus, Photinus's opponent and one of Julian's bêtes noires. Diodore's writings are mainly lost, however, so that examining his position requires a move forward in time to his disciple Theodore of Mopsuestia's *Response* to Julian's *Against the Galileans*, and to Gregory's *Theological Orations*.

Myth and Allegory: Diodore of Tarsus and Theodore of Mopsuestia

Julian had attacked Diodore of Tarsus, then resident in Antioch, and his teachings in *Against the Galileans* and in a letter to Photinus.[79] In that letter, Julian had accused Diodore of using his philosophical training to spin fictional fables or myths about the Galilean whom he invented as a god. According to Julian, Diodore had read the stories about the Galilean literally, as historical truth, to argue, allegorically as it were, for his divinity, so that part of Diodore's argument addressed the appropriate (or inappropriate) relationship between literary compositions and their allegorical interpretation, between the *lexis* (the historical and literal sense) and the *dianoia* (meaning) of myths. What exactly Diodore had argued is difficult to reconstruct, but the main points can be constructed from surviving fragments and the later work of Diodore's prominent Antiochene disciple Theodore, later bishop of Mopsuestia, a contemporary of John Chrysostom, with whom he had studied under Libanius. At some point before 378, Diodore had written his *Commentary on the Psalms*. He wrote in the preface that the scriptures, while divinely inspired, were formulated to instruct and illuminate even when taken literally (*kata lexin*), so that it is neither necessary nor advisable to become "distracted by words, and to be preoccupied with thoughts alien [to the literal] to the point of no longer

---

79. Jul. *Ep*. 90 (Wright 55).

understanding [the literal meaning]." Nevertheless, through *theōria,* or interpretation, a higher, better meaning could be discovered.[80] Diodore intended his exposition of that higher meaning to help his audience sing the Psalms with deep understanding rather than "superficially by merely pursing their lips." Diodore's *theōria,* aiming to preserve the text while nevertheless revealing its deeper meaning, offers a middle way between those who departed from the historical and strictly literal sense of the text and, searching for a deeper meaning, fell into the faulty allegorical method of "Hellenism, which misreads one thing for another and introduces monstrosities," and those who, defending the literal meaning as the only acceptable one, were "dragged down to Judaism, . . . forced to deal with the letters only."[81]

John Chrysostom composed his anti-Julianic treatise *On Babylas and against the Hellenes* around 379 or 380, and at that time Diodore's disciple Theodore, still in Antioch, also wrote his point-by-point rebuttal of Julian's *Against the Galileans* (mentioned above in Chapter 7); John and Theodore probably responded to a pagan revival in the city after the death of Valens.[82] The few surviving fragments suggest that Theodore used the same method the emperor had also employed in *Against the Galileans* to rebut him: an exegetical commentary, in which he cited passages of Julian's text that explicated scripture and countered with his own exegesis, arguing that Julian, in emphasizing the contradictions of scripture, exposed his limited comprehension of the meaning of words rather than proving the fictional nature of the scripture, an argument Gregory had also made.[83] Just prior to composing his refutation, Theodore too had written the *Commentary on the Psalms.* There he appears to have used the same exegetical methods as in his *Response to Julian.*[84] True Christians used allegory (which he called *theōria*) so that it adhered to the literal and historical reality of the written word while presenting a better and more beautiful sense of that text. Julian and the other Christians Theodore opposed employed allegorical methods (which he called *allēgoria* when using it polemically) that led them far away from the literal sense of the written word. Julian had used allegory to circumvent the pernicious embarrassment of his myths, and false Christians veered too far from the literal, so that they corrupted divine meaning, thus imitat-

---

80. For Diodore's use of *theōria* and *historia,* F. Thome, *Historia,* 97–119.

81. For the identification of Diodore as author, the manuscript tradition, and a discussion of the *Commentary on Psalms,* F. Thome, *Historia,* 84–90, 97–119. The text is Mariès, "Extraits," who edited and translated the text while convalescing.

82. Theodore of Mopsuestia, *Replica a Giuliano,* ed. and trans. Guida, 9–17, for the biographical data; as mentioned above in Chapter 7, this was probably the first point-by-point refutation of the *CG.* In 553, Diodore and Theodore were condemned as heretics and their writings dispersed, so that they survive only in fragments. For the date of the response and its manuscripts, ibid., 34–53.

83. Jul. *CG* Fr. 1.39a–b; F. Thome, *Historia,* 164–87, analyzes Theodore's criticism of Julian's allegorical method.

84. See the preface to the commentary, *Théodore de Mopsueste: Fragments,* ed. and trans. van Rompay, 1–18, xxxvii–xlvii; F. Thome, *Historia,* 124–49.

ing Julian; Gregory made a similar argument in *Oration* 4.116-19. In sum, as Felix Thome has now shown, both Diodore and Theodore developed their exegetical methods in direct response to Julian.[85]

Further, while composing his *Response* to Julian's *Against the Galileans* about 380, Theodore, again following Diodore, also wrote his first treatise *Against Eunomius* (now lost), refuting Eunomius's contemporary *Apology of the Apology* in response to Basil's *Against Eunomius*.[86] Theodore thus countered Eunomius at the same time he rebutted Julian's *Against the Galileans*. This was hardly coincidence. Much like Gregory in 364, Theodore between 379 and 381 used the Christian allegorical method (*theōria*) he had developed against Julian also against Eunomius, who presumably represented a similar challenge to the right interpretation of sacred texts and the meaning of words when applied to the divine. In 380, Gregory also rebutted Eunomius, sharpening the arguments he had used against Julian before in 364.[87]

Gregory's Theological Orations:
Against Eunomius to Advise Theodosius

Gregory's five *Theological Orations* (*Or.* 27-31), delivered in Constantinople in July and August 380, have received much attention from modern theologians because they represent his most comprehensive formulation of the Trinity.[88] Rather than provide a succinct statement of his concept of the Trinity as he had done in *Oration* 2, Gregory now formulated his views in a series of counterarguments responding to his opponents, creating, in Christopher Beeley's words, "the impres-

---

85. Grillmeier, *Christ,* vol. 1, 353-55, already posited a connection between Diodore's counter to Julian and his exegetical method, though he focused on Christology rather than exegesis. F. Thome's work (esp. *Historia*), inspired by Guida, succeeded in showing such a relationship. As far as I know, the parallel to Eunomius has not been discussed.

86. Both works are fragmentary; Vaggione, "Some Neglected Fragments," points out that Theodore's anti-Eunomian work of 379/81 was in all likelihood the first of a total of three books against Eunomius in defense of Basil; Devreesse, *Essai,* 49-50, and 53-93 for the exegetical method.

87. That Gregory's exegetical method (similar to Diodore's and Theodore's) led him to different conclusions about the Son, especially after 380, is a different matter. In one of his first Constantinopolitan orations, *Or.* 22.13, Gregory addressed the Christological debates between Diodore and Apollinarius in Antioch, sparked by Diodore's defense of the divinity of Christ against Julian. These Christological debates became central, and Gregory eventually took a different stance from Apollinarius and Diodore, with whom he also disagreed about the successor of Meletius at Antioch; Beeley, *Gregory,* 46-48, 60-61, and 128-32, 136-38, 285-92, 304-5 for Gregory's opposition to Diodore's Christology, including Mary as *theotokos,* and the extent of his agreement with Apollinarius.

88. *Grégoire de Nazianze: Discours Théologiques 27-31,* ed. and trans. Gallay and Jourjon. I use the English translation by Wickham and Williams in Gregory of Nazianzus, *Faith,* intro. Norris, 217-99, with modifications. (Italian translation *Gregorio di Nazianzo: Tutte le orazioni,* ed. Moreschini, 644-779.) For the sequence of the orations and possible later alterations, especially to *Or.* 28, Gregory of Nazianzus, *Faith,* intro. Norris, 76, 386-87; for dating and the context, McGuckin, *St. Gregory,* 277-310.

sion of a momentous theological showdown."[89] Among those whom Gregory wrestled to the ground, though he never explicitly named them, were homoians such as Constantinople's Bishop Demophilus, homoiousians whose positions on the divinity of the Spirit differed from his, and most of all Eunomius, recalled from Naxos and residing again in Chalcedon, and his followers.

Orations 27–31 were written under circumstances markedly different from those of *Orations* 4 and 5, though all these orations were connected: in both instances, a hostile emperor had just died under dramatic circumstances, to be succeeded by what Gregory hoped might be a more congenial one. In 378, the emperor Valens, a staunch Arian who by then had become the Apostate redivivus for Gregory, Basil, and others, had been killed near Adrianople, in Thrace, in a battle with Goths.[90] Valentinian's son and successor Gratian chose Theodosius, a high-ranking army officer, to succeed Valens and made him Augustus on January 19, 379. As in 363 and 364, the death of an emperor caused a (brief) destabilization, with military matters in dire need of containment. It also meant a rearrangement of the court and its top personnel, which entailed significant realignments in questions of religion and the church's own top personnel: that is, the bishops, especially those of imperial residences.[91] As a result, everyone jostled for position and sought to put his best doctrinal foot forward to win over the new emperor, who continued campaigning against the Goths and entered Constantinople only on November 24, 380. Eunomius returned from exile with his *Apology of the Apology* in hand. Gregory had arrived in Constantinople from Seleucia, in Isauria, in 379 at the instigation of Meletius of Antioch and quite possibly Diodore, who by then had become bishop of Tarsus, not far from Seleucia; Gregory referred to Diodore's (Antiochene) Christological debate with Apollinarius in one of his earliest Constantinopolitan orations.[92] On February 27, 380, the new emperor declared, in his famous edict addressed to the people of Constantinople, that the faith he embraced and prescribed

---

89. Beeley, *Gregory*, 39; his work is a salutary corrective of scholars' exclusive engagement with these orations.

90. Rousseau (*Basil*, 278–85, 351–53) notes that doctrinal differences did not prevent Valens from using Basil for his political purposes regarding Armenia; Van Dam, *Kingdom*, 118–35.

91. In keeping with the religious realignments following imperial deaths, Gratian issued an edict recalling (select) Christians from exile who had been sent there by Valens and allowed all to worship freely, except the Manicheans, the Eunomians (the edict appears to have affected his followers' right to assemble, but not Eunomius, who returned to Constantinople and Chalcedon), and the followers of Photinus. This edict is not extant but is reported in Soz. *HE* 7.1.3, Socr. *HE* 5.2.1, Thdt. *HE* 5.2.1; *CTh* 16.5.5 withdraws the freedom to assemble. Vaggione, *Eunomius*, 305–10, argues for two edicts, one by Valens issued prior to Adrianople and leading to a "loosening up" of the Nicene situation in Antioch and Constantinople for select persons, and a general recall by Gratian just after Valens's death that would have allowed Eunomius to return from Naxos.

92. Gr. Naz. *Or.* 22.13, *On Peace*, delivered 379; *Grégoire de Nazianze: Discours 20–23*, ed. and trans. Mossay, 194.

to *cunctos populos* as *religio Romanorum* was that of Damasus of Rome and Peter of Alexandria. Gregory thus pronounced his *Theological Orations* in July and August 380 in Constantinople knowing that the new emperor did not share the religious leanings of his precursor, Valens, and that there was now room to maneuver. By November 27, three days after arriving in the city, Theodosius installed Gregory as the new bishop of Constantinople.[93]

The majority of Christians in Constantinople and in the East did not share Theodosius's theological leanings, and Gregory engaged and rebutted their views in these orations while awaiting the emperor's arrival. In their conventional sequence, Gregory's *Orations* 27 and 28 present arguments about theological and exegetical methods and their relevance to the incomprehensibility of God, given his nature and that of human beings. *Orations* 29 and 30 defend the divinity of the Son against those who proffer logical and scriptural objections, and *Oration* 31 concludes with a discussion of the divinity of the Spirit against those same objections.[94] The orations, that is, consider the correct use of *logoi*, the epistemological possibilities when (Greek) rhetoric and philosophy are applied to the *Logos*, and the dangers of applying mistaken notions of both. *Oration* 27, the first of the *Theological Orations*, is a *psogos* and sets the agenda for the four to follow.[95]

"I shall address my word ["discourse"] to those whose cleverness is in words . . . against [their] education, hearing, and thought"—Gregory opened his *Theological Orations* attacking Eunomius and his ilk by echoing the phrase he had used to present Julian's philosophers on his metaphorical stage.[96] Such people delight in an entirely pointless strife of words. Mere sophists and word-gamesters, whose facility with words is sadly unmatched by their deeds, they seek nonetheless to undermine "every path to true religion except one, the setting and solving of logical problems," so that they risk turning the great mystery of the faith into an insignificant little art (*technydrion*). They "are like the promoters of wrestling bouts in the theaters, and not even the sort of bouts that are conducted in accordance with the rules

---

93. *CTh* 16.1.2; Socr. *HE* 4.32–35, 5.2; Soz. *HE* 6.37. For the accession of Theodosius, Matthews, *Western Aristocracies*, 88–100. McGuckin, *St. Gregory*, 233–36, argues that Theodosius's Nicene leanings were known as early as 378, certainly by 379, based on Gratian and Theodosius's joint decree, *CTh* 16.5.5, reversing the toleration of the earlier decree but without naming names. Matthews, *Western Aristocracies*, 121–22, cannot discern Theodosian religious actions until early 380; Vaggione, *Eunomius*, 314–22, offers a salutary reminder of the continuities of religious policy between Valens and Theodosius and the extent of the maneuvers immediately following Theodosius's accession. For the difficult reconstruction of who sent Gregory to Constantinople and when (e.g., 378 or 379), Beeley, *Gregory*, 33; McGuckin, *St. Gregory*, 236–38; Van Dam, *Kingdom*, 138–42.

94. Gautier, *Retraite*, 375–77, 394, considers *Or*. 31 a separate work.

95. Gregory of Nazianzus, *Faith*, intro. Norris, 53–85; Demoen, *Pagan and Biblical Exempla*, 115–19. Copyists of the manuscript entitled the oration *Against the Eunomians*.

96. Gr. Naz. *Or*. 27.1: πρὸς τοὺς ἐν λόγῳ κομψοὺς ὁ λόγος. . . . καὶ παίδευσιν καὶ ἀκουὴν καὶ διάνοιαν. Compare *Or*. 4.42: οἱ τὰ κομψὰ λαρυγγίζοντες.

of the sport and lead to the victory of one of the antagonists, but the sort that are stage-managed to give the uncritical audience visual spectacles and compel their applause." The city is abuzz with their arguments, and no place, not even the women's quarters, is free of their intrusive disputes, so that "'the great mystery' of our faith is in danger of becoming a mere social accomplishment" (*Or.* 27.1–2). Such disputes are fodder for those who have no faith in the strength of their arguments, outsiders (pagans) who "hunt for . . . our weakness." Continuous and divisive "discussions of the 'generation' and the 'creation' of God, or of God's 'production from nonbeing,' and such dissection, distinctions, and analyses" provide them with the best arguments against "us." Disputing such questions everywhere and before everyone only demonstrates "that we are less reverent than those who worship demons and venerate obscene tales and objects. They would sooner give their blood than disclose certain words to noninitiates": Christians, in contrast, fight against each other like "madmen who set fire to their own houses, tear their own children limb from limb, or reject their own parents" (*Or.* 27.4–6).

Gregory aims in this oration to point out by whom, on what occasion, in front of which audience, and in what manner theology ought to be practiced. "Not everyone, I tell you, not everyone can philosophize about God" (*Or.* 27.3)—only those who have been purified in body and soul and are in the process of continuing purification, and who have been properly educated and "tested and [have] a sound foundation in learning [*theōria*]."[97] There is a due season for theology, just as there is one for all other pursuits, as anyone who is a true philosopher (one who knew the basic rhetorical rules about proper time, place, tenor, and audience as laid out by Aristotle) was fully aware, whereas mere sophists and word-gamesters paraded the mysteries in front of those who should not hear them. "How, I ask you, will such a discussion be interpreted by the man who subscribes to a creed of adulteries and infanticides, who worships the passions, who is incapable of conceiving anything higher than the body, who fabricated his own gods only the other day, and gods that are distinguished by their utter vileness? What sort of construction will he put on it? . . . Will he not appropriate our theology to defend his own gods and passions?" (*Or.* 27.6). To use philosophy falsely in speaking about the mysteries of the Christians and to parade disputes before all plays into the hands of those who only the other day acted as Julian did. Precisely such a civil war among Christians, caused by men who love strife of words, had brought down God's punishment in the form of Julian in the first place.

To counter such misuses, Gregory set out to "smooth the theologian in us, like a statue, into beauty," beginning with a few questions addressed to his opponents,

---

97. *Theōria* also denoted typological prefiguration of future events; see F. Thome's discussion (*Historia*, passim) of Diodore's and Theodore's use of the term.

"so fond of talking and the dialectic method" (*Or.* 27.7, 8).[98] Inviting his opponents, represented by Eunomius, to use Aristotelian dialectical methods in order to direct attacks instead against "the silence of Pythagoras, or the Orphic beans, or the extraordinarily pretentious 'He said it' [of the *Golden Verses*], [against] Plato's ideas . . . , Epicurus's atheism . . . , Aristotle's mean conception of Providence," or to areas of Christian *logoi* where they might do good, Gregory employs the same Aristotelian dialectics to attack Eunomius's notion—as Gregory framed it—that humans may comprehend the divine (*Or.* 27.10).[99] Eunomius had argued that God the Father's unbegotten essence cannot be understood in name only (*ouk onomati monon*), as if it were merely a human invention (*kat' epinoian*), but must be seen as a literal description reflecting God's essential reality (*Apol.* 8).[100] Eunomius gave absolute priority to the essential characteristic of God as unbegotten, because, as Eunomius pointed out in response to Basil, who had rejected his unveiling of that naked truth, God was earlier and longer unbegotten than Father, because he existed as such prior to the Son.[101]

In Gregory's view, such an argument, despite its merits, revealed Eunomius's fatal flaw: he insisted that he comprehended accurately the essence of God. Gregory, in a Socratic dialogue citing scripture, responded that God's house had many mansions, so that there are many ways toward him, principally those of reason and study, and if there is only one way, then it is that of virtue—and Eunomius and those like him, who rush to philosophy falsely understood, have neither, for they mistake gossip and sensationalism for reason and study (*logou kai theōrias, Or.* 27.8).

But even if—Gregory proposes to Eunomius for the sake of argument—"[you have] reached the heights, gone beyond them, higher, if you like, than the clouds, so that you have looked on things not to be seen . . . ; so that, a second Elijah, you have been raised up; so that, a second Moses, you have been judged worthy to see God"; so that Eunomius had indeed been sufficiently purified to be allowed to see

---

98. Gr. Naz. *Or.* 4.102; Dillon, "Image," on the rules of such exegesis.

99. Norris (Gregory of Nazianzus, *Faith,* intro. Norris, 17–35) demonstrates Gregory's reliance on Plato's *Phaedo* and *Phaedrus,* and on Aristotle's *Organon* and *Rhetoric,* especially Aristotle's epistemological principles about language. Norris also highlights Gregory's use of Hermogenes, in particular his *stasis* theory, which presents argumentative strategies for cases, situations, or positions (*staseis*), often structured as interrogations. This forms what Norris calls Gregory's "philosophical rhetoric." See also Kennedy, "Later Greek Philosophy," especially his discussion of the later Greek rhetorical-philosophical corpus at pp. 193–96.

100. Predicated on Eunomius's understanding of Plato's argument in *Cra.* 430a–431e, according to which the god gave things names that reveal his nature; Gregory of Nazianzus, *Faith,* intro. Norris, 34 n. 167.

101. Eun. *Apol.* 3.4–5; *Apol. apol.* 182.2–6, 186.3–10, 192.20–193.1; *Eunomius: The Extant Works,* ed. and trans. Vaggione, 102–3.

and perceive and perhaps even comprehend God, all this does not explain or justify his precipitous appointment of others as theologians and his unleashing of "the most effeminate specimens of the male sex" against "us" as the new dialecticians (*Or.* 27.9). As it stands, his opponents' entirely misguided philosophy resulted in a correspondingly misguided *ēthos*, rejecting hospitality, brotherly love, care of the poor, singing of psalms, abstinence, and mastery of passion, choosing licentiousness instead (*Or.* 27.7).

Philosophy falsely understood and thus falsely applied to the divine by the wrong person yielded flawed ethics, reflecting misguided notions of the divine, which led to civil war and disaster instead of harmony, unity, and peace—Gregory now reiterated and augmented the themes of *Oration* 2, elaborated against Julian in *Oration* 4, in these subsequent *Theological Orations*. Only Gregory and those like him—truly divinely inspired prophets purified by long and arduous devotion to *logoi*, who led the true philosophical life and manifestly embodied true *ēthos*—could know how to employ the hermeneutical tools of *logoi* to unveil the truth of the divine to the extent possible to humans. Such men—that is, Gregory—demonstrate the true understanding of the Trinity that flows from purified comprehension and thereby teach and guide others to the divine, as he shows in the subsequent *Theological Orations*.

Oration 28 begins with Gregory's central counterargument. "So we must begin again with this in mind. To know God is hard; to describe him, impossible, as a Hellenic theologian philosophized [Pl. *Ti.* 28c]. . . . No—to tell of God is not possible, so my argument runs, but to know him is even less possible. For language may show the known, if not adequately, at least faintly, to a person not entirely deaf or dull of mind." But for all human beings, regardless of their advancement in purity, "to grasp so great a matter [*pragma*] mentally [*dianoiai*] is utterly beyond possibility."[102] Now, as Gregory hastens to add, to be unable to comprehend God does not mean it is impossible to know him. To realize God's transcendence means that one cannot understand the nature of God, not that one questions his existence. "That God, the creative and sustaining cause of all, exists, sight and instinctive law inform us." Looking at the well-ordered world around us that functions like a harmonious instrument makes that clear enough. Nevertheless, even observing well-ordered and divinely created nature and then applying to what is observed all methods of deductive argument, thus approaching knowledge of the divine by analogy, cannot lead us to comprehend the nature of the divine, because "whatever we imagine or figure to ourselves or reason delineates is not the reality of God" (*Or.* 28.5–7).

---

102. Gr. Naz. *Or.* 28.4: τὸ . . . πρᾶγμα τῇ διανοίᾳ περιλαβεῖν πάντως ἀδύνατον. Gregory of Nazianzus, *Faith*, intro. Norris, 135, and 53–71, for Gregory's audience, which Norris defines as later Arians. Narkevics "*Skiagraphia*," discusses the orations' technical theological aspects.

To rephrase it, as Gregory does in *Oration* 29, human conception cannot grasp God's essential nature, because our physical, bodily condition imposes limits on the human mind and human conceptual faculties (*Or.* 28.11, 21; compare Proclus, above). Thus the human mind is too small a tool to grasp God's essence, so large a construction that "no one has yet discovered or shall ever discover what God is in his nature and essence" (*Or.* 28.17, 21). Even though "all truth, all philosophy, to be sure, is obscure, hard to trace out," however, the right person working in the right way can, in some sense, really and truly know God. For example, to understand the lunar cycles does not mean to comprehend equally what moves them; to claim such a link is mistaken inductive logic. To underscore that point Gregory presents a long list of phenomena in nature for which "reason has no explanation . . . , except the will of God" (*Or.* 28.25, 26). In other words, understanding part of a phenomenon does not necessarily permit comprehension of the whole. It does, however, permit operations of inference by accurate syllogistic argument to prove the existence of a force guiding (say) nature, without thereby positing an understanding of that nature in its complete essence—the counterargument to Eunomius laid out in a series of dialectical moves.

Eunomius, according to Gregory, made conceptual mistakes by applying an imprecise and often faulty logic, both inductive and deductive, and by being similarly imprecise about the workings of homonyms and synonyms. These mistakes affected his grasp of the signifying power of language. He mistook aspects or qualities for essence. If Eunomius and his followers knew so clearly what God is not—*agennētos*—then by their own logic they should be able to say precisely what he is (*Or.* 28.5, 9); but they cannot, because doing so requires a *theōria* quite beyond them. Or, as Gregory had said earlier, citing Plato's *Timaeus* (28c), God's nature cannot be fully expressed in human language. Thus, Eunomius's deductions about the meaning of (human) names when applied to the divine can never encompass the full reality of God.

This is so because according to Gregory the facts (*pragmata*) determine the names (*onomata*), and not the other way around. Reality precedes language, as Aristotle had argued in *On Interpretation* (16a–b), since language is the product of (human) invention (*kata thesin*). For example, Gregory's opponents argue that a name can be the same yet refer to different realities, so that the Son participates in the name "God" qua homonym but differs in essence. To prove their point the opponents adduce "the Greek word for 'dog' [*kyōn*], which, as a real homonym, can be used in the proper sense for the land as well as the sea animal [i.e., dogfish]": one word; two different realities.

True, Gregory rejoins, there are such words, but the homonym, the name per se, permits no deduction about the priority of their respective natures. Neither a dog nor a dogfish is more or less dog, but they are certainly not the same animal. Homonyms used to deduce true essence can be deceiving, particularly if stripped of proper context (*Or.* 29.14).[103] (See Gregory's interpretation, at *Or.* 4.102, of Julian's use of the word "speak Greek," *hellēnizein*.) Names designate relations, not essences, and are therefore not linked in a deep sense to underlying facts, realities, or essences. "I accept the *pragmata* [objects] without fearing the *onomata* [names]" (*Or.* 31.7). This means that "God is of one essence, one nature, one appellative [*klēsis*], even if the names differ according to the different concepts [*epinoiai*] one has regarding him" (*Or.* 29.13).[104]

Most of Gregory's opponents' arguments exhibit a lack of the contextual, because they fail to employ terms in their proper relational fashion. "'But,' they say, 'if the Son is the same in substance as the Father, and the Father is unbegotten, then the Son must be unbegotten too.' True—provided that unbegottenness constitutes God's being.... But supposing the difference lies outside the substance of God: What validity has your argument got? ... Surely it is clear that if we are looking, if look we can, for what God's being consists in, a personal characteristic must be left out of the account." "Seeing that only logical equivalents can be used interchangeably," "unbegotten" and "God" cannot be used as synonyms. To do so, as Gregory suggests Eunomius has done, equates a condition with a privation, which cannot be done, "since conditions are prior to privations, and privations take away conditions," as Aristotle demonstrates, using the example of blindness, which he shows is a privation, requiring a prior state of seeing; so it follows that possession (sight) precedes privation (blindness). Thus, to claim the Father is un-begotten presupposes "begotten" as a prior, meaning that the Son would have preceded the Father, clearly an absurdity (to which Eunomius had already responded by pointing out that negation, un-begotten, need not equal privation; but that did not perturb Gregory: *Or.* 29.12; Arist. *Cat.* 12a).[105]

Such imprecision and logical inaccuracies had far-reaching consequences in Gregory's view because they distorted and cheapened the Trinity and its inherent causal relationship between Father, Son, and Holy Spirit. As Plato understood (in contrast to Eunomius), cause usually but not always precedes effect (*Or.* 29.3). "I wonder if you have noticed the important truth that, as a non-Christian writer puts it, 'the Sun has the same place in things of sense [*en aisthētois*] as God has in things ideal [*en noētois*]'" (*Or.* 28.30; Plato *R.* 508c). Gregory read this passage, familiar from Julian's *Hymn to King Helios*, as indicating that the Sun is not prior to its light: they coexisted as coessentials. In a similar manner God is a prior cause, but he coexists with the Son because he eternally caused himself as well as the three *hy-*

---

103. Gregory of Nazianzus, *Faith*, intro. Norris, 28–32, 148–49.

104. Names do not reveal meanings, but it is meanings that count. "Two times seven" and "fourteen" have the same meaning, though the words differ; but those who use the words have no stronger claim than those who infer their logical meaning: *Or.* 31.24, 28.4, and 31.10, 19–20.

105. Gregory of Nazianzus, *Faith*, intro. Norris, 148, lists further Aristotelian references.

postaseis, since the Father as the first cause assured the eternal existence of all three in their specificity. As Gregory formulated it in *Oration* 29.16, "'The Father' is the name neither of an essence nor of an activity, you experts, but of a relation, and the way in which the Father exists with respect to the Son, and the Son to the Father."[106] So Eunomius, the great (Aristotelian) dialectician (*technologos*), did not grasp even the first principles of grammar and logic, of the meaning of words in relation to their context, or of causation and effect (*Or.* 29.15, 21; 27.2, 31.18).[107]

Although much more could be said about Gregory's counterarguments, his points (for the purpose of this discussion) are evident. His opponents made mistakes because of their insufficient comprehension of *logoi*, resulting from their inappropriate *paideia*.[108] Because their *paideia* had not been the right kind—not least because of their unacceptably low social origins—Eunomius and others like him had rushed toward what they considered philosophy and *logoi*, assuming that the quick and dirty road would suffice. Not so. Not so, because the quick and dirty road precluded the true goal of *paideia*—the purification of the philosophical life achieved by discipline and long study, which alone could lead to the one thing that "gives fullness to reasoning [*logos*]": faith.[109]

Eunomius lacked the purity that allows for kinship, close converse—even unity—with the divine (*oikeiōsis*), which in turn engenders faith; faith then gives that fullness to reason that pure reason cannot have; only faith combined with true reasoning can yield the true understanding of philosophy, which in turn permits a true knowledge of the Trinity within the limits of human comprehension. That true knowledge must then be imparted to all in the right manner, so as to lead them, too, to unity with the divine. This Eunomius did not possess. (Or if he did, he was unable to impart it properly to his followers; see *Or.* 27.9.)

Gregory in contrast had ascended the mountain like Moses. "I ascend the mountain with eagerness—or, to speak truer, at once with eagerness and with fear, [eager] because of my hope and [fearful] because of my frailty—to enter into the cloud and to converse with God as God commands. If there is an Aaron, may he

---

106. Gr. Naz. *Or.* 25.15–16. In *Or.* 30.1. and 31.23 and 33, Gregory argues that God is the prior cause, anticipating Proclus's notion that the gods create (*poiein*) by naming.

107. Gr. Naz. *Or.* 4.104, 102; Gregory of Nazianzus, *Faith*, intro. Norris, 59, 98–105. Gr. Naz. *Or.* 30 offers additional examples of Eunomius's lacking *paideia*. "I cannot understand how what is common to two things could be the particular property of one of them alone. Nor, I think, can anyone else"—the same argument Gregory uses against Julian's hijacking of Greekness (*Or.* 30.12); "deeds [*erga*] are a demonstration [*apodeixis*] of disposition [*diatheseōs*]"—the tenor of *Oration* 4 (*Or.* 30.6); "You do not understand the signified [τὰ σημαινόμενα]," using the example that "until" is not "the logical contrary of what lies in the future" (*Or.* 30.4; also 8).

108. For example, his attacks against pagan symbols such as statues and their false signifying powers (e.g., *Or.* 28.14–15); or his examples of his opponents' misuse of grammar and logic when applied to scripture and to the meaning of names of the divine (e.g., *Or.* 29.18).

109. Gr. Naz. *Or.* 29.21: ἡ γὰρ πίστις τοῦ καθ' ἡμᾶς λόγου πλήρωσις.

ascend with me and stand close, and be willing to remain outside the cloud if necessary. If there is a Nadab . . . or any one of the elders, let him ascend, but let him remain at a distance in accordance with the worth of his purity. If there are those from the multitude and those who are unworthy of such height and such contemplation [*theōria*] . . . , let them not approach . . . ; it is dangerous" (*Or.* 28.2). Gregory was sufficiently pure and fully prepared, and he did indeed ascend close enough to the divine—"What happened to me, my friends and initiates [*mystai*] and fellow lovers of the truth? I was running to comprehend God, and so I ascended the mountain, and penetrated the cloud and entered [it] far from matter and material things and focused insofar as I could inward toward myself. Then when I looked I barely saw the back parts of God [Ex. 33:23], . . . only that part of [God's nature] that is farthest away and comes down to us. . . . And in this way then shall you do theology, even if you are Moses and 'a god to Pharaoh,' even if you were lifted 'to the third heaven' like Paul and heard 'unspeakable words,' even if you are above him at the status or in the order of an angel or archangel!" For not all beings, however exalted they are, however closely affiliated to God, may comprehend God in his entirety (*Or.* 28.3; and see *Or.* 2.92–95).

God's incomprehensibility was Gregory's main point in *Oration* 28, but his secondary point, interwoven with the first, was equally crucial: only purity as practiced by Gregory and his fellow initiates permits an ascent to the heights to be close enough to God to comprehend his back parts, to achieve that knowledge of the divine that God has meant to come down to us. Thus, his philosophical life and the purity he had gained as a result permitted him to apprehend God, to have the true incomprehensibility of his greatness revealed to him. For all others the true and solid words of scripture are like rocks: their misuse is dangerous for themselves and for others. His *logos,* however, is engraved in "durable tablets of stone and on both sides, because one part of the Law is visible and the other hidden: the one is for the multitude and for those who remain below, and the other for the few and those who have ascended up high" (*Or.* 28.2).

In these orations Gregory once again advocated a middle ground, arguing that the primacy of the historical and literal must not occlude allegorical readings by those who have reached the appropriate purification—to rest purely on the literal level is wrong and misguided, but to overreach in the opposite direction, toward Julianic allegory, is supremely dangerous, as Gregory's opponents demonstrated; their faulty philosophy corresponded to and was exposed by their equally faulty way of life. True philosophy and the correct conduct of life (*ēthos*) resulting from it permitted true purification, which in turn led the initiate to ascend to God, even to become divine to the extent possible for a human leaving all matter and material things behind, like Moses the prophet on the mountain. Such close converse with God revealed true allegorical reading of scripture: as with Moses' tablets, the literal was for all, but God revealed the hidden meaning only to those few who could read and interpret it because they had seen God through faith, achieved in the long process of purification. Thus, in Christian writings "the outer form [the visible or literal] is never unseemly, and the hidden is marvelous, sublime, and magnificent for those who have penetrated the profundity" (*Or.* 4.118). False use of philosophy and an incorrect *ēthos* leads to civil war and *apostasis*. On January 10, 381, Theodosius issued an edict that reaffirmed the Nicene tenets of his faith and prohibited heretics (as defined by Gregory) from assembling inside the cities.[110]

APOSTASIS VERSUS *THEŌSIS;*
OR, TRUE *OIKEIŌSIS PROS THEON*

Gregory, in his *Oration* 4 against Julian, coined the term *theōsis,* nearly untranslatable, but connoting divinization or deification of the human individual—the process described in the section preceding this one. The term was Gregory's conscious innovation, and the concept of deification it crystallized had a stellar career in the orthodox Byzantine and later Russian tradition, especially in the "discourse of sainthood" and that of "priestly (or saintly) mediation that is distinctive of Eastern Christian ethics."[111] Despite scholarly attention to and clarification of *theōsis,* especially in the work of Norman Russell, engagement with Gregory's neologism and his conceptual framework has remained unsatisfactory. None of the modern scholarly discussions pay attention to Julian's writings, or to the intellectual interconnectedness of Julian's and Eunomius's arguments that Gregory (and Diodore and Theodore) perceived, thus omitting the foil against which Gregory coined the term and developed the concept. Indeed, most scholarly discussions of *theōsis* do not even focus on Gregory beyond pointing to his neologism and expressing reservations about his intentions. Norman Russell, for example, notes Gregory's innovation but discusses it under the generalized heading "Cappadocian Thought," even though he acknowledges Gregory's distinctiveness. As a result, the decisive influence of Gregory's concept of deification on that of Maximus the Confessor, John of Damascus, and Simeon the New Theologian remains unexplored.

Indeed, as I mentioned above in Chapter 4, scholarly treatments generally see Gregory's use of the term *theōsis* and the concept as an example of Christian Platonism and seek to integrate it with the scant biblical references to human assimilation to the divine. Such an approach flattens the impact of Gregory's statements. Presupposing Platonic concepts according to which Gregory must have advocated imitation of Christ, rather than incorporation into him, led Russell to posit that

---

110. *CTh* 16.5.6 = *CJ* 1.1.2; Van Dam, *Kingdom,* 142–46.
111. Maslov, "*Oikeiosis,*" manuscript pp. 2 and 4.

Gregory's concept of *theōsis* should be seen as metaphorical rather than realistic. This interpretation reverses what Gregory actually said.[112] In other words, the idea that Gregory could have applied the notion of deification to individual persons (rather than to humanity as a whole, deified through Christ's incarnation) brings him—so modern scholars apparently fear—perilously close to pagan notions of *apotheōsis* and the theurgic operation associated with Julian (the emperor and the theurgist).[113] *Theōsis*, the process of close affiliation of humans and the divine, continues to be a troubling concept for scholars, especially those of a Western scholarly tradition imprinted by the stark dualism between man and God posited by Augustine.[114] Closer analysis of the manner in which Gregory used the term *theōsis* in Oration 4, however, shows that the term crystallized semantically everything Gregory had said repeatedly on earlier occasions, in particular in Oration 2, *On the Priesthood* (*Or.* 2.3, 17, 91), when discussing kinship, affiliation, or parentage with (that is, participation in) the divine or the Good—or becoming God's own: *oikeōsis pros theon*.

Becoming God's Own and the Unity of the Politeia

Gregory, influenced by (Roman) Stoic (rather than Platonic or Platonizing) concepts, as Boris Maslov has shown (see also Chapter 4 above), understood *theōsis* as *oikeiōsis pros theon,* as a process of continuing ethical perfection and hence purification through the philosophical life, which demanded that the divinely inspired philosopher guide everyone, the multitude (*hoi polloi*), toward kinship with God, making them God's own through his mediation.[115] The charge of "those who are

---

112. N. Russell, *Doctrine of Deification*, 213–25 for Gregory, and 233–37 for the assertion that Maximus developed the concept "in a completely new way." Russell's amalgamation of the Platonic and the biblical and the quotation are at p. 224; for the vocabulary of deification, ibid., 121–54, 333–44; Wittung, "Resources," 294–309, discusses the history of the term; Winslow, *Dynamics*, 171–99, 179 the neologism, and at 173 also the conflation of the Platonic and the biblical. Molac, *Douleur*, 31–78, 104–61, includes a discussion of man as God's *eikōn* in *theōsis*. McGuckin, "Strategic Adaptation," 101–2, excludes from Gregory's concept "the reassertion of any divine element within creaturely nature," though he grants a language of "'kinship' or 'affinity' with the divine nature." None of these scholars refers to *Or.* 4 beyond citing the two occurrences of the term *theōsis*, with the exception of Molac, *Douleur*, 21–22, who mentions Gregory's reference to Julian's display of *eikones* (and misses the argument).

113. As N. Russell's appendix demonstrates (*Doctrine of Deification*, 333–44), Christian writers were fully aware of that parallel and sought to distance themselves from such associations through their choice of vocabulary.

114. Winslow, *Dynamics*, 179–80; N. Russell, *Doctrine of Deification*, 223–24. The term is often linked to Athanasius's concept of *theopoiēsis*, a term Gregory does not use. See Markus's judicious remarks in *Christianity*, 165: even though "Christians necessarily repudiated any divinization of the world," including "the pagan Stoic cosmic religion," "a residual sense of the holiness of the natural world as a whole was never lost in Eastern theology, . . . [which] remained inhospitable to the stark way of opposing regenerate with unregenerate nature which dogged Western theology."

115. Maslov's analysis ("Oikeiosis," manuscript pp. 9–12, 17–18) of the Platonic assimilation to God, *homoiōsis theōi*, details the limits of that framework for Gregory.

higher than the multitude in their virtue and their *oikeiōsis pros theon*" is "to approach God and lead others toward him."[116] The philosopher-priest who has ascended the mountain and comprehended as much of God as is humanly possible must "mold the figure and furnish the image and serve as a manufacturer to the world above, and furthermore, [he] will become a god and produce God."[117]

Oikeiōsis pros theon, as Gregory spelled out in *Oration* 2, required the purified philosopher's active involvement in the divinely created *politeia*, both to achieve his own purification and ascent to the divine and to fulfill his divine mandate, to mold the entire *politeia* toward God as God's own. Implicit in such a mandate was Gregory's understanding of the cosmos as a harmonious universe governed by well-ordered forces created by the most philanthropic God. This notion (see *Oration* 28.25–26) Gregory also shared with Julian. "The best thing is consent and mutual agreement between cities, nations, households, and individuals, who all follow the law and order of nature that divided and bound together all and have made this entire world one out of many."[118]

Kinship with the divine led to ever-widening circles of altruism extending outward from love of self to that of one's parents to encompass the whole of humanity—what both Julian and Gregory expressed in the words *oikeiōsis* and *philanthrōpia*. Recourse to the self, self-love, focusing inward to the self as Gregory formulated in *Oration* 28.3, was this nexus of kinship: to cite G. B. Kerferd, "the process by which we search for and achieve a sense of personal identity." That meant not withdrawal but "the assimilation or relating of one's environment to one's self as an extension or continuation of the primary process of the construction of the self," so that all nature was *oikeios*, proper to the self, and the self thus proper to nature, understood as God. It was a logic of expansion rather than escape.[119] The cosmological dimension of that nature has been remarked (above, Chapter 4): because Reason (*Logos*), in the original Stoic concept, governs all, and because Reason is identical to Nature (*Physis*), every act of engagement with Nature in the form of altruistic ethical behavior is also a conscious act of linking self, other, and *kosmos* in *oikeiōsis pros theon*.[120] To

---

116. Gr. Naz. *Or.* 2.3: ὅσοι τῶν πολλῶν εἰσιν ἀνωτέρω κατ' ἀρετὴν καὶ τὴν πρὸς τὸν θεὸν οἰκείωσιν, and 2.71: ἐγγίσαι θεῷ καὶ προσαγαγεῖν ἄλλους.

117. Gr. Naz. *Or.* 2.73: τὸν ἀναπλάσοντα τὸ πλάσμα καὶ παραστήσοντα τὴν εἰκόνα καὶ τῷ ἄνω κόσμῳ δημιουργήσοντα καὶ τὸ μεῖζον εἰπεῖν θεὸν ἐσόμενον καὶ θεοποιήσοντα.

118. Gr. Naz. *Or.* 4.120: Ἄριστον ὁμόνοια καὶ τὸ συμφρονεῖν ἀλλήλοις πόλεις καὶ δήμους καὶ οἰκίας καὶ τοὺς καθ' ἕκαστον, νόμῳ καὶ τάξει φύσεως ἑπομένους ἢ πάντα διεῖλέ τε καὶ συνέδησε καὶ τὸ πᾶν τοῦτο κόσμον ἕνα ἐκ πλειόνων πεποίηκε.

119. Kerferd, "Search," 178–79; Bees, *Oikeiosislehre*, 248–49, and 285 for Platonic and Stoic thoughts about the self and nature; Reydams-Schils (*Roman Stoics*, 2–13, 53–113) discusses scholarly assessments of the Stoic definition of "pro-cosmic" (that is, pro-Roman) values.

120. Bees, *Oikeiosislehre*, 183, 227. *Sympatheia*, or linking cosmos, nature, and individual, shaped how *oikeiōsis* became part of Neoplatonic thought through what Hadot, "Apport," 118–21, has called a

cite Julian's *Epistle to the Priest Theodorus* (*Ep.* 89a): "All men ... are related [*syngeneis*] to all other men" (291d), because the gods created them as well as their customs and laws, for "when Zeus ordered all things, drops of sacred blood fell from heaven, out of which grew the human race. Therefore we are all related" (292a–b).

Julian and Gregory shared this view of the cosmos as a united, harmonious, and essentially benevolent being. *Kosmos* was, for them, the Roman body politic, encompassing all created and living beings, from the very fabric of the earth and insects, other animals, and man up to the highest divinity. Gregory's notion of the *oikoumenē*, however, reached further, to the limits of the earth (though it could be argued that the same was true for Julian, who also considered realms beyond the limits of empire his purview, as indicated by his civilizing mission to Persia). Whereas for Julian this cosmos was held together by an uninterrupted sequence of intermediary powers and activities, Gregory's uniting force was the *Logos* in the Trinity. The active *oikeiōsis* of Julian's imperial rule, conceptualized as *philanthrōpia*, dictated his educational mediation as a divinely inspired philosopher-priest and emperor, granted knowledge of the divine to guide those in his keep toward the ethical life proper (*oikeios*) to his divinities. That had been the argument of Julian's *Epistle to the Priest Theodorus*, and most certainly that of his hymns, both *To the Mother of the Gods* and *To King Helios*, where the instruction he provided by reading the literal *paradoxa* of the myth allegorically gave ethical guidelines for all, enhanced by sacrifices, rituals, and festivities, whose ethical foundation he likewise revealed.

As the emperor said in the *Hymn to the Mother of the Gods*, the gods, as a gesture of their divine love, wished to teach humans through rites and symbols "to ... break the rush toward the infinite [i.e., the disorder of matter] in ourselves and to imitate the gods our leaders and return back to the defined and uniform, and, if it be possible, to the One" (169c)—a return the Christians had rejected, thereby disrupting the divinely ordered unity.[121] As *mystagōgos* (that is, as initiate almost "perfect in theurgy," *en theourgiai teleiotēta*), as philosopher, *pontifex maximus*, and emperor, Julian was to guide the *koina* of the Romans so that "very many souls [are] lifted up" (172d), because they had correctly "followed the sacred rites, ... [so that] straightway the divine light illumines our souls [*ellampei to theion phōs*]" (178b), even if only the "blessed theurgists" (*theourgois ... tois makariois*) could fully penetrate the depth of the *mysterium* (172d). Philosophers thus blessed—including Julian—could reach the presence of the divine (*tēs epiphaneias ... tōn theōn*), which enabled them, as god's slaves, to guide everyone else to virtue and salvation, according to their abilities, with the help of myths, statues, and sacrifices,

---

rehabilitation of corporality and the sensible world as a well-functioning body where everything has its place; Gurtler, "Sympathy."

121. G. Shaw, *Theurgy*, 143–61.

"for the gods command me to purify everything as far as possible, and I obey them with enthusiasm."[122]

Julian used the term *theoō*, "deify," from which Gregory derived the noun *theōsis*, to emphasize that the purified soul in a state of deification could also transform the body by proper ethical behavior and by sacred rites—a statement unusual for a pure Platonist and replicated only by Gregory among Julian's contemporaries in the sense that increasing progress to the divine purified soul and body both.[123] This is significant, because Gregory, in the context of Julian's use of *oikeiōsis pros theon* and *theon poiein parousias*, developed his counterconcept of *oikeiōsis pros theon*, understood as *theōsis*, in Oration 4. Gregory's concept differed from Julian's as Gregory's notion of *theōria* differed from Julian's use of *allēgoria*—nearly the same, except for some subtle, though important, differences.

For Gregory, the behavior of Julian's gods demonstrated their falseness and that of their myths and of the philosophers upholding and interpreting them. That behavior promoted, in those *oikeioi* to them, an *ēthos* antithetical to harmony, unity, and benevolently ordered oneness. When Julian deserted Christ for the teachings of his false philosophers, he broke the *oikeiōsis* uniting all, in favor of excluding Christians, driven by his desire for self-aggrandizement and propelled by his self-centered innovations. All Julian's *erga* had therefore resulted in "civil war . . . more unnatural than war waged on foreigners, as the eating of one's own flesh is more to be shunned than the eating of the flesh of another" (*Or.* 4.109, 2.91).

Gregory's first explicit use of the term *theōsis* occurs at the center of Oration 4, at the moment of Julian's *apostasia* (*Or.* 4.52–73).[124] He begins with the negative use of the term *theoō*. The philosophers whom Julian followed, who led him to desert Christ, were so concerned with their self-centered love for glory in the eyes of men that they sought to deify themselves.[125] Empedocles had thrown himself into Etna,

---

122. Jul. *Ep.* 26 (Wright 8), *To Maximus of Ephesus*, written in December 361 from Constantinople.

123. See Jul. *Or.* 5.177d–178c: "And to the question of what food is permitted I will only say this. The divine law does not allow all kinds of food to all men, but takes into account what is possible to human nature. . . . But at the season of the highest festivals we ought to exert [our own will] to the utmost, so that we may attain to what is beyond our ordinary physical powers. . . . For it is by all means more effective for the salvation of the soul itself that one ought to pay greater heed to its safety than to the safety of the body. And moreover, the body too seems thereby to share insensibly in that great and marvelous benefit. For when the soul abandons herself wholly to the gods . . . and then follows the sacred rites, . . . the divine light illuminates our souls. And thus endowed with divinity [*theōtheisthai*] they impart a certain vigor . . . [and] by the rite of purification not only the soul alone but the body as well is greatly benefited."

124. I think that Gregory consciously placed the use of his neologism at such a prominent place, the center of his *Or.* 4, because he was aware that this neologism would be controversial: it described, after all, a relationship between God and man based on a term not found in scripture, like *homoousios*, which Gregory used so infrequently. Not surprisingly, Gregory used his innovative term while advocating a middle way between strict literal adherence to scripture and Julianic allegory.

125. Gr. Naz. *Or.* 4.59: ἑαυτὸν θεώσας.

expecting to be deified by posterity through this ruse that would make his body disappear, but the sandal he left behind outed him as a vainglorious (*kenodoxos*) pseudo-philosopher who lacked common sense. Persons like Empedocles who faked deification to achieve glory among men were Julian's moral and ethical exemplars (*Or.* 4.59). Indeed, as Gregory alleged in *Oration* 5.14, Julian sought to stage his own death in Persia as a fake *theōsis* by throwing himself into the Tigris, only to be rescued by one of his eunuchs. Like his exemplars he placed vain, self-centered desire for personal fame, noxious self-love,[126] above all else—certainly above any altruistic act on behalf of his neighbors, thus embodying the very opposite of the true philosopher's voluntary subordination of self to others (*oikeiōsis*).[127] And Julian, as was apparent in his rebellion against Constantius, had chosen this path by his own will (*prohairesis: Or.* 4.47).[128]

Martyrs and True Philosophers

Gregory's exemplars were models of altruistic behavior, of voluntary subjection of self to the laws demanding love of others as God's own. Model philosophers of Gregory's day, Christians, they were overlooked entirely by Julian in his vain search for vain exemplars. These men and women preferred to suffer in obscurity for the sake of *eusebeia*. For them, pleasing men counted for nothing; all that mattered was to acquire honor with God.[129] "Even more than that," Gregory adds, as "true philosophers and lovers of God," they embraced "kinship [*oikeiōsis*] with the beautiful ["the noble," "the Good"] for the sake of the beautiful itself."[130]

Gregory used the noun *theōsis* for the first time in his short invective against Julian (*Or.* 4.67–78), in a brief *synkrisis* contrasting exemplars of the Christian philosophical life with the most famous philosophers of the past (*Or.* 4.71–72; above, Chapter 8). Again, the motivation of those philosophers was earthly glory, manifest in their mistaken *ēthos*—in Socrates' case, by love of boys rather than of truth; in Plato's disciples by greed rather than altruism when they refused to ransom Plato

---

126. Gr. Naz. *Or.* 4.59: ὑπὸ τῆς αὐτῆς νόσου καὶ φιλαυτίας.

127. Julian also mentioned Empedotimus's death in the context of the veneration of statues, *Ep.* 89b.295b, *To the Priest Theodorus*. Empedotimus, or at least his story, appears to be an invention of Heraclides Ponticus frs. 90–96 (Wehrli); Julian may have read about it in a commentary on Plato; Kurmann, *Gregor von Nazianz*, 200–201.

128. See Kurmann's astute remarks (*Gregor von Nazianz*, 162), referring to moral choice; Gregory of Nazianzus, *Contro Giuliano*, trans. and comm. Lugaresi, 287.

129. Gr. Naz. *Or.* 4.60: τῆς δὲ παρὰ θεοῦ τιμῆς.

130. Gr. Naz. *Or.* 4.60: μᾶλλον δὲ καὶ ὑπὲρ ταύτην οἵ γε ἀληθῶς φιλόσοφοι καὶ φιλόθεοι τὴν πρὸς τὸ καλὸν οἰκείωσιν ἀγαπῶντες δι' αὐτὸ τὸ καλόν. In the passage that follows, *Or.* 4.61, Gregory attacks Julian's anti-Christian legislation as preventing martyrdom. Note the anti-Cynic criticism, focusing on self-centeredness in contrast to altruism. Jul. *Or.* 5.178b, *theōtheisthai*; Pl. *R.* 500c; Gr. Naz. *Or.* 4.71, 73, 124; *Or.* 2.3, 8.5, 21.1, 28.31.

from slavery; in Diogenes' loquacity; in Epicurus's love of pleasure (cf. *Or.* 4.70);[131] and in Julian's reckless disregard for the well-being of the army and the entire *oikoumenē* when he marched ahead of his soldiers, imagining himself another Epaminondas and another Scipio, full of pride in his self-restraint, discipline, and asceticism, because he shared his soldiers' food only to be killed in battle, imperiling all.[132]

Christian philosophers, in contrast, men and women without homes and means, with bodies scarcely of blood and flesh, "know no measure in their ascent and deification."[133] Their physical bodies dissolve not spuriously like Empedocles', but by their purification through asceticism, leaving matter behind. They achieve a true focus on the essentials of the self not by a (Platonic) moving to the self and away from others, but by selflessly disregarding the limits of their person and self, for love of their kin and for the sake of the *Logos*. Christian ascetics "lose sight of their nature only where it is necessary to make oneself kin with God through chastity and mastery [of self]."[134]

Combatants such as Paul, Steven, Luke, Andrew, or Thecla were Gregory's true heroes. As voluntary victims for Christ, they resisted fire, iron, and beasts "as if their bodies were those of another, or as if they had none." Those were the true philosophical exemplars, the true philosophers of Julian's and Gregory's time—those whom Gregory, the survivor, and his family and friends had emulated by risking martyrdom resisting Julian (so that they resembled Marc of Arethusa and other almost-martyrs of the time). Gregory and his kin had been willing and ready, and if God had chosen not to accept their self-sacrifice, then it was for a good reason: so that Gregory could expound his will to all in the present and future, thereby securing the realm by preventing another Julian (*Or.* 4.73).[135]

To emulate the martyrs past and present and their *ēthos* of voluntary subjection of the self to others did not constitute a rejection of human material nature as corrupt—quite to the contrary. The *erga* of these martyrs and of Gregory and his kin manifested how Christian *theōsis* sanctified soul and body by transforming both rather than requiring that one leave the body behind for the selfish aims of the soul.

---

131. Crates acted ὡς ἄν τις οὐ φιλόσοφος μᾶλλον ἢ φιλόδοξος, *Or.* 4.72. Kurmann, *Gregor von Nazianz*, 249, notes Gregory's contrasting of Heraclitus's κατήφεια (*Or.* 4.72) and the tear of the ascetic, which "purifies the sin of the world" (τὸ δάκρυον ἁμαρτίας κόσμου καθάρσιον, *Or.* 4.71); Socrates' *paiderastia* contrasts with Christian ἀπαθὴς ἔρως.

132. Plutarch's *Parallel Lives*; see Kurmann, *Gregor von Nazianz*, 216–40.

133. Gr. Naz. *Or.* 4.71: μηδὲν μέτρον εἰδότων ἀναβάσεως καὶ θεώσεως.

134. Gr. Naz. *Or.* 4.73: κἀνταῦθα μόνον ἐπιλανθανομένων τῆς φύσεως οὗ δεῖ θεὸν οἰκειοῦσθαι δι' ἁγνείας καὶ καρτερίας.

135. Another echo of Tacitus and Pliny's argument that if all were to follow Thrasea Paetus's example, no one would be left to run the empire; S. Elm, "*Persona*," for bibliography.

"Their bodies alone can bring about [miracles] like their sanctified souls when touched and honored, and even small drops of their blood and the small symbols of their suffering have the same efficacy as their bodies" (*Or.* 4.69). These, then, the remains of the martyrs, are not vile miasma, but the true symbols and signs of divine presence intended to aid all in strengthening their own affiliation with God; they are the proper recipients of festivals and honors.

Christian ascetic philosophical life transforms body and soul, in analogy to divine *oikeiōsis* vis-à-vis all creation. Such *oikeiōsis* may take the form of dissolving one's body entirely through martyrdom, a dissolution that paradoxically sanctifies rather than diminishes the physical self, unlike the fake rejection of the physical represented by Empedocles. Such proper disregard of self in favor of the other and in subordination to others is the aim of Christian life, the *ēthos* of *oikeiōsis* as Gregory emphasized in the last sentence of *Oration* 4: "One of the beautiful things we have achieved, another we hold on to, and still another we aim at until we reach the *telos* of divinization for which we are born and to which we are propelled—those of us, at any rate, who are advanced in our way of thinking and expect something worthy of God's magnanimity."[136]

The Humanity of the Logos

What made possible the true linking of *kosmos* and humanity, body and soul, in kinship with the divine, was the Trinity Julian had voluntarily abandoned. By considering Christ a mere human, setting his own impure rites against Christ's sacrifice, his "bloody sacrifice against the blood that purifies the world," Julian had set war against peace, (physical) dissolution against (physically saving) death, insurrection against Resurrection (*Or.* 4.68). In so doing, Julian had willfully disregarded his own place in the proper order of things, failing, in his self-centered search for self-aggrandizing glory, to recognize his cosmically required duty to subordinate himself to the true higher authority of the one he had misconstrued as merely human. Julian's choice was important—it had initiated the evil course that God, in his infinite goodness and wisdom, had permitted Julian to embrace.[137] Julian had willfully chosen to reject his proper place by rebelling against those to whom he owed subjection—his emperor and his God—and by choosing personal *apostasia* he had sought to disrupt the eternal chain of *oikeiōsis*.

---

136. Gr. Naz. *Or.* 4.124: Καὶ δεῖ τὸ μὲν ἡμῖν ἐξηνύσθαι τῶν καλῶν, τοῦ δὲ ἔχεσθαι μέχρι τοῦ τέλους καὶ τῆς θεώσεως, ἐφ' ᾗ γεγόναμεν καὶ πρὸς ἣν ἐπειγόμεθα, οἵ γε διαβατικοὶ τὴν διάνοιαν καί τι τῆς τοῦ Θεοῦ μεγαλονοίας ἐλπίζοντες ἄξιον. Gr. Naz. *Ep.* 6, *Carm.* 1.2.10.630, *Or.* 2.14–16, 8.5; N. Russell, *Doctrine of Deification*, 214–19.

137. In *Or.* 4.99 Gregory contrasts Julian's laws, which assume one ethical standard for all, with "our" laws, which permit the free choice of ethical conduct appropriate to each, guided by the mediator (that is, Gregory's dual ethics: above, Chapter 4). Free choice is central to *oikeiōsis* and thus also to Gregory's views on the nature of evil.

Julian had made his mistaken choice because he had misconstrued the significance of Christ's humanity. Instead of realizing that Christ's assumption of humanity was living proof of his most altruistic *oikeiōsis,* Julian, like some other so-called Christians at the time, had misinterpreted Christ's humanity to deny him full divinity. Persons who did so failed to understand that only the Son's full divinity could make *theōsis* possible. Only as full Son of God can the *Logos* effect the physical transformation that leads to *theōsis,* because only in him as Son could God assume humanity so that humans might become divine: "Let us become like Christ, since Christ has become like us. Let us become gods for his sake, since he became human for ours."[138] God through his Son had "assumed our condition" to allow this economy of salvation to unfold (*Or.* 14.15). For us "who had ignored the great mystery of the union," "the Savior and Master of all, the creator and ruler of this entire world, the Son of the highest Father, the *Logos,* mediator and high priest and participant in the Father's throne" had assumed the form of a slave and had even ascended the Cross, "taking my sin with him so that it would be annihilated" (*Or.* 4.78).

Christ's incarnation was the prototype of man's salvation and of his *theōsis.* Christ incarnate was the supreme *paradoxon,* signifying salvation, by mixing ontologically distinct, even contradictory, essences, divine and human, heaven and earth, God and man, "two disparate elements, tied together by the relationship of familiarity that the mediator entertains toward both of them."[139] This historical chain, prefigured and fulfilled, must not be disrupted, for example by lessening the Son's divinity vis-à-vis the Father (doing so also denied that Mary was *theotokos*).[140] For decreasing the Son's full divinity negates the miraculous chain of full *oikeiōsis:* "If I worshipped a creature, I would not be called a Christian. Why is Christianity precious? Is it not that Christ is God?" (*Or.* 37.17).

Christ's full divinity together with his full humanity, expressed in the Trinity as one, was the paradoxical *paradeigma* of *theōsis,* the kinship between God and man that made man's individual salvation possible (*Or.* 2.37–38). Because of that kinship, *oikeiōsis pros theon,* man's individual salvation was predicated on his altruistic, voluntary submission to others and his continuing efforts to progress toward the divine by purification of soul and body. This was all the more important for those

---

138. Gr. Naz. *Or.* 1.5: Γενώμεθα θεοὶ δι' αὐτόν, ἐπειδὴ κἀκεῖνος δι' ἡμᾶς ἄνθρωπος. As Gregory's term implies, this is not Athanasius's *theopoiēsis:* "The *Logos* of God itself became human in order that we may be made divine" (αὐτὸς γὰρ [ὁ τοῦ θεοῦ Λόγος] ἐνανθρώπησεν, ἵνα ἡμεῖς θεοποιηθῶμεν, *De incarnatione* 2.54, *PG* 25.192). Gregory's *theōsis* differs from Athanasius's somewhat automatic deification, the obverse of Christ's incarnation. Gregory's *oikeiōsis,* an ongoing process, required active participation (see S. Elm, "Inscriptions and Conversions"); he rarely used *theopoiein*. This further supports Beeley's view (*Gregory,* 277–93) that we need not assume Athanasian influence on Gregory.

139. Gr. Naz. *Or.* 2.23: συνεδέθη τὰ διεστῶτα τῇ πρὸς ἄμφω τοῦ μεσιτεύοντος οἰκειότητι.

140. Because she would not have borne God in the fullest sense in the Son. Gr. Naz. *Ep.* 101.16; 102.4, *To Cledonius;* F. Thome, *Historia,* 29.

who had already advanced further and guided others to the divine. Their voluntary and ongoing subordination to God's *oikeiōsis* meant submission to others, less ethically advanced, to guide them as mediators to God as God's own. The main point of the incarnation thus was God's philanthropic intention to unite humans to his own nature as constituted by the unity of everything that was the Trinity, the all as one (*Or.* 2.37)—a central theme of *Oration* 4. The harmoniously united Christian *oikoumenē* mirrored the unity of the Trinity to which it was *oikeios* (*Or.* 4.15; see also 4.12–19, 2.3), achieved through *logoi* created by and sacrificed to the *Logos*, the "*telos* of divinization for which we are born and to which we are propelled" (*Or.* 4.124).[141]

Julian had disrupted that divine unity by claiming *logoi* for himself and by falsely associating them with Hellenic religion (by making *logoi Hellēnikoi* to exclude Galileans). That was his desertion or apostasy. Eunomius and others like him had disrupted the chain in denying Christ full divinity, and Photinus and other Sabellians in lessening Christ's full humanity. True harmony and true kinship with the divine were predicated on the correct understanding of the Trinity as one in the full humanity and divinity of all its participants, each according to what was proper to it in its correct hierarchical relation. Such true understanding was exemplified and made manifest in the correct harmony of the *oikoumenē* properly understood as *Rhōmaia*, an understanding embodied by Constantius as exemplar of appropriate *eusebeia*. Those who followed the example of Julian instead ought henceforth to be considered merely *Hellēnes*, practitioners of all that was *hellēnizein*, namely the wrong use of *logoi* as proper to the wrong gods. Their voluntary rejection of universal kinship with God placed those persons well and truly "on the outside" (*hoi exō*); they were *allotrioi*, strangers and foreign to "us," the family of the civilized. (And *Hellēn* in due course became the equivalent of "pagan.")

ORATION 6, ON PEACE: UNITY AND CONCORD

Christians were Gregory's intended audience for *Oration* 4—well-informed, sophisticated, highly educated Christians, who knew Julian and were aware of (or had connections to persons privy to) Julian's secrets, much like Gregory. It was an audience capable of judging Gregory's *stēlographia* with all its allusions and references to Julian's deeds and thoughts. These were also the Christians who had been most affected by Julian's measures regarding *logoi*, the *hiera*, and the polis; like Gregory, they could now once more run free. They also included persons who had prospered under Julian, for whom Gregory's invective had offered an apology. The audience included Caesarius and others in Constantinople and Antioch, but also Gregory's educated friends in and near Nazianzus such as Helladius and Eulalius, the magis-

---

141. For unity, Gr. Naz. *Or.* 2.37–38, 29.19, 31.20, 37.2 and 4, 38.1 and 13; *Epp.* 101, 102.

trates Caesarius and Lollianus, in short, those detailed in Chapter 5.[142] Some of these friends and brothers were still in open opposition to Gregory the Elder when Gregory completed *Oration* 4.

In that oration's opening hymn, Gregory had invited the *philochristoi* emperors, most prominent among them Constantius, as well as different Christian groups to join the celebration. The first invitees were those advanced in *oikeiōsis pros theon* who had resisted Julian.[143] Other Christians, in contrast, had not comprehended the workings of divine Providence because of the "poverty and superficiality of their soul[s]," and had become attracted to the imperial impiety. Still others had simply been too stupefied by the theater of this world to resist the lure of appearances (*Or.* 4.9). The *thauma* of Julian's death persuaded all these persons, however opportunistic, of the truth (though some of them still deserved to be shunned forever: *Or.* 4.8, 11), and all were now reunited.[144] But *Oration* 4 also addressed one group at Nazianzus that even the wonder of Julian's death could not move to unity and harmony (*Or.* 4.10). One of Gregory's goals in the oration was to offer them a platform for reconciliation that would allow all concerned to maintain face.[145]

Gregory's praise for Constantius and Marc of Arethusa corroborates Brennecke's suggestion that the conciliatory platform of *Oration* 4 was in essence homoian, intended to reestablish a modus operandi much like that in effect at the time of Constantius's death. Such a platform represented the mainstream at that time.[146] *Oration* 2 and a close reading of *Oration* 4, however, indicate this platform was homoian as understood by Gregory, vindicating his father but also opening a middle road between the extremes of Eunomius and Photinus as he saw them. Given that Gregory's imagined audience for *Oration* 4 reached well beyond Nazianzus, his presentation of Constantius as the template of a Christian *basileus* is significant. Though much of what Gregory praised in the generic framework of a *Fürstenspiegel* was specific to Constantius, it was equally applicable to what we can reconstruct of Jovian's policies: to return to the status quo ante Julian. Jovian, a dynastic newcomer, consciously evoked ties to Constantius. On September 16, 363, he promulgated an

---

142. Gr. Naz. *Carm.* 2.2.1 (*Ad Hellenium*); *Epp.* 14, 15; McLynn, "Among the Hellenists," 220–38.

143. "Dedicated . . . to fasting, weeping and praying, day and night," they "endured great battles," and their renown is so great that they have become a positive "spectacle [*theatron*] for the cosmos— 'for the angels and for men,' to use the words of the Apostle Paul" (*Or.* 4.7; 1 Cor 4:9); Gregory echoes these words in *Or.* 18.32 to describe his father's fate under Julian.

144. Gr. Naz. *Or.* 2.40–42, 49; see above, Chapter 8. As Julian's *Ep.* 114 (Wright 41) to the citizens of Bostra suggests, the number of converts had been significant.

145. Bernardi, ed. and trans., *Grégoire de Nazianze: Discours 4–5*, 23–37; Kurmann, *Gregor von Nazianz*, 6–12; Gregory of Nazianzus, *Contro Giuliano*, trans. and comm. Lugaresi, 39–44.

146. Ath. *Hist. aceph.* 4.2 (Athanasius of Alexandria, *Histoire "acephale,"* ed. and trans. Martin and Albert, 153); Soz. *HE* 6.3–4; Brennecke, *Studien*, 158–81. The accord of the council of Constantinople had not been and would not be officially reversed.

edict announcing his wish to emulate Constantius's religious policy of *homonoia* and *eirēnē*, concord and peace.[147] Religious tolerance for all may have been the imperial intent, and as far as Christians were concerned, the minimalist homoian formula was well suited for that. According to Ammianus, Jovian had accepted sacrifices and the predictions of haruspices upon his elevation as Augustus while also signaling that he was beyond doubt Christian, and there were no purges of non-Christian top personnel.[148] Themistius's praise in his famous *Oration* 5, given on January 1, 364, in Ancyra at the celebration of Jovian's consulship, reflects such tolerance of everyone's choosing his own path to God.[149]

Christian sources reveal that in the late summer of 363 numerous delegations rushed to meet the emperor as soon as he crossed back into the Roman realm. Apparently homoians, as the majority and Julian's principal target, were the exception, presumably able to rest on their laurels without special pleas, as confirmed by Jovian's pronouncement that Constantius's policies should be upheld. The homoiousians, who had done well under neither Constantius nor Julian, wished to strengthen their position and to regain episcopal sees lost in 360 and 361. Thus, in the fall of 363, they gathered in a synod in Antioch under the leadership of Meletius, formulating a letter to Jovian asking that Meletius be restored as bishop of Antioch, and clarifying the homoiousian position in relation to the homoians from whom Meletius had distanced himself in 361. The foil here—according to the motto My Enemy's Enemy Is My Friend—against which Meletius set his position as closer to the homoian than Constantius had realized, was the position of Eunomius and his followers, prominently represented in Antioch.[150] Eunomius's followers, who had flourished under Julian, sent to Edessa two bishops charged with safeguarding their positions.[151]

Gregory fit *Oration* 4 well into this scenario. He praised Constantius as an ideal Christian ruler, thus praising his Christian successor Jovian, and aligned his own

---

147. Soz. *HE* 6.3.3. Ephraem *Carm. Nisib.* 21.14.21 also saw Jovian as a new Constantius; Socr. *HE* 3.25.4, 11; Griffith, "Ephraem the Syrian's Hymns," 251–56; Lenski, *Failure*, 14–20.

148. Amm. Marc. 15.6.1; Haehling, *Religionszugehörigkeit*, 548–55.

149. Them. *Or.* 5.67a–b; Amm. Marc. 21.16.20, 25.10.14.

150. Socr. *HE* 3.25.6–18; Soz. *HE* 6.4.6–11; Jer. *Chron. a.* 364. Brennecke, *Studien*, 173–78, suggests that Meletius's independent formulation of the relationship between *hypostaseis* and *ousia*, based on a notion of *homoousios*, may also have responded to Athanasius's *Tomus ad Antiochenos* of 362, but he too considers Meletius's formulation primarily anti-Eunomian. Bernardi (ed. and trans., *Grégoire de Nazianze: Discours 4–5*, 27–35) and Calvet-Sébasti (*Grégoire de Nazianze: Discours 6–12*, ed. and trans. Calvet-Sébasti, 30–31) argue that the formulations of this Antiochene synod were the creed signed by Gregory the Elder.

151. For a positive portrayal of Jovian in the homoian historiography, see frs. 38–40 in Anhang 7, *Philostorgius: Kirchengeschichte*, ed. Bidez and Winkelmann, 237–38. For Eunomius's mission to Jovian, Philost. *HE* 8.6; Brennecke, *Studien*, 169. For the homoiousian bishops, Socr. *HE* 3.25, Brennecke, *Studien*, 168. The Nicene historians preserve traces of a homoian and a different Athanasian tradition regarding this period; Socr. *HE* 3.24.1, 25.2; Soz. *HE* 6.4.3; Brennecke, *Studien*, 159 n. 3.

father's homoian credentials with those of the almost-martyred Marc of Arethusa. Gregory advised Jovian and his successor Valens (during whose rule Gregory completed *Oration* 4 after Jovian died on February 16, 364) to emulate Constantius's comportment. But that admonition, implicit in Gregory's panegyric for Constantius, that the new emperor (or emperors) should aim primarily for the unity among Christians that Constantius's concord had achieved, addressed first the opponents of that unity in Nazianzus. The literary formulations Gregory used to imply that his advice was for the new emperors, thereby suggesting that he was close to the good emperor and resisted the bad to the point of martyrdom (which is not to say that he really thought he was influencing current imperial policy), added authority to his persuasion of his peers and friends at Nazianzus.[152]

Although Gregory appealed to the homoian consensus in his offer of reconciliation, it was on his terms, which indicates that he also had in mind the *oikoumenē* at large when formulating his new platform. First, the simplicity of a Constantius no longer sufficed. Scripture could not merely be read literally. To arrive at its deeper meaning—to comprehend the Trinity as fully as humanly possible—required a precise understanding of Greek philosophy (that is, *logoi*), which if rightly done permitted even the use of nonscriptural (man-made, humanly invented, *thesei*) language to describe divine things, such as *homoousios* or *theōsis*. A simple rejection of Greek learning, philosophy, and the true philosophical life was no longer tenable. Second, to read scripture properly required the right *theōria*, attainable only by a correct understanding of philosophy and by leading the true philosophical life, rejecting the false sophistication of *technologoi* such as Eunomius, whose misuse of philosophical techniques (à la Julian) had led him to preserve the Father's transcendence only at the expense of the Son's divinity (something implicit in the homoian position). Gregory's position differed from all three—homoian, literal, and the *akribēs* position of Eunomius—by insisting on the monarchy of the Father that by its hierarchical relation ensured the full divinity and full humanity of the Son.[153]

Concord and Oikeiōsis pros Theon

Oration 4 might have done the trick. By late 364 Gregory, with his *Oration* 6, *On Peace,* celebrated the reconciliation of his father's opponents.[154] When *Oration* 6 is

---

152. Regali, "Intenti," 404–9, suggested that Gregory's conciliatory tone vis-à-vis the homoians aimed at a broader coalition capable of directing the new emperor's Christian policies. I agree entirely but am less sanguine that Gregory hoped to influence concrete measures. Rather, I think he used Jovian's policy of returning to Constantius to effect change in Nazianzus, though what was good for Nazianzus was also good for the *oikoumenē* and vice versa.

153. Hil. *Syn.* 11, *PL* 10.488A; Brennecke, *Studien,* 104, 176–78. Interesting, though focusing on Marius Victorinus, is Abramowski, "Trinitarische und christologische Hypostasenformeln," 41–47.

154. For the context, above, Chapter 5; McLynn, "Gregory the Peacemaker," 194–216; McGuckin, *St. Gregory,* 135–40.

read in the context of *Oration 4*, something not usually done, a synopsis of the essential elements of *Oration 4*'s theology is evident, highlighting and elaborating the central points. For example, in *Oration 6* Gregory presented a full formulation of his understanding of the Trinity, phrased succinctly in *Orations 1* and *2* and only implied in *Oration 4*. That formulation was deeply embedded in the tenets of *oikeiōsis pros theon;* it used the controversial terms *ousia* and *hypostasis*.[155]

Gregory begins, "Eagerness has loosened my tongue," bound while the Evil instigated "our members [to rebel] against us, and the great and precious body of Christ was so divided and shattered that almost 'our bones were dispersed to the doors of Hades' [Ps 140:7]." Now sufficiently purified by the philosophy founded on deeds, Gregory was willing to break the silence such division imposed on him.[156] He offered his oration of peace to the reunited community and to God as the "most proper sacrifice, a more precious gift than gold, ... than incense and holocausts, than the thousands of 'fat lambs' with which an elementary Law ruled the infant Israel.... That is what I bring to God: I consecrate to him the one thing that I have preserved for myself, in which I am rich.... I have clung to the word alone as servant to the Word, and never out of my own will could I neglect this good."[157]

Gregory spelled out the terms of his sacrifice, the modus of reconciliation, lest anyone think "that I consider any kind of peace satisfactory."[158] He reiterated his definition of the Trinity three times, insisting that it "is with us firm and unshaken, just as it is in its very nature, and to take away something from the Trinity, or to consider [one of its parts] foreign to it, is to us the equivalent of doing away with the whole."[159] The unity of the Trinity and therefore the absence of division are the leitmotifs of *Oration 6*, because the person who had caused division among Christians was no more, thanks to the divine pedagogue's altruistic benevolence (*Or*. 6.7–8). With its series of allusions to *Oration 4*, *Oration 6* becomes yet another paragon of literary *damnatio memoriae*, because Julian, never mentioned, highlights by his obvious absence his all-too-recent presence, never to be forgotten.

The essential Greek civic virtues, good order, unity, and harmony, are proper to

---

155. McGuckin, *St. Gregory*, 139 n. 192, comments that Gregory in *Or*. 6 "strangely, does not have Christology to the fore," which unduly separates Gregory's Christology from his Trinitarian teachings. McGuckin suggests that Gregory added *Or*. 6.22 in the late 380s; in my reading it fits in the text, and I see no reason for a later insertion.

156. Gr. Naz. *Or*. 6.1: τὸ μέγα καὶ τίμιον σῶμα Χριστοῦ διῃρεῖτο καὶ διεκόπτετο ... τῇ δι' ἔργων φιλοσοφίᾳ.

157. Gr. Naz. *Or*. 6.4–5: τῷ Θεῷ χαριστήριον θυσίαν οἰκειοτάτην ... τοῦτο προσφέρω Θεῷ, τοῦτο ἀνατίθημι ὃ μόνον ἐμαυτῷ κατέλιπον, ᾧ πλουτῶ μόνῳ ... τοῦ λόγου δὲ περιέχομαι μόνου ὡς Λόγου θεραπευτής, καὶ οὐκ ἄν ποτε ἑκὼν τούτου τοῦ κτήματος ἀμελήσαιμι.

158. Gr. Naz. *Or*. 6.20: καὶ μηδεὶς οἰέσθω με λέγειν ὅτι πᾶσαν εἰρήνην ἀγαπητέον. Jovian's peace had not been a satisfactory one, Gr. Naz. *Or*. 5.15.

159. Gr. Naz. *Or*. 6.11: παρ' ἡμῖν ἡ Τριὰς καὶ ἀσάλευτος, οὐδέν γε ἐν αὐτῇ τῇ φύσει, καὶ τὸ περικόψαι τι τῶν Τριῶν ἢ ἀποξενῶσαι ἴσον ἡμῖν καὶ τὸ πᾶν ἀνελεῖν.

Christians, because they are (their) God's essential qualities. Like peace, they are attached to the Good and to God (*Or.* 6.20). Indeed, nothing is further from God's nature than rupture and division (*lysis* and *stasis*), and Peace and Love are among the appellatives God favors most because "he presents himself to us through the mediation of names so that we may lay claim to the virtues that appertain to him." Names are of divine origin but mediated through human invention.[160]

Gregory preceded his definition of the Trinity as one, at the center of the oration, by evoking the entire *kosmos*—the angels, the divinely created order of nature, and the history of Israel—to demonstrate that Christianity, peace, and the harmonious order of everything in the correct sequence of subordination are one and the same, and *stasis*, rebellion, and discord are proper to those on the outside.[161] Some angelic powers revolted by choice, and they were punished, so that order was maintained and all participated "in unity as the gift of the admirable and saintly Trinity ... [that] is in effect one God—and we have faith in that—no less on account of [the Trinity's] concord than on account of the sameness of substance."[162] *Homonoia* and good order are essential components of the chain of *oikeiōsis* linking everything and everyone to the divine. And they are central to Gregory's formulation of the Trinity. Because concord, harmony, and kinship function as integrative metaphors, in which the Father-Son relation (that is, Christology) is subsumed, Gregory shifts the focus so that the relational element that orders and links all three participants in the Trinity, including the Spirit, supersedes causality. The contextual relation implied in these names matters more than the causal link they also connote (as Eunomius had not grasped). Thus the Son as first link in the chain of *oikeiōsis* is both fully divine and fully human, for he fully assumed our humanity and was fully affiliated with God as one. Somewhat analogously to the One revealing itself through statues, humans can worship the One in a manner appropriate to them and thereby achieve greater proximity to the divine: the Son assumed our humanity so that man could comprehend

---

160. Gr. Naz. *Or.* 6.12: ἡμῖν παρέχων διὰ τῶν ὀνομάτων ὡς Θεοῦ τούτων μεταποιεῖσθαι τῶν ἀρετῶν. Scholars have expressed discomfort at Gregory's (monarchic) conceptualization of the Father as first essence; Cross, "Divine Monarchy," 106–7. But see Gr. Naz. *Or.* 29.4, 30.1, 31.23 and 33, where Gregory's argument that God is the prior cause anticipates Proclus's notion that the gods create by naming (*poiein*): Gregory's God eternally caused himself as well as the three *hypostaseis*, and as first cause the Father assures the eternal existence of all three in their specificity; see also *Or.* 25.15–16.

161. Gr. Naz. *Or.* 6.12: "God is the most beautiful and the most elevated of all that exists, unless one prefers to place him above all being or to place all being completely into him, from whom it also [proceeds] to all others [εἰ μή τῳ φίλον καὶ ὑπὲρ τὴν οὐσίαν ἄγειν αὐτόν, ἢ ὅλον ἐν αὐτῷ τιθέναι τὸ εἶναι, παρ' οὗ καὶ τοῖς ἄλλοις]. Second, let us consider all that at the beginning has come from God and is around him: I am speaking of the angelic and celestial powers, which are lights and reflections, because they have first enjoyed the divine light and have been illuminated by it."

162. Gr. Naz. *Or.* 6.13: καὶ ἀστασίαστον, τὸ ἓν εἶναι λαβόντες παρὰ τῆς ἐπαινετῆς καὶ ἁγίας Τριάδος. . . . Ἐπεὶ κἀκείνη εἷς Θεός ἐστί τε καὶ εἶναι πιστεύεται, οὐχ ἧττον διὰ τὴν ὁμόνοιαν ἢ τὴν τῆς οὐσίας ταὐτότητα.

the divine to the extent possible. "The soul, created according to God's image, [should take heed] to preserve its nobility to the extent possible by taking him as model and by making itself his own as much as possible."[163]

Emulating the divinely ordered harmony and concord proper to the Trinity should be easy, because it is natural: the entire cosmos reveals the golden mean, harmony and peace, the divine laws of creation.[164] The artistic Logos (*ho technitēs Logos*) has bound the whole together through his *eunoia,* his benevolence, so "that all forms one *kosmos* [order] . . . of an inaccessible beauty, and nothing more splendid or more magnificent can be conceived." Such ruptures of that natural harmony as earthquakes, floods, eclipses, and harsh seasons are God's punishment for the sinners whose *stasis* has disrupted that divine order (*Or.* 6.14–15; Pl. *Ti.* 36a).[165] Here Gregory resumes the history of the people of Israel, not to argue about cultural borrowing but to compare the stele represented by the disastrous effects of Israel's revolt on its people, cities, armies, households, and friends to his own *stēlographia* of Julian's revolt (*Or.* 6.17–18). Israel prospered as long as it listened to its divinely inspired priests and remained in harmony with God. But when it revolted against God by ignoring his Son, God in man, it brought down "the iron rod that had threatened them from afar—I mean that power and that empire that dominate them today—and what happened, and how have they suffered?"[166]

Christians who are divided are worse than rebellious Jews, however, because they "return, as one says, to their own vomit" after they have been instructed how to behave better. To persevere in division as a Christian is thus a matter of choice and lack of discipline rather than of ignorance; as such it is far worse than the behavior of those who vacillate between good and bad for lack of proper guidance. The lack of discipline requires imposition of order by law, as if by a tyrant, since free choice has failed. Gregory had already shown in *Oration* 4.99 that imposed order is not optimal, when he contrasted Julian's misguided efforts to impose one set of ethical behavior by law with Christian free choice: Julian had not recognized, according to Gregory, that a dual ethics was necessary because humans differ in their capacity to behave ethically (*Or.* 6.19–20, responding to Julian's snide remark in *Against the Galileans,* and in *Caesars,* that Christ's teachings responded to all crime with washing).[167]

---

163. Gr. Naz. *Or.* 6.14: ψυχήν, ἵν' ὡς μάλιστα τὸ εὐγενὲς αὐτῇ διασῴζηται διὰ τῆς πρὸς αὐτὰ νεύσεως καὶ ὡς ἐφικτὸν ὁμοιώσεως. *Or.* 37.1 and 3, 14.15, 19.13, 34.10.

164. When observing the relation between air and the earth, the seasons, the alternation of night and day, and so on.

165. For an excellent discussion of Gregory's vocabulary contrasting *stasis* and *homonoia,* see *Grégoire de Nazianze: Discours 6–12,* ed. and trans. Calvet-Sébasti, 33–36.

166. The Temple destroyed, the city razed—a fate so miserable that whenever Gregory reads the Book of Lamentations to remind himself to remain humble, he cries bitter tears of lamentation.

167. See above, Chapter 4, for dual ethics in the context of *oikeiōsis.*

The Trinity and the True—Mixed—Philosophical Life

After such admonitions regarding the effects of disrupting *oikeiōsis pros theon,* Gregory embraced his brothers with open arms and administered the most potent *pharmakon* of all, the Trinity,

> showing reverence to the Father, the Son, and the Holy Spirit, recognizing in the Son the Father, in the Spirit the Son, into whom we have been baptized . . . , with whom we are united, distinguishing them before uniting, and uniting before dividing them, recognizing that the Three are not like One—because the names are not without *hypostaseis* or attributed only to one *hypostasis,* as if the richness is for us in the names and not the objects [or realities]—but that the Three are One. In effect, they are One not because of their *hypostaseis* but because of their divinity. The One is revered in the Three and the Three summed up in the One, all to be revered, all regal, on one sole throne, of one unique glory, above the world, above time, uncreated, invisible, intangible, incomprehensible, alone to know the order residing in it, but worthy of being honored and served by us in the same manner; it alone penetrates into the Holy of the Holies, leaving all creatures outside; those separated by the first veil, the others by the second—that is, the celestial and angelic creatures separated by the first veil of divinity, the creatures that we are separated from the celestial powers by the second veil.[168]

Gregory's definition remained firm and unshaken, even if he subsequently adjusted, amplified, and rendered more precise various elements of his formulation, which became foundational to later Christian thinking. That formulation now was accepted by all in Nazianzus (*Or.* 6.11). It is illuminating that Gregory begins by distinguishing the three persons or *hypostaseis* before uniting them, stressing against Photinus and the so-called Sabellians their distinct characteristics.[169] "The

---

168. Gr. Naz. *Or.* 6.22: προσκυνοῦντες Πατέρα καὶ Υἱὸν καὶ ἅγιον Πνεῦμα. ἐν Υἱῷ τὸν Πατέρα, ἐν Πνεύματι τὸν Υἱὸν γινώσκοντες, εἰς ἃ βεβαπτίσμεθα, εἰς ἃ πεπιστεύκαμεν, οἷς συντετάγμεθα, πρὶν συνάψαι διαιροῦντες, καὶ πρὶν διελεῖν συνάπτοντες οὔτε τὰ Τρία ὡς ἕνα—οὐ γὰρ ἀνυπόστατα τὰ ὀνόματα, ἢ κατὰ μιᾶς ὑποστάσεως, ὡς εἶναι τὸν πλοῦτον ἡμῖν ἐν ὀνόμασιν ἀλλ' οὐ πράγμασι—καὶ τὰ Τρία ἕν. Ἓν γὰρ οὐχ ὑποστάσει ἀλλὰ θεότητι. Μονὰς ἐν Τριάδι προσκυνουμένη καὶ Τριὰς εἰς Μονάδα ἀνακεφαλαιουμένη, πᾶσα προσκυνητή, βασιλικὴ πᾶσα, ὁμόθρονος, ὁμόδοξος, ὑπερκόσμιος, ὑπέρχρονος, ἄκτιστος, ἀόρατος, ἀναφής, ἀπερίληπτος, πρὸς μὲν ἑαυτὴν ὅπως ἔχει τάξεως αὐτῇ μόνῃ γινωσκομένη, σεπτὴ δ' ἡμῖν ὁμοίως καὶ λατρευτή, καὶ μόνη τοῖς Ἁγίοις τῶν Ἁγίων ἐμβατεύουσα, τὴν δὲ κτίσιν πᾶσαν ἐκτὸς ἐῶσα, τὴν μὲν τῷ πρώτῳ, τὴν δὲ τῷ δευτέρῳ διειργομένην καταπετάσματι, πρώτῳ μὲν τὴν οὐράνιον καὶ ἀγγελικὴν ἀπὸ τῆς θεότητος, δευτέρῳ δὲ τὴν ἡμετέραν ἀπὸ τῶν οὐρανίων. See Beeley, *Gregory,* 190–91, 201–17; Gautier, *Retraite,* 300–302. Again, Beeley argues in the context of this passage that Athanasius's influence need not be assumed, *pace* Gautier and *Grégoire de Nazianze: Discours 6–12,* ed. and trans. Calvet-Sébasti, 23–24, 27–29; Ayres, *Nicaea,* 174–77. For Gregory's distinction between the intended meaning of scriptural texts and their different expressions, *Or.* 30.17, *Or.* 31, Narkevics, "Skiagraphia," 109–12.

169. To alter the essential characteristics of each *hypostasis,* to take away anything from Father, Son, or Spirit individually, destroys the whole.

Three are not like one," as he reiterated when he arrived in Constantinople in *Oration* 20.6. Next, instead of addressing the question of the equality or dissimilarity of the Father and the Son, as one might expect, Gregory focuses on the relation of the Three, beginning with the One. The Father, in Gregory's conception, is unique because he is above all existence, the first cause of all others. The Son is unique because he is caused by the Father as his own distinct *hypostasis* (as is the Spirit proceeding from the Father), but they are eternally related because of their divinity, a differentiation the homoians had not maintained rigorously enough—the Father is unbegotten, but he eternally begets the Son, who also creates eternally because he is equal in divinity to the Father. Only because the Father is Father, and hence the source of all, can he create the unity that eternally unites him with the Son and the Spirit: they are equal in divinity because they are ontologically the same. However, without the Son as Son, the Father's paternity would lose its meaning: *oikeiōsis,* good order, requires the hierarchical arrangement expressed in the Son as Son. The equality of all three is ontological and also the result of the Father, who is its cause: it is an equality based on subordination and dependence—as a good son's relation to his father demands. Subordination does not oppose equality, but equal divinity and subordination go hand in hand—this is also the central point of *oikeiōsis pros theon* or *theōsis:* an unbroken chain of divinity, expressed in a chain of subordination down to the very last and lowest link.

Rather than arguing, as Eunomius did, that the Son and the Spirit cannot be of the same essence with the Father because they are created, Gregory stresses that they are of the same essence precisely because they are created. The eternal act of creation expresses their equal divine nature; this is why they are One. But each is also distinct, because it is the function of the Son (and the Spirit) to express a particular relation to the Father. To maintain that internal hierarchical arrangement of the Trinity is important; the Son and Spirit must not be commingled with the Father. Among other things, that hierarchical order stands paradigmatic of good order, the appropriate subordination that is silently revealed in the divinely ordered cosmos. The well-functioning empire of the Romans as Christian mirrors that divine cosmos, permitting man, in turn, to know God the creator by deduction.[170]

---

170. Gregory explored these themes further in *Or.* 22 and 23, *On Peace,* and in *Or.* 28. His definition of the Trinity in *Or.* 6 also deals with the relation between *onomata* and *pragmata.* Names imitate divine *dynamis.* They are divinely created to act as intermediaries between humans and the divine, so that men can imitate divine *dynamis* by imitating what the name contains: for example, Peace and Love. Again, what matters are the *pragmata,* the realities the names denote, and not the names per se. The passage cited acknowledges that the term *hypostasis* is a homonym because one name, "God," denotes three distinct realities, Father, Son, Spirit. It is also a synonym, denoting one essence. Gregory has not yet arrived at his language theory at the conclusion of the *Theological Orations,* because Eunomius's *Apology of the Apology* has not yet forced him to outline his understanding of God's names as *kat' epinoian,*

In this context Gregory outlined again the *ēthos* required of the true philosopher as leader of all in *Oration* 6.2, echoing the passages in *Epistle* 6, *To Basil,* in which he had described life at Annesi, the true philosophical life, as asceticism. Its characteristics were those of the true philosophers of his day Gregory had contrasted with Julian's misguided philosophers: purification through vigils, tears, silence, fasts, prayers, psalms, and recitations of doxology to bring the mind closer to God, combined with disregard of hair and clothes, measured demeanor, steadfast gaze, moderate laughter, words guided by reason, silence more precious than *logoi,* and "moderation in mingling with the community as well as in retreat. The one has as its aim to teach the others; the other, the initiation into the mystery of the Spirit. The one safeguards what is not common in the community; the other, brotherly love and philanthropy in the unmixed life."[171]

The passage is one of several in which Gregory discusses the famous mixed life scholars have generally discussed in relation to eremitical, or anchoretic, and communal monastic, or cenobitic, life.[172] I want to highlight that I consider the central element of Gregory's mixed life what I have discussed as Gregory's true philosophical life in Chapters 4–6. For Gregory, the mixed life—a central theme in the study of early monasticism as it relates to episcopal office[173]—was the ideal the philosopher as mediator had to achieve in his continuing progress to the divine so that he could strengthen the link of *theōsis* in all others in his care, initiating and furthering their progress back to the divine source of all. Altruistic *oikeiōsis* achieved by subordinating the (philosopher's) self to the other (through ordination as priest) is the essential condition both for the philosopher's *theōsis* and that of his kin, his spiritual

---

describing the distinctive characteristics (*idiotētes*) of God, *Or.* 29.13, 30.18–19. Cross, "Divine Monarchy," 109–16, is important, though he focuses only on *Or.* 31; idem, "Gregory of Nyssa," discusses the Platonic implications of Gregory's language; Narkevics, "*Skiagraphia,*" 97–109.

171. Gr. Naz. *Or.* 6.2: μέτρα τῆς εἰς τὸ κοινὸν ἐπιμιξίας καὶ ὑποχωρήσεως, τῆς μὲν τοὺς ἄλλους παιδαγωγούσης, τῆς δὲ τῷ Πνεύματι μυσταγωγούσης, καὶ τῆς μὲν ἐν τῷ κοινῷ τὸ ἄκοινον φυλαττούσης, τῆς δὲ ἐν τῷ ἀμίκτῳ τὸ φιλάδελφον καὶ φιλάνθρωπον. This is the famous passage that Rufinus translated to suggest that the schismatics at Nazianzus were monks loyal to Basil and Eustathius of Sebaste, so that Gregory was torn between loyalty to Basil and the monks, and Gregory the Elder; above, Chapter 6. McLynn ("Gregory the Peacemaker," 196–200, 211–16) has shown that Gregory merely compares the unity he saw at Annesi with the division at home; idem, "Among the Hellenists," 225–33.

172. Gautier (*Retraite,* 89–112, 22–28, 54–69, 82) most recently discussed the mixed life in Gregory's oeuvre in terms of *anachōrēsis* and the coenobitic life. He mentions the Stoic component of Gregory's philosophical life—i.e., its turn outward toward others. *Pace* Gautier (p. 90), I think Gregory demanded intermittent retreat for philosopher-priests because they had to progress in purification; McGuckin, *St. Gregory,* 87, 93–101, 145–52, 190, 204–6; and 138–39 for *Or.* 6; S. Elm, "Gregory's Women," 171–75, 190–91 for his children; and eadem, "Inscriptions and Conversions," for the role of light and illumination in the progress to the divine.

173. Sterk, *Renouncing the World,* passim.

children. The *erga* of that life are plentiful: richness in poverty, transcendence of the human condition, "poor for the Kingdom [*basileia*] and kings because of their poverty" (*Or.* 6.2)—philosophy as leadership, or the ideal orthodox bishop.

Oration 6 follows *Oration* 4 with a synopsis of its main ideas, stressing the theological significance of *Oration* 4: Gregory presents a seamless whole that ties together imperial and episcopal philosophical leadership and a cohesive vision of Rome as a properly ordered, universal power that mirrors the well-ordered subordination of the Trinity as One. Integral to that proper Roman Christian order—in which the subordination of the advanced philosopher to the greater good of those in his care reflected the equality of the Father and his subordinate but divine Son—was Greek learning, stripped of all its negative elements represented by Julian. Julian as Gregory constructed him was the antithesis of the true philosopher as ruler defined by Plato in the *Laws* and *Republic*: a tyrant who playacted as emperor without realizing that he performed transient theater. His rule and his laws were illegitimate, unjust, and transient, because they were based on Julian's myths and their fanciful allegories, not on the lasting deeds of a divinely inspired system. Constantius's rule had been divinely inspired and lasting; his *eusebeia* granted unity, concord, and security of the realm, because—instructed by the bishops and priests who advised him—he knew that Christianity and Rome were one. Julian had chosen to rebel against him and against God, the source of everything, because of his selfish love of fame and honor, instilled in him by false philosophers whose teachings he had embraced because he had permitted evil to grow within him. His philosophical life (so called) disregarded the first demand of *oikeiōsis*: voluntary submission of the self to others for their benefit. Consequently, he had misunderstood the divine entirely. That he mistook the divine was manifest in his numerous mistakes in the language that denotes the divine—as in his false interpretation of the word *hellēnizein*. Julian's mistakes were also perpetrated by others who falsely applied to the Trinity philosophy wrongly understood. They too created dissension rather than preserving unity by disrupting the chain of well-ordered *oikeiōsis pros theon*, predicated on proper unity, equality, and subordination in *eutaxia*, for which the Trinity stood paradigmatic. Persons who did not grasp the interconnectedness of One in Three, good order, and the Roman *oikoumenē* as Christian could rule and lead no better than Julian had done. Those who acted and thought as Julian had were not *oikeioi* to the *oikoumenē* of Christian Romans, but were, as *Hellēnes* and heretics, forever *allotrioi*. To demonstrate how to be and how not to be a Christian Roman, especially a Christian Roman leader, had therefore been God's plan in sending Julian. Gregory as his prophet explained it: how to guide the universal Christian *oikoumenē* to the One as Three, from the correct comprehension of the divine and subordination as equality, justified war, just legislation, and the rule of law to the manner in which the city, the agora, and the theater should properly function as Christian.

10

Gregory's Second Strike, *Oration* 5

Here is our stele for you, higher and more visible than the Stelae of Hercules. Those are merely planted in one place and are visible only for those who go there. This stele, instead, cannot but move about and make itself known to all; it will be read even in the future, of that I am certain, to shame you and your works [sa stēliteuousan], and to teach everyone not to attempt such a rebellion against God, lest they may be punished in like manner for having committed similar crimes.[1]

—GREGORY OF NAZIANZUS, ORATION 5.42

"'The first of my declamatory strikes is completed and brought to an end.' . . . 'Now [on to] another target I do not know anyone else has already hit.'"[2] Gregory begins his second oration against Julian innocuously enough, seamlessly interweaving a quotation from Homer's *Odyssey* (22.5–6) with one from Proverbs (3:11–12) to alert his audience to what is to come. But in fact Gregory's opening sentence encapsulates everything he represents. The context of the seemingly innocuous remark Gregory quotes from Homer—my first strike is complete—is the brief pause before Odysseus's second and final attack on the suitors who were still alive.[3] Having already demonstrated his superior fighting skill in his first strike, Gregory as Odysseus will now kill all who have usurped his house: Julian and his followers. Gregory's second strike will have such force because the "artful *Logos* and administrator of

---

1. Gr. Naz. *Or.* 5.42: Αὕτη σοι παρ' ἡμῶν στήλη, τῶν Ἡρακλείων στηλῶν ὑψηλοτέρα τε καὶ περιφανεστέρα, . . . ἣν καὶ ὁ μέλλων ὑπολήψεται χρόνος, εὖ οἶδα, σέ τε καὶ τὰ σὰ στηλιτεύουσαν καὶ τοὺς λοιποὺς πάντας παιδεύουσαν μή τινα τοιαύτην κατὰ θεοῦ τολμᾶν ἐπανάστασιν, ἵνα μὴ τὰ ὅμοια δράσαντες τῶν ἴσων καὶ ἀντιτύχωσιν.

2. Gr. Naz. *Or.* 5.1: Οὗτος μὲν δὴ τῶν ἐμῶν λόγων ὁ πρῶτος ἄεθλος ἐκτετέλεσται καὶ διήνυσται. . . . νῦν αὖτε σκοπὸν ἄλλον, ὃν οὐκ οἶδ' εἴ τις βέβληκεν, ἤδη τοῦ λόγου προστησόμεθα.

3. Gregory returned to the same Homeric episode in *Or.* 5.39, quoting the words of Odysseus's chief cowherd while attacking Ctesippus (*Od.* 22.290). The editions used are Bernardi, ed. and trans., *Grégoire de Nazianze: Discours 4–5 contre Julien;* and Gregory of Nazianzus, *La morte di Giuliano l'Apostata: Orazione 5*, trans. and comm. Lugaresi (see 88–89, 173–74).

our destiny" has already righted God's balance (Prov. 16:11), according to which the punishment for evil, "those scourges he knows to use to educate" (Prov. 3:11–12), is meted out sooner or later, without fail. The persecutor and Apostate had received his just punishment and was dead. Gregory's first strike had, however, not been sufficient to eliminate all suitors who had so insidiously invaded his home—Odysseus's house (if Gregory's claim to own Greek *logoi* has not become obvious, here it is in a nutshell)—or there would have been no reason for him to pursue a discussion of Julian's divine visions, his Persian campaign, the circumstances of his death, and his apotheosis.

At the time of *Oration* 5 Julian and what he represented was as urgent a topic of debate as it had been immediately after his demise, if not more. This was so because Gregory composed *Oration* 5 during the troublesome period of Procopius's usurpation. Procopius was Julian's cousin and, as *comes*, had been in Persia in charge of a small army that was to divert Shapur's attention away from the main force while Julian advanced to Ctesiphon. He had been among those considered as Julian's successor, had accompanied his bier to Tarsus, and, as last scion of the Flavian dynasty, had a stronger claim to legitimacy than either Jovian or the Pannonian Valens—and rumor had it that Julian on his deathbed had appointed Procopius as successor. On September 28, 365, Procopius declared himself Augustus in Constantinople. He found significant support in the city's Christian and non-Christian elite circles and quickly gained control over Thrace and Bithynia (where Caesarius was then one of the highest financial officials).[4] Procopius's usurpation brought several issues into sharp focus. How had Julian (and Procopius) comported themselves in Persia, and what did the Persian campaign and the peace treaty ending it signify? How had Julian died, who was his legitimate successor, and how much legitimating force should Julian's (purported) endorsement of Procopius assume? How relevant was a dynastic connection to Constantine and Constantius? Whom should the true Christian public official support as emperor? The Arian Pannonian Valens, or the Christian scion of Constantine and Constantius's dynasty who, like Julian, presented himself with a beard and was Julian's cousin? In sum, how should Julian be remembered and memorialized?[5]

Oration 5 engaged these questions head on, becoming in effect the most political of the first six orations (and the last in the series I discuss). As I indicated in Chapter 8, Gregory's *Oration* 5, though thematically linked to *Oration* 4, was a sep-

---

4. For a detailed treatment of the usurpation, Lenski, *Failure*, 68–115.
5. For theories of memory and memorialization, especially those of Maurice Halbwachs, J. Assmann, *Religion;* A. Assmann, *Erinnerungsräume;* Haverkamp and Lachmann, eds., *Memoria,* esp. ix–xxvii. See E. Elm, "Damnatio," 5–34, 156–76, for the tension in Roman concepts of memory between preservation and erasure, the de-, re-, and hyper-semanticization of signs; also Varner, *Mutilation.*

arate oration, entering the debate about Julian's legacy and how he ought to be remembered urgently relevant to all members of the ruling elites, pagan and Christian, because of Procopius's usurpation. As far as the consequences of Julian's failed Persian campaign are concerned, Antiochene voices, represented by Libanius (and later Ammianus) carried a particular weight. Antioch was close to Persia, and Persia close to the Antiochenes' watchful eye; the city had nearly been lost to Persia almost a century earlier. The intended audience of Gregory's oration, thus, may well have had a particularly Antiochene bent.[6] But Procopius's usurpation also highlighted Julian's own legitimacy as Roman emperor, duly declared *divus*, divinized, by the Roman senate. How then should a hypothetical Christian ranking official react to topics such as Persia, Julian's *apotheōsis*, and arguments that pitched Valens's legitimacy against that of Procopius? To put it simply, Gregory's *Oration* 5 offered the appropriate talking points. What then were the debates assessing Julian and his aftermath in which Gregory's oration intervened, from both the pagan and the Christian vantage? Themistius's praise of Julian's direct successor, Jovian, is the appropriate starting point for answers; for once more, pagan and Christian voices crossed the pagan-Christian divide.

THE PAGAN CONTEXT

Themistius's Hypatikos *for Jovian*

On February 17, 364, Jovian died of carbon monoxide poisoning in Dardastana, a *mansio* about equidistant from Ancyra and Nicaea, barely six weeks after Themistius had praised his first consulship in Ancyra. The rule Themistius had so hopefully celebrated lasted barely eight months. Themistius's themes, however, outlasted the emperor. In Themistius's view Jovian had "adopt[ed] . . . in the sight of all" and restored "philosophy . . . to the palace once more."[7] On the basis of that philosophy, Themistius then addressed the war in Persia, Jovian's accession, the peace treaty he had concluded, and the question of the appropriate imperial position on ways to worship—themes that affected Jovian's legitimacy and that of his rule, and would also affect his successors Valentinian and, especially, Valens.

According to Themistius, Jovian had been elected with unbecoming haste. Nevertheless, he had demonstrated by hesitation and restraint that he had not lusted for power. His quick rise resulted from dire circumstances beyond his responsibility. Thus, he conformed to the Platonic ideal of the ruler and had been legitimately

---

6. For the sack of Antioch in the third century, see Dodgeon and Lieu, eds., *Roman Eastern Frontier*, 51–54.

7. Them. *Or*. 5.63c–d: φιλοσοφίαν . . . κατὰ τὸν παρόντα χρόνον ἐπανάγεις αὖθις εἰς τὰ βασίλεια . . . ἐν τοῖς ἁπάντων ὀφθαλμοῖς συμπαραλαμβάνων φιλοσοφίαν.

elected, as further demonstrated by a succession that had required neither bloody purges nor the suppression of a rebellious army. (See also *Or.* 5.70d.)[8] In addition, Shapur had acknowledged him benevolently and had been prepared to negotiate peace (*Or.* 5.65c–d, 66a–d), which had been the right move to safeguard the realm (*Or.* 5.69b–c). Jovian enhanced the *securitas rei publicae* further by his judicious selection of Friends and advisors, including Themistius (*Or.* 5.63c, 67a–b). Indeed, Jovian's choice of Christian and non-Christian advisors, and of Themistius's political philosophy above all, manifested his praiseworthy attitude toward religion.

> It is as if all the competitors in a race are hastening toward the same awarder of the prize, but not all in the same lane, some going by this route, others by that.... Thus you realize that, while there exists only one awarder of prizes, mighty and true, there is no one road leading to him, but one is more difficult to travel, another more direct, one steep, and another more level.[9] All roads, however, tend alike toward that one place of rest, and our competition and our zealousness arise from no reason other than our travel by different routes. If you allow only one path, closing off the rest, you fence off the broad field of competition.... We behaved worse toward one another than the Persians [toward us]; the written disputes of the two religious factions issuing from the city [i.e., the inside] were more damaging than the attacks [of the Persians].... Let the scale find its own balance: do not force down one side or the other, and let prayers for your rule rise to heaven from every quarter.[10]

This passage and the one that follows have received a great deal of scholarly attention. Praise in the context of a panegyric reflected the imperial political program but also expressed the speaker's ideals and hopes; it was thus a plea rather than the

---

8. Themistius appears to slight Procopius at *Or.* 5.65c by comparing the situation after Julian's demise to the aftermath of the death of Alexander: the Romans rightly chose Ptolemy (= Jovian) as successor, whereas the Macedonians had elevated Alexander's mentally impaired half-brother, Arrhidaeus (= Procopius). Themistius addressed the aftermath of Procopius's usurpation in *Or.* 7.

9. This passage may allude to Prodicus's *Choice of Hercules;* Gregory evoked the many ways to reach God in *Or.* 27.9, also emphasizing the choice between the easy and the hard road: the Eunomians chose the easy one.

10. Them. *Or.* 5.68d–69c: ὥσπερ δὲ ἐπὶ τὸν αὐτὸν ἀθλοθέτην ἵενται μὲν ἅπαντες οἱ σταδιεῖς, οὐ μὴν ἅπαντες τὸν αὐτὸν δρόμον, ἀλλ' οἱ μὲν ἔνθεν, οἱ δὲ ἔνθεν.... οὕτως ἕνα μὲν ὑπολαμβάνεις τὸν μέγαν καὶ ἀληθινὸν ἀγωνοθέτην, ὁδὸν δ' ἐπ' αὐτὸν οὐ μίαν φέρειν, ἀλλὰ τὴν μὲν δυσπορωτέραν, τὴν δὲ εὐθυτέραν, καὶ τὴν μὲν τραχεῖαν, τὴν δὲ ὁμαλήν. συντετάσθαι δὲ ὅμως ἁπάσας πρὸς τὴν μίαν ἐκείνην καταγωγήν, καὶ τὴν ἅμιλλαν ἡμῖν καὶ προθυμίαν οὐκ ἀλλαχόθεν ὑπάρχειν, ἀλλ' ἐκ τοῦ μὴ τὴν αὐτὴν πάντας βαδίζειν. εἰ δὲ μίαν μὲν ἀτραπὸν ἐάσεις, ἀποικοδομήσεις δὲ τὰς λοιπάς, ἐμφράξεις τὴν εὐρυχωρίαν τοῦ ἀγωνίσματος.... χείρους Περσῶν ἀλλήλοις ἦμεν, χαλεπώτεραι ἦσαν τῶν ἐπιδρομῶν αἱ γραφαὶ ἐξ ἑκατέρας θρησκείας παρὰ τῆς πόλεως.... ἔα μένειν τὴν τρυτάνην ἐφ' ἑαυτῆς, μὴ καθελκύσῃς ἐπὶ θάτερα τὴν ῥοπήν, ἁπανταχόθεν φοιτᾶν εἰς τὸν οὐρανὸν τὰς ὑπὲρ τῶν σκήπτρων τῶν σῶν ἱκεσίας. *Themistii Orationes,* ed. Schenkl, Downey, and Norman, vols. 2 and 3; Themistius, *Politics,* trans. Heather and Moncur, 168–69, with my modifications; German trans. Leppin and Portmann, *Themistios: Staatsreden,* 100–112; Amm. Marc. 25.10.11; Vanderspoel, *Themistius,* 135–54.

mirror of existing legislation (though it is possible that Jovian had issued a decree of religious tolerance, now lost, that Themistius summarized).¹¹ Themistius's evocation of ideal imperial comportment in religion did coincide with what we know of Jovian's behavior. He removed from the inner circle those who had opposed his election but kept others regardless of their religion, while his Christian policy was one of cautious continuity. According to Themistius, the "new Constantine" (*Or.* 5.71b) ascertained—"as divine law [*nomos empsychos*] that has come down at last from up high, as an outpouring of the everlasting Good . . . who looks in every way towards Him" (*Or.* 5.64b; Arist. *Pol.* 1284a11–15)—

> that the participation in ritual is for all men, in this respect emulating God, who made the favorable disposition toward piety a common attribute of human nature but lets the manner of worship depend on individual inclination. He who applies compulsion removes the liberty granted by God. . . . Consider that the creator of the universe also takes pleasure in such diversity. He wishes the Syrians to organize their affairs in one way, and the Greeks [*Hellēnes*] in another, the Egyptians in another, and does not wish there to be uniformity among the Syrians themselves but has already fragmented them into small groups. No individual has exactly the same beliefs as his neighbor, but one man believes this and another that. Why then do we use force when it is ineffectual?¹²

Themistius, in praising Jovian, did not spare Julian. In his view, Jovian grasped the essence of Greek religion far better than Julian, because he knew that the gods of the Greeks and Romans were truly universal: they permitted everyone—including Syrians, (that is, Christians with all their different factions)—to pursue their own path to the divine, each group with its own appropriate ritual. Julian had not grasped this, as his exclusionary attitude toward Galileans had shown; for him, ultimately, full and complete diversity had been less important than the unifying force he attributed to the universal gods of the Greeks and the Romans. Jovian instead understood the essence of Greek religion as well as Empedocles,¹³ because he knew

---

11. For a discussion of Jovian's religious laws and Themistius's view, Themistius, *Politics*, ed. and trans. Heather and Moncur, 33–35, 154–58, 169, *pace* Vanderspoel, *Themistius*, 148–53, who argues that Jovian had not yet adopted religious toleration; Wirth, "Jovian," 369–74; *Themistios: Staatsreden*, ed. and trans. Leppin and Portmann, 12–13, 100–101; and Rosen, *Julian*, 374, 376.

12. Them. *Or.* 5.68a, 70a: τὸ τῆς ἁγιστείας μέρος εἰς ἅπαντας εἶναι νομοθετεῖς, καὶ ταύτῃ ζηλῶν τὸν θεόν, ὅς τὸ μὲν ἔχειν πρὸς εὐσέβειαν ἐπιτηδείως τῆς φύσεως κοινὸν ἐποίησε τῆς ἀνθρωπίνης, τὸν τρόπον δὲ τῆς θεραπείας ἐξῆψε τῆς ἐν ἑκάστῳ βουλήσεως. ὁ δὲ προσάγων ἀνάγκην ἀφαιρεῖται τὴν ἐξουσίαν, ἣν ὁ θεὸς συνεχώρησεν. . . . [70a] ταύτῃ νόμιζε γάνυσθαι τῇ ποικιλίᾳ καὶ τὸν τοῦ παντὸς ἀρχηγέτην· ἄλλως Σύρους ἐθέλει πολιτεύεσθαι, ἄλλως Ἕλληνας, ἄλλως Αἰγυπτίους, καὶ οὐδ' αὐτοὺς Σύρους ὁμοίως, ἀλλ' ἤδη κατακεκερμάτισται εἰς μικρά. εἰς γὰρ οὐδεὶς τῷ πέλας τὰ αὐτὰ ὑπείληφεν ἀκριβῶς, ἀλλ' ὁ μὲν τοδί, ὁ δὲ τοδί. τί οὖν βιαζόμεθα τὰ ἀμήχανα; "Syrians" stands for Christians; Dagron, *Empire romain*, 159–60; Ruggini, *Simboli*, 180–82; Themistius, *Politics*, ed. and trans. Heather and Moncur, 170 n. 106.

13. Themistius added "I do not mean the ancient one," which has led scholars to differ with regard to the Empedocles referred to. Dagron (*Empire romain*, 159–63) and Vanderspoel (*Themistius*, 25–26)

how to distinguish temples from "the haunts of impostors," and "lawful sacrifices" (*thysias ennomous*) from "magic arts" (*tois goēteuousin*, *Or.* 5.70b–c; that Julian mistook magic for sacrifice anticipates Ammianus's criticism of his excessive reliance on un-Roman divinatory practices). At the same time, Themistius stressed that Christians also represented but one religious custom that likewise ought not to be favored to the detriment of those of either the Greeks or the Egyptians. Julian's mistake should not be repeated under a different premise; to declare one among the many roads leading to God the only one, and thus fence off all others, was not proper to the divine creator, who had purposely created diverse approaches to him. The good order and harmonious unity created by different ethnicities and their *nomoi*, as one, reflected divine harmony and unity. That was the essence of Rome's harmonizing universality, and Jovian represented it well.[14]

The majority of modern scholars do not share Themistius's positive picture of Jovian—in a panegyric written by a Constantinopolitan. They tend to follow the Antioch-centered assessment of Libanius and Ammianus. Modern historians have, further, accepted the perspective of the Alexandria-centered, Nicene, Christian historiographic tradition, beginning with Epiphanius and followed by Rufinus, which focused on Athanasius's supposed conversion of Jovian to the Nicene faith. This view of Jovian differs markedly from the homoian historiographic view, wherein Jovian is the restorer of Constantius's homoian position, as supported by Gregory's *Orations* 4 and 6.[15] It was this homoian or Arian Jovian whom Valentinian (made Augustus February 25, 364) and his brother, Valens (coruler from March 28, 364), succeeded. None of these emperors voiced any doubt about Julian's legitimacy as emperor; religious tolerance evidently applied to Roman rulers. Procopius, ordered by Jovian to accompany Julian's bier to Tarsus (a risky move, given the significance of such a ceremonial act for the continuity of the reign), began construction there of the mausoleum the deceased emperor had requested.[16] The Roman senate officially attested that Julian "inter divos relatus est": that is, affirmed his official apotheosis.[17] Valentinian and Valens spent lavishly on the completion of the mausoleum.

---

think that this is a swipe against Christ, whereas Ruggini (*Simboli*, 177–87) reads this as criticism of Julian, as do I: the Christian Jovian knew Greek religion better than Julian, the new Empedocles; Themistius, *Politics*, ed. and trans. Heather and Moncur, 170 n. 109.

14. Though he addressed Julian, Libanius concurred when he stressed in *Or.* 12.15 that each city and place differ in praising the gods.

15. Eutr. 10.17, writing for the homoian Valens, agreed with Themistius. Jovian was the legitimate successor, and his handling of the Persian disaster was necessary, albeit shameful; Amm. Marc. 25.5.4–9; Lib. *Ep.* 1193.5; for the Nicene voices, Epiph. *Haer.* 61.11; Rufin. *HE* 11.31; Wirth, "Jovian," 353–84, offers a revision of previous scholarly assessments; Brennecke, *Studien*, 159–73.

16. Amm. Marc. 25.9.12.

17. Eutr. 10.16.2; Symm. *Rel.* 40.3; Ruggini, "Apoteosi," 433–35, 455; Matthews, *Roman Empire*, 180–203.

Julian and not the short-lived Jovian was the link connecting them to the long chain of their precursors.[18] Theodosius ordered that Julian's sarcophagus be transferred from Tarsus to Constantinople and laid to rest in Constantine's mausoleum in the Church of the Apostles that Constantius had completed. There, among Christian emperors and their wives, in the grand mausoleum of the dynasty to which he had belonged and that he had represented, Julian found his final resting place next to Helena, honored with an epitaph that ended with a verse from the *Iliad*. Whoever erased his name from inscriptions and statues did so at a much later time.[19] So much for Gregory's *damnatio memoriae* and the centuries of Christian defamation of the Apostate: these affected Julian's *Nachleben* but not his legitimacy.

Libanius's Monody *and His* Epitaphius: *Julian Remembered*

However clearly the emperors demonstrated and continued to demonstrate that Julian had been legitimate, the debate about the topics Themistius had raised in his praise of Jovian persisted. Who had been responsible for Julian's death? Was the peace treaty truly necessary and appropriate? What role should religion play in the *oikoumenē*, and what role had it played in the Persian campaign?[20] Libanius had asked for a copy of Themistius's *hypatikos* for Jovian, but his orations lamenting and praising the deceased Julian show that he (and, later on, Ammianus) saw things differently.[21] Libanius completed his *Monody* on the dead emperor by the spring of 364, and his *Epitaphius*, in all probability written for the occasion of the deceased emperor's birthday, in late May or early June 365.[22] By that time, Valentinian and Valens, residing outside Naissus, had divided the empire and its army. Valens had returned to Constantinople, and Valentinian to Milan. In 365, Valentinian had to engage the Alamanni, because the situation on the Western frontier had deteriorated significantly.[23] Earlier, between March and April 364, Valentinian had con-

---

18. Lib. *Or.* 24.10; Amm. Marc. 26.1.4–5, 4.2; Lenski, *Failure*, 18–33; Rosen, *Julian*, 391.

19. For the inscription on the grave, Zonaras 13.13.24; Zosimus 3.34.4; the verse is *Il.* 3.179; Lib. *Or.* 59.12. Some manuscripts credit Libanius with the authorship of the epitaph, placing it at the end of *Or.* 18; *Libanii opera*, ed. Foerster, vol. 2, 317. C. Mango, "Three Imperial Byzantine Sarcophagi"; Basset, *Urban Image*, 32. For erasures, Conti, *Inschriften*, nos. 28, 32, 35, 136, 170, 174; private erasures of imperial names would have been highly irregular.

20. Martig, *Studi*, 11–14.

21. Lib. *Ep.* 1193.5 implicitly criticized Themistius as magnifying little things; Amm. Marc. 25.5.4–9.

22. The orations are dated between 363 and 368; Wiemer's dating (*Libanios*, 251–55, 260–66) of *Or.* 17 to spring or early summer 364 and of *Or.* 18 as prior to the earthquake on July 21, 365, represents the consensus, *pace* Felgentreu, "Zur Datierung," 206–17, who assumes the end of Maximus's incarceration in the summer of 366 as *terminus ante quem;* G. Kelly, "Ammianus," 142–47; Martig, *Studi;* 19–23; Wintjes, *Leben*, 20.

23. Amm. Marc. 26.5.1–4, 27.1–2. Themistius defended Jovian's peace even more emphatically in *Or.* 8.114c–d, his praise of Valens and Valentinian's first joint consulate delivered January 1, 365, because of the worsening Western situation.

demned Maximus of Ephesus to a hefty fine, and when he had been unable to pay, he was left to bake in the sun before being thrown in prison, not to be released until 366. According to Eunapius, Priscus suffered a similar fate. All these events found their echo in Libanius's two orations. On July 21, 365, an earthquake and a subsequent tsunami devastated the eastern littoral of the Mediterranean, and on September 28, 365, Procopius declared himself Augustus in Constantinople, calamities that appeared to corroborate all of Libanius's dire predictions for the future of the realm after Julian's demise.[24]

Libanius's *Monody* (*Oration* 17) was a prose version of the poetic lament (*thrēnos*) that expressed an author's personal sorrow and sadness, unlike an *epitaphios logos*, which praised the virtues of the deceased to console his relatives.[25] Libanius in his *Monody* asked the question that touched him most deeply (and that Menander Rhetor considered a crucial topos of the genre: "to rail against the gods"): Why had the gods on whom Julian had lavished his attention decreed his life so brief and transient, while permitting Constantine, who had fought them tooth and nail, to rule for nearly forty years?[26] The transience of Julian's rule prevented the happiness he brought to the *oikoumenē* from taking root; why had the gods decreed such a fate (*Or.* 17.4–5, 8–10)?[27] Doubts about the wisdom of the Persian campaign surface: true, Julian had failed to balance crime against punishment when marching to fight Shapur; in hindsight, diplomacy would have been better (*Or.* 17.19–20). The Persian campaign had been heroic, however, and Julian's courage was not diminished by his certainty (which Libanius had shared) that the gods marched alongside his army, assuring its victory (*Or.* 17.5–6). Such certainty had made Julian rash, but the gods ought to have been more merciful and forgiving (*Or.* 17.6, 23–24). Who was the Persian horseman who launched the fatal lance (*Or.* 17.23, 32)? Now Julian had gone to a better place. All that remained for the Muses, the philosophers and rhetoricians, the peasants and the magistrates, the poor and those depending on justice—indeed, the entire cosmos—was to lament the dark times ahead: earthquakes and conflagrations would ravage the realm (*Or.* 17.23–29).[28] Only the (Western) bar-

---

24. Eun. *VS* 7.4.11–5.8; Lib. *Or.* 18.287; Them. *Or.* 7.100b-c; Matthews, *Roman Empire*, 191–203; Martig, *Studi*, 19. For earthquakes as portents, G. Kelly, "Ammianus," 143–48. Dagron, *Empire romain*, 71 n. 207, considers the repressive measures against Maximus and other Friends of Julian a response to Procopius's usurpation and has them begin September 365.

25. For monodies for persons (rather than destroyed cities), Men. Rh. *Treatise* 2.16 (*Menander Rhetor*, ed. and trans. Russell and Wilson, 200–206; *Peri epideiktikōn*, ed. Spengel, 434.10–437.4).

26. For the literary aspects of *Or.* 17 and 18, Libanius, *Kaiserreden*, trans. and comm. Fatouros, Krischer, and Portmann, 127–31; Wiemer, *Libanios*, 247–48.

27. Here follows a brief summary of Julian's youth, rise, and rule: *Or.* 17.14–21.

28. Perhaps an allusion to the burning of the Traianaeum, completed by Julian, and its library in the fall of 363. The *Suda* 401 [Adler vol. 2, 638] blamed Jovian's wife, Charito, for the fire, though she

barians (*Or.* 17.30)²⁹ and those who had already removed Julian's images from the palace and the marketplaces and had ended the sacrifices rejoiced. But they could remove as many images as they liked—this would not end the lament, the tears, the sadness, which would be everlasting (*Or.* 17.34–35). Libanius had lost his friend, and sorrow nearly robbed him of his rational faculties. Would madness not have been better than mourning without consolation (*Or.* 17.38)?

The *Monody* had presumably been shared only with a small audience of friends and companions. When Libanius set about composing the *Epitaphius* (*Or.* 18) about a year later, the intended audience was that of his *Hypaticus* (*Or.* 12) celebrating Julian's consulate: that is, all who mattered in the empire. Libanius chose the appropriate genre, which—to console the audience—called for the praise of the deceased's native land, noble birth, physical beauty, youth, education, marriage, and, more than those, his virtues, deeds, good fortune, and his end.³⁰ Libanius changed his emphasis and his interpretation of key events, in part responding to the different demands of genre and audience, and in part to accommodate insights gained in preparing the *Epitaphius* not yet available when he composed the *Monody*. Rumors and debates, moreover, had not ceased in the interim.³¹ It also created the impression that Libanius had not sought to approach Jovian's court, as he had in fact done.³²

---

did not visit Antioch while Jovian was emperor; Zon. 13.14, *PG* 134.1160; Cedrenus *PG* 121.588C; Joh. Ant. fr. 181 (John of Antioch, *Fragments*, in *Excerpta historica*, vol. 2, *Excerpta de virtutibus et vitiis*, ed. Büttner-Wobst, 201–2).

29. Whose delegates Julian had dismissed; Lib. *Or.* 12.78; Amm. Marc. 22.7.7–8.

30. For the genre *epitaphios logos*, Men. Rh. *Treatise* 2.9 (*Menander Rhetor*, ed. and trans. Russell and Wilson, 170–78; *Peri epideiktikōn*, ed. Spengel, 419.11–422.4). For the audience of Lib. *Or.* 12, Wiemer, *Libanios*, 154–59, 256–58 for that of *Or.* 17, and 266–68 for *Or.* 18; he argues for publication only after Valens's death. Lib. *Or.* 18.4 and 6 state what public he had in mind; Felgentreu, "Zur Datierung," 215–16; Criscuolo, "Giuliano."

31. For the historical aspects of the genre Libanius used his earlier orations, Julian's *Epistle to the Athenians*, personal letters such as *Ep.* 98, in which Julian detailed aspects of the campaign, and Julian's lost *Bellum Gallicum*. Libanius also used the correspondence and field notes of friends who had participated in the campaign, deploring their slow delivery of promised materials. Jul. *Ep.* 98 (Wright 58); Lib. *Epp.* 1220.7, 1434.1; *Epp.* 802, 811, *To Julian*; *Epp.* 1434, 1508, to friends. For Julian's lost work on his Gallic campaigns, Lib. *Or.* 13.25; Eun. *Hist.* 9.

32. For Libanius's efforts to gain access to Jovian, Wintjes, *Leben*, 151–62. The debate about Ammianus's sources continues: Sabbah, *Méthode*, 170–71, 255–66, thinks that Ammianus as historian consciously resisted the persuasive temptation of Libanius's works, especially *Or.* 18, concluding that Ammianus did not use Libanius on the Persian campaign; but he sees points of contact with Themistius (pp. 347–66, for example, countering Themistius's *Or.* 5) and with Gregory's invectives (pp. 369–72); Martig, *Studi*, 21–24. G. Kelly, *Ammianus*, 156–58, 254–55, elaborates T. D. Barnes's important suggestion (*Ammianus*, 49–53, 79–94) that Ammianus was brought up Christian and used Christian texts. Kelly does not discuss Gregory's two orations, but I think Ammianus was aware of them, either directly or through Libanius. Kelly (pp. 92–100) demonstrates how Ammianus used the tsunami as a metaphor

The *Epitaphius* became more influential than the *Monody;* Ammianus Marcellinus was presumably aware of it. It is no surprise that the *Epitaphius* echoes Julian's positions. Libanius held Constantius responsible for the massacre of Julian's family, his imprisonment at Macellum, and the inferiority of his initial Christian education. Gallus's elevation as Caesar had only one redeeming virtue: it permitted Julian to pursue true philosophy. At first this pursuit had been a secret, but all who were close to him (such as Libanius) could readily imagine how Julian would cure the *oikoumenē* of its ills if he could join power to his newfound wisdom (*Or.* 18.7–24). Libanius mentions Julian's Athenian sojourn and his reluctant acceptance of the rank of Caesar, and then describes his successful campaigns in the West in detail, reflecting Julian's *Epistle to the Athenians* and presumably his lost work on the Gallic wars (*Or.* 18.26–97). The Rhine army's elevation of Julian to Augustus in Paris was entirely legitimate: Libanius affords pride of place to Julian's reluctant acceptance of the army's wishes, and to his gratitude and obedience to Constantius (*Or.* 18.90–106).[33] Constantius's death and proper burial further highlight Julian's filial piety; he honored Constantius and his memory, just as Jovian and Valens honored his (*Or.* 18.98–121).

Libanius's presentation of Julian's deeds as Augustus begins with the restitution of the cult of the gods and the reforms at court (*Or.* 18.131–40), followed by the purges of the *agentes in rebus,* the reform of the *cursus publicus,* and legislative acts in favor of the cities, especially regarding the *curiales* (*Or.* 18.141–54)—circles of imperial activity extending outward whose structure parallels what Gregory employed in *Oration* 4. Indeed, the structural parallels between Gregory's *Oration* 4 and Libanius's *Epitaphius* reflect the demands of the genre: invective is the inverse of orations of praise, of which the *epitaphios logos* is a specific form. Both genres trace the trajectory from birth, youth, and education to deeds and virtues, albeit with diametrically opposed aims and intentions.

Before addressing Julian's sojourn in Antioch, his home turf, Libanius praised Julian's deeds for *logoi,* "the siblings of the divine rites [*hiera*]," such as his orations *Against the Uneducated Cynics* and the *Hymn to the Mother of the Gods* (*Or.* 18.157–65). While in Antioch (*Or.* 18.163–203), Julian displayed his religiosity, ascetic personal habits, generosity toward friends and enemies alike for all to see, as well as his disciplined administration and just legislation, and his philosophical aversion to the theater and the hippodrome. He blessed all with more outstanding gifts to *logoi,* especially *Against the Galileans.* Like a new Proteus, Julian was "at the same time priest, writer, diviner, judge, soldier, and savior of all."[34]

---

proving that Jovian and his successors were far less able than Julian; see also Kelly's discussion of allusion at pp. 165–221.

33. Libanius, *Kaiserreden,* trans. and comm. Fatouros, Krischer, and Portmann, 183–89.

34. Lib. *Or.* 18.176: πάντα δὲ ἐπόνει μόνος τὰς Πρωτέως μεταβολὰς ἐν τοῖς πραττομένοις παριών, ὁ αὐτὸς ἱερεύς, λογογράφος, μάντις, δικαστής, στρατιώτης, διὰ πάντων σωτήρ. See *Or.* 12.91.

After a brief summary of the events prompting the *Misopogon*,[35] Libanius devoted a third of the oration to the march toward Ctesiphon and Julian's death (*Or.* 18.204–80).[36] In contrast to the *Monody*, Libanius now no longer questioned the wisdom of the enterprise. Julian's heroic conduct is the principal theme: he was victorious when he perished. Constantius's hesitant tactics and Persian defeats are the foil Libanius uses to showcase Julian as the superior *stratēgos* (*Or.* 18.205–11). Julian had not acted rashly (as he had done in the *Monody*), had not misread oracles and divine portents, and had not vainly sought to emulate Alexander. He had been forced, instead, to confront Shapur because of Constantius's mistakes, rooted in the failures of Constantine. (See Chapter 7.) As he had done from Paris to Naissus, Julian advanced rapidly yet with circumspection. Filling the Euphrates with ships, he went from victory to glorious victory all the way to Ctesiphon (*Or.* 18.212–44). There the situation required a decisive act. Finding himself and the army between two rivers, a devastated countryside behind them and the Persians ahead, Julian did not hesitate but pressed forward. He crossed the Tigris, attacked, and almost captured Ctesiphon—a glorious victory, after which Julian initiated the retreat. He burned the ships in a well-thought-out move to free hands that would otherwise be engaged in moving ships upstream; it also motivated the soldiers by removing a means of rest. The orderly return to Rome continued—Libanius makes no mention of food shortages or the desolate situation of the army—until the fatal moment in the heat of battling the pursuing Persians when Julian was fatally wounded (*Or.* 18.244–64).

"Shall I veil the rest with silence? . . . I must speak and put an end to the untrue reports regarding his death."[37] The details of Libanius's account of that day and night, as well as his literary framing of Julian's death as that of another Socrates—calm, composed, serene—anticipate Ammianus (*Or.* 18.272–73).[38] But for our purpose another point is crucial: Libanius now identified a culprit. In the *Monody* he had declared that a Persian lance wounded the emperor fatally. Now he concluded that this could not have been the case, because no Persian ever claimed the reward offered (*Or.* 18.274). Instead, Romans must "search for the murderer among ourselves. Those who reaped no advantage if he remained alive—those who did not live according to the laws—had already plotted against him in the past and now seized the opportunity to kill him; their tendency toward injustice, which they could not

---

35. In this context Libanius mentions an episode when Julian executed ten soldiers (*Or.* 18.199), perhaps the one to which Gregory referred in the context of the *donativum* (*Or.* 4.83).

36. Libanius's sources for this part differ from those of Ammianus. Ammianus was present, but it is possible that he and Libanius (and Eunapius and Zosimus) used Oribasius's *Hypomnema*. Sabbah, *Méthode*, 200, 261–66; den Boeft, den Hengst, and Teitler, eds., *Philological and Historical Commentary on Ammianus Marcellinus 23*, xii–xiv; Matthews, *Roman Empire*, 161–75.

37. Lib. *Or.* 18.267: βούλεσθε σιγήσω τὰ λοιπά. . . . ῥητέον δὴ καὶ δόξαν οὐκ ἀληθῆ περὶ τῆς τελευτῆς παυστέον.

38. Amm. Marc. 25.3.15, evoking Pl. *Phd.*; also Pl. *Ap.* 42a.

exercise under his rule, and especially the honors he paid to the gods, which they strenuously opposed, brought them to this."[39] To accuse a Christian member of the army of having murdered the emperor in battle was a grave accusation indeed.[40]

To hammer home the gravity of that accusation—if that were necessary—Libanius left no doubt that the Persian campaign, previously victorious, turned disastrous as a result of Julian's death (Or. 18.276). Jovian, another weak and indecisive ruler, did everything he could to placate the Persian king and never even contemplated battle (a point Ammianus also stressed). Libanius could only marvel that Shapur had not demanded more cities and provinces—indeed, Antioch and even Constantinople (Or. 18.277–80). And the disasters did not end there. The entire *oikoumenē* was turned upside down. Why had the gods decreed such a fate for Julian and the *oikoumenē*, only just recovering from the fatal disease (Or. 18.281)? The *synkrisis* with others who died prematurely allowed Libanius to demonstrate that every one of Julian's deeds and the virtues they represented had now been reverted. Demagogues who spoke against the gods were revered, and priests and philosophers (such as Maximus) tortured in the scorching sun and imprisoned (Or. 18.286–87). Teachers of rhetoric were dismissed as if they were murderers; *curiales* shirked their duties; abject poverty reigned, and barbarians were sharpening their swords to attack the realm, whose cities were ravaged by earthquakes (Or. 18.288–92). Few consolations remained. Julian's writings, including his letters (which Libanius may in fact have published) survived him as his true immortal children,[41] and his many portraits in the cities and temples were venerated as if they were gods, "so evidently has he been received among the gods, so clearly did they consider him a partaker in the power of the divine." After all, the gods "themselves [have] given him part of their power."[42] To him, the child of the gods, the disciple of the gods, the companion and trusted friend of the gods who spurned all pleasure except *logoi*, Libanius offered his *logos* (Or. 18.308).

Ugo Criscuolo (wishing to soften Gilbert Dagron's view of Libanius as the voice of a pagan opposition he rightly considers less hardened than it would become under Theodosius) argued against reading Libanius's *Epitaphius* as a political state-

---

39. Lib. Or. 18.275: παρ' ἡμῖν αὐτοῖς τὸν σφαγέα ζητεῖν. οἷς γὰρ οὐκ ἐλυσιτέλει ζῶν, οὗτοι δὲ ἦσαν οἱ ζῶντες οὐ κατὰ τοὺς νόμους, πάλαι τε ἐπεβούλευον καὶ τότε δυνηθέντες εἰργάσαντο τῆς τε ἄλλης ἀδικίας αὐτοὺς ἀναγκαζούσης οὐκ ἐχούσης ἐπὶ τῆς ἐκείνου βασιλείας ἐξουσίαν καὶ μάλιστά γε τοῦ τιμᾶσθαι τοὺς θεούς, οὗ τὸ ἐναντίον ἐζήτουν.

40. In Or. 24.6, *To the Emperor Theodosius I*, Libanius asserted that a "Taienos," a Tayy Arab or Saracen, was the culprit; Amm. Marc. 25.6.6 remains uncertain but also hints at a Roman (Christian); den Boeft, Drijvers, et al., *Philological and Historical Commentary on Ammianus Marcellinus 25*, 206–7; Matthews, *Roman Empire*, 182–83.

41. Gregory also called his writings his children: S. Elm, "Gregory's Women," 190–91.

42. Lib. Or. 18.302–5: οὕτως ἀτεχνῶς παρ' ἐκείνους τε ἀναβέβηκε καὶ τῆς τῶν κρειττόνων δυνάμεως παρ' αὐτῶν ἐκείνων μετείληφε.

ment, because Libanius merely opposed two pasts, the glorious one under Julian and that under Constantius, without considering the present, much less the bleak future.[43] As the comparison of themes in Themistius's *Oration* 5 and in Libanius's *Epitaphius* has already indicated, however, and as Gregory's *Oration* 5 further demonstrates, the *Epitaphius* was not the nostalgic musings of a man withdrawn from public life, but instead it directly engaged current affairs. Julian's legacy was at stake. Rome's relations with Persia had been severely damaged; a legitimate, victorious Roman emperor had been murdered in battle, and the resulting peace treaty had yielded significant territories and exposed Antioch, and even Constantinople, to a continuous Persian threat. For all these reasons, redress was required. (And Libanius himself, Ammianus, Eutropius, Festus, Eunapius, and others revisited these arguments again and again to press their views.)[44] Furthermore, earthquakes, barbarian attacks, and other calamities demonstrated the cosmic upheaval Julian's death (and not his life) had caused. In fact, in the *Epitaphius* Libanius formulated the providential explanation of Julian's fate that had eluded him when he composed the *Monody*. For him Julian was a tragic hero like those celebrated by Sophocles, destined to play the part the gods had allotted him in their divinely preordained drama. For reasons known only to them, the gods wished to ruin Rome. Julian had been a good man caught inexorably in the inopportune moment the gods had assigned him. For those who were not so close to him (as Libanius) and who were not initiated, Julian may have resembled Xerxes, who had brought about his own death by willfully disregarding the signs that foretold his end (*Or.* 18.117).[45] Julian, in truth, discerned the deeper meaning of divine portents and, divinely chosen, understood the gods' ultimate plan, hidden from the many: to destroy Rome. Thus, he acted as he did. As divinely elected and fully initiated, and as the gods' chosen protagonist in their providential tragedy, he also reaped the ultimate reward. The gods let Julian die young, beautiful, and glorious, and gave him everlasting life as one of their own.

GREGORY'S SECOND STRIKE AGAINST THE PAGANS

The relationship between Libanius's *Orations* 17 and 18 and Gregory's *Orations* 4 and 5 against Julian has received much scholarly attention, with assessments ranging from Asmus's suggestion that Gregory's "stele of shame" countered Libanius's

---

43. Criscuolo, "Giuliano," 272–75; Dagron, *Empire romain*, 75–77.
44. Some themes, such as Constantius's negligence and the constant Persian threat for Antioch, echo Lib. *Or.* 12.52–53, 71–74.
45. Libanius also described Constantius as a new Xerxes, because as a Christian he did not comprehend divine portents either. Themistius *Or.* 5.67b evoked Darius and Xerxes to praise Jovian's choice of advisors.

"stele of honor" to Bernardi's rejection of any connection between these works.[46] These assessments (discussed in Chapter 8) assume, however, that Gregory's *Orations* 4 and 5 essentially formed two parts of one work. Indeed, *Oration* 4 resembles Libanius's *Epitaphius* only insofar as they both address Julian's youth, rise, and rule similarly, because of the structural demands of their genres, but to opposite ends. In *Oration* 5, although Gregory again addressed, as demanded by the genre, Julian's character, comportment, and Friends, and how the empire should be ruled as Christian, and not as Julian did it, four themes are now the central focus: Julian's incapacity to read divine portents, as shown by the fate of the Temple in Jerusalem (*Or.* 5.3–7); his conduct of the Persian campaign (*Or.* 5.8–12); Julian's death and *apotheōsis* (*Or.* 5.13–14, 19–24); and Jovian's peace treaty and the nature of a just war (*Or.* 5.15). The oration concludes with a discussion, constituting more than a third of the oration, of appropriate Christian imperial comportment and conduct (*Or.* 5.25–38). Once it is considered on its own terms, the convergence of *Oration* 5 and Libanius's *Epitaphius* emerges clearly.[47] Even if one does not accept a direct relationship (considering only verbatim quotations irrefutable proof), Gregory, in 365, countered arguments and accusations such as those Libanius voiced in his orations, in particular his *Epitaphius,* arguments that assumed added relevance once Procopius (whom Libanius supported) had begun his usurpation.[48]

---

46. Asmus, "Invektiven," 326–29, 358–67; Bernardi, ed. and trans., *Grégoire de Nazianze: Discours 4-5 contre Julien,* 11–12, 22; Regali, "Intenti," 401; Gregory of Nazianzus, *La morte di Giuliano l'Apostata: Orazione 5,* trans. and comm. Lugaresi 14–15. Martig, *Studi,* 14–17, 20–24, points out that Libanius's arguments were well known by the late fourth and the early fifth century, thus making a direct dependence—which she rejects—superfluous. All except Lugaresi consider *Or.* 4 and 5 as one, so that arguments against Gregory's awareness of Libanius's work always include, if not focus on, *Or.* 4.

47. Lugaresi (Gregory of Nazianzus, *La morte di Giuliano l'Apostata: Orazione 5,* trans. and comm. Lugaresi, 19 n. 21) lists a number of places where Gregory says, "so they say," "as declared by many of those who are of his side," "what now all say and think," "according to others," etc., which Lugaresi reads as referring to Libanius. For many scholars, verbatim quotations are the litmus test of awareness: e.g., Wiemer, *Libanios,* 257 n. 44. Coulie notes ("Chaînes," 137 and passim), however, that fourth-century authors such as Gregory rarely cite their contemporaries directly. Rather, they cite only classic, normative figures and texts, and allude to them subsequently; allusion (the tacit but manifest reference to an author, a work, or a "courant de pénsee déterminé") is the norm. In his autobiographical *Or.* 1.133, 135, and 138, Libanius indicated that his *Epitaphius* was no secret. Wiemer (*Libanios,* 266–67, with n. 106) assumes a public reading for a restricted audience. Lugaresi (Gregory of Nazianzus, *La morte di Giuliano l'Apostata: Orazione 5,* trans. and comm. Lugaresi, 14–23) offers additional proof that Gregory engaged Libanius directly; even if he had no access to a written version of Libanius's *Epitaphius,* he knew the *Hypaticus,* aspects of which reappear in *Or.* 17 and 18 (for example, Julian's dismissal of the diplomatic solution Shapur II had offered, *Or.* 17.5–6). Gr. Naz. *Ep.* 236 shows that he knew Libanius.

48. Lib. *Or.* 1.163 relates that he was suspected of having composed a panegyric for Procopius; two of his students had joined Procopius's cause, Andronicus (3: *PLRE,* vol. 1, 64–65) and Hyperechius (1: ibid., 449–50).

The Failed Prophet and the Temple in Jerusalem

Gregory advanced with unusual conciseness *in medias res*. After a brief allusion to the just fate that had befallen the persecutor, he immediately addressed Julian's ability to comprehend the divine will, which would manifest his divine origin and election, as shown by "the portent, famous everywhere, which not even the atheists refused to believe": Julian's attempt to rebuild the Temple in Jerusalem (*Or.* 5.3-5). Just as Julian was about to set out for Persia, the Temple in Jerusalem he had ordered rebuilt was destroyed by an earthquake and fire. Could God have delivered a clearer sign predicting the emperor's fate and that of his army than to make the earth once again reject a temple restored by Julian? Could one imagine a more dire portent?[49] Yet he, who made so much of his divine inspiration, failed to read the ominous sign that so clearly foretold the end of him who had vainly ignored God (*Or.* 5.1-2).

Julian had declared in *Against the Galileans* that the God of Moses was ancient and true, even though his followers mistakenly considered their God the universal God of all, despite his being responsible only for the people of a small territory. Nevertheless, because as true God the one of Moses, whom the Galileans had deserted, deserved the veneration and sacrifices due him, Julian, in an undated letter excerpted by John Lydus, pronounced his intention to rebuild "with all zeal the Temple of the Most High God." Further, he added in his *Epistle to the Priest Theodorus*, of early 363, that he was rebuilding the Temple, which had been destroyed three times.[50] These remarks, Ephraem of Nisibis's *Hymns* 1 and 4 *Against Julian*, and Gregory's *Oration* 5 are the earliest sources on the project. With the addition of the information of Ammianus's later account, it appears that orders for the reconstruction were given in January 363 and that the earthquake and subsequent fire that halted the project occurred about March, when Julian began to move east, though a fifth-century Syriac source suggests a later date, May 19, 363, which is also possible.[51]

---

49. All agreed that earthquakes were a bad omen; thus Ammianus 23.1.17 relates how Julian's priests used earthquakes in Constantinople to dissuade him from the Persian war. Indeed, beginning with Julian's arrival in Antioch, Ammianus 23.2.6-3.3 lists an intensifying series of inauspicious omens the emperor ignored: collapsing porticoes and haystacks, the burning of the Temple of Apollo in Rome, etc.

50. Jul. *Ep.* 134 fr. in John Lydus *Mens.* 4.110; *Ep.* 89b.295c; *Ep.* 89a.454a-b; *CG* frs. 86.354b, 87.356c-d. The authenticity of Julian's *Ep.* 204, *To the Community of the Jews*, remains in doubt; van Nuffelen, "Deux fausses lettres," 132-36, suggested that it should be dated between 429 and 450.

51. Amm. Marc. 23.1.2-3; Ephraem Syrus *Hymns c. Jul.* 1.13-20, 4.18-23 (Ephraem the Syrian, *Hymnen De Paradiso und Contra Julianum*, ed. Beck, vol. 1 [CSCO 175], 73-75, 89-90; German trans. vol. 2 [CSCO 176], 67-69, 84-85; English trans. in Lieu, *Emperor Julian*, 96-134). For the letter purportedly sent by Cyril of Jerusalem, preserved in Syriac, Brock, "Rebuilding"; Wainwright, "Letter," argues for the historicity of the letter's details if not its authorship; trans. Drijvers, *Cyril*, 191-93, who considers it a fifth-century construct connected to the Syriac *Julian Romance* but based on a Jerusalem source: ibid., 137-52.

Gregory, in his account of Julian's Persian campaign, placed the destruction of the Temple strategically, at the beginning, to emphasize his principal point: that Julian the Apostate could not comprehend even the most obvious divine portents and oracles. He was not divinely chosen, and he could not see even what was plain to everyone: that the fate of the buildings he believed sacred and wished to renew revealed the powerlessness of those he falsely considered gods and foretold the fate the only true God had decreed for him. Here Gregory again adduced the physical arrangement of the city and its significance—as he had those of the imperial portraits in the agora in *Oration* 4—to further his argument. When earthquake and fire leveled what the Jews had considered a work of piety, they sought refuge in a Christian temple: that is where the sacred now resided in the polis. The theme of divisiveness and misconstrued *oikeiōsis*, indicating wrong governance, also returns. Julian's final outrage had been to set Jews against Christians (by reconstructing the Temple, whose destruction was a principal point in Christian arguments for their predestined role as the true chosen people) after he had increased his own violence against the Christians, "like wave following wave." Drawing his inspiration from his mistaken reading of divine teachings and their hidden meaning—this time Jewish secret teachings—he declared the moment opportune "to return to their home, to reconstruct the Temple, and to renew the force of their traditions, and he hid his project under the fiction of an act of benevolence," as if Julian understood the providential history of Jews and Christians better than the divine creator and originator of that history.[52]

The Jews, as malleable as Julian, supported the enterprise enthusiastically.[53] But when earthquake and fire struck just as the rebuilding had begun, all rushed in horror to a Christian temple, though—according to Gregory's sources—it could not save all, because it too began to burn, so that the wounded became "a living stele for the threats and actions of God against sinners."[54] For those who could see, God added even further signs, as if the earthquake and fire had not been sufficient. A cross appeared in the sky above Jerusalem as a cosmic symbol of triumph, and a cross also marked the clothes of those present that day (*Or.* 5.4).[55] "Thus heaven and earth; and did the air not provide a sign in these opportune circumstances, and

---

52. Gr. Naz. *Or.* 5.3: κατελθεῖν εἰς τὴν ἑαυτῶν καὶ τὸν νεὼν ἀναδείμασθαι καὶ τῶν πατρίων τὸ κράτος ἀνανεώσασθαι, καὶ ἀποκρυπτόμενος εὐνοίας πλάσματι τὴν ἐπίνοιαν.

53. Gr. Naz. *Or.* 5.3: τὴν παλαιάν τε αὐτῶν κουφότητα. As acts of piety women sold their jewelry and even moved earth by hand (*Or.* 5.4).

54. Gr. Naz. *Or.* 5.4: στήλην . . . ἔμψυχον τῆς τοῦ θεοῦ κατὰ τῶν ἁμαρτωλῶν ἀπειλῆς καὶ κινήσεως.

55. According to one of Gregory's sources, those present preserved their clothes; others affirmed that the cross reappeared whenever they told the story. Rufin. *HE* 10.40 and the Syriac Ps.-Cyril letter, but not Ephraem, also have the story of the Cross on the clothes; Gregory of Nazianzus, *La morte di Giuliano l'Apostata: Orazione 5*, trans. and comm. Lugaresi, 180–81.

was it not made holy by the signs of the Passion?"⁵⁶ Those in Jerusalem, unlike Julian, read the signs correctly. Many "invoked the God of the Christians and sought to placate him with many benedictions and supplications," and many "ran to our priests": Julian's act had led to the conversion of the city to Christ and thus to a new unity—the opposite of what Julian had intended.

> Given such things, what say the wise [*sophoi*] of this world who magnify their talents, carry their long beards about, and wave their elegant philosopher's coat in front of our eyes? Oppose me with your arguments, you who write these long discourses and compose those incredible stories, you who remain openmouthed looking upward, and who lie regarding the heavenly things, and who connect births and things to come to the movement of the stars.⁵⁷

Everything Julian had considered and proclaimed a divine sign and portent, a symbol of divine will, from the stars to sacrifices and from statues to oracles and temples, was false. To argue that Julian had truly understood divine signs, even ominous portents, better than the masses because he comprehended the deeper meaning hidden behind the literal was false: his death had been proof, if any further proof was needed. "I too have something to say to you that I gather from the stars: the star [that went from the East to Bethlehem] manifested the coming of Christ;⁵⁸ that [star] was Christ's victory crown."

Scholars have studied these passages in the context of Julian's attitude toward Jews and his intentions regarding the Temple; Jewish attitudes, in particular of those in Antioch, vis-à-vis Julian and this project;⁵⁹ and for the project's implication for the legal status of Jerusalem, officially Aelia Capitolina.⁶⁰ Discussions of Gregory's

---

56. Gr. Naz. *Or.* 5.7: Ἀρ' οὖν γῆ μὲν οὕτω καὶ οὐρανός, ἀὴρ δὲ οὐκ ἐπισημαίνει τοῖς τοιούτοις καιροῖς οὐδὲ ἡγιάσθη τότε τοῖς σημείοις τοῦ πάθους;

57. Gr. Naz. *Or.* 5.5: Πρὸς ταῦτα τί φήσουσιν οἱ τοῦ αἰῶνος τούτου σοφοὶ καὶ τὰ παρ' αὐτοῖς ἀποσεμνύνοντες, οἱ τὰς βαθείας ὑπήνας ἕλκοντες καὶ τὸ κομψὸν περισύροντες ἡμῖν τριβώνιον; Ἀντιδιήγησαί μοι καὶ σὺ τὰ σά, ὁ τοὺς μακροὺς λόγους γράφων καὶ τὰς ἀπίστους συντιθεὶς ἱστορίας καὶ κεχηνὼς πρὸς τὰ ἄνω καὶ τῶν οὐρανίων καταψευδόμενος καὶ πλέκων ἐκ τῆς τῶν ἀστέρων κινήσεως τὰς γενέσεις καὶ τὰ συμβαίνοντα.

58. Gr. Naz. *Or.* 5.5: τὴν Χριστοῦ παρουσίαν ἀνεδήλωσεν.

59. Scholars debate whether Julian intended the Temple project as a means to win the support of Antioch's important Jewish community for his Persian war, as suggested by J. Chrys. *Jud.* 5.11, *PG* 48.900–901 (but not by Gregory or Ammianus); Lugaresi (Gregory of Nazianzus, *La morte di Giuliano l'Apostata: Orazione 5*, trans. and comm. Lugaresi, 39–41) notes the near-absolute silence of the Jewish sources regarding the Temple: e.g., *Bereshit Rabba* 64.10.

60. Jews were not permitted to enter Jerusalem or its municipal territory after it became Aelia Capitolina as a consequence of the Bar Kochba revolt and Hadrian's decree; Hadrian's new colony Aelia Capitolina consisted mainly of Latin-speaking veterans; D.C. 59.12; Eus. *HE* 4.6.4. Jews were permitted to enter the city once a year to mourn the ruined Temple and had to pay a certain sum to do so; *Itinerarium Burdigalense* 591; Jer. *Comm. in Soph.* 1.16, *PL* 25.1354A–B. It is possible that the ban on Jews en-

attitude toward Jews, how it compared to that of John Chrysostom, and the evolution of Jewish-Christian relations in the later fourth and early fifth century also cite this passage, often in connection with Ephraem's *Hymns*.[61] Scholars engaged in such enormously important and complex issues, however, understandably overlook the relevance of the passage in the economy of Gregory's *Oration 5*, in part because *Oration 5* has received no scholarly attention in its own right, except in Lugaresi's commentary (Gregory of Nazianzus, *La morte di Giuliano l'Apostata: Orazione 5*).

Gregory's principal point—compared to which the Temple's identity as that in Jerusalem (and, consequently, Christian-Jewish relations themselves) are secondary—is that Julian could not interpret divine will, read oracles, or understand portents because he was not divinely elected, divinely born, or in any way close to the divine. Thus, he was not a true philosopher, nor a true mantic or prophet, but merely an evil Apostate who got what he deserved. Furthermore, only those who were truly divinely chosen, purified, and legitimately entrusted with the *hiera* could alter the sacred topography of a city. To erect temples (of any kind) required divine authorization (because of the divine *dynamis* of all such places, whether pagan, Jewish, Christian).[62] All Julian's attempts to do so had failed, from the building of the sanc-

---

tering Aelia Capitolina was renewed under Constantine, instigated by local bishops. However, it was not rigorously enforced, as Gregory's episode also shows; see Drijvers, *Cyril*, 1–11. Julian effectively nullified Hadrian's decree by explicitly inviting Jews back.

61. For Drijvers, *Cyril*, 130, "this restoration project is one of the most amazing endeavors of Julian's short reign and one with a great impact. It elicited fierce reactions from Christian authors and had a great influence on the opinion formed of Julian's reign by his Christian contemporaries as well as later generations. The source material on the event is relatively vast." *Or.* 5 is one source. Without diminishing the centrality of the topic, it is worth noting that for Ammianus the project was not particularly exceptional, and that the reactions of contemporary Christians, before John Chrysostom, were not that fierce. For Gregory, the Temple is just one of several failed temple projects. Ephraem's *Hymns* employ more biblical imagery than *Or.* 5, particularly from the Book of Daniel (e.g., *Hymn* 1.24–25, Dan 4:16–17; also *Hymn* 4.20, Dan 9:4–27), to show the interrelation of the failed restoration, the fate of the Jews, and that of Julian (Griffith, "Ephraem," 250), whereas Gregory blamed Julian alone. Most modern studies reflect later Christian sources, beginning with John Chrysostom, especially *Jud. et Gent.* 17, *PG* 48.835–88 (Mayer, *Homilies*, 462, also 405–9), and his portrayal of Jewish-Christian relations in Antioch. Drijvers, *Cyril*, 131–52; Gregory of Nazianzus, *La morte di Giuliano l'Apostata: Orazione 5*, trans. and comm. Lugaresi, 27–51; and Hahn, "Kaiser Julian." Vinson, "Gregory Nazianzen's Homily 15," 187–92, connects Gregory's *Or.* 15, dating it to late 362, with Julian's attempts to rebuild the Temple, which she sees as Julian's wish to forge a pagan-Jewish alliance. As her discussion of the Christianization of the Jewish cult of the Maccabees in Antioch shows, it was John Chrysostom who alleged that the Jews supported Julian. In the later fourth century, hostile Christian sources associate Jews with Julian to accuse them of influencing Julian to reverse the preordained history of the Messiah, in which the destruction of the Temple corroborates Christian truth. It is important to keep this later context in mind; Gregory did not make that link. For the Christianization of the Maccabeans in Antioch, also Rutgers, "Importance."

62. Gr. Naz. *Or.* 4.25–27 relates the collapse of Mamas's shrine. This passage may be read as foreshadowing the Jerusalem fiasco. To destroy pagan temples was no small matter: Eus. *VC* 3.30.4 shows how God had to order Constantine to destroy the Temple of Venus erected over the site of Christ's bur-

tuary for Mamas, to the rebuilding of Apollo's temple at Daphne, to the rebuilding of the Temple at Jerusalem. Psalm 9:7, which Gregory read in conjunction with the celestial signs, predicted that cities that revolt "against us" would be destroyed (*Or.* 5.6). This had happened to the Temple, already destroyed once, and its reconstruction now divinely prevented. Furthermore, Jerusalem, as a result of Julian's blasphemy, was an even more Christian city, united by divine design—here, that the Temple in Jerusalem rather than another sanctuary was at stake signifies the preordained history prefigured in the Old Covenant and actualized in the New.[63] Thus, Julian's intent to reverse divine providence and incite Jews against Christians by renewing the polis Jerusalem as their home, restoring the Temple, and reinstituting old traditions came to nothing.

The question mattered: Whose *hiera* were true *hiera* and therefore belonged in the cities—those of the ancient pagans and Jews, or those of the true creator of everything, "the artful *Logos*," Christ? But just as important was Gregory's point that Julian's wish to memorialize in his grandiose public monuments the grandiosity of his rule—what Ammianus called "imperii sui memoriam magnitudine operum gestiens propagare"—exposed in fact the opposite: failure of his building projects (Gregory mentions one Christian, one Jewish, and one pagan temple) memorialized Julian's false divinity and failed prophesies. In this passage Gregory echoed Eusebius's concept of political theology as the connection between demonically inspired public sanctuaries, rituals, and oracles and Greek Roman rule, now narrowing the focus on Julian as sole representative of everything demonic. In the case of the Mamas sanctuary, the wrong person had sought to worship the right God; in the case of the Jerusalem Temple, the same demonically inspired person intended to counteract that God's decisions; likewise in the case of the Apollo sanctuary, this time by worshipping a god that was none.[64] Gregory may have denounced Julian's failed sacred building projects in this way in direct rejoinder to Libanius, to whose *Epitaphius* he may have alluded when claiming that his *logos* refuted the works of Porphyry "they" had praised as divine revelation (*Or.* 5.41).[65] Gregory's

---

ial; Thdt. *HE* 5.21.1 also evokes divine will in the destruction of the Temple of Zeus in Apamea; Fowden, "Bishops"; Emmel, Gotter, and Hahn, "From Temple to Church."

63. Lugaresi (Gregory of Nazianzus, *La morte di Giuliano l'Apostata: Orazione 5*, trans. and comm. Lugaresi, 43–48) has an excellent discussion of Gregory's semantics of sacred space: Julian and Gregory debated in effect the "re-sacralization of the political space" (p. 48), where it is important to keep in mind that the political space never lost its sacred *dynamis*; at stake was which *hiera* in the political space were of universal and continuing sacredness.

64. Johnson, *Ethnicity*, 156–70; and above, Chapter 7. Gregory did not mention the episode of the Temple in *Or.* 4, though he could have done so in the context of Mamas (*Or.* 4.25–27). It is possible that Gregory had not yet heard of the disaster when composing *Or.* 4; he may allude to the destroyed Temple in *Or.* 6.17–18 without directly mentioning it, in keeping with the *damnatio* motif.

65. Lib. *Or.* 18.178 praises Julian's *CG* as superior to that of "the old man from Tyre": i.e., Porphyry.

Julian was the opposite of Libanius's as "priest, writer, diviner, judge, soldier, and savior of all," residing as god among gods (*Or.* 18.176). Having swiftly dispatched Julian the priest and diviner, Gregory addressed Julian the soldier and savior before turning to Julian as eternal resident among the gods.

The Persian War and Its Commander

"Such was the status of these things," the reconstruction of the Temple brought to an end and Jerusalem's citizens baptized, when Gregory turned to Julian's gravest misjudgment of the divine will, his "most sage and most philanthropic"[66] endeavor with the most devastating consequences: the Persian campaign (*Or.* 5.8–15). Again, Gregory, in his presentation of the war, counters Libanius (*Or.* 18.204–67), addressing in particular one intensely controversial tactical element, Julian's decision to burn the fleet. Echoing Libanius's *Monody* and reflecting the discussion of threats to the Western frontier mentioned in his *Hypaticus* (*Or.* 12.77) and later by Ammianus, Gregory accused Julian of having embarked on his march to Persia rashly, careless because he thought the Christians had been dealt with and because he had succeeded earlier against the Western barbarians.[67] Mocking Julian's faith in his divine calling and the victory he believed it guaranteed (a faith that Libanius shared when he said that Julian had proceeded with "the gods at his side, a small but powerful army": *Or.* 17.5), Gregory declared that Julian had put more faith in irrational audacity than in the army as he marched at the head of two armies, one of hoplites and the other of *daimones* (*Or.* 5.8).[68]

Just War   Julian mistook audacity for courage. To do so had grave consequences, because it blinded him to the demands of just war, a theory of which Gregory proceeded to develop. To act defensively was justified: to protect territories in one's possession against intruders, "that is the first and highest care of those who have intelligence [*nous*]." One must never place defense of territories on an equal footing with the conquest of lands not in one's possession, however. A war of aggression may be risked only if the circumstances are absolutely favorable. What could be more misguided than to risk everything to gain, potentially, nothing? Julian looked to the Trajans and Hadrians but overlooked their being prudent and courageous in equal measure. And he forgot Carus and Valerian, who paid a price for senseless

---

66. Gr. Naz. *Or.* 5.8: βουλὴν συνετωτάτην τε καὶ φιλανθρωποτάτην.

67. For reconstructions of the Persian campaign, Matthews, *Roman Empire*, 161–79; den Boeft, den Hengst, and Teitler, *Philological and Historical Commentary on Ammianus Marcellinus 23*, vii–xiv; Marcone, "Significato"; Bowersock, *Julian*, 107–8; Blockley, *East Roman Foreign Policy*, 8–30; Rosen, *Julian*, 345–63; Dodgeon and Lieu collect further primary sources in *Roman Eastern Frontier*, 231–74; comments ibid. 390–94.

68. Lib. *Or.* 18.40–90 for Julian in Gaul; *Or.* 18.167–69, 12.88–89, 13.49 for the religious aspects of the Persian campaign.

aggression: they were "destroyed at the summit of their fortune in Persian territory" (*Or.* 5.8).⁶⁹ In contrast to the accusations of hesitancy, indecisiveness, and lack of fortitude Julian (and Libanius) had leveled against Constantius, Gregory praises such a defensive policy as the sole right and just one. Deliberate defense of territory, in combination with an attack when it was risk-free, was the only justification of war. (Note that Gregory does not exclude territorial expansion outright.) Such a comparison of just war as conducted by Constantius, a true leader capable of true deeds securely anchored in reality because he was Christian, and unjust aggressive war incited by a delusional leader moored in demonically inspired (pagan) fictions, is the dominant theme of Gregory's version of the advance into Persia to Ctesiphon.

Fiction versus Reality: The Burning Fleet "He took on this enterprise, having set in motion every kind of charlatanry of divination, magic, and open and hidden sacrifice, with the sole result that in short time all this was brought to ruin."⁷⁰ Julian advanced along the Euphrates, leaving devastation in his wake, until he reached nearly the confluence of Euphrates and Tigris. Now, with the army before Ctesiphon, "having come close to that city already appeared to him in part a victory" (*Or.* 5.9), and the emperor began to contemplate the return. Gregory succinctly summarized what Libanius and then Ammianus narrated in far greater detail to arrive at the juncture he meant to emphasize: that at Ctesiphon—not after Julian's death—things began to go badly. Caught between the rivers and the cities Coche (Al-Mada'in) and Ctesiphon and their defenders, Julian, the army, and the supply ships advanced, evading Coche by an ancient canal they reactivated; but they did not attack Ctesiphon.⁷¹ The Persians retreated strategically, attacking the Romans from elevated positions.⁷² Julian was caught—surrounded—and no longer knew where to turn (*Or.* 5.10). At this point, a high-ranking Persian came to him and persuaded him to pursue an aggressive strategy and augment his fighting power by burning the fleet. Now all disasters struck at once. Julian burned the fleet, and with it all provisions, so that morale deteriorated precipitously because this appeared to all an act of self-immolation (*Or.* 5.11–12).

As François Paschoud has noted, Gregory's account is very close to that of Libanius's *Epitaphius,* including the mention of a Persian emissary sent to Julian, whose

---

69. Julian *Caes.* 328a praises Trajan's use of force against the Parthians only when provoked; Eutr. 9.18.1; Fest. 24.2; *SHA V. Cari* 8.2–7; Carus, who perished near Ctesiphon in 283, became the exemplar for fatal Roman hybris because he wanted to extend the territory into Persia beyond what was appropriate; see also Aur. Vict. 38.3–6; Martig, *Studi,* 27–28. Julian praised him (*Or.* 1.18a). Valerian had been captured alive (and enslaved) by the Persians while defending Edessa in 260.

70. Gr. Naz. *Or.* 5.9: Ἀλλ' οὖν ἔδοξε ταῦτα καὶ τῆς ὁρμῆς ἦν, πᾶσαν μαντείας καὶ γοητείας ῥητῆς τε καὶ ἀρρήτου θυσίας τερατείαν εἰς ἓν ἀγαγών, ἵν' ἐν βραχεῖ πᾶσα καταλυθῇ.

71. Ammianus 24.6.2 identified Coche as Seleucia.

72. Amm. Marc. 24.7.7.

conciliatory offers Julian rejected (to Libanius's barely concealed horror).[73] Gregory's interpretation differs entirely: his Julian was delusional. Instead of pushing decisively through the dangerous position at Ctesiphon by marching inland and burning the fleet to facilitate that advance, Julian, malleable as he was (Gregory refers to Julian's *kouphotēs*, the term with which he described the Jews in *Or.* 5.3), followed the Persian's advice—the ultimate, fatal loss of any sense of reality. He did not realize that the Persian was an impostor pretending to be an enemy of Shapur to lure Julian into disaster (as Zopyrus had done to aid Darius's capture of Babylon: Hdt. 3.153–60), promising Julian an easy retreat (through territories Julian's army had previously burned, Gregory sarcastically implied), for which the fleet with its essential provisions was superfluous baggage and could easily be burned. Thus disaster befell the army: not because of its cowardice (*anandria*) but because of Julian's levity (*Or.* 5.12). The resulting circumstances were so dire that only Julian's death offered the slightest hope of salvation—the reverse of Libanius's arguments.

Julian's Death and Apotheosis   Gregory's account of Julian's death continues to underscore the emperor's delusional fiction as a fatal loss of any sense of the real, countering at the same time accusations of Christian complicity in Julian's demise (*Or.* 5.13–14). As Gregory's emphasis on the army's true courage indicates, in contrast to Julian's audacity masquerading as courage, he had to tread carefully. He did not intend to criticize, or to be seen to criticize, the conduct of Rome's army, whatever the number of Christians who served in it, a theme already evident in *Oration* 4.64–65 and 82–84, where Gregory accused Julian of having weakened the army by removing the right flags and standards and by duplicitously linking donatives and sacrifices. Julian, not the army, was the culprit. Gregory reemphasized the point in relating three stages of Julian's death: his wounding, the immediate aftermath, and the funeral (*Or.* 5.16–18). Gregory, showcasing his mastery in shaping the issues, does not mention Julian's death at all.

By presenting his audience with several versions of Julian's final battle and the manner in which he was wounded, Gregory elided the issue of the culprit: "There is no unanimity of affirmation" (*Or.* 5.13). Some said that Julian had been hit by a Persian arrow while he rushed about, just as Cyrus had lost the victory he had won over his brother, Artaxerxes, by his derring-do (X. *An.* 1.8.26–27)—Gregory shaped his account by alluding to several classic Persian war narratives, above all Herodotus, as has already become apparent. Others reported that Julian had leapt onto a small hill to survey his army, and when it appeared to him far to exceed its actual size, he had shouted that it was a shame to lead so mighty a force back to Rome, upon which an incensed Roman soldier (aware of the true situation) stabbed him. Still others

---

73. Lib. *Or.* 18.244–47; Amm. Marc. 24.6.1–2; Zos. 3.24.2; and *Zosime: Histoire nouvelle*, ed. Paschoud, vol. 2, 167–73.

thought that a "comic barbarian, one of those who accompany the troops" to entertain them, or a Saracen had wielded that sword.[74] Julian, in the grip of delusion, did not even realize that his grave wound was fatal: the great haruspex could not read even his own exposed entrails (*Or*. 5.13). Thus, it was irrelevant who and what had wounded him, whether a Roman arrow, a Roman sword, or that of a comic barbarian or Saracen (possibilities also mentioned by Libanius and Ammianus, with the exception of the comic barbarian).[75]

Julian's survey of his army, so rudely interrupted by—perhaps—the comic barbarian, evokes again the theme of Julian as *histrio*, a bad actor, starring in a comedy of his own making with tragic consequence for all. Gregory's telling (or rather, not telling) of Julian's death continues in that vein; what Libanius had framed as the tragic death of a new Socrates, of the philosopher as hero, Gregory dramatizes in the comic mode. Indeed (as mentioned in Chapter 9 in the context of *theōsis* [*Or.* 4.59]), Gregory's Julian, severely wounded and felled near the river Tigris, recalled that others later considered divine had vanished without trace, such as Empedocles, whose faked disappearance had been ruined only by his sandal caught on Etna. Helped by some of his friends and fellow initiates, Julian thus had himself thrown into the river to ensure his deification, or *apotheōsis*. Had it not been for a disgruntled eunuch (he had famously purged many of them from Constantius's court) who spread the word, his apotheosis might well have succeeded: "This is how this man had governed; this is how he had led the army, and this is how he lost his life," not as a philosopher emulating Socrates but as a fake—a complete rejection of Julian's myth of his divine origin and Libanius's assertion of his everlasting place among gods (*Or*. 5.14).[76]

Gregory's framing of Julian's end, sidestepping the question of who wielded the fatal weapon to focus on the emperor as bad actor, countering Libanius's tragic hero, leaves no doubt about the responsibility of Julian's successor to conclude a peace "in a situation of extreme danger." That man, Jovian, was entirely worthy of absolute power, above all because of his piety (*eusebeia*).[77] His inheritance of a defeat more than justified his actions. He could not engage the Persians in any further battle,

---

74. The comic barbarian is probably Gregory's deliberate misreading of a *scurra barbarus*, a non-Roman soldier with the army. The *SHA Tyr. Trig.* 30.24–26 mentions a *scurra Persicus* in Zenobia's service who was considered her guard, accompanying her after her defeat in the triumph in Rome; *SHA Alex. Sev.* 61.3; Amm. Marc. 29.4.4; Matthews, *Roman Empire*, 507 n. 3.

75. Some appear to have wondered why Christians in the army, in particular in high command, did not stop Julian. Soz. *HE* 6.1.14 and Thdt. *HE* 3.25.6 also have the story of the incensed soldier, probably depending on Gregory.

76. As Lugaresi notes (Gregory of Nazianzus, *La morte di Giuliano l'Apostata: Orazione 5*, trans. and comm. Lugaresi, 61–62), this had the added advantage of denying Julian any last words; Libanius's dying Julian in the *Monody* railed against the gods; Amm. Marc. 24.6.17, 25.3.7 for the location. Later Christian accounts made much of Julian's hasty, disorganized death, a bad sign for the afterlife; Thdt. *HE* 3.25.7; Philost. *HE* 7.15; John Malalas *Chron.* 954 (Dindorf); Soz. *HE* 6.2.10–12.

77. Gr. Naz. *Or*. 5.15: ἀληθῶς τυραννίδος ἄξιος.

not because he lacked courage, but because the army was in disarray and he had to consider the long road back. Therefore he concluded this peace, "as shameful as it was unworthy of Roman might, to state the issue concisely."[78] Because the Persians controlled the situation, Jovian had to salvage what he could. The mild demands of the Persians, relatively speaking, reflected their ability to measure their success and to use restraint in victory. Jovian, in sum, had done the best he could. "If someone attributes the blame for that situation to him, absolving that other one from all responsibility, for me he is one who wants to dispute while knowing absolutely nothing about what has happened."[79] Gregory, citing Herodotus on the tyrant of Samos, pointed to the cobbler as cause of the boots' failings, not the one who had to wear them (Or. 5.15; Hdt. 6.1.2).

The funeral cortege that accompanied Julian's corpse back to Rome stood as emblem of the ruler's life and afterlife. Gregory, evoking the traditional elements of the *pompa funebris* honoring a deceased emperor, juxtaposed that cortege with the *translatio* of Constantius, who had ended his life in a saintly manner and "had left to us the power." Julian's funeral was shameful burlesque; Constantius's was pious, dignified, imperial, sanctified (Or. 5.16–18). "Our emperor" had been accompanied by all the united people, the court, and all "our" solemn rites, vigils, and illuminated torches. "Even this [account] reached the ears of the people: after the corpse [of Constantius] had crossed the Taurus and had reached the security of his paternal city [Constantinople] . . . , there were those who heard a voice from heaven, as if singing psalms, accompanying the cortege—angelic powers, I think—as a sign of honor rendered him for his piety and as a reward for his funeral."[80] This miracle certified Constantius's true apotheosis, his everlasting resting place among divine souls in the celestial heights (as Gregory had already affirmed in the opening hymn of *Oration* 4). To persons who questioned that, arguing that Constantius upset orthodox faith, Gregory argued that such upset resulted merely from the stupidity of persons who governed in Constantius's name and, taking advantage of his simple soul, allowed their zeal to become a hindrance—a ringing defense of Constantius's and his father's homoian faith, shared by Jovian and Valens (Or. 5.16, 4.36).[81]

Julian's corpse instead was accompanied by mimes, flute players, and dancers.

---

78. Gr. Naz. Or. 5.15: ἐπὶ ταῖς συνθήκαις ταύταις συνέβησαν, ταῖς οὕτως αἰσχραῖς τε καὶ ἀναξίαις τῆς Ῥωμαίων χειρός.

79. Gr. Naz. Or. 5.15: ἵν' εἴπω τὸ συντομώτατον, ὧν εἴ τις, ἐκεῖνον ἀφεὶς τῆς αἰτίας, τοῦτον καταμέμφοιτο, λίαν ἐστὶν ἀγνώμων ἔμοιγε λογιστὴς τῶν τότε συμβεβηκότων.

80. Gr. Naz. Or. 5.16: καὶ τοῦτο διεδόθη ταῖς τῶν πολλῶν ἀκοαῖς ὅτι, ἐπειδὴ τὸν Ταῦρον ὑπερβάλλοι τὸ σῶμα πρὸς τὴν πατρῴαν αὐτῷ πόλιν διασῳζόμενον . . . φωνή τις ἐκ τῶν ἄκρων ἔστιν οἷς ἐξηκούετο, οἷον ψαλλόντων τε καὶ παραπεμπόντων, ἀγγελικῶν οἶμαι δυνάμεων, γέρας τῆς εὐσεβείας ἐκείνῳ καὶ ἀντίδοσις ἐπιτάφιος.

81. For daytime funerals, CTh 9.17.5; for Julian's funeral, Amm. Marc. 25.9.12–13, 10.5; Lib. Or. 18.306; Zos. 3.34.3–4; for that of Constantius, Amm. Marc. 21.16.20–21; Philost. HE 6.6a–7a; Mac-

Rather than sing hymns, the populace lining the roads made jokes. Furthermore, explicitly violating Julian's own law, the funeral cortege traveled during the day, so that the sun had to watch the corpse of its so-called son. Julian's shameful end led to a shameful and degrading *translatio*. Tarsus, Paul's city, refused to accept his corpse, so that he was buried outside it, in a mausoleum, a "site without honor" (*temenos atimon*), not worthy to be looked at by the pious (*Or.* 5.18). Such shame and dishonor made official *apotheōsis* inconceivable; in fact, such grave violations of proper imperial decorum alone should have made *apotheōsis* impossible. No matter the decrees of the Roman senate attesting Julian's acceptance among the *divi* and the proclamations of admirers such as Libanius, Julian was not among the divine beings; his soul would not last forever; he had not been received by the one true God. (And praying to his statues was useless; see Lib. *Or.* 18.304.)[82]

Gregory, as his depiction of Constantius's funeral with its angelic choir indicates, did not reject notions of Roman imperial *apotheōsis*. Eutropius attests, with the same formula for all, "Inter divos relatus est," that Constantine, Constantius, and Jovian were also officially deified, as were, for that matter, Valens, Valentinian, Gratian, Valentinian II, and Theodosius I.[83] This was not an argument against imperial funerals or imperial *apotheōsis*, just as in *Oration 4* Gregory had not argued against imperial representation, including *proskynēsis*, in the agora, nor against any other form of imperial ceremonial per se: at stake was the correct Christian use of imperial representation in all its facets. Here, *apotheōsis* was a function of just and moral personal behavior, of *eusebeia*, as much as victorious conduct of just wars and good administration at home. Julian lacked every attribute and character trait requisite for *aeterna memoria* and for *apotheōsis*. Julian had no saving grace, not even his dynastic connection to Constantius and Constantine: Valens, though homoian, must be preferred to Procopius; Julian the emperor (of whom Procopius was a direct reminder) had to be erased from memory and replaced by the Apostate.

Gregory's *Oration 5*, beginning with Julian's failed restoration of the Temple in Jerusalem, the examination of his mistaken assumption that his Persian war was divinely sanctioned, leading to his shameful death and funeral, was meant to invalidate every claim Julian and his followers had made that he was divine, specially chosen by the gods, and, thus, as a true Roman emperor, received among the gods, residing in the sphere of the stars, his *memoria* eternal. Had Julian been divine, he would have been able to read divine signs, but he had been wrong every time he

---

Cormack, *Art*, 132–34, 330–31; Gregory of Nazianzus, *La morte di Giuliano l'Apostata: Orazione 5*, trans. and comm. Lugaresi, 117–213; Dagron, *Naissance*, 401–8.

82. Ruggini, "Apoteosi," 455–61, and *Simboli*, 237–39, 260–65; Straub, "Himmelfahrt."

83. Eutr. 10.16.2 (Julian), 10.18.2 (Jovian; cf. *CTh* 1.6.2); Eutropius used the same formula for Antoninus Pius: "inter divos relatus et merito consecratus." The practice continued until Anastasius; Ruggini, "Apoteosi," 432–36, 438–39; Lenski, *Failure*, 20 n. 37.

pretended to do so. He was no prophet (*mantis*); his writings were wrong; his sacrifices were demonically inspired, and he had failed entirely as a military leader. Gregory, echoing Themistius's criticism of Julian's mistaken interpretation of Greek religion, which Jovian, as new Empedocles, understood far better than his predecessor, defended Jovian, his legitimacy as ruler, and his actions in Persia, from the peace treaty to saving the army that remained: he had preserved peace, unity, and the security of the *oikoumenē* at a time of gravest danger. Gregory, again echoing Themistius, comparing Jovian favorably with Constantius, defined and praised just war and just imperial conduct: *eusebeia* was the central imperial virtue, and the accusation that Constantius had disrupted orthodoxy was entirely secondary; merely the result of misguided courtiers he had failed to curtail. The same, by implication, was true of his successors Jovian and Valens, also homoian. The religious dimension of Julian's rule, Persian campaign, and end were Gregory's central themes because they affected the memory of the emperor and his deeds, including his legislation and the legacy of his war. And the memory of these key aspects of Julian's reign directly affected the legitimacy of the rulers who followed him, none of whom belonged to his dynasty, so that they derived their legitimacy from the circumstances of their election and the efficacy of their rule. Thus Gregory countered every proclamation of Libanius's *Epitaphius,* insisting that Julian's death had been a salvation: his life spelled Rome's ruin, his claim of deep insight into divine signs and symbols false. Both Gregory and Libanius reflect an evident need to explain Julian's brief reign in providential terms, and they agree that his short reign was divine punishment. For Libanius, Julian's life had been a short reprieve before the body politic relapsed into its divinely preordained sickness and inevitable ruin; for Gregory, Julian's rule had been punishment for Christian arrogance and misrule, mercifully brief yet an everlasting warning. Indeed, both Gregory and Libanius believed that Julian should be remembered, but they differed on what his memory ought to signify—who read divine will correctly.[84]

Julian the Man—Manqué

Divine will and how to read it, who was in truth a prophet, also forms the context of Gregory's famous depiction of Julian's person and character at Athens, the second episode of *Oration* 5 that has received scholarly attention (*Or.* 5.23).[85] It occurs in the section following the funeral (according to the rules of the genre), in a summary of the virtues and characteristics of the deceased that match them to his external comportment (*Or.* 5.19–22). The themes are well known. In marked contrast

---

84. Ammianus, too, attributed Julian's failures to his un-Roman sacrificial excess, which made him misread oracles, and thus led him to the wrong philosophical friends; see above, Chapters 4 and 7. Divine will and its interpretation were also central to Ephraem's *Hymns c. Jul.* 2.2–4, 9, 15; 3.9–14; 4.26.

85. Socr. *HE* 3.23.18–26 reiterates Gregory's description; divine signs, Gr. Naz. *Or.* 5.25.

to Libanius's Julian, Gregory's was the antithesis of a divinely chosen philosopher as leader. Julian chose high administrators according to personal attachment rather than merit; his legislation—supposedly superior to Rhadamanthys's in the underworld (Lib. *Or.* 17.26–27)—was capricious. Although he surrounded himself with philosophers as advisors—in principle a good thing—he treated them capriciously, too, praising them one day, dismissing them the next. Though he sought to imitate true philosopher-kings, whose immovable faces revealed their control of their passions (Gregory anticipates Ammianus's depiction of Constantius, 16.10.9–10), he was so immune to rage, Gregory sarcastically observes, that the law courts were filled with his screaming rages, which drowned out even the victims of judicial torture.[86] And, deriding "our habits," he went about with "old women" huffing and puffing to light the fires on the altars, offering the pitiful sight of a Roman emperor with ridiculously puffed-out cheeks, a sight not even Athena could stomach once she observed herself playing the flute she had invented (*Or.* 5.19–22).[87]

Julian's comportment and his physiognomy reflected his internal vices, his vacillating, malleable character.[88] Others recognized him for what he truly was only after the fact, whereas Gregory even as a young man in Athens had seen through him. He had met Julian when, after Gallus's death, "having demanded and obtained permission from the emperor," Julian came to Athens for one noble reason, "to know Greece and its schools personally"—a defense of Gregory's view of Athens—and for an evil one, "to consult the priests and the impostors there regarding his destiny."[89] He ought to have consulted instead the oracle Gregory, who was far more *mantikos* than the oracle at Eleusis. When Gregory laid eyes on Julian in Athens, he saw a man remarkably similar to the emperor's own presentation of his person in the *Misopogon,* who was the obverse of Gregory's ideal philosopher (a man such as himself) in *Oration* 6.2: "I saw nothing indicating anything good." His neck and shoulders twitched and trembled; his eyes roamed; he was constantly scurrying about, screwing up his face. He laughed noisily and inappropriately; his speech was marred by wheezing and snuffling; his questions were incoherent, and his arguments devoid of logic (*Or.* 5.23).[90]

---

86. Jul. *CG* fr. 36; *Or.* 9.184a; 192a on a philosopher's *apatheia;* Brown, *Power and Persuasion,* 69–89.

87. Association with "old women" was a standard slur (see also Pl. *Tht.* 176b) Julian *Ep.* 89b.295d also used to deride Christian prophecies. Amm. Marc. 22.14.3 criticized Julian's *mulierculi* in the context of Julian's sacerdotal zeal; Lib. *Or.* 12.80–82, 18.126–27.

88. For the widespread use of physiognomy and its significance for constructing manliness, Gleason, *Making Men.*

89. Gr. Naz. *Or.* 5.23: τὸν βασιλέα τοῦτο αὐτὸ παραιτησάμενος, ... ὁ μὲν εὐπρεπέστερος, καθ' ἱστορίαν τῆς Ἑλλάδος καὶ τῶν ἐκεῖσε παιδευτηρίων ... ὥστε τοῖς ἐκεῖ θύταις καὶ ἀπατεῶσι περὶ τῶν καθ' ἑαυτὸν συγγενέσθαι.

90. This passage, cited in nearly all monographs on Julian, scholars have read psychologically, but they have also dismissed it as pure rhetoric; Gregory of Nazianzus, *La morte di Giuliano l'Apostata:*

Such physiognomic traits revealed to the discerning physician of the soul the true diagnosis: "I saw him before the deeds as I came to know him after the deeds. And if some of those who were with me then and heard me then could be with me now, they could attest to this without difficulty. Turning to them, immediately after having seen these things, I exclaimed, 'What a disaster is the Roman Empire nurturing here!' And while voicing this premonition I prayed at the same time to be a bad prophet [*pseudomantis*]."[91] Alas, earthquakes, fires, tsunamis, "about which there is now so much talk," substantiate the disasters Gregory's physiognomic diagnosis had predicted (*Or.* 5.24). As Gavin Kelly has pointed out, Julian's death and Procopius's revolt are the subtext of most fourth- and fifth-century discussion of the providential implications of the tsunami of July 21, 365, and in my view Gregory's *Oration* 5 forms part of those discussions.[92]

So much, then, for Libanius's savior (*Or.* 18.4), "different from the gods because he eats food as humans do, but close to them in the practice of virtue and in the care of the soul."[93] "That is what we have to tell, we the Galileans, we the despised, the venerators of the Cross, the disciples of fishermen and of the uneducated, as they say; we who assemble with old women and sing psalms with them, we who consume ourselves through fasting and reduce ourselves to near-starvation, we who pass the nights uselessly with vigils.... Where are the grammarians? Where are the counselors? From one of our *a-sophoi* [Paul], at least as he appears to you, I take the chant of victory. Where are the sacrifices and the initiations and the mysteries? ... Where are the prodigies of divination, ... the much-promised glorious Babylon? Where is that entire universe seen in a drop of sacrificial blood? ... Where are the gods who marched ahead of the army and next to it, who fought before it and with it? ... All disappeared like a dream."[94]

Orazione 5, trans. and comm. Lugaresi, 71–79; Rosen, *Julian*, 14–15 for the *Misopogon*, and 18–19 for the passage.

91. Gr. Naz. *Or.* 5.24: Τοῦτον πρὸ τῶν ἔργων ἐθεασάμην ὃν καὶ ἐπὶ τῶν ἔργων ἐγνώρισα. Καὶ εἴ μοι παρῆσάν τινες τῶν τηνικαῦτα συνόντων καὶ ἀκουσάντων, οὐ χαλεπῶς ἂν ἐμαρτύρησαν· οἷς, ἐπειδὴ ταῦτα ἐθεασάμην, εὐθὺς ἐφθεγξάμην· "Οἷον κακὸν ἡ Ῥωμαίων τρέφει," καὶ προαγορεύσας καὶ γενέσθαι ψευδόμαντις ἐμαυτοῦ κατευξάμενος, probably alluding to Theognis 39–40 and the city giving birth to a tyrant.

92. Amm. Marc. 26.10.15; Them. *Or.* 7.86b. G. Kelly, "Ammianus," 143–48, discusses Christian sources but not *Or.* 5. While Gregory probably referred to that tsunami here, he often mentioned earthquakes, common in seismically active Asia Minor. In *Or.* 21.33, Gregory stated that the earth refused to receive Julian's corpse, whereas Libanius saw earthquakes as a sign of the earth mourning the emperor; Kurmann, *Gregor von Nazianz*, 99; Wiemer, *Libanios*, 262–66.

93. Lib. *Or.* 16.18: τῶν θεῶν τῷ μὲν σῖτον ἐσθίειν διέστηκεν, ἐν δὲ τῇ τῆς ἀρετῆς ἀσκήσει καὶ τῇ τῆς ψυχῆς ἐπιμελείᾳ πλησίον αὐτῶν ἐστι.

94. Gr. Naz. *Or.* 5.25: Ταῦτα τῶν Γαλιλαίων ἡμῶν, ταῦτα τῶν ἀτίμων τὰ διηγήματα· ταῦτα οἱ τὸν ἐσταυρωμένον προσκυνοῦντες ἡμεῖς, ταῦτα οἱ τῶν ἁλιέων μαθηταὶ καὶ τῶν ἀπαιδεύτων, ὡς αὐτοὶ λέγουσι· ταῦτα οἱ τοῖς γραϊδίοις συγκαθεζόμενοι καὶ συμψάλλοντες· ταῦτα οἱ ταῖς μακραῖς νηστείαις

Providence and Governance

The final chapters of *Oration* 5 (25–34) lead up to and return to the theme that so preoccupied Libanius, and Gregory in *Oration* 4: the providential lessons of Julian's rule and its end.[95] For Gregory, Julian, though in no way connected to the divine—indeed the epitome of *allotriotēs* in relation to God—had been a divine sign, a *sēmeion* sent to teach the *oikoumenē* of the Romans a lesson: But which lesson (*Or.* 5.33–34)?[96] In Libanius's view Julian had been an excellent servant of the gods who had done all he was meant to do to cure the world and halt the spread of disease by guiding the *oikoumenē* and its inhabitants back to the gods. Alas, humanity had lost its capacity to listen and to read the gods' will, and the gods had allowed Julian to die young and gloriously so that they could prolong their harsh lesson; times had to get even worse before they could get better.[97]

To decipher God's will was not easy for Gregory either.[98] By the time of *Oration* 5, Gregory's emphasis on the providential explanation in *Oration* 4—that Julian was punishment for misuse of power—had shifted. Now the principal divine lesson was restraint in victory as a proper recognition of divine justice (as the Persians had practiced it). Echoing Themistius's *Oration* 5, Gregory contends that reconciliation, tolerance, and mildness toward those subjugated had to be paramount in an empire governed as Christian (*Or.* 5.36–38). "Like children we have been corrected. Let us not forget the tempest in times of calm or infirmity in times of good health . . . , now that we show ourselves exalted and inflated with pride and ready to return to the same sins for which we have been disgraced. . . . [Knowing that it is easier to bemoan prosperity lost than to preserve what one has,] let us seek

---

ἐκτετηγμένοι καὶ ἡμιθνῆτες· ταῦτα οἱ μάτην ἀγρυπνοῦντες ἡμεῖς. . . . Ποῦ εἰσιν οἱ γραμματικοί; Ποῦ εἰσιν οἱ σύμβουλοι;᾽Εκ τῶν παρ' ἡμῖν τινος ἀσόφων ὡς γοῦν ὑμῖν δοκεῖ λαμβάνω τὸν ἐπινίκιον. Ποῦ αἱ θυσίαι καὶ τελεταὶ καὶ μυστήρια; . . . Ποῦ τέχνη κατὰ τῶν ἐντόμων ἐπαινουμένη; . . . Ποῦ Βαβυλὼν ἡ ἔνδοξος θρυλλουμένη καὶ οἰκουμένη πᾶσα περινοουμένη δι' ὀλίγου καὶ ἐναγοῦς αἵματος; . . . Ποῦ δὲ οἱ προπεμπόμενοι καὶ παραπέμποντες καὶ προπολεμοῦντες καὶ συμπολεμοῦντες θεοί; . . . Οἴχεται πάντα, διέψευσται, διερρύηκεν, ὄναρ ἐφάνη τῶν ἀσεβῶν τὰ κομπάσματα.

95. In *Or.* 5.25–32, as in *Or.* 4.12–19, Gregory chanted another victory hymn, now summarizing the key themes of *Or.* 4: Julian's ingratitude, his sacrifices, his hatred of martyrs, whose tombs he burned, his laws aimed at "closing our mouths" (τὰς γλώσσας ἡμῶν ἐμφράξοντες), "the discourses of an emperor and sophist" (τοὺς λόγους . . . τοὺς βασιλικούς τε καὶ σοφιστικούς), for which he used divinatory and magic books, and his ridiculous gods; Gregory of Nazianzus, *La morte di Giuliano l'Apostata: Orazione 5*, trans. and comm. Lugaresi, 227–44; Demoen, *Pagan and Biblical Exempla*, 189–92, 211–31.

96. Athanasius's view that Julian had been merely a passing cloud was a minority opinion; Gregory of Nazianzus, *La morte di Giuliano l'Apostata: Orazione 5*, trans. and comm. Lugaresi, 80.

97. Jul. *Or.* 7.227c–234c; Lib. *Or.* 17.36–37; 18.2, 4, 21–23, 122–25, 281–83, 285, 287, 298; see Martig, *Studi*, 131–46.

98. Aug. *Civ. Dei* 5.21 also grappled with the concept: "dat felicitatem in regno caelorum solis piis; regnum vero terrenum et piis et impiis, sicut ei placet, cui nihil iniuste placet."

to be masters of ourselves, and let us regulate our circumstances wisely."[99] Gregory knows that men like their revenge, especially well-deserved revenge, and they do not like to hear of restraint. "I know that I will pronounce a difficult discourse hard to accept for the many ... but one that is nevertheless worth hearing and accepting. Let us not abuse the situation; let us not rejoice in our power; let us not become cruel toward those who have done us injustice, lest we commit the same crimes as those of which we have accused them.... Let us show what Christ has taught us!"[100]

Christians must not confiscate goods, bring false accusations to the tribunals, send persons capriciously into exile, or punish them by torture. God has already exacted revenge in just measure on their behalf, and the actions of Christians ought not to interfere with that divine judgment. "Peoples and cities already inveigh against the persecutors in the theaters, the marketplaces, the assemblies. The old is blessed; the new, shamed [*stēliteuein*] even by those who have participated in the persecution.... What more do we want?"[101] Here, uniquely in his orations, Gregory skillfully embeds a mention of Julian's name, *Ioulianos,* in a list of paradigmatic offenders of divine will—inspired by Homer's *Odyssey:* Tantalus, Tityus, and Ixion.[102] Those now in command ought not to offend the divine will in like manner by ingratitude and revenge, questioning the just measure of God's punishment by behaving with extreme and unnecessary harshness: scourges and whips belong to the hereafter.

This was a severe condemnation of practices such as those Valens had used against Maximus of Ephesus and other Friends and followers of Julian. Valentinian and Valens's purges had in fact been drastic in contrast to those of Jovian, who had shown tolerance and restraint, removing only a few persons, such as Alexander of Heliopolis, the governor of Syria known from the *Misopogon*. Valens's and Valentinian's purges began when the emperors fell ill with fever in Constantinople just after Valens's proclamation as Augustus on March 28, 364. Fearing that

99. Gr. Naz. *Or.* 5.34: ὡς παῖδες ἐσωφρονίσθημεν. Μὴ ἐπιλαθώμεθα τῆς ζάλης ἐν τῇ γαλήνῃ, μηδὲ τῆς ἀρρωστίας ἐν τῷ καιρῷ τῆς ὑγιείας.... γενώμεθα ἡμῶν αὐτῶν καὶ σωφρόνως τὸν καιρὸν διαθώμεθα.

100. Gr. Naz. *Or.* 5.36: χαλεπὸν μὲν οἶδα λόγον ἐρῶν καὶ δυσπαράδεκτον τοῖς πολλοῖς, ... ἀκουσθῆναι δὲ ὅμως καὶ προσδεχθῆναι ἄξιον. Μὴ ἀπλήστως χρησώμεθα τῷ καιρῷ. μὴ κατατρυφήσωμεν τῆς ἐξουσίας, μὴ πικροὶ γενώμεθα τοῖς ἠδικηκόσι, μὴ ὧν κατέγνωμεν, ταῦτα πράξωμεν, ... δείξωμεν.... τί δὲ ἡμᾶς ἐκπαιδεύει Χριστός;

101. Gr. Naz. *Or.* 5.37: Δήμοις καταβοῶνται καὶ πόλεσιν οἱ διώξαντες ἐν θεάτροις, ἐν ἀγοραῖς, ἐν συλλόγοις. Τὰ παλαιὰ μακαρίζεται, τὰ νέα στηλιτεύεται καὶ παρ' αὐτῶν τῶν συνδιωξάντων.... Τούτων τί μεῖζον ἐπιζητοῦμεν; Demoen, *Pagan and Biblical Exempla,* 120–22, for Gregory's use of old and new.

102. Gr. Naz. *Or.* 5.38: οἷς ἀδικίαν κολάζουσι Τάνταλος, Τιτυός, Ἰξίων. Ἰουλιανός, ταύτης ὁ βασιλεὺς ὑμῶν τῆς φατρίας, μετ' ἐκείνων ἀριθμηθήσεται. Homer *Od.* 10.513–14; Tantalus, 11.582–92; and Tityus, 11.576–81, whose liver was eaten. Ixion is mentioned in Pindar *P.* 2.39–76; he was bound on a burning wheel and rolled through the sky. Gregory mentioned Julian's name again only in *Carm.* 1.2.1.458, *PG* 37.557; Gregory of Nazianzus, *Contro Giuliano,* trans. and comm. Lugaresi, 224–25.

their fever had been caused by the sorcery of Julian's friends, they began to remove them. Noel Lenski has presented an impressive list of officeholders, including Aurelius Victor, Saturninius Secundus Salutius, and Modestus, prefect of Constantinople, whose careers were interrupted, albeit in some instances only briefly. (Salutius was removed in 365 but recalled in 366 to help Valens against Procopius; Modestus was forced out in 364 but later also recalled.) Many leading officials were charged with peculation, flogged, fined, had their properties confiscated, and were exiled, such as Salutius, Claudius Mamertinus, Oribasius, and Julian's teacher Nicocles. Libanius rightly bemoaned that none of "our" friends had any influence at court; his *Epitaphius* also alludes to an edict demanding payment as punishment for sacrifices.[103] Gregory concurred entirely with Libanius's judgment. Measures such as those used, for example, against the philosopher Maximus were harsh, excessive, inappropriate, and an offense against God's will that did not reflect good (Christian) governance.[104]

Festivals and the City   To practice restraint in victory was not the same as not to celebrate. Of course, public celebrations were called for after Julian's demise, but as with all other acts of public representation, imperial ceremonial, and governance, these had to reflect appropriate Christian decorum: retaliations should be moderate, and so too celebrations. How then should a Christian polis conduct its festivals? Note that a central strand of Gregory's arguments in both *Orations* 4 and 5 is to use Julian's actions to demonstrate how to Christianize the city and what it stood for: to locate properly the *hiera* (inside or outside the city), to recognize that divine authorization was required not only to erect but also to destroy temples and churches, to honor in the agora and the tribunals those to whom honor was due, and to celebrate appropriately in public (*Or.* 5.35). According to Gregory, Julian's festivals, as he had made evident in his *Misopogon* and in all his public acts, were dominated by expensive sacrifices, incense, sumptuously dressed priests conducting pompous processions, hymns, and raucous feasts—in sum, by a combination of greed and *asebeia* (*Or.* 5.29)—and they excluded Christians from all the central sites of the polis and its affairs.[105] Now this will be reversed to give public

---

103. Ammianus despised Valens's circle of Friends and advisors (26.6.7–8, 6.17, 7.7, 8.14) and denounced especially the cruelty of the purges (26.10.13–14); for the fever and the resulting accusation of sorcery, 26.4.4. Lib. *Or.* 18.286–89 criticizes Valens's cruel treatment of the philosophers; *Or.* 18.286 mentions the payments for sacrifices Jovian had permitted; *CTh* 9.16.7. For Libanius's lack of Friends at court, *Ep.* 1459; Lenski, *Failure*, 25–26, 105–8; Matthews, *Roman Empire*, 201–3.

104. *Pace* Lugaresi (Gregory of Nazianzus, *La morte di Giuliano l'Apostata: Orazione 5*, trans. and comm. Lugaresi, 81–82), who reads this as expressing Gregory's hope Valens would not interfere in the affairs of the church.

105. Jul. *Mis.* 361d–362a describes the festival honoring Apollo he had expected to see at Daphne; *Ep.* 64 (Bidez) = fr. 176.

festivals their true sacred dimension. "First and foremost, Brothers, let us not celebrate by the splendor of our body, by costly changes of clothes, by revels and great drinking bouts.... Do not decorate your streets with flowers or your tables with the shame of perfumes. Do not garland your porticoes, illuminate your houses with lamps, or have them resound with instruments. This is the custom by which the Greeks celebrate their festivals during the sacred months; but we do not honor God in such manner."[106] When Christians celebrate, their lamps are "visions and conceptions of the divine."[107] Their priests and kings, both anointed, are their perfume. Their shepherds, their teachers, and those who are pure and elected are their flowers, incense, and altars. Hymns and psalms are their music; prayers, their theatrical applause. Instead of laughing they meditate; instead of drinking they listen to discourses; instead of levity they maintain decorum, and their dance is that of David, "which I consider to be a symbol of the decorous and intricate journey toward God."[108]

The topic was of great relevance: public festivals were central to the constitution of the polis and the *politeia,* and, like the theater, they were intrinsic to religion and the gods. Gregory takes every occasion to insist on the sacred content of civic and imperial rituals, rites, and sites, providing precise guidelines how to remove their Greek characteristics and to emphasize their true sacredness as Christian; for him the artful *Logos* is at the origin of all, festivals included. In other words, Gregory conceived the festivals evoked here as public celebrations linked to the polis and its space, in counterpoint to Julian's denial of Christian political and public space; these are not instances of secularization.[109] Though liturgical elements are present, this is not a call for a theoretical, contemplative communication with the divine either. The context leaves little doubt: the description of the festival falls between Gregory's exhortation to be mindful of the result of past abuses of power and his harsh condemnation of Valens's excessive retributions. To conduct a public festival the right, sacred, Christian way is among the duties of those who govern.[110]

---

106. Gr. Naz. *Or.* 5.35: Πρῶτον μέν, ἀδελφοί, πανηγυρίσωμεν μὴ φαιδρότητι σώματος, μηδὲ ἐσθῆτος ἐξαλλαγαῖς καὶ πολυτελείαις, μηδὲ κώμοις καὶ μέθαις, . . . μηδὲ ἄνθεσι στέψωμεν ἀγυιάς, μηδὲ μύρων αἰσχύναις τραπέζας μηδὲ πρόθυρα καλλωπίζετε· μὴ τῷ αἰσθητῷ φωτὶ καταλαμπέσθωσαν αἱ οἰκίαι, μηδὲ συναυλίαις καὶ κρότοις περιηχείσθωσαν. Οὗτος μὲν γὰρ Ἑλληνικῆς ἱερομηνίας ὁ νόμος· ἡμεῖς δὲ μὴ τούτοις τὸν θεὸν γεραίρωμεν.

107. Gr. Naz. *Or.* 5.35: θείοις λέγω θεωρήμασι καὶ νοήμασιν.

108. Gr. Naz. *Or.* 5.35: τοὺς ἱεροὺς καὶ εὐώδεις ποιμένας καὶ διδασκάλους καὶ τοῦ λαοῦ ὅσον καθαρόν τε καὶ ἔκκριτον, . . . ἣν ἡγοῦμαι τῆς εὐκινήτου καὶ πολυστρόφου κατὰ θεὸν πορείας εἶναι μυστήριον.

109. For the secularization of festivals and cities, Markus, *End of Ancient Christianity,* 107–23, with a theoretical discussion of the secular on pp. 1–19.

110. Gregory repeated his characterization of Christian public celebrations in *Or.* 38.4–5, and again, now positively, in *Or.* 21.9 for Athanasius's triumphant *adventus* into Alexandria after the murder of George.

PROCOPIUS VERSUS VALENS

Who, then, was Gregory's implicit audience, and who his real one, to use Wolfgang Iser's distinction?[111] As before—especially in *Oration 4*—Gregory wrote *Oration 5* with the emperor and his advisors as his implicit audience, whereas the real audience was probably narrower and closer to home. Gregory's two audiences overlapped: he engaged directly such pagan arguments as those proffered by Themistius, with whom he agreed, and Libanius, whom he opposed. Other members of the elites, including those at court, pagan as well as Christian, presumably also engaged in such discussions. Gregory's direct engagement of these arguments could easily serve to advise Christian members of the elites now entrusted with governing the empire—some at court, others his peers and friends in Cappadocia, Constantinople, and Antioch—how to argue and act. They evidently needed such advice urgently, and indeed, here the historical context becomes crucial: Procopius's revolt and the legitimacy of Valens. But before considering the historical circumstances of the years 364 and 365/6, including the whereabouts of Caesarius and Basil, Gregory's conclusion to *Oration 5* merits examination.

Gregory, warning against offending God by exacting excessive revenge, concluded with a list of offenders of the divine that included Julian by name—the only time (with one exception) he mentions the emperor directly (in contrast to Constantius, whose name appears several times in these orations alone). Gregory explicitly inscribed Julian into the column of shame as an offender against God.[112] Immediately thereafter he presented Julian with his "gift of welcome to match the hoof" the suitors had given Odysseus when he had been a beggar in his own house, citing the cowherd's boast as he killed Ctesippus (*Or.* 5.39; Hom. *Od.* 22.290). "That is what we give you, [the "most excellent and most intelligent,"] we the excluded from *logoi* because of your great and wonderful legislation." Instead of being condemned to silence, as beggars in their own home, "we" speak loudly and freely to confound "your" stupidity. The "we" here are Basil and Gregory, now also named explicitly. "This Basil and Gregory say to you, the opponents and adversaries of your endeavor—you thought so yourself and persuaded others of it, honoring us with your threats and inspiring us to greater fervor in our piety. Knowing that we, through our lives, our *logoi,* and our mutual harmony, were already distinguished and known in Greece, you considered us worthy of the honor of the Cyclops [Polyphemus, who

---

111. Iser, *Implizite Leser*; for general remarks about Gregory's audience, Demoen, *Pagan and Biblical Exempla*, 64–70.

112. For Constantius, *Or.* 4.3.1, 21.1, 88.2; for Julian, *Carm.* 1.2.1.458. Lugaresi (Gregory of Nazianzus, *Contro Giuliano*, trans. and comm. Lugaresi, 224–25) interprets Gregory's avoidance of Julian's name as de facto *damnatio memoriae,* extending beyond the literary conventions of the Second Sophistic not to name names. Libanius never mentions Jovian.

promised to eat Odysseus last: *Od.* 9.369–70], and you set us apart as the last victims of your persecution, planning perhaps to offer us to the demons as a great and splendid offering to thank them for your victory [had you returned from Persia]; or you hoped, having calculated badly, to drag us down with you into the abyss" (*Or.* 5.39).

Julian, Basil, Gregory: Basil and Gregory sign with their autographs the stele memorializing the infamy of him who wished to silence and to shame them, overwriting and thus erasing everything he had done. "Here is our stele for you, higher and more visible than the Stelae of Hercules, ... to shame you and all your works [*sa stēliteuousan*], and to teach everyone not to dare such a rebellion against God, lest they may be punished in like manner for having committed similar crimes" (*Or.* 5.42). Evoking once again the Maccabees of *Oration* 15, Gregory declares himself, his father and mother, and Basil to have been among the direct victims of Julian's persecutions, like two others, unnamed, who resisted torture and threats (*Or.* 5.40).

Nothing, of course, had happened to Gregory, Basil, or for that matter Caesarius under Julian—quite the contrary. Basil and Gregory advanced to become presbyters, and Caesarius's career also prospered. It is not at all implausible that Julian had known both Gregory and Basil. After all, Caesarius was his physician, and later tradition, at least, considered Basil so close to the emperor that Julian had personally invited him to court.[113] It is impossible not to think of Tacitus and Pliny under Trajan: like them, Gregory needed to explain how very threatened he and Basil had been, how close they had come to being martyred by Julian (their Domitian), while others, in contrast, had indeed suffered such a fate. But to be killed by Domitian (to stay with the analogy), required closeness to the tyrant, a harsh fate, to be sure, but also a marker of elite status: both Tacitus and Pliny presented themselves as personally under threat, and so did Gregory.[114] Julian had singled out him and Basil because he had known them and their *logoi* well, at least since their time at Athens. Their closeness to Julian and their fame were in fact what had prevented them from joining other martyrs, ready though they had been: Julian had saved them for last because they were his greatest prize.

Endowed with such authority, as personally chosen victims, almost, Basil and Gregory together countered "the lies and ravings of Porphyry that you praised as if they were divine voices, or your *Misopogon,* also called *Antiochikos logos:* both writings belong to the *logos* Christians consider most unworthy" (*Or.* 5.41). These writings were once considered great only because an emperor wrote them, but now

---

113. Julian's letter inviting Basil to court, *Ep.* 32 (Wright 26), may have addressed another Basil (see above, Chapters 3 and 4), but later tradition created an entire correspondence between them, *Epp.* 40–41 (*Saint Basile: Lettres,* ed. and trans. Courtonne, vol. 1, 94–98). For Gregory and Basil's Athenian connection, Gr. Naz. *Or.* 10.2, 43.22; McLynn, "Gregory Nazianzen's Basil," 181–83.

114. Sailor, *Writing and Empire,* 10–33; E. Elm, "Damnatio," 251–96.

that beard, which had been for Julian a proud sign of his asceticism and true philosophical life, was ridiculed. After all, Julian's asceticism had been run of the mill, especially when compared with the true philosophical life of Christians. What damage does it do the state (*koinon*) if one person vomits? But to incite a revolt against Christians, to innovate as Julian has done, harms the entire Roman Empire.

Misopogon *and* Oration 5

Gregory's citation here of Julian's oration by its title and his allusion to passages in that oration (for example, to Julian's account of his episode of vomiting in Lutetia when describing his ascetic habits: 340b–342a) proves, according to scholarly consensus, that Gregory had not read and did not know the *Misopogon* (or *Against the Galileans*, to which the reference to Porphyry's writing could allude, unless it responds only to Libanius). This is so because the *Misopogon* does not appear to affect the overall argument of *Oration* 5 (nor that of *Oration* 4, since both are considered one). Furthermore, there are no verbatim citations of the *Misopogon*, so that even Lugaresi thinks Gregory did not know that text, though he has splendidly established the link between Gregory's *Oration* 5 and Libanius's two works, also without verbatim citations. Most scholars believe that Gregory added these titles hastily at the end for little apparent reason.[115] Gregory may well have added the entire concluding section (*Or.* 5.39–42) hastily, but, in my view, for very good reasons. At this point, however, I turn briefly to the question of scholars' assessments of the relation between Gregory's *Oration* 5 and the *Misopogon*, and the verbatim citation as standard of proof as it relates to a pagan-Christian dialogue.

Oration 5 engaged specific arguments, to which the *Misopogon* relates only tangentially, thus making a direct engagement superfluous. Things differ with respect to *Oration* 4, however, as shown by Chapters 8 and 9 above (supported by Lugaresi's

---

115. Asmus, "Invektiven," 357, considers the reference to the *Misopogon* and *Antiochikos* (which the Post-Nicene Fathers of the Church translation renders into English as "Antichrist") a later addition to the manuscript and thus not part of the original oration, a suggestion Bernardi and Lugaresi reject. This passage is usually cited to argue that Gregory cannot have read Julian; Gregory of Nazianzus, *La morte di Giuliano l'Apostata: Orazione 5*, trans. and comm. Lugaresi, 258–61; Bernardi, ed. and trans., *Grégoire de Nazianze: Discours 4–5 contre Julien*, 46–50; Kurmann, *Gregor von Nazianz*, 25 n. 17, with bibliography. Moreschini's point (*Filosofia*, 175–77) that *Or.* 4 and 5 are a direct counter not to the *Misopogon* but to all of Julian's action is true, but that need not exclude that he knew individual writings. McGuckin's observation (*St. Gregory*, 132) that Gregory showed the orations to Basil and added his name as endorsement is important, especially given reluctance among some modern scholars to associate both saints with invectives. As for Julian's *CG*, Lugaresi (Gregory of Nazianzus, *La morte di Giuliano l'Apostata: Orazione 5*, trans. and comm. Lugaresi, 260) suggests Gregory did not know it when writing *Or.* 5, because he refers only to Porphyry, or that he knew Libanius's praise of the *CG* only in *Or.* 18. Caesarius appears to have left the court about the time of the *CG*'s completion, and it may not have circulated widely before Julian left for Persia. Still, Gregory and his audience knew what Julian thought about Christianity even without the *CG*.

commentary, which notes a plethora of allusions to the *Misopogon*). Both Gregory's *Oration* 4 and the *Misopogon* depart deliberately—in a sophisticated rhetorical turn—from classic invective, to which they nonetheless remain structurally beholden. Neither the *Misopogon* nor Gregory's *Oration* 4 has received a systematic, in-depth analysis of its structure, despite the invaluable work of Lugaresi, Criscuolo, Kurmann, Wiemer, Long, and Gleason, and neither work has ever been read systematically in comparison with the other. Both *Misopogon* and *Oration* 4 reveal, however, within the structure of the invective, a further structural similarity, in that both engage and comment on what is required of the just ruler, as defined in Plato's *Laws*. This could be entirely coincidental, or, in Gregory's case, a general response to what he may have heard about Julian; I read it as Gregory's deliberate engagement of Julian's self-presentation. There are many points of direct allusion—names, exemplars—some of which I discuss in the text or notes, and many more that Lugaresi and Kurmann note in their commentaries. A systematic comparison would add more, but it has as yet not been undertaken, because according to one group of scholars Gregory cannot have read the *Misopogon*, while other scholars do not consider Gregory's orations relevant beyond their function as a repository of gossip about Julian. In these arguments, the presence or absence of verbatim citations becomes crucial. Because Gregory does not cite Julian or Libanius verbatim, he cannot have had detailed knowledge of their works and arguments.[116] At the same time, scholars who posit such lack of awareness, corroborated by the lack of verbatim citation, agree that Gregory, Libanius, and Julian followed the literary conventions of the Second Sophistic; they also concur that these conventions prescribe that contemporaries, including enemies, not be named and their works not cited but merely alluded to (creating a specific form of literary *damnatio memoriae* in the case of opponents). Why then must Gregory cite Libanius and Julian verbatim to have known their work and arguments? Julian, Libanius, and Gregory cite verbatim and name persons they consider normative, authentic sources of divinely inspired wisdom—Homer, Hesiod, Plato, Aristotle, Zeno, scriptures, good emperors—and only in signal exceptions speak their own names or those of their opponents. (Note that Julian names but does not cite Iamblichus and Porphyry.) All else is conveyed by allusions to the shared heritage, to gods, heroic persons—Minos, Rhadamanthys, Darius, Cyrus, uneducated Cynics, and so on.[117] The methods of modern scholarly discourse, to which verbatim citations are central, do not apply.

---

116. Wiemer, *Libanios*, 257 n. 44, rejects the suggestion of Mattera, "Libanio," that the *Monody* may have prompted *Or.* 4, because "Mattera kann nur inhaltliche Parallelen anführen...; wörtliche Übereinstimmungen gibt es nicht."

117. Sabbah's incisive remarks (*Méthode*, 115-55, 371-72) are equally relevant for Gregory's work; Demoen, *Pagan and Biblical Exempla*, 21-23, 35-51, 189-92, 201-6.

Gregory may well never have read the *Misopogon,* publicly posted in Antioch, and may have added the citation and reference hastily to the end of *Oration* 5. But he need not have read that work, or any of Julian's writings, to understand perfectly what Julian wanted. Allusions, official pronouncements, hearsay from Caesarius and others, and Julian's self-presentation as bearded philosopher on his coins would have sufficed, because the logic and economy of *paideia,* as common currency, after all, made such allusions sufficient to know the essence of a person's presentation, even without reading his work. Gregory knew exactly what Julian, Libanius, Themistius and other pagans stood for, and he engaged their positions directly. Conversely, pagans knew their Gregory, as paradigmatic of their Christian contemporaries and friends. But to show this requires that scholars at least read the work of these contemporaries to discern whether they were in dialogue with each other. Perhaps scholars use verbatim citations to reify what they want to preserve—genealogies of influence that minimize interdependence, interaction, and dialogue. Libanius belongs to a genealogical line linking him—for scholarly purposes—to Julian and Ammianus; Porphyry and Iamblichus lead to Proclus; Gregory follows Origen, connects with Basil and Gregory of Nyssa, and leads on to John Chrysostom, Socrates, and Sozomen. Eusebius and Themistius are the odd men out (one as pagan advocate of Christian emperors, the other as doctrinally suspect Christian historian), and the absence of verbatim citations is proof positive that to read across these genealogies is, after all, not called for. Be this as it may, Gregory did add a verbatim citation of the double title of Julian's *Misopogon* to his conclusion of *Oration* 5, a rare occurrence indeed.

Procopius's Revolt

Why did Gregory cite the title *Misopogon,* or *Antiochikos logos,* and add a short reference to Julian's beard and his ascetic habits (including the vomiting incident)? The citation occurs just after Gregory has mentioned himself, Basil, and Julian by name, presenting the stele of infamy, overwriting every one of Julian's deeds and words, to remind future generations never to revolt as he had done. Gregory and Basil at that moment are formally introduced by name as persons whom Julian knew personally and had personally singled out as the ultimate sacrifice because of the power of their *logoi.* As an endorsement, this is hard to top. Gregory claimed all the markers of prestige: sufficient closeness to the tyrant to be under his personal threat and spared martyrdom by divine design (Julian's death). How much more authority could Gregory-Odysseus's *logoi* carry?

Gregory's audience, as his citation proves, was familiar with the *Misopogon,* or *Beard Hater,* perhaps because they had links to Antioch, as the oration's engagement with Libanius also implies. Moreover, the themes discussed in *Oration* 5 imply as audience persons engaged in public office, primarily Christians. Among those addressed, exhorted, and criticized were persons—including Valens—directly involved in the judicial harassment of Julian's Friends.[118] However, Gregory's sustained praise of Constantius and Jovian as good emperors, including his defense of them as homoian, indicate that the target of Gregory's criticism was not Valens as ruler, but only Julian and others who wore beards and represented themselves as ascetic philosopher-emperors.

In the fall of 365, Valens left Constantinople for Antioch to engage Persia, having issued an edict on May 5 revoking Julian's amnesty and sending home again the bishops whom Constantius had exiled and Julian had recalled.[119] En route, he spent several weeks in Caesarea, primarily to wait out a heat wave, but perhaps also to address Rome's relations with Armenia, much impaired as a result of Jovian's peace treaty, in which Jovian had to cede all influence in that region.[120] By early October or thereabout, Valens learned of Procopius's usurpation in Constantinople and turned back toward Galatia to winter in Ancyra. Procopius, supposedly hiding in Chalcedon prior to his revolt, quickly managed to gain control of Thrace and of the harbors along the Bosporus, thus rupturing all communication between Valens and Valentinian, the senior Augustus. By the fall of 365, Procopius had extended his control to Bithynia. Indeed, by the time he engaged Valens's force in the winter of 365, Procopius had become a formidable adversary, particularly, as Noel Lenski has pointed out, because Valentinian had left his brother to fend for himself. Procopius in fact emerged victorious in direct battle with Valens, taking Cyzicus and thus gaining control over the Hellespont and then Asiana while Valens retreated to Ancyra. Only in the spring of 366 had Valens assembled sufficient troops for a decisive action, which resulted finally in Procopius's capture and decapitation, on May 27, 366.[121]

Procopius's usurpation, unusual because it occurred without instigation by the army, found significant support among elite circles, both Christian and non-Christian. Valens had not been popular, in part because of his brutish, humble Pannonian origin and in part because to finance another war he had demanded funds from the landed elites, especially those residing in Constantinople.[122] Valens had no connection to Constantine's and Constantius's imperial dynasty, the second longest to rule up to that time.[123] Procopius, in contrast, could claim such a connection, and he made the most of it, even if the link was through Julian's mother. Indeed, sup-

---

118. To expose members of the elites publicly to juridical cruelty was considered especially savage, and Gregory is no exception in denouncing such practices; Lenski, *Failure*, 103–15.

119. Ath. *Hist. aceph.* 5.1 (Athanasius of Alexandria, *Histoire "acephale,"* ed. and trans. Martin and Albert, 158); Soz. *HE* 6.12.5; Brennecke, *Studien*, 209.

120. Amm. Marc. 25.7.12 for Armenia. The peace treaty was a compromise, returning to Persia about half the territory Rome had gained after 299; but Rome lost its claim to protect Armenia when called upon, so that Armenia was now exposed to Persian control; Lenski, *Failure*, 161–64.

121. Lenski, *Failure*, 68–82.

122. Amm. Marc. 26.6.9.

123. MacCormack, *Art*, 185–88, for the imperial propaganda of the new Flavians.

port for Procopius did not follow pagan-versus-Christian lines, but persons rallied for Procopius and against Valens for a variety of reasons, among which religion was the least important. (Eunomius, for example, was a strong supporter of Procopius.) Particularly in Constantinople, many high-ranking persons with close ties to Constantius and to Julian rallied to the usurper.[124] In addition, not least because of Valens's harsh reprisals, Procopius gained strong support among Julian's close friends; that Libanius in faraway Antioch was later accused of having composed Procopius's panegyric "serves to highlight the kind of person contemporaries associated with the rebel."[125] Procopius's coins, struck while he controlled the Hellespont and Bithynia, make this clear. They show him as Christian and also portray him as a bearded, lean-faced, ascetic philosopher: as Constantius's and Julian's legitimate heir.[126]

Gregory, in his conclusion citing the *Misopogon,* dismantled precisely such an emperor as a bearded, lean-faced, ascetic philosopher—referring as much to the dead emperor as to his living relative now claiming the throne as heir to Constantius and Julian (*Or.* 5.40).[127] The whole of Gregory's *Oration* 5 counters Libanius and his arguments—that is, the arguments of persons allied with Procopius. Gregory praised Constantius and Jovian, and though he criticized Valens's harshness, the overwhelming critique of Julian makes it clear that for Gregory the true and legitimate heir to Constantius (and hence also the corrective heir to Julian) was Valens, and no one else. Valens's propaganda also emphasized that he was Constantius's legitimate successor: Jovian had been a legitimate successor to Julian, and Valens to Jovian—a link displayed, for example, in the official care and expense lavished on Julian's mausoleum.[128] Once he had subdued Procopius, Valens proceeded with far greater clemency and mildness toward Procopius's supporters than he had with Julian's; too many of Procopius's supporters were persons loyal to the Constantinian dynasty that Valens too considered his legitimate root.[129]

Gregory, in short, took a clear position and was well informed. Indeed, Caesarius had rejoined the imperial administration, probably already under Jovian. According to Gregory, Valentinian and Valens competed for Caesarius's friendship, which suggests that Caesarius assumed the position of treasurer responsible for the

---

124. Philost. *HE* 9.5.8 says that Procopius was hiding in Chalcedon with Eunomius; Amm. Marc. 26.6.5 has him hide with Strategius, a close friend and court official of Julian; Matthews, *Roman Empire,* 192–97, 199–200; Vaggione, *Eunomius,* 292–97; Lenski, *Failure,* 110–11.

125. Lenski, *Failure,* 109.

126. Pearce, *Roman Imperial Coinage,* vol. 9, 209–16, 192–93, 239–41, 250–52; Lenski, *Failure,* 100.

127. Jul. *Mis.* 340c; Amm. Marc. 26.7.11, 26.8.7–9. I think Caesarius was in residence in Nicaea under Procopius, though he could have arrived there after Procopius's execution; Matthews, *Roman Empire,* 200.

128. Lib. *Or.* 24.10.

129. For the lenient purges after the revolt, Lenski, *Failure,* 111–13.

imperial finances, residing in Nicaea, as early as 364—which means that he held that position while Procopius controlled the city and Bithynia. (And Caesarius would certainly have known what Procopius's coins represented.) Caesarius occupied that position until his death in 368/9: his public career, which had begun under Constantius, continued under Julian, Jovian, Procopius, and Valens.[130]

Thus, the contours of Gregory's real audience emerge. One person who needed advice on how to behave while Procopius was in power may well have been Caesarius. As Gregory's correspondence indicates, and as has been mentioned already above, a number of his friends belonged to the Constantinopolitan elites and were active in Valens's administration. (And although we do not know what they did while Procopius claimed power, those residing in areas a usurper controlled tended to support him.) Under Valens, Sophronius was *magister officiorum;* Aburgius became quaestor about 369; Flavius Saturninus, *magister militum* and consul; Cledonius held an office at court during Valens's reign; a certain Julian (not the emperor), whom Gregory had known since Athens, had become *peraequator* in Bithynia and Galatia in 363. (It is not clear what he did under Valens.)[131] They and others like them may well have been those for whose benefit Gregory argued, persons who may not in fact have objected at all to the Christian Constantinian Procopius in Constantinople, with the result that all of Gregory's and Basil's combined authority was required to persuade them that Valens, and not Procopius, was eminently worthy of ruling (and that Themistius and Gregory were worthy of advising the ruler of the realm, and not those who argued like Libanius)—by pointing out how Julian ought to be remembered and why, and why they had better yield to such persuasion.

Valens and Basil

Gregory would not have been Gregory, however, if his very political *Oration* 5 did not have a theological subtext. In Gregory there is never a distinction between what we call "political" today and what we think of, on the whole, as theological. When Gregory praised Constantius's funeral and apotheosis, he explicitly chastised those who had criticized Constantius's homoian accord. "If indeed he seemed to have dis-

---

130. Gr. Naz. *Or.* 7.14–15; *Carm.* 2.1.11.368. The precise nature of that office is difficult to ascertain, most likely *comes thesaurorum* or *rationalis rerum privatarum;* Coulie, *Richesses,* 140; *Grégoire de Nazianze: Discours 6–12,* ed. and trans. Calvet-Sébasti, 49–50; McGuckin, *St. Gregory,* 155–57, 162–63; Van Dam, *Families,* 62, and "Self-representation," 121–22.

131. For Sophronius, Gr. Naz. *Epp.* 37, 39, and Saturninus (*PLRE,* vol. 1, Flavius Saturninus 10, p. 807—i.e., not Saturninius Secundus Salutius), *Ep.* 181, dating from the same period; see *Epp.* 37–39, written on behalf of Eudoxius. For Gregory's other connections to the Constantinopolitan elite and to provincial officeholders, *Carm.* 2.2.3, *Ad Vitalianum,* PG 37.1480A–1505C, esp. vv. 181–84; *Epp.* 193, 194, *To Vitalianus; Epp.* 24, 38, *To Themistius;* Hauser-Meury, *Prosopographie,* s.vv., 110–11, 153–54, 156–57, 179–80. As McLynn has pointed out ("Other Olympias," 245 n. 75), Gregory's correspondence after 381 includes additional Constantinopolitan court officials: i.e., Modares, Procopius, Postumianus, and Victor.

turbed the right teaching [*orthodoxa*], even that accusation should be directed to the stupidity and false teachings of those who exercised power in his name, who—controlling a simple soul not steadfast in its piety, which thus did not anticipate the dangers—guided him where they wanted and, under the pretense of precision [*akribeia*], turned zeal into something bad."[132] The characterization of Constantius as simple is one we have encountered before. Less common, indeed surprising in light of earlier characterizations, is the observation that Constantius was not steadfast in his *eusebeia* and thus was open to the influence of those in his circle who used *akribeia* to confound him. "Precision" (*akribeia*) and "zeal" (*spoudē, zēlos*) are watchwords Gregory most often employs to allude to Eunomius, but Constantius had not been Eunomius's supporter. It may well be that Gregory's defense of the deceased Constantius, whose apotheosis he had just affirmed, was designed, rather, to provide arguments in support of Valens, by analogy with Constantius.

Valens has entered history as the arch–Arian heretic, in no small part because Gregory later characterized him as pseudo-Christian and as Julian redivivus (*Or.* 42.3, 43.44–46); he became also Gregory's and Basil's declared enemy, as epitomized in the famous standoff between emperor and bishop, Valens and Basil, in Basil's church as portrayed by Gregory (*Or.* 43.52–53, 31–32).[133] The occasion of that famous portrayal was Gregory's funeral oration for Basil, in January 382, in which Gregory described the encounter, which had occurred in 372, in the same church in Caesarea where Gregory now spoke. But what can we infer about Gregory and Basil's attitude toward Valens in 365 and 366, at the time of *Oration* 5? Does external evidence support the view that Gregory defended Valens against Procopius?

As Brennecke has shown, Valens, not at all tolerant of Julian's supporters, followed Jovian in supporting Constantius's homoian agreement of 360, with the intention of restoring and maintaining harmony and peace among Christians.[134] That Valens would more or less follow in what he considered Constantius's footsteps became evident as early as late 364, when he flatly rejected a delegation of bishops who had met at Lampsacus and who supported homoiousians such as Macedonius's followers (he had died in the interim) and Eustathius against Eudoxius and especially Eunomius: Basil had used scribes provided by Eustathius to arm him with arguments against Eunomius in time for that meeting.[135] This delegation rejected the

---

132. Gr. Naz. *Or.* 5.16: Καὶ γὰρ εἰ τὴν ὀρθὴν δόξαν παρακινεῖν ἔδοξεν, ἀλλὰ καὶ τοῦτο τῆς τῶν ὑποδυναστευόντων σκαιότητος καὶ κακοδοξίας τὸ ἔγκλημα, οἳ ἁπλῆν καὶ ἀπαγῆ εἰς εὐσέβειαν παραλαβόντες ψυχήν, οὐ προορωμένην τὰ βάραθρα, ἀπήγαγον ᾗπερ ἐβούλοντο καὶ προσχήματι ἀκριβείας τὸν ζῆλον κακίαν εἰργάσαντο. Gr. Naz. *Or.* 4.36; Brennecke, *Studien*, 226–27.

133. Beginning with Rufinus, the Nicene historiography considered Valens an apostate like Julian, perhaps inspired by Gregory's description of the emperor; Rufin. *HE* 11.2–9; Socr. *HE* 4.2.6, 1, 15–18; Soz. *HE* 6.7.10, 13, 15, 16, 18–21; Thdt. *HE* 4.13–15; Brennecke, *Studien*, 185.

134. Lenski, *Failure*, 243.

135. Bas. *Ep.* 223; Rousseau, *Basil*, 102.

accord of 360, including its elevation of Eunomius to the position of bishop. Valens in turn repudiated them, urging them to reconcile with Eudoxius, though his full response came only in the spring of 365, when he issued the edict stipulating that bishops sent home and into exile by Constantius and recalled by Julian should once again leave; he added—because he had to finance another Persian campaign—that he would fine magistrates who failed to ensure compliance three hundred pounds in gold.[136]

Shortly after issuing that edict, Valens proceeded to Antioch, pausing in Caesarea to wait out a heat wave. In anticipation of that visit, Gregory wrote to Basil, by then in Annesi, and urged him to return to Caesarea to reconcile with Eusebius and to assume his priestly duties.[137] Eusebius, bishop of Caesarea, had been a staunch homoian and for that reason had suffered Julian's reprisals when that emperor paused in Caesarea on his way to Antioch and to fight against the Persians. Basil supported Eustathius and the decisions of Lampsacus, even though he began to distance himself from the *homoiousios* at that time. As he pointed out in a letter to Maximus the Philosopher (*Ep.* 9, not Maximus of Ephesus), Basil was prepared to accept the term *homoios,* but only if it was understood to mean "like in essence," *homoios kat' ousian* (*homoiousios,* in sum), "without variation" (*aparallaktōs*). The accord of Constantinople had not been specific enough when it accepted merely *homoios.* In addition, Basil had shifted his emphasis further, as Philip Rousseau has pointed out: "I have therefore myself adopted the phrase 'of the same substance' [*to homoousion*], because I think that this term is less open to perversion." Basil addressed this letter, and others written at the same time that concerned the same theological issues, to wealthy "citizens of this world," his peers actively engaged in public life, precisely those whom Gregory's *Oration* 5 addressed and sought to persuade at that time.[138]

In fact, from Gregory's perspective, Basil, the conspicuous cosigner of *Oration* 5, was among those to be persuaded to accept Valens's homoian policies. As Basil's letter just cited indicates, Basil supported Eustathius's *homoiousios* position and thus the delegates from Lampsacus whom Valens had repudiated, even if he now began to favor a more definitively *homoousios* interpretation, which was indeed gaining ground at the time thanks to the increasing influence of Meletius in Antioch.[139] Nevertheless, Basil was still prepared to accept the *homoios,* and Gregory's letter urged him to reconcile with the homoian Eusebius in Caesarea (just as those in Nazianzus

---

136. I follow Brennecke, *Studien,* 184–86, 202–9, 212–14; *pace,* in some aspects, McGuckin, *St. Gregory,* 140–44. According to Ath. *Hist. aceph.* 5.1–10 (Athanasius of Alexandria, *Histoire "acephale,"* ed. and trans. Martin and Albert, 158), Valens's edict reached Alexandria on May 5; Rousseau, *Basil,* 88–89, 135–36; Vaggione, *Eunomius,* 290–92.

137. Gr. Naz. *Ep.* 19; also *Epp.* 16–18; McGuckin, *St. Gregory,* 131–35.

138. Trans. Rousseau, *Basil,* 102.

139. Brennecke, *Studien,* 173–78; Ayres, *Nicaea,* 167–71, 188–90.

had reconciled with the homoian elder Gregory). That was also what Valens strove for: after all, reconciliation and forgiveness were the highest good, even if words to such effect were not always well received (*Or.* 5.36; Valens was still infirm in his faith, after all, easily detracted by the likes of Eunomius).

Eusebius had, in fact, written directly to Gregory at that time in anticipation of the imperial presence. With Basil in Annesi (and in opposition), Eusebius had asked the "most learned" (*logiōtatos*) Gregory instead to act as his advisor and voice should the emperor's presence require a public debate of matters of theology; the prospect of "these wild beasts that are rushing on the church" caused some trepidation.[140] Gregory replied, with a philosopher's *parrhēsia*, that he felt exceedingly honored to have been invited to the *synodoi*. He could be of assistance, however, only if Basil too was present—his "most honorable brother Basil, whom I have elected from the beginning [and still now hold] as my soul mate in terms of life, of thought, and of his most exalted philosophy."[141] So long as Eusebius dishonored Basil, Gregory could not accept the honor of this invitation. Eusebius, as Gregory's *Epistles* 17 and 18 reveal, was offended by his refusal to come. Gregory replied that the bishop ought to take the advice he had sought: Did he wish the frank counsel of a friend, or that of a sycophant? Gregory reiterated that peace was the order of the day, and when Eusebius invited him again, Gregory came. Eusebius appears to have relented on Basil as well. Gregory's letter to Basil, asking him to return to duty, indicated that Eusebius's apology was already en route and that Basil could therefore anticipate Eusebius. That way, he and Gregory could be seen as having won beautifully and philosophically, showing restraint in victory. Basil's signing *Oration* 5, and thus presumably approving its content, shows that he too was persuaded and did as Gregory had suggested: as "sage architect of the words and teachings . . . of the truth,"[142] Basil returned and reconciled with the homoian Eusebius and thus also with the homoian Valens—and if the likes of Gregory and Basil (eminently authoritative voices, as the conclusion of Gregory's *Oration* 5 had proved) considered Valens legitimate, who could disagree?[143]

Emperors, bishops, philosopher-priests as advisors, and their elite peers are the focus of *Orations* 4 and 5, each with different emphasis, but both also always

---

140. *Logiōtatos*, Gr. Naz. *Ep.* 17 (*Saint Grégoire de Nazianze: Lettres*, ed. Gallay, vol. 1, 25); wild beasts, *Ep.* 18, (ibid., 26). Homoiousians apparently initiated a number of local synods at the time, so that Eusebius's anticipation of a public debate in the emperor's presence was well founded; Brennecke, *Studien*, 218; T. D. Barnes, *Athanasius*, 161–62.

141. Gr. Naz. *Ep.* 16.4: τῷ τιμιωτάτῳ ἀδελφῷ Βασιλείῳ, . . . ὃν καὶ βίου καὶ λόγου κοινωνὸν καὶ τῆς ὑψηλοτάτης φιλοσοφίας εἱλόμην τ' ἀπ' ἀρχῆς καὶ νῦν ἔχω. Trans. McGuckin, *St. Gregory,* 141; and *Epp.* 17–19.

142. Gr. Naz. *Ep.* 19: τοῦ σοφοῦ τῶν τοιούτων ἀρχιτέκτονος λόγων τε καὶ δογμάτων.

143. Basil became bishop under Valens and enjoyed excellent relations with many court officials and a number of benefits; Lenski, *Failure,* 254–55.

concerned with the Trinity to which terms such as *homoios, homoios kat' ousian,* and *homoousios* refer. Even *Oration* 5, almost entirely engaging pagan arguments about the legitimacy of Jovian and Valens vis-à-vis Julian, carried its central arguments into the theological realm, for there was no distinction between the correct understanding of the Trinity and just governance. The active philosopher's duty, as priest and bishop, was to give advice to those who governed—fellow bishops, public officials, and emperors—at every opportunity, predicated on steadfast *eusebeia* sustained by the right teachings on the Trinity, which only those sufficiently purified could give: active philosophers such as Gregory.

This is the central message that endured; this the point Gregory illustrated so vividly when he opposed Valens and Basil (both deceased by the time of *Oration* 43) nearly two decades later. Valens, though by then a heretic and an apostate, was still a Roman emperor, and Basil, the metropolitan bishop, remained first and foremost the philosopher. Now—transposed from the agora and the theater into the church—Gregory presented a direct confrontation, brilliantly choreographed to showcase an aspect of imperial ceremonial then in the making, as Neil McLynn has splendidly shown: how the emperor ought to perform in the sacred space of the new temple.[144]

> The emperor entered the holy place with his bodyguard (it was the feast of Epiphany, and crowded) and took his place among the people, thus making a token gesture of unity.... But when he came inside, he was thunderstruck by the singing of psalms that assailed his ears and saw the ocean of people and the whole well-ordered array around the *bēma* [the raised platform on which the liturgy was performed].... Basil stood completely still, facing his people, as scripture says of Samuel [1 Sam 19:20], with no movement of his body or his eyes or in his mind, as if nothing unusual had occurred, transformed, so to speak, into a stele dedicated to God and the *bēma,* while his followers stood around him in fear and reverence. When the emperor saw this spectacle, which he could relate to no previous experience, he reacted as an ordinary man would—his vision and his mind were filled with darkness and dizziness from the shock.... For he started trembling, and had one of those from the platform not reached out his hand and steadied him, he would have taken a fall worthy of tears.[145]

---

144. McLynn, "Transformation," 250–56. The actual event occurred on January 6, 372, when Valens was in Caesarea to celebrate the New Year festivities after Roman forces had defeated the Persians in Armenia, thus restoring the relations harmed by the peace treaty of 363; Amm. Marc. 29.1.1–4. Lenski, *Failure,* 253–54.

145. Gr. Naz. *Or.* 43.52: Εἰς γὰρ τὸ ἱερὸν εἰσελθὼν μετὰ πάσης τῆς περὶ αὐτὸν δορυφορίας—ἦν δὲ ἡμέρα τῶν Ἐπιφανίων καὶ ἀθροίσιμος—καὶ τοῦ λαοῦ μέρος γενόμενος, οὕτως ἀφοσιοῦται τὴν ἕνωσιν.... Ἐπειδὴ γὰρ ἔνδον ἐγένετο καὶ τὴν ἀκοὴν προσβαλλούσῃ τῇ ψαλμῳδίᾳ κατεβροντήθη, τοῦ τε λαοῦ τὸ πέλαγος εἶδε καὶ πᾶσαν τὴν εὐκοσμίαν, ὅση τε περὶ τὸ βῆμα καὶ ὅση πλησίον.... τὸν μὲν τοῦ λαοῦ προτεταγμένον ὄρθιον, οἷον τὸν Σαμουὴλ ὁ λόγος γράφει, ἀκλινῆ καὶ τὸ σῶμα καὶ τὴν ὄψιν καὶ τὴν διάνοιαν ὥσπερ οὐδενὸς καινοῦ γεγονότος, ἀλλ' ἐστηλωμένον, ἵν' οὕτως εἴπω, θεῷ καὶ τῷ βήματι,

Here, unity, steadfastness, imperial comportment, a well-ordered *politeia* subordinate to its true ruler confronted the one who only pretended to unite and thus to rule, who trembles and twitches (like Julian had), and thus reveals that his imperial comportment is but skin-deep. The bishop is the firm stele, the emperor, without (and even with) proper *eusebeia,* but an ordinary man, a *laos* standing beneath the *bēma.* How better to impose oneself as a Christian bishop on a Christian emperor as if writing on stone? After Julian, emperor, philosopher, and priest must never again be one and the same person. Good emperors ought to be philosophers as rulers to the degree possible, advised at all times by true philosophers as priests, without whose guiding hand they are sure to tremble and fall.

Gregory's *Oration* 5 directly engaged contemporary debates on how Julian ought to be memorialized, particularly salient at a time when his relative Procopius claimed the position of Augustus against Valens by stressing his relation to the dynasty of Constantius and Julian against the Pannonian newcomer. Gregory's arguments once again echo those of Themistius: for him Valens, though homoian, was the legitimate ruler, because Jovian had been legitimately chosen. Jovian and Valens represented the true connection to Constantius and his house; and Julian, and thus Procopius, the infamous aberration. *Oration* 5 is linked to *Oration* 4 by the theme of dishonoring and dismantling Julian, making him into the Apostate to be remembered as a negative exemplar for all time. In that capacity the Julian in both orations serves as God's and Gregory's teaching tool to demonstrate for all what actions, thoughts, and behavior, public and private, had to be abandoned as Hellenic, a characteristic Julian now epitomizes, so that all else, all *logoi,* now characterized as *orthoi*—right thoughts, actions, and behavior—are properly "ours," Christian. Although both *Orations* 4 and 5 implicitly address emperors, Jovian and especially Valens, their direct, real audience was public officials—in *Oration* 5 those in actual administrative positions, whereas in *Oration* 4 those more directly involved with questions of the right teaching of the Trinity, though the addressees overlapped. Both orations, in sum, show Gregory as fully active political philosopher, advising those who govern, administer, and rule, thus acting as mediator between them and the divine, to which he will guide them, mindful of the demands *oikeiōsis pros theon* or *theōsis* placed upon him as a member of the elites and slave of God.

τοὺς δὲ περὶ αὐτὸν ἑστηκότας ἐν φόβῳ τινὶ καὶ σεβάσματι, ἐπειδὴ ταῦτα εἶδε καὶ πρὸς οὐδὲν παράδειγμα ἐδύνατο θεωρεῖν τὰ ὁρώμενα, ἔπαθέ τι ἀνθρώπινον· σκότου καὶ δίνης πληροῦται τὴν ὄψιν καὶ τὴν ψυχὴν ἐκ τοῦ θάμβους.... Περιτρέπει γὰρ καί, εἰ μή τις τῶν ἐκ τοῦ βήματος ὑποσχὼν τὴν χεῖρα τὴν περιτροπὴν ἔστησε, κἂν κατηνέχθη πτῶμα δακρύων ἄξιον.

Conclusion

Visions of Rome

Batter my heart, three-person'd God; for you
As yet but knock; breathe, shine, and seek to mend;
That I may rise, and stand, o'erthrow me, and bend
Your force, to break, blow, burn, and make me new.[1]

—JOHN DONNE, HOLY SONNETS

Il potassio . . . è gemello del sodio, ma reagisce con l'aria e con l'acqua con anche maggiore energia: è noto a tutti (ed era noto anche a me) che a contatto con l'acqua . . . si infiamma. Perciò trattai il mio mezzo pisello come una santa reliquia. . . . Presi il pallone ormai vuoto, lo posi sotto il rubinetto ed aprii l'acqua. Si udì un rapido tonfo, del collo del pallone uscì una vampa diretto verso la finestra che era vicina . . . e le tende di questa presero fuoco. . . . Io pensavo ad un'altra morale, più terrena e concreta . . . : che occorre diffidare del quasi-uguale (il sodio è quasi uguale al potassio: ma col sodio non sarebbe successo nulla), del praticamente identico, del pressapoco, dell'oppure. . . . Le differenze possono essere piccole, ma portare a conseguenze radicalmente diverse.[2]

—PRIMO LEVI, IL SISTEMA PERIODICO

This book, about the power of words to fashion a world and about the radical consequences of small differences, also addresses the corollary: that words can be so powerful and the consequences of small differences so radical because of profound similarities. All the principals of this book were intellectual twins, affiliated (*oikeioi*) with one another and with the empire in which they lived and that they governed by their common *paideia*, literally how they were raised. Indeed, though they exercised power to different degrees, all the principals of this book (most of whom

---

1. John Donne, *Holy Sonnets*, 14; Chambers, ed., *Poems of John Donne*, vol. 1, 165.
2. Levi, *Sistema*, "Potassio," 61, 63.

were bishops) had one dominant concern: how to govern the *oikoumenē* of the Romans the right way. To govern the *oikoumenē,* to assure the power of the Romans and the security and well-being of everyone, they had to understand a few foundational matters. Did one comprehend correctly the will of the divine creator of everything and the laws he had issued governing the cosmos and the *politeia*? Did one have proper command of the methods of advanced learning and progressive purification to deduce how the divine bridged the deep divide separating it from humanity, so that one could lead all those in one's care to the divine, whence all had originated? By Julian and Gregory's time the question was how to guarantee the salvation implicit in the return to the divine, becoming God, to all and not merely to those of higher purity. This was so because all, as Romans, were subjects of those who had been divinely mandated to rule them, and that rule included the safeguarding of everything sacred. So how should Rome's diversity be ordered to ensure that one universal way, accessible to all, could lead each person, body and soul, in his own way and according to his capacity, to the one supreme divinity? What did Rome's universalism mean?

GOVERNING THE *OIKOUMENĒ*

Those who participated in these debates fought for their vision of Rome, a vision predicated on the true and right understanding of all that was old and therefore time-honored and good, thus innovating (a notion all considered fundamentally abhorrent) the right way to restore the entire world, to re-form what the supreme Divine Being had originated in the beginning. To develop their vision, they all debated, interpreted, and commented on laws regulating good governance formulated by the divinely inspired writers all considered normative, especially Homer, Plato, Aristotle, Zeno, and Pythagoras. Plato emerges as the central figure. His *Laws, Republic, Timaeus, Cratylus,* and other writings, such as *Phaedo* and *Phaedrus,* the *Gorgias* or *Theaetetus,* combined with Aristotle's *Politics, Nicomachean Ethics,* and *Categories*—as they understood all these works in the fourth century—provide the substrate of almost every writing discussed. This was so because in these works the fundamental questions had been addressed in a normative way: how the cosmos had been created, what linked the divine with matter, what the heuristic function of language was when applied to the divine, how one should govern the *politeia*. Furthermore, these normative texts—subjected to stringent tests to determine their authenticity, including the figurative reading of their paradoxical elements to disclose their divinely intended deep truths to the initiated—underwent a continuous process of interpretation by each new generation. Into this matrix, the *paideia* common to all the elite since birth, Christians—especially after Constantine made the religion legal—inserted the writings they also now considered normative: the Christian scriptures, the Septuagint, and the New Testament writings that became canonical during Gregory's lifetime. Constantine's edict legalizing Christianity gave juridical expression to a social status quo: by the end of the third century many members of the elites were Christian; by the time of Constantine their religion could no longer be considered none, for their God had made his power manifest. But Constantine's edict was a caesura nonetheless: Christians were now those who governed.

In the eyes of those Christians, members of the elite, the God who truly mandated divinely born philosophers to rule or to advise those who ruled was the Christian God. He had created the Roman *oikoumenē* and *logoi*. Therefore, both belonged from the beginning to Christians, followers of the *Logos,* divinely ordained to lead others in accord with the *eutaxia* of the cosmos represented by their *eugeneia*. Gregory, that is, stands for all those bishops, presbyters, or readers known to us; there were many others, some of a different social background, but we know little or next to nothing of them. Those we know were elite men, and it is they, as Christians, who shaped and formed the New Rome. Some became known as Fathers of the Church; others, often more influential at the time, were eventually considered heretical. They are known to us because they wrote, and their writings were preserved; they wrote because they belonged to the educated elites. Thus, their concerns were those of elite men: how to govern and to advise others who exercised greater power and influence then they did. These men, the bishops and influential Christian members of the elites with clerical functions (whatever their clerical status: hence the interchangeability of titles such as "bishop" and "presbyter"), thus had to acquire authority and prestige among their peers to gain access to the centers of power—to the imperial court, wherever it happened to be located—in Antioch, and increasingly in Constantinople, and in the Western residences Milan, Sirmium, and eventually Ravenna. They achieved such prestige in the same way as their precursors and their peers who did not choose a clerical path. From the perspective of social history, prominent members of the Christian elites, whether clergy or the holders of positions in the imperial administration, profited from the general rise of elites in the fourth century and the early fifth, a rise reflected in the expansion of the Constantinopolitan senate. Caesarius was a paradigm of the "new men"—Peter Heather's term—but so was Gregory, who also made it to Constantinople, and so were others who moved to and between the New Rome, Antioch, and Alexandria: Eusebius, Eustathius, Aetius, Eunomius, Diodore, Eudoxius, Acacius, George, and eventually Demophilus and all the others who populate these pages. These men owed their membership in that club to their families and connections, but one could enter the select group and further enhance one's standing in it vis-à-vis one's peers by expertise in *paideia*: that is, by demonstrating mastery of Greek philosophy, its intellectual techniques, and the way of life on which such expertise rested. Oral demonstrations of such expertise were publicized in writing.

By writing oneself a particular persona, one gained authority and prestige. Gregory's persona was that of a man torn between philosophical retreat and active involvement in the *politeia*—he wrote himself as "stuttering" when it came to church and other politics, as Raymond Van Dam has said, from his first orations presenting his normative demands for the role of a Christian leader. Why—unless to do so gained him authority and prestige among his peers, all of them in positions of leadership to varying degrees? A key element of his persona was evidently that of the true philosopher leading the true philosophical life. Gregory's contemporaries, most prominent among them the emperors, also considered themselves philosophers. Thus, one gained authority by demonstrable expertise as a true philosopher, divinely born, especially if the philosopher-as-author could write himself into close connection with good emperors, as their advisor, and distance himself by his stance of fearless *parrhēsia,* risking martyrdom, from the bad ones. Gregory's authorial methods are thus, mutatis mutandis, those of a Dio Chrysostom, a Seneca, Pliny, or Tacitus. They tap into the prestige shared, for example, by persons such as Porphyry and Iamblichus, who influenced policy as divinely chosen philosophers, considered so by others. As Dominic O'Meara has shown, philosophers were ipso facto active in that they taught and advised their disciples who entered public careers, and because they themselves acted as advisors to those who ruled, their heightened purification—achieved through contemplation—granting them the closer affiliation with the divine that in turn required them to advise the emperor for the benefit of all.

Here enter the peers, the reason for the fierceness of these debates and for the emphasis on the small differences by which the debaters separated themselves from their competitors in the *agōn.* If all agreed that there was one way to the divine and that philosophers, having achieved greater union with the transcendent divine than most, must—as mediators between God and man—advise the sovereign (himself a philosopher, but one who ruled), then who should be that advisor? What divinity truly stood at the beginning and hence governed everything? And once that question was answered, then how had that divinity communicated its will to those now entrusted to guide those they advised, so that all in their care could be saved and brought closer to that divine? If it was the Christian God, then in what configuration? Who truly comprehended the Trinity? Hence the fierce arguments among philosophers who sought to achieve closeness to the sovereign in order to advise him and those close to him at court. The men known as bishops and their presbyters, who advised them, in the debates commonly subsumed under the headings "orthodoxy" and "heresy," fiercely argued how exactly and by which techniques elements of the scriptures, especially those on the Trinity, should be inserted into the classical matrix, showcasing the expertise of those involved in that process. Alliances were fluid. Christian members of the empirewide elites (the bishops), though ostensibly divided sharply between orthodox, or Nicene, and heterodox, or Arian (a divide still underlying much modern scholarship, despite increasing nuances and perception of fluidities), shared a great deal. They gained the emperor's ear and lost it, were removed from and called back to court when a new emperor arrived, found supporters and opponents among Christians as well as non-Christians (Themistius and Gregory, Julian and Eunomius), flourished or were sent home under Arian (i.e., homoian), pagan, moderately Arian, extreme Arian, and Nicene emperors.[3] In short, the bishops behaved more or less like other members of the high imperial administration and the lower—within their brief as philosophers and public officials in charge of episcopal sees.

AUTHORITY AND KINSHIP OF THE ELITES

Methodologically speaking, this means that the model of late Roman Christian leadership (the bishop) is rooted not so much in the prescriptions of the New Testament and their Jewish antecedents, however constructed, but in the social reality of Greek Roman elite men. Their positions, with all the traditional accoutrements of elite status—in flux as a result of Constantine and Constantius's, or in fact Diocletian's, reforms—each individual's place in that fine-tuned hierarchy (whose nuances Jane Austen illustrates even more vividly than Pierre Bourdieu's or Peter Berger's and Thomas Luckmann's analysis), determined how they integrated the prescriptions of Christian scriptures on the leadership of men and their souls into long-debated paradigms of governance.[4] In other words, to showcase one's mastery of Plato and Aristotle while insinuating that one had persuaded a Constantius or Valens how to rule gave one the authority required to guide others as bishop—that, and a family already among the notables, or one's own superior expertise graciously acknowledged by the emperor. All these had to be marshaled to persuade one's peers of one's legitimate authority (for example, in the agonistic forum also known as the synod).

Julian and Gregory represent these processes. Though one was the emperor and the other a member of the provincial elite, acting as advisor to his father, the local bishop—not a metropolitan bishop, either, so that the son, to gain the prestige he considered his due, had to look farther afield than his peer Basil, who was associated with and succeeded a bishop in a metropolis—both men were on a par as di-

---

3. Gregory's attitude toward homoians, Arians, which may strike scholars as more positive than expected from the theologian who formulated the enduring orthodox Nicene definition of the Trinity, reflects the demands of his time. For Gregory, *eutaxia*, good order, and harmonious unity were paramount. In the 360s, the homoian formulation represented a compromise that could accommodate a variety of different positions. Gregory's own formulation, though not advocating a homoian position, likewise offered a middle ground, acceptable to many and preserving good order and harmony. Gregory's formulation was thus closer to the homoian middle than to the extremes represented by Eunomius and Photinus.

4. I have benefited enormously from the classics, Bourdieu, *Esquisse d'une théorie de la pratique*, and *Distinction: Critique sociale du jugement*; Berger and Luckmann, *Gesellschaftliche Konstruktion der Wirklichkeit*; and Schmidt, *Symbolische Gewalt*. To understand what codes shaped Julian's and Gregory's self-presentation, and what makes late Roman power and its administration distinct, I also profited greatly from Clendinnen, *Ambivalent Conquests* (I thank Neil McLynn for this reference); Hämäläinen, *Comanche Empire*; DeLay, *War of a Thousand Deserts*; and from Waal, *Peacemaking among Primates*.

vinely chosen and purified philosophers, highly trained at Athens and practicing a strict ascetic life. (At least, one wrote as if he was on equal footing with the ruler of the known world.) Both were entirely men of their time. They shared with each other and their elite contemporaries far more than divided them. This is why "le differenze possono essere piccole, ma portare a conseguenze radicalmente diverse."

Both considered their true philosophical life divinely authorized and therefore deduced that their philosophical approximation to the divine made them better helmsmen to keep the ship of the *politeia* on true course than their fathers or father figures. Both considered the cosmos a well-ordered, beneficial whole, the expression of divine affiliation with man created by divine *philanthrōpia*. Both subscribed to a notion of Stoic *oikeiōsis* that demanded their engagement on behalf of everyone in their care. It is a notion the Aristotelian Platonist Themistius expressed in his *Oration 6, On Philadelphia or Philanthrōpia*, delivered before the Constantinopolitan senate in the presence of Valens, praising him and his brother, Valentinian, for their division of the empire.[5] The emperors' mutual brotherly affection was a mark (*sēmeion*) of the essential imperial virtue, *philanthrōpia* (*Or.* 6.74b). For, "goodwill toward one's family members is the beginning and the principle of goodwill toward all humanity. For nature, privileging man above the rest of the animals and binding us together with all our kith and kin, has laid down the first principle from those nearby and from the family hearth, so that he who loves his brother will also love his household; he who loves his family will love his native land; and he who loves this will also love mankind. It is impossible, once caught in the doorway of nature, not also to become obedient to her prompting."[6] For Julian as for Themistius, who pronounced these words about the time Gregory formulated his key concept of *theōsis*, in his *Oration* 4, the transcendent divine was also kin to humanity, so that material aspects of the cosmos, including sacrifices and man's physical body, became essential for the salvation of the soul. This paradigm of adoptive kinship made greater closeness to the divine in practice available to everyone rather than the privilege of the select few who practice Platonic *homoiōsis theōi*.

The similarity to Julian is evident. Themistius's *oikeiōsis*, however, was far

---

5. The oration was delivered in December 364, when Gregory composed *Or.* 4; Themistius, *Politics*, ed. Heather and Moncur, 173–79 (transl. idem, with my modifications); Rousseau, *Basil*, 221–22, discusses the importance of nature in Basil, pointing to the Stoic background: "Human nature, in both its potential and its destiny, should make a life of virtue easy." Gregory of Nyssa's Platonizing view of the material world is less positive; *Theaet.* 176a–b; Plotinus *Enn.* 1.2; Merki, *ΟΜΟΙΩΣΙΣ ΘΕΩΙ*, 126–28. For Merki, Gregory of Nyssa considers *physis* as "im Grunde nichts anderes als *eikôn theou* oder *homoiôsis theôi* als ursprünglicher Zustand" (p. 96).

6. Them. *Or.* 6.76c–d: ἀλλ' ὅτι σημεῖόν ἐστι φιλαδελφία φιλανθρωπίας, καὶ ὥσπερ ἀρχὴ καὶ στοιχεῖον τῆς πρὸς ἅπαντας ἀνθρώπους εὐνοίας ἡ πρὸς τοὺς συγγόνους καὶ ὁμοσπόρους. . . . ἅπαν συνδέουσα τὸ ὁμόφυλον ἐκ τῶν ἐγγύθεν καὶ ἀφ' ἑστίας καταβέβληται τὰ προοίμια. . . . καὶ οὐκ ἔνεστιν ἐν τοῖς προθύροις τῆς φύσεως ἑαλωκότα μὴ γενέσθαι καὶ προϊούσης κατήκοον.

closer to Gregory's than Julian's, because even though Julian also considered such *oikeiōsis* foundational—it was this *oikeiōsis* with the gods that the Galileans had left, after all—and even though he too saw himself as an active philosopher working for the benefit of all, he saw sacrifices to the gods of the Greeks and the Romans as the sole material way of opening salvation to all souls and bodies, offering, as Iamblichus had done, a humbler affiliation with the divine to all while reserving the highest approximation to the initiated, purified philosopher. Themistius thought that many ways had been divinely intended to lead to the One, including those of the Christians whom he called Syrians, and here he differed from Julian. Gregory concurred, except that for him (and here he was closer to Julian again) only the Christian *oikeiōsis,* prefigured in the Trinity, led to salvation: the bloodless sacrifices of words to the Word. Because Julian, following Iamblichus, considered sacrifices, statues of the gods, and the rituals associated with them the means that permitted all to strengthen their affiliation with the divine, however humble, Julian the philosopher-as-emperor was in effect a more Platonic (withdrawn) philosopher than Gregory, because he offered closeness to the divine to all while preserving the particular affiliation of the select few, the purified divinely chosen philosophers making god present. Gregory instead was a far more active philosopher in the Aristotelian sense, mixed with that of Stoic *oikeiōsis:* because only progressive purification could strengthen the affiliation, body and soul, of all with the divine, he, as advanced and far more purified philosopher, closer to the divine than most, had to act as mediator and teacher to all in his care to strengthen their link, however tenuous, with the divine. In this, however, he could administer a *pharmakon* whose efficacy trumped all else: the Trinity, the paradoxical fusion of two ontologically distinct matters, divine and human.

The saving power manifested in the Trinity, in the *Logos* incarnate, granted that all could become God if they followed the ethical demands of the Trinity as taught them by their divinely inspired mediators, such as Gregory. And here another crucial aspect comes to the fore. For Gregory, true *oikeiōsis* and thus the true philosophical life consisted in the voluntary submission of the self to the demands of the other—to the public good. Such submission—as God's slave—paradoxically does not reflect inequality; subordination does not detract from equal potency or power: indeed the contrary. In Gregory's case, philosophical submission as son and priest enhances his standing as mediator for the divine Son of the divine Father, whose relation to the Father is likewise one of hierarchical subordination as full equal, as one in essence (which, incidentally, is not a bad metaphor for ruling a multiethnic empire).

COMPETING UNIVERSALISMS

Such similarities and the small but significant differences between Julian's and Gregory's thought demonstrate the intrinsic link between philosophy, theology, religion, and governance or politics: they were one and the same for everyone concerned. Though it is a truism that politics and religion were not separated in the Roman Empire, the appearance of Christianity on the imperial scene nonetheless prompts most scholars to write as if they were in practice separate entities. One example is the common description of the changing topography of late Roman cities as a process by which public spheres previously denominated religious were secularized. To discuss Gregory's repudiation of what he saw as Julian's attempts to exclude Christians from the city center—the actual and metaphorical locus of participation in the administration and governance of the empire, so that the army forms part of those sites—using such terminology is inappropriate, because the sacred is never removed. What occurs is the demand for a shift from places associated with what is now considered the wrong divine to others deemed appropriate to the right God. For Gregory divine power, even if negative, demonic, continues to reside in temples and statues, so that to speak of the profanation of sacred space is more to the point, as in his insistence that only a divine decree—such as an earthquake or a fire—can appropriately destroy a temple.[7] The same orations that illustrate Gregory's definition of the correct hermeneutical approaches to comprehending God, the Trinity, also show how he intends Christian theater to function—his *Oration 4* is the *skēnē* of the right Christian theater—how one should honor the Christian emperor in the agora, how to celebrate festivals, what colors a Christian army must fly, and what kind of war it ought to fight (a defensive one, unless territories can be gained without risk), and how the emperor ought to interact with the bishop in the churches. Everything is permeated with the correct form of the sacred, namely the Christian one, from the highest imperial virtue, *eusebeia,* to the correct adornment of porticoes during the festivals. Plato's *Laws,* delineating how the philosopher-as-ruler should treat the service of the gods, and his *Republic,* defining the good ruler as philosopher, form the old matrix, into which Gregory inserted the new.

Gregory of Nazianzus, Gregory the Theologian, formulated a vision of Rome as a Christian empire. It was a vision in which Christianity represented and guaranteed the universal claims of the Roman *oikoumenē*. Created by the *Logos,* One as Three, universal (*katholikos*) Christianity was the true expression of Rome's well-ordered greatness, where all were related to each other and to the divine. Gregory's universal Roman Christianity was deeply embedded in everything that had made Greek Rome great, and it integrated the new into the old such that the new represented all that was good and superior in the old: correct innovation. His universal vision encompassed everyone in the *oikoumenē,* from the emperor to the slave, because each had his proper place, and all could be saved through the power of the Trinity and the healing mediation of those who administered it correctly, philoso-

---

7. Moderns also know the power of objects, albeit by a different name; Vinken, *Flaubert,* 350–418.

phers as leaders such as Gregory. Gregory's comprehensive vision, formulated in intense negotiation with competing universal claims, endured because it was broader in its reach, truly encompassing many—but certainly not all. To be Roman became synonymous with being orthodox Christian—whether that orthodoxy was formulated in the Old Rome or the New, in Alexandria, Milan, or Ravenna. All those not orthodox Christians became *allotrioi,* outsiders; it was a universality that excluded. For those *oikeioi,* who were affiliated with the universal Roman Trinity, Gregory offered harmony and *eutaxia,* good order—each his own place as part of the whole. It should come as no surprise that his influence was monumental and lasting, for bishops like Gregory the Great and Photius, for emperors like Justinian and Constantine VII Porphyrogenitus, but also for the scribes who filled unused manuscript pages with his poems as they remembered them from their schooldays—the same schooldays in which Julian still reigned supreme as the evil Apostate.[8] However central Julian the emperor and Gregory the Theologian may have been, though, this book has shown that in the end it was the Roman Empire—its inhabitants, institutions, administration, and its intellectual foundations—that made Christianity universal, because as Gregory said, Christianity had been from the beginning Roman.

8. Rapp, "Antiochos Manuscript."

BIBLIOGRAPHY

PRIMARY SOURCES

Ammianus Marcellinus. *History.* 3 vols. Ed. and trans. J. C. Rolfe. Cambridge, Mass., 1950.

Apostolic Constitutions. Ed. M. Metzger under the title *Les Constitutions apostoliques.* 3 vols. Paris 1985–87.

Aretaeus. *The Extant Works of Aretaeus the Cappadocian.* Ed. F. Adams. London 1856.

Artemii Passio. In *Die Schriften des Johannes von Damaskos,* ed. B. Kotter, vol. 5, 185–245. Berlin 1988. [See also the partial editions in Philostorgius, *Kirchengeschichte,* ed. Bidez and Winkelmann; and by J. Bidez in his *Philostorgius: The Ordeal of Artemius,* trans. M. Vermes, in *From Constantine to Julian: Pagan and Byzantine Views,* ed. S. Lieu and D. Montserrat, 210–62 (London 1996).]

Athanasius of Alexandria. *Histoire "acephale" et index syriaque des Lettres festales d'Athanase d'Alexandrie.* Ed. and trans. A. Martin and M. Albert. Paris 1985.

———. *Werke.* 3 vols. Ed. H. G. Opitz. Berlin 1934–41.

Aurelius Victor. *Liber de Caesaribus of Sextus Aurelius Victor.* Trans. H. W. Bird. Liverpool 1994.

———. *Livre des Césars.* Ed. and trans. P. Dufraigne. Paris 1975.

Basil of Caesarea. *Basile de Césarée: Contre Eunome.* 2 vols. Ed. and trans. B. Sesboüé. Paris 1982–83.

———. *Saint Basil: The Letters.* 4 vols. Ed. and trans. R. J. Deferrari. Cambridge, Mass., 1926–34. [Reprint 1970–72.]

———. *Saint Basile: Lettres.* 3 vols. Ed. and trans. Y. Courtonne. Paris 1957–66.

Callimachus. *Opera.* Ed. R. Pfeiffer. Vol. 1, *Fragmenta.* Oxford 1949.

Chaldean Oracles. Ed. R. Majerick. Leiden 1989.

Chronicon Paschale, A.D. 284–628. Ed. and trans. Michael Whitby and Mary Whitby. Liverpool 1989.

Claudius Mamertinus. *Claudio Mamertino: Panegírico (Gratiarum actio) al emperador Juliano.* Ed. and trans. M. P. García Ruiz. Pamplona 2006.
Codex Theodosianus. See *The Theodosian Code.*
Commentaria in Aristotelem Graeca. 6 vols. Berlin 1883–1902. [Reprint 1956–60.]
Cyril of Alexandria. *Cyrille d'Alexandrie: Contre Julien.* Ed. and trans. P. Burguière and P. Évieux. Paris 1985.
Dio Chrysostom. *Dion Chrysostomos: Oratio 6.* Ed. and trans. G. Krapinger. Graz 1996.
Epiphanius. *Ancoratus und Panarion.* 3 vols. Ed. K. Holl. Berlin 1915–33. [2nd ed. J. Dummer (Berlin 1980–85).]
Ephraem the Syrian. *Hymnen De Paradiso und Contra Julianum.* 2 vols. Ed. E. Beck. Louvain 1957.
Eunapius. *Philostratus and Eunapius: The Lives of the Sophists.* Ed. and trans. W. C. Wright. London 1922. [Reprint 1998.]
Eunomius of Cyzicus. *The Extant Works.* Ed. and trans. R. Vaggione. Oxford 1987.
Eusebius of Caesarea. *Eusèbe de Césarée: La préparation évangélique, livres 1, 3, 11.* Ed. and trans. É. des Places [3], J. Sirinelli [1], and G. Favrelle [11]. Paris 1974–82. [*Eusèbe de Césarée: La préparation évangélique, livres 15.* Ed. J. Sirinelli, É. des Places, et al. 10 vols. Paris 1974–91.]
———. *Eusebio di Cesarea: Dimostrazione evangelica.* Ed. and trans. P. Carrara. Milan 2000.
———. *Life of Constantine: Introduction, Translation, and Commentary.* Ed. and trans. A. Cameron and S. Hall. Oxford 1999.
———. *The Preparation of the Gospel.* Trans. E. H. Gifford. 2 vols. Grand Rapids 1981.
Eustathius of Antioch. *Eustathii Antiocheni, Patris Nicaeni, opera quae supersunt omnia.* Ed. J. H. Declerck. Turnhout 2002.
Eutropius. *The Breviarium ab urbe condita of Eutropius.* Trans. H. W. Bird. Liverpool 1993.
———. *Eutrope: Abrégé d'histoire romaine.* Ed. and trans. J. Hellegouarc'h. Paris 1999.
———. *Eutropii Breviarium ab urbe condita.* Ed. C. Santini. Leipzig 1979.
Festus. *The Breviarium of Festus: A Critical Edition with Historical Commentary.* Ed. and trans. J. A. Eadie. London 1967.
Galen. *Claudii Galeni opera omnia.* Ed. K. G. Kühn. 20 vols. Leipzig 1822–33. [Reprint Hildesheim 1964.]
———. *De usu partium libri 17.* Vols. 3 and 4 of *Opera omnia,* ed. Kühn. Leipzig 1822.
———. *On the Doctrines of Hippocrates and Plato.* 3 vols. Ed. and trans. P. De Lacy. Berlin 1978–84.
———. *On the Elements according to Hippocrates.* Ed. and trans. P. De Lacy. Berlin 1996.
———. *On Examinations by Which the Best Physicians Are Recognized.* Arabic text ed. and English trans. A. Z. Iskandar. Berlin 1988.
———. *On the Natural Faculties.* Trans. A. J. Brock. London 1916.
———. *On the Passions and Errors of the Soul.* Trans. P. W. Harkins. Columbus 1963.
———. *On Semen.* Ed. and trans. P. De Lacy. Berlin 1992.
The Greek Anthology. 5 vols. Ed. W. R. Paton. London 1916. [Reprint 1993.]
Gregory the Great. *Grégoire le Grand: Règle pastorale.* 2 vols. Intro. B. Judic, ed. F. Rommel, and trans. C. Morel. Paris 1992.
Gregory of Nazianzus. *Briefe.* Ed. and trans. M. Wittig. Stuttgart 1981.

———. *Contro Giuliano l'Apostata: Orazione 4*. Trans. with comm. L. Lugaresi. Florence 1993.
———. *Faith Gives Fullness to Reasoning: The Five Theological Orations of Gregory Nazianzen*. Intro. F. W. Norris, trans. L. Wickham and F. Williams. Leiden 1991.
———. *Funeral Orations by Saint Gregory Nazianzen and Saint Ambrose*. Trans. L. P. McCauley. New York 1953.
———. *Grégoire de Nazianze: Discours 1–3*. Ed. and trans. J. Bernardi. Paris 1978.
———. *Grégoire de Nazianze: Discours 4–5 contre Julien*. Ed. and trans. J. Bernardi. Paris 1983.
———. *Grégoire de Nazianze: Discours 6–12*. Ed. and trans. M.-A. Calvet-Sébasti. Paris 1995.
———. *Grégoire de Nazianze: Discours 20–23*. Ed. and trans. J. Mossay. Paris 1980.
———. *Grégoire de Nazianze: Discours 24–26*. Ed. and trans. J. Mossay. Paris 1981.
———. *Grégoire de Nazianze: Discours 32–37*. Ed. C. Moreschini and trans. P. Gallay. Paris 1985.
———. *Grégoire de Nazianze: Discours Théologiques 27–31*. Ed. and trans. P. Gallay and M. Jourjon. Paris 1978.
———. *Gregorio di Nazianzo: Tutte le orazioni*. Ed. and trans. C. Moreschini; notes C. Sani and M. Vincelli. Milan 2000.
———. *Gregorio Nazianzeno: Ad Olimpiade, carmen II, 2, 6*. Ed. and trans. L. Bacci. Pisa 1996.
———. *Gregorio Nazianzeno: Fuga e Autobiografia*. Ed. and trans. L. Viscanti. Rome 1987.
———. *Gregorio Nazianzeno: Poesie*. 2 vols. Ed. and trans. C. Moreschini, I. Costa, and C. Crimi. Rome 1994–99.
———. *Gregory of Nazianzus: Autobiographical Poems*. Ed. and trans. C. White. New York 1996.
———. *Gregor von Nazianz: De vita sua*. Ed. and trans. C. Jungck. Heidelberg 1974.
———. *La morte di Giuliano l'Apostata: Orazione 5*. Trans. with comm. L. Lugaresi. Florence 1997.
———. *Saint Grégoire de Nazianze: Lettres*. Ed. P. Gallay. 2 vols. Paris 1964–67.
———. *Tyrannii Rufini orationum Gregorii Nazianzeni novem interpretatio*. Ed. A. Engelbrecht. Vienna 1910.
Gregory of Nyssa. *Gregorii Nysseni opera*. 11 vols. Ed. W. Jaeger et al. Berlin and Leiden 1921–2009.
Gregory the Presbyter. *Vita Sancti Gregorii Theologi*. Ed. and trans. X. Lequeux. Corpus Christianorum, Series Graeca. Vol. 44. Turnhout 2001.
Hermias of Alexandria. *Hermias Alexandrinus in Platonis Phaedrum commentarii*. Ed. C. Lucarini. Berlin 2010.
———. *Kommentar zu Platons Phaidros*. Trans. H. Bernard. Tübingen 1997.
Hierocles. *Hierokles: Kommentar zum Pythagoreischen Goldenen Gedicht*. Ed. and trans. F. W. Köhler. Stuttgart 1974, 1983.
Hilary of Poitiers. *Hilaire de Poitiers: Contre Constance*. Ed. and trans. A. Rocher. Paris 1987.
———. *Hilarius von Poitiers: Collectanea antiariana Parisina*. In *Hilarius von Poitiers: Opera*, ed. A. L. Feder, 41–187. Vienna 1916.
Himerius. *Himerii declamationes et orationes cum deperditarum fragmentis*. Ed. A. Colonna. Rome 1951.

———. *Man and the Word: The Orations of Himerius.* Ed. and trans. R. J. Penella. Berkeley and Los Angeles 2007.
Hippocrates. *Hippocrate: Airs, eaux, lieux.* Ed. and trans. J. Jouanna. Paris 1996.
Iamblichus. *De anima: Text, Translation and Commentary.* Ed. J. F. Finamore and J. M. Dillon. Leiden 2002.
———. *De mysteriis.* Trans. E. C. Clarke, J. M. Dillon, and J. P. Hershbell. Atlanta 2003.
———. *Exhortation to Philosophy, Including the Letters of Iamblichus and Proclus' Commentary on the Chaldean Oracles.* Trans. T. Moore Johnson. Grand Rapids 1988.
———. *Iamblichi Chalcidensis in Platonis dialogos commentariorum fragmenta.* Ed. and trans. J. M. Dillon. Leiden 1973.
———. *Jamblique: Vie de Pythagore.* Ed. and trans. L. Brisson and A. P. Segonds. Paris 1996.
———. *On the Pythagorean Life.* Trans. G. Clark. Liverpool 1989.
———. *On the Pythagorean Way of Life.* Ed. and trans. J. Dillon and J. Hershbell. Atlanta 1991.
John Chrysostom. *Discours sur Babylas.* Ed. and trans., with introduction and notes, by M. A. Schatkin, with C. Blanc and B. Gillet. Paris 1990.
———. *Jean Chrysostome, Sur le sacerdoce: Dialogue et homélie.* Ed. and trans. A.-M. Malingrey. Paris 1980.
John Malalas. *The Chronicle of John Malalas.* Trans. E. Jeffreys, M. Jeffreys, and R. Scott. Melbourne 1986.
———. *Chronographia.* Ed. J. Thurn. Berlin 2000.
John of Antioch. *Fragments.* In *Excerpta historica iussu Imp. Constantini Porphyrogeniti confecta*, vol. 2, *Excerpta de virtutibus et vitiis*, ed. T. Büttner-Wobst. Berlin 1906.
Julian. *L'empereur Julien: Œuvres complètes.* 2 vols. Ed. and trans. J. Bidez, G. Rochefort, and C. Lacombrade. Paris 1932–64.
———. *L'epistolario di Giuliano imperatore.* Trans. and comm. M. Caltabiano. Naples 1991.
———. *Giuliano l'Apostata: Autobiografia, Messaggio agli Ateniesi.* Ed. and trans. I. Labriola. Florence 1975.
———. *Giuliano imperatore: Al Cinico Eraclio.* Ed. and trans. R. Guido. Lecce 2000.
———. *Giuliano imperatore: Alla Madre degli dèi.* Ed. and trans. V. Ugenti. Lecce 1992.
———. *Giuliano imperatore: Alla Madre degli dèi e altri discorsi.* Intro. J. Fontaine, ed. C. Prato, trans. A. Marcone. Milan 1987.
———. *Giuliano imperatore: Contro i Cinici ignoranti.* Ed. and trans. C. Prato and D. Micalella. Lecce 1988.
———. *Giuliano imperatore: Contra Galilaeos.* Ed. and trans. E. Masaracchia. Rome 1990.
———. *Giuliano imperatore: Epistola a Temistio.* Ed. C. Prato and A. Fornaro. Lecce 1984.
———. *Giuliano imperatore: Misopogon.* Ed. and trans. C. Prato and D. Micalella. Lecce 1979.
———. *Giuliano imperatore: Simposio i Cesari.* Ed. and trans. R. Sardiello. Lecce 2000.
———. *Imperatoris Caesaris Flavii Claudii Iuliani epistulae, leges, poemata, fragmenta varia.* Ed. J. Bidez and F. Cumont. Paris 1922.
———. *Iuliani imperatoris librorum contra Christianos quae supersunt.* Ed. K. J. Neumann. Leipzig 1880.
———. *La prima orazione di Giuliano a Costanzo.* Ed. and trans. I. Tantillo. Rome 1997.

———. *The Works of the Emperor Julian.* Ed. and trans. W. C. Wright. 3 vols. 2nd ed. London 1962-69.
Libanius. *Kaiserreden.* Trans. and comm. G. Fatouros, T. Krischer, and W. Portmann. Stuttgart 2002.
———. *Libanii opera.* Ed. R. Foerster. 12 vols. Leipzig 1903-27. [Reprint: Hildesheim 1963-85.]
———. *Libanios, Antiochikos (Or. XI): Zur heidnischen Renaissance in der Spätantike.* Trans. and comm. G. Fatouros and T. Krischer. Vienna 1992.
———. *Libanius: Autobiography and Selected Letters.* 2 vols. Ed. and trans. A. F. Norman. Cambridge, Mass., 1992.
———. *Libanius, Imaginary Speeches: A Selection of Declamations.* Ed. and trans. D. A. Russell. London 1996.
———. *Selected Letters of Libanius: From the Age of Constantius and Julian.* Trans. S. Bradbury. Liverpool 2004.
———. *Selected Orations.* Ed. and trans. A. F. Norman. 2 vols. London and Cambridge, Mass., 1969-77.
Marcellus of Ankara. *Markell von Ancyra: Die Fragmente und der Brief an Julius von Rom.* Ed. and trans. M. Vinzent. Leiden 1997.
I martirii di S. Teodoto e di S. Ariadne con un' appendice sul testo originale del martirio di S. Eleuterio. Ed. P. Franchi de' Cavalieri, 61-87. Rome 1901.
Menander Rhetor. *Peri epideiktikōn.* In *Rhetores Graeci,* ed. L. Spengel, vol. 3, 331-446. Leipzig 1856. [Reprint Frankfurt a.M. 1966.]
———. *Treatise.* Ed. and trans. D. A. Russell and N. G. Wilson. Oxford 1981.
Origen. *Origène, Philocalie 1-20: Sur les écritures.* Ed. and trans. M. Harl. Paris 1983.
———. *Origène, Philocalie 21-27: Sur le libre arbitre.* Ed. and trans. É. Junod. Paris 1976.
———. *Origen's Contra Celsum libri VIII.* Ed. and trans. M. Marcovich. Leiden 2001.
Philostorgius. *Kirchengeschichte, mit dem Leben des Lucian von Antiochien und den Fragmenten eines arianischen Historiographen.* 2nd ed. Ed. J. Bidez and F. Winkelmann. Berlin 1972.
Plato. *Platonis opera.* Vol. 4. Ed. J. Burnet. Oxford 1902. [Reprint 1989.]
Pliny the Younger. *Epistularum libri decem.* Ed. R. A. B. Mynors. Oxford 1963.
Plutarch. *Lives.* Vol. 7. Ed. and trans. B. Perrin. London and Cambridge, Mass., 1919.
———. *Moralia.* 15 vols. Ed. and trans. F. C. Babbitt et al. Cambridge, Mass., 1936-2005.
Porphyry. *Porphyre: La vie de Plotin.* Ed. and trans. L. Brisson. Paris 1982-92.
———. *Porphyre: Vie de Pythagore; Lettre à Marcella.* Ed. and trans. E. des Places. Paris 1982.
———. *Porphyrii philosophi fragmenta.* Ed. A. Smith. Arabic fragments ed. D. Wasserstein. Stuttgart 1993.
———. *Porphyry: On Abstinence from Killing Animals.* Trans. G. Clark. London 2000.
Proclus. *The Elements of Theology.* Ed. and trans. E. R. Dodds. Oxford 1933.
Pseudo-Hippocrates. *De flatibus I.* In *Hippocrates,* ed. and trans. W. H. S. Jones, vol. 2, 226-28. London 1959.
Salutius [Sallustius]. *Saloustios: Des dieux et du monde.* Ed. and trans. G. Rochefort. Paris 1960.

School of Aristotle. *Die Schule des Aristoteles: Texte und Kommentare.* Part 1, *Dikaiarchos.* Ed. F. Wehrli. 2nd ed. Basel 1967.
Socrates. *Sokrates: Kirchengeschichte.* Ed. G. C. Hansen. Berlin 1995.
Soranus. *Soranos d'Ephèse: Maladies des femmes.* 4 vols. Ed. and trans. P. Burguière, D. Gourevitch, and Y. Malinas. Paris 1988–2000.
Sozomen. *Sozomenus: Kirchengeschichte.* Ed. J. Bidez and G. C. Hansen. Berlin 1960.
Themistius. *Politics, Philosophy, and Empire in the Fourth Century: Select Orations of Themistius.* Ed. and trans. P. Heather and D. Moncur. Liverpool 2001.
———. *The Private Orations of Themistius.* Ed. and trans. R. J. Penella. Berkeley and Los Angeles 2000.
———. *Risâlat: Epistula Themistii De re publica gerenda.* Ed. and trans. I Shahîd in *Themistii orationes,* ed. H. Schenkl, G. Downey, and A. F. Norman, vol. 3, 83–119. Leipzig 1974.
———. *Themistii orationes.* Ed. W. Dindorf. Hildesheim 1961.
———. *Themistii orationes.* Ed. H. Schenkl, G. Downey, and A. F. Norman. 3 vols. Leipzig 1965–74.
———. *Themistios: Staatsreden.* Trans. H. Leppin and W. Portmann. Stuttgart 1998.
———. *Themistius: On Aristotle's "On the Soul."* Trans. R. B. Todd. London 1996.
Theodore of Mopsuestia. *Teodoro di Mopsuestia: Replica a Giuliano Imperatore.* Ed. and trans. A. Guida. Florence 1994.
———. *Théodore de Mopsueste: Fragments syriaques du Commentaire des Psaumes (Psaume 118 et Psaume 138–148).* Ed. and trans. L. van Rompay. Louvain 1982.
The Theodosian Code and Novels and the Sirmondian Constitutions. Trans. C. Pharr. Princeton 1952.
Zosimus. *Zosime: Histoire nouvelle.* Ed. F. Paschoud. 3 vols. Paris 1971–89.

SECONDARY LITERATURE

Abramowski, L. "Trinitarische und christologische Hypostasenformeln." *Th&Ph* 54 (1979): 38–49.
Alexandre, M. "Clément d'Alexandrie et les loisirs." In *Les loisirs et l'héritage de la culture classique: Actes du XIIIe Congrès de l'Association Guillaume Budé, Dijon, 27–31 août 1993,* ed. J.-M. André, J. Dangel, and P. Demont, 170–89. Brussels 1996.
Allen, D. S. *The World of Prometheus: The Politics of Punishing in Democratic Athens.* Princeton 2000.
Ameling, W. "Die jüdischen Gemeinden im antiken Kleinasien." In *Jüdische Gemeinden und Organisationsformen von der Antike bis zur Gegenwart,* ed. R. Jütte and A. P. Kustermann, 29–55. Vienna 1996.
Anastos, M. V. "Basil's *Kata Eunomiou:* A Critical Analysis." In *Basil of Caesarea: Christian, Humanist, Ascetic: A Sixteen-Hundredth Anniversary Symposium,* ed. P. J. Fedwick, part 1, 67–136. Toronto 1981.
Anderson, G. *Sage, Saint, and Sophist: Holy Men and Their Associates in the Early Roman Empire.* London 1994.
Ando, C. *Imperial Ideology and Provincial Loyalty in the Roman Empire.* Berkeley and Los Angeles 2000.

André, J.-M. *L'otium dans la vie morale et intellectuelle romaine des origines à l'époque augustéenne*. Paris 1966.
Andreotti, R. "Kaiser Julians Gesetzgebung und Verwaltung." In *Julian Apostata*, ed. R. Klein, 130–90. Darmstadt 1978.
———. "L'opera legislativa ed amministrativa dell'imperatore Giuliano." *NRS* 14 (1930): 236–73.
Arce, J. J. "Algunos problemas de la numismática del emperador Fl. Cl. Iuliano." *AEA* 45–47 (1972–74): 477–96.
———. *Estudios sobre el emperador Fl. Cl. Juliano: Fuentes literarias, epigrafía, numismática*. Madrid 1984.
———. "Reconstrucción de templos en época del emperador Juliano (361–363)." *RSA* 5 (1975): 201–13.
Argov, E. I. "Giving the Heretic a Voice: Philostorgius of Borissus and Greek Ecclesiastical Historiography." *Athenaeum* 89 (2001): 497–524.
Arjava, A. "Paternal Power in Late Antiquity." *JRS* 88 (1998): 147–65.
———. *Women and Law in Late Antiquity*. Oxford 1996.
Asmus, R. "Die Invektiven des Gregorius von Nazianz im Lichte der Werke des Kaisers Julian." *ZKG* 31 (1910): 325–67.
Assmann, A. *Erinnerungsräume: Formen und Wandlungen des kulturellen Gedächtnisses*. 3rd ed. Munich 2006.
Assmann, J. *Religion und kulturelles Gedächtnis: Zehn Studien*. 3rd ed. Munich 2007.
Athanassiadi-Fowden, P. "A Contribution to Mithraic Theology: The Emperor Julian's *Hymn to King Helios*." *JThS* 28 (1977): 360–71.
———. *Julian and Hellenism: An Intellectual Biography*. Oxford 1981.
Atherton, C. *The Stoics on Ambiguity*. Cambridge 1993.
Ayres, L. *Nicaea and Its Legacy: An Approach to Fourth-Century Trinitarian Theology*. Oxford 2004.
Ballériaux, O. "Thémistius et le Néoplatonisme: Le *nous pathêtikos* et l'immoralité de l'âme." *RPhA* 12 (1994): 171–200.
Banaji, J. *Agrarian Change in Late Antiquity: Gold, Labour, and Aristocratic Dominance*. Oxford 2001.
Banchich, T. M. "Julian's School Laws: *Cod. Theod.* 13.3.5 and *Ep.* 42." *AncW* 24 (1993): 5–14.
Barceló, P. *Constantius II. und seine Zeit: Die Anfänge des Staatskirchentums*. Stuttgart 2004.
Barnes, M. R. "The Background and Use of Eunomius' Causal Language." In *Arianism after Arius: Essays on the Development of the Fourth-Century Trinitarian Conflicts*, ed. M. R. Barnes and D. H. Williams, 217–36. Edinburgh 1993.
———. "The Fourth Century as Trinitarian Canon." In *Christian Origins: Theology, Rhetoric, and Community*, ed. L. Ayres and G. Jones, 47–67. London 1998.
———. *The Power of God. Dynamis in Gregory of Nyssa's Trinitarian Theology*. Washington, D.C., 2001.
Barnes, T. D. *Ammianus Marcellinus and the Representation of Historical Reality*. Ithaca 1998.
———. *Athanasius and Constantius: Theology and Politics in the Constantinian Empire*. Cambridge, Mass., 1993.

———. "Christians and Pagans in the Reign of Constantius." In *L'église et l'empire au IVe siècle*, ed. A. Dihle, 301–37. Geneva 1989.
———. "Himerius and the Fourth Century." *CPh* 82 (1987): 206–25.
Barton, C. A. *Roman Honor: The Fire in the Bones*. Berkeley and Los Angeles 2001.
Bartsch, S. *Actors in the Audience: Theatricality and Doublespeak from Nero to Hadrian*. Cambridge, Mass., 1994.
Bassett, S. *The Urban Image of Late Antique Constantinople*. Cambridge 2004.
Baynes, N. H. "The Thought-World of East Rome." In *Byzantine Studies and Other Essays*, 24–46. London 1955.
Beatrice, P. F. *Anonymi Monophysitae Theosophia: An Attempt at Reconstruction*. Leiden 2001.
———. "Towards a New Edition of Porphyry's Fragments against the Christians." In *ΣΟΦΙΗΣ ΜΑΙΗΤΟΡΕΣ, Chercheurs de sagesse: Hommage à Jean Pépin*, ed. M.-O. Goulet-Cazé, G. Madec, and D. O'Brien, 347–55. Paris 1992.
———. "The Word 'Homoousios' from Hellenism to Christianity." *ChHist* 71 (2002): 243–72.
Beeley, C. A. *Gregory of Nazianzus on the Trinity and the Knowledge of God: In Your Light We Shall See Light*. Oxford 2008.
Bees, R. *Die Oikeiosislehre der Stoa*. Vol. 1, *Rekonstruktion ihres Inhalts*. Würzburg 2004.
Benedetti, I. "Giuliano in Antiochia nell'orazione xviii di Libanio." *Athenaeum* 59 (1981): 166–79.
Benner, M. *The Emperor Says: Studies in the Rhetorical Style in Edicts of the Early Empire*. Gothenburg 1975.
Béranger, J. "Étude sur saint Ambroise: L'image de l'état dans les sociétés animales, *Exameron* 5.15.51–52, 21.66–72." In *Principatus: Études de notions et d'histoire politiques dans l'antiquité gréco-romaine*, ed. J. Béranger, F. Paschoud, and P. Ducrey, 303–30. Geneva 1973.
———. "Julien l'Apostat et l'hérédité du pouvoir impérial." In *Bonner Historia Augusta Colloquium 1970*, ed. J. Straub, 75–93. Bonn 1972.
———. "Le réfus du pouvoir: Recherches sur l'aspect idéologique du principat." In *Principatus: Études de notions et d'histoire politiques dans l'antiquité gréco-romaine*, ed. J. Béranger, F. Paschoud, and P. Ducrey, 165–90. Geneva 1973.
Berchman, R. M. *Porphyry against the Christians*. Leiden 2005.
Berg, G. O. *Metaphor and Comparison in the Dialogues of Plato*. Berlin 1904.
van den Berg, R. "Live Unnoticed! The Invisible Neoplatonic Politician." In *The Philosopher and Society in Late Antiquity: Essays in Honour of Peter Brown*, ed. A. Smith, 101–15. Swansea 2005.
Berger, P. L., and T. Luckmann. *Die gesellschaftliche Konstruktion der Wirklichkeit: Eine Theorie der Wissenssoziologie*. Frankfurt a.M. 1994. [Reprint of the 5th ed. (1977).]
Bernardi, J. "Nouvelles perspectives sur la famille de Grégoire de Nazianze." *VChr* 38 (1984): 352–59.
———. *La prédication des Pères cappadociens: Le prédicateur et son auditoire*. Paris 1968.
———. "Un réquisitoire: Les *Invectives contre Julien* de Grégoire de Nazianze." In *L'empereur Julien*, vol. 1, *De l'histoire à la légende (331–1715)*, ed. R. Braun and J. Richer, 89–98. Paris 1978.
———. *Saint Grégoire de Nazianze: Le théologien et son temps, 330–390*. Paris 1995.

———, ed. and trans. *Grégoire de Nazianze: Discours 1–3*. Paris 1978.
———, ed. and trans. *Grégoire de Nazianze: Discours 4–5 contre Julien*. Paris 1983.
Berrens, S. *Sonnenkult und Kaisertum von den Severern bis zu Constantin I. (193–337 n.Chr.)*. Stuttgart 2004.
Bidez, J. *La vie de l'empereur Julien*. Paris 1930.
———. *Vie de Porphyre*. Ghent 1913.
Bienert, W. A. "Sabellius und Sabellianismus als historisches Problem." In *Logos: Festschrift Luise Abramowski*, ed. H. C. Brennecke, E. L. Grasmück, and C. Markschies, 124–39. Berlin 1993.
Billerbeck, M. "The Ideal Cynic from Epictetus to Julian." In *The Cynics: The Cynic Movement in Antiquity and Its Legacy*, ed. R. B. Branham and M.-O. Goulet-Cazé, 205–21. Berkeley and Los Angeles 1996.
Blázquez, J. M. "La Academia de Atenas como foco de formación humanística para paganos y cristianos: Los casos de Juliano, Basilio y Gregorio Nacianceno." *Gerión* 19 (2001): 595–628.
Bleckmann, B. "Constantina, Vetranio und Gallus Caesar." *Chiron* 24 (1994): 29–68.
———. *Die Reichskrise des 3. Jhd. in der spätantiken und byzantinischen Geschichtsschreibung: Untersuchungen zu den nachdionischen Quellen der Chronik des Johannes Zonaras*. Munich 1992.
Blockley, R. C. *East Roman Foreign Policy: Formation and Conduct from Diocletian to Anastasius*. Leeds 1992.
———. *The Fragmentary Classicising Historians of the Later Roman Empire: Eunapius, Olympiodorus, Priscus and Malchus*. Volume 2. Liverpool 1981
———. "The Panegyric of Claudius Mamertinus on the Emperor Julian." *AJPh* 93 (1972): 437–50.
Blok, J. H. "Becoming Citizens. Some Notes on the Semantics of 'Citizen' in Archaic Greece and Classical Athens." *Klio* 87 (2005): 7–40.
Bloomer, W. M. "Schooling in Persona: Imagination and Subordination in Roman Education." *ClAnt* 16 (1997): 57–78.
Blumenthal, H. J. *Aristotle and Neoplatonism in Late Antiquity: Interpretations of the "De Anima."* London 1996.
den Boeft, J., D. den Hengst, and H. C. Teitler, eds. *Philological and Historical Commentary on Ammianus Marcellinus 21*. Groningen 1991.
———. *Philological and Historical Commentary on Ammianus Marcellinus 23*. Groningen 1998.
den Boeft, J., J. W. Drijvers, D. den Hengst, and H. C. Teitler, eds. *Philological and Historical Commentary on Ammianus Marcellinus 22*. Groningen 1995.
———. *Philological and Historical Commentary on Ammianus Marcellinus 25*. Leiden 2005.
den Boer, W. *Some Minor Roman Historians*. Leiden 1972.
Bogner, H. "Kaiser Julians 5. Rede." *Philologus* 79 (1924): 258–79.
Børtnes, J. "Eros Transformed: Same-Sex Love and Divine Desire—Reflections on the Erotic Vocabulary in St. Gregory of Nazianzus's Speech on St. Basil the Great." In *Greek Biography and Panegyric in Late Antiquity*, ed. T. Hägg and P. Rousseau, 180–93. Berkeley and Los Angeles 2000.

Bouffartigue, J. "Le Cynisme dans le cursus philosophique au VIe siècle: Le témoignage de l'empereur Julien." In *Le Cynisme ancien et ses prolongements: Actes du Colloque international du CNRS, Paris, 22–25 juillet 1991*, ed. M.-O. Goulet-Cazé and R. Goulet, 339–58. Paris 1993.

———. "Du prétendu parti païen au prétendu fléau de Dieu: Observations sur l'action antichrétienne de l'empereur Julien." In *Giuliano imperatore: Le sue idee, i suoi amici, i suoi avversari—Atti del Convegno internazionale di studi, Lecce, 10–12 dicembre 1998*, ed. A. Filippo and R. Guido, 59–87. Lecce 1998.

———. *L'empereur Julien et la culture de son temps.* Paris 1992.

———. "Philosophie et antichristianisme chez l'empereur Julien." In *Hellénisme et christianisme*, ed. M. Narcy and É. Rebillard, 111–31. Villeneuve-d'Ascq 2004.

Bourdieu, P. *La distinction: Critique sociale du jugement.* Paris 1979.

———. *Esquisse d'une théorie de la pratique.* 2nd ed. Paris 2000.

Bowersock, G. W. "From Emperor to Bishop: The Self-conscious Transformation of Political Power in the Fourth Century." *CPh* 81 (1986): 298–307.

———. *Greek Sophists in the Roman Empire.* Oxford 1969.

———. *Julian the Apostate.* Cambridge, Mass., 1978.

Boylan, M. "The Galenic and Hippocratic Challenges to Aristotle's Conception Theory." *JHB* 17 (1984): 83–112.

Bradbury, S. "Constantine and the Problem of Anti-pagan Legislation in the Fourth Century." *CPh* 89 (1994): 120–39.

———. "The Date of Julian's *Letter to Themistius*." *GRBS* 28 (1987): 235–51.

———. "Julian's Pagan Revival and the Decline of Blood Sacrifice." *Phoenix* 49 (1995): 331–56.

Branham, R. B. "Defacing the Currency: Diogenes' Rhetoric and the Invention of Cynicism." In *The Cynics: The Cynic Movement in Antiquity and Its Legacy*, ed. R. B. Branham and M.-O. Goulet-Cazé, 81–104. Berkeley and Los Angeles 1996.

Branham, R. B., and M.-O. Goulet-Cazé, eds. *The Cynics: The Cynic Movement in Antiquity and Its Legacy.* Berkeley and Los Angeles 1996.

Brauch, T. "The Prefect of Constantinople for 362 A.D.: Themistius." *Byzantion* 63 (1993): 37–78.

———. "Themistius and the Emperor Julian." *Byzantion* 63 (1993): 79–115.

Braun, R., and J. Richer, eds. *L'empereur Julien.* Vols. 1, *De l'histoire à la légende (331–1715)*, and 2, *De la légende au mythe (de Voltaire à nos jours).* Paris 1978–81.

Breitenbach, A. "Der unfreiwillige Hochzeitsgast: Die verschiedenen Berufungen des Gregor von Nazianz und das Schweigen über seine Taufe." In *Corona Coronaria*, ed. S. Harwardt and J. Schwind, 31–48. Hildesheim 2005.

Brennecke, H. C. *Hilarius von Poitiers und die Bischofsopposition gegen Konstantius II.: Untersuchungen zur dritten Phase des Arianischen Streites (337–361).* Berlin 1984.

———. *Studien zur Geschichte der Homöer: Der Osten bis zum Ende der homöischen Reichskirche.* Tübingen 1988.

Brock, S. P. "The Rebuilding of the Temple under Julian: A New Source." *PalEQ* 108 (1976): 103–7.

Brown, P. "Aspects of the Christianization of the Roman Aristocracy." *JRS* 51 (1961): 1–11.
———. *Authority and the Sacred: Aspects of the Christianisation of the Roman World*. Cambridge 1995.
———. *The Body and Society: Men, Women, and Sexual Renunciation in Early Christianity*. New York 1988.
———. "Christianization and Religious Conflict." In *The Cambridge Ancient History*, vol. 13, *The Late Empire, A.D. 337–425*, ed. A. Cameron and P. Garnsey, 632–64. Cambridge 1998.
———. *Poverty and Leadership in the Later Roman Empire*. Hanover 2002.
———. *Power and Persuasion in Late Antiquity: Towards a Christian Empire*. Madison, Wisc., 1992.
Browning, R. *The Emperor Julian*. London 1975.
de Bruyn, T. S. "Flogging a Son: The Emergence of the *pater flagellans* in Latin Christian Discourse." *JECS* 7 (1999): 249–90.
Buck, D. F. "Eunapius on Julian's Acclamation as Augustus." *AHB* 7 (1993): 73–80.
Burrus, V. *Begotten, Not Made: Conceiving Manhood in Late Antiquity*. Stanford 2000.
Burton, P. J. "The Summoning of the Magna Mater to Rome." *Historia* 45 (1996): 36–63.
Cadiou, R. "Le problème des relations scolaires entre saint Basile et Libanios." *REG* 79 (1966): 143–53.
Calderone, S. "Teologia politica, successione dinastica e *consecratio* in età costantiniana." In *Le culte des souverains dans l'empire romain*, ed. W. den Boer, 215–61. Geneva 1973.
Callahan, J. F. "Greek Philosophy and Cappadocian Cosmology." *DOP* 12 (1952): 30–57.
Caltabiano, M. "Giuliano imperatore nelle *Res gestae* di Ammiano Marcellino: Tra panegirico e storia." In *Giuliano imperatore: Le sue idee, i suoi amici, i suoi avversari—Atti del Convegno internazionale di studi, Lecce, 10–12 dicembre 1998*, ed. A. Filippo and R. Guido, 335–55. Lecce 1998.
Camelot, T. "Amour des letters et désir de Dieu chez Grégoire de Nazianze: Les *logoi* au service du *Logos*." In *Littérature et religion: Mélanges offerts à M. le chanoine Joseph Coppin*, 23–30. Lille 1966.
Cameron, Alan. "Wandering Poets: A Literary Movement in Byzantine Egypt." *Historia* 14 (1965): 470–509.
Cameron, Averil. *Christianity and the Rhetoric of Empire: The Development of Christian Discourse*. Berkeley and Los Angeles 1991.
Camplani, A., and M. Zambon. "Il sacrificio come problema in alcune correnti filosofiche di età imperiale." *AnnSE* 19 (2002): 59–99.
Caner, D. F. "Notions of 'Strict Discipline' and Apostolic Tradition in Early Definitions of Orthodox Monasticism." In *Orthodoxie, christianisme, histoire / Orthodoxy, Christianity, History*, ed. S. Elm, É. Rebillard, and A. Romano, 23–34. Rome 2000.
———. *Wandering, Begging Monks: Spiritual Authority and the Promotion of Monasticism in Late Antiquity*. Berkeley and Los Angeles 2001.
Carotenuto, E. "Six Constantinian Documents (Eus. H.E. 10, 5–7)." *VChr* 56 (2002): 56–74.
Carrié, J.-M. "Le gouverneur romain à l'époque tardive: Orientations de l'enquête." *Antiquité Tardive* 6 (1998): 17–30.
Carriker, A. J. *The Library of Eusebius of Caesarea*. Leiden 2003.

Cartledge, P. "Greek Political Thought: The Historical Context." In *The Cambridge History of Greek and Roman Political Thought,* ed. C. Rowe and M. Schofield, 11–22. Cambridge 2005.
Casana, J. "The Archaeological Landscape of Late Roman Antioch." In *Culture and Society in Later Roman Antioch,* ed. I. Sandwell and J. Huskinson, 102–25. Oxford 2004.
Casson, L. *Travel in the Ancient World.* Toronto 1974.
Cavalcanti, E. *Studi Eunomiani.* Rome 1976.
Chambers, E. W., ed. *Poems of John Donne.* Vol. 1. London 1896.
Charles, D. *Aristotle on Meaning and Essence.* Oxford 2000.
Clark, E. A. *The Origenist Controversy: The Cultural Construction of an Early Christian Debate.* Princeton 1992.
———. "Rewriting Early Christian History: Augustine's Representation of Monica." In *Portraits of Spiritual Authority: Religious Power in Early Christianity, Byzantium, and the Christian Orient,* ed. J. W. Drijvers and J. W. Watt, 3–23. Leiden 1999.
Clark, G. "Philosophic Lives and the Philosophical Life: Porphyry and Iamblichus." In *Greek Biography and Panegyric in Late Antiquity,* ed. T. Hägg and P. Rousseau, 29–51. Berkeley and Los Angeles 2000.
Clarke, E. C. *Iamblichus' "De Mysteriis": A Manifesto of the Miraculous.* Aldershot 2001.
Clendinnen, I. *Ambivalent Conquests: Maya and Spaniard in Yucatan, 1517–1570.* Cambridge 1987.
Coleman, K. "Fatal Charades: Roman Executions Staged as Mythological Enactments." *JRS* 80 (1990): 44–73.
Colpe, C. "*Civilitas graeca* und *eupistia hellenike:* Kennworte zur Religionspolitik des Kaisers Julian." In *Stimuli: Exegese und ihre Hermeneutik in Antike und Christentum,* ed. G. Schollgen and C. Scholten, 308–28. Munich 1996.
Colpi, B. *Die paideia des Themistios: Ein Beitrag zur Geschichte der Bildung im vierten Jahrhundert nach Christus.* Bern 1987.
Conti, S. *Die Inschriften Kaiser Julians.* Stuttgart 2004.
Cooper, J. M. *Reason and Emotion: Essays on Ancient Moral Psychology and Ethical Theory.* Princeton 1999.
Corcoran, S. *The Empire of the Tetrarchs: Imperial Pronouncements and Government,* A.D. 284–324. Oxford 1996.
Cordes, P. *Iatros: Das Bild des Arztes in der griechischen Literatur von Homer bis Aristoteles.* Stuttgart 1994.
Cosi, D. M. *Casta mater Idaea: Giuliano l'Apostata e l'etica della sessualità.* Venice 1986.
Coulie, B. "Chaînes d'allusions dans les discourses IV et V de Grégoire de Nazianze." *JöByz* 32 (1982): 137–43.
———. *Les richesses dans l'oeuvre de saint Grégoire de Nazianze: Étude littéraire et historique.* Louvain-la-Neuve 1985.
Courcelle, P. P. *"Connais-toi toi-même" de Socrate à saint Bernard.* 3 vols. Paris 1974–75.
Cribiore, R. *Gymnastics of the Mind: Greek Education in Hellenistic and Roman Egypt.* Princeton 2001.
———. *The School of Libanius in Late Antique Antioch.* Princeton 2007.
Criscuolo, U. "A proposito di Gregorio di Nazianzo, *Or.* 4.96." *Koinonia* 11 (1987): 43–52.

———. "Giuliano nell'*Epitafio* di Libanio." In *Giuliano imperatore: Le sue idee, i suoi amici, i suoi avversari—Atti del Convegno internazionale di studi, Lecce, 10-12 dicembre 1998*, ed. A. Filippo and R. Guido, 266-91. Lecce 1998.
———. "Gregorio di Nazianzo e Giuliano." In *Talariscos: Studia Graeca Antonio Garzya sexagenario a discipulis oblata*, ed. U. Criscuolo, 165-208. Naples 1987.
———. "Sull'epistola di Giuliano imperatore al filosofo Temistio." *Koinonia* 7 (1983): 89-111.
———. "Sull'epistola 10 di Gregorio di Nazianzo." *Koinonia* 9 (1985): 115-20.
Cross, R. "Divine Monarchy in Gregory of Nazianzus." *JECS* 14 (2006): 105-16.
———. "Gregory of Nyssa on Universals." *VChr* 56 (2002): 372-410.
Cumont, F. *Textes et monuments figurés relatifs aux Mystères de Mithra*. 2 vols. Brussels 1896-99.
Cuneo, P. Ombretta. *La legislazione di Costantino II, Costanzo II e Costante (337-361)*. Milan 1997.
Cuntz, O., ed. *Itineraria Antonini Augusti et Burdigalense; Accedit tabula geographica*. Itineraria Romana, vol. 1. Stuttgart 1929. [Reprint: 1990.]
Curran, J. R. *Pagan City and Christian Capital: Rome in the Fourth Century*. Oxford 2000.
Curta, F. "Atticism, Homer, Neoplatonism, and *Fürstenspiegel*: Julian's Second Panegyric to Constantius." *GRBS* 36 (1995): 177-211.
Dagron, G. *Empereur et prêtre: Étude sur le "Césaropapisme" byzantin*. Paris 1996.
———. *L'empire romain d'Orient au IVe siècle et les traditions politiques de l'hellénisme: Le témoignage de Thémistios*. Paris 1968.
———. *Naissance d'une capitale: Constantinople et ses institutions de 330 à 451*. 2nd ed. Paris 1984.
Daley, B. E. *Gregory of Nazianzus*. London 2006.
Daly, L. J. "'In a Borderland': Themistius' Ambivalence toward Julian." *ByzZ* 73 (1980): 1-11.
———. "Themistius' Refusal of a Magistracy (*Or*. 34, cc. XIII-XIV)." *Byzantion* 53 (1983): 164-212.
Daniélou, J. "Eunome l'Arien et l'éxegèse néoplatonicienne du *Cratyle*." *REG* 69 (1956): 412-32.
Dawson, D. *Allegorical Readers and Cultural Revisions in Ancient Alexandria*. Berkeley and Los Angeles 1992.
———. "Allegorical Reading and the Embodiment of the Soul in Origen." In *Christian Origins: Theology, Rhetoric and Community*, ed. L. Ayres and G. Jones, 26-43. London 1998.
Deichgräber, K. *Medicus gratiosus: Untersuchungen zu einem griechischen Arztbild*. Mainz 1970.
Delatte, L., S. Govaerts, and J. Denooz, eds. *Index du Corpus hermeticum*. Rome 1977.
DeLay, B. *War of a Thousand Deserts*. New Haven 2008.
Demoen, K. "The Attitude towards Greek Poetry in the Verse of Gregory Nazianzus." In *Early Christian Poetry: A Collection of Essays*, ed. J. den Boeft and A. Hilhorst, 235-52. Leiden 1993.
———. *Pagan and Biblical Exempla in Gregory Nazianzen: A Study in Rhetoric and Hermeneutic*. Turnhout 1996.

Demont, P. *La cité grecque archaïque et classique et l'idéal de tranquillité.* Paris 1990.

———. "Les problèmes du loisir en Grèce." In *Les loisirs et l'héritage de la culture classique: Actes du XIIIe Congrès de l'Association Guillaume Budé, Dijon, 27–31 août 1993*, ed. J.-M. André, J. Dangel, and P. Demont, 9–36. Brussels 1996.

Devreesse, R. *Essai sur Théodore de Mopsueste.* Vatican City 1948.

Di Paola, L. *Viaggi, trasporti e istituzioni. Studi sul cursus publicus.* Messina 1999.

Dickey, E. *Latin Forms of Address: From Plautus to Apuleius.* Oxford 2002.

Dierlmeier, F. *Die Oikeiosis-Lehre Theophrasts.* Leipzig 1937.

Digeser, E. "Apollo at Daphne and the Great Persecution." *CPh* 99 (2004): 57–77.

———. *The Making of a Christian Empire: Lactantius and Rome.* Ithaca 2000.

———. "The Power of Religious Rituals: A Philosophical Quarrel on the Eve of the Great Persecution." In *The Power of Religion in Late Antiquity*, ed. A. Cain and N. Lenski, 81–92. Farnham 2009.

Dillon, J. "Image, Symbol and Analogy: Three Basic Concepts of Neoplatonic Allegorical Exegesis." In *The Golden Chain: Studies in the Development of Platonism and Christianity*, 247–62. Aldershot 1990.

———. "Looking on the Light." In *The Golden Chain: Studies in the Development of Platonism and Christianity*, 125–56. Aldershot 1990.

———. "The Magical Power of Names in Origen and Later Platonism." In *The Golden Chain: Studies in the Development of Platonism and Christianity*, 203–16. Aldershot 1990.

———. "Philosophy as a Profession in Late Antiquity." In *The Philosopher and Society in Late Antiquity: Essays in Honour of Peter Brown*, ed. A. Smith, 1–17. Swansea 2005.

———. "The Theology of Julian's 'Hymn to King Helios.'" *Itaca* 14–15 (1998–99): 103–15.

Dionisotti, A. C. "From Ausonius' Schooldays? A Schoolbook and Its Relations." *JRS* 72 (1982): 83–125.

Divjak, J. "Der sogenannte Kalender des Filocalus." In *Textsorten und Textkritik: Tagungsbeiträge*, ed. A. Primmer, K. Smolak, and D. Weber, 19–38. Vienna 2002.

Dodgeon, M. H., and S. L. Lieu, eds. *The Roman Eastern Frontier and the Persian Wars (AD 226–363).* London 1991.

Döring, K. "Kaiser Julians Plädoyer für den Kynismus." *RhM* 140 (1997): 386–400.

Dörnemann, M. *Krankheit und Heilung in der Theologie der frühen Kirchenväter.* Tübingen 2003.

Dossetti, G. L. *Il simbolo di Nicea e di Costantinopoli: Edizione critica.* Freiburg 1967.

Douglass, L. "A New Look at the *Itinerarium Burdigalense*." *JECS* 4 (1996): 313–33.

Downey, G. *A History of Antioch in Syria: From Seleucus to the Arab Conquest.* Princeton 1961.

Drake, H. A. *Constantine and the Bishops: The Politics of Intolerance.* Baltimore 2000.

———. "The Eusebian Template." In *The Greek Strand in Islamic Political Thought*, ed. E. Gannagé, 75–88. Beirut 2005.

———. *In Praise of Constantine: A Historical Study and New Translation of Eusebius' Tricennial Orations.* Berkeley and Los Angeles 1976.

Drecoll, C. *Die Liturgien im römischen Kaiserreich des 3. und 4. Jhdt. n.Chr.* Stuttgart 1997.

Drecoll, V. H. *Die Entwicklung der Trinitätslehre des Basilius von Caesarea.* Göttingen 1996.

Drijvers, J. W. "Ammianus Marcellinus 23.1.2–3: The Rebuilding of the Temple in Jerusalem."

In *Cognitio Gestorum: The Historiographic Art of Ammianus Marcellinus,* ed. J. den Boeft, D. den Hengst, and H. C. Teitler, 19–26. Amsterdam 1992.

———. *Cyril of Jerusalem: Bishop and City.* Leiden 2004.

Drinkwater, J. F. "The 'Pagan Underground,' Constantius II's 'Secret Service,' and the Survival and the Usurpation of Julian the Apostate." In *Studies in Latin Literature and Roman History,* ed. C. Deroux, vol. 3, 348–87. Brussels 1983.

Droge, A. J. *Homer or Moses? Early Christian Interpretations of the History of Culture.* Tübingen 1989.

Dünzl, F. "Die Absetzung des Bischofs Meletius von Antiochien, 361 n.Chr." *JbAC* 43 (2000): 71–93.

Eck, W. "Der Einfluss der konstantinischen Wende auf die Auswahl der Bischöfe im 4. und 5. Jahrhundert." *Chiron* 8 (1978): 561–85.

Edwards, M. J. *Origen against Plato.* Aldershot 2002.

Efthymiadis, S. "Two Gregories and Three Genres: Autobiography, Autohagiography, and Hagiography." In *Gregory of Nazianzus: Images and Reflections,* ed. J. Børtnes and T. Hägg, 239–56. Copenhagen 2006.

Ehling, K. "Der Ausgang des Perserfeldzuges in der Münzpropaganda des Jovian." *Klio* 78 (1996): 186–91.

———. "Kaiser Julian, der Senat und die Stadt Rom." *ZPE* 137 (2001): 292–96.

Eitrem, S. "Zur Apotheose." *SO* 11 (1937): 11–34.

Elia, F. "Sui *privilegia urbis Constantinopolitanae*." In *Politica retorica e simbolismo del primato: Roma e Constantinopoli (secoli IV–VII),* ed. F. Elia, 78–105. Catania 2002.

Elm, E. "Die *Damnatio memoriae.*" Habilitationsschrift, Marburg 2010.

———. "'Du bist wie jener Gott': Die Darstellung Kaiser Konstantins in der 'Vita Constantini' des Eusebius von Caesarea." *GLP* 19 (2004): 33–44.

———. *Die Macht der Weisheit: Das Bild des Bischofs in der "Vita Augustini" des Possidius und anderen spätantiken und frühmittelalterlichen Bischofsviten.* Leiden 2003.

Elm, S. "Der Asket als *vir publicus:* Die Bedeutung von Augustinus' Konzept des *Christus iustus et iustificans* für den spätantiken Asketen als Bischof." In *Recht, Macht, Gerechtigkeit,* ed. J. Mehlhausen, 192–201. Gütersloh 1999.

———. "The Diagnostic Gaze: Gregory of Nazianzus' Theory of Orthodox Priesthood in His Orations 6 *De Pace* and 2 *Apologia de Fuga Sua*." In *Orthodoxie, christianisme, histoire / Orthodoxy, Christianity, History,* ed. S. Elm, É. Rebillard, and A. Romano, 83–100. Rome 2000.

———. "The Dog That Did Not Bark: Doctrine and Patriarchal Authority in the Conflict between Theophilus of Alexandria and John Chrysostom of Constantinople." In *Christian Origins: Theology, Rhetoric and Community,* ed. L. Ayres and G. Jones, 68–93. London 1998.

———. "Family Men: Masculinity and Philosophy in Late Antiquity." In *Transformations of Late Antiquity: Essays for Peter Brown,* ed. P. Rousseau and M. Papoutsakis, 279–302. Farnham 2009.

———. "Gregory of Nazianzus's *Life of Julian* Revisited (*Or.* 4 and 5): The Art of Governance by Invective." In *From the Tetrarchs to the Theodosians: Later Roman History and Culture, 284–450 CE,* ed. S. McGill, C. Sogno, and E. Watts, 169–80. Cambridge 2010.

———. "Gregory's Women: Creating a Philosopher's Family." In *Gregory of Nazianzus: Images and Reflections,* ed. J. Børtnes and T. Hägg, 171–91. Copenhagen 2006.

———. "Hellenism and Historiography: Emperor Julian and Gregory of Nazianzus in Dialogue." *Journal of Medieval and Early Modern Studies* 33 (2003): 493–515.

———. "Inscriptions and Conversions: Gregory of Nazianzus on Baptism (*Or.* 38–40)." In *Conversion in Late Antiquity and the Early Middle Ages: Seeing and Believing,* ed. K. Mills and A. Grafton, 1–35. Rochester 2003.

———. "Marking the Self in Late Antiquity: Inscriptions, Baptism, and the Conversion of Mimes." In *Stigmata,* ed. B. Menken and B. Vinken, 47–68. Paderborn 2004.

———. "Orthodoxy and the True Philosophical Life: Julian and Gregory of Nazianzus." *Studia Patristica* 37 (2001): 69–85.

———. "Paul as Seen by Gregory of Nazianzus: Some Aspects of His Greek Antiochene and Syrian *Nachleben.*" in *San Paolo letto da Oriente,* ed. F. Bonaghi and E. Virginio, 109–18. Milan 2010.

———. "Die *persona* des Senators in der Kaiserzeit: Tacitus' *Agricola* und Plinius' Bithynia." *Phoenix,* forthcoming.

———. "'Pierced by Bronze Needles': Anti-Montanist Charges of Ritual Stigmatization in Their Fourth-Century Context." *JECS* 4 (1996): 409–39.

———. "The Polemical Use of Genealogies: Jerome's Classification of Pelagius and Evagrius Ponticus." *Studia Patristica* 33 (1996): 311–18.

———. "A Programmatic Life: Gregory of Nazianzus' *Orations* 42 and 43 and the Constantinopolitan Elites." *Arethusa* 33 (2000): 411–27.

———. "Translating Culture: Gregory of Nazianzus, Hellenism, and the Claim to *Romanitas.*" In *Intermedien: Zur kulturellen und artistischen Übertragung,* ed. A. Kleihues, B. Naumann, and E. Pankow, 17–26. Zurich 2010.

———. *Virgins of God: The Making of Asceticism in Late Antiquity.* Oxford 1994.

Emmel, S., U. Gotter, and J. Hahn. "From Temple to Church: Analysing a Late Antique Phenomenon of Transformation." In *From Temple to Church: Destruction and Renewal of Local Cultic Topography in Late Antiquity,* ed. J. Hahn, S. Emmel, and U. Gotter, 1–22. Leiden 2008.

Entralgo, P. Laín. *The Therapy of the Word in Classical Antiquity.* New Haven 1970.

Erler, M. "Interpretieren als Gottesdienst: Proklus' Hymnen vor dem Hintergrund seines Kratyloskommentars." In *Proclus et son influence: Actes du colloque de Neuchâtel, juin 1985,* ed. G. Boss and G. Seel, 179–217. Zurich 1987.

———. "*Philologia medicans:* Wie die Epikureer die Texte ihres Meisters lasen." In *Vermittlung und Tradierung von Wissen in der griechischen Kultur,* ed. W. Kullmann and J. Althoff, 281–303. Tübingen 1993.

Étienne, R. "Flavius Sallustius et Secundus Salutius." *REAug* 65 (1975): 104–13.

Eyben, E. "Fathers and Sons." In *Marriage, Divorce, and Children in Ancient Rome,* ed. B. Rawson, 112–43. Oxford 1991.

Fauth, W. *Helios Megistos: Zur synkretistischen Theologie der Spätantike.* Leiden 1995.

Fedwick, P. J. *Bibliotheca Basiliana universalis: A Study of the Manuscript Tradition of the Works of Basil of Caesarea.* Vol. 1, *The Letters.* Turnhout 1993.

Felgentreu, F. "Zur Datierung der 18. Rede des Libanios." *Klio* 86 (2004): 206–17.
Fernández, S. *Cristo médico, según Orígenes: La actividad médica como metáfora de la acción divina.* Rome 1999.
Festugière, A.-J. *Antioche païenne et chrétienne.* Paris 1959.
———. "Julien à Macellum." *JRS* 47 (1957): 53–58.
———. *La révélation d'Hermès Trismégiste.* 3 vols. Paris 1981.
Fiedler, W. *Analogiemodelle bei Aristoteles: Untersuchungen zu den Vergleichen zwischen den einzelnen Wissenschaften und Künsten.* Amsterdam 1978.
Fiedrowicz, M. *Apologie im frühen Christentum: Die Kontroverse um den christlichen Wahrheitsanspruch in den ersten Jahrhunderten.* Paderborn 2000.
Finn, R. *Almsgiving in the Later Roman Empire: Christian Promotion and Practice, 313–450.* Oxford 2006.
Folliet, G. "'Deificari in otio': Augustin, *Epistula* X, 2." *RecAug* 2 (1962): 225–36.
Fontenrose, J. *The Delphic Oracle.* Berkeley and Los Angeles 1978.
———. *Didyma: Apollo's Oracle, Cult, and Companions.* Berkeley and Los Angeles 1988.
Fortenbaugh, W. W. *Aristotle on Emotions: A Contribution to Philosophical Psychology, Rhetoric, Poetics, and Ethics.* London 1975.
Foussard, J.-C. "Julien philosophe." In *L'empereur Julien*, vol. 1, *De l'histoire à la légende (331–1715)*, ed. R. Braun and J. Richer, 189–212. Paris 1978.
Fowden, G. "Bishops and Temples in the Eastern Empire." *JThS* 29 (1978): 53–78.
———. "The Last Days of Constantine. Oppositional Versions and Their Influence." *JRS* 84 (1994): 146–70.
———. "The Pagan Holy Man in Late Antique Society." *JHS* 102 (1982): 33–59.
Franchi de' Cavalieri, P. *I martirii di S. Teodoto e di S. Ariadne, con un' appendice sul testo originale del martirio di S. Eleuterio.* Studi e Testi 6. Rome 1901.
Francis, J. A. *Subversive Virtue: Asceticism and Authority in the Second-Century Pagan World.* University Park 1995.
Frantz, A. *Late Antiquity, A.D. 267–700.* Vol. 24 of *The Athenian Agora.* Princeton 1988.
French, D. R. "Maintaining Boundaries: The Status of Actresses in Early Christian Society." *VChr* 52 (1998): 293–318.
Gaca, K. L. *The Making of Fornication: Eros, Ethics, and Political Reform in Greek Philosophy and Early Christianity.* Berkeley and Los Angeles 2003.
Gallay, P. *La vie de saint Grégoire de Nazianze.* Lyon 1943.
Gangloff, A. *Dion Chrysostome et les mythes: Hellénisme, communication et philosophie politique.* Grenoble 2006.
García, M. D. Garrido. *Las homilías In hexaemeron de Basilios de Cesarea: Una respuesta a la política religiosa del emperador Juliano?* Louvain-la-Neuve 2000.
Garnsey, P. *Famine and Food Supply: Responses to Risk and Crisis.* Cambridge 1988.
Garnsey, P., and C. Humfress. *The Evolution of the Late Antique World.* Cambridge 2001.
Garzya, A. "Ideali e conflitti di cultura alla fine del mondo antico." In *Storia e interpretazione di testi bizantini: Saggi e ricerche*, 301–20. London 1974.
———. "Sul rapporto fra teoria e prassi nella grecità tardoantica e medievale." In *Il mandarino e il quotidiano: Saggi sulla letteratura tardoantica e bizantina*, 201–19. Naples 1983.

———. "Sur l'idée de *scholè* dans l'hellénisme tardif." In *Les loisirs et l'héritage de la culture classique: Actes du XIIIe Congrès de l'Association Guillaume Budé, Dijon, 27–31 août 1993*, ed. J.-M. André, J. Dangel, and P. Demont, 211–17. Brussels 1996.

Gasparro, G. Sfameni. "Le interpretazioni gnostiche e misteriosofiche del mito di Attis." In *Studies in Gnosticism and Hellenistic Religions Presented to Gilles Quispel*, ed. R. van den Broek, 376–411. Leiden 1981.

———. *Soteriology and Mystic Aspects in the Cult of Cybele and Attis*. Leiden 1985.

Gautier, F. *La retraite et le sacerdoce chez Grégoire de Nazianze*. Turnhout 2002.

Geffcken, J. *Kaiser Julianus*. Leipzig 1914.

Gehrke, H.-J. "Das Verhältnis von Politik und Philosophie in den Werken des Demetrios von Phaleron." *Chiron* 8 (1978): 149–93.

Germino, E. *Scuola e cultura nella legislazione di Giuliano l'Apostata*. Naples 2004.

Gerson, L. *Aristotle and Other Platonists*. Ithaca 2005.

Ginzburg, C. "Myth: Distance and Deceit." In *Wooden Eyes: Nine Reflections on Distance*, trans. M. Ryle and K. Soper, 25–61. New York 2001.

Girardi, M. "'Semplicità' e ortodossia nel dibattito antiariano di Basilio di Cesarea: La raffigurazione dell'eretico." *VetChr* 15 (1978): 51–74.

Gleason, M. W. "Festive Satire: Julian's *Misopogon* and the New Year at Antioch." *JRS* 76 (1986): 106–19.

———. *Making Men: Sophists and Self-Presentation in Ancient Rome*. Princeton 1995.

Gombrich, E. H. *Meditations on a Hobby-Horse and Other Essays on the Theory of Art*. London 1963.

Goody, J. *Representations and Contradictions: Ambivalence towards Images, Theatre, Fiction, Relics and Sexuality*. Oxford 1997.

Gottschalk, H. B. "Aristotelian Philosophy in the Roman World from the Time of Cicero to the End of the Second Century." In *ANRW* 2.36.2, ed. W. Haase, 1079–1174. Berlin 1987.

———. "Demetrius of Phalerum: A Politician among Philosophers and a Philosopher among Politicians." In *Demetrius of Phalerum: Text, Translation, and Discussion*, ed. W. W. Fortenbaugh and E. Schütrumpf, 367–80. New Brunswick 2000.

Gottwald, R. *De Gregorio Nazianzeno Platonico*. Bratislava 1906.

Goulet, R. "Hypothèses récentes sur le traité de Porphyre *Contre les Chrétiens*." In *Hellénisme et christianisme*, ed. M. Narcy and É. Rebillard, 61–109. Villeneuve-d'Ascq 2004.

———. *Macarios de Magnésie: Le Monogénès*. 2 vols. Paris 2003.

———. "Prohérésius le païen et quelques remarques sur la chronologie d'Eunape de Sardes." *Antiquité Tardive* 8 (2000): 209–22.

———. "Les vies de philosophes dans l'antiquité tardive et leur portée mystérique." In *Les Actes apocryphes des apôtres: Christianisme et monde païen*, ed. F. Bovon, M. van Esbroeck, et al., 161–208. Geneva 1981.

Gregg, R. C., and D. E. Groh. *Early Arianism: A View of Salvation*. Philadelphia 1981.

Gregory, T. E. "Julian and the Last Oracle at Delphi." *GRBS* 24 (1983): 355–66.

Griffin, M. "*De Beneficiis* and Roman Society." *JRS* 93 (2003): 92–113.

Griffith, S. "Ephraem the Syrian's Hymns 'Against Julian': Meditations on History and Imperial Power." *VChr* 41 (1987): 238–66.

Grillmeier, A. *Christ in Christian Tradition*. Vol. 1, *From the Apostolic Age to Chalcedon (451)*. Trans. J. Bowden. 2nd ed. Atlanta 1975.

Grubbs, J. Evans. *Law and Family in Late Antiquity: The Emperor Constantine's Marriage Legislation*. Oxford 1995.

Guida, A. "Frammenti inediti del 'Contro i Galilei' di Giuliano e della Replica di Teodoro di Mopsuestia." *Prometheus* 9 (1983): 139–63.

———. "Per un' edizione della Replica di Teodoro di Mopsuestia al 'Contro i Galilei' dell'imperatore Giuliano." In *Paideia Cristiana: Studi in Onore di Mario Naldini*, ed. C. Burini, 87–102. Rome 1994.

———, ed. *Un anonimo panegirico per l'imperatore Giuliano (Anon. Paneg. Iul. Imp.)*. Florence 1990.

Guido, R. "La nozione di *philia* in Giuliano imperatore." In *Giuliano imperatore: Le sue idée, i suoi amici, i suoi avversari—Atti del Convegno internazionale di studi, Lecce, 10–12 dicembre 1998*, ed. A. Filippo and R. Guido, 114–44. Lecce 1998.

Guignet, M. *Saint Grégoire de Nazianze et la rhétorique*. Paris 1911.

Gunderson, E. "The Ideology of the Arena." *ClAnt* 15 (1996): 113–51.

Gurtler, G. M. "Sympathy: Stoic Materialism and the Platonic Soul." In *Neoplatonism and Nature: Studies in Plotinus' Enneads*, ed. M. F. Wagner, 241–76. Albany 2002.

Hadot, P. "L'apport du néoplatonisme à la philosophie de la nature en Occident." In *Tradition und Gegenwart: Eranos Jahrbuch 1968*, 91–132. Zurich 1970.

———. *Exercices spirituels et philosophie antique*. Paris 1981.

———. "Philosophie, dialectique, rhétorique dans l'antiquité." *StudPhil* 39 (1980): 139–66.

———. "Théologie, exégese, révélation, écriture dans la philosophie grecque." In *Les règles de l'interprétation*, ed. M. Tardieu, 13–34. Paris 1987.

von Haehling, R. *Die Religionszugehörigkeit der hohen Amtsträger des römischen Reiches seit Constantins I. Alleinherrschaft bis zum Ende der Theodosianischen Dynastie (324–450 bzw. 455 n.Chr.)*. Bonn 1978.

Haensch, R. "Inscriptions as Sources of Knowledge for Religions and Cults in the Roman World of Imperial Times." In *A Companion to Roman Religion*, ed. J. Rüpke, 176–87. Oxford 2007.

———. "Die Rolle der Bischöfe im 4. Jahrhundert: Neue Anforderungen und neue Antworten." *Chiron* 37 (2007): 153–81.

———. "Römische Amtsinhaber als Vorbild für christliche Bischöfe." In *The Representation and Perception of Roman Imperial Power*, ed. L. de Blois et al., 117–31. Amsterdam 2003.

Hagedorn, D., ed. *Der Hiobkommentar des Arianers Julian*. Berlin 1973.

Hahn, J. *Gewalt und religiöser Konflikt: Studien zu den Auseinandersetzungen zwischen Christen, Heiden und Juden im Osten des römischen Reiches (von Konstantin bis Theodosius II)*. Berlin 2004.

———. "Kaiser Julian und ein dritter Tempel? Idee, Wirklichkeit, Wirkung eines gescheiterten Projekts." In *Zerstörungen des Jerusalemer Tempels: Geschehen—Wahrnehmung—Bewältigung*, ed. J. Hahn and C. Ronning, 237–62. Tübingen 2002.

———. *Der Philosoph und die Gesellschaft: Selbstverständnis, öffentliches Auftreten und populäre Erwartungen in der hohen Kaiserzeit*. Stuttgart 1989.

———. "Philosophen zwischen Kaiserzeit und Spätantike: Das 3. Jahrhundert n.Chr." In

Crises and the Roman Empire, ed. O. Hekster, G. De Kleijn, and D. Slootjes, 397–412. Leiden 2007.
Halfmann, H. *Itinera principum: Geschichte und Typologie der Kaiserreise im römischen Reich*. Stuttgart 1986.
Hall, S. G. "'Contra Eunomium I': Introducción y Traducción." In *El "Contra Eunomium I" en la producción literaria de Gregorio de Nisa*, ed. L. F. Mateo-Seco and J. L. Bastero, 21–135. Pamplona 1988.
Hämäläinen, P. *The Comanche Empire*. New Haven 2008.
Hammerstaedt, J. "Le Cynisme littéraire a l'époque impériale." In *Le Cynisme ancien et ses prolongements: Actes du Colloque international du CNRS, Paris, 22–25 juillet 1991*, ed. M.-O. Goulet-Cazé and R. Goulet, 399–418. Paris 1993.
———. "Der Kyniker Oenomaus von Gadara." In *ANRW* 2.36.4, ed. W. Haase, 2834–65. Berlin 1990.
———. *Die Orakelkritik des Kynikers Oenomaus*. Frankfurt a.M. 1988.
Hanson, R. P. C. *The Search for the Christian Doctrine of God: The Arian Controversy, 318–381*. Edinburgh 1988.
Hardy, B. C. "The Emperor Julian and His School Law." *ChHist* 38 (1968): 131–43.
Harlow, M. "In the Name of the Father: Procreation, Paternity and Patriarchy." In *Thinking Men: Masculinity and Its Self-Representation in the Classical Tradition*, ed. L. Foxhall and J. Salmon, 155–69. London 1998.
von Harnack, A. *Porphyrius gegen die Christen: 15 Bücher, Zeugnisse, Fragmente und Referate*. Berlin 1916.
Harris, W. V. *Restraining Rage: The Ideology of Anger Control in Classical Antiquity*. Cambridge, Mass., 2001.
Harrison, V. "Some Aspects of St. Gregory (Nazianzen) the Theologian's Soteriology." *Greek Orthodox Theological Review* 34 (1989): 11–18.
Hauser-Meury, M. M. *Prosopographie zu den Schriften Gregors von Nazianz*. Bonn 1960.
Haverkamp, A., and R. Lachmann, eds. *Memoria: Vergessen und Erinnern*. Munich 1993.
Heath, M. *Hermogenes "On Issues": Strategies of Argument in Later Greek Rhetoric*. Oxford 1995.
———. *Menander: A Rhetor in Context*. Oxford 2004.
Heather, P. "New Men for New Constantines? Creating an Imperial Elite in the Eastern Mediterranean." In *New Constantines: The Rhythm of Imperial Renewal in Byzantium, 4th–13th Centuries*, ed. P. Magdalino, 11–33. Aldershot 1994.
———. "Themistius: A Political Philosopher." In *The Propaganda of Power: The Role of Panegyric in Late Antiquity*, ed. Mary Whitby, 125–50. Leiden 1998.
Hemelrijk, E. A. "City Patronesses in the Roman Empire." *Historia* 53 (2004): 209–45.
Henck, N. "Constantius' *paideia*, Intellectual Milieu and Promotion of the Liberal Arts." *PCPhS* 47 (2001): 172–87.
———. "From Macellum to Milan: The Movements of Julian the Apostate from A.D. 348 to 355." *Kodai* 10 (1999/2000): 105–16.
———. "Images of Constantius II: *Ho philanthrōpos basileus* and Imperial Propaganda in the Mid-Fourth Century A.D." D.Phil. thesis, University of Oxford, 1998.
Hild, F., and H. Hellenkemper, eds. *Tabula Imperii Byzantini*. Vol. 5, *Kilikien und Isaurien*. 2 vols. Vienna 1990.

Hild, F., and M. Restle, eds. *Tabula Imperii Byzantini*. Vol. 2, *Kappadokien (Kappadokia, Charsianon, Sebasteia und Lykandos)*. Vienna 1981.
Hildebrand, S. M. "A Reconsideration of the Development of Basil's Trinitarian Theology: The Dating of *Ep.* 9 and *Contra Eunomium.*" *VChr* 58 (2004): 393–406.
Hirschle, M. *Sprachphilosophie und Namensmagie im Neuplatonismus: Mit einem Exkurs zu "Demokrit" B 142*. Meisenheim am Glan 1979.
Hollerich, M. J. *Eusebius of Caesarea's "Commentary on Isaiah."* Oxford 1997.
Holman, S. R. *The Hungry Are Dying: Beggars and Bishops in Roman Cappadocia*. Oxford 2001.
Hose, M. "Konstruktion von Autorität: Julians Hymnen." In C. Schäfer, ed., *Kaiser Julian "Apostata" und die philosophische Reaktion gegen das Christentum*, 157–75. Berlin 2008.
Huber, G. "*Bios theoretikos* und *bios praktikos* bei Aristoteles und Platon." In *Arbeit, Musse, Meditation: Betrachtungen zur Vita activa und Vita contemplativa*, ed. B. Vickers, 21–34. Zurich 1985.
Huber-Rebenich, G., and M. Chronz. "Cyrill von Alexandrien: Ein Forschungsvorhaben." In *Heiden und Christen im 5. Jahrhundert*, ed. J. van Oort and D. Wyrwa, 66–87. Louvain 1998.
Hübner, R. M. *Die Schrift des Apollinarius von Laodicea gegen Photin (Pseudo-Athanasius, Contra Sabellianos) und Basilius von Caesarea*. Berlin 1989.
Hübner, S. *Der Klerus in der Gesellschaft des spätantiken Kleinasiens*. Stuttgart 2005.
Humfress, C. *Orthodoxy and the Courts in Late Antiquity*. Oxford 2007.
Humphries, M. "*In Nomine Patris*: Constantine the Great and Constantius II in Christological Polemic." *Historia* 46 (1997): 448–64.
Hyland, A. *Equus: The Horse in the Roman World*. London 1990.
Innes, D., and M. Winterbottom. *Sopatros the Rhetor: Studies in the Text of the Diaíresis Zētēmatōn*. London 1988.
Iser, W. *Der implizite Leser: Kommunikationsformen des Romans von Bunyan bis Beckett*. 3rd ed. Munich 1994.
Iskander, A. Z. "An Attempted Reconstruction of the Late Alexandrian Medical Curriculum." *MedHist* 20 (1976): 235–58.
Johnson, A. P. *Ethnicity and Argument in Eusebius' "Praeparatio evangelica."* Oxford 2006.
Johnston, S. I. *Hekate soteira: A Study of Hekate's Role in the Chaldean Oracles and Related Literature*. Atlanta 1989.
Jones, A. H. M. *The Later Roman Empire, 284–602: A Social Economic and Administrative Survey*. 2nd ed. Baltimore 1986.
———. "Notes on the Genuineness of the Constantinian Documents in Eusebius' *Life of Constantine.*" *JEH* 5 (1954): 196–200.
Jones, C. P. "Greek Drama in the Roman World." In *Theater and Society in the Classical World*, ed. R. Scodel, 39–52. Ann Arbor 1993.
———. *The Roman World of Dio Chrysostom*. Cambridge, Mass., 1978.
———. "Themistius and *The Speech to the King.*" *CPh* 92 (1997): 149–52.
Jouan, F. "Le Diogène de Dion Chrysostome." In *Le Cynisme ancien et ses prolongements: Actes du Colloque international du CNRS, Paris, 22–25 juillet 1991*, ed. M.-O. Goulet-Cazé and R. Goulet, 381–97. Paris 1993.

———. "Le loisir chez Dion Chrysostome." In *Les loisirs et l'héritage de la culture classique: Actes du XIIIe Congrès de l'Association Guillaume Budé, Dijon, 27–31 août 1993*, ed. J.-M. André, J. Dangel, and P. Demont, 129–36. Brussels 1996.
Jouanna, J. "Le médecin modèle du législateur dans les *Lois* de Platon." *Ktéma* 3 (1978): 79–89.
———. "Réflexions sur la notion d'*aërgiē/argiē* vel *argia* à l'époque archaïque et classique à partir du traité hippocratique des *Airs, eaux, lieux* (c. 16)." In *Les loisirs et l'héritage de la culture classique: Actes du XIIIe Congrès de l'Association Guillaume Budé, Dijon, 27–31 août 1993*, ed. J.-M. André, J. Dangel, and P. Demont, 54–64. Brussels 1996.
Junod, É. "Basile de Cesarée et Grégoire de Nazianze sont-ils les compilateurs de la *Philocalie* d'Origène?" In *Mémorial Dom Jean Gribomont (1920—1986)*, 349–60. Rome 1988.
———. "Particularités de la *Philocalie*." In *Origeniana: Premier Colloque international des études origèniennes*, ed. H. Crouzel, G. Lomiento, and J. Rius-Camps, 181–97. Bari 1975.
Just, P. *Imperator et Episcopus: Zum Verhältnis von Staatsgewalt und christlicher Kirche zwischen dem 1. Konzil von Nicaea (325) und dem 1. Konzil von Konstantinopel (381)*. Stuttgart 2003.
Kabiersch, J. *Untersuchungen zum Begriff der "philanthropia" bei dem Kaiser Julian*. Wiesbaden 1960.
Kaegi, W. E. "The Emperor Julian's Assessment of the Significance and Function of History." *PAPHS* 108 (1964): 29–38.
Kaldellis, A. *Hellenism in Byzantium: The Transformations of Greek Identity and the Reception of the Classical Tradition*. Cambridge 2007.
Karamboula, D. *Staatsbegriffe in der frühbyzantinischen Zeit*. Vienna 1993.
Kaster, R. A. "Controlling Reason: Declamation in Rhetorical Education at Rome." In *Education in Greek and Roman Antiquity*, ed. Y. L. Too, 316–37. Leiden 2001.
———. *Guardians of Language: The Grammarian and Society in Late Antiquity*. Berkeley and Los Angeles 1988.
Kazhdan, A., and G. Constable. *People and Power in Byzantium: An Introduction to Modern Byzantine Studies*. Washington, D.C., 1982.
Kelly, C. *Ruling the Later Roman Empire*. Cambridge, Mass., 2004.
Kelly, G. "Ammianus and the Great Tsunami." *JRS* 94 (2004): 141–67.
———. *Ammianus Marcellinus: The Allusive Historian*. Cambridge 2008.
———. "Constantius II, Julian, and the Example of Marcus Aurelius (Ammianus Marcellinus XXI, 16, 11–12)." *Latomus* 64 (2005): 409–16.
Kennedy, G. A. "Later Greek Philosophy and Rhetoric." *Ph&Rh* 13 (1980): 181–97.
Kenny, A. *Aristotle on the Perfect Life*. Oxford 1992.
Kent, J. P. C. "An Introduction to the Coinage of Julian the Apostate (A.D. 360–363)." *NC* 19 (1959): 109–17.
———. *The Roman Imperial Coinage*. Vol. 8, *The Family of Constantine I*. London 1981.
Ker, J. "Nocturnal Writers in Imperial Rome: The Culture of 'lucubratio.'" *CPh* 99 (2004): 209–42.
Kerferd, G. B. "The Search for Personal Identity in Stoic Thought." *BRL* 55 (1972): 177–96.
Kertsch, M. "Das Motiv des Blitzes in der griechischen Literatur der Kaiserzeit." *WS* 13 (1979): 166–74.

———. "Zur interschiedlichen ethischen Bewertung von 'Natur/äusserer Zwang' und 'freier Willensentschluss' bei Heiden und Christen im Hintergrund einer Aussage Gregors von Nazianz." *WS* 18 (1984): 187–93.
King, H. *Hippocrates' Woman: Reading the Female Body in Ancient Greece*. London 1998.
Klein, R. *Constantius II. und die christliche Kirche*. Darmstadt 1977.
———. "Julians Rhetoren—und Unterrichtsgesetz." *RQA* 76 (1981): 73–94.
———. "Die Kämpfe um die Nachfolge nach dem Tod Constantins des Grossen." *ByzF* 6 (1979): 101–50.
———, ed. *Julian Apostata*. Darmstadt 1978.
Kloft, H. *Liberalitas principis: Studien zur Prinzipatsideologie*. Cologne 1970.
Knorr, U. W. *Basilius der Grosse: Sein Beitrag zur christlichen Durchdringung Kleinasiens*. Tübingen 1968.
Kobusch, T. "Name und Sein: Zu den sprachphilosophischen Grundlagen der Schrift *Contra Eunomium* des Gregor von Nyssa." In *El "Contra Eunomium I" en la producción literaria de Gregorio de Nisa*, ed. L. F. Mateo-Seco and J. L. Bastero, 247–68. Pamplona 1988.
Koch, W. "Comment l'empereur Julien tâcha fonder une église païenne." *RBPh* 6 (1927): 123–46; and 7 (1928): 49–82, 511–50, 1363–85.
Kokolakis, M. "Pantomimus and the Treatise *Peri Orcheseos (De Saltatione)*." *Platon* 11 (1959): 3–56.
Kolb, A. "Kaiser Julians Innenpolitik: Grundlegende Reformen oder traditionelle Verwaltung? Das Beispiel des *cursus publicus*." *Historia* 47 (1998): 342–59.
Kolb, F. *Herrscherideologie in der Spätantike*. Berlin 2001.
Konstan, D. *Friendship in the Classical World*. Cambridge 1996.
———. "How to Praise a Friend: St. Gregory of Nazianzus's Funeral Oration for St. Basil the Great." In *Greek Biography and Panegyric in Late Antiquity*, ed. T. Hägg and P. Rousseau, 160–79. Berkeley and Los Angeles 2000.
Kopecek, T. "The Cappadocian Fathers and Civic Patriotism." *ChHist* 43 (1974): 293–303.
———. *A History of Neo-Arianism*. 2 vols. Cambridge, Mass., 1979.
———. "The Social Class of the Cappadocian Fathers." *ChHist* 42 (1973): 453–66.
Koster, S. *Die Invektive in der griechischen und römischen Literatur*. Meisenheim am Glan 1980.
Koziol, G. "Truth and Its Consequences: Why Carolingianists Don't Speak of Myth." In *Myth in Early Northwest Europe*, ed. S. Glosecki, 71–104. Ithaca 2007.
Krueger, D. "Diogenes the Cynic among the Fourth-Century Fathers." *VChr* 47 (1993): 24–49.
Kullmann, W. "Aristote et le loisir." In *Les loisirs et l'héritage de la culture classique: Actes du XIIIe Congrès de l'Association Guillaume Budé, Dijon, 27–31 août 1993*, ed. J.-M. André, J. Dangel, and P. Demont, 104–12. Brussels 1996.
Kurmann, A. *Gregor von Nazianz, Oratio 4 gegen Julian: Ein Kommentar*. Basel 1988.
Laks, A. "Legislation and Demiurgy: On the Relationship between Plato's *Republic* and *Laws*." *ClAnt* 9 (1990): 209–29.
Lane Fox, R. "The Itinerary of Alexander: Constantius to Julian." *CQ* 47 (1997): 239–52.
———. "Movers and Shakers." In *The Philosopher and Society in Late Antiquity: Essays in Honour of Peter Brown*, ed. A. Smith, 19–50. Swansea 2005.

———. *Pagans and Christians.* New York 1987.
Lanza, D. "La critica aristotelica a Platone e i due piani della *Politica.*" *Athenaeum* 49 (1971): 355–92.
Le Boulluec, A. *La notion d'hérésie dans la literature grecque, II–III siècles.* 2 vols. Paris 1985.
Le Nain de Tillemont, L.-S. *Mémoires pour servir à l'histoire ecclésiastique des six premiers siècles.* 16 vols. Brussels 1706–28.
Lee, T.-S. *Die griechische Tradition der aristotelischen Syllogistik in der Spätantike: Eine Untersuchung über die Kommentare zu den "Analytica Priora" von Alexander Aphrodisiensis, Ammonius und Philoponus.* Göttingen 1984.
Lendon, J. E. *Empire of Honour: The Art of Government in the Roman World.* Oxford 1997.
Lenski, N. *Failure of Empire: Valens and the Roman State in the Fourth Century* A.D. Berkeley and Los Angeles 2002.
———. "Were Valentinian, Valens and Jovian Confessors before Julian the Apostate?" *ZAC* 6 (2002): 253–76.
Leppin, H. "Constantius II. und das Heidentum." *Athenaeum* 87 (1999): 457–80.
———. *Von Constantin dem Grossen zu Theodosius II: Das christliche Kaisertum bei den Kirchenhistorikern Socrates, Sozomenus und Theodoret.* Göttingen 1996.
Levi, P. *Il sistema periodico.* Turin 1975.
Lewy, H. *Chaldean Oracles and Theurgy: Mysticism, Magic and Platonism in the Later Roman Empire.* New ed. Ed. M. Tardieu. Paris 1978.
Leyerle, B. *Theatrical Shows and Ascetic Lives: John Chrysostom's Attack on Spiritual Marriage.* Berkeley and Los Angeles 2001.
Leyser, C. *Authority and Asceticism from Augustine to Gregory the Great.* Oxford 2000.
Lieberman, S. "Roman Legal Institutions in Early Rabbinics and in the *Acta Martyrum.*" *Jewish Quarterly Review* 35 (1944): 1–57.
Liebeschuetz, J. H. W. G. *Antioch: City and Imperial Administration in the Later Roman Empire.* Oxford 1972.
———. *The Decline and Fall of the Roman City.* Oxford 2001.
van Liefferinge, C. *La Théurgie: Des oracles chaldaïques à Proclus.* Liège 1999.
Lienhard, J. T. "Did Athanasius Reject Marcellus?" In *Arianism after Arius: Essays on the Development of the Fourth-Century Trinitarian Conflicts,* ed. M. R. Barnes and D. H. Williams, 65–80. Edinburgh 1993.
Lieu, S. N. C., ed. *The Emperor Julian: Panegyric and Polemic—Claudius Mamertinus, John Chrysostom, Ephrem the Syrian.* Liverpool 1989.
Lieu, S. N. C., and D. Montserrat, eds. *From Constantine to Julian: Pagan and Byzantine Views.* London 1996.
Lim, R. "Converting the Un-Christianizable: The Baptism of Stage Performers in Late Antiquity." In *Conversion in Late Antiquity and the Early Middle Ages: Seeing and Believing,* ed. K. Mills and A. Grafton, 84–126. Rochester 2003.
———. *Public Disputation, Power, and Social Order in Late Antiquity.* Berkeley and Los Angeles 1995.
von Lingenthal, K. E. Z. *Geschichte des griechisch-römischen Rechts.* 3rd ed. Berlin 1892.
Lizzi Testa, R. "The Bishop as *Vir Venerabilis:* Fiscal Privileges and Status Definition in Late Antiquity." *Studia Patristica* 37 (2001): 125–44.

———. *Il potere episcopale nell'Oriente romano: Rappresentazione ideologica e realtà politica (IV–V sec. d.C.)*. Rome 1987.
Lloyd, A. C. *The Anatomy of Neoplatonism*. Oxford 1990.
———. "Neoplatonic Logic and Aristotelian Logic I and II." *Phronesis* 1 (1955): 58–72; and 2 (1955–56): 146–60.
Löhr, W. A. "A Sense of Tradition: The Homoiousian Church Party." In *Arianism after Arius: Essays on the Development of the Fourth-Century Trinitarian Conflicts*, ed. M. R. Barnes and D. H. Williams, 81–100. Edinburgh 1993.
———. "Some Observations on Karl-Heinz Schwarte's 'Diokletian's Christengesetz.'" *VChr* 56 (2002): 75–95.
Long, A. A. *Hellenistic Philosophy: Stoics, Epicureans, Sceptics*. London 1974.
———. "Soul and Body in Stoicism." *Phronesis* 27 (1982): 34–57.
Long, J. "Structures of Irony in Julian's *Misopogon*." *AncW* 24 (1993): 15–23.
Longrigg, J. *Greek Rational Medicine: Philosophy and Medicine from Alcmaeon to the Alexandrians*. London 1993.
Loofs, F. "Gregor von Nazianz." *Realenzyklopädie für Protestantische Theologie und Kirche* 7 (1899): 138–46.
Lugaresi, L. "Ambivalenze della rappresentazione: Riflessioni patristiche su riti e spettacoli." *ZAC* 7 (2003): 281–309.
———. "Spettacoli e vita cristiana nelle orazioni di Gregorio Nazianzeno." *AnnSE* 15 (1998): 441–66.
———. "Tra evento e rappresentazione: Per un' interpretazione della polemica contro gli spettacoli nei primi secoli cristiani." *RSLR* 30 (1994): 437–63.
Lutterbach, H. "Der *Christus medicus* und die *Sancti medici*: Das wechselvolle Verhältnis zweier Grundmotive christlicher Frömmigkeit zwischen Spätantike und früher Neuzeit." *Saeculum* 47 (1996): 239–81.
Lyman, R. "Arians and Manichees on Christ." *JThS* 40 (1989): 493–503.
———. *Christology and Cosmology: Models of Divine Activity in Origen, Eusebius, and Athanasius*. Oxford 1993.
———. "Heresiology: The Invention of 'Heresy' and 'Schism.'" In *The Cambridge History of Christianity*, vol. 2, *Constantine to c. 600*, ed. A. Casiday and F. W. Norris, 296–313. Cambridge 2007.
———. "The Politics of Passing: Justin Martyr's Conversion as a Problem of 'Hellenization.'" In *Conversion in Late Antiquity and the Early Middle Ages: Seeing and Believing*, ed. K. Mills and A. Grafton, 36–60. Rochester 2003.
———. "A Topography of Heresy: Mapping the Rhetorical Creation of Arianism." In *Arianism after Arius. Essays on the Development of the Fourth-Century Trinitarian Conflicts*, ed. M. R. Barnes and D. H. Williams, 45–63. Edinburgh 1993.
MacCormack, S. G. *Art and Ceremony in Late Antiquity*. Berkeley and Los Angeles 1981.
Macé, C. "À propos d'une édition récente de Grégoire de Nazianze." *AC* 77 (2008): 243–56.
Malingrey, A. M. *Philosophia: Étude d'un groupe de mots dans la littérature grecque, des présocratiques au IVe siècle après J.-C.* Paris 1961.
Malosse, P.-L. "Enquête sur les relations entre Julien et Gallus." *Klio* 86 (2004): 185–96.

———. "Noblesse, sottise et tragédie: Le regard porté par Julien sur sa propre famille." *QS* 54 (2001): 41–67.
Mango, C. "Three Imperial Byzantine Sarcophagi Discovered in 1750." *DOP* 16 (1962): 397–402.
Marasco, G. *Filostorgio: Cultura, fede e politica in uno storico ecclesiastico del V secolo.* Rome 2005.
Marcone, A. "Giuliano e lo stile dell'imperatore tardoantico." In *Giuliano imperatore: Le sue idee, i suoi amici, i suoi avversari—Atti del Convegno internazionale di studi, Lecce, 10–12 dicembre 1998,* ed. A. Filippo and R. Guido, 43–58. Lecce 1998.
———. "Un panegirico rovesciato: Pluralità di modelli e contaminazione letteraria nel 'Misopogon' giulianeo." *REAug* 30 (1984): 226–39.
———. "Il significato della spedizione di Giuliano contro la Persia." *Athenaeum* 57 (1979): 334–56.
Mariès, L. "Extraits du commentaire de Diodore de Tarse sur les Psaumes: Préface du commentaire—Prologue du Psaume CXVIII." *RecSR* 9 (1919): 79–101.
Marincola, J. *Authority and Tradition in Ancient Historiography.* Cambridge 1997.
Markus, R. A. *Christianity in the Roman World.* London 1974.
———. *The End of Ancient Christianity.* Cambridge 1990.
———. "Gregory the Great's *rector* and His Genesis." In *Grégoire le Grand,* ed. J. Fontaine, R. Gillet, and S. Pellistrandi, 137–46. Paris 1986.
Martig, I. Benedetti. *Studi sulla Guerra Persiana nell'Orazione funebre per Giuliano di Libanio.* Florence 1990.
Martin, A. *Athanase d'Alexandrie et l'église d'Égypte au IVe siècle (328–373).* Rome 1996.
Martin, D. B. "The Construction of the Ancient Family: Methodological Considerations." *JRS* 86 (1996): 40–60.
———. *The Corinthian Body.* New Haven 1995.
Martin, J. *Antike Rhetorik: Technik und Methode.* Munich 1974.
Martschukat, J., and S. Patzold, eds. *Geschichtswissenschaft und "performative turn": Ritual, Inszenierung und Performanz vom Mittelalter bis zur Neuzeit.* Cologne 2003.
Maslov, B. R. "*Oikeiosis pros theon*: Gregory of Nazianzus' Concept of Divinization and the Heteronomous Subject of Eastern Christian Penance." *ZAC/JAC* 16 (2012).
Mathews, T. F. *The Clash of Gods: A Reinterpretation of Early Christian Art.* Princeton 1993.
Mattera, L. "Libanio, *Or.* 17, e Gregorio di Nazianzo, *Or.* 4." *Koinonia* 15 (1991): 139–43.
Matthews, J. F. *The Journey of Theophanes: Travel, Business, and Daily Life in the Roman East.* New Haven 2006.
———. *Laying Down the Law: A Study of the Theodosian Code.* New Haven 2000.
———. "The Letters of Symmachus." In *Latin Literature of the Fourth Century,* ed. J. W. Binns, 58–99. London 1974.
———. *The Roman Empire of Ammianus.* Baltimore 1989.
———. *Western Aristocracies and Imperial Court, A.D. 364–425.* Oxford 1975.
Mau, G. *Die Religionsphilosophie Kaiser Julians in seinen Reden auf König Helios und die Göttermutter.* Leipzig 1907.
Mayer, W. *The Homilies of St John Chrysostom: Provenance, Reshaping the Foundations.* Rome 2005.

Mayhew, R. *Aristotle's Criticism of Plato's "Republic."* Lanham 1997.
Mazza, M. "Filosofia religiosa ed '*imperium*' in Giuliano." In *Giuliano imperatore: Atti del Convegno della S.I.S.A.C. (Messina, 3 aprile 1984)*, ed. B. Gentili, 39–108. Urbino 1986.
———. "Giuliano; o, Dell'utopia religiosa: Il tentativo di fondare una chiesa pagana?" *Rudiae* 10 (1998): 17–42.
McCarthy, K. *Slaves, Masters and the Art of Authority in Plautine Comedy.* Princeton 2000.
McGuckin, J. "Autobiography as Apologia in St. Gregory of Nazianzus." *Studia Patristica* 37 (2001): 160–77.
———. "Gregory of Nazianzus: The Rhetorician as Poet." In *Gregory of Nazianzus: Images and Reflections*, ed. J. Børtnes and T. Hägg, 191–212. Copenhagen 2006.
———. *St. Gregory of Nazianzus: An Intellectual Biography.* Crestwood 2001.
———. "The Strategic Adaptation of Deification in the Cappadocians." In *Partakers of the Divine Nature: The History and Development of Deification in the Christian Traditions*, ed. M. J. Christensen and J. A. Wittung, 95–114. Madison, N.J., 2007.
McLynn, N. "Among the Hellenists: Gregory and the Sophists." In *Gregory of Nazianzus: Images and Reflections*, ed. J. Børtnes and T. Hägg, 213–38. Copenhagen 2006.
———. *Christian Politics and Religious Culture in Late Antiquity.* Farnham 2009.
———. "*Curiales* into Churchmen: The Case of Gregory Nazianzen." In *Le trasformazioni delle élites in età tardoantica*, ed. R. Lizzi Testa, 277–95. Rome 2006.
———. "Disciplines of Discipleship in Late-Antique Education: Augustine and Gregory." In *Augustine and the Disciplines: From Cassiacum to Confessions*, ed. K. Pollman and M. Vessey, 25–48. Oxford 2005.
———. "'*Genere Hispanus*': Theodosius, Spain and Nicene Orthodoxy." In *Hispania in Late Antiquity: Current Perspectives*, ed. K. Bowes and M. Kulikowski, 77–120. Leiden 2005.
———. "Gregory Nazianzen's Basil: The Literary Construction of a Christian Friendship." *Studia Patristica* 37 (2001): 178–93.
———. "Gregory the Peacemaker: A Study of Oration Six." *Kyoyo-Ronso* 101 (1996): 183–216.
———. "Moments of Truth: Gregory of Nazianzus and Theodosius I." In *From the Tetrarchs to the Theodosians: Later Roman History and Culture, 284–450 CE*, ed. S. McGill, C. Sogno, and E. Watts, 215–39. Cambridge 2010.
———. "The Other Olympias: Gregory Nazianzen and the Family of Vitalianus." *ZAC* 2 (1998): 227–46.
———. "A Self-Made Holy Man: The Case of Gregory Nazianzen." In *The "Holy Man" Revisited (1971–1997): Charisma, Texts and Communities in Late Antiquity*, ed. S. Elm and N. Janowitz. *JECS*, Special Issue 6 (1998): 463–83.
———. "The Transformation of Imperial Churchgoing in the Fourth Century." In *Approaching Late Antiquity: The Transformation from Early to Late Empire*, ed. S. Swain and M. Edwards, 235–70. Oxford 2004.
———. "The Use and Abuse of Eudoxius of Germanicia." *Kyoyo-Ronso* 110 (1999): 69–99.
———. "The Voice of Conscience: Gregory Nazianzen in Retirement." In *Vescovi e pastori in epoca Teodosiana: In occasione del XVI centenario della consacrazione episcopale di S. Agostino, 396-1996—XXV Incontro di studiosi dell'antichita cristiana*, vol. 2: 299–308. Rome 1997.

———. "What Was the *Philocalia* of Origen?" In *Meddelanden från Collegium Patristicum Lundense* 20 (2005): 32–43.
Meredith, A. "Porphyry and Julian against the Christians." In *ANRW* 2.23.2, ed. H. Temporini and W. Haase, 1119–48. Berlin 1980.
Merkelbach, R., and J. Stauber. "'Unsterbliche Kaiserpriester': Drei Dokumente der heidnischen Reaktion." *EA* 31 (1999): 157–64.
Merki, H. *ΟΜΟΙΩΣΙΣ ΘΕΩΙ: Von der platonischen Angleichung an Gott zur Gottähnlichkeit bei Gregor von Nyssa*. Freiburg 1952.
Meyer, E. A. "The Epigraphic Habit in the Roman Empire: The Evidence of Epitaphs." *JRS* 80 (1990): 74–96.
Migl, J. *Die Ordnung der Ämter: Prätorianerpräfektur und Vikariat in der Regionalverwaltung des römischen Reiches von Konstantin bis zur Valentinianischen Dynastie*. Frankfurt a.M. 1994.
Millar, F. *The Emperor in the Roman World, 31 BC–AD 337*. Ithaca 1977.
Miller, P. Cox. "Strategies of Representation in Collective Biography: Constructing the Subject as Holy." In *Greek Biography and Panegyric in Late Antiquity*, ed. T. Hägg and P. Rousseau, 209–54. Berkeley and Los Angeles 2000.
Mitchell, S. *Anatolia: Land, Men, and Gods in Asia Minor*. 2 vols. Oxford 1993.
———. "The Cult of Theos Hypsistos between Pagans, Jews, and Christians." In *Pagan Monotheism in Late Antiquity*, ed. P. Athanassiadi and M. Frede, 81–148. Oxford 1999.
Molac, P. *Douleur et transfiguration: Une lecture du cheminement spirituel de saint Grégoire de Nazianze*. Paris 2006.
Moreschini, C. *Filosofia e letteratura in Gregorio di Nazianzo*. Milan 1997.
———. "Rufino traduttore di Gregorio di Nazianzeno." In *Rufino di Concordia e il suo tempo*, vol. 1, ed. A. Quacquarelli, 227–85. Udine 1987.
Mortley, R. *From Word to Silence*. Vols. 1, *The Rise and Fall of Logos*, and 2, *The Way of Negation, Christian and Greek*. Bonn 1986.
Moscadi, A. "Le lettere dell'archivio di Teofane." *Aegyptus* 50 (1970): 88–154.
Mossay, J. "La date de l'*Oratio* II de Grégoire de Nazianze et celle de son ordination." *Muséon* 77 (1964): 175–86.
———. "Nazianze, Nenezi, Bekârlar." *Byzantion* 71 (2001): 438–50.
Müller, F. L. *Die beiden Satiren des Kaisers Julianus Apostata (Symposion oder Caesares und Antiochikos oder Misopogon)*. Stuttgart 1998.
Näf, B. *Senatorisches Standesbewußtsein in spätrömischer Zeit*. Freiburg 1995.
Narkevics, E. "*Skiagraphia*: Outlining the Conception of God in Gregory's *Theological Orations*." In *Gregory of Nazianzus: Images and Reflections*, ed. J. Børtnes and T. Hägg, 83–112. Copenhagen 2006.
Nasemann, B. *Theurgie und Philosophie in Jamblichs "De mysteriis."* Stuttgart 1991.
Näsström, B.-M. *"O Mother of the Gods and Men": Some Aspects of the Religious Thoughts in Emperor Julian's Discourse on the Mother of the Gods*. Lund 1990.
Neri, V. "Ammianus' Definition of Christianity as *absoluta et simplex religio*." In *Cognitio Gestorum: The Historiographic Art of Ammianus Marcellinus*, ed. J. den Boeft, D. den Hengst, and H. C. Teitler, 59–65. Amsterdam 1992.
Nesselrath, H.-G. "Die Christen und die heidnische Bildung: Das Beispiel des Sokrates

Scholasticus (Hist. Eccl. 3,16)." In *Leitbilder der Spätantike—Eliten und Leitbilder*, ed. J. Dummer and M. Vielberg, 79–100. Stuttgart 1999.
Neumeister, C. *Grundsätze der forensischen Rhetorik, gezeigt an Gerichtsreden Ciceros*. Munich 1964.
Nicholson, O. "The 'Pagan Churches' of Maximinus Daia and Julian the Apostate." *JEH* 45 (1994): 1–10.
Nock, A. D. "The Emperor's Divine *comes*." *JRS* 37 (1947): 102–16. [Reprinted in *Essays on Religions and the Ancient World*, vol. 2, ed. Z. Stewart, 2nd ed. (Oxford 1986): 653–75.]
Noethlichs, K. L. "Kirche, Recht und Gesellschaft in der Jahrhundertmitte." In *L'église et l'empire au IVe siècle*, ed. A. Dihle, 251–99. Geneva 1989.
Noreña, C. F. "The Communication of the Emperor's Virtues." *JRS* 91 (2001): 146–68.
North, H. F. *Sophrosyne: Self-Knowledge and Self-Restraint in Greek Literature*. Ithaca 1966.
Norton, P. *Episcopal Elections, 25–600: Hierarchy and Popular Will in Late Antiquity*. Oxford 2007.
van Nuffelen, P. "Deux fausses lettres de Julien l'Apostat (la lettre aux Juifs, *Ep*. 51 [Wright], et la lettre à Arsacius, *Ep*. 84 [Bidez])." *VChr* 55 (2001): 131–50.
Nussbaum, M. C. "Therapeutic Arguments: Epicurus and Aristotle." In *The Norms of Nature: Studies in Hellenistic Ethics*, ed. M. Schofield and G. Striker, 31–74. Cambridge 1986.
———. *The Therapy of Desire: Theory and Practice in Hellenistic Ethics*. Princeton 1994.
———. *Upheavals of Thought: The Intelligence of Emotions*. Cambridge 2001.
Nutton, V. "Galen and Medical Autobiography." *PCPhS* 18 (1972): 50–62.
———. "Two Notes on Immunities: *Digest* 27.1.6.10 and 11." *JRS* 61 (1971): 52–63.
Olivar, A. *La predicación cristiana antigua*. Barcelona 1991.
O'Meara, D. "Neoplatonist Conceptions of the Philosopher-King." In *Plato and Platonism*, ed. J. M. van Ophuijsen, 278–91. Washington, D.C., 1999.
———. "A Neoplatonist Ethics for High-Level Officials: Sopatros' Letter to Himerios." In *The Philosopher and Society in Late Antiquity: Essays in Honour of Peter Brown*, ed. A. Smith, 91–100. Swansea 2005.
———. *Platonopolis: Platonic Political Philosophy in Late Antiquity*. Oxford 2003.
O'Meara, J. J. "Porphyry's *Philosophy from Oracles* in Eusebius' *Preparation for the Gospel* and Augustine's *Dialogues from Cassiciacum*." *RecAug* 6 (1969): 103–39.
Pack, E. *Städte und Steuern in der Politik Julians: Untersuchungen zu den Quellen eines Kaiserbildes*. Brussels 1986.
Parker, R. "Law and Religion." In *The Cambridge Companion to Ancient Greek Law*, ed. D. Cohen and R. Gagarin, 61–81. Cambridge 2005.
Parkin, T. G. *Old Age in the Roman World: A Cultural and Social History*. Baltimore 2003.
Parvis, S. *Marcellus of Ancyra and the Lost Years of the Arian Controversy, 325–345*. Oxford 2006.
Patlagean, E. *Pauvreté économique et pauvreté sociale à Byzance, 4e–7e siècles*. Paris 1977.
Patrucco, M. Forlin, and S. Roda. "Crisi di potere e autodifesa di classe: Aspetti del tradizionalismo delle aristocrazie." In *Società romana e impero tardoantico*, vol. 1, *Istituzioni, ceti, economie*, ed. A. Giardina, 245–72. Rome 1986.
Patterson, L. G. "*De libero arbitrio* and Methodius' Attack on Origen." *Studia Patristica* 14 (1976): 160–66.

Pearce, J. W. E. *The Roman Imperial Coinage.* Vol. 9, *Valentinian I–Theodosius I.* London 1951.
Penella, R. J. *Greek Philosophers and Sophists in the Fourth Century* A.D.: *Studies in Eunapius of Sardis.* Leeds 1990.
Petit, P. *Les étudiants de Libanius.* Paris 1957.
Pietri, C. "La politique de Constance II: Un premier 'Césaropapisme' ou l'*imitatio Constantini*?" In *L'église et l'empire au IVe siècle,* ed. A. Dihle, 113–78. Geneva 1989.
Pigeaud, J. *La maladie de l'âme: Étude sur la relation de l'âme et du corps dans la tradition médico-philosophique antique.* Paris 1981.
Plagnieux, J. *Saint Grégoire de Nazianze théologien.* Paris 1952.
Pohlenz, M. *Grundfragen der stoischen Philosophie.* Göttingen 1940.
Portmann, W. "Die politische Krise zwischen den Kaisern Constantius II. und Constans." *Historia* 48 (1999): 301–29.
Potter, D. *Prophets and Emperors: Human and Divine Authority from Augustus to Theodosius.* Cambridge, Mass., 1994.
Pottier, B. *Dieu et le Christ selon Grégoire de Nysse: Étude systématique du "Contre Eunome" avec traduction inédite des extraits d'Eunome.* Namur 1994.
Pouchet, R. *Basile le Grand et son univers d'amis d'après sa correspondance: Une stratégie de communion.* Rome 1992.
Praechter, K. "Maximus (40)." In *Realenzyklopädie der Klassischen Altertumswissenschaft,* vol. 14, ed. A. F. von Pauly, G. Wissowa, et al., cols. 2563–70. Stuttgart 1930.
Price, S. R. F. *Rituals and Power: The Roman Imperial Cult in Asia Minor.* Cambridge 1984.
Prostmeier, F. R. "'Die Wolke der Gottlosigkeit': Gültigkeit und politische Relevanz des traditionellen Wirklichkeitsverständnisses in der Polemik gegen das Christentum bei Kaiser Julian." *JbAC* 44 (2001): 33–57.
Pyykkö, V. *Die griechischen Mythen bei den grossen Kappadokiern und bei Johannes Chrysostomus.* Turku 1991.
Quasten, J. *Patrology.* Vol. 3, *The Golden Age of Greek Patristic Literature.* Utrecht 1974.
Rabel, R. J. "Diseases of the Soul in Stoic Psychology." *GRBS* 22 (1981): 385–93.
Rademaker, A. M. "*Sôphrosynê*: Polysemy, Prototypicality and Persuasive Use of an Ancient Greek Value Term." PhD dissertation, University of Leiden, 2004.
Raeder, H. "Kaiser Julian als Philosoph und religiöser Reformator." In *Julian Apostata,* ed. R. Klein, 206–40. Darmstadt 1978.
Rapp, C. "The Antiochos Manuscript at Keio University: A Preliminary Description." In *Codices Keioenses: Essays on Western Manuscripts and Early Printed Books in Keio University Library,* ed. T. Matsuda, 11–29. Tokyo 2005.
———. "The Elite Status of Bishops in Late Antiquity in Ecclesiastical, Spiritual, and Social Context." *Arethusa* 33 (2000): 379–99.
———. *Holy Bishops in Late Antiquity: The Nature of Christian Leadership in an Age of Transition.* Berkeley and Los Angeles 2005.
———. "Imperial Ideology in the Making: Eusebius of Caesarea on Constantine as 'Bishop.'" *JThS* 49 (1998): 685–95.
———. "Ritual Brotherhood in Byzantium." *Traditio* 52 (1997): 285–326.
Rebenich, S. *Hieronymus und sein Kreis: Prosopographische und sozialgeschichtliche Untersuchungen.* Stuttgart 1992.

Rebillard, S. Abrams. "Speaking for Salvation: Gregory of Nazianzus as Poet and Priest in His Autobiographical Poems." PhD dissertation, Brown University, 2003.
Recanati, F. *Meaning and Force: The Pragmatics of Performative Utterances.* Cambridge 1987.
Rees, R. "Private Lives of Public Figures in Latin Prose Panegyrics." In *The Propaganda of Power: The Role of Panegyric in Late Antiquity,* ed. Mary Whitby, 77–101. Leiden 1998.
Regali, M. "Il carmen II.2.3 di Gregorio Nazianzeno nei suoi rapporti con le declamazioni." *Studia Patristica* 18 (1989): 529–37.
———. "Intenti programmatici e datazione delle 'Invectivae in Iulianum' di Gregorio di Nazianzo." *CrSt* 1 (1980): 401–10.
Renucci, P. *Les idées politiques et le gouvernement de l'empereur Julien.* Brussels 2000.
Reydams-Schils, G. *The Roman Stoics: Self, Responsibility, and Affection.* Chicago 2005.
Richlin, A. "Gender and Rhetoric: Producing Manhood in the Schools." In *Roman Eloquence: Rhetoric in Society and Literature,* ed. W. J. Dominik, 90–110. London 1997.
Riedweg, C. "Mit Stoa und Platon gegen die Christen: Philosophische Argumentationsstrukturen in Julians *Contra Galilaeos.*" In *Zur Rezeption der hellenistischen Philosophie in der Spätantike,* ed. T. Fuhrer and M. Erler, 55–81. Stuttgart 1999.
———. "Porphyrios über Christus und die Christen: *De philosophia ex oraculis haurienda* und *Contra Christianos* im Vergleich." In *L'apologétique chrétienne gréco-latine à l'époque prénicénienne,* ed. A. Wlosok, 151–203. Geneva 2005.
———. *Ps.-Justin (Markell von Ankyra?), "Ad Graecos de vera religione" (bisher "Cohortatio ad Graecos").* Basel 1992.
Rijlaarsdam, J. C. *Platon über die Sprache:. Ein Kommentar zum "Kratylos," mit einem Anhang über die Quelle der Zeichentheorie Ferdinand de Saussures.* Utrecht 1978.
Rist, J. M. "Basil's 'Neoplatonism': Its Background and Nature." In *Basil of Caesarea: Christian, Humanist, Ascetic—A Sixteen-Hundredth Anniversary Symposium,* part 1, ed. P. J. Fedwick, 137–200. Toronto 1981.
———. "Mysticism and Transcendence in Later Platonism." *Hermes* 92 (1964): 213–25.
Rizzi, M. "La cittadinanza paradossale dei cristiani (*Ad Diognetum* 5–6): Le trasformazioni cristiane di un *topos* retorico." *Annali di Scienze Religiose* 1 (1996): 221–60.
———. "Problematiche politiche nel dibattito tra Celso e Origene." In *Discorsi di verità: Paganesimo, giudaismo e cristianesimo a confronto nel "Contro Celso" di Origene,* ed. L. Perrone, 171–212. Rome 1998.
Robert, L. "Héracles à Pergame et une épigramme de l'*Anthologie* XVI, 91." *Revue Philologique* 58 (1984): 7–18.
Roda, S. "Fuga nel privato e nostalgia del potere nel IV sec. d.C.: Nuovi accenti di un'antica ideologica." In *Le trasformazioni della cultura nella tarda antichità: Atti del Convegno tenuto a Catania, Univ. degli Studi, 27 settembre–2 ottobre 1982,* ed. C. Giuffrida, 95–108. Rome 1985.
Rosen, K. "Beobachtungen zur Erhebung Julians, 360–361 n.Chr." *AClass* 12 (1969): 121–49.
———. *Julian: Kaiser, Gott und Christenhaßer.* Stuttgart 2006.
———. "Kaiser Julian auf dem Weg vom Christentum zum Heidentum." *JbAC* 40 (1997): 126–46.
Roueché, C. *Aphrodisias in Late Antiquity: The Late Roman and Byzantine Inscriptions.* London 1989.

———. "The Functions of the Governor in Late Antiquity: Some Observations." *Antiquité Tardive* 6 (1998): 31–36.
Rousseau, P. "Antony as Teacher in the Greek *Life*." In *Greek Biography and Panegyric in Late Antiquity*, ed. T. Hägg and P. Rousseau, 89–109. Berkeley and Los Angeles 2000.
———. *Basil of Caesarea*. Berkeley and Los Angeles 1994.
———. "Basil of Caesarea, *Contra Eunomium*: The Main Preoccupations." In *The Idea of Salvation*, ed. D. W. Dockrill and R. G. Tanner, 77–94. Armidale 1988.
Rowe, G. *Princes and Political Cultures: The New Tiberian Senatorial Decrees*. Ann Arbor 2002.
Rubenson, S. "The Cappadocians on the Areopagus." In *Gregory of Nazianzus: Images and Reflections*, ed. J. Børtnes and T. Hägg, 113–32. Copenhagen 2006.
Ruether, R. Radford. *Gregory of Nazianzus: Rhetor and Philosopher*. Oxford 1969.
Ruggini, L. Cracco. "Apoteosi e politica senatoria nel IV secolo d.C.: Il dittico dei Symmachi al British Museum." *RSI* 89 (1977): 425–89.
———. "'*Felix temporum repartio*': Realtà socio-economiche in movimento durante un ventennio di regno (Costanzo II Augusto, 337–361 d.C.)." In *L'église et l'empire au IVe siècle*, ed. A. Dihle, 179–249. Geneva 1989.
———. *Simboli di battaglia ideologica nel tardo ellenismo (Roma, Atene, Costantinopoli: Numa, Empedocle, Cristo)*. Pisa 1972.
———. "Sofisti greci nell'impero Romano." *Athenaeum* 49 (1971): 402–45.
Russell, D. A. *Criticism in Antiquity*. Berkeley and Los Angeles 1981.
———. *Greek Declamation*. Cambridge 1983.
———. "The Panegyrists and Their Teachers." In *The Propaganda of Power: The Role of Panegyric in Late Antiquity*, ed. Mary Whitby, 17–50. Leiden 1998.
Russell, N. *The Doctrine of Deification in the Greek Patristic Tradition*. Oxford 2004.
Rutgers, L. V. "The Importance of Scripture in the Conflict between Jews and Christians: The Example of Antioch." In *The Use of Sacred Books in the Ancient World*, ed L. V. Rutgers and P. W. van den Horst, 287–303. Louvain 1998.
Sabbah, G. *La méthode d'Ammien Marcellin: Recherches sur la construction du discours historique dans les "Res Gestae."* Paris 1978.
Saffrey, H. D. "Connaissance et inconnaissance de Dieu: Porphyre et la théosophie de Tübingen." In *Recherches sur le néoplatonisme après Plotin*, 11–30. Paris 1990.
Saïd, S. *Sophiste et tyran; ou, Le problème du Prométhée enchaîné*. Paris 1985.
Sailor, D. "Becoming Tacitus: Significance and Inconsequentiality in the Prologue of *Agricola*." *ClAnt* 23 (2004): 139–77.
———. *Writing and Empire in Tacitus*. Cambridge 2008.
Saller, R. P. "The Age of Roman Men at Marriage and Its Consequences in the Roman Family." *CPh* 82 (1987): 21–34.
———. *Patriarchy, Property and Death in the Roman Family*. Cambridge 1994.
Sallis, J. *Being and Logos: The Way of Platonic Dialogue*. Atlantic Highlands 1986.
Salzman, M. R. *The Making of a Christian Aristocracy: Social and Religious Change in the Western Roman Empire*. Cambridge, Mass., 2002.
Sanders, G. "Kybele und Attis." In *Die orientalischen Religionen im Römerreich*, ed. M. J. Vermaseren, 264–97. Leiden 1981.

Saracino, S. "La politica culturale dell'imperatore Giuliano attraverso il *Cod. Th.* XIII 3, 5 e l'*Ep.* 61." *Aevum* 76 (2002): 123–41.
Sarris, P. "Rehabilitating the Great Estate: Aristocratic Property and Economic Growth in the Late-Antique East." In *Recent Research on the Late-Antique Countryside,* ed. W. Bowden, L. Lavan, and C. Machado, 55–71. Leiden 2004.
Schäfer, C., ed. *Kaiser Julian "Apostata" und die philosophische Reaktion gegen das Christentum.* Berlin 2008.
Scheidel, W. "Progress and Problems in Roman Demography." In *Debating Roman Demography,* ed. Scheidel, 13–32. Leiden 2001.
Scherberg, B. *Das Vater-Sohn-Verhältnis in der griechischen und römischen Komödie.* Tübingen 1995.
Schlange-Schöningen, H. *Kaisertum und Bildungswesen im spätantiken Konstantinopel.* Stuttgart 1995.
Schlinkert, D. *Ordo senatorius und nobilitas: Die Konstitution des Senatsadels in der Spätantike, mit einem Appendix über den praepositus sacri cubiculi, den "allmächtigen" Eunuchen am kaiserlichen Hof.* Stuttgart 1996.
Schmidt, R., ed. *Symbolische Gewalt: Herrschaftsanalyse nach Pierre Bourdieu.* Constance 2008.
Schmidt-Hofner, S. *Reagieren und Gestalten: Der Regierungsstil des spätrömischen Kaisers am Beispiel der Gesetzgebung Valentinians I.* Munich 2008.
Schniewind, A. "The Social Concern of the Plotinian Sage." In *The Philosopher and Society in Late Antiquity: Essays in Honour of Peter Brown,* ed. A. Smith, 51–64. Swansea 2005.
Scholl, R. *Historische Beiträge zu den julianischen Reden des Libanios.* Stuttgart 1994.
Scholz, P. *Der Philosoph und die Politik: Die Ausbildung der philosophischen Lebensform und die Entwicklung des Verhältnisses von Philosophie und Politik im 4. und 3. Jh. v.Chr.* Stuttgart 1998.
Schott, J. M. "Founding Platonopolis: The Platonic *Politeia* in Porphyry, Iamblichus, and Eusebius." *JECS* 11 (2003): 501–31.
———. "Porphyry on Christians and Others: 'Barbarian Wisdom,' Identity Politics, and Anti-Christian Polemics on the Eve of the Great Persecution." *JECS* 13 (2005): 277–314.
Schouler, B. "Loisir et travail dans les conceptions morales des sophistes grecs du IVe siècle de notre ère." In *Les loisirs et l'héritage de la culture classique: Actes du XIIIe Congrès de l'Association Guillaume Budé, Dijon, 27–31 août 1993,* ed. J.-M. André, J. Dangel, and P. Demont, 198–210. Brussels 1996.
———. *La tradition hellénique chez Libanios.* Paris 1984.
Schroeder, F. M., and R. B. Todd, eds. *Two Greek Aristotelian Commentators on the Intellect: The "De intellectu" Attributed to Alexander of Aphrodisias and Themistius' Paraphrase of Aristotle, "De anima" 3.4–8.* Toronto 1990.
Scicolone, S. "Le accezioni dell'appellativo Galilaioi in Giuliano." *Aevum* 56 (1982): 71–80.
Sedley, D. "The Idea of Godlikeness." In *Plato,* vol. 2, *Ethics, Politics, Religion and the Soul,* ed. Gail Fine, 309–28. Oxford 1999.
Seeck, O. *Regesten der Kaiser und Päpste für die Jahre 311 bis 476 n.Chr.: Vorarbeit zu einer Prosopographie der christlichen Kaiserzeit.* Stuttgart 1919. [Reprint: Frankfurt a.M. 1964.]

Seibt, K. *Die Theologie des Markell von Ankyra.* Berlin 1994.
Sessa, K. M. *The Formation of Papal Authority in Late Antique Italy: Roman Bishops and the Domestic Sphere.* Cambridge 2011.
Shahîd, I. *Byzantium and the Arabs in the Fourth Century.* Washington, D.C., 1984.
Shaw, B. D. "The Family in Late Antiquity: The Experience of Augustine." *P&P* 115 (1987): 3–51.
———. "Latin Funerary Epigraphy and Family Life in the Later Roman Empire." *Historia* 33 (1984): 457–97.
Shaw, G. *Theurgy and the Soul: The Neoplatonism of Iamblichus.* University Park 1995.
Siegel, R. E. *Galen on Psychology, Psychopathology, and Function and Diseases of the Nervous System: An Analysis of His Doctrines, Observations and Experiments.* Basel 1973.
Simonetti, M. *La crisi Ariana nel IV secolo.* Rome 1975.
Sinko, T. "De Gregorii Nazanzieni laudibus Macchabaeorum." *Eos* 13 (1907): 1–29.
———. *De traditione orationum Gregorii Nazianzeni.* 2 vols. Krakow 1917–23.
Sironen, E. *The Late Roman and Early Byzantine Inscriptions of Athens and Attica.* Helsinki 1997.
Skeat, T. C., ed. *Papyri from Panopolis in the Chester Beatty Library.* Vol. 10. Dublin 1964.
Small, J. P. *Wax Tablets of the Mind: Cognitive Studies of Memory and Literacy in Classical Antiquity.* New York 1997.
Smith, A. "Porphyry and the *Platonic Theology.*" In *Proclus et la Théologie Platonicienne,* ed. A.-Ph. Segonds and C. Steel, 177–88. Louvain 2000.
———, ed. *The Philosopher and Society in Late Antiquity: Essays in Honour of Peter Brown.* Swansea 2005.
Smith, R. *Julian's Gods: Religion and Philosophy in the Thought and Action of Julian the Apostate.* London 1995.
———. "Telling Tales: Ammianus' Narrative of the Persian Expedition of Julian." In *The Late Roman World and Its Historian: Interpreting Ammianus Marcellinus,* ed. J. W. Drijvers and D. Hunt, 89–104. London 1999.
Smith, R. R. R. "Late Roman Philosopher Portraits from Aphrodisias." *JRS* 80 (1990): 127–55.
Soler, E. "D'Apollonios de Tyane à l'empereur Julien: L'importance d'Antioche comme lieu de pèlerinage et centre philosophique grecs." In *Antioche de Syrie: Histoire, images et traces de la ville antique,* ed. B. Cabouret, 381–99. Dordrecht 2004.
Somers, V. *Histoire des collections complètes des discours de Grégoire de Nazianze.* Louvain-le-Neuve 1997.
Sorabji, R., ed. *Aristotle and After.* London 1997.
———. *Emotion and Peace of Mind: From Stoic Agitation to Christian Temptation.* Oxford 2000.
Sotinel, C. "Le récruitement des évêques en Italie aux IVe et Ve siècles." In *Vescovi e pastori in epoca Teodosiana: In occasione del XVI centenario della consacrazione episcopale di S. Agostino, 396–1996—XXV Incontro di studiosi dell'antichità cristiana,* vol. 2, 197–204. Rome 1997.
Spanneut, M. *Le stoïcisme des Pères de l'Église: De Clément de Rome à Clément d'Alexandrie.* 2nd ed. Paris 1957.

Špidlík, T. *Grégoire de Nazianze: Introduction à l'étude de sa doctrine spirituelle*. Rome 1971.
———. "La theoria et la praxis chez Grégoire de Nazianze." *Studia Patristica* 14 (1976): 358–64.
Spoerl, K. M. "The Schism at Antioch since Cavallera." In *Arianism after Arius: Essays on the Development of the Fourth-Century Trinitarian Conflicts*, ed. M. R. Barnes and D. H. Williams, 101–26. Edinburgh 1993.
von Staden, H. "Body, Soul, and Nerve: Epicurus, Herophilus, Erasistratus, the Stoics, and Galen." In *Psyche and Soma: Physicians and Metaphysicians on the Mind-Body Problem from Antiquity to the Enlightenment*, ed. J. P. Wright and P. Potter, 79–116. Oxford 2000.
———. "Character and Competence: Personal and Professional Conduct in Greek Medicine." In *Médecine et morale dans l'antiquité*, ed. H. Flashar and J. Jouanna, 157–210. Geneva 1997.
———. "L'idéal de tranquillité et la construction du passé dans la Seconde Sophistique: Aelius Aristides." In *Les loisirs et l'héritage de la culture classique: Actes du XIIIe Congrès de l'Association Guillaume Budé, Dijon, 27–31 août 1993*, ed. J.-M. André, J. Dangel, and P. Demont, 147–61. Brussels 1996.
———. "Stoic Theory of Perception and Its 'Platonic' Critics." In *Studies in Perception: Interrelations in the History of Philosophy and Science*, ed. P. K. Machamer and R. G. Turnbull, 96–137. Columbus 1978.
Stead, C. *Divine Substance*. Oxford 1977.
———. "Logic and the Application of Names to God." In *El "Contra Eunomium I" en la producción literaria de Gregorio de Nisa*, ed. L. F. Mateo-Seco and J. L. Bastero, 303–20. Pamplona 1988.
Sterk, A. *Renouncing the World Yet Leading the Church: The Monk-Bishop in Late Antiquity*. Cambridge, Mass., 2004.
Straub, J. "Die Himmelfahrt des Iulianus Apostata." *Gymnasium* 69 (1962): 310–26.
Studer, B. "Der Pesonenbegriff in der frühen kirchenamtlichen Trinitätslehre." *Th&Ph* 57 (1982): 161–70.
Sussman, L. A. "Sons and Fathers in the *Major Declamations* Ascribed to Quintilian." *Rhetorica* 13 (1995): 179–92.
Swain, S. *Hellenism and Empire: Language, Classicism, and Power in the Greek World, A.D. 50–250*. Oxford 1996.
Swift, L. J., and J. H. Oliver. "Constantius II on Flavius Philippus." *AJPh* 83 (1962): 247–64.
Szidat, J. *Historischer Kommentar zu Ammianus Marcellinus, Buch XX–XXI*. Parts 1–3. Stuttgart 1977–96.
———. "Die Usurpation Iulians: Ein Sonderfall?" In *Usurpation in der Spätantike*, ed. F. Paschoud and J. Szidat, 63–70. Stuttgart 1997.
———. "Zur Ankunft Julians in Sirmium 361 n.Chr. auf seinem Zug gegen Constantius II." *Historia* 24 (1975): 375–78.
Szymusiak, J. "Les sites de Nazianze et Karbala." In *Épektasis: Mélanges patristiques offerts au Cardinal Jean Daniélou*, ed. J. Fontaine and C. Kannengiesser, 545–48. Paris 1972.
Tabacco, R. "Il tiranno nelle declamazioni di scuola in lingua latina." *MAT* 5.9 (1985): 1–141.
Talbert, R. J. A., ed. *Barrington Atlas of the Greek and Roman World*. Princeton 2000.

Taormina, D. P. *Jamblique critique de Plotin et de Porphyre: Quatre études.* Paris 1999.
Thomas, Y. P. "Droit domestique et droit politique à Rome: Remarques sur le pécule et les honores des fils de famille." *MEFRA* 94 (1982): 527–80.
———. "*Vitae necisque potestas:* Le père, la cité, la mort." In *Du châtiment dans la cité: Supplices corporels et peine de mort dans le monde antique,* ed. Thomas, 499–548. Rome 1984.
Thome, F. *Historia contra Mythos: Die Schriftauslegung Diodors von Tarsus und Theodors von Mopsuestia im Widerstreit zu Kaiser Julians und Salustius' allegorischem Mythenverständnis.* Bonn 2004.
Thome, J. *Psychotherapeutische Aspekte in der Philosophie Platons.* Hildesheim 1995.
Tollefsen, T. T. "*Theosis* according to Gregory." In *Gregory of Nazianzus: Images and Reflections,* ed. J. Børtnes and T. Hägg, 257–70. Copenhagen 2006.
Tougher, S. "In Praise of an Empress: Julian's *Speech of Thanks* to Eusebia." In *The Propaganda of Power: The Role of Panegyric in Late Antiquity,* ed. Mary Whitby, 105–23. Leiden 1998.
———. *Julian the Apostate.* Edinburgh 2007.
———. "Julian's Bull Coinage: Kent Revisited." *CQ* 54 (2004): 327–30.
Treucker, B. *Politische und sozialgeschichtliche Studien zu den Basilius-Briefen.* Munich 1961.
Trisoglio, F. "La figura dell'eretico in Gregorio di Nazianzo." *Augustinianum* 25 (1985): 793–832.
Turcan, R. *Mithras Platonicus.* Leiden 1975.
Ulrich, J. *Die Anfänge der abendländischen Rezeption des Nizänums.* Berlin 1994.
———. "Nicaea and the West." *VChr* 51 (1997): 10–24.
Urbainczyk, T. *Socrates of Constantinople: Historian of Church and State.* Ann Arbor 1997.
Vaggione, R. *Eunomius of Cyzicus and the Nicene Revolution.* Oxford 2000.
———. "Of Monks and Lounge Lizards: 'Arians,' Polemics and Asceticism in the Roman East." In *Arianism after Arius: Essays on the Development of the Fourth-Century Trinitarian Conflicts,* ed. M. R. Barnes and D. H. Williams, 181–214. Edinburgh 1993.
———. "Some Neglected Fragments of Theodore of Mopsuestia's *Contra Eunomium*." *JThS* 31 (1980): 403–70.
Van Dam, R. *Becoming Christian: The Conversion of Roman Cappadocia.* Philadelphia 2003.
———. "Emperor, Bishops, and Friends in Late-Antique Cappadocia." *JThS* 37 (1986): 53–76.
———. *Families and Friends in Late Roman Cappadocia.* Philadelphia 2003.
———. *Kingdom of Snow: Roman Rule and Greek Culture in Cappadocia.* Philadelphia 2002.
———. "Self-Representation in the Will of Gregory of Nazianzus." *JThS* 46 (1995): 118–48.
Vanderspoel, J. "The Fourth-Century Philosopher Maximus of Byzantium." *AHB* 1 (1987): 71–74.
———. *Themistius and the Imperial Court: Oratory, Civic Duty, and Paideia from Constantius to Theodosius.* Ann Arbor 1995.
Varner, E. R. *Mutilation and Transformation: Damnatio memoriae and Roman Imperial Portraiture.* Leiden 2004.
Vatsend, K. *Die Rede Julians auf Kaiserin Eusebia: Abfassungszeit, Gattungszugehörigkeit, panegyrische Topoi und Vergleiche, Zweck.* Oslo 2000.

Vérilhac, A.-M. "L'image de la femme dans les épigrammes funéraires grecques." In *La femme dans le monde méditerranéen*, vol. 1, *Antiquité*, ed. Vérilhac, 85–112. Lyon 1985.
Vermaseren, M. J. *Cybele and Attis: The Myth and the Cult.* London 1977.
Villegas, N. Gómez. *Gregorio de Nazianzo en Constantinopla: Ortodoxia, heterodoxia y régimen teodosiano en una capital cristiana.* Madrid 2000.
Vinken, B. *Flaubert: Durchkreuzte Moderne.* Frankfurt a.M. 2009.
Vinson, M. "Gregory Nazianzen's Homily 15 and the Genesis of the Christian Cult of the Maccabean Martyrs." *Byzantion* 64 (1994): 166–92.
Vinzent, M. "Gottes Wesen, Logos, Weisheit und Kraft, bei Asterius von Kappadokien und Markell von Ancyra." *VChr* 47 (1993): 170–91.
———. *Pseudo-Athanasius, "Contra Arianos" IV: Eine Schrift gegen Asterius von Kappadokien, Eusebius von Cäsarea, Markell von Ancyra und Photin von Sirmium.* Leiden 1996.
Voelke, A.-J. *La philosophie comme thérapie de l'âme: Études de philosophie hellénistique.* Paris 1993.
Vogler, C. *Constance II et l'administration impériale.* Strasbourg 1979.
Volkmann, R. E. *Die Rhetorik der Griechen und Römer in systematischer Übersicht.* 2nd ed. Leipzig 1885. [Reprint: Hildesheim 1963.]
de Waal, F. B. M. *Peacemaking among Primates.* Cambridge, Mass., 1989.
Wainwright, P. "A Letter Attributed to Cyril of Jerusalem on the Building of the Temple." *VChr* 40 (1986): 286–93.
Wallace-Hadrill, A. "*Civilis Princeps*: Between Citizen and King." *JRS* 72 (1982): 32–48.
———. "The Emperor and His Virtues." *Historia* 30 (1981): 298–323.
Wallis, R. T. *Neoplatonism.* With foreword and bibliography by L. P. Gerson. 2nd ed. London 1995.
Wallraff, M. *Christus versus Sol: Sonnenverehrung und Christentum in der Spätantike.* Münster 2001.
Watts, E. J. *City and School in Late-Antique Athens and Alexandria.* Berkeley and Los Angeles 2006.
Webb, R. *Ekphrasis, Imagination and Persuasion in Ancient Rhetorical Theory and Practice.* Farnham 2009.
———. "The *Progymnasmata* as Practice." In *Education in Greek and Roman Antiquity*, ed. Y. L. Too, 289–316. Leiden 2001.
———. "The Protean Performer: Mimesis and Identity in Late-Antique Discussions of the Theater." In *Performing Ecstasies: Music, Dance, and Ritual in the Mediterranean*, ed. L. del Giudice and N. van Deusen, 3–11. Ottawa 2005.
Wehrli, F. "Der Arztvergleich bei Platon." *MH* 8 (1951): 179–80.
Weiss, J.-P. "Julien, Rome et les Romains." In *L'empereur Julien*, vol. 1, *De l'histoire à la légende (331–1715)*, ed. R. Braun and J. Richer, 125–40. Paris 1978.
Wells, L. *The Greek Language of Healing from Homer to New Testament Times.* Berlin 1998.
Whitby, M. "Images of Constantius." In *The Late Roman World and Its Historian: Interpreting Ammianus Marcellinus*, ed. J. W. Drijvers and D. Hunt, 77–88. London 1999.
White, C. *Christian Friendship in the Fourth Century.* Cambridge 1992.
Whitmarsh, T. *Greek Literature and the Roman Empire: The Politics of Imitation.* Oxford 2001.

Whittaker, J. "ΕΠΕΚΕΙΝΑ ΝΟΥ ΚΑΙ ΟΥΣΙΑΣ." *VChr* 23 (1969): 91–104.
Wickham, C. *Framing the Early Middle Ages: Europe and the Mediterranean, 400—800.* Oxford 2005.
Wickham, L. R. "The Date of Eunomius' Apology: A Reconsideration." *JThS* 20 (1969): 231–40.
———. "The *Syntagmation* of Aetius the Anomean." *JThS* 19 (1968): 523–69.
Widdicombe, P. *The Fatherhood of God from Origen to Athanasius.* Oxford 1994.
Wiemer, H.-U. "Ein Kaiser verspottet sich selbst: Literarische Form und historische Bedeutung von Julians Misopogon." In *Imperium Romanum: Studien zur Geschichte und Rezeption,* ed. P. Kneissl and V. Losemann, 733–55. Stuttgart 1998.
———. *Libanios und Julian: Studien zum Verhältnis von Rhetorik und Politik im vierten Jhd. nach Christus.* Munich 1995.
———. "Libanius on Constantine." *CQ* 44 (1994): 511–24.
Wildberg, C. "Three Neoplatonic Introductions to Philosophy: Ammonius, David and Elias." *Hermes* 149 (1990): 33–51.
Wilhelm, A. *Beiträge zur griechischen Inschriftenkunde, mit einem Anhange über die öffentliche Aufzeichnung von Urkunden.* Vienna 1909.
Williams, D. H. *Ambrose of Milan and the End of the Nicene-Arian Conflicts.* Oxford 1995.
Williams, R. *Arius: Heresy and Tradition.* London 1987.
———. Review of *Eunomius: The Extant Works,* ed. and trans. R. Vaggione (Oxford 1987). *Scottish Journal of Theology* 45 (1992): 101–11.
Williamson, C. "Monuments of Bronze: Roman Legal Documents on Bronze Tablets." *ClAnt* 6 (1987): 160–83.
Winkelmann, F. "Konstantins Religionspolitik und ihre Motive im Urteil der literarischen Quellen des 4. und 5. Jhrdts." *Acta Antiqua* 9 (1961): 239–56.
Winslow, D. F. *The Dynamics of Salvation: A Study of Gregory of Nazianzus.* Philadelphia 1979.
Wintjes, J. *Das Leben des Libanius.* Rahden 2005.
Wirbelauer, E., and C. Fleer. "*Totius orbis Augustus:* Claudius Mamertinus als praefectus praetorio der Kaiser Julian und Valentinian." In *Historische Interpretation,* ed. M. Weinmann-Walser, 191–201. Stuttgart 1995.
Wirth, G. "Jovian: Kaiser und Karikatur." In *Vivarium: Festschrift Theodor Klauser,* ed. E. Dassmann and K. Thraede, 353–84. Münster 1984.
———. "Themistius und Constantius." *ByzF* 6 (1979): 293–317.
Wischmeyer, W. "Theos Hypsistos: Neues zu einer alten Debatte." *ZAC* 9 (2005): 149–68.
Witt, R. E. "Jamblichus as a Forerunner of Julian." In *De Jamblique à Proclus,* ed. H. Dörrie, 35–64. Geneva 1975.
Wittung, J. A. "Resources on *Theosis,* with Select Primary Sources in Translation." In *Partakers of the Divine Nature: The History and Development of Deification in the Christian Traditions,* ed. M. J. Christensen and J. A. Wittung, 294–309. Madison, N.J., 2007.
Wlosok, A., ed. *L'apologétique chrétienne gréco-latine à l'époque prénicénienne.* Geneva 2005.
Wolf, P. *Vom Schulwesen der Spätantike: Libanius-Interpretationen.* Baden 1951.
Woods, D. "Julian, Gallienus, and the Solar Bull." *AJN* 12 (2000): 157–69.
Wörner, M. H. *Performatives und sprachliches Handeln: Ein Beitrag zu J. L. Austins Theorie der Sprechakte.* Hamburg 1978.

Wright, W. "An Ancient Syrian Martyrology." *Journal of Sacred Literature* 8 (1866): 423–32.
Wyss, B. "Gregor II (Gregor von Nazianz)." *RAC* 12: 793–863.
Ysebaert, J. *Greek Baptismal Terminology: Its Origins and Early Development.* Nijmegen 1962.
Zachhuber, J. "The Antiochene Synod of A.D. 363 and the Beginnings of Neo-Nicenism." *ZAC* 4 (2000): 83–101.
———. "Basil and the Three-Hypostases Tradition: Reconsidering the Origins of Cappadocian Theology." *ZAC* 5 (2001): 65–85.
Ziadé, R. *Les martyrs Maccabées: De l'histoire juive au culte Chrétien—Les homélies de Grégoire de Nazianze et de Jean Chrysostome.* Leiden 2007.

INDEX

Ablabius (rhetorician), 207n95
Aburgius (notary), 68
Aburgius (quaestor), 472
Acacius (bishop of Caesarea), 55, 238, 375n133; in Christological debates, 46, 47, 49; debate with Meletius, 108; Gregory's attack on, 229
actors, civic status of, 352n60
Adamantius sophist, 207n95
Aedesius (philosopher?): Julian's studies with, 92; Themistius on, 94; theurgy of, 95
Aelius Aristides, 20n15; on Cynics, 138; on philosophical life, 81n79
Aerius (deacon), feeding of poor, 205
Aesop, 112
Aetius (bishop), 44, 45, 48, 235–45; bishops supporting, 239, 240; career of, 235–36; opponents of, 102n64; consecration of bishops, 238–39; and Constantius, 243, 244; death of, 244; divine calling of, 243; engagement as physician, 241; episcopal status of, 240n107, 259; and Eudoxius, 236, 237; and Eunomius, 236, 238n102; exile of, 49, 237; and Flavian dynasty, 244; and Gallus Caesar, 243–44; Gregory's denunciation of, 233; homoianism of, 229; at Julian's court, 57, 107, 235, 238, 239; Julian's support of, 259, 318; on *Logos*, 397; philosophical life of, 239–45, 241, 244; rehabilitation of, 239; study with Leontius, 235; *Syntagmation*, 237; understanding of Trinity, 245–58; as uneducated Cynic, 241

agency, individual, 3n4
agōn Solis (festival), 287
agora: Christian access to, 355, 463, 464, 486; in Gregory's *Oration 4*, 353–55; imperial images in, 353, 457
Alexander the Great, successors of, 436n8
Alexander of Aphrodisias (philosopher), 227n47
Alexander of Heliopolis, consularis Syriae, 331, 462
Alexandria: philosophical schools of, 253; riots (361), 89; role in *paideia*, 89–90
allegory: Christian, 385–86, 389, 401, 402–3; Gregory on, 380–87, 400, 412–13; Julian's use of, 402, 417
allotrioi (strangers): exclusion from Roman universalism, 379, 487; Gregory's concern with, 225; Julian's followers as, 432; in Nazianzus schism, 150, 189, 190, 199, 201, 209; trickery of, 202, 208
Ambrose (bishop of Milan), 17; on Greek language, 387n36
Ammianus Marcellinus: on Antioch, 270, 271, 272, 274, 328; on bishops, 41n95, 65, 148; on Chalcedon, 358; on Constantius, 96n3, 459; on earthquakes, 447n49; on *Epistle to the Athenians*, 62n5; on Gallus, 30; on Jovian, 438; on Julian's acclamation, 63; on Julian's administration, 360n88; on Julian's monuments, 451; on Julian's reception, 270, 271; on Julian's reforms, 89; on Julian's reli-

529

Ammianus Marcellinus *(continued)*
gious practice, 284, 438, 458n84; knowledge of Gregory, 441n32; on Maximus of Ephesus, 91, 92; on oracles, 277nn29,32; on Persian campaigns, 281, 282, 284; on Procopius, 244n125, 471n124; rediscovery of, 337; *Res gestae*, 91, 92, 337; sources of, 443n36; on temple burning, 277, 316; on temple of Jerusalem, 450n61; use of Christian texts, 441n32; on Valens's circle, 463n103; on west-east routes, 19

Ammonius Sacchas (philosopher), 253

Amphilochius (uncle of Gregory), 27n45; school of, 150

Amphilochius the Younger, 226n43

Ando, Clifford, 63

Annesi: ascetics of, 204; Basil of Caesarea at, 27–28, 58, 149, 153, 183

anomoians, 228, 230n62

anthropology, 172–73

Antioch: Christians of, 277–81; church of Paulinus at, 281; *curiales* of, 30, 275n21; drought of 361/62, 273, 274, 275, 276; famine in, 271, 272, 273–75, 281, 284, 328, 329n240; grain supply for, 274–75, 327n229; Great Church of, 279, 280; Greekness of, 271, 330; Iamblichan philosophy at, 275; as imperial headquarters, 272n7; Jewish community of, 449n59, 450n61; Julian in, 265, 269, 270–72, 282, 442; Julian's intentions for, 292n91; Julian's invective against, 327–31, 362; love of theater, 361, 383n21; New Year festivities (363), 328; origin story of, 330; on *ousia*, 43; pagan revival in, 402; Persian threat to, 435, 445n44; public library of, 302n127; ridicule of Julian, 327–29, 337; temple fire at, 271, 272, 275–77, 279, 284, 316, 369

Antioch, council of (341), 38–39; dedication creed, 39, 43; fourth creed of, 42n99, 43, 46, 47n110, 50

Antioch, synod of (362), 281

Antioch, synod of (363), 424

Antiochus IV Epiphanes, Maccabean resistance to, 152–53, 341–42

apatheia, Clement on, 180n120

Apollinaris (bishop of Laodicaea), 150n15; *Contra Sabellianos,* 233

Apollo: aid to Zeus-Helios, 333; festivals of, 463n105; Know Thyself command, 110; oracles of, 116–17, 123, 276–77, 290; temple at Antioch, 275–77, 279, 284, 369; temple at Daphne, 276–77, 451; temple at Rome, 447n49

Apollo Musagetes: Helios as, 298; statue of, 276, 277

apologētikos logos (genre), 76

Apostolic Constitutions, 151n17, 242n116; bishops' duties in, 155n31

apotaktitai, 227. *See also* renunciators, Christian

apotheōsis, 178; imperial, 457; Julian's, 435, 446, 455–57; *theōsis* and, 414

apragmosynē (freedom from care), 84

Arcadius, Emperor: censoring of Eunomius, 241–42

Aretaeus of Cappadocia (physician), 196

aretē, public displays of, 25

Arethusa, anti-Christian violence in, 357

Arian Historiographer, 277, 278, 279n36, 280

Arianism, 35; Gregory on, 184, 185, 206, 209, 228. *See also* homoians

Arianzus, Gregory at, 21

Arinthaeus (military officer), 68

Aristotle: on divine Ideas, 129n136; on *dynamis,* 245n134; on dynastic succession, 85; on emotions, 174n99; on ether, 128; on friendship, 107n79; on governance, 2; Gregory's use of, 165, 407n99; ideal ruler of, 85, 86; on *mimēsis,* 351n57; physician metaphors of, 171, 172; on privation, 254; on the soul, 128n134, 173n96; Themistius on, 84–85, 98–99; on tyranny, 352n63. Works: *Categories,* 246, 254; *Nicomachean Ethics,* 171; *On Interpretation,* 409; *Politics,* 84, 165

Arius, 40; in Gregory's *Oration 2*, 184, 185, 206, 228

Arles, Constantius at, 29

Armenia, relations with Rome, 470

army, Roman: banners of, 358–59, 486; Christians in, 358–59, 454, 455n75; under Julian, 358–59, 419; soldiers, 358–59, 454, 455n75; soldiers' bonus in, 359, 443n35

Artemii Passio (9th century), 278

the arts, divine origin of, 394–95, 396

asceticism: in Asia Minor, 205n86; Egyptian, 223; Gregory's, 8, 9; Julian's, 467; for laity, 167n76; non-Christian, 224; in philosophical life, 158, 431; zealous, 203–6. *See also* retreat, philosophical

Asclepius: in creative realm, 298, 299; descent to earth, 320; subordination to Helios, 299

Asmus, R., 445, 467n115

Asterius, 53

INDEX 531

Athanasius (bishop of Alexandria): on Antony, 224n38; on automatic deification, 421n138; in Christological debates, 37, 40, 43; on Constantius, 31; deposition of, 34; Gregory on, 157; on Julian, 461n96; Photinus and, 234; on *theopoiēsis*, 414n114; on Trinity, 261n171; use of *stēlographia*, 345n35

Athens, cult of Cybele in, 119

Attis: castration of, 118, 127, 130, 131, 133, 135; created nature of, 133; as creative force, 125, 126, 127–31, 133; descent through galaxy, 129–31, 132, 133; as *Logos*, 126, 127, 131, 288, 289, 300; mediating function of, 132; as noeric god, 130; as *ousia*, 126, 127; resurrection of, 127, 136; transgression of, 130

Attis myth: Christian criticism of, 118, 119n111; cosmological aspects of, 134; in Julian's *Hymn to the Mother of the Gods*, 118–36; *paradoxa* of, 127–28, 136; rites of, 133–36; universal wisdom in, 119. *See also* Cybele; Mother of the Gods

Augustine (bishop of Hippo Regius): *City of God*, 347, 385; on human/divine dualism, 414; on theater, 352n62

Augustus, Emperor: Roman *oikoumenē* under, 361

Aurelian, Emperor, 291; *heliogenesis* of, 290n84

Aurelius Victor: Julian's use of, 286n68; removal from office, 463

Babylas (martyr), 376n140; homoianism of, 280; remains of, 277, 278, 279, 369

barbarians, goodness of, 330, 331

Barceló, P., 30n59

Bar Kochba revolt, 449n60

Barnes, Michel R., 230, 254n157, 258

Barnes, T. D., 441n32

Basil (bishop of Ancyra), 42, 49; in Christological debates, 46, 47; and Constantius, 47, 59; following formulation of Constantinople, 236; homoiousian views of, 148, 149, 233–34, 237; influence on Constantius, 45n105; on *ousia*, 44, 47, 48; supporters of, 46

Basil (bishop of Caesarea), 4; at Annesi, 27–28, 58, 149, 153, 183; on asceticism, 167n76; in Athens, 23, 24–26; authority of, 483; consecration of Gregory, 157; correspondence with Gregory, 27, 207, 208, 220, 221–23, 223n34; correspondence with Libanius, 26; death of father, 193; on *erēmia*, 221; and Eudoxius, 239; and Eusebius of Caesarea in Cappadocia, 205, 474–75; and Eustathius, 220n21, 474; excerpting of Origen, 22n23; and formulation of Constantinople, 55–56; friendship with Gregory, 24–26, 204, 205, 221–22, 342n26; Gregory's funeral oration for, 157, 473; and homoiousios, 205; Julian's invitation to, 57, 69, 466n113; Julian's knowledge of, 466; Julian's threat to, 469; knowledge of Julian, 68–69; on language, 396, 398n68; monastic followers of, 204n83; and Neoplatonism, 224n37; and nonscriptural terminology, 389n41; oration against Sabellians, 234; ordination of, 215, 222; philosophical life of, 205, 209, 223, 239; refutation of Eunomius, 230–31, 254, 396, 403; signing of Gregory's *Oration 5*, 465, 466, 474, 475; use of *tachygraphoi*, 230, 473; and Valens, 476. Works: *Contra Eunomium*, 230–31, 403; *De Spiritu Sanctu*, 229n59; *Epistle 2*, 221–22

basileus, as philosopher, 86. *See also* philosopher-kings

Bassidius Lauricius (*comes*), 46

Baynes, Norman H., 167

Beeley, Christopher A., 7n22, 155, 230n61; on Gregory's *Theological Orations*, 403–4; on Gregory's theology, 184n3, 229–30; on Trinity, 235

Benedict XVI, Pope: *Deus Caritas Est*, 326n225

Berger, Peter, 483

Bernardi, Jean, 175n103, 176n105, 445; on Gregory's portrait of Julian, 339; on persecution, 365n103

Berrens, S., 292n92Bidez, Jean, 363n99

bios praktikos: versus *bios theōrētikos*, 71–73, 81, 161; in Neoplatonism, 103–5; Porphyry on, 105. *See also* philosophical life

bishops: access to court, 240; advice to emperors, 482–83; anomoian, 239, 240; association with sees, 240; authority of, 7, 9n30, 481, 483; convocation in Seleucia (359), 46–47; delegation to Constantinople, 46; diversity among, 240; duties of, 155n31; exile of, 43n100, 47, 474; function of, 3, 240; homoiousian, 148–50; imperial approval over, 41; *paideia* of, 36; pastoral functions of, 240; philosophical life of, 240–41, 259; as political philosophers, 377, 483; relations with Constantius, 31, 33–40, 59; relations with Julian, 65, 148, 151, 238–39; rural, 240n108; under Valens, 470, 473

bishops, Eastern: Christological debates of, 34–39, 40; consensus among, 34, 35–36, 39, 41, 42–53; factions among, 34–36; and formulation of Constantinople, 49, 50, 52, 55–57
bishops, Western, 150; under Constantius, 42–43; and formulation of Constantinople, 47–48, 54, 63; at Sirmium, 42–43
Bloomer, M., 198
Bogner, H., 130n140
Bouffartigue, Jean, 113; on *Against the Galileans*, 317n189; on Cybele, 135; on *Hymn to King Helios*, 294n97; on Julian's *Oration 5*, 119n112; on Porphyry, 305
Bourdieu, Pierre, 483
Bowersock, G. W., 63n7, 338; on trials at Chalcedon, 358
Braun, R., 340n16
Brennecke, Hanns-Christof, 47n114, 49n124; on Babylas, 280; on Meletius, 424n150; on Valens, 473
Brown, Peter, 51; on body and soul, 180n121; on Eustathius, 205; on *paideia*, 7n23
Bryaxis (sculptor), 276–77
Burrus, Virginia, 242n113

Caesarea: Gregory in, 21; Julian's punishment of, 357
Caesarea Maritima: Gregory in, 21–23
Caesarius (brother of Gregory), 8, 12; at Alexandria, 23, 57, 58; at Constantinople, 225; education of, 21; imperial treasurer position, 471–72; intestate death of, 193nn38–39, 194; under Julian, 66, 68, 148, 152, 154, 273, 364, 466; in Nazianzus, 225, 337n5; as new man, 481; in Nicaea, 472; during Procopius's usurpation, 434; public honors for, 225–26; as public man, 219; "second philosophy" of, 103n69; senate seat of, 26, 225n40; and Valens, 471
Calendar of Philocalus, 135
Cameron, Averil, 11n33
Candidianus (judge), 68, 151
Caner, Daniel, 209
Cappadocia, emperors in, 20n14
Caracalla, Emperor, journeys of, 20n10
Carterius (*paidagōgos*), 21
Carus (Praetorian prefect), Persian campaign of, 453–54
causality: in Greek philosophy, 38; Julian's, 127–31, 334; theological debates concerning, 36, 38

Celsus (philosopher), 97; work against Christians, 302n130
Chalcedon: judges at, 64, 358; strategic importance of, 244n125
Charito (wife of Jovian), 440n28
choice (*prohairesis*), 169, 170, 179
Choricius (rhetorician), 198n64
Christ: in *Against the Galileans*, 317, 318, 319–20; alignment with creation, 185, 186; as *allotrios*, 261; beginning of, 258; as begotten, 255; causation of, 36, 38; in chain of *oikeiōsis*, 427; creative capacity of, 256; *dynamis* of, 256; as *energeia* of God, 257–58; humanity of, 421–22, 427–28; *hypostasis* of, 430; incarnation of, 178; innovations of, 320; in Julian's *Caesars*, 285–86; as *Logos*, 42, 127, 186, 233, 234, 261, 262, 341, 373; as mediator, 214n2; as *Monogenēs*, 261, 262, 317; and *oikeios pros theon*, 262; *ousia* of, 38, 39, 44, 245, 256, 261, 400; as physician, 171; sacrifice of, 253
Christianity: boundary with paganism, 11; canonical writings of, 480–81; civilizing impact of, 372; claim to Roman *oikoumenē*, 365–66, 379–80, 432; as Greek wisdom, 318; as inferior myth, 304; innovation in, 121–22, 308–9; in Julian's *Oration 7*, 111–14; Julian's plagiarism of, 327; legalization of, 10, 11; as myth, 384; Roman character of, 1; and Roman imperial power, 372–74; threat to Roman *oikoumenē*, 305, 306; universal, 486, 487
Christianity, Eastern: asceticism in, 167n76; under Constantius II, 33–40; divinization in, 177–78
Christians: abandonment of Greekness, 309; access to agora, 355, 463, 464, 486; of Antioch, 277–81; complicity in Julian's death, 454; of Constantinople, 405; desertion of Roman *oikoumenē*, 320–21; *eugeneia* of, 481; exclusion from Greek language, 387–88, 390, 392; under Gratian, 404n91; Great Persecution of, 276; under Julian, 321, 326, 340, 355–64, 390, 417, 437, 486; possession of truth, 388; in Roman army, 358–59, 454, 455n75
Christological debates, 12, 120; among Eastern bishops, 34–40; Constans and, 39; between Diodore and Apollinarius, 403n87, 404; Eunomius in, 245–48; Julian's knowledge of, 60, 317, 318; sources for, 36n77. *See also* formulation of Constantinople; homoians; homoiousians

Chrysanthius (priest), 66n21; theurgy of, 95
Chrysanthius of Sardis, 91, 92
Chrysipp, 179n116, 323, 370n116
Cicero, on philosophical life, 73n53, 74n59
cities, late Roman: Christianization of, 463–64; festivals of, 463–64; origin narratives of, 330n244; religious practices of, 438n14; role of theater in, 350; sacred topography of, 450, 451; secularized, 486; welcoming of Julian, 270
citizenship, and social mobility, 20n15
Claudius II Gothicus, Emperor, 287; Mythical founder of Flavians, 115, 289, 292
Claudius Mamertinus, 64n16, 342n27; exile of, 463
Cledonius (imperial official), 207, 472
Clement: on *apatheia*, 180n120; on kinship with the divine, 179
clergy, late-antique: Gregory on, 17; immunity from taxation, 56; Julian's edict on, 57; social status of, 8n25. *See also* bishops; priesthood
Commodus, Emperor: Olympic festivals under, 276n24
Constans, Emperor, 32; acclamation of, 33; acts of governance, 34; and Christological debates, 39; control of Roman West, 28n52; episcopal supporters of, 40, 41; murder of, 29, 41, 42, 236
Constantia (sister of Constantius), 29
Constantine I, Emperor: Julian on, 285, 286; legalization of Christianity, 481; mausoleum of, 439; succession of, 32–33
Constantine II, Emperor, 32; acts of governance, 34; rule over West, 33
Constantinople: bishops' delegation to (359), 46; Christians of, 405; under Constantius, 96; cult of Cybele in, 119, 123, 135; episcopal leadership of, 40; intellectual life of, 96–97; *paideia* of, 96; reception of Julian, 88–89. *See also* formulation of Constantinople; senate, Constantinopolitan
Constantius II, Emperor: advisors of, 59; amnesty under, 28; anhomoian views of, 237; and Antioch, 331; antipagan legislation of, 306n149; appointment of bishops, 40; as Augustus of East, 33; and Basil of Ancyra, 47; burial of, 64, 65, 457; campaigns against Persians, 29, 41, 46, 48–49, 53, 272, 281, 372, 443; as Christian *basileus*, 423; Christian Rome of, 372; coins of, 82; concept of empire, 81–82; consensus building under, 35, 39–53, 58–59, 81, 237, 374, 377, 472; con-

solidation of rule, 31; Constantinople under, 96; corruption by Christianity, 80; death of, 56, 64, 148, 376n138; engagement against Silvanius, 78n68; in *Epistle to the Athenians*, 62, 77–80, 331; *eusebeia* of, 367, 372, 473; exile of Julian, 62; and formulation of Constantinople, 45, 48; Gallus and, 77, 367, 368, 369; Gregory on, 339, 366–70, 371–73, 423, 424–25, 470, 472–73; *haplotēs* of, 374n130; historiographical traditions on, 31–32, 48, 58; honoring of Caesarius, 225–26; iconography of, 367n105; interest in *paideia*, 96; Julian and, 53, 77–78, 79, 80, 92, 365–77; in Julian's *Caesars*, 285, 371; on *logoi*, 379; murders by, 77; *oikoumenē* under, 29; *philanthrōpia* of, 367, 375; relations with bishops, 33–40, 59; religious policies of, 32–42, 58–59; remarriage of, 63; *Romanitas* of, 373; service toward *Logos*, 388; sole rulership, 28–32, 41, 42, 54; successors of, 83n87; on taxation of clergy, 56; and Themistius, 80–82, 92, 96; and Theophilus the Indian, 243; universalism of, 122n17; veneration of martyrs, 331n247; and Vetranio, 29n54; view of philosophical life, 81, 85, 221, 224, 227; Western campaigns of, 30
correspondence, imperial, 70n38
Cosi, D. M., 130n140; on Porphyry, 250n140
cosmology: Epicurus's, 129n136; Gregory's, 215n3, 415, 416, 427; Julian's, 125–27, 132n143, 295–300, 312, 324n218, 334, 484; in Roman universalism, 2, 123
cosmos: as good, 180; harmonious, 416, 428; hierarchical order of, 430; intelligent/intelligible, 295–97; link with humanity, 420; *politeia* as, 416; role of kinship in, 199; as single entity, 172n92; Zeus as, 251n146
Coulie, B., 446n47
court, Julian's, 57–58, 66–67, 68; Aetius at, 57, 107, 235, 238, 239; Cynics at, 107; Eustathius at, 106–7; purges of, 89
Crates: Delphic commands to, 117; use of myth, 113n95
Criscuolo, Ugo, 342; on Gregory's *Oration 5*, 343; on Libanius, 444–45
Ctesiphon, Julian at, 332, 434, 453–54
cursus publicus: access to, 20, 91; Julian's reform of, 360, 442
Cybele: cosmological significance of, 135; cult of, 119, 121n115, 135; in Roman universalism, 118, 120; as *theotokos*, 301, 335. *See also* Attis myth; Mother of the gods

Cynics: emulation of Diogenes, 110; false, 108n82, 110, 111; at Julian's court, 107; Julian's orations to, 67, 136–39, 164; sexual ethics of, 109; use of myth, 113
Cyprian (bishop of Carthage), Gregory on, 157
Cyril (bishop of Jerusalem), 447n51; conflict with Acacius, 46

Dagron, Gilbert, 97, 444
daimones: Iamblichus on, 132n143; threat to humans, 94
Daley, B. E., 5n15
damnatio memoriae: Gregory's practice of, 347, 426, 439; literary, 468; on statues, 353
Darius, as used by Gregory, 454
"dated creed," 44, 45, 47
deification. See *apotheōsis;* divinization
Demiurge: in *Against the Galileans,* 313, 314, 315; Helios as, 129, 294n98, 299; intellect of, 252; Platonic, 104, 313, 314
Demoen, K., 13n38
Demophilus (bishop of Constantinople), 404
Demosthenes, 12, 25, 141, 162n59, 243, 341n20
Dexippus, 245n133
dialektikon (refutation), 76, 159
Dianius (bishop of Caesarea), 49, 50, 52; and formulation of Constantinople, 148, 149; Gregory the Elder's support for, 204
Dillon, J., 293n95
Diocaesarea. See Nazianzus
Dio Chrysostom: on philosophical life, 81n79; on rhetoric, 97n45; use of myth, 112n92. Works: *On Tyranny,* 109, 110; *Oration 4 On Kingship,* 138; *Third Oration on Kingship,* 290
Diocletian, Emperor, consultation of oracle, 276, 277n32
Diodore (bishop of Tarsus), 305; on allegory, 401; *Commentary on the Psalms,* 401–2; condemnation as heretic, 402n82; debate with Apollinarius, 403n87, 404; exegetical method of, 403; manuscript tradition of, 402n81; response to Julian, 306n146
Diogenes: *chreiai* of, 108n82; death of, 164n65; Delphic commands to, 117; emulation of, 110, 232; *enkrateia* of, 109; *erga* of, 138; Julian on, 138; philosophical life of, 139; use of myth, 113n95
Diogenes Laertius, 185n7
Dionysus: birth of, 385n29; in creative realm, 298–99; divinity of, 116n105; as ideal ruler, 114; subordination to Helios, 299

the divine: in *Against the Galileans,* 313; *agennētos* essence of, 120, 130, 245, 246–47, 254, 257n163, 261, 288, 295; archetypes of, 128n132; ascent to, 249–50, 253–54; communication with philosophers, 482; conversion to, 220n19; cultic practices regarding, 308; ethnic approaches to, 307–8, 309, 333; fatal mistakes concerning, 379; grammatical issues concerning, 37–39; as Greek, 397; in Greek language, 120; Greek philosophy's approach to, 308–9; Gregory on, 18, 176–81, 199, 200, 411–12, 462; Gregory's family and, 219; Gregory's relationship with, 18, 186–87, 217–19, 220; human kinship with, 98, 105, 127, 128, 130, 138, 170, 176–81, 182, 200, 263, 313, 315n179, 317, 333, 339, 366, 379; *hypostaseis* of, 126, 127–28, 132, 133; Iamblichus on, 94, 249, 485; images of, 124, 252; in Julian's philosophical life, 26, 89, 176, 432; leaders' kinship with, 106, 167, 170; material realm and, 125; mediation with, 214, 215; mysteries of, 94; myths' revelation of, 113–14, 116; names of, 246–54, 261n171, 399; offenders against, 462, 465; Oneness of, 333–34; philosophers' access to, 3, 94; philosophers' duty toward, 167; philosophers' guidance to, 214, 253–54; Platonic assimilation to, 178; representation in statues, 124; in Roman *oikoumenē,* 2, 7, 10, 19, 366; in Roman universalism, 10, 120–21; souls' reflection of, 129n135; sun's manifestation of, 297–98; symbols of, 134–36; theurgic approaches to, 116; unbroken chain of, 430. See also *oikeiōsis pros theon; ousia*
divinization: in Eastern Christianity, 177–78, 413; fakery in, 417–18; Gregory on, 413
Domitian, Emperor, 466
donativum (soldiers' bonus), 359, 443n35
Drijvers, J. W., 450n61

earthquakes, as portents, 460n92
East, Roman: balance with West, 82; debates on philosophical life, 214; euergetism in, 191; under Gallus, 29–30; growth of, 8; on Julian's accession, 67
Ecdicius (prefect of Egypt), 302
edicts, imperial: honoring of, 70
education, Roman, 197–98. See also *paideia*
Eleusinian Mysteries, Julian's initiation into, 217
Eleusius (bishop of Cyzicus), 231, 238n100
elites: authority of, 483–85; Constantinopolitan,

INDEX 535

472; hierarchy among, 483; juridical cruelty toward, 470n118; kinship among, 483–85; *paideia* of, 7, 479, 480, 481
elites, Christian: under Julian, 60, 66–67, 87, 106, 154; in Roman leadership, 7–8
elites, Roman: ancestral cities of, 20–21; Christian leaders among, 7–8; governance under, 11; Gregory's appeal to, 9; on innovation, 122
emotions: Aristotle on, 174n99; disorders of, 172; in Greek philosophy, 172n89
Empedocles, 173n93, 417–18, 437–38
Empedotimus (philosopher), 418n137
emperors: access to, 59; in Cappadocia, 20n14; consensus among, 142n179; correspondence of, 69; embodiment of law, 355–56; images of, 70n39, 354; persecution under, 364; as philosopher-kings, 105, 482; as philosophers, 86–87; philosophical leisure of, 73; as *pontifex maximus*, 332n248; rivalry among, 35–36, 39; worship of, 354
emperors, Christian, 354, 373–77; advisors of, 374, 482–83; approval over bishops, 41; Gregory and, 425, 446; in Gregory's *Oration 4*, 423; relationship with priests, 377; in sacred space, 476–77
energeia: effects of, 258; of God, 44, 245; of Helios, 297; of statues, 277n29
Ephraem (bishop of Nisibis), 447; *Hymns*, 450
Epictetus, on *koinōnia*, 178
Epicureans, Julian on, 128n131
Epicurus: on *apragmosynē*, 84; cosmology of, 129n136
epinoia (cognition), 261n171
epitaphios logos (genre), 441n30
erēmia: Basil on, 221; philosophical life in, 99, 170. *See also* retreat, philosophical
essence. *See ousia*
ethnicity: and approach to the divine, 307–8, 309, 333; presiding gods of, 314–15; and *Romanitas*, 395–96; and Roman universalism, 2, 330
Eudoxius (bishop of Constantinople), 44, 49, 53; in Christological debates, 46, 57; consecration of bishops, 238–39; exile of, 45; Gregory's attack on, 229; homoian supporters of, 237
Eudoxius (rhetorician), 226n43
euergetism, 191
eugeneia, Roman celebration of, 191
Eugenius (father of Themistius), 97n45, 98
Eulalius (bishop of Nazianzus), 207

Eunapius of Sardis: on Julian, 282n52; *Lives of Philosophers and Sophists*, 92–93, 95, 98n48; philosophical life of, 220
Eunomius (bishop of Cyzicus), 49, 53, 57, 236–45; and Aetius, 236; on *agraphos* God, 389; *akribeia* of, 473; anti-Cynic attacks on, 242; Asianic style of, 242; Basil's refutation of, 230–31, 254, 396, 403; bishops supporting, 239, 240; career of, 236; censoring of, 241–42; and Constantius, 237–38; corpus of works, 241; as deacon, 236; dialectical methods of, 407; divine calling of, 243, 244–45; episcopal duties of, 244, 245; episcopal status of, 259; and Eudoxius, 236, 237; exile of, 237, 244n126; and Flavian dynasty, 244; *genea* of, 371; under Gratian, 404n91; Gregory of Nyssa and, 229n59, 230, 241–42, 242nn113–14; Gregory's denunciation of, 229, 233, 404, 405, 407–11; heresy of, 11; homoianism of, 229; homoiousians and, 238, 245; imperial sponsors of, 12; and Julian, 57, 238, 239, 259, 300, 318; on *Logos*, 397; mission to Jovian, 424; misuse of philosophical techniques, 425; as *notarius*, 236; opponents of, 258, 259; philosophical life of, 239–45; and Procopius, 244, 471; relations with Aetius, 238n102; scholarship on, 229n58; *spoudē* of, 241; technical vocabulary of, 256n159; theory of language, 255n157, 262, 400, 409, 430n170; on unbegotten God, 407; understanding of *mimēsis*, 263n176; understanding of Trinity, 245–58, 260–61, 263, 380; use of Methodius, 256–57; use of Plato, 407n100; Valens and, 473, 474
—*Apology*, 238, 239, 241, 242, 245, 294; the *agennētos* in, 247, 254, 261; critics of, 254; divine names in, 246–54, 255; Gregory's response to, 258, 259–62; heuristic strategies of, 246; language of negation in, 254n154; language theory in, 400; Neoplatonism of, 246, 247; refutations of, 230; Trinity in, 255–58, 260–61, 400
—*Apology of the Apology*, 241n112, 254, 403, 404, 430n170
Eusebia, Empress: death of, 63n10; Julian's address to, 61
Eusebius (bishop of Caesarea in Cappadocia), 149; and Basil of Caesarea, 205, 474–75; correspondence with Gregory, 475; Gregory the Elder's support for, 204; on Eustathius, 205

536 INDEX

Eusebius (bishop of Caesarea Maritima, Church Historian), 37–39; cosmogony of, 310–11; cosmology of, 295n101; on divine power, 299n118; on images of the divine, 252; Julian's knowledge of, 311n166; Julian's response to, 253, 300, 305, 315–16; on oracles, 253n152; on *ousia*, 37, 38; political theology of, 451; mention of Oenomaeus's works, 116; rebuttal of Porphyry, 307, 309–12; on Roman *oikoumenē*, 306; textual exegesis by, 309
—*Demonstratio Evangelica*, 305, 311
—*In Praise of Constantine*, 372
—*Praeparatio Evangelica*, 249–52, 256, 295, 305; composition of, 307; descent in, 310–11; Judaism in, 311, 312; Julian's response to, 253, 305, 315–16, 320; pagan learning in, 318; sacrifice in, 310; tripartite theology of, 310; use of *Cratylus*, 393
Eusebius (bishop of Nicomedia and Constantinople), 34, 50; and Constantine, 32, 33; at Constantius's court, 243; at Council of Antioch, 38–39; death of, 40; Julian's studies with, 90; on *ousia*, 37, 38
Eusebius (bishop of Vercelli), 43, 150
Eusebius (eunuch), 77
Eusebius of Myndus (philosopher): Julian's studies with, 92; on *logos*, 95
Eustathius (bishop of Sebaste), 55, 68; asceticism of, 205, 223–24; Basil of Caesarea and, 220n21, 474; feeding of poor, 226; homoiousian views of, 148, 204; monastic supporters of, 204, 209; philosophical life of, 209, 226
Eustathius (philosopher): embassy to Shapur, 96, 107; at Julian's court, 106–7
Eustochius (rhetorician), 25, 151
Euthalius (deacon), 207–12
Eutropius: on Antoninus Pius, 457n83; on Jovian, 438n15
Euzoius (bishop of Antioch), 22, 55, 238, 278–80; homoianism of, 280

faith, unquestioning, 391
fatherhood, medical concept of, 196
fathers: sons' care of, 191; sons' *mimēsis* of, 197–98
father-son relationship: anthropology of, 195; conflict in, 192; declamations on, 198n64; discipline in, 194–95, 198–99; educational aspects of, 197–98; in Gregory's *Oration 2*, 183–200; masculinity in, 196–97; medical concepts of, 196–97; mutual obligations in, 199; nurturing in, 197; in *Romanitas*, 191; socialization in, 197; sons as fathers in, 196–200; sons like fathers in, 190–96; tyranny in, 187–90, 194
Fauth, W., 293n95
festivals, public: at Antioch, 328; Christian, 486; following Julian's death, 463
Flavian dynasty: immorality of, 123; Julian's relationship to, 76, 114, 286n68, 289, 292, 365–71; murdered, 33; Procopius and, 470
Flavius Claudius Julianus. *See* Julian, Emperor
Flavius Sallustius, 284
foreigners. *See allotrioi*
formulation of Constantinople, 44–50, 186; Eastern bishops and, 49, 50, 55–57; homoian signers of, 228; homoiousian support for, 149; opposition to, 53–59; Valens's support for, 473; Western bishops and, 47–48, 54, 63
Foussard, J.-C., 119n112
free will (*autoexousios*), 169, 170, 171, 179
funerals, daytime, 456n81, 457

Galen: on inner/outer connection, 173; on physician-philosophers, 171n88; *On Semen*, 196n54
Galileans (Christians), 110, 111, 117; anti-Christian topos of, 112n94; desertion of *oikeiōsis*, 485; exclusion from Roman *oikoumenē*, 143; Julian on, 151, 272, 301, 437; *philanthrōpia* of, 325. *See also* Christians
Gallus (Cybele myth). *See* Attis
Gallus (river), 129
Gallus Caesar: and Aetius, 235–36; Constantius and, 77, 367, 368, 369; downfall of, 78n69; elevation as Caesar, 442; in *Epistle to the Athenians*, 77, 78, 79–80; execution of, 30, 236; exile of, 62; at Macellum, 368–69; rule of Roman East, 29–30; temper of, 368n110; and Theophilus the Indian, 243–44
Gangra: bishops' assembly at, 205; zealots of, 209
Gautier, Francis, 215n5, 223, 339n13, 431n172
Gaza, anti-Christian violence in, 357
genealogies, literary, 469
generative realm, and material realm, 125, 126
George (bishop of Alexandria), 43, 44–45, 47, 149; and Aetius, 244n124; and Constantius, 374n130; debate with Meletius, 108; Julian's studies with, 90; library of, 301–2, 305; murder of, 357
Germinius (bishop of Sirmium), 43

Gleason, Maud, 196; on *Misopogon*, 328
God: *agraphos*, 389; creation of inventors, 394; design for Julian, 338, 365, 368–69, 371, 373–74, 406, 461; *dynamis* of, 245, 256; *energeia* of, 244, 245; as First Cause, 234, 260, 261, 262, 295, 411, 430; incomprehensibility of, 405, 408–9, 412; Israel's rebelliousness against, 428; of Moses, 313, 314–16; names for, 246; *philanthrōpia* of, 338; Platonic assimilation to, 414n115; transcendence of, 52, 408, 425; unbegotten essence of, 245, 246–47, 254, 255–56, 261, 317, 396, 400, 407, 410, 430; will of, 258. *See also* the divine
gods, Greco-Roman: *agalmata* of, 324; appropriate veneration of, 378; communication with humans, 125; creative, 314; in *Epistle to the Athenians*, 64, 65, 66, 77, 78–80; Heraclius's rejection of, 111; hierarchy of, 378; influence after Constantine, 2, 13; Julian's relationship with, 66, 286; language of, 385n29; *logoi* of, 349; names of, 248, 251, 315n180, 393n55; naming by, 399n73, 427n160; need for reverence, 325n219; *noeric*, 131, 314; *noetic*, 314; *oikeiōsis* with, 327; origin of, 304; *philanthrōpia* of, 325, 326; role in philosophical life, 87; role in *Romanitas*, 10–11; sacrificial practices for, 392; statues of, 123–25, 135, 249–54, 276, 277, 399, 485; theatrical representations of, 351; unifying force of, 437
Golden Verses, 391, 407
the Good: choice in, 169, 170; Neoplatonists' performance of, 104; Plato on, 290, 294–95
Gorgonia (sister of Gregory), *sōphrosynē* of, 219
Goulet, R., 303n132
governance: Aristotelian, 161; by Christian elites, 465; Christian Roman, 338, 380, 461–62; classical topoi of, 161; competing visions of, 480; good versus tyrannical, 189; in Greek philosophy, 2–3; in Gregory's *Oration 4*, 344; normative texts for, 480; by the pious, 347; Platonic, 161; role of Trinity in, 476; of Roman *oikoumenē*, 480–83
Gratian, Emperor: Christians under, 404n91
Great Goddess. *See* Cybele; Mother of the Gods
Greek language: Christians' exclusion from, 387–88, 390, 392; common use of, 394, 395; Gregory on, 387–88; identity with Greek religion, 391; Julian's possession of, 392–93, 397, 401, 410; Julian's syllogisms concerning, 392–93

Greekness: of Antioch, 271, 330; Christians abandonment of, 309; combination with *Romanitas*, 121, 122–23, 142, 289, 290–91; Gregory on, 337; Herodotus on, 378–79; as *logoi*, 296, 338, 391–92; in *paideia*, 330; of Roman *oikoumenē*, 142, 289, 290–91; in Roman universalism, 142
Gregory (bishop of Alexandria) 34, 39
Gregory of Nazianzus (bishop of Constantinople), 1, 3, 10; access to news, 68–69, 364; advice to emperors, 425; at Annesi, 27n46, 58, 153, 183; anti-Cynic topoi of, 117n107, 164, 232–33; appeal to homoians, 423, 425; on Arianism, 209, 228; at Arianzus, 21; asceticism of, 8, 9, 204, 209n103; in Athens, 23–27, 150n16, 151, 162–63; attitude toward homoians, 483n3; attitude toward Jews, 449–50; authorial strategy of, 364, 482; authority of, 8, 9, 264, 482, 483; avoidance of *ousia* terminology, 211; baptism of, 151n17, 217, 218n12; brothers of, 200, 201; in Caesarea in Cappadocia and Maritima, 21–23; and Caesarius's estate, 193n39, 194; character of, 5–6; Christianization of, 22, 24; Christian opponents of, 225; citation practice of, 468; civic pride of, 21; and community of Nazianzus, 187–90; competitiveness of, 25; composition methods, 154n30; concept of *oikeiōsis*, 262, 386, 418, 420; at Constantinople, 225; and Constantinopolitan elites, 472; on Constantius, 339, 366–70, 371–73, 423, 424–25, 470; correspondence, 151; correspondence with Basil of Caesarea, 27, 207, 208, 220, 221–23, 223n34; correspondence with Eusebius of Caesarea, 475; cosmology of, 215n3, 415, 416, 427; in crisis of 362–63, 219, 223, 224; date of birth, 21n18; denunciation of Eunomius, 11n33, 229–30, 233, 258, 259–62, 317–18, 405, 407–11; denunciation of Photinus, 233–35; discursive style of, 175; on the divine, 18, 176–81, 199, 200, 411–12, 462; divine calling of, 186–87, 217–19, 220; as divinely chosen mediator, 263–64, 485; on earthquakes, 460n92; ecclesiastical career of, 5–6; editions of, 6n19; education of, 21–26; *enkyklia paideia*, 175; episcopacy of Constantinople, 157; estates of, 21n19; on *eutaxia*, 483n3; exegetical method of, 403n87; family of, 21; father's demands on, 158; flight from Nazianzus, 148, 153–54, 159–60, 164; friendships at Nazianzus, 207–12; friendship with

Gregory of Nazianzus *(continued)*
　Basil of Caesarea, 24–26, 204, 205, 221–22, 342n26; friends in Athens, 25; funeral eulogies by, 50, 51, 191, 219, 341n19; on Greekness, 337; on Hercules, 114n101; historiographic identity of, 10, 27; in history of ideas, 9–14; homoiousian leanings of, 205; influence of, 4–5, 10, 177n107, 413, 487; initiation into philosophy, 217; innovations of, 156, 186, 202, 211, 225, 390, 413; installation at Constantinople, 405; invectives against Julian, 273, 422, 441n32; and Julian's accession, 67–69; on Julian's apostasy, 340, 389, 395, 417, 420; on Julian's death, 11, 337; Julian's impact on, 13, 60–61, 225; Julian's knowledge of, 466, 469; Julian's response to, 300; Julian's threat to, 469; knowledge of Julian, 61, 68–69, 343, 364; knowledge of Julian's writings, 341n22, 351, 467n115; knowledge of Origen, 22–23, 24; knowledge of Themistius, 226; *logoi* of, 163, 206–7, 269, 341, 349–50, 379; on Maccabean martyrs, 152–53, 341–42, 376; on Marc of Arethusa, 339; mastery of normative texts, 161–62; on Maximus the Cynic, 157; mediation for father, 203; meeting with Julian, 459; as Moses, 214; mother's influence on, 217–18; on nature of evil, 420n137; at Nazianzus, 26, 28, 49–50, 337n5; Nicene orthodoxy of, 11, 206, 228, 483n3; on *oikeiōsis pros theon*, 259–65, 269, 324, 413–22, 425–28; ordination of, 26, 58, 148, 151n17, 153n27, 206; *paideia* of, 341; *parrhēsia* of, 475; *patria potestas* over, 192–93, 194, 198n67, 200n69; persona of, 481–82; persuasive powers of, 326; philosophical family of, 219, 263; philosophical life of, 151, 153, 208–9, 215–28; philosophical retreat of, 168, 199, 216, 218, 219, 223, 239, 260, 314n19; as physician of soul, 213; poems of, 157, 216, 487; as political philosopher, 263, 362, 365, 376, 477; on polytheism, 234, 235; as presbyter, 9, 151n17; prestige among peers, 9; in public life, 188, 220; refusal of office, 157, 158–63, 183, 201; refusal of Sasima episcopacy, 157, 158–63, 183, 201; relationship with father, 9, 183–200, 263, 264; relationship with mother, 188; retirement of, 5–6, 21, 216, 218, 219, 223; rhetorical activities of, 26, 28, 150–52, 206–7, 208; sacred descent of, 218–19, 263–64; scholarship on, 4–5, 13; on "second philosophy," 103;

self-presentation of, 5, 6, 483n4; shipwreck survival, 216–17, 220; social status of, 8, 10; Stoic influences on, 414; submission to authority, 190, 199; teachers of, 23, 163; on Themistius, 226; on *theōsis*, 177, 262n173, 339, 377, 386, 413–22, 484; on true and false philosophers, 182–83; understanding of *mimēsis*, 263n176; use of Aristotle, 407n99; use of Plato, 407n99; use of Plotinus, 295n103; use of syllogism, 409; use of tachygraphs, 154n30; and Valens, 157n36, 472, 473; view of baptism, 217–18; vision of Rome, 486–87; warrior metaphors of, 212, 214, 222–23, 263, 340; writings on Julian, 269–70; on zealots, 204, 209
—*Ad Vitalianus*, 192
—*De vita sua*, 26, 194, 206
—*Epistle 1*, 222
—*Epistle 8*, 222
—*Epistle 10 to Candidianus*, 151; *logoi* in, 341
—*Epistle 17*, 475
—*Epistle 18*, 475
—*Epistle 58*, 208
—*Orations*, 4; audience of, 161, 208; circulation of, 154; composition of, 156n35; engagement with Julian, 60; *epinikia* of, 340; Eunomian controversies in, 230; history in, 338–39; manuscript tradition of, 154n30; as *panēgyrismos*, 340; as performance pieces, 339–40, 348; philosophical life in, 161; relationship with father in, 188; rhetorical genres of, 155n30
—*Oration 1*, 201–2; Day of Resurrection in, 154n29, 181; Trinity in, 211
—*Oration 2 Apology for His Flight to Pontus*, 7, 17–19, 58, 59; anti-Cynic topoi of, 259; as *apologētikos logos*, 159; Arius in, 184, 185, 206, 228; art of persuasion in, 171, 174–75; audience of, 154, 163; calligrapher metaphor of, 211–12; care of self in, 179; Christian civil war in, 228; Christian leadership in, 153–81, 187, 189–90, 232, 259; codes of aptitude in, 161, 164, 166–81; composition of, 153n27, 164, 239; cosmos in, 215n3; disobedience in, 160; divine calling in, 217–19; editions of, 154; engagement with Christological debates, 258; father-son relationships in, 183–200; flight from Nazianzus in, 153–54, 159–60, 164; Julian in, 60, 151, 154; kinship with the divine in, 176–81, 199, 200; martyrdom in, 342; Moses in, 214; myth in, 384n25;

oikeiōsis pros theon in, 259–65, 269, 414, 415; *paideia* in, 159–60; pastoral aspects of, 165, 175; *patria potestas* in, 192–94; Paul in, 260; *pharmakeia* in, 169, 170, 172–76, 181; *philochristoi* in, 185; *philopatores* in, 185; philosophical life in, 153–65, 216, 217; philosophical retreat in, 160–62, 165, 168, 170, 206; physician metaphors in, 166–76, 180–81, 200; political theory in, 161, 188–89; priesthood in, 262; purpose of, 181; refusal of office in, 158–63; response to Eunomius, 258, 259–62, 317–18; on ridicule of Christians, 346n36; Sabellius in, 184, 185, 206; *sōphrosynē* in, 174–75; soul in, 166–76, 181, 212; structure of, 165n69; teachers in, 232; Trinity in, 183, 184–87, 210, 231–33, 297, 422; uneducated philosophers in, 164, 259–60; use of Aristotle, 165; zealots in, 211

—*Oration 3*: Gregory's friends in, 210, 211; Trinity in, 211

—*Oration 4 Against Julian*, 231, 265, 344–65; agora in, 353–55; allegory in, 380–87; apostasy in, 389, 395, 417, 420; army in, 358–59, 419; audience of, 344, 374, 422–23, 477; Christian emperors in, 373; Christian reconciliation in, 423; civil war in, 214; composition of, 342–43, 396; Constantius in, 366–70, 371–73, 423, 424–25; countervision for Rome, 365–66; *Cratylus* in, 393–96; *epinikion* of, 344, 345, 388–89, 423; Eunomius in, 371; God's Providence in, 461; Greek language in, 387–88, 401; Gregory's theology in, 230; *Hellēnikos* in, 380; homoian aspects of, 423; homonyms in, 392, 397; image worship in, 354–55; imperial portraits in, 448; invective of, 346, 366, 468; inventors in, 401; Julian's *asebeia* in, 380; Julian's illegitimacy in, 354–57, 377; Julian's life in, 343n28, 346; Julian's philosophy in, 368–69, 376, 391; Julian's plagiarism in, 381–82; language theory in, 389–93, 396, 400–401; law in, 355–58; and Libanius's writings, 442, 445–46; *logoi* in, 349–50; *Logos* in, 348; Marc of Arethusa in, 375; martyrdom in, 342, 461n95; Maximus of Ephesus in, 370; and *Misopogon*, 468; myth in, 381–87; normative texts in, 161; *oikeiōsis* in, 386, 418, 420; *oikoumenē* in, 361–62; *paideia* in, 349–50; persecution in, 364–65; as philippic, 341; philosopher-leader in, 341; philosophical life in, 363; political philosophy in, 362, 365, 376; public governance in, 344; relationship to *Oration 5*, 446, 477; relationship to *Oration 6*, 425–26; rhetorical strategies of, 370n116; Roman Empire in, 355–65; *Romanitas* in, 393–96; sacrifice in, 348, 349, 362–63; statues in, 385; as *stēlographia*, 345, 346–48, 355, 389; theater in, 348–53, 486; themes of, 345, 461n95; theodicy in, 366; *theōsis* in, 177, 386, 413–22, 484; Trinity in, 344, 349, 475–76; true and false enemies in, 359–65

—*Oration 5 Against Julian*, 156, 265, 445–64; audience of, 344, 469–70, 472, 474, 477; Basil's signing of, 465, 466, 474, 475; Christian emperors in, 446; composition of, 342–43, 434; conclusion of, 465, 467–72, 471; Constantius in, 456, 472–75; God's Providence in, 461–62; Jews in, 448–50; Jovian in, 455–56; Julian's afterlife in, 347; Julian's *apotheōsis* in, 446; Julian's character in, 446, 458–60; Julian's death in, 343n28, 454–57; and Libanius's writings, 445, 470; *Misopogon* and, 466–69, 471; normative texts in, 161; offenses against the divine in, 462; opening of, 433–34; Persian campaign in, 446, 452–54; as philippic, 341; political issues of, 434–35; public festivals in, 463–64; relationship to *Oration 4*, 446, 477; revenge in, 462–63, 465; as *stēlographia*, 345; Temple of Jerusalem in, 446, 447–51, 457; themes of, 469–70; theology of, 472, 476; Trinity in, 475–76; victory hymn in, 461n95;

—*Oration 6 On Peace*, 156, 341n19, 422–32; Christian discord in, 428; cosmos in, 427; dual ethics in, 428; *eusebeia* in, 210; ideal philosopher in, 459; Israel's revolt in, 428; *koinōnia* in, 201; *oikeiōsis pros theon* in, 425–28; *paideia* in, 429–32; philosophical life in, 429–32; relationship to *Oration 4*, 425–26; Rufinus's translation of, 203; theological significance of, 432; Trinity in, 202–3, 426–30; zealots in, 204

—*Oration 15 In Praise of the Maccabees*, 152–53, 376, 466; Julian in, 180

—*Oration 20 On Theology and the Installation of Bishops*, 157

—*Oration 21*, 157; Constantius in, 375n132

—*Oration 24*, 157

—*Oration 25*, Constantius in, 375n132

—*Oration 42*, 157

—*Oration 43*, 150, 157

—*Theological Orations (Orations 27–31)*, 229–30, 403–15; allegory in, 412–13; Christian

Gregory of Nazianzus
—*Theological Orations (continued)*
civil war in, 406; Christ's divinity in, 405; composition of, 404; correct *logoi* in, 406; the divine in, 411–12; divinity of Spirit in, 405; Eunomius in, 261, 404, 405, 407–10, 411; God's essence in, 411; homoiousians in, 404; homonyms in, 409–10; incomprehensibility of God in, 405, 408–9, 412; incorrect *paideia* in, 411; law in, 412; Moses in, 411–12; names in, 409; *oikeiōsis pros theon*, 413–22; pagan symbols in, 411n108; philosophical life in, 412; practical theology in, 406; theological disputes in, 405–6; theory of language in, 409, 430n170; *theōsis* in, 262n173; Trinity in, 403, 408, 410–11

Gregory of Nazianzus the Elder, 9, 42, 50–53; as Abraham, 183, 187–90, 202, 218–19; advisors of, 52–53; appointment as bishop, 50; birth date, 50n126; civic rank of, 21, 26, 51; conversion of, 51, 52; death of, 187; demands on Gregory, 158; embodiment of priesthood, 187; *eusebeia* of, 202; and Eusebius of Caesarea in Cappadocia, 149n10; family obedience to, 199–200; fatherly tyranny of, 187, 190, 194; Gregory's mediation for, 203; *haplotēs* of, 202, 349; and homoianism, 201, 210; under Julian, 210; marriage of, 50; *megalopsychia* of, 200, 202, 376; opponents of, 199, 201–12, 264, 374, 423; opposition to Julian, 148n2, 376; *philanthrōpia* of, 375; *philoteknia* of, 200; scholarly portrayals of, 187–88; signing of formulation of Constantinople, 49n124, 50, 52, 56, 58, 148, 150, 154, 201, 374; sons' reconciliation with, 201; worship of *Theos Hypsistos*, 50

Gregory of Nyssa, 4, 178n111; on Aetius, 241; on Eunomius, 229n59, 230, 241–42, 254n156; on material world, 484n5; on *Theos Hypsistos*, 51; use of *Cratylus*, 254n156; use of Plotinus, 295n103

Gregory the Great, on the priesthood, 17

Gurtler, Gary M., 179

Hadrian, Emperor: Jewish policy of, 316n184
Hagia Sophia, dedication of, 49, 53
Heather, Peter, 481
Hecate-Semele, 370, in theurgic cosmology, 130n138, 132n144
Hecebolius (rhetor), 90
Helena (wife of Julian), 30; death of, 110

Helios: as Apollo Musagetes, 298; benefits to mankind, 290; creative capacity of, 293, 317, 335; as Demiurge, 129, 294n98, 299; *energeia* of, 297; Julian's cult of, 89, 114–16, 117; manifestations of, 291; as mediator with the divine, 288, 293–99; as middle cosmos, 296–97, 298, 299; as second king, 297; as Third Creator, 132; threefold activity of, 297–99, 300. *See also* Zeus-Helios

Helladius (brother of Eulalius), 207n98
Hellenism, inheritors of, 11. *See also* Greekness
Hellenius (*peraequator*, friend of Gregory), 25, 207, 208
Hera, as power of air, 252n150
Heraclides Ponticus, 418n137
Heraclius (Cynic), 102; analogy of Zeus and Pan, 108–10, 111, 114; *parrhēsia* of, 108, 110, 112; rejection of gods, 111
Hercules, as philosopher-king, 114n101, 286
Hermogenes, Gregory's use of, 407n99
Hermogenes (*magister equitum*), 40
Herodotus: on Greekness, 378–79; Gregory's use of, 454, 456
Hesiod, myths of, 383
hēsychazōn. *See* retreat, philosophical
heterousians, 228–29
Hierocles (Stoic philosopher), 178, 391n49
Hilary (bishop of Poitiers), 43; and formulation of Constantine, 54; on Julian, 65n18
Himerius (rhetorician), 23; Asianic style of, 242n114; at Constantinople, 96; Gregory's studies with, 163; at Julian's court, 68; Julian's studies with, 91; on philosophical retreat, 163n60; pride in native city, 25n37
Hippocratic Corpus, inner/outer connection in, 173
Hippolytus of Rome, *Refutation of All Heresies*, 130n140
Homer: Gregory's use of, 433–34, 462, 465–66; myths of, 383, 384
homoians, 55; of Antioch, 278, 279, 280, 281; at Constantius's court, 243; differences among, 228–29; Gregory's appeal to, 423, 425; Gregory's attitude toward, 229, 483n3; as heretics, 202; Jovian and, 424; under Julian, 318, 376; martyrs, 376n140; of Nazianzus, 183; opposition to Photinus, 234; signing of formulation of Constantinople, 228; support for Eudoxius, 236. *See also* Arianism; formulation of Constantinople

homoiousians, 148–50; demise of, 239; in

INDEX   541

Gregory's *Theological Orations*, 404; Jovian and, 424; local synods of, 475n140; monks, 204; of Nazianzus, 183
homonyms: *dynamis* of, 392, 397; Eunomius' use of, 409; Gregory on, 392, 397, 409–10; Julian's use of, 397
Household, 68, 99, 113, 154, 222n29, 236, 242, 361, 415, 428, 484,
humanity: kinship with the divine, 105, 127, 128, 130, 138, 170, 176–81; *koinōnia* of, 178
hymns: compositional guidelines for, 118n110; *physikoi*, 288n77
hypostaseis: *allotrioi*, 184; banning of term, 261n171; bishops' debates concerning, 38, 39, 45, 48, 148–49; Julian on, 126, 127–28, 132, 133; Stoic use of, 261n171; of Trinity, 184–86, 211, 261, 297, 410, 429

Iambe (inventor of poetry), 394
Iamblichus: cosmology of, 295–96; disciples of, 92, 93, 94, 95; on the divine, 94, 249, 485; Julian's use of, 125n124, 292, 293, 294, 332, 333; on matter, 133n146; on retreat and participation, 93–94; on ritual, 312n168; on sacrifice, 284; on theurgy, 125n123.
—Works: *Commentary on the Chaldean Oracles*, 125, 132; *Commentary on Alcibiades*, 295–96; *Ignatian Epistles*, 242n116
innovation: in Christianity, 121–22; correct and incorrect, 122, 486; Gregory's, 156, 186, 202, 211, 225, 390, 413; John Lydus on, 102n62; in late Roman antiquity, 10; Plato's, 101; Roman elites on, 122; Themistius's, 101–2; threat to *oikoumenē*, 123
invective (genre), 346
inventors, 396; Gregory on, 401; of language, 398, 401; traditions concerning, 394–95
Isaac, Rabbi, 70n40
Iser, Wolfgang, 465
Isis, cult of, 89

Jerusalem, legal status of, 449. *See also* Temple at Jerusalem
Jews: of Antioch, 449n59; Gregory's attitude toward, 449–50; Hadrian's policy on, 316n184; John Chrysostom and, 450; Julian and, 447–49, 451; rebelliousness against God, 428
John Chrysostom: attitude toward Jews, 450; on Babylas, 277, 278, 279, 402; Gregory's influence on, 17

John Lydus, 447; on innovation, 102n62
John of Damascus, 413
Johnson, Aaron, 372
John the Baptist, Julian on, 316–17, 318
Jovian, Emperor: advisors of, 436, 437, 445n45; attitude toward religion, 436–38; coinage of, 336–37; death of, 425; edict on religion, 424; *eusebeia* of, 455, 458; Gregory on, 455–56, 470; and homoians, 424, 438; legitimacy of, 435–36, 458, 471; Themistius's *Hypatikos* for, 435–39; ties to Constantius, 423; treaty with Shapur II, 337, 340, 434, 436, 439, 444, 454, 458
Jovinus (military officer), 68
Judaism: Eusebius on, 311, 312; Julian on, 304; Plato's borrowings from, 311, 312
Julian (bishop of Cilicia), *Commentary on Job*, 241, 242–43
Julian (tax assessor), 25
Julian Constantius, *comes* (uncle of Julian, Emperor), 33, 137, 163n60, 275
Julian of Eclanum, 18n3
Julian, Emperor: known as the Apostate, 1; access to, 66; acquaintance with Gregory, 469; address to Eusebia, 61; administration of, 4, 89, 360n88, 459; advance on Constantinople, 63–64; *adventus* into cities, 270; *adventus* into Constantinople, 88–89; advisors of, 105, 459; anti-Cynic *topoi* of, 109n84, 324; in Antioch, 265, 269, 270–72, 282, 337; Antiochene writings of, 272, 273; and Antioch famine, 273–75; *apotheōsis* of, 435, 446, 455–57; army under, 358–59, 419; asceticism of, 467; *asebeia* of, 380; *askēsis* of, 332; at Athens, 69, 77n68; attitude toward *logoi*, 265, 348–49, 381, 387, 390–91, 422, 442; as Augustus, 53–54, 442; building projects of, 450–51; and burning of temple, 277–78; as Caesar, 30, 43, 49, 61, 74n57, 77; at Caesarea, 137; and Caesareans, 149, 357; campaigns as Caesar, 54, 63, 71, 442; and causality, 334; celebration of Saturnalia, 285; Christian audience of, 334; and Christian civil war, 269; Christian elites under, 60, 66–67, 87, 107, 154; and Christian observances, 65, 115; and Christians of Antioch, 278; Christians under, 321, 326, 340, 355–64, 390, 417, 437, 486; Christian upbringing of, 366; on Christ's humanity, 421; churches under, 356–57; citation practice of, 468; civil discord under, 417, 420; civilizing mission to Persia,

542   INDEX

Julian, Emperor *(continued)*
416; coinage of, 65, 66, 70, 284–85; conception of Roman *oikoumenē*, 287, 289, 292, 332, 335; concepts of leadership, 71–87; in Constantinople, 270, 271n5; and Constantinopolitan senate, 106; and Constantius, 53, 77–78, 79, 80, 365–77, 418; and Constantius's Persian campaign, 53; conversion to paganism, 369n113, 370n115; correspondence of, 69–70, 71, 73–75; correspondence with Julian Constantius, 137; cosmology of, 125–27, 132n143, 295–300, 312, 324n218, 334, 484; court of, 57–58, 66–67, 68, 442; crisis of *koinōnia* under, 182; cult of Helios, 89, 114–16, 117; death of, 156, 316, 332, 336, 423, 443–44, 454–57; death of father, 116; desire for *oikeiōsis pros theon,* 332; dissimulation by, 352–53, 368–69, 374, 381; divine mandate of, 142, 270, 271, 286–327; as divine punishment, 338, 365, 373–74, 406, 461; dynastic legitimacy of, 76, 77, 78, 79, 88n1, 365, 435, 438, 439, 442; and dynastic succession, 78n70; edict on clergy, 57; edict on grain, 274, 275n21; edicts on Galileans, 301; edicts on teachers, 139–43, 148, 149n7, 151, 152, 227, 269, 318, 325n220, 342n27, 357, 383n16, 387n36; effect on *oikeiōsis pros theon,* 362; embodiment of *imperium Romanum*, 270; *enkrateia* of, 110; in Ephesus, 92; *eudaimonia* of, 330; *eugeneia* of, 366; *eusebeia* of, 287; and Eusebius of Caesarea in Cappadocia, 149; executions under, 64; exegetical method of, 403n85; exile of, 62, 368; fourth consulate of, 282, 292, 328; funeral of, 454, 456–57; God's design for, 338, 365, 368–69, 371, 373–74; Gregory's knowledge of, 61, 68–69, 343, 364; in Gregory's orations, 337–44; Gregory the Elder under, 210; as guardian of law, 355–58; historiography of, 10, 61, 338–39, 340; in history of ideas, 9–14; as *histrio,* 455; impact on Gregory, 13, 60–61, 225; on imperial correspondence, 69; imperial law under, 355–58, 359–60; initiation into cults, 121n115, 217; innovations of, 332, 333, 335; inscriptions of, 70–71, 293; intent toward Christians, 321, 326; invention of pagan church, 382; invitation to Basil of Caesarea, 57, 69, 466n113; and Jews, 447–49, 451; knowledge of Aristotle's *Politics,* 84n92; knowledge of Basil of Caesarea, 466; knowledge of Celsus, 305n142; knowledge of Christological debates, 60, 317, 318; knowledge of Eusebius of Caesarea, 311n166; knowledge of Gregory, 466; knowledge of Porphyry, 113n98, 250n140, 304, 307n152; knowledge of Sabellian controversy, 317; knowledge of scripture, 316; knowledge of theological debates, 12n34; leadership style, 66; legacy of, 435, 444–45; as legislator, 378; loyalty to Constantius, 80; on Lutetia, 330n243; at Macellum, 69, 91, 368–69, 442; malleability of, 448, 454, 459; on Marcus Aurelius, 329; marriage to Helena, 30; on martyrdom, 331, 359n85, 360, 364–65, 461n95; mausoleum of, 438–39, 456; Maximus's advice to, 105; memorialization of, 434, 477; as mime, 340; misreading of portents, 446, 448–49, 450, 457–58; Mithraism of, 291n89; mother's estate, 78; as *mystagōgos,* 416; at Naissus, 64, 67, 75; at Nazianzus, 147–48, 269; as new Hercules, 285, 286; in Nicene sources, 281; in Nicomedia, 92; official images of, 355n71, 358, 444; open-mindedness of, 107; orations on philosophical life, 106; orations to Cynics, 67, 136–39, 164; origin myth of, 117, 136, 142, 285, 289, 292, 301, 390n46, 455; on *paideia,* 86, 141; *paideia* of, 283, 361; panegyrics to Constantius, 30, 61, 63, 73, 77n68, 78, 301, 367; on *parrhēsia,* 108; in Pergamon, 92; Persian campaign of, 136–37, 147, 271–72, 273, 281–86, 321, 359–60, 443–44, 452–54, 457; Persian emissaries to, 453; *philanthrōpia* of, 306, 322, 359, 372n122, 416; as philosopher, 70–71, 289; as philosopher-king, 142, 305, 327–35, 347, 459, 485; philosophical circles of, 90–107; on philosophical labor, 177; philosophical life of, 71, 74–75, 79, 89, 90–106, 227, 292, 332, 432; as *philostratiōtēs,* 358; physiognomy of, 459–60; plagiarization of Christianity, 327, 381–82; political program of, 359–62; as *pontifex maximus,* 118, 123, 273–81, 283, 284, 321, 331–32, 416; practice of *philia,* 107; practice of sacrifice, 65, 89, 284, 287n69, 348, 349, 362–63, 438, 458n88, 461n95, 485; proclamations, 70; as public enemy, 56, 62n4; purity of, 270; reading of omens, 282; reception in the West, 3n5; reform of *cursus publicus,* 360, 442; relationship to Flavian dynasty, 76, 114, 285, 286n68, 289, 292, 365–71; relationship with bishops, 65, 148, 151, 238–39; relation-

ship with gods, 286; reliance on Providence, 385n27; reorganizations under, 64, 66–67, 86–87, 89–90, 360, 442; Roman *oikoumenē* under, 270, 361–62; on Roman universalism, 11, 327–35; scholarship on, 3–4, 12–13; on scripture, 402; security of Empire under, 359–62; self-presentation of, 66, 468, 483n4; sex life of, 110n86; Shapur II's advances to, 283; and shrine of Mamas, 368, 450–51; sole rulership of, 65, 75, 106; on statues, 123–25, 135, 249, 277, 324–25, 385; study of Neoplatonism, 92; submission to law, 329n239; successors of, 458; support for Aetius, 259, 318; support for Eunomius, 259, 318; teachers of, 69, 83, 91–92, 95, 139n168, 244n124; and Temple of Jerusalem, 273n10, 447–51, 457; theatricality of, 348–55, 361, 382–83, 432, 455; Themistius on, 107n76; Thracian origin of, 394; as tool of God, 337, 350; tripartite cosmology of, 297–99, 300, 324n218; understanding of divine will, 271; understanding of *Romanitas*, 119; use of allegory, 402, 417; use of imperial portraits, 354; use of oracles, 292n89; victory at Strasbourg, 63; vision of Rome, 10, 332; Western reception of, 340n16; wounding of, 454–55; on zealots, 209
—*Against the Galileans*, 287, 303–6, 312–21; audience of, 319; baptism in, 319; censoring of, 303; Christian illegitimacy in, 306; Christ in, 317, 318, 319–20; composition of, 300–301; Constantius in, 366; cosmology of, 312; Demiurge in, 313, 314, 315; descent narrative of, 312; Diodore of Tarsus in, 401; engagement with Christian apologias, 312–21; ethnicity in, 250, 314–15; exegesis of, 315; fragments of, 303, 320; God of Moses in, 447; Greek learning in, 349; Gregory's response to, 428; John the Baptist in, 316–17, 318; Judaism in, 304, 311n166; *logoi* in, 442; Moses in, 313–14, 315, 316; myth in, 312–13, 317; *oikeiōsis* in, 323; origin of gods in, 304; pagan-Christian relations in, 278; Photinus in, 233; plan of, 303–4; *Praeparatio Evangelica*'s influence, 307n151; *Pronoia* in, 315; and Quellenkritik, 302; refutations of, 302–3, 306; response to Eusebius in, 253, 305, 315–16, 320; sacrifice in, 319; salvation in, 318; salvation of *koina* in, 306; Theodore's rebuttal of, 305n146, 402, 403; title of, 300n121; veneration of tombs in, 319
—*Bellum Gallicum*, 441n31, 442

—*Caesars*, 272; Augustus in, 361; Christ in, 285–86; Constantius in, 285, 371; date of, 286n68; Gregory's response to, 428
—*Epistle 49*, 249
—*Epistle 54*, 301n123
—*Epistle 61 The Law Regarding Teachers*, 139–43; manuscript tradition of, 140n169
—*Epistle 84 To Arsacius*, 326
—*Epistle 89*, 326; human-divine relations in, 323n212
—*Epistle 98*, 441n31
—*Epistle to the Athenians*, 30n59, 61–64, 77–80, 119, 442; as *apologētikos logos*, 62, 75–76, 159; Athens in, 75, 76, 79; Constantius in, 62, 77–80, 331, 366; declaration of intent in, 75; *dialektikon* of, 76–77; exile in, 368; Gallus in, 77, 78, 79–80; gods in, 64, 65, 66, 77, 78–80; Libanius on, 283n55; military conditions in, 73; military in, 358; philosophical retreat in, 160–61; publication of, 61n1; *recusatio* in, 79, 109; statue worship in, 354
—*Epistle to Themistius*, 64n13, 66, 80–87, 105; Constantius in, 86; knowledge of God in, 85; modern philosophers on, 109n84; *paideia* in, 86; philosophical life in, 83–86, 106
—*Epistle to the Priest Theodorus*, 124, 290n83, 321–27; date of, 321n203; kinship in, 416; "Know Thyself" in, 324; moral philosophy of, 323; *oikeiōsis pros theon* in, 323, 326; *philanthrōpia* in, 322–23, 324–25; priesthood in, 321, 325; statues in, 324–25; Temple of Jerusalem in, 447
—*Hymn to King Helios*, 272, 286–99, 313, 320, 344; creative process in, 298, 395; dedication of, 287; First Cause in, 294–95, 298, 299, 300; Greek language in, 395; intelligent/intelligible cosmos in, 295–97; mixture of Greece and Rome in, 291; *oikeiōsis* in, 416; the One in, 294; *ousia* in, 288; patron-client terminology of, 289n79; political philosophy of, 293–94; prior cause in, 410; Roman *oikoumenē* in, 287; scholarly treatment of, 289n78; structure of, 288n75, 293; use of Iamblichus, 292, 293, 294, 296; use of Plato, 290, 291, 294–95, 296; Zeus-Helios in, 288–97
—*Misopogon*, 272, 275, 315, 462; Antioch in, 327–31, 362, 384; *eirōnia* of, 330; festivals in, 463; Gregory's knowledge of, 351, 466–69; and Gregory's *Oration 5*, 471; homoian references in, 280; imperial *sōphrosynē* in, 329–30; invective in, 468; Libanius on, 443;

544 INDEX

Julian, Emperor
—*Misopogon (continued)*
  public posting of, 347; temple fire in, 277; theater in, 352; use of Plato, 329
—*Oration 5 Hymn to the Mother of the Gods*, 287, 344; Attis myth in, 118–36; causal language of, 127–31; cosmology of, 125–27; galaxy in, 129–30; Helios in, 132–33; Intellect in, 252n150; intent of, 134; Libanius on, 442; Mother of the Gods in, 131–34, 301; *oikeiōsis* in, 416; *ousia* in, 120; purification in, 417n123; ritual in, 134–36; *Romanitas* in, 119; soul in, 128–29; sources for, 125n124; statues in, 123–25, 135, 249, 324; symbols of the divine in, 134–36; themes of, 119; theurgy in, 124; universal divinity in, 120–21
—*Oration 6 Against the Uneducated Cynics*, 108n81, 136–39, 176–77, 178; "Know Thyself" in, 176; Libanius on, 442; *ousia* in, 137; philosophical life in, 117, 138; sources for, 138n165
—*Oration 7 Against the Cynic Heraclius*, 106–18, 119, 285, 384; Christianity in, 111–14; composition of, 117n107; divine mysteries in, 113–14; oracles in, 310; origin myth of, 117, 136; parts of philosophy in, 113; philosophical retreat in, 111; sacred myths in, 111–14, 117; sacred symbols in, 116–18; sources of, 113n98; theurgy in, 116–18; true philosophers in, 117; Zeus-Helios in, 114–16, 117
—*Oration 8 Consolation to Himself*, 111n90
Julius (bishop of Rome), 34–35

Kaldellis, A, 339n11
Kalendae Ianuariae, celebrations of, 282n53
Kelly, Gavin, 460
Kerferd, G. B., 415
"Know Thyself" (maxim), 110; Julian on, 137, 176, 324; Porphyry on, 93n23
Koinon/koina
Kronos, myth of, 383, 387n34
Kurmann, Alois, 345

labor: classical view of, 72; philosophical, 177
Lampsacus, council of (364), 230, 244n125, 473, 474
language: Basil of Caesarea on, 396, 398n68; common use of, 394; divine origin of, 396–401; human and divine, 393; inventors of, 398, 401. *See also* Greek language
language theory: Eunomius's, 255n157, 262, 400, 409, 430n160; Gregory's, 389–93, 396, 400–401, 409, 430n170; modern, 399n68; Stoic, 398n71
law: emperors' embodiment of, 355–56; Julian's submission to, 329n239; written and divine, 389
leadership: Aristotelian, 171; classical topoi of, 161; Platonic, 171; preparation for, 189. *See also* rulers, ideal
leadership, Christian: aptitude for, 161, 164, 166–81; characteristics of, 166; dual ethics of, 167; foreign, 56, 150, 189, 190, 199, 201; in Gregory's *Oration 2*, 153–81, 187, 189–90, 232, 259; Gregory's orations on, 157; kinship with divinity, 167, 170; normative texts of, 161–62, 334, 480–81; as philosophical life, 155n32, 240, 262; responsibilities of, 165; sins of, 166
legitimacy: Jovian's, 435–36, 458, 471; Valens's, 434, 435, 465, 471, 475
legitimacy, dynastic: Julian's, 76, 77, 78, 79, 88n1, 365, 435, 438, 439, 442; versus philosophical, 166n70
leisure, philosophical, 71–73; Aristotelian, 81; Julian on, 84; Symmachus on, 74n59. *See also* retreat, philosophical
Le Nain de Tillemont, L.-S., 49n124
Lenski, Noel, 463
Leonas (*comes*), 46
Leontius (bishop of Caesarea), 51, 202; Aetius's study with, 235; and Eunomius, 236
Leyerle, Blake, 350
Libanius: access to Jovian, 441; on Antioch, 275, 330; on Caesarea, 22; citation practice of, 468; on cities' religious practices, 438n14; at Constantinople, 96; on Constantius, 445; correspondence with Basil of Caesarea, 26; on earthquakes, 460n92; on Jovian, 438, 444; and Julian's accession, 67, 68; on Julian's administration, 89, 360n88; on Julian's death, 336, 343; on Julian's legitimacy, 442; on Julian's mandate, 271; on Julian's *Oration 6*, 118n109; Julian's studies with, 91, 92; on Persian campaigns, 282; on philosophical retreat, 163n60; and Procopius, 446n48; on punishment of cities, 328n236; sources of, 443n36; on theater, 351; and Themistius, 97–98, 439n21; on zealots, 209
—*Oration 12 Hypaticus on the Emperor as Consul*, 282–83, 286, 452; audience of, 441; Julian's religious practice in, 284
—*Oration 17 Monody*, 343, 440–41, 443, 445,

452; composition of, 441; influence of, 442
—*Oration 18 Epitaphius,* 302, 441, 442–45, 446n47, 451; Gregory's response to, 458; Julian as savior in, 460; Julian's divinity in, 343; Persian campaign in, 453; sacrifice in, 463
—*Oration 59,* 372n121
Licinius, Emperor, victory over Maximinus Daia, 276
Lizzi, Rita, 160–61, 188
Lloyd, A. C., 120n114
logoi: as Christian, 379; Christian mistakes concerning, 349; divine creation of, 481; *dynamis* of, 389, 397–98; freedom of, 345, 388; of the gods, 349; Greekness as, 338, 391–92, 396; Gregory on, 163, 341, 349–50, 379; Gregory's practice of, 206–7; hermeneutic techniques of, 390, 408; as highest good, 388n38; Julian's attitude toward, 265, 348–49, 381, 387, 390–91, 422, 442; and *Logos,* 380; ownership of, 11, 390, 395; proper use of, 395; and Roman dominance, 378, 379; the sacred and, 348, 349, 378, 391, 396; teaching of, 387n36; theological implications of, 387–413; in understanding of Trinity, 349
Logos: application of Greek philosophy to, 405; Attis as, 126, 127, 131, 288, 289, 300; Christ as, 42, 127, 186, 233, 234, 261, 262, 341, 373; Constantius's service toward, 388; debates concerning, 36, 37; fostering of invention, 395; governing of soul, 173–74, 176; humanity of, 420–22; *logoi* and, 380; physical factors affecting, 173; and *Romanitas,* 393–96; the sacred as, 349, 351; Stoic concept of, 415; therapeutic, 174; of Trinity, 181
Long, A. A., 179n116
Lucian of Samosata: on Cynics, 138; on theater, 351. Works: *Council of the Gods,* 285, 286n68; *Peregrinus,* 202n77
Lucifer (bishop of Calaris), 43, 55, 281; anti-homoianism of, 150; opposition to Gregory the Elder, 56
Luckmann, Thomas, 483
Lugaresi, Leonardo, 69, 228n51, 341; on Constantius, 367n105; on Gregory's *Oration 5,* 343, 446n47, 450, 455n76, 463n104, 465n112; on *Misopogon,* 467–68; on theater, 351

Maccabean martyrs: Christianization of cult, 450n61; Gregory on, 152–53, 341–42, 376, 466

Macedonius (bishop of Constantinople), 40, 47; *ptōchotropheia* of, 226
Macrobius, 113n98
Magna mater, Roman cult of, 119. *See also* Attis; Cybele; Mother of the Gods
Magnentius (usurper): murder of Constans, 29; suicide of, 41, 42
Mamas (martyr), shrine of, 368–69, 450–51
mansiones, 20
Marc (bishop of Arethusa), 45, 53; aid to Julian, 368; Arethusans' attack on, 375–76; destruction of temple, 375, 376; Gregory on, 339, 423; homoianism of, 375, 376; at Sirmium, 375n133
Marcellus (bishop of Ancyra), 34, 35n75, 186n7; in Christological debates, 37, 39, 40, 42, 43; Cyril's use of, 305; fragments of, 233n76; language of power, 38n81
Marcone, A., 128n131
Marcus Aurelius, Emperor, 329
Mardonius (eunuch), 90, 330
Maris (bishop of Chalcedon), 49
Markus, R. A., 414n114
Martig, I. Benedetti, 446n46
martyrdom: Gregory on, 342; Julian on, 331, 359n85, 364–65, 369, 461n95
martyrs: as philosophical exemplars, 419; remains of, 420. *See also* Babylas
Mary, Virgin: as *theotokos,* 133, 421
masculinity, late Roman concept of, 196–97
Maslov, Boris, 178, 414
materiality, 397–98; the divine and, 125; generative realm and, 125, 126; Gregory of Nyssa on, 484n5
matter, prior cause of, 256
Matthews, John F., 70, 405n93
Mau, Georg, 288n75, 297
Maximinus Daia, Emperor, 276
Maximus (Cynic), Gregory on, 157
Maximus of Byzantium, 107n77
Maximus of Ephesus (philosopher), 106, 227, 325, 369, 474; advice to Julian, 105; dispute with Themistius, 107–8; execution of, 92n18; Gregory on, 370; imprisonment of, 440, 444; philosophical life of, 91–92, 95–96; social status of, 103; theurgy of, 95
Maximus the Confessor, 413, 414n112; Gregory's influence on, 177n107
Mazza, M., 326n225
McGuckin, John, 21, 23n26, 178n109; on Christian controversies, 228; on Constantius,

McGuckin, John *(continued)*
339n11, 375; on Gregory's baptism, 151n17, 217, 218n12; on Gregory's character, 188; on Gregory's correspondence, 221n24; on Gregory's *Orations,* 426n155, 467n115; on Gregory's philosophical life, 223; on Gregory the Elder, 193n42, 203n79, 204n84; on kinship with the divine, 177; on *theōsis,* 414n112

McLynn, Neil, 24, 27n45, 201; on Basil of Caesarea, 476; on Eudoxius, 239n104; on Gregory's correspondence, 207; on Gregory's rhetorical activities, 206; on homoians, 150; on Lucifer of Calaris, 56

Meletius (bishop of Antioch), 49, 404; exile of, 55, 108, 280; homoiousianism of, 474; petition to Jovian, 424; return of, 281

memory, Roman concepts of, 434n5. See also *damnatio memoriae*

Menander Rhetor, 440; on hymns, 118n110

Merki, H., 177n106, 178n111

Methodius (bishop of Olympus), Eusebius's use of, 256–57

Milan, synod of (355), 42

military virtues, Roman, 88n1

mimēsis: Aristotle on, 351n57; Gregory's understanding of, 263n176; of *ousia,* 248; sons', 197–98; theatrical, 351–52

Minos, as just legislator, 341, 353

mints, imperial control of, 70n43

Mitchell, Stephen, 50

Mithraism, 121n115; Julian's, 291n89

Modestus (prefect of Constantinople), 463

monks: bishops, 7; overzealous, 203–6; support for Eustathius of Sebaste, 204, 209; tax benefits for, 208

monodies, 440n25

Moreschini, C., 152n23

Mortley, Raoul, 246, 254n155

Moses: in *Against the Galileans,* 313–14, 315, 316; Eusebius on, 311; God of, 313, 314–16; Gregory as, 214; in Gregory's *Theological Orations,* 411–12; on names, 250, 254; *philanthrōpia* of, 322

Mossay, J., 156n35

Mother of the Gods: arrival in Rome, 123–24; in causation, 132; in Julian's *Oration 5,* 131–34, 300; love for Attis, 133; as *parthenos amētōr,* 131–32; rituals of, 180, 253; *Romanitas* and, 120, 123–25; sanctuary at Pessinus, 137; spread of cult, 121–22; statue of, 123–24, 135, 249, 324. See also Attis myth; Cybele

Mursa, battle of, 29

mysteries, divine, 94; Julian and, 113–14, 217

myth: in *Against the Galileans,* 312–13; allegorical readings of, 317, 383–86; for children, 111, 114, 303, 383; Christianity as, 384; Cynics' use of, 113; *dianoia* of, 114, 129, 383, 401; divine inspiration of, 383; ethical function of, 112, 113, 114, 386–87; Eusebius on, 310, 311; as fiction, 381–87; Gregory on, 381–87, 400; Heraclius's misunderstanding of, 111; hidden meaning in, 384; Homeric, 383; Julian's concept of, 383–84, 390, 401; in Julian's *Oration 7,* 111–14, 117; *lexis* of, 114, 383, 401; origins of, 114–16; *paradoxa* of, 113–14, 123, 129, 253, 263, 301, 313, 383; Plato on, 112n92; in *progymnasmata,* 112n93; relevance to philosophy, 112, 124; revelation of the divine, 113–14, 116; sacred, 111–14; *stasis* in, 386; theurgy and, 124; true meanings of, 114, 383–86

names: appellative power of, 393n55, 394n58; artful creation of, 398, 399; deductive power of, 253; divine, 246–54, 261n171, 362, 399; *dynamis* of, 430n170; Eunomius on, 246–54, 255; of gods, 248, 251, 393n55; as imitations, 248; Moses on, 250, 254; and *ousia,* 246–54, 257, 258, 398; Plato on, 247–49, 250, 251, 253, 397–98; sounds of, 248; in Stoicism, 398

Naucratius (brother of Basil), 27

Nazianzus, 18–21; *allotrioi* of, 150, 189, 190, 199, 201, 209; in *Antonine Itinerary,* 19n9; city status of, 21n16; environs of, 19–20; Gregory's friendships at, 207–12; Gregory the Elder's opponents at, 199, 201–12; homoians of, 183; homoiousians of, 183; under Julian, 60; Julian at, 147–48; *koinōnia* in, 201; as *mansio,* 20, 60; municipal officers of, 27n45; schism in, 56, 150, 152, 156, 183, 201–12, 342n27

negation, and privation, 246–47, 254n154

Neoplatonism, 92–94; active life in, 95–96, 103–5; Basil of Caesarea and, 224n37; Eunomius's use of, 247; the Good in, 104; Julian's study of, 92; *oikeiōsis* in, 415n120; political aspects of, 98n48, 292n92; school at Aphrodisias, 104n70

Nero, Emperor, 352, 353n64

Neumann, K. J., 303n133

New Covenant, preordained history of, 451

Nicaea, council of (325), 35, 45; *ousia* in, 37–38

Nicobulus (nephew of Gregory), 236
Nicocles (grammarian), 90; exile of, 463
Nicomedes (relative of Gregory), 207–8
Nicomedia, pagan philosophers of, 92n17
Nonna (mother of Gregory of Nazianzus), 50, 52, 191; divine vision of, 217n8; Gregory's identification with, 188; offering of Gregory to God, 217–18
Norris, F. W., 407n99, 408n102
Norton, Peter, 7
Nous (Divine Intellect), 37; *dynamis* of, 248; illumination from, 298; Rhea as, 252n150
Numa (king of Rome), 291
Nussbaum, Martha, 172n90

Oenomaus of Gadara, 116; on oracles, 310
oikeiōsis (kinship), 199; altruistic, 431–32; with the beautiful, 418; Christian, 386; free choice in, 420n137; Galileans' desertion of, 485; Gregory's concept of, 262; under Julian, 360, 416–17; in Julian's works, 323–24; in Neoplatonism, 415n120; Origen on, 179–80; with pagan gods, 327; in Stoicism, 178–79, 220, 326n223, 485; Themistius's, 484–85
oikeiōsis pros theon, 176–81, 182, 200, 324; chain of, 420, 421, 427; Christ's, 262; concord in, 425–28; disruptions to, 429; in *Epistle to the Priest Theodorus*, 323, 326; in Gregory's *Oration 2*, 259–65, 269, 414, 415; in Gregory's *Oration 6*, 425–28; in Gregory's *Theological Orations*, 413–22; Julian's desire for, 332; Julian's effect on, 362, 420; pagan rejection of, 422; *philanthrōpia* in, 324, 326n224; philosophers' role in, 415; political involvement as, 225; salvation through, 421; self and other in, 415; Stoic, 323; unity in, 432
oikoumenē: Hebrews in, 316; integration with God, 264; philosopher leaders of, 264; threat of innovation to, 123; universal, 82; Zeus-Helios's establishment of, 333
oikoumenē, Christian: danger from schism, 374; harmony of, 422; Julian's effect on, 371; leadership of, 153–81; universal, 432
oikoumenē, Roman: active philosophy in, 264; *allotrioi* outside, 379, 487; under Augustus, 361; Christian claim to, 365–66, 379–80, 432; Christian desertion of, 320–21; Christian governance of, 461–62; Christian threat to, 305, 306; Christian vision of, 335; under Constantius, 29; correct governance of, 480–83; the divine in, 2, 7, 10, 19, 366, 481; divine punishment of, 365; ethnic hierarchy of, 330; following Julian's death, 332, 444; Galileans' exclusion from, 143; goodness of, 180; Greekness of, 142, 289, 290–91; harmony of, 422; Helios's role in, 298, 299; in *Hymn to King Helios*, 287; under Julian, 270, 361–62, 365; Julian's conception of, 289, 292, 332, 335; leaders of, 8; mirroring of Christian cosmos, 430; role of Trinity in, 486–87; safeguarding of, 35; theological warfare in, 214; true understanding of, 348
Olivar, A., 156n35
O'Meara, Dominic, 3n2, 98n48, 292n90; on active philosophers, 482; on Platonists, 103
The One: assimilation of diversity into, 334; as creator, 128n132, 130n138; emanations from, 126–27, 132; as First Cause, 317; in *Hymn to King Helios*, 294; *hypostasis* of, 126; unity of, 333
oracles: Ammianus on, 277nn29,32; of Apollo, 116–17, 123, 276–77, 290; Diocletian's consultation of, 276, 277n32; Eusebius on, 253n152; Julian on, 310; Julian's consultation of, 292n89, 459; on Julian's death, 336n1; Oenomaus of Gadara on, 310
Oribasius (physician): exile of, 463; *Hypomnema*, 443n35
Origen: on Christ as physician, 171; Gregory's knowledge of, 22–23, 24; on meanings of reality, 399n75; on *oikeiōsis*, 179–80; *Philocalia*, 22
origin narratives, Mediterranean, 310
Orpheus, 113, 383, 384; association with Julian, 394n60
orthodoxy, Nicene, 35; Gregory's, 11, 206, 228, 483n3
Orthodoxy, Russian: Gregory's influence in, 7n22, 413
ousia (essence): versus accident, 257–58; Aristotelian, 38; Attis as, 126, 127; avoidance of, 43, 44; bishops' debates concerning, 36, 37–38, 148; of Christ, 38, 39, 44, 245, 256, 261, 400; communality of, 255; council of Antioch on, 43; of God the Father, 38; Gregory's avoidance of term, 211; in *Hymn to King Helios*, 288; in Julian's orations, 120, 137; *mimēsis* of, 248; names and, 246–54, 257, 258, 398; negative definition of, 246; prior cause of, 120, 128, 129, 256, 410. *See also* the divine
Ovid, Cybele and Attis in, 118n110

548   INDEX

paidagōgoi, 21n21, 214
paideia: among Constantius's administrators, 102n65; bishops', 36; Christian, 142; Christian attitudes toward, 349; of Constantinople, 96; cultural notions of, 9n30; of elites, 7, 479, 480, 481; in explication of scripture, 36; Greekness in, 330; Gregory's, 341; in Gregory's orations, 349–50, 411; *instrumentarium* of, 14; intellectual formation through, 75; Julian on, 86, 141; Julian's, 283, 361; as marker of status, 73; nuances of, 13–14; right and wrong use of, 11, 12; role of Alexandria in, 89–90; social capital from, 264
Pan, masturbation and, 109
panegyrics, Christian imperial, 372
parainesis (moral exhortation), 112
parrhēsia (frank speech): Heraclius's, 108, 110, 112; of philosophers, 482; priests', 157; public displays of, 108
Paschoud, François, 453
patria potestas, 192–94; mutual obligations of, 194–95; property under, 193. *See also* father-son relationships
patronage, late-antique, 6n18; terminology of, 289n79
Paul (bishop of Constantinople), 40; exile of, 34; on Gregory's *Oration 2*, 260
Paul, Apostle: leadership of, 232; on nature of Christ, 258
Penella, Robert, 95
Persian campaigns: Constantius's, 29, 41, 46, 48–49, 53, 272, 281, 372, 443; fiction versus reality in, 453–54; in Gregory's *Oration 5*, 446, 452–54; Julian's, 136–37, 147, 271–72, 273, 281–86, 321, 359–60, 443–44, 452–54, 457; justness of, 452–53; Libanius on, 282; Themistius on, 435; Valerian's, 452–53
persuasion, Gregory on, 171, 174–75
pharmakeia: of philosophers, 169, 170, 172–76, 181, 182; and Trinity, 260, 262, 338, 349, 429, 485; words as, 172–76
philanthrōpia: civic virtue of, 322n205; Constantius's, 367; divine, 322, 484; of Galileans, 325; of God, 338; of the gods, 325, 326; as imperial virtue, 372n122; Julian's, 306, 322, 359, 372n122, 416; in *oikeiōsis pros theon*, 324, 326n224
philarchia (hunger for power), 74, 161
Philo, on names, 251n144
philosopher-kings: emperors as, 105; Hercules as, 114n101, 286; Julian as, 142, 305, 327–35,

347, 459, 485; Platonic, 72, 103, 104, 214, 486. *See also* rulers, ideal
philosophers: abstention from sacrifice, 94n26; assimilation with the divine, 138; characteristics of, 138n165; Christian versus non-Christian, 252; contribution to common good, 110; differences among, 310n163; divinely chosen, 219, 259, 481, 484; divine parentage of, 115n103, 482; duty toward the divine, 167; emperors as, 86–87; ethical training for, 138; guidance to the divine, 214, 253–54; involvement in *politeia*, 108, 110–11, 167; knowledge of God, 223n35; knowledge of Greek, 139; as mediators, 333; modesty of, 176; outer appearances of, 222n29; *parrhēsia* of, 482; *pharmakeia* of, 169, 170, 172–76, 181, 182; as physicians of soul, 166–71, 172, 180–81, 182, 212; political, 108, 110–11, 167, 223n35, 377, 483; as priests, 137; role in civic harmony, 157, 103; self-control of, 139; souls of, 104, 249; theurgy of, 254; true and false, 99–100, 117, 166, 167, 182–83; uneducated, 164–65, 259–60; union with the divine, 3, 94
philosophical life: active, 99–106, 219–25, 480–81, 482; ambition and, 103; among Gregory's friends, 209; Aristotelian, 95, 161–62, 215, 220, 227; asceticism in, 158, 431; bishops', 240–41, 259; Christian ascetic, 419–20; Christian leadership as, 155n32, 240, 262; Christian versus pagan, 418–19; Cicero on, 73n53, 74n59; classical matrix of, 71–75, 156, 159, 171, 300, 480; Constantius on, 81, 85, 221, 224, 227; correct practice of, 139, 142; debates over, 86, 214; in *Epistle to Themistius*, 83–86, 106; in Gregory's orations, 153–65, 216, 217, 363, 412, 431; Julian's, 71, 74–75, 79, 89, 90–106, 227, 292, 332, 432; in Julian's orations, 138–39; *koinon* in, 222; of Maximus of Ephesus, 91–92, 95–96; mixed, 429–32; as model for priesthood, 153–65; Plato on, 93, 161–62, 220; in *politeia*, 157; purification of, 411, 414; role of gods in, 87; in Roman West, 74n59; second level of, 103, 105; Themistius's, 81–84, 85–86, 92, 101, 121, 220, 221, 224. *See also* leisure, philosophical; retreat, philosophical
philosophical life, Gregory's, 151, 153, 208–9, 215–28; active, 223–24, 485; authority in, 264; mixed, 431; Themistius as model for, 225–28

philosophy: causality in, 38; Christian rejection of, 349–50; equation with medicine, 171n88; in explication of scripture, 36, 38, 156; governance in, 2–3; Hebrew influence on, 312; parts of, 113; relevance of myth to, 112, 124; second level of, 103, 105; in the shade versus in the open, 99–106, 219–25

Philostorgius, 229n57, 239n105; on Aetius, 236, 243; on Babylus, 277, 278, 279; *Ecclesiastical History*, 242, 243; on Eunomius, 237n93, 238; on Eusebius of Nicomedia, 32, 243

Phoenicians, impiety of, 310

Photinus (bishop of Sirmium), 42, 48, 186n7; Gregory's attack on, 229, 233–35; homoian opposition to, 234; Julian on, 233, 305, 318; on names, 253; theology of, 233–35; on Trinity, 400, 429

Photius, on Eunapius, 282n52

physei/thesei, debates on, 397–401

physicians: of the body, 168, 169; social status of, 171; of the soul, 166–71, 172, 180–81, 182, 200, 213

piety: innovating, 210; limits of, 185

Plato: on appearance and reality, 129n135; borrowings from Judaism, 311, 312; cosmogony of, 312; Demiurge of, 104, 313, 314; on the Good, 290, 294–95; on governance, 2, 84; Gregory's reliance on, 407n99; in *Hymn to King Helios*, 290, 291, 294–95, 296; ideal ruler of, 74, 85, 160; influence on governance, 480; and innovation, 101; in *Misopogon*, 329; on myth, 112n92; on names, 247–49, 250, 251, 253, 397–98; on philosopher-kings, 72, 103, 104, 214, 486; on philosophical life, 93; physician metaphors of, 168, 171, 172; on the sacred, 379; on sophists, 100; on suicide, 79n71; Themistius on, 99. Works: *Alcibiades I*, 125n124; *Cratylus*, 247–49, 250, 251, 253, 254n156, 315n180, 393–96; *Gorgias*, 370n116; *Laws*, 84, 103, 292n90, 329, 332, 383n16; *Phaedo*, 79; *Republic*, 103, 104, 290, 295, 329, 383; *Theaetetus*, 72; *Timaeus*, 104, 172n92, 299, 312, 313–14, 409

Platonism: and the Bible, 177, 178; Christian, 413

Plotinus, 93, 132n143; on ascent to the divine, 249; disciples of, 95; Gregory's use of, 295n103; on matter, 126

pneuma, in Greek philosophy, 173n94

politeia: citizenship in, 348; as cosmos, 416; Greek and Roman combined, 121; household tropes of, 195n49; under Julian, 361, 387; philosophers' involvement in, 108, 110–11, 167; philosophical life in, 157; physician metaphor of, 168n77; role of festivals in, 464; veneration of gods in, 378

political theory, Christian: Roman themes in, 2

polytheism, Gregory on, 234, 235

Pomponius, Sextus, 194n46

Porphyrius (*katholikos* of Egypt), 302

Porphyry: on the active life, 105; Christian refutations of, 302, 305; Eusebius's rebuttal of, 307, 309–12; on Judaism, 309; Julian's knowledge of, 113n98, 250n140, 304, 307n152; on the maxim "Know Thyself," 93n23; on name of Zeus, 251n146; on names, 253n153; on philosophical retreat, 93, 94; on ritual and purification, 307–8; reconstruction of works, 303n132; on sacrifice, 284; textual exegesis of, 307; theurgy of, 125n123, 250n141. Works: *Against the Christians*, 253, 302; *On the Statues*, 125n123, 249, 250, 251–52, 308

priesthood, Christian: Gregory the Elder's embodiment of, 187; mediating function of, 262, 324; philosophical life in, 153–65. *See also* bishops; leadership, Christian

priesthood, pagan: avoidance of innovation, 322; in *Epistle to the Priest Theodorus*, 321, 325; Julian's regulation of, 325n220, 381; philosophical life of, 325

priests, Christian: *parrhēsia* of, 157; sacramental role of, 176n105. *See also* clergy, late-antique

priests, pagan: Julian's letters to, 321

Priscus (philosopher), 23; and Julian, 71, 91

privation: blindness as, 410; negation and, 246–47, 254n154

Proclus: on names, 248n138, 251n145, 399; on philosophers' souls, 104; on theurgy, 94

Procopius, usurper: at Chalcedon, 244n125, 471n124; decapitation of, 470; Eunomius and, 244; and Flavian dynasty, 470; Libanius and, 446n48; and Shapur, 434; supporters of, 470–71; usurpation of Valens, 342n27, 434, 440n24, 446, 460, 469–72, 477

Prodicus, *Choice of Hercules*, 436n9

progymnasmata (education), 197

Prohaeresius (rhetorician), 23; Christian community under, 24n32; Gregory's studies with, 163; under Julian's edict, 142n180; Julian's studies with, 91

prostitutes, male, 196n53

Proverbs (Old Testament), Gregory's use of, 433–34
Providence: in Gregory's *Oration 5*, 461–62; imperial power through, 334; Julian's reliance on, 385n27
Prudentius, on Cybele, 119n111
Ps.-Athanasius, *Contra Sabellianos*, 233n77
Ps.-Maximus the Confessor, 7n22
purification: of philosophical life, 411, 414; of souls, 128–29, 136, 143
Pythagoras, 391
Pythiodorus (priest), 276

Quasten, Johannes, 338

Rapp, Claudia, 244n127; *Holy Bishops in Late Antiquity*, 7
Rapsaces (Assyrian), 381
reality: first principles of, 120; levels of, 399, 400
recusatio, ritual of, 213
Renucci, P., 294n97
renunciators, Christian, 110, 111, 116, 117, 227
retreat, philosophical, 72; versus active life, 99–106, 219–25; in *Against the Cynic Heraclius*, 111; Basil of Caesarea's, 223, 239; choice in, 73; classical topos of, 188; in *Epistle to the Athenians*, 160–61; Gregory's, 168, 199, 216, 218, 219, 223, 239, 260, 341n19; in Gregory's *Oration 2*, 160–62, 165, 168, 170, 206; Himerius on, 163n60; and involvement, 75, 93–94, 117, 167; Julian on, 74, 79, 84, 111; Libanius on, 163n60; places for, 381; Porphyry on, 93, 94; purity gained in, 264; tranquility in, 216. *See also bios praktikos*; philosophical life
Reydams-Schils, G., 415n119
Rhea, as Intellect, 252n150
Rheginus (friend of Gregory), 208
rhetoric: and baptism, 151n17; competition in, 25–26; and forensic advocacy, 76n63; and philosophy, 97n45
rhetoricians, remuneration of, 97n45
Richer, J., 340n16
Riedweg, C., 303n132
Rimini, council of (359), 45–46
Rist, J. M., 224n37
ritual: Eunomian practices, 263n176 Iamblichus on, 312n168; in Julian's works, 134–36; purpose of, 134n149
Roman Empire: diversity of, 338, 480; divine power of, 2, 7; law of, 355–58; life expectancy in, 193n37; pagan versus Christian in, 3; relations with Armenia, 470; service aristocracy of, 8; west-east routes of, 19. *See also oikoumenē*, Roman
Romanitas: Christian abandonment of, 11; civic virtues of, 191; combination with *Hellēnismos*, 121, 122–23, 142, 289, 290–91; Constantius's, 373; ethnicities under, 395–96; father-son relationships in, 191; Julian's understanding of, 119, 265; *Logos* as, 393–96; Mother of the Gods in, 120, 123–25; role of gods in, 10–11; universal, 395–96
Rousseau, P., 240n107, 484n5
Rubenson, Samuel, 23, 23n28
Rufinus: on Cybele, 119n111; translation of Gregory, 17
rulers, ideal, 71–73; Aristotle's, 85, 86; consensus with ruled, 142n179; Dionysus as, 114; Julian on, 333; Plato's, 74, 85, 160. *See also* philosopher-kings
Russell, D. A., 198
Russell, Norman, 177–78; on *theōsis*, 413–14

Sabbah, G., 468n17
Sabellians, 209; denunciations of, 233–34, 235; Julian's knowledge of, 317; on Trinity, 255, 429
Sabellius (theologian), 41, 206; excommunication of, 186n7
the sacred: Julian's actions toward, 382; *logoi* and, 348, 349, 378, 391, 396; reverence toward, 379. *See also* the divine
sacred space: Christian emperors in, 476–77; Gregory on, 451n63; profanation of, 486
sacrifice: efficacy of, 284; Eusebius on, 310; Gregory on, 348, 349, 362–63, 369n113; Hebrew practice of, 319; Julian's practice of, 65, 89, 284, 287n69, 348, 349, 362–63, 438, 458n88, 461n95, 485; philosophers' abstention from, 94n26; Porphyry on, 249, 251; Presocratics on, 369n112; punishment for, 66n20, 463
salvation: in *Against the Galileans*, 318; debates concerning, 37; of physical body, 180; as return to the divine, 300; through Julian's death, 458; through *oikeiōsis pros theon*, 421
Samuel (prophet), emulation of, 232, 259
Sasima, see of: Gregory's refusal of, 157, 158–63, 183, 201
Saturnalia, 286n68; Julian's celebration of, 285
Saturninius Secundus Salutius, (PPO) 285, 376;

On the Gods and the World, 287; removal from office, 463
Saturninus, Flavius, (consul) 472
scriptures: allegorical reading of, 401; in classical matrix, 482; Julian on, 402; literal reading of, 389, 401–2; philosophy in explication of, 36, 38, 156; proper reading of, 425
Second Sophistic, literary conventions of, 468
Seleucia, council of (359), 46–47
self: relationship to cosmos, 415; subjection to others, 418–22, 431, 432, 485
self-definition, Christian: Roman aspects of, 2
senate, Constantinopolitan: delegation to Rome, 96; development of, 80n76, 481; Julian and, 106; recruitment into, 82, 97; Themistius's *adlectio* to, 80–82, 96, 97, 100, 101, 105
Serapis, cult of, 89
Serdica, council of (343), 39, 40, 41
Sextus Empiricus, 192, 193; on language, 398n71
Shapur II (ruler of Persia): advances to Julian, 283; campaigns against Constantius, 29, 48–49, 53, 272; campaigns against Julian, 136–37, 147, 272, 273, 440, 443–44; Eustathius's embassy to, 96, 107; and Procopius, 434; treaty with Jovian, 337, 340, 434, 436, 439, 444, 456, 458. *See also* Persian campaigns
Silvanus (master of infantry), revolt of, 30
Simon the New Theologian, 413
Sinko, T., 155n30
Sirmium, convocations of bishops at, 42, 43, 44
Smith, R., 109n84, 294n97, 301n125; on Julian's upbringing, 317n189
Socrates (historian), 244n125, 341
Sol Invictus, Roman worship of, 290, 291, 292, 334. *See also* Helios; Zeus-Helios
Sopater (son of Sopater), 103, 105, 209
Sophronius (magistrate), 25, 472
Sophronius (notary), 68
sōphrosynē: Gregory on, 174–75; imperial, 195n50; under Julian, 387
Soranus of Ephesus (physician), 197
Sosipatra (philosopher), 107
soul: Aristotle on, 128n134, 173n96; ascent of, 135, 222; divine origin of, 127; and emotions, 172; governance by *Logos*, 173–74, 176; in Gregory's *Oration 2,* 166–76, 181, 212; Julian on, 128–29, 132n143; link to God, 180; material elements of, 173; mediating function of, 181; philosophers', 104, 249; physicians of, 166–71, 172, 180–81, 182, 200; prior existence of, 129n135; purification of, 128–29, 136, 143; reflection of the divine, 129n135; severance from body, 221n27; stewardship of, 212; Stoic view of, 173n97; striving toward nobility, 170; symbiosis with body, 180n121; Themistius on, 227n47; without beginning, 257n163
Stagirius (rhetorician), 25n36, 26n42, 151; Attic training of, 150n16
statues: of Apollo Musagetes, 276, 277; divine power of, 251, 252; in *Epistle to the Priest Theodorus,* 324; erasures from, 353; representation of divinity, 354; sacred fear of, 324; symbolic power of, 123–25; usefulness of, 251, 252
stelae, public proclamations on, 347
stēlographia, Gregory's writings as, 345, 346–48, 355, 364, 389, 422, 428, 466
Sterk, A., 7n20, 167n76, 205n88
Stoicism: chain of being in, 179n116; influence on Gregory, 414; language theory of, 398n71; *Logos* of, 415; names in, 398; *oikeiōsis* in, 178–79, 220, 323, 326n223, 485; on passion, 172; on the soul, 173n97; use of *hypostasis,* 261n171
storms at sea, literary motif of, 217n8
sun: coexistence with light, 410; in imagery of kingship, 290; manifestation of the divine, 297–98; Roman worship of, 290, 291, 292, 334; as symbol of empire, 289. *See also* Helios; Zeus-Helios
syllogisms: Gregory's use of, 409; Julian's, 392–93; training in use of, 397
Symmachus: on Julian, 67; on leisure, 74n59
synkrisis (in *apologētikos logos*), 76, 159
synonyms: *dynamis* of, 397; Eunomius's, 409

Tantillo, I., 63n7
Taurus (prefect), 45n107
teachers: Christian, 141–42; in Gregory's *Oration 2,* 232; Julian's edicts on, 139–43, 148, 149n7, 151, 152, 227, 269, 318, 325n220, 342n27, 357, 383n16, 387n36; registers of, 140; restrictions on, 141–42
Temple at Jerusalem, 446; destruction of, 447–49; Julian's rebuilding attempts, 273n10, 447–51, 457
temples: of Apollo, 275–77, 279, 284, 369, 447n49, 451; Julian's edicts on, 140; Marc of Arethusa's destruction of, 375, 376; restitutions to, 65, 275n23, 331, 357n76

theater: Antioch's love for, 361, 383n21; barbarians and, 384n24; Christian, 486; in Gregory's *Oration 4*, 348–53; hyperrealism of, 352; inculcation of classical culture, 350–51; Julian's polemic on, 383n21; role in Roman cities, 350

Themistius (philosopher), 12; *adlectio* to Constantinopolitan senate, 80–82, 96, 97, 100, 101, 105; on Aedesius, 94; on Aristotle, 84–85, 98–99; and Basil the Elder, 226n45; correspondence of, 83, 98n46; dispute with Maximus, 107–8; on embodiment of law, 355–56; exposure to Neoplatonism, 99n52; on friendship, 107n79; Gregory on, 226; innovations of, 101–2; involvement in *politeia*, 101; on Julian, 107n76; Julian's studies with, 83, 91; Libanius on, 439n21; as model for Gregory, 225–28; on new men, 243; *oikeiōsis* of, 484–85; opponents of, 97–103; orations of, 98–100; patrons of, 106; on Persian campaigns, 435; philosophical life of, 81–84, 85–86, 92, 101, 121, 220, 221, 224; on Plato, 99; as political philosopher, 98, 101–2, 224, 243, 436; proconsulship of, 100n57; recruitment of senators, 82, 97; relationship with Libanius, 97–98; on rhetoric, 97n45; on the soul, 227n47; students of, 100n55; supporters of, 102; vocabulary of office, 100n58. Works: *Oration 5 Hypatikos* for Jovian, 435–39, 445, 461; *Oration 6 On Philadelphia*, 484; *Oration 22 On Friendship*, 99; *Oration 23*, 100; *Risâlat*, 83n89. *See also* Julian, *Epistle to Themistius*

Theodora, Empress, 33n69

Theodore (bishop of Mopsuestia), 241, 401; condemnation as heretic, 402n82; exegetical method of, 403; rebuttal of Julian, 305n146, 402, 403. Works: *Against Eunomius*, 403; *Commentary on the Psalms*, 402

Theodoret (bishop of Cyrrhus), use of Arian Historiographer, 279n36

Theodorus (priest), 321; Julian's mandate to, 325; relationship with Julian, 322

Theodosian Code, 140, 141

Theodosius I, Emperor, 157; bishops under, 404; consecration of Gregory, 374, 405; edict on religion, 404; and Gregory, 5–6; theology of, 405, 413

Theodosius II, Emperor: censoring of Julian, 303

theology, Christian: imperial influence over, 12; Roman themes in, 2. *See also* Christological debates; orthodoxy, Nicene; *ousia*; Trinity

Theophanes, sons' letter to, 191, 192, 194

Theophilus the Indian, 243, 281; and Gallus Caesar, 243–44

Theophrastus, on philosophical life, 73n53

Theos Hypsistos, 50–51

theōsis: *apostasis* versus, 413–22; Gregory of Nazianzus on, 177, 262n173, 339, 377, 386, 413–22, 484; role of *Logos* in, 421–22; scholarly discussions of, 413–14; transformation through, 419, 421; Trinity and, 421–22

Thespesius (rhetorician), 22

theurgy, 94; Julian's use of, 116–18, 124, 370, 414; and Maximus of Ephesus, 95; and myth, 124; perfection in, 134; philosophers', 254; Porphyry's, 250n141

Thome, Felix, 403

Thrasea Paetus, Roman senator, 419n135

Tollefsen, T. T., 177n106

tombs, veneration of, 319. *See also* martyrs

Traianeum, burning of, 440n28

Trajan, Emperor, on Christianity, 326n225

Trinity: concord proper to, 428; correct comprehension of, 183, 184, 374; errors concerning, 231–33, 261–62; Eunomius's understanding of, 245–58, 260–61, 263, 380, 400; *eusebeia* through, 476; falsification of, 264, 350, 401; familial aspects of, 263; Greek philosophy in comprehending of, 425; in Gregory's *Oration 1*, 211; in Gregory's *Oration 2*, 184–87, 210, 231–33, 297, 422; in Gregory's *Oration 3*, 211; in Gregory's *Oration 4*, 344, 349; in Gregory's *Oration 6*, 202–3, 426–30; in Gregory's *Theological Orations*, 403, 408, 410–11; hierarchical order of, 430, 432; *hypostaseis* of, 184–86, 211, 261, 297, 410, 429; Nicene definition of, 483n3; as Oneness, 262; *pharmakon* of, 260, 262, 338, 349, 429, 485; Photinus on, 400, 429; role in governance, 476; role in kinship with divine, 420; role in Roman *oikoumenē*, 486–87; Sabellians on, 255, 429; *theōsis* and, 421–22. *See also* Christological debates

tsunami (July 21, 365), 460

tyranny: in father-son relationships, 187–90, 194; in governance, 189

universalism: competing views of, 485–87; and governance, 2–3. *See also oikoumenē*

INDEX 553

universalism, Christian, 308–9; innovation in, 122; Roman ideology in, 1–2
universalism, Roman, 1, 287; approach to the divine in, 480; Christian claim to, 306, 486, 487; Constantius's, 122n17; cosmic dimension of, 2, 123; Cybele in, 118, 120; the divine in, 10, 120–21; ethnical hierarchies of, 2; exclusion of *allotrioi* from, 379, 487; Greek nature of, 318; harmonizing aspects of, 438; Julian's, 11, 327–35; mirroring of Trinity, 432; *Romanitas/Hellēnismos* in, 142
Ursacius (bishop of Singidunum), 43

Vaggione, Richard, 230, 258; on Gratian, 404n91; on *Logos,* 397; on Theodosius I, 405n93
Valens (bishop of Mursa), 43, 46n108
Valens, Emperor: at Antioch, 474; apostasy of, 201, 404, 473; Arianism of, 342n27, 457, 473; and Basil of Caesarea, 476; bishops under, 470, 473; and Caesarius, 471; death of, 404; division of empire, 439; and Eunomius, 473, 474; Gregory on, 157n36, 472, 473; and Julian's mausoleum, 438; legitimacy of, 434, 435, 465, 471, 475; in Nicene historiography, 473n133; officials under, 472; *philanthrōpia* of, 484; Procopius's usurpation of, 342n27, 434, 440n24, 446, 460, 469–72, 477; purges of, 462–63, 464; reconciliation under, 475; religious policy of, 405n93; Themistius on, 439n23; unpopularity of, 470
Valentinian I, Emperor: and Caesarius, 471; division of empire, 439; and Julian's mausoleum, 438; legitimacy of, 435; *philanthrōpia* of, 484; purges of, 462–63; Themistius on, 439n23
Valentinian II, Emperor: censoring of Julian, 303
Valerian, Emperor: Persian campaign of, 452–53
Van Dam, Raymond, 5, 20n10, 244n127, 482; on Gregory's mother, 188; on Gregory's portrait of Julian, 338; on Trinity, 262–63
van Nuffelen, Peter, 326
Vetranio, rebellion of, 29

Victor (military officer), 68
Vinson, M., 152n23, 450n61
Vinzent, M., 234n80

war, civil, 214, 222, 225, 227–28; Aetius in, 259; Gregory's preparation for, 213; in Gregory's *Theological Orations,* 406; Julian and, 269; Nicenes and non-Nicenes in, 228; role of false philosophy in, 408, 413; theological causes of, 212
war, just or justified, 2, 283, 446, 452–53, 457–58
Watts, E. J., 91n12
West, Roman: balance with East, 82; civic inscriptions of, 191n26; decline of, 6; philosophical life in, 74n59
Wiemer, Hans-Ulrich, 274–75, 468n16
Winslow, Donald, 177
wisdom, *pharmakeia* of, 169, 170
Wittung, J. A., 177n106
words: *dynamis* of, 247–48; as *pharmakeia,* 172–76. *See also logoi*
Wulfila (bishop), 243

Xenarchus of Seleucia, 128n133, 129n136
Xerxes (Persian ruler), 445n45

zealots: opposition to Gregory the Elder, 203–6; resistance to innovation, 206
Zeno (physician), 90n5
Zeno (Stoic), on ignorance, 172, 323, 349, 468, 480
Zeus: commandment on *philanthrōpia,* 322; as cosmos, 251n146; in *Hymn to King Helios,* 288; name of, 251n146; and Pan, 108–10, 111, 114; philanthropic divinities of, 320; representations of, 252, 308
Zeus-Helios: civilizing impact of, 291, 298; as common father, 326; as founder of Rome, 291; human approach to, 333; Julian on, 114–16, 117, 132, 142, 270, 272, 288–97; as mediator, 293–99; as one god, 297; as origin of creation, 292; unity under, 320, 333; universal community of, 320, 321
Zosimus, 135

TEXT
10/12/5 Minion Pro

DISPLAY
Minion Pro

COMPOSITOR
Integrated Composition Systems

INDEXER
Roberta Engleman

CARTOGRAPHER
Bill Nelson

PRINTER AND BINDER
Maple-Vail Book Manufacturing Group

www.ingramcontent.com/pod-product-compliance
Lightning Source LLC
Chambersburg PA
CBHW021130230426
43667CB00005B/77